C HOW TO PROGRAM
SEVENTH EDITION

Deitel Series Page

How To Program Series

Android How to Program
C++ How to Program, 8/E
C How to Program, 7/E
Java™ How to Program, 9/E
Java™ How to Program, Late Objects Version, 8/E
Internet & World Wide Web How to Program, 5/E
Visual C++® 2008 How to Program, 2/E
Visual Basic® 2010 How to Program
Visual C#® 2010 How to Program, 3/E

Simply Series

Simply C++: An App-Driven Tutorial Approach
Simply Java™ Programming: An App-Driven
  Tutorial Approach
Simply C#: An App-Driven Tutorial Approach
Simply Visual Basic® 2010: An App-Driven
  Approach, 4/E

CourseSmart Web Books

www.deitel.com/books/CourseSmart/

C++ How to Program, 5/E, 6/E, 7/E & 8/E
Simply C++: An App-Driven Tutorial Approach
Java™ How to Program, 6/E, 7/E, 8/E & 9/E
Simply Visual Basic 2010: An App-Driven
  Approach, 4/E

(continued from previous column)
Visual Basic® 2010 How to Program
Visual Basic® 2008 How to Program
Visual C#® 2010 How to Program, 4/E
Visual C#® 2008 How to Program, 3/E

Deitel Developer Series

AJAX, Rich Internet Applications and Web
  Development for Programmers
Android for Programmers: An App-Driven
  Approach
C++ for Programmers
C# 2010 for Programmers
iPhone® for Programmers: An App-Driven
Java™ for Programmers, 2/e
JavaScript for Programmers

LiveLessons Video Learning P

www.deitel.com/books/LiveLessons

Android App Development Fundamenta
C++ Fundamentals
Java™ Fundamentals
C# 2010 Fundamentals
iPhone® App Development Fundamen
JavaScript Fundamentals
Visual Basic Fundamentals

To receive updates on Deitel publications, Resource Centers, training courses, partner offer
please register for the free *Deitel Buzz Online* e-mail newsletter at:

    www.deitel.com/newsletter/subscribe.html

and join the Deitel communities on Twitter®

    @deitel

Facebook®

    facebook.com/DeitelFan

and Google+

    gplus.to/deitel

To communicate with the authors, send e-mail to:

    deitel@deitel.com

For information on government and corporate *Dive-Into Series* on-site seminars offered l
Associates, Inc. worldwide, visit:

    www.deitel.com/training/

or write to

    deitel@deitel.com

For continuing updates on Prentice Hall/Deitel publications visit:

    www.deitel.com
    www.pearsoninternationaleditions.com/deitel

Visit the Deitel Resource Centers that will help you master programming languages, so
ment, Android and iPhone/iPad app development, and Internet- and web-related topic

    www.deitel.com/ResourceCenters.html

C HOW TO PROGRAM

SEVENTH EDITION

Paul Deitel
Deitel & Associates, Inc.

Harvey Deitel
Deitel & Associates, Inc.

International Edition contributions by
Mohit P. Tahiliani
National Institute of Technology Karnataka,
Surathkal

DEITEL

PEARSON

Boston   Columbus   Indianapolis   New York   San Francisco   Upper Saddle River
Amsterdam   Cape Town   Dubai   London   Madrid   Milan   Munich   Paris   Montreal   Toronto
Delhi   Mexico City   Sao Paulo   Sydney   Hong Kong   Seoul   Singapore   Taipei   Tokyo

Editorial Director: *Marcia J. Horton*
Editor-in-Chief: *Michael Hirsch*
Associate Editor: *Carole Snyder*
Vice President, Marketing: *Patrice Jones*
Marketing Manager: *Yezan Alayan*
Marketing Coordinator: *Kathryn Ferranti*
Vice President, Production: *Vince O'Brien*
Managing Editor: *Jeff Holcomb*
Associate Managing Editor: *Robert Engelhardt*
Publisher, International Edition: *Angshuman Chakraborty*
Acquisitions Editor, International Edition: *Somnath Basu*
Publishing Assistant, International Edition: *Shokhi Shah*
Print and Media Editor, International Edition: *Ashwitha Jayakumar*
Project Editor, International Edition: *Jayashree Arunachalam*
Publishing Administrator, International Edition: *Hema Mehta*
Senior Manufacturing Controller, Production, International Edition: *Trudy Kimber*
Cover Photo Credit: *kentoh / Shutterstock.com <http://Shutterstock.com>*
Media Editor: *Daniel Sandin.*

Pearson Education Limited
Edinburgh Gate
Harlow
Essex CM20 2JE
England

and Associated Companies throughout the world

Visit us on the World Wide Web at:
www.pearsoninternationaleditions.com

© Pearson Education Limited 2013

The right of Paul Deitel and Harvey Deitel to be identified as authors of this work has been asserted by them in accordance with the Copyright, Designs and Patents Act 1988.

Authorized adaptation from the United States edition, entitled C How to Program, 7th edition, *ISBN 978-0-13-299044-8 by* Paul Deitel and Harvey Deitel *published by Pearson Education* © *2013.*

ISBN 10: 0-273-77684-3
ISBN 13: 978-0-273-77684-0

British Library Cataloguing-in-Publication Data
A catalogue record for this book is available from the British Library

10 9 8 7 6 5 4 3 2
14 13

Typeset in AGaramond-Regular by GEX Publishing Services
Printed and bound by Courier Westford in The United States of America

The publisher's policy is to use paper manufactured from sustainable forests.

In Memory of Dennis Ritchie,
creator of the C programming language
and co-creator of the UNIX operating system.

Paul and Harvey Deitel

Trademarks

Contents

Appendices E through H are PDF documents posted online at the book's Companion Website (located at **www.pearsoninternationaleditions.com/deitel**).

8   C Characters and Strings   362

9   C Formatted Input/Output   407

10   C Structures, Unions, Bit Manipulation and Enumerations   433

11   C File Processing — 469

12   C Data Structures — 504

13   C Preprocessor — 545

14 Other C Topics   557

15 C++ as a Better C; Introducing Object Technology   575

16 Introduction to Classes, Objects and Strings   614

17 Classes: A Deeper Look, Part 1   651

18 Classes: A Deeper Look, Part 2   686

19 Operator Overloading; Class string   723

20   Object-Oriented Programming: Inheritance   771

21   Object-Oriented Programming: Polymorphism   806

Appendices E through H are PDF documents posted online at the book's Companion Website (located at www.pearsoninternationaleditions.com/deitel).

Preface

Welcome to the C programming language—and to C++, too! This book presents leading-edge computing technologies for college students, instructors and software development professionals.

At the heart of the book is the Deitel signature "live-code approach." We present concepts in the context of complete working programs, rather than in code snippets. Each code example is followed by one or more sample executions. Read the online Before You Begin section (www.deitel.com/books/chtp7/chtp7_BYB.pdf) to learn how to set up your computer to run the hundreds of code examples. All the source code is available at www.deitel.com/books/chtp7/ and www.pearsoninternationaleditions.com/deitel. Use the source code we provide to *run every program* as you study it.

We believe that this book and its support materials will give you an informative, challenging and entertaining introduction to C. As you read the book, if you have questions, send an e-mail to deitel@deitel.com—we'll respond promptly. For book updates, visit www.deitel.com/books/chtp7/, join our communities on Facebook (www.deitel.com/deitelfan), Twitter (@deitel) and Google+ (gplus.to/deitel), and subscribe to the *Deitel Buzz Online* newsletter (www.deitel.com/newsletter/subscribe.html).

New and Updated Features

Here are some key features of *C How to Program, 7/e*:

- *Coverage of the New C standard.* The previous edition of the book conformed to "standard C" and included a detailed appendix on the C99 standard. The New C Standard was approved just before *C How to Program, 7/e* went to publication. The new standard incorporates both C99 and the more recent C1X—now referred to as C11 or simply "the C standard" since its approval in 2011. Support for the new standard varies by compiler. The vast majority of our readership uses either the GNU gcc compiler—which supports several of the key features in the new standard—or the Microsoft Visual C++ compiler. Microsoft supports only a limited subset of the features that were added to C in C99 and C11—primarily the features that are also required by the C++ standard. To accommodate all of our readers, we placed the discussion of the new standard in optional, easy-to-use-or-omit sections and in Appendix F, Introduction to the New C Standard. We've also replaced various deprecated capabilities with newer preferred versions as a result of the new C standard.

- *New Chapter 1.* The new Chapter 1 engages students with intriguing facts and figures to get them excited about studying computers and computer programming. The chapter includes a table of some of the research made possible by computers and the Internet, current technology trends and hardware discussion, the data hierarchy, a new section on social networking, a table of business and technology publications and websites that will help you stay up to date with the latest technology news and trends, and updated exercises. We've included test-drives that show how to run a command-line C program on Microsoft Windows, Linux and Mac OS X.

- *Secure C Programming Sections.* We've added notes about secure C programming to many of the C programming chapters. We've also posted a Secure C Programming Resource Center at www.deitel.com/SecureC/. For more details, see the section "A Note About Secure C Programming" in this Preface.

- *Focus on Performance Issues.* C (and C++) are favored by designers of performance-intensive applications such as operating systems, real-time systems, embedded systems and communications systems, so we focus intensively on performance issues.

- *"Making a Difference" Exercise Sets.* We encourage you to use computers and the Internet to research and solve problems that really matter. These exercises are meant to increase awareness of important issues the world is facing. We hope you'll approach them with your own values, politics and beliefs.

- *All Code Tested on Windows and Linux.* We've tested every example and exercise program using Visual C++ and GNU gcc in Windows and Linux, respectively.

- *Updated Coverage of C++ and Object-Oriented Programming.* We updated Chapters 15–24 on object-oriented programming in C++ with material from our textbook *C++ How to Program, 8/e.*

- *Sorting: A Deeper Look.* Sorting places data in order, based on one or more sort keys. We begin our presentation of sorting with a simple algorithm in Chapter 6— in Appendix E, we present a deeper look. We consider several algorithms and compare them with regard to their memory consumption and processor demands. For this purpose, we introduce Big O notation, which indicates how hard an algorithm may have to work to solve a problem. Through examples and exercises, Appendix E discusses the selection sort, insertion sort, recursive merge sort, recursive selection sort, bucket sort and recursive Quicksort. Sorting is an interesting problem because different sorting techniques achieve the same final result but they can vary hugely in their consumption of memory, CPU time and other system resources.

- *Titled Programming Exercises.* All the programming exercises are titled to help instructors tune assignments for their classes.

- *Debugger Appendices.* We've updated the Visual C++® and GNU gdb debugging appendices.

- *Order of Evaluation.* We added cautions about order of evaluation issues.

- *Additional Exercises.* We added more function pointer exercises. We also added a Fibonacci exercise project that improves the Fibonacci recursion example (tail recursion).

- *C++-Style // Comments.* We use the newer, more concise C++-style // comments in preference to C's older style /*...*/ comments.

- *C Standard Library.* Section 1.7 references P.J. Plauger's Dinkumware website (www.dinkumware.com/manuals/default.aspx) where students can find thorough searchable documentation for the C Standard Library functions.

A Note About Secure C Programming

Throughout this book, we focus on C programming *fundamentals*. When we write each *How to Program* book, we search the corresponding language's standards document for the features that we feel novices need to learn in a first programming course, and features that existing programmers need to know to *begin* working in that language. We must also cover programming fundamentals *and* computer-science fundamentals for novice programmers—our core audience.

Industrial-strength coding techniques in any programming language are beyond the scope of an introductory textbook. For that reason, our Secure C Programming sections present some key issues and techniques, and provide links and references so you can continue learning.

Experience has shown that it's difficult to build industrial-strength systems that stand up to attacks from viruses, worms, etc. Today, via the Internet, such attacks can be instantaneous and global in scope. Software vulnerabilities often come from simple programming issues. Building security into software from the start of the development cycle can greatly reduce costs and vulnerabilities.

The CERT® Coordination Center (www.cert.org) was created to analyze and respond promptly to attacks. CERT—the Computer Emergency Response Team—publishes and promotes secure coding standards to help C programmers and others implement industrial-strength systems that avoid the programming practices that open systems to attacks. The CERT standards evolve as new security issues arise.

We've upgraded our code (as appropriate for an introductory book) to conform to various CERT recommendations. If you'll be building C systems in industry, consider reading *The CERT C Secure Coding Standard* (Robert Seacord, Addison-Wesley Professional, 2009) and *Secure Coding in C and C++* (Robert Seacord, Addison-Wesley Professional, 2006). The CERT guidelines are available free online at www.securecoding.cert.org. Mr. Seacord, a technical reviewer for the C portion of this book, provided specific recommendations on each of our new Secure C Programming sections. Mr. Seacord is the Secure Coding Manager at CERT at Carnegie Mellon University's Software Engineering Institute (SEI) and an adjunct professor in the Carnegie Mellon University School of Computer Science.

The Secure C Programming sections at the ends of Chapters 2–13 discuss many important topics, including testing for arithmetic overflows, using unsigned integer types, new more secure functions in the C standard's Annex K, the importance of checking the status information returned by standard-library functions, range checking, secure random-number generation, array bounds checking, techniques for preventing buffer overflows, input validation, avoiding undefined behaviors, choosing functions that return status information vs. using similar functions that do not, ensuring that pointers are always NULL or contain valid addresses, using C functions vs. using preprocessor macros, and more.

Web-Based Materials

This book is supported by substantial online materials. The book's Companion Website (www.pearsoninternationaleditions.com/deitel) contains source code for all the code examples and the following appendices in *searchable* PDF format:

- Appendix E, Sorting: A Deeper Look
- Appendix F, Introduction to the New C Standard

- Appendix G, Using the Visual Studio Debugger
- Appendix H, Using the GNU Debugger

Dependency Charts

Figures 1 and 2 show the dependencies among the chapters to help instructors plan their syllabi. *C How to Program, 7/e* is appropriate for CS1 and CS2 courses, and intermediate-level C and C++ programming courses. The C++ part of the book assumes that you've studied the C part.

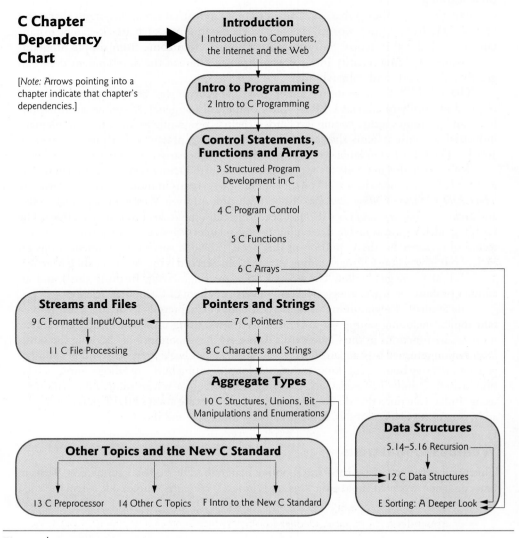

Fig. 1 | C chapter dependency chart.

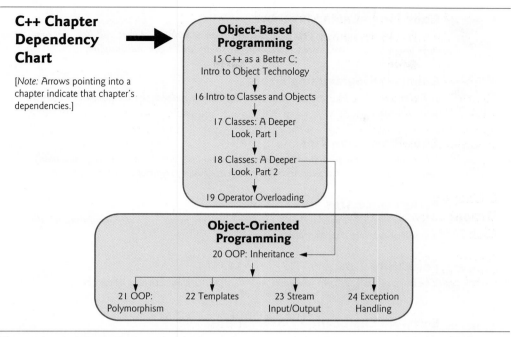

Fig. 2 | C++ chapter dependency chart.

Teaching Approach

C How to Program, 7/e, contains a rich collection of examples. We focus on good software engineering and stressing program clarity.

Syntax Shading. For readability, we syntax shade the code, similar to the way most IDEs and code editors syntax color code. Our syntax-shading conventions are:

```
comments appear like this
keywords appear like this
constants and literal values appear like this
all other code appears in black
```

Code Highlighting. We place gray rectangles around the key code.

Using Fonts for Emphasis. We place the key terms and the index's page reference for each defining occurrence in bold blue text for easy reference. We emphasize on-screen components in the **bold Helvetica** font (e.g., the **File** menu) and C program text in the Lucida font (for example, int x = 5;).

Objectives. The opening quotes are followed by a list of chapter objectives.

Illustrations/Figures. Abundant charts, tables, line drawings, UML diagrams, programs and program output are included.

Programming Tips. We include programming tips to help you focus on important aspects of program development. These tips and practices represent the best we've gleaned from a combined seven decades of programming and teaching experience.

Good Programming Practices

The Good Programming Practices *call attention to techniques that will help you produce programs that are clearer, more understandable and more maintainable.*

Common Programming Errors

Pointing out these Common Programming Errors *reduces the likelihood that you'll make them.*

Error-Prevention Tips

These tips contain suggestions for exposing and removing bugs from your programs; many describe aspects of C that prevent bugs from getting into programs in the first place.

Performance Tips

These tips highlight opportunities for making your programs run faster or minimizing the amount of memory that they occupy.

Portability Tips

The Portability Tips *help you write code that will run on a variety of platforms.*

Software Engineering Observations

The Software Engineering Observations *highlight architectural and design issues that affect the construction of software systems, especially large-scale systems.*

Summary Bullets. We present a section-by-section, bullet-list summary of the chapter.

Terminology. We include an alphabetized list of the important terms defined in each chapter with the page number of each term's defining occurrence for easy reference.

Self-Review Exercises and Answers. Extensive self-review exercises *and* answers are included for self-study.

Exercises. Each chapter concludes with a substantial set of exercises including:
- simple recall of important terminology and concepts
- identifying the errors in code samples
- writing individual program statements
- writing small portions of C functions and C++ member functions and classes
- writing complete programs
- implementing major projects

Index. We've included an extensive index, which is especially useful when you use the book as a reference. Defining occurrences of key terms are highlighted with a bold blue page number.

Software Used in *C How to Program, 7/e*

We wrote *C How to Program, 7/e* using Microsoft's free Visual C++ Express Edition (which can compile both C and C++ programs and can be downloaded from www.microsoft.com/

express/downloads/) and the free GNU C and C++ compilers (`gcc.gnu.org/install/binaries.html`), which are already installed on most Linux systems and can be installed on Mac OS X and Windows systems. Apple includes GNU C and C++ in their Xcode development tools, which Mac OS X users can download from `developer.apple.com/technologies/tools/xcode.html`.

For other free C and C++ compilers, visit:

```
www.thefreecountry.com/compilers/cpp.shtml
www.compilers.net/Dir/Compilers/CCpp.htm
www.freebyte.com/programming/cpp/#cppcompilers
en.wikipedia.org/wiki/List_of_compilers#C.2B.2B_compilers
```

CourseSmart Web Books

Today's students and instructors have increasing demands on their time and money. Pearson has responded to that need by offering digital texts and course materials online through CourseSmart. CourseSmart allows faculty to review course materials online, saving time and costs. It offers students a high-quality digital version of the text for less than the cost of a print copy. Students receive the same content offered in the print textbook enhanced by search, note-taking and printing tools. For more information, visit `www.coursesmart.co.uk`

Instructor Resources

The following supplements are available to *qualified instructors only* through Pearson Education's Instructor Resource Center `www.pearsoninternationaleditions.com/deitel`

- *PowerPoint® slides* containing all the code and figures in the text, plus bulleted items that summarize key points.
- *Test Item File* of multiple-choice questions (approximately two per book section)

- *Solutions Manual* with solutions to most of the end-of-chapter exercises. Please check the Instructor Resource Center to determine which exercises have solutions.

Please do not write to us requesting access to the Pearson Instructor's Resource Center. Access is restricted to college instructors teaching from the book. Instructors may obtain access only through their Pearson representatives. If you're not a registered faculty member, contact your Pearson representative.

Solutions are *not* provided for "project" exercises. Check out our Programming Projects Resource Center for lots of additional exercise and project possibilities (www.deitel.com/ProgrammingProjects/).

Acknowledgments

We'd like to thank Abbey Deitel and Barbara Deitel for long hours devoted to this project. We're fortunate to have worked with the dedicated team of publishing professionals at Pearson. We appreciate the guidance, savvy and energy of Michael Hirsch, Editor-in-Chief of Computer Science. Carole Snyder and Bob Engelhardt did a marvelous job managing the review and production processes, respectively.

C How to Program, 7/e *Reviewers*
We wish to acknowledge the efforts of our reviewers. Under tight deadlines, they scrutinized the text and the programs and provided countless suggestions for improving the presentation: Dr. John F. Doyle (Indiana University Southeast), Hemanth H.M. (Software Engineer at SonicWALL), Vytautus Leonavicius (Microsoft), Robert Seacord (Secure Coding Manager at SEI/CERT, author of *The CERT C Secure Coding Standard* and technical expert for the international standardization working group for the programming language C) and José Antonio González Seco (Parliament of Andalusia).

Other Recent Editions Reviewers
William Albrecht (University of South Florida), Ian Barland (Radford University), Ed James Beckham (Altera), John Benito (Blue Pilot Consulting, Inc. and Convener of ISO WG14—the Working Group responsible for the C Programming Language Standard), Alireza Fazelpour (Palm Beach Community College), Mahesh Hariharan (Microsoft), Kevin Mark Jones (Hewlett Packard), Lawrence Jones, (UGS Corp.), Don Kostuch (Independent Consultant), Xiaolong Li (Indiana State University), William Mike Miller (Edison Design Group, Inc.), Tom Rethard (The University of Texas at Arlington), Benjamin Seyfarth (University of Southern Mississippi), Gary Sibbitts (St. Louis Community College at Meramec), William Smith (Tulsa Community College) and Douglas Walls (Senior Staff Engineer, C compiler, Sun Microsystems).

Well, there you have it! C is a powerful programming language that will help you write high-performance programs quickly and effectively. C scales nicely into the realm of enterprise systems development to help organizations build their business-critical and mission-critical information systems. As you read the book, we would sincerely appreciate your comments, criticisms, corrections and suggestions for improving the text. Please address all correspondence to:

```
deitel@deitel.com
```

We'll respond promptly, and post corrections and clarifications on:

> www.deitel.com/books/chtp7/

We hope you enjoy working with *C How to Program, Seventh Edition* as much as we enjoyed writing it!

Paul Deitel
Harvey Deitel
January 2012

The publishers wish to thank Atriya Sen, of the Indian Statistical Institute, Kolkata, for reviewing the content of the International Edition.

About the Authors

Paul Deitel, CEO and Chief Technical Officer of Deitel & Associates, Inc., is a graduate of MIT, where he studied Information Technology. Through Deitel & Associates, Inc., he has delivered hundreds of programming courses to industry clients, including Cisco, IBM, Siemens, Sun Microsystems, Dell, Lucent Technologies, Fidelity, NASA at the Kennedy Space Center, the National Severe Storm Laboratory, White Sands Missile Range, Rogue Wave Software, Boeing, SunGard Higher Education, Stratus, Cambridge Technology Partners, One Wave, Hyperion Software, Adra Systems, Entergy, CableData Systems, Nortel Networks, Puma, iRobot, Invensys and many more. He and his co-author, Dr. Harvey M. Deitel, are the world's best-selling programming-language textbook/professional book/video authors.

Dr. Harvey Deitel, Chairman and Chief Strategy Officer of Deitel & Associates, Inc., has 50 years of experience in the computer field. Dr. Deitel earned B.S. and M.S. degrees from MIT and a Ph.D. from Boston University. He has extensive college teaching experience, including earning tenure and serving as the Chairman of the Computer Science Department at Boston College before founding Deitel & Associates, Inc., in 1991 with his son, Paul Deitel. The Deitels' publications have earned international recognition, with translations published in Chinese, Korean, Japanese, German, Russian, Spanish, French, Polish, Italian, Portuguese, Greek, Urdu and Turkish. Dr. Deitel has delivered hundreds of professional programming seminars to major corporations, academic institutions, government organizations and the military.

Corporate Training from Deitel & Associates, Inc.

Deitel & Associates, Inc., founded by Paul Deitel and Harvey Deitel, is an internationally recognized authoring, corporate training and software development organization specializing in computer programming languages, object technology, Android and iPhone app development and Internet and web software technology. The company offers instructor-led training courses delivered at client sites worldwide on major programming languages and platforms, including C, C++, Visual C++®, Java™, Visual C#®, Visual Basic®, XML®, Python®, object technology, Internet and web programming, Android app development, Objective-C and iPhone app development and a growing list of additional programming and software development courses. The company's clients include many of the world's largest companies, government agencies, branches of the military, and academic institutions.

Through its 36-year publishing partnership with Prentice Hall/Pearson, Deitel & Associates, Inc., publishes leading-edge programming college textbooks, professional books and *LiveLessons* video courses. Deitel & Associates, Inc. and the authors can be reached at:

```
deitel@deitel.com
```

To learn more about Deitel's *Dive Into Series* Corporate Training curriculum, visit:

```
www.deitel.com/training/
```

To request a proposal for worldwide on-site, instructor-led training at your company or organization, e-mail `deitel@deitel.com`.

Individuals wishing to purchase Deitel books and *LiveLessons* video training can do so through `www.deitel.com`. Bulk orders by corporations, the government, the military and academic institutions should be placed directly with Pearson.

Introduction to Computers, the Internet and the Web

1

Objectives

In this chapter, you'll learn:

- Basic computer concepts.

- The different types of programming languages.

- The history of the C programming language.

- The purpose of the C Standard Library.

- The elements of a typical C program development environment.

- To test-drive a C application in Windows, Linux and Mac OS X.

- Some basics of the Internet and the World Wide Web.

Outline

1.1 Introduction

Welcome to C and C++! C is a concise yet powerful computer programming language that's appropriate for technically oriented people with little or no programming experience and for experienced programmers to use in building substantial software systems. *C How to Program, Seventh Edition*, is an effective learning tool for each of these audiences.

The core of the book emphasizes effective software engineering through the proven methodologies of *structured programming* in C and *object-oriented programming* in C++. The book presents hundreds of *complete working programs* and shows the outputs produced when those programs are run on a computer. We call this the "live-code approach." All of these example programs may be downloaded from our website www.deitel.com/books/chtp7/.

Most people are familiar with the exciting tasks that computers perform. Using this textbook, you'll learn how to command computers to perform those tasks. It's **software** (i.e., the instructions you write to command computers to perform actions and make decisions) that controls computers (often referred to as **hardware**).

1.2 Computers and the Internet in Industry and Research

These are exciting times in the computer field. Many of the most influential and successful businesses of the last two decades are technology companies, including Apple, IBM, Hewlett Packard, Dell, Intel, Motorola, Cisco, Microsoft, Google, Amazon, Facebook, Twitter, Groupon, Foursquare, Yahoo!, eBay and many more. These companies are major employers of people who study computer science, computer engineering, information systems or related disciplines. At the time of this writing, Apple was the most valuable company in the world. Figure 1.1 provides a few examples of the ways in which computers are used in research and industry.

Name	Description
Electronic health records	These might include a patient's medical history, prescriptions, immunizations, lab results, allergies, insurance information and more. Making this information available to health care providers across a secure network improves patient care, reduces the probability of error and increases overall efficiency of the health care system.
Human Genome Project	The Human Genome Project was founded to identify and analyze the 20,000+ genes in human DNA. The project used computer programs to analyze complex genetic data, determine the sequences of the billions of chemical base pairs that make up human DNA and store the information in databases which have been made available over the Internet to researchers in many fields.
AMBER™ Alert	The AMBER (America's Missing: Broadcast Emergency Response) Alert System is used to find abducted children. Law enforcement notifies TV and radio broadcasters and state transportation officials, who then broadcast alerts on TV, radio, computerized highway signs, the Internet and wireless devices. AMBER Alert recently partnered with Facebook, whose users can "Like" AMBER Alert pages by location to receive alerts in their news feeds.
World Community Grid	People worldwide can donate their unused computer processing power by installing a free secure software program that allows the World Community Grid (www.worldcommunitygrid.org) to harness unused capacity. This computing power, accessed over the Internet, is used in place of expensive supercomputers to conduct scientific research projects that are making a difference—providing clean water to third-world countries, fighting cancer, growing more nutritious rice for regions fighting hunger and more.
Medical imaging	X-ray computed tomography (CT) scans, also called CAT (computerized axial tomography) scans, take X-rays of the body from hundreds of different angles. Computers are used to adjust the intensity of the X-rays, optimizing the scan for each type of tissue, then to combine all of the information to create a 3D image. MRI scanners use a technique called magnetic resonance imaging, also to produce internal images non-invasively.
One Laptop Per Child (OLPC)	One Laptop Per Child (one.laptop.org) is providing low-power, inexpensive, Internet-enabled laptops to children in third-world countries—enabling learning and reducing the digital divide.

Fig. 1.1 | A few uses for computers. (Part 1 of 3.)

Name	Description
Cloud computing	Cloud computing allows you to use software, hardware and information stored in the "cloud"—i.e., accessed on remote computers via the Internet and available on demand—rather than having it stored on your personal computer. These services allow you to increase or decrease resources to meet your needs at any given time, so they can be more cost effective than purchasing expensive hardware to ensure that you have enough storage and processing power to meet your needs at their peak levels. Business applications often are expensive, and require significant hardware to run them and knowledgeable support staff to ensure that they're running properly and securely. Using cloud computing services shifts the burden of managing these applications from the business to the service provider, saving businesses money.
GPS	Global Positioning System (GPS) devices use a network of satellites to retrieve location-based information. Multiple satellites send time-stamped signals to the GPS device, which calculates the distance to each satellite based on the time the signal left the satellite and the time the signal arrived. This information is used to determine the exact location of the device. GPS devices can provide step-by-step directions and help you locate nearby businesses (restaurants, gas stations, etc.) and points of interest. GPS is used in numerous location-based Internet services such as check-in apps to help you find your friends (e.g., Foursquare and Facebook), exercise apps such as RunKeeper that track the time, distance and average speed of your outdoor jog, dating apps that help you find a match nearby and apps that dynamically update changing traffic conditions.
Robots	Robots can be used for day-to-day tasks (e.g., iRobot's Roomba vacuuming robot), entertainment (e.g., robotic pets), military combat, deep sea and space exploration (e.g., NASA's Mars rover) and more. RoboEarth (www.roboearth.org) is "a World Wide Web for robots." It allows robots to learn from each other by sharing information and thus improving their abilities to perform tasks, navigate, recognize objects and more.
E-mail, Instant Messaging, Video Chat and FTP	Internet-based servers support all of your online messaging. E-mail messages go through a mail server that also stores the messages. Instant Messaging (IM) and Video Chat apps, such as AIM, Skype, Yahoo! Messenger and others allow you to communicate with others in real time by sending your messages and live video through servers. FTP (file transfer protocol) allows you to exchange files between multiple computers (e.g., a client computer such as your desktop and a file server) over the Internet.
Internet TV	Internet TV set-top boxes (such as Apple TV, Google TV and TiVo) allow you to access an enormous amount of content on demand, such as games, news, movies, television shows and more, and they help ensure that the content is streamed to your TV smoothly.

Fig. 1.1 | A few uses for computers. (Part 2 of 3.)

Name	Description
Game programming	Analysts expect global video game revenues to reach $91 billion by 2015 (www.vg247.com/2009/06/23/global-industry-analysts-predicts-gaming-market-to-reach-91-billion-by-2015/). The most sophisticated games can cost as much as $100 million to develop. Activision's *Call of Duty: Black Ops*—one of the best-selling games of all time—earned $360 million in just one day (www.forbes.com/sites/insertcoin/2011/03/11/call-of-duty-black-ops-now-the-best-selling-video-game-of-all-time/)! Online *social gaming*, which enables users worldwide to compete with one another over the Internet, is growing rapidly. Zynga—creator of popular online games such as *Farmville* and *Mafia Wars*—was founded in 2007 and already has over 200 million monthly users. To accommodate the growth in traffic, Zynga is adding nearly 1,000 servers each week (techcrunch.com/2010/09/22/zynga-moves-1-petabyte-of-data-daily-adds-1000-servers-a-week/)!

Fig. 1.1 | A few uses for computers. (Part 3 of 3.)

1.3 Hardware and Software

In use today are more than a billion general-purpose computers, and billions more *embedded* computers are used in cell phones, smartphones, tablet computers, home appliances, automobiles and more. Computers can perform computations and make logical decisions phenomenally faster than human beings can. Many of today's personal computers can perform billions of calculations in one second—more than a human can perform in a lifetime. *Supercomputers* are already performing *thousands of trillions (quadrillions) of instructions per second!* In 2011, Fujitsu announced that its "K" supercomputer can perform over 10 quadrillion calculations per second (10 *petaflops*)! To put that in perspective, *the K supercomputer can perform in one second more than 1,000,000 calculations for every person on the planet!* And—these "upper limits" are growing quickly!

Computers process data under the control of sequences of instructions called **computer programs**. These programs guide the computer through ordered actions specified by people called computer **programmers**. The programs that run on a computer are referred to as **software**. In this book, you'll learn key programming methodologies that are enhancing programmer productivity, thereby reducing software development costs—*structured programming* (in C) and *object-oriented programming* in C++.

A computer consists of various devices referred to as hardware (e.g., the keyboard, screen, mouse, hard disks, memory, DVD drives and processing units). Computing costs are *dropping dramatically*, owing to rapid developments in hardware and software technologies. Computers that might have filled large rooms and cost millions of dollars decades ago are now inscribed on silicon chips smaller than a fingernail, costing perhaps a few dollars each. Ironically, silicon is one of the most abundant materials—it's an ingredient in common sand. Silicon-chip technology has made computing so economical that computers have become a commodity.

1.3.1 Moore's Law

Every year, you probably expect to pay at least a little more for most products and services. The opposite has been the case in the computer and communications fields, especially with regard to the costs of hardware supporting these technologies. For many decades, hardware costs have fallen rapidly. Every year or two, the capacities of computers have approximately *doubled* inexpensively. This remarkable trend often is called Moore's Law, named for the person who identified it, Gordon Moore, co-founder of Intel—the leading manufacturer of the processors in today's computers and embedded systems. Moore's Law and related observations apply especially to the amount of memory that computers have for programs, the amount of secondary storage (such as disk storage) they have to hold programs and data over longer periods of time, and their processor speeds—the speeds at which computers execute their programs (i.e., do their work). Similar growth hpas occurred in the communications field, in which costs have plummeted as enormous demand for communications bandwidth (i.e., information-carrying capacity) has attracted intense competition. We know of no other fields in which technology improves so quickly and costs fall so rapidly. Such phenomenal improvement is truly fostering the *Information Revolution*.

1.3.2 Computer Organization

Regardless of differences in physical appearance, computers can be envisioned as divided into various **logical units** or sections (Fig. 1.2).

Logical unit	Description
Input unit	This "receiving" section obtains information (data and computer programs) from **input devices** and places it at the disposal of the other units for processing. Most information is entered into computers through keyboards, touch screens and mouse devices. Other forms of input include receiving voice commands, scanning images and barcodes, reading from secondary storage devices (such as hard drives, DVD drives, Blu-ray Disc™ drives and USB flash drives—also called "thumb drives" or "memory sticks"), receiving video from a webcam and having your computer receive information from the Internet (such as when you download videos from YouTube™ or e-books from Amazon). Newer forms of input include position data from a GPS device, and motion and orientation information from an accelerometer in a smartphone or game controller (such as Microsoft® Kinect™, Wii™ Remote and PlayStation® Move).
Output unit	This "shipping" section takes information that the computer has processed and places it on various **output devices** to make it available for use outside the computer. Most information that's output from computers today is displayed on screens, printed on paper, played as audio or video on PCs and media players (such as Apple's popular iPods) and giant screens in sports stadiums, transmitted over the Internet or used to control other devices, such as robots and "intelligent" appliances.

Fig. 1.2 | Logical units of a computer. (Part 1 of 2.)

Logical unit	Description
Memory unit	This rapid-access, relatively low-capacity "warehouse" section retains information that has been entered through the input unit, making it immediately available for processing when needed. The memory unit also retains processed information until it can be placed on output devices by the output unit. Information in the memory unit is *volatile*—it's typically lost when the computer's power is turned off. The memory unit is often called either **memory** or **primary memory**. Typical main memories on desktop and notebook computers contain between 1 and 8 GB (GB stands for gigabytes; a gigabyte is approximately one billion bytes).
Arithmetic and logic unit (ALU)	This "manufacturing" section performs *calculations*, such as addition, subtraction, multiplication and division. It also contains the *decision* mechanisms that allow the computer, for example, to compare two items from the memory unit to determine whether they're equal. In today's systems, the ALU is usually implemented as part of the next logical unit, the CPU.
Central processing unit (CPU)	This "administrative" section coordinates and supervises the operation of the other sections. The CPU tells the input unit when information should be read into the memory unit, tells the ALU when information from the memory unit should be used in calculations and tells the output unit when to send information from the memory unit to certain output devices. Many of today's computers have multiple CPUs and, hence, can perform many operations simultaneously. A **multi-core processor** implements multiple processors on a single integrated-circuit chip—a *dual-core processor* has two CPUs and a *quad-core processor* has four CPUs. Today's desktop computers have processors that can execute billions of instructions per second.
Secondary storage unit	This is the long-term, high-capacity "warehousing" section. Programs or data not actively being used by the other units normally are placed on secondary storage devices (e.g., your *hard drive*) until they're again needed, possibly hours, days, months or even years later. Information on secondary storage devices is *persistent*—it's preserved even when the computer's power is turned off. Secondary storage information takes much longer to access than information in primary memory, but the cost per unit of secondary storage is much less than that of primary memory. Examples of secondary storage devices include CD drives, DVD drives and flash drives, some of which can hold up to 512 GB. Typical hard drives on desktop and notebook computers can hold up to 2 TB (TB stands for terabytes; a terabyte is approximately one trillion bytes).

Fig. 1.2 | Logical units of a computer. (Part 2 of 2.)

1.4 Data Hierarchy

Data items processed by computers form a **data hierarchy** that becomes larger and more complex in structure as we progress from bits to characters to fields, and so on. Figure 1.3

illustrates a portion of the data hierarchy. Figure 1.4 summarizes the data hierarchy's levels.

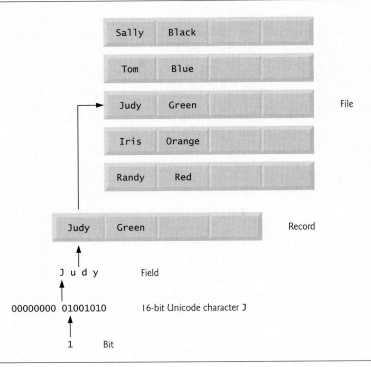

Fig. 1.3 | Data hierarchy.

Level	Description
Bits	The smallest data item in a computer can assume the value 0 or the value 1. Such a data item is called a bit (short for "binary digit"—a digit that can assume one of two values). It's remarkable that the impressive functions performed by computers involve only the simplest manipulations of 0s and 1s—*examining a bit's value, setting a bit's value* and *reversing a bit's value* (from 1 to 0 or from 0 to 1).
Characters	It's tedious for people to work with data in the low-level form of bits. Instead, they prefer to work with *decimal digits* (0–9), *letters* (A–Z and a–z), and *special symbols* (e.g., $, @, %, &, *, (,), –, +, ", :, ? and /). Digits, letters and special symbols are known as characters. The computer's character set is the set of all the characters used to write programs and represent data items. Computers process only 1s and 0s, so every character is represented as a pattern of 1s and 0s. The Unicode character set contains characters for many of the world's languages. C supports several character sets, including 16-bit Unicode® characters

Fig. 1.4 | Levels of the data hierarchy. (Part 1 of 2.)

Level	Description
Characters (cont.)	that are composed of two bytes, each composed of eight bits. See Appendix B for more information on the ASCII (American Standard Code for Information Interchange) character set—the popular subset of Unicode that represents uppercase and lowercase letters, digits and some common special characters.
Fields	Just as characters are composed of bits, fields are composed of characters or bytes. A field is a group of characters or bytes that conveys meaning. For example, a field consisting of uppercase and lowercase letters could be used to represent a person's name, and a field consisting of decimal digits could represent a person's age.
Records	Several related fields can be used to compose a record. In a payroll system, for example, the record for an employee might consist of the following fields (possible types for these fields are shown in parentheses): • Employee identification number (a whole number) • Name (a string of characters) • Address (a string of characters) • Hourly pay rate (a number with a decimal point) • Year-to-date earnings (a number with a decimal point) • Amount of taxes withheld (a number with a decimal point) Thus, a record is a group of related fields. In the preceding example, all the fields belong to the same employee. A company might have many employees and a payroll record for each one.
Files	A file is a group of related records. [*Note:* More generally, a file contains arbitrary data in arbitrary formats. In some operating systems, a file is viewed simply as a *sequence of bytes*—any organization of the bytes in a file, such as organizing the data into records, is a view created by the application programmer.] It's not unusual for an organization to have many files, some containing billions, or even trillions, of characters of information.
Database	A database is an electronic collection of data that's organized for easy access and manipulation. The most popular database model is the relational database in which data is stored in simple *tables*. A table includes *records* and *fields*. For example, a table of students might include first name, last name, major, year, student ID number and grade point average. The data for each student is a record, and the individual pieces of information in each record are the fields. You can search, sort and manipulate the data based on its relationship to multiple tables or databases. For example, a university might use data from the student database in combination with databases of courses, on-campus housing, meal plans, etc.

Fig. 1.4 | Levels of the data hierarchy. (Part 2 of 2.)

1.5 Programming Languages

Programmers write instructions in various programming languages, some directly understandable by computers and others requiring intermediate *translation* steps.

Machine Languages

Any computer can directly understand only its own **machine language**, defined by its hardware architecture. Machine languages generally consist of numbers (ultimately reduced to 1s and 0s). Such languages are cumbersome for humans.

Assembly Languages

Programming in machine language was simply too slow and tedious for most programmers. Instead, they began using Englishlike *abbreviations* to represent elementary operations. These abbreviations formed the basis of **assembly languages**. *Translator programs* called **assemblers** were developed to convert assembly-language programs to machine language. Although assembly-language code is clearer to humans, it's incomprehensible to computers until translated to machine language.

High-Level Languages

To speed the programming process even further, **high-level languages** were developed in which single statements could be written to accomplish substantial tasks. High-level languages allow you to write instructions that look almost like everyday English and contain commonly used mathematical expressions. Translator programs called **compilers** convert high-level language programs into machine language.

The process of compiling a large high-level language program into machine language can take a considerable amount of computer time. **Interpreter** programs were developed to execute high-level language programs directly (without the need for compilation), although more slowly than compiled programs. **Scripting languages** such as JavaScript and PHP are processed by interpreters.

Performance Tip 1.1

Interpreters have an advantage over compilers in Internet scripting. An interpreted program can begin executing as soon as it's downloaded to the client's machine, without needing to be compiled before it can execute. On the downside, interpreted scripts generally run slower than compiled code.

1.6 The C Programming Language

C evolved from two previous languages, BCPL and B. BCPL was developed in 1967 by Martin Richards as a language for writing operating systems and compilers. Ken Thompson modeled many features in his B language after their counterparts in BCPL, and in 1970 he used B to create early versions of the UNIX operating system at Bell Laboratories.

The C language was evolved from B by Dennis Ritchie at Bell Laboratories and was originally implemented in 1972. C initially became widely known as the development language of the UNIX operating system. Many of today's leading operating systems are written in C and/or C++. C is mostly hardware independent—with careful design, it's possible to write C programs that are **portable** to most computers.

Built for Performance

C is widely used to develop systems that demand performance, such as operating systems, embedded systems, real-time systems and communications systems (Figure 1.5).

Application	Description
Operating systems	C's portability and performance make it desirable for implementing operating systems, such as Linux and portions of Microsoft's Windows and Google's Android. Apple's OS X is built in Objective-C, which was derived from C. We discuss some key popular desktop/notebook operating systems and mobile operating systems in Section 1.12.
Embedded systems	The vast majority of the microprocessors produced each year are embedded in devices other than general-purpose computers. These embedded systems include navigation systems, smart home appliances, home security systems, smartphones, robots, intelligent traffic intersections and more. C is one of the most popular programming languages for developing embedded systems, which typically need to run as fast as possible and conserve memory. For example, a car's anti-lock brakes must respond immediately to slow or stop the car without skidding; game controllers used for video games should respond instantaneously to prevent any lag between the controller and the action in the game, and to ensure smooth animations.
Real-time systems	Real-time systems are often used for "mission-critical" applications that require nearly instantaneous response times. For example, an air-traffic-control system must constantly monitor the positions and velocities of the planes and report that information to air-traffic controllers without delay so that they can alert the planes to change course if there's a possibility of a collision.
Communications systems	Communications systems need to route massive amounts of data to their destinations quickly to ensure that things such as audio and video are delivered smoothly and without delay.

Fig. 1.5 | Some popular performance-oriented C applications.

By the late 1970s, C had evolved into what's now referred to as "traditional C." The publication in 1978 of Kernighan and Ritchie's book, *The C Programming Language,* drew wide attention to the language. This became one of the most successful computer science books of all time.

Standardization
The rapid expansion of C over various types of computers (sometimes called hardware platforms) led to many variations that were similar but often incompatible. This was a serious problem for programmers who needed to develop code that would run on several

platforms. It became clear that a standard version of C was needed. In 1983, the X3J11 technical committee was created under the American National Standards Committee on Computers and Information Processing (X3) to "provide an unambiguous and machine-independent definition of the language." In 1989, the standard was approved as ANSI X3.159-1989 in the United States through the **American National Standards Institute (ANSI)**, then worldwide through the **International Standards Organization (ISO)**. We call this simply Standard C. This standard was updated in 1999—its standards document is referred to as *INCITS/ISO/IEC 9899-1999* and often referred to simply as C99. Copies may be ordered from the American National Standards Institute (www.ansi.org) at web-store.ansi.org/ansidocstore.

The New C Standard

We also introduce the new C standard (referred to as C11), which was approved as this book went to publication. The new standard refines and expands the capabilities of C. Not all popular C compilers support the new features. Of those that do, most implement only a subset of the new features. We've integrated into the text (and appendices) in easy-to-include-or-omit sections many of the new features implemented in leading compilers.

Portability Tip 1.1

Because C is a hardware-independent, widely available language, applications written in C often can run with little or no modification on a range of different computer systems.

1.7 C Standard Library

As you'll learn in Chapter 5, C programs consist of pieces called functions. You can program all the functions that you need to form a C program, but most C programmers take advantage of the rich collection of existing functions called the C Standard Library. Thus, there are really two parts to learning how to program in C—learning the C language itself and learning how to use the functions in the C Standard Library. Throughout the book, we discuss many of these functions. P. J. Plauger's book *The Standard C Library* is must reading for programmers who need a deep understanding of the library functions, how to implement them and how to use them to write portable code. We use and explain many C library functions throughout this text. Visit the following website for the C Standard Library documentation:

```
www.dinkumware.com/manuals/#Standard%20C%20Library
```

C How to Program, 7/e encourages a *building-block approach* to creating programs. Avoid "reinventing the wheel." Instead, use existing pieces—this is called software reuse. When programming in C you'll typically use the following building blocks:

- C Standard Library functions
- Functions you create yourself
- Functions other people (whom you trust) have created and made available to you

The advantage of creating your own functions is that you'll know exactly how they work. You'll be able to examine the C code. The disadvantage is the time-consuming effort that goes into designing, developing and debugging new functions.

Performance Tip 1.2

Using Standard C library functions instead of writing your own comparable versions can improve program performance, because these functions are carefully written to perform efficiently.

Portability Tip 1.2

Using Standard C library functions instead of writing your own comparable versions can improve program portability, because these functions are used in virtually all Standard C implementations.

1.8 C++ and Other C-Based Languages

C++ was developed by Bjarne Stroustrup at Bell Laboratories. It has its roots in C, providing a number of features that "spruce up" the C language. More important, it provides capabilities for **object-oriented programming**. **Objects** are essentially reusable software **components** that model items in the real world. Using a modular, object-oriented design and implementation approach can make software development groups more productive.

Chapters 15–24 present a condensed treatment of C++ selected from our book *C++ How to Program, 8/e*. As you study C++, check out our online C++ Resource Center at www.deitel.com/cplusplus/. Figure 1.6 introduces several other popular C-based programming languages.

Programming language	Description
Objective-C	Objective-C is an object-oriented language based on C. It was developed in the early 1980s and later acquired by NeXT, which in turn was acquired by Apple. It has become the key programming language for the Mac OS X operating system and all iOS-based devices (such as iPods, iPhones and iPads).
Visual C#	Microsoft's three primary object-oriented programming languages are Visual Basic, Visual C++ (based on C++) and C# (based on C++ and Java, and developed for integrating the Internet and the web into computer applications).
Java	Sun Microsystems in 1991 funded an internal corporate research project which resulted in the C++-based object-oriented programming language called Java. A key goal of Java is to enable the writing of programs that will run on a broad variety of computer systems and computer-controlled devices. This is sometimes called "write once, run anywhere." Java is used to develop large-scale enterprise applications, to enhance the functionality of web servers (the computers that provide the content we see in our web browsers), to provide applications for consumer devices (smartphones, television set-top boxes and more) and for many other purposes.

Fig. 1.6 | Popular C-based programming languages. (Part 1 of 2.)

Programming language	Description
PHP	PHP—an object-oriented, open-source (see Section 1.12) scripting language based on C and supported by a community of users and developers—is used by many websites including Wikipedia and Facebook. PHP is *platform independent*—implementations exist for all major UNIX, Linux, Mac and Windows operating systems. PHP also supports many databases, including MySQL. Other languages similar in concept to PHP are Perl and Python.
JavaScript	JavaScript—developed by Netscape—is the most widely used scripting language. It's primarily used to add programmability to web pages—for example, animations and interactivity with the user. It's provided with all major web browsers.

Fig. 1.6 | Popular C-based programming languages. (Part 2 of 2.)

1.9 Object Technology

Building software quickly, correctly and economically remains an elusive goal at a time when demands for new and more powerful software are soaring. *Objects*, or more precisely the *classes* objects come from, are essentially *reusable* software components. There are date objects, time objects, audio objects, video objects, automobile objects, people objects, etc. Almost any *noun* can be reasonably represented as a software object in terms of *attributes* (e.g., name, color and size) and *behaviors* (e.g., calculating, moving and communicating). Software developers are discovering that using a modular, object-oriented design-and-implementation approach can make software-development groups much more productive than was possible with earlier techniques—object-oriented programs are often easier to understand, correct and modify.

The Automobile as an Object
Let's begin with a simple analogy. Suppose you want to *drive a car and make it go faster by pressing its accelerator pedal*. What must happen before you can do this? Well, before you can drive a car, someone has to *design* it. A car typically begins as engineering drawings, similar to the *blueprints* that describe the design of a house. These drawings include the design for an accelerator pedal. The pedal *hides* from the driver the complex mechanisms that actually make the car go faster, just as the brake pedal hides the mechanisms that slow the car, and the steering wheel *hides* the mechanisms that turn the car. This enables people with little or no knowledge of how engines, braking and steering mechanisms work to drive a car easily.

Before you can drive a car, it must be *built* from the engineering drawings that describe it. A completed car has an *actual* accelerator pedal to make the car go faster, but even that's not enough—the car won't accelerate on its own (hopefully!), so the driver must *press* the pedal to accelerate the car.

Methods and Classes
Let's use our car example to introduce some key object-oriented programming concepts. Performing a task in a program requires a **method**. The method houses the program state-

ments that actually perform its tasks. It hides these statements from its user, just as a car's accelerator pedal hides from the driver the mechanisms of making the car go faster. In object-oriented programming languages, we create a program unit called a **class** to house the set of methods that perform the class's tasks. For example, a class that represents a bank account might contain one method to *deposit* money to an account, another to *withdraw* money from an account and a third to *inquire* what the account's current balance is. A class is similar in concept to a car's engineering drawings, which house the design of an accelerator pedal, steering wheel, and so on.

Instantiation

Just as someone has to *build a car* from its engineering drawings before you can actually drive a car, you must *build an object* from a class before a program can perform the tasks that the class's methods define. The process of doing this is called *instantiation*. An object is then referred to as an **instance** of its class.

Reuse

Just as a car's engineering drawings can be *reused* many times to build many cars, you can *reuse* a class many times to build many objects. Reuse of existing classes when building new classes and programs saves time and effort. Reuse also helps you build more reliable and effective systems, because existing classes and components often have gone through extensive *testing*, *debugging* and *performance tuning*. Just as the notion of *interchangeable parts* was crucial to the Industrial Revolution, reusable classes are crucial to the software revolution that has been spurred by object technology.

Messages and Method Calls

When you drive a car, pressing its gas pedal sends a *message* to the car to perform a task—that is, to go faster. Similarly, you *send messages to an object*. Each message is implemented as a **method call** that tells a method of the object to perform its task. For example, a program might call a particular bank-account object's *deposit* method to increase the account's balance.

Attributes and Instance Variables

A car, besides having capabilities to accomplish tasks, also has *attributes*, such as its color, its number of doors, the amount of gas in its tank, its current speed and its record of total miles driven (i.e., its odometer reading). Like its capabilities, the car's attributes are represented as part of its design in its engineering diagrams (which, for example, include an odometer and a fuel gauge). As you drive an actual car, these attributes are carried along with the car. Every car maintains its *own* attributes. For example, each car knows how much gas is in its own gas tank, but *not* how much is in the tanks of *other* cars.

An object, similarly, has attributes that it carries along as it's used in a program. These attributes are specified as part of the object's class. For example, a bank-account object has a *balance attribute* that represents the amount of money in the account. Each bank-account object knows the balance in the account it represents, but *not* the balances of the *other* accounts in the bank. Attributes are specified by the class's **instance variables**.

Encapsulation

Classes **encapsulate** (i.e., wrap) attributes and methods into objects—an object's attributes and methods are intimately related. Objects may communicate with one another, but normally they're not allowed to know how other objects are implemented—implementation details are *hidden* within the objects themselves. This **information hiding** is crucial to good software engineering.

Inheritance

A new class of objects can be created quickly and conveniently by **inheritance**—the new class absorbs the characteristics of an existing class, possibly customizing them and adding unique characteristics of its own. In our car analogy, an object of class "convertible" certainly *is an* object of the more *general* class "automobile," but more *specifically*, the roof can be raised or lowered.

1.10 Typical C Program Development Environment

C systems generally consist of several parts: a program development environment, the language and the C Standard Library. The following discussion explains the typical C development environment shown in Fig. 1.7.

C programs typically go through six phases to be executed (Fig. 1.7). These are: **edit, preprocess, compile, link, load** and **execute**. Although *C How to Program, Seventh Edition* is a generic C textbook (written independently of the details of any particular operating system), we concentrate in this section on a typical Linux-based C system. [*Note:* The programs in this book will run with little or no modification on most current C systems, including Microsoft Windows-based systems.] If you're not using a Linux system, refer to the documentation for your system or ask your instructor how to accomplish these tasks in your environment. Check out our C Resource Center at `www.deitel.com/C` to locate "getting started" tutorials for popular C compilers and development environments.

1.10.1 Phase 1: Creating a Program

Phase 1 consists of editing a file. This is accomplished with an **editor program**. Two editors widely used on Linux systems are `vi` and `emacs`. Software packages for the C/C++ integrated program development environments such as Eclipse and Microsoft Visual Studio have editors that are integrated into the programming environment. You type a C program with the editor, make corrections if necessary, then store the program on a secondary storage device such as a hard disk. C program file names should end with the `.c` extension.

1.10.2 Phases 2 and 3: Preprocessing and Compiling a C Program

In Phase 2, the you give the command to **compile** the program. The compiler translates the C program into machine language-code (also referred to as **object code**). In a C system, a **preprocessor** program executes automatically before the compiler's translation phase begins. The C preprocessor obeys special commands called **preprocessor directives**, which indicate that certain manipulations are to be performed on the program before compilation. These manipulations usually consist of including other files in the file to be compiled and performing various text replacements. The most common preprocessor directives are discussed in the early chapters; a detailed discussion of preprocessor features appears in Chapter 13.

In Phase 3, the compiler translates the C program into machine-language code. A **syntax error** occurs when the compiler cannot recognize a statement because it violates the

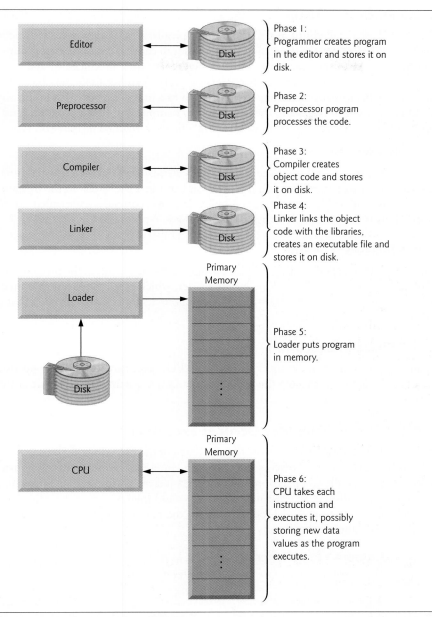

Fig. 1.7 | Typical C development environment.

rules of the language. The compiler issues an error message to help you locate and fix the incorrect statement. The C Standard does not specify the wording for error messages issued by the compiler, so the error messages you see on your system may differ from those on other systems. Syntax errors are also called **compile errors**, or **compile-time errors**.

1.10.3 Phase 4: Linking

The next phase is called **linking**. C programs typically contain references to functions defined elsewhere, such as in the standard libraries or in the private libraries of groups of programmers working on a particular project. The object code produced by the C compiler typically contains "holes" due to these missing parts. A linker links the object code with the code for the missing functions to produce an **executable image** (with no missing pieces). On a typical Linux system, the command to compile and link a program is called **gcc** (the GNU C compiler). To compile and link a program named welcome.c, type

```
gcc welcome.c
```

at the Linux prompt and press the *Enter* key (or *Return* key). [*Note:* Linux commands are case sensitive; make sure that each c is lowercase and that the letters in the filename are in the appropriate case.] If the program compiles and links correctly, a file called a.out is produced. This is the executable image of our welcome.c program.

1.10.4 Phase 5: Loading

The next phase is called **loading**. Before a program can be executed, the program must first be placed in memory. This is done by the **loader**, which takes the executable image from disk and transfers it to memory. Additional components from shared libraries that support the program are also loaded.

1.10.5 Phase 6: Execution

Finally, the computer, under the control of its CPU, **executes** the program one instruction at a time. To load and execute the program on a Linux system, type ./a.out at the Linux prompt and press *Enter*.

1.10.6 Problems That May Occur at Execution Time

Programs do not always work on the first try. Each of the preceding phases can fail because of various errors that we'll discuss. For example, an executing program might attempt to divide by zero (an illegal operation on computers just as in arithmetic). This would cause the computer to display an error message. You would then return to the edit phase, make the necessary corrections and proceed through the remaining phases again to determine that the corrections work properly.

> **Common Programming Error 1.1**
>
> *Errors such as division-by-zero occur as a program runs, so they are called runtime errors or execution-time errors. Divide-by-zero is generally a fatal error, i.e., one that causes the program to terminate immediately without successfully performing its job. Nonfatal errors allow programs to run to completion, often producing incorrect results.*

1.10.7 Standard Input, Standard Output and Standard Error Streams

Most C programs input and/or output data. Certain C functions take their input from **stdin** (the **standard input stream**), which is normally the keyboard, but stdin can be connected to another stream. Data is often output to **stdout** (the **standard output stream**), which is normally the computer screen, but stdout can be connected to another stream.

When we say that a program prints a result, we normally mean that the result is displayed on a screen. Data may be output to devices such as disks and printers. There's also a **standard error stream** referred to as `stderr`. The `stderr` stream (normally connected to the screen) is used for displaying error messages. It's common to route regular output data, i.e., `stdout`, to a device other than the screen while keeping `stderr` assigned to the screen so that the user can be immediately informed of errors.

1.11 Test-Driving a C Application in Windows, Linux and Mac OS X

In this section, you'll run and interact with your first C application. You'll begin by running a guess-the-number game, which randomly picks a number from 1 to 1000 and prompts you to guess it. If your guess is correct, the game ends. If your guess is not correct, the application indicates whether your guess is higher or lower than the correct number. There's no limit on the number of guesses you can make but you should be able to guess any of the numbers in this range correctly in 10 or fewer tries. There's some nice computer science behind this game—in Section 6.8, Searching Arrays, you'll explore the *binary search* technique.

For this test-drive only, we've modified this application from the exercise you'll be asked to create in Chapter 5. Normally this application *randomly* selects the correct answers. The modified application uses the same sequence of correct answers every time you execute the program (though this may vary by compiler), so you can use the same guesses we use in this section and see the same results.

We'll demonstrate running a C application using the Windows **Command Prompt**, a shell on Linux and a **Terminal** window in Mac OS X. The application runs similarly on all three platforms. After you perform the test drive for your platform, you can try the *randomized* version of the game, which we've provided with each test drive's version of the example in a subfolder named `randomized_version`.

Many development environments are available in which you can compile, build and run C applications, such as GNU C, Dev C++, Microsoft Visual C++, CodeLite, Net-Beans, Eclipse, Xcode, etc. Consult your instructor for information on your specific development environment. Most C++ development environments can compile both C and C++ programs.

In the following steps, you'll run the application and enter various numbers to guess the correct number. The elements and functionality that you see in this application are typical of those you'll learn to program in this book. We use fonts to distinguish between features you see on the screen (e.g., the **Command Prompt**) and elements that are not directly related to the screen. We emphasize screen features like titles and menus (e.g., the **File** menu) in a semibold **sans-serif Helvetica** font, and to emphasize filenames, text displayed by an application and values you should enter into an application (e.g., `GuessNumber` or `500`) we use a sans-serif `Lucida` font. As you've noticed, the **defining** occurrence of each key term is set in **bold blue type**. For the Windows version of the test drive in this section, we've modified the background color of the **Command Prompt** window to make the **Command Prompt** windows more readable. To modify the **Command Prompt** colors on your system, open a **Command Prompt** by selecting **Start > All Programs > Accessories > Command Prompt**, then right click the title bar and select **Properties**. In the **"Command Prompt" Properties** dialog box that appears, click the **Colors** tab, and select your preferred text and background colors.

1.11.1 Running a C Application from the Windows Command Prompt

1. *Checking your setup.* It's important to read the Before You Begin section at www.deitel.com/books/chtp7/ to make sure that you've copied the book's examples to your hard drive correctly.

2. *Locating the completed application.* Open a **Command Prompt** window. To change to the directory for the completed **GuessNumber** application, type cd C:\examples\ch01\GuessNumber\Windows, then press *Enter* (Fig. 1.8). The command cd is used to change directories.

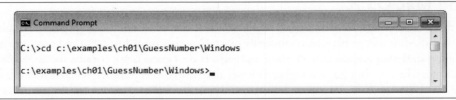

Fig. 1.8 | Opening a **Command Prompt** window and changing the directory.

3. *Running the GuessNumber application.* Now that you are in the directory that contains the **GuessNumber** application, type the command GuessNumber (Fig. 1.9) and press *Enter*. [*Note:* GuessNumber.exe is the actual name of the application; however, Windows assumes the .exe extension by default.]

Fig. 1.9 | Running the **GuessNumber** application.

4. *Entering your first guess.* The application displays "Please type your first guess.", then displays a question mark (?) as a prompt on the next line (Fig. 1.9). At the prompt, enter 500 (Fig. 1.10).

Fig. 1.10 | Entering your first guess.

5. *Entering another guess.* The application displays "Too high. Try again.", meaning that the value you entered is greater than the number the application chose as

the correct guess. So, you should enter a lower number for your next guess. At the prompt, enter 250 (Fig. 1.11). The application again displays "Too high. Try again.", because the value you entered is still greater than the number that the application chose.

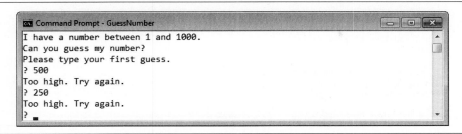

Fig. 1.11 | Entering a second guess and receiving feedback.

6. ***Entering additional guesses.*** Continue to play the game by entering values until you guess the correct number. The application will display "Excellent! You guessed the number!" (Fig. 1.12).

7. ***Playing the game again or exiting the application.*** After you guess correctly, the application asks if you'd like to play another game (Fig. 1.12). At the prompt, entering 1 causes the application to choose a new number and displays the message "Please type your first guess." followed by a question-mark prompt (Fig. 1.13), so you can make your first guess in the new game. Entering 2 ends the application and returns you to the application's directory at the **Command Prompt**

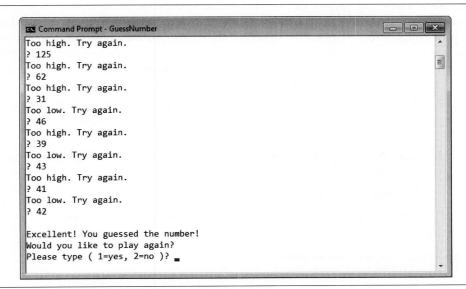

Fig. 1.12 | Entering additional guesses and guessing the correct number.

(Fig. 1.14). Each time you execute this application from the beginning (i.e., *Step 3*), it will choose the same numbers for you to guess.

8. *Close the Command Prompt window.*

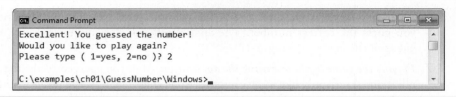

```
Command Prompt - GuessNumber
Excellent! You guessed the number!
Would you like to play again?
Please type ( 1=yes, 2=no )? 1

I have a number between 1 and 1000.
Can you guess my number?
Please type your first guess.
?
```

Fig. 1.13 | Playing the game again.

```
Command Prompt
Excellent! You guessed the number!
Would you like to play again?
Please type ( 1=yes, 2=no )? 2

C:\examples\ch01\GuessNumber\Windows>
```

Fig. 1.14 | Exiting the game.

1.11.2 Running a C Application Using GNU C with Linux

For this test drive, we assume that you know how to copy the examples into your home directory. Please see your instructor if you have any questions regarding copying the files to your Linux system. Also, for the figures in this section, we use a bold font to point out the user input required by each step. The prompt in the shell on our system uses the tilde (~) character to represent the home directory, and each prompt ends with the dollar-sign ($) character. The prompt will vary among Linux systems.

1. **Checking your setup.** It's important to read the Before You Begin section at www.deitel.com/books/chtp7/ to make sure that you've copied the book's examples to your hard drive correctly.

2. **Locating the completed application.** From a Linux shell, change to the completed **GuessNumber** application directory (Fig. 1.15) by typing

   ```
   cd examples/ch01/GuessNumber/GNU
   ```

   then pressing *Enter*. The command cd is used to change directories.

```
~$ cd examples/ch01/GuessNumber/GNU
~/examples/ch01/GuessNumber/GNU$
```

Fig. 1.15 | Changing to the **GuessNumber** application's directory.

3. *Compiling the GuessNumber application.* To run an application on the GNU C++ compiler, you must first compile it by typing

```
gcc GuessNumber.c -o GuessNumber
```

as in Fig. 1.16. This command compiles the application and produces an executable file called GuessNumber.

```
~/examples/ch01/GuessNumber/GNU$ gcc GuessNumber.c -o GuessNumber
~/examples/ch01/GuessNumber/GNU$
```

Fig. 1.16 | Compiling the **GuessNumber** application using the gcc command.

4. *Running the GuessNumber application.* To run the executable file GuessNumber, type ./GuessNumber at the next prompt, then press *Enter* (Fig. 1.17).

```
~/examples/ch01/GuessNumber/GNU$ ./GuessNumber

I have a number between 1 and 1000.
Can you guess my number?
Please type your first guess.
?
```

Fig. 1.17 | Running the **GuessNumber** application.

5. *Entering your first guess.* The application displays "Please type your first guess.", then displays a question mark (?) as a prompt on the next line (Fig. 1.17). At the prompt, enter 500 (Fig. 1.18).

```
~/examples/ch01/GuessNumber/GNU$ ./GuessNumber

I have a number between 1 and 1000.
Can you guess my number?
Please type your first guess.
? 500
Too high. Try again.
?
```

Fig. 1.18 | Entering an initial guess.

6. *Entering another guess.* The application displays "Too high. Try again.", meaning that the value you entered is greater than the number the application chose as the correct guess (Fig. 1.18). At the next prompt, enter 250 (Fig. 1.19). This time the application displays "Too low. Try again.", because the value you entered is less than the correct guess.

7. *Entering additional guesses.* Continue to play the game (Fig. 1.20) by entering values until you guess the correct number. When you guess correctly, the application displays "Excellent! You guessed the number!"

```
~/examples/ch01/GuessNumber/GNU$ ./GuessNumber

I have a number between 1 and 1000.
Can you guess my number?
Please type your first guess.
? 500
Too high. Try again.
? 250
Too low. Try again.
?
```

Fig. 1.19 | Entering a second guess and receiving feedback.

```
Too low. Try again.
? 375
Too low. Try again.
? 437
Too high. Try again.
? 406
Too high. Try again.
? 391
Too high. Try again.
? 383
Too low. Try again.
? 387
Too high. Try again.
? 385
Too high. Try again.
? 384

Excellent! You guessed the number!
Would you like to play again?
Please type ( 1=yes, 2=no )?
```

Fig. 1.20 | Entering additional guesses and guessing the correct number.

8. ***Playing the game again or exiting the application.*** After you guess the correct number, the application asks if you'd like to play another game. At the prompt, entering 1 causes the application to choose a new number and displays the message "Please type your first guess." followed by a question-mark prompt (Fig. 1.21) so that you can make your first guess in the new game. Entering 2 ends the application and returns you to the application's directory in the shell (Fig. 1.22). Each time you execute this application from the beginning (i.e., *Step 4*), it will choose the same numbers for you to guess.

```
Excellent! You guessed the number!
Would you like to play again?
Please type ( 1=yes, 2=no )? 1

I have a number between 1 and 1000.
Can you guess my number?
Please type your first guess.
?
```

Fig. 1.21 | Playing the game again.

```
Excellent! You guessed the number!
Would you like to play again?
Please type ( 1=yes, 2=no )? 2

~/examples/ch01/GuessNumber/GNU$
```

Fig. 1.22 | Exiting the game.

1.11.3 Running a C Application Using GNU C with Mac OS X

For the figures in this section, we use a bold font to point out the user input required by each step. You'll use Mac OS X's **Terminal** window to perform this test dive. To open a **Terminal** window, click the Spotlight Search icon in the upper-right corner of your screen, then type Terminal to locate the **Terminal** application. Under **Applications** in the Spotlight Search results, select **Terminal** to open a **Terminal** window. The prompt in a **Terminal** window has the form *hostName*:~ *userFolder*$ to represent your user directory. For the figures in this section we remove the *hostName*: part and used the generic name userFolder to represent your user account's folder.

1. *Checking your setup.* It's important to read the Before You Begin section at www.deitel.com/books/chtp7/ to make sure that you've copied the book's examples to your hard drive correctly. We assume that the examples are located in your user account's Documents/examples folder.

2. *Locating the completed application.* In the **Terminal** window, change to the completed **GuessNumber** application directory (Fig. 1.23) by typing

   ```
   cd Documents/examples/ch01/GuessNumber/GNU
   ```

   then pressing *Enter*. The command cd is used to change directories.

```
hostName:~ userFolder$ cd Documents/examples/ch01/GuessNumber/GNU
hostName:GNU$
```

Fig. 1.23 | Changing to the **GuessNumber** application's directory.

3. *Compiling the GuessNumber application.* To run an application on the GNU C compiler, you must first compile it by typing

   ```
   gcc GuessNumber.c -o GuessNumber
   ```

   as in Fig. 1.24. This command compiles the application and produces an executable file called GuessNumber.

```
hostName:GNU~ userFolder$ gcc GuessNumber.c -o GuessNumber
hostName:GNU~ userFolder$
```

Fig. 1.24 | Compiling the **GuessNumber** application using the gcc command.

4. *Running the GuessNumber application.* To run the executable file GuessNumber, type ./GuessNumber at the next prompt, then press *Enter* (Fig. 1.25).

```
hostName:GNU~ userFolder$ ./GuessNumber

I have a number between 1 and 1000.
Can you guess my number?
Please type your first guess.
?
```

Fig. 1.25 | Running the **GuessNumber** application.

5. *Entering your first guess.* The application displays "Please type your first guess.", then displays a question mark (?) as a prompt on the next line (Fig. 1.25). At the prompt, enter 500 (Fig. 1.26).

```
hostName:GNU~ userFolder$ ./GuessNumber

I have a number between 1 and 1000.
Can you guess my number?
Please type your first guess.
? 500
Too low. Try again.
?
```

Fig. 1.26 | Entering an initial guess.

6. *Entering another guess.* The application displays "Too low. Try again." (Fig. 1.26), meaning that the value you entered is greater than the number the application chose as the correct guess. At the next prompt, enter 750 (Fig. 1.27). Again the application displays "Too low. Try again.", because the value you entered is less than the correct guess.

```
hostName:GNU~ userFolder$ ./GuessNumber

I have a number between 1 and 1000.
Can you guess my number?
Please type your first guess.
? 500
Too low. Try again.
? 750
Too low. Try again.
?
```

Fig. 1.27 | Entering a second guess and receiving feedback.

7. *Entering additional guesses.* Continue to play the game (Fig. 1.28) by entering values until you guess the correct number. When you guess correctly, the application displays "Excellent! You guessed the number!"

8. *Playing the game again or exiting the application.* After you guess the correct number, the application asks if you'd like to play another game. At the prompt,

```
Too low. Try again.
? 825
Too high. Try again.
? 788
Too low. Try again.
? 806
Too low. Try again.
? 815
Too high. Try again.
? 811
Too high. Try again.
? 808

Excellent! You guessed the number!
Would you like to play again?
Please type ( 1=yes, 2=no )?
```

Fig. 1.28 | Entering additional guesses and guessing the correct number.

entering 1 causes the application to choose a new number and displays the message "`Please type your first guess.`" followed by a question-mark prompt (Fig. 1.29) so you can make your first guess in the new game. Entering 2 ends the application and returns you to the application's folder in the **Terminal** window (Fig. 1.30). Each time you execute this application from the beginning (i.e., *Step 3*), it will choose the same numbers for you to guess.

```
Excellent! You guessed the number!
Would you like to play again?
Please type ( 1=yes, 2=no )? 1

I have a number between 1 and 1000.
Can you guess my number?
Please type your first guess.
?
```

Fig. 1.29 | Playing the game again.

```
Excellent! You guessed the number!
Would you like to play again?
Please type ( 1=yes, 2=no )? 2

hostName:GNU~ userFolder$
```

Fig. 1.30 | Exiting the game.

1.12 Operating Systems

Operating systems are software systems that make using computers more convenient for users, application developers and system administrators. They provide services that allow each application to execute safely, efficiently and *concurrently* (i.e., in parallel) with other applications. The software that contains the core components of the operating system is called the **kernel**. Popular desktop operating systems include Linux, Windows and Mac OS X. Popular mobile operating systems used in smartphones and tablets include Google's Android, Apple's iOS (for iPhone, iPad and iPod Touch devices), BlackBerry OS and Windows Phone 7. You can develop applications in C for all four of the following key operating systems, including several of the latest mobile operating systems.

1.12.1 Windows—A Proprietary Operating System

In the mid-1980s, Microsoft developed the **Windows operating system**, consisting of a graphical user interface built on top of DOS—an enormously popular personal-computer operating system that users interacted with by *typing* commands. Windows borrowed from many concepts (such as icons, menus and windows) developed by Xerox PARC and popularized by early Apple Macintosh operating systems. Windows 7 is Microsoft's latest operating system—its features include enhancements to the user interface, faster startup times, further refinement of security features, touch-screen and multitouch support, and more. Windows is a *proprietary* operating system—it's controlled by Microsoft exclusively. Windows is by far the world's most widely used operating system.

1.12.2 Linux—An Open-Source Operating System

The Linux operating system is perhaps the greatest success of the *open-source* movement. **Open-source software** departs from the *proprietary* software development style that dominated software's early years. With open-source development, individuals and companies *contribute* their efforts in developing, maintaining and evolving software in exchange for the right to use that software for their own purposes, typically at no charge. Open-source code is often scrutinized by a much larger audience than proprietary software, so errors often get removed faster. Open source also encourages more innovation. Enterprise systems companies, such as IBM, Oracle and many others, have made significant investments in Linux open-source development.

Some key organizations in the open-source community are the Eclipse Foundation (the Eclipse Integrated Development Environment helps programmers conveniently develop software), the Mozilla Foundation (creators of the Firefox web browser), the Apache Software Foundation (creators of the Apache web server used to develop web-based applications) and SourceForge (which provides the tools for managing open-source projects—it has over 322,000 of them under development). Rapid improvements to computing and communications, decreasing costs and open-source software have made it much easier and more economical to create a software-based business now than just a decade ago. A great example is Facebook, which was launched from a college dorm room and built with open-source software.

The **Linux** kernel is the core of the most popular open-source, freely distributed, full-featured operating system. It's developed by a loosely organized team of volunteers and is popular in servers, personal computers and embedded systems. Unlike that of proprietary operating systems like Microsoft's Windows and Apple's Mac OS X, Linux source code (the program code) is available to the public for examination and modification and is free to download and install. As a result, Linux users benefit from a community of developers actively debugging and improving the kernel, an absence of licensing fees and restrictions, and the ability to completely customize the operating system to meet specific needs.

A variety of issues—such as Microsoft's market power, the small number of user-friendly Linux applications and the diversity of Linux distributions, such as Red Hat Linux, Ubuntu Linux and many others—have prevented widespread Linux use on desktop computers. Linux *has* become extremely popular on servers and in embedded systems, such as Google's Android-based smartphones.

1.12.3 Apple's Mac OS X; Apple's iOS for iPhone®, iPad® and iPod Touch® Devices

Apple, founded in 1976 by Steve Jobs and Steve Wozniak, quickly became a leader in personal computing. In 1979, Jobs and several Apple employees visited Xerox PARC (Palo Alto Research Center) to learn about Xerox's desktop computer that featured a graphical user interface (GUI). That GUI served as the inspiration for the Apple Macintosh, launched with much fanfare in a memorable Super Bowl ad in 1984.

The Objective-C programming language, created by Brad Cox and Tom Love at Stepstone in the early 1980s, added capabilities for object-oriented programming (OOP) to the C programming language. Steve Jobs left Apple in 1985 and founded NeXT Inc. In 1988, NeXT licensed Objective-C from StepStone and developed an Objective-C compiler and libraries which were used as the platform for the NeXTSTEP operating system's user interface and Interface Builder—used to construct graphical user interfaces.

Jobs returned to Apple in 1996 when Apple bought NeXT. Apple's Mac OS X operating system is a descendant of NeXTSTEP. Apple's proprietary operating system, iOS, is derived from Apple's Mac OS X and is used in the iPhone, iPad and iPod Touch devices.

1.12.4 Google's Android

Android—the fastest growing mobile and smartphone operating system—is based on the Linux kernel and Java. Experienced Java programmers can quickly dive into Android development. One benefit of developing Android apps is the openness of the platform. The operating system is open source and free.

The Android operating system was developed by Android, Inc., which was acquired by Google in 2005. In 2007, the Open Handset Alliance™—a consortium of 34 companies initially and 84 by 2011—was formed to continue developing Android. As of June 2011, more than 500,000 Android smartphones were being activated each day![1] Android smartphones are now outselling iPhones in the United States.[2] The Android operating system is used in numerous smartphones (such as the Motorola Droid, HTC EVO™ 4G, Samsung Vibrant™ and many more), e-reader devices (such as the Barnes and Noble Nook™), tablet computers (such as the Dell Streak and the Samsung Galaxy Tab), in-store touch-screen kiosks, cars, robots, multimedia players and more.

---

1.   news.cnet.com/8301-13506_3-20074956-17/google-500000-android-devices-activated-each-day/.
2.   www.pcworld.com/article/196035/android_outsells_the_iphone_no_big_surprise.html.

1.13 The Internet and World Wide Web

The Internet—a global network of computers—was made possible by the *convergence of computing and communications technologies*. In the late 1960s, ARPA (the Advanced Research Projects Agency) rolled out blueprints for networking the main computer systems of about a dozen ARPA-funded universities and research institutions. Academic research was about to take a giant leap forward. ARPA proceeded to implement the **ARPANET**, which eventually evolved into today's **Internet**. It rapidly became clear that communicating quickly and easily via electronic mail was the key early benefit of the ARPANET. This is true even today on the Internet, which facilitates communications of all kinds among the world's Internet users.

Packet Switching
A primary goal for ARPANET was to allow *multiple* users to send and receive information simultaneously over the *same* communications paths (e.g., phone lines). The network operated with a technique called **packet switching**, in which digital data was sent in small bundles called **packets**. The packets contained *address*, *error-control* and *sequencing* information. The address information allowed packets to be *routed* to their destinations. The sequencing information helped in *reassembling* the packets—which, because of complex routing mechanisms, could actually arrive out of order—into their original order for presentation to the recipient. Packets from different senders were intermixed on the *same* lines to efficiently use the available bandwidth. This packet-switching technique greatly reduced transmission costs, as compared with the cost of *dedicated* communications lines.

The network was designed to operate without centralized control. If a portion of the network failed, the remaining working portions would still route packets from senders to receivers over alternative paths for reliability.

TCP/IP
The protocol (i.e., set of rules) for communicating over the ARPANET became known as TCP—the **Transmission Control Protocol**. TCP ensured that messages were properly routed from sender to receiver and that they arrived intact.

As the Internet evolved, organizations worldwide were implementing their own networks. One challenge was to get these different networks to communicate. ARPA accomplished this with the development of IP—the **Internet Protocol**, truly creating a network of networks, the current architecture of the Internet. The combined set of protocols is now commonly called TCP/IP.

World Wide Web, HTML, HTTP
The **World Wide Web** allows you to execute web-based applications and to locate and view multimedia-based documents on almost any subject over the Internet. The web is a relatively recent creation. In 1989, Tim Berners-Lee of CERN (the European Organization for Nuclear Research) began to develop a technology for sharing information via hyperlinked text documents. Berners-Lee called his invention the **HyperText Markup Language (HTML)**. He also wrote communication protocols to form the backbone of his new information system, which he called the World Wide Web. In particular, he wrote the **Hypertext Transfer Protocol (HTTP)**—a communications protocol used to send information over the web. The **URL (Uniform Resource Locator)** specifies the address (i.e.,

location) of the web page displayed in the browser window. Each web page on the Internet is associated with a unique URL. **Hypertext Transfer Protocol Secure (HTTPS)** is the standard for transferring encrypted data on the web.

Mosaic, Netscape, Emergence of Web 2.0

Web use exploded with the availability in 1993 of the Mosaic browser, which featured a user-friendly graphical interface. Marc Andreessen, whose team at the National Center for Supercomputing Applications developed Mosaic, went on to found Netscape, the company that many people credit with igniting the explosive Internet economy of the late 1990s.

In 2003 there was a noticeable shift in how people and businesses were using the web and developing web-based applications. The term **Web 2.0** was coined by Dale Dougherty of O'Reilly Media[3] in 2003 to describe this trend. Generally, Web 2.0 companies use the web as a platform to create collaborative, community-based sites (e.g., social networking sites, blogs, wikis).

Companies with Web 2.0 characteristics are Google (web search), YouTube (video sharing), Facebook (social networking), Twitter (microblogging), Groupon (social commerce), Foursquare (mobile check-in), Salesforce (business software offered as online services "in the cloud"), Craigslist (mostly free classified listings), Flickr (photo sharing), Skype (Internet telephony and video calling and conferencing) and Wikipedia (a free online encyclopedia).

Web 2.0 *involves* the users—not only do they create content, but they help organize it, share it, remix it, critique it, update it, etc. Web 2.0 is a *conversation*, with everyone having the opportunity to speak and share views. Companies that understand Web 2.0 realize that their products and services are conversations as well.

Architecture of Participation

Web 2.0 embraces an **architecture of participation**—a design that encourages user interaction and community contributions. You, the user, are the most important aspect of Web 2.0—so important, in fact, that in 2006, *TIME* magazine's "Person of the Year" was "You."[4] The article recognized the social phenomenon of Web 2.0—the shift away from a *powerful few* to an *empowered many*. Popular blogs now compete with traditional media powerhouses, and many Web 2.0 companies are built almost entirely on user-generated content. For websites like Facebook®, Twitter™, YouTube, eBay® and Wikipedia® users create the content, while the companies provide the *platforms* on which to enter, manipulate and share the information.

1.14 Some Key Software Development Terminology

Figure 1.31 lists a number of buzzwords that you'll hear in the software development community. We've created Resource Centers on most of these topics, with more on the way.

---

3. T. O'Reilly, "What is Web 2.0: Design Patterns and Business Models for the Next Generation of Software." September 2005 <http://www.oreillynet.com/pub/a/oreilly/tim/news/2005/09/30/what-is-web-20.html?page=1>.
4. L. Grossman, "TIME's Person of the Year: You." *TIME*, December 2006 <http://www.time.com/time/magazine/article/0,9171,1569514,00.html>.

Technology	Description
Ajax	Ajax is one of the premier Web 2.0 software technologies. Ajax helps Internet-based applications perform like desktop applications—a difficult task, given that such applications suffer transmission delays as data is shuttled back and forth between your computer and servers on the Internet.
Agile software development	Agile software development is a set of methodologies that try to get software implemented faster and using fewer resources than previous methodologies. Check out the Agile Alliance (www.agilealliance.org) and the Agile Manifesto (www.agilemanifesto.org).
Refactoring	Refactoring involves reworking programs to make them clearer and easier to maintain while preserving their correctness and functionality. It's widely employed with agile development methodologies. Many IDEs include *refactoring tools* to do major portions of the reworking automatically.
Design patterns	Design patterns are proven architectures for constructing flexible and maintainable object-oriented software. The field of design patterns tries to enumerate those recurring patterns, encouraging software designers to *reuse* them to develop better-quality software using less time, money and effort.
LAMP	MySQL is an open-source database management system. PHP is the most popular open-source server-side Internet "scripting" language for developing Internet-based applications. LAMP is an acronym for the set of open-source technologies that many developers use to build web applications—it stands for Linux, Apache, MySQL and PHP (or Perl or Python—two other languages used for similar purposes).
Software as a Service (SaaS)	Software has generally been viewed as a product; most software still is offered this way. If you want to run an application, you buy a software package from a software vendor—often a CD, DVD or web download. You then install that software on your computer and run it as needed. As new versions of the software appear, you upgrade your software, often requiring significant time and at considerable expense. This process can become cumbersome for organizations with tens of thousands of systems that must be maintained on a diverse array of computer equipment. With Software as a Service (SaaS), the software runs on servers elsewhere on the Internet. When that server is updated, all clients worldwide see the new capabilities—no local installation is needed. You access the service through a browser. Browsers are quite portable, so you can run the same applications on a wide variety of computers from anywhere in the world. Salesforce.com, Google, and Microsoft's Office Live and Windows Live all offer SaaS. SaaS is a capability of cloud computing.
Platform as a Service (PaaS)	Platform as a Service (PaaS), another capability of cloud computing, provides a computing platform for developing and running applications as a service over the web, rather than installing the tools on your computer. PaaS providers include Google App Engine, Amazon EC2, Bungee Labs and more.
Software Development Kit (SDK)	Software Development Kits (SDKs) include the tools and documentation developers use to program applications.

Fig. 1.31 | Software technologies.

Figure 1.32 describes software product-release categories.

Version	Description
Alpha	An *alpha* version is the earliest release of a software product that's still under active development. Alpha versions are often buggy, incomplete and unstable and are released to a relatively small number of developers for testing new features, getting early feedback, etc.
Beta	*Beta* versions are released to a larger number of developers later in the development process after most major bugs have been fixed and new features are nearly complete. Beta software is more stable, but still subject to change.
Release candidates	*Release candidates* are generally *feature complete* and (supposedly) bug free and ready for use by the community, which provides a diverse testing environment—the software is used on different systems, with varying constraints and for a variety of purposes. Any bugs that appear are corrected, and eventually the final product is released to the general public. Software companies often distribute incremental updates over the Internet.
Continuous beta	Software that's developed using this approach generally does not have version numbers (for example, Google search or Gmail). The software, which is hosted in the cloud (not installed on your computer), is constantly evolving so that users always have the latest version.

Fig. 1.32 | Software product-release terminology.

1.15 Keeping Up-to-Date with Information Technologies

Figure 1.33 lists key technical and business publications that will help you stay up-to-date with the latest news and trends and technology. You can also find a growing list of Internet- and web-related Resource Centers at www.deitel.com/resourcecenters.html.

Publication	URL
ACM TechNews	technews.acm.org/
ACM Transactions on Accessible Computing	www.gccis.rit.edu/taccess/index.html
ACM Transactions on Internet Technology	toit.acm.org/
Bloomberg BusinessWeek	www.businessweek.com
CNET	news.cnet.com
Communications of the ACM	cacm.acm.org/
Computer World	www.computerworld.com
Engadget	www.engadget.com
eWeek	www.eweek.com

Fig. 1.33 | Technical and business publications. (Part 1 of 2.)

Publication	URL
Fast Company	www.fastcompany.com/
Fortune	money.cnn.com/magazines/fortune/
IEEE Computer	www.computer.org/portal/web/computer
IEEE Internet Computing	www.computer.org/portal/web/internet/home
InfoWorld	www.infoworld.com
Mashable	mashable.com
PCWorld	www.pcworld.com
SD Times	www.sdtimes.com
Slashdot	slashdot.org/
Smarter Technology	www.smartertechnology.com
Technology Review	technologyreview.com
Techcrunch	techcrunch.com
Wired	www.wired.com

Fig. 1.33 | Technical and business publications. (Part 2 of 2.)

1.16 Web Resources

This section provides links to our C and related Resource Centers that will be useful to you as you learn C. These Resource Centers include various C resources, including blogs, articles, whitepapers, compilers, development tools, downloads, FAQs, tutorials, webcasts, wikis and links to resources for C game programming with the Allegro libraries. For updates on Deitel publications, Resource Centers, training courses, partner offers and more, follow us on Facebook® at www.facebook.com/deitelfan/ and on Twitter® @deitel.

Deitel & Associates Websites

www.deitel.com/books/chtp7/
The Deitel & Associates *C How to Program, 7/e* site. Here you'll find links to the book's examples and other resources.

www.deitel.com/C/
www.deitel.com/visualcplusplus/
www.deitel.com/codesearchengines/
www.deitel.com/programmingprojects/
Check these Resource Centers for compilers, code downloads, tutorials, documentation, books, e-books, articles, blogs, RSS feeds and more that will help you develop C applications.

www.deitel.com
Check this site for updates, corrections and additional resources for all Deitel publications.

www.deitel.com/newsletter/subscribe.html
Subscribe here for the *Deitel® Buzz Online* e-mail newsletter to follow the Deitel & Associates publishing program, including updates and errata to *C How to Program, 7/e*.

Terminology

Self-Review Exercises

1.1 Fill in the blanks in each of the following:

a) Computers process data under the control of sequences of instructions called computer _____.

b) _____ is a type of computer language that uses Englishlike abbreviations for machine-language instructions.

c) _____ languages are most convenient to the programmer for writing programs quickly and easily.

d) The only language a computer can directly understand is that computer's _____.

e) The programs that translate high-level language programs into machine language are called _____.

f) With _____ development, individuals and companies contribute their efforts in developing, maintaining and evolving software in exchange for the right to use that software for their own purposes, typically at no charge.

g) C is widely known as the development language of the _____ operating system.

1.2 Fill in the blanks in each of the following sentences about the C environment.

a) C programs are normally typed into a computer using a(n) _____ program.

b) In a C system, a(n) _____ program automatically executes before the translation phase begins.

c) The two most common kinds of preprocessor directives are _____ and _____.

d) The _____ program combines the output of the compiler with various library functions to produce an executable image.

e) The _____ program transfers the executable image from disk to memory.

1.3 Fill in the blanks in each of the following statements (based on Section 1.9):

a) Objects have the property of _____—although objects may know how to communicate with one another across well-defined interfaces, they normally are not allowed to know how other objects are implemented.

b) In object-oriented programming languages, we create _____ to house the set of methods that perform tasks.

c) With _____, new classes of objects are derived by absorbing characteristics of existing classes, then adding unique characteristics of their own.

d) The size, shape, color and weight of an object are considered _____ of the object's class.

Answers to Self-Review Exercises

1.1 a) programs. b) Assembly language. c) High-level. d) machine language. e) compilers. f) open-source. g) UNIX.

1.2 a) editor. b) preprocessor. c) including other files in the file to be compiled, performing various text replacements. d) linker. e) loader.

1.3 a) information hiding. b) classes. c) inheritance. d) attributes.

Exercises

1.4 Categorize each of the following items as either a form of input or output:

a) scanning images

b) printing images

c) scanning a barcode

d) receiving a video from a webcam

e) displaying a message on a giant screen

f) receiving a voice command

1.5 Fill in the blanks in each of the following statements:

a) The process of instructing the computer to solve a problem is called _____.

b) What type of computer language uses Englishlike abbreviations for machine-language instructions? _____.

c) The level of computer language at which it's most convenient to write programs quickly and easily is _____.

d) The only language that a computer directly understands is called that computer's _____.

e) Web 2.0 embraces a(n) _____—a design that encourages user interaction and community contributions.

1.6 Fill in the blanks in each of the following statements:

a) _____ is now used to develop large-scale enterprise applications, to enhance the functionality of web servers, to provide applications for consumer devices and for many other purposes.

b) _____ initially became widely known as the development language of the UNIX operating system.

c) The _____ programming language was developed by Bjarne Stroustrup in the early 1980s at Bell Laboratories.

1.7 Discuss the meaning of each of the following names:

a) `stdin`

b) `stdout`

c) `stderr`

1.8 Why is so much attention today focused on object-oriented programming?

1.9 *(Internet in Industry and Research)* Figure 1.1 provides examples of how computers and the Internet are being used in industry and research. Find three additional examples and describe how each is using the Internet and the web.

1.10 *(Global Positioning System)* Describe the benefits of the Global Positioning System.

1.11 *(Internet Negatives)* Besides their numerous benefits, the Internet and the web have several downsides, such as privacy issues, identity theft, spam and malware. Research some of the negative aspects of the Internet. List five problems and describe what could possibly be done to help solve each.

1.12 *(Watch as an Object)* You are probably wearing on your wrist one of the most common types of objects—a watch. Discuss how each of the following terms and concepts applies to the notion of a watch: object, attributes, behaviors, class, inheritance (consider, for example, an alarm clock), messages, encapsulation and information hiding.

Making a Difference

1.13 *(Test-Drive: Carbon Footprint Calculator)* Some scientists believe that carbon emissions, especially from the burning of fossil fuels, contribute significantly to global warming and that this can be combatted if individuals take steps to limit their use of carbon-based fuels. Organizations and individuals are increasingly concerned about their "carbon footprints." Websites such as TerraPass

```
www.terrapass.com/carbon-footprint-calculator/
```

and Carbon Footprint

```
www.carbonfootprint.com/calculator.aspx
```

provide carbon footprint calculators. Test-drive these calculators to estimate your carbon footprint. Exercises in later chapters will ask you to program your own carbon footprint calculator. To prepare for this, use the web to research the formulas for calculating carbon footprints.

1.14 *(Test-Drive: Body Mass Index Calculator)* By recent estimates, two-thirds of the people in the United States are overweight and about half of those are obese. This causes significant increases in illnesses such as diabetes and heart disease. To determine whether a person is overweight or obese, you can use a measure called the body mass index (BMI). The United States Department of Health and Human Services provides a BMI calculator at www.nhlbisupport.com/bmi/. Use it to calculate your own BMI. An exercise in Chapter 2 will ask you to program your own BMI calculator. To prepare for this, use the web to research the formulas for calculating BMI.

1.15 *(Gender Neutrality)* Many people want to eliminate sexism in all forms of communication. You've been asked to create a program that can process a paragraph of text and replace gender-specific words with gender-neutral ones. Assuming that you've been given a list of gender-specific words and their gender-neutral replacements (e.g., replace "wife" with "spouse," "man" with "person," "daughter" with "child" and so on), explain the procedure you'd use to read through a paragraph of text and manually perform these replacements. How might your procedure generate a strange term like "woperchild?" In Chapter 4, you'll learn that a more formal term for "procedure" is "algorithm," and that an algorithm specifies the steps to be performed and the order in which to perform them.

1.16 *(Privacy)* Some online e-mail services save all e-mail correspondence for some period of time. Suppose a disgruntled employee were to post all of the e-mail correspondences for millions of people, including yours, on the Internet. Discuss the issues.

1.17 *(Programmer Responsibility and Liability)* As a programmer in industry, you may develop software that could affect people's health or even their lives. Suppose a software bug in one of your programs causes a cancer patient to receive an excessive dose during radiation therapy and that the person is severely injured or dies. Discuss the issues.

1.18 *(2010 "Flash Crash")* An example of the consequences of our excessive dependence on computers was the so-called "flash crash" which occurred on May 6, 2010, when the U.S. stock market fell precipitously in a matter of minutes, wiping out trillions of dollars of investments, and then recovered within minutes. Research online the causes of this crash and discuss the issues it raises.

1.19 *(Making a Difference Projects)* The following is a list of just a few worldwide organizations that are working to make a difference. Visit these sites and our Making a Difference Resource Center at www.deitel.com/makingadifference. Prepare a top-10 list of programming projects that you think could indeed "make a difference."

- www.imaginecup.com/
  The *Microsoft Image Cup* is a global competition in which students use technology to try to solve some of the world's most difficult problems, such as environmental sustainability, ending hunger, emergency response, literacy and combating HIV/AIDS. Visit www.imaginecup.com/about for more information about the competition and to learn about the projects developed by previous winners. You can also find several project ideas submitted by worldwide charitable organizations at www.imaginecup.com/students/imagine-cup-solve-this. For additional ideas for programming projects that can make a difference, search the web for "making a difference" and visit the following websites:

- www.un.org/millenniumgoals
  The United Nations Millennium Project seeks solutions to major worldwide issues such as environmental sustainability, gender equality, child and maternal health, universal education and more.

- www.ibm.com/smarterplanet/
  The IBM® Smarter Planet website discusses how IBM is using technology to solve issues related to business, cloud computing, education, sustainability and more.

- www.gatesfoundation.org/Pages/home.aspx
  The Bill and Melinda Gates Foundation provides grants to organizations that work to alleviate hunger, poverty and disease in developing countries. In the United States, the foundation focuses on improving public education, particularly for people with few resources.

- www.nethope.org/
  NetHope is a collaboration of humanitarian organizations worldwide working to solve technology problems such as connectivity, emergency response and more.

- www.rainforestfoundation.org/home
  The Rainforest Foundation works to preserve rainforests and to protect the rights of the indigenous people who call the rainforests home. The site includes a list of things you can do to help.

- www.undp.org/
  The United Nations Development Programme (UNDP) seeks solutions to global challenges such as crisis prevention and recovery, energy and the environment and democratic governance.

- www.unido.org
  The United Nations Industrial Development Organization (UNIDO) seeks to reduce poverty, give developing countries the opportunity to participate in global trade, and promote energy efficiency and sustainability.

- www.usaid.gov/
  USAID promotes global democracy, health, economic growth, conflict prevention, humanitarian aid and more.

- www.toyota.com/ideas-for-good/
  Toyota's Ideas for Good website describes several Toyota technologies that are making a difference—including their Advanced Parking Guidance System, Hybrid Synergy Drive®, Solar Powered Ventilation System, T.H.U.M.S. (Total Human Model for Safety) and Touch Tracer Display. You can participate in the Ideas for Good challenge by submitting a short essay or video describing how these technologies can be used for other good purposes.

2

Introduction to C Programming

What's in a name?
That which we call a rose
By any other name would
smell as sweet.
—William Shakespeare

"Take some more tea," the
March Hare said to Alice, very
earnestly. "I've had nothing yet,"
Alice replied in an offended
tone: "so I can't take more." "You
mean you can't take less," said
the Hatter: "it's very easy to take
more than nothing."
—Lewis Carroll

High thoughts must have high
language.
—Aristophanes

Objectives

In this chapter, you'll:

- Write simple computer programs in C.
- Use simple input and output statements.
- Use the fundamental data types.
- Learn computer memory concepts.
- Use arithmetic operators.
- Learn the precedence of arithmetic operators.
- Write simple decision-making statements.

2.1 Introduction

The C language facilitates a structured and disciplined approach to computer-program design. In this chapter we introduce C programming and present several examples that illustrate many important features of C. Each example is analyzed one statement at a time. In Chapters 3 and 4 we present an introduction to structured programming in C. We then use the structured approach throughout the remainder of the C portion of the text.

2.2 A Simple C Program: Printing a Line of Text

C uses some notations that may appear strange to people who have not programmed computers. We begin by considering a simple C program. Our first example prints a line of text. The program and its screen output are shown in Fig. 2.1.

```
1   // Fig. 2.1: fig02_01.c
2   // A first program in C.
3   #include <stdio.h>
4
5   // function main begins program execution
6   int main( void )
7   {
8      printf( "Welcome to C!\n" );
9   } // end function main
```

```
Welcome to C!
```

Fig. 2.1 | A first program in C.

Comments

Even though this program is simple, it illustrates several important features of the C language. Lines 1 and 2

```
// Fig. 2.1: fig02_01.c
// A first program in C
```

begin with //, indicating that these two lines are **comments**. You insert comments to **document programs** and improve program readability. Comments do *not* cause the computer to perform any action when the program is run. Comments are *ignored* by the C compiler and do *not* cause any machine-language object code to be generated. The preceding comment simply describes the figure number, file name and purpose of the program. Comments also help other people read and understand your program.

You can also use /*...*/ **multi-line comments** in which everything from /* on the first line to */ at the end of the last line is a comment. We prefer // comments because they're shorter and they eliminate common programming errors that occur with /*...*/ comments, especially when the closing */ is omitted.

#include *Preprocessor Directive*
Line 3

```
#include <stdio.h>
```

is a directive to the C preprocessor. Lines beginning with # are processed by the preprocessor *before* compilation. Line 3 tells the preprocessor to include the contents of the **standard input/output header** (**<stdio.h>**) in the program. This header contains information used by the compiler when compiling calls to standard input/output library functions such as printf (line 8). We explain the contents of headers in more detail in Chapter 5.

Blank Lines and White Space
Line 4 is simply a blank line. You use blank lines, space characters and tab characters (i.e., "tabs") to make programs easier to read. Together, these characters are known as **white space**. White-space characters are normally ignored by the compiler.

The main *Function*
Line 6

```
int main( void )
```

is a part of every C program. The parentheses after main indicate that main is a program building block called a **function**. C programs contain one or more functions, one of which *must* be main. Every program in C begins executing at the function main. Functions can *return* information. The keyword int to the left of main indicates that main "returns" an integer (whole-number) value. We'll explain what it means for a function to "return a value" when we demonstrate how to create your own functions in Chapter 5. For now, simply include the keyword int to the left of main in each of your programs. Functions also can *receive* information when they're called upon to execute. The void in parentheses here means that main does *not* receive any information. In Chapter 14, we'll show an example of main receiving information.

Good Programming Practice 2.1
Every function should be preceded by a comment describing the purpose of the function.

A left brace, {, begins the **body** of every function (line 7). A corresponding **right brace** ends each function (line 9). This pair of braces and the portion of the program between the braces is called a *block*. The block is an important program unit in C.

An Output Statement
Line 8

```
printf( "Welcome to C!\n" );
```

instructs the computer to perform an **action**, namely to print on the screen the **string of characters** marked by the quotation marks. A string is sometimes called a **character string**, a **message** or a **literal**. The entire line, including the `printf` function (the "`f`" stands for "formatted"), its **argument** within the parentheses and the semicolon (`;`), is called a **statement**. Every statement must end with a semicolon (also known as the **statement terminator**). When the preceding `printf` statement is executed, it prints the message `Welcome to C!` on the screen. The characters normally print exactly as they appear between the double quotes in the `printf` statement.

Escape Sequences

Notice that the characters \n were not printed on the screen. The backslash (\) is called an **escape character**. It indicates that `printf` is supposed to do something out of the ordinary. When encountering a backslash in a string, the compiler looks ahead at the next character and combines it with the backslash to form an **escape sequence**. The escape sequence \n means **newline**. When a newline appears in the string output by a `printf`, the newline causes the cursor to position to the beginning of the next line on the screen. Some common escape sequences are listed in Fig. 2.2.

Escape sequence	Description
\n	Newline. Position the cursor at the beginning of the next line.
\t	Horizontal tab. Move the cursor to the next tab stop.
\a	Alert. Produces a sound or visible alert without changing the current cursor position.
\\	Backslash. Insert a backslash character in a string.
\"	Double quote. Insert a double-quote character in a string.

Fig. 2.2 | Some common escape sequences .

Because the backslash has special meaning in a string, i.e., the compiler recognizes it as an escape character, we use a double backslash (\\) to place a single backslash in a string. Printing a double quote also presents a problem because double quotes mark the boundaries of a string—such quotes are not printed. By using the escape sequence \" in a string to be output by `printf`, we indicate that `printf` should display a double quote. The right brace, }, (line 9) indicates that the end of `main` has been reached.

Good Programming Practice 2.2

Add a comment to the line containing the right brace, }, that closes every function, including `main`*.*

We said that `printf` causes the computer to perform an **action**. As any program executes, it performs a variety of actions and makes **decisions**. Section 2.6 discusses decision making. Chapter 3 discusses this **action/decision model** of programming in depth.

The Linker and Executables

Standard library functions like `printf` and `scanf` are *not* part of the C programming language. For example, the compiler *cannot* find a spelling error in `printf` or `scanf`. When the compiler compiles a printf statement, it merely provides space in the object program for a "call" to the library function. But the compiler does *not* know where the library functions are—the *linker* does. When the linker runs, it locates the library functions and inserts the proper calls to these library functions in the object program. Now the object program is complete and ready to be executed. For this reason, the linked program is called an executable. If the function name is misspelled, the *linker* will spot the error, because it will not be able to match the name in the C program with the name of any known function in the libraries.

Common Programming Error 2.1

Mistyping the name of the output function printf as print in a program.

Good Programming Practice 2.3

Indent the entire body of each function one level of indentation (we recommend three spaces) within the braces that define the body of the function. This indentation emphasizes the functional structure of programs and helps make programs easier to read.

Good Programming Practice 2.4

Set a convention for the size of indent you prefer and then uniformly apply that convention. The tab key may be used to create indents, but tab stops may vary.

Using Multiple printfs

The printf function can print Welcome to C! several different ways. For example, the program of Fig. 2.3 produces the same output as the program of Fig. 2.1. This works because each printf resumes printing where the previous printf stopped printing. The first printf (line 8) prints Welcome followed by a space, and the second printf (line 9) begins printing on the *same* line immediately following the space.

```
1   // Fig. 2.3: fig02_03.c
2   // Printing on one line with two printf statements.
3   #include <stdio.h>
4
5   // function main begins program execution
6   int main( void )
7   {
8      printf( "Welcome " );
9      printf( "to C!\n" );
10  } // end function main
```

```
Welcome to C!
```

Fig. 2.3 | Printing on one line with two printf statements.

One printf can print *several* lines by using additional newline characters as in Fig. 2.4. Each time the \n (newline) escape sequence is encountered, output continues at the beginning of the next line.

```
1   // Fig. 2.4: fig02_04.c
2   // Printing multiple lines with a single printf.
3   #include <stdio.h>
4
5   // function main begins program execution
6   int main( void )
7   {
8      printf( "Welcome\nto\nC!\n" );
9   } // end function main
```

```
Welcome
to
C!
```

Fig. 2.4 | Printing multiple lines with a single printf.

2.3 Another Simple C Program: Adding Two Integers

Our next program uses the Standard Library function scanf to obtain two integers typed by a user at the keyboard, computes the sum of these values and prints the result using printf. The program and sample output are shown in Fig. 2.5. [In the input/output dialog of Fig. 2.5, we emphasize the numbers entered by the user in **bold**.]

```
1   // Fig. 2.5: fig02_05.c
2   // Addition program.
3   #include <stdio.h>
4
5   // function main begins program execution
6   int main( void )
7   {
8      int integer1; // first number to be entered by user
9      int integer2; // second number to be entered by user
10     int sum; // variable in which sum will be stored
11
12     printf( "Enter first integer\n" ); // prompt
13     scanf( "%d", &integer1 ); // read an integer
14
15     printf( "Enter second integer\n" ); // prompt
16     scanf( "%d", &integer2 ); // read an integer
17
18     sum = integer1 + integer2; // assign total to sum
19
20     printf( "Sum is %d\n", sum ); // print sum
21  } // end function main
```

```
Enter first integer
45
Enter second integer
72
Sum is 117
```

Fig. 2.5 | Addition program.

The comment in lines 1–2 states the purpose of the program. As we stated earlier, every program begins execution with `main`. The left brace { (line 7) marks the beginning of the body of `main`, and the corresponding right brace } (line 21) marks the end of `main`.

Variables and Variable Definitions
Lines 8–10

```
int integer1; // first number to be entered by user
int integer2; // second number to be entered by user
int sum; // variable in which sum will be stored
```

are **definitions**. The names `integer1`, `integer2` and `sum` are the names of **variables**— locations in memory where values can be stored for use by a program. These definitions specify that variables `integer1`, `integer2` and `sum` are of type `int`, which means that they'll hold **integer** values, i.e., whole numbers such as 7, –11, 0, 31914 and the like.

All variables must be defined with a name and a data type *before* they can be used in a program. For readers using the Microsoft Visual C++ compiler, note that we're placing our variable definitions immediately after the left brace that begins the body of `main`. The C standard allows you to place each variable definition *anywhere* in `main` before that variable's first use in the code. Some compilers, such as GNU `gcc`, have implemented this capability. We'll address this issue in more depth in later chapters.

The preceding definitions could have been combined into a single definition statement as follows:

```
int integer1, integer2, sum;
```

but that would have made it difficult to describe the variables with corresponding comments as we did in lines 8–10.

Identifiers and Case Sensitivity
A variable name in C is any valid **identifier**. An identifier is a series of characters consisting of letters, digits and underscores (_) that does *not* begin with a digit. C is **case sensitive**— uppercase and lowercase letters are *different* in C, so `a1` and `A1` are *different* identifiers.

Common Programming Error 2.2
Using a capital letter where a lowercase letter should be used (for example, typing `Main` instead of `main`).

Error-Prevention Tip 2.1
Avoid starting identifiers with the underscore character (_) to prevent conflicts with compiler-generated identifiers and standard library identifiers.

Good Programming Practice 2.5
Choosing meaningful variable names helps make a program self-documenting—that is, fewer comments are needed.

Good Programming Practice 2.6
The first letter of an identifier used as a simple variable name should be a lowercase letter. Later in the text we'll assign special significance to identifiers that begin with a capital letter and to identifiers that use all capital letters.

Good Programming Practice 2.7

Multiple-word variable names can help make a program more readable. Separate the words with underscores as in total_commissions, *or, if you run the words together, begin each word after the first with a capital letter as in* totalCommissions. *The latter style is preferred.*

Syntax Errors

We discussed what syntax errors are in Chapter 1. Recall that the Microsoft Visual C++ compiler requires variable definitions to be placed *after* the left brace of a function and *before* any executable statements. Therefore, in the program in Fig. 2.5, inserting the definition of integer1 *after* the first printf would cause a syntax error in Visual C++.

Common Programming Error 2.3

Placing variable definitions among executable statements causes syntax errors in the Microsoft Visual C++ Compiler.

Prompting Messages

Line 12

```
printf( "Enter first integer\n" ); // prompt
```

displays the literal "Enter first integer" and positions the cursor to the beginning of the next line. This message is called a **prompt** because it tells the user to take a specific action.

The scanf Function and Formatted Inputs

The next statement

```
scanf( "%d", &integer1 ); // read an integer
```

uses **scanf** (the "f" stands for "formatted") to obtain a value from the user. The function reads from the *standard input*, which is usually the keyboard. This scanf has two arguments, "%d" and &integer1. The first, the **format control string**, indicates the *type* of data that should be entered by the user. The **%d conversion specifier** indicates that the data should be an integer (the letter d stands for "decimal integer"). The % in this context is treated by scanf (and printf as we'll see) as a special character that begins a conversion specifier. The second argument of scanf begins with an ampersand (&)—called the **address operator**—followed by the variable name. The &, when combined with the variable name, tells scanf the location (or address) in memory at which the variable integer1 is stored. The computer then stores the value that the user enters for integer1 at that location. The use of ampersand (&) is often confusing to novice programmers or to people who have programmed in other languages that do not require this notation. For now, just remember to precede each variable in every call to scanf with an ampersand. Some exceptions to this rule are discussed in Chapters 6 and 7. The use of the ampersand will become clear after we study *pointers* in Chapter 7.

Good Programming Practice 2.8

Place a space after each comma (,) to make programs more readable.

When the computer executes the preceding scanf, it waits for the user to enter a value for variable integer1. The user responds by typing an integer, then pressing the *Enter* key to send the number to the computer. The computer then assigns this number, or value, to the variable `integer1`. Any subsequent references to `integer1` in this program will use this same value. Functions `printf` and `scanf` facilitate interaction between the user and the computer. Because this interaction resembles a dialogue, it's often called **interactive computing**.

Line 15

```
printf( "Enter second integer\n" ); // prompt
```

displays the message `Enter second integer` on the screen, then positions the cursor to the beginning of the next line. This `printf` also prompts the user to take action.

Line 16

```
scanf( "%d", &integer2 ); // read an integer
```

obtains a value for variable `integer2` from the user.

Assignment Statement
The assignment statement in line 18

```
sum = integer1 + integer2; // assign total to sum
```

calculates the total of variables `integer1` and `integer2` and assigns the result to variable `sum` using the assignment operator `=`. The statement is read as, "`sum` *gets* the value of `integer1 + integer2`." Most calculations are performed in assignments. The `=` operator and the `+` operator are called *binary* operators because each has *two* operands. The `+` operator's two operands are `integer1` and `integer2`. The `=` operator's two operands are `sum` and the value of the expression `integer1 + integer2`.

Good Programming Practice 2.9
Place spaces on either side of a binary operator. This makes the operator stand out and makes the program more readable.

Common Programming Error 2.4
A calculation in an assignment statement must be on the right *side of the* = *operator. It's a compilation error to place a calculation on the* left *side of an assignment operator.*

Printing with a Format Control String
Line 20

```
printf( "Sum is %d\n", sum ); // print sum
```

calls function `printf` to print the literal `Sum is` followed by the numerical value of variable `sum` on the screen. This `printf` has two arguments, `"Sum is %d\n"` and `sum`. The first argument is the format control string. It contains some literal characters to be displayed, and it contains the conversion specifier `%d` indicating that an integer will be printed. The second argument specifies the value to be printed. Notice that the conversion specifier for an integer is the same in both `printf` and `scanf`—this is the case for most C data types.

Calculations in `printf` Statements
Calculations can also be performed inside `printf` statements. We could have combined the previous two statements into the statement

```
printf( "Sum is %d\n", integer1 + integer2 );
```

The right brace, `}`, at line 21 indicates that the end of function `main` has been reached.

Common Programming Error 2.5

Forgetting to precede a variable in a scanf *statement with an ampersand when that variable should, in fact, be preceded by an ampersand results in an execution-time error. On many systems, this causes a "segmentation fault" or "access violation." Such an error occurs when a user's program attempts to access a part of the computer's memory to which it does not have access privileges. The precise cause of this error will be explained in Chapter 7.*

Common Programming Error 2.6

Preceding a variable included in a printf *statement with an ampersand when, in fact, that variable should not be preceded by an ampersand.*

2.4 Memory Concepts

Variable names such as integer1, integer2 and sum actually correspond to locations in the computer's memory. Every variable has a name, a type and a value.

In the addition program of Fig. 2.5, when the statement (line 13)

```
scanf( "%d", &integer1 ); // read an integer
```

is executed, the value entered by the user is placed into a memory location to which the name integer1 has been assigned. Suppose the user enters the number 45 as the value for integer1. The computer will place 45 into location integer1, as shown in Fig. 2.6.

integer1   45

Fig. 2.6 | Memory location showing the name and value of a variable.

Whenever a value is placed in a memory location, the value *replaces* the previous value in that location; thus, this process is said to be **destructive**.

Returning to our addition program again, when the statement (line 16)

```
scanf( "%d", &integer2 ); // read an integer
```

executes, suppose the user enters the value 72. This value is placed into location integer2, and memory appears as in Fig. 2.7. These locations are not necessarily adjacent in memory.

Once the program has obtained values for integer1 and integer2, it adds these values and places the total into variable sum. The statement (line 18)

```
sum = integer1 + integer2; // assign total to sum
```

integer1   45

integer2   72

Fig. 2.7 | Memory locations after both variables are input.

that performs the addition also *replaces* whatever value was stored in sum. This occurs when the calculated total of integer1 and integer2 is placed into location sum (destroying the value already in sum). After sum is calculated, memory appears as in Fig. 2.8. The values of integer1 and integer2 appear exactly as they did *before* they were used in the calculation. They were used, but not destroyed, as the computer performed the calculation. Thus, when a value is *read* from a memory location, the process is said to be **nondestructive**.

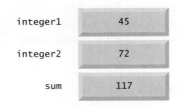

Fig. 2.8 | Memory locations after a calculation.

2.5 Arithmetic in C

Most C programs perform calculations using the C arithmetic operators (Fig. 2.9). Note the use of various special symbols not used in algebra. The asterisk (*) indicates *multiplication* and the **percent sign** (%) denotes the *remainder operator*, which is introduced below. In algebra, to multiply *a* times *b*, we simply place these single-letter variable names side by side, as in *ab*. In C, however, if we were to do this, ab would be interpreted as a single, two-letter name (or identifier). Therefore, C (and many other programming languages) require that multiplication be explicitly denoted by using the * operator, as in a * b. The arithmetic operators are all *binary* operators. For example, the expression 3 + 7 contains the binary operator + and the operands 3 and 7.

C operation	Arithmetic operator	Algebraic expression	C expression
Addition	+	$f + 7$	f + 7
Subtraction	−	$p - c$	p − c
Multiplication	*	bm	b * m
Division	/	x / y or $\dfrac{x}{y}$ or $x \div y$	x / y
Remainder	%	$r \bmod s$	r % s

Fig. 2.9 | Arithmetic operators.

Integer Division and the Remainder Operator
Integer division yields an integer result. For example, the expression 7 / 4 evaluates to 1 and the expression 17 / 5 evaluates to 3. C provides the **remainder operator**, **%**, which yields the *remainder* after integer division. The remainder operator is an integer operator that can be used only with integer operands. The expression x % y yields the remainder after x is divided by y. Thus, 7 % 4 yields 3 and 17 % 5 yields 2. We'll discuss many interesting applications of the remainder operator.

> **Common Programming Error 2.7**
>
> *An attempt to divide by zero is normally undefined on computer systems and generally results in a* fatal error, *i.e., an error that causes the program to terminate immediately without having successfully performed its job.* Nonfatal errors *allow programs to run to completion, often producing incorrect results.*

Arithmetic Expressions in Straight-Line Form

Arithmetic expressions in C must be written in **straight-line form** to facilitate entering programs into the computer. Thus, expressions such as "a divided by b" must be written as a/b so that all operators and operands appear in a straight line. The algebraic notation

$$\frac{a}{b}$$

is generally not acceptable to compilers, although some special-purpose software packages do support more natural notation for complex mathematical expressions.

Parentheses for Grouping Subexpressions

Parentheses are used in C expressions in the same manner as in algebraic expressions. For example, to multiply a times the quantity b + c we write a * (b + c).

Rules of Operator Precedence

C applies the operators in arithmetic expressions in a precise sequence determined by the following **rules of operator precedence**, which are generally the same as those in algebra:

1. Operators in expressions contained within pairs of parentheses are evaluated first. Parentheses are said to be at the "highest level of precedence." In cases of **nested, or embedded, parentheses**, such as

    ```
    ( ( a + b ) + c )
    ```

    the operators in the *innermost* pair of parentheses are applied first.

2. Multiplication, division and remainder operations are applied next. If an expression contains several multiplication, division and remainder operations, evaluation proceeds from left to right. Multiplication, division and remainder are said to be on the same level of precedence.

3. Addition and subtraction operations are evaluated next. If an expression contains several addition and subtraction operations, evaluation proceeds from left to right. Addition and subtraction also have the same level of precedence, which is lower than the precedence of the multiplication, division and remainder operations.

4. The assignment operator (=) is evaluated last.

The rules of operator precedence specify the order C uses to evaluate expressions.[1] When we say evaluation proceeds from left to right, we're referring to the **associativity** of the operators. We'll see that some operators associate from right to left. Figure 2.10 summarizes these rules of operator precedence for the operators we've seen so far.

---

1. We use simple examples to explain the order of evaluation of expressions. Subtle issues occur in more complex expressions that you'll encounter later in the book. We'll discuss these issues as they arise.

Operator(s)	Operation(s)	Order of evaluation (precedence)
( )	Parentheses	Evaluated first. If the parentheses are nested, the expression in the *innermost* pair is evaluated first. If there are several pairs of parentheses "on the same level" (i.e., not nested), they're evaluated left to right.
* / %	Multiplication Division Remainder	Evaluated second. If there are several, they're evaluated left to right.
+ –	Addition Subtraction	Evaluated third. If there are several, they're evaluated left to right.
=	Assignment	Evaluated last.

Fig. 2.10 | Precedence of arithmetic operators.

Sample Algebraic and C Expressions

Now let's consider several expressions in light of the rules of operator precedence. Each example lists an algebraic expression and its C equivalent. The following expression calculates the arithmetic mean (average) of five terms.

Algebra: $m = \dfrac{a + b + c + d + e}{5}$

C: `m = ( a + b + c + d + e ) / 5;`

The parentheses are required to group the additions because division has higher precedence than addition. The entire quantity (a + b + c + d + e) should be divided by 5. If the parentheses are erroneously omitted, we obtain a + b + c + d + e / 5, which evaluates incorrectly as

$a + b + c + d + \dfrac{e}{5}$

The following expression is the equation of a straight line:

Algebra: $y = mx + b$

C: `y = m * x + b;`

No parentheses are required. The multiplication is evaluated first because multiplication has a higher precedence than addition.

The following expression contains remainder (%), multiplication, division, addition, subtraction and assignment operations:

Algebra: $z = pr \% q + w/x - y$

C: `z = p * r % q + w / x - y;`
              6   1   2   4   3   5

The circled numbers indicate the order in which C evaluates the operators. The multiplication, remainder and division are evaluated first in left-to-right order (i.e., they associate from left to right) because they have higher precedence than addition and subtraction. The addition and subtraction are evaluated next. They're also evaluated left to right. Finally, the result is assigned to the variable z.

Not all expressions with several pairs of parentheses contain nested parentheses. For example, the following expression does *not* contain nested parentheses—instead, the parentheses are said to be "on the same level."

```
a * ( b + c ) + c * ( d + e )
```

Evaluation of a Second-Degree Polynomial

To develop a better understanding of the rules of operator precedence, let's see how C evaluates a second-degree polynomial.

The circled numbers under the statement indicate the order in which C performs the operations. There's no arithmetic operator for exponentiation in C, so we've represented x^2 as x * x. The C Standard Library includes the pow ("power") function to perform exponentiation. Because of some subtle issues related to the data types required by pow, we defer a detailed explanation of pow until Chapter 4.

Suppose variables a, b, c and x in the preceding second-degree polynomial are initialized as follows: a = 2, b = 3, c = 7 and x = 5. Figure 2.11 illustrates the order in which the operators are applied.

Step 1.	y = 2 * 5 * 5 + 3 * 5 + 7; 2 * 5 is 10	*(Leftmost multiplication)*
Step 2.	y = 10 * 5 + 3 * 5 + 7; 10 * 5 is 50	*(Leftmost multiplication)*
Step 3.	y = 50 + 3 * 5 + 7; 3 * 5 is 15	*(Multiplication before addition)*
Step 4.	y = 50 + 15 + 7; 50 + 15 is 65	*(Leftmost addition)*
Step 5.	y = 65 + 7; 65 + 7 is 72	*(Last addition)*
Step 6.	y = 72	*(Last operation—place 72 in y)*

Fig. 2.11 | Order in which a second-degree polynomial is evaluated.

As in algebra, it's acceptable to place unnecessary parentheses in an expression to make the expression clearer. These are called **redundant parentheses**. For example, the preceding statement could be parenthesized as follows:

```
y = ( a * x * x ) + ( b * x ) + c;
```

2.6 Decision Making: Equality and Relational Operators

Executable statements either perform actions (such as calculations or input or output of data) or make **decisions** (we'll soon see several examples of these). We might make a decision in a program, for example, to determine whether a person's grade on an exam is greater than or equal to 60 and whether the program should print the message "Congratulations! You passed." This section introduces a simple version of C's **if statement** that allows a program to make a decision based on the truth or falsity of a statement of fact called a **condition**. If the condition is **true** (i.e., the condition is met), the statement in the body of the if statement is executed. If the condition is **false** (i.e., the condition isn't met), the body statement isn't executed. Whether the body statement is executed or not, after the if statement completes, execution proceeds with the next statement after the if statement.

Conditions in if statements are formed by using the **equality operators** and **relational operators** summarized in Fig. 2.12. The relational operators all have the same level of precedence and they associate left to right. The equality operators have a lower level of precedence than the relational operators and they also associate left to right. [*Note:* In C, a condition may actually be *any expression that generates a zero (false) or nonzero (true) value.*]

Common Programming Error 2.8

A syntax error occurs if the two symbols in any of the operators ==, !=, >= and <= are separated by spaces.

Common Programming Error 2.9

Confusing the equality operator == with the assignment operator. To avoid this confusion, the equality operator should be read "double equals" and the assignment operator should be read "gets" or "is assigned the value of." As you'll see, confusing these operators may not cause an easy-to-recognize compilation error, but may cause extremely subtle logic errors.

Algebraic equality or relational operator	C equality or relational operator	Example of C condition	Meaning of C condition
Equality operators			
=	==	x == y	x is equal to y
≠	!=	x != y	x is not equal to y
Relational operators			
>	>	x > y	x is greater than y
<	<	x < y	x is less than y
≥	>=	x >= y	x is greater than or equal to y
≤	<=	x <= y	x is less than or equal to y

Fig. 2.12 | Equality and relational operators.

Figure 2.13 uses six if statements to compare two numbers entered by the user. If the condition in any of these if statements is true, the printf statement associated with that if executes. The program and three sample execution outputs are shown in the figure.

```c
1   // Fig. 2.13: fig02_13.c
2   // Using if statements, relational
3   // operators, and equality operators.
4   #include <stdio.h>
5
6   // function main begins program execution
7   int main( void )
8   {
9      int num1; // first number to be read from user
10     int num2; // second number to be read from user
11
12     printf( "Enter two integers, and I will tell you\n" );
13     printf( "the relationships they satisfy: " );
14
15     scanf( "%d%d", &num1, &num2 ); // read two integers
16
17     if ( num1 == num2 ) {
18        printf( "%d is equal to %d\n", num1, num2 );
19     } // end if
20
21     if ( num1 != num2 ) {
22        printf( "%d is not equal to %d\n", num1, num2 );
23     } // end if
24
25     if ( num1 < num2 ) {
26        printf( "%d is less than %d\n", num1, num2 );
27     } // end if
28
29     if ( num1 > num2 ) {
30        printf( "%d is greater than %d\n", num1, num2 );
31     } // end if
32
33     if ( num1 <= num2 ) {
34        printf( "%d is less than or equal to %d\n", num1, num2 );
35     } // end if
36
37     if ( num1 >= num2 ) {
38        printf( "%d is greater than or equal to %d\n", num1, num2 );
39     } // end if
40  } // end function main
```

```
Enter two integers, and I will tell you
the relationships they satisfy: 3 7
3 is not equal to 7
3 is less than 7
3 is less than or equal to 7
```

Fig. 2.13 | Using if statements, relational operators, and equality operators. (Part I of 2.)

```
Enter two integers, and I will tell you
the relationships they satisfy: 22 12
22 is not equal to 12
22 is greater than 12
22 is greater than or equal to 12
```

```
Enter two integers, and I will tell you
the relationships they satisfy: 7 7
7 is equal to 7
7 is less than or equal to 7
7 is greater than or equal to 7
```

Fig. 2.13 | Using if statements, relational operators, and equality operators. (Part 2 of 2.)

The program uses scanf (line 15) to input two numbers. Each conversion specifier has a corresponding argument in which a value will be stored. The first %d converts a value to be stored in the variable num1, and the second %d converts a value to be stored in the variable num2.

Good Programming Practice 2.10

Although it's allowed, there should be no more than one statement per line in a program.

Common Programming Error 2.10

Placing commas (when none are needed) between conversion specifiers in the format control string of a scanf statement.

Comparing Numbers
The if statement in lines 17–19

```
if ( num1 == num2 ) {
    printf( "%d is equal to %d\n", num1, num2 );
}
```

compares the values of variables num1 and num2 to test for equality. If the values are equal, the statement in line 18 displays a line of text indicating that the numbers are equal. If the conditions are true in one or more of the if statements starting in lines 21, 25, 29, 33 and 37, the corresponding body statement displays an appropriate line of text. Indenting the body of each if statement and placing blank lines above and below each if statement enhances program readability.

Common Programming Error 2.11

Placing a semicolon immediately to the right of the right parenthesis after the condition in an if statement.

A left brace, {, begins the body of each if statement (e.g., line 17). A corresponding right brace, }, ends each if statement's body (e.g., line 19). Any number of statements can be placed in the body of an if statement.[2]

Good Programming Practice 2.11

A lengthy statement may be spread over several lines. If a statement must be split across lines, choose breaking points that make sense (such as after a comma in a comma-separated list). If a statement is split across two or more lines, indent all subsequent lines. It's not correct to split identifiers.

Figure 2.14 lists from highest to lowest the precedence of the operators introduced in this chapter. Operators are shown top to bottom in decreasing order of precedence. The equals sign is also an operator. All these operators, with the exception of the assignment operator =, associate from left to right. The assignment operator (=) associates from right to left.

Good Programming Practice 2.12

Refer to the operator precedence chart when writing expressions containing many operators. Confirm that the operators in the expression are applied in the proper order. If you're uncertain about the order of evaluation in a complex expression, use parentheses to group expressions or break the statement into several simpler statements. Be sure to observe that some of C's operators such as the assignment operator (=) associate from right to left *rather than from left to right.*

Operators				Associativity
( )				left to right
*	/	%		left to right
+	-			left to right
<	<=	>	>=	left to right
==	!=			left to right
=				right to left

Fig. 2.14 | Precedence and associativity of the operators discussed so far.

Some of the words we've used in the C programs in this chapter—in particular int and if—are keywords or reserved words of the language. Figure 2.15 contains the C keywords. These words have special meaning to the C compiler, so you must be careful not to use these as identifiers such as variable names.

In this chapter, we've introduced many important features of the C programming language, including displaying data on the screen, inputting data from the user, performing calculations and making decisions. In the next chapter, we build upon these techniques as we introduce structured programming. You'll become more familiar with indentation techniques. We'll study how to specify the *order in which statements are executed*—this is called flow of control.

---

2. Using braces to delimit the body of an if statement is optional when the body contains only one statement. Many programmers consider it good practice to always use these braces. In Chapter 3, we'll explain the issues.

Keywords			
auto	double	int	struct
break	else	long	switch
case	enum	register	typedef
char	extern	return	union
const	float	short	unsigned
continue	for	signed	void
default	goto	sizeof	volatile
do	if	static	while

Keywords added in C99 standard

_Bool _Complex _Imaginary inline restrict

Keywords added in C11 draft standard

_Alignas _Alignof _Atomic _Generic _Noreturn _Static_assert _Thread_local

Fig. 2.15 | C's keywords.

2.7 Secure C Programming

We mentioned *The CERT C Secure Coding Standard* in the Preface and indicated that we would follow certain guidelines that will help you avoid programming practices that open systems to attacks.

Avoid Single-Argument printfs[3]

One such guideline is to *avoid using* printf *with a single string argument*. If you need to display a string that *terminates with a newline*, use the **puts function**, which displays its string argument followed by a newline character. For example, in Fig. 2.1, line 8

```
printf( "Welcome to C!\n" );
```

should be written as:

```
puts( "Welcome to C!" );
```

We did not include \n in the preceding string because puts adds it automatically.

If you need to display a string *without* a terminating newline character, use printf with *two* arguments—a "%s" format control string and the string to display. The **%s conversion specifier** is for displaying a string. For example, in Fig. 2.3, line 8

```
printf( "Welcome " );
```

should be written as:

```
printf( "%s", "Welcome " );
```

---

3. For more information, see CERT C Secure Coding rule FIO30-C (www.securecoding.cert.org/confluence/display/seccode/FIO30-C.+Exclude+user+input+from+format+strings). In Chapter 6's Secure C Programming section, we'll explain the notion of user input as referred to by this CERT guideline.

Although the printfs in this chapter as written are actually *not* insecure, these changes are responsible coding practices that will eliminate certain security vulnerabilities as we get deeper into C—we'll explain the rationale later in the book. From this point forward, we use these practices in the chapter examples and you should use them in your exercise solutions.

scanf *and* printf, scanf_s *and* printf_s
We introduced scanf and printf in this chapter. We'll be saying more about these in subsequent Secure C Coding Guidelines sections. We'll also discuss scanf_s and printf_s, which were introduced in C11.

Summary

Section 2.1 Introduction
- The C language facilitates a structured and disciplined approach to computer-program design.

Section 2.2 A Simple C Program: Printing a Line of Text
- Comments begin with //. Comments document programs and improve program readability. C also supports older-style multi-line comments that begin with /* and end with */.
- Comments do not cause the computer to perform any action when the program is run. They're ignored by the C compiler and do not cause any machine-language object code to be generated.
- Lines beginning with # are processed by the preprocessor before the program is compiled. The #include directive tells the preprocessor to include the contents of another file.
- The <stdio.h> header contains information used by the compiler when compiling calls to standard input/output library functions such as printf.
- The function main is a part of every C program. The parentheses after main indicate that main is a program building block called a function. C programs contain one or more functions, one of which must be main. Every program in C begins executing at the function main.
- Functions can return information. The keyword int to the left of main indicates that main "returns" an integer (whole-number) value.
- Functions can receive information when they're called upon to execute. The void in parentheses after main indicates that main does not receive any information.
- A left brace, {, begins the body of every function. A corresponding right brace, }, ends each function. This pair of braces and the portion of the program between the braces is called a block.
- The printf function instructs the computer to display information on the screen.
- A string is sometimes called a character string, a message or a literal.
- Every statement must end with a semicolon (also known as the statement terminator).
- In \n, the backslash (\) is called an escape character. When encountering a backslash in a string, the compiler looks ahead at the next character and combines it with the backslash to form an escape sequence. The escape sequence \n means newline.
- When a newline appears in the string output by a printf, the newline causes the cursor to position to the beginning of the next line on the screen.
- The double backslash (\\) escape sequence can be used to place a single backslash in a string.
- The escape sequence \" represents a literal double-quote character.

Section 2.3 Another Simple C Program: Adding Two Integers
- A variable is a location in memory where a value can be stored for use by a program.

- Variables of type int hold integer values, i.e., whole numbers such as 7, −11, 0, 31914.
- All variables must be defined with a name and a data type before they can be used in a program.
- A variable name in C is any valid identifier. An identifier is a series of characters consisting of letters, digits and underscores (_) that does not begin with a digit.
- C is case sensitive—uppercase and lowercase letters are different in C.
- Micosoft Visual C++ requires variable definitions in C programs to be placed after the left brace of a function and before *any* executable statements. GNU gcc and some other compilers do not have this restriction.
- A syntax error is caused when the compiler cannot recognize a statement. The compiler normally issues an error message to help you locate and fix the incorrect statement. Syntax errors are violations of the language. Syntax errors are also called compile errors, or compile-time errors.
- Standard Library function scanf can be used to obtain input from the standard input, which is usually the keyboard.
- The scanf format control string indicates the type(s) of data that should be input.
- The %d conversion specifier indicates that the data should be an integer (the letter d stands for "decimal integer"). The % in this context is treated by scanf (and printf) as a special character that begins a conversion specifier.
- The arguments that follow scanf's format control string begin with an ampersand (&)—called the address operator in C—followed by a variable name. The ampersand, when combined with a variable name, tells scanf the location in memory at which the variable is located. The computer then stores the value for the variable at that location.
- Most calculations are performed in assignment statements.
- The = operator and the + operator are binary operators—each has two operands.
- In a printf that specifies a format control string as its first argument the conversion specifiers indicate placeholders for data to output.

Section 2.4 Memory Concepts
- Variable names correspond to locations in the computer's memory. Every variable has a name, a type and a value.
- Whenever a value is placed in a memory location, the value replaces the previous value in that location; thus, placing a new value into a memory location is said to be destructive.
- When a value is read from a memory location, the process is said to be nondestructive.

Section 2.5 Arithmetic in C
- In algebra, if we want to multiply *a* times *b*, we can simply place these single-letter variable names side by side as in *ab*. In C, however, if we were to do this, ab would be interpreted as a single, two-letter name (or identifier). Therefore, C (like other programming languages, in general) requires that multiplication be explicitly denoted by using the * operator, as in a * b.
- Arithmetic expressions in C must be written in straight-line form to facilitate entering programs into the computer. Thus, expressions such as "a divided by b" must be written as a/b, so that all operators and operands appear in a straight line.
- Parentheses are used to group terms in C expressions in much the same manner as in algebraic expressions.
- C evaluates arithmetic expressions in a precise sequence determined by the following rules of operator precedence, which are generally the same as those followed in algebra.

- Multiplication, division and remainder operations are applied first. If an expression contains several multiplication, division and remainder operations, evaluation proceeds from left to right. Multiplication, division and remainder are said to be on the same level of precedence.

- Addition and subtraction operations are evaluated next. If an expression contains several addition and subtraction operations, evaluation proceeds from left to right. Addition and subtraction also have the same level of precedence, which is lower than the precedence of the multiplication, division and remainder operators.

- The rules of operator precedence specify the order C uses to evaluate expressions. The associativity of the operators specifies whether they evaluate from left to right or from right to left.

Section 2.6 Decision Making: Equality and Relational Operators
- Executable C statements either perform actions or make decisions.

- C's if statement allows a program to make a decision based on the truth or falsity of a statement of fact called a condition. If the condition is met (i.e., the condition is true) the statement in the body of the if statement executes. If the condition isn't met (i.e., the condition is false) the body statement does not execute. Whether the body statement is executed or not, after the if statement completes, execution proceeds with the next statement after the if statement.

- Conditions in if statements are formed by using the equality operators and relational operators.

- The relational operators all have the same level of precedence and associate left to right. The equality operators have a lower level of precedence than the relational operators and they also associate left to right.

- To avoid confusing assignment (=) and equality (==), the assignment operator should be read "gets" and the equality operator should be read "double equals."

- In C programs, white-space characters such as tabs, newlines and spaces are normally ignored. So, statements may be split over several lines. It's not correct to split identifiers.

- Keywords (or reserved words) have special meaning to the C compiler, so you cannot use them as identifiers such as variable names.

Section 2.7 Secure C Programming
- One practice to help avoid leaving systems open to attacks is to avoid using printf with a single string argument.

- To display a string followed by a newline character, use the puts function, which displays it's string argument followed by a newline character.

- To display a string without a trailing newline character, you can use printf the format string argument "%s" followed by a second argument representing the string to display. The conversion specification %s is for displaying a string.

Terminology

Self-Review Exercises

2.1 Fill in the blanks in each of the following.
a) Every C program begins execution at the function _____.
b) Every function's body begins with _____ and ends with _____.
c) Every statement ends with a(n) _____.
d) The _____ standard library function displays information on the screen.
e) The escape sequence \n represents the _____ character, which causes the cursor to position to the beginning of the next line on the screen.
f) The _____ Standard Library function is used to obtain data from the keyboard.
g) The conversion specifier _____ is used in a scanf format control string to indicate that an integer will be input and in a printf format control string to indicate that an integer will be output.
h) Whenever a new value is placed in a memory location, that value overrides the previous value in that location. This process is said to be _____.
i) When a value is read from a memory location, the value in that location is preserved; this process is said to be _____.
j) The _____ statement is used to make decisions.

2.2 State whether each of the following is *true* or *false*. If *false*, explain why.
a) Function printf always begins printing at the beginning of a new line.
b) Comments cause the computer to display the text after // on the screen when the program is executed.
c) The escape sequence \n when used in a printf format control string causes the cursor to position to the beginning of the next line on the screen.
d) All variables must be defined before they're used.
e) All variables must be given a type when they're defined.

    f)   C considers the variables number and NuMbEr to be identical.

    g)   Definitions can appear anywhere in the body of a function.

    h)   All arguments following the format control string in a printf function must be preceded by an ampersand (&).

    i)   The remainder operator (%) can be used only with integer operands.

    j)   The arithmetic operators *, /, %, + and - all have the same level of precedence.

    k)   A program that prints three lines of output must contain three printf statements.

2.3   Write a single C statement to accomplish each of the following:

    a)   Define the variables c, thisVariable, q76354 and number to be of type int.

    b)   Prompt the user to enter an integer. End your prompting message with a colon (:) followed by a space and leave the cursor positioned after the space.

    c)   Read an integer from the keyboard and store the value entered in integer variable a.

    d)   If number is not equal to 7, print "The variable number is not equal to 7."

    e)   Print the message "This is a C program." on one line.

    f)   Print the message "This is a C program." on two lines so that the first line ends with C.

    g)   Print the message "This is a C program." with each word on a separate line.

    h)   Print the message "This is a C program." with the words separated by tabs.

2.4   Write a statement (or comment) to accomplish each of the following:

    a)   State that a program will calculate the sum of four integers.

    b)   Define the variables p, q, r, s and sum to be of type int.

    c)   Prompt the user to enter four integers.

    d)   Read four integers from the keyboard and store them in the variables p, q, r and s.

    e)   Compute the sum of the four integers contained in variables p, q, r and s, and assign the result to the variable sum.

    f)   Print "The sum is" followed by the value of the integer variable sum.

2.5   Using the statements you wrote in Exercise 2.4, write a complete program that calculates the sum of four integers.

2.6   Identify and correct the errors in each of the following statements:

    a)   `printf( "The value is %d\n", &number );`

    b)   `scanf( "%d%d", &number1, number2 );`

    c)
```
if ( c < 7 );{
    printf( "C is less than 7\n" );
}
```

    d)
```
if ( c => 7 ) {
    printf( "C is greater than or equal to 7\n" );
}
```

Answers to Self-Review Exercises

2.1   a) main. b) left brace ({), right brace (}). c) semicolon. d) printf. e) newline. f) scanf. g) %d. h) destructive. i) nondestructive. j) if.

2.2   a)   False. Function printf always begins printing where the cursor is positioned, and this may be anywhere on a line of the screen.

    b)   False. Comments do not cause any action to be performed when the program is executed. They're used to document programs and improve their readability.

    c)   True.

    d)   True.

    e)   True.

    f)   False. C is case sensitive, so these variables are unique.

g) False. A variable's definition must appear before its first use in the code. In Microsoft Visual C++, variable definitions must appear immediately following the left brace that begins the body of main. Later in the book we'll discuss this in more depth as we encounter additional C features that can affect this issue.

h) False. Arguments in a printf function ordinarily should not be preceded by an ampersand. Arguments following the format control string in a scanf function ordinarily should be preceded by an ampersand. We'll discuss exceptions to these rules in Chapter 6 and Chapter 7.

i) True.

j) False. The operators *, / and % are on the same level of precedence, and the operators + and - are on a lower level of precedence.

k) False. A printf statement with multiple \n escape sequences can print several lines.

2.3 a) `int c, thisVariable, q76354, number;`
   b) `printf( "Enter an integer: " );`
   c) `scanf( "%d", &a );`
   d) `if ( number != 7 ) {`
       `printf( "The variable number is not equal to 7.\n" );`
       `}`
   e) `printf( "This is a C program.\n" );`
   f) `printf( "This is a C\nprogram.\n" );`
   g) `printf( "This\nis\na\nC\nprogram.\n" );`
   h) `printf( "This\tis\ta\tC\tprogram.\n" );`

2.4 a) `/* Calculate the sum of four integers */`
   b) `int p, q, r, s, sum;`
   c) `printf( "Enter four integers: " );`
   d) `scanf( "%d%d%d%d", &p, &q, &r, &s );`
   e) `sum = p + q + r + s;`
   f) `printf( "The sum is %d\n", sum );`

2.5 See below.

```
I    /* Calculate the sum of four integers */
2    #include <stdio.h>
3
4    int main( void )
5    {
6       int p, q, r, s, sum; /* declare variables */
7
8       printf( "Enter four integers: " );  /* prompt */
9       scanf( "%d%d%d%d", &p, &q, &r, &s );      /* read four integers */
10      sum = p + q + r + s; /* add values */
11      printf( "The sum is %d\n", sum ); /* display result */
12      return 0;
13   } /* end function main */
```

2.6 a) Error: &number.
   Correction: Eliminate the &. We discuss exceptions to this later.
   b) Error: number2 does not have an ampersand.
   Correction: number2 should be &number2. Later in the text we discuss exceptions to this.
   c) Error: Semicolon after the right parenthesis of the condition in the if statement.
   Correction: Remove the semicolon after the right parenthesis. [*Note:* The result of this error is that the printf statement will be executed whether or not the condition in the

if statement is true. The semicolon after the right parenthesis is considered an empty statement—a statement that does nothing.]

d) Error: => is not an operator in C.
Correction: The relational operator => should be changed to >= (greater than or equal to).

Exercises

2.7 Identify and correct the errors in each of the following statements. (*Note:* There may be more than one error per statement.)

a) `scanf( "d", value );`

b) `printf( "The product of %d and %d is %d"\n, x, y );`

c) `firstNumber + secondNumber = sumOfNumbers`

d) `if ( number => largest )`
     `largest == number;`

e) `*/ Program to determine the largest of three integers /*`

f) `Scanf( "%d", anInteger );`

g) `printf( "Remainder of %d divided by %d is\n", x, y, x % y );`

h) `if ( x = y );`
     `printf( %d is equal to %d\n", x, y );`

i) `print( "The sum is %d\n," x + y );`

j) `Printf( "The value you entered is: %d\n, &value );`

2.8 Fill in the blanks in each of the following:

a) _____ are used to document a program and improve its readability.

b) The function used to display information on the screen is _____.

c) A C statement that makes a decision is _____.

d) Calculations are normally performed by _____ statements.

e) The _____ function inputs values from the keyboard.

2.9 Write a single C statement or line that accomplishes each of the following:

a) State that a program performs scientific calculations (i.e., use text that helps to document a program).

b) Print the message "C Language" with double quotes.

c) Write a statement that performs the subtraction of two numbers stored in variables a and b respectively, and stores the result in a variable called difference.

d) Write a statement which initializes the value of A to an integer number 7.

2.10 State which of the following are *true* and which are *false*. If *false*, explain your answer.

a) C operators are evaluated from left to right.

b) The following are all valid variable names: _under_bar_, m928134, t5, j7, her_sales, his_account_total, a, b, c, z, z2.

c) The statement printf("a = 5;"); is a typical example of an assignment statement.

d) A valid arithmetic expression containing no parentheses is evaluated from left to right.

e) The following are all invalid variable names: 3g, 87, 67h2, h22, 2h.

2.11 Fill in the blanks in each of the following:

a) What arithmetic operations are on the same level of precedence as multiplication? _____.

b) When parentheses are nested, which set of parentheses is evaluated first in an arithmetic expression? _____.

c) A location in the computer's memory that may contain different values at various times throughout the execution of a program is called a _____.

2.12 What, if anything, prints when each of the following statements is performed? If nothing prints, then answer "Nothing." Assume a = 3, b = 9 and c = 18.

    a) printf("%d", a * b /c);
    b) printf("%d", c % b);
    c) scanf("%d", &a);
    d) p = a * b * c;
    e) printf("%d + %d = %d", a + b, a + a, c);
    f) /* q = a % c; */
    g) printf("(a + b) + c = %d\n a + (b + c) = %d", (a + b) + c, a + (b + c));
    h) a = c / 6;
    i) printf("%d\n%d", a, a);

2.13 Which, if any, of the following C statements contain variables whose values are replaced?

    a) printf("%d", x + y);
    b) scanf("%d", &x);
    c) printf("\n");
    d) x = (a * b) % c / d;

2.14 Given the equation $z = \dfrac{ax^2 + bx^2}{3}$, which of the following, if any, are correct C statements for this equation?

    a) z = a * x * x + b * x * x / 3 ;
    b) z = a *(x * x) + (b * x) * x / 3;
    c) z =((a *(x * x))+ (b * (x * x))) / 3;
    d) z = a *(x * x) + (b * x) * (x / 3);
    e) z = a * x * (x + b) * x * x / 3 ;
    f) z = a * (x * x) + b * (x * x) / 3 ;

2.15 State the order of evaluation of the operators in each of the following C statements and show the value of p after each statement is performed.

    a) p = 1 + 3 * 15 % 5;
    b) p = (((4 + 3) - 5) * 7) % 3;
    c) p = 6 % ((2 - 1) * 6);

2.16 *(Arithmetic)* Write a program that asks the user to enter two numbers, obtains them from the user and prints their sum, square of the sum, cube of the sum, difference, square of the difference and cube of the difference.

2.17 *(Printing Values with* `printf`*)* Write a program that prints the numbers 1 to 4 on the same line. Write the program using the following methods.

    a) Using one `printf` statement with no conversion specifiers.
    b) Using one `printf` statement with four conversion specifiers.
    c) Using four `printf` statements.

2.18 *(Comparing Integers)* Write a program that asks the user to enter the length and the breadth of a rectangle and obtains the numbers from the user. If the length and the breadth are equal, print the message "It is a Square" else print the message "It is not a Square". Use only the single-selection form of the `if` statement you learned in this chapter.

2.19 *(Arithmetic, Largest Value and Smallest Value)* Write a program that inputs three different integers from the keyboard, then prints the sum, the average, the product, the smallest and the largest of these numbers. Use only the single-selection form of the `if` statement you learned in this chapter. The screen dialogue should appear as follows:

```
Enter three different integers: 13 27 14
Sum is 54
Average is 18
Product is 4914
Smallest is 13
Largest is 27
```

2.20   *(Area and perimeter of a square)* Write a program that reads in the side of a square and prints the square's area and perimeter. Perform each of these calculations inside the `printf` statement(s).

2.21   *(Shapes with Asterisks)* Write a program that prints the following shapes with asterisks.

```
*********         ***               *                    *
*       *        *   *             ***                  *  *
*       *       *     *           *****                *    *
*       *       *     *             *                 *      *
*       *       *     *             *                *        *
*       *       *     *             *                *        *
*       *       *     *             *                 *      *
*       *        *   *              *                  *    *
*********         ***               *                    *
```

2.22   What does the following code print?

```
printf( "*****\n*\n*\n*\n*\n*\n *****\n" );
```

2.23   *(Largest and Smallest Integers)* Write a program that reads in three integers and then determines and prints the largest and the smallest integers in the group. Use only the programming techniques you have learned in this chapter.

2.24   *(Odd or Even)* Write a program that reads an integer and determines and prints whether it's odd or even. [*Hint:* Use the remainder operator. An even number is a multiple of two. Any multiple of two leaves a remainder of zero when divided by 2.]

2.25   Print your initials in block letters down the page. Construct each block letter out of the letter it represents, as shown below.

```
PPPPPPPPP
     P       P
     P       P
     P       P
      P P

   JJ
  J
 J
  J
   JJJJJJJ
DDDDDDDDD
D        D
D        D
 D      D
   DDDDD
```

2.26   *(Multiples)* Write a program that reads in two integers and determines and prints whether the first is a multiple of the second. [*Hint:* Use the remainder operator.]

2.27   *(Pyramid Pattern of Asterisks)* Display the following pyramid pattern with five `printf` statements and then display the same pattern using a single `printf` statement.

```
    *
   ***
  *****
 *******
*********
```

2.28 Distinguish between the terms fatal error and nonfatal error. Why might you prefer to experience a fatal error rather than a nonfatal error?

2.29 *(Integer Value of a Character)* Here's a peek ahead. In this chapter you learned about integers and the type int. C can also represent uppercase letters, lowercase letters and a considerable variety of special symbols. C uses small integers internally to represent each different character. The set of characters a computer uses together with the corresponding integer representations for those characters is called that computer's character set. You can print the integer equivalent of uppercase A, for example, by executing the statement

```
printf( "%d", 'A' );
```

Write a C program that prints the integer equivalents of some uppercase letters, lowercase letters, digits and special symbols. As a minimum, determine the integer equivalents of the following: A B C a b c 0 1 2 $ * + / and the blank character.

2.30 *(Separating Digits in an Integer)* Write a program that inputs one five-digit number, separates the number into its individual digits and prints the digits separated from one another by three spaces each. [*Hint:* Use combinations of integer division and the remainder operation.] For example, if the user types in 42139, the program should print

```
4   2   1   3   9
```

2.31 *(Table of Squares and Cubes)* Using only the techniques you learned in this chapter, write a program that calculates the squares and cubes of the numbers from 0 to 10 and uses tabs to print the following table of values:

```
number  square  cube
0       0       0
1       1       1
2       4       8
3       9       27
4       16      64
5       25      125
6       36      216
7       49      343
8       64      512
9       81      729
10      100     1000
```

Making a Difference

2.32 *(Body Mass Index Calculator)* We introduced the body mass index (BMI) calculator in Exercise 1.14. The formulas for calculating BMI are

$$BMI = \frac{weightInPounds \times 703}{heightInInches \times heightInInches}$$

or

$$BMI = \frac{weightInKilograms}{heightInMeters \times heightInMeters}$$

Create a BMI calculator application that reads the user's weight in pounds and height in inches (or, if you prefer, the user's weight in kilograms and height in meters), then calculates and displays the user's body mass index. Also, the application should display the following information from the Department of Health and Human Services/National Institutes of Health so the user can evaluate his/her BMI:

```
BMI VALUES
Underweight: less than 18.5
Normal:      between 18.5 and 24.9
Overweight:  between 25 and 29.9
Obese:       30 or greater
```

[*Note:* In this chapter, you learned to use the int type to represent whole numbers. The BMI calculations when done with int values will both produce whole-number results. In Chapter 4 you'll learn to use the double type to represent numbers with decimal points. When the BMI calculations are performed with doubles, they'll both produce numbers with decimal points—these are called "floating-point" numbers.]

2.33   *(Car-Pool Savings Calculator)* Research several car-pooling websites. Create an application that calculates your daily driving cost, so that you can estimate how much money could be saved by car pooling, which also has other advantages such as reducing carbon emissions and reducing traffic congestion. The application should input the following information and display the user's cost per day of driving to work:

    a) Total miles driven per day.
    b) Cost per gallon of gasoline.
    c) Average miles per gallon.
    d) Parking fees per day.
    e) Tolls per day.

3

Structured Program Development in C

Let's all move one place on.
—Lewis Carroll

The wheel is come full circle.
—William Shakespeare

All the evolution we know of proceeds from the vague to the definite.
—Charles Sanders Peirce

Objectives

In this chapter, you'll:

- Use basic problem-solving techniques.

- Develop algorithms through the process of top-down, stepwise refinement.

- Use the if selection statement and the if...else selection statement to select actions.

- Use the while repetition statement to execute statements in a program repeatedly.

- Use counter-controlled repetition and sentinel-controlled repetition.

- Learn structured programming.

- Use increment, decrement and assignment operators.

3.1 Introduction

Before writing a program to solve a particular problem, we must have a thorough understanding of the problem and a carefully planned solution approach. The next two chapters discuss techniques that facilitate the development of structured computer programs. In Section 4.12, we present a summary of the structured programming techniques developed here and in Chapter 4.

3.2 Algorithms

The solution to any computing problem involves executing a series of actions in a specific order. A **procedure** for solving a problem in terms of

1. the **actions** to be executed, and

2. the **order** in which these actions are to be executed

is called an **algorithm**. The following example demonstrates that correctly specifying the order in which the actions are to be executed is important.

Consider the "rise-and-shine algorithm" followed by one junior executive for getting out of bed and going to work: (1) Get out of bed, (2) take off pajamas, (3) take a shower, (4) get dressed, (5) eat breakfast, (6) carpool to work. This routine gets the executive to work well prepared to make critical decisions. Suppose that the *same* steps are performed in a slightly different *order*: (1) Get out of bed, (2) take off pajamas, (3) get dressed, (4) take a shower, (5) eat breakfast, (6) carpool to work. In this case, our junior executive shows up for work soaking wet. Specifying the order in which statements are to be executed in a computer program is called **program control**. In this and the next chapter, we investigate C's program control capabilities.

3.3 Pseudocode

Pseudocode is an artificial and informal language that helps you develop algorithms. The pseudocode we present here is particularly useful for developing algorithms that will be converted to structured C programs. Pseudocode is similar to everyday *English*; it's convenient and user friendly although it's *not* an actual computer programming language.

Pseudocode programs are *not* executed on computers. Rather, they merely help you "think out" a program before attempting to write it in a programming language like C.

Pseudocode consists purely of characters, so you may conveniently type pseudocode programs into a computer using an editor program. A carefully prepared pseudocode program may be easily converted to a corresponding C program. This is done in many cases simply by replacing pseudocode statements with their C equivalents.

Pseudocode consists only of *action* statements—those that are executed when the program has been converted from pseudocode to C and is run in C. Definitions are *not* executable statements—they're simply messages to the compiler. For example, the definition

```
int i;
```

tells the compiler the type of variable i and instructs the compiler to reserve space in memory for the variable. But this definition does *not* cause any action—such as input, output, a calculation or a comparison—to occur when the program is executed. Some programmers choose to list each variable and briefly mention the purpose of each at the beginning of a pseudocode program.

3.4 Control Structures

Normally, statements in a program are executed one after the other in the order in which they're written. This is called **sequential execution**. Various C statements we'll soon discuss enable you to specify that the next statement to be executed may be *other* than the next one in sequence. This is called **transfer of control**.

During the 1960s, it became clear that the indiscriminate use of transfers of control was the root of a great deal of difficulty experienced by software development groups. The finger of blame was pointed at the **goto statement** that allows you to specify a transfer of control to one of many possible destinations in a program. The notion of so-called structured programming became almost synonymous with "**goto elimination.**"

The research of Bohm and Jacopini[1] had demonstrated that programs could be written *without* any goto statements. The challenge of the era was for programmers to shift their styles to "goto-less programming." It was not until well into the 1970s that the programming profession started taking structured programming seriously. The results were impressive, as software development groups reported reduced development times, more frequent on-time delivery of systems and more frequent within-budget completion of software projects. Programs produced with structured techniques were clearer, easier to debug and modify and more likely to be bug free in the first place.

Bohm and Jacopini's work demonstrated that all programs could be written in terms of only three **control structures**, namely the **sequence structure**, the **selection structure** and the **repetition structure**. The sequence structure is simple—unless directed otherwise, the computer executes C statements one after the other in the order in which they're written. The flowchart segment of Fig. 3.1 illustrates C's sequence structure.

---

1. C. Bohm and G. Jacopini, "Flow Diagrams, Turing Machines, and Languages with Only Two Formation Rules," *Communications of the ACM*, Vol. 9, No. 5, May 1966, pp. 336–371.

Flowcharts

A flowchart is a *graphical* representation of an algorithm or of a portion of an algorithm. Flowcharts are drawn using certain special-purpose symbols such as *rectangles, diamonds, rounded rectaingles*, and *small circles*; these symbols are connected by arrows called flowlines.

Like pseudocode, flowcharts are useful for developing and representing algorithms, although pseudocode is preferred by most programmers. Flowcharts clearly show how control structures operate; that's what we use them for in this text.

Consider the flowchart for the sequence structure in Fig. 3.1. We use the **rectangle** symbol, also called the **action symbol**, to indicate any type of action including a calculation or an input/output operation. The flowlines in the figure indicate the *order* in which the actions are performed—first, `grade` is added to `total`, then 1 is added to `counter`. C allows us to have as many actions as we want in a sequence structure. As we'll soon see, *anywhere a single action may be placed, we may place several actions in sequence*.

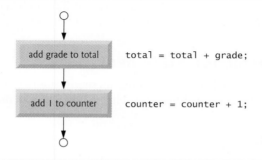

Fig. 3.1 | Flowcharting C's sequence structure.

When drawing a flowchart that represents a complete algorithm, a **rounded rectangle** symbol containing the word "Begin" is the first symbol used in the flowchart; a rounded rectangle symbol containing the word "End" is the last symbol used. When drawing only a *portion* of an algorithm as in Fig. 3.1, the rounded rectangle symbols are omitted in favor of using **small circle** symbols, also called **connector symbols**.

Perhaps the most important flowcharting symbol is the **diamond symbol**, also called the **decision symbol**, which indicates that a *decision* is to be made. We'll discuss the diamond symbol in the next section.

Selection Statements in C

C provides three types of selection structures in the form of statements. The `if` selection statement (Section 3.5) either *selects* (performs) an action if a condition is *true* or *skips* the action if the condition is *false*. The `if...else` selection statement (Section 3.6) performs an action if a condition is *true* and performs a different action if the condition is *false*. The `switch` selection statement (discussed in Chapter 4) performs one of *many* different actions, depending on the value of an expression. The `if` statement is called a **single-selection statement** because it selects or ignores a single action. The `if...else` statement is called a **double-selection statement** because it selects between two different actions. The `switch` statement is called a **multiple-selection statement** because it selects among many different actions.

Repetition Statements in C

C provides three types of *repetition structures* in the form of statements, namely while (Section 3.7), do...while, and for (both discussed in Chapter 4).

That's all there is. C has only seven control statements: sequence, three types of selection and three types of repetition. Each C program is formed by combining as many of each type of control statement as is appropriate for the algorithm the program implements. As with the sequence structure of Fig. 3.1, we'll see that the flowchart representation of each control statement has two small circle symbols, one at the *entry point* to the control statement and one at the *exit point*. These **single-entry/single-exit control statements** make it easy to build clear programs. The control-statement flowchart segments can be attached to one another by connecting the exit point of one control statement to the entry point of the next. This is much like the way in which a child stacks building blocks, so we call this **control-statement stacking**. We'll learn that there's only one other way control statements may be connected—a method called control-statement *nesting*. Thus, any C program we'll ever need to build can be constructed from only *seven* different types of control statements combined in only two ways. This is the essence of simplicity.

3.5 The if Selection Statement

Selection statements are used to choose among alternative courses of action. For example, suppose the passing grade on an exam is 60. The pseudocode statement

> *If student's grade is greater than or equal to 60*
> *Print "Passed"*

determines whether the condition "student's grade is greater than or equal to 60" is true or false. If the condition is true, then "Passed" is printed, and the next pseudocode statement in order is "performed" (remember that pseudocode isn't a real programming language). If the condition is false, the printing is ignored, and the next pseudocode statement in order is performed. The second line of this selection structure is indented. Such indentation is optional, but it's highly recommended, as it helps emphasize the inherent structure of structured programs. The C compiler ignores white-space characters such as blanks, tabs and newlines used for indentation and vertical spacing.

The preceding pseudocode *If* statement may be written in C as

```
if ( grade >= 60 ) {
   printf( "Passed\n" );
} // end if
```

Notice that the C code corresponds closely to the pseudocode (of course you'll also need to declare the int variable grade). This is one of the properties of pseudocode that makes it such a useful program development tool.

The flowchart of Fig. 3.2 illustrates the single-selection if statement. This flowchart contains what is perhaps the most important flowcharting symbol—the diamond symbol, also called the decision symbol, which indicates that a decision is to be made. The decision symbol contains an expression, such as a condition, that can be either true or false. The decision symbol has *two* flowlines emerging from it. One indicates the direction to take when the expression in the symbol is true and the other the direction to take when the expression is false. Decisions can be based on conditions containing relational or equality operators. In fact, a decision can be based on *any* expression—if the expression evaluates to *zero*, it's treated as false, and if it evaluates to *nonzero*, it's treated as true.

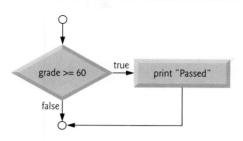

Fig. 3.2 | Flowcharting the single-selection if statement.

The if statement, too, is a *single-entry/single-exit* statement. We'll soon learn that the flowcharts for the remaining control structures can also contain (besides small circle symbols and flowlines) only rectangle symbols to indicate the actions to be performed, and diamond symbols to indicate decisions to be made. This is the *action/decision model of programming* we've been emphasizing.

We can envision seven bins, each containing only control-statement flowcharts of one of the seven types. These flowchart segments are empty—nothing is written in the rectangles and nothing in the diamonds. Your task, then, is assembling a program from as many of each type of control statement as the algorithm demands, combining them in only *two* possible ways (*stacking* or *nesting*), and then filling in the *actions* and *decisions* in a manner appropriate for the algorithm. We'll discuss the variety of ways in which actions and decisions may be written.

3.6 The if...else Selection Statement

The if selection statement performs an indicated action only when the condition is true; otherwise the action is skipped. The if...else selection statement allows you to specify that *different* actions are to be performed when the condition is true and when it's false. For example, the pseudocode statement

> *If student's grade is greater than or equal to 60*
>> *Print "Passed"*
> *else*
>> *Print "Failed"*

prints *Passed* if the student's grade is greater than or equal to 60 and *Failed* if the student's grade is less than 60. In either case, after printing occurs, the next pseudocode statement in sequence is "performed." The body of the *else* is also indented.

Good Programming Practice 3.1

Indent both body statements of an if...else statement.

Good Programming Practice 3.2

If there are several levels of indentation, each level should be indented the same *additional amount of space.*

The preceding pseudocode *If...else* statement may be written in C as

```
if ( grade >= 60 ) {
   puts( "Passed" );
} // end if
else {
   puts( "Failed" );
} // end else
```

The flowchart of Fig. 3.3 illustrates the flow of control in the if...else statement. Once again, besides small circles and arrows, the only symbols in the flowchart are rectangles (for actions) and a diamond (for a decision).

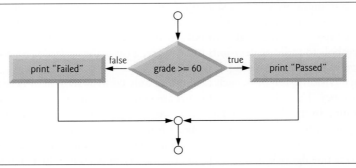

Fig. 3.3 | Flowcharting the double-selection if...else statement.

C provides the **conditional operator (?:)**, which is closely related to the if...else statement. The conditional operator is C's only *ternary* operator—it takes *three* operands. These together with the conditional operator form a **conditional expression**. The first operand is a *condition*. The second operand is the value for the entire conditional expression if the condition is *true* and the operand is the value for the entire conditional expression if the condition is *false*. For example, the puts statement

```
puts( grade >= 60 ? "Passed" : "Failed" );
```

contains as its second argument a conditional expression that evaluates to the string "Passed" if the condition grade >= 60 is true and to the string "Failed" if the condition is false. The puts statement performs in essentially the same way as the preceding if...else statement.

The second and third operands in a conditional expression can also be actions to be executed. For example, the conditional expression

```
grade >= 60 ? puts( "Passed" ) : puts( "Failed" );
```

is read, "If grade is greater than or equal to 60, then puts("Passed"), otherwise puts("Failed")." This, too, is comparable to the preceding if...else statement. We'll see that conditional operators can be used in some places where if...else statements cannot.

Nested *if...else Statements*

Nested if...else statements test for multiple cases by placing if...else statements *inside* if...else statements. For example, the following pseudocode statement will print A for exam grades greater than or equal to 90, B for grades greater than or equal to 80 (but less than 90), C for grades greater than or equal to 70 (but less than 80), D for grades greater than or equal to 60 (but less than 70), and F for all other grades.

> *If student's grade is greater than or equal to 90*
> > *Print "A"*
>
> *else*
> > *If student's grade is greater than or equal to 80*
> > > *Print "B"*
> >
> > *else*
> > > *If student's grade is greater than or equal to 70*
> > > > *Print "C"*
> > >
> > > *else*
> > > > *If student's grade is greater than or equal to 60*
> > > > > *Print "D"*
> > > >
> > > > *else*
> > > > > *Print "F"*

This pseudocode may be written in C as

```c
if ( grade >= 90 ) {
    puts( "A" );
} // end if
else {
    if ( grade >= 80 ) {
        puts("B");
    } // end if
    else {
        if ( grade >= 70 ) {
            puts("C");
        } // end if
        else {
            if ( grade >= 60 ) {
                puts( "D" );
            } // end if
            else {
                puts( "F" );
            } // end else
        } // end else
    } // end else
} // end else
```

If the variable grade is greater than or equal to 90, all four conditions will be true, but only the puts statement after the first test will by executed. After that puts is executed, the else part of the "outer" if...else statement is skipped.

You may prefer to write the preceding `if` statement as

```
if ( grade >= 90 ) {
   puts( "A" );
} // end if
else if ( grade >= 80 ) {
   puts( "B" );
} // end else if
else if ( grade >= 70 ) {
   puts( "C" );
} // end else if
else if ( grade >= 60 ) {
   puts( "D" );
} // end else if
else {
   puts( "F" );
} // end else
```

As far as the C compiler is concerned, both forms are equivalent. The latter form is popular because it avoids the deep indentation of the code to the right. Such indentation often leaves little room on a line, forcing lines to be split and decreasing program readability.

The `if` selection statement expects only one statement in its body—if you have only one statement in the `if`'s body, you do *not* need the enclose it in braces. To include several statements in the body of an `if`, you must enclose the set of statements in braces ({ and }). A set of statements contained within a pair of braces is called a **compound statement** or a **block**.

Software Engineering Observation 3.1

A compound statement can be placed anywhere in a program that a single statement can be placed.

The following example includes a compound statement in the `else` part of an `if...else` statement.

```
if ( grade >= 60 ) {
   puts( "Passed." );
} // end if
else {
   puts( "Failed." );
   puts( "You must take this course again." );
} // end else
```

In this case, if grade is less than 60, the program executes *both* `puts` statements in the body of the `else` and prints

```
Failed.
You must take this course again.
```

The braces surrounding the two statements in the `else` clause are important. Without them, the statement

```
puts( "You must take this course again." );
```

would be *outside* the body of the `else` part of the `if` and would execute regardless of whether the grade was less than 60.

A *syntax error* is caught by the compiler. A *logic error* has its effect at execution time. A *fatal logic error* causes a program to fail and terminate prematurely. A *nonfatal logic error* allows a program to continue executing but to produce incorrect results.

Just as a compound statement can be placed anywhere a single statement can be placed, it's also possible to have no statement at all, i.e., the empty statement. The empty statement is represented by placing a semicolon (;) where a statement would normally be.

Common Programming Error 3.1

Placing a semicolon after the condition in an if statement as in if (grade >= 60); leads to a logic error in single-selection if statements and a syntax error in double-selection if statements.

Error-Prevention Tip 3.1

Typing the beginning and ending braces of compound statements before typing the individual statements within the braces helps avoid omitting one or both of the braces, preventing syntax errors and logic errors (where both braces are indeed required).

3.7 The while Repetition Statement

A **repetition statement** (also called an **iteration statement**) allows you to specify that an action is to be repeated while some condition remains true. The pseudocode statement

> *While there are more items on my shopping list*
> *Purchase next item and cross it off my list*

describes the repetition that occurs during a shopping trip. The condition, "there are more items on my shopping list" may be true or false. If it's true, then the action, "Purchase next item and cross it off my list" is performed. This action will be performed *repeatedly* while the condition remains true. The statement(s) contained in the *while* repetition statement constitute the body of the *while*. The *while* statement body may be a single statement or a compound statement.

Eventually, the condition will become false (when the last item on the shopping list has been purchased and crossed off the list). At this point, the repetition terminates, and the first pseudocode statement *after* the repetition structure is executed.

Common Programming Error 3.2

Not providing in the body of a while statement an action that eventually causes the condition in the while to become false. Normally, such a repetition structure will never terminate—an error called an "infinite loop."

Common Programming Error 3.3

Spelling the keyword while with an uppercase W, as in While (remember that C is a case-sensitive language).

As an example of a **while** statement, consider a program segment designed to find the first power of 3 larger than 100. Suppose the integer variable product has been initialized to 3. When the following while repetition statement finishes executing, product will contain the desired answer:

```
product = 3;
while ( product <= 100 ) {
   product = 3 * product;
} // end while
```

The flowchart of Fig. 3.4 illustrates the flow of control in the while repetition statement. Once again, note that (besides small circles and arrows) the flowchart contains only a rectangle symbol and a diamond symbol. The flowchart clearly shows the repetition. The flowline emerging from the rectangle wraps back to the decision, which is tested each time through the loop until the decision eventually becomes false. At this point, the while statement is exited and control passes to the next statement in the program.

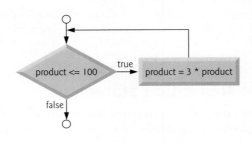

Fig. 3.4 | Flowcharting the while repetition statement.

When the while statement is entered, the value of product is 3. The variable product is repeatedly multiplied by 3, taking on the values 9, 27 and 81 successively. When product becomes 243, the condition in the while statement, product <= 100, becomes false. This terminates the repetition, and the final value of product is 243. Program execution continues with the next statement after the while.

3.8 Formulating Algorithms Case Study 1: Counter-Controlled Repetition

To illustrate how algorithms are developed, we solve several variations of a class-averaging problem. Consider the following problem statement:

> *A class of ten students took a quiz. The grades (integers in the range 0 to 100) for this quiz are available to you. Determine the class average on the quiz.*

The class average is equal to the sum of the grades divided by the number of students. The algorithm for solving this problem on a computer must input each of the grades, perform the averaging calculation, and print the result.

Let's use pseudocode to list the actions to execute and specify the order in which these actions should execute. We use **counter-controlled repetition** to input the grades one at a time. This technique uses a variable called a **counter** to specify the number of times a set of statements should execute. In this example, repetition terminates when the counter exceeds 10. In this section we simply present the pseudocode algorithm (Fig. 3.5) and the corresponding C program (Fig. 3.6). In the next section we show how pseudocode algorithms are *developed*. Counter-controlled repetition is often called **definite repetition** because the number of repetitions is known *before* the loop begins executing.

---

1 *Set total to zero*
2 *Set grade counter to one*
3
4 *While grade counter is less than or equal to ten*
5   *Input the next grade*
6   *Add the grade into the total*
7   *Add one to the grade counter*
8
9 *Set the class average to the total divided by ten*
10 *Print the class average*

Fig. 3.5 | Pseudocode algorithm that uses counter-controlled repetition to solve the class-average problem.

```
1   // Fig. 3.6: fig03_06.c
2   // Class average program with counter-controlled repetition.
3   #include <stdio.h>
4
5   // function main begins program execution
6   int main( void )
7   {
8      unsigned int counter; // number of grade to be entered next
9      int grade; // grade value
10     int total; // sum of grades entered by user
11     int average; // average of grades
12
13     // initialization phase
14     total = 0; // initialize total
15     counter = 1; // initialize loop counter
16
17     // processing phase
18     while ( counter <= 10 ) { // loop 10 times
19        printf( "%s", "Enter grade: " ); // prompt for input
20        scanf( "%d", &grade ); // read grade from user
21        total = total + grade; // add grade to total
22        counter = counter + 1; // increment counter
23     } // end while
24
25     // termination phase
26     average = total / 10; // integer division
27
28     printf( "Class average is %d\n", average ); // display result
29  } // end function main
```

Fig. 3.6 | Class-average problem with counter-controlled repetition. (Part 1 of 2.)

```
Enter grade: 98
Enter grade: 76
Enter grade: 71
Enter grade: 87
Enter grade: 83
Enter grade: 90
Enter grade: 57
Enter grade: 79
Enter grade: 82
Enter grade: 94
Class average is 81
```

Fig. 3.6 | Class-average problem with counter-controlled repetition. (Part 2 of 2.)

The algorithm mentions a total and a counter. A **total** is a variable used to accumulate the sum of a series of values. A counter is a variable (line 8) used to *count*—in this case, to count the number of grades entered. Because the counter variable is used to count from 1 to 10 in this program (all positive values), we declared the variable as an `unsigned int`, which can store only non-negative values (that is, 0 and higher). Variables used to store totals should normally be initialized to zero *before* being used in a program; otherwise the sum would include the previous value stored in the total's memory location. Counter variables are normally initialized to zero or one, depending on their use (we'll present examples of each). An uninitialized variable contains a "garbage" value—the value last stored in the memory location reserved for that variable.

Common Programming Error 3.4

If a counter or total isn't initialized, the results of your program will probably be incorrect. This is an example of a logic error.

Error-Prevention Tip 3.2

Initialize all counters and totals.

The averaging calculation in the program produced an integer result of 81. Actually, the sum of the grades in this example is 817, which when divided by 10 should yield 81.7, i.e., a number with a *decimal point*. We'll see how to deal with such numbers (called *floating-point* numbers) in the next section.

3.9 Formulating Algorithms with Top-Down, Stepwise Refinement Case Study 2: Sentinel-Controlled Repetition

Let's generalize the class-average problem. Consider the following problem:

> *Develop a class-averaging program that will process an* arbitrary *number of grades each time the program is run.*

In the first class-average example, the number of grades (10) was known in advance. In this example, no indication is given of how many grades are to be entered. The program must process an *arbitrary* number of grades. How can the program determine when to stop the input of grades? How will it know when to calculate and print the class average?

One way to solve this problem is to use a special value called a **sentinel value** (also called a **signal value**, a **dummy value**, or a **flag value**) to indicate "end of data entry." The user types in grades until all *legitimate* grades have been entered. The user then types the sentinel value to indicate "the last grade has been entered." Sentinel-controlled repetition is often called **indefinite repetition** because the number of repetitions isn't known *before* the loop begins executing.

Clearly, the sentinel value must be chosen so that it *cannot* be confused with an acceptable input value. Because grades on a quiz are normally *nonnegative* integers, –1 is an acceptable sentinel value for this problem. Thus, a run of the class-average program might process a stream of inputs such as 95, 96, 75, 74, 89 and –1. The program would then compute and print the class average for the grades 95, 96, 75, 74, and 89 (–1 is the sentinel value, so it should *not* enter into the averaging calculation).

Top-Down, Stepwise Refinement

We approach the class-average program with a technique called **top-down, stepwise refinement**, a technique that's essential to the development of well-structured programs. We begin with a pseudocode representation of the **top**:

> *Determine the class average for the quiz*

The top is a single statement that conveys the program's overall function. As such, the top is, in effect, a *complete* representation of a program. Unfortunately, the top rarely conveys a sufficient amount of detail for writing the C program. So we now begin the *refinement* process. We divide the top into a series of smaller tasks and list these in the order in which they need to be performed. This results in the following **first refinement**.

> *Initialize variables*
> *Input, sum, and count the quiz grades*
> *Calculate and print the class average*

Here, only the *sequence structure* has been used—the steps listed are to be executed in order, one after the other.

Software Engineering Observation 3.2

Each refinement, as well as the top itself, is a complete specification of the algorithm; only the level of detail varies.

Second Refinement

To proceed to the next level of refinement, i.e., the **second refinement**, we commit to specific variables. We need a running total of the numbers, a count of how many numbers have been processed, a variable to receive the value of each grade as it's input and a variable to hold the calculated average. The pseudocode statement

> *Initialize variables*

may be refined as follows:

> *Initialize total to zero*
> *Initialize counter to zero*

Notice that only the total and counter need to be initialized; the variables average and grade (for the calculated average and the user input, respectively) need not be initialized because their values will be written over by the process of destructive read-in discussed in Chapter 2. The pseudocode statement

Input, sum, and count the quiz grades

requires a *repetition structure* that successively inputs each grade. Because we do not know in advance how many grades are to be processed, we'll use sentinel-controlled repetition. The user will enter legitimate grades one at a time. After the last legitimate grade is typed, the user will type the sentinel value. The program will test for this value after each grade is input and will terminate the loop when the sentinel is entered. The refinement of the preceding pseudocode statement is then

Input the first grade
While the user has not as yet entered the sentinel
    Add this grade into the running total
    Add one to the grade counter
    Input the next grade (possibly the sentinel)

Notice that in pseudocode, we do *not* use braces around the set of statements that form the body of the *while* statement. We simply indent all these statements under the *while* to show that they all belong to the *while*. Again, pseudocode is an informal program development aid.

The pseudocode statement

Calculate and print the class average

may be refined as follows:

If the counter is not equal to zero
    Set the average to the total divided by the counter
    Print the average
else
    Print "No grades were entered"

Notice that we're being careful here to test for the possibility of *division by zero*—a **fatal** error that if undetected would cause the program to fail (often called "**crashing**"). The complete second refinement is shown in Fig. 3.7.

Common Programming Error 3.5
An attempt to divide by zero causes a fatal error.

Good Programming Practice 3.3
When performing division by an expression whose value could be zero, explicitly test for this case and handle it appropriately in your program (such as printing an error message) rather than allowing the fatal error to occur.

In Fig. 3.5 and Fig. 3.7, we include some completely blank lines in the pseudocode for readability. Actually, the blank lines separate these programs into their various phases.

```
 1    Initialize total to zero
 2    Initialize counter to zero
 3
 4    Input the first grade
 5    While the user has not as yet entered the sentinel
 6        Add this grade into the running total
 7        Add one to the grade counter
 8        Input the next grade (possibly the sentinel)
 9
10    If the counter is not equal to zero
11        Set the average to the total divided by the counter
12        Print the average
13    else
14        Print "No grades were entered"
```

Fig. 3.7 | Pseudocode algorithm that uses sentinel-controlled repetition to solve the class-average problem.

Software Engineering Observation 3.3

Many programs can be divided logically into three phases: an initialization phase *that initializes the program variables; a* processing phase *that inputs data values and adjusts program variables accordingly; and a* termination phase *that calculates and prints the final results.*

The pseudocode algorithm in Fig. 3.7 solves the more general class-averaging problem. This algorithm was developed after only two levels of refinement. Sometimes more levels are necessary.

Software Engineering Observation 3.4

You terminate the top-down, stepwise refinement process when the pseudocode algorithm is specified in sufficient detail for you to be able to convert the pseudocode to C. Implementing the C program is then normally straightforward.

The C program and a sample execution are shown in Fig. 3.8. Although only integer grades are entered, the averaging calculation is likely to produce a number *with a decimal point*. The type int cannot represent such a number. The program introduces the data type **float** to handle numbers with decimal points (called **floating-point numbers**) and introduces a special operator called a *cast operator* to handle the averaging calculation. These features are explained after the program is presented.

```
1    // Fig. 3.8: fig03_08.c
2    // Class-average program with sentinel-controlled repetition.
3    #include <stdio.h>
4
```

Fig. 3.8 | Class-average program with sentinel-controlled repetition. (Part 1 of 3.)

```c
5   // function main begins program execution
6   int main( void )
7   {
8      unsigned int counter; // number of grades entered
9      int grade; // grade value
10     int total; // sum of grades
11
12     float average; // number with decimal point for average
13
14     // initialization phase
15     total = 0; // initialize total
16     counter = 0; // initialize loop counter
17
18     // processing phase
19     // get first grade from user
20     printf( "%s", "Enter grade, -1 to end: " ); // prompt for input
21     scanf( "%d", &grade ); // read grade from user
22
23     // loop while sentinel value not yet read from user
24     while ( grade != -1 ) {
25        total = total + grade; // add grade to total
26        counter = counter + 1; // increment counter
27
28        // get next grade from user
29        printf( "%s", "Enter grade, -1 to end: " ); // prompt for input
30        scanf("%d", &grade); // read next grade
31     } // end while
32
33     // termination phase
34     // if user entered at least one grade
35     if ( counter != 0 ) {
36
37        // calculate average of all grades entered
38        average = ( float ) total / counter; // avoid truncation
39
40        // display average with two digits of precision
41        printf( "Class average is %.2f\n", average );
42     } // end if
43     else { // if no grades were entered, output message
44        puts( "No grades were entered" );
45     } // end else
46  } // end function main
```

```
Enter grade, -1 to end: 75
Enter grade, -1 to end: 94
Enter grade, -1 to end: 97
Enter grade, -1 to end: 88
Enter grade, -1 to end: 70
Enter grade, -1 to end: 64
Enter grade, -1 to end: 83
Enter grade, -1 to end: 89
Enter grade, -1 to end: -1
Class average is 82.50
```

Fig. 3.8 | Class-average program with sentinel-controlled repetition. (Part 2 of 3.)

```
Enter grade, -1 to end: -1
No grades were entered
```

Fig. 3.8 | Class-average program with sentinel-controlled repetition. (Part 3 of 3.)

Notice the compound statement in the `while` loop (line 24) in Fig. 3.8. Once again, the braces are *necessary* to ensure that all four statements are executed within the loop. Without the braces, the last three statements in the body of the loop would fall *outside* the loop, causing the computer to interpret this code incorrectly as follows.

```
while ( grade != -1 )
    total = total + grade; // add grade to total
counter = counter + 1; // increment counter
printf( "%s", "Enter grade, -1 to end: " ); // prompt for input
scanf( "%d", &grade ); // read next grade
```

This would cause an *infinite loop* if the user did not input -1 for the first grade.

Good Programming Practice 3.4

In a sentinel-controlled loop, the prompts requesting data entry should explicitly remind the user what the sentinel value is.

Converting Between Types Explicitly and Implicitly

Averages do not always evaluate to integer values. Often, an average is a value such as 7.2 or −93.5 that contains a fractional part. These values are referred to as floating-point numbers and can be represented by the data type `float`. The variable `average` is defined to be of type `float` (line 12) to capture the fractional result of our calculation. However, the result of the calculation `total / counter` is an integer because `total` and `counter` are *both* integer variables. Dividing two integers results in **integer division** in which any fractional part of the calculation is **truncated** (i.e., lost). Because the calculation is performed *first*, the fractional part is lost *before* the result is assigned to `average`. To produce a floating-point calculation with integer values, we must create temporary values that are floating-point numbers. C provides the unary **cast operator** to accomplish this task. Line 38

```
average = ( float ) total / counter;
```

includes the cast operator (`float`), which creates a *temporary* floating-point copy of its operand, `total`. The value stored in `total` is still an integer. Using a cast operator in this manner is called **explicit conversion**. The calculation now consists of a floating-point value (the temporary `float` version of `total`) divided by the `unsigned int` value stored in `counter`. C evaluates arithmetic expressions only in which the data types of the operands are *identical*. To ensure that the operands are of the *same* type, the compiler performs an operation called **implicit conversion** on selected operands. For example, in an expression containing the data types `unsigned int` and `float`, copies of `unsigned int` operands are made and converted to `float`. In our example, after a copy of `counter` is made and converted to `float`, the calculation is performed and the result of the floating-point division is assigned to `average`. C provides a set of rules for convertion of operands of different types. We discuss this further in Chapter 5.

Cast operators are available for *most* data types—they're formed by placing parentheses around a type name. Each cast operator is a **unary operator**, i.e., an operator that takes only one operand. In Chapter 2, we studied the binary arithmetic operators. C also supports unary versions of the plus (+) and minus (-) operators, so you can write expressions such as -7 or +5. Cast operators associate from right to left and have the same precedence as other unary operators such as unary + and unary -. This precedence is one level higher than that of the **multiplicative operators** *, / and **%**.

Formatting Floating-Point Numbers

Figure 3.8 uses the printf conversion specifier %.2f (line 41) to print the value of average. The f specifies that a floating-point value will be printed. The .2 is the **precision** with which the value will be displayed—with 2 digits to the right of the decimal point. If the %f conversion specifier is used (without specifying the precision), the **default precision** of 6 is used—exactly as if the conversion specifier %.6f had been used. When floating-point values are printed with precision, the printed value is **rounded** to the indicated number of decimal positions. The value in memory is unaltered. When the following statements are executed, the values 3.45 and 3.4 are printed.

```
printf( "%.2f\n", 3.446 ); // prints 3.45
printf( "%.1f\n", 3.446 ); // prints 3.4
```

Common Programming Error 3.6

Using precision in a conversion specification in the format control string of a scanf *statement is wrong. Precisions are used only in* printf *conversion specifications.*

Notes on Floating-Point Numbers

Although floating-point numbers are not always "100% precise," they have numerous applications. For example, when we speak of a "normal" body temperature of 98.6, we do not need to be precise to a large number of digits. When we view the temperature on a thermometer and read it as 98.6, it may actually be 98.5999473210643. The point here is that calling this number simply 98.6 is fine for most applications. We'll say more about this issue later.

Another way floating-point numbers develop is through division. When we divide 10 by 3, the result is 3.3333333… with the sequence of 3s repeating infinitely. The computer allocates only a *fixed* amount of space to hold such a value, so the stored floating-point value can be only an *approximation*.

Common Programming Error 3.7

Using floating-point numbers in a manner that assumes they're represented precisely can lead to incorrect results. Floating-point numbers are represented only approximately by most computers.

Error-Prevention Tip 3.3

Do not compare floating-point values for equality.

3.10 Formulating Algorithms with Top-Down, Stepwise Refinement Case Study 3: Nested Control Statements

Let's work another complete problem. We'll once again formulate the algorithm using pseudocode and top-down, stepwise refinement, and write a corresponding C program. We've seen that control statements may be *stacked* on top of one another (in sequence) just as a child stacks building blocks. In this case study we'll see the only other structured way control statements may be connected in C, namely through **nesting** of one control statement *within* another.

Consider the following problem statement:

> *A college offers a course that prepares students for the state licensing exam for real estate brokers. Last year, 10 of the students who completed this course took the licensing examination. Naturally, the college wants to know how well its students did on the exam. You've been asked to write a program to summarize the results. You've been given a list of these 10 students. Next to each name a 1 is written if the student passed the exam and a 2 if the student failed.*
>
> *Your program should analyze the results of the exam as follows:*
>
> *1. Input each test result (i.e., a 1 or a 2). Display the prompting message "Enter result" each time the program requests another test result.*
>
> *2. Count the number of test results of each type.*
>
> *3. Display a summary of the test results indicating the number of students who passed and the number who failed.*
>
> *4. If more than eight students passed the exam, print the message "Bonus to instructor!"*

After reading the problem statement carefully, we make the following observations:

1. The program must process 10 test results. A counter-controlled loop will be used.

2. Each test result is a number—either a 1 or a 2. Each time the program reads a test result, the program must determine whether the number is a 1 or a 2. We test for a 1 in our algorithm. If the number is not a 1, we assume that it's a 2. (An exercise at the end of the chapter considers the consequences of this assumption.)

3. Two counters are used—one to count the number of students who passed the exam and one to count the number of students who failed the exam.

4. After the program has processed all the results, it must decide whether more than 8 students passed the exam.

Let's proceed with top-down, stepwise refinement. We begin with a pseudocode representation of the top:

Analyze exam results and decide whether instructor should receive a bonus

Once again, it's important to emphasize that the top is a *complete* representation of the program, but several refinements are likely to be needed before the pseudocode can be naturally evolved into a C program. Our first refinement is

Initialize variables
Input the ten quiz grades and count passes and failures
Print a summary of the exam results and decide whether instructor should receive a bonus

Here, too, even though we have a *complete* representation of the entire program, further refinement is necessary. We now commit to specific variables. Counters are needed to record the passes and failures, a counter will be used to control the looping process, and a variable is needed to store the user input. The pseudocode statement

Initialize variables

may be refined as follows:

Initialize passes to zero
Initialize failures to zero
Initialize student to one

Notice that only the counters and totals are initialized. The pseudocode statement

Input the ten quiz grades and count passes and failures

requires a loop that successively inputs the result of each exam. Here it's known *in advance* that there are precisely ten exam results, so counter-controlled looping is appropriate. Inside the loop (i.e., **nested within the loop**) a double-selection statement will determine whether each exam result is a pass or a failure and will increment the appropriate counters accordingly. The refinement of the preceding pseudocode statement is then

While student counter is less than or equal to ten
    Input the next exam result

    If the student passed
        Add one to passes
    else
        Add one to failures

    Add one to student counter

Notice the use of blank lines to set off the *If...else* to improve program readability. The pseudocode statement

Print a summary of the exam results and decide whether instructor should receive a bonus

may be refined as follows:

Print the number of passes4
Print the number of failures
If more than eight students passed
    Print "Bonus to instructor!"

The complete second refinement appears in Fig. 3.9. We use blank lines to set off the `while` statement for program readability.

This pseudocode is now sufficiently refined for conversion to C. The C program and two sample executions are shown in Fig. 3.10. We've taken advantage of a feature of C that allows initialization to be incorporated into definitions (lines 9–11). Such initialization occurs at compile time. Also, notice that when you output an unsigned int you use the **%u** conversion specifier (lines 33–34).

```
 1   Initialize passes to zero
 2   Initialize failures to zero
 3   Initialize student to one
 4
 5   While student counter is less than or equal to ten
 6       Input the next exam result
 7
 8       If the student passed
 9           Add one to passes
10       else
11           Add one to failures
12
13       Add one to student counter
14
15   Print the number of passes
16   Print the number of failures
17   If more than eight students passed
18       Print "Bonus to instructor!"
```

Fig. 3.9 | Pseudocode for examination-results problem.

Software Engineering Observation 3.5

Experience has shown that the most difficult part of solving a problem on a computer is developing the algorithm for the solution. Once a correct algorithm has been specified, the process of producing a working C program is normally straightforward.

Software Engineering Observation 3.6

Many programmers write programs without ever using program development tools such as pseudocode. They feel that their ultimate goal is to solve the problem on a computer and that writing pseudocode merely delays the production of final outputs.

```c
 1   // Fig. 3.10: fig03_10.c
 2   // Analysis of examination results.
 3   #include <stdio.h>
 4
 5   // function main begins program execution
 6   int main( void )
 7   {
 8      // initialize variables in definitions
 9      unsigned int passes = 0; // number of passes
10      unsigned int failures = 0; // number of failures
11      unsigned int student = 1; // student counter
12      int result; // one exam result
13
```

Fig. 3.10 | Analysis of examination results. (Part 1 of 2.)

```
14        // process 10 students using counter-controlled loop
15        while ( student <= 10 ) {
16
17           // prompt user for input and obtain value from user
18           printf( "%s", "Enter result ( 1=pass,2=fail ): " );
19           scanf( "%d", &result );
20
21           // if result 1, increment passes
22           if ( result == 1 ) {
23              passes = passes + 1;
24           } // end if
25           else { // otherwise, increment failures
26              failures = failures + 1;
27           } // end else
28
29           student = student + 1; // increment student counter
30        } // end while
31
32        // termination phase; display number of passes and failures
33        printf( "Passed %u\n", passes );
34        printf( "Failed %u\n", failures );
35
36        // if more than eight students passed, print "Bonus to instructor!"
37        if ( passes > 8 ) {
38           puts( "Bonus to instructor!" );
39        } // end if
40     } // end function main
```

```
Enter Result (1=pass,2=fail): 1
Enter Result (1=pass,2=fail): 2
Enter Result (1=pass,2=fail): 2
Enter Result (1=pass,2=fail): 1
Enter Result (1=pass,2=fail): 1
Enter Result (1=pass,2=fail): 1
Enter Result (1=pass,2=fail): 2
Enter Result (1=pass,2=fail): 1
Enter Result (1=pass,2=fail): 1
Enter Result (1=pass,2=fail): 2
Passed 6
Failed 4
```

```
Enter Result (1=pass,2=fail): 1
Enter Result (1=pass,2=fail): 1
Enter Result (1=pass,2=fail): 1
Enter Result (1=pass,2=fail): 2
Enter Result (1=pass,2=fail): 1
Enter Result (1=pass,2=fail): 1
Enter Result (1=pass,2=fail): 1
Enter Result (1=pass,2=fail): 1
Enter Result (1=pass,2=fail): 1
Enter Result (1=pass,2=fail): 1
Passed 9
Failed 1
Bonus to instructor!
```

Fig. 3.10 | Analysis of examination results. (Part 2 of 2.)

3.11 Assignment Operators

C provides several assignment operators for abbreviating assignment expressions. For example, the statement

```
c = c + 3;
```

can be abbreviated with the **addition assignment operator** += as

```
c += 3;
```

The += operator adds the value of the expression on the *right* of the operator to the value of the variable on the *left* of the operator and stores the result in the variable on the *left* of the operator. Any statement of the form

variable = variable operator expression;

where *operator* is one of the binary operators +, -, *, / or % (or others we'll discuss in Chapter 10), can be written in the form

variable operator= expression;

Thus the assignment c += 3 adds 3 to c. Figure 3.11 shows the arithmetic assignment operators, sample expressions using these operators and explanations.

Assignment operator	Sample expression	Explanation	Assigns
Assume: int c = 3, d = 5, e = 4, f = 6, g = 12;			
+=	c += 7	c = c + 7	10 to c
-=	d -= 4	d = d - 4	1 to d
*=	e *= 5	e = e * 5	20 to e
/=	f /= 3	f = f / 3	2 to f
%=	g %= 9	g = g % 9	3 to g

Fig. 3.11 | Arithmetic assignment operators.

3.12 Increment and Decrement Operators

C also provides the unary **increment operator**, ++, and the unary **decrement operator**, --, which are summarized in Fig. 3.12. If a variable c is to be incremented by 1, the increment operator ++ can be used rather than the expressions c = c + 1 or c += 1. If increment or decrement operators are placed *before* a variable (i.e., *prefixed*), they're referred to as the **preincrement** or **predecrement** operators, respectively. If increment or decrement operators are placed *after* a variable (i.e., *postfixed*), they're referred to as the **postincrement** or **postdecrement** operators, respectively. Preincrementing (predecrementing) a variable causes the variable to be incremented (decremented) by 1, then its new value is used in the expression in which it appears. Postincrementing (postdecrementing) the variable causes the current value of the variable to be used in the expression in which it appears, then the variable value is incremented (decremented) by 1.

Operator	Sample expression	Explanation
++	++a	Increment a by 1, then use the new value of a in the expression in which a resides.
++	a++	Use the current value of a in the expression in which a resides, then increment a by 1.
--	--b	Decrement b by 1, then use the new value of b in the expression in which b resides.
--	b--	Use the current value of b in the expression in which b resides, then decrement b by 1.

Fig. 3.12 | Increment and decrement operators

Figure 3.13 demonstrates the difference between the preincrementing and the postincrementing versions of the ++ operator. Postincrementing the variable c causes it to be incremented *after* it's used in the printf statement. Preincrementing the variable c causes it to be incremented *before* it's used in the printf statement.

```
1   // Fig. 3.13: fig03_13.c
2   // Preincrementing and postincrementing.
3   #include <stdio.h>
4
5   // function main begins program execution
6   int main( void )
7   {
8      int c; // define variable
9
10     // demonstrate postincrement
11     c = 5; // assign 5 to c
12     printf( "%d\n", c ); // print 5
13     printf( "%d\n", c++ ); // print 5 then postincrement
14     printf( "%d\n\n", c ); // print 6
15
16     // demonstrate preincrement
17     c = 5; // assign 5 to c
18     printf( "%d\n", c ); // print 5
19     printf( "%d\n", ++c ); // preincrement then print 6
20     printf( "%d\n", c ); // print 6
21  } // end function main
```

```
5
5
6

5
6
6
```

Fig. 3.13 | Preincrementing and postincrementing.

The program displays the value of c before and after the ++ operator is used. The decrement operator (--) works similarly.

Good Programming Practice 3.5

Unary operators should be placed directly next to their operands with no intervening spaces.

The three assignment statements in Fig. 3.10

```
passes = passes + 1;
failures = failures + 1;
student = student + 1;
```

can be written more concisely with *assignment operators* as

```
passes += 1;
failures += 1;
student += 1;
```

with *preincrement operators* as

```
++passes;
++failures;
++student;
```

or with *postincrement operators* as

```
passes++;
failures++;
student++;
```

It's important to note here that when incrementing or decrementing a variable in a statement by *itself*, the preincrement and postincrement forms have the *same* effect. It's only when a variable appears in the context of a larger expression that preincrementing and postincrementing have *different* effects (and similarly for predecrementing and post-decrementing). Of the expressions we've studied thus far, only a simple variable name may be used as the operand of an increment or decrement operator.

Common Programming Error 3.8

Attempting to use the increment or decrement operator on an expression other than a simple variable name is a syntax error, e.g., writing ++(x + 1).

Error-Prevention Tip 3.4

C generally does not specify the order in which an operator's operands will be evaluated (although we'll see exceptions to this for a few operators in Chapter 4). Therefore you should use increment or decrement operators only in statements in which one variable is incremented or decremented by itself.

Figure 3.14 lists the precedence and associativity of the operators introduced to this point. The operators are shown top to bottom in decreasing order of precedence. The second column indicates the associativity of the operators at each level of precedence. Notice that the conditional operator (?:), the unary operators increment (++), decrement (--), plus (+), minus (-) and casts, and the assignment operators =, +=, -=, *=, /= and %= associate from right to left. The third column names the various groups of operators. All other operators in Fig. 3.14 associate from left to right.

Operators	Associativity	Type
++ *(postfix)* -- *(postfix)*	right to left	postfix
+ - *(type)* ++ *(prefix)* -- *(prefix)*	right to left	unary
* / %	left to right	multiplicative
+ -	left to right	additive
< <= > >=	left to right	relational
== !=	left to right	equality
?:	right to left	conditional
= += -= *= /= %=	right to left	assignment

Fig. 3.14 | Precedence and associativity of the operators encountered so far in the text.

3.13 Secure C Programming

Arithmetic Overflow
Figure 2.5 presented an addition program which calculated the sum of two int values (line 18) with the statement

```
sum = integer1 + integer2; // assign total to sum
```

Even this simple statement has a potential problem—adding the integers could result in a value that's *too large* to store in an int variable. This is known as **arithmetic overflow** and can cause undefined behavior, possibly leaving a system open to attack.

The maximum and minimum values that can be stored in an int variable are represented by the constants INT_MAX and INT_MIN, respectively, which are defined in the header <limits.h>. There are similar constants for the other integral types that we'll be introducing in Chapter 4. You can see your platform's values for these constants by opening the header <limits.h> in a text editor.

It's considered a good practice to ensure that *before* you perform arithmetic calculations like the one in line 18 of Fig. 2.5, they will *not* overflow. The code for doing this is shown on the CERT website www.securecoding.cert.org—just search for guideline "INT32-C." The code uses the && (logical AND) and || (logical OR) operators, which are introduced in the Chapter 4. In industrial-strength code, you should perform checks like these for *all* calculations. In later chapters, we'll show other programming techniques for handling such errors.

Unsigned Integers
In Fig. 3.6, line 8 declared as an unsigned int the variable counter because it's used to count *only non-negative values*. In general, counters that should store only non-negative values should be declared with unsigned before the integer type. Variables of unsigned types can represent values from 0 to approximately twice the positive range of the corresponding signed integer types. You can determine your platform's maximum unsigned int value with the constant UINT_MAX from <limits.h>.

The class-averaging program in Fig. 3.6 could have declared as unsigned int the variables grade, total and average. Grades are normally values from 0 to 100, so the total and average should each be greater than or equal to 0. We declared those variables as ints because we can't control what the user actually enters—the user could enter *negative* values. Worse yet, the user could enter a value that's not even a number. (We'll show how to deal with such inputs later in the book.)

Sometimes sentinel-controlled loops use invalid values to terminate a loop. For example, the class-averaging program of Fig. 3.8 terminates the loop when the user enters the sentinel -1 (an invalid grade), so it would be improper to declare variable grade as an unsigned int. As you'll see, the end-of-file (EOF) indicator—which is introduced in the next chapter and is often used to terminate sentinel-controlled loops—is also a negative number. For more information, see Chapter 5, "Integer Security" of Robert Seacord's book *Secure Coding in C and C++*.

scanf_s *and* printf_s

The C11 standard's Annex K introduces more secure versions of printf and scanf called printf_s and scanf_s. Annex K is designated as *optional*, so not every C vendor will implement it.

Microsoft implemented its own versions of printf_s and scanf_s prior to the publication of the C11 standard and immediately began issuing warnings for every scanf call. The warnings say that scanf is *deprecated*—it should no longer be used—and that you should consider using scanf_s instead.

Many organizations have coding standards that require code to compile *without warning messages*. There are two ways to eliminate Visual C++'s scanf warnings—you can use scanf_s instead of scanf or you can disable these warnings. For the input statements we've used so far, Visual C++ users can simply replace scanf with scanf_s. You can disable the warning messages in Visual C++ as follows:

1. Type *Alt F7* to display the **Property Pages** dialog for your project.

2. In the left column, expand **Configuration Properties > C/C++** and select **Preprocessor**.

3. In the right column, at the end of the value for **Preprocessor Definitions**, insert

```
;_CRT_SECURE_NO_WARNINGS
```

4. Click **OK** to save the changes.

You'll no longer receive warnings on scanf (or any other functions that Microsoft has deprecated for similar reasons). For industrial-strength coding, disabling the warnings is discouraged. We'll say more about how to use scanf_s and printf_s in a later Secure C Coding Guidelines section.

Summary

Section 3.1 Introduction
- Before writing a program to solve a particular problem, you must have a thorough understanding of the problem and a carefully planned approach to solving the problem.

Section 3.2 Algorithms
- The solution to any computing problem involves executing a series of actions in a specific order.

- A procedure for solving a problem in terms of the actions to be executed, and the order in which these actions are to be executed, is called an algorithm.
- The order in which actions are to be executed is important.

Section 3.3 Pseudocode

- Pseudocode is an artificial and informal language that helps you develop algorithms.
- Pseudocode is similar to everyday English; it's not an actual computer programming language.
- Pseudocode programs help you "think out" a program.
- Pseudocode consists purely of characters; you may type pseudocode using an editor.
- Carefully prepared pseudocode programs may be converted easily to corresponding C programs.
- Pseudocode consists only of action statements.

Section 3.4 Control Structures

- Normally, statements in a program execute one after the other in the order in which they're written. This is called sequential execution.
- Various C statements enable you to specify that the next statement to execute may be other than the next one in sequence. This is called transfer of control.
- Structured programming has become almost synonymous with "goto elimination."
- Structured programs are clearer, easier to debug and modify and more likely to be bug free.
- All programs can be written in terms of sequence, selection and repetition control structures.
- Unless directed otherwise, the computer automatically executes C statements in sequence.
- A flowchart is a graphical representation of an algorithm. Flowcharts are drawn using rectangles, diamonds, rounded rectangles and small circles, connected by arrows called flowlines.
- The rectangle (action) symbol indicates any type of action including a calculation or an input/ output operation.
- Flowlines indicate the order in which the actions are performed.
- When drawing a flowchart that represents a complete algorithm, a rounded rectangle containing the word "Begin" is the first symbol used; a rounded rectangle symbol containing the word "End" is the last symbol used. When drawing only a portion of an algorithm, we omit the rounded rectangle symbols in favor of using small circle symbols, also called connector symbols.
- The diamond (decision) symbol indicates that a decision is to be made.
- The if selection statement either performs (selects) an action if a condition is true or skips the action if the condition is false. The if...else selection statement performs an action if a condition is true and performs a different action if the condition is false. The switch selection statement performs one of many different actions depending on the value of an expression.
- The if statement is called a single-selection statement because it selects or ignores a single action.
- The if...else statement is called a double-selection statement because it selects between two different actions.
- The switch statement is called a multiple-selection statement because it selects among many different actions.
- C provides three types of repetition statements (also called iteration statements), namely while, do...while and for.
- Control-statement flowchart segments can be attached to one another with control-statement stacking—connecting the exit point of one control statement to the entry point of the next.
- There's only one other way control statements may be connected—control-statement nesting.

Section 3.5 The *if* Selection Statement

- Selection structures are used to choose among alternative courses of action.

- The decision symbol contains an expression, such as a condition, that can be either true or false. The decision symbol has two flowlines emerging from it. One indicates the direction to be taken when the expression is true; the other indicates the direction when the expression is false.

- A decision can be based on any expression—if the expression evaluates to zero, it's treated as false, and if it evaluates to nonzero, it's treated as true.

- The if statement is a single-entry/single-exit structure.

Section 3.6 The *if...else* Selection Statement

- C provides the conditional operator (?:) which is closely related to the if...else statement.

- The conditional operator is C's only ternary operator—it takes three operands. The first operand is a condition. The second operand is the value for the conditional expression if the condition is true, and the third operand is the value for the conditional expression if the condition is false.

- The values in a conditional expression can also be actions to execute.

- Nested if...else statements test for multiple cases by placing if...else statements inside if...else statements.

- The if selection statement expects only one statement in its body. To include several statements in the body of an if, you must enclose the set of statements in braces ({ and }).

- A set of statements contained within a pair of braces is called a compound statement or a block.

- A syntax error is caught by the compiler. A logic error has its effect at execution time. A fatal logic error causes a program to fail and terminate prematurely. A nonfatal logic error allows a program to continue executing but to produce incorrect results.

Section 3.7 The *while* Repetition Statement

- The while repetition statement specifies that an action is to be repeated while a condition is true. Eventually, the condition will become false. At this point, the repetition terminates, and the first statement after the repetition statement executes.

Section 3.8 Formulating Algorithms Case Study 1: Counter-Controlled Repetition

- Counter-controlled repetition uses a variable called a counter to specify the number of times a set of statements should execute.

- Counter-controlled repetition is often called definite repetition because the number of repetitions is known before the loop begins executing.

- A total is a variable used to accumulate the sum of a series of values. Variables used to store totals should normally be initialized to zero before being used in a program; otherwise the sum would include the previous value stored in the total's memory location.

- A counter is a variable used to count. Counter variables are normally initialized to zero or one, depending on their use.

- An uninitialized variable contains a "garbage" value—the value last stored in the memory location reserved for that variable.

Section 3.9 Formulating Algorithms with Top-Down, Stepwise Refinement Case Study 2: Sentinel-Controlled Repetition

- A sentinel value (also called a signal value, a dummy value, or a flag value) is used in a sentinel-controlled loop to indicate the "end of data entry."

- Sentinel-controlled repetition is often called indefinite repetition because the number of repetitions is not known before the loop begins executing.

- The sentinel value must be chosen so that it cannot be confused with an acceptable input value.

- In top-down, stepwise refinement, the top is a statement that conveys the program's overall function. It's a complete representation of a program. In the refinement process, we divide the top into smaller tasks and list these in execution order.

- The type `float` represents numbers with decimal points (called floating-point numbers).

- When two integers are divided any fractional part of the result is truncated.

- To produce a floating-point calculation with integer values, you must cast the integers to floating-point numbers. C provides the unary cast operator `(float)` to accomplish this task.

- Cast operators perform explicit conversions.

- Most computers can evaluate arithmetic expressions only in which the operands' data types are identical. To ensure this, the compiler performs an operation called implicit conversion on selected operands.

- Cast operators are available for most data types. A cast operator is formed by placing parentheses around a type name. The cast operator is a unary operator—it takes only one operand.

- Cast operators associate from right to left and have the same precedence as other unary operators such as unary + and unary -. This precedence is one level higher than that of *, / and %.

- The `printf` conversion specifier `%.2f` specifies that a floating-point value will be displayed with two digits to the right of the decimal point. If the `%f` conversion specifier is used (without specifying the precision), the default precision of 6 is used.

- When floating-point values are printed with precision, the printed value is rounded to the indicated number of decimal positions for display purposes.

Section 3.11 Assignment Operators

- C provides several assignment operators for abbreviating assignment expressions.

- The `+=` operator adds the value of the expression on the right of the operator to the value of the variable on the left of the operator and stores the result in the variable on the left of the operator.

- Any statement of the form

    variable = variable operator expression;

    where *operator* is one of the binary operators +, -, *, / or % (or others we'll discuss in Chapter 10), can be written in the form

    variable operator= expression;

Section 3.12 Increment and Decrement Operators

- C provides the unary increment operator, ++, and the unary decrement operator, --.

- If increment or decrement operators are placed before a variable, they're referred to as the preincrement or predecrement operators, respectively. If increment or decrement operators are placed after a variable, they're referred to as the postincrement or postdecrement operators, respectively.

- Preincrementing (predecrementing) a variable causes it to be incremented (decremented) by 1, then the new value of the variable is used in the expression in which it appears.

- Postincrementing (postdecrementing) a variable uses the current value of the variable in the expression in which it appears, then the variable value is incremented (decremented) by 1.

- When incrementing or decrementing a variable in a statement by itself, the preincrement and postincrement forms have the same effect. When a variable appears in the context of a larger expression, preincrementing and postincrementing have different effects (and similarly for predecrementing and postdecrementing).

Section 3.13 Secure C Programming

- Adding integers can result in a value that's too large to store in an int variable. This is known as arithmetic overflow and can cause unpredictable runtime behavior, possibly leaving a system open to attack.

- The maximum and minimum values that can be stored in an int variable are represented by the constants INT_MAX and INT_MIN, respectively, from the header <limits.h>.

- It's considered a good practice to ensure that arithmetic calculations will not overflow before you perform the calculation. In industrial-strength code, you should perform checks for all calculations that can result on overflow or underflow.

- In general, any integer variable that should store only non-negative values should be declared with unsigned before the integer type. Variables of unsigned types can represent values from 0 to approximately double the positive range of the corresponding signed integer type.

- You can determine your platform's maximum unsigned int value with the constant UINT_MAX from <limits.h>.

- The C11 standard's Annex K introduces more secure versions of printf and scanf called printf_s and scanf_s. Annex K is designated as optional, so not every C compiler vendor will implement it.

- Microsoft implemented its own versions of printf_s and scanf_s prior to the C11 standard's publication and immediately began issuing warnings for every scanf call. The warnings say that scanf is deprecated—it should no longer be used—and that you should consider using scanf_s instead.

- Many organizations have coding standards that require code to compile without warning messages. There are two ways to eliminate Visual C++'s scanf warnings. You can either start using scanf_s immediately or disable this warning message.

Terminology

Self-Review Exercises

3.1   Fill in the blanks in each of the following questions.

a) A procedure for solving a problem in terms of the actions to be executed and the order in which the actions should be executed is called a(n) _____.

b) Specifying the execution order of statements by the computer is called _____.

c) All programs can be written in terms of three types of control statements: _____, _____ and _____.

d) The _____ selection statement is used to execute one action when a condition is true and another action when that condition is false.

e) Several statements grouped together in braces ({ and }) are called a(n) _____.

f) The _____ repetition statement specifies that a statement or group of statements is to be executed repeatedly while some condition remains true.

g) Repetition of a set of instructions a specific number of times is called _____ repetition.

h) When it's not known in advance how many times a set of statements will be repeated, a(n) _____ value can be used to terminate the repetition.

3.2   Write four different C statements that each subtracts 1 from integer variable p.

3.3   Write a single C statement to accomplish each of the following:

a) Multiply the variable product by 2 using the *= operator.

b) Multiply the variable product by 2 using the = and * operators.

c) Test if the value of the variable count is greater than 10. If it is, print "Count is greater than 10."

d) Calculate the remainder after q is divided by divisor and assign the result to q. Write this statement two different ways.

e) Print the value 123.4567 with two digits of precision. What value is printed?

f) Print the floating-point value 3.14159 with three digits to the right of the decimal point. What value is printed?

3.4   Write a C statement to accomplish each of the following tasks:
a) Define variables `product` and `p` to be of type `int`.
b) Set variable `p` to 1.
c) Set variable `product` to 1.
d) Multiply variable `p` with variable `product` and assign the result to variable `product`.
e) Print `"The product is: "` followed by the value of variable `product`.

3.5   Combine the statements that you wrote in Exercise 3.4 into a program that calculates the product of the integers from 1 to 10. Use the `while` statement to loop through the calculation and increment statements. The loop should terminate when the value of `p` becomes 11.

3.6   Write single C statements that
a) Input unsigned integer variable `x` with `scanf`. Use the conversion specifier `%u`.
b) Input unsigned integer variable `y` with `scanf`. Use the conversion specifier `%u`.
c) Set unsigned integer variable `i` to 1.
d) Set unsigned integer variable `power` to 1.
e) Multiply unsigned integer variable `power` by `x` and assign the result to `power`.
f) Increment variable `i` by 1.
g) Test `i` to see if it's less than or equal to `y` in the condition of a `while` statement.
h) Output unsigned integer variable `power` with `printf`. Use the conversion specifier `%u`.

3.7   Write a C program that uses the statements in Exercise 3.6 to calculate `x` raised to the `y` power. The program should have a `while` repetition control statement.

3.8   Identify and correct the errors in each of the following:
a) ```
    if (p != 0);
        x = x / p;
    ```
b)  ```
    while (p > 0) {
        x = x / p;
        p--;
    }
    ```
c) ```
    while (d != 10) {
        sum += d;
        d++
    }
    ```

**3.9**    What's wrong with the following `while` repetition statement (assume `z` has value 100), which is supposed to calculate the sum of the integers from 100 down to 1?
```
while (z >= 0)
    sum += z;
```

## Answers to Self-Review Exercises

**3.1**    a) Algorithm. b) Program control. c) Sequence, selection, repetition. d) `if...else`. e) Compound statement or block. f) `while`. g) Counter-controlled or definite. h) Sentinel.

**3.2**    
```
p = p - 1;
p -= 1;
--p;
p--;
```

**3.3**    a) `product *= 2;`
b) `product = product * 2;`
c) ```
   if ( count > 10 )
       puts( "Count is greater than 10." );
   ```
d) ```
   q %= divisor;
   q = q % divisor;
   ```
   ```

e) `printf( "%.2f", 123.4567 );`
123.46 is displayed.

f) `printf( "%.3f\n", 3.14159 );`
3.142 is displayed.

3.4   a) `int product, p;`

b) `p = 1;`

c) `product = 1;`

d) `product = p * product;`

e) `printf( "The product is:%d \n ", product);`

3.5   See below.

```c
/* Calculate the product of the integers from 1 to 10 */
#include <stdio.h>

int main( void )
{
    int product, p; /* define variables product and p */
    p = 1;   /* initialize p */
    product = 1; /* initialize product */
    while ( p <= 10 ) { /* loop while p is less than or equal to 10 */
        product *= p; /* multiply p with product */
        ++p; /* increment p */
    } /* end while */
    printf( "The product is: %d\n", product ); /* display product */
    return 0;
} /* end main function */
```

The product is 3628800.

3.6   a) `scanf( "%u", &x );`

b) `scanf( "%u", &y );`

c) `i = 1;`

d) `power = 1;`

e) `power *= x;`

f) `++i;`

g) `while ( i <= y )`

h) `printf( "%d", power );`

3.7   See top of next page.

```c
// raise x to the y power
#include <stdio.h>

int main( void )
{
    unsigned int x, y, i, power; // define variables

    i = 1; // set i
    power = 1; // set power
    printf( "%s", "Enter first integer: " );
    scanf( "%u", &x ); // read value for x from user
    printf( "%s", "Enter second integer: " );
    scanf( "%u", &y ); // read value for y from user

```

```
15      while ( i <= y ) { // loop while i is less than or equal to y
16         power *= x; // multiply power by x
17         ++i; // increment i
18      } // end while
19
20      printf( "%u\n", power ); // display power
21    } // end main function
```

3.8   a) Error: Semicolon after the `if` loop results in logical error.
        Correction: Remove semicolon after the `if` loop condition.
    b) Error: Opening brace of the `while` body is (.
        Correction: Opening brace of `while` body must be replaced with {.
    c) Error: Missing semicolon after the statement d++.
        Correction: Add semicolon after the statement d++.

3.9   The value of the variable z is never changed in the `while` statement. Therefore, an infinite loop is created. To prevent the infinite loop, z must be decremented so that it eventually becomes 0.

Exercises

3.10   Identify and correct the errors in each of the following. [*Note:* There may be more than one error in each piece of code.]

    a)
```
if ( age >= 65 );
    puts( "Age is greater than or equal to 65" );
else
    puts( "Age is less than 65" );
```
    b)
```
int x = 1, total;

while ( x <= 10 ) {
   total += x;
   ++x;
}
```
    c)
```
While ( x <= 100 )
   total += x;
   ++x;
```
    d)
```
while ( y > 0 ) {
   printf( "%d\n", y );
   ++y;
}
```

3.11   Fill in the blanks in each of the following:
    a) The solution to any problem involves performing a series of actions in a specific _____.
    b) A synonym for procedure is _____.
    c) A variable that accumulates the sum of several numbers is a(n) _____.
    d) A special value used to indicate "end of data entry" is called a(n) _____, a(n) _____, a(n) _____ or a(n) _____ value.
    e) A(n) _____ is a graphical representation of an algorithm.
    f) In a flowchart, the order in which the steps should be performed is indicated by _____ symbols.

g) Rectangle symbols correspond to calculations that are normally performed by statements and input/output operations that are normally performed by calls to the _____ and _____ Standard Library functions.

h) The item written inside a decision symbol is called a(n) _____.

3.12 What does the following program print?

```
1    #include <stdio.h>
2
3    int main( void )
4    {
5       unsigned int p = 1, result = 0, q;
6
7       while ( p <= 9 ) {
8          q = p * p * p;
9          printf( "%d\n", q );
10         result += q;
11         ++p;
12      } // end while
13
14      printf( "Total is %d\n", result );
15   } // end main
```

3.13 Write a single pseudocode statement that indicates each of the following:
a) Display the message "Enter five numbers".
b) Obtain the values for variables a, b, c, d and e from keyboard.
c) Calculate the average of variables a, b, c, d and e assign it to variable avg.
d) Display the average of five numbers.

3.14 Formulate a pseudocode algorithm for each of the following:
a) Obtain two numbers from the keyboard, compute their sum and display the result.
b) Obtain two numbers from the keyboard, and determine and display which (if either) is the larger of the two numbers.
c) Obtain a series of positive numbers from the keyboard, and determine and display their sum. Assume that the user types the sentinel value -1 to indicate "end of data entry."

3.15 State which of the following are *true* and which are *false*. If a statement is *false*, explain why.
a) Experience has shown that the most difficult part of solving a problem on a computer is producing a working C program.
b) A sentinel value must be a value that cannot be confused with a legitimate data value.
c) Flowlines indicate the actions to be performed.
d) Conditions written inside decision symbols always contain arithmetic operators (i.e., +, -, *, /, and %).
e) In top-down, stepwise refinement, each refinement is a complete representation of the algorithm.

For Exercises 3.16–3.20, perform each of these steps:

1. Read the problem statement.
2. Formulate the algorithm using pseudocode and top-down, stepwise refinement.
3. Write a C program.
4. Test, debug and execute the C program.

3.16 *(Gas Mileage)* Drivers are concerned with the mileage obtained by their automobiles. One driver has kept track of several tankfuls of gasoline by recording miles driven and gallons used for each tankful. Develop a program that will input the miles driven and gallons used for each tankful. The program should calculate and display the miles per gallon obtained for each tankful. After processing all input information, the program should calculate and print the combined miles per gallon obtained for all tankfuls. Here is a sample input/output dialog:

```
Enter the gallons used (-1 to end): 12.8
Enter the miles driven: 287
The miles/gallon for this tank was 22.421875

Enter the gallons used (-1 to end): 10.3
Enter the miles driven: 200
The miles/gallon for this tank was 19.417475

Enter the gallons used (-1 to end): 5
Enter the miles driven: 120
The miles/gallon for this tank was 24.000000

Enter the gallons used (-1 to end): -1

The overall average miles/gallon was 21.601423
```

3.17   *(Credit Limit Calculator)* Develop a C program that will determine if a department store customer has exceeded the credit limit on a charge account. For each customer, the following facts are available:

    a) Account number
    b) Balance at the beginning of the month
    c) Total of all items charged by this customer this month
    d) Total of all credits applied to this customer's account this month
    e) Allowed credit limit

    The program should input each fact, calculate the new balance (= *beginning balance + charges – credits*), and determine whether the new balance exceeds the customer's credit limit. For those customers whose credit limit is exceeded, the program should display the customer's account number, credit limit, new balance and the message "Credit limit exceeded." Here is a sample input/output dialog:

```
Enter account number (-1 to end): 100
Enter beginning balance: 5394.78
Enter total charges: 1000.00
Enter total credits: 500.00
Enter credit limit: 5500.00
Account:      100
Credit limit: 5500.00
Balance:      5894.78
Credit Limit Exceeded.

Enter account number (-1 to end): 200
Enter beginning balance: 1000.00
Enter total charges: 123.45
Enter total credits: 321.00
Enter credit limit: 1500.00

Enter account number (-1 to end): 300
Enter beginning balance: 500.00
Enter total charges: 274.73
Enter total credits: 100.00
Enter credit limit: 800.00

Enter account number (-1 to end): -1
```

3.18   *(Sales Commission Calculator)* One large chemical company pays its salespeople on a commission basis. The salespeople receive $200 per week plus 9% of their gross sales for that week. For example, a salesperson who sells $5000 worth of chemicals in a week receives $200 plus 9% of $5000, or a total of $650. Develop a program that will input each salesperson's gross sales for last week and will calculate and display that salesperson's earnings. Process one salesperson's figures at a time. Here is a sample input/output dialog:

```
Enter sales in dollars (-1 to end): 5000.00
Salary is: $650.00

Enter sales in dollars (-1 to end): 1234.56
Salary is: $311.11

Enter sales in dollars (-1 to end): -1
```

3.19   *(Interest Calculator)* The simple interest on a loan is calculated by the formula

```
interest = principal * rate * days / 365;
```

The preceding formula assumes that rate is the annual interest rate, and therefore includes the division by 365 (days). Develop a program that will input principal, rate and days for several loans, and will calculate and display the simple interest for each loan, using the preceding formula. Here is a sample input/output dialog:

```
Enter loan principal (-1 to end): 1000.00
Enter interest rate: .1
Enter term of the loan in days: 365
The interest charge is $100.00

Enter loan principal (-1 to end): 1000.00
Enter interest rate: .08375
Enter term of the loan in days: 224
The interest charge is $51.40

Enter loan principal (-1 to end): -1
```

3.20   *(Salary Calculator)* Develop a program that will determine the gross pay for each of several employees. The company pays "straight time" for the first 40 hours worked by each employee and pays "time-and-a-half" for all hours worked in excess of 40 hours. You're given a list of the employees of the company, the number of hours each employee worked last week and the hourly rate of each employee. Your program should input this information for each employee and should determine and display the employee's gross pay. Here is a sample input/output dialog:

```
Enter # of hours worked (-1 to end): 39
Enter hourly rate of the worker ($00.00): 10.00
Salary is $390.00

Enter # of hours worked (-1 to end): 40
Enter hourly rate of the worker ($00.00): 10.00
Salary is $400.00

Enter # of hours worked (-1 to end): 41
Enter hourly rate of the worker ($00.00): 10.00
Salary is $415.00

Enter # of hours worked (-1 to end): -1
```

3.21 *(Preincrementing vs. Postincrementing)* Write a program that demonstrates the difference between preincrementing and postincrementing using the increment operator ++.

3.22 *(Printing Numbers from a Loop)* Write a program that utilizes looping to print the numbers from 1 to 20 in two columns such that two consecutive numbers are printed side by side on the same line with four spaces between them.

3.23 *(Find the Smallest Number)* The process of finding the smallest number (i.e., the minimum of a group of numbers) is used frequently in computer applications. For example, a program that determines the winner of a coding contest would input the execution time of the code written by each student. The student whose code takes minimum time to execute wins the contest. Write a pseudocode program and then a program that inputs a series of 21 non-negative numbers and determines and prints the smallest of the numbers. *Hint:* Your program should use three variables as follows:

counter: A counter to count to 21 (i.e., to keep track of how many numbers have been input and to determine when all 21 numbers have been processed)

number: The current number input to the program

smallest: The smallest number found so far

3.24 *(Tabular Output)* Write a program that uses looping to print the following table of values. Use the tab escape sequence, \t, in the printf statement to separate the columns with tabs.

N	0.25*N	0.50*N	0.75*N
10.000000	2.500000	5.000000	7.500000
20.000000	5.000000	10.000000	15.000000
30.000000	7.500000	15.000000	22.500000
40.000000	10.000000	20.000000	30.000000
50.000000	12.500000	25.000000	37.500000
60.000000	15.000000	30.000000	45.000000
70.000000	17.500000	35.000000	52.000000
80.000000	20.000000	40.000000	60.000000
90.000000	22.500000	45.000000	67.500000
100.000000	25.000000	50.000000	75.000000

3.25 *(Tabular Output)* Write a program that utilizes looping to produce the following table of values:

N	N - 3	N + 3	N * 3
9	6	12	27
18	15	21	54
27	24	30	81
36	33	39	108
45	42	48	135

3.26 *(Find the Two Smallest Numbers)* Using an approach similar to Exercise 3.23, find the *two* smallest values of the 21 numbers. [*Note:* You may input each number only *once*.]

3.27 *(Validating User Input)* Modify the program in Figure 3.10 to validate its inputs. On any input, if the value entered is other than 1 or 2, keep looping until the user enters a correct value.

3.28 What does the following program print?

```
1   #include <stdio.h>
2
3   int main( void )
4   {
```

```
5        unsigned int count = 30; // initialize count
6
7        while ( count >= 1 ) { // loop 30 times
8
9           // output line of text
10          puts( count % 5 ? "^^^^^^^^^^" : "xxxxxxxxxx" );
11          ---count; // decrement count
12       } // end while
13    } // end function main
```

3.29   What does the following program print?

```
1     #include <stdio.h>
2
3     int main( void )
4     {
5        unsigned int row = 10; // initialize row
6        unsigned int column; // define column
7
8        while ( row >= 1 ) { // loop until row < 1
9           column = 1; // set column to 1 as iteration begins
10
11          while ( column <= 10 ) { // loop 10 times
12             printf( "%s", row % 2 ? "<": ">" ); // output
13             ++column; // increment column
14          } // end inner while
15
16          --row; // decrement row
17          puts( "" ); // begin new output line
18       } // end outer while
19    } // end function main
```

3.30   *(Dangling Else Problem)* Determine the output for each of the following when x is 9 and y is 11, and when x is 11 and y is 9. The compiler ignores the indentation in a C program. Also, the compiler always associates an else with the previous if unless told to do otherwise by the placement of braces {}. Because, on first glance, you may not be sure which if an else matches, this is referred to as the "dangling else" problem. We eliminated the indentation from the following code to make the problem more challenging. [*Hint:* Apply indentation conventions you have learned.]

```
a)  if ( x < 10 )
    if ( y > 10 )
    puts( "*****" );
    else
    puts( "#####" );
    puts( "$$$$$" );
b)  if ( x < 10 ) {
    if ( y > 10 )
    puts( "*****" );
    }
    else {
    puts( "#####" );
    puts( "$$$$$" );
    }
```

3.31   *(Another Dangling Else Problem)* Modify the following code to produce the output shown. Use proper indentation techniques. You may not make any changes other than inserting braces. The compiler ignores the indentation in a program. We eliminated the indentation from the following code to make the problem more challenging. [*Note:* It's possible that no modification is necessary.]

```
if ( y == 8 )
if ( x == 5 )
puts( "@@@@@" );
else
puts( "#####" );
puts( "$$$$$" );
puts( "&&&&&" );
```

a)   Assuming x = 5 and y = 8, the following output is produced.

```
@@@@@
$$$$$
&&&&&
```

b)   Assuming x = 5 and y = 8, the following output is produced.

```
@@@@@
```

c)   Assuming x = 5 and y = 8, the following output is produced.

```
@@@@@
&&&&&
```

d)   Assuming x = 5 and y = 7, the following output is produced. [*Note:* The last three puts statements are all part of a compound statement.]

```
#####
$$$$$
&&&&&
```

3.32   *(Rectangle of Plus Symbols)* Write a program that reads in the length and the breadth of a rectangle and then prints that rectangle out of the plus symbols. For example, if your program reads a length of 3 and a breadth of 12, it should print

```
++++++++++++
++++++++++++
++++++++++++
```

3.33   *(Hollow Rectangle of Plus Symbols)* Modify the program you wrote in Exercise 3.32 so that it prints a hollow rectangle. For example, if your program reads a length of 3 and a breadth of 12, it should print

```
++++++++++++
+          +
++++++++++++
```

3.34 *(Palindrome Tester)* A palindrome is a number or a text phrase that reads the same backward as forward. For example, each of the following five-digit integers is a palindrome: 12321, 55555, 45554 and 11611. Write a program that reads in a five-digit integer and determines whether or not it's a palindrome. [*Hint*: Use the division and remainder operators to separate the number into its individual digits.]

3.35 *(Printing the Decimal Equivalent of a Binary Number)* Input an integer (5 digits or fewer) containing only 0s and 1s (i.e., a "binary" integer) and print its decimal equivalent. [*Hint*: Use the remainder and division operators to pick off the "binary" number's digits one at a time from right to left. Just as in the decimal number system, in which the rightmost digit has a positional value of 1, and the next digit left has a positional value of 10, then 100, then 1000, and so on, in the binary number system the rightmost digit has a positional value of 1, the next digit left has a positional value of 2, then 4, then 8, and so on. Thus the decimal number 234 can be interpreted as 4 * 1 + 3 * 10 + 2 * 100. The decimal equivalent of binary 1101 is 1 * 1 + 0 * 2 + 1 * 4 + 1 * 8 or 1 + 0 + 4 + 8 or 13.]

3.36 *(How Fast is Your Computer?)* How can you determine how fast your own computer really operates? Write a program with a `while` loop that counts from 1 to 1,000,000,000 by 1s. Every time the count reaches a multiple of 100,000,000, print that number on the screen. Use your watch to time how long each 100 million repetitions of the loop takes.

3.37 *(Detecting Multiples of 10)* Write a program that prints 100 asterisks, one at a time. After every tenth asterisk, your program should print a newline character. [*Hint*: Count from 1 to 100. Use the remainder operator to recognize each time the counter reaches a multiple of 10.]

3.38 *(Counting 7s)* Write a program that reads an integer (5 digits or fewer) and determines and prints how many digits in the integer are 7s.

3.39 *(Checkerboard Pattern of Asterisks)* Write a program that displays the following checkerboard pattern:

```
* * * * * * * *
 * * * * * * * *
* * * * * * * *
 * * * * * * * *
* * * * * * * *
 * * * * * * * *
* * * * * * * *
 * * * * * * * *
```

Your program must use only three output statements, one of each of the following forms:

```
printf( "%s", "* " );
printf( "%s", " " );
puts( "" ); // outputs a newline
```

3.40 *(Multiples of 2 with an Infinite Loop)* Write a program that keeps printing the multiples of the integer 2, namely 2, 4, 8, 16, 32, 64, and so on. Your loop should not terminate (i.e., you should create an infinite loop). What happens when you run this program?

3.41 *(Surface area of a Cone)* Write a program that reads the radius of a circle at the bottom of the cone (as a `float` value), the lateral height of the cone (as a `float` value) and computes and prints the total surface area of a right circular cone. Use the value 3.14159 for π.

3.42 What's wrong with the following statement? Rewrite it to accomplish what the programmer was probably trying to do.

```
printf( "%d", --( a - b ) );
```

3.43 *(Sides of a Triangle)* Write a program that reads three nonzero integer values and determines and prints whether they could represent the sides of a triangle.

3.44 *(Sides of a Right Triangle)* Write a program that reads three nonzero integers and determines and prints whether they could be the sides of a right triangle.

3.45 *(Factorial)* The factorial of a nonnegative integer n is written $n!$ (pronounced "n factorial") and is defined as follows:

$n! = n \cdot (n - 1) \cdot (n - 2) \cdot \ldots \cdot 1$ (for values of n greater than or equal to 1)

and

$n! = 1$ (for $n = 0$).

For example, $5! = 5 \cdot 4 \cdot 3 \cdot 2 \cdot 1$, which is 120.

a) Write a program that reads a nonnegative integer and computes and prints its factorial.

b) Write a program that estimates the value of the mathematical constant e by using the formula:

$$e = 1 + \frac{1}{1!} + \frac{1}{2!} + \frac{1}{3!} + \ldots$$

c) Write a program that computes the value of e^x by using the formula

$$e^x = 1 + \frac{x}{1!} + \frac{x^2}{2!} + \frac{x^3}{3!} + \ldots$$

Making a Difference

3.46 *(World-Population-Growth Calculator)* Use the web to determine the current world population and the annual world population growth rate. Write an application that inputs these values, then displays the estimated world population after one, two, three, four and five years.

3.47 *(Target-Heart-Rate Calculator)* While exercising, you can use a heart-rate monitor to see that your heart rate stays within a safe range suggested by your trainers and doctors. According to the American Heart Association (AHA), the formula for calculating your *maximum heart rate* in beats per minute is 220 minus your age in years. Your *target heart rate* is a range that's 50–85% of your maximum heart rate. [*Note:* These formulas are estimates provided by the AHA. Maximum and target heart rates may vary based on the health, fitness and gender of the individual. *Always consult a physician or qualified health care professional before beginning or modifying an exercise program.*] Create a program that reads the user's birthday and the current day (each consisting of the month, day and year). Your program should calculate and display the person's age (in years), the person's maximum heart rate and the person's target-heart-rate range.

3.48 *(Enforcing Privacy with Cryptography)* The explosive growth of Internet communications and data storage on Internet-connected computers has greatly increased privacy concerns. The field of cryptography is concerned with coding data to make it difficult (and hopefully—with the most advanced schemes—impossible) for unauthorized users to read. In this exercise you'll investigate a simple scheme for *encrypting* and *decrypting* data. A company that wants to send data over the Internet has asked you to write a program that will encrypt it so that it may be transmitted more securely. All the data is transmitted as four-digit integers. Your application should read a four-digit integer entered by the user and *encrypt* it as follows: Replace each digit with the result of adding 7 to the digit and getting the remainder after dividing the new value by 10. Then swap the first digit with the third, and swap the second digit with the fourth. Then print the encrypted integer. Write a separate application that inputs an encrypted four-digit integer and *decrypts* it (by reversing the encryption scheme) to form the original number. [*Optional reading project:* Research "public key cryptography" in general and the PGP (Pretty Good Privacy) specific public key scheme. You may also want to investigate the RSA scheme, which is widely used in industrial-strength applications.]

4

C Program Control

Objectives

In this chapter, you'll learn:

- The essentials of counter-controlled repetition.

- To use the `for` and `do...while` repetition statements to execute statements repeatedly.

- To understand multiple selection using the `switch` selection statement.

- To use the `break` and `continue` statements to alter the flow of control.

- To use the logical operators to form complex conditional expressions in control statements.

- To avoid the consequences of confusing the equality and assignment operators.

4.1 Introduction

You should now be comfortable with writing simple, complete C programs. In this chapter, repetition is considered in greater detail, and additional repetition control statements, namely the `for` and the `do...while`, are presented. The `switch` multiple-selection statement is introduced. We discuss the `break` statement for exiting immediately from certain control statements, and the `continue` statement for skipping the remainder of the body of a repetition statement and proceeding with the next iteration of the loop. The chapter discusses logical operators used for combining conditions, and summarizes the principles of structured programming as presented in Chapters 3 and 4.

4.2 Repetition Essentials

Most programs involve repetition, or looping. A loop is a group of instructions the computer executes repeatedly while some **loop-continuation condition** remains true. We've discussed two means of repetition:

1. Counter-controlled repetition
2. Sentinel-controlled repetition

Counter-controlled repetition is sometimes called *definite repetition* because we know *in advance* exactly how many times the loop will be executed. Sentinel-controlled repetition is sometimes called *indefinite repetition* because it's *not known* in advance how many times the loop will be executed.

In counter-controlled repetition, a **control variable** is used to count the number of repetitions. The control variable is incremented (usually by 1) each time the group of instructions is performed. When the value of the control variable indicates that the correct number of repetitions has been performed, the loop terminates and execution continues with the statement after the repetition statement.

Sentinel values are used to control repetition when:

1. The precise number of repetitions isn't known in advance, and
2. The loop includes statements that obtain data each time the loop is performed.

The sentinel value indicates "end of data." The sentinel is entered after all regular data items have been supplied to the program. Sentinels must be distinct from regular data items.

4.3 Counter-Controlled Repetition

Counter-controlled repetition requires:

1. The name of a control variable (or loop counter).

2. The initial value of the control variable.

3. The increment (or decrement) by which the control variable is modified each time through the loop.

4. The condition that tests for the final value of the control variable (i.e., whether looping should continue).

Consider the simple program shown in Fig. 4.1, which prints the numbers from 1 to 10. The definition

```
unsigned int counter = 1; // initialization
```

names the control variable (counter), defines it to be an integer, reserves memory space for it, and sets it to an initial value of 1.

```
1  // Fig. 4.1: fig04_01.c
2  // Counter-controlled repetition.
3  #include <stdio.h>
4
5  // function main begins program execution
6  int main( void )
7  {
8     unsigned int counter = 1; // initialization
9
10    while ( counter <= 10 ) { // repetition condition
11       printf ( "%u\n", counter ); // display counter
12       ++counter; // increment
13    } // end while
14 } // end function main
```

```
1
2
3
4
5
6
7
8
9
10
```

Fig. 4.1 | Counter-controlled repetition.

The definition and initialization of counter could also have been written as

```
unsigned int counter;
counter = 1;
```

The definition is *not* executable, but the assignment *is*. We use both methods of setting the values of variables.

The statement

```
++counter; // increment
```

increments the loop counter by 1 each time the loop is performed. The loop-continuation condition in the while statement tests whether the value of the control variable is less than or equal to 10 (the last value for which the condition is true). The body of this while is performed even when the control variable is 10. The loop terminates when the control variable *exceeds* 10 (i.e., counter becomes 11).

You could make the program in Fig. 4.1 more concise by initializing counter to 0 and by replacing the while statement with

```
while ( ++counter <= 10 )
    printf( "%u\n", counter );
```

This code saves a statement because the incrementing is done directly in the while condition before the condition is tested. Also, this code eliminates the need for the braces around the body of the while because the while now contains only *one* statement. Coding in such a condensed fashion takes some practice. Some programmers feel that this makes the code too cryptic and error prone.

Common Programming Error 4.1

Floating-point values may be approximate, so controlling counting loops with floating-point variables may result in imprecise counter values and inaccurate termination tests.

Error-Prevention Tip 4.1

Control counting loops with integer values.

Good Programming Practice 4.1

Too many levels of nesting can make a program difficult to understand. As a rule, try to avoid using more than three levels of nesting.

Good Programming Practice 4.2

The combination of vertical spacing before and after control statements and indentation of the bodies of control statements within the control-statement headers gives programs a two-dimensional appearance that greatly improves program readability.

4.4 for Repetition Statement

The for repetition statement handles all the details of counter-controlled repetition. To illustrate its power, let's rewrite the program of Fig. 4.1. The result is shown in Fig. 4.2.

The program operates as follows. When the for statement begins executing, the control variable counter is initialized to 1. Then, the loop-continuation condition counter <= 10 is checked. Because the initial value of counter is 1, the condition is satisfied, so the printf statement (line 13) prints the value of counter, namely 1. The control variable counter is then incremented by the expression ++counter, and the loop begins again with the loop-continuation test. Because the control variable is now equal to 2, the final value is not exceeded, so the program performs the printf statement again. This process continues until the control variable counter is incremented to its final value of 11—this causes the

```
1   // Fig. 4.2: fig04_02.c
2   // Counter-controlled repetition with the for statement.
3   #include <stdio.h>
4
5   // function main begins program execution
6   int main( void )
7   {
8      unsigned int counter; // define counter
9
10     // initialization, repetition condition, and increment
11     //  are all included in the for statement header.
12     for ( counter = 1; counter <= 10; ++counter ) {
13        printf( "%u\n", counter );
14     } // end for
15  } // end function main
```

Fig. 4.2 | Counter-controlled repetition with the for statement.

loop-continuation test to fail, and repetition terminates. The program continues by performing the first statement after the for statement (in this case, the end of the program).

for *Statement Header Components*

Figure 4.3 takes a closer look at the for statement of Fig. 4.2. Notice that the for statement "does it all"—it specifies each of the items needed for counter-controlled repetition with a control variable. If there's more than one statement in the body of the for, braces are required to define the body of the loop.

The C standard allows you to declare the control variable in the initialization section of the for header (as in int counter = 1). We show a complete code example of this in Appendix F. This feature is not supported in Microsoft Visual C++.

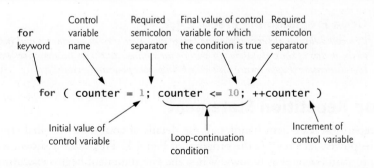

Fig. 4.3 | for statement header components.

Off-By-One Errors

Notice that Fig. 4.2 uses the loop-continuation condition counter <= 10. If you incorrectly wrote counter < 10, then the loop would be executed only 9 times. This is a common logic error called an **off-by-one error**.

Error-Prevention Tip 4.2
Using the final value in the condition of a while *or* for *statement and using the* <= *relational operator can help avoid off-by-one errors. For a loop used to print the values 1 to 10, for example, the loop-continuation condition should be* counter <= 10 *rather than* counter < 11 *or* counter < 10.

General Format of a **for** Statement
The general format of the for statement is

```
for ( expression1; expression2; expression3 ) {
    statement
}
```

where *expression1* initializes the loop-control variable, *expression2* is the loop-continuation condition, and *expression3* increments the control variable. In most cases, the for statement can be represented with an equivalent while statement as follows:

```
expression1;
while ( expression2 ) {
    statement
    expression3;
}
```

There's an exception to this rule, which we discuss in Section 4.9.

Comma-Separated Lists of Expressions
Often, *expression1* and *expression3* are comma-separated lists of expressions. The commas as used here are actually **comma operators** that guarantee that lists of expressions evaluate from left to right. The value and type of a comma-separated list of expressions are the value and type of the rightmost expression in the list. The comma operator is most often used in the for statement. Its primary use is to enable you to use multiple initialization and/or multiple increment expressions. For example, there may be two control variables in a single for statement that must be initialized and incremented.

Software Engineering Observation 4.1
Place only expressions involving the control variables in the initialization and increment sections of a for *statement. Manipulations of other variables should appear either before the loop (if they execute only once, like initialization statements) or in the loop body (if they execute once per repetition, like incrementing or decrementing statements).*

Expressions in the **for** Statement's Header Are Optional
The three expressions in the for statement are *optional*. If *expression2* is omitted, C *assumes* that the condition is *true*, thus creating an *infinite loop*. You may omit *expression1* if the control variable is initialized elsewhere in the program. *expression3* may be omitted if the increment is calculated by statements in the body of the for statement or if no increment is needed.

Increment Expression Acts Like a Standalone Statement
The increment expression in the for statement acts like a stand-alone C statement at the end of the body of the for. Therefore, the expressions

```
counter = counter + 1
counter += 1
++counter
counter++
```

are all equivalent in the increment part of the for statement. Some C programmers prefer the form counter++ because the incrementing occurs *after* the loop body is executed, and the postincrementing form seems more natural. Because the variable being preincremented or postincremented here does *not* appear in a larger expression, both forms of incrementing have the *same* effect. The two semicolons in the for statement are required.

Common Programming Error 4.2
Using commas instead of semicolons in a for *header is a syntax error.*

Common Programming Error 4.3
Placing a semicolon immediately to the right of a for *header makes the body of that* for *statement an empty statement. This is normally a logic error.*

4.5 for Statement: Notes and Observations

1. The initialization, loop-continuation condition and increment can contain arithmetic expressions. For example, if x = 2 and y = 10, the statement

```
for ( j = x; j <= 4 * x * y; j += y / x )
```

is equivalent to the statement

```
for ( j = 2; j <= 80; j += 5 )
```

2. The "increment" may be negative (in which case it's really a *decrement* and the loop actually counts *downward*).

3. If the loop-continuation condition is initially *false*, the loop body does *not* execute. Instead, execution proceeds with the statement following the for statement.

4. The control variable is frequently printed or used in calculations in the body of a loop, but it need not be. It's common to use the control variable for controlling repetition while never mentioning it in the body of the loop.

5. The for statement is flowcharted much like the while statement. For example, Fig. 4.4 shows the flowchart of the for statement

```
for ( counter = 1; counter <= 10; ++counter )
    printf( "%u", counter );
```

This flowchart makes it clear that the initialization occurs only once and that incrementing occurs *after* the body statement is performed.

Error-Prevention Tip 4.3
Although the value of the control variable can be changed in the body of a for *loop, this can lead to subtle errors. It's best not to change it.*

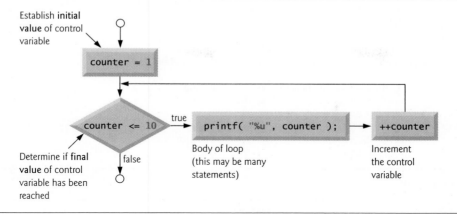

Fig. 4.4 | Flowcharting a typical for repetition statement.

4.6 Examples Using the for Statement

The following examples show methods of varying the control variable in a for statement.

1. Vary the control variable from 1 to 100 in increments of 1.

```
for ( i = 1; i <= 100; ++i )
```

2. Vary the control variable from 100 to 1 in increments of -1 (*decrements* of 1).

```
for ( i = 100; i >= 1; --i )
```

3. Vary the control variable from 7 to 77 in steps of 7.

```
for ( i = 7; i <= 77; i += 7 )
```

4. Vary the control variable from 20 to 2 in steps of -2.

```
for ( i = 20; i >= 2; i -= 2 )
```

5. Vary the control variable over the following sequence of values: 2, 5, 8, 11, 14, 17.

```
for ( j = 2; j <= 17; j += 3 )
```

6. Vary the control variable over the following sequence of values: 44, 33, 22, 11, 0.

```
for ( j = 44; j >= 0; j -= 11 )
```

Application: Summing the Even Integers from 2 to 100
Figure 4.5 uses the for statement to sum all the even integers from 2 to 100. Each iteration of the loop (lines 11–13) adds control variable number's value to variable sum.

```
1   // Fig. 4.5: fig04_05.c
2   // Summation with for.
3   #include <stdio.h>
4
```

Fig. 4.5 | Summation with for. (Part 1 of 2.)

```
 5   // function main begins program execution
 6   int main( void )
 7   {
 8      unsigned int sum = 0; // initialize sum
 9      unsigned int number; // number to be added to sum
10
11      for ( number = 2; number <= 100; number += 2 ) {
12         sum += number; // add number to sum
13      } // end for
14
15      printf( "Sum is %u\n", sum ); // output sum
16   } // end function main
```

```
Sum is 2550
```

Fig. 4.5 │ Summation with `for`. (Part 2 of 2.)

The body of the `for` statement in Fig. 4.5 could actually be merged into the rightmost portion of the `for` header by using the *comma operator* as follows:

```
for ( number = 2; number <= 100; sum += number, number += 2 )
   ; // empty statement
```

The initialization `sum = 0` could also be merged into the initialization section of the `for`.

Good Programming Practice 4.3

Although statements preceding a for *and statements in the body of a* for *can often be merged into the* for *header, avoid doing so, because it makes the program more difficult to read.*

Good Programming Practice 4.4

Limit the size of control-statement headers to a single line if possible.

Application: Compound-Interest Calculations

The next example computes compound interest using the `for` statement. Consider the following problem statement:

> *A person invests $1000.00 in a savings account yielding 5% interest. Assuming that all interest is left on deposit in the account, calculate and print the amount of money in the account at the end of each year for 10 years. Use the following formula for determining these amounts:*
>
> $$a = p(1 + r)^n$$
>
> *where*
>
> > *p is the original amount invested (i.e., the principal)*
> > *r is the annual interest rate*
> > *n is the number of years*
> > *a is the amount on deposit at the end of the nth year.*

This problem involves a loop that performs the indicated calculation for each of the 10 years the money remains on deposit. The solution is shown in Fig. 4.6.

```
 1   // Fig. 4.6: fig04_06.c
 2   // Calculating compound interest.
 3   #include <stdio.h>
 4   #include <math.h>
 5
 6   // function main begins program execution
 7   int main( void )
 8   {
 9      double amount; // amount on deposit
10      double principal = 1000.0; // starting principal
11      double rate = .05; // annual interest rate
12      unsigned int year; // year counter
13
14      // output table column heads
15      printf( "%4s%21s\n", "Year", "Amount on deposit" );
16
17      // calculate amount on deposit for each of ten years
18      for ( year = 1; year <= 10; ++year ) {
19
20         // calculate new amount for specified year
21         amount = principal * pow( 1.0 + rate, year );
22
23         // output one table row
24         printf( "%4u%21.2f\n", year, amount );
25      } // end for
26   } // end function main
```

```
Year     Amount on deposit
   1               1050.00
   2               1102.50
   3               1157.63
   4               1215.51
   5               1276.28
   6               1340.10
   7               1407.10
   8               1477.46
   9               1551.33
  10               1628.89
```

Fig. 4.6 | Calculating compound interest.

The for statement executes the body of the loop 10 times, varying a control variable from 1 to 10 in increments of 1. Although C does *not* include an exponentiation operator, we can use the Standard Library function pow for this purpose. The function pow(x, y) calculates the value of x raised to the yth power. It takes two arguments of type double and returns a double value. Type double is a floating-point type like float, but typically a variable of type double can store a value of *much greater magnitude* with *greater precision* than float. The header <math.h> (line 4) should be included whenever a math function such as pow is used. Actually, this program would malfunction without the inclusion of math.h, as the linker would be unable to find the pow function.[1] Function **pow** requires

1.   On many Linux/UNIX C compilers, you must include the -lm option (e.g., gcc -lm fig04_06.c) when compiling Fig. 4.6. This links the math library to the program.

two `double` arguments, but variable `year` is an integer. The `math.h` file includes information that tells the compiler to convert the value of `year` to a temporary `double` representation *before* calling the function. This information is contained in something called pow's function prototype. Function prototypes are explained in Chapter 5. We also provide a summary of the `pow` function and other math library functions in Chapter 5.

A Caution about Using Type **float** *or* **double** *for Monetary Amounts*
Notice that we defined the variables `amount`, `principal` and `rate` to be of type `double`. We did this for simplicity because we're dealing with fractional parts of dollars.

> **Error-Prevention Tip 4.4**
> *Do not use variables of type* `float` *or* `double` *to perform monetary calculations. The impreciseness of floating-point numbers can cause errors that will result in incorrect monetary values. [In this chapter's exercises, we explore the use of integers to perform precise monetary calculations.]*

Here is a simple explanation of what can go wrong when using `float` or `double` to represent dollar amounts. Two `float` dollar amounts stored in the machine could be 14.234 (which with `%.2f` prints as 14.23) and 18.673 (which with `%.2f` prints as 18.67). When these amounts are added, they produce the sum 32.907, which with `%.2f` prints as 32.91. Thus your printout could appear as

```
  14.23
+ 18.67
-------
  32.91
```

Clearly the sum of the individual numbers as printed should be 32.90! You've been warned!

Formatting Numeric Output
The conversion specifier `%21.2f` is used to print the value of the variable `amount` in the program. The 21 in the conversion specifier denotes the *field width* in which the value will be printed. A field width of 21 specifies that the value printed will appear in 21 print positions. The 2 specifies the *precision* (i.e., the number of decimal positions). If the number of characters displayed is *less than* the field width, then the value will automatically be *right justified* in the field. This is particularly useful for aligning floating-point values with the same precision (so that their decimal points align vertically). To *left justify* a value in a field, place a - (minus sign) between the % and the field width. The minus sign may also be used to left justify integers (such as in `%-6d`) and character strings (such as in `%-8s`). We'll discuss the powerful formatting capabilities of `printf` and `scanf` in detail in Chapter 9.

4.7 `switch` Multiple-Selection Statement

In Chapter 3, we discussed the `if` single-selection statement and the `if...else` double-selection statement. Occasionally, an algorithm will contain a *series of decisions* in which a variable or expression is tested separately for each of the constant integral values it may assume, and different actions are taken. This is called *multiple selection*. C provides the `switch` multiple-selection statement to handle such decision making.

The switch statement consists of a series of case labels, an optional default case and statements to execute for each case. Figure 4.7 uses switch to count the number of each different letter grade students earned on an exam.

```c
1   // Fig. 4.7: fig04_07.c
2   // Counting letter grades with switch.
3   #include <stdio.h>
4
5   // function main begins program execution
6   int main( void )
7   {
8      int grade; // one grade
9      unsigned int aCount = 0; // number of As
10     unsigned int bCount = 0; // number of Bs
11     unsigned int cCount = 0; // number of Cs
12     unsigned int dCount = 0; // number of Ds
13     unsigned int fCount = 0; // number of Fs
14
15     puts( "Enter the letter grades." );
16     puts( "Enter the EOF character to end input." );
17
18     // loop until user types end-of-file key sequence
19     while ( ( grade = getchar() ) != EOF ) {
20
21        // determine which grade was input
22        switch ( grade ) { // switch nested in while
23
24           case 'A': // grade was uppercase A
25           case 'a': // or lowercase a
26              ++aCount; // increment aCount
27              break; // necessary to exit switch
28
29           case 'B': // grade was uppercase B
30           case 'b': // or lowercase b
31              ++bCount; // increment bCount
32              break; // exit switch
33
34           case 'C': // grade was uppercase C
35           case 'c': // or lowercase c
36              ++cCount; // increment cCount
37              break; // exit switch
38
39           case 'D': // grade was uppercase D
40           case 'd': // or lowercase d
41              ++dCount; // increment dCount
42              break; // exit switch
43
44           case 'F': // grade was uppercase F
45           case 'f': // or lowercase f
46              ++fCount; // increment fCount
47              break; // exit switch
48
```

Fig. 4.7 | Counting letter grades with switch. (Part 1 of 2.)

```
49                case '\n': // ignore newlines,
50                case '\t': // tabs,
51                case ' ': // and spaces in input
52                    break; // exit switch
53
54                default: // catch all other characters
55                    printf( "%s", "Incorrect letter grade entered." );
56                    puts( " Enter a new grade." );
57                    break; // optional; will exit switch anyway
58            } // end switch
59        } // end while
60
61        // output summary of results
62        puts( "\nTotals for each letter grade are:" );
63        printf( "A: %u\n", aCount ); // display number of A grades
64        printf( "B: %u\n", bCount ); // display number of B grades
65        printf( "C: %u\n", cCount ); // display number of C grades
66        printf( "D: %u\n", dCount ); // display number of D grades
67        printf( "F: %u\n", fCount ); // display number of F grades
68    } // end function main
```

```
Enter the letter grades.
Enter the EOF character to end input.
a
b
c
C
A
d
f
C
E
Incorrect letter grade entered. Enter a new grade.
D
A
b
^Z ——————— Not all systems display a representation of the EOF character

Totals for each letter grade are:
A: 3
B: 2
C: 3
D: 2
F: 1
```

Fig. 4.7 | Counting letter grades with switch. (Part 2 of 2.)

Reading Character Input

In the program, the user enters letter grades for a class. In the while header (line 19),

```
while ( ( grade = getchar() ) != EOF )
```

the parenthesized assignment (grade = getchar()) executes first. The getchar function (from <stdio.h>) reads one character from the keyboard and stores that character in the integer variable grade. Characters are normally stored in variables of type **char**. However, an important feature of C is that characters can be stored in any integer data type because they're usually represented as one-byte integers in the computer. Thus, we can treat a character as either an integer or a character, depending on its use. For example, the statement

```
printf( "The character (%c) has the value %d.\n", 'a', 'a' );
```

uses the conversion specifiers %c and %d to print the character a and its integer value, respectively. The result is

```
The character (a) has the value 97.
```

The integer 97 is the character's numerical representation in the computer. Many computers today use the ASCII (American Standard Code for Information Interchange) character set in which 97 represents the lowercase letter 'a'. A list of the ASCII characters and their decimal values is presented in Appendix B. Characters can be read with scanf by using the conversion specifier %c.

Assignments as a whole actually have a value. This value is assigned to the variable on the left side of the =. The value of the assignment expression grade = getchar() is the character that's returned by getchar and assigned to the variable grade.

The fact that assignments have values can be useful for setting several variables to the same value. For example,

```
a = b = c = 0;
```

first evaluates the assignment c = 0 (because the = operator associates from right to left). The variable b is then assigned the value of the assignment c = 0 (which is 0). Then, the variable a is assigned the value of the assignment b = (c = 0) (which is also 0). In the program, the value of the assignment grade = getchar() is compared with the value of EOF (a symbol whose acronym stands for "end of file"). We use EOF (which normally has the value -1) as the sentinel value. The user types a system-dependent keystroke combination to mean "end of file"—i.e., "I have no more data to enter." EOF is a symbolic integer constant defined in the <stdio.h> header (we'll see in Chapter 6 how symbolic constants are defined). If the value assigned to grade is equal to EOF, the program terminates. We've chosen to represent characters in this program as ints because EOF has an integer value (again, normally -1).

Portability Tip 4.1
The keystroke combinations for entering EOF (end of file) are system dependent.

Portability Tip 4.2
Testing for the symbolic constant EOF [rather than −1 makes programs more portable. The C standard states that EOF is a negative integral value (but not necessarily −1). Thus, EOF could have different values on different systems.

Entering the EOF Indicator
On Linux/UNIX/Mac OS X systems, the EOF indicator is entered by typing

<Ctrl> d

on a line by itself. This notation *<Ctrl> d* means to press the *Enter* key and then simultaneously press both the *Ctrl* key and the *d* key. On other systems, such as Microsoft Windows, the EOF indicator can be entered by typing

> *<Ctrl> z*

You may also need to press *Enter* on Windows.

The user enters grades at the keyboard. When the *Enter* key is pressed, the characters are read by function getchar one character at a time. If the character entered is not equal to EOF, the switch statement (line 22–58) is entered.

switch Statement Details

Keyword switch is followed by the variable name grade in parentheses. This is called the **controlling expression**. The value of this expression is compared with each of the **case** labels. Assume the user has entered the letter C as a grade. C is automatically compared to each case in the switch. If a match occurs (case 'C':), the statements for that case are executed. In the case of the letter C, cCount is incremented by 1 (line 36), and the switch statement is exited immediately with the break statement.

The break statement causes program control to continue with the first statement after the switch statement. The break statement is used because the cases in a switch statement would otherwise run together. If break is *not* used anywhere in a switch statement, then each time a match occurs in the statement, the statements for *all* the remaining cases will be executed. (This feature is rarely useful, although it's perfect for programming Exercise 4.38—the iterative song *The Twelve Days of Christmas!*) If no match occurs, the default case is executed, and an error message is printed.

switch Statement Flowchart

Each case can have one or more actions. The switch statement is different from all other control statements in that braces are *not* required around multiple actions in a case of a switch. The general switch multiple-selection statement (using a break in each case) is flowcharted in Fig. 4.8. The flowchart makes it clear that each break statement at the end of a case causes control to immediately exit the switch statement.

Common Programming Error 4.4

Forgetting a break statement when one is needed in a switch statement is a logic error.

Software Engineering Observation 4.2

Provide a default case in switch statements. Cases not explicitly tested in a switch are ignored. The default case helps prevent this by focusing you on the need to process exceptional conditions. Sometimes no default processing is needed.

Good Programming Practice 4.5

Although the case clauses and the default case clause in a switch statement can occur in any order, it's common to place the default clause last.

Good Programming Practice 4.6

In a switch statement when the default clause is last, the break statement isn't required. You may prefer to include this break for clarity and symmetry with other cases.

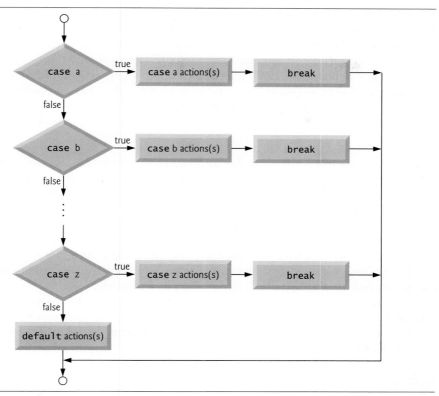

Fig. 4.8 | switch multiple-selection statement with breaks.

Ignoring Newline, Tab and Blank Characters in Input

In the switch statement of Fig. 4.7, the lines

```
case '\n': // ignore newlines,
case '\t': // tabs,
case ' ': // and spaces in input
    break; // exit switch
```

cause the program to skip newline, tab and blank characters. Reading characters one at a time can cause some problems. To have the program read the characters, you must send them to the computer by pressing the *Enter* key. This causes the newline character to be placed in the input after the character we wish to process. Often, this newline character must be specially processed to make the program work correctly. By including the preceding cases in our switch statement, we prevent the error message in the default case from being printed each time a newline, tab or space is encountered in the input.

Error-Prevention Tip 4.5

Remember to provide processing capabilities for newline (and possibly other white-space) characters in the input when processing characters one at a time.

Listing several case labels together (such as case 'D': case 'd': in Fig. 4.7) simply means that the *same* set of actions is to occur for either of these cases.

Constant Integral Expressions

When using the switch statement, remember that each individual case can test only a constant integral expression—i.e., any combination of character constants and integer constants that evaluates to a constant integer value. A character constant can be represented as the specific character in single quotes, such as 'A'. Characters *must* be enclosed within single quotes to be recognized as character constants—characters in double quotes are recognized as strings. Integer constants are simply integer values. In our example, we've used character constants. Remember that characters are represented as small integer values.

Notes on Integral Types

Portable languages like C must have flexible data type sizes. Different applications may need integers of different sizes. C provides several data types to represent integers. In addition to int and char, C provides types short int (which can be abbreviated as short) and long int (which can be abbreviated as long). The C standard specifies the minimum range of values for each integer type, but the actual range may be greater and depends on the implementation. For short ints the minimum range is –32767 to +32767. For most integer calculations, long ints are sufficient. The minimum range of values for long ints is –2147483647 to +2147483647. The range of values for an int greater than or equal to that of a short int and less than or equal to that of a long int. On many of today's platforms, ints and long ints represent the same range of values. The data type signed char can be used to represent integers in the range –127 to +127 or any of the characters in the computer's character set. See section 5.2.4.2 of the C standard document for the complete list of signed and unsigned integer-type ranges.

4.8 do...while Repetition Statement

The do...while repetition statement is similar to the while statement. In the while statement, the loop-continuation condition is tested at the beginning of the loop *before* the body of the loop is performed. The do...while statement tests the loop-continuation condition *after* the loop body is performed. Therefore, the loop body will be executed *at least once*. When a do...while terminates, execution continues with the statement after the while clause. It's not necessary to use braces in the do...while statement if there's only one statement in the body. However, the braces are usually included to avoid confusion between the while and do...while statements. For example,

```
while ( condition )
```

is normally regarded as the header to a while statement. A do...while with no braces around the single-statement body appears as

```
do
    statement
while ( condition );
```

which can be confusing. The last line—while(*condition*);—may be misinterpreted as a while statement containing an empty statement. Thus, to avoid confusion, the do...while with one statement is often written as follows:

```
do {
    statement
} while ( condition );
```

Good Programming Practice 4.7

To eliminate the potential for ambiguity, you may want to include braces in do...while statements, even if they're not necessary.

Common Programming Error 4.5

Infinite loops are caused when the loop-continuation condition in a repetition statement never becomes false. To prevent this, make sure there's not a semicolon immediately after a while or for statement's header. In a counter-controlled loop, make sure the control variable is incremented (or decremented) in the loop. In a sentinel-controlled loop, make sure the sentinel value is eventually input.

Figure 4.9 uses a do...while statement to print the numbers from 1 to 10. The control variable counter is preincremented in the loop-continuation test.

```c
// Fig. 4.9: fig04_09.c
// Using the do...while repetition statement.
#include <stdio.h>

// function main begins program execution
int main( void )
{
   unsigned int counter = 1; // initialize counter

   do {
      printf( "%u  ", counter ); // display counter
   } while ( ++counter <= 10 ); // end do...while
} // end function main
```

```
1 2 3 4 5 6 7 8 9 10
```

Fig. 4.9 | Using the do...while repetition statement.

do...while *Statement Flowchart*

Figure 4.10 shows the do...while statement flowchart, which makes it clear that the loop-continuation condition does not execute until after the action is performed *at least once*.

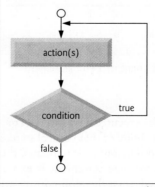

Fig. 4.10 | Flowcharting the do...while repetition statement.

4.9 break and continue Statements

The break and continue statements are used to alter the flow of control. Section 4.7 showed how break can be used to terminate a switch statement's execution. This section discusses how to use break in a repetition statement.

break *Statement*

The break statement, when executed in a while, for, do...while or switch statement, causes an *immediate exit* from that statement. Program execution continues with the next statement. Common uses of the break statement are to escape early from a loop or to skip the remainder of a switch statement (as in Fig. 4.7). Figure 4.11 demonstrates the break statement in a for repetition statement. When the if statement detects that x has become 5, break is executed. This terminates the for statement, and the program continues with the printf after the for. The loop fully executes only four times.

```c
 1   // Fig. 4.11: fig04_11.c
 2   // Using the break statement in a for statement.
 3   #include <stdio.h>
 4
 5   // function main begins program execution
 6   int main( void )
 7   {
 8      unsigned int x; // counter
 9
10      // loop 10 times
11      for ( x = 1; x <= 10; ++x ) {
12
13         // if x is 5, terminate loop
14         if ( x == 5 ) {
15            break; // break loop only if x is 5
16         } // end if
17
18         printf( "%u ", x ); // display value of x
19      } // end for
20
21      printf( "\nBroke out of loop at x == %u\n", x );
22   } // end function main
```

```
1 2 3 4
Broke out of loop at x == 5
```

Fig. 4.11 | Using the break statement in a for statement.

continue *Statement*

The continue statement, when executed in a while, for or do...while statement, skips the remaining statements in the body of that control statement and performs the next iteration of the loop. In while and do...while statements, the loop-continuation test is evaluated immediately *after* the continue statement is executed. In the for statement, the increment expression is executed, then the loop-continuation test is evaluated. Earlier, we said that the while statement could be used in most cases to represent the for statement.

The one exception occurs when the increment expression in the while statement *follows* the continue statement. In this case, the increment is *not* executed before the repetition-continuation condition is tested, and the while does *not* execute in the same manner as the for. Figure 4.12 uses the continue statement in a for statement to skip the printf statement and begin the next iteration of the loop.

```c
1   // Fig. 4.12: fig04_12.c
2   // Using the continue statement in a for statement.
3   #include <stdio.h>
4
5   // function main begins program execution
6   int main( void )
7   {
8      unsigned int x; // counter
9
10     // loop 10 times
11     for ( x = 1; x <= 10; ++x ) {
12
13        // if x is 5, continue with next iteration of loop
14        if ( x == 5 ) {
15           continue; // skip remaining code in loop body
16        } // end if
17
18        printf( "%u ", x ); // display value of x
19     } // end for
20
21     puts( "\nUsed continue to skip printing the value 5" );
22  } // end function main
```

```
1 2 3 4 6 7 8 9 10
Used continue to skip printing the value 5
```

Fig. 4.12 | Using the continue statement in a for statement.

Software Engineering Observation 4.3

Some programmers feel that break and continue violate the norms of structured programming. The effects of these statements can be achieved by structured programming techniques we'll soon learn, so these programmers do not use break and continue.

Performance Tip 4.1

The break and continue statements, when used properly, perform faster than the corresponding structured techniques that we'll soon learn.

Software Engineering Observation 4.4

There's a tension between achieving quality software engineering and achieving the best-performing software. Often one of these goals is achieved at the expense of the other. For all but the most performance-intensive situations, apply the following guidelines: First, make your code simple and correct; then make it fast and small, but only if necessary.

4.10 Logical Operators

So far we've studied only simple conditions, such as counter <= 10, total > 1000, and number != sentinelValue. We've expressed these conditions in terms of the *relational operators*, >, <, >= and <=, and the *equality operators*, == and !=. Each decision tested precisely *one* condition. To test multiple conditions in the process of making a decision, we had to perform these tests in separate statements or in nested if or if...else statements. C provides *logical operators* that may be used to form more complex conditions by combining simple conditions. The logical operators are && (logical AND), || (logical OR) and ! (logical NOT also called **logical negation**). We'll consider examples of each of these operators.

Logical AND (&&) Operator

Suppose we wish to ensure that two conditions are *both* true before we choose a certain path of execution. In this case, we can use the logical operator && as follows:

```
if ( gender == 1 && age >= 65 )
    ++seniorFemales;
```

This if statement contains two *simple* conditions. The condition gender == 1 might be evaluated, for example, to determine whether a person is a female. The condition age >= 65 is evaluated to determine whether a person is a senior citizen. The two simple conditions are evaluated first because == and >= are have *higher* precedence than &&. The if statement then considers the combined condition gender == 1 && age >= 65, which is *true* if and only if *both* of the simple conditions are *true*. Finally, if this combined condition is true, then the count of seniorFemales is incremented by 1. If *either or both* of the simple conditions are *false*, then the program skips the incrementing and proceeds to the statement following the if.

Figure 4.13 summarizes the && operator. The table shows all four possible combinations of zero (false) and nonzero (true) values for expression1 and expression2. Such tables are often called **truth tables**. *C evaluates all expressions that include relational operators, equality operators, and/or logical operators to 0 or 1. Although C sets a true value to 1, it accepts *any* nonzero value as true.*

expression1	expression2	expression1 && expression2
0	0	0
0	nonzero	0
nonzero	0	0
nonzero	nonzero	1

Fig. 4.13 | Truth table for the logical AND (&&) operator.

Logical OR (||) Operator

Now let's consider the || (logical OR) operator. Suppose we wish to ensure at some point in a program that *either or both* of two conditions are *true* before we choose a certain path of execution. In this case, we use the || operator, as in the following program segment:

```
if ( semesterAverage >= 90 || finalExam >= 90 )
    puts( "Student grade is A" );
```

This statement also contains two simple conditions. The condition `semesterAverage >= 90` is evaluated to determine whether the student deserves an "A" in the course because of a solid performance throughout the semester. The condition `finalExam >= 90` is evaluated to determine whether the student deserves an "A" in the course because of an outstanding performance on the final exam. The `if` statement then considers the combined condition

```
semesterAverage >= 90 || finalExam >= 90
```

and awards the student an "A" if *either or both* of the simple conditions are *true*. The message "`Student grade is A`" is *not* printed only when *both* of the simple conditions are *false* (zero). Figure 4.14 is a truth table for the logical OR operator (`||`).

expression1	expression2	expression1 || expression2
0	0	0
0	nonzero	1
nonzero	0	1
nonzero	nonzero	1

Fig. 4.14 | Truth table for the logical OR (`||`) operator.

The `&&` operator has a *higher* precedence than `||`. Both operators associate from left to right. An expression containing `&&` or `||` operators is evaluated *only* until truth or falsehood is known. Thus, evaluation of the condition

```
gender == 1 && age >= 65
```

will stop if `gender` is not equal to 1 (i.e., the entire expression is false), and continue if `gender` is equal to 1 (i.e., the entire expression could still be true if `age >= 65`). This performance feature for the evaluation of logical AND and logical OR expressions is called short-circuit evaluation.

Performance Tip 4.2

In expressions using operator &&, make the condition that's most likely to be false the left-most condition. In expressions using operator ||, make the condition that's most likely to be true the leftmost condition. This can reduce a program's execution time.

Logical Negation (!) Operator

C provides `!` (logical negation) to enable you to "reverse" the meaning of a condition. Unlike operators `&&` and `||`, which combine *two* conditions (and are therefore *binary* operators), the logical negation operator has only a *single* condition as an operand (and is therefore a *unary* operator). The logical negation operator is placed before a condition when we're interested in choosing a path of execution if the original condition (without the logical negation operator) is *false*, such as in the following program segment:

```
if ( !( grade == sentinelValue ) )
    printf( "The next grade is %f\n", grade );
```

The parentheses around the condition `grade == sentinelValue` are needed because the logical negation operator has a higher precedence than the equality operator. Figure 4.15 is a truth table for the logical negation operator.

expression	!expression
0	1
nonzero	0

Fig. 4.15 | Truth table for operator ! (logical negation).

In most cases, you can avoid using logical negation by expressing the condition differently with an appropriate relational operator. For example, the preceding statement may also be written as follows:

```
if ( grade != sentinelValue )
   printf( "The next grade is %f\n", grade );
```

Summary of Operator Precedence and Associativity

Figure 4.16 shows the precedence and associativity of the operators introduced to this point. The operators are shown from top to bottom in decreasing order of precedence.

Operators					Associativity	Type
++ *(postfix)*	-- *(postfix)*				right to left	postfix
+	-	!	++ *(prefix)*	-- *(prefix)*	*(type)*	right to left	unary
*	/	%			left to right	multiplicative
+	-				left to right	additive
<	<=	>	>=		left to right	relational
==	!=				left to right	equality
&&					left to right	logical AND
||					left to right	logical OR
?:					right to left	conditional
=	+=	-=	*=	/= %=	right to left	assignment
,					left to right	comma

Fig. 4.16 | Operator precedence and associativity.

The _Bool Data Type

The C standard includes a **boolean type**—represented by the keyword **_Bool**—which can hold only the values 0 or 1. Recall C's convention of using zero and nonzero values to represent false and true—the value 0 in a condition evaluates to false, while any nonzero value evaluates to true. Assigning any non-zero value to a _Bool sets it to 1. The standard also includes the **<stdbool.h>** header, which defines **bool** as a shorthand for the type _Bool, and **true** and **false** as named representations of 1 and 0, respectively. At preprocessor time, bool, true and false are replaced with _Bool, 1 and 0. Section F.8 presents an example that uses bool, true and false. The example uses a programmer-defined function, a concept we introduce in Chapter 5. You can study the example now, but might wish to revisit it after reading Chapter 5. Microsoft Visual C++ does *not* implement the _Bool data type.

4.11 Confusing Equality (==) and Assignment (=) Operators

There's one type of error that C programmers, no matter how experienced, tend to make so frequently that we felt it was worth a separate section. That error is accidentally swapping the operators == (equality) and = (assignment). What makes these swaps so damaging is the fact that they do *not* ordinarily cause *compilation errors*. Rather, statements with these errors ordinarily compile correctly, allowing programs to run to completion while likely generating incorrect results through *runtime logic errors*.

Two aspects of C cause these problems. One is that any expression in C that produces a value can be used in the decision portion of any control statement. If the value is 0, it's treated as false, and if the value is nonzero, it's treated as true. The second is that assignments in C produce a value, namely the value that's assigned to the variable on the left side of the assignment operator. For example, suppose we intend to write

```
if ( payCode == 4 )
    printf( "%s", "You get a bonus!" );
```

but we accidentally write

```
if ( payCode = 4 )
    printf( "%s", "You get a bonus!" );
```

The first if statement properly awards a bonus to the person whose paycode is equal to 4. The second if statement—the one with the error—evaluates the assignment expression in the if condition. This expression is a simple assignment whose value is the constant 4. Because any nonzero value is interpreted as "true," the condition in this if statement is always true, and not only is the value of payCode inadvertently set to 4, but the person always receives a bonus regardless of what the actual paycode is!

Common Programming Error 4.6

Using operator == for assignment or using operator = for equality is a logic error.

lvalues *and* rvalues

You'll probably be inclined to write conditions such as x == 7 with the variable name on the left and the constant on the right. By reversing these terms so that the constant is on the left and the variable name is on the right, as in 7 == x, then if you accidentally replace the == operator with =, you'll be protected by the compiler. The compiler will treat this as a *syntax error*, because only a variable name can be placed on the left-hand side of an assignment expression. This will prevent the potential devastation of a runtime logic error.

Variable names are said to be *lvalues* (for "left values") because they can be used on the *left* side of an assignment operator. Constants are said to be *rvalues* (for "right values") because they can be used on only the *right* side of an assignment operator. *lvalues* can also be used as *rvalues*, but not vice versa.

Error-Prevention Tip 4.6

When an equality expression has a variable and a constant, as in x == 1, you may prefer to write it with the constant on the left and the variable name on the right (e.g., 1 == x as protection against the logic error that occurs when you accidentally replace operator == with =).

Confusing == and = in Standalone Statements

The other side of the coin can be equally unpleasant. Suppose you want to assign a value to a variable with a simple statement such as

```
x = 1;
```

but instead write

```
x == 1;
```

Here, too, this is not a syntax error. Rather the compiler simply evaluates the conditional expression. If x is equal to 1, the condition is true and the expression returns the value 1. If x is not equal to 1, the condition is false and the expression returns the value 0. Regardless of what value is returned, there's no assignment operator, so the value is simply *lost*, and the value of x remains *unaltered*, probably causing an execution-time logic error. Unfortunately, we do not have a handy trick available to help you with this problem! Many compilers, however, will issue a *warning* on such a statement.

Error-Prevention Tip 4.7

After you write a program, text search it for every = and check that it's used properly.

4.12 Structured Programming Summary

Just as architects design buildings by employing the collective wisdom of their profession, so should programmers design programs. Our field is younger than architecture is, and our collective wisdom is considerably sparser. We've learned a great deal in a mere six decades. Perhaps most important, we've learned that structured programming produces programs that are easier (than unstructured programs) to understand and therefore are easier to test, debug, modify, and even prove correct in a mathematical sense.

Chapters 3 and 4 have concentrated on C's control statements. Each statement has been presented, flowcharted and discussed separately with examples. Now, we summarize the results of Chapters 3 and 4 and introduce a simple set of rules for the formation and properties of structured programs.

Figure 4.17 summarizes the control statements discussed in Chapters 3 and 4. Small circles are used in the figure to indicate the *single entry point* and the *single exit point* of each statement. Connecting individual flowchart symbols arbitrarily can lead to unstructured programs. Therefore, the programming profession has chosen to combine flowchart symbols to form a limited set of control statements, and to build only structured programs by properly combining control statements in two simple ways. For simplicity, only *single-entry/single-exit* control statements are used—there's only one way to enter and only one way to exit each control statement. Connecting control statements in sequence to form structured programs is simple—the exit point of one control statement is connected directly to the entry point of the next—i.e., the control statements are simply placed one after another in a program—we've called this "control-statement stacking." The rules for forming structured programs also allow for control statements to be nested.

Figure 4.18 shows the rules for forming structured programs. The rules assume that the rectangle flowchart symbol may be used to indicate *any* action including input/output. Figure 4.19 shows the simplest flowchart.

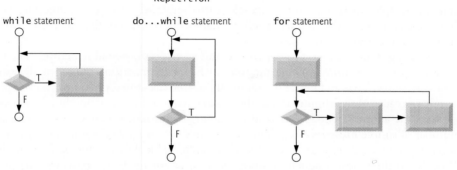

Fig. 4.17 | C's single-entry/single-exit sequence, selection and repetition statements.

> ### Rules for forming structured programs
>
> 1) Begin with the "simplest flowchart" (Fig. 4.19).
> 2) Any rectangle (action) can be replaced by *two* rectangles (actions) in sequence.
> 3) Any rectangle (action) can be replaced by *any* control statement (sequence, `if`, `if...else`, `switch`, `while`, `do...while` or `for`).
> 4) Rules 2 and 3 may be applied as often as you like and in *any* order.

Fig. 4.18 | Rules for forming structured programs.

Fig. 4.19 | Simplest flowchart.

Applying the rules of Fig. 4.18 always results in a structured flowchart with a neat, building-block appearance. Repeatedly applying Rule 2 to the simplest flowchart (Fig. 4.19) results in a structured flowchart containing many rectangles *in sequence* (Fig. 4.20). Rule 2 generates a stack of control statements; so we call Rule 2 the **stacking rule**.

Rule 3 is called the **nesting rule**. Repeatedly applying Rule 3 to the simplest flowchart results in a flowchart with neatly nested control statements. For example, in Fig. 4.21, the rectangle in the simplest flowchart is first replaced with a double-selection (`if...else`) statement. Then Rule 3 is applied again to both of the rectangles in the double-selection statement, replacing each of these rectangles with double-selection statements. The dashed box around each of the double-selection statements represents the rectangle that was replaced in the original flowchart.

Rule 4 generates larger, more involved, and more deeply nested structures. The flowcharts that emerge from applying the rules in Fig. 4.18 constitute the set of all possible structured flowcharts and hence the set of all possible structured programs.

It's because of the elimination of the `goto` statement that these building blocks never overlap one another. The beauty of the structured approach is that we use only a small number of simple *single-entry/single-exit* pieces, and we assemble them in only *two* simple ways. Figure 4.22 shows the kinds of stacked building blocks that emerge from applying Rule 2 and the kinds of nested building blocks that emerge from applying Rule 3. The figure also shows the kind of overlapped building blocks that cannot appear in structured flowcharts (because of the elimination of the `goto` statement).

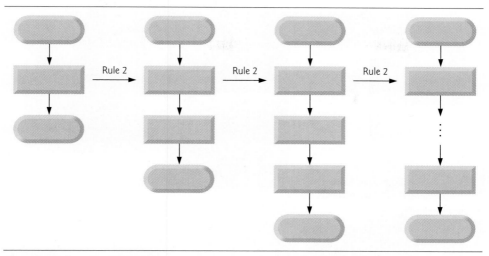

Fig. 4.20 | Repeatedly applying Rule 2 of Fig. 4.18 to the simplest flowchart.

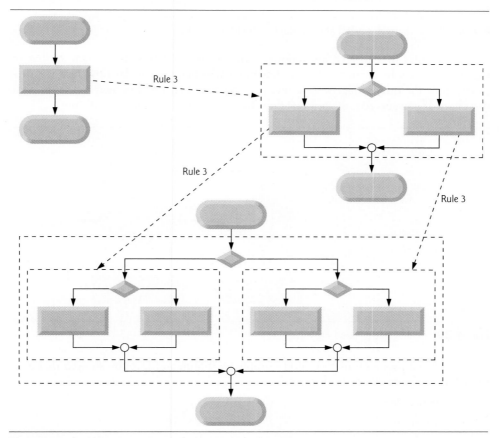

Fig. 4.21 | Applying Rule 3 of Fig. 4.18 to the simplest flowchart.

Stacked building blocks

Nested building blocks

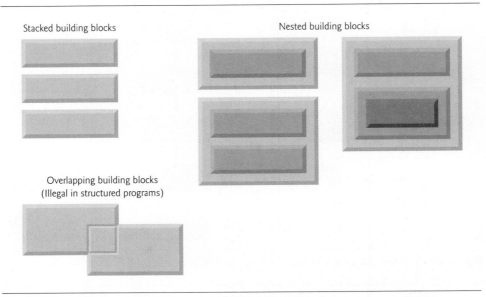

Overlapping building blocks
(Illegal in structured programs)

Fig. 4.22 | Stacked, nested and overlapped building blocks.

If the rules in Fig. 4.18 are followed, an unstructured flowchart (such as that in Fig. 4.23) *cannot* be created. If you're uncertain whether a particular flowchart is structured, apply the rules of Fig. 4.18 in reverse to try to reduce the flowchart to the simplest flowchart. If you succeed, the original flowchart is structured; otherwise, it's not.

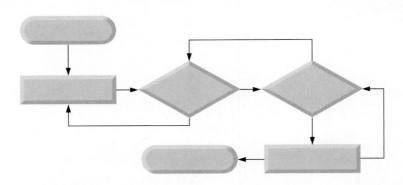

Fig. 4.23 | An unstructured flowchart.

Structured programming promotes simplicity. Bohm and Jacopini showed that only three forms of control are needed:

- Sequence
- Selection
- Repetition

Sequence is straightforward. Selection is implemented in one of three ways:

- `if` statement (single selection)
- `if...else` statement (double selection)
- `switch` statement (multiple selection)

It's straightforward to prove that the simple `if` statement is sufficient to provide *any* form of selection—everything that can be done with the `if...else` statement and the `switch` statement can be implemented with one or more `if` statements.

Repetition is implemented in one of three ways:

- `while` statement
- `do...while` statement
- `for` statement

It's straightforward to prove that the `while` statement is sufficient to provide *any* form of repetition. Everything that can be done with the `do...while` statement and the `for` statement can be done with the `while` statement.

Combining these results illustrates that any form of control ever needed in a C program can be expressed in terms of only *three* forms of control:

- sequence
- `if` statement (selection)
- `while` statement (repetition)

And these control statements can be combined in only *two* ways—*stacking* and *nesting*. Indeed, structured programming promotes simplicity.

In Chapters 3 and 4, we discussed how to compose programs from control statements containing actions and decisions. In Chapter 5, we introduce another program structuring unit called the function. We'll learn to compose large programs by combining functions, which, in turn, are composed of control statements. We'll also discuss how using functions promotes software reusability.

4.13 Secure C Programming

Checking Function scanf's Return Value

Figure 4.6 used the math library function pow, which calculates the value of its first argument raised to the power of its second argument and *returns* the result as a `double` value. The calculation's result was then used in the statement that called pow.

Many functions return values indicating whether they executed successfully. For example, function scanf returns an `int` indicating whether the input operation was successful. If an input failure occurs, scanf returns the value EOF (defined in `<stdio.h>`); otherwise, it returns the number of items that were read. If this value does *not* match the number you intended to read, then scanf was unable to complete the input operation.

Consider the following statement from Fig. 3.6

```
scanf( "%d", &grade ); // read grade from user
```

which expects to read one `int` value. If the user enters an integer, scanf returns 1 indicating that one value was indeed read. If the user enters a string, such as `"hello"`, scanf returns 0 indicating that it was unable to read the input as an integer. In this case, the variable grade does *not* receive a value.

Function scanf can read multiple inputs, as in

```
scanf( "%d%d", &number1, &number2 ); // read two integers
```

If the input is successful, scanf will return 2 indicating that two values were read. If the user enters a string for the first value, scanf will return 0 and neither number1 nor number2 will receive values. If the user enters an integer followed by a string, scanf will return 1 and only number1 will receive a value.

To make your input processing more robust, check scanf's return value to ensure that the number of inputs read matches the number of inputs expected. Otherwise, your program will use the values of the variables as if scanf completed successfully. This could lead to logic errors, program crashes or even attacks.

Range Checking

Even if a scanf operates successfully, the values read might still be *invalid*. For example, grades are typically integers in the range 0–100. In a program that inputs such grades, you should **validate** the grades by using **range checking** to ensure that they are values from 0 to 100. You can then ask the user to reenter any value that's out of range. If a program requires inputs from a specific set of values (e.g., non-sequential product codes), you can ensure that each input matches a value in the set. For more information, see Chapter 5, "Integer Security" of Robert Seacord's book *Secure Coding in C and C++*.

Summary

Section 4.2 Repetition Essentials
- Most programs involve repetition, or looping. A loop is a group of instructions the computer executes repeatedly while some loop-continuation condition remains true.
- Counter-controlled repetition is sometimes called definite repetition because we know in advance exactly how many times the loop will execute.
- Sentinel-controlled repetition is sometimes called indefinite repetition because it's not known in advance how many times the loop will execute; the loop includes statements that obtain data each time the loop is performed.
- In counter-controlled repetition, a control variable is used to count the number of repetitions. The control variable is incremented (or decremented) each time the group of instructions is performed. When the correct number of repetitions has been performed, the loop terminates, and the program resumes execution with the statement after the repetition statement.
- The sentinel value indicates "end of data." The sentinel is entered after all regular data items have been supplied to the program. Sentinels must be distinct from regular data items.

Section 4.3 Counter-Controlled Repetition
- Counter-controlled repetition requires the name of a control variable (or loop counter), the initial value of the control variable, the increment (or decrement) by which the control variable is modified each time through the loop, and the condition that tests for the final value of the control variable (i.e., whether looping should continue).

Section 4.4 **for** Repetition Statement
- The for repetition statement handles all the details of counter-controlled repetition.

- When the `for` statement begins executing, its control variable is initialized. Then, the loop-continuation condition is checked. If the condition is true, the loop's body executes. The control variable is then incremented, and the loop begins again with the loop-continuation condition. This process continues until the loop-continuation condition fails.

- The general format of the `for` statement is

    > `for` (*expression1*; *expression2*; *expression3*)
    >   *statement*

    where *expression1* initializes the loop-control variable, *expression2* is the loop-continuation condition, and *expression3* increments the control variable.

- In most cases, the `for` statement can be represented with an equivalent `while` statement as in:

    > *expression1*;
    >
    > `while` (*expression2*) {
    >   *statement*
    >   *expression3*;
    > }

- The comma operator guarantees that lists of expressions evaluate from left to right. The value of the entire expression is that of the rightmost expression.

- The three expressions in the `for` statement are optional. If *expression2* is omitted, C assumes that the condition is true, thus creating an infinite loop. One might omit *expression1* if the control variable is initialized elsewhere in the program. *expression3* might be omitted if the increment is calculated by statements in the body of the `for` statement or if no increment is needed.

- The increment expression in the `for` statement acts like a stand-alone C statement at the end of the body of the `for`.

- The two semicolons in the `for` statement are required.

Section 4.5 for *Statement: Notes and Observations*

- The initialization, loop-continuation condition and increment can contain arithmetic expressions.

- The "increment" may be negative (in which case it's really a decrement and the loop actually counts downward).

- If the loop-continuation condition is initially false, the body portion of the loop isn't performed. Instead, execution proceeds with the statement following the `for` statement.

Section 4.6 Examples Using the **for** *Statement*

- Function `pow` performs exponentiation. The function `pow(x, y)` calculates the value of x raised to the yth power. It takes two arguments of type `double` and returns a `double` value.

- Type `double` is a floating-point type much like `float`, but typically a variable of type `double` can store a value of much greater magnitude with greater precision than `float`.

- The header `<math.h>` should be included whenever a math function such as `pow` is used.

- The conversion specifier `%21.2f` denotes that a floating-point value will be displayed right justified in a field of 21 characters with two digits to the right of the decimal point.

- To left justify a value in a field, place a - (minus sign) between the `%` and the field width.

Section 4.7 **switch** *Multiple-Selection Statement*

- Occasionally, an algorithm will contain a series of decisions in which a variable or expression is tested separately for each of the constant integral values it may assume, and different actions are taken. This is called multiple selection. C provides the `switch` statement to handle this.

- The switch statement consists of a series of case labels, an optional default case and statements to execute for each case.

- The getchar function (from the standard input/output library) reads and returns one character from the keyboard.

- Characters are normally stored in variables of type char. Characters can be stored in any integer data type because they're usually represented as one-byte integers in the computer. Thus, we can treat a character as either an integer or a character, depending on its use.

- Many computers today use the ASCII (American Standard Code for Information Interchange) character set in which 97 represents the lowercase letter 'a'.

- Characters can be read with scanf by using the conversion specifier %c.

- Assignment expressions as a whole actually have a value. This value is assigned to the variable on the left side of the =.

- The fact that assignment statements have values can be useful for setting several variables to the same value, as in a = b = c = 0;.

- EOF is often used as a sentinel value. EOF is a symbolic integer constant defined in <stdio.h>.

- On Linux/UNIX systems and many others, the EOF indicator is entered by typing <*Ctrl*> *d*. On other systems, such as Microsoft Windows, the EOF indicator can be entered by typing <*Ctrl*> *z*.

- Keyword switch is followed by the controlling expression in parentheses. The value of this expression is compared with each of the case labels. If a match occurs, the statements for that case execute. If no match occurs, the default case executes.

- The break statement causes program control to continue with the statement after the switch. The break statement prevents the cases in a switch statement from running together.

- Each case can have one or more actions. The switch statement is different from all other control statements in that braces are not required around multiple actions in a case of a switch.

- Listing several case labels together simply means that the same set of actions is to occur for any of these cases.

- Remember that the switch statement can be used only for testing a constant integral expression—i.e., any combination of character constants and integer constants that evaluates to a constant integer value. A character constant can be represented as the specific character in single quotes, such as 'A'. Characters must be enclosed within single quotes to be recognized as character constants. Integer constants are simply integer values.

- C provides several data types to represent integers. In addition to int and char, C provides types short int (which can be abbreviated as short) and long int (which can be abbreviated as long). The C standard specifies the minimum range of values for each integer type, but the actual range may be greater and depends on the implementation. For short ints the minimum range is –32767 to +32767. The minimum range of values for long ints is –2147483647 to +2147483647. The range of values for an int greater than or equal to that of a short int and less than or equal to that of a long int. On many of today's platforms, ints and long ints represent the same range of values. The data type signed char can be used to represent integers in the range –127 to +127 or any of the characters in the computer's character set. See section 5.2.4.2 of the C standard document for the complete list of signed and unsigned integer-type ranges.

Section 4.8 do...while Repetition Statement
- The do...while statement tests the loop-continuation condition *after* the loop body is performed. Therefore, the loop body will be executed at least once. When a do...while terminates, execution continues with the statement after the while clause.

Section 4.9 **break** *and* **continue** *Statements*

- The break statement, when executed in a while, for, do...while or switch statement, causes immediate exit from that statement. Program execution continues with the next statement.

- The continue statement, when executed in a while, for or do...while statement, skips the remaining statements in the body of that control statement and performs the next iteration of the loop. In while and do...while statements, the loop-continuation test is evaluated immediately after the continue statement is executed. In the for statement, the increment expression is executed, then the loop-continuation test is evaluated.

Section 4.10 *Logical Operators*

- Logical operators may be used to form complex conditions by combining simple conditions. The logical operators are && (logical AND), || (logical OR) and ! (logical NOT, or logical negation).

- A condition containing the && (logical AND) operator is true if and only if both of the simple conditions are true.

- C evaluates all expressions that include relational operators, equality operators, and/or logical operators to 0 or 1. Although C sets a true value to 1, it accepts *any* nonzero value as true.

- A condition containing the || (logical OR) operator is true if either or both of the simple conditions are true.

- The && operator has a higher precedence than ||. Both operators associate from left to right.

- An expression containing && or || operators is evaluated only until truth or falsehood is known.

- C provides ! (logical negation) to enable you to "reverse" the meaning of a condition. Unlike the binary operators && and ||, which combine two conditions, the unary logical negation operator has only a single condition as an operand.

- The logical negation operator is placed before a condition when we're interested in choosing a path of execution if the original condition (without the logical negation operator) is false.

- In most cases, you can avoid using logical negation by expressing the condition differently with an appropriate relational operator.

Section 4.11 *Confusing Equality (==) and Assignment (=) Operators*

- Programmers often accidentally swap the operators == (equality) and = (assignment). What makes these swaps so damaging is that they do not ordinarily cause syntax errors. Rather, statements with these errors ordinarily compile correctly, allowing programs to run to completion while likely generating incorrect results through runtime logic errors.

- You may be inclined to write conditions such as x == 7 with the variable name on the left and the constant on the right. By reversing these terms so that the constant is on the left and the variable name is on the right, as in 7 == x, then if you accidentally replace the == operator with =, you'll be protected by the compiler. The compiler will treat this as a syntax error, because only a variable name can be placed on the left-hand side of an assignment statement.

- Variable names are said to be *lvalues* (for "left values") because they *can* be used on the left side of an assignment operator.

- Constants are said to be *rvalues* (for "right values") because they can be used *only* on the right side of an assignment operator. *lvalues* can also be used as *rvalues*, but not vice versa.

Terminology

Self-Review Exercises

4.1   Fill in the blanks in each of the following statements.
a) Counter-controlled repetition is also known as _____ repetition because it's known in advance how many times the loop will be executed.
b) Sentinel-controlled repetition is also known as _____ repetition because it's not known in advance how many times the loop will be executed.
c) In counter-controlled repetition, a(n) _____ is used to count the number of times a group of instructions should be repeated.
d) The _____ statement, when executed in a repetition statement, causes the next iteration of the loop to be performed immediately.
e) The _____ statement, when executed in a repetition statement or a switch, causes an immediate exit from the statement.
f) The _____ is used to test a particular variable or expression for each of the constant integral values it may assume.

4.2   State whether the following are *true* or *false*. If the answer is *false*, explain why.
a) The default case is required in the switch selection statement.
b) The break statement is required in the default case of a switch selection statement.
c) The expression (x > y && a < b) is true if either x > y is true or a < b is true.
d) An expression containing the || operator is true if either or both of its operands is true.

4.3   Write a statement or a set of statements to accomplish each of the following tasks:
a) Calculate the product of even integers between 1 and 10 using a for statement. Assume the integer variables product and count have been defined.
b) Print the value 912.19852012 in a field width of 18 characters with precisions of 2, 4, 5 and 6. Left justify the output. What are the four values that print?
c) Calculate the value of x raised to the power of y using the pow function. Assume x = 3.75 and y = 2. Print the result with a precision of 1 in a field width of 5 positions. What is the value that prints? Repeat the same for x = 4.12 and y = 4.
d) Print the multiples of 3 between 1 to 45 using a while loop and the variable p. Assume that the variable p has been defined, but not initialized. Print only three integers per line. [*Hint:* Use the calculation p % 3. When the value of this is 0, print a newline character, otherwise print a tab character.]
e) Repeat Exercise 4.3(d) using a for statement.

4.4   Find the error in each of the following code segments and explain how to correct it.
a)
```
x = 1;
while ( x <= 10 );
    ++x;
}
```

b)
```c
for ( y = .1; y != 1.0; y += .1 )
    printf( "%f\n", y );
```
c)
```c
switch ( n ) {
    case 1:
        puts( "The number is 1" );
    case 2:
        puts( "The number is 2" );
        break;
    default:
        puts( "The number is not 1 or 2" );
        break;
}
```
d) The following code should print the values 1 to 10.
```c
n = 1;
while ( n < 10 )
    printf( "ud ", n++ );
```

Answers to Self-Review Exercises

4.1   a) definite. b) indefinite. c) control variable or counter. d) `continue`. e) `break`. f) `switch` selection statement.

4.2   a) False. The `default` case is optional. If no default action is needed, then there's no need for a `default` case.
b) False. The `break` statement is used to exit the `switch` statement. The `break` statement is not required in *any* case.
c) False. Both of the relational expressions must be true in order for the entire expression to be true when using the `&&` operator.
d) True.

4.3   a)
```c
product = 1;
for ( count = 2; count <= 10; count += 2 )
    product *= count;
```
b)
```c
printf( "%-18.2f\n", 912.19852012 );  /* prints 912.19     */
printf( "%-18.4f\n", 912.19852012 );  /* prints 912.1985    */
printf( "%-18.5f\n", 912.19852012 );  /* prints 912.19852   */
printf( "%-18.6f\n", 912.19852012 );  /* prints 912.198520  */
```
c)
```c
printf( "%5.1f\n", pow( 3.75, 2 ) );  /* prints 14.1 */
printf( "%5.1f\n", pow( 4.12, 4 ) );  /* prints 288.1 */
```
d)
```c
p = 1;
count = 0;
while ( p <= 45 ) {
    if (p % 3 == 0){
    printf( "%d", p );
    count++;
        if ( count % 3 == 0 )
            printf( "\n" );
        else
```

```
                    printf( "\t" );
    }
        p++;
    }
e)  count = 0;
    for (p = 1; p <= 45; p++ ) {
        if (p % 3 == 0){
        printf( "%d", p );
        count++;
        if ( count % 3 == 0 )
            printf( "\n" );
        else
            printf( "\t" );
    }
    }
```

4.4   a) Error: The semicolon after the while header causes an infinite loop.
Correction: Replace the semicolon with a { or remove both the ; and the }.

b) Error: Using a floating-point number to control a for repetition statement.
Correction: Use an integer, and perform the proper calculation to get the values you desire.

```
for ( y = 1; y != 10; ++y )
    printf( "%f\n", ( float ) y / 10 );
```

c) Error: Missing break statement in the statements for the first case.
Correction: Add a break statement at the end of the statements for the first case. This is not necessarily an error if you want the statement of case 2: to execute every time the case 1: statement executes.

d) Error: Improper relational operator used in the while repetition-continuation condition.
Correction: Use <= rather than <.

Exercises

4.5   Find the error in each of the following. (*Note:* There may be more than one error.)

a)
```
For ( x = 100, x >= 1, ++x )
    printf( "%d\n", x );
```

b) The following code should print whether a given integer is odd or even:
```
switch ( value % 2 ) {
    case 0:
        puts( "Even integer" );
    case 1:
        puts( "Odd integer" );
}
```

c) The following code should input an integer and a character and print them. Assume the user types as input 100 A.
```
scanf( "%d", &intVal );
charVal = getchar();
printf( "Integer: %d\nCharacter: %c\n", intVal, charVal );
```

d)
```
for ( x = .000001; x == .0001; x += .000001 ) {
    printf( "%.7f\n", x );
}
```

e) The following code should output the odd integers from 999 to 1:
```
for ( x = 999; x >= 1; x += 2 ) {
    printf( "%d\n", x );
}
```

f) The following code should output the even integers from 2 to 100:
```
counter = 2;

Do {
    if ( counter % 2 == 0 ) {
        printf( "%u\n", counter );
    }

    counter += 2;
} While ( counter < 100 );
```

g) The following code should sum the integers from 100 to 150 (assume total is initialized to 0):
```
for ( x = 100; x <= 150; ++x ); {
    total += x;
}
```

4.6   State which values of the control variable p are printed by each of the following for statements:

a)
```
for ( p = 1; p <= 21; p += 4 ) {
    printf( "%d\n", p );
}
```

b)
```
for ( p = 27; p >= 2; p -= 3 ) {
    printf( "%d\n", p );
}
```

c)
```
for ( p = 1; p <= 30; p *= 4 ) {
    printf( "%d\n", p );
}
```

d)
```
for ( p = 51; p >= 1; p /= 2 ) {
    printf( "%d\n", p );
}
```

e)
```
for ( p = 15; p >= 11; --p ) {
    printf( "%d\n", p );
}
```

4.7   Write for statements that print the following sequences of values:
a) 2, 4, 6, 8, 10, 12, 14
b) 9, 18, 27, 36, 45, 54
c) 75, 66, 57, 48, 39, 30
d) 53, 64, 75, 86, 97

4.8   What does the following program do

```
1   #include <stdio.h>
2   // function main begins program execution
3   int main( void )
4   {
5      unsigned int a;
6      unsigned int b;
7      unsigned int i;
8      unsigned int j;
9      // prompt user for input
10     printf( "%s", "Enter two unsigned integers in the range 1-9: " );
11     scanff( "%u%u", &a, &b ); // read values for a and b
12
13     for ( i = 1; i <= b; i++ ) { // count from 1 to b
14
15         for ( j = 1; j <= a; j++ ) { // count from 1 to a
16             printf( "%s", "+" ); // output +
17         } // end inner for
18         if ((i % 2) == 0)
19         printf("\n");// begin new line
20         else
21         printf("\t");// give a tab
22     } // end outer for
23  } // end function main
```

4.9   *(Multiply a Sequence of Integers)* Write a program that multiplies a sequence of integers. Assume that the first integer read with scanf specifies the number of values remaining to be entered. Your program should read only one value each time scanf is executed. A typical input sequence might be

       3   20   5   12

where the 3 indicates that the subsequent three values are to be multiplied.

4.10   *(Sum a Sequence of Integers)* Write a program that calculates and prints the average of several integers. Assume the last value read with scanf is the sentinel 0000. A typical input sequence might be

       12   25   47   0000

4.11   *(Find the Largest)* Write a program that finds the largest of several integers. Assume that the first value read specifies the number of values remaining.

4.12   *(Calculating the Sum of Multiples)* Write a program that calculates and prints the sum of the multiples of 3 from 1 to 45.

4.13 *(Calculating the Product of Even Integers)* Write a program that calculates and prints the product of the even integers from 4 to 20.

4.14 *(Factorials)* The *factorial* function is used frequently in probability problems. The factorial of a positive integer n (written $n!$ and pronounced "n factorial") is equal to the product of the positive integers from 1 to n. Write a program that evaluates the factorials of the integers from 1 to 5. Print the results in tabular format. What difficulty might prevent you from calculating the factorial of 20?

4.15 *(Modified Compound-Interest Program)* Modify the compound-interest program of Section 4.6 to repeat its steps for an investment of $5000, for 15 years, and for interest rates of 10.0%, 10.5%, 11.0%, 11.5%, and 12.0%. Use a for loop to vary the interest rate.

4.16 *(Triangle-Printing Program)* Write a program that prints the following patterns separately, one below the other. Use for loops to generate the patterns. All asterisks (*) should be printed by a single printf statement of the form printf("%s", "*"); (this causes the asterisks to print side by side). [*Hint:* The last two patterns require that each line begin with an appropriate number of blanks.]

```
(A)                (B)                (C)                (D)
*                  **********         **********                  *
**                 *********          *********                  **
***                ********           ********                  ***
****               *******            *******                  ****
*****              ******             ******                  *****
******             *****              *****                  ******
*******            ****               ****                  *******
********           ***                ***                  ********
*********          **                 **                  *********
**********         *                  *                  **********
```

4.17 *(Calculating Credit Limits)* Collecting money becomes increasingly difficult during periods of recession, so companies may tighten their credit limits to prevent their accounts receivable (money owed to them) from becoming too large. In response to a prolonged recession, one company has cut its customers' credit limits in half. Thus, if a particular customer had a credit limit of $2000, it's now $1000. If a customer had a credit limit of $5000, it's now $2500. Write a program that analyzes the credit status of three customers of this company. For each customer you're given:

a) The customer's account number

b) The customer's credit limit before the recession

c) The customer's current balance (i.e., the amount the customer owes the company).

Your program should calculate and print the new credit limit for each customer and should determine (and print) which customers have current balances that exceed their new credit limits.

4.18 *(Bar Chart Printing Program)* One interesting application of computers is drawing graphs and bar charts (sometimes called "histograms"). Write a program that reads five numbers (each between 1 and 30). For each number read, your program should print a line containing that number of adjacent asterisks. For example, if your program reads the number seven, it should print *******.

4.19 *(Calculating Sales)* A pharmaceutical company sells five different types of drugs. The profit on selling each drug is shown in the following table:

Drug Type	Profit
1	$9.3
2	$12.75
3	$3.99
4	$15.13
5	$0.99

Write a program that asks the accountant to enter:
a) Drug type
b) Quantity sold for one day

Your program should use a switch statement to help determine the profit on each drug type. Your program should calculate and display the total profit on the drugs sold last month.

4.20 *(Truth Tables)* Complete the following truth tables by filling in each blank with 0 or 1.

Condition1	Condition2	Condition1 && Condition2
0	0	0
0	nonzero	0
nonzero	0	_____
nonzero	nonzero	_____

Condition1	Condition2	Condition1 || Condition2
0	0	0
0	nonzero	1
nonzero	0	_____
nonzero	nonzero	_____

Condition1	!Condition1
0	1
nonzero	_____

4.21 Rewrite the program of Fig. 4.2 so that the increment of the variable counter is done in the body of the for loop instead of in the for statement.

4.22 *(Average Grade)* Modify the program of Fig. 4.7 so that it calculates the average grade for the class.

4.23 *(Calculating the Compound Interest with Integers)* Modify the program of Fig. 4.6 so that it uses only integers to calculate the compound interest. [*Hint:* Treat all monetary amounts as integral numbers of pennies. Then "break" the result into its dollar portion and cents portion by using the division and remainder operations, respectively. Insert a period.]

4.24 Assume a = 3, b = 6, c = 8 and d = 9. What does each of the following statements print?
a) `printf( "%d", d == 9 );`
b) `printf( "%d\t%d", a == 3, c == 1 );`
c) `printf( "%d", b != 4 && d > d );`
d) `printf( "%d", c >= d || a <= b );`
e) `printf( "%d\n%d", a != 1 && d >= 9, b == 1 || c <= 9 );`
f) `printf( "%d\t%d\t%d", !a, b + c > d || 2 * a >= c, b == 6 );`
g) `printf( "%d\t%d\n%d\t%d", a + c - 11, b + d - 14, !(a + c), !(b + d) );`
h) `printf( "%d", !( b < d ) );`
i) `printf( "%d", !( a != b ) );`
j) `printf( "%d", !( a + b > d ) );`

4.25   *(Table of Decimal, Binary, Octal and Hexadecimal Equivalents)* Write a program that prints a table of the binary, octal and hexadecimal equivalents of the decimal numbers in the range 1 through 256. If you're not familiar with these number systems, read Appendix C before you attempt this exercise. [*Note:* You can display an integer as an octal or hexadecimal value with the conversion specifiers %o and %X, respectively.]

4.26   *(Calculating the Value of π)* Calculate the value of π from the infinite series

$$\pi = 4 - \frac{4}{3} + \frac{4}{5} - \frac{4}{7} + \frac{4}{9} - \frac{4}{11} + \cdots$$

Print a table that shows the value of π approximated by one term of this series, by two terms, by three terms, and so on. How many terms of this series do you have to use before you first get 3.14? 3.141? 3.1415? 3.14159?

4.27   *(Pythagorean Triples)* A right triangle can have sides that are all integers. The set of three integer values for the sides of a right triangle is called a Pythagorean triple. These three sides must satisfy the relationship that the sum of the squares of two of the sides is equal to the square of the hypotenuse. Find all Pythagorean triples for side1, side2, and the hypotenuse all no larger than 500. Use a triple-nested for loop that simply tries all possibilities. This is an example of "brute-force" computing. It's not aesthetically pleasing to many people. But there are many reasons why these techniques are important. First, with computing power increasing at such a phenomenal pace, solutions that would have taken years or even centuries of computer time to produce with the technology of just a few years ago can now be produced in hours, minutes or even seconds. Recent microprocessor chips can process a billion instructions per second! Second, as you'll learn in more advanced computer science courses, there are large numbers of interesting problems for which there's no known algorithmic approach other than sheer brute force. We investigate many kinds of problem-solving methodologies in this book. We'll consider many brute-force approaches to various interesting problems.

4.28   *(Calculating Weekly Pay)* A company pays its employees as managers (who receive a fixed weekly salary), hourly workers (who receive a fixed hourly wage for up to the first 40 hours they work and "time-and-a-half"—i.e., 1.5 times their hourly wage—for overtime hours worked), commission workers (who receive $250 plus 5.7% of their gross weekly sales), or pieceworkers (who receive a fixed amount of money for each of the items they produce—each pieceworker in this company works on only one type of item). Write a program to compute the weekly pay for each employee. You do not know the number of employees in advance. Each type of employee has its own pay code: Managers have paycode 1, hourly workers have code 2, commission workers have code 3 and pieceworkers have code 4. Use a switch to compute each employee's pay based on that employee's paycode. Within the switch, prompt the user (i.e., the payroll clerk) to enter the appropriate facts your program needs to calculate each employee's pay based on that employee's paycode. [*Note:* You can input values of type double using the conversion specifier %1f with scanf.]

4.29   *(De Morgan's Laws)* In this chapter, we discussed the logical operators &&, ||, and !. De Morgan's Laws can sometimes make it more convenient for us to express a logical expression. These laws state that the expression !(*condition1* && *condition2*) is logically equivalent to the expression (!*condition1* || !*condition2*). Also, the expression !(*condition1* || *condition2*) is logically equivalent to the expression (!*condition1* && !*condition2*). Use De Morgan's Laws to write equivalent expressions for each of the following, and then write a program to show that both the original expression and the new expression in each case are equivalent.

a) !(x < 5) && !(y >= 7)
b) !(a == b) || !(g != 5)
c) !((x <= 8) && (y > 4))
d) !((i > 4) || (j <= 6))

4.30 *(Replacing switch with if...else)* Rewrite the program of Fig. 4.7 by replacing the switch statement with a nested if...else statement; be careful to deal with the default case properly. Then rewrite this new version by replacing the nested if...else statement with a series of if statements; here, too, be careful to deal with the default case properly (this is more difficult than in the nested if...else version). This exercise demonstrates that switch is a convenience and that any switch statement can be written with only single-selection statements.

4.31 *(Diamond-Printing Program)* Write a program that prints the following diamond shape. You may use printf statements that print either a single asterisk (*) or a single blank. Maximize your use of repetition (with nested for statements) and minimize the number of printf statements.

```
        *
       ***
      *****
     *******
    *********
     *******
      *****
       ***
        *
```

4.32 *(Modified Diamond-Printing Program)* Modify the program you wrote in Exercise 4.31 to read an odd number in the range 1 to 19 to specify the number of rows in the diamond. Your program should then display a diamond of the appropriate size.

4.33 *(Character Equivalent of ASCII Values)* Write a program that prints a table of all the character equivalents of the ASCII values in the range 65 to 90.

4.34 Describe the process you would use to replace a do...while loop with an equivalent while loop. What problem occurs when you try to replace a while loop with an equivalent do...while loop? Suppose you have been told that you must remove a while loop and replace it with a do...while. What additional control statement would you need to use and how would you use it to ensure that the resulting program behaves exactly as the original?

4.35 A criticism of the break statement and the continue statement is that each is unstructured. Actually, break statements and continue statements can always be replaced by structured statements, although doing so can be awkward. Describe in general how you would remove any break statement from a loop in a program and replace that statement with some structured equivalent. [*Hint:* The break statement leaves a loop from within the body of the loop. The other way to leave is by failing the loop-continuation test. Consider using in the loop-continuation test a second test that indicates "early exit because of a 'break' condition."] Use the technique you developed here to remove the break statement from the program of Fig. 4.11.

4.36 What does the following program segment do?

```
1    for ( a = 3; a >= 1; --a ) {
2       for ( b = 6; b >= 1; --b ) {
3          for ( c = 6; c >= 1; --c )
4             printf( "#" );
5          printf( "\t" );
6       }
7       printf( "\n" );
8    }
```

4.37   Describe in general how you would remove any `continue` statement from a loop in a program and replace that statement with some structured equivalent. Use the technique you developed here to remove the `continue` statement from the program of Fig. 4.12.

4.38   *("The Twelve Days of Christmas" Song)* Write a program that uses repetition and `switch` statements to print the song "The Twelve Days of Christmas." One `switch` statement should be used to print the day (i.e., "first," "second," etc.). A separate `switch` statement should be used to print the remainder of each verse.

Making a Difference

4.39   *(World Population Growth)* World population has grown considerably over the centuries. Continued growth could eventually challenge the limits of breathable air, drinkable water, arable cropland and other limited resources. There's evidence that growth has been slowing in recent years and that world population could peak some time this century, then start to decline.

For this exercise, research world population growth issues online. *Be sure to investigate various viewpoints.* Get estimates for the current world population and its growth rate (the percentage by which it's likely to increase this year). Write a program that calculates world population growth each year for the next 75 years, *using the simplifying assumption that the current growth rate will stay constant.* Print the results in a table. The first column should display the year from year 1 to year 75. The second column should display the anticipated world population at the end of that year. The third column should display the numerical increase in the world population that would occur that year. Using your results, determine the year in which the population would be double what it is today, if this year's growth rate were to persist.

4.40   *(Tax Plan Alternatives; The "FairTax")* There are many proposals to make taxation fairer. Check out the FairTax initiative in the United States at

> www.fairtax.org/site/PageServer?pagename=calculator

Research how the proposed FairTax works. One suggestion is to eliminate income taxes and most other taxes in favor of a 23% consumption tax on all products and services that you buy. Some FairTax opponents question the 23% figure and say that because of the way the tax is calculated, it would be more accurate to say the rate is 30%—check this carefully. Write a program that prompts the user to enter expenses in various categories (e.g., housing, food, clothing, transportation, education, health care, vacations), then prints the estimated FairTax that person would pay.

5

C Functions

Form ever follows function.
—Louis Henri Sullivan

O! call back yesterday, bid time return.
—William Shakespeare

Answer me in one word.
—William Shakespeare

There is a point at which methods devour themselves.
—Frantz Fanon

Objectives

In this chapter, you'll:

- Construct programs modularly from small pieces called functions.

- Use common math functions in the C standard library.

- Create new functions.

- Use the mechanisms that pass information between functions.

- Learn how the function call/ return mechanism is supported by the function call stack and stack frames.

- Use simulation techniques based on random number generation.

- Write and use functions that call themselves.

5.1 Introduction

Most computer programs that solve real-world problems are much larger than the programs presented in the first few chapters. Experience has shown that the best way to develop and maintain a large program is to construct it from smaller pieces or **modules**, each of which is more manageable than the original program. This technique is called **divide and conquer**. This chapter describes some key features of the C language that facilitate the design, implementation, operation and maintenance of large programs.

5.2 Program Modules in C

Modules in C are called **functions**. C programs are typically written by combining new functions you write with *prepackaged* functions available in the **C standard library**. We discuss both kinds of functions in this chapter. The C standard library provides a rich collection of functions for performing common *mathematical calculations*, *string manipulations*, *character manipulations*, *input/output*, and many other useful operations. This makes your job easier, because these functions provide many of the capabilities you need.

Good Programming Practice 5.1
Familiarize yourself with the rich collection of functions in the C standard library.

Software Engineering Observation 5.1
Avoid reinventing the wheel. When possible, use C standard library functions instead of writing new functions. This can reduce program development time.

Portability Tip 5.1
Using the functions in the C standard library helps make programs more portable.

The C language and the standard library are *both* specified by the C standard, and they're both provided with standard C systems (with the exception that some of the libraries are designated as optional). The functions printf, scanf and pow that we've used in previous chapters are standard library functions.

You can write functions to define specific tasks that may be used at many points in a program. These are sometimes referred to as **programmer-defined functions**. The actual statements defining the function are written only once, and the statements are hidden from other functions.

Functions are **invoked** by a **function call**, which specifies the function name and provides information (as arguments) that the function needs to perform its designated task. A common analogy for this is the hierarchical form of management. A boss (the **calling function** or **caller**) asks a worker (the **called function**) to perform a task and report back when the task is done (Fig. 5.1). For example, a function needing to display information on the screen calls the worker function printf to perform that task, then printf displays the information and reports back—or **returns**—to the calling function when its task is completed. The boss function does *not* know how the worker function performs its designated tasks. The worker may call other worker functions, and the boss will be unaware of this. We'll soon see how this "hiding" of implementation details promotes good software engineering. Figure 5.1 shows a boss function communicating with several worker functions in a hierarchical manner. Note that Worker1 acts as a boss function to worker4 and worker5. Relationships among functions may differ from the hierarchical structure shown in this figure.

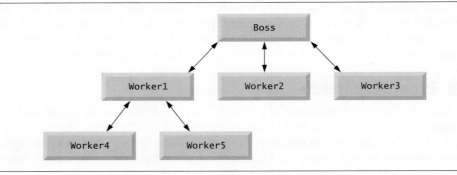

Fig. 5.1 | Hierarchical boss-function/worker-function relationship.

5.3 Math Library Functions

Math library functions allow you to perform certain common mathematical calculations. We use some of them here to introduce the concept of functions. Later in the book, we'll discuss many of the other functions in the C standard library.

Functions are normally used in a program by writing the name of the function followed by a left parenthesis followed by the **argument** (or a comma-separated list of arguments) of the function followed by a right parenthesis. For example, to calculate and print the square root of 900.0 you might write

```
printf( "%.2f", sqrt( 900.0 ) );
```

When this statement executes, the math library function sqrt is *called* to calculate the square root of the number contained in the parentheses (900.0). The number 900.0 is the *argument* of the sqrt function. The preceding statement would print 30.00. The sqrt function takes an argument of type `double` and returns a result of type `double`. All functions in the math library that return floating-point values return the data type `double`. Note that `double` values, like `float` values, can be output using the `%f` conversion specification.

Error-Prevention Tip 5.1
Include the math header by using the preprocessor directive `#include <math.h>` when using functions in the math library.

Function arguments may be constants, variables, or expressions. If `c1 = 13.0`, `d = 3.0` and `f = 4.0`, then the statement

```
printf( "%.2f", sqrt( c1 + d * f ) );
```

calculates and prints the square root of 13.0 + 3.0 * 4.0 = 25.0, namely 5.00.

Figure 5.2 summarizes a small sample of the C math library functions. In the figure, the variables x and y are of type `double`. The C11 standard adds a wide range of floating-point and complex-number capabilities.

Function	Description	Example
`sqrt( x )`	square root of *x*	`sqrt( 900.0 )` is 30.0 `sqrt( 9.0 )` is 3.0
`cbrt( x )`	cube root of *x* (C99 and C11 only)	`cbrt( 27.0 )` is 3.0 `cbrt( -8.0 )` is -2.0
`exp( x )`	exponential function e^x	`exp( 1.0 )` is 2.718282 `exp( 2.0 )` is 7.389056
`log( x )`	natural logarithm of *x* (base *e*)	`log( 2.718282 )` is 1.0 `log( 7.389056 )` is 2.0
`log10( x )`	logarithm of *x* (base 10)	`log10( 1.0 )` is 0.0 `log10( 10.0 )` is 1.0 `log10( 100.0 )` is 2.0
`fabs( x )`	absolute value of *x* as a floating-point number	`fabs( 13.5 )` is 13.5 `fabs( 0.0 )` is 0.0 `fabs( -13.5 )` is 13.5
`ceil( x )`	rounds *x* to the smallest integer not less than *x*	`ceil( 9.2 )` is 10.0 `ceil( -9.8 )` is -9.0
`floor( x )`	rounds *x* to the largest integer not greater than *x*	`floor( 9.2 )` is 9.0 `floor( -9.8 )` is -10.0
`pow( x, y )`	*x* raised to power *y* (x^y)	`pow( 2, 7 )` is 128.0 `pow( 9, .5 )` is 3.0
`fmod( x, y )`	remainder of *x/y* as a floating-point number	`fmod( 13.657, 2.333 )` is 1.992
`sin( x )`	trigonometric sine of *x* (*x* in radians)	`sin( 0.0 )` is 0.0
`cos( x )`	trigonometric cosine of *x* (*x* in radians)	`cos( 0.0 )` is 1.0
`tan( x )`	trigonometric tangent of *x* (*x* in radians)	`tan( 0.0 )` is 0.0

Fig. 5.2 | Commonly used math library functions.

5.4 Functions

Functions allow you to modularize a program. All variables defined in function definitions are local variables—they can be accessed *only* in the function in which they're defined. Most functions have a list of **parameters** that provide the means for communicating information between functions. A function's parameters are also *local variables* of that function.

Software Engineering Observation 5.2
In programs containing many functions, main is often implemented as a group of calls to functions that perform the bulk of the program's work.

There are several motivations for "functionalizing" a program. The *divide-and-conquer* approach makes program development more manageable. Another motivation is **software reusability**—using existing functions as *building blocks* to create new programs. Software reusability is a major factor in the *object-oriented programming* movement that you'll learn more about when you study languages derived from C, such as C++, Java and C# (pronounced "C sharp"). With good function naming and definition, programs can be created from standardized functions that accomplish specific tasks, rather than being built by using customized code. This is known as **abstraction**. We use abstraction each time we use standard library functions like printf, scanf and pow. A third motivation is to avoid repeating code in a program. Packaging code as a function allows the code to be executed from other locations in a program simply by calling the function.

Software Engineering Observation 5.3
Each function should be limited to performing a single, well-defined task, and the function name should express that task. This facilitates abstraction and promotes software reusability.

Software Engineering Observation 5.4
If you cannot choose a concise name that expresses what the function does, it's possible that your function is attempting to perform too many diverse tasks. It's usually best to break such a function into several smaller functions—this is sometimes called decomposition.

5.5 Function Definitions

Each program we've presented has consisted of a function called main that called standard library functions to accomplish its tasks. We now consider how to write *custom* functions. Consider a program that uses a function square to calculate and print the squares of the integers from 1 to 10 (Fig. 5.3).

```
1   // Fig. 5.3: fig05_03.c
2   // Creating and using a programmer-defined function.
3   #include <stdio.h>
4
5   int square( int y ); // function prototype
6
```

Fig. 5.3 | Creating and using a programmer-defined function. (Part 1 of 2.)

```
7   // function main begins program execution
8   int main( void )
9   {
10     int x; // counter
11
12     // loop 10 times and calculate and output square of x each time
13     for ( x = 1; x <= 10; ++x ) {
14        printf( "%d  ", square( x ) ); // function call
15     } // end for
16
17     puts( "" );
18  } // end main
19
20  // square function definition returns the square of its parameter
21  int square( int y ) // y is a copy of the argument to the function
22  {
23     return y * y; // returns the square of y as an int
24  } // end function square
```

```
1   4   9   16   25   36   49   64   81   100
```

Fig. 5.3 | Creating and using a programmer-defined function. (Part 2 of 2.)

Function square is invoked or called in main within the printf statement (line 14)

```
printf( "%d  ", square( x ) ); // function call
```

Function square receives a *copy* of the value of x in the parameter y (line 21). Then square calculates y * y. The result is passed back returned to function printf in main where square was invoked (line 14), and printf displays the result. This process is repeated 10 times using the for statement.

The definition of function square (lines 21–24) shows that square expects an integer parameter y. The keyword int preceding the function name (line 21) indicates that square *returns* an integer result. The **return** statement in square passes the value of the expression y * y (that is, the result of the calculation) back to the calling function.

Line 5

```
int square( int y ); // function prototype
```

is a **function prototype**. The int in parentheses informs the compiler that square expects to *receive* an integer value from the caller. The int to the *left* of the function name square informs the compiler that square *returns* an integer result to the caller. The compiler refers to the function prototype to check that any calls to square (line 14) contain the *correct return type*, the *correct number of arguments* and the *correct argument types*, and that the *arguments are in the correct order*. Function prototypes are discussed in detail in Section 5.6.

The format of a function definition is

```
return-value-type function-name( parameter-list )
{
    definitions
    statements
}
```

The *function-name* is any valid identifier. The *return-value-type* is the data type of the result returned to the caller. The *return-value-type* void indicates that a function does *not* return a value. Together, the *return-value-type*, *function-name* and *parameter-list* are sometimes referred to as the function **header**.

Error-Prevention Tip 5.2

Check that your functions that are supposed to return values do so. Check that your functions that are not supposed to return values do not.

The *parameter-list* is a comma-separated list that specifies the parameters received by the function when it's called. If a function does *not* receive any values, *parameter-list* is void. A type *must* be listed *explicitly* for each parameter.

Common Programming Error 5.1

Specifying function parameters of the same type as double x, y instead of double x, double y results in a compilation error.

Common Programming Error 5.2

Placing a semicolon after the right parenthesis enclosing the parameter list of a function definition is a syntax error.

Common Programming Error 5.3

Defining a parameter again as a local variable in a function is a compilation error.

Good Programming Practice 5.2

Although it's not incorrect to do so, do not use the same names for a function's arguments and the corresponding parameters in the function definition. This helps avoid ambiguity.

The *definitions* and *statements* within braces form the **function body**, which is also referred to as a **block**. Variables can be declared in any block, and blocks can be nested.

Common Programming Error 5.4

Defining a function inside another function is a syntax error.

Good Programming Practice 5.3

Choosing meaningful function names and meaningful parameter names makes programs more readable and helps avoid excessive use of comments.

Software Engineering Observation 5.5

Small functions promote software reusability.

Software Engineering Observation 5.6

Programs should be written as collections of small functions. This makes programs easier to write, debug, maintain and modify.

Software Engineering Observation 5.7

A function requiring a large number of parameters may be performing too many tasks. Consider dividing the function into smaller functions that perform the separate tasks. The function header should fit on one line if possible.

Software Engineering Observation 5.8

The function prototype, function header and function calls should all agree in the number, type, and order of arguments and parameters, and in the type of return value.

There are three ways to return control from a called function to the point at which a function was invoked. If the function does *not* return a result, control is returned simply when the function-ending right brace is reached, or by executing the statement

```
return;
```

If the function *does* return a result, the statement

```
return expression;
```

returns the value of *expression* to the caller.

`main`'s Return Type

Notice that `main` has an `int` return type. The return value of `main` is used to indicate whether the program executed correctly. In earlier versions of C, we'd explicitly place

```
return 0;
```

at the end of `main`—0 indicates that a program ran successfully. The C standard indicates that `main` implicitly returns 0 if you to omit the preceding statement—as we've done throughout this book. You can explicitly return non-zero values from `main` to indicate that a problem occured during your program's execution. For information on how to report a program failure, see the documentation for your particular operating-system environment.

Function `maximum`

Our second example uses a programmer-defined function `maximum` to determine and return the largest of three integers (Fig. 5.4). The integers are input with `scanf` (line 15). Next, they're passed to `maximum` (line 19), which determines the largest integer. This value is returned to main by the `return` statement in `maximum` (line 36). The value returned is then printed in the `printf` statement (line 19).

```
1   // Fig. 5.4: fig05_04.c
2   // Finding the maximum of three integers.
3   #include <stdio.h>
4
5   int maximum( int x, int y, int z ); // function prototype
6
7   // function main begins program execution
8   int main( void )
9   {
```

Fig. 5.4 | Finding the maximum of three integers. (Part 1 of 2.)

```
10    int number1; // first integer entered by the user
11    int number2; // second integer entered by the user
12    int number3; // third integer entered by the user
13
14    printf( "%s", "Enter three integers: " );
15    scanf( "%d%d%d", &number1, &number2, &number3 );
16
17    // number1, number2 and number3 are arguments
18    // to the maximum function call
19    printf( "Maximum is: %d\n", maximum( number1, number2, number3 ) );
20 } // end main
21
22 // Function maximum definition
23 // x, y and z are parameters
24 int maximum( int x, int y, int z )
25 {
26    int max = x; // assume x is largest
27
28    if ( y > max ) { // if y is larger than max,
29       max = y; // assign y to max
30    } // end if
31
32    if ( z > max ) { // if z is larger than max,
33       max = z; // assign z to max
34    } // end if
35
36    return max; // max is largest value
37 } // end function maximum
```

```
Enter three integers: 22 85 17
Maximum is: 85
```

```
Enter three integers: 47 32 14
Maximum is: 47
```

```
Enter three integers: 35 8 79
Maximum is: 79
```

Fig. 5.4 | Finding the maximum of three integers. (Part 2 of 2.)

5.6 Function Prototypes: A Deeper Look

An important feature of C is the function prototype. This feature was borrowed from C++. The compiler uses function prototypes to validate function calls. Early versions of C did *not* perform this kind of checking, so it was possible to call functions improperly without the compiler detecting the errors. Such calls could result in fatal execution-time errors or nonfatal errors that caused subtle, difficult-to-detect problems. Function prototypes correct this deficiency.

Good Programming Practice 5.4

Include function prototypes for all functions to take advantage of C's type-checking capabilities. Use #include preprocessor directives to obtain function prototypes for the standard library functions from the headers for the appropriate libraries, or to obtain headers containing function prototypes for functions developed by you and/or your group members.

The function prototype for `maximum` in Fig. 5.4 (line 5) is

```
int maximum( int x, int y, int z ); // function prototype
```

It states that `maximum` takes three arguments of type `int` and returns a result of type `int`. Notice that the function prototype is the same as the first line of `maximum`'s definition.

Good Programming Practice 5.5

Parameter names are sometimes included in function prototypes (our preference) for documentation purposes. The compiler ignores these names.

Common Programming Error 5.5

Forgetting the semicolon at the end of a function prototype is a syntax error.

Compilation Errors

A function call that does not match the function prototype is a *compilation* error. An error is also generated if the function prototype and the function definition disagree. For example, in Fig. 5.4, if the function prototype had been written

```
void maximum( int x, int y, int z );
```

the compiler would generate an error because the `void` return type in the function prototype would differ from the `int` return type in the function header.

Argument Coercion and "Usual Arithmetic Conversion Rules"

Another important feature of function prototypes is the **coercion of arguments**, i.e., the forcing of arguments to the appropriate type. For example, the math library function `sqrt` can be called with an integer argument even though the function prototype in `<math.h>` specifies a `double` parameter, and the function will still work correctly. The statement

```
printf( "%.3f\n", sqrt( 4 ) );
```

correctly evaluates `sqrt(4)` and prints the value `2.000`. The function prototype causes the compiler to convert a *copy* of the integer value 4 to the `double` value `4.0` before the *copy* is passed to `sqrt`. In general, *argument values that do not correspond precisely to the parameter types in the function prototype are converted to the proper type before the function is called.* These conversions can lead to incorrect results if C's **usual arithmetic conversion rules** are not followed. These rules specify how values can be converted to other types without losing data. In our `sqrt` example above, an `int` is automatically converted to a `double` without changing its value (because `double` can represent a much larger range of values than `int`). However, a `double` converted to an `int` *truncates* the fractional part of the `double` value, thus changing the original value. Converting large integer types to small integer types (e.g., `long` to `short`) may also result in changed values.

The usual arithmetic conversion rules automatically apply to expressions containing values of two data types (also referred to as **mixed-type expressions**), and are handled for you by the compiler. In a mixed-type expression, the compiler makes a temporary copy of the value that needs to be converted then converts the copy to the "highest" type in the expression—the original value remains unchanged. The usual arithmetic conversion rules for a mixed-type expression containing at least one floating-point value are:

- If one of the values is a `long double`, the other is converted to a `long double`.
- If one of the values is a `double`, the other is converted to a `double`.
- If one of the values is a `float`, the other is converted to a `float`.

If the mixed-type expression contains only integer types, then the usual arithmetic conversions specify a set of integer promotion rules. In *most* cases, the integer types lower in Fig. 5.5 are converted to types higher in the figure. Section 6.3.1 of the C standard document specifies the complete details of arithmetic operands and the usual arithmetic conversion rules. Figure 5.5 lists the floating-point and integer data types with each type's `printf` and `scanf` conversion specifications.

Data type	printf conversion specification	scanf conversion specification
Floating-point types		
long double	%Lf	%Lf
double	%f	%lf
float	%f	%f
Integer types		
unsigned long long int	%llu	%llu
long long int	%lld	%lld
unsigned long int	%lu	%lu
long int	%ld	%ld
unsigned int	%u	%u
int	%d	%d
unsigned short	%hu	%hu
short	%hd	%hd
char	%c	%c

Fig. 5.5 | Arithmetic data types and their conversion specifications.

Converting values to *lower* types in Fig. 5.5 can result in incorrect values, so the compiler typically issues warnings for such cases. A value can be converted to a lower type *only* by explicitly assigning the value to a variable of lower type or by using a *cast* operator. Arguments in a function call are converted to the parameter types specified in a function prototype as if the arguments were being assigned directly to variables of those types. If our `square` function that uses an `int` parameter (Fig. 5.3) is called with a floating-point argument, the argument is converted to `int` (a lower type), and `square` usually returns an incorrect value. For example, `square(4.5)` returns 16, not 20.25.

Common Programming Error 5.6

Converting from a higher data type in the promotion hierarchy to a lower type can change the data value. Many compilers issue warnings in such cases.

If there's no function prototype for a function, the compiler forms its own function prototype using the first occurrence of the function—either the function definition or a call to the function. This typically leads to warnings or errors, depending on the compiler.

Error-Prevention Tip 5.3

Always include function prototypes for the functions you define or use in your program to help prevent compilation errors and warnings.

Software Engineering Observation 5.9

A function prototype placed outside any function definition applies to all calls to the function appearing after *the function prototype in the file. A function prototype placed in a function applies only to calls made in that function.*

5.7 Function Call Stack and Stack Frames

To understand how C performs function calls, we first need to consider a data structure (i.e., collection of related data items) known as a **stack**. Think of a stack as analogous to a pile of dishes. When a dish is placed on the pile, it's normally placed at the *top* (referred to as **pushing** the dish onto the stack). Similarly, when a dish is removed from the pile, it's normally removed from the *top* (referred to as **popping** the dish off the stack). Stacks are known as **last-in, first-out (LIFO) data structures**—the *last* item pushed (inserted) on the stack is the *first* item popped (removed) from the stack.

An important mechanism for computer science students to understand is the **function call stack** (sometimes referred to as the **program execution stack**). This data structure—working "behind the scenes"—supports the function call/return mechanism. It also supports the creation, maintenance and destruction of each called function's automatic variables. We explained the last-in, first-out (LIFO) behavior of stacks with our dish-stacking example. As we'll see in Figs. 5.7–5.9, this LIFO behavior is *exactly* what a function does when returning to the function that called it.

As each function is called, it may call other functions, which may call other functions—all *before* any function returns. Each function eventually must return control to the function that called it. So, we must keep track of the return addresses that each function needs to return control to the function that called it. The function call stack is the perfect data structure for handling this information. Each time a function calls another function, an entry is *pushed* onto the stack. This entry, called a **stack frame**, contains the *return address* that the called function needs in order to return to the calling function. It also contains some additional information we'll soon discuss. If the called function returns, instead of calling another function before returning, the stack frame for the function call is *popped*, and control transfers to the return address in the popped stack frame.

Each called function *always* finds the information it needs to return to its caller at the *top* of the call stack. And, if a function makes a call to another function, a stack frame for the new function call is simply pushed onto the call stack. Thus, the return address required by the newly called function to return to its caller is now located at the *top* of the stack.

The stack frames have another important responsibility. Most functions have *automatic variables*—parameters and some or all of their local variables. Automatic variables need to exist while a function is executing. They need to remain active if the function makes calls to other functions. But when a called function returns to its caller, the called function's automatic variables need to "go away." The called function's stack frame is a perfect place to reserve the memory for automatic variables. That stack frame exists only as long as the called function is active. When that function returns—and no longer needs its local automatic variables—its stack frame is *popped* from the stack, and those local automatic variables are no longer known to the program.

Of course, the amount of memory in a computer is finite, so only a certain amount of memory can be used to store stack frames on the function call stack. If more function calls occur than can have their stack frames stored on the function call stack, a *fatal* error known as **stack overflow** occurs.

Function Call Stack in Action

Now let's consider how the call stack supports the operation of a square function called by main (lines 8–13 of Fig. 5.6). First the operating system calls main—this pushes a stack frame onto the stack (shown in Fig. 5.7). The stack frame tells main how to return to the operating system (i.e., transfer to return address R1) and contains the space for main's automatic variable (i.e., a, which is initialized to 10).

Function main—before returning to the operating system—now calls function square in line 12 of Fig. 5.6. This causes a stack frame for square (lines 16–19) to be pushed onto the function call stack (Fig. 5.8). This stack frame contains the return address that square needs to return to main (i.e., R2) and the memory for square's automatic variable (i.e., x).

```
1   // Fig. 5.6: fig05_06.c
2   // Demonstrating the function call stack
3   // and stack frames using a function square.
4   #include <stdio.h>
5
6   int square( int ); // prototype for function square
7
8   int main()
9   {
10     int a = 10; // value to square (local automatic variable in main)
11
12     printf( "%d squared: %d\n", a, square( a ) ); // display a squared
13  } // end main
14
15  // returns the square of an integer
16  int square( int x ) // x is a local variable
17  {
18     return x * x; // calculate square and return result
19  } // end function square
```

```
10 squared: 100
```

Fig. 5.6 | Demonstrating the function call stack and stack frames using a function square.

Step 1: Operating system invokes `main` to execute application

Fig. 5.7 | Function call stack after the operating system invokes `main` to execute the program.

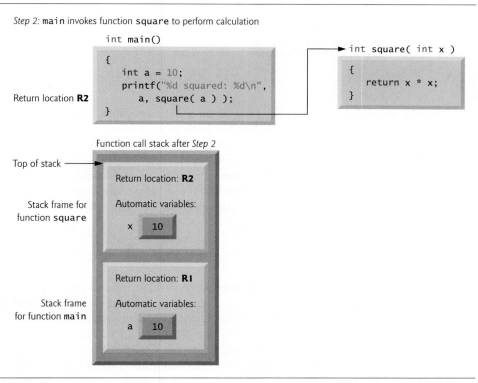

Step 2: `main` invokes function `square` to perform calculation

Fig. 5.8 | Function call stack after `main` invokes `square` to perform the calculation.

After `square` calculates the square of its argument, it needs to return to `main`—and no longer needs the memory for its automatic variable `x`. So the stack is popped—giving `square` the return location in `main` (i.e., R2) and losing `square`'s automatic variable. Figure 5.9 shows the function call stack *after* `square`'s stack frame has been popped.

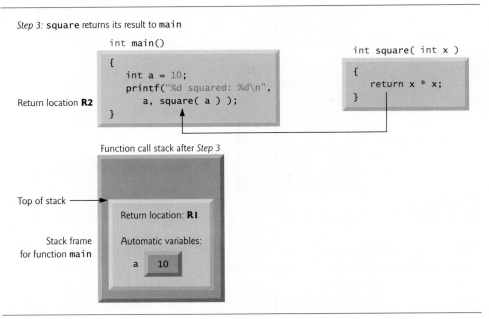

Step 3: `square` returns its result to `main`

Fig. 5.9 | Function call stack after function `square` returns to `main`.

Function `main` now displays the result of calling `square` (line 12). Reaching the closing right brace of `main` causes its stack frame to be popped from the stack, gives `main` the address it needs to return to the operating system (i.e., R1 in Fig. 5.7) and causes the memory for `main`'s automatic variable (i.e., a) to become unavailable.

You've now seen how valuable the stack data structure is in implementing a key mechanism that supports program execution. Data structures have many important applications in computer science. We discuss stacks, queues, lists, trees and other data structures in Chapter 12.

5.8 Headers

Each standard library has a corresponding **header** containing the function prototypes for all the functions in that library and definitions of various *data types* and constants needed by those functions. Figure 5.10 lists alphabetically some of the standard library headers that may be included in programs. The C standard includes additional headers. The term "macros" that's used several times in Fig. 5.10 is discussed in detail in Chapter 13.

You can create custom headers. Programmer-defined headers should also use the `.h` filename extension. A programmer-defined header can be included by using the `#include` preprocessor directive. For example, if the prototype for our square function was located

Header	Explanation
`<assert.h>`	Contains information for adding diagnostics that aid program debugging.
`<ctype.h>`	Contains function prototypes for functions that test characters for certain properties, and function prototypes for functions that can be used to convert lowercase letters to uppercase letters and vice versa.
`<errno.h>`	Defines macros that are useful for reporting error conditions.
`<float.h>`	Contains the floating-point size limits of the system.
`<limits.h>`	Contains the integral size limits of the system.
`<locale.h>`	Contains function prototypes and other information that enables a program to be modified for the current locale on which it's running. The notion of locale enables the computer system to handle different conventions for expressing data such as dates, times, currency amounts and large numbers throughout the world.
`<math.h>`	Contains function prototypes for math library functions.
`<setjmp.h>`	Contains function prototypes for functions that allow bypassing of the usual function call and return sequence.
`<signal.h>`	Contains function prototypes and macros to handle various conditions that may arise during program execution.
`<stdarg.h>`	Defines macros for dealing with a list of arguments to a function whose number and types are unknown.
`<stddef.h>`	Contains common type definitions used by C for performing calculations.
`<stdio.h>`	Contains function prototypes for the standard input/output library functions, and information used by them.
`<stdlib.h>`	Contains function prototypes for conversions of numbers to text and text to numbers, memory allocation, random numbers, and other utility functions.
`<string.h>`	Contains function prototypes for string-processing functions.
`<time.h>`	Contains function prototypes and types for manipulating the time and date.

Fig. 5.10 | Some of the standard library headers.

in the header `square.h`, we'd include that header in our program by using the following directive at the top of the program:

```
#include "square.h"
```

Section 13.2 presents additional information on including headers.

5.9 Passing Arguments By Value and By Reference

In many programming languages, there are two ways to pass arguments—**pass-by-value** and **pass-by-reference**. When arguments are *passed by value*, a *copy* of the argument's value is made and passed to the called function. Changes to the copy do *not* affect an original variable's value in the caller. When an argument is *passed by reference*, the caller allows the called function to *modify* the original variable's value.

Pass-by-value should be used whenever the called function does not need to modify the value of the caller's original variable. This prevents the accidental **side effects** (variable modifications) that so greatly hinder the development of correct and reliable software systems. Pass-by-reference should be used only with *trusted* called functions that need to modify the original variable.

In C, all arguments are passed by value. As we'll see in Chapter 7, it's possible to simulate pass-by-reference by using the *address operator* and the *indirection operator*. In Chapter 6, we'll see that array arguments are automatically passed by reference for performance reasons. We'll see in Chapter 7 that this is *not* a contradiction. For now, we concentrate on pass-by-value.

5.10 Random Number Generation

We now take a brief and, hopefully, entertaining diversion into *simulation* and *game playing*. In this and the next section, we'll develop a nicely structured game-playing program that includes multiple functions. The program uses most of the control statements we've studied. The *element of chance* can be introduced into computer applications by using the C standard library function rand from the <stdlib.h> header.

Consider the following statement:

```
i = rand();
```

The rand function generates an integer between 0 and RAND_MAX (a symbolic constant defined in the <stdlib.h> header). Standard C states that the value of RAND_MAX must be at least 32767, which is the maximum value for a two-byte (i.e., 16-bit) integer. The programs in this section were tested on Microsoft Visual C++ with a maximum RAND_MAX value of 32767 and on GNU gcc with a maximum RAND_MAX value of 2147483647. If rand truly produces integers *at random*, every number between 0 and RAND_MAX has an equal chance (or probability) of being chosen each time rand is called.

The range of values produced directly by rand is often different from what's needed in a specific application. For example, a program that simulates coin tossing might require only 0 for "heads" and 1 for "tails." A dice-rolling program that simulates a six-sided die would require random integers from 1 to 6.

Rolling a Six-Sided Die

To demonstrate rand, let's develop a program to simulate 20 rolls of a six-sided die and print the value of each roll. The function prototype for function rand is in <stdlib.h>. We use the remainder operator (%) in conjunction with rand as follows

```
rand() % 6
```

to produce integers in the range 0 to 5. This is called scaling. The number 6 is called the scaling factor. We then shift the range of numbers produced by adding 1 to our previous result. The output of Fig. 5.11 confirms that the results are in the range 1 to 6—the actual random values chosen might vary by compiler.

```
1   // Fig. 5.11: fig05_11.c
2   // Shifted, scaled random integers produced by 1 + rand() % 6.
3   #include <stdio.h>
4   #include <stdlib.h>
```

Fig. 5.11 | Shifted, scaled random integers produced by 1 + rand() % 6. (Part 1 of 2.)

```
 5
 6   // function main begins program execution
 7   int main( void )
 8   {
 9      unsigned int i; // counter
10
11      // loop 20 times
12      for ( i = 1; i <= 20; ++i ) {
13
14         // pick random number from 1 to 6 and output it
15         printf( "%10d", 1 + ( rand() % 6 ) );
16
17         // if counter is divisible by 5, begin new line of output
18         if ( i % 5 == 0 ) {
19            puts( "" );
20         } // end if
21      } // end for
22   } // end main
```

6	6	5	5	6
5	1	1	5	3
6	6	2	4	2
6	2	3	4	1

Fig. 5.11 | Shifted, scaled random integers produced by 1 + rand() % 6. (Part 2 of 2.)

Rolling a Six-Sided Die 6,000,000 Times

To show that these numbers occur approximately with *equal likelihood*, let's simulate 6,000,000 rolls of a die with the program of Fig. 5.12. Each integer from 1 to 6 should appear approximately 1,000,000 times.

```
 1   // Fig. 5.12: fig05_12.c
 2   // Rolling a six-sided die 6,000,000 times.
 3   #include <stdio.h>
 4   #include <stdlib.h>
 5
 6   // function main begins program execution
 7   int main( void )
 8   {
 9      unsigned int frequency1 = 0; // rolled 1 counter
10      unsigned int frequency2 = 0; // rolled 2 counter
11      unsigned int frequency3 = 0; // rolled 3 counter
12      unsigned int frequency4 = 0; // rolled 4 counter
13      unsigned int frequency5 = 0; // rolled 5 counter
14      unsigned int frequency6 = 0; // rolled 6 counter
15
16      unsigned int roll; // roll counter, value 1 to 6000000
17      int face; // represents one roll of the die, value 1 to 6
```

Fig. 5.12 | Rolling a six-sided die 6,000,000 times. (Part 1 of 2.)

```
18
19      // loop 6000000 times and summarize results
20      for ( roll = 1; roll <= 6000000; ++roll ) {
21         face = 1 + rand() % 6; // random number from 1 to 6
22
23         // determine face value and increment appropriate counter
24         switch ( face ) {
25
26            case 1: // rolled 1
27               ++frequency1;
28               break;
29
30            case 2: // rolled 2
31               ++frequency2;
32               break;
33
34            case 3: // rolled 3
35               ++frequency3;
36               break;
37
38            case 4: // rolled 4
39               ++frequency4;
40               break;
41
42            case 5: // rolled 5
43               ++frequency5;
44               break;
45
46            case 6: // rolled 6
47               ++frequency6;
48               break; // optional
49         } // end switch
50      } // end for
51
52      // display results in tabular format
53      printf( "%s%13s\n", "Face", "Frequency" );
54      printf( "    1%13u\n", frequency1 );
55      printf( "    2%13u\n", frequency2 );
56      printf( "    3%13u\n", frequency3 );
57      printf( "    4%13u\n", frequency4 );
58      printf( "    5%13u\n", frequency5 );
59      printf( "    6%13u\n", frequency6 );
60   } // end main
```

```
Face    Frequency
   1       999702
   2      1000823
   3       999378
   4       998898
   5      1000777
   6      1000422
```

Fig. 5.12 | Rolling a six-sided die 6,000,000 times. (Part 2 of 2.)

As the program output shows, by scaling and shifting we've used the rand function to realistically simulate the rolling of a six-sided die. Note the use of the %s conversion specifier to print the character strings "Face" and "Frequency" as column headers (line 53). After we study arrays in Chapter 6, we'll show how to replace this 26-line switch statement elegantly with a single-line statement.

Randomizing the Random Number Generator
Executing the program of Fig. 5.11 again produces

6	6	5	5	6
5	1	1	5	3
6	6	2	4	2
6	2	3	4	1

Notice that *exactly the same sequence of values* was printed. How can these be *random* numbers? Ironically, this *repeatability* is an important characteristic of function rand. When *debugging* a program, this repeatability is essential for proving that corrections to a program work properly.

Function rand actually generates **pseudorandom numbers**. Calling rand repeatedly produces a sequence of numbers that *appears* to be random. However, the sequence repeats itself each time the program is executed. Once a program has been thoroughly debugged, it can be conditioned to produce a *different* sequence of random numbers for each execution. This is called **randomizing** and is accomplished with the standard library function **srand**. Function srand takes an unsigned integer argument and **seeds** function rand to produce a different sequence of random numbers for each execution of the program.

We demonstrate function srand in Fig. 5.13. Function srand takes an unsigned int value as an argument. The conversion specifier %u is used to read an unsigned int value with scanf. The function prototype for srand is found in <stdlib.h>.

Let's run the program several times and observe the results. Notice that a *different* sequence of random numbers is obtained each time the program is run, provided that a *different* seed is supplied.

To randomize *without* entering a seed each time, use a statement like

```
srand( time( NULL ) );
```

This causes the computer to read its clock to obtain the value for the seed automatically. Function time returns the number of seconds that have passed since midnight on January 1, 1970. This value is converted to an unsigned integer and used as the seed to the random number generator. The function prototype for time is in <time.h>. We'll say more about NULL in Chapter 7.

```
1   // Fig. 5.13: fig05_13.c
2   // Randomizing the die-rolling program.
3   #include <stdlib.h>
4   #include <stdio.h>
5
```

Fig. 5.13 | Randomizing the die-rolling program. (Part 1 of 2.)

```
6   // function main begins program execution
7   int main( void )
8   {
9      unsigned int i; // counter
10     unsigned int seed; // number used to seed the random number generator
11
12     printf( "%s", "Enter seed: " );
13     scanf( "%u", &seed ); // note %u for unsigned int
14
15     srand( seed );   // seed the random number generator
16
17     // loop 10 times
18     for ( i = 1; i <= 10; ++i ) {
19
20        // pick a random number from 1 to 6 and output it
21        printf( "%10d", 1 + ( rand() % 6 ) );
22
23        // if counter is divisible by 5, begin a new line of output
24        if ( i % 5 == 0 ) {
25           puts( "" );
26        } // end if
27     } // end for
28  } // end main
```

```
Enter seed: 67
        6         1         4         6         2
        1         6         1         6         4
```

```
Enter seed: 867
        2         4         6         1         6
        1         1         3         6         2
```

```
Enter seed: 67
        6         1         4         6         2
        1         6         1         6         4
```

Fig. 5.13 | Randomizing the die-rolling program. (Part 2 of 2.)

Generalized Scaling and Shifting of Random Numbers

The values produced directly by rand are always in the range:

```
0  ≤  rand()  ≤  RAND_MAX
```

As you know, the following statement simulates rolling a six-sided die:

```
face = 1 + rand() % 6;
```

This statement always assigns an integer value (at random) to the variable face in the range $1 \leq$ face ≤ 6. The *width* of this range (i.e., the number of consecutive integers in the range) is 6 and the *starting number* in the range is 1. Referring to the preceding statement, we see that the width of the range is determined by the number used to *scale* rand with the *remainder operator* (i.e., 6), and the *starting number* of the range is equal to the number (i.e., 1) that's added to rand % 6. We can generalize this result as follows:

```
n = a + rand() % b;
```

where a is the shifting value (which is equal to the *first* number in the desired range of consecutive integers) and b is the *scaling factor* (which is equal to the *width* of the desired range of consecutive integers). In the exercises, we'll see that it's possible to choose integers at random from sets of values other than ranges of consecutive integers.

Common Programming Error 5.7

Using srand in place of rand to generate random numbers.

5.11 Example: A Game of Chance

One of the most popular games of chance is a dice game known as "craps," which is played in casinos and back alleys throughout the world. The rules of the game are straightforward:

> *A player rolls two dice. Each die has six faces. These faces contain 1, 2, 3, 4, 5, and 6 spots. After the dice have come to rest, the sum of the spots on the two upward faces is calculated. If the sum is 7 or 11 on the first throw, the player wins. If the sum is 2, 3, or 12 on the first throw (called "craps"), the player loses (i.e., the "house" wins). If the sum is 4, 5, 6, 8, 9, or 10 on the first throw, then that sum becomes the player's "point." To win, you must continue rolling the dice until you "make your point." The player loses by rolling a 7 before making the point.*

Figure 5.14 simulates the game of craps and Fig. 5.15 shows several sample executions.

```c
1   // Fig. 5.14: fig05_14.c
2   // Simulating the game of craps.
3   #include <stdio.h>
4   #include <stdlib.h>
5   #include <time.h> // contains prototype for function time
6
7   // enumeration constants represent game status
8   enum Status { CONTINUE, WON, LOST };
9
10  int rollDice( void ); // function prototype
11
12  // function main begins program execution
13  int main( void )
14  {
15     int sum; // sum of rolled dice
16     int myPoint; // player must make this point to win
17
18     enum Status gameStatus; // can contain CONTINUE, WON, or LOST
19
20     // randomize random number generator using current time
21     srand( time( NULL ) );
22
```

Fig. 5.14 | Simulating the game of craps. (Part 1 of 3.)

```
23       sum = rollDice(); // first roll of the dice
24
25       // determine game status based on sum of dice
26       switch( sum ) {
27
28          // win on first roll
29          case 7: // 7 is a winner
30          case 11: // 11 is a winner
31             gameStatus = WON; // game has been won
32             break;
33
34          // lose on first roll
35          case 2: // 2 is a loser
36          case 3: // 3 is a loser
37          case 12: // 12 is a loser
38             gameStatus = LOST; // game has been lost
39             break;
40
41          // remember point
42          default:
43             gameStatus = CONTINUE; // player should keep rolling
44             myPoint = sum; // remember the point
45             printf( "Point is %d\n", myPoint );
46             break; // optional
47       } // end switch
48
49       // while game not complete
50       while ( CONTINUE == gameStatus ) { // player should keep rolling
51          sum = rollDice(); // roll dice again
52
53          // determine game status
54          if ( sum == myPoint ) { // win by making point
55             gameStatus = WON; // game over, player won
56          } // end if
57          else {
58             if ( 7 == sum ) { // lose by rolling 7
59                gameStatus = LOST; // game over, player lost
60             } // end if
61          } // end else
62       } // end while
63
64       // display won or lost message
65       if ( WON == gameStatus ) { // did player win?
66          puts( "Player wins" );
67       } // end if
68       else { // player lost
69          puts( "Player loses" );
70       } // end else
71    } // end main
72
73    // roll dice, calculate sum and display results
74    int rollDice( void )
75    {
```

Fig. 5.14 | Simulating the game of craps. (Part 2 of 3.)

```
76      int die1; // first die
77      int die2; // second die
78      int workSum; // sum of dice
79
80      die1 = 1 + ( rand() % 6 ); // pick random die1 value
81      die2 = 1 + ( rand() % 6 ); // pick random die2 value
82      workSum = die1 + die2; // sum die1 and die2
83
84      // display results of this roll
85      printf( "Player rolled %d + %d = %d\n", die1, die2, workSum );
86      return workSum; // return sum of dice
87   } // end function rollRice
```

Fig. 5.14 | Simulating the game of craps. (Part 3 of 3.)

Player wins on the first roll

```
Player rolled 5 + 6 = 11
Player wins
```

Player wins on a subsequent roll

```
Player rolled 4 + 1 = 5
Point is 5
Player rolled 6 + 2 = 8
Player rolled 2 + 1 = 3
Player rolled 3 + 2 = 5
Player wins
```

Player loses on the first roll

```
Player rolled 1 + 1 = 2
Player loses
```

Player loses on a subsequent roll

```
Player rolled 6 + 4 = 10
Point is 10
Player rolled 3 + 4 = 7
Player loses
```

Fig. 5.15 | Sample runs for the game of craps.

In the rules of the game, notice that the player must roll *two* dice on the first roll, and must do so later on all subsequent rolls. We define a function rollDice to roll the dice and compute and print their sum. Function rollDice is defined *once*, but it's called from *two* places in the program (lines 23 and 51). Interestingly, rollDice takes no arguments, so we've indicated void in the parameter list (line 74). Function rollDice does return the sum of the two dice, so a return type of int is indicated in its function header and in its function prototype.

Enumerations

The game is reasonably involved. The player may win or lose on the first roll, or may win or lose on any subsequent roll. Variable gameStatus, defined to be of a new type—enum Status—stores the current status. Line 8 creates a programmer-defined type called an **enumeration**. An enumeration, introduced by the keyword **enum**, is a set of integer constants represented by identifiers. **Enumeration constants** are sometimes called symbolic constants. Values in an enum start with 0 and are incremented by 1. In line 8, the constant CONTINUE has the value 0, WON has the value 1 and LOST has the value 2. It's also possible to assign an integer value to each identifier in an enum (see Chapter 10). The *identifiers* in an enumeration must be *unique*, but the *values* may be *duplicated*.

Common Programming Error 5.8

Assigning a value to an enumeration constant after it has been defined is a syntax error.

Good Programming Practice 5.6

Use only uppercase letters in the names of enumeration constants to make these constants stand out in a program and to indicate that enumeration constants are not *variables.*

When the game is won, either on the first roll or on a subsequent roll, gameStatus is set to WON. When the game is lost, either on the first roll or on a subsequent roll, gameStatus is set to LOST. Otherwise gameStatus is set to CONTINUE and the game continues.

Game Ends on First Roll

After the first roll, if the game is over, the while statement (lines 50–62) is skipped because gameStatus is not CONTINUE. The program proceeds to the if...else statement at lines 65–70, which prints "Player wins" if gameStatus is WON and "Player loses" otherwise.

Game Ends on a Subsequent Roll

After the first roll, if the game is *not* over, then sum is saved in myPoint. Execution proceeds with the while statement because gameStatus is CONTINUE. Each time through the while, rollDice is called to produce a new sum. If sum matches myPoint, gameStatus is set to WON to indicate that the player won, the while-test fails, the if...else statement prints "Player wins" and execution terminates. If sum is equal to 7 (line 58), gameStatus is set to LOST to indicate that the player lost, the while-test fails, the if...else statement prints "Player loses" and execution terminates.

Control Architecture

Note the program's interesting control architecture. We've used two functions—main and rollDice—and the switch, while, nested if...else and nested if statements. In the exercises, we'll investigate various interesting characteristics of the game of craps.

5.12 Storage Classes

In Chapters 2–4, we used identifiers for variable names. The attributes of variables include *name*, *type*, *size* and *value*. In this chapter, we also use identifiers as names for user-defined functions. Actually, each identifier in a program has other attributes, including storage class, storage duration, scope and linkage.

C provides the **storage class specifiers** auto, register[1], extern and **static**.[2] An identifier's **storage class** determines its storage duration, scope and linkage. An identifier's **storage duration** is the period during which the identifier *exists in memory*. Some exist briefly, some are repeatedly created and destroyed, and others exist for the program's entire execution. An identifier's **scope** is *where* the identifier can be referenced in a program. Some can be referenced throughout a program, others from only portions of a program. An identifier's **linkage** determines for a multiple-source-file program whether the identifier is known *only* in the current source file or in *any* source file with proper declarations. This section discusses storage classes and storage duration. Section 5.13 discusses scope. Chapter 14 discusses identifier linkage and programming with multiple source files.

The storage-class specifiers can be split **automatic storage duration** and **static storage duration**. Keyword **auto** is used to declare variables of automatic storage duration. Variables with automatic storage duration are created when the block in which they're defined is entered; they exist while the block is active, and they're destroyed when the block is exited.

Local Variables
Only variables can have automatic storage duration. A function's local variables (those declared in the parameter list or function body) normally have automatic storage duration. Keyword auto explicitly declares variables of automatic storage duration. Local variables have automatic storage duration by *default*, so keyword auto is rarely used. For the remainder of the text, we'll refer to variables with automatic storage duration simply as **automatic variables**.

Performance Tip 5.1

Automatic storage is a means of conserving memory, because automatic variables exist only when they're needed. They're created when a function is entered and destroyed when the function is exited.

Static Storage Class
Keywords extern and static are used in the declarations of identifiers for variables and functions of *static storage duration*. Identifiers of static storage duration exist from the time at which the program begins execution until the program terminates. For static variables, storage is allocated and initialized *only once, before the program begins execution*. For functions, the name of the function exists when the program begins execution. However, even though the variables and the function names exist from the start of program execution, this does *not* mean that these identifiers can be accessed throughout the program. Storage duration and scope (*where* a name can be used) are separate issues, as we'll see in Section 5.13.

There are several types of identifiers with static storage duration: *external identifiers* (such as global variables and function names) and local variables declared with the storage-class specifier static. Global variables and function names are of storage class extern by default. Global variables are created by placing variable declarations *outside* any function definition, and they retain their values throughout the execution of the program. Global variables and functions can be referenced by any function that follows their declarations

---

1.   Keyword register is archaic and should not be used.
2.   The new C standard adds the storage class specifier _Thread_local, which is beyond this book's scope.

or definitions in the file. This is one reason for using function prototypes—when we include `stdio.h` in a program that calls `printf`, the function prototype is placed at the start of our file to make the name `printf` known to the rest of the file.

Software Engineering Observation 5.10

Defining a variable as global rather than local allows unintended side effects to occur when a function that does not need access to the variable accidentally or maliciously modifies it. In general, global variables should be avoided except in certain situations with unique performance requirements (as discussed in Chapter 14).

Software Engineering Observation 5.11

Variables used only in a particular function should be defined as local variables in that function rather than as external variables.

Local variables declared with the keyword `static` are still known *only* in the function in which they're defined, but unlike automatic variables, `static` local variables *retain* their value when the function is exited. The next time the function is called, the `static` local variable contains the value it had when the function last exited. The following statement declares local variable `count` to be `static` and initializes it to 1.

```
static int count = 1;
```

All numeric variables of static storage duration are initialized to zero by default if you do not explicitly initialize them.

Keywords `extern` and `static` have special meaning when explicitly applied to external identifiers. In Chapter 14 we discuss the explicit use of `extern` and `static` with external identifiers and multiple-source-file programs.

5.13 Scope Rules

The **scope of an identifier** is the portion of the program in which the identifier can be referenced. For example, when we define a local variable in a block, it can be referenced *only* following its definition in that block or in blocks nested within that block. The four identifier scopes are function scope, file scope, block scope, and function-prototype scope.

Labels (identifiers followed by a colon such as `start:`) are the *only* identifiers with **function scope**. Labels can be used *anywhere* in the function in which they appear, but cannot be referenced outside the function body. Labels are used in `switch` statements (as `case` labels) and in `goto` statements (see Chapter 14). Labels are implementation details that functions hide from one another. This hiding—more formally called **information hiding**—is a means of implementing the **principle of least privilege**—a fundamental principle of good software engineering. In the context of an application, the principle states that code should be granted *only* the amount of privilege and access that it needs to accomplish its designated task, but no more.

An identifier declared outside any function has **file scope**. Such an identifier is "known" (i.e., accessible) in all functions from the point at which the identifier is declared until the end of the file. Global variables, function definitions, and function prototypes placed outside a function all have file scope.

Identifiers defined inside a block have **block scope**. Block scope ends at the terminating right brace (`}`) of the block. Local variables defined at the beginning of a function have block scope, as do function parameters, which are considered local variables by the function. *Any block may contain variable definitions.* When blocks are nested, and an identifier in an outer block has the *same* name as an identifier in an inner block, the identifier in the outer block is *hidden* until the inner block terminates. This means that while executing in the inner block, the inner block sees the value of its own local identifier and *not* the value of the identically named identifier in the enclosing block. Local variables declared static still have block scope, even though they exist from before program startup. Thus, storage duration does *not* affect the scope of an identifier.

The only identifiers with **function-prototype scope** are those used in the parameter list of a function prototype. As mentioned previously, function prototypes do *not* require *names* in the parameter list—only *types* are required. If a name is used in the parameter list of a function prototype, the compiler *ignores* the name. Identifiers used in a function prototype can be reused elsewhere in the program without ambiguity.

Common Programming Error 5.9
Accidentally using the same name for an identifier in an inner block as is used for an identifier in an outer block, when in fact you want the identifier in the outer *block to be active for the duration of the inner block.*

Error-Prevention Tip 5.4
Avoid variable names that hide names in outer scopes.

Figure 5.16 demonstrates scoping issues with global variables, automatic local variables and static local variables. A global variable x is defined and initialized to 1 (line 9). This global variable is hidden in any block (or function) in which a variable named x is defined. In main, a local variable x is defined and initialized to 5 (line 14). This variable is then printed to show that the global x is hidden in main. Next, a new block is defined in main with another local variable x initialized to 7 (line 19). This variable is printed to show that it hides x in the outer block of main. The variable x with value 7 is automatically destroyed when the block is exited, and the local variable x in the outer block of main is printed again to show that it's no longer hidden.

```
1   // Fig. 5.16: fig05_16.c
2   // Scoping.
3   #include <stdio.h>
4
5   void useLocal( void ); // function prototype
6   void useStaticLocal( void ); // function prototype
7   void useGlobal( void ); // function prototype
8
9   int x = 1; // global variable
10
11  // function main begins program execution
12  int main( void )
13  {
```

Fig. 5.16 | Scoping. (Part 1 of 3.)

```
14      int x = 5; // local variable to main
15
16      printf("local x in outer scope of main is %d\n", x );
17
18      { // start new scope
19        int x = 7; // local variable to new scope
20
21        printf( "local x in inner scope of main is %d\n", x );
22      } // end new scope
23
24      printf( "local x in outer scope of main is %d\n", x );
25
26      useLocal(); // useLocal has automatic local x
27      useStaticLocal(); // useStaticLocal has static local x
28      useGlobal(); // useGlobal uses global x
29      useLocal(); // useLocal reinitializes automatic local x
30      useStaticLocal(); // static local x retains its prior value
31      useGlobal(); // global x also retains its value
32
33      printf( "\nlocal x in main is %d\n", x );
34   } // end main
35
36   // useLocal reinitializes local variable x during each call
37   void useLocal( void )
38   {
39      int x = 25; // initialized each time useLocal is called
40
41      printf( "\nlocal x in useLocal is %d after entering useLocal\n", x );
42      ++x;
43      printf( "local x in useLocal is %d before exiting useLocal\n", x );
44   } // end function useLocal
45
46   // useStaticLocal initializes static local variable x only the first time
47   // the function is called; value of x is saved between calls to this
48   // function
49   void useStaticLocal( void )
50   {
51      // initialized once before program startup
52      static int x = 50;
53
54      printf( "\nlocal static x is %d on entering useStaticLocal\n", x );
55      ++x;
56      printf( "local static x is %d on exiting useStaticLocal\n", x );
57   } // end function useStaticLocal
58
59   // function useGlobal modifies global variable x during each call
60   void useGlobal( void )
61   {
62      printf( "\nglobal x is %d on entering useGlobal\n", x );
63      x *= 10;
64      printf( "global x is %d on exiting useGlobal\n", x );
65   } // end function useGlobal
```

Fig. 5.16 | Scoping. (Part 2 of 3.)

```
local x in outer scope of main is 5
local x in inner scope of main is 7
local x in outer scope of main is 5

local x in useLocal is 25 after entering useLocal
local x in useLocal is 26 before exiting useLocal

local static x is 50 on entering useStaticLocal
local static x is 51 on exiting useStaticLocal

global x is 1 on entering useGlobal
global x is 10 on exiting useGlobal

local x in useLocal is 25 after entering useLocal
local x in useLocal is 26 before exiting useLocal

local static x is 51 on entering useStaticLocal
local static x is 52 on exiting useStaticLocal

global x is 10 on entering useGlobal
global x is 100 on exiting useGlobal

local x in main is 5
```

Fig. 5.16 | Scoping. (Part 3 of 3.)

The program defines three functions that each take no arguments and return nothing. Function useLocal defines an automatic variable x and initializes it to 25 (line 39). When useLocal is called, the variable is printed, incremented, and printed again before exiting the function. Each time this function is called, automatic variable x is *reinitialized* to 25. Function useStaticLocal defines a static variable x and initializes it to 50 in line 52 (recall that the storage for static variables is allocated and initialized *only once, before the program begins execution*). Local variables declared as static *retain* their values even when they're out of scope. When useStaticLocal is called, x is printed, incremented, and printed again before exiting the function. In the next call to this function, static local variable x will contain the value 51. Function useGlobal does not define any variables. Therefore, when it refers to variable x, the global x (line 9) is used. When useGlobal is called, the global variable is printed, multiplied by 10, and printed again before exiting the function. The next time function useGlobal is called, the global variable still has its modified value, 10. Finally, the program prints the local variable x in main again (line 33) to show that none of the function calls modified the value of x because the functions all referred to variables in other scopes.

5.14 Recursion

The programs we've discussed are generally structured as functions that call one another in a disciplined, hierarchical manner. For some types of problems, it's useful to have functions call themselves. A recursive **function** is a function that *calls itself* either directly or indirectly through another function. Recursion is a complex topic discussed at length in upper-level computer science courses. In this section and the next, simple examples of recursion are presented. This book contains an extensive treatment of recursion, which is spread throughout Chapters 5–8 and 12 and Appendix F. Figure 5.21, in Section 5.16, summarizes the recursion examples and exercises in the book.

We consider recursion conceptually first, then examine several programs containing recursive functions. Recursive problem-solving approaches have a number of elements in common. A recursive function is called to solve a problem. The function actually knows how to solve only the *simplest* case(s), or so-called **base case**(s). If the function is called with a base case, the function simply returns a result. If the function is called with a more complex problem, the function divides the problem into two conceptual pieces: a piece that the function knows how to do and a piece that it does not know how to do. To make recursion feasible, the latter piece must resemble the original problem, but be a slightly simpler or smaller version. Because this new problem looks like the original problem, the function launches (calls) a fresh copy of itself to go to work on the smaller problem—this is referred to as a **recursive call** or the **recursion step**. The recursion step also includes the keyword return, because its result will be combined with the portion of the problem the function knew how to solve to form a result that will be passed back to the original caller.

The recursion step executes while the original call to the function has not yet finished executing. The recursion step can result in many more such recursive calls, as the function keeps dividing each problem it's called with into two conceptual pieces. For the recursion to terminate, each time the function calls itself with a slightly simpler version of the original problem, this sequence of smaller problems must eventually *converge on the base case*. When the function recognizes the base case, it returns a result to the previous copy of the function, and a sequence of returns ensues all the way up the line until the original call of the function eventually returns the final result to main. All of this sounds quite exotic compared to the kind of problem solving we've been using with conventional function calls to this point. It can take a great deal of practice writing recursive programs before the process will appear natural. As an example of these concepts at work, let's write a recursive program to perform a popular mathematical calculation.

Recursively Calculating Factorials

The factorial of a nonnegative integer n, written $n!$ (pronounced "n factorial"), is the product

$$n \cdot (n-1) \cdot (n-2) \cdot \ldots \cdot 1$$

with $1!$ equal to 1, and $0!$ defined to be 1. For example, $5!$ is the product $5 * 4 * 3 * 2 * 1$, which is equal to 120.

The factorial of an integer, number, greater than or equal to 0 can be calculated *iteratively* (nonrecursively) using a for statement as follows:

```
factorial = 1;
for ( counter = number; counter >= 1; --counter )
    factorial *= counter;
```

A *recursive* definition of the factorial function is arrived at by observing the following relationship:

$$n! = n \cdot (n-1)!$$

For example, 5! is clearly equal to 5 * 4! as is shown by the following:

$$5! = 5 \cdot 4 \cdot 3 \cdot 2 \cdot 1$$
$$5! = 5 \cdot (4 \cdot 3 \cdot 2 \cdot 1)$$
$$5! = 5 \cdot (4!)$$

The evaluation of 5! would proceed as shown in Fig. 5.17. Figure 5.17(a) shows how the succession of recursive calls proceeds until 1! is evaluated to be 1 (i.e., the *base case*), which terminates the recursion. Figure 5.17(b) shows the values returned from each recursive call to its caller until the final value is calculated and returned.

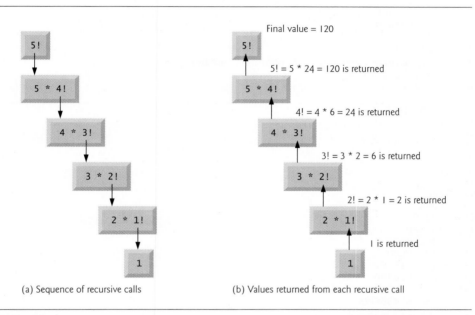

(a) Sequence of recursive calls   (b) Values returned from each recursive call

Fig. 5.17 | Recursive evaluation of 5!.

Figure 5.18 uses recursion to calculate and print the factorials of the integers 0–10 (the choice of the type unsigned long long int will be explained momentarily).

```
 1   // Fig. 5.18: fig05_18.c
 2   // Recursive factorial function.
 3   #include <stdio.h>
 4
 5   unsigned long long int factorial( unsigned int number );
 6
 7   // function main begins program execution
 8   int main( void )
 9   {
10       unsigned int i; // counter
11
```

Fig. 5.18 | Recursive factorial function. (Part 1 of 2.)

```
12      // during each iteration, calculate
13      // factorial( i ) and display result
14      for ( i = 0; i <= 21; ++i ) {
15          printf( "%u! = %llu\n", i, factorial( i ) );
16      } // end for
17   } // end main
18
19   // recursive definition of function factorial
20   unsigned long long int factorial( unsigned int number )
21   {
22      // base case
23      if ( number <= 1 ) {
24          return 1;
25      } // end if
26      else { // recursive step
27          return ( number * factorial( number - 1 ) );
28      } // end else
29   } // end function factorial
```

```
0! = 1
1! = 1
2! = 2
3! = 6
4! = 24
5! = 120
6! = 720
7! = 5040
8! = 40320
9! = 362880
10! = 3628800
11! = 39916800
12! = 479001600
13! = 6227020800
14! = 87178291200
15! = 1307674368000
16! = 20922789888000
17! = 355687428096000
18! = 6402373705728000
19! = 121645100408832000
20! = 2432902008176640000
21! = 14197454024290336768
```

Fig. 5.18 | Recursive factorial function. (Part 2 of 2.)

The recursive factorial function first tests whether a *terminating condition* is true, i.e., whether number is less than or equal to 1. If number is indeed less than or equal to 1, factorial returns 1, no further recursion is necessary, and the program terminates. If number is greater than 1, the statement

```
return number * factorial( number - 1 );
```

expresses the problem as the product of number and a recursive call to factorial evaluating the factorial of number - 1. The call factorial(number - 1) is a slightly simpler problem than the original calculation factorial(number).

Function `factorial` (lines 20–29) receives an `unsigned int` and returns a result of type `unsigned long long int`. The C standard specifies that a variable of type `unsigned long long int` can hold a value at least as large as 18,446,744,073,709,551,615. As can be seen in Fig. 5.18, factorial values become large quickly. We've chosen the data type `unsigned long long int` so the program can calculate larger factorial values. The conversion specifier `%11u` is used to print `unsigned long long int` values. Unfortunately, the `factorial` function produces large values so quickly that even `unsigned long long int` does not help us print very many factorial values before the maximum value of a `unsigned long long int` variable is exceeded.

Even when we use `unsigned long long int`, we still can't calculate factorials beyond 21! This points to a weakness in C (and most other procedural programming languages)— namely that the language is not easily *extended* to handle the unique requirements of various applications. As we'll see later in the book, C++ is an *extensible* language that, through "classes," allows us to create new data types, including ones that could hold arbitrarily large integers if we wish.

Common Programming Error 5.10

Forgetting to return a value from a recursive function when one is needed.

Common Programming Error 5.11

Either omitting the base case, or writing the recursion step incorrectly so that it does not converge on the base case, will cause infinite recursion, eventually exhausting memory. This is analogous to the problem of an infinite loop in an iterative (nonrecursive) solution. Infinite recursion can also be caused by providing an unexpected input.

5.15 Example Using Recursion: Fibonacci Series

The Fibonacci series

0, 1, 1, 2, 3, 5, 8, 13, 21, …

begins with 0 and 1 and has the property that each subsequent Fibonacci number is the sum of the previous two Fibonacci numbers.

The series occurs in nature and, in particular, describes a form of spiral. The ratio of successive Fibonacci numbers converges to a constant value of 1.618…. This number, too, repeatedly occurs in nature and has been called the *golden ratio* or the *golden mean*. Humans tend to find the golden mean aesthetically pleasing. Architects often design windows, rooms, and buildings whose length and width are in the ratio of the golden mean. Postcards are often designed with a golden mean length/width ratio.

The Fibonacci series may be defined recursively as follows:

fibonacci(0) = 0
fibonacci(1) = 1
fibonacci(n) = fibonacci(n – 1) + fibonacci(n – 2)

Figure 5.19 calculates the nth Fibonacci number recursively using function `fibonacci`. Notice that Fibonacci numbers tend to become large quickly. Therefore, we've chosen the data type `unsigned int` for the parameter type and the data type `unsigned long long int` for the return type in function fibonacci. In Fig. 5.19, each pair of output lines shows a separate run of the program.

```c
1   // Fig. 5.19: fig05_19.c
2   // Recursive fibonacci function
3   #include <stdio.h>
4
5   unsigned long long int fibonacci( unsigned int n ); // function prototype
6
7   // function main begins program execution
8   int main( void )
9   {
10     unsigned long long int result; // fibonacci value
11     unsigned int number; // number input by user
12
13     // obtain integer from user
14     printf( "%s", "Enter an integer: " );
15     scanf( "%u", &number );
16
17     // calculate fibonacci value for number input by user
18     result = fibonacci( number );
19
20     // display result
21     printf( "Fibonacci( %u ) = %llu\n", number, result );
22   } // end main
23
24   // Recursive definition of function fibonacci
25   unsigned long long int fibonacci( unsigned int n )
26   {
27     // base case
28     if ( 0 == n || 1 == n ) {
29        return n;
30     } // end if
31     else { // recursive step
32        return fibonacci( n - 1 ) + fibonacci( n - 2 );
33     } // end else
34   } // end function fibonacci
```

```
Enter an integer: 0
Fibonacci( 0 ) = 0
```

```
Enter an integer: 1
Fibonacci( 1 ) = 1
```

```
Enter an integer: 2
Fibonacci( 2 ) = 1
```

```
Enter an integer: 3
Fibonacci( 3 ) = 2
```

Fig. 5.19 | Recursive fibonacci function. (Part 1 of 2.)

```
Enter an integer: 10
Fibonacci( 10 ) = 55
```

```
Enter an integer: 20
Fibonacci( 20 ) = 6765
```

```
Enter an integer: 30
Fibonacci( 30 ) = 832040
```

```
Enter an integer: 40
Fibonacci( 40 ) = 102334155
```

Fig. 5.19 | Recursive fibonacci function. (Part 2 of 2.)

The call to fibonacci from main is *not* a recursive call (line 18), but all subsequent calls to fibonacci are recursive (line 32). Each time fibonacci is invoked, it immediately tests for the *base case*—n is equal to 0 or 1. If this is true, n is returned. Interestingly, if n is greater than 1, the recursion step generates *two* recursive calls, each a slightly simpler problem than the original call to fibonacci. Figure 5.20 shows how function fibonacci would evaluate fibonacci(3).

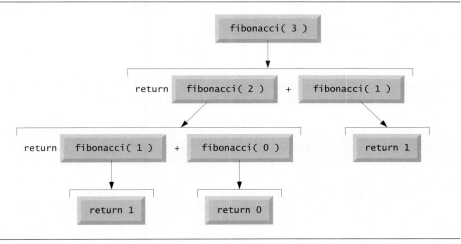

Fig. 5.20 | Set of recursive calls for fibonacci(3).

Order of Evaluation of Operands
This figure raises some interesting issues about the *order* in which C compilers will evaluate the operands of operators. This is a different issue from the order in which operators are applied to their operands, namely the order dictated by the rules of operator precedence. Figure 5.20 shows that while evaluating fibonacci(3), *two* recursive calls will be made, namely fibonacci(2) and fibonacci(1). But in what order will these calls be made? You might simply assume the operands will be evaluated left to right. For optimization reasons,

C does *not* specify the order in which the operands of most operators (including +) are to be evaluated. Therefore, you should make no assumption about the order in which these calls will execute. The calls could in fact execute `fibonacci(2)` first and then `fibonacci(1)`, or the calls could execute in the reverse order, `fibonacci(1)` then `fibonacci(2)`. In this and most other programs, the final result would be the same. But in some programs the evaluation of an operand may have *side effects* that could affect the final result of the expression. C specifies the order of evaluation of the operands of *only four* operators— namely &&, ||, the comma (,) operator and ?:. The first three of these are binary operators whose operands are guaranteed to be evaluated *left to right*. [*Note:* The commas used to separate the arguments in a function call are *not* comma operators.] The last operator is C's only *ternary* operator. Its leftmost operand is *always* evaluated *first*; if the leftmost operand evaluates to nonzero, the middle operand is evaluated next and the last operand is ignored; if the leftmost operand evaluates to zero, the third operand is evaluated next and the middle operand is ignored.

Common Programming Error 5.12

Writing programs that depend on the order of evaluation of the operands of operators other than &&, ||, ?:, and the comma (,) operator can lead to errors because compilers may not necessarily evaluate the operands in the order you expect.

Portability Tip 5.2

Programs that depend on the order of evaluation of the operands of operators other than &&, ||, ?:, and the comma (,) operator can function differently on different compilers.

Exponential Complexity

A word of caution is in order about recursive programs like the one we use here to generate Fibonacci numbers. Each level of recursion in the `fibonacci` function has a *doubling* effect on the number of calls—the number of recursive calls that will be executed to calculate the nth Fibonacci number is on the order of 2^n. This rapidly gets out of hand. Calculating only the 20th Fibonacci number would require on the order of 2^{20} or about a million calls, calculating the 30th Fibonacci number would require on the order of 2^{30} or about a billion calls, and so on. Computer scientists refer to this as *exponential complexity*. Problems of this nature humble even the world's most powerful computers! Complexity issues in general, and exponential complexity in particular, are discussed in detail in the upper-level computer science course generally called "Algorithms."

The example we showed in this section used an intuitively appealing solution to calculate Fibonacci numbers, but there are better approaches. Exercise 5.48 asks you to investigate recursion in more depth and propose alternate approaches to implementing the recursive Fibonacci algorithm.

5.16 Recursion vs. Iteration

In the previous sections, we studied two functions that can easily be implemented either recursively or iteratively. In this section, we compare the two approaches and discuss why you might choose one approach over the other in a particular situation.

- Both iteration and recursion are based on a *control structure*: Iteration uses a *repetition structure*; recursion uses a *selection structure*.

- Both iteration and recursion involve *repetition*: Iteration explicitly uses a *repetition statement*; recursion achieves repetition through *repeated function calls*.

- Iteration and recursion each involve a *termination test*: Iteration terminates when the *loop-continuation condition fails*; recursion when a *base case is recognized*.

- Iteration with counter-controlled repetition and recursion each *gradually approach termination*: Iteration keeps modifying a counter until the counter assumes a value that makes the *loop-continuation condition fail*; recursion keeps producing simpler versions of the original problem until the *base case is reached*.

- Both iteration and recursion can occur *infinitely*: An *infinite loop* occurs with iteration if the loop-continuation test *never* becomes false; *infinite recursion* occurs if the recursion step does *not* reduce the problem each time in a manner that *converges on the base case*.

Recursion has many negatives. It *repeatedly* invokes the mechanism, and consequently the *overhead, of function calls*. This can be expensive in both processor time and memory space. Each recursive call causes *another copy* of the function (actually only the function's variables) to be created; this can *consume considerable memory*. Iteration normally occurs within a function, so the overhead of repeated function calls and extra memory assignment is omitted. So why choose recursion?

Software Engineering Observation 5.12

Any problem that can be solved recursively can also be solved iteratively (nonrecursively). A recursive approach is normally chosen in preference to an iterative approach when the recursive approach more naturally mirrors the problem and results in a program that's easier to understand and debug. Another reason to choose a recursive solution is that an iterative solution may not be apparent.

Most programming textbooks introduce recursion much later than we've done here. We feel that recursion is a sufficiently rich and complex topic that it's better to introduce it earlier and spread the examples over the remainder of the text. Figure 5.21 summarizes by chapter the 31 recursion examples and exercises in the text.

Chapter	Recursion examples and exercises
Chapter 5	Factorial function
	Fibonacci function
	Greatest common divisor
	Sum of two integers
	Multiply two integers
	Raising an integer to an integer power
	Towers of Hanoi
	Recursive main
	Printing keyboard inputs in reverse
	Visualizing recursion

Fig. 5.21 | Recursion examples and exercises in the text. (Part 1 of 2.)

Chapter	Recursion examples and exercises
Chapter 6	Sum the elements of an array
	Print an array
	Print an array backward
	Print a string backward
	Check whether a string is a palindrome
	Minimum value in an array
	Linear search
	Binary search
	Eight Queens
Chapter 7	Maze traversal
Chapter 8	Printing a string input at the keyboard backward
Chapter 12	Linked list insert
	Linked list delete
	Search a linked list
	Print a linked list backward
	Binary tree insert
	Preorder traversal of a binary tree
	Inorder traversal of a binary tree
	Postorder traversal of a binary tree
Appendix E	Selection sort
	Quicksort

Fig. 5.21 | Recursion examples and exercises in the text. (Part 2 of 2.)

Let's close this chapter with some observations that we make repeatedly throughout the book. Good software engineering is important. High performance is important. Unfortunately, these goals are often at odds with one another. Good software engineering is key to making more manageable the task of developing the larger and more complex software systems we need. High performance is key to realizing the systems of the future that will place ever greater computing demands on hardware. Where do functions fit in here?

Performance Tip 5.2

Functionalizing programs promotes good software engineering. But it has a price. A heavily functionalized program—as compared to a monolithic (i.e., one-piece) program without functions—makes potentially large numbers of function calls, and these consume execution time on a computer's processor(s). Although monolithic programs may perform better, they're more difficult to program, test, debug, maintain, and evolve.

Performance Tip 5.3

Today's hardware architectures are tuned to make function calls efficient, and today's hardware processors are incredibly fast. For the vast majority of applications and software systems you'll build, concentrating on good software engineering will be more important than programming for high performance. Nevertheless, in many C applications and systems, such as game programming, real-time systems, operating systems and embedded systems, performance is crucial, so we include performance tips throughout the book.

5.17 Secure C Programming

Secure Random Numbers

In Section 5.10, we introduced the rand function for generating pseudorandom numbers. The C standard library does not provide a secure random-number generator. According to the C standard document's description of function rand, "There are no guarantees as to the quality of the random sequence produced and some implementations are known to produce sequences with *distressingly* non-random low-order bits." The CERT guideline MSC30-C indicates that implementation-specific random-number generation functions must be used to ensure that the random numbers produced are *not predictable*—this is extremely important, for example, in cryptography and other security applications. The guideline presents several platform-specific random-number generators that are considered to be secure. For example, Microsoft Windows provides the CryptGenRandom function, and POSIX based systems (such as Linux) provide a random function that produces more secure results. For more information, see guideline MSC30-C at https://www.securecoding.cert.org. If you're building industrial-strength applications that require random numbers, you should investigate for your platform the recommended function(s) to use.

Summary

Section 5.1 Introduction
- The best way to develop and maintain a large program is to divide it into several smaller program modules, each more manageable than the original program. Modules are written as functions in C.

Section 5.2 Program Modules in C
- A function is invoked by a function call. The function call mentions the function by name and provides information (as arguments) that the called function needs to perform its task.
- The purpose of information hiding is to give functions access only to the information they need to complete their tasks. This is a means of implementing the principle of least privilege, one of the most important principles of good software engineering.

Section 5.3 Math Library Functions
- A function os normally invoked in a program by writing the function's name followed by a left parenthesis followed by the argument (or a comma-separated list of arguments) of the function followed by a right parenthesis.
- Data type double is a floating-point type like float. A variable of type double can store a value of much greater magnitude and precision than float can store.
- Each argument of a function may be a constant, a variable, or an expression.

Section 5.4 Functions
- A local variable is known only in a function definition. Other functions are not allowed to know the names of a function's local variables, nor is any function allowed to know the implementation details of any other function.

Section 5.5 Function Definitions
* The general format for a function definition is

```
return-value-type function-name( parameter-list )
{
        definitions
        statements
}
```

The *return-value-type* states the type of the value returned to the calling function. If a function does not return a value, the *return-value-type* is declared as void. The *function-name* is any valid identifier. The *parameter-list* is a comma-separated list containing the definitions of the variables that will be passed to the function. If a function does not receive any values, *parameter-list* is declared as void. The function body is the set of definitions and statements that constitute the function.

* The arguments passed to a function should match in number, type and order with the parameters in the function definition.

* When a program encounters a function call, control is transferred from the point of invocation to the called function, the statements of the called function are executed and control returns to the caller.

* A called function can return control to the caller in one of three ways. If the function does not return a value, control is returned when the function-ending right brace is reached, or by executing the statement

```
return;
```

If the function does return a value, the statement

```
return expression;
```

returns the value of *expression*.

Section 5.6 Function Prototypes: A Deeper Look
* A function prototype declares the function's return type and declares the number, types, and order of the parameters the function expects to receive.

* Function prototypes enable the compiler to verify that functions are called correctly.

* The compiler ignores variable names mentioned in the function prototype.

* Arguments in a mixed-type expression are converted to the same type via the C standard's usual arithmetic conversion rules.

Section 5.7 Function Call Stack and Stack Frames
* Stacks are known as last-in, first-out (LIFO) data structures—the last item pushed (inserted) on the stack is the first item popped (removed) from the stack.

* A called function must know how to return to its caller, so the return address of the calling function is pushed onto the program execution stack when the function is called. If a series of function calls occurs, the successive return addresses are pushed onto the stack in last-in, first-out order so that the last function to execute will be the first to return to its caller.

* The program execution stack contains the memory for the local variables used in each invocation of a function during a program's execution. This data is known as the stack frame of the function call. When a function call is made, the stack frame for that function call is pushed onto the program execution stack. When the function returns to its caller, the stack frame for this function call is popped off the stack and those local variables are no longer known to the program.

* The amount of memory in a computer is finite, so only a certain amount of memory can be used to store stack frames on the program execution stack. If there are more function calls than can

have their stack frames stored on the program execution stack, an error known as a stack overflow occurs. The application will compile correctly, but its execution causes a stack overflow.

Section 5.8 Headers
- Each standard library has a corresponding header containing the function prototypes for all the functions in that library, as well as definitions of various symbolic constants needed by those functions.
- You can create and include your own headers.

Section 5.9 Passing Arguments By Value and By Reference
- When an argument is passed by value, a copy of the variable's value is made and the copy is passed to the called function. Changes to the copy in the called function do not affect the original variable's value.
- All calls in C are call-by-value.
- It's possible to simulate call-by-reference by using address operators and indirection operators.

Section 5.10 Random Number Generation
- Function `rand` generates an integer between 0 and `RAND_MAX` which is defined by the C standard to be at least 32767.
- The function prototypes for `rand` and `srand` are contained in `<stdlib.h>`.
- Values produced by `rand` can be scaled and shifted to produce values in a specific range.
- To randomize a program, use the C standard library function `srand`.
- The `srand` function call is ordinarily inserted in a program only after it has been thoroughly debugged. While debugging, it's better to omit `srand`. This ensures repeatability, which is essential to proving that corrections to a random number generation program work properly.
- To randomize without the need for entering a seed each time, we use `srand(time(NULL))`.
- The general equation for scaling and shifting a random number is

    ```
    n = a + rand() % b;
    ```

  where a is the shifting value (i.e., the first number in the desired range of consecutive integers) and b is the scaling factor (i.e,. the width of the desired range of consecutive integers).

Section 5.11 Example: A Game of Chance
- An enumeration, introduced by the keyword `enum`, is a set of integer constants represented by identifiers. Values in an `enum` start with 0 and are incremented by 1. It's also possible to assign an integer value to each identifier in an `enum`. The identifiers in an enumeration must be unique, but the values may be duplicated.

Section 5.12 Storage Classes
- Each identifier in a program has the attributes storage class, storage duration, scope and linkage.
- C provides four storage classes indicated by the storage class specifiers: `auto`, `register`, `extern` and `static`.
- An identifier's storage duration is when that identifier exists in memory.

Section 5.13 Scope Rules
- An identifier's scope is where the identifier can be referenced in a program.
- An identifier's linkage determines for a multiple-source-file program whether an identifier is known only in the current source file or in any source file with proper declarations.

- Variables with automatic storage duration are created when the block in which they're defined is entered, exist while the block is active and are destroyed when the block is exited. A function's local variables normally have automatic storage duration.

- Keywords extern and static are used to declare identifiers for variables and functions of static storage duration.

- Static storage duration variables are allocated and initialized once, before the program begins execution.

- There are two types of identifiers with static storage duration: external identifiers (such as global variables and function names) and local variables declared with the storage-class specifier static.

- Global variables are created by placing variable definitions outside any function definition. Global variables retain their values throughout the execution of the program.

- Local static variables retain their value between calls to the function in which they're defined.

- All numeric variables of static storage duration are initialized to zero if you do not explicitly initialize them.

- An identifier can have function scope, file scope, block scope or function-prototype scope.

- Labels are the only identifiers with function scope. Labels can be used anywhere in the function in which they appear but cannot be referenced outside the function body.

- An identifier declared outside any function has file scope. Such an identifier is "known" in all functions from the point at which it's declared until the end of the file.

- Identifiers defined inside a block have block scope. Block scope ends at the terminating right brace (}) of the block.

- Local variables defined at the beginning of a function have block scope, as do function parameters, which are considered local variables by the function.

- Any block may contain variable definitions. When blocks are nested, and an identifier in an outer block has the same name as an identifier in an inner block, the identifier in the outer block is "hidden" until the inner block terminates.

- The only identifiers with function-prototype scope are those used in the parameter list of a function prototype. Identifiers used in a function prototype can be reused elsewhere in the program without ambiguity.

Section 5.14 Recursion

- A recursive function is a function that calls itself either directly or indirectly.

- If a recursive function is called with a base case, the function simply returns a result. If it's called with a more complex problem, the function divides the problem into two conceptual pieces: a piece that the function knows how to do and a slightly smaller version of the original problem. Because this new problem looks like the original problem, the function launches a recursive call to work on the smaller problem.

- For recursion to terminate, each time the recursive function calls itself with a slightly simpler version of the original problem, the sequence of smaller and smaller problems must converge on the base case. When the function recognizes the base case, the result is returned to the previous function call, and a sequence of returns ensues all the way up the line until the original call of the function eventually returns the final result.

- Standard C does not specify the order in which the operands of most operators (including +) are to be evaluated. Of C's many operators, the standard specifies the order of evaluation of the operands of only the operators &&, ||, the comma (,) operator and ?:. The first three of these are binary operators whose two operands are evaluated left to right. The last operator is C's only ternary operator. Its leftmost operand is evaluated first; if it evaluates to nonzero, the middle operand is evaluated next and the last operand is ignored; if the leftmost operand evaluates to zero, the third operand is evaluated next and the middle operand is ignored.

Section 5.16 Recursion vs. Iteration

- Both iteration and recursion are based on a control structure: Iteration uses a repetition structure; recursion uses a selection structure.

- Both iteration and recursion involve repetition: Iteration explicitly uses a repetition structure; recursion achieves repetition through repeated function calls.

- Iteration and recursion each involve a termination test: Iteration terminates when the loop-continuation condition fails; recursion terminates when a base case is recognized.

- Iteration and recursion can occur infinitely: An infinite loop occurs with iteration if the loop-continuation test never becomes false; infinite recursion occurs if the recursion step does not reduce the problem in a manner that converges on the base case.

- Recursion repeatedly invokes the mechanism, and consequently the overhead, of function calls. This can be expensive in both processor time and memory space.

Terminology

abstraction 190
argument (of a function) 188
auto 211
automatic storage duration 211
automatic variable 211
base case 216
block 192
block scope 212
C standard library 187
call a function 188
called 191
called function 188
caller 188
calling function 188
coercion of arguments 195
divide and conquer 187
enum 210
enumeration 210
enumeration constant 210
file scope 212
function 187
function body 192
function call 188
function call stack 197
function prototype 191
function-prototype scope 213
function scope 212
header 192
information hiding 212
invoke a function 188
last-in, first-out (LIFO) 197

linkage of an identifier 211
local variable 190
mixed-type expression 195
module 187
parameter 190
parameter list 192
pass-by-reference 201
pass-by-value 201
pop off a stack 197
principle of least privilege 212
program execution stack 197
programmer-defined function 188
pseudorandom numbers 205
push onto a stack 197
randomizing 205
recursion step 216
recursive call 216
recursive function 215
return from a function 188
return statement 191
return value type 192
scaling 202
scaling factor 202
scope 211
scope of an identifier 212
seed the rand function 205
shift 202
shifting value 207
side effect 201
simulate 202
software reusability 190

stack 197
stack frame 197
stack overflow 198
standard library header 200
static 211

static storage duration 211
storage class of an identifier 211
storage class specifier 211
storage duration 211
usual arithmetic conversion rules 195

Self-Review Exercises

5.1 Answer each of the following:
   a) A program module in C is called a(n) _____.
   b) A function is invoked with a(n) _____.
   c) A variable that's known only within the function in which it's defined is called a(n) _____.
   d) The _____ statement in a called function is used to pass the value of an expression back to the calling function.
   e) Keyword _____ is used in a function header to indicate that a function does not return a value or to indicate that a function contains no parameters.
   f) The _____ of an identifier is the portion of the program in which the identifier can be used.
   g) The three ways to return control from a called function to a caller are _____, _____ and _____.
   h) A(n) _____ allows the compiler to check the number, types, and order of the arguments passed to a function.
   i) The _____ function is used to produce random numbers.
   j) The _____ function is used to set the random number seed to randomize a program.
   k) The storage-class specifiers are _____, _____, _____ and _____.
   l) Variables declared in a block or in the parameter list of a function are assumed to be of storage class _____ unless specified otherwise.
   m) A non-static variable defined outside any block or function is a(n) _____ variable.
   n) For a local variable in a function to retain its value between calls to the function, it must be declared with the _____ storage-class specifier.
   o) The four possible scopes of an identifier are _____, _____, _____ and _____.
   p) A function that calls itself either directly or indirectly is a(n) _____ function.
   q) A recursive function typically has two components: one that provides a means for the recursion to terminate by testing for a(n) _____ case, and one that expresses the problem as a recursive call for a slightly simpler problem than the original call.

5.2 For the following program, state the scope (either function scope, file scope, block scope or function-prototype scope) of each of the following elements:
   a) The variable a in main.
   b) The function square.
   c) The variable b in square.
   d) The function main.
   e) The function prototype for square.
   f) The identifier b in the function prototype for square.

```
1   #include <stdio.h>
2   int square( int b );
3
```

```
4   int main( void )
5   {
6       int a;
7       a = 1;
8       while (a <= 5) {
9           printf( "%d\n", square( a ) );
10          a++;
11      }
12  int square( int b )
13  {
14      return b * b;
15  }
```

5.3   Write a program that tests whether the examples of the math library function calls shown in Fig. 5.2 actually produce the indicated results.

5.4   Give the function header for each of the following functions.
  a) Function `unique` that takes two integer arguments, a and n, and returns an integer result.
  b) Function `compare` that takes two floating point arguments, n and m, and does not return a value.
  c) Function `binary` takes two double-precision floating-point arguments x and y, and an integer argument z, and returns double-precision floating-point result.
  d) Function `swap` that does not receive any arguments and does not return a value. [*Note:* Such functions are commonly used to display instructions to a user.]

5.5   Give the function prototype for each of the following:
  a) The function described in Exercise 5.4(a).
  b) The function described in Exercise 5.4(b).
  c) The function described in Exercise 5.4(c).
  d) The function described in Exercise 5.4(d).

5.6   Write a declaration for an integer number that should be maintained in a register. Initialize the number to 1.

5.7   Find the error in each of the following program segme nts and explain how the error can be corrected (see also Exercise 5.46):
  a)
```
int g( void )
{
    printf( "%s", Inside function g\n" );
    int h( void )
    {
        printf( "%s", Inside function h\n" );
    }
}
```
  b)
```
int sum( int x, int y )
{
    int result;
    result = x + y;
}
```
  c)
```
void f( float a );
{
    float a;
    printf( "%f", a );
}
```

d) int sum(int n)
```
{
    if ( 0 == n ) {
        return 0; //
    }
    else {
        n + sum( n - 1 );
    }
}
```

e) void product(void)
```
{
    int a, b, c, result;
    printf( "%s", "Enter three integers: " )
    scanf( "%d%d%d", &a, &b, &c );
    result = a * b * c;
    printf( "Result is %d", result );
    return result;
}
```

Answers to Self-Review Exercises

5.1   a) function. b) function call. c) local variable. d) return. e) void. f) Scope. g) return; or return expression; or encountering the closing right brace of a function. h) function prototype. i) rand. j) srand. k) auto, register, extern, static. l) auto. m) external, global. n) static. o) function scope, file scope, block scope, function-prototype scope. p) recursive. q) base.

5.2   a) Block scope. b) File scope. c) Block scope. d) File scope. e) File scope. f) Function-prototype scope.

5.3   See below. [*Note:* On most Linux systems, you must use the -1m option when compiling this program.]

```
1   // ex05_03.c
2   // Testing the math library functions
3   #include <stdio.h>
4   #include <math.h>
5
6   // function main begins program execution
7   int main( void )
8   {
9       // calculates and outputs the square root
10      printf( "sqrt(%.1f) = %.1f\n", 900.0, sqrt( 900.0 ) );
11      printf( "sqrt(%.1f) = %.1f\n", 9.0, sqrt( 9.0 ) );
12
13      // calculates and outputs the exponential function e to the x
14      printf( "exp(%.1f) = %f\n", 1.0, exp( 1.0 ) );
15      printf( "exp(%.1f) = %f\n", 2.0, exp( 2.0 ) );
16
17      // calculates and outputs the logarithm (base e)
18      printf( "log(%f) = %.1f\n", 2.718282, log( 2.718282 ) );
19      printf( "log(%f) = %.1f\n", 7.389056, log( 7.389056 ) );
20
21      // calculates and outputs the logarithm (base 10)
22      printf( "log10(%.1f) = %.1f\n", 1.0, log10( 1.0 ) );
23      printf( "log10(%.1f) = %.1f\n", 10.0, log10( 10.0 ) );
24      printf( "log10(%.1f) = %.1f\n", 100.0, log10( 100.0 ) );
```

```
25
26        // calculates and outputs the absolute value
27        printf( "fabs(%.1f) = %.1f\n", 13.5, fabs( 13.5 ) );
28        printf( "fabs(%.1f) = %.1f\n", 0.0, fabs( 0.0 ) );
29        printf( "fabs(%.1f) = %.1f\n", -13.5, fabs( -13.5 ) );
30
31        // calculates and outputs ceil( x )
32        printf( "ceil(%.1f) = %.1f\n", 9.2, ceil( 9.2 ) );
33        printf( "ceil(%.1f) = %.1f\n", -9.8, ceil( -9.8 ) );
34
35        // calculates and outputs floor( x )
36        printf( "floor(%.1f) = %.1f\n", 9.2, floor( 9.2 ) );
37        printf( "floor(%.1f) = %.1f\n", -9.8, floor( -9.8 ) );
38
39        // calculates and outputs pow( x, y )
40        printf( "pow(%.1f, %.1f) = %.1f\n", 2.0, 7.0, pow( 2.0, 7.0 ) );
41        printf( "pow(%.1f, %.1f) = %.1f\n", 9.0, 0.5, pow( 9.0, 0.5 ) );
42
43        // calculates and outputs fmod( x, y )
44        printf( "fmod(%.3f/%.3f) = %.3f\n", 13.657, 2.333,
45           fmod( 13.657, 2.333 ) );
46
47        // calculates and outputs sin( x )
48        printf( "sin(%.1f) = %.1f\n", 0.0, sin( 0.0 ) );
49
50        // calculates and outputs cos( x )
51        printf( "cos(%.1f) = %.1f\n", 0.0, cos( 0.0 ) );
52
53        // calculates and outputs tan( x )
54        printf( "tan(%.1f) = %.1f\n", 0.0, tan( 0.0 ) );
55     } // end main
```

```
sqrt(900.0) = 30.0
sqrt(9.0) = 3.0
exp(1.0) = 2.718282
exp(2.0) = 7.389056
log(2.718282) = 1.0
log(7.389056) = 2.0
log10(1.0) = 0.0
log10(10.0) = 1.0
log10(100.0) = 2.0
fabs(13.5) = 13.5
fabs(0.0) = 0.0
fabs(-13.5) = 13.5
ceil(9.2) = 10.0
ceil(-9.8) = -9.0
floor(9.2) = 9.0
floor(-9.8) = -10.0
pow(2.0, 7.0) = 128.0
pow(9.0, 0.5) = 3.0
fmod(13.657/2.333) = 2.010
sin(0.0) = 0.0
cos(0.0) = 1.0
tan(0.0) = 0.0
```

5.4   a) `int unique( int a, int n )`
       b) `void compare( float n, float m)`
       c) `double binary( double x, double y, int z)`
       d) `void swap( void )`

5.5   a) `int unique( int a, int n );`
       b) `void compare( float n, float m);`

    c) `double binary( double x, double y, int z);`
    d) `void swap( void );`

5.6 `register int number = 1;`

5.7
    a) Error: Function h is defined in function g.
        Correction: Move the definition of h out of the definition of g.

    b) Error: The body of the function is supposed to return an integer, but does not.
        Correction: Delete variable `result` and place the following statement in the function:

```
return x + y;
```

    c) Error: Semicolon after the right parenthesis that encloses the parameter list, and redefining the parameter a in the function definition.
        Correction: Delete the semicolon after the right parenthesis of the parameter list, and delete the declaration `float a;` in the function body.

    d) Error: The result of `n + sum( n - 1 )` is not returned; sum returns an improper result.
        Correction: Rewrite the statement in the `else` clause as

```
return n + sum( n - 1 );
```

    e) Error: The function returns a value when it's not supposed to.
        Correction: Eliminate the `return` statement.

Exercises

5.8 Show the value of p after each of the following statements is performed:
    a) `p = sqrt( 25.5 );`
    b) `p = cbrt( 82.0 );`
    c) `p = floor( 98.52 );`
    d) `p = exp( 5 );`
    e) `p = pow( 3, 5 );`
    f) `p = fabs( 12.76 );`
    g) `p = abs( -ceil( -15 + sqrt( 16.05 ) ) );`

5.9 *(Baggage Counter Charges)* A baggage counter charges a \$0.50 minimum fee to deposit a bag for up to three hours and an additional \$0.25 per hour for each hour *or part thereof* over three hours. The maximum charge for any given 6-hour period is \$1.00. Assume that no bags are deposited for longer than 6 hours at a time. Write a program that will calculate and print the baggage counter charges for each of five customers who deposited their bags at this counter. You should enter the hours deposited for each customer. Your program should print the results in a tabular format, and should calculate and print the total of all receipts of a day. The program should use the function `calculateCharges` to determine the charge for each customer. Your outputs should appear in the following format:

Customers	Hours	Charge($)
1	1	0.50
2	1.8	0.50
3	2.0	0.50
4	4.0	0.75
5	6.0	1.00
TOTAL	14.8	3.25

5.10 *(Rounding Numbers)* An application of function `floor` is rounding a value to the nearest integer. The statement

```
y = floor( x + .5 );
```

will round the number x to the nearest integer and assign the result to y. Write a program that reads several numbers and uses the preceding statement to round each of these numbers to the nearest integer. For each number processed, print both the original number and the rounded number.

5.11 *(Rounding Numbers)* Function `floor` may be used to round a number to a specific decimal place. The statement

    y = floor(x * 10 + .5) / 10;

rounds x to the tenths position (the first position to the right of the decimal point). The statement

    y = floor(x * 100 + .5) / 100;

rounds x to the hundredths position (the second position to the right of the decimal point). Write a program that defines four functions to round a number x in various ways

- a) `roundToInteger( number )`
- b) `roundToTenths( number )`
- c) `roundToHundreths( number )`
- d) `roundToThousandths( number )`

For each value read, your program should print the original value, the number rounded to the nearest integer, the number rounded to the nearest tenth, the number rounded to the nearest hundredth, and the number rounded to the nearest thousandth.

5.12 Answer each of the following questions.
- a) What does it mean to choose numbers "at random"?
- b) Why is the rand function useful for simulating games of chance?
- c) Why would you randomize a program by using srand? Under what circumstances is it desirable not to randomize?
- d) Why is it often necessary to scale and/or shift the values produced by rand?

5.13 Write statements that assign random integers to the variable *n* in the following ranges:
- a) $1 \leq n \leq 2$
- b) $1 \leq n \leq 100$
- c) $0 \leq n \leq 9$
- d) $1000 \leq n \leq 1112$
- e) $-1 \leq n \leq 1$
- f) $-3 \leq n \leq 11$

5.14 For each of the following sets of integers, write a single statement that will print a number at random from the set.
- a) 6, 12, 18, 24, 30.
- b) 4, 9, 16, 24, 36.
- c) 5, 10, 15, 20, 25.

5.15 *(Area of Ellipse Calculation)* Define a function called `areaOfEllipse` that calculates the area of an ellipse when the other two radiuses are given. The function should take two arguments of type `double` and return the area of the ellipse as a `double`. Test your program with the radius values specified in Fig. 5.22.

Ellipse	Radius 1	Radius 2
1	5.0	7.0
2	19.0	12.0
3	23.0	9.0
4	13.0	10.0
5	4.0	14.0

Fig. 5.22 | Sample Ellipse radiuses values for Exercise 5.15.

5.16 *(Exponentiation)* Write a function integerPower(base, exponent) that returns the value of

baseexponent

For example, integerPower(3, 4) = 3 * 3 * 3 * 3. Assume that exponent is a positive, nonzero integer, and base is an integer. Function integerPower should use for to control the calculation. Do not use any math library functions.

5.17 *(Factors)* Write a function factor that determines for three integers whether the last two integers are factors of the first. The function should take three integer arguments and return 1 (true) if the last two integers are factors of the first, and 0 (false) otherwise.

5.18 *(Uppercase or Lowercase)* Write a program that inputs a series of characters and passes them one at a time to function case, which uses the ASCII values to determine whether the given character is in uppercase or lowercase. The function should take an integer argument and return 1 if the character is uppercase and 0 otherwise.

5.19 *(Rectangle of Hashes)* Write a function that displays a solid rectangle of hashes whose length and breadth are specified in integer parameters length and breadth. For example, if length is 2 and breadth is 4, the function displays:

```
####
####
```

5.20 *(Displaying a Rectangle of any Character)* Modify the function created in Exercise 5.19 to form the rectangle out of whatever character is contained in character parameter fillCharacter. Thus if length is 2, breadth is 4 and fillCharacter is "M", then this function should print:

```
MMMM
MMMM
```

5.21 *(Project: Drawing Shapes with Characters)* Use techniques similar to those developed in Exercises 5.19–5.20 to produce a program that graphs a wide range of shapes.

5.22 *(Separating Digits)* Write program segments that accomplish each of the following:
   a) Calculate the integer part of the quotient when integer a is divided by integer b.
   b) Calculate the integer remainder when integer a is divided by integer b.
   c) Use the program pieces developed in a) and b) to write a function that inputs an integer between 1 and 32767 and prints it as a series of digits,with two spaces between each digit. For example, the integer 4562 should be printed as:

```
4  5  6  2
```

5.23 *(Distance in Meters)* Write a function that takes the distance travelled by a car as two integer arguments (for kilometers and meters) and returns the total distance travelled in meters. Use this function to calculate the total distance travelled (in meters) by three cars.

5.24 *(Temperature Conversions)* Implement the following integer functions:
   a) Function celsius returns the Celsius equivalent of a Fahrenheit temperature.
   b) Function fahrenheit returns the Fahrenheit equivalent of a Celsius temperature.
   c) Use these functions to write a program that prints charts showing the Fahrenheit equivalents of all Celsius temperatures from 0 to 100 degrees, and the Celsius equivalents of

all Fahrenheit temperatures from 32 to 212 degrees. Print the outputs in a tabular format that minimizes the number of lines of output while remaining readable.

5.25 *(Find the Maximum)* Write a function that returns the largest of five floating-point numbers.

5.26 *(Perfect Numbers)* An integer number is said to be a *perfect number* if its factors, including 1 (but not the number itself), sum to the number. For example, 6 is a perfect number because 6 = 1 + 2 + 3. Write a function perfect that determines whether parameter number is a perfect number. Use this function in a program that determines and prints all the perfect numbers between 1 and 1000. Print the factors of each perfect number to confirm that the number is indeed perfect. Challenge the power of your computer by testing numbers much larger than 1000.

5.27 *(Prime Numbers)* An integer is said to be *prime* if it's divisible by only 1 and itself. For example, 2, 3, 5 and 7 are prime, but 4, 6, 8 and 9 are not.

  a) Write a function that determines whether a number is prime.
  b) Use this function in a program that determines and prints all the prime numbers between 1 and 10,000. How many of these 10,000 numbers do you really have to test before being sure that you have found all the primes?
  c) Initially you might think that $n/2$ is the upper limit for which you must test to see whether a number is prime, but you need go only as high as the square root of n. Rewrite the program, and run it both ways. Estimate the performance improvement.

5.28 *(Changing the Case)* Write a function that takes an alphabet and returns the alphabet with its case changed. For example, given the character Z, the function should return z.

5.29 *(Least Common Multiple)* The *least common multiple (LCM)* of two integers is the smallest integer that is a multiple of both the numbers. Write function lcm that returns the least common multiple of two integers..

5.30 *(Quality Points for Student's Grades)* Write a function qualityPoints that inputs a student's average and returns 4 it's 90–100, 3 if it's 80–89, 2 if it's 70–79, 1 if it's 60–69, and 0 if the average is lower than 60.

5.31 *(Coin Tossing)* Write a program that simulates coin tossing. For each toss of the coin the program should print Heads or Tails. Let the program toss the coin 100 times, and count the number of times each side of the coin appears. Print the results. The program should call a separate function flip that takes no arguments and returns 0 for tails and 1 for heads. [*Note:* If the program realistically simulates the coin tossing, then each side of the coin should appear approximately half the time for a total of approximately 50 heads and 50 tails.]

5.32 *(Guess the Alphabet)* Write a C program that plays the game of "guess the alphabet" as follows: Your program chooses the alphabet to be guessed by selecting an alphabet at random in the range A to Z. The program then types:

```
I have selected a character between A and Z
Try to guess the character selected by me!
What is your guess?
```

The player then types a first guess. The program responds with one of the following:

```
1. Great! Your guess is right!
2. Way ahead! Please try again.
3. Way behind! Please try again.
```

If the player's guess is incorrect, your program should loop until the player finally gets the character right. Your program should keep telling the player Way ahead or Way behind till the player guesses the correct answer. [*Note:* The searching technique employed in this problem is called binary search. We'll say more about this in the next problem.]

5.33 *(Guess the Alphabet Modification)* Modify the program of Exercise 5.32 to count the number of guesses the player makes. If the number is 5 or fewer, print Either you know the secret or you are lucky! If the player guesses the number in 5 tries, then print I guess you know the secret! If the player makes more than 5 guesses, then print You should be able to do better! Why should it take no more than 5 guesses? Show why any character between A to Z can be guessed in 5 or fewer tries.

5.34 *(Recursive Exponentiation)* Write a recursive function power(base, exponent) that when invoked returns

$$\text{base}^{\text{exponent}}$$

For example, power(3, 4) = 3 * 3 * 3 * 3. Assume that exponent is an integer greater than or equal to 1. *Hint:* The recursion step would use the relationship

$$\text{base}^{\text{exponent}} = \text{base} * \text{base}^{\text{exponent}-1}$$

and the terminating condition occurs when exponent is equal to 1 because

$$\text{base}^1 = \text{base}$$

5.35 *(Fibonacci)* The Fibonacci series

0, 1, 1, 2, 3, 5, 8, 13, 21, ...

begins with the terms 0 and 1 and has the property that each succeeding term is the sum of the two preceding terms. a) Write a *nonrecursive* function fibonacci(n) that calculates the nth Fibonacci number. Use unsigned int for the function's parameter and unsigned long long int for its return type. b) Determine the largest Fibonacci number that can be printed on your system.

5.36 *(Towers of Hanoi)* Every budding computer scientist must grapple with certain classic problems, and the Towers of Hanoi (see Fig. 5.23) is one of the most famous of these. Legend has it that in a temple in the Far East, priests are attempting to move a stack of disks from one peg to another. The initial stack had 64 disks threaded onto one peg and arranged from bottom to top by decreasing size. The priests are attempting to move the stack from this peg to a second peg under the constraints that exactly one disk is moved at a time, and at no time may a larger disk be placed

Fig. 5.23 | Towers of Hanoi for the case with four disks.

above a smaller disk. A third peg is available for temporarily holding the disks. Supposedly the world will end when the priests complete their task, so there's little incentive for us to facilitate their efforts.

Let's assume that the priests are attempting to move the disks from peg 1 to peg 3. We wish to develop an algorithm that will print the precise sequence of disk-to-disk peg transfers.

If we were to approach this problem with conventional methods, we'd rapidly find ourselves hopelessly knotted up in managing the disks. Instead, if we attack the problem with recursion in mind, it immediately becomes tractable. Moving n disks can be viewed in terms of moving only $n - 1$ disks (and hence the recursion) as follows:

a) Move $n - 1$ disks from peg 1 to peg 2, using peg 3 as a temporary holding area.
b) Move the last disk (the largest) from peg 1 to peg 3.
c) Move the $n - 1$ disks from peg 2 to peg 3, using peg 1 as a temporary holding area.

The process ends when the last task involves moving $n = 1$ disk, i.e., the base case. This is accomplished by trivially moving the disk without the need for a temporary holding area.

Write a program to solve the Towers of Hanoi problem. Use a recursive function with four parameters:

a) The number of disks to be moved
b) The peg on which these disks are initially threaded
c) The peg to which this stack of disks is to be moved
d) The peg to be used as a temporary holding area

Your program should print the precise instructions it will take to move the disks from the starting peg to the destination peg. For example, to move a stack of three disks from peg 1 to peg 3, your program should print the following series of moves:

1 → 3 (This means move one disk from peg 1 to peg 3.)
1 → 2
3 → 2
1 → 3
2 → 1
2 → 3
1 → 3

5.37 *(Towers of Hanoi: Iterative Solution)* Any program that can be implemented recursively can be implemented iteratively, although sometimes with considerably more difficulty and considerably less clarity. Try writing an iterative version of the Towers of Hanoi. If you succeed, compare your iterative version with the recursive version you developed in Exercise 5.36. Investigate issues of performance, clarity, and your ability to demonstrate the correctness of the programs.

5.38 *(Visualizing Recursion)* It's interesting to watch recursion "in action." Modify the factorial function of Fig. 5.18 to print its local variable and recursive call parameter. For each recursive call, display the outputs on a separate line and add a level of indentation. Do your utmost to make the outputs clear, interesting and meaningful. Your goal here is to design and implement an output format that helps a person understand recursion better. You may want to add such display capabilities to the many other recursion examples and exercises throughout the text.

5.39 *(Recursive Greatest Common Divisor)* The greatest common divisor of integers x and y is the largest integer that evenly divides both x and y. Write a recursive function gcd that returns the greatest common divisor of x and y. The gcd of x and y is defined recursively as follows: If y is equal to 0, then gcd(x, y) is x; otherwise gcd(x, y) is gcd(y, x % y), where % is the remainder operator.

5.40 *(Recursive main)* Can main be called recursively? Write a program containing a function main. Include static local variable count initialized to 1. Postincrement and print the value of count each time main is called. Run your program. What happens?

5.41   *(Distance Between Points)* Write a function `distance` that calculates the distance between two points *(x1, y1)* and *(x2, y2)*. All numbers and return values should be of type `double`.

5.42   What does the following program do?

```
1   #include <stdio.h>
2
3   // function main begins program execution
4   int main( void )
5   {
6      int c; // variable to hold character input by user
7
8      if ( ( c = getchar() ) != EOF ) {
9         main();
10        printf( "%c", c );
11     } // end if
12  } // end main
```

5.43   What does the following program do?

```
1   #include <stdio.h>
2
3   unsigned int mystery( unsigned int a, unsigned int b ); // function prototype
4
5   // function main begins program execution
6   int main( void )
7   {
8      unsigned int x; // first integer
9      unsigned int y; // second integer
10
11     printf( "%s", "Enter two positive integers: " );
12     scanf( "%u%u", &x, &y );
13
14     printf( "The result is %u\n", mystery( x, y ) );
15  } // end main
16
17  // Parameter b must be a positive integer
18  // to prevent infinite recursion
19  unsigned int mystery( unsigned int a, unsigned int b )
20  {
21     // base case
22     if ( 1 == b ) {
23        return a;
24     } // end if
25     else { // recursive step
26        return a + mystery( a, b - 1 );
27     } // end else
28  } // end function mystery
```

5.44   After you determine what the program of Exercise 5.43 does, modify the program to function properly after removing the restriction of the second argument's being nonnegative.

5.45   *(Testing Math Library Functions)* Write a program that tests the math library functions in Fig. 5.2. Exercise each of these functions by having your program print out tables of return values for a diversity of argument values.

5.46 Find the error in each of the following program segments and explain how to correct it:

a)
```
double cube( float ); // function prototype
cube( float number ) // function definition
{
    return number * number * number;
}
```

b)
```
int randomNumber = srand();
```

c)
```
double y = 123.45678;
int x;
x = y;
printf( "%f\n", (double) x );
```

d)
```
double square( double number )
{
    double number;
    return number * number;
}
```

e)
```
int sum( int n )
{
    if ( 0 == n ) {
        return 0;
    }
    else {
        return n + sum( n );
    }
}
```

5.47 *(Craps Game Modification)* Modify the craps program of Fig. 5.14 to allow *wagering*. Package as a function the portion of the program that runs one game of craps. Initialize variable bankBalance to 1000 dollars. Prompt the player to enter a wager. Use a while loop to check that wager is less than or equal to bankBalance, and if not, prompt the user to reenter wager until a valid wager is entered. After a correct wager is entered, run one game of craps. If the player wins, increase bankBalance by wager and print the new bankBalance. If the player loses, decrease bankBalance by wager, print the new bankBalance, check whether bankBalance has become zero, and if so print the message, "Sorry. You busted!" As the game progresses, print various messages to create some "chatter" such as, "Oh, you're going for broke, huh?" or "Aw cmon, take a chance!" or "You're up big. Now's the time to cash in your chips!"

5.48 *(Research Project: Improving the Recursive Fibonacci Implementation)* In Section 5.15, the recursive algorithm we used to calculate Fibonacci numbers was intuitively appealing. However, recall that the algorithm resulted in the exponential explosion of recursive function calls. Research the recursive Fibonacci implementation online. Study the various approaches, including the iterative version in Exercise 5.35 and versions that use only so-called "tail recursion." Discuss the relative merits of each.

Making a Difference

5.49 *(Global Warming Facts Quiz)* The controversial issue of global warming has been widely publicized by the film *An Inconvenient Truth*, featuring former Vice President Al Gore. Mr. Gore and a U.N. network of scientists, the Intergovernmental Panel on Climate Change, shared the 2007 Nobel Peace Prize in recognition of "their efforts to build up and disseminate greater knowledge about man-made climate change." Research *both* sides of the global warming issue online (you might want to search for phrases like "global warming skeptics"). Create a five-question multiple-choice quiz on global warming, each question having four possible answers (numbered 1–4). Be objective and try to fairly represent both sides of the issue. Next, write an application that administers the quiz, calculates the number of correct answers (zero through five) and returns a message to the user. If the user correctly answers five questions, print "Excellent"; if four, print "Very good"; if three or fewer, print "Time to brush up on your knowledge of global warming," and include a list of some of the websites where you found your facts.

Computer-Assisted Instruction

As computer costs decline, it becomes feasible for every student, regardless of economic circumstance, to have a computer and use it in school. This creates exciting possibilities for improving the educational experience of all students worldwide as suggested by the next five exercises. [*Note:* Check out initiatives such as the One Laptop Per Child Project (www.laptop.org). Also, research "green" laptops—what are some key "going green" characteristics of these devices? Look into the Electronic Product Environmental Assessment Tool (www.epeat.net) which can help you assess the "greenness" of desktops, notebooks and monitors to help you decide which products to purchase.]

5.50 *(Computer-Assisted Instruction)* The use of computers in education is referred to as *computer-assisted instruction* (*CAI*). Write a program that will help an elementary school student learn multiplication. Use the rand function to produce two positive one-digit integers. The program should then prompt the user with a question, such as

```
How much is 6 times 7?
```

The student then inputs the answer. Next, the program checks the student's answer. If it's correct, display the message "Very good!" and ask another multiplication question. If the answer is wrong, display the message "No. Please try again." and let the student try the same question repeatedly until the student finally gets it right. A separate function should be used to generate each new question. This function should be called once when the application begins execution and each time the user answers the question correctly.

5.51 *(Computer-Assisted Instruction: Reducing Student Fatigue)* One problem in CAI environments is student fatigue. This can be reduced by varying the computer's responses to hold the student's attention. Modify the program of Exercise 5.50 so that various comments are displayed for each answer as follows:

Possible responses to a correct answer:

```
Very good!
Excellent!
Nice work!
Keep up the good work!
```

Possible responses to an incorrect answer:

```
No. Please try again.
Wrong. Try once more.
Don't give up!
No. Keep trying.
```

Use random-number generation to choose a number from 1 to 4 that will be used to select one of the four appropriate responses to each correct or incorrect answer. Use a switch statement to issue the responses.

5.52 *(Computer-Assisted Instruction: Monitoring Student Performance)* More sophisticated computer-assisted instruction systems monitor the student's performance over a period of time. The decision to begin a new topic is often based on the student's success with previous topics. Modify the program of Exercise 5.51 to count the number of correct and incorrect responses typed by the student. After the student types 10 answers, your program should calculate the percentage that are correct. If the percentage is lower than 75%, display "Please ask your teacher for extra help.", then reset the program so another student can try it. If the percentage is 75% or higher, display "Congratulations, you are ready to go to the next level!", then reset the program so another student can try it.

5.53 *(Computer-Assisted Instruction: Difficulty Levels)* Exercises 5.50– through Exercise 5.52 developed a computer-assisted instruction program to help teach an elementary-school student multiplication. Modify the program to allow the user to enter a difficulty level. At a difficulty level of 1, the program should use only single-digit numbers in the problems; at a difficulty level of 2, numbers as large as two digits, and so on.

5.54 *(Computer-Assisted Instruction: Varying the Types of Problems)* Modify the program of Exercise 5.53 to allow the user to pick a type of arithmetic problem to study. An option of 1 means addition problems only, 2 means subtraction problems only, 3 means multiplication problems only and 4 means a random mixture of all these types.

6

C Arrays

*Now go, write it
before them in a table,
and note it in a book.*
—Isaiah 30:8

*To go beyond is as
wrong as to fall short.*
—Confucius

*Begin at the beginning, … and
go on till you come to the end:
then stop.*
—Lewis Carroll

Objectives

In this chapter, you'll learn:

- To use the array data structure to represent lists and tables of values.

- To define an array, initialize an array and refer to individual elements of an array.

- To define symbolic constants.

- To pass arrays to functions.

- To use arrays to store, sort and search lists and tables of values.

- To define and manipulate multidimensional arrays.

6.1 Introduction

This chapter serves as an introduction to data structures. Arrays are data structures consisting of related data items of the same type. In Chapter 10, we discuss C's notion of struct (structure)—a data structure consisting of related data items of possibly different types. Arrays and structures are "static" entities in that they remain the same size throughout program execution (they may, of course, be of automatic storage class and hence created and destroyed each time the blocks in which they're defined are entered and exited).

6.2 Arrays

An array is a group of *contiguous* memory locations that all have the *same type*. To refer to a particular location or element in the array, we specify the array's name and the position number of the particular element in the array.

Figure 6.1 shows an integer array called c, containing 12 elements. Any one of these elements may be referred to by giving the array's name followed by the *position number* of the particular element in square brackets ([]). The first element in every array is the zeroth element. An array name, like other variable names, can contain only letters, digits and underscores and cannot begin with a digit.

c[0]	-45
c[1]	6
c[2]	0
c[3]	72
c[4]	1543
c[5]	-89
c[6]	0
c[7]	62
c[8]	-3
c[9]	1
c[10]	6453
c[11]	78

All elements of this array share the array name, c

Position number of the element within array c

Fig. 6.1 | 12-element array.

The position number within square brackets is called a **subscript**. A subscript must be an integer or an integer expression. For example, if a = 5 and b = 6, then the statement

```
c[ a + b ] += 2;
```

adds 2 to array element c[11]. A subscripted array name is an *lvalue*—it can be used on the left side of an assignment.

Let's examine array c (Fig. 6.1) more closely. The array's name is c. Its 12 elements are referred to as c[0], c[1], c[2], ..., c[10] and c[11]. The value stored in c[0] is -45, the value of c[1] is 6, c[2] is 0, c[7] is 62 and c[11] is 78. To print the sum of the values contained in the first three elements of array c, we'd write

```
printf( "%d", c[ 0 ] + c[ 1 ] + c[ 2 ] );
```

To divide the value of element 6 of array c by 2 and assign the result to the variable x, write

```
x = c[ 6 ] / 2;
```

The brackets used to enclose the subscript of an array are actually considered to be an *operator* in C. They have the same level of precedence as the *function call operator* (i.e., the parentheses that are placed after a function name to call that function). Figure 6.2 shows the precedence and associativity of the operators introduced to this point in the text.

Operators	Associativity	Type
[] () ++ *(postfix)* -- *(postfix)*	left to right	highest
+ - ! ++ *(prefix)* -- *(prefix)* *(type)*	right to left	unary
* / %	left to right	multiplicative
+ -	left to right	additive
< <= > >=	left to right	relational
== !=	left to right	equality
&&	left to right	logical AND
||	left to right	logical OR
?:	right to left	conditional
= += -= *= /= %=	right to left	assignment
,	left to right	comma

Fig. 6.2 | Operator precedence and associativity.

6.3 Defining Arrays

Arrays occupy space in memory. You specify the type of each element and the number of elements each array requires so that the computer may reserve the appropriate amount of memory. The following definition reserves 12 elements for integer array c, which has subscripts in the range 0–11.

```
int c[ 12 ];
```

The definition

```
int b[ 100 ], x[ 27 ];
```

reserves 100 elements for integer array b and 27 elements for integer array x. These arrays have subscripts in the ranges 0–99 and 0–26, respectively.

Arrays may contain other data types. For example, an array of type char can store a character string. Character strings and their similarity to arrays are discussed in Chapter 8. The relationship between pointers and arrays is discussed in Chapter 7.

6.4 Array Examples

This section presents several examples that demonstrate how to define and initialize arrays, and how to perform many common array manipulations.

Defining an Array and Using a Loop to Initialize the Array's Elements

Like any other variables, uninitialized array elements contain garbage values. Figure 6.3 uses for statements to initialize the elements of a 10-element integer array n to zeros and print the array in tabular format. The first printf statement (line 16) displays the column heads for the two columns printed in the subsequent for statement.

Notice that the variable i is declared to be of type size_t (line 9), which according to the C standard represents an unsigned integral type. This type is recommended for any variable that represents an array's size or an array's subscripts. Type size_t is defined in header <stddef.h>, which is often included by other headers (such as <stdio.h>). [*Note:* If you attempt to compile Fig. 6.3 and receive errors, simply include <stddef.h> in your program.]

```
 1   // Fig. 6.3: fig06_03.c
 2   // Initializing the elements of an array to zeros.
 3   #include <stdio.h>
 4
 5   // function main begins program execution
 6   int main( void )
 7   {
 8      int n[ 10 ]; // n is an array of 10 integers
 9      size_t i; // counter
10
11      // initialize elements of array n to 0
12      for ( i = 0; i < 10; ++i ) {
13         n[ i ] = 0; // set element at location i to 0
14      } // end for
15
16      printf( "%s%13s\n", "Element", "Value" );
17
18      // output contents of array n in tabular format
19      for ( i = 0; i < 10; ++i ) {
20         printf( "%7u%13d\n", i, n[ i ] );
21      } // end for
22   } // end main
```

Fig. 6.3 | Initializing the elements of an array to zeros. (Part 1 of 2.)

Element	Value
0	0
1	0
2	0
3	0
4	0
5	0
6	0
7	0
8	0
9	0

Fig. 6.3 | Initializing the elements of an array to zeros. (Part 2 of 2.)

Initializing an Array in a Definition with an Initializer List

The elements of an array can also be initialized when the array is defined by following the definition with an equals sign and braces, {}, containing a comma-separated list of array initializers. Figure 6.4 initializes an integer array with 10 values (line 9) and prints the array in tabular format.

```
1   // Fig. 6.4: fig06_04.c
2   // Initializing the elements of an array with an initializer list.
3   #include <stdio.h>
4
5   // function main begins program execution
6   int main( void )
7   {
8      // use initializer list to initialize array n
9      int n[ 10 ] = { 32, 27, 64, 18, 95, 14, 90, 70, 60, 37 };
10     size_t i; // counter
11
12     printf( "%s%13s\n", "Element", "Value" );
13
14     // output contents of array in tabular format
15     for ( i = 0; i < 10; ++i ) {
16        printf( "%7u%13d\n", i, n[ i ] );
17     } // end for
18  } // end main
```

Element	Value
0	32
1	27
2	64
3	18
4	95
5	14
6	90
7	70
8	60
9	37

Fig. 6.4 | Initializing the elements of an array with an initializer list.

If there are *fewer* initializers than elements in the array, the remaining elements are initialized to zero. For example, the elements of the array n in Fig. 6.3 could have been initialized to zero as follows:

```
int n[ 10 ] = { 0 }; // initializes entire array to zeros
```

This *explicitly* initializes the first element to zero and initializes the remaining nine elements to zero because there are fewer initializers than there are elements in the array. It's important to remember that arrays are *not* automatically initialized to zero. You must at least initialize the first element to zero for the remaining elements to be automatically zeroed. Array elements are initialized before program startup for `static` arrays and at runtime for *automatic* arrays.

Common Programming Error 6.1
Forgetting to initialize the elements of an array.

The array definition

```
int n[ 5 ] = { 32, 27, 64, 18, 95, 14 };
```

causes a syntax error because there are six initializers and *only* five array elements.

Common Programming Error 6.2
Providing more initializers in an array initializer list than there are elements in the array is a syntax error.

If the array size is *omitted* from a definition with an initializer list, the number of elements in the array will be the number of elements in the initializer list. For example,

```
int n[] = { 1, 2, 3, 4, 5 };
```

would create a five-element array initialized with the indicated values.

Specifying an Array's Size with a Symbolic Constant and Initializing Array Elements with Calculations

Figure 6.5 initializes the elements of a 10-element array s to the values 2, 4, 6, ..., 20 and prints the array in tabular format. The values are generated by multiplying the loop counter by 2 and adding 2.

```
1   // Fig. 6.5: fig06_05.c
2   // Initializing the elements of array s to the even integers from 2 to 20.
3   #include <stdio.h>
4   #define SIZE 10 // maximum size of array
5
6   // function main begins program execution
7   int main( void )
8   {
9      // symbolic constant SIZE can be used to specify array size
10     int s[ SIZE ]; // array s has SIZE elements
11     size_t j; // counter
```

Fig. 6.5 | Initialize the elements of array s to the even integers from 2 to 20. (Part 1 of 2.)

```
12
13      for ( j = 0; j < SIZE; ++j ) { // set the values
14         s[ j ] = 2 + 2 * j;
15      } // end for
16
17      printf( "%s%13s\n", "Element", "Value" );
18
19      // output contents of array s in tabular format
20      for ( j = 0; j < SIZE; ++j ) {
21         printf( "%7u%13d\n", j, s[ j ] );
22      } // end for
23   } // end main
```

```
Element        Value
     0             2
     1             4
     2             6
     3             8
     4            10
     5            12
     6            14
     7            16
     8            18
     9            20
```

Fig. 6.5 | Initialize the elements of array s to the even integers from 2 to 20. (Part 2 of 2.)

The **#define** preprocessor directive is introduced in this program. Line 4

```
#define SIZE 10
```

defines a symbolic constant SIZE whose value is 10. A symbolic constant is an identifier that's replaced with replacement text by the C preprocessor before the program is compiled. When the program is preprocessed, all occurrences of the symbolic constant SIZE are replaced with the replacement text 10. Using symbolic constants to specify array sizes makes programs more scalable. In Fig. 6.5, we could have the first for loop (line 13) fill a 1000-element array by simply changing the value of SIZE in the #define directive from 10 to 1000. If the symbolic constant SIZE had not been used, we'd have to change the program in *three* separate places. As programs get larger, this technique becomes more useful for writing clear, maintainable programs.

Common Programming Error 6.3

Ending a #define or #include preprocessor directive with a semicolon. Remember that preprocessor directives are not *C statements.*

If the #define preprocessor directive in line 4 is terminated with a semicolon, the preprocessor replaces all occurrences of the symbolic constant SIZE in the program with the text 10;. This may lead to syntax errors at compile time, or logic errors at execution time. Remember that the preprocessor is *not* the C compiler.

Software Engineering Observation 6.1

Defining the size of each array as a symbolic constant makes programs more scalable.

Common Programming Error 6.4

Assigning a value to a symbolic constant in an executable statement is a syntax error. A symbolic constant is not a variable. The compiler does not reserve space for symbolic constants as it does for variables that hold values at execution time.

Good Programming Practice 6.1

Use only uppercase letters for symbolic constant names. This makes these constants stand out in a program and reminds you that symbolic constants are not *variables.*

Good Programming Practice 6.2

In multiword symbolic constant names, separate the words with underscores for readability.

Summing the Elements of an Array

Figure 6.6 sums the values contained in the 12-element integer array a. The for statement's body (line 16) does the totaling.

```c
1   // Fig. 6.6: fig06_06.c
2   // Computing the sum of the elements of an array.
3   #include <stdio.h>
4   #define SIZE 12
5
6   // function main begins program execution
7   int main( void )
8   {
9      // use an initializer list to initialize the array
10     int a[ SIZE ] = { 1, 3, 5, 4, 7, 2, 99, 16, 45, 67, 89, 45 };
11     size_t i; // counter
12     int total = 0; // sum of array
13
14     // sum contents of array a
15     for ( i = 0; i < SIZE; ++i ) {
16        total += a[ i ];
17     } // end for
18
19     printf( "Total of array element values is %d\n", total );
20  } // end main
```

```
Total of array element values is 383
```

Fig. 6.6 | Computing the sum of the elements of an array.

Using Arrays to Summarize Survey Results

Our next example uses arrays to summarize the results of data collected in a survey. Consider the problem statement.

Forty students were asked to rate the quality of the food in the student cafeteria on a scale of 1 to 10 (1 means awful and 10 means excellent). Place the 40 responses in an integer array and summarize the results of the poll.

This is a typical array application (see Fig. 6.7). We wish to summarize the number of responses of each type (i.e., 1 through 10). The array `responses` (line 17) is a 40-element array of the students' responses. We use an 11-element array `frequency` (line 14) to count the number of occurrences of each response. We ignore `frequency[0]` because it's logical to have response 1 increment `frequency[1]` rather than `frequency[0]`. This allows us to use each response directly as the subscript in the `frequency` array.

Good Programming Practice 6.3

Strive for program clarity. Sometimes it may be worthwhile to trade off the most efficient use of memory or processor time in favor of writing clearer programs.

Performance Tip 6.1

Sometimes performance considerations far outweigh clarity considerations.

```c
1   // Fig. 6.7: fig06_07.c
2   // Analyzing a student poll.
3   #include <stdio.h>
4   #define RESPONSES_SIZE 40 // define array sizes
5   #define FREQUENCY_SIZE 11
6
7   // function main begins program execution
8   int main( void )
9   {
10     size_t answer; // counter to loop through 40 responses
11     size_t rating; // counter to loop through frequencies 1-10
12
13     // initialize frequency counters to 0
14     int frequency[ FREQUENCY_SIZE ] = { 0 };
15
16     // place the survey responses in the responses array
17     int responses[ RESPONSES_SIZE ] = { 1, 2, 6, 4, 8, 5, 9, 7, 8, 10,
18        1, 6, 3, 8, 6, 10, 3, 8, 2, 7, 6, 5, 7, 6, 8, 6, 7, 5, 6, 6,
19        5, 6, 7, 5, 6, 4, 8, 6, 8, 10 };
20
21     // for each answer, select value of an element of array responses
22     // and use that value as subscript in array frequency to
23     // determine element to increment
24     for ( answer = 0; answer < RESPONSES_SIZE; ++answer ) {
25        ++frequency[ responses [ answer ] ];
26     } // end for
27
28     // display results
29     printf( "%s%17s\n", "Rating", "Frequency" );
30
31     // output the frequencies in a tabular format
32     for ( rating = 1; rating < FREQUENCY_SIZE; ++rating ) {
33        printf( "%6d%17d\n", rating, frequency[ rating ] );
34     } // end for
35  } // end main
```

Fig. 6.7 | Analyzing a student poll. (Part 1 of 2.)

```
Rating        Frequency
  1               2
  2               2
  3               2
  4               2
  5               5
  6              11
  7               5
  8               7
  9               1
 10               3
```

Fig. 6.7 | Analyzing a student poll. (Part 2 of 2.)

The for loop (line 24) takes the responses one at a time from the array responses and increments one of the 10 counters (frequency[1] to frequency[10]) in the frequency array. The key statement in the loop is line 25

```
++frequency[ responses[ answer ] ];
```

which increments the appropriate frequency counter depending on the value of responses[answer]. When the counter variable answer is 0, responses[answer] is 1, so ++frequency[responses[answer]]; is interpreted as

```
++frequency[ 1 ];
```

which increments array element one. When answer is 1, responses[answer] is 2, so ++frequency[responses[answer]]; is interpreted as

```
++frequency[ 2 ];
```

which increments array element two. When answer is 2, responses[answer] is 6, so ++frequency[responses[answer]]; is interpreted as

```
++frequency[ 6 ];
```

which increments array element six, and so on. Regardless of the number of responses processed in the survey, only an 11-element array is required (ignoring element zero) to summarize the results. If the data contained invalid values such as 13, the program would attempt to add 1 to frequency[13]. This would be outside the bounds of the array. *C has no array bounds checking to prevent the program from referring to an element that does not exist.* Thus, an executing program can "walk off" either end of an array without warning—a security problem that we discuss in Section 6.11. You should ensure that all array references remain within the bounds of the array.

Common Programming Error 6.5
Referring to an element outside the array bounds.

Error-Prevention Tip 6.1
When looping through an array, the array subscript should never go below 0 and should always be less than the total number of elements in the array (size − 1). Make sure the loop-terminating condition prevents accessing elements outside this range.

> **Error-Prevention Tip 6.2**
> *Programs should validate the correctness of all input values to prevent erroneous information from affecting a program's calculations.*

Graphing Array Element Values with Histograms

Our next example (Fig. 6.8) reads numbers from an array and graphs the information in the form of a bar chart or histogram—each number is printed, then a bar consisting of that many asterisks is printed beside the number. The nested for statement (line 20) draws the bars. Note the use of puts("") to end each histogram bar (line 24).

```c
1   // Fig. 6.8: fig06_08.c
2   // Displaying a histogram.
3   #include <stdio.h>
4   #define SIZE 10
5
6   // function main begins program execution
7   int main( void )
8   {
9      // use initializer list to initialize array n
10     int n[ SIZE ] = { 19, 3, 15, 7, 11, 9, 13, 5, 17, 1 };
11     size_t i; // outer for counter for array elements
12     int j; // inner for counter counts *s in each histogram bar
13
14     printf( "%s%13s%17s\n", "Element", "Value", "Histogram" );
15
16     // for each element of array n, output a bar of the histogram
17     for ( i = 0; i < SIZE; ++i ) {
18        printf( "%7u%13d        ", i, n[ i ]) ;
19
20        for ( j = 1; j <= n[ i ]; ++j ) { // print one bar
21           printf( "%c", '*' );
22        } // end inner for
23
24        puts( "" ); // end a histogram bar
25     } // end outer for
26  } // end main
```

```
Element        Value        Histogram
      0           19        ********************
      1            3        ***
      2           15        ***************
      3            7        *******
      4           11        ***********
      5            9        *********
      6           13        *************
      7            5        *****
      8           17        *****************
      9            1        *
```

Fig. 6.8 | Displaying a histogram.

Rolling a Die 6,000,000 Times and Summarizing the Results in an Array
In Chapter 5, we stated that we'd show a more elegant method of writing the dice-rolling program of Fig. 5.12. The problem was to roll a single six-sided die 6,000,000 times to test whether the random number generator actually produces random numbers. An array version of this program is shown in Fig. 6.9.

```c
1   // Fig. 6.9: fig06_09.c
2   // Roll a six-sided die 6,000,000 times
3   #include <stdio.h>
4   #include <stdlib.h>
5   #include <time.h>
6   #define SIZE 7
7
8   // function main begins program execution
9   int main( void )
10  {
11     size_t face; // random die value 1 - 6
12     unsigned int roll; // roll counter 1-6,000,000
13     unsigned int frequency[ SIZE ] = { 0 }; // clear counts
14
15     srand( time( NULL ) ); // seed random number generator
16
17     // roll die 6,000,000 times
18     for ( roll = 1; roll <= 6000000; ++roll ) {
19        face = 1 + rand() % 6;
20        ++frequency[ face ]; // replaces entire switch of Fig. 5.8
21     } // end for
22
23     printf( "%s%17s\n", "Face", "Frequency" );
24
25     // output frequency elements 1-6 in tabular format
26     for ( face = 1; face < SIZE; ++face ) {
27        printf( "%4d%17d\n", face, frequency[ face ] );
28     } // end for
29  } // end main
```

Face	Frequency
1	999753
2	1000773
3	999600
4	999786
5	1000552
6	999536

Fig. 6.9 | Roll a six-sided die 6,000,000 times.

Using Character Arrays to Store and Manipulate Strings
We've discussed only integer arrays. However, arrays are capable of holding data of *any* type. We now discuss storing *strings* in character arrays. So far, the only string-processing capability we have is outputting a string with printf. A string such as "hello" is really an array of individual characters in C.

Character arrays have several unique features. A character array can be initialized using a string literal. For example,

```
char string1[] = "first";
```

initializes the elements of array string1 to the individual characters in the string literal "first". In this case, the size of array string1 is determined by the compiler based on the length of the string. The string "first" contains five characters *plus* a special *string-termination character* called the **null character**. Thus, array string1 actually contains *six* elements. The character constant representing the null character is '\0'. All strings in C end with this character. A character array representing a string should always be defined large enough to hold the number of characters in the string and the terminating null character.

Character arrays also can be initialized with individual character constants in an initializer list, but this can be tedious. The preceding definition is equivalent to

```
char string1[] = { 'f', 'i', 'r', 's', 't', '\0' };
```

Because a string is really an array of characters, we can access individual characters in a string directly using array subscript notation. For example, string1[0] is the character 'f' and string1[3] is the character 's'.

We also can input a string directly into a character array from the keyboard using scanf and the conversion specifier %s. For example,

```
char string2[ 20 ];
```

creates a character array capable of storing a string of *at most 19 characters* and a *terminating null character*. The statement

```
scanf( "%19s", string2 );
```

reads a string from the keyboard into string2. The name of the array is passed to scanf without the preceding & used with nonstring variables. The & is normally used to provide scanf with a variable's *location* in memory so that a value can be stored there. In Section 6.5, when we discuss passing arrays to functions, we'll see that the value of an array name *is the address of the start of the array*; therefore, the & is not necessary. Function scanf will read characters until a *space, tab, newline* or *end-of-file indicator* is encountered. The string string2 should be no longer than 19 characters to leave room for the terminating null character. If the user types 20 or more characters, your program may crash or create a security vulnerability. For this reason, we used the conversion specifier %19s so that scanf reads a maximum of 19 characters and does not write characters into memory beyond the end of the array string2.

It's your responsibility to ensure that the array into which the string is read is capable of holding any string that the user types at the keyboard. Function scanf does *not* check how large the array is. Thus, scanf can write beyond the end of the array.

A character array representing a string can be output with printf and the %s conversion specifier. The array string2 is printed with the statement

```
printf( "%s\n", string2 );
```

Function printf, like scanf, does *not* check how large the character array is. The characters of the string are printed until a terminating null character is encountered. [Consider what would print if, for some reason, the terminating null character were missing.]

Figure 6.10 demonstrates initializing a character array with a string literal, reading a string into a character array, printing a character array as a string and accessing individual characters of a string. The program uses a for statement (line 23) to loop through the string1 array and print the individual characters separated by spaces, using the %c conversion specifier. The condition in the for statement is true while the counter is less than the size of the array and the terminating null character has *not* been encountered in the string. In this program, we read only strings that do not contain whitespace characters. We'll show how to read strings with whitespace characters in Chapter 8. Notice that lines 18–19 contain two string literals separated only by whitespace. The compiler automatically combines such string literals into one—this is helpful for making long string literals more readable.

```c
1  // Fig. 6.10: fig06_10.c
2  // Treating character arrays as strings.
3  #include <stdio.h>
4  #define SIZE 20
5
6  // function main begins program execution
7  int main( void )
8  {
9     char string1[ SIZE ]; // reserves 20 characters
10    char string2[] = "string literal"; // reserves 15 characters
11    size_t i; // counter
12
13    // read string from user into array string1
14    printf( "%s", "Enter a string (no longer than 19 characters): " );
15    scanf( "%19s", string1 ); // input no more than 19 characters
16
17    // output strings
18    printf( "string1 is: %s\nstring2 is: %s\n"
19            "string1 with spaces between characters is:\n",
20            string1, string2 );
21
22    // output characters until null character is reached
23    for ( i = 0; i < SIZE && string1[ i ] != '\0'; ++i ) {
24       printf( "%c ", string1[ i ] );
25    } // end for
26
27    puts( "" );
28 } // end main
```

```
Enter a string (no longer than 19 characters): Hello there
string1 is: Hello
string2 is: string literal
string1 with spaces between characters is:
H e l l o
```

Fig. 6.10 | Treating character arrays as strings.

Static Local Arrays and Automatic Local Arrays

Chapter 5 discussed the storage-class specifier static. A static local variable exists for the *duration* of the program but is *visible* only in the function body. We can apply static to a local array definition so the array is *not* created and initialized each time the function is called and the array is *not* destroyed each time the function is exited in the program. This reduces program execution time, particularly for programs with frequently called functions that contain large arrays.

Performance Tip 6.2

In functions that contain automatic arrays where the function is in and out of scope frequently, make the array static *so it's not created each time the function is called.*

Arrays that are static are initialized once at program startup. If you do not explicitly initialize a static array, that array's elements are initialized to *zero* by default.

Figure 6.11 demonstrates function staticArrayInit (lines 21–40) with a local static array (line 24) and function automaticArrayInit (lines 43–62) with a local automatic array (line 46). Function staticArrayInit is called twice (lines 12 and 16). The local static array in the function is initialized to zero before program startup (line 24). The function prints the array, adds 5 to each element and prints the array again. The second time the function is called, the static array contains the values stored during the first function call.

Function automaticArrayInit is also called twice (lines 13 and 17). The elements of the automatic local array in the function are initialized with the values 1, 2 and 3 (line 46). The function prints the array, adds 5 to each element and prints the array again. The second time the function is called, the array elements are initialized to 1, 2 and 3 again because the array has automatic storage duration.

Common Programming Error 6.6

Assuming that elements of a local static *array are initialized to zero every time the function in which the array is defined is called.*

```
1   // Fig. 6.11: fig06_11.c
2   // Static arrays are initialized to zero if not explicitly initialized.
3   #include <stdio.h>
4
5   void staticArrayInit( void ); // function prototype
6   void automaticArrayInit( void ); // function prototype
7
8   // function main begins program execution
9   int main( void )
10  {
11     puts( "First call to each function:" );
12     staticArrayInit();
13     automaticArrayInit();
14
15     puts( "\n\nSecond call to each function:" );
16     staticArrayInit();
17     automaticArrayInit();
18  } // end main
19
20  // function to demonstrate a static local array
21  void staticArrayInit( void )
22  {
```

Fig. 6.11 | Static arrays are initialized to zero if not explicitly initialized. (Part 1 of 3.)

```
23        // initializes elements to 0 first time function is called
24        static int array1[ 3 ];
25        size_t i; // counter
26
27        puts( "\nValues on entering staticArrayInit:" );
28
29        // output contents of array1
30        for ( i = 0; i <= 2; ++i ) {
31            printf( "array1[ %u ] = %d  ", i, array1[ i ] );
32        } // end for
33
34        puts( "\nValues on exiting staticArrayInit:" );
35
36        // modify and output contents of array1
37        for ( i = 0; i <= 2; ++i ) {
38            printf( "array1[ %u ] = %d  ", i, array1[ i ] += 5 );
39        } // end for
40    } // end function staticArrayInit
41
42    // function to demonstrate an automatic local array
43    void automaticArrayInit( void )
44    {
45        // initializes elements each time function is called
46        int array2[ 3 ] = { 1, 2, 3 };
47        size_t i; // counter
48
49        puts( "\n\nValues on entering automaticArrayInit:" );
50
51        // output contents of array2
52        for ( i = 0; i <= 2; ++i ) {
53            printf("array2[ %u ] = %d  ", i, array2[ i ] );
54        } // end for
55
56        puts( "\nValues on exiting automaticArrayInit:" );
57
58        // modify and output contents of array2
59        for ( i = 0; i <= 2; ++i ) {
60            printf( "array2[ %u ] = %d  ", i, array2[ i ] += 5 );
61        } // end for
62    } // end function automaticArrayInit
```

```
First call to each function:

Values on entering staticArrayInit:
array1[ 0 ] = 0  array1[ 1 ] = 0  array1[ 2 ] = 0
Values on exiting staticArrayInit:
array1[ 0 ] = 5  array1[ 1 ] = 5  array1[ 2 ] = 5

Values on entering automaticArrayInit:
array2[ 0 ] = 1  array2[ 1 ] = 2  array2[ 2 ] = 3
Values on exiting automaticArrayInit:
array2[ 0 ] = 6  array2[ 1 ] = 7  array2[ 2 ] = 8
```

Fig. 6.11 | Static arrays are initialized to zero if not explicitly initialized. (Part 2 of 3.)

```
Second call to each function:

Values on entering staticArrayInit:
array1[ 0 ] = 5  array1[ 1 ] = 5  array1[ 2 ] = 5
Values on exiting staticArrayInit:
array1[ 0 ] = 10  array1[ 1 ] = 10  array1[ 2 ] = 10

Values on entering automaticArrayInit:
array2[ 0 ] = 1  array2[ 1 ] = 2  array2[ 2 ] = 3
Values on exiting automaticArrayInit:
array2[ 0 ] = 6  array2[ 1 ] = 7  array2[ 2 ] = 8
```

Fig. 6.11 | Static arrays are initialized to zero if not explicitly initialized. (Part 3 of 3.)

6.5 Passing Arrays to Functions

To pass an array argument to a function, specify the array's name without any brackets. For example, if array hourlyTemperatures has been defined as

```
int hourlyTemperatures[ HOURS_IN_A_DAY ];
```

the function call

```
modifyArray( hourlyTemperatures, HOURS_IN_A_DAY )
```

passes array hourlyTemperatures and its size to function modifyArray.

Recall that all arguments in C are passed *by value*. C automatically passes arrays to functions *by reference* (again, we'll see in Chapter 7 that this is *not* a contradiction)—the called functions can modify the element values in the callers' original arrays. The name of the array evaluates to the address of the first element of the array. Because the starting address of the array is passed, the called function knows precisely where the array is stored. Therefore, when the called function modifies array elements in its function body, it's modifying the actual elements of the array in their *original* memory locations.

Figure 6.12 demonstrates that an array name is really the *address* of the first element of the array by printing array, &array[0] and &array using the **%p** conversion specifier—a special conversion specifier for printing addresses. The %p conversion specifier normally outputs addresses as hexadecimal numbers, but this is compiler dependent. Hexadecimal (base 16) numbers consist of the digits 0 through 9 and the letters A through F (these letters are the hexadecimal equivalents of the decimal numbers 10–15). Appendix C provides an in-depth discussion of the relationships among binary (base 2), octal (base 8), decimal (base 10; standard integers) and hexadecimal integers. The output shows that array, &array and &array[0] have the same value, namely 0012FF78. The output of this program is system dependent, but the addresses are always identical for a particular execution of this program on a particular computer.

> **Performance Tip 6.3**
>
> *Passing arrays by reference makes sense for performance reasons. If arrays were passed by value, a copy of each element would be passed. For large, frequently passed arrays, this would be time consuming and would consume storage for the copies of the arrays.*

```
1   // Fig. 6.12: fig06_12.c
2   // Array name is the same as the address of the array's first element.
3   #include <stdio.h>
4
5   // function main begins program execution
6   int main( void )
7   {
8      char array[ 5 ]; // define an array of size 5
9
10     printf( "      array = %p\n&array[0] = %p\n   &array = %p\n",
11        array, &array[ 0 ], &array );
12  } // end main
```

```
      array = 0012FF78
 &array[0] = 0012FF78
    &array = 0012FF78
```

Fig. 6.12 | Array name is the same as the address of the array's first element.

Software Engineering Observation 6.2

It's possible to pass an array by value (by using a simple trick we explain in Chapter 10).

Although entire arrays are passed by reference, individual array elements are passed by *value* exactly as simple variables are. Such simple single pieces of data (such as individual ints, floats and chars) are called **scalars**. To pass an element of an array to a function, use the subscripted name of the array element as an argument in the function call. In Chapter 7, we show how to pass scalars (i.e., individual variables and array elements) to functions by reference.

For a function to receive an array through a function call, the function's parameter list *must* specify that an array will be received. For example, the function header for function modifyArray (that we called earlier in this section) might be written as

```
void modifyArray( int b[], int size )
```

indicating that modifyArray expects to receive an array of integers in parameter b and the number of array elements in parameter size. The *size* of the array is *not* required between the array brackets. If it's included, the compiler checks that it's greater than zero, then ignores it. Specifying a negative size is a compilation error. Because arrays are automatically passed by reference, when the called function uses the array name b, it will be referring to the array in the caller (array hourlyTemperatures in the preceding call). In Chapter 7, we introduce other notations for indicating that an array is being received by a function. As we'll see, these notations are based on the intimate relationship between arrays and pointers in C.

Difference Between Passing an Entire Array and Passing an Array Element

Figure 6.13 demonstrates the difference between passing an entire array and passing an array element. The program first prints the five elements of integer array a (lines 20–22). Next, a and its size are passed to function modifyArray (line 27), where each of a's elements is multiplied by 2 (lines 53–55). Then a is reprinted in main (lines 32–34). As the output shows, the elements of a are indeed modified by modifyArray. Now the program prints the value of a[3] (line 38) and passes it to function modifyElement (line 40). Function modifyElement multiplies its argument by 2 (line 63) and prints the new value. When a[3] is reprinted in main (line 43), it has not been modified, because individual array elements are passed by value.

There may be situations in your programs in which a function should *not* be allowed to modify array elements. C provides the type qualifier **const** (for "constant") that can be used to prevent modification of array values in a function. When an array parameter is preceded by the const qualifier, the array elements become constant in the function body, and any attempt to modify an element of the array in the function body results in a compile-time error. This enables you to correct a program so it does not attempt to modify array elements.

```c
 1   // Fig. 6.13: fig06_13.c
 2   // Passing arrays and individual array elements to functions.
 3   #include <stdio.h>
 4   #define SIZE 5
 5
 6   // function prototypes
 7   void modifyArray( int b[], size_t size );
 8   void modifyElement( int e );
 9
10   // function main begins program execution
11   int main( void )
12   {
13      int a[ SIZE ] = { 0, 1, 2, 3, 4 }; // initialize array a
14      size_t i; // counter
15
16      puts( "Effects of passing entire array by reference:\n\nThe "
17         "values of the original array are:" );
18
19      // output original array
20      for ( i = 0; i < SIZE; ++i ) {
21         printf( "%3d", a[ i ] );
22      } // end for
23
24      puts( "" );
25
26      // pass array a to modifyArray by reference
27      modifyArray( a, SIZE );
28
29      puts( "The values of the modified array are:" );
30
31      // output modified array
32      for ( i = 0; i < SIZE; ++i ) {
33         printf( "%3d", a[ i ] );
34      } // end for
35
```

Fig. 6.13 | Passing arrays and individual array elements to functions. (Part 1 of 2.)

```
36      // output value of a[ 3 ]
37      printf( "\n\n\nEffects of passing array element "
38         "by value:\n\nThe value of a[3] is %d\n", a[ 3 ] );
39
40      modifyElement( a[ 3 ] ); // pass array element a[ 3 ] by value
41
42      // output value of a[ 3 ]
43      printf( "The value of a[ 3 ] is %d\n", a[ 3 ] );
44   } // end main
45
46   // in function modifyArray, "b" points to the original array "a"
47   // in memory
48   void modifyArray( int b[], size_t size )
49   {
50      size_t j; // counter
51
52      // multiply each array element by 2
53      for ( j = 0; j < size; ++j ) {
54         b[ j ] *= 2; // actually modifies original array
55      } // end for
56   } // end function modifyArray
57
58   // in function modifyElement, "e" is a local copy of array element
59   // a[ 3 ] passed from main
60   void modifyElement( int e )
61   {
62      // multiply parameter by 2
63      printf( "Value in modifyElement is %d\n", e *= 2 );
64   } // end function modifyElement
```

```
Effects of passing entire array by reference:

The values of the original array are:
  0  1  2  3  4
The values of the modified array are:
  0  2  4  6  8


Effects of passing array element by value:

The value of a[3] is 6
Value in modifyElement is 12
The value of a[ 3 ] is 6
```

Fig. 6.13 | Passing arrays and individual array elements to functions. (Part 2 of 2.)

Using the const Qualifier with Array Parameters

Figure 6.14 demonstrates the const qualifier. Function tryToModifyArray (line 19) is defined with parameter const int b[], which specifies that array b is *constant* and *cannot* be modified. The output shows the error messages produced by the compiler—the errors may be different for your compiler. Each of the function's three attempts to modify array elements results in the compiler error "l-value specifies a const object." The const qualifier is discussed in additional contexts in Chapter 7.

```
1   // Fig. 6.14: fig06_14.c
2   // Using the const type qualifier with arrays.
3   #include <stdio.h>
4
5   void tryToModifyArray( const int b[] ); // function prototype
6
7   // function main begins program execution
8   int main( void )
9   {
10     int a[] = { 10, 20, 30 }; // initialize array a
11
12     tryToModifyArray( a );
13
14     printf("%d %d %d\n", a[ 0 ], a[ 1 ], a[ 2 ] );
15  } // end main
16
17  // in function tryToModifyArray, array b is const, so it cannot be
18  // used to modify the original array a in main.
19  void tryToModifyArray( const int b[] )
20  {
21     b[ 0 ] /= 2; // error
22     b[ 1 ] /= 2; // error
23     b[ 2 ] /= 2; // error
24  } // end function tryToModifyArray
```

```
fig06_14.c(21) : error C2166: l-value specifies const object
fig06_14.c(22) : error C2166: l-value specifies const object
fig06_14.c(23) : error C2166: l-value specifies const object
```

Fig. 6.14 | Using the const type qualifier with arrays.

Software Engineering Observation 6.3

The const type qualifier can be applied to an array parameter in a function definition to prevent the original array from being modified in the function body. This is another example of the principle of least privilege. A function should not be given the capability to modify an array in the caller unless it's absolutely necessary.

6.6 Sorting Arrays

Sorting data (i.e., placing the data into a particular order such as ascending or descending) is one of the most important computing applications. A bank sorts all checks by account number so that it can prepare individual bank statements at the end of each month. Telephone companies sort their lists of accounts by last name and, within that, by first name to make it easy to find phone numbers. Virtually every organization must sort some data, and in many cases massive amounts of it. Sorting data is an intriguing problem which has attracted some of the most intense research efforts in the field of computer science. In this chapter we discuss what is perhaps the simplest known sorting scheme. In Chapter 12 and Appendix E, we investigate more complex schemes that yield better performance.

Performance Tip 6.4

Often, the simplest algorithms perform poorly. Their virtue is that they're easy to write, test and debug. More complex algorithms are often needed to realize maximum performance.

Figure 6.15 sorts the values in the elements of the 10-element array a (line 10) into ascending order. The technique we use is called the **bubble sort** or the **sinking sort** because the smaller values gradually "bubble" their way upward to the top of the array like air bubbles rising in water, while the larger values sink to the bottom of the array. The technique is to make several passes through the array. On each pass, successive pairs of elements (element 0 and element 1, then element 1 and element 2, etc.) are compared. If a pair is in increasing order (or if the values are identical), we leave the values as they are. If a pair is in decreasing order, their values are swapped in the array.

```c
// Fig. 6.15: fig06_15.c
// Sorting an array's values into ascending order.
#include <stdio.h>
#define SIZE 10

// function main begins program execution
int main( void )
{
   // initialize a
   int a[ SIZE ] = { 2, 6, 4, 8, 10, 12, 89, 68, 45, 37 };
   int pass; // passes counter
   size_t i; // comparisons counter
   int hold; // temporary location used to swap array elements

   puts( "Data items in original order" );

   // output original array
   for ( i = 0; i < SIZE; ++i ) {
      printf( "%4d", a[ i ] );
   } // end for

   // bubble sort
   // loop to control number of passes
   for ( pass = 1; pass < SIZE; ++pass ) {

      // loop to control number of comparisons per pass
      for ( i = 0; i < SIZE - 1; ++i ) {

         // compare adjacent elements and swap them if first
         // element is greater than second element
         if ( a[ i ] > a[ i + 1 ] ) {
            hold = a[ i ];
            a[ i ] = a[ i + 1 ];
            a[ i + 1 ] = hold;
         } // end if
      } // end inner for
   } // end outer for
```

Fig. 6.15 | Sorting an array's values into ascending order. (Part 1 of 2.)

```
38
39       puts( "\nData items in ascending order" );
40
41       // output sorted array
42       for ( i = 0; i < SIZE; ++i ) {
43          printf( "%4d", a[ i ] );
44       } // end for
45
46       puts( "" );
47   } // end main
```

```
Data items in original order
   2    6    4    8   10   12   89   68   45   37
Data items in ascending order
   2    4    6    8   10   12   37   45   68   89
```

Fig. 6.15 | Sorting an array's values into ascending order. (Part 2 of 2.)

First the program compares a[0] to a[1], then a[1] to a[2], then a[2] to a[3], and so on until it completes the pass by comparing a[8] to a[9]. Although there are 10 elements, only nine comparisons are performed. Because of the way the successive comparisons are made, a large value may move down the array many positions on a single pass, but a small value may move up only one position.

On the first pass, the largest value is guaranteed to sink to the bottom element of the array, a[9]. On the second pass, the second-largest value is guaranteed to sink to a[8]. On the ninth pass, the ninth-largest value sinks to a[1]. This leaves the smallest value in a[0], so only *nine* passes of the array are needed to sort the array, even though there are *ten* elements.

The sorting is performed by the nested for loops (lines 24–37). If a swap is necessary, it's performed by the three assignments

```
hold = a[ i ];
a[ i ] = a[ i + 1 ];
a[ i + 1 ] = hold;
```

where the extra variable hold *temporarily* stores one of the two values being swapped. The swap cannot be performed with only the two assignments

```
a[ i ] = a[ i + 1 ];
a[ i + 1 ] = a[ i ];
```

If, for example, a[i] is 7 and a[i + 1] is 5, after the first assignment both values will be 5 and the value 7 will be lost—hence the need for the extra variable hold.

The chief virtue of the bubble sort is that it's easy to program. However, it runs slowly because every exchange moves an element only one position closer to its final destination. This becomes apparent when sorting large arrays. In the exercises, we'll develop more efficient versions of the bubble sort. Far more efficient sorts than the bubble sort have been developed. We'll investigate a few of these in the exercises. More advanced courses investigate sorting and searching in greater depth.

6.7 Case Study: Computing Mean, Median and Mode Using Arrays

We now consider a larger example. Computers are commonly used for survey data analysis to compile and analyze the results of surveys and opinion polls. Figure 6.16 uses array response initialized with 99 responses to a survey. Each response is a number from 1 to 9. The program computes the mean, median and mode of the 99 values. Figure 6.17 contains a sample run of this program. This example includes most of the common manipulations usually required in array problems, including passing arrays to functions.

```c
 1  // Fig. 6.16: fig06_16.c
 2  // Survey data analysis with arrays:
 3  // computing the mean, median and mode of the data.
 4  #include <stdio.h>
 5  #define SIZE 99
 6
 7  // function prototypes
 8  void mean( const unsigned int answer[] );
 9  void median( unsigned int answer[] );
10  void mode( unsigned int freq[], unsigned const int answer[] ) ;
11  void bubbleSort( int a[] );
12  void printArray( unsigned const int a[] );
13
14  // function main begins program execution
15  int main( void )
16  {
17     unsigned int frequency[ 10 ] = { 0 }; // initialize array frequency
18
19     // initialize array response
20     unsigned int response[ SIZE ] =
21        { 6, 7, 8, 9, 8, 7, 8, 9, 8, 9,
22          7, 8, 9, 5, 9, 8, 7, 8, 7, 8,
23          6, 7, 8, 9, 3, 9, 8, 7, 8, 7,
24          7, 8, 9, 8, 9, 8, 9, 7, 8, 9,
25          6, 7, 8, 7, 8, 7, 9, 8, 9, 2,
26          7, 8, 9, 8, 9, 8, 9, 7, 5, 3,
27          5, 6, 7, 2, 5, 3, 9, 4, 6, 4,
28          7, 8, 9, 6, 8, 7, 8, 9, 7, 8,
29          7, 4, 4, 2, 5, 3, 8, 7, 5, 6,
30          4, 5, 6, 1, 6, 5, 7, 8, 7 };
31
32     // process responses
33     mean( response );
34     median( response );
35     mode( frequency, response );
36  } // end main
37
38  // calculate average of all response values
39  void mean( const unsigned int answer[] )
40  {
```

Fig. 6.16 | Survey data analysis with arrays: computing the mean, median and mode of the data. (Part 1 of 4.)

```
41        size_t j; // counter for totaling array elements
42        unsigned int total = 0; // variable to hold sum of array elements
43
44        printf( "%s\n%s\n%s\n", "*********", "  Mean", "*********" );
45
46        // total response values
47        for ( j = 0; j < SIZE; ++j ) {
48           total += answer[ j ];
49        } // end for
50
51        printf( "The mean is the average value of the data\n"
52                "items. The mean is equal to the total of\n"
53                "all the data items divided by the number\n"
54                "of data items ( %u ). The mean value for\n"
55                "this run is: %u / %u = %.4f\n\n",
56                SIZE, total, SIZE, ( double ) total / SIZE );
57     } // end function mean
58
59  // sort array and determine median element's value
60  void median( unsigned int answer[] )
61  {
62        printf( "\n%s\n%s\n%s\n%s",
63                "*********", "  Median", "*********",
64                "The unsorted array of responses is" );
65
66        printArray( answer ); // output unsorted array
67
68        bubbleSort( answer ); // sort array
69
70        printf( "%s", "\n\nThe sorted array is" );
71        printArray( answer ); // output sorted array
72
73        // display median element
74        printf( "\n\nThe median is element %u of\n"
75                "the sorted %u element array.\n"
76                "For this run the median is %u\n\n",
77                SIZE / 2, SIZE, answer[ SIZE / 2 ] );
78     } // end function median
79
80  // determine most frequent response
81  void mode( unsigned int freq[], const unsigned int answer[] )
82  {
83        size_t rating; // counter for accessing elements 1-9 of array freq
84        size_t j; // counter for summarizing elements 0-98 of array answer
85        unsigned int h; // counter for diplaying histograms freq array values
86        unsigned int largest = 0; // represents largest frequency
87        unsigned int modeValue = 0; // represents most frequent response
88
89        printf( "\n%s\n%s\n%s\n",
90                "*********", "  Mode", "*********" );
```

Fig. 6.16 | Survey data analysis with arrays: computing the mean, median and mode of the data. (Part 2 of 4.)

```
91
92      // initialize frequencies to 0
93      for ( rating = 1; rating <= 9; ++rating ) {
94         freq[ rating ] = 0;
95      } // end for
96
97      // summarize frequencies
98      for ( j = 0; j < SIZE; ++j ) {
99         ++freq[ answer[ j ] ];
100     } // end for
101
102     // output headers for result columns
103     printf( "%s%11s%19s\n\n%54s\n%54s\n\n",
104             "Response", "Frequency", "Histogram",
105             "1    1    2    2", "5    0    5    0    5" );
106
107     // output results
108     for ( rating = 1; rating <= 9; ++rating ) {
109        printf( "%8u%11u          ", rating, freq[ rating ] );
110
111        // keep track of mode value and largest frequency value
112        if ( freq[ rating ] > largest ) {
113           largest = freq[ rating ];
114           modeValue = rating;
115        } // end if
116
117        // output histogram bar representing frequency value
118        for ( h = 1; h <= freq[ rating ]; ++h ) {
119           printf( "%s", "*" );
120        } // end inner for
121
122        puts( "" ); // being new line of output
123     } // end outer for
124
125     // display the mode value
126     printf( "\nThe mode is the most frequent value.\n"
127             "For this run the mode is %u which occurred"
128             " %u times.\n", modeValue, largest );
129  } // end function mode
130
131  // function that sorts an array with bubble sort algorithm
132  void bubbleSort( unsigned int a[] )
133  {
134     unsigned int pass; // pass counter
135     size_t j; // comparison counter
136     unsigned int hold; // temporary location used to swap elements
137
138     // loop to control number of passes
139     for ( pass = 1; pass < SIZE; ++pass ) {
140
```

Fig. 6.16 | Survey data analysis with arrays: computing the mean, median and mode of the data. (Part 3 of 4.)

```
141          // loop to control number of comparisons per pass
142          for ( j = 0; j < SIZE - 1; ++j ) {
143
144             // swap elements if out of order
145             if ( a[ j ] > a[ j + 1 ] ) {
146                hold = a[ j ];
147                a[ j ] = a[ j + 1 ];
148                a[ j + 1 ] = hold;
149             } // end if
150          } // end inner for
151       } // end outer for
152    } // end function bubbleSort
153
154    // output array contents (20 values per row)
155    void printArray( const unsigned int a[] )
156    {
157       size_t j; // counter
158
159       // output array contents
160       for ( j = 0; j < SIZE; ++j ) {
161
162          if ( j % 20 == 0 ) { // begin new line every 20 values
163             puts( "" );
164          } // end if
165
166          printf( "%2u", a[ j ] );
167       } // end for
168    } // end function printArray
```

Fig. 6.16 | Survey data analysis with arrays: computing the mean, median and mode of the data. (Part 4 of 4.)

```
********
  Mean
********
The mean is the average value of the data
items. The mean is equal to the total of
all the data items divided by the number
of data items ( 99 ). The mean value for
this run is: 681 / 99 = 6.8788


********
 Median
********
The unsorted array of responses is
  6 7 8 9 8 7 8 9 8 9 7 8 9 5 9 8 7 8 7 8
  6 7 8 9 3 9 8 7 8 7 7 8 9 8 9 8 9 7 8 9
  6 7 8 7 8 7 9 8 9 2 7 8 9 8 9 8 9 7 5 3
  5 6 7 2 5 3 9 4 6 4 7 8 9 6 8 7 8 9 7 8
  7 4 4 2 5 3 8 7 5 6 4 5 6 1 6 5 7 8 7
```

Fig. 6.17 | Sample run for the survey data analysis program. (Part 1 of 2.)

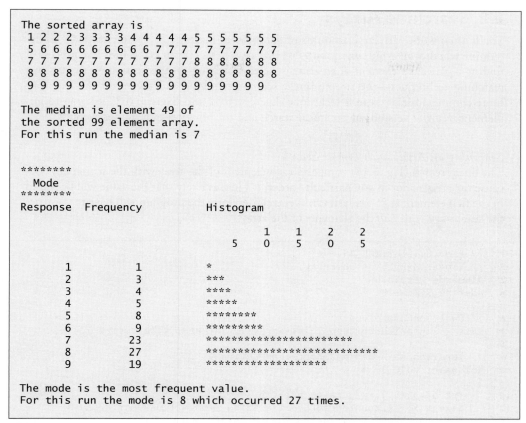

```
The sorted array is
1 2 2 2 3 3 3 3 4 4 4 4 4 5 5 5 5 5 5 5
5 6 6 6 6 6 6 6 6 7 7 7 7 7 7 7 7 7 7 7
7 7 7 7 7 7 7 7 7 7 7 7 8 8 8 8 8 8 8 8
8 8 8 8 8 8 8 8 8 8 8 8 8 8 8 8 8 8 8 8
9 9 9 9 9 9 9 9 9 9 9 9 9 9 9 9 9 9 9

The median is element 49 of
the sorted 99 element array.
For this run the median is 7


********
  Mode
********
Response  Frequency      Histogram

                              1     1     2     2
                        5     0     5     0     5

        1         1      *
        2         3      ***
        3         4      ****
        4         5      *****
        5         8      ********
        6         9      *********
        7        23      ***********************
        8        27      ***************************
        9        19      *******************

The mode is the most frequent value.
For this run the mode is 8 which occurred 27 times.
```

Fig. 6.17 | Sample run for the survey data analysis program. (Part 2 of 2.)

Mean

The *mean* is the *arithmetic average* of the 99 values. Function mean (Fig. 6.16, lines 39–57) computes the mean by totaling the 99 elements and dividing the result by 99.

Median

The median is the *middle* value. Function median (lines 60–78) determines the median by calling function bubbleSort (defined in lines 132–152) to sort the array of responses into ascending order, then picking answer[SIZE / 2] (the middle element) of the sorted array. When the number of elements is even, the median should be calculated as the mean of the two middle elements. Function median does not currently provide this capability. Function printArray (lines 155–168) is called to output the response array.

Mode

The *mode* is the *value that occurs most frequently* among the 99 responses. Function mode (lines 81–129) determines the mode by counting the number of responses of each type, then selecting the value with the greatest count. This version of function mode does not handle a tie (see Exercise 6.14). Function mode also produces a histogram to aid in determining the mode graphically.

6.8 Searching Arrays

You'll often work with large amounts of data stored in arrays. It may be necessary to determine whether an array contains a value that matches a certain key value. The process of finding a particular element of an array is called searching. In this section we discuss two searching techniques—the simple linear search technique and the more efficient (but more complex) binary search technique. Exercise 6.32 and Exercise 6.33 ask you to implement *recursive* versions of the linear search and the binary search, respectively.

Searching an Array with Linear Search

The linear search (Fig. 6.18) compares each element of the array with the search key. Because the array is not in any particular order, it's just as likely that the value will be found in the first element as in the last. On average, therefore, the program will have to compare the search key with *half* the elements of the array.

```c
1   // Fig. 6.18: fig06_18.c
2   // Linear search of an array.
3   #include <stdio.h>
4   #define SIZE 100
5
6   // function prototype
7   size_t linearSearch( const int array[], int key, size_t size );
8
9   // function main begins program execution
10  int main( void )
11  {
12     int a[ SIZE ]; // create array a
13     size_t x; // counter for initializing elements 0-99 of array a
14     int searchKey; // value to locate in array a
15     size_t element; // variable to hold location of searchKey or -1
16
17     // create some data
18     for ( x = 0; x < SIZE; ++x ) {
19        a[ x ] = 2 * x;
20     } // end for
21
22     puts( "Enter integer search key:" );
23     scanf( "%d", &searchKey );
24
25     // attempt to locate searchKey in array a
26     element = linearSearch( a, searchKey, SIZE );
27
28     // display results
29     if ( element != -1 ) {
30        printf( "Found value in element %d\n", element );
31     } // end if
32     else {
33        puts( "Value not found" );
34     } // end else
35  } // end main
```

Fig. 6.18 | Linear search of an array. (Part 1 of 2.)

```
36
37   // compare key to every element of array until the location is found
38   // or until the end of array is reached; return subscript of element
39   // if key is found or -1 if key is not found
40   size_t linearSearch( const int array[], int key, size_t size )
41   {
42      size_t n; // counter
43
44      // loop through array
45      for ( n = 0; n < size; ++n ) {
46
47         if ( array[ n ] == key ) {
48            return n; // return location of key
49         } // end if
50      } // end for
51
52      return -1; // key not found
53   } // end function linearSearch
```

```
Enter integer search key:
36
Found value in element 18
```

```
Enter integer search key:
37
Value not found
```

Fig. 6.18 | Linear search of an array. (Part 2 of 2.)

Searching an Array with Binary Search

The linear searching method works well for *small* or *unsorted* arrays. However, for *large* arrays linear searching is *inefficient*. If the array is sorted, the high-speed binary search technique can be used.

The binary search algorithm eliminates from consideration *one-half* of the elements in a sorted array after each comparison. The algorithm locates the *middle* element of the array and compares it to the search key. If they're equal, the search key is found and the array subscript of that element is returned. If they're not equal, the problem is reduced to searching *one-half* of the array. If the search key is less than the middle element of the array, the *first half* of the array is searched, otherwise the *second half* is searched. If the search key is not found in the specified subarray (piece of the original array), the algorithm is repeated on one-quarter of the original array. The search continues until the search key is equal to the middle element of a subarray, or until the subarray consists of one element that's not equal to the search key (i.e., the search key is not found).

In a worst case-scenario, searching an array of 1023 elements takes *only* 10 comparisons using a binary search. Repeatedly dividing 1,024 by 2 yields the values 512, 256, 128, 64, 32, 16, 8, 4, 2 and 1. The number 1,024 (2^{10}) is divided by 2 only 10 times to get the value 1. Dividing by 2 is equivalent to one comparison in the binary search algorithm. An array of 1,048,576 (2^{20}) elements takes a maximum of *only* 20 comparisons to find the search key. An array of one billion elements takes a maximum of *only* 30 comparisons to find the search key. This is a tremendous increase in performance over the linear search that required comparing the search key to an average of half of the array elements. For a one-billion-element array, this is a difference between an average of 500 million comparisons and a maximum of 30 comparisons! The maximum comparisons for any array can be determined by finding the first power of 2 greater than the number of array elements.

Figure 6.19 presents the *iterative* version of function binarySearch (lines 42–72). The function receives four arguments—an integer array b to be searched, an integer searchKey, the low array subscript and the high array subscript (these define the portion of the array to be searched). If the search key does *not* match the middle element of a subarray, the low subscript or high subscript is modified so that a smaller subarray can be searched. If the search key is *less than* the middle element, the high subscript is set to middle - 1 and the search is continued on the elements from low to middle - 1. If the search key is *greater than* the middle element, the low subscript is set to middle + 1 and the search is continued on the elements from middle + 1 to high. The program uses an array of 15 elements. The first power of 2 greater than the number of elements in this array is 16 (2^4), so no more than 4 comparisons are required to find the search key. The program uses function printHeader (lines 75–94) to output the array subscripts and function printRow (lines 98–118) to output each subarray during the binary search process. The middle element in each subarray is marked with an asterisk (*) to indicate the element to which the search key is compared.

```c
1    // Fig. 6.19: fig06_19.c
2    // Binary search of a sorted array.
3    #include <stdio.h>
4    #define SIZE 15
5
6    // function prototypes
7    size_t binarySearch(const int b[], int searchKey, size_t low, size_t high);
8    void printHeader( void );
9    void printRow( const int b[], size_t low, size_t mid, size_t high );
10
11   // function main begins program execution
12   int main( void )
13   {
14      int a[ SIZE ]; // create array a
15      size_t i; // counter for initializing elements of array a
16      int key; // value to locate in array a
17      size_t result; // variable to hold location of key or -1
18
19      // create data
20      for ( i = 0; i < SIZE; ++i ) {
21         a[ i ] = 2 * i;
22      } // end for
23
24      printf( "%s", "Enter a number between 0 and 28: " );
25      scanf( "%d", &key );
```

Fig. 6.19 | Binary search of a sorted array. (Part 1 of 4.)

```
26
27      printHeader();
28
29      // search for key in array a
30      result = binarySearch( a, key, 0, SIZE - 1 );
31
32      // display results
33      if ( result != -1 ) {
34         printf( "\n%d found in array element %d\n", key, result );
35      } // end if
36      else {
37         printf( "\n%d not found\n", key );
38      } // end else
39   } // end main
40
41   // function to perform binary search of an array
42   size_t binarySearch(const int b[], int searchKey, size_t low, size_t high)
43   {
44      int middle; // variable to hold middle element of array
45
46      // loop until low subscript is greater than high subscript
47      while ( low <= high ) {
48
49         // determine middle element of subarray being searched
50         middle = ( low + high ) / 2;
51
52         // display subarray used in this loop iteration
53         printRow( b, low, middle, high );
54
55         // if searchKey matched middle element, return middle
56         if ( searchKey == b[ middle ] ) {
57            return middle;
58         } // end if
59
60         // if searchKey less than middle element, set new high
61         else if ( searchKey < b[ middle ] ) {
62            high = middle - 1; // search low end of array
63         } // end else if
64
65         // if searchKey greater than middle element, set new low
66         else {
67            low = middle + 1; // search high end of array
68         } // end else
69      } // end while
70
71      return -1; // searchKey not found
72   } // end function binarySearch
73
74   // Print a header for the output
75   void printHeader( void )
76   {
77      unsigned int i; // counter
78
```

Fig. 6.19 | Binary search of a sorted array. (Part 2 of 4.)

```
79      puts( "\nSubscripts:" );
80
81      // output column head
82      for ( i = 0; i < SIZE; ++i ) {
83         printf( "%3u ", i );
84      } // end for
85
86      puts( "" ); // start new line of output
87
88      // output line of - characters
89      for ( i = 1; i <= 4 * SIZE; ++i ) {
90         printf( "%s", "-" );
91      } // end for
92
93      puts( "" ); // start new line of output
94   } // end function printHeader
95
96   // Print one row of output showing the current
97   // part of the array being processed.
98   void printRow( const int b[], size_t low, size_t mid, size_t high )
99   {
100     size_t i; // counter for iterating through array b
101
102     // loop through entire array
103     for ( i = 0; i < SIZE; ++i ) {
104
105        // display spaces if outside current subarray range
106        if ( i < low || i > high ) {
107           printf( "%s", "    " );
108        } // end if
109        else if ( i == mid ) { // display middle element
110           printf( "%3d*", b[ i ] ); // mark middle value
111        } // end else if
112        else { // display other elements in subarray
113           printf( "%3d ", b[ i ] );
114        } // end else
115     } // end for
116
117     puts( "" ); // start new line of output
118   } // end function printRow
```

```
Enter a number between 0 and 28: 25

Subscripts:
  0   1   2   3   4   5   6   7   8   9  10  11  12  13  14
------------------------------------------------------------
  0   2   4   6   8  10  12  14* 16  18  20  22  24  26  28
                             16  18  20  22* 24  26  28
                                         24  26* 28
                                         24*

25 not found
```

Fig. 6.19 | Binary search of a sorted array. (Part 3 of 4.)

```
Enter a number between 0 and 28: 8
Subscripts:
 0   1   2   3   4   5   6   7   8   9  10  11  12  13  14
----------------------------------------------------------
 0   2   4   6   8  10  12  14* 16  18  20  22  24  26  28
 0   2   4   6*  8  10  12
             8  10* 12
             8*

8 found in array element 4
```

```
Enter a number between 0 and 28: 6
Subscripts:
 0   1   2   3   4   5   6   7   8   9  10  11  12  13  14
----------------------------------------------------------
 0   2   4   6   8  10  12  14* 16  18  20  22  24  26  28
 0   2   4   6*  8  10  12

6 found in array element 3
```

Fig. 6.19 | Binary search of a sorted array. (Part 4 of 4.)

6.9 Multidimensional Arrays

Arrays in C can have multiple subscripts. A common use of multiple-subscripted arrays, which the C standard refers to as **multidimensional arrays**, is to represent tables of values consisting of information arranged in *rows* and *columns*. To identify a particular table element, we must specify two subscripts: The *first* (by convention) identifies the element's *row* and the *second* (by convention) identifies the element's *column*. Tables or arrays that require two subscripts to identify a particular element are called **double-subscripted arrays**. Multidimensional arrays can have more than two subscripts.

Figure 6.20 illustrates a double-subscripted array, a. The array contains three rows and four columns, so it's said to be a 3-by-4 array. In general, an array with m rows and n columns is called an m-by-n array.

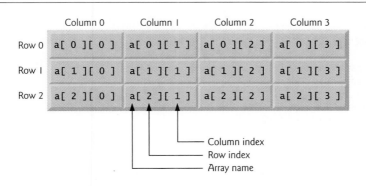

Fig. 6.20 | Double-subscripted array with three rows and four columns.

Every element in array a is identified in Fig. 6.20 by an element name of the form a[i][j]; a is the name of the array, and i and j are the subscripts that uniquely identify each element in a. The names of the elements in row 0 all have a first subscript of 0; the names of the elements in column 3 all have a second subscript of 3.

Common Programming Error 6.7

Referencing a double-subscripted array element as a[x, y] *instead of* a[x][y] *is a logic error. C interprets* a[x, y] *as* a[y] *(because the comma in this context is treated as a comma operator), so this programmer error is* not *a syntax error.*

A multidimensional array can be initialized when it's defined, much like a single-subscripted array. For example, a double-subscripted array int b[2][2] could be defined and initialized with

```
int b[ 2 ][ 2 ] = { { 1, 2 }, { 3, 4 } };
```

The values are grouped by row in braces. The values in the first set of braces initialize row 0 and the values in the second set of braces initialize row 1. So, the values 1 and 2 initialize elements b[0][0] and b[0][1], respectively, and the values 3 and 4 initialize elements b[1][0] and b[1][1], respectively. *If there are not enough initializers for a given row, the remaining elements of that row are initialized to 0.* Thus,

```
int b[ 2 ][ 2 ] = { { 1 }, { 3, 4 } };
```

would initialize b[0][0] to 1, b[0][1] to 0, b[1][0] to 3 and b[1][1] to 4. Figure 6.21 demonstrates defining and initializing double-subscripted arrays.

```c
1   // Fig. 6.21: fig06_21.c
2   // Initializing multidimensional arrays.
3   #include <stdio.h>
4
5   void printArray( int a[][ 3 ] ); // function prototype
6
7   // function main begins program execution
8   int main( void )
9   {
10     // initialize array1, array2, array3
11     int array1[ 2 ][ 3 ] = { { 1, 2, 3 }, { 4, 5, 6 } };
12     int array2[ 2 ][ 3 ] = { 1, 2, 3, 4, 5 };
13     int array3[ 2 ][ 3 ] = { { 1, 2 }, { 4 } };
14
15     puts( "Values in array1 by row are:" );
16     printArray( array1 );
17
18     puts( "Values in array2 by row are:" );
19     printArray( array2 );
20
21     puts( "Values in array3 by row are:" );
22     printArray( array3 );
23  } // end main
```

Fig. 6.21 | Initializing multidimensional arrays. (Part 1 of 2.)

```
24
25   // function to output array with two rows and three columns
26   void printArray( int a[][ 3 ] )
27   {
28      size_t i; // row counter
29      size_t j; // column counter
30
31      // loop through rows
32      for ( i = 0; i <= 1; ++i ) {
33
34         // output column values
35         for ( j = 0; j <= 2; ++j ) {
36            printf( "%d ", a[ i ][ j ] );
37         } // end inner for
38
39         printf( "\n" ); // start new line of output
40      } // end outer for
41   } // end function printArray
```

```
Values in array1 by row are:
1 2 3
4 5 6
Values in array2 by row are:
1 2 3
4 5 0
Values in array3 by row are:
1 2 0
4 0 0
```

Fig. 6.21 | Initializing multidimensional arrays. (Part 2 of 2.)

The program defines three arrays of two rows and three columns (six elements each). The definition of array1 (line 11) provides six initializers in two sublists. The first sublist initializes *row 0* of the array to the values 1, 2 and 3; and the second sublist initializes *row 1* of the array to the values 4, 5 and 6.

If the braces around each sublist are removed from the array1 initializer list, the compiler initializes the elements of the first row followed by the elements of the second row. The definition of array2 (line 12) provides five initializers. The initializers are assigned to the first row, then the second row. Any elements that do *not* have an explicit initializer are initialized to zero automatically, so array2[1][2] is initialized to 0.

The definition of array3 (line 13) provides three initializers in two sublists. The sublist for the first row *explicitly* initializes the first two elements of the first row to 1 and 2. The third element is initialized to *zero*. The sublist for the second row explicitly initializes the first element to 4. The last two elements are initialized to *zero*.

The program calls printArray (lines 26–41) to output each array's elements. The function definition specifies the array parameter as const int a[][3]. When we receive a single-subscripted array as a parameter, the array brackets are *empty* in the function's parameter list. The first subscript of a multidimensional array is not required either, but all subsequent subscripts are required. The compiler uses these subscripts to determine the locations in memory of elements in multidimensional arrays. All array elements are stored consecutively in memory regardless of the number of subscripts. In a double-subscripted array, the first row is stored in memory followed by the second row.

Providing the subscript values in a parameter declaration enables the compiler to tell the function how to locate an element in the array. In a double-subscripted array, each row is basically a single-subscripted array. To locate an element in a particular row, the compiler must know *how many elements are in each row* so that it can skip the proper number of memory locations when accessing the array. Thus, when accessing a[1][2] in our example, the compiler knows to skip the three elements of the first row to get to the second row (row 1). Then, the compiler accesses element 2 of that row.

Many common array manipulations use for repetition statements. For example, the following statement sets all the elements in row 2 of array a in Fig. 6.20 to zero:

```
for ( column = 0; column <= 3; ++column ) {
   a[ 2 ][ column ] = 0;
}
```

We specified row 2, so the first subscript is always 2. The loop varies only the second (column) subscript. The preceding for statement is equivalent to the assignment statements:

```
a[ 2 ][ 0 ] = 0;
a[ 2 ][ 1 ] = 0;
a[ 2 ][ 2 ] = 0;
a[ 2 ][ 3 ] = 0;
```

The following nested for statement determines the total of all the elements in array a.

```
total = 0;
for ( row = 0; row <= 2; ++row ) {
   for ( column = 0; column <= 3; ++column ) {
      total += a[ row ][ column ];
   }
}
```

The for statement totals the elements of the array one row at a time. The outer for statement begins by setting row (i.e., the row subscript) to 0 so that the elements of that row may be totaled by the inner for statement. The outer for statement then increments row to 1, so the elements of that row can be totaled. Then, the outer for statement increments row to 2, so the elements of the third row can be totaled. When the nested for statement terminates, total contains the sum of all the elements in the array a.

Two-Dimensional Array Manipulations

Figure 6.22 performs several other common array manipulations on 3-by-4 array studentGrades using for statements. Each row of the array represents a student and each column represents a grade on one of the four exams the students took during the semester. The array manipulations are performed by four functions. Function minimum (lines 41–60) determines the lowest grade of any student for the semester. Function maximum (lines 63–82) determines the highest grade of any student for the semester. Function average (lines 85–96) determines a particular student's semester average. Function printArray (lines 99–118) outputs the double-subscripted array in a neat, tabular format.

```
1    // Fig. 6.22: fig06_22.c
2    // Double-subscripted array manipulations.
3    #include <stdio.h>
4    #define STUDENTS 3
5    #define EXAMS 4
6
7    // function prototypes
8    int minimum( int grades[][ EXAMS ], size_t pupils, size_t tests );
9    int maximum( int grades[][ EXAMS ], size_t pupils, size_t tests );
10   double average( const int setOfGrades[], size_t tests );
11   void printArray( int grades[][ EXAMS ], size_t pupils, size_t tests );
12
13   // function main begins program execution
14   int main( void )
15   {
16      size_t student; // student counter
17
18      // initialize student grades for three students (rows)
19      int studentGrades[ STUDENTS ][ EXAMS ] =
20         { { 77, 68, 86, 73 },
21           { 96, 87, 89, 78 },
22           { 70, 90, 86, 81 } };
23
24      // output array studentGrades
25      puts( "The array is:" );
26      printArray( studentGrades, STUDENTS, EXAMS );
27
28      // determine smallest and largest grade values
29      printf( "\n\nLowest grade: %d\nHighest grade: %d\n",
30         minimum( studentGrades, STUDENTS, EXAMS ),
31         maximum( studentGrades, STUDENTS, EXAMS ) );
32
33      // calculate average grade for each student
34      for ( student = 0; student < STUDENTS; ++student ) {
35         printf( "The average grade for student %u is %.2f\n",
36            student, average( studentGrades[ student ], EXAMS ) );
37      } // end for
38   } // end main
39
40   // Find the minimum grade
41   int minimum( int grades[][ EXAMS ], size_t pupils, size_t tests )
42   {
43      size_t i; // student counter
44      size_t j; // exam counter
45      int lowGrade = 100; // initialize to highest possible grade
46
47      // loop through rows of grades
48      for ( i = 0; i < pupils; ++i ) {
49
50         // loop through columns of grades
51         for ( j = 0; j < tests; ++j ) {
52
53            if ( grades[ i ][ j ] < lowGrade ) {
```

Fig. 6.22 | Double-subscripted array manipulations. (Part 1 of 3.)

```
54              lowGrade = grades[ i ][ j ];
55           } // end if
56        } // end inner for
57     } // end outer for
58
59     return lowGrade; // return minimum grade
60  } // end function minimum
61
62  // Find the maximum grade
63  int maximum( int grades[][ EXAMS ], size_t pupils, size_t tests )
64  {
65     size_t i; // student counter
66     size_t j; // exam counter
67     int highGrade = 0; // initialize to lowest possible grade
68
69     // loop through rows of grades
70     for ( i = 0; i < pupils; ++i ) {
71
72        // loop through columns of grades
73        for ( j = 0; j < tests; ++j ) {
74
75           if ( grades[ i ][ j ] > highGrade ) {
76              highGrade = grades[ i ][ j ];
77           } // end if
78        } // end inner for
79     } // end outer for
80
81     return highGrade; // return maximum grade
82  } // end function maximum
83
84  // Determine the average grade for a particular student
85  double average( const int setOfGrades[], size_t tests )
86  {
87     size_t i; // exam counter
88     int total = 0; // sum of test grades
89
90     // total all grades for one student
91     for ( i = 0; i < tests; ++i ) {
92        total += setOfGrades[ i ];
93     } // end for
94
95     return ( double ) total / tests; // average
96  } // end function average
97
98  // Print the array
99  void printArray( int grades[][ EXAMS ], size_t pupils, size_t tests )
100 {
101    size_t i; // student counter
102    size_t j; // exam counter
103
104    // output column heads
105    printf( "%s", "              [0]  [1]  [2]  [3]" );
106
```

Fig. 6.22 | Double-subscripted array manipulations. (Part 2 of 3.)

```
107        // output grades in tabular format
108        for ( i = 0; i < pupils; ++i ) {
109
110           // output label for row
111           printf( "\nstudentGrades[%d] ", i );
112
113           // output grades for one student
114           for ( j = 0; j < tests; ++j ) {
115              printf( "%-5d", grades[ i ][ j ] );
116           } // end inner for
117        } // end outer for
118     } // end function printArray
```

```
The array is:
                 [0]   [1]   [2]   [3]
studentGrades[0] 77    68    86    73
studentGrades[1] 96    87    89    78
studentGrades[2] 70    90    86    81

Lowest grade: 68
Highest grade: 96
The average grade for student 0 is 76.00
The average grade for student 1 is 87.50
The average grade for student 2 is 81.75
```

Fig. 6.22 | Double-subscripted array manipulations. (Part 3 of 3.)

Functions minimum, maximum and printArray each receive three arguments—the studentGrades array (called grades in each function), the number of students (rows of the array) and the number of exams (columns of the array). Each function loops through array grades using nested for statements. The following nested for statement is from the function minimum definition:

```
// loop through rows of grades
for ( i = 0; i < pupils; ++i ) {
   // loop through columns of grades
   for ( j = 0; j < tests; ++j ) {
      if ( grades[ i ][ j ] < lowGrade ) {
         lowGrade = grades[ i ][ j ];
      } // end if
   } // end inner for
} // end outer for
```

The outer for statement begins by setting i (i.e., the row subscript) to 0 so the elements of that row (i.e., the grades of the first student) can be compared to variable lowGrade in the body of the inner for statement. The inner for statement loops through the four grades of a particular row and compares each grade to lowGrade. If a grade is less than lowGrade, lowGrade is set to that grade. The outer for statement then increments the row subscript to 1. The elements of that row are compared to variable lowGrade. The outer for statement then increments the row subscript to 2. The elements of that row are compared to variable lowGrade. When execution of the *nested* statement is complete, lowGrade contains the smallest grade in the double-subscripted array. Function maximum works similarly to function minimum.

Function average (lines 85–96) takes two arguments—a single-subscripted array of test results for a particular student called setOfGrades and the number of test results in the array. When average is called, the first argument studentGrades[student] is passed. This causes the address of one row of the double-subscripted array to be passed to average. The argument studentGrades[1] is the starting address of row 1 of the array. Remember that a double-subscripted array is basically an array of single-subscripted arrays and that the name of a single-subscripted array is the address of the array in memory. Function average calculates the sum of the array elements, divides the total by the number of test results and returns the floating-point result.

6.10 Variable-Length Arrays

In early versions of C, all arrays had constant size. But what if you don't know an array's size at compilation time? To handle this, you'd have to use dynamic memory allocation with malloc and related functions. The C standard allows you to handle arrays of unknown size using variable-length arrays (VLAs). These are not arrays whose size can change—that would compromise the integrity of nearby locations in memory. A variable-length array is an array whose length, or size, is defined in terms of an expression evaluated at execution time. The program of Fig. 6.23 declares and prints several VLAs. [*Note:* This feature is not supported in Microsoft Visual C++.]

```
1   // Fig. 6.23: figG_14.c
2   // Using variable-length arrays in C99
3   #include <stdio.h>
4
5   // function prototypes
6   void print1DArray( int size, int arr[ size ] );
7   void print2DArray( int row, int col, int arr[ row ][ col ] );
8
9   int main( void )
10  {
11     int arraySize; // size of 1-D array
12     int row1, col1, row2, col2; // number of rows and columns in 2-D arrays
13
14     printf( "%s", "Enter size of a one-dimensional array: " );
15     scanf( "%d", &arraySize );
16
17     printf( "%s", "Enter number of rows and columns in a 2-D array: " );
18     scanf( "%d %d", &row1, &col1 );
19
20     printf( "%s",
21        "Enter number of rows and columns in another 2-D array: " );
22     scanf( "%d %d", &row2, &col2 );
23
24     int array[ arraySize ]; // declare 1-D variable-length array
25     int array2D1[ row1 ][ col1 ]; // declare 2-D variable-length array
26     int array2D2[ row2 ][ col2 ]; // declare 2-D variable-length array
27
```

Fig. 6.23 | Using variable-length arrays in C99. (Part 1 of 3.)

```
28      // test sizeof operator on VLA
29      printf( "\nsizeof(array) yields array size of %d bytes\n",
30         sizeof( array ) );
31
32      // assign elements of 1-D VLA
33      for ( int i = 0; i < arraySize; ++i ) {
34         array[ i ] = i * i;
35      } // end for
36
37      // assign elements of first 2-D VLA
38      for ( int i = 0; i < row1; ++i ) {
39         for ( int j = 0; j < col1; ++j ) {
40            array2D1[ i ][ j ] = i + j;
41         } // end for
42      } // end for
43
44      // assign elements of second 2-D VLA
45      for ( int i = 0; i < row2; ++i ) {
46         for ( int j = 0; j < col2; ++j ) {
47            array2D2[ i ][ j ] = i + j;
48         } // end for
49      } // end for
50
51      puts( "\nOne-dimensional array:" );
52      print1DArray( arraySize, array ); // pass 1-D VLA to function
53
54      puts( "\nFirst two-dimensional array:" );
55      print2DArray( row1, col1, array2D1 ); // pass 2-D VLA to function
56
57      puts( "\nSecond two-dimensional array:" );
58      print2DArray( row2, col2, array2D2 ); // pass other 2-D VLA to function
59   } // end main
60
61   void print1DArray( int size, int array[ size ] )
62   {
63      // output contents of array
64      for ( int i = 0; i < size; i++ ) {
65         printf( "array[%d] = %d\n", i, array[ i ] );
66      } // end for
67   } // end function print1DArray
68
69   void print2DArray( int row, int col, int arr[ row ][ col ] )
70   {
71      // output contents of array
72      for ( int i = 0; i < row; ++i ) {
73         for ( int j = 0; j < col; ++j ) {
74            printf( "%5d", arr[ i ][ j ] );
75         } // end for
76
77         puts( "" );
78      } // end for
79   } // end function print2DArray
```

Fig. 6.23 | Using variable-length arrays in C99. (Part 2 of 3.)

```
Enter size of a one-dimensional array: 6
Enter number of rows and columns in a 2-D array: 2 5
Enter number of rows and columns in another 2-D array: 4 3

sizeof(array) yields array size of 24 bytes

One-dimensional array:
array[0] = 0
array[1] = 1
array[2] = 4
array[3] = 9
array[4] = 16
array[5] = 25

First two-dimensional array:
    0    1    2    3    4
    1    2    3    4    5

Second two-dimensional array:
    0    1    2
    1    2    3
    2    3    4
    3    4    5
```

Fig. 6.23 | Using variable-length arrays in C99. (Part 3 of 3.)

First, we prompt the user for the desired sizes for a one-dimensional array and two two-dimensional arrays (lines 14–22). Lines 24–26 then declare VLAs of the appropriate size. This is valid as long as the variables representing the array sizes are of an integral type.

After declaring the arrays, we use the sizeof operator in lines 29–30 to make sure that our VLA is of the proper length. In early versions of C sizeof was always a compile-time operation, but when applied to a VLA, sizeof operates at runtime. The output window shows that the sizeof operator returns a size of 24 bytes—four times that of the number we entered because the size of an int on our machine is 4 bytes.

Next we assign values to the elements of our VLAs (lines 33–49). We use i < array-Size as our loop-continuation condition when filling the one-dimensional array. As with fixed-length arrays, *there is no protection against stepping outside the array bounds.*

Lines 61–67 define function print1DArray that takes a one-dimensional VLA. The syntax for passing VLAs as parameters to functions is the same as with a normal, fixed-length array. We use the variable size in the declaration of the array parameter, but no checking is performed other than the variable being defined and of integral type—it's purely documentation for the programmer.

Function print2DArray (lines 69–79) takes a variable-length two-dimensional array and displays it to the screen. Recall from Section 6.9 that, all but the first subscript of a multidimensional array must be specified when declaring a function parameter. The same restriction holds true for VLAs, except that the sizes can be specified by variables. The initial value of col passed to the function is used to convert from two-dimensional indices to offsets into the contiguous memory the array is stored in, just as with a fixed-size array. Changing the value of col inside the function will not cause any changes to the indexing, but passing an incorrect value to the function will.

6.11 Secure C Programming

Bounds Checking for Array Subscripts

It's important to ensure that every subscript you use to access an array element is within the array's bounds—that is, greater than or equal to 0 and less than the number of array elements. A two-dimensional array's row and column subscripts must be greater than or equal to 0 and less than the numbers of rows and columns, respectively. This extends to arrays with additional dimensions as well.

Allowing programs to read from or write to array elements outside the bounds of arrays are common security flaws. Reading from out-of-bounds array elements can cause a program to crash or even appear to execute correctly while using bad data. Writing to an out-of-bounds element (known as a *buffer overflow*) can corrupt a program's data in memory, crash a program and allow attackers to exploit the system and execute their own code.

As we stated in the chapter, *C provides no automatic bounds checking for arrays*, so you must provide your own. For techniques that help you prevent such problems, see CERT guideline ARR30-C at www.securecoding.cert.org.

scanf_s

Bounds checking is also important in string processing. When reading a string into a char array, scanf does *not* prevent buffer overflows. If the number of characters input is greater than or equal to the array's length, scanf will write characters—including the string's terminating null character ('\0')—beyond the end of the array. This might *overwrite* other variables' values, and eventually the program might overwrite the string's '\0' if it writes to those other variables.

Functions determine where strings end by looking for their terminating '\0' character. For example, function printf outputs a string by reading characters from the beginning of the string in memory and continuing until the string's '\0' is encountered. If the '\0' is missing, printf might read far beyond the end of the string until it encounters some other '\0' in memory.

The C standard's optional Annex K provides new, more secure, versions of many string-processing and input/output functions, including scanf_s—a version of scanf that performs additional checks to ensure that it *does not* write beyond the end of a character array used to store a string. Assuming that myString is a 20-character array, the statement

```
scanf_s( "%19s", myString, 20 );
```

reads a string into myString. Function scanf_s requires two arguments for *each* %s in the format string—a character array in which to place the input string and the number of array elements. The second of these arguments is used by scanf_s to prevent buffer overflows. For example, it's possible to supply a field width for %s that's too long for the underlying character array, or to simply omit the field width entirely. If the number of characters input plus the terminating null character is larger than the number of array elements, the %s conversion would fail. Because the preceding statement contains only one conversion specifier, scanf_s would return 0 indicating that no conversions were performed, and myString would be unaltered.

In general, if your compiler supports the functions from the C standard's optional Annex K, you should use them. We discuss additional Annex K functions in later Secure C Programming sections.

Don't Use Strings Read from the User as Format-Control Strings
You might have noticed that throughout this book, we never use single-argument printfs. Instead we use one of the following forms:

- When we need to output a '\n' after the string, we use function puts (which automatically outputs a '\n' after its single string argument), as in

```
puts( "Welcome to C!" );
```

- When we need the cursor to remain on the same line as the string, we use function printf, as in

```
printf( "%s", "Enter first integer: " );
```

Because we were displaying *string literals*, we certainly could have used the one-argument form of printf, as in

```
printf( "Welcome to C!\n" );
printf( "Enter first integer: " );
```

When printf evaluates the format-control string in its first (and possibly its only) argument, the function performs tasks based on the conversion specifier(s) in that string. If the format-control string were obtained from the user, an attacker could supply malicious conversion specifiers that would be "executed" by the formatted output function. Now that you know how to read strings into *character arrays*, it's important to note that you should *never* use as a printf's format-control string a character array that might contain user input. For more information, see CERT guideline FIO30-C at www.securecoding.cert.org.

Summary

Section 6.1 Introduction
- Arrays are data structures consisting of related data items of the same type.
- Arrays are "static" entities in that they remain the same size throughout program execution.

Section 6.2 Arrays
- An array is a group of memory locations related by the fact that they all have the same name and the same type.
- To refer to a particular location or element in the array, specify the array's name and the position number of the particular element in the array.
- The first element in every array is the zeroth element. Thus, the first element of array c is referred to as c[0], the second element is referred to as c[1], the seventh element is referred to as c[6], and, in general, the *i*th element is referred to as c[i - 1].
- An array name, like other variable names, can contain only letters, digits and underscores and cannot begin with a digit.
- The position number contained within square brackets is more formally called a subscript. A subscript must be an integer or an integer expression.
- The brackets used to enclose the subscript of an array are actually considered to be an operator in C. They have the same level of precedence as the function call operator.

Section 6.3 Defining Arrays

- Arrays occupy space in memory. You specify the type of each element and the number of elements in the array so that the computer may reserve the appropriate amount of memory.

- An array of type char can be used to store a character string.

Section 6.4 Array Examples

- Type size_t represents an unsigned integral type. This type is recommended for any variable that represents an array's size or an array's subscripts. The header <stddef.h> defines size_t and is often included by other headers (such as <stdio.h>).

- The elements of an array can be initialized when the array is defined by following the definition with an equals sign and braces, {}, containing a comma-separated list of initializers. If there are fewer initializers than elements in the array, the remaining elements are initialized to zero.

- The statement int n[10] = {0}; explicitly initializes the first element to zero and initializes the remaining nine elements to zero because there are fewer initializers than there are elements in the array. It's important to remember that automatic arrays are not automatically initialized to zero. You must at least initialize the first element to zero for the remaining elements to be automatically zeroed. This method of initializing the array elements to 0 is performed before program startup for static arrays and at runtime for automatic arrays.

- If the array size is omitted from a definition with an initializer list, the number of elements in the array will be the number of elements in the initializer list.

- The #define preprocessor directive can be used to define a symbolic constant—an identifier that the preprocessor replaces with replacement text before the program is compiled. When the program is preprocessed, all occurrences of the symbolic constant are replaced with the replacement text. Using symbolic constants to specify array sizes makes programs more scalable.

- C has no array bounds checking to prevent a program from referring to an element that does not exist. Thus, an executing program can "walk off" the end of an array without warning. You should ensure that all array references remain within the bounds of the array.

- A string such as "hello" is really a static array of individual characters in C.

- A character array can be initialized using a string literal. In this case, the size of the array is determined by the compiler based on the length of the string.

- Every string contains a special string-termination character called the null character. The character constant representing the null character is '\0'.

- A character array representing a string should always be defined large enough to hold the number of characters in the string and the terminating null character.

- Character arrays also can be initialized with individual character constants in an initializer list.

- Because a string is really an array of characters, we can access individual characters in a string directly using array subscript notation.

- You can input a string directly into a character array from the keyboard using scanf and the conversion specifier %s. The name of the character array is passed to scanf without the preceding & used with nonstring variables.

- Function scanf reads characters from the keyboard until the first white-space character is encountered—it does not check the array size. Thus, scanf can write beyond the end of the array.

- A character array representing a string can be output with printf and the %s conversion specifier. The characters of the string are printed until a terminating null character is encountered.

- A static local variable exists for the duration of the program but is visible only in the function body. We can apply static to a local array definition so that the array is not created and initialized each time the function is called and the array is not destroyed each time the function is exited in the program. This reduces program execution time, particularly for programs with frequently called functions that contain large arrays.

- Arrays that are static are automatically initialized once before program startup. If you do not explicitly initialize a static array, that array's elements are initialized to zero by the compiler.

Section 6.5 Passing Arrays to Functions

- To pass an array argument to a function, specify the name of the array without any brackets.

- Unlike char arrays that contain strings, other array types do not have a special terminator. For this reason, the size of an array is passed to a function, so that the function can process the proper number of elements.

- C automatically passes arrays to functions by reference—the called functions can modify the element values in the callers' original arrays. The name of the array evaluates to the address of the first element of the array. Because the starting address of the array is passed, the called function knows precisely where the array is stored. Therefore, when the called function modifies array elements in its function body, it's modifying the actual elements of the array in their original memory locations.

- Although entire arrays are passed by reference, individual array elements are passed by value exactly as simple variables are.

- Such simple single pieces of data (such as individual ints, floats and chars) are called scalars.

- To pass an element of an array to a function, use the subscripted name of the array element as an argument in the function call.

- For a function to receive an array through a function call, the function's parameter list must specify that an array will be received. The size of the array is not required between the array brackets. If it's included, the compiler checks that it's greater than zero, then ignores it.

- When an array parameter is preceded by the const qualifier, the elements of the array become constant in the function body, and any attempt to modify an element of the array in the function body results in a compile-time error.

Section 6.6 Sorting Arrays

- Sorting data (i.e., placing the data into a particular order such as ascending or descending) is one of the most important computing applications.

- One sorting technique is called the bubble sort or the sinking sort, because the smaller values gradually "bubble" their way upward to the top of the array like air bubbles rising in water, while the larger values sink to the bottom of the array. The technique is to make several passes through the array. On each pass, successive pairs of elements are compared. If a pair is in increasing order (or if the values are identical), we leave the values as they are. If a pair is in decreasing order, their values are swapped in the array.

- Because of the way the successive comparisons are made, a large value may move down the array many positions on a single pass, but a small value may move up only one position.

- The chief virtue of the bubble sort is that it's easy to program. However, the bubble sort runs slowly. This becomes apparent when sorting large arrays.

Section 6.7 Case Study: Computing Mean, Median and Mode Using Arrays

- The mean is the arithmetic average of a set of values.

- The median is the "middle value" in a sorted set of values.

- The mode is the value that occurs most frequently in a set of values.

Section 6.8 Searching Arrays

- The process of finding a particular element of an array is called searching.

- The linear search compares each element of the array with the search key. Because the array is not in any particular order, it's just as likely that the value will be found in the first element as in the last. On average, therefore, the search key will be compared with half the elements of the array.

- The linear searching method works well for small or unsorted arrays. For sorted arrays, the high-speed binary search technique can be used.

- The binary search algorithm eliminates from consideration one-half of the elements in a sorted array after each comparison. The algorithm locates the middle element of the array and compares it to the search key. If they're equal, the search key is found and the array subscript of that element is returned. If they're not equal, the problem is reduced to searching one-half of the array. If the search key is less than the middle element of the array, the first half of the array is searched, otherwise the second half is searched. If the search key is not found in the specified subarray (piece of the original array), the algorithm is repeated on one-quarter of the original array. The search continues until the search key is equal to the middle element of a subarray, or until the subarray consists of one element that's not equal to the search key (i.e., the search key is not found).

- When using a binary search, the maximum number of comparisons required for any array can be determined by finding the first power of 2 greater than the number of array elements.

Section 6.9 Multidimensional Arrays

- A common use of multidimensional arrays is to represent tables of values consisting of information arranged in rows and columns. To identify a particular table element, we must specify two subscripts: The first (by convention) identifies the element's row and the second (by convention) identifies the element's column.

- Tables or arrays that require two subscripts to identify a particular element are called double-subscripted arrays.

- Multidimensional arrays can have more than two subscripts.

- A multidimensional array can be initialized when it's defined, much like a single-subscripted array. The values are grouped by row in braces. If there are not enough initializers for a given row, the remaining elements of that row are initialized to 0.

- The first subscript of a multidimensional array parameter declaration is not required, but all subsequent subscripts are required. The compiler uses these subscripts to determine the locations in memory of elements in multidimensional arrays. All array elements are stored consecutively in memory regardless of the number of subscripts. In a double-subscripted array, the first row is stored in memory followed by the second row.

- Providing the subscript values in a parameter declaration enables the compiler to tell the function how to locate an array element. In a double-subscripted array, each row is basically a single-subscripted array. To locate an element in a particular row, the compiler must know how many elements are in each row so that it can skip the proper number of memory locations when accessing the array.

Section 6.10 Variable-Length Arrays

- A variable-length array is an array whose length, or size, is defined in terms of an expression evaluated at execution time.

- When applied to a variable-length array, `sizeof` operates at runtime.

- As with fixed-length arrays, there is no protection against stepping outside the array bounds of variable-length arrays.

- The syntax for passing variable-length arrays as parameters to functions is the same as with a normal, fixed-length array.

Terminology

#define preprocessor directive
array 245
array initializer 248
binary search 272
bubble sort 265
const keyword 262
double-subscripted array 277
element 245
key value 272
linear search 272
m-by-*n* array 277
multidimensional array 277
name 246
null character 256

position number 245
replacement text 250
scalable 250
scalar 261
search key 272
searching 272
sinking sort 265
subscript 246
survey data analysis 267
symbolic constant 250
table 277
value 246
variable-length array 284
zeroth element 245

Self-Review Exercises

6.1 Answer each of the following:
a) Lists and tables of values are stored in _____.
b) The number used to refer to a particular element of an array is called its _____.
c) A(n) _____ should be used to specify the size of an array because it makes the program more scalable.
d) The process of placing the elements of an array in order is called _____ the array.
e) Determining whether an array contains a certain key value is called _____ the array.
f) An array that uses two subscripts is referred to as a(n) _____ array.

6.2 State whether the following are *true* or *false*. If the answer is *false*, explain why.
a) An array can store many different types of values.
b) An array subscript can be of data type double.
c) If there are fewer initializers in an initializer list than the number of elements in the array, C automatically initializes the remaining elements to the last value in the list of initializers.
d) It's an error if an initializer list contains more initializers than there are elements in the array.
e) An individual array element that's passed to a function as an argument of the form a[i] and modified in the called function will contain the modified value in the calling function.

6.3 Follow the instructions below regarding an array called construction.
a) Define a symbolic constant LENGTH to be replaced with the replacement text 5.
b) Define an array with LENGTH elements of type integer and initialize the elements to 10.
c) Name the second element from the beginning of the array.
d) Refer to last element of the array.
e) Assign the value 625 to array element two.
f) Assign the value 56 to the second element of the array.
g) Print all the elements of the array, using a for repetition statement. Assume the integer variable a has been defined as a control variable for the loop. Show the output.

6.4 Write statements to accomplish the following:
a) Define matrix to be an integer array and to have 2 rows and 2 columns. Assume the symbolic constant LENGTH has been defined to be 2.
b) How many elements does the array table contain? Print the total number of elements.
c) Use a for repetition statement to initialize each element of matrix to the product of its subscripts. Assume the integer variables a and b are defined as control variables.

   d) Print the values of each element of array `matrix`. Assume the matrix was initialized with the definition:

```
int matrix [ LENGTH ][ LENGTH ] =
   { { 1 }, { } };
```

6.5 Find the error in each of the following program segments and correct the error.

   a) `#define SIZE 100;`

   b) `SIZE = 10;`

   c) *Assume* `int b[ 10 ] = { 0 }, i;`
```
      for ( i = 0; i <= 10; ++i ) {
         b[ i ] = 1;
      }
```

   d) `#include <stdio.h>;`

   e) *Assume* `int a[ 2 ][ 2 ] = { { 1, 2 }, { 3, 4 } };`
```
      a[ 1, 1 ] = 5;
```

   f) `#define VALUE = 120`

Answers to Self-Review Exercises

6.1 a) arrays. b) subscript. c) symbolic constant. d) sorting. e) searching. f) double-subscripted.

6.2 a) False. An array can store only values of the same type.

   b) False. An array subscript must be an integer or an integer expression.

   c) False. C automatically initializes the remaining elements to zero.

   d) True.

   e) False. Individual elements of an array are passed by value. If the entire array is passed to a function, then any modifications to the elements will be reflected in the original.

6.3 a) `#define LENGTH 5`

   b) `int construction [ LENGTH ] = { 10 };`

   c) `construction [ 1 ]`

   d) `construction [ 4 ]`

   e) `construction [ 2 ] = 625;`

   f) `construction [ 1 ] = 56;`

   g) `for ( a = 0; a < LENGTH; a++ )`
```
      printf( "construction [%d] = %d\n", a, construction [ a ] );
```

   Output:
```
   construction [0] = 10
   construction [1] = 56
   construction [2] = 625
   construction [3] = 10
   construction [4] = 10
```

6.4 a) `int matrix [ LENGTH ][ LENGTH ];`

   b) Four elements. `printf( "%d\n", LENGTH * LENGTH );`

```
c) for ( a = 0; a < LENGTH; a++ )
       for ( b = 0; b < LENGTH; b++ )
           matrix [ a ][ b ] = a * b;

d) for ( a = 0; a < LENGTH; a++ )
       for ( b = 0; b < LENGTH; b++ )
           printf( "table[%d][%d] = %d\n", a, b, table[ a ][ b ] );
```

Output:

```
table[0][0] = 1
table[0][1] = 0
table[1][0] = 0
table[1][1] = 0
```

6.5   a) Error: Semicolon at the end of the #define preprocessor directive.
Correction: Eliminate semicolon.

b) Error: Assigning a value to a symbolic constant using an assignment statement.
Correction: Assign a value to the symbolic constant in a #define preprocessor directive without using the assignment operator as in #define SIZE 10.

c) Error: Referencing an array element outside the bounds of the array (b[10]).
Correction: Change the final value of the control variable to 9.

d) Error: Semicolon at the end of the #include preprocessor directive.
Correction: Eliminate semicolon.

e) Error: Array subscripting done incorrectly.
Correction: Change the statement to a[1][1] = 5;

f) Error: Assigning a value to a symbolic constant using an assignment statement.
Correction: Assign a value to the symbolic constant in a #define preprocessor directive without using the assignment operator as in #define VALUE 120.

Exercises

6.6   Fill in the blanks in each of the following:

a) C stores lists of values in _____.

b) The elements of an array are related by the fact that they _____.

c) When referring to an array element, the position number contained within square brackets is called a(n) _____.

d) The names of the five elements of array p are _____, _____, _____, _____ and _____.

e) The contents of a particular element of an array is called the _____ of that element.

f) Naming an array, stating its type and specifying the number of elements in the array is called _____ the array.

g) The process of placing the elements of an array into either ascending or descending order is called _____.

h) In a double-subscripted array, the first subscript identifies the _____ of an element and the second subscript identifies the _____ of an element.

    i)   An *m*-by-*n* array contains _____ rows, _____ columns and _____ elements.

    j)   The name of the element in row 3 and column 5 of array d is _____.

6.7   State which of the following are *true* and which are *false*. If *false*, explain why.

    a)   To refer to a particular location or element within an array, we specify the name of the array and the value of the particular element.

    b)   An array definition reserves space for the array.

    c)   To indicate that 100 locations should be reserved for integer array p, write

```
p[ 100 ];
```

    d)   A C program that initializes the elements of a 15-element array to zero must contain one for statement.

    e)   A C program that totals the elements of a double-subscripted array must contain nested for statements.

    f)   The mean, median and mode of the following set of values are 5, 6 and 7, respectively: 1, 2, 5, 6, 7, 7, 7.

6.8   Write statements to accomplish each of the following:

    a)   Display the value of the eleventh element of an integer array arrayInt.

    b)   Input a value into the element that is present in the 5th row and 6th column of the double-subscripted integer array matrix.

    c)   Initialize each of the 4 elements of the double-subscripted integer array doubleArray to 2.

    d)   Multiply the elements of the integer array intArray of 50 elements.

    e)   Copy array p into the fiftieth portion of array q. Assume int p[50], q[100];

    f)   Determine and print the sum and difference values contained in 50-element integer array m.

6.9   Consider a 2-by-5 integer array t.

    a)   Write a definition for t.

    b)   How many rows does t have?

    c)   How many columns does t have?

    d)   How many elements does t have?

    e)   Write the names of all the elements in the second row of t.

    f)   Write the names of all the elements in the third column of t.

    g)   Write a single statement that sets the element of t in row 1 and column 2 to zero.

    h)   Write a series of statements that initialize each element of t to zero. Do not use a repetition structure.

    i)   Write a nested for statement that initializes each element of t to zero.

    j)   Write a statement that inputs the values for the elements of t from the terminal.

    k)   Write a series of statements that determine and print the smallest value in array t.

    l)   Write a statement that displays the elements of the first row of t.

    m) Write a statement that totals the elements of the fourth column of t.

    n)   Write a series of statements that print the array t in tabular format. List the column subscripts as headings across the top and list the row subscripts at the left of each row.

6.10 *(Sales Commissions)* Use a single-subscripted array to solve the following problem: A pharmaceutical company pays its medical representatives (MRs) on a commission basis. The MRs receive a fixed salary of $1000 per month plus 6% of their gross sales for that month. For example, a MR who grosses $15,000 in sales in a month receives $1000 plus 6% of $15,000, or a total of $1900. Write a C program (using an array of counters) that determines how many of the MRs earned commissions in each of the following ranges (assume that each MR's commission is truncated to an integer amount):

    a) $0 – 120

    b) $121 – 240

    c) $241 – 360

    d) $361 – 480

e) $481 – 600

f) $601 – 720

g) $721 – 840

h) $841 – 960

i) $960 and above

6.11 *(Bubble Sort)* The bubble sort presented in Fig. 6.15 is inefficient for large arrays. Make the following simple modifications to improve its performance.

a) After the first pass, the largest number is guaranteed to be in the highest-numbered element of the array; after the second pass, the two highest numbers are "in place," and so on. Instead of making nine comparisons on every pass, modify the bubble sort to make eight comparisons on the second pass, seven on the third pass and so on.

b) The data in the array may already be in the proper or near-proper order, so why make nine passes if fewer will suffice? Modify the sort to check at the end of each pass whether any swaps have been made. If none has been made, then the data must already be in the proper order, so the program should terminate. If swaps have been made, then at least one more pass is needed.

6.12 Write loops that perform each of the following single-subscripted array operations:

a) Read the 7 values of an integer array `weeklyConsumption` from the keyboard.

b) Initialize the 25 elements of an integer array `multiply to ones`.

c) Subtract 1 from each of the 25 elements of an integer array `multiply`.

d) Print the first 10 values of an integer array `multiply` in row format.

6.13 Find the error(s) in each of the following statements:

a) Assume: `char str[ 5 ];`

```
scanf( "%s", str ); // User types hello
```

b) Assume: `int a[ 3 ];`

```
printf( "$d  %d  %d\n", a[ 1 ], a[ 2 ], a[ 3 ] );
```

c) `double f[ 3 ] = { 1.1, 10.01, 100.001, 1000.0001 };`

d) Assume: `double d[ 2 ][ 10 ];`

```
d[ 1, 9 ] = 2.345;
```

6.14 *(Mean, Median and Mode Program Modifications)* Modify the program of Fig. 6.16 so function `mode` is capable of handling a tie for the mode value. Also modify function `median` so the two middle elements are averaged in an array with an even number of elements.

6.15 *(Duplicate Elimination)* Use a single-subscripted array to solve the following problem. Read in 10 characters, each of which is between A and Z, inclusive. As each character is read, print it only if it's not a duplicate of a character already read. Provide for the "worst case" in which all 10 characters are different. Use the smallest possible array to solve this problem.

6.16 Label the elements of 2-by-3 double-subscripted array `commission` to indicate the order in which they're set to one by the following program segment:

```
for ( row = 0; row <= 1; row++ ) {
   for ( column = 0; column <= 2; column++ ) {
      commission[ row ][ column ] = 1;
   }
}
```

6.17 What does the following program do?

```
1   /*  ex06_17.c */
2   /* What does this program do? */
3   #include <stdio.h>
4   #define MAX 5
```

```
 5
 6    int functionName ( const int a[], size_t b ); /* function prototype */
 7
 8    /* function main begins program execution */
 9    int main( void )
10    {
11       int c; /* holds return value of functionName */
12
13       /* initialize array p */
14       int p[ MAX ] = { 1, 2, 3, 4, 5 };
15
16       c = functionName( p, MAX );
17
18       printf( "Result is %d\n", c );
19    } /* end main */
20
21    /* what does this function do? */
22    int functionName( const int a[], size_t b )
23    {
24       /* base case */
25       if ( 1 == b ) {
26          return a[ 0 ];
27       } /* end if */
28       else { /* recursion step */
29          return a[ b - 1 ] * functionName ( a, b - 1 );
30       } /* end else */
31    } /* end functionName */
```

6.18   What does the following program do?

```
 1    /* ex06_18.c */
 2    /* What does this program do? */
 3    #include <stdio.h>
 4    #define MAX 12
 5
 6    /* function prototype */
 7    void functionName( const int b[], size_t startSubscript, size_t size );
 8
 9    /* function main begins program execution */
10    int main( void )
11    {
12       int p[ MAX ] = { 9, 1, 2, 1, 9, 8, 5, 3, 6, 5, 0, 7 }; /* initialize p */
13
14       puts( "Answer is:" );
15       functionName ( P, 0, MAX );
16       puts( "" );
17    } /* end main */
18
19    /* What does this function do? */
20    void functionName( const int b[], size_t startSubscript, size_t size )
21    {
22       if ( startSubscript < size ) {
23          functionName( b, startSubscript + 1, size );
24          printf( "%d  ", b[ startSubscript ] * 2);
25       } /* end if */
26    } /* end functionName */
```

6.19   *(Dice Rolling)* Write a program that simulates the rolling of two dice. The program should use rand twice to roll the first die and second die, respectively. The sum of the two values should then be calculated. [*Note:* Because each die can show an integer value from 1 to 6, then the sum of the two values will vary from 2 to 12, with 7 being the most frequent sum and 2 and 12 the least frequent sums.] Figure 6.24 shows the 36 possible combinations of the two dice. Your program should roll the two dice 36,000 times. Use a single-subscripted array to tally the numbers of times each possible sum appears. Print the results in a tabular format. Also, determine if the totals are reasonable; i.e., there are six ways to roll a 7, so approximately one-sixth of all the rolls should be 7.

	1	2	3	4	5	6
1	2	3	4	5	6	7
2	3	4	5	6	7	8
3	4	5	6	7	8	9
4	5	6	7	8	9	10
5	6	7	8	9	10	11
6	7	8	9	10	11	12

Fig. 6.24 | Dice-rolling outcomes.

6.20 *(Game of Craps)* Write a program that runs 1000 games of craps (without human intervention) and answers each of the following questions:

a) How many games are won on the first roll, second roll, …, twentieth roll and after the twentieth roll?

b) How many games are lost on the first roll, second roll, …, twentieth roll and after the twentieth roll?

c) What are the chances of winning at craps? [*Note:* You should discover that craps is one of the fairest casino games. What do you suppose this means?]

d) What's the average length of a game of craps?

e) Do the chances of winning improve with the length of the game?

6.21 *(Airline Reservations System)* A small airline has just purchased a computer for its new automated reservations system. The president has asked you to program the new system. You'll write a program to assign seats on each flight of the airline's only plane (capacity: 10 seats).

Your program should display the following menu of alternatives:

```
Please type 1 for "first class"
Please type 2 for "economy"
```

If the person types 1, then your program should assign a seat in the first class section (seats 1–5). If the person types 2, then your program should assign a seat in the economy section (seats 6–10). Your program should then print a boarding pass indicating the person's seat number and whether it's in the first class or economy section of the plane.

Use a single-subscripted array to represent the seating chart of the plane. Initialize all the elements of the array to 0 to indicate that all seats are empty. As each seat is assigned, set the corresponding element of the array to 1 to indicate that the seat is no longer available.

Your program should, of course, never assign a seat that has already been assigned. When the first class section is full, your program should ask the person if it's acceptable to be placed in the economy section (and vice versa). If yes, then make the appropriate seat assignment. If no, then print the message "Next flight leaves in 3 hours."

6.22 *(Total Sales)* Use a double-subscripted array to solve the following problem. A company has four salespeople (1 to 4) who sell five different products (1 to 5). Once a day, each salesperson passes in a slip for each different type of product sold. Each slip contains:

a) The salesperson number
b) The product number
c) The total dollar value of that product sold that day

Thus, each salesperson passes in between 0 and 5 sales slips per day. Assume that the information from all of the slips for last month is available. Write a program that will read all this information for last month's sales and summarize the total sales by salesperson by product. All totals should be stored in the double-subscripted array `sales`. After processing all the information for last month, print the results in tabular format with each column representing a particular salesperson and each row representing a particular product. Cross total each row to get the total sales of each product for last month; cross total each column to get the total sales by salesperson for last month. Your tabular printout should include these cross totals to the right of the totaled rows and to the bottom of the totaled columns.

6.23 *(Turtle Graphics)* The Logo language made the concept of *turtle graphics* famous. Imagine a mechanical turtle that walks around the room under the control of a C program. The turtle holds a pen in one of two positions, up or down. While the pen is down, the turtle traces out shapes as it moves; while the pen is up, the turtle moves about freely without writing anything. In this problem you'll simulate the operation of the turtle and create a computerized sketchpad as well.

Use a 50-by-50 array `floor` which is initialized to zeros. Read commands from an array that contains them. Keep track of the current turtle position at all times and whether the pen is currently up or down. Assume that the turtle always starts at position 0, 0 of the floor with its pen up. The set of turtle commands your program must process are shown in Fig. 6.25. Suppose that the turtle is somewhere near the center of the floor. The following "program" would draw and print a 12-by-12 square:

```
2
5,12
3
5,12
3
5,12
3
5,12
1
6
9
```

As the turtle moves with the pen down, set the appropriate elements of array `floor` to 1s. When the 6 command (print) is given, wherever there's a 1 in the array, display an asterisk, or some other character you choose. Wherever there's a zero, display a blank. Write a program to implement the turtle graphics capabilities discussed here. Write several turtle graphics programs to draw interesting shapes. Add other commands to increase the power of your turtle graphics language.

Command	Meaning
1	Pen up
2	Pen down
3	Turn right

Fig. 6.25 | Turtle commands. (Part 1 of 2.)

Command	Meaning
4	Turn left
5, 10	Move forward 10 spaces (or a number other than 10)
6	Print the 50-by-50 array
9	End of data (sentinel)

Fig. 6.25 | Turtle commands. (Part 2 of 2.)

6.24 *(Knight's Tour)* One of the more interesting puzzlers for chess buffs is the Knight's Tour problem, originally proposed by the mathematician Euler. The question is this: Can the chess piece called the knight move around an empty chessboard and touch each of the 64 squares once and only once? We study this intriguing problem in depth here.

The knight makes L-shaped moves (over two in one direction and then over one in a perpendicular direction). Thus, from a square in the middle of an empty chessboard, the knight can make eight different moves (numbered 0 through 7) as shown in Fig. 6.26.

Fig. 6.26 | The eight possible moves of the knight.

a) Draw an 8-by-8 chessboard on a sheet of paper and attempt a Knight's Tour by hand. Put a 1 in the first square you move to, a 2 in the second square, a 3 in the third, and so on. Before starting the tour, estimate how far you think you'll get, remembering that a full tour consists of 64 moves. How far did you get? Were you close to the estimate?

b) Now let's develop a program that will move the knight around a chessboard. The board itself is represented by an 8-by-8 double-subscripted array board. Each square is initialized to zero. We describe each of the eight possible moves in terms of both its horizontal and vertical components. For example, a move of type 0 as shown in Fig. 6.26 consists of moving two squares horizontally to the right and one square vertically upward. Move 2 consists of moving one square horizontally to the left and two squares vertically upward. Horizontal moves to the left and vertical moves upward are indicated with negative numbers. The eight moves may be described by two single-subscripted arrays, horizontal and vertical, as follows:

```
horizontal[ 0 ] = 2
horizontal[ 1 ] = 1
horizontal[ 2 ] = -1
horizontal[ 3 ] = -2
horizontal[ 4 ] = -2
horizontal[ 5 ] = -1
horizontal[ 6 ] = 1
horizontal[ 7 ] = 2

vertical[ 0 ] = -1
vertical[ 1 ] = -2
vertical[ 2 ] = -2
vertical[ 3 ] = -1
vertical[ 4 ] = 1
vertical[ 5 ] = 2
vertical[ 6 ] = 2
vertical[ 7 ] = 1
```

Let the variables currentRow and currentColumn indicate the row and column of the knight's current position on the board. To make a move of type moveNumber, where moveNumber is between 0 and 7, your program uses the statements

```
currentRow += vertical[ moveNumber ];
currentColumn += horizontal[ moveNumber ];
```

Keep a counter that varies from 1 to 64. Record the latest count in each square the knight moves to. Remember to test each potential move to see if the knight has already visited that square. And, of course, test every potential move to make sure that the knight does not land off the chessboard. Now write a program to move the knight around the chessboard. Run the program. How many moves did the knight make?

c) After attempting to write and run a Knight's Tour program, you have probably developed some valuable insights. We'll use these to develop a *heuristic* (or strategy) for moving the knight. Heuristics do not guarantee success, but a carefully developed heuristic greatly improves the chance of success. You may have observed that the outer squares are in some sense more troublesome than the squares nearer the center of the board. In fact, the most troublesome, or inaccessible, squares are the four corners.

Intuition may suggest that you should attempt to move the knight to the most troublesome squares first and leave open those that are easiest to get to, so that when the board gets congested near the end of the tour, there will be a greater chance of success.

We develop an "accessibility heuristic" by classifying each square according to how accessible it is and always moving the knight to the square (within the knight's L-shaped moves, of course) that's most inaccessible. We label a double-subscripted array accessibility with numbers indicating from how many squares each particular square is accessible. On a blank chessboard, the center squares are therefore rated as 8s, the corner squares are rated as 2s, and the other squares have accessibility numbers of 3, 4, or 6 as follows:

```
2  3  4  4  4  4  3  2
3  4  6  6  6  6  4  3
4  6  8  8  8  8  6  4
4  6  8  8  8  8  6  4
4  6  8  8  8  8  6  4
4  6  8  8  8  8  6  4
3  4  6  6  6  6  4  3
2  3  4  4  4  4  3  2
```

Now write a version of the Knight's Tour program using the accessibility heuristic. At any time, the knight should move to the square with the lowest accessibility number. In case of a tie, the knight may move to any of the tied squares. Therefore, the tour may begin in any of the four corners. [*Note:* As the knight moves around the chessboard, your program should reduce the accessibility numbers as more and more squares become occupied. In this way, at any given time during the tour, each available square's accessibility number will remain equal to precisely the number of squares from which that square may be reached.] Run this version of your program. Did you get a full tour? (*Optional:* Modify the program to run 64 tours, one from each square of the chessboard. How many full tours did you get?)

d) Write a version of the Knight's Tour program which, when encountering a tie between two or more squares, decides what square to choose by looking ahead to those squares reachable from the "tied" squares. Your program should move to the square for which the next move would arrive at a square with the lowest accessibility number.

6.25 *(Knight's Tour: Brute-Force Approaches)* In Exercise 6.24 we developed a solution to the Knight's Tour problem. The approach used, called the "accessibility heuristic," generates many solutions and executes efficiently.

As computers continue increasing in power, we'll be able to solve many problems with sheer computer power and relatively unsophisticated algorithms. Let's call this approach brute-force problem solving.

a) Use random number generation to enable the knight to walk around the chess board (in its legitimate L-shaped moves, of course) at random. Your program should run one tour and print the final chessboard. How far did the knight get?

b) Most likely, the preceding program produced a relatively short tour. Now modify your program to attempt 1,000 tours. Use a single-subscripted array to keep track of the number of tours of each length. When your program finishes attempting the 1000 tours, it should print this information in a tabular format. What was the best result?

c) Most likely, the preceding program gave you some "respectable" tours but no full tours. Now "pull all the stops out" and simply let your program run until it produces a full tour. [*Caution:* This version of the program could run for hours on a powerful computer.] Once again, keep a table of the number of tours of each length and print this table when the first full tour is found. How many tours did your program attempt before producing a full tour? How much time did it take?

d) Compare the brute-force version of the Knight's Tour with the accessibility-heuristic version. Which required a more careful study of the problem? Which algorithm was more difficult to develop? Which required more computer power? Could we be certain (in advance) of obtaining a full tour with the accessibility-heuristic approach? Could we be certain (in advance) of obtaining a full tour with the brute-force approach? Argue the pros and cons of brute-force problem solving in general.

6.26 *(Eight Queens)* Another puzzler for chess buffs is the Eight Queens problem. Simply stated: Is it possible to place eight queens on an empty chessboard so that no queen is "attacking" any other—that is, so that no two queens are in the same row, the same column, or along the same diagonal? Use the kind of thinking developed in Exercise 6.24 to formulate a heuristic for solving the Eight Queens problem. Run your program. [*Hint:* It's possible to assign a numeric value to each square of the chessboard indicating how many squares of an empty chessboard are "eliminated" once a queen is placed in that square. For example, each of the four corners would be assigned the value 22, as in Fig. 6.27.]

Once these "elimination numbers" are placed in all 64 squares, an appropriate heuristic might be: Place the next queen in the square with the smallest elimination number. Why is this strategy intuitively appealing?

6.27 *(Eight Queens: Brute-Force Approaches)* In this problem you'll develop several brute-force approaches to solving the Eight Queens problem introduced in Exercise 6.26.

a) Solve the Eight Queens problem, using the random brute-force technique developed in Exercise 6.25.

Fig. 6.27 | The 22 squares eliminated by placing a queen in the upper-left corner.

b) Use an exhaustive technique (i.e., try all possible combinations of eight queens on the chessboard).
c) Why do you suppose the exhaustive brute-force approach may not be appropriate for solving the Eight Queens problem?
d) Compare and contrast the random brute-force and exhaustive brute-force approaches in general.

6.28 *(Duplicate Elimination)* In Chapter 12, we explore the high-speed binary search tree data structure. One feature of a binary search tree is that duplicate values are discarded when insertions are made into the tree. This is referred to as duplicate elimination. Write a program that produces 20 random numbers between 1 and 20. The program should store all nonduplicate values in an array. Use the smallest possible array to accomplish this task.

6.29 *(Knight's Tour: Closed Tour Test)* In the Knight's Tour, a full tour occurs when the knight makes 64 moves touching each square of the chessboard once and only once. A closed tour occurs when the 64th move is one move away from the location in which the knight started the tour. Modify the Knight's Tour program you wrote in Exercise 6.24 to test for a closed tour if a full tour has occurred.

6.30 *(The Sieve of Eratosthenes)* A prime integer is any integer greater than 1 that can be divided evenly only by itself and 1. The Sieve of Eratosthenes is a method of finding prime numbers. It works as follows:
a) Create an array with all elements initialized to 1 (true). Array elements with prime subscripts will remain 1. All other array elements will eventually be set to zero.
b) Starting with array subscript 2 (subscript 1 is not prime), every time an array element is found whose value is 1, loop through the remainder of the array and set to zero every element whose subscript is a multiple of the subscript for the element with value 1. For array subscript 2, all elements beyond 2 in the array that are multiples of 2 will be set to zero (subscripts 4, 6, 8, 10, and so on.). For array subscript 3, all elements beyond 3 in the array that are multiples of 3 will be set to zero (subscripts 6, 9, 12, 15, and so on.).

When this process is complete, the array elements that are still set to 1 indicate that the subscript is a prime number. Write a program that uses an array of 1,000 elements to determine and print the prime numbers between 1 and 999. Ignore element 0 of the array.

Recursion Exercises

6.31 *(Greatest Common Divisor)* The *greatest common divisor* (GCD) of two integers is the largest integer that evenly divides each of the two numbers. Write a recursive function gcd that returns the greatest common divisor of two integers.

6.32   *(Linear Search)* Modify the program of Fig. 6.18 to use a recursive linearSearch function to perform the linear search of the array. The function should receive an integer array, the size of the array and the search key as arguments. If the search key is found, return the array subscript; otherwise, return –1.

6.33   *(Binary Search)* Modify the program of Fig. 6.19 to use a recursive binarySearch function to perform the binary search of the array. The function should receive an integer array, the starting subscript, the ending subscript and the search key as arguments. If the search key is found, return the array subscript; otherwise, return –1.

6.34   *(Eight Queens)* Modify the Eight Queens program you created in Exercise 6.26 to solve the problem recursively.

6.35   *(Print Half of the Array)* Write a recursive function printHalfArray that takes an array and the size of the array as arguments, prints half of the array, and returns nothing. The function should stop processing and return when it receives an array of size zero.

6.36   *(Print a String Backward)* Write a recursive function stringReverse that takes a character array as an argument, prints it back to front and returns nothing. The function should stop processing and return when the terminating null character of the string is encountered.

6.37   *(Find the Maximum Value in an Array)* Write a recursive function recursiveMaximum that takes an integer array and the array size as arguments and returns the largest element of the array. The function should stop processing and return when it receives an array of one element.

6.38   *(Project: Sudoku Puzzles)* In Appendix D, Game Programming: Solving Sudoku, we'll discuss various simple solution strategies and suggest what to do when these fail. We'll also present various approaches for programming Sudoku puzzle creators and solvers in C. Unfortunately, Standard C does not include graphics and GUI (graphical user interface) capabilities, so our representation of the board won't be as elegant as we could make it in Java and other programming languages that support these capabilities. You may want to revisit your Sudoku programs after you study a game programming library such as Allegro, which offers capabilities that will help you add graphics and even sounds to your Sudoku programs.

Be sure to check out our Sudoku Resource Center at www.deitel.com/sudoku for downloads, tutorials, books, e-books and more that will help you master the game. And—not for the faint of heart—try fiendishly difficult Sudokus with tricky twists, a circular Sudoku and a variant of the puzzle with five interlocking grids.

7

C Pointers

Objectives

In this chapter, you'll learn:

- Pointers and pointer operators.

- To use pointers to pass arguments to functions by reference.

- The close relationships among pointers, arrays and strings.

- To use pointers to functions.

- To define and use arrays of strings.

7.1 Introduction

In this chapter, we discuss one of the most powerful features of the C programming language, the pointer.[1] Pointers are among C's most difficult capabilities to master. Pointers enable programs to simulate pass-by-reference, to pass functions between functions, and to create and manipulate dynamic data structures, i.e., data structures that can grow and shrink at execution time, such as linked lists, queues, stacks and trees. This chapter explains basic pointer concepts. Chapter 10 examines the use of pointers with structures. Chapter 12 introduces dynamic memory management techniques and presents examples of creating and using dynamic data structures.

7.2 Pointer Variable Definitions and Initialization

Pointers are variables whose values are *memory addresses*. Normally, a variable directly contains a specific value. A pointer, on the other hand, contains an *address* of a variable that contains a specific value. In this sense, a variable name *directly* references a value, and a pointer *indirectly* references a value (Fig. 7.1). Referencing a value through a pointer is called indirection.

Declaring Pointers
Pointers, like all variables, must be defined before they can be used. The definition

```
int *countPtr, count;
```

---

1. Pointers and pointer-based entities such as arrays and strings, when misused intentionally or accidentally, can lead to errors and security breaches. See our Secure C Programming Resource Center (www.deitel.com/SecureC/) for articles, books, white papers and forums on this important topic.

Fig. 7.1 | Directly and indirectly referencing a variable.

specifies that variable `countPtr` is of type `int *` (i.e., a pointer to an integer) and is read (right to left), "`countPtr` is a pointer to `int`" or "`countPtr` points to an object of type `int`." Also, the variable `count` is defined to be an `int`, *not* a pointer to an `int`. The `*` applies *only* to `countPtr` in the definition. When `*` is used in this manner in a definition, it indicates that the variable being defined is a pointer. Pointers can be defined to point to objects of any type. To prevent the ambiguity of declaring pointer and non-pointer variables in the same declaration as shown above, you should always declare only one variable per declaration.

 Common Programming Error 7.1
The asterisk (*) notation used to declare pointer variables does not *distribute to all variable names in a declaration. Each pointer must be declared with the * prefixed to the name; e.g., if you wish to declare* xPtr *and* yPtr *as* int *pointers, use* int *xPtr, *yPtr;.

 Good Programming Practice 7.1
We prefer to include the letters Ptr *in pointer variable names to make it clear that these variables are pointers and thus need to be handled appropriately.*

Initializing and Assigning Values to Pointers
Pointers should be initialized when they're defined, or they can be assigned a value. A pointer may be initialized to `NULL`, `0` or an address. A pointer with the value `NULL` points to *nothing*. `NULL` is a *symbolic constant* defined in the `<stddef.h>` header (and several other headers, such as `<stdio.h>`). Initializing a pointer to `0` is equivalent to initializing a pointer to `NULL`, but `NULL` is preferred. When `0` is assigned, it's first converted to a pointer of the appropriate type. The value `0` is the *only* integer value that can be assigned directly to a pointer variable. Assigning a variable's address to a pointer is discussed in Section 7.3.

 Error-Prevention Tip 7.1
Initialize pointers to prevent unexpected results.

7.3 Pointer Operators

The &, or **address operator**, is a unary operator that returns the *address* of its operand. For example, assuming the definitions

```
int y = 5;
int *yPtr;
```

the statement

```
yPtr = &y;
```

assigns the *address* of the variable y to pointer variable yPtr. Variable yPtr is then said to "point to" y. Figure 7.2 shows a schematic representation of memory after the preceding assignment is executed.

Fig. 7.2 | Graphical representation of a pointer pointing to an integer variable in memory.

Pointer Representation in Memory

Figure 7.3 shows the representation of the pointer in memory, assuming that integer variable y is stored at location 600000, and pointer variable yPtr is stored at location 500000. The operand of the address operator must be a variable; the address operator *cannot* be applied to constants or expressions.

Fig. 7.3 | Representation of y and yPtr in memory.

The Indirection (*) Operator

The unary * operator, commonly referred to as the **indirection operator** or **dereferencing operator**, returns the *value* of the object to which its operand (i.e., a pointer) points. For example, the statement

```
printf( "%d", *yPtr );
```

prints the value of variable y, namely 5. Using * in this manner is called **dereferencing a pointer**.

Common Programming Error 7.2

Dereferencing a pointer that has not been properly initialized or that has not been assigned to point to a specific location in memory is an error. This could cause a fatal execution-time error, or it could accidentally modify important data and allow the program to run to completion with incorrect results.

Demonstrating the & and * Operators

Figure 7.4 demonstrates the pointer operators & and *. The printf conversion specifier %p outputs the memory location as a *hexadecimal* integer on most platforms. (See Appendix C for more information on hexadecimal integers.) Notice that the *address* of a and the *value* of aPtr are identical in the output, thus confirming that the address of a is indeed assigned to the pointer variable aPtr (line 11). The & and * operators are complements of one another—when they're both applied consecutively to aPtr in either order (line 21), the same result is printed. Figure 7.5 lists the precedence and associativity of the operators introduced to this point.

```c
1   // Fig. 7.4: fig07_04.c
2   // Using the & and * pointer operators.
3   #include <stdio.h>
4
5   int main( void )
6   {
7      int a; // a is an integer
8      int *aPtr; // aPtr is a pointer to an integer
9
10     a = 7;
11     aPtr = &a; // set aPtr to the address of a
12
13     printf( "The address of a is %p"
14             "\nThe value of aPtr is %p", &a, aPtr );
15
16     printf( "\n\nThe value of a is %d"
17             "\nThe value of *aPtr is %d", a, *aPtr );
18
19     printf( "\n\nShowing that * and & are complements of "
20             "each other\n&*aPtr = %p"
21             "\n*&aPtr = %p\n", &*aPtr, *&aPtr );
22  } // end main
```

```
The address of a is 0028FEC0
The value of aPtr is 0028FEC0

The value of a is 7
The value of *aPtr is 7

Showing that * and & are complements of each other
&*aPtr = 0028FEC0
*&aPtr = 0028FEC0
```

Fig. 7.4 | Using the & and * pointer operators.

Operators								Associativity	Type
()	[]	++ *(postfix)*	-- *(postfix)*					left to right	postfix
+	-	++	--	!	*	&	*(type)*	right to left	unary
*	/	%						left to right	multiplicative
+	-							left to right	additive
<	<=	>	s>=					left to right	relational
==	!=							left to right	equality
&&								left to right	logical AND
||								left to right	logical OR

Fig. 7.5 | Operator precedence and associativity. (Part 1 of 2.)

Operators	Associativity	Type
?:	right to left	conditional
= += -= *= /= %=	right to left	assignment
,	left to right	comma

Fig. 7.5 | Operator precedence and associativity. (Part 2 of 2.)

7.4 Passing Arguments to Functions by Reference

There are two ways to pass arguments to a function—pass-by-value and pass-by-reference. *All arguments in C are passed by value.* As we saw in Chapter 5, return may be used to return one value from a called function to a caller (or to return control from a called function without passing back a value). Many functions require the capability to *modify variables in the caller* or to pass a pointer to a large data object to avoid the overhead of passing the object by value (which incurs the time and memory overheads of making a copy of the object).

In C, you use pointers and the indirection operator to *simulate* pass-by-reference. When calling a function with arguments that should be modified, the *addresses* of the arguments are passed. This is normally accomplished by applying the address operator (&) to the variable (in the caller) whose value will be modified. As we saw in Chapter 6, arrays are *not* passed using operator & because C automatically passes the starting location in memory of the array (the name of an array is equivalent to &arrayName[0]). When the address of a variable is passed to a function, the indirection operator (*) may be used in the function to modify the value at that location in the caller's memory.

Pass-By-Value

The programs in Figs. 7.6 and 7.7 present two versions of a function that cubes an integer—cubeByValue and cubeByReference. Figure 7.6 passes the variable number by value to function cubeByValue (line 14). The cubeByValue function cubes its argument and passes the new value back to main using a return statement. The new value is assigned to number in main (line 14).

```
1   // Fig. 7.6: fig07_06.c
2   // Cube a variable using pass-by-value.
3   #include <stdio.h>
4
5   int cubeByValue( int n ); // prototype
6
7   int main( void )
8   {
9       int number = 5; // initialize number
10
11      printf( "The original value of number is %d", number );
12
```

Fig. 7.6 | Cube a variable using pass-by-value. (Part 1 of 2.)

```
13        // pass number by value to cubeByValue
14        number = cubeByValue( number );
15
16        printf( "\nThe new value of number is %d\n", number );
17     } // end main
18
19     // calculate and return cube of integer argument
20     int cubeByValue( int n )
21     {
22        return n * n * n; // cube local variable n and return result
23     } // end function cubeByValue
```

```
The original value of number is 5
The new value of number is 125
```

Fig. 7.6 | Cube a variable using pass-by-value. (Part 2 of 2.)

Pass-By-Reference

Figure 7.7 passes the variable number by reference (line 15)—the address of number is passed—to function cubeByReference. Function cubeByReference takes as a parameter a pointer to an int called nPtr (line 21). The function *dereferences* the pointer and cubes the value to which nPtr points (line 23), then assigns the result to *nPtr (which is really number in main), thus changing the value of number in main. Figures 7.8 and 7.9 analyze graphically and step-by-step the programs in Figs. 7.6 and 7.7, respectively.

```
1     // Fig. 7.7: fig07_07.c
2     // Cube a variable using pass-by-reference with a pointer argument.
3
4     #include <stdio.h>
5
6     void cubeByReference( int *nPtr ); // function prototype
7
8     int main( void )
9     {
10        int number = 5; // initialize number
11
12        printf( "The original value of number is %d", number );
13
14        // pass address of number to cubeByReference
15        cubeByReference( &number );
16
17        printf( "\nThe new value of number is %d\n", number );
18     } // end main
19
20     // calculate cube of *nPtr; actually modifies number in main
21     void cubeByReference( int *nPtr )
22     {
23        *nPtr = *nPtr * *nPtr * *nPtr; // cube *nPtr
24     } // end function cubeByReference
```

Fig. 7.7 | Cube a variable using pass-by-reference with a pointer argument. (Part 1 of 2.)

```
The original value of number is 5
The new value of number is 125
```

Fig. 7.7 | Cube a variable using pass-by-reference with a pointer argument. (Part 2 of 2.)

A function receiving an *address* as an argument must define a *pointer parameter* to receive the address. For example, in Fig. 7.7 the header for function cubeByReference (line 21) is:

> void cubeByReference(int *nPtr)

The header specifies that cubeByReference *receives* the *address* of an integer variable as an argument, stores the address locally in nPtr and does not return a value.

The function prototype for cubeByReference (line 6) contains int * in parentheses. As with other variable types, it's *not* necessary to include names of pointers in function prototypes. Names included for documentation purposes are ignored by the C compiler.

For a function that expects a single-subscripted array as an argument, the function's prototype and header can use the pointer notation shown in the parameter list of function cubeByReference (line 21). The compiler does not differentiate between a function that receives a pointer and one that receives a single-subscripted array. This, of course, means that the function must "know" when it's receiving an array or simply a single variable for which it's to perform pass-by-reference. When the compiler encounters a function parameter for a single-subscripted array of the form int b[], the compiler converts the parameter to the pointer notation int *b. The two forms are interchangeable.

Error-Prevention Tip 7.2
Use pass-by-value to pass arguments to a function unless the caller explicitly requires the called function to modify the value of the argument variable in the caller's environment. This prevents accidental modification of the caller's arguments and is another example of the principle of least privilege.

7.5 Using the const Qualifier with Pointers

The **const qualifier** enables you to inform the compiler that the value of a particular variable should not be modified.

Software Engineering Observation 7.1
The const qualifier can be used to enforce the principle of least privilege in software design. This can reduce debugging time and improper side effects, making a program easier to modify and maintain.

Over the years, a large base of legacy code was written in early versions of C that did not use const because it was not available. For this reason, there are significant opportunities for improvement by reengineering old C code.

Six possibilities exist for using (or not using) const with function parameters—two with pass-by-value parameter passing and four with pass-by-reference parameter passing. How do you choose one of the six possibilities? Let the principle of least privilege be your guide. Always award a function enough access to the data in its parameters to accomplish its specified task, but absolutely no more.

Step 1: Before main calls cubeByValue:

```
int main( void )
{
    int number = 5;

    number = cubeByValue( number );
}
```

number

5

```
int cubeByValue( int n )
{
    return n * n * n;
}
```

n

undefined

Step 2: After cubeByValue receives the call:

```
int main( void )
{
    int number = 5;

    number = cubeByValue( number );
}
```

number

5

```
int cubeByValue( int n )
{
    return n * n * n;
}
```

n

5

Step 3: After cubeByValue cubes parameter n and before cubeByValue returns to main:

```
int main( void )
{
    int number = 5;

    number = cubeByValue( number );
}
```

number

5

```
int cubeByValue( int n )
{
                  125
    return n * n * n;
}
```

n

5

Step 4: After cubeByValue returns to main and before assigning the result to number:

```
int main( void )
{
    int number = 5;
            125
    number = cubeByValue( number );
}
```

number

5

```
int cubeByValue( int n )
{
    return n * n * n;
}
```

n

undefined

Step 5: After main completes the assignment to number:

```
int main( void )
{
    int number = 5;
      125            125
    number = cubeByValue( number );
}
```

number

125

```
int cubeByValue( int n )
{
    return n * n * n;
}
```

n

undefined

Fig. 7.8 | Analysis of a typical pass-by-value.

Step 1: Before `main` calls `cubeByReference`:

```
int main( void )                    number
{
    int number = 5;                   5

    cubeByReference( &number );
}
```

```
void cubeByReference( int *nPtr )
{
    *nPtr = *nPtr * *nPtr * *nPtr;
}
                                    nPtr

                              undefined
```

Step 2: After `cubeByReference` receives the call and before `*nPtr` is cubed:

```
int main( void )                    number
{
    int number = 5;                   5

    cubeByReference( &number );
}
```

```
void cubeByReference( int *nPtr )
{
    *nPtr = *nPtr * *nPtr * *nPtr;
}
                                    nPtr

call establishes this pointer
```

Step 3: After `*nPtr` is cubed and before program control returns to `main`:

```
int main( void )                    number
{
    int number = 5;                  125

    cubeByReference( &number );
}
```

```
void cubeByReference( int *nPtr )
{                                   125
    *nPtr = *nPtr * *nPtr * *nPtr;
}
                                    nPtr
called function modifies caller's
variable
```

Fig. 7.9 | Analysis of a typical pass-by-reference with a pointer argument.

In Chapter 5, we explained that *all function calls in C are pass-by-value*—a copy of the argument in the function call is made and passed to the function. If the copy is modified in the function, the original value in the caller does *not* change. In many cases, a value passed to a function is modified so the function can accomplish its task. However, in some instances, the value should *not* be altered in the called function, even though it manipulates only a *copy* of the original value.

Consider a function that takes a single-subscripted array and its size as arguments and prints the array. Such a function should loop through the array and output each array element individually. The size of the array is used in the function body to determine the high subscript of the array, so the loop can terminate when the printing is completed. Neither the size of the array nor its contents should change in the function body.

 Error-Prevention Tip 7.3
If a variable does not (or should not) change in the body of a function to which it's passed, the variable should be declared `const` to ensure that it's not accidentally modified.

If an attempt is made to modify a value that's declared `const`, the compiler catches it and issues either a warning or an error, depending on the particular compiler.

Common Programming Error 7.3

Being unaware that a function is expecting pointers as arguments for pass-by-reference and passing arguments by value. Some compilers take the values assuming they're pointers and dereference the values as pointers. At runtime, memory-access violations *or* segmentation faults *are often generated. Other compilers catch the mismatch in types between arguments and parameters and generate error messages.*

There are four ways to pass a pointer to a function: a non-constant pointer to non-constant data, a constant pointer to nonconstant data, a non-constant pointer to constant data, and a constant pointer to constant data. Each of the four combinations provides different access privileges. These are discussed in the next several examples.

7.5.1 Converting a String to Uppercase Using a Non-Constant Pointer to Non-Constant Data

The highest level of data access is granted by a non-constant pointer to non-constant data. In this case, the data can be modified through the dereferenced pointer, and the pointer can be modified to point to other data items. A declaration for a non-constant pointer to non-constant data does not include const. Such a pointer might be used to receive a string as an argument to a function that processes (and possibly modifies) each character in the string. Function convertToUppercase of Fig. 7.10 declares its parameter, a *non-constant pointer to non-constant data* called sPtr (char *sPtr), in line 19. The function processes the array string (pointed to by sPtr) one character at a time. C standard library function toupper (line 22) from the <ctype.h> header is called to convert each character to its corresponding uppercase letter—if the original character is not a letter or is already uppercase, toupper returns the original character. Line 23 moves the pointer to the next character in the string.

```
1   // Fig. 7.10: fig07_10.c
2   // Converting a string to uppercase using a
3   // non-constant pointer to non-constant data.
4   #include <stdio.h>
5   #include <ctype.h>
6
7   void convertToUppercase( char *sPtr ); // prototype
8
9   int main( void )
10  {
11     char string[] = "cHaRaCters and $32.98"; // initialize char array
12
13     printf( "The string before conversion is: %s", string );
14     convertToUppercase( string );
15     printf( "\nThe string after conversion is: %s\n", string );
16  } // end main
17
18  // convert string to uppercase letters
19  void convertToUppercase( char *sPtr )
20  {
```

Fig. 7.10 | Converting a string to uppercase using a non-constant pointer to non-constant data. (Part 1 of 2.)

```
21      while ( *sPtr != '\0' ) { // current character is not '\0'
22          *sPtr = toupper( *sPtr ); // convert to uppercase
23          ++sPtr; // make sPtr point to the next character
24      } // end while
25  } // end function convertToUppercase
```

```
The string before conversion is: cHaRaCters and $32.98
The string after conversion is: CHARACTERS AND $32.98
```

Fig. 7.10 | Converting a string to uppercase using a non-constant pointer to non-constant data. (Part 2 of 2.)

7.5.2 Printing a String One Character at a Time Using a Non-Constant Pointer to Constant Data

A non-constant pointer to constant data *can be modified* to point to any data item of the appropriate type, but the *data* to which it points *cannot be modified*. Such a pointer might be used to receive an array argument to a function that will process each element without modifying the data. For example, function printCharacters (Fig. 7.11) declares parameter sPtr to be of type const char * (line 21). The declaration is read from *right to left* as "sPtr is a pointer to a character constant." The function uses a for statement to output each character in the string until the null character is encountered. After each character is printed, pointer sPtr is incremented to point to the next character in the string.

```
 1  // Fig. 7.11: fig07_11.c
 2  // Printing a string one character at a time using
 3  // a non-constant pointer to constant data.
 4
 5  #include <stdio.h>
 6
 7  void printCharacters( const char *sPtr );
 8
 9  int main( void )
10  {
11      // initialize char array
12      char string[] = "print characters of a string";
13
14      puts( "The string is:" );
15      printCharacters( string );
16      puts( "" );
17  } // end main
18
19  // sPtr cannot modify the character to which it points,
20  // i.e., sPtr is a "read-only" pointer
21  void printCharacters( const char *sPtr )
22  {
```

Fig. 7.11 | Printing a string one character at a time using a non-constant pointer to constant data. (Part 1 of 2.)

```
23      // loop through entire string
24      for ( ; *sPtr != '\0'; ++sPtr ) { // no initialization
25         printf( "%c", *sPtr );
26      } // end for
27   } // end function printCharacters
```

```
The string is:
print characters of a string
```

Fig. 7.11 | Printing a string one character at a time using a non-constant pointer to constant data. (Part 2 of 2.)

Figure 7.12 illustrates the attempt to compile a function that receives a non-constant pointer (xPtr) to constant data. This function attempts to modify the data pointed to by xPtr in line 18—which results in a compilation error. The actual error message you see will be compiler specific.

```
 1   // Fig. 7.12: fig07_12.c
 2   // Attempting to modify data through a
 3   // non-constant pointer to constant data.
 4   #include <stdio.h>
 5   void f( const int *xPtr ); // prototype
 6
 7   int main( void )
 8   {
 9      int y; // define y
10
11      f( &y ); // f attempts illegal modification
12   } // end main
13
14   // xPtr cannot be used to modify the
15   // value of the variable to which it points
16   void f( const int *xPtr )
17   {
18      *xPtr = 100; // error: cannot modify a const object
19   } // end function f
```

```
c:\examples\ch07\fig07_12.c(18) : error C2166: l-value specifies const object
```

Fig. 7.12 | Attempting to modify data through a non-constant pointer to constant data.

As you know, arrays are aggregate data types that store related data items of the same type under one name. In Chapter 10, we'll discuss another form of aggregate data type called a **structure** (sometimes called a **record** in other languages). A structure is capable of storing related data items of *different* data types under one name (e.g., storing information about each employee of a company). When a function is called with an array as an argument, the array is automatically passed to the function *by reference*. However, structures are always passed *by value*—a *copy* of the entire structure is passed. This requires the execution-time overhead of making a copy of each data item in the structure and storing it on the computer's *function call stack*. When structure data must be passed to a function, we can use pointers to constant data to get the performance of pass-by-reference and the protection of pass-by-value. When a pointer to a structure is passed, only a copy of the *address* at which the structure is stored must be made. On a machine with four-byte addresses, a copy of four bytes of memory is made rather than a copy of a possibly large structure.

> **Performance Tip 7.1**
>
> *Pass large objects such as structures using pointers to constant data to obtain the performance benefits of pass-by-reference and the security of pass-by-value.*

If memory is low and execution efficiency is a concern, use pointers. If memory is in abundance and efficiency is not a major concern, pass data by value to enforce the principle of least privilege. Remember that some systems do not enforce const well, so pass-by-value is still the best way to prevent data from being modified.

7.5.3 Attempting to Modify a Constant Pointer to Non-Constant Data

A constant pointer to non-constant data always points to the *same* memory location, and the data at that location *can be modified* through the pointer. This is the default for an array name. An array name is a constant pointer to the beginning of the array. All data in the array can be accessed and changed by using the array name and array subscripting. A constant pointer to non-constant data can be used to receive an array as an argument to a function that accesses array elements using only array subscript notation. Pointers that are declared const must be initialized when they're defined (if the pointer is a function parameter, it's initialized with a pointer that's passed to the function). Figure 7.13 attempts to modify a constant pointer. Pointer ptr is defined in line 12 to be of type int * const. The definition is read from *right to left* as "ptr is a constant pointer to an integer." The pointer is initialized (line 12) with the address of integer variable x. The program attempts to assign the address of y to ptr (line 15), but the compiler generates an error message.

```
1   // Fig. 7.13: fig07_13.c
2   // Attempting to modify a constant pointer to non-constant data.
3   #include <stdio.h>
4
5   int main( void )
6   {
7      int x; // define x
8      int y; // define y
9
10     // ptr is a constant pointer to an integer that can be modified
11     // through ptr, but ptr always points to the same memory location
12     int * const ptr = &x;
13
14     *ptr = 7; // allowed: *ptr is not const
15     ptr = &y; // error: ptr is const; cannot assign new address
16  } // end main
```

Fig. 7.13 | Attempting to modify a constant pointer to non-constant data. (Part 1 of 2.)

```
c:\examples\ch07\fig07_13.c(15) : error C2166: 1-value specifies const object
```

Fig. 7.13 | Attempting to modify a constant pointer to non-constant data. (Part 2 of 2.)

7.5.4 Attempting to Modify a Constant Pointer to Constant Data

The *least* access privilege is granted by a **constant pointer to constant data**. Such a pointer always points to the *same* memory location, and the data at that memory location *cannot be modified*. This is how an array should be passed to a function that only looks at the array using array subscript notation and does *not* modify the array. Figure 7.14 defines pointer variable ptr (line 13) to be of type const int *const, which is read from *right to left* as "ptr is a constant pointer to an integer constant." The figure shows the error messages generated when an attempt is made to *modify* the *data* to which ptr points (line 16) and when an attempt is made to *modify* the *address* stored in the pointer variable (line 17).

```
 1   // Fig. 7.14: fig07_14.c
 2   // Attempting to modify a constant pointer to constant data.
 3   #include <stdio.h>
 4
 5   int main( void )
 6   {
 7      int x = 5; // initialize x
 8      int y; // define y
 9
10      // ptr is a constant pointer to a constant integer. ptr always
11      // points to the same location; the integer at that location
12      // cannot be modified
13      const int *const ptr = &x; // initialization is OK
14
15      printf( "%d\n", *ptr );
16      *ptr = 7; // error: *ptr is const; cannot assign new value
17      ptr = &y; // error: ptr is const; cannot assign new address
18   } // end main
```

```
c:\examples\ch07\fig07_14.c(16) : error C2166: 1-value specifies const object
c:\examples\ch07\fig07_14.c(17) : error C2166: 1-value specifies const object
```

Fig. 7.14 | Attempting to modify a constant pointer to constant data.

7.6 Bubble Sort Using Pass-by-Reference

Let's improve the bubble sort program of Fig. 6.15 to use two functions—bubbleSort and swap. Function bubbleSort sorts the array. It calls function swap (line 50) to exchange the array elements array[j] and array[j + 1] (Fig. 7.15). Remember that C enforces *information hiding* between functions, so swap does not have access to individual array elements in bubbleSort. Because bubbleSort *wants* swap to have access to the array elements to be swapped, bubbleSort passes each of these elements *by reference* to swap—the *address* of each array element is passed explicitly. Although entire arrays are automatically passed by reference, individual array elements are *scalars* and are ordinarily passed by value. Therefore, bubbleSort uses the address operator (&) on each of the array elements in the swap call (line 50) to effect pass-by-reference as follows

```
swap( &array[ j ], &array[ j + 1 ] );
```

Function swap receives &array[j] in pointer variable element1Ptr (line 58). Even though swap—because of information hiding—is *not* allowed to know the name array[j], swap may use *element1Ptr as a *synonym* for array[j]—when swap references *element1Ptr, it's *actually* referencing array[j] in bubbleSort. Similarly, when swap references *element2Ptr, it's *actually* referencing array[j + 1] in bubbleSort. Even though swap is not allowed to say

```
int hold = array[ j ];
array[ j ] = array[ j + 1 ];
array[ j + 1 ] = hold;
```

precisely the *same* effect is achieved by lines 60 through 62

```
int hold = *element1Ptr;
*element1Ptr = *element2Ptr;
*element2Ptr = hold;
```

```c
1   // Fig. 7.15: fig07_15.c
2   // Putting values into an array, sorting the values into
3   // ascending order and printing the resulting array.
4   #include <stdio.h>
5   #define SIZE 10
6
7   void bubbleSort( int * const array, size_t size ); // prototype
8
9   int main( void )
10  {
11     // initialize array a
12     int a[ SIZE ] = { 2, 6, 4, 8, 10, 12, 89, 68, 45, 37 };
13
14     size_t i; // counter
15
16     puts( "Data items in original order" );
17
18     // loop through array a
19     for ( i = 0; i < SIZE; ++i ) {
20        printf( "%4d", a[ i ] );
21     } // end for
22
23     bubbleSort( a, SIZE ); // sort the array
24
25     puts( "\nData items in ascending order" );
26
27     // loop through array a
28     for ( i = 0; i < SIZE; ++i ) {
29        printf( "%4d", a[ i ] );
30     } // end for
```

Fig. 7.15 | Putting values into an array, sorting the values into ascending order and printing the resulting array. (Part 1 of 2.)

```
31
32      puts( "" );
33   } // end main
34
35   // sort an array of integers using bubble sort algorithm
36   void bubbleSort( int * const array, size_t size )
37   {
38      void swap( int *element1Ptr, int *element2Ptr ); // prototype
39      unsigned int pass; // pass counter
40      size_t j; // comparison counter
41
42      // loop to control passes
43      for ( pass = 0; pass < size - 1; ++pass ) {
44
45         // loop to control comparisons during each pass
46         for ( j = 0; j < size - 1; ++j ) {
47
48            // swap adjacent elements if they're out of order
49            if ( array[ j ] > array[ j + 1 ] ) {
50               swap( &array[ j ], &array[ j + 1 ] );
51            } // end if
52         } // end inner for
53      } // end outer for
54   } // end function bubbleSort
55
56   // swap values at memory locations to which element1Ptr and
57   // element2Ptr point
58   void swap( int *element1Ptr, int *element2Ptr )
59   {
60      int hold = *element1Ptr;
61      *element1Ptr = *element2Ptr;
62      *element2Ptr = hold;
63   } // end function swap
```

```
Data items in original order
   2   6   4   8  10  12  89  68  45  37
Data items in ascending order
   2   4   6   8  10  12  37  45  68  89
```

Fig. 7.15 | Putting values into an array, sorting the values into ascending order and printing the resulting array. (Part 2 of 2.)

Several features of function bubbleSort should be noted. The function header (line 36) declares array as int * const array rather than int array[] to indicate that bubble-Sort receives a single-subscripted array as an argument (again, these notations are interchangeable). Parameter size is declared const to enforce the principle of least privilege. Although parameter size receives a copy of a value in main, and modifying the copy cannot change the value in main, bubbleSort does *not* need to alter size to accomplish its task. The size of the array remains fixed during the execution of function bubbleSort. Therefore, size is declared const to ensure that it's *not* modified.

The prototype for function swap (line 38) is included in the body of function bubbleSort because bubbleSort is the only function that calls swap. Placing the prototype in bubbleSort restricts proper calls of swap to those made from bubbleSort. Other functions that attempt to call swap do *not* have access to a proper function prototype, so the compiler generates one automatically. This normally results in a prototype that does *not* match the function header (and generates a compilation warning or error) because the compiler assumes int for the return type and the parameter types.

Software Engineering Observation 7.2

Placing function prototypes in the definitions of other functions enforces the principle of least privilege by restricting proper function calls to the functions in which the prototypes appear.

Function bubbleSort receives the size of the array as a parameter (line 36). The function must know the size of the array to sort the array. When an array is passed to a function, the memory address of the first element of the array is received by the function. The address, of course, does *not* convey the number of elements in the array. Therefore, you must pass the array size to the function. Another common practice is to pass a pointer to the beginning of the array and a pointer to the location just beyond the end of the array—as you'll learn in Section 7.8, the difference of the two pointers is the length of the array and the resulting code is simpler.

In the program, the size of the array is explicitly passed to function bubbleSort. There are two main benefits to this approach—*software reusability* and *proper software engineering*. By defining the function to receive the array size as an argument, we enable the function to be used by any program that sorts single-subscripted integer arrays of any size.

Software Engineering Observation 7.3

When passing an array to a function, also pass the size of the array. This helps make the function reusable in many programs.

We could have stored the array's size in a global variable that's accessible to the entire program. This would be more efficient, because a copy of the size is not made to pass to the function. However, other programs that require an integer array-sorting capability may not have the same global variable, so the function cannot be used in those programs.

Software Engineering Observation 7.4

Global variables usually violate the principle of least privilege and can lead to poor software engineering. Global variables should be used only to represent truly shared resources, such as the time of day.

The size of the array could have been programmed directly into the function. This restricts the use of the function to an array of a specific size and significantly reduces its reusability. Only programs processing single-subscripted integer arrays of the specific size coded into the function can use the function.

7.7 sizeof Operator

C provides the special unary operator **sizeof** to determine the size in bytes of an array (or any other data type). When applied to the name of an array as in Fig. 7.16 (line 15), the sizeof operator returns the total number of bytes in the array as type size_t. Variables of type float on this computer are stored in 4 bytes of memory, and array is defined to have 20 elements. Therefore, there are a total of 80 bytes in array.

Performance Tip 7.2

sizeof *is a compile-time operator, so it does not incur any execution-time overhead.*

```c
1   // Fig. 7.16: fig07_16.c
2   // Applying sizeof to an array name returns
3   // the number of bytes in the array.
4   #include <stdio.h>
5   #define SIZE 20
6
7   size_t getSize( float *ptr ); // prototype
8
9   int main( void )
10  {
11     float array[ SIZE ]; // create array
12
13     printf( "The number of bytes in the array is %u"
14             "\nThe number of bytes returned by getSize is %u\n",
15             sizeof( array ), getSize( array ) );
16  } // end main
17
18  // return size of ptr
19  size_t getSize( float *ptr )
20  {
21     return sizeof( ptr );
22  } // end function getSize
```

```
The number of bytes in the array is 80
The number of bytes returned by getSize is 4
```

Fig. 7.16 | Applying sizeof to an array name returns the number of bytes in the array.

The number of elements in an array also can be determined with sizeof. For example, consider the following array definition:

```c
double real[ 22 ];
```

Variables of type double normally are stored in 8 bytes of memory. Thus, array real contains a total of 176 bytes. To determine the number of elements in the array, the following expression can be used:

```c
sizeof( real ) / sizeof( real[ 0 ] )
```

The expression determines the number of bytes in array real and divides that value by the number of bytes used in memory to store the first element of array real (a double value).

Even though function getSize receives an array of 20 elements as an argument, the function's parameter ptr is simply a pointer to the array's first element. When you use sizeof with a pointer, it returns the *size of the pointer*, not the size of the item to which it points. The size of a pointer on our system is 4 bytes, so getSize returned 4. Also, the calculation shown above for determining the number of array elements using sizeof works *only* when using the actual array, *not* when using a pointer to the array.

Determining the Sizes of the Standard Types, an Array and a Pointer

Figure 7.17 calculates the number of bytes used to store each of the standard data types. *The results of this program are implementation dependent and often differ across platforms and sometimes across different compilers on the same platform.*

```
 1   // Fig. 7.17: fig07_17.c
 2   // Using operator sizeof to determine standard data type sizes.
 3   #include <stdio.h>
 4
 5   int main( void )
 6   {
 7      char c;
 8      short s;
 9      int i;
10      long l;
11      long long ll;
12      float f;
13      double d;
14      long double ld;
15      int array[ 20 ]; // create array of 20 int elements
16      int *ptr = array; // create pointer to array
17
18      printf( "     sizeof c = %u\tsizeof(char)   = %u"
19              "\n    sizeof s = %u\tsizeof(short) = %u"
20              "\n    sizeof i = %u\tsizeof(int) = %u"
21              "\n    sizeof l = %u\tsizeof(long) = %u"
22              "\n   sizeof ll = %u\tsizeof(long long) = %u"
23              "\n    sizeof f = %u\tsizeof(float) = %u"
24              "\n    sizeof d = %u\tsizeof(double) = %u"
25              "\n   sizeof ld = %u\tsizeof(long double) = %u"
26              "\n sizeof array = %u"
27              "\n   sizeof ptr = %u\n",
28              sizeof c, sizeof( char ), sizeof s, sizeof( short ), sizeof i,
29              sizeof( int ), sizeof l, sizeof( long ), sizeof ll,
30              sizeof( long long ), sizeof f, sizeof( float ), sizeof d,
31              sizeof( double ), sizeof ld, sizeof( long double ),
32              sizeof array, sizeof ptr );
33   } // end main
```

```
    sizeof c = 1      sizeof(char)   = 1
    sizeof s = 2      sizeof(short) = 2
    sizeof i = 4      sizeof(int) = 4
    sizeof l = 4      sizeof(long) = 4
   sizeof ll = 8      sizeof(long long) = 8
    sizeof f = 4      sizeof(float) = 4
    sizeof d = 8      sizeof(double) = 8
   sizeof ld = 8      sizeof(long double) = 8
 sizeof array = 80
   sizeof ptr = 4
```

Fig. 7.17 | Using operator sizeof to determine standard data type sizes.

Portability Tip 7.1

The number of bytes used to store a particular data type may vary between systems. When writing programs that depend on data type sizes and that will run on several computer systems, use sizeof *to determine the number of bytes used to store the data types.*

Operator sizeof can be applied to any variable name, type or value (including the value of an expression). When applied to a variable name (that's *not* an array name) or a constant, the number of bytes used to store the specific type of variable or constant is returned. The parentheses are required when a type is supplied as sizeof's operand.

7.8 Pointer Expressions and Pointer Arithmetic

Pointers are valid operands in arithmetic expressions, assignment expressions and comparison expressions. However, not all the operators normally used in these expressions are valid in conjunction with pointer variables. This section describes the operators that can have pointers as operands, and how these operators are used.

A limited set of arithmetic operations may be performed on pointers. A pointer may be *incremented* (++) or *decremented* (--), an integer may be *added* to a pointer (+ or +=), an integer may be *subtracted* from a pointer (- or -=) and one pointer may be subtracted from another—this last operation is meaningful only when *both* pointers point to elements of the *same* array.

Assume that array int v[5] has been defined and its first element is at location 3000 in memory. Assume pointer vPtr has been initialized to point to v[0]—i.e., the value of vPtr is 3000. Figure 7.18 illustrates this situation for a machine with 4-byte integers. Variable vPtr can be initialized to point to array v with either of the statements

```
vPtr = v;
vPtr = &v[ 0 ];
```

Portability Tip 7.2

Because the results of pointer arithmetic depend on the size of the objects a pointer points to, pointer arithmetic is machine dependent.

Fig. 7.18 | Array v and a pointer variable vPtr that points to v.

In conventional arithmetic, 3000 + 2 yields the value 3002. This is normally *not* the case with pointer arithmetic. When an integer is added to or subtracted from a pointer, the pointer is *not* incremented or decremented simply by that integer, but by that integer times the size of the object to which the pointer refers. The number of bytes depends on the object's data type. For example, the statement

```
vPtr += 2;
```

would produce 3008 (3000 + 2 * 4), assuming an integer is stored in 4 bytes of memory. In the array v, vPtr would now point to v[2] (Fig. 7.19). If an integer is stored in 2 bytes of memory, then the preceding calculation would result in memory location 3004 (3000 + 2 * 2). If the array were of a different data type, the preceding statement would increment the pointer by twice the number of bytes that it takes to store an object of that data type. When performing pointer arithmetic on a character array, the results will be consistent with regular arithmetic, because each character is 1 byte long.

Fig. 7.19 | The pointer vPtr after pointer arithmetic.

If vPtr had been incremented to 3016, which points to v[4], the statement

```
vPtr -= 4;
```

would set vPtr back to 3000—the beginning of the array. If a pointer is being incremented or decremented by one, the increment (++) and decrement (--) operators can be used. Either of the statements

```
++vPtr;
vPtr++;
```

increments the pointer to point to the *next* location in the array. Either of the statements

```
--vPtr;
vPtr--;
```

decrements the pointer to point to the *previous* element of the array.

Pointer variables may be subtracted from one another. For example, if vPtr contains the location 3000, and v2Ptr contains the address 3008, the statement

```
x = v2Ptr - vPtr;
```

would assign to x the *number of array elements* from vPtr to v2Ptr, in this case 2 (not 8). Pointer arithmetic is undefined unless performed on an array. We cannot assume that two variables of the same type are stored contiguously in memory unless they're adjacent elements of an array.

Common Programming Error 7.4

Using pointer arithmetic on a pointer that does not refer to an element in an array.

Common Programming Error 7.5

Subtracting or comparing two pointers that do not refer to elements in the same *array.*

Common Programming Error 7.6

Running off either end of an array when using pointer arithmetic.

A pointer can be assigned to another pointer if both have the same type. The exception to this rule is the **pointer to void** (i.e., **void ***), which is a generic pointer that can represent *any* pointer type. All pointer types can be assigned a pointer to void, and a pointer to void can be assigned a pointer of any type. In both cases, a cast operation is *not* required.

A pointer to void *cannot* be dereferenced. Consider this: The compiler knows that a pointer to int refers to 4 bytes of memory on a machine with 4-byte integers, but a pointer to void simply contains a memory location for an *unknown* data type—the precise number of bytes to which the pointer refers is *not* known by the compiler. The compiler *must* know the data type to determine the number of bytes to be dereferenced for a particular pointer.

Common Programming Error 7.7

Assigning a pointer of one type to a pointer of another type if neither is of type void * is a syntax error.

Common Programming Error 7.8

Dereferencing a void * pointer is a syntax error.

Pointers can be compared using equality and relational operators, but such comparisons are meaningless unless the pointers point to elements of the *same* array. Pointer comparisons compare the addresses stored in the pointers. A comparison of two pointers pointing to elements in the same array could show, for example, that one pointer points to a higher-numbered element of the array than the other pointer does. A common use of pointer comparison is determining whether a pointer is NULL.

7.9 Relationship between Pointers and Arrays

Arrays and pointers are intimately related in C and often may be used interchangeably. An *array name* can be thought of as a *constant pointer*. Pointers can be used to do any operation involving array subscripting.

Assume that integer array b[5] and integer pointer variable bPtr have been defined. Because the array name (without a subscript) is a pointer to the first element of the array, we can set bPtr equal to the address of the first element in array b with the statement

```
bPtr = b;
```

This statement is equivalent to taking the address of the array's first element as follows:

```
bPtr = &b[ 0 ];
```

Array element b[3] can alternatively be referenced with the pointer expression

```
*( bPtr + 3 )
```

The 3 in the expression is the **offset** to the pointer. When the pointer points to the array's first element, the offset indicates which array element should be referenced, and the offset value is identical to the array subscript. This notation is referred to as **pointer/offset notation**. The parentheses are necessary because the precedence of * is higher than the precedence of +. Without the parentheses, the above expression would add 3 to the value of the expression *bPtr (i.e., 3 would be added to b[0], assuming bPtr points to the beginning of the array). Just as the array element can be referenced with a pointer expression, the address

```
&b[ 3 ]
```

can be written with the pointer expression

```
bPtr + 3
```

The array itself can be treated as a pointer and used in pointer arithmetic. For example, the expression

```
*( b + 3 )
```

also refers to the array element b[3]. In general, all subscripted array expressions can be written with a pointer and an offset. In this case, pointer/offset notation was used with the name of the array as a pointer. The preceding statement does not modify the array name in any way; b still points to the first element in the array.

Pointers can be subscripted like arrays. If bPtr has the value b, the expression

```
bPtr[ 1 ]
```

refers to the array element b[1]. This is referred to as **pointer/subscript notation**.

Remember that an array name is essentially a constant pointer; it always points to the beginning of the array. Thus, the expression

```
b += 3
```

is *invalid* because it attempts to modify the value of the array name with pointer arithmetic.

Common Programming Error 7.9
Attempting to modify an array name with pointer arithmetic is a compilation error.

Figure 7.20 uses the four methods we've discussed for referring to array elements—array subscripting, pointer/offset with the array name as a pointer, **pointer subscripting**, and pointer/offset with a pointer—to print the four elements of the integer array b.

```
1   // Fig. 7.20: fig07_20.cpp
2   // Using subscripting and pointer notations with arrays.
3   #include <stdio.h>
4   #define ARRAY_SIZE 4
5
6   int main( void )
7   {
```

Fig. 7.20 | Using subscripting and pointer notations with arrays. (Part 1 of 3.)

```
 8      int b[] = { 10, 20, 30, 40 }; // create and initialize array b
 9      int *bPtr = b; // create bPtr and point it to array b
10      size_t i; // counter
11      size_t offset; // counter
12
13      // output array b using array subscript notation
14      puts( "Array b printed with:\nArray subscript notation" );
15
16      // loop through array b
17      for ( i = 0; i < ARRAY_SIZE; ++i ) {
18         printf( "b[ %u ] = %d\n", i, b[ i ] );
19      } // end for
20
21      // output array b using array name and pointer/offset notation
22      puts( "\nPointer/offset notation where\n"
23            "the pointer is the array name" );
24
25      // loop through array b
26      for ( offset = 0; offset < ARRAY_SIZE; ++offset ) {
27         printf( "*( b + %u ) = %d\n", offset, *( b + offset ) );
28      } // end for
29
30      // output array b using bPtr and array subscript notation
31      puts( "\nPointer subscript notation" );
32
33      // loop through array b
34      for ( i = 0; i < ARRAY_SIZE; ++i ) {
35         printf( "bPtr[ %u ] = %d\n", i, bPtr[ i ] );
36      } // end for
37
38      // output array b using bPtr and pointer/offset notation
39      puts( "\nPointer/offset notation" );
40
41      // loop through array b
42      for ( offset = 0; offset < ARRAY_SIZE; ++offset ) {
43         printf( "*( bPtr + %u ) = %d\n", offset, *( bPtr + offset ) );
44      } // end for
45   } // end main
```

```
Array b printed with:
Array subscript notation
b[ 0 ] = 10
b[ 1 ] = 20
b[ 2 ] = 30
b[ 3 ] = 40

Pointer/offset notation where
the pointer is the array name
*( b + 0 ) = 10
*( b + 1 ) = 20
*( b + 2 ) = 30
*( b + 3 ) = 40
```

Fig. 7.20 | Using subscripting and pointer notations with arrays. (Part 2 of 3.)

```
Pointer subscript notation
bPtr[ 0 ] = 10
bPtr[ 1 ] = 20
bPtr[ 2 ] = 30
bPtr[ 3 ] = 40

Pointer/offset notation
*( bPtr + 0 ) = 10
*( bPtr + 1 ) = 20
*( bPtr + 2 ) = 30
*( bPtr + 3 ) = 40
```

Fig. 7.20 | Using subscripting and pointer notations with arrays. (Part 3 of 3.)

String Copying with Arrays and Pointers

To further illustrate the interchangeability of arrays and pointers, let's look at the two string-copying functions—copy1 and copy2—in the program of Fig. 7.21. Both functions copy a string into a character array. After a comparison of the function prototypes for copy1 and copy2, the functions appear identical. They accomplish the same task, but they're implemented differently.

Function copy1 uses *array subscript notation* to copy the string in s2 to the character array s1. The function defines counter variable i as the array subscript. The for statement header (line 29) performs the entire copy operation—its body is the empty statement. The header specifies that i is initialized to zero and incremented by one on each iteration of the loop. The expression s1[i] = s2[i] copies one character from s2 to s1. When the null character is encountered in s2, it's assigned to s1, and the value of the assignment becomes the value assigned to the left operand (s1). The loop terminates when the null character is assigned from s2 to s1 (false).

```
1    // Fig. 7.21: fig07_21.c
2    // Copying a string using array notation and pointer notation.
3    #include <stdio.h>
4    #define SIZE 10
5
6    void copy1( char * const s1, const char * const s2 ); // prototype
7    void copy2( char *s1, const char *s2 ); // prototype
8
9    int main( void )
10   {
11      char string1[ SIZE ]; // create array string1
12      char *string2 = "Hello"; // create a pointer to a string
13      char string3[ SIZE ]; // create array string3
14      char string4[] = "Good Bye"; // create a pointer to a string
15
16      copy1( string1, string2 );
17      printf( "string1 = %s\n", string1 );
18
```

Fig. 7.21 | Copying a string using array notation and pointer notation. (Part 1 of 2.)

```
19        copy2( string3, string4 );
20        printf( "string3 = %s\n", string3 );
21   } // end main
22
23   // copy s2 to s1 using array notation
24   void copy1( char * const s1, const char * const s2 )
25   {
26        size_t i; // counter
27
28        // loop through strings
29        for ( i = 0; ( s1[ i ] = s2[ i ] ) != '\0'; ++i ) {
30             ; // do nothing in body
31        } // end for
32   } // end function copy1
33
34   // copy s2 to s1 using pointer notation
35   void copy2( char *s1, const char *s2 )
36   {
37        // loop through strings
38        for ( ; ( *s1 = *s2 ) != '\0'; ++s1, ++s2 ) {
39             ; // do nothing in body
40        } // end for
41   } // end function copy2
```

```
string1 = Hello
string3 = Good Bye
```

Fig. 7.21 | Copying a string using array notation and pointer notation. (Part 2 of 2.)

Function copy2 uses *pointers and pointer arithmetic* to copy the string in s2 to the character array s1. Again, the for statement header (line 38) performs the entire copy operation. The header does not include any variable initialization. As in function copy1, the expression (*s1 = *s2) performs the copy operation. Pointer s2 is dereferenced, and the resulting character is assigned to the dereferenced pointer *s1. After the assignment in the condition, the pointers are incremented to point to the next element of array s1 and the next character of string s2, respectively. When the null character is encountered in s2, it's assigned to the dereferenced pointer s1 and the loop terminates.

The first argument to both copy1 and copy2 must be an array large enough to hold the string in the second argument. Otherwise, an error may occur when an attempt is made to write into a memory location that's not part of the array. Also, the second parameter of each function is declared as const char * (a constant string). In both functions, the second argument is copied into the first argument—characters are read from it one at a time, but the characters are *never modified*. Therefore, the second parameter is declared to point to a constant value so that the *principle of least privilege* is enforced—neither function requires the capability of modifying the second argument, so neither function is provided with that capability.

7.10 Arrays of Pointers

Arrays may contain pointers. A common use of an **array of pointers** is to form an **array of strings**, referred to simply as a **string array**. Each entry in the array is a string, but in C a string is essentially a pointer to its first character. So each entry in an array of strings is actually a pointer to the first character of a string. Consider the definition of string array suit, which might be useful in representing a deck of cards.

```
const char *suit[ 4 ] = { "Hearts", "Diamonds", "Clubs", "Spades"
};
```

The suit[4] portion of the definition indicates an array of 4 elements. The char * portion of the declaration indicates that each element of array suit is of type "pointer to char." Qualifier const indicates that the strings pointed to by each element pointer will not be modified. The four values to be placed in the array are "Hearts", "Diamonds", "Clubs" and "Spades". Each is stored in memory as a *null-terminated character string* that's one character longer than the number of characters between quotes. The four strings are 7, 9, 6 and 7 characters long, respectively. Although it appears as though these strings are being placed in the suit array, only pointers are actually stored in the array (Fig. 7.22). Each pointer points to the first character of its corresponding string. Thus, even though the suit array is *fixed* in size, it provides access to character strings of *any length*. This flexibility is one example of C's powerful data-structuring capabilities.

Fig. 7.22 | Graphical representation of the suit array.

The suits could have been placed in a two-dimensional array, in which each row would represent a suit and each column would represent a letter from a suit name. Such a data structure would have to have a fixed number of columns per row, and that number would have to be as large as the largest string. Therefore, considerable memory could be wasted when storing a large number of strings of which most were shorter than the longest string. We use string arrays to represent a deck of cards in the next section.

7.11 Case Study: Card Shuffling and Dealing Simulation

In this section, we use random number generation to develop a card shuffling and dealing simulation program. This program can then be used to implement programs that play specific card games. To reveal some subtle performance problems, we've intentionally used suboptimal shuffling and dealing algorithms. In this chapter's exercises and in Chapter 10, we develop more efficient algorithms.

Using the top-down, stepwise refinement approach, we develop a program that will shuffle a deck of 52 playing cards and then deal each of the 52 cards. The top-down approach is particularly useful in attacking larger, more complex problems than you've seen in earlier chapters.

We use 4-by-13 double-subscripted array deck to represent the deck of playing cards (Fig. 7.23). The rows correspond to the *suits*—row 0 corresponds to hearts, row 1 to diamonds, row 2 to clubs and row 3 to spades. The columns correspond to the *face* values of the cards—columns 0 through 9 correspond to ace through ten respectively, and columns 10 through 12 correspond to jack, queen and king. We shall load string array suit with character strings representing the four suits, and string array face with character strings representing the thirteen face values.

Fig. 7.23 | Double-subscripted array representation of a deck of cards.

This simulated deck of cards may be *shuffled* as follows. First the array deck is cleared to zeros. Then, a row (0–3) and a column (0–12) are each chosen *at random*. The number 1 is inserted in array element deck[row][column] to indicate that this card will be the first one dealt from the shuffled deck. This process continues with the numbers 2, 3, …, 52 being randomly inserted in the deck array to indicate which cards are to be placed second, third, …, and fifty-second in the shuffled deck. As the deck array begins to fill with card numbers, it's possible that a card will be selected again—i.e., deck[row] [column] will be nonzero when it's selected. This selection is simply ignored and other rows and columns are repeatedly chosen at random until an *unselected* card is found. Eventually, the numbers 1 through 52 will occupy the 52 slots of the deck array. At this point, the deck of cards is fully shuffled.

This shuffling algorithm can execute *indefinitely* if cards that have already been shuffled are repeatedly selected at random. This phenomenon is known as **indefinite postponement**. In this chapter's exercises, we discuss a better shuffling algorithm that eliminates the possibility of indefinite postponement.

Performance Tip 7.3

Sometimes an algorithm that emerges in a "natural" way can contain subtle performance problems, such as indefinite postponement. Seek algorithms that avoid indefinite postponement.

To deal the first card, we search the array for deck[row][column] equal to 1. This is accomplished with nested for statements that vary row from 0 to 3 and column from 0 to

12. What card does that element of the array correspond to? The `suit` array has been pre-loaded with the four suits, so to get the suit, we print the character string `suit[row]`. Similarly, to get the face value of the card, we print the character string `face[column]`. We also print the character string `" of "`. Printing this information in the proper order enables us to print each card in the form `"King of Clubs"`, `"Ace of Diamonds"` and so on.

Let's proceed with the top-down, stepwise refinement process. The *top* is simply

> *Shuffle and deal 52 cards*

Our *first refinement* yields:

> *Initialize the suit array*
> *Initialize the face array*
> *Initialize the deck array*
> *Shuffle the deck*
> *Deal 52 cards*

"Shuffle the deck" may be expanded as follows:

> *For each of the 52 cards*
>   *Place card number in randomly selected unoccupied slot of deck*

"Deal 52 cards" may be expanded as follows:

> *For each of the 52 cards*
>   *Find card number in deck array and print face and suit of card*

Incorporating these expansions yields our complete *second refinement*:

> *Initialize the suit array*
> *Initialize the face array*
> *Initialize the deck array*
>
> *For each of the 52 cards*
>   *Place card number in randomly selected unoccupied slot of deck*
>
> *For each of the 52 cards*
>   *Find card number in deck array and print face and suit of card*

"Place card number in randomly selected unoccupied slot of deck" may be expanded as:

> *Choose slot of deck randomly*
>
> *While chosen slot of deck has been previously chosen*
>   *Choose slot of deck randomly*
>
> *Place card number in chosen slot of deck*

"Find card number in deck array and print face and suit of card" may be expanded as:

> *For each slot of the deck array*
>   *If slot contains card number*
>   *Print the face and suit of the card*

Incorporating these expansions yields our *third refinement*:

> *Initialize the suit array*
> *Initialize the face array*
> *Initialize the deck array*
>
> *For each of the 52 cards*
>   *Choose slot of deck randomly*
>
>   *While slot of deck has been previously chosen*
>   *Choose slot of deck randomly*
>
>   *Place card number in chosen slot of deck*
>
> *For each of the 52 cards*
>   *For each slot of deck array*
>   *If slot contains desired card number*
>   *Print the face and suit of the card*

This completes the refinement process. This program is more efficient if the shuffle and deal portions of the algorithm are combined so that each card is dealt as it's placed in the deck. We've chosen to program these operations separately because normally cards are dealt after they're shuffled (not while they're being shuffled).

The card shuffling and dealing program is shown in Fig. 7.24, and a sample execution is shown in Fig. 7.25. Conversion specifier %s is used to print strings of characters in the calls to printf. The corresponding argument in the printf call must be a pointer to char (or a char array). The format specification "%5s of %-8s" (line 74) prints a character string *right justified* in a field of five characters followed by " of " and a character string *left justified* in a field of eight characters. The *minus sign* in %-8s signifies left justification.

There's a weakness in the dealing algorithm. Once a match is found, the two inner for statements continue searching the remaining elements of deck for a match. We correct this deficiency in this chapter's exercises and in a Chapter 10 case study.

```c
1   // Fig. 7.24: fig07_24.c
2   // Card shuffling and dealing.
3   #include <stdio.h>
4   #include <stdlib.h>
5   #include <time.h>
6
7   #define SUITS 4
8   #define FACES 13
9   #define CARDS 52
10
11  // prototypes
12  void shuffle( unsigned int wDeck[][ FACES ] ); // shuffling modifies wDeck
13  void deal( unsigned int wDeck[][ FACES ], const char *wFace[],
14     const char *wSuit[] ); // dealing doesn't modify the arrays
15
16  int main( void )
17  {
```

Fig. 7.24 | Card shuffling and dealing. (Part 1 of 3.)

```
18    // initialize suit array
19    const char *suit[ SUITS ] =
20       { "Hearts", "Diamonds", "Clubs", "Spades" };
21
22    // initialize face array
23    const char *face[ FACES ] =
24       { "Ace", "Deuce", "Three", "Four",
25         "Five", "Six", "Seven", "Eight",
26         "Nine", "Ten", "Jack", "Queen", "King" };
27
28    // initialize deck array
29    unsigned int deck[ SUITS ][ FACES ] = { 0 };
30
31    srand( time( NULL ) ); // seed random-number generator
32
33    shuffle( deck ); // shuffle the deck
34    deal( deck, face, suit ); // deal the deck
35 } // end main
36
37 // shuffle cards in deck
38 void shuffle( unsigned int wDeck[][ FACES ] )
39 {
40    size_t row; // row number
41    size_t column; // column number
42    size_t card; // counter
43
44    // for each of the cards, choose slot of deck randomly
45    for ( card = 1; card <= CARDS; ++card ) {
46
47       // choose new random location until unoccupied slot found
48       do {
49          row = rand() % SUITS;
50          column = rand() % FACES;
51       } while( wDeck[ row ][ column ] != 0 ); // end do...while
52
53       // place card number in chosen slot of deck
54       wDeck[ row ][ column ] = card;
55    } // end for
56 } // end function shuffle
57
58 // deal cards in deck
59 void deal( unsigned int wDeck[][ FACES ], const char *wFace[],
60    const char *wSuit[] )
61 {
62    size_t card; // card counter
63    size_t row; // row counter
64    size_t column; // column counter
65
66    // deal each of the cards
67    for ( card = 1; card <= CARDS; ++card ) {
68       // loop through rows of wDeck
69       for ( row = 0; row < SUITS; ++row ) {
```

Fig. 7.24 | Card shuffling and dealing. (Part 2 of 3.)

```
70              // loop through columns of wDeck for current row
71              for ( column = 0; column < FACES; ++column ) {
72                  // if slot contains current card, display card
73                  if ( wDeck[ row ][ column ] == card ) {
74                      printf( "%5s of %-8s%c", wFace[ column ], wSuit[ row ],
75                          card % 2 == 0 ? '\n' : '\t' ); // 2-column format
76                  } // end if
77              } // end for
78          } // end for
79      } // end for
80  } // end function deal
```

Fig. 7.24 | Card shuffling and dealing. (Part 3 of 3.)

```
 Nine of Hearts        Five of Clubs
Queen of Spades       Three of Spades
Queen of Hearts         Ace of Clubs
 King of Hearts         Six of Spades
 Jack of Diamonds      Five of Spades
Seven of Hearts        King of Clubs
Three of Clubs        Eight of Hearts
Three of Diamonds      Four of Diamonds
Queen of Diamonds      Five of Diamonds
  Six of Diamonds      Five of Hearts
  Ace of Spades         Six of Hearts
 Nine of Diamonds     Queen of Clubs
Eight of Spades        Nine of Clubs
Deuce of Clubs          Six of Clubs
Deuce of Spades        Jack of Clubs
 Four of Clubs        Eight of Clubs
 Four of Spades       Seven of Spades
Seven of Diamonds     Seven of Clubs
 King of Spades         Ten of Diamonds
 Jack of Hearts         Ace of Hearts
 Jack of Spades         Ten of Clubs
Eight of Diamonds     Deuce of Diamonds
  Ace of Diamonds      Nine of Spades
 Four of Hearts       Deuce of Hearts
 King of Diamonds      Ten of Spades
Three of Hearts        Ten of Hearts
```

Fig. 7.25 | Sample run of card dealing program.

7.12 Pointers to Functions

A **pointer to a function** contains the *address* of the function in memory. In Chapter 6, we saw that an array name is really the address in memory of the first element of the array. Similarly, a function name is really the starting address in memory of the code that performs the function's task. Pointers to functions can be *passed* to functions, *returned* from functions, *stored* in arrays and *assigned* to other function pointers.

To illustrate the use of pointers to functions, Fig. 7.26 presents a modified version of the bubble sort program in Fig. 7.15. The new version consists of main and functions bubble, swap, ascending and descending. Function bubbleSort receives a pointer to a function—either function `ascending` or function `descending`—as an *argument*, in addition to an integer array and the size of the array. The program prompts the user to choose whether the array should be sorted in *ascending* or in *descending* order. If the user enters 1, a pointer to function `ascending` is passed to function `bubble`, causing the array to be sorted into *increasing* order. If the user enters 2, a pointer to function `descending` is passed to function `bubble`, causing the array to be sorted into *decreasing* order. The output of the program is shown in Fig. 7.27.

```c
// Fig. 7.26: fig07_26.c
// Multipurpose sorting program using function pointers.
#include <stdio.h>
#define SIZE 10

// prototypes
void bubble( int work[], size_t size, int (*compare)( int a, int b ) );
int ascending( int a, int b );
int descending( int a, int b );

int main( void )
{
   int order; // 1 for ascending order or 2 for descending order
   size_t counter; // counter

   // initialize unordered array a
   int a[ SIZE ] = { 2, 6, 4, 8, 10, 12, 89, 68, 45, 37 };

   printf( "%s", "Enter 1 to sort in ascending order,\n"
          "Enter 2 to sort in descending order: " );
   scanf( "%d", &order );

   puts( "\nData items in original order" );

   // output original array
   for ( counter = 0; counter < SIZE; ++counter ) {
      printf( "%5d", a[ counter ] );
   } // end for

   // sort array in ascending order; pass function ascending as an
   // argument to specify ascending sorting order
   if ( order == 1 ) {
      bubble( a, SIZE, ascending );
      puts( "\nData items in ascending order" );
   } // end if
   else { // pass function descending
      bubble( a, SIZE, descending );
      puts( "\nData items in descending order" );
   } // end else

   // output sorted array
   for ( counter = 0; counter < SIZE; ++counter ) {
      printf( "%5d", a[ counter ] );
   } // end for
```

Fig. 7.26 | Multipurpose sorting program using function pointers. (Part 1 of 2.)

```
45
46       puts( "\n" );
47    } // end main
48
49    // multipurpose bubble sort; parameter compare is a pointer to
50    // the comparison function that determines sorting order
51    void bubble( int work[], size_t size, int (*compare)( int a, int b ) )
52    {
53       unsigned int pass; // pass counter
54       size_t count; // comparison counter
55
56       void swap( int *element1Ptr, int *element2ptr ); // prototype
57
58       // loop to control passes
59       for ( pass = 1; pass < size; ++pass ) {
60
61          // loop to control number of comparisons per pass
62          for ( count = 0; count < size - 1; ++count ) {
63
64             // if adjacent elements are out of order, swap them
65             if ( (*compare)( work[ count ], work[ count + 1 ] ) ) {
66                swap( &work[ count ], &work[ count + 1 ] );
67             } // end if
68          } // end for
69       } // end for
70    } // end function bubble
71
72    // swap values at memory locations to which element1Ptr and
73    // element2Ptr point
74    void swap( int *element1Ptr, int *element2Ptr )
75    {
76       int hold; // temporary holding variable
77
78       hold = *element1Ptr;
79       *element1Ptr = *element2Ptr;
80       *element2Ptr = hold;
81    } // end function swap
82
83    // determine whether elements are out of order for an ascending
84    // order sort
85    int ascending( int a, int b )
86    {
87       return b < a; // should swap if b is less than a
88    } // end function ascending
89
90    // determine whether elements are out of order for a descending
91    // order sort
92    int descending( int a, int b )
93    {
94       return b > a; // should swap if b is greater than a
95    } // end function descending
```

Fig. 7.26 | Multipurpose sorting program using function pointers. (Part 2 of 2.)

```
Enter 1 to sort in ascending order,
Enter 2 to sort in descending order: 1

Data items in original order
    2    6    4    8   10   12   89   68   45   37
Data items in ascending order
    2    4    6    8   10   12   37   45   68   89
```

```
Enter 1 to sort in ascending order,
Enter 2 to sort in descending order: 2

Data items in original order
    2    6    4    8   10   12   89   68   45   37
Data items in descending order
   89   68   45   37   12   10    8    6    4    2
```

Fig. 7.27 | The outputs of the bubble sort program in Fig. 7.26.

The following parameter appears in the function header for `bubble` (line 51)

```
int (*compare)( int a, int b )
```

This tells `bubble` to expect a parameter (`compare`) that's a pointer to a function that receives two integer parameters and returns an integer result. Parentheses are needed around `*compare` to group the `*` with `compare` to indicate that `compare` is a *pointer*. If we had not included the parentheses, the declaration would have been

```
int *compare( int a, int b )
```

which declares a function that receives two integers as parameters and returns a pointer to an integer.

The function prototype for `bubble` is shown in line 7. The third parameter in the prototype could have been written as

```
int (*)( int, int );
```

without the function-pointer name and parameter names.

The function passed to `bubble` is called in an `if` statement (line 65) as follows:

```
if ( (*compare)( work[ count ], work[ count + 1 ] ) )
```

Just as a pointer to a variable is dereferenced to access the value of the variable, *a pointer to a function is dereferenced to use the function.*

The call to the function could have been made without dereferencing the pointer as in

```
if ( compare( work[ count ], work[ count + 1 ] ) )
```

which uses the pointer directly as the function name. We prefer the first method of calling a function through a pointer because it explicitly illustrates that `compare` is a pointer to a function that's dereferenced to call the function. The second method of calling a function through a pointer makes it appear as if `compare` is an *actual* function. This may be confusing to a programmer reading the code who would like to see the definition of function `compare` and finds that it's *never defined* in the file.

Using Function Pointers to Create a Menu-Driven System

A common use of **function pointers** is in text-based *menu-driven systems*. A user is prompted to select an option from a menu (possibly from 1 to 5) by typing the menu item's number. Each option is serviced by a different function. Pointers to each function are stored in an array of pointers to functions. The user's choice is used as a subscript in the array, and the pointer in the array is used to call the function.

Figure 7.28 provides a generic example of the mechanics of defining and using an array of pointers to functions. We define three functions—function1, function2 and function3—that each take an integer argument and return nothing. We store pointers to these three functions in array f, which is defined in line 14.

```c
1   // Fig. 7.28: fig07_28.c
2   // Demonstrating an array of pointers to functions.
3   #include <stdio.h>
4
5   // prototypes
6   void function1( int a );
7   void function2( int b );
8   void function3( int c );
9
10  int main( void )
11  {
12     // initialize array of 3 pointers to functions that each take an
13     // int argument and return void
14     void (*f[ 3 ])( int ) = { function1, function2, function3 };
15
16     size_t choice; // variable to hold user's choice
17
18     printf( "%s", "Enter a number between 0 and 2, 3 to end: " );
19     scanf( "%u", &choice );
20
21     // process user's choice
22     while ( choice >= 0 && choice < 3 ) {
23
24        // invoke function at location choice in array f and pass
25        // choice as an argument
26        (*f[ choice ])( choice );
27
28        printf( "%s", "Enter a number between 0 and 2, 3 to end: " );
29        scanf( "%u", &choice );
30     } // end while
31
32     puts( "Program execution completed." );
33  } // end main
34
35  void function1( int a )
36  {
37     printf( "You entered %d so function1 was called\n\n", a );
38  } // end function1
39
```

Fig. 7.28 | Demonstrating an array of pointers to functions. (Part 1 of 2.)

```
40   void function2( int b )
41   {
42      printf( "You entered %d so function2 was called\n\n", b );
43   } // end function2
44
45   void function3( int c )
46   {
47      printf( "You entered %d so function3 was called\n\n", c );
48   } // end function3
```

```
Enter a number between 0 and 2, 3 to end: 0
You entered 0 so function1 was called

Enter a number between 0 and 2, 3 to end: 1
You entered 1 so function2 was called

Enter a number between 0 and 2, 3 to end: 2
You entered 2 so function3 was called

Enter a number between 0 and 2, 3 to end: 3
Program execution completed.
```

Fig. 7.28 | Demonstrating an array of pointers to functions. (Part 2 of 2.)

The definition is read beginning at the leftmost set of parentheses, "f is an array of 3 pointers to functions that each take an int as an argument and return void." The array is initialized with the names of the three functions. When the user enters a value between 0 and 2, the value is used as the subscript into the array of pointers to functions. In the function call (line 26), f[choice] selects the pointer at location choice in the array. The *pointer is dereferenced to call the function*, and choice is passed as the argument to the function. Each function prints its argument's value and its function name to demonstrate that the function is called correctly. In this chapter's exercises, you'll develop several text-based, menu-driven systems.

7.13 Secure C Programming

printf_s, scanf_s and Other Secure Functions
Earlier Secure C Programming sections presented printf_s and scanf_s, and mentioned other more secure versions of standard library functions that are described by Annex K of the C standard. A key feature of functions like printf_s and scanf_s that makes them more secure is that they have *runtime constraints* requiring their pointer arguments to be non-NULL. The functions check these runtime constraints *before* attempting to use the pointers. Any NULL pointer argument is considered to be a *constraint violation* and causes the function to fail and return a status notification. In a scanf_s, if any of the pointer arguments (including the format-control string) are NULL, the function returns EOF. In a printf_s, if the format-control string or any argument that corresponds to a %s is NULL, the function stops outputting data and returns a negative number. For complete details of the Annex K functions, see the C standard document or your compiler's library documentation.

Other CERT Guidelines Regarding Pointers

Misused pointers lead to many of the most common security vulnerabilities in systems today. CERT provides various guidelines to help you prevent such problems. If you're building industrial-strength C systems, you should familiarize yourself with the *CERT C Secure Coding Standard* at `www.securecoding.cert.org`. The following guidelines apply to pointer programming techniques that we presented in this chapter:

- EXP34-C: Dereferencing `NULL` pointers typically causes programs to crash, but CERT has encountered cases in which dereferencing `NULL` pointers can allow attackers to execute code.

- DCL13-C: Section 7.5 discussed uses of `const` with pointers. If a function parameter points to a value that will not be changed by the function, `const` should be used to indicate that the data is constant. For example, to represent a pointer to a string that will not be modified, use `const char *` as the pointer parameter's type.

- MSC16-C: This guideline discusses techniques for encrypting function pointers to help prevent attackers from overwriting them and executing attack code.

Summary

Section 7.2 Pointer Variable Definitions and Initialization

- A pointer contains an address of another variable that contains a value. In this sense, a variable name *directly* references a value, and a pointer *indirectly* references a value.

- Referencing a value through a pointer is called indirection.

- Pointers can be defined to point to objects of any type.

- Pointers should be initialized either when they're defined or in an assignment statement. A pointer may be initialized to `NULL`, 0 or an address. A pointer with the value `NULL` points to nothing. Initializing a pointer to 0 is equivalent to initializing a pointer to `NULL`, but `NULL` is preferred. The value 0 is the only integer value that can be assigned directly to a pointer variable.

- `NULL` is a symbolic constant defined in the `<stddef.h>` header (and several other headers).

Section 7.3 Pointer Operators

- The &, or address operator, is a unary operator that returns the address of its operand.

- The operand of the address operator must be a variable.

- The indirection operator * returns the value of the object to which its operand points.

- The `printf` conversion specifier %p outputs a memory location as a hexadecimal integer on most platforms.

Section 7.4 Passing Arguments to Functions by Reference

- All arguments in C are passed by value.

- C provides the capabilities for simulating pass-by-reference using pointers and the indirection operator. To pass a variable by reference, apply the address operator (&) to the variable's name.

- When the address of a variable is passed to a function, the indirection operator (*) may be used in the function to modify the value at that location in the caller's memory.

- A function receiving an address as an argument must define a pointer parameter to receive the address.

- The compiler does not differentiate between a function that receives a pointer and one that receives a single-subscripted array. A function must "know" when it's receiving an array vs. a single variable passed by reference.

- When the compiler encounters a function parameter for a single-subscripted array of the form int b[], the compiler converts the parameter to the pointer notation int *b.

Section 7.5 Using the const Qualifier with Pointers

- The const qualifier indicates that the value of a particular variable should not be modified.

- If an attempt is made to modify a value that's declared const, the compiler catches it and issues either a warning or an error, depending on the particular compiler.

- There are four ways to pass a pointer to a function: a non-constant pointer to non-constant data, a constant pointer to non-constant data, a non-constant pointer to constant data, and a constant pointer to constant data.

- With a non-constant pointer to non-constant data, the data can be modified through the dereferenced pointer, and the pointer can be modified to point to other data items.

- A non-constant pointer to constant data can be modified to point to any data item of the appropriate type, but the data to which it points cannot be modified.

- A constant pointer to non-constant data always points to the same memory location, and the data at that location can be modified through the pointer. This is the default for an array name.

- A constant pointer to constant data always points to the same memory location, and the data at that memory location cannot be modified.

Section 7.7 sizeof Operator

- Unary operator sizeof determine the size in bytes of a variable or type at compilation time.

- When applied to the name of an array, sizeof returns the total number of bytes in the array.

- Type size_t is an integral type (unsigned int or unsigned long int) returned by operator sizeof. Type size_t is defined in header <stddef.h>.

- Operator sizeof can be applied to any variable name, type or value.

- The parentheses used with sizeof are required if a type name is supplied as its operand.

Section 7.8 Pointer Expressions and Pointer Arithmetic

- A limited set of arithmetic operations may be performed on pointers. A pointer may be incremented (++) or decremented (--), an integer may be added to a pointer (+ or +=), an integer may be subtracted from a pointer (- or -=) and one pointer may be subtracted from another.

- When an integer is added to or subtracted from a pointer, the pointer is incremented or decremented by that integer times the size of the object to which the pointer refers.

- Two pointers to elements of the same array may be subtracted from one another to determine the number of elements between them.

- A pointer can be assigned to another pointer if both have the same type. An exception is the pointer of type void * which can represent any pointer type. All pointer types can be assigned a void * pointer, and a void * pointer can be assigned a pointer of any type.

- A void * pointer cannot be dereferenced.

- Pointers can be compared using equality and relational operators, but such comparisons are meaningless unless the pointers point to elements of the same array. Pointer comparisons compare the addresses stored in the pointers.

- A common use of pointer comparison is determining whether a pointer is NULL.

Section 7.9 Relationship between Pointers and Arrays
- Arrays and pointers are intimately related in C and often may be used interchangeably.

- An array name can be thought of as a constant pointer.

- Pointers can be used to do any operation involving array subscripting.

- When a pointer points to the beginning of an array, adding an offset to the pointer indicates which element of the array should be referenced, and the offset value is identical to the array subscript. This is referred to as pointer/offset notation.

- An array name can be treated as a pointer and used in pointer arithmetic expressions that do not attempt to modify the address of the pointer.

- Pointers can be subscripted exactly as arrays can. This is referred to as pointer/subscript notation.

- A parameter of type const char * typically represents a constant string.

Section 7.10 Arrays of Pointers
- Arrays may contain pointers. A common use of an array of pointers is to form an array of strings. Each entry in the array is a string, but in C a string is essentially a pointer to its first character. So, each entry in an array of strings is actually a pointer to the first character of a string.

Section 7.12 Pointers to Functions
- A pointer to a function contains the address of the function in memory. A function name is really the starting address in memory of the code that performs the function's task.

- Pointers to functions can be passed to functions, returned from functions, stored in arrays and assigned to other function pointers.

- A pointer to a function is dereferenced to call the function. A function pointer can be used directly as the function name when calling the function.

- A common use of function pointers is in text-based, menu-driven systems.

Terminology

Self-Review Exercises

7.1   Answer each of the following:
a) A pointer variable contains as its value the _____ of another variable.
b) The three values that can be used to initialize a pointer are _____, _____ and _____.
c) The only integer that can be assigned to a pointer is _____.

7.2   State whether the following are *true* or *false*. If the answer is *false*, explain why.
a) The address operator (&) can be applied only to constants, to expressions and to variables declared with the storage-class `register`.
b) A pointer that's declared to be `void` can be dereferenced.
c) Pointers of different types may not be assigned to one another without a cast operation.

7.3   Answer each of the following. Assume that single-precision floating-point numbers are stored in 4 bytes, and that the starting address of the array is at location 1002500 in memory. Each part of the exercise should use the results of previous parts where appropriate.
a) Define an array of type `float` called `numbers` with 10 elements, and initialize the elements to the values `0.0, 1.1, 2.2, ..., 9.9`. Assume the symbolic constant `SIZE` has been defined as `10`.
b) Define a pointer, `nPtr`, that points to an object of type `float`.
c) Print the elements of array `numbers` using array subscript notation. Use a `for` statement and assume the integer control variable `i` has been defined. Print each number with 1 position of precision to the right of the decimal point.
d) Give two separate statements that assign the starting address of array `numbers` to the pointer variable `nPtr`.
e) Print the elements of array `numbers` using pointer/offset notation with the pointer `nPtr`.
f) Print the elements of array `numbers` using pointer/offset notation with the array name as the pointer.
g) Print the elements of array `numbers` by subscripting pointer `nPtr`.
h) Refer to element 4 of array `numbers` using array subscript notation, pointer/offset notation with the array name as the pointer, pointer subscript notation with `nPtr` and pointer/offset notation with `nPtr`.
i) Assuming that `nPtr` points to the beginning of array `numbers`, what address is referenced by `nPtr + 8`? What value is stored at that location?
j) Assuming that `nPtr` points to `numbers[5]`, what address is referenced by `nPtr -= 4`? What's the value stored at that location?

7.4   For each of the following, write a statement that performs the indicated task. Assume that integer variables `a` and `b` are defined and that `a` is initialized to `100`.
a) Define the variable `ptr` to be a pointer to an object of type `int`.
b) Assign the address of variable `a` to pointer variable `ptr`.
c) Assign the value of the object pointed to by `ptr` to variable `b`.
d) Print the value of the object pointed to by `ptr`.
e) Print the address stored in `ptr`. Use the `%p` conversion specifier. The value printed is same or it is different as the address of `a`?
f) Print the value of `b`.
g) Print the address of `a`. Use the `%p` conversion specifier.

7.5   Do each of the following:
a) Write the function header for a function called `number` that takes two pointers to integer numbers `p` and `q` as parameters and returns an integer.
b) Write the function prototype for the function in part (a).

c) Write the function header for a function called `value` that does not return anything and that takes as parameter a pointer to function `rect`. Function `rect` takes two floating-point parameters and returns a floating-point number.

d) Write the function prototype for the function in part (c).

7.6 Find the error in each of the following program segments. Assume

```
int *zPtr; // zPtr will reference array z
int *aPtr = NULL;
void *sPtr = NULL;
int number, i;
int z[ 5 ] = { 1, 2, 3, 4, 5 };
sPtr = z;
```

a) ++zptr;

b) // use pointer to get first value of array; assume zPtr is initialized
   number = zPtr;

c) // assign array element 2 (the value 3) to number;
       assume zPtr is initialized
   number = *zPtr[2];

d) // print entire array z; assume zPtr is initialized
   for (i = 0; i <= 5; ++i) {
       printf("%d ", zPtr[i]);
   }

e) // assign the value pointed to by sPtr to number
   number = *sPtr;

f) ++z;

Answers to Self-Review Exercises

7.1 a) address. b) 0, NULL, an address. c) 0.

7.2 a) False. The address operator can be applied only to variables. The address operator cannot be applied to variables declared with storage class `register`. b) False. A pointer to `void` cannot be dereferenced, because there's no way to know exactly how many bytes of memory to dereference. c) False. Pointers of type `void` can be assigned pointers of other types, and pointers of type `void` can be assigned to pointers of other types.

7.3 a) `float numbers[ SIZE ] = { 0.0, 1.1, 2.2, 3.3, 4.4, 5.5, 6.6, 7.7, 8.8, 9.9 };`
  b) `float *nPtr;`
  c) `for ( i = 0; i < SIZE; ++i ) {`
       `printf( "%.1f ", numbers[ i ] );`
     `}`
  d) `nPtr = numbers;`
     `nPtr = &numbers[ 0 ];`
  e) `for ( i = 0; i < SIZE; ++i ) {`
       `printf( "%.1f ", *( nPtr + i ) );`
     `}`
  f) `for ( i = 0; i < SIZE; ++i ) {`
       `printf( "%.1f ", *( numbers + i ) );`
     `}`
  g) `for ( i = 0; i < SIZE; ++i ) {`
       `printf( "%.1f ", nPtr[ i ] );`
     `}`

h) `numbers[ 4 ]`
   `*( numbers + 4 )`
   `nPtr[ 4 ]`
   `*( nPtr + 4 )`

i) The address is 1002500 + 8 * 4 = 1002532. The value is 8.8.

j) The address of `numbers[ 5 ]` is 1002500 + 5 * 4 = 1002520.
   The address of `nPtr -= 4` is 1002520 - 4 * 4 = 1002504.
   The value at that location is 1.1.

7.4   a) `int *Ptr;`
   b) `Ptr = &a;`
   c) `b = *ptr;`
   d) `printf( "the value of *fptr is %d\n", *Ptr );`
   e) `printf( "the address stored in ptr is %p\n", Ptr );`
      The value is the same.
   f) `printf( "the value of b is %d\n", b );`
   g) `printf( "the address of a is %p\n", &a );`

7.5   a) `int number( int *p, int *q )`
   b) `int number( int *p, int *q );`
   c) `void value(float (*rect)( float, float ) )`
   d) `void value(float (*rect)( float, float ) );`

7.6   a) Error: `zPtr` has not been initialized.
      Correction: Initialize `zPtr` with `zPtr = z;` before performing the pointer arithmetic.
   b) Error: The pointer is not dereferenced.
      Correction: Change the statement to `number = *zPtr;`
   c) Error: `zPtr[ 2 ]` is not a pointer and should not be dereferenced.
      Correction: Change `*zPtr[ 2 ]` to `zPtr[ 2 ]`.
   d) Error: Referring to an array element outside the array bounds with pointer subscripting.
      Correction: Change the operator `<=` in the `for` condition to `<`.
   e) Error: Dereferencing a void pointer.
      Correction: To dereference the pointer, it must first be cast to an integer pointer.
      Change the statement to `number = *( ( int * ) sPtr );`
   f) Error: Trying to modify an array name with pointer arithmetic.
      Correction: Use a pointer variable instead of the array name to accomplish pointer arithmetic, or subscript the array name to refer to a specific element.

Exercises

7.7   Answer each of the following:
   a) The _____ operator returns the location in memory where its operand is stored.
   b) The _____ operator returns the value of the object to which its operand points.
   c) To simulate pass-by-reference when passing a nonarray variable to a function, it's necessary to pass the _____ of the variable to the function.

7.8   State whether the following are *true* or *false*. If *false*, explain why.
   a) Two pointers that point to different arrays cannot be compared meaningfully.
   b) Because the name of an array is a pointer to the first element of the array, array names may be manipulated in precisely the same manner as pointers.

7.9   Answer each of the following. Assume that unsigned integers are stored in 2 bytes and that the starting address of the array is at location 1002500 in memory.

    a) Define an array of type unsigned int called values with five elements, and initialize the elements to the even integers from 2 to 10. Assume the symbolic constant SIZE has been defined as 5.

    b) Define a pointer vPtr that points to an object of type unsigned int.

    c) Print the elements of array values using array subscript notation. Use a for statement and assume integer control variable i has been defined.

    d) Give two separate statements that assign the starting address of array values to pointer variable vPtr.

    e) Print the elements of array values using pointer/offset notation.

    f) Print the elements of array values using pointer/offset notation with the array name as the pointer.

    g) Print the elements of array values by subscripting the pointer to the array.

    h) Refer to element 5 of array values using array subscript notation, pointer/offset notation with the array name as the pointer, pointer subscript notation, and pointer/offset notation.

    i) What address is referenced by vPtr + 3? What value is stored at that location?

    j) Assuming vPtr points to values[4], what address is referenced by vPtr -= 4? What value is stored at that location?

7.10 For each of the following, write a single statement that performs the indicated task. Assume that integer variables one and two have been defined and that two has been initialized to 600 and one has been initialized to 500.

    a) Print the value of one.

    b) Print the value of two.

    c) Define the variable m to be a pointer to an object of type int.

    d) Assign the address of variable two to pointer variable m.

    e) Assign the value of the object pointed to by m to variable two.

    f) Print the address stored in m. Is the value printed different as the address of two? Use the %p conversion specifier.

    g) Print the value of the object pointed to by m.

7.11 Do each of the following:

    a) Write the function header for function add, which takes two floating-point array parameters firstNumber and secondNumber and returns a floating-point value.

    b) Write the function prototype for the function in part (a).

    c) Write the function header for function first, which takes a double array parameter number and does not return a value.

    d) Write the function prototype for the function described in part (c).

Note: Exercises 7.12–7.15 are reasonably challenging. Once you have done these problems, you ought to be able to implement most popular card games easily.

7.12 *(Card Shuffling and Dealing)* Modify the program in Fig. 7.24 so that the card-dealing function deals a five-card poker hand. Then write the following additional functions:

    a) Determine whether the hand contains a pair.

    b) Determine whether the hand contains two pairs.

    c) Determine whether the hand contains three of a kind (e.g., three jacks).

    d) Determine whether the hand contains four of a kind (e.g., four aces).

    e) Determine whether the hand contains a flush (i.e., all five cards of the same suit).

    f) Determine whether the hand contains a straight (i.e., five cards of consecutive face values).

7.13 *(Project: Card Shuffling and Dealing)* Use the functions developed in Exercise 7.12 to write a program that deals two five-card poker hands, evaluates each, and determines which is the better hand.

7.14 *(Project: Card Shuffling and Dealing)* Modify the program developed in Exercise 7.13 so that it can simulate the dealer. The dealer's five-card hand is dealt "face down" so the player cannot see it. The program should then evaluate the dealer's hand, and based on the quality of the hand, the dealer should draw one, two or three more cards to replace the corresponding number of un-needed cards in the original hand. The program should then reevaluate the dealer's hand. [*Caution:* This is a difficult problem!]

7.15 *(Project: Card Shuffling and Dealing)* Modify the program developed in Exercise 7.14 so that it can handle the dealer's hand automatically, but the player is allowed to decide which cards of the player's hand to replace. The program should then evaluate both hands and determine who wins. Now use this new program to play 20 games against the computer. Who wins more games, you or the computer? Have one of your friends play 20 games against the computer. Who wins more games? Based on the results of these games, make appropriate modifications to refine your poker-playing program (this, too, is a difficult problem). Play 20 more games. Does your modified program play a better game?

7.16 *(Card Shuffling and Dealing Modification)* In the card shuffling and dealing program of Fig. 7.24, we intentionally used an inefficient shuffling algorithm that introduced the possibility of indefinite postponement. In this problem, you'll create a high-performance shuffling algorithm that avoids indefinite postponement.

Modify the program of Fig. 7.24 as follows. Begin by initializing the deck array as shown in Fig. 7.29. Modify the shuffle function to loop row-by-row and column-by-column through the array, touching every element once. Each element should be swapped with a randomly selected element of the array. Print the resulting array to determine whether the deck is satisfactorily shuffled (as in Fig. 7.30, for example). You may want your program to call the shuffle function several times to ensure a satisfactory shuffle.

Unshuffled deck array												
	0	1	2	3	4	5	6	7	8	9	10	11	12
0	1	2	3	4	5	6	7	8	9	10	11	12	13
1	14	15	16	17	18	19	20	21	22	23	24	25	26
2	27	28	29	30	31	32	33	34	35	36	37	38	39
3	40	41	42	43	44	45	46	47	48	49	50	51	52

Fig. 7.29 | Unshuffled deck array.

Sample shuffled deck array												
	0	1	2	3	4	5	6	7	8	9	10	11	12
0	19	40	27	25	36	46	10	34	35	41	18	2	44
1	13	28	14	16	21	30	8	11	31	17	24	7	1
2	12	33	15	42	43	23	45	3	29	32	4	47	26
3	50	38	52	39	48	51	9	5	37	49	22	6	20

Fig. 7.30 | Sample shuffled deck array.

Although the approach in this problem improves the shuffling algorithm, the dealing algorithm still requires searching the deck array for card 1, then card 2, then card 3, and so on. Worse yet, even after the dealing algorithm locates and deals the card, the algorithm still searches through the remainder of the deck. Modify the program of Fig. 7.24 so that once a card is dealt, no further attempts are made to match that card number, and the program immediately proceeds with dealing the next card. In Chapter 10, we develop a dealing algorithm that requires only one operation per card.

7.17 *(Simulation: The Tortoise and the Hare)* In this problem, you'll recreate one of the truly great moments in history, namely the classic race of the tortoise and the hare. You'll use random number generation to develop a simulation of this memorable event.

Our contenders begin the race at "square 1" of 70 squares. Each square represents a possible position along the race course. The finish line is at square 70. The first contender to reach or pass square 70 is rewarded with a pail of fresh carrots and lettuce. The course weaves its way up the side of a slippery mountain, so occasionally the contenders lose ground.

There's a clock that ticks once per second. With each tick of the clock, your program should adjust the position of the animals according to the rules of Fig. 7.31.

Animal	Move type	Percentage of the time	Actual move
Tortoise	Fast plod	50%	3 squares to the right
	Slip	20%	6 squares to the left
	Slow plod	30%	1 square to the right
Hare	Sleep	20%	No move at all
	Big hop	20%	9 squares to the right
	Big slip	10%	12 squares to the left
	Small hop	30%	1 square to the right
	Small slip	20%	2 squares to the left

Fig. 7.31 | Tortoise and hare rules for adjusting positions.

Use variables to keep track of the positions of the animals (i.e., position numbers are 1–70). Start each animal at position 1 (i.e., the "starting gate"). If an animal slips left before square 1, move the animal back to square 1. Generate the percentages in the preceding table by producing a random integer, i, in the range $1 \leq i \leq 10$. For the tortoise, perform a "fast plod" when $1 \leq i \leq 5$, a "slip" when $6 \leq i \leq 7$, or a "slow plod" when $8 \leq i \leq 10$. Use a similar technique to move the hare.

Begin the race by printing

```
BANG !!!!!
AND THEY'RE OFF !!!!!
```

Then, for each tick of the clock (i.e., each repetition of a loop), print a 70-position line showing the letter T in the position of the tortoise and the letter H in the position of the hare. Occasionally, the contenders will land on the same square. In this case, the tortoise bites the hare and your program should print OUCH!!! beginning at that position. All print positions other than the T, the H, or the OUCH!!! (in case of a tie) should be blank.

After each line is printed, test whether either animal has reached or passed square 70. If so, then print the winner and terminate the simulation. If the tortoise wins, print TORTOISE WINS!!! YAY!!! If the hare wins, print Hare wins. Yuch. If both animals win on the same tick of the clock, you may want to favor the turtle (the "underdog"), or you may want to print It's a tie. If neither animal wins, perform the loop again to simulate the next tick of the clock. When you're ready to run your program, assemble a group of fans to watch the race. You'll be amazed at how involved your audience gets!

7.18 *(Card Shuffling and Dealing Modification)* Modify the card shuffling and dealing program of Fig. 7.24 so the shuffling and dealing operations are performed by the same function (shuffle-AndDeal). The function should contain one nested looping structure that's similar to function shuffle in Fig. 7.24.

7.19 What does this program do?

```
 1   #include <stdio.h>
 2   void guess( char *a, const char *b ); /* prototype */
 3   int main( void )
 4   {
 5      char first[ 80 ]; /* create char array */
 6      char second[ 80 ]; /* create char array */
 7   printf( "Enter two strings: " );
 8     scanf( "%s%s" , first, second );
 9      guess( first, second );
10      printf("%s", first );
11      return 0; /* indicates successful termination */
12   } /* end main */
13
14   /* What does this function do? */
15   void guess( char *a, const char *b )
16   {
17      while ( *a != '\0' ) {
18         a++;
19      } /* end while */
20
21      for ( ; *a != *b; a++, b-- ) {
22         ; /* empty statement */
23      } /* end for */} /* end function guess */
24   /* end function guess */
```

7.20 What does this program do?

```
 1   #include <stdio.h>
 2   int guess1( const char *s ); /* prototype */
 3   int main( void )
 4   {
 5      char a[ 80 ], b[ 80 ]; /* create char array */
 6      int m, n;
 7      printf( "Enter the first string: ");
 8      scanf( "%s", a );
 9      printf( "Enter the second string: ");
10      scanf( "%s", b );
11      m = guess1( a );
12      n = guess1( b );
13      printf( "L%d\n", m );
14      printf( "%d\n", n );
15      printf( "%d\n", m + n );
16       return 0; /* indicates successful termination */
17   } /* end main */
18   /* What does this function do? */
19   int guess1( const char *s )
```

```
20      {
21          int a; /* counter */
22           /* loop through string */
23          for ( a = 0; *s != '\0'; s++ ) {
24          a++;
25      } /* end for */
26          return a;
27   } /* end function guess1 */
```

7.21   Find the error in each of the following program segments. If the error can be corrected, explain how.

    a) `int *number;`
        `printf( "%d\n", *number );`
    b) `float *realPtr;`
        `long *integerPtr;`
        `integerPtr = realPtr;`
    c) `int * x, y;`
        `x = y;`
    d) `char s[] = "this is a character array";`
        `int count;`
        `for ( ; *s != '\0'; ++s)`
           `printf( "%c ", *s );`
    e) `short *numPtr, result;`
        `void *genericPtr = numPtr;`
        `result = *genericPtr + 7;`
    f) `float x = 19.34;`
        `float xPtr = &x;`
        `printf( "%f\n", xPtr );`
    g) `char *s;`
        `printf( "%s\n", s );`

7.22   *(Maze Traversal)* The following grid is a double-subscripted array representation of a maze.

```
# # # # # # # # # # #
# . . . # . . . . . #
. . # . # . # # # . #
# # # . # . . . # . #
# . . . . # # # . # . .
# # # # . # . # . # . #
# . . # . # . # . # . #
# # . # . # . # . # . #
# . . . . . . . # . # .
# # # # # . # # # . # .
# . . . . . # . . . # .
# # # # # # # # # # #
```

The # symbols represent the walls of the maze, and the periods (.) represent squares in the possible paths through the maze.

    There's a simple algorithm for walking through a maze that guarantees finding the exit (assuming there's an exit). If there's not an exit, you'll arrive at the starting location again. Place your right hand on the wall to your right and begin walking forward. Never remove your hand from the wall. If the maze turns to the right, you follow the wall to the right. As long as you do not remove your hand from the wall, eventually you'll arrive at the exit of the maze. There may be a shorter path than the one you have taken, but you're guaranteed to get out of the maze.

Write recursive function `mazeTraverse` to walk through the maze. The function should receive as arguments a 12-by-12 character array representing the maze and the starting location of the maze. As `mazeTraverse` attempts to locate the exit from the maze, it should place the character X in each square in the path. The function should display the maze after each move so the user can watch as the maze is solved.

7.23 *(Generating Mazes Randomly)* Write a function `mazeGenerator` that takes as an argument a double-subscripted 12-by-12 character array and randomly produces a maze. The function should also provide the starting and ending locations of the maze. Try your function `mazeTraverse` from Exercise 7.22 using several randomly generated mazes.

7.24 *(Mazes of Any Size)* Generalize functions `mazeTraverse` and `mazeGenerator` of Exercises 7.22–7.23 to process mazes of any width and height.

7.25 *(Arrays of Pointers to Functions)* Rewrite the program of Fig. 6.22 to use a menu-driven interface. The program should offer the user four options as follows:

```
Enter a choice:
   0  Print the array of grades
   1  Find the minimum grade
   2  Find the maximum grade
   3  Print the average on all tests for each student
   4  End program
```

One restriction on using arrays of pointers to functions is that all the pointers must have the same type. The pointers must be to functions of the same return type that receive arguments of the same type. For this reason, the functions in Fig. 6.22 must be modified so that they each return the same type and take the same parameters. Modify functions `minimum` and `maximum` to print the minimum or maximum value and return nothing. For option 3, modify function `average` of Fig. 6.22 to output the average for each student (not a specific student). Function `average` should return nothing and take the same parameters as `printArray`, `minimum` and `maximum`. Store the pointers to the four functions in array `processGrades` and use the choice made by the user as the subscript into the array for calling each function.

7.26 What does this program do?

```
1   #include<stdio.h>
2   #include<string.h>
3   void guess2(char *a);
4   int main()
5   {
6      char a[20]; /* string */
7      printf("Enter the string\n");
8      gets(a);
9      guess2(a);
10     return 0;
11     }
12  void guess2(char *a)
13  {
14     char reverse[20]; /* reversed string */
15     char *m = a;
16     char *n = reverse;
17
18     while(*m!='\0')
19  {
20         m++;
21     }
```

```
21          m--;          /* move to the last character of given string */
22      while(m>=&a[0])
23  {
24          *n++ = *m--;
25  }
26          *n = '\0';
27          printf("string = %s", reverse);
28  }
```

Special Section: Building Your Own Computer

In the next several exercises, we take a temporary diversion away from the world of high-level language programming. We "peel open" a computer and look at its internal structure. We introduce machine-language programming and write several machine-language programs. To make this an especially valuable experience, we then build a computer (through the technique of software-based *simulation*) on which you can execute your machine-language programs!

7.27 *(Machine-Language Programming)* Let's create a computer we'll call the Simpletron. As its name implies, it's a simple machine, but as we'll soon see, it's a powerful one as well. The Simpletron runs programs written in the only language it directly understands—that is, Simpletron Machine Language, or SML for short.

The Simpletron contains an *accumulator*—a "special register" in which information is put before the Simpletron uses that information in calculations or examines it in various ways. All information in the Simpletron is handled in terms of *words*. A word is a signed four-digit decimal number such as +3364, -1293, +0007, -0001 and so on. The Simpletron is equipped with a 100-word memory, and these words are referenced by their location numbers 00, 01, ..., 99.

Before running an SML program, we must *load* or place the program into memory. The first instruction (or statement) of every SML program is always placed in location 00.

Each instruction written in SML occupies one word of the Simpletron's memory, so instructions are signed four-digit decimal numbers. We assume that the sign of an SML instruction is always plus, but the sign of a data word may be either plus or minus. Each location in the Simpletron's memory may contain either an instruction, a data value used by a program or an unused (and hence undefined) area of memory. The first two digits of each SML instruction are the *operation code*, which specifies the operation to be performed. SML operation codes are summarized in Fig. 7.32.

Operation code	Meaning
Input/output operations:	
#define READ 10	Read a word from the terminal into a specific location in memory.
#define WRITE 11	Write a word from a specific location in memory to the terminal.
Load/store operations:	
#define LOAD 20	Load a word from a specific location in memory into the accumulator.
#define STORE 21	Store a word from the accumulator into a specific location in memory.

Fig. 7.32 | Simpletron Machine Language (SML) operation codes. (Part 1 of 2.)

Operation code	Meaning
Arithmetic operations:	
#define ADD 30	Add a word from a specific location in memory to the word in the accumulator (leave result in accumulator).
#define SUBTRACT 31	Subtract a word from a specific location in memory from the word in the accumulator (leave result in accumulator).
#define DIVIDE 32	Divide a word from a specific location in memory into the word in the accumulator (leave result in accumulator).
#define MULTIPLY 33	Multiply a word from a specific location in memory by the word in the accumulator (leave result in accumulator).
Transfer-of-control operations:	
#define BRANCH 40	Branch to a specific location in memory.
#define BRANCHNEG 41	Branch to a specific location in memory if the accumulator is negative.
#define BRANCHZERO 42	Branch to a specific location in memory if the accumulator is zero.
#define HALT 43	Halt—i.e., the program has completed its task.

Fig. 7.32 | Simpletron Machine Language (SML) operation codes. (Part 2 of 2.)

The last two digits of an SML instruction are the *operand,* which is the address of the memory location containing the word to which the operation applies. Now let's consider several simple SML programs. The following SML program reads two numbers from the keyboard, and computes and prints their sum.

The instruction +1007 reads the first number from the keyboard and places it into location 07 (which has been initialized to zero). Then +1008 reads the next number into location 08. The *load* instruction, +2007, puts the first number into the accumulator, and the *add* instruction, +3008, adds the second number to the number in the accumulator. *All SML arithmetic instructions leave their results in the accumulator.* The *store* instruction, +2109, places the result back into memory location 09, from which the *write* instruction, +1109, takes the number and prints it (as a signed four-digit decimal number). The *halt* instruction, +4300, terminates execution.

Example 1 Location	Number	Instruction
00	+1007	*(Read A)*
01	+1008	*(Read B)*
02	+2007	*(Load A)*
03	+3008	*(Add B)*
04	+2109	*(Store C)*
05	+1109	*(Write C)*
06	+4300	*(Halt)*
07	+0000	*(Variable A)*
08	+0000	*(Variable B)*
09	+0000	*(Result C)*

The following SML program reads two numbers from the keyboard, and determines and prints the larger value. Note the use of the instruction +4107 as a conditional transfer of control, much the same as C's if statement.

Example 2 Location	Number	Instruction
00	+1009	*(Read A)*
01	+1010	*(Read B)*
02	+2009	*(Load A)*
03	+3110	*(Subtract B)*
04	+4107	*(Branch negative to 07)*
05	+1109	*(Write A)*
06	+4300	*(Halt)*
07	+1110	*(Write B)*
08	+4300	*(Halt)*
09	+0000	*(Variable A)*
10	+0000	*(Variable B)*

Now write SML programs to accomplish each of the following tasks.

a) Use a sentinel-controlled loop to read positive integers and compute and print their sum.

b) Use a counter-controlled loop to read seven numbers, some positive and some negative, and compute and print their average.

c) Read a series of numbers and determine and print the largest number. The first number read indicates how many numbers should be processed.

7.28 *(A Computer Simulator)* It may at first seem outrageous, but in this problem you're going to build your own computer. No, you won't be soldering components together. Rather, you'll use the powerful technique of *software-based simulation* to create a *software model* of the Simpletron. You'll not be disappointed. Your Simpletron simulator will turn the computer you're using into a Simpletron, and you'll actually be able to run, test and debug the SML programs you wrote in Exercise 7.27.

When you run your Simpletron simulator, it should begin by printing:

```
*** Welcome to Simpletron! ***
*** Please enter your program one instruction ***
*** (or data word) at a time. I will type the ***
*** location number and a question mark (?).  ***
*** You then type the word for that location. ***
*** Type the sentinel -99999 to stop entering ***
*** your program. ***
```

Simulate the memory of the Simpletron with a single-subscripted array memory that has 100 elements. Now assume that the simulator is running, and let's examine the dialog as we enter the program of Example 2 of Exercise 7.27:

```
00 ? +1009
01 ? +1010
02 ? +2009
03 ? +3110
04 ? +4107
05 ? +1109
06 ? +4300
```

```
07 ? +1110
08 ? +4300
09 ? +0000
10 ? +0000
11 ? -99999
*** Program loading completed ***
*** Program execution begins  ***
```

The SML program has now been placed (or loaded) into the array `memory`. Now the Simpletron executes the SML program. It begins with the instruction in location 00 and continues sequentially, unless directed to some other part of the program by a transfer of control.

Use the variable `accumulator` to represent the accumulator register. Use the variable `instructionCounter` to keep track of the location in memory that contains the instruction being performed. Use the variable `operationCode` to indicate the operation currently being performed—i.e., the left two digits of the instruction word. Use the variable `operand` to indicate the memory location on which the current instruction operates. Thus, if an instrucion has an `operand`, it's the rightmost two digits of the instruction currently being performed. Do not execute instructions directly from memory. Rather, transfer the next instruction to be performed from memory to a variable called `instructionRegister`. Then "pick off" the left two digits and place them in the variable `operationCode`, and "pick off" the right two digits and place them in `operand`.

When Simpletron begins execution, the special registers are initialized as follows:

```
accumulator              +0000
instructionCounter          00
instructionRegister      +0000
operationCode               00
operand                     00
```

Now let's "walk through" the execution of the first SML instruction, +1009 in memory location 00. This is called an *instruction execution cycle*.

The `instructionCounter` tells us the location of the next instruction to be performed. We *fetch* the contents of that location from `memory` by using the C statement

```
instructionRegister = memory[ instructionCounter ];
```

The operation code and the operand are extracted from the instruction register by the statements

```
operationCode = instructionRegister / 100;
operand = instructionRegister % 100;
```

Now the Simpletron must determine that the operation code is actually a *read* (versus a *write*, a *load*, and so on). A `switch` differentiates among the twelve operations of SML.

The `switch` statement simulates the behavior of various SML instructions as follows (we leave the others to the reader):

read: `scanf( "%d", &memory[ operand ] );`
load: `accumulator = memory[ operand ];`
add: `accumulator += memory[ operand ];`
Various branch instructions: We'll discuss these shortly.
halt: This instruction prints the message

```
      *** Simpletron execution terminated ***
```

then prints the name and contents of each register as well as the complete contents of memory. Such a printout is often called a *computer dump*. To help you program your dump function, a sample dump format is shown in Fig. 7.33. A dump after executing a Simpletron program would show the actual values of instructions and data values at the moment execution terminated. You can print leading 0s in front of an integer that is shorter than its field width by placing the 0 formatting flag before the field width in the format specifier as in `"%02d"`. You can place a + or - sign before a value with the + formatting flag. So to produce a number of the form +0000, you can use the format specifier `"%+05d"`.

```
REGISTERS:
accumulator              +0000
instructionCounter          00
instructionRegister      +0000
operationCode               00
operand                     00

MEMORY:
         0      1      2      3      4      5      6      7      8      9
 0   +0000  +0000  +0000  +0000  +0000  +0000  +0000  +0000  +0000  +0000
10   +0000  +0000  +0000  +0000  +0000  +0000  +0000  +0000  +0000  +0000
20   +0000  +0000  +0000  +0000  +0000  +0000  +0000  +0000  +0000  +0000
30   +0000  +0000  +0000  +0000  +0000  +0000  +0000  +0000  +0000  +0000
40   +0000  +0000  +0000  +0000  +0000  +0000  +0000  +0000  +0000  +0000
50   +0000  +0000  +0000  +0000  +0000  +0000  +0000  +0000  +0000  +0000
60   +0000  +0000  +0000  +0000  +0000  +0000  +0000  +0000  +0000  +0000
70   +0000  +0000  +0000  +0000  +0000  +0000  +0000  +0000  +0000  +0000
80   +0000  +0000  +0000  +0000  +0000  +0000  +0000  +0000  +0000  +0000
90   +0000  +0000  +0000  +0000  +0000  +0000  +0000  +0000  +0000  +0000
```

Fig. 7.33 | Sample Simpletron dump format.

Let's proceed with the execution of our program's first instruction, namely the +1009 in location 00. As we've indicated, the switch statement simulates this by performing the C statement

```
scanf( "%d", &memory[ operand ] );
```

A question mark (?) should be displayed on the screen before the scanf is executed to prompt the user for input. The Simpletron waits for the user to type a value and then press the *Return* key. The value is then read into location 09.

At this point, simulation of the first instruction is completed. All that remains is to prepare the Simpletron to execute the next instruction. Because the instruction just performed was not a transfer of control, we need merely increment the instruction counter register as follows:

```
++instructionCounter;
```

This completes the simulated execution of the first instruction. The entire process (i.e., the instruction execution cycle) begins anew with the fetch of the next instruction to be executed.

Now let's consider how the branching instructions—the transfers of control—are simulated. All we need to do is adjust the value in the instruction counter appropriately. Therefore, the unconditional branch instruction (40) is simulated within the switch as

```
instructionCounter = operand;
```

The conditional "branch if accumulator is zero" instruction is simulated as

```
if ( accumulator == 0 ) {
    instructionCounter = operand;
}
```

At this point, you should implement your Simpletron simulator and run the SML programs you wrote in Exercise 7.27. You may embellish SML with additional features and provide for these in your simulator.

Your simulator should check for various types of errors. During the program loading phase, for example, each number the user types into the Simpletron's memory must be in the range -9999 to +9999. Your simulator should use a while loop to test that each number entered is in this range, and, if not, keep prompting the user to reenter the number until a correct number is entered.

During the execution phase, your simulator should check for serious errors, such as attempts to divide by zero, attempts to execute invalid operation codes and accumulator overflows (i.e., arithmetic operations resulting in values larger than +9999 or smaller than -9999). Such serious errors are called *fatal errors*. When a fatal error is detected, print an error message such as:

```
*** Attempt to divide by zero ***
*** Simpletron execution abnormally terminated ***
```

and should print a full computer dump in the format we've discussed previously. This will help the user locate the error in the program.

Implementation Note: When you implement the Simpletron Simulator, define the memory array and all the registers as variables in main. The program should contain three other functions—load, execute and dump. Function load reads the SML instructions from the user at the keyboard. (Once you study file processing in Chapter 11, you'll be able to read the SML instruction from a file.) Function execute executes the SML program currently loaded in the memory array. Function dump displays the contents of memory and all of the registers stored in main's variables. Pass the memory array and registers to the other functions as necessary to complete their tasks. Functions load and execute need to modify variables that are defined in main, so you'll need to pass those variables to the functions by reference using pointers. So, you'll need to modify the statements we showed throughout this problem description to use the appropriate pointer notations.

7.29 *(Modifications to the Simpletron Simulator)* In Exercise 7.28, you wrote a software simulation of a computer that executes programs written in Simpletron Machine Language (SML). In this exercise, we propose several modifications and enhancements to the Simpletron Simulator. In Exercises 12.26 and 12.27, we propose building a compiler that converts programs written in a high-level programming language (a variation of BASIC) to Simpletron Machine Language. Some of the following modifications and enhancements may be required to execute the programs produced by the compiler.

a) Extend the Simpletron Simulator's memory to contain 1000 memory locations to enable the Simpletron to handle larger programs.

b) Allow the simulator to perform remainder calculations. This requires an additional Simpletron Machine Language instruction.

c) Allow the simulator to perform exponentiation calculations. This requires an additional Simpletron Machine Language instruction.

d) Modify the simulator to use hexadecimal values rather than integer values to represent Simpletron Machine Language instructions.

e) Modify the simulator to allow output of a newline. This requires an additional Simpletron Machine Language instruction.

f) Modify the simulator to process floating-point values in addition to integer values.

g) Modify the simulator to handle string input. [*Hint:* Each Simpletron word can be divided into two groups, each holding a two-digit integer. Each two-digit integer represents the ASCII decimal equivalent of a character. Add a machine-language instruction that will input a string and store it beginning at a specific Simpletron memory location. The first half of the word at that location will be a count of the number of characters in the string (i.e., the length of the string). Each succeeding half word contains one ASCII character expressed as two decimal digits. The machine-language instruction converts each character into its ASCII equivalent and assigns it to a half word.]

h) Modify the simulator to handle output of strings stored in the format of part (g). [*Hint:* Add a machine-language instruction that prints a string beginning at a specified Simpletron memory location. The first half of the word at that location is the length of the string in characters. Each succeeding half word contains one ASCII character expressed as two decimal digits. The machine-language instruction checks the length and prints the string by translating each two-digit number into its equivalent character.]

Array of Function Pointer Exercises

7.30   *(Calculating Area of Square, Area of Rectangle, Perimeter of Square and Perimeter of Rectangle)* Using the techniques you learned in Fig. 7.28, create a text-based, menu-driven program that allows the user to choose whether to calculate the area of a square, the area of a rectangle, the perimeter of a square or the perimeter of a rectangle. The program should then input a side (for square) or length and breadth (for rectangle) from the user, perform the appropriate calculation and display the result. The corresponding functions should each display the result of the calculation.

7.31   *(Swapping Two Numbers)* Using the techniques you learned in Fig. 7.28, create a text-based, menu-driven program that allows the user to choose whether to swap two integers or to swap two floating point numbers. The program should then input either two integer values or two floating point values from the user, swap both the values and display the result. The corresponding functions should each display the values before swapping and the values after swapping.

Making a Difference

7.32   *(Polling)* The Internet and the web are enabling more people to network, join a cause, voice opinions, and so on. The U.S. presidential candidates in 2008 used the Internet intensively to get out their messages and raise money for their campaigns. In this exercise, you'll write a simple polling program that allows users to rate five social-consciousness issues from 1 (least important) to 10 (most important). Pick five causes that are important to you (e.g., political issues, global environmental issues). Use a one-dimensional array topics (of type char *) to store the five causes. To summarize the survey responses, use a 5-row, 10-column two-dimensional array responses (of type int), each row corresponding to an element in the topics array. When the program runs, it should ask the user to rate each issue. Have your friends and family respond to the survey. Then have the program display a summary of the results, including:
   a) A tabular report with the five topics down the left side and the 10 ratings across the top, listing in each column the number of ratings received for each topic.
   b) To the right of each row, show the average of the ratings for that issue.
   c) Which issue received the highest point total? Display both the issue and the point total.
   d) Which issue received the lowest point total? Display both the issue and the point total.

7.33   *(Carbon Footprint Calculator: Arrays of Function Pointers)* Using arrays of function pointers, as you learned in this chapter, you can specify a set of functions that are called with the same types of arguments and return the same type of data. Governments and companies worldwide are becoming increasingly concerned with carbon footprints (annual releases of carbon dioxide into the atmosphere) from buildings burning various types of fuels for heat, vehicles burning fuels for power, and the like. Many scientists blame these greenhouse gases for the phenomenon called global warming. Create three functions that help calculate the carbon footprint of a building, a car and a bicycle, respectively. Each function should input appropriate data from the user, then calculate and display the carbon footprint. (Check out a few websites that explain how to calculate carbon footprints.) Each function should receive no parameters and return void. Write a program that prompts the user to enter the type of carbon footprint to calculate, then calls the corresponding function in the array of function pointers. For each type of carbon footprint, display some identifying information and the object's carbon footprint.

8

C Characters and Strings

Objectives

In this chapter, you'll:

- Use the functions of the character-handling library (<ctype.h>).

- Use the string-conversion functions of the general utilities library (<stdlib.h>).

- Use the string and character input/output functions of the standard input/output library (<stdio.h>).

- Use the string-processing functions of the string-handling library (<string.h>).

- Use the memory-processing functions of the string-handling library (<string.h>).

8.1 Introduction

This chapter introduces the C standard library functions that facilitate string and character processing. The functions enable programs to process characters, strings, lines of text and blocks of memory. The chapter discusses the techniques used to develop editors, word processors, page-layout software, computerized typesetting systems and other kinds of text-processing software. The text manipulations performed by formatted input/output functions like printf and scanf can be implemented using the functions discussed in this chapter.

8.2 Fundamentals of Strings and Characters

Characters are the fundamental building blocks of source programs. Every program is composed of a sequence of characters that—when grouped together meaningfully—is interpreted by the computer as a series of instructions used to accomplish a task. A program may contain **character constants**. A character constant is an int value represented as a character in single quotes. The value of a character constant is the integer value of the character in the machine's **character set**. For example, 'z' represents the integer value of z, and '\n' the integer value of newline (122 and 10 in ASCII, respectively).

A **string** is a series of characters treated as a single unit. A string may include letters, digits and various special characters such as +, -, *, / and $. String literals, or string constants, in C are written in double quotation marks as follows:

```
"John Q. Doe"              (a name)
"99999 Main Street"        (a street address)
"Waltham, Massachusetts"   (a city and state)
"(201) 555-1212"           (a telephone number)
```

A string in C is an array of characters ending in the **null character** (`'\0'`). A string is accessed via a *pointer* to the first character in the string. The value of a string is the address of its first character. Thus, in C, it's appropriate to say that a **string is a pointer**—in fact, a pointer to the string's first character. In this sense, strings are like arrays, because an array is also a pointer to its first element.

A *character array* or a *variable of type char ** can be initialized with a string in a definition. The definitions

```
char color[] = "blue";
const char *colorPtr = "blue";
```

each initialize a variable to the string `"blue"`. The first definition creates a 5-element array `color` containing the characters `'b'`, `'l'`, `'u'`, `'e'` and `'\0'`. The second definition creates pointer variable `colorPtr` that points to the string `"blue"` somewhere in memory.

Portability Tip 8.1

When a variable of type char * is initialized with a string literal, some compilers may place the string in a location in memory where it cannot be modified. If you might need to modify a string literal, it should be stored in a character array to ensure modifiability on all systems.

The preceding array definition could also have been written

```
char color[] = { 'b', 'l', 'u', 'e', '\0' };
```

When defining a character array to contain a string, the array must be large enough to store the string *and* its terminating null character. The preceding definition automatically determines the size of the array based on the number of initializers in the initializer list.

Common Programming Error 8.1

Not allocating sufficient space in a character array to store the null character that terminates a string is an error.

Common Programming Error 8.2

Printing a "string" that does not contain a terminating null character is an error.

Error-Prevention Tip 8.1

When storing a string of characters in a character array, be sure that the array is large enough to hold the largest string that will be stored. C allows strings of any length to be stored. If a string is longer than the character array in which it's to be stored, characters beyond the end of the array will overwrite data in memory following the array.

A string can be stored in an array using scanf. For example, the following statement stores a string in character array word[20]:

```
scanf( "%19s", word );
```

The string entered by the user is stored in word. Variable word is an array, which is, of course, a pointer, so the & is not needed with argument word. Recall from Section 6.4 that function scanf will read characters until a space, tab, newline or end-of-file indicator is encountered. So, it's possible that, without the field width 19 in the conversion specifier %19s, the user input could exceed 19 characters and that your program might crash! For this reason, you should *always* use a field width when using *scanf* to read into a char array. The field width 19 in the preceding statement ensures that scanf reads a *maximum* of 19 characters and saves the last character for the string's terminating null character. This prevents scanf from writing characters into memory beyond the end of s. (For reading input lines of arbitrary length, there's a nonstandard—yet widely supported—function readline, usually included in stdio.h.) For a character array to be printed properly as a string, the array must contain a terminating null character.

Common Programming Error 8.3

Processing a single character as a string. A string is a pointer—probably a respectably large integer. However, a character is a small integer (ASCII values range 0–255). On many systems this causes an error, because low memory addresses are reserved for special purposes such as operating-system interrupt handlers—so "access violations" occur.

Common Programming Error 8.4

Passing a character as an argument to a function when a string is expected (and vice versa) is a compilation error.

8.3 Character-Handling Library

The **character-handling library** (<ctype.h>) includes several functions that perform useful tests and manipulations of character data. Each function receives an unsigned char (represented as an int) or EOF as an argument. As we discussed in Chapter 4, characters are often manipulated as integers, because a character in C is a one-byte integer. EOF normally has the value −1. Figure 8.1 summarizes the functions of the character-handling library.

Prototype	Function description
int isblank(int c);	Returns a true value if c is a *blank character* that separates words in a line of text and 0 (false) otherwise. [*Note:* This function is not available in Microsoft Visual C++.]
int isdigit(int c);	Returns a true value if c is a *digit* and 0 (false) otherwise.
int isalpha(int c);	Returns a true value if c is a *letter* and 0 otherwise.
int isalnum(int c);	Returns a true value if c is a *digit* or a *letter* and 0 otherwise.

Fig. 8.1 | Character-handling library (<ctype.h>) functions. (Part 1 of 2.)

Prototype	Function description
`int isxdigit( int c );`	Returns a true value if c is a *hexadecimal digit character* and 0 otherwise. (See Appendix C for a detailed explanation of binary numbers, octal numbers, decimal numbers and hexadecimal numbers.)
`int islower( int c );`	Returns a true value if c is a *lowercase letter* and 0 otherwise.
`int isupper( int c );`	Returns a true value if c is an *uppercase letter* and 0 otherwise.
`int tolower( int c );`	If c is an *uppercase letter*, `tolower` returns c as a *lowercase letter*. Otherwise, `tolower` returns the argument unchanged.
`int toupper( int c );`	If c is a *lowercase letter*, `toupper` returns c as an *uppercase letter*. Otherwise, `toupper` returns the argument unchanged.
`int isspace( int c );`	Returns a true value if c is a *whitespace character*—newline (`'\n'`), space (`' '`), form feed (`'\f'`), carriage return (`'\r'`), horizontal tab (`'\t'`) or vertical tab (`'\v'`)—and 0 otherwise.
`int iscntrl( int c );`	Returns a true value if c is a *control character* and 0 otherwise.
`int ispunct( int c );`	Returns a true value if c is a *printing character other than a space, a digit, or a letter* and returns 0 otherwise.
`int isprint( int c );`	Returns a true value if c is a *printing character including a space* and returns 0 otherwise.
`int isgraph( int c );`	Returns a true value if c is a *printing character other than a space* and returns 0 otherwise.

Fig. 8.1 | Character-handling library (`<ctype.h>`) functions. (Part 2 of 2.)

8.3.1 Functions `isdigit`, `isalpha`, `isalnum` and `isxdigit`

Figure 8.2 demonstrates functions `isdigit`, `isalpha`, `isalnum` and `isxdigit`. Function `isdigit` determines whether its argument is a digit (0–9). Function `isalpha` determines whether its argument is an uppercase (A–Z) or lowercase letter (a–z). Function `isalnum` determines whether its argument is an uppercase letter, a lowercase letter or a digit. Function `isxdigit` determines whether its argument is a hexadecimal digit (A–F, a–f, 0–9).

```c
// Fig. 8.2: fig08_02.c
// Using functions isdigit, isalpha, isalnum, and isxdigit
#include <stdio.h>
#include <ctype.h>

int main( void )
{
   printf( "%s\n%s%s\n%s%s\n\n", "According to isdigit: ",
      isdigit( '8' ) ? "8 is a " : "8 is not a ", "digit",
      isdigit( '#' ) ? "# is a " : "# is not a ", "digit" );

   printf( "%s\n%s%s\n%s%s\n%s%s\n%s%s\n\n",
      "According to isalpha:",
```

Fig. 8.2 | Using functions `isdigit`, `isalpha`, `isalnum` and `isxdigit`. (Part 1 of 2.)

```
14            isalpha( 'A' ) ? "A is a " : "A is not a ", "letter",
15            isalpha( 'b' ) ? "b is a " : "b is not a ", "letter",
16            isalpha( '&' ) ? "& is a " : "& is not a ", "letter",
17            isalpha( '4' ) ? "4 is a " : "4 is not a ", "letter" );
18
19         printf( "%s\n%s%s\n%s%s\n%s%s\n\n",
20            "According to isalnum:",
21            isalnum( 'A' ) ? "A is a " : "A is not a ",
22            "digit or a letter",
23            isalnum( '8' ) ? "8 is a " : "8 is not a ",
24            "digit or a letter",
25            isalnum( '#' ) ? "# is a " : "# is not a ",
26            "digit or a letter" );
27
28         printf( "%s\n%s%s\n%s%s\n%s%s\n%s%s\n%s%s\n",
29            "According to isxdigit:",
30            isxdigit( 'F' ) ? "F is a " : "F is not a ",
31            "hexadecimal digit",
32            isxdigit( 'J' ) ? "J is a " : "J is not a ",
33            "hexadecimal digit",
34            isxdigit( '7' ) ? "7 is a " : "7 is not a ",
35            "hexadecimal digit",
36            isxdigit( '$' ) ? "$ is a " : "$ is not a ",
37            "hexadecimal digit",
38            isxdigit( 'f' ) ? "f is a " : "f is not a ",
39            "hexadecimal digit" );
40    } // end main
```

```
According to isdigit:
8 is a digit
# is not a digit

According to isalpha:
A is a letter
b is a letter
& is not a letter
4 is not a letter

According to isalnum:
A is a digit or a letter
8 is a digit or a letter
# is not a digit or a letter

According to isxdigit:
F is a hexadecimal digit
J is not a hexadecimal digit
7 is a hexadecimal digit
$ is not a hexadecimal digit
f is a hexadecimal digit
```

Fig. 8.2 | Using functions isdigit, isalpha, isalnum and isxdigit. (Part 2 of 2.)

Figure 8.2 uses the conditional operator (?:) to determine whether the string " is a " or the string " is not a " should be printed in the output for each character tested. For example, the expression

```
isdigit( '8' ) ? "8 is a " : "8 is not a "
```

indicates that if '8' is a digit, the string "8 is a " is printed, and if '8' is not a digit (i.e., isdigit returns 0), the string "8 is not a " is printed.

8.3.2 Functions islower, isupper, tolower and toupper

Figure 8.3 demonstrates functions islower, isupper, tolower and toupper. Function islower determines whether its argument is a lowercase letter (a–z). Function isupper determines whether its argument is an uppercase letter (A–Z). Function tolower converts an uppercase letter to a lowercase letter and returns the lowercase letter. If the argument is *not* an uppercase letter, tolower returns the argument *unchanged*. Function toupper converts a lowercase letter to an uppercase letter and returns the uppercase letter. If the argument is *not* a lowercase letter, toupper returns the argument *unchanged*.

```c
 1  // Fig. 8.3: fig08_03.c
 2  // Using functions islower, isupper, tolower, toupper
 3  #include <stdio.h>
 4  #include <ctype.h>
 5
 6  int main( void )
 7  {
 8     printf( "%s\n%s%s\n%s%s\n%s%s\n%s%s\n\n",
 9        "According to islower:",
10        islower( 'p' ) ? "p is a " : "p is not a ",
11        "lowercase letter",
12        islower( 'P' ) ? "P is a " : "P is not a ",
13        "lowercase letter",
14        islower( '5' ) ? "5 is a " : "5 is not a ",
15        "lowercase letter",
16        islower( '!' ) ? "! is a " : "! is not a ",
17        "lowercase letter" );
18
19     printf( "%s\n%s%s\n%s%s\n%s%s\n%s%s\n\n",
20        "According to isupper:",
21        isupper( 'D' ) ? "D is an " : "D is not an ",
22        "uppercase letter",
23        isupper( 'd' ) ? "d is an " : "d is not an ",
24        "uppercase letter",
25        isupper( '8' ) ? "8 is an " : "8 is not an ",
26        "uppercase letter",
27        isupper( '$' ) ? "$ is an " : "$ is not an ",
28        "uppercase letter" );
29
30     printf( "%s%c\n%s%c\n%s%c\n%s%c\n",
31        "u converted to uppercase is ", toupper( 'u' ),
32        "7 converted to uppercase is ", toupper( '7' ),
33        "$ converted to uppercase is ", toupper( '$' ),
34        "L converted to lowercase is ", tolower( 'L' ) );
35  } // end main
```

Fig. 8.3 | Using functions islower, isupper, tolower and toupper. (Part 1 of 2.)

```
According to islower:
p is a lowercase letter
P is not a lowercase letter
5 is not a lowercase letter
! is not a lowercase letter

According to isupper:
D is an uppercase letter
d is not an uppercase letter
8 is not an uppercase letter
$ is not an uppercase letter

u converted to uppercase is U
7 converted to uppercase is 7
$ converted to uppercase is $
L converted to lowercase is l
```

Fig. 8.3 | Using functions islower, isupper, tolower and toupper. (Part 2 of 2.)

8.3.3 Functions isspace, iscntrl, ispunct, isprint and isgraph

Figure 8.4 demonstrates functions isspace, iscntrl, ispunct, isprint and isgraph. Function isspace determines whether a character is one of the following whitespace characters: space (' '), form feed ('\f'), newline ('\n'), carriage return ('\r'), horizontal tab ('\t') or vertical tab ('\v'). Function iscntrl determines whether a character is one of the following **control characters**: horizontal tab ('\t'), vertical tab ('\v'), form feed ('\f'), alert ('\a'), backspace ('\b'), carriage return ('\r') or newline ('\n'). Function ispunct determines whether a character is a **printing character** other than a space, a digit or a letter, such as $, #, (,), [,], {, }, ;, : or %. Function isprint determines whether a character can be displayed on the screen (including the space character). Function isgraph is the same as isprint, except that the space character is not included.

```c
 1   // Fig. 8.4: fig08_04.c
 2   // Using functions isspace, iscntrl, ispunct, isprint, isgraph
 3   #include <stdio.h>
 4   #include <ctype.h>
 5
 6   int main( void )
 7   {
 8      printf( "%s\n%s%s%s\n%s%s%s\n%s%s\n\n",
 9         "According to isspace:",
10         "Newline", isspace( '\n' ) ? " is a " : " is not a ",
11         "whitespace character", "Horizontal tab",
12         isspace( '\t' ) ? " is a " : " is not a ",
13         "whitespace character",
14         isspace( '%' ) ? "% is a " : "% is not a ",
15         "whitespace character" );
16
17      printf( "%s\n%s%s%s\n%s%s\n\n", "According to iscntrl:",
18         "Newline", iscntrl( '\n' ) ? " is a " : " is not a ",
```

Fig. 8.4 | Using functions isspace, iscntrl, ispunct, isprint and isgraph. (Part 1 of 2.)

```
19          "control character", iscntrl( '$' ) ? "$ is a " :
20          "$ is not a ", "control character" );
21
22      printf( "%s\n%s%s\n%s%s\n%s%s\n\n",
23          "According to ispunct:",
24          ispunct( ';' ) ? "; is a " : "; is not a ",
25          "punctuation character",
26          ispunct( 'Y' ) ? "Y is a " : "Y is not a ",
27          "punctuation character",
28          ispunct( '#' ) ? "# is a " : "# is not a ",
29          "punctuation character" );
30
31      printf( "%s\n%s%s\n%s%s%s\n\n", "According to isprint:",
32          isprint( '$' ) ? "$ is a " : "$ is not a ",
33          "printing character",
34          "Alert", isprint( '\a' ) ? " is a " : " is not a ",
35          "printing character" );
36
37      printf( "%s\n%s%s\n%s%s%s\n", "According to isgraph:",
38          isgraph( 'Q' ) ? "Q is a " : "Q is not a ",
39          "printing character other than a space",
40          "Space", isgraph( ' ' ) ? " is a " : " is not a ",
41          "printing character other than a space" );
42  } // end main
```

```
According to isspace:
Newline is a whitespace character
Horizontal tab is a whitespace character
% is not a whitespace character

According to iscntrl:
Newline is a control character
$ is not a control character

According to ispunct:
; is a punctuation character
Y is not a punctuation character
# is a punctuation character

According to isprint:
$ is a printing character
Alert is not a printing character

According to isgraph:
Q is a printing character other than a space
Space is not a printing character other than a space
```

Fig. 8.4 | Using functions isspace, iscntrl, ispunct, isprint and isgraph. (Part 2 of 2.)

8.4 String-Conversion Functions

This section presents the string-conversion functions from the general utilities library (<stdlib.h>). These functions convert strings of digits to integer and floating-point values. Figure 8.5 summarizes the string-conversion functions. The C standard also includes strtoll and strtoull for converting strings to long long int and unsigned long long int, respectively. Note the use of const to declare variable nPtr in the function headers (read from right to left as "nPtr is a pointer to a character constant"); const specifies that the argument value will not be modified.

Function prototype	Function description
double strtod(const char *nPtr, char **endPtr);	
	Converts the string nPtr to double.
long strtol(const char *nPtr, char **endPtr, int base);	
	Converts the string nPtr to long.
unsigned long strtoul(const char *nPtr, char **endPtr, int base);	
	Converts the string nPtr to unsigned long.

Fig. 8.5 | String-conversion functions of the general utilities library.

8.4.1 Function strtod

Function strtod (Fig. 8.6) converts a sequence of characters representing a floating-point value to double. The function returns 0 if it's unable to convert any portion of its first argument to double. The function receives two arguments—a string (char *) and a pointer to a string (char **). The string argument contains the character sequence to be converted to double—any whitespace characters at the beginning of the string are ignored. The function uses the char ** argument to modify a char * in the calling function (stringPtr) so that it points to the *location of the first character after the converted portion of the string* or to the entire string if no portion can be converted. Line 14

```
    d = strtod( string, &stringPtr );
```

indicates that d is assigned the double value converted from string, and stringPtr is assigned the location of the first character after the converted value (51.2) in string.

```
 1   // Fig. 8.6: fig08_06.c
 2   // Using function strtod
 3   #include <stdio.h>
 4   #include <stdlib.h>
 5
 6   int main( void )
 7   {
 8      // initialize string pointer
 9      const char *string = "51.2% are admitted"; // initialize string
10
11      double d; // variable to hold converted sequence
12      char *stringPtr; // create char pointer
13
14      d = strtod( string, &stringPtr );
15
```

Fig. 8.6 | Using function strtod. (Part I of 2.)

```
16      printf( "The string \"%s\" is converted to the\n", string );
17      printf( "double value %.2f and the string \"%s\"\n", d, stringPtr );
18   } // end main
```

```
The string "51.2% are admitted" is converted to the
double value 51.20 and the string "% are admitted"
```

Fig. 8.6 | Using function strtod. (Part 2 of 2.)

8.4.2 Function strtol

Function **strtol** (Fig. 8.7) converts to long int a sequence of characters representing an integer. The function returns 0 if it's unable to convert any portion of its first argument to long int. The function receives three arguments—a string (char *), a pointer to a string and an integer. The string argument contains the character sequence to be converted to double—any whitespace characters at the beginning of the string are ignored. The function uses the char ** argument to modify a char * in the calling function (remainderPtr) so that it points to the *location of the first character after the converted portion of the string* or to the entire string if no portion can be converted. The integer specifies the *base* of the value being converted. Line 13

```
    x = strtol( string, &remainderPtr, 0 );
```

indicates that x is assigned the long value converted from string. The second argument, remainderPtr, is assigned the remainder of string after the conversion. Using NULL for the second argument causes the *remainder of the string to be ignored.* The third argument, 0, indicates that the value to be converted can be in octal (base 8), decimal (base 10) or hexadecimal (base 16) format. The base can be specified as 0 or any value between 2 and 36. (See Appendix C for a detailed explanation of the octal, decimal and hexadecimal number systems.) Numeric representations of integers from base 11 to base 36 use the characters A–Z to represent the values 10 to 35. For example, hexadecimal values can consist of the digits 0–9 and the characters A–F. A base-11 integer can consist of the digits 0–9 and the character A. A base-24 integer can consist of the digits 0–9 and the characters A–N. A base-36 integer can consist of the digits 0–9 and the characters A–Z. The function returns 0 if it's unable to convert any portion of its first argument to a long int value.

```
1    // Fig. 8.7: fig08_07.c
2    // Using function strtol
3    #include <stdio.h>
4    #include <stdlib.h>
5
6    int main( void )
7    {
8       const char *string = "-1234567abc"; // initialize string pointer
9
10      char *remainderPtr; // create char pointer
11      long x; // variable to hold converted sequence
12
```

Fig. 8.7 | Using function strtol. (Part 1 of 2.)

```
13      x = strtol( string, &remainderPtr, 0 );
14
15      printf( "%s\"%s\"\n%s%ld\n%s\"%s\"\n%s%ld\n",
16          "The original string is ", string,
17          "The converted value is ", x,
18          "The remainder of the original string is ",
19          remainderPtr,
20          "The converted value plus 567 is ", x + 567 );
21   } // end main
```

```
The original string is "-1234567abc"
The converted value is -1234567
The remainder of the original string is "abc"
The converted value plus 567 is -1234000
```

Fig. 8.7 | Using function strtol. (Part 2 of 2.)

8.4.3 Function strtoul

Function strtoul (Fig. 8.8) converts to unsigned long int a sequence of characters representing an unsigned long int value. The function works identically to function strtol. The statement

```
      x = strtoul( string, &remainderPtr, 0 );
```

in line 12 of Fig. 8.8 indicates that x is assigned the unsigned long int value converted from string. The second argument, &remainderPtr, is assigned the remainder of string after the conversion. The third argument, 0, indicates that the value to be converted can be in octal, decimal or hexadecimal format.

```
 1   // Fig. 8.8: fig08_08.c
 2   // Using function strtoul
 3   #include <stdio.h>
 4   #include <stdlib.h>
 5
 6   int main( void )
 7   {
 8      const char *string = "1234567abc"; // initialize string pointer
 9      unsigned long int x; // variable to hold converted sequence
10      char *remainderPtr; // create char pointer
11
12      x = strtoul( string, &remainderPtr, 0 );
13
14      printf( "%s\"%s\"\n%s%lu\n%s\"%s\"\n%s%lu\n",
15          "The original string is ", string,
16          "The converted value is ", x,
17          "The remainder of the original string is ",
18          remainderPtr,
19          "The converted value minus 567 is ", x - 567 );
20   } // end main
```

Fig. 8.8 | Using function strtoul. (Part I of 2.)

```
The original string is "1234567abc"
The converted value is 1234567
The remainder of the original string is "abc"
The converted value minus 567 is 1234000
```

Fig. 8.8 | Using function `strtoul`. (Part 2 of 2.)

8.5 Standard Input/Output Library Functions

This section presents several functions from the standard input/output library (`<stdio.h>`) specifically for manipulating character and string data. Figure 8.9 summarizes the character and string input/output functions of the standard input/output library.

Function prototype	Function description
`int getchar( void );`	Inputs the next character from the standard input and returns it as an integer.
`char *fgets( char *s, int n, FILE *stream);`	
	Inputs characters from the specified stream into the array s until a *newline* or *end-of-file* character is encountered, or until n - 1 bytes are read. In this chapter, we specify the stream as `stdin`—the *standard input stream*, which is typically used to read characters from the keyboard. A *terminating null character* is appended to the array. Returns the string that was read into s.
`int putchar( int c );`	Prints the character stored in c and returns it as an integer.
`int puts( const char *s );`	Prints the string s followed by a *newline* character. Returns a nonzero integer if successful, or EOF if an error occurs.
`int sprintf( char *s, const char *format, ... );`	
	Equivalent to `printf`, except the output is stored in the array s instead of printed on the screen. Returns the number of characters written to s, or EOF if an error occurs. [*Note:* We mention the more secure related functions snprintf and snprintf_s in the Secure C Programming section of this chapter and in Appendix F.]
`int sscanf( char *s, const char *format, ... );`	
	Equivalent to `scanf`, except the input is read from the array s rather than from the keyboard. Returns the number of items successfully read by the function, or EOF if an error occurs.

Fig. 8.9 | Standard input/output library character and string functions.

8.5.1 Functions fgets and putchar

Figure 8.10 uses functions `fgets` and `putchar` to read a line of text from the standard input (keyboard) and recursively output the characters of the line in reverse order. Function `fgets` reads characters from the *standard input* into its first argument—an array of chars—until a *newline* or the *end-of-file* indicator is encountered, or until the maximum number of characters is read. The maximum number of characters is one fewer than the value specified in fgets's second argument. The third argument specifies the *stream* from which to read characters—in this case, we use the *standard input stream* (stdin). A null character ('\0') is appended to the array when reading terminates. Function putchar prints its character argument. The program calls *recursive* function reverse to print the line of text backward. If the first character of the array received by reverse is the null character '\0', reverse returns. Otherwise, reverse is called again with the address of the subarray beginning at element sPtr[1], and character sPtr[0] is output with putchar when the recursive call is completed. The order of the two statements in the else portion of the if statement causes reverse to walk to the terminating null character of the string before a character is printed. As the recursive calls are completed, the characters are output in reverse order.

```c
 1   // Fig. 8.10: fig08_10.c
 2   // Using functions fgets and putchar
 3   #include <stdio.h>
 4   #define SIZE 80
 5
 6   void reverse( const char * const sPtr ); // prototype
 7
 8   int main( void )
 9   {
10      char sentence[ SIZE ]; // create char array
11
12      puts( "Enter a line of text:" );
13
14      // use fgets to read line of text
15      fgets( sentence, SIZE, stdin );
16
17      puts( "\nThe line printed backward is:" );
18      reverse( sentence );
19   } // end main
20
21   // recursively outputs characters in string in reverse order
22   void reverse( const char * const sPtr )
23   {
24      // if end of the string
25      if ( '\0' == sPtr[ 0 ] ) { // base case
26         return;
27      } // end if
28      else { // if not end of the string
29         reverse( &sPtr[ 1 ] ); // recursion step
30         putchar( sPtr[ 0 ] ); // use putchar to display character
31      } // end else
32   } // end function reverse
```

```
Enter a line of text:
Characters and Strings

The line printed backward is:
sgnirtS dna sretcarahC
```

Fig. 8.10 | Using functions fgets and putchar. (Part 1 of 2.)

```
Enter a line of text:
able was I ere I saw elba

The line printed backward is:
able was I ere I saw elba
```

Fig. 8.10 | Using functions `fgets` and `putchar`. (Part 2 of 2.)

8.5.2 Function getchar

Figure 8.11 uses functions `getchar` and `puts` to read characters from the standard input into character array `sentence` and display the characters as a string. Function `getchar` reads a character from the *standard input* and returns the character as an integer. As you know, function `puts` takes a string as an argument and displays the string followed by a newline character. The program stops inputting characters when either 79 characters have been read or when `getchar` reads the *newline* character entered by the user to end the line of text. A *null character* is appended to array `sentence` (line 20) so that the array may be treated as a string. Then, line 24 uses `puts` to display the string contained in `sentence`.

```
1   // Fig. 8.11: fig08_11.c
2   // Using function getchar.
3   #include <stdio.h>
4   #define SIZE 80
5
6   int main( void )
7   {
8      int c; // variable to hold character input by user
9      char sentence[ SIZE ]; // create char array
10     int i = 0; // initialize counter i
11
12     // prompt user to enter line of text
13     puts( "Enter a line of text:" );
14
15     // use getchar to read each character
16     while ( i < SIZE - 1 && ( c = getchar() ) != '\n' ) {
17        sentence[ i++ ] = c;
18     } // end while
19
20     sentence[ i ] = '\0'; // terminate string
21
22     // use puts to display sentence
23     puts( "\nThe line entered was:" );
24     puts( sentence );
25  } // end main
```

```
Enter a line of text:
This is a test.

The line entered was:
This is a test.
```

Fig. 8.11 | Using function `getchar`.

8.5.3 Function sprintf

Figure 8.12 uses function sprintf to print formatted data into array s—an array of characters. The function uses the same conversion specifiers as printf (see Chapter 9 for a detailed discussion of formatting). The program inputs an int value and a double value to be formatted and printed to array s. Array s is the first argument of sprintf. [*Note:* If your system supports snprintf_s, then use that in preference to sprintf. If your system doesn't support snprintf_s but does support snprintf, then use that in preference to sprintf. We discuss each of these functions in Appendix F.]

```c
1   // Fig. 8.12: fig08_12.c
2   // Using function sprintf
3   #include <stdio.h>
4   #define SIZE 80
5
6   int main( void )
7   {
8      char s[ SIZE ]; // create char array
9      int x; // x value to be input
10     double y; // y value to be input
11
12     puts( "Enter an integer and a double:" );
13     scanf( "%d%lf", &x, &y );
14
15     sprintf( s, "integer:%6d\ndouble:%8.2f", x, y );
16
17     printf( "%s\n%s\n",
18             "The formatted output stored in array s is:", s );
19  } // end main
```

```
Enter an integer and a double:
298 87.375
The formatted output stored in array s is:
integer:   298
double:   87.38
```

Fig. 8.12 | Using function sprintf.

8.5.4 Function sscanf

Figure 8.13 uses function sscanf to read formatted data from character array s. The function uses the same conversion specifiers as scanf. The program reads an int and a double from array s and stores the values in x and y, respectively. The values of x and y are printed. Array s is the first argument of sscanf.

```c
1   // Fig. 8.13: fig08_13.c
2   // Using function sscanf
3   #include <stdio.h>
4
```

Fig. 8.13 | Using function sscanf. (Part 1 of 2.)

```
 5   int main( void )
 6   {
 7      char s[] = "31298 87.375"; // initialize array s
 8      int x; // x value to be input
 9      double y; // y value to be input
10
11      sscanf( s, "%d%lf", &x, &y );
12      printf( "%s\n%s%6d\n%s%8.3f\n",
13              "The values stored in character array s are:",
14              "integer:", x, "double:", y );
15   } // end main
```

```
The values stored in character array s are:
integer: 31298
double:  87.375
```

Fig. 8.13 | Using function `sscanf`. (Part 2 of 2.)

8.6 String-Manipulation Functions of the String-Handling Library

The string-handling library (`<string.h>`) provides many useful functions for manipulating string data (copying strings and concatenating strings), comparing strings, searching strings for characters and other strings, tokenizing strings (separating strings into logical pieces) and determining the length of strings. This section presents the string-manipulation functions of the string-handling library. The functions are summarized in Fig. 8.14. Every function—except for `strncpy`—appends the *null character* to its result. [*Note:* Each of these functions has a more secure version described in the optional Annex K of the C11 standard. We mention these in the Secure C Programming section of this chapter and in Appendix F.]

Function prototype	Function description
`char *strcpy( char *s1, const char *s2 )`	
	Copies string s1 into array s1. The value of s1 is returned.
`char *strncpy( char *s1, const char *s2, size_t n )`	
	Copies at most n characters of string s2 into array s1. The value of s1 is returned.
`char *strcat( char *s1, const char *s2 )`	
	Appends string s2 to array s1. The first character of s2 *overwrites the terminating null character* of s1. The value of s1 is returned.
`char *strncat( char *s1, const char *s2, size_t n )`	
	Appends at most n characters of string s2 to array s1. The first character of s2 *overwrites the terminating null character* of s1. The value of s1 is returned.

Fig. 8.14 | String-manipulation functions of the string-handling library.

Functions strncpy and strncat specify a parameter of type size_t. Function strcpy copies its second argument (a string) into its first argument—a character array that *you must ensure is large enough* to store the string and its terminating null character, which is also copied. Function strncpy is equivalent to strcpy, except that strncpy specifies the number of characters to be copied from the string into the array. *Function strncpy does not necessarily copy the terminating null character of its second argument. This occurs only if the number of characters to be copied is at least one more than the length of the string.* For example, if "test" is the second argument, a *terminating null character* is written only if the third argument to strncpy is at least 5 (four characters in "test" plus a terminating null character). If the third argument is larger than 5, null characters are appended to the array until the total number of characters specified by the third argument are written.

Error-Prevention Tip 8.2

When using functions from the string-handling library, include the <string.h> header.

Common Programming Error 8.5

Not appending a terminating null character to the first argument of a strncpy when the third argument is less than or equal to the length of the string in the second argument.

8.6.1 Functions strcpy and strncpy

Figure 8.15 uses strcpy to copy the entire string in array x into array y and uses strncpy to copy the first 14 characters of array x into array z. A *null character* ('\0') is appended to array z, because the call to strncpy in the program *does not write a terminating null character* (the third argument is less than the string length of the second argument).

```c
 1   // Fig. 8.15: fig08_15.c
 2   // Using functions strcpy and strncpy
 3   #include <stdio.h>
 4   #include <string.h>
 5   #define SIZE1 25
 6   #define SIZE2 15
 7
 8   int main( void )
 9   {
10      char x[] = "Happy Birthday to You"; // initialize char array x
11      char y[ SIZE1 ]; // create char array y
12      char z[ SIZE2 ]; // create char array z
13
14      // copy contents of x into y
15      printf( "%s%s\n%s%s\n",
16         "The string in array x is: ", x,
17         "The string in array y is: ", strcpy( y, x ) );
18
19      // copy first 14 characters of x into z. Does not copy null
20      // character
21      strncpy( z, x, SIZE2 - 1 );
22
```

Fig. 8.15 | Using functions strcpy and strncpy. (Part 1 of 2.)

```
23      z[ SIZE2 - 1 ] = '\0'; // terminate string in z
24      printf( "The string in array z is: %s\n", z );
25   } // end main
```

```
The string in array x is: Happy Birthday to You
The string in array y is: Happy Birthday to You
The string in array z is: Happy Birthday
```

Fig. 8.15 | Using functions strcpy and strncpy. (Part 2 of 2.)

8.6.2 Functions strcat and strncat

Function **strcat** appends its second argument (a string) to its first argument (a character array containing a string). The first character of the second argument replaces the null ('\0') that terminates the string in the first argument. *You must ensure that the array used to store the first string is large enough to store the first string, the second string and the terminating null character copied from the second string.* Function **strncat** appends a specified number of characters from the second string to the first string. A terminating null character is automatically appended to the result. Figure 8.16 demonstrates function strcat and function strncat.

```
1    // Fig. 8.16: fig08_16.c
2    // Using functions strcat and strncat
3    #include <stdio.h>
4    #include <string.h>
5
6    int main( void )
7    {
8       char s1[ 20 ] = "Happy "; // initialize char array s1
9       char s2[] = "New Year "; // initialize char array s2
10      char s3[ 40 ] = ""; // initialize char array s3 to empty
11
12      printf( "s1 = %s\ns2 = %s\n", s1, s2 );
13
14      // concatenate s2 to s1
15      printf( "strcat( s1, s2 ) = %s\n", strcat( s1, s2 ) );
16
17      // concatenate first 6 characters of s1 to s3. Place '\0'
18      // after last character
19      printf( "strncat( s3, s1, 6 ) = %s\n", strncat( s3, s1, 6 ) );
20
21      // concatenate s1 to s3
22      printf( "strcat( s3, s1 ) = %s\n", strcat( s3, s1 ) );
23   } // end main
```

```
s1 = Happy
s2 = New Year
strcat( s1, s2 ) = Happy New Year
strncat( s3, s1, 6 ) = Happy
strcat( s3, s1 ) = Happy Happy New Year
```

Fig. 8.16 | Using functions strcat and strncat.

8.7 **Comparison Functions of the String-Handling Library**

This section presents the string-handling library's string-comparison functions, `strcmp` and `strncmp`. Figure 8.17 contains their prototypes and a brief description of each function.

Function prototype	Function description
`int strcmp( const char *s1, const char *s2 );`	
	Compares the string s1 with the string s2. The function returns 0, less than 0 or greater than 0 if s1 is equal to, less than or greater than s2, respectively.
`int strncmp( const char *s1, const char *s2, size_t n );`	
	Compares up to n characters of the string s1 with the string s2. The function returns 0, less than 0 or greater than 0 if s1 is equal to, less than or greater than s2, respectively.

Fig. 8.17 | String-comparison functions of the string-handling library.

Figure 8.18 compares three strings using `strcmp` and `strncmp`. Function `strcmp` compares its first string argument with its second string argument, character by character. The function returns 0 if the strings are equal, a *negative value* if the first string is less than the second string and a *positive value* if the first string is greater than the second string. Function `strncmp` is equivalent to `strcmp`, except that `strncmp` compares up to a specified number of characters. Function `strncmp` does *not* compare characters following a null character in a string. The program prints the integer value returned by each function call.

```c
 1   // Fig. 8.18: fig08_18.c
 2   // Using functions strcmp and strncmp
 3   #include <stdio.h>
 4   #include <string.h>
 5
 6   int main( void )
 7   {
 8      const char *s1 = "Happy New Year"; // initialize char pointer
 9      const char *s2 = "Happy New Year"; // initialize char pointer
10      const char *s3 = "Happy Holidays"; // initialize char pointer
11
12      printf("%s%s\n%s%s\n%s%s\n\n%s%2d\n%s%2d\n%s%2d\n\n",
13         "s1 = ", s1, "s2 = ", s2, "s3 = ", s3,
14         "strcmp(s1, s2) = ", strcmp( s1, s2 ),
15         "strcmp(s1, s3) = ", strcmp( s1, s3 ),
16         "strcmp(s3, s1) = ", strcmp( s3, s1 ) );
17
18      printf("%s%2d\n%s%2d\n%s%2d\n",
19         "strncmp(s1, s3, 6) = ", strncmp( s1, s3, 6 ),
20         "strncmp(s1, s3, 7) = ", strncmp( s1, s3, 7 ),
21         "strncmp(s3, s1, 7) = ", strncmp( s3, s1, 7 ) );
22   } // end main
```

Fig. 8.18 | Using functions `strcmp` and `strncmp`. (Part 1 of 2.)

```
s1 = Happy New Year
s2 = Happy New Year
s3 = Happy Holidays
strcmp(s1, s2) =  0
strcmp(s1, s3) =  1
strcmp(s3, s1) = -1
strncmp(s1, s3, 6) =  0
strncmp(s1, s3, 7) =  6
strncmp(s3, s1, 7) = -6
```

Fig. 8.18 | Using functions `strcmp` and `strncmp`. (Part 2 of 2.)

Common Programming Error 8.6

Assuming that `strcmp` and `strncmp` return 1 when their arguments are equal is a logic error. Both functions return 0 (strangely, the equivalent of C's false value) for equality. Therefore, when comparing two strings for equality, the result of function `strcmp` or `strncmp` should be compared with 0 to determine whether the strings are equal.

To understand just what it means for one string to be "greater than" or "less than" another, consider the process of alphabetizing a series of last names. The reader would, no doubt, place "Jones" before "Smith," because the first letter of "Jones" comes before the first letter of "Smith" in the alphabet. But the alphabet is more than just a list of 26 letters—it's an ordered list of characters. Each letter occurs in a specific position within the list. "Z" is more than merely a letter of the alphabet; "Z" is specifically the 26th letter of the alphabet.

How do the string comparison functions know that one particular letter comes before another? All characters are represented inside the computer as **numeric codes** in character sets such as ASCII and Unicode; when the computer compares two strings, it actually compares the numeric codes of the characters in the strings.

8.8 Search Functions of the String-Handling Library

This section presents the functions of the string-handling library used to *search strings* for characters and other strings. The functions are summarized in Fig. 8.19. The functions `strcspn` and `strspn` return `size_t`. [*Note:* Function `strtok` has a more secure version described in optional Annex K of the C11 standard. We mention this in the Secure C Programming section of this chapter and in Appendix F.]

Function prototypes and descriptions
`char *strchr( const char *s, int c );`   *Locates* the first occurrence of character `c` in string `s`. If `c` is found, a pointer to `c` in `s` is returned. Otherwise, a `NULL` pointer is returned.
`size_t strcspn( const char *s1, const char *s2 );`   Determines and returns the length of the initial segment of string `s1` consisting of characters *not* contained in string `s2`.

Fig. 8.19 | Search functions of the string-handling library. (Part 1 of 2.)

Function prototypes and descriptions

`size_t strspn( const char *s1, const char *s2 );`

Determines and returns the length of the initial segment of string s1 consisting *only* of characters contained in string s2.

`char *strpbrk( const char *s1, const char *s2 );`

Locates the first occurrence in string s1 of any character in string s2. If a character from string s2 is found, a pointer to the character in string s1 is returned. Otherwise, a NULL pointer is returned.

`char *strrchr( const char *s, int c );`

Locates the last occurrence of c in string s. If c is found, a pointer to c in string s is returned. Otherwise, a NULL pointer is returned.

`char *strstr( const char *s1, const char *s2 );`

Locates the first occurrence in string s1 of string s2. If the string is found, a pointer to the string in s1 is returned. Otherwise, a NULL pointer is returned.

`char *strtok( char *s1, const char *s2 );`

A sequence of calls to strtok breaks string s1 into *tokens*—logical pieces such as words in a line of text—separated by characters contained in string s2. The first call contains s1 as the first argument, and subsequent calls to continue tokenizing the same string contain NULL as the first argument. A pointer to the current token is returned by each call. If there are no more tokens when the function is called, NULL is returned.

Fig. 8.19 | Search functions of the string-handling library. (Part 2 of 2.)

8.8.1 Function strchr

Function strchr searches for the *first occurrence* of a character in a string. If the character is found, strchr returns a pointer to the character in the string; otherwise, strchr returns NULL. Figure 8.20 searches for the first occurrences of 'a' and 'z' in "This is a test".

```
1   // Fig. 8.20: fig08_20.c
2   // Using function strchr
3   #include <stdio.h>
4   #include <string.h>
5
6   int main( void )
7   {
8      const char *string = "This is a test"; // initialize char pointer
9      char character1 = 'a'; // initialize character1
10     char character2 = 'z'; // initialize character2
11
12     // if character1 was found in string
13     if ( strchr( string, character1 ) != NULL ) {
14        printf( "\'%c\' was found in \"%s\".\n",
15           character1, string );
16     } // end if
```

Fig. 8.20 | Using function strchr. (Part 1 of 2.)

```
17      else { // if character1 was not found
18         printf( "\'%c\' was not found in \"%s\".\n",
19            character1, string );
20      } // end else
21
22      // if character2 was found in string
23      if ( strchr( string, character2 ) != NULL ) {
24         printf( "\'%c\' was found in \"%s\".\n",
25            character2, string );
26      } // end if
27      else { // if character2 was not found
28         printf( "\'%c\' was not found in \"%s\".\n",
29            character2, string );
30      } // end else
31   } // end main
```

```
'a' was found in "This is a test".
'z' was not found in "This is a test".
```

Fig. 8.20 | Using function strchr. (Part 2 of 2.)

8.8.2 Function strcspn

Function **strcspn** (Fig. 8.21) determines the length of the initial part of the string in its first argument that does *not* contain any characters from the string in its second argument. The function returns the length of the segment.

```
1   // Fig. 8.21: fig08_21.c
2   // Using function strcspn
3   #include <stdio.h>
4   #include <string.h>
5
6   int main( void )
7   {
8      // initialize two char pointers
9      const char *string1 = "The value is 3.14159";
10     const char *string2 = "1234567890";
11
12     printf( "%s%s\n%s%s\n\n%s\n%s%u\n",
13        "string1 = ", string1, "string2 = ", string2,
14        "The length of the initial segment of string1",
15        "containing no characters from string2 = ",
16        strcspn( string1, string2 ) );
17  } // end main
```

```
string1 = The value is 3.14159
string2 = 1234567890

The length of the initial segment of string1
containing no characters from string2 = 13
```

Fig. 8.21 | Using function strcspn.

8.8.3 Function `strpbrk`

Function **strpbrk** searches its first string argument for the *first occurrence* of any character in its second string argument. If a character from the second argument is found, `strpbrk` returns a pointer to the character in the first argument; otherwise, `strpbrk` returns NULL. Figure 8.22 shows a program that locates the first occurrence in `string1` of any character from `string2`.

```
1   // Fig. 8.22: fig08_22.c
2   // Using function strpbrk
3   #include <stdio.h>
4   #include <string.h>
5
6   int main( void )
7   {
8      const char *string1 = "This is a test"; // initialize char pointer
9      const char *string2 = "beware"; // initialize char pointer
10
11     printf( "%s\"%s\"\n'%c'%s\n\"%s\"\n",
12        "Of the characters in ", string2,
13        *strpbrk( string1, string2 ),
14        " appears earliest in ", string1 );
15  } // end main
```

```
Of the characters in "beware"
'a' appears earliest in
"This is a test"
```

Fig. 8.22 | Using function `strpbrk`.

8.8.4 Function `strrchr`

Function **strrchr** searches for the *last occurrence* of the specified character in a string. If the character is found, `strrchr` returns a pointer to the character in the string; otherwise, `strrchr` returns NULL. Figure 8.23 shows a program that searches for the last occurrence of the character `'z'` in the string `"A zoo has many animals including zebras"`.

```
1   // Fig. 8.23: fig08_23.c
2   // Using function strrchr
3   #include <stdio.h>
4   #include <string.h>
5
6   int main( void )
7   {
8      // initialize char pointer
9      const char *string1 = "A zoo has many animals including zebras";
10
11     int c = 'z'; // character to search for
12
```

Fig. 8.23 | Using function `strrchr`. (Part 1 of 2.)

```
13      printf( "%s\n%s'%c'%s\"%s\"\n",
14          "The remainder of string1 beginning with the",
15          "last occurrence of character ", c,
16          " is: ", strrchr( string1, c ) );
17   } // end main
```

```
The remainder of string1 beginning with the
last occurrence of character 'z' is: "zebras"
```

Fig. 8.23 | Using function strrchr. (Part 2 of 2.)

8.8.5 Function strspn

Function strspn (Fig. 8.24) determines the length of the *initial part* of the string in its first argument that contains only characters from the string in its second argument. The function returns the length of the segment.

```
1    // Fig. 8.24: fig08_24.c
2    // Using function strspn
3    #include <stdio.h>
4    #include <string.h>
5
6    int main( void )
7    {
8        // initialize two char pointers
9        const char *string1 = "The value is 3.14159";
10       const char *string2 = "aehi lsTuv";
11
12       printf( "%s%s\n%s%s\n\n%s\n%s%u\n",
13           "string1 = ", string1, "string2 = ", string2,
14           "The length of the initial segment of string1",
15           "containing only characters from string2 = ",
16           strspn( string1, string2 ) );
17   } // end main
```

```
string1 = The value is 3.14159
string2 = aehi lsTuv

The length of the initial segment of string1
containing only characters from string2 = 13
```

Fig. 8.24 | Using function strspn.

8.8.6 Function strstr

Function **strstr** searches for the *first occurrence* of its second string argument in its first string argument. If the second string is found in the first string, a pointer to the location of the string in the first argument is returned. Figure 8.25 uses strstr to find the string "def" in the string "abcdefabcdef".

```
1   // Fig. 8.25: fig08_25.c
2   // Using function strstr
3   #include <stdio.h>
4   #include <string.h>
5
6   int main( void )
7   {
8      const char *string1 = "abcdefabcdef"; // string to search
9      const char *string2 = "def"; // string to search for
10
11     printf( "%s%s\n%s%s\n\n%s\n%s%s\n",
12        "string1 = ", string1, "string2 = ", string2,
13        "The remainder of string1 beginning with the",
14        "first occurrence of string2 is: ",
15        strstr( string1, string2 ) );
16  } // end main
```

```
string1 = abcdefabcdef
string2 = def

The remainder of string1 beginning with the
first occurrence of string2 is: defabcdef
```

Fig. 8.25 | Using function strstr.

8.8.7 Function strtok

Function **strtok** (Fig. 8.26) is used to break a string into a series of tokens. A token is a sequence of characters separated by delimiters (usually *spaces* or *punctuation marks*, but a delimiter can be *any character*). For example, in a line of text, each word can be considered a token, and the spaces and punctuation separating the words can be considered delimiters.

```
1   // Fig. 8.26: fig08_26.c
2   // Using function strtok
3   #include <stdio.h>
4   #include <string.h>
5
6   int main( void )
7   {
8      // initialize array string
9      char string[] = "This is a sentence with 7 tokens";
10     char *tokenPtr; // create char pointer
11
12     printf( "%s\n%s\n\n%s\n",
13        "The string to be tokenized is:", string,
14        "The tokens are:" );
15
16     tokenPtr = strtok( string, " " ); // begin tokenizing sentence
17
```

Fig. 8.26 | Using function strtok. (Part 1 of 2.)

```
18      // continue tokenizing sentence until tokenPtr becomes NULL
19      while ( tokenPtr != NULL ) {
20         printf( "%s\n", tokenPtr );
21         tokenPtr = strtok( NULL, " " ); // get next token
22      } // end while
23   } // end main
```

```
The string to be tokenized is:
This is a sentence with 7 tokens

The tokens are:
This
is
a
sentence
with
7
tokens
```

Fig. 8.26 | Using function `strtok`. (Part 2 of 2.)

Multiple calls to `strtok` are required to *tokenize a string*—i.e., break it into tokens (assuming that the string contains more than one token). The first call to `strtok` contains two arguments: a string to be tokenized, and a string containing characters that separate the tokens. In line 16, the statement

```
tokenPtr = strtok( string, " " ); // begin tokenizing sentence
```

assigns `tokenPtr` a pointer to the first token in `string`. The second argument, `" "`, indicates that tokens are separated by spaces. Function `strtok` searches for the first character in `string` that's not a delimiting character (space). This begins the first token. The function then finds the next delimiting character in the string and *replaces it with a null (`'\0'`) character* to terminate the current token. Function `strtok` saves a pointer to the next character following the token in `string` and returns a pointer to the current token.

Subsequent `strtok` calls in line 21 continue tokenizing `string`. These calls *contain NULL as their first argument.* The `NULL` argument indicates that the call to `strtok` should continue tokenizing from the location in `string` saved by the last call to `strtok`. If no tokens remain when `strtok` is called, `strtok` returns `NULL`. You can change the delimiter string in each new call to `strtok`. Figure 8.26 uses `strtok` to tokenize the string `"This is a sentence with 7 tokens"`. Each token is printed separately. Function `strtok` *modifies the input string* by placing `'\0'` at the end of each token; therefore, a *copy* of the string should be made if the string will be used again in the program after the calls to `strtok`. [*Note:* Also see CERT recommendation STR06-C.]

8.9 Memory Functions of the String-Handling Library

The string-handling library functions presented in this section manipulate, compare and search blocks of memory. The functions treat blocks of memory as character arrays and can manipulate any block of data. Figure 8.27 summarizes the memory functions of the string-handling library. In the function discussions, "object" refers to a block of data.

[*Note:* Each of these functions has a more secure version described in optional Annex K of the C11 standard. We mention these in the Secure C Programming section of this chapter and in Appendix F.]

Function prototype	Function description
`void *memcpy( void *s1, const void *s2, size_t n );`	
	Copies n characters from the object pointed to by s2 into the object pointed to by s1. A pointer to the resulting object is returned.
`void *memmove( void *s1, const void *s2, size_t n );`	
	Copies n characters from the object pointed to by s2 into the object pointed to by s1. The copy is performed as if the characters were first copied from the object pointed to by s2 into a *temporary array* and then from the temporary array into the object pointed to by s1. A pointer to the resulting object is returned.
`int memcmp( const void *s1, const void *s2, size_t n );`	
	Compares the first n characters of the objects pointed to by s1 and s2. The function returns 0, less than 0 or greater than 0 if s1 is equal to, less than or greater than s2.
`void *memchr( const void *s, int c, size_t n );`	
	Locates the first occurrence of c (converted to unsigned char) in the first n characters of the object pointed to by s. If c is found, a pointer to c in the object is returned. Otherwise, NULL is returned.
`void *memset( void *s, int c, size_t n );`	
	Copies c (converted to unsigned char) into the *first n characters* of the object pointed to by s. A pointer to the result is returned.

Fig. 8.27 | Memory functions of the string-handling library.

The pointer parameters are declared void * so they can be used to manipulate memory for *any* data type. In Chapter 7, we saw that a pointer to any data type can be assigned directly to a pointer of type void *, and a pointer of type void * can be assigned directly to a pointer to any data type. For this reason, these functions can receive pointers to any data type. Because a void * pointer cannot be dereferenced, each function receives a size argument that specifies the number of characters (bytes) the function will process. For simplicity, the examples in this section manipulate character arrays (blocks of characters). The functions in Fig. 8.27 *do not* check for terminating null characters.

8.9.1 Function memcpy

Function **memcpy** copies a specified number of characters from the object pointed to by its second argument into the object pointed to by its first argument. The function can receive a pointer to any type of object. The result of this function is *undefined* if the two objects overlap in memory (i.e., if they are parts of the same object)—in such cases, use memmove. Figure 8.28 uses memcpy to copy the string in array s2 to array s1.

Performance Tip 8.1

memcpy is more efficient than strcpy when you know the size of the string you are copying.

```
1   // Fig. 8.28: fig08_28.c
2   // Using function memcpy
3   #include <stdio.h>
4   #include <string.h>
5
6   int main( void )
7   {
8      char s1[ 17 ]; // create char array s1
9      char s2[] = "Copy this string"; // initialize char array s2
10
11     memcpy( s1, s2, 17 );
12     printf( "%s\n%s\"%s\"\n",
13        "After s2 is copied into s1 with memcpy,",
14        "s1 contains ", s1 );
15  } // end main
```

```
After s2 is copied into s1 with memcpy,
s1 contains "Copy this string"
```

Fig. 8.28 | Using function memcpy.

8.9.2 Function memmove

Function **memmove**, like memcpy, *copies a specified number of bytes* from the object pointed to by its second argument into the object pointed to by its first argument. Copying is performed as if the bytes were copied from the second argument into a temporary character array, then copied from the temporary array into the first argument. This allows characters from one part of a string to be copied into another part of the *same* string. Figure 8.29 uses memmove to copy the last 10 bytes of array x into the first 10 bytes of array x.

Common Programming Error 8.7

String-manipulation functions other than memmove *that copy characters have undefined results when copying takes place between parts of the* same *string.*

```
1   // Fig. 8.29: fig08_29.c
2   // Using function memmove
3   #include <stdio.h>
4   #include <string.h>
5
6   int main( void )
7   {
8      char x[] = "Home Sweet Home"; // initialize char array x
9
```

Fig. 8.29 | Using function memmove. (Part 1 of 2.)

```
10      printf( "%s%s\n", "The string in array x before memmove is: ", x );
11      printf( "%s%s\n", "The string in array x after memmove is: ",
12        (char *) memmove( x, &x[ 5 ], 10 ) );
13    } // end main
```

```
The string in array x before memmove is: Home Sweet Home
The string in array x after memmove is: Sweet Home Home
```

Fig. 8.29 | Using function memmove. (Part 2 of 2.)

8.9.3 Function memcmp

Function memcmp (Fig. 8.30) *compares the specified number of characters* of its first argument with the corresponding characters of its second argument. The function returns a value greater than 0 if the first argument is *greater than* the second, returns 0 if the arguments are equal and returns a value less than 0 if the first argument is less than the second.

```
1    // Fig. 8.30: fig08_30.c
2    // Using function memcmp
3    #include <stdio.h>
4    #include <string.h>
5
6    int main( void )
7    {
8       char s1[] = "ABCDEFG"; // initialize char array s1
9       char s2[] = "ABCDXYZ"; // initialize char array s2
10
11      printf( "%s%s\n%s%s\n\n%s%2d\n%s%2d\n%s%2d\n",
12         "s1 = ", s1, "s2 = ", s2,
13         "memcmp( s1, s2, 4 ) = ", memcmp( s1, s2, 4 ),
14         "memcmp( s1, s2, 7 ) = ", memcmp( s1, s2, 7 ),
15         "memcmp( s2, s1, 7 ) = ", memcmp( s2, s1, 7 ) );
16   } // end main
```

```
s1 = ABCDEFG
s2 = ABCDXYZ

memcmp( s1, s2, 4 ) =  0
memcmp( s1, s2, 7 ) = -1
memcmp( s2, s1, 7 ) =  1
```

Fig. 8.30 | Using function memcmp.

8.9.4 Function memchr

Function memchr searches for the *first occurrence of a byte*, represented as unsigned char, in the specified number of bytes of an object. If the byte is found, a pointer to the byte in the object is returned; otherwise, a NULL pointer is returned. Figure 8.31 searches for the character (byte) 'r' in the string "This is a string".

```
 1   // Fig. 8.31: fig08_31.c
 2   // Using function memchr
 3   #include <stdio.h>
 4   #include <string.h>
 5
 6   int main( void )
 7   {
 8      const char *s = "This is a string"; // initialize char pointer
 9
10      printf( "%s\'%c\'%s\"%s\"\n",
11         "The remainder of s after character ", 'r',
12         " is found is ", (char *) memchr( s, 'r', 16 ) );
13   } // end main
```

```
The remainder of s after character 'r' is found is "ring"
```

Fig. 8.31 | Using function memchr.

8.9.5 Function memset

Function memset copies the value of the byte in its second argument into the first n bytes of the object pointed to by its first argument, where n is specified by the third argument. Figure 8.32 uses memset to copy 'b' into the first 7 bytes of string1.

Performance Tip 8.2

Use memset to set an array's values to 0 rather than looping through the array's elements and assigning 0 to each element. For example, in Fig. 6.3, we could have initialized the 10-element array n with memset(n, 0, 10);. Many hardware architectures have a block copy or clear instruction that the compiler can use to optimize memset for high performance zeroing of memory.

```
 1   // Fig. 8.32: fig08_32.c
 2   // Using function memset
 3   #include <stdio.h>
 4   #include <string.h>
 5
 6   int main( void )
 7   {
 8      char string1[ 15 ] = "BBBBBBBBBBBBBB"; // initialize string1
 9
10      printf( "string1 = %s\n", string1 );
11      printf( "string1 after memset = %s\n",
12         (char *) memset( string1, 'b', 7 ) );
13   } // end main
```

```
string1 = BBBBBBBBBBBBBB
string1 after memset = bbbbbbbBBBBBBB
```

Fig. 8.32 | Using function memset.

8.10 Other Functions of the String-Handling Library

The two remaining functions of the string-handling library are `strerror` and `strlen`. Figure 8.33 summarizes the `strerror` and `strlen` functions.

Function prototype	Function description
`char *strerror( int errornum );`	
	Maps `errornum` into a full text string in a compiler- and locale-specific manner (e.g. the message may appear in different languages based on its location). A pointer to the string is returned.
`size_t strlen( const char *s );`	
	Determines the length of string s. The number of characters preceding the terminating null character is returned.

Fig. 8.33 | Other functions of the string-handling library.

8.10.1 Function `strerror`

Function **strerror** takes an error number and creates an error message string. A pointer to the string is returned. Figure 8.34 demonstrates `strerror`.

```
1   // Fig. 8.34: fig08_34.c
2   // Using function strerror
3   #include <stdio.h>
4   #include <string.h>
5
6   int main( void )
7   {
8      printf( "%s\n", strerror( 2 ) );
9   } // end main
```

```
No such file or directory
```

Fig. 8.34 | Using function `strerror`.

8.10.2 Function `strlen`

Function **strlen** takes a string as an argument and returns the number of characters in the string—the terminating null character is not included in the length. Figure 8.35 demonstrates function `strlen`.

```
1   // Fig. 8.35: fig08_35.c
2   // Using function strlen
3   #include <stdio.h>
4   #include <string.h>
```

Fig. 8.35 | Using function `strlen`. (Part 1 of 2.)

```
 5
 6   int main( void )
 7   {
 8      // initialize 3 char pointers
 9      const char *string1 = "abcdefghijklmnopqrstuvwxyz";
10      const char *string2 = "four";
11      const char *string3 = "Boston";
12
13      printf("%s\"%s\"%s%u\n%s\"%s\"%s%u\n%s\"%s\"%s%u\n",
14         "The length of ", string1, " is ", strlen( string1 ),
15         "The length of ", string2, " is ", strlen( string2 ),
16         "The length of ", string3, " is ", strlen( string3 ) );
17   } // end main
```

```
The length of "abcdefghijklmnopqrstuvwxyz" is 26
The length of "four" is 4
The length of "Boston" is 6
```

Fig. 8.35 | Using function strlen. (Part 2 of 2.)

8.11 Secure C Programming

Secure String-Processing Functions
In this chapter, we presented functions sprintf, strcpy, strncpy, strcat, strncat, strtok, strlen, memcpy, memmove and memset. More secure versions of these and many other string-processing and input/output functions are described by the C11 standard's optional Annex K. If your C compiler supports Annex K, you should use the secure versions of these functions. Among other things, the more secure versions help prevent buffer overflows by requiring an additional parameter that specifies the number of elements in the target array and by ensuring that pointer arguments are non-NULL.

Reading Numeric Inputs and Input Validation
It's important to validate the data that you input into a program. For example, when you ask the user to enter an integer in the range 1–100 then attempt to read that integer using scanf, there are several possible problems. The user could enter an integer that's outside the program's required range, an integer that's outside the allowed range for integers on that computer, a non-integer numeric value or a non-numeric value.

You can use various functions that you learned in this chapter to fully validate such input. For example, you could

- use fgets to read the input as a line of text
- convert the string to a number using strtol and ensure that the conversion was successful, then
- ensure that the value is in range.

For more information and techniques for converting input to numeric values, see CERT guideline INT05-C at www.securecoding.cert.org.

Summary

Section 8.2 Fundamentals of Strings and Characters

- Characters are the fundamental building blocks of source programs. Every program is composed of a sequence of characters that—when grouped together meaningfully—is interpreted by the computer as a series of instructions used to accomplish a task.

- A character constant is an int value represented as a character in single quotes. The value of a character constant is the character's integer value in the machine's character set.

- A string is a series of characters treated as a single unit. A string may include letters, digits and various special characters such as +, -, *, / and $. String literals, or string constants, in C are written in double quotation marks.

- A string in C is an array of characters ending in the null character ('\0').

- A string is accessed via a pointer to its first character. The value of a string is the address of its first character.

- A character array or a variable of type char * can be initialized with a string in a definition.

- When defining a character array to contain a string, the array must be large enough to store the string and its terminating null character.

- A string can be stored in an array using scanf. Function scanf will read characters until a space, tab, newline or end-of-file indicator is encountered.

- For a character array to be printed as a string, the array must contain a terminating null character.

Section 8.3 Character-Handling Library

- Function islower determines whether its argument is a lowercase letter (a–z).

- Function isupper determines whether its argument is an uppercase letter (A–Z).

- Function isdigit determines whether its argument is a digit (0–9).

- Function isalpha determines whether its argument is an uppercase letter (A–Z) or a lowercase letter (a–z).

- Function isalnum determines whether its argument is an uppercase letter (A–Z), a lowercase letter (a–z) or a digit (0–9).

- Function isxdigit determines whether its argument is a hexadecimal digit (A–F, a–f, 0–9).

- Function toupper converts a lowercase letter to uppercase and returns the uppercase letter.

- Function tolower converts an uppercase letter to lowercase and returns the lowercase letter.

- Function isspace determines whether its argument is one of the following whitespace characters: ' ' (space), '\f', '\n', '\r', '\t' or '\v'.

- Function iscntrl determines whether its argument is one of the following control characters: '\t', '\v', '\f', '\a', '\b', '\r' or '\n'.

- Function ispunct determines whether its argument is a printing character other than a space, a digit or a letter.

- Function isprint determines whether its argument is any printing character including the space character.

- Function isgraph determines whether its argument is a printing character other than the space character.

Section 8.4 String-Conversion Functions

- Function strtod converts a sequence of characters representing a floating-point value to double. The function receives two arguments—a string (char *) and a pointer to char *. The string con-

tains the character sequence to be converted, and the location specified by the pointer to char *
is assigned the address of the remainder of the string after the conversion, or to the entire string
if no portion of the string can be converted.

- Function strtol converts a sequence of characters representing an integer to long. The function
  receives three arguments—a string (char *), a pointer to char * and an integer. The string contains
  the character sequence to be converted, the location specified by the pointer to char * is assigned
  the address of the remainder of the string after the conversion, or to the entire string if no portion
  of the string can be converted. The integer specifies the base of the value being converted.

- Function strtoul converts a sequence of characters representing an integer to unsigned long
  int. The function works identically to strtol.

Section 8.5 Standard Input/Output Library Functions

- Function fgets reads characters until a newline character or the end-of-file indicator is encountered. The arguments to fgets are an array of type char, the maximum number of characters that
  can be read and the stream from which to read. A null character ('\0') is appended to the array
  after reading terminates.

- Function putchar prints its character argument.

- Function getchar reads a single character from the standard input and returns it as an integer. If
  the end-of-file indicator is encountered, getchar returns EOF.

- Function puts takes a string (char *) as an argument and prints the string followed by a newline
  character.

- Function sprintf uses the same conversion specifications as function printf to print formatted
  data into an array of type char.

- Function sscanf uses the same conversion specifications as function scanf to read formatted data
  from a string.

Section 8.6 String-Manipulation Functions of the String-Handling Library

- Function strcpy copies its second argument (a string) into its first argument (a character array).
  You must ensure that the array is large enough to store the string and its terminating null character.

- Function strncpy is equivalent to strcpy, except that a call to strncpy specifies the number of
  characters to be copied from the string into the array. The terminating null character will be copied only if the number of characters to be copied is one more than the length of the string.

- Function strcat appends its second string argument—including the terminating null character—to its first string argument. The first character of the second string replaces the null ('\0')
  character of the first string. You must ensure that the array used to store the first string is large
  enough to store both the first string and the second string.

- Function strncat appends a specified number of characters from the second string to the first
  string. A terminating null character is appended to the result.

Section 8.7 Comparison Functions of the String-Handling Library

- Function strcmp compares its first string argument to its second string argument, character by
  character. It returns 0 if the strings are equal, returns a negative value if the first string is less than
  the second and returns a positive value if the first string is greater than the second.

- Function strncmp is equivalent to strcmp, except that strncmp compares a specified number of
  characters. If one of the strings is shorter than the number of characters specified, strncmp compares characters until the null character in the shorter string is encountered.

Section 8.8 Search Functions of the String-Handling Library

- Function strchr searches for the first occurrence of a character in a string. If the character is found, strchr returns a pointer to the character in the string; otherwise, strchr returns NULL.

- Function strcspn determines the length of the initial part of the string in its first argument that does not contain any characters from the string in its second argument. The function returns the length of the segment.

- Function strpbrk searches for the first occurrence in its first argument of any character in its second argument. If a character from the second argument is found, strpbrk returns a pointer to the character; otherwise, strpbrk returns NULL.

- Function strrchr searches for the last occurrence of a character in a string. If the character is found, strrchr returns a pointer to the character in the string; otherwise, strrchr returns NULL.

- Function strspn determines the length of the initial part of the string in its first argument that contains only characters from the string in its second argument. The function returns the length of the segment.

- Function strstr searches for the first occurrence of its second string argument in its first string argument. If the second string is found in the first string, a pointer to the location of the string in the first argument is returned.

- A sequence of calls to strtok breaks the first string s1 into tokens that are separated by characters contained in the second string s2. The first call contains s1 as the first argument, and subsequent calls to continue tokenizing the same string contain NULL as the first argument. A pointer to the current token is returned by each call. If there are no more tokens when the function is called, a NULL pointer is returned.

Section 8.9 Memory Functions of the String-Handling Library

- Function memcpy copies a specified number of characters from the object to which its second argument points into the object to which its first argument points. The function can receive a pointer to any type of object. Function memcpy manipulates the bytes of the object as characters.

- Function memmove copies a specified number of bytes from the object pointed to by its second argument to the object pointed to by its first argument. Copying is accomplished as if the bytes were copied from the second argument to a temporary character array and then copied from the temporary array to the first argument.

- Function memcmp compares the specified number of characters of its first and second arguments.

- Function memchr searches for the first occurrence of a byte, represented as unsigned char, in the specified number of bytes of an object. If the byte is found, a pointer to the byte is returned; otherwise, a NULL pointer is returned.

- Function memset copies its second argument, treated as an unsigned char, to a specified number of bytes of the object pointed to by the first argument.

Section 8.10 Other Functions of the String-Handling Library

- Function strerror maps an integer error number into a full text string in a locale specific manner. A pointer to the string is returned.

- Function strlen takes a string as an argument and returns the number of characters in the string—the terminating null character is not included in the length of the string.

Terminology

Self-Review Exercises

8.1　Write a single statement to accomplish each of the following. Assume that variables c (which stores a character), x, y and z are of type int, variables d, e and f are of type double, variable ptr is of type char * and arrays s1[100] and s2[100] are of type char.

- a) Convert the character stored in variable c to an uppercase letter. Assign the result to variable c.
- b) Determine whether the value of variable c is a digit. Use the conditional operator as shown in Figs. 8.2–8.4 to print " is a " or " is not a " when the result is displayed.
- c) Determine whether the value of variable c is a control character. Use the conditional operator to print " is a " or " is not a " when the result is displayed.
- d) Read a line of text into array s1 from the keyboard. Do not use scanf.
- e) Print the line of text stored in array s1. Do not use printf.
- f) Assign ptr the location of the last occurrence of c in s1.
- g) Print the value of variable c. Do not use printf.
- h) Determine whether the value of c is a letter. Use the conditional operator to print " is a " or " is not a " when the result is displayed.
- i) Read a character from the keyboard and store the character in variable c.
- j) Assign ptr the location of the first occurrence of s2 in s1.

k) Determine whether the value of variable c is a printing character. Use the conditional operator to print " is a " or " is not a " when the result is displayed.
l) Read three double values into variables d, e and f from the string "1.27 10.3 9.432".
m) Copy the string stored in array s2 into array s1.
n) Assign ptr the location of the first occurrence in s1 of any character from s2.
o) Compare the string in s1 with the string in s2. Print the result.
p) Assign ptr the location of the first occurrence of c in s1.
q) Use sprintf to print the values of integer variables x, y and z into array s1. Each value should be printed with a field width of 7.
r) Append 10 characters from the string in s2 to the string in s1.
s) Determine the length of the string in s1. Print the result.
t) Assign ptr to the location of the first token in s2. Tokens in the string s2 are separated by commas (,).

8.2   Show two different methods of initializing character array skill with the string "PROGRAMMING".

8.3   What, if anything, prints when each of the following C statements is performed? If the statement contains an error, describe the error and indicate how to correct it. Assume the following variable definitions:

```
char a[ 100 ] = "computer", b[ 100 ] = "science", c[ 100 ], *ptr;
```

a) printf("%s", strcpy(c, b));
b) printf("%u", strlen(c));
c) printf("%u", strlen(a) + strlen(b));
d) printf("%c%s", toupper(a[6]), &b[1]);
e) printf("%s", strcat(strcat(strcpy(c, a), " and "), b));

8.4   Find the error in each of the following program segments and explain how to correct it:
a)
```
char s[ 10 ];
strncpy( s, "hello", 5 );
printf( "%s\n", s );
```
b) printf("%s", 'a');
c)
```
char s[ 12 ];
strcpy( s, "Welcome Home" );
```
d)
```
if ( strcmp( string1, string2 ) ) {
    puts( "The strings are equal" );
}
```

Answers to Self-Review Exercises

8.1   a) c = toupper(c);
b) printf("'%c'%sdigit\n", c, isdigit(c) ? " is a " : " is not a ");
c) printf("'%c'%scontrol character\n",
         c, iscntrl(c) ? " is a " : " is not a ");
d) fgets(s1, 100, stdin);
e) puts(s1);
f) ptr = strrchr(s1, c);
g) putchar(c);
h) printf("'%c'%sletter\n", c, isalpha(c) ? " is a " : " is not a ");
i) c = getchar();
j) ptr = strstr(s1, s2);

k) `printf( "'%c'%sprinting character\n",`
   `    c, isprint( c ) ? " is a " : " is not a " );`
l) `sscanf( "1.27 10.3 9.432", "%f%f%f", &d, &e, &f );`
m) `strcpy( s1, s2 );`
n) `ptr = strpbrk( s1, s2 );`
o) `printf( "strcmp( s1, s2 ) = %d\n", strcmp( s1, s2 ) );`
p) `ptr = strchr( s1, c );`
q) `sprintf( s1, "%7d%7d%7d", x, y, z );`
r) `strncat( s1, s2, 10 );`
s) `printf( "strlen(s1) = %u\n", strlen( s1 ) );`
t) `ptr = strtok( s2, "," );`

8.2 `char skill[] = "PROGRAMMING";`
`char skill[] = { 'P', 'R', 'O', 'G', 'R', 'A', 'M', 'M', 'I','N', 'G', '\0' };`

8.3 a) `science`
b) `3`
c) `15`
d) `Escience`
e) `computer and science`

8.4 a) Error: Function `strncpy` does not write a terminating null character to array s, because its third argument is equal to the length of the string "hello".
Correction: Make the third argument of `strncpy` 6, or assign `'\0'` to `s[ 5 ]`.
b) Error: Attempting to print a character constant as a string.
Correction: Use `%c` to output the character, or replace `'a'` with `"a"`.
c) Error: Character array s is not large enough to store the terminating null character.
Correction: Declare the array with more elements.
d) Error: Function `strcmp` returns 0 if the strings are equal; therefore, the condition in the `if` statement is false, and the `printf` will not be executed.
Correction: Compare the result of `strcmp` with 0 in the condition.

Exercises

8.5 *(Character Testing)* Write a program that inputs a character from the keyboard and tests it with each of the functions in the character-handling library. The program should print the value returned by each function.

8.6 *(Converting Uppercase Strings to Lowercase and vice versa)* Write a program that inputs a line of text into char array p[100]. Output the uppercase letters of the line in lowercase letters and vice versa.

8.7 *(Converting Strings to Integers for Calculations)* Write a program that inputs two strings that represent integers, converts the strings to integers and prints the greatest common divisor (GCD) of two values.

8.8 *(Converting Strings to Floating-Point for Calculations)* Write a program that inputs three strings that represent floating-point values, converts the strings to double values, multiplies the values and prints the average of the three values.

8.9 *(Concatenating Strings)* Write a program that takes two strings from the user, uses the function `strcat` to concatenate two strings and prints the concatenated string.

8.10 *(Concatenating a Part of a String)* Write a program that uses function `strncat` to concatenate two strings input by the user. The program should input the number of characters to be concatenated from second string to the first string.

8.11 *(Random Sentences)* Write a program that uses random number generation to create sentences. The program should use four arrays of pointers to char called article, noun, verb and preposition. The program should create a sentence by selecting a word at random from each array in the following order: article, noun, verb, preposition, article and noun. As each word is picked, it should be concatenated to the previous words in an array large enough to hold the entire sentence. The words should be separated by spaces. When the final sentence is output, it should start with a capital letter and end with a period. The program should generate 20 such sentences. The arrays should be filled as follows: The article array should contain the articles "the", "a", "one", "some" and "any"; the noun array should contain the nouns "boy", "girl", "dog", "town" and "car"; the verb array should contain the verbs "drove", "jumped", "ran", "walked" and "skipped"; the preposition array should contain the prepositions "to", "from", "over", "under" and "on".

After the preceding program is written and working, modify it to produce a short story consisting of several of these sentences. (How about the possibility of a random term paper writer?)

8.12 *(Limericks)* A limerick is a humorous five-line verse in which the first and second lines rhyme with the fifth, and the third line rhymes with the fourth. Using techniques similar to those developed in Exercise 8.11, write a program that produces random limericks. Polishing this program to produce good limericks is a challenging problem, but the result will be worth the effort!

8.13 *(Pig Latin)* Write a program that encodes English-language phrases into pig Latin. Pig Latin is a form of coded language often used for amusement. Many variations exist in the methods used to form pig-Latin phrases. For simplicity, use the following algorithm:

To form a pig-Latin phrase from an English-language phrase, tokenize the phrase into words with function strtok. To translate each English word into a pig-Latin word, place the first letter of the English word at the end of the English word and add the letters "ay". Thus the word "jump" becomes "umpjay", the word "the" becomes "hetay" and the word "computer" becomes "omputercay". Blanks between words remain as blanks. Assume the following: The English phrase consists of words separated by blanks, there are no punctuation marks, and all words have two or more letters. Function printLatinWord should display each word. [*Hint:* Each time a token is found in a call to strtok, pass the token pointer to function printLatinWord, and print the pig-Latin word. *Note:* We've provided simplified rules for converting words to pig Latin here. For more detailed rules and variations, visit en.wikipedia.org/wiki/Pig_latin.]

8.14 *(Tokenizing Telephone Numbers)* Write a program that inputs a telephone number as a string in the form (555) 555-5555. The program should use function strtok to extract the area code as a token, the first three digits of the phone number as a token and the last four digits of the phone number as a token. The seven digits of the phone number should be concatenated into one string. The program should convert the area-code string to int and convert the phone-number string to long. Both the area code and the phone number should be printed.

8.15 *(Alphabetic Order)* Write a program that takes characters from the user and prints them in alphabetical order.

8.16 *(Searching for Substrings)* Write a program that inputs a line of text and a search string from the keyboard. Using function strstr, locate the first occurrence of the search string in the line of text, and assign the location to variable searchPtr of type char *. If the search string is found, print the remainder of the line of text beginning with the search string. Then, use strstr again to locate the next occurrence of the search string in the line of text. If a second occurrence is found, print the remainder of the line of text beginning with the second occurrence. [*Hint:* The second call to strstr should contain searchPtr + 1 as its first argument.]

8.17 *(Counting Words and Characters in a String)* Write a program that inputs several lines of text, counts the total number of words and total number of characters in the text and prints the result.

8.18 *(First Occurrence of a Character)* Write a program that inputs a string and three search characters and uses function strchr to determine the first occurrence of each character in the string. Print whether the characters are found or not.

8.19 *(First Occurrence of a Character from Another String)* Write a program that inputs two strings and uses function strpbrk to search its first string for the first occurrence of any character from the second string.

8.20 *(Counting the Number of Words in a String)* Write a program that inputs several lines of text and uses strtok to count the total number of words in each line. Print the average number of words in each line. Assume that the words are separated by either spaces or newline characters.

8.21 *(Alphabetizing a List of Strings)* Use the string-comparison functions and the techniques for sorting arrays to write a program that alphabetizes a list of strings. Use the names of 10 or 15 towns in your area as data for your program.

8.22 The chart in Appendix B shows the numeric code representations for the characters in the ASCII character set. Study this chart and then state whether each of the following is *true* or *false*.
   a) The symbol "@" comes before the uppercase as well as lowercase characters.
   b) The paranthesis "]" comes after the paranthesis "}".
   c) The letter "m" comes after the letter "M".
   d) The backslash symbol "\" comes between "(" and ")".
   e) If a sort program sorts strings into descending sequence, then the program will place the symbol for a left parenthesis before the symbol for a right parenthesis.

8.23 *(Strings Starting with "Mo")* Write a program that reads a series of strings and prints only those beginning with the letters "Mo".

8.24 *(Strings Ending with "top")* Write a program that reads a series of strings and prints only those that end with the letters "top".

8.25 *(Printing Letters for a Set of ASCII Codes)* Write a program that inputs two ASCII codes and prints all the corresponding characters between first ASCII code and second ASCII code.

8.26 *(Write Your Own Character-Handling Functions)* Using the ASCII character chart in Appendix B as a guide, write your own versions of the character-handling functions in Fig. 8.1.

8.27 *(Write Your String Conversion Functions)* Write your own versions of the functions in Fig. 8.5 for converting strings to numbers.

8.28 *(Write Your Own String Copy and Concatenation Functions)* Write two versions of each of the string-copy and string-concatenation functions in Fig. 8.14. The first version should use array subscripting, and the second should use pointers and pointer arithmetic.

8.29 *(Write Your Own String Comparison Functions)* Write two versions of each string-comparison function in Fig. 8.17. The first version should use array subscripting, and the second should use pointers and pointer arithmetic.

8.30 *(Write Your Own String Length Function)* Write two versions of function strlen in Fig. 8.33. The first version should use array subscripting, and the second should use pointers and pointer arithmetic.

Special Section: Advanced String-Manipulation Exercises

The preceding exercises are keyed to the text and designed to test the reader's understanding of fundamental string-manipulation concepts. This section contains intermediate and advanced problems that you should find challenging yet enjoyable. They vary considerably in difficulty. Some require an hour or two of programming. Others are useful for lab assignments that might require two or three weeks of study and implementation. Some are challenging term projects.

8.31   *(Text Analysis)* The availability of computers with string-manipulation capabilities has resulted in some rather interesting approaches to analyzing the writings of great authors. Much attention has been focused on whether William Shakespeare ever lived. Some scholars find substantial evidence that Christopher Marlowe actually penned the masterpieces attributed to Shakespeare. Researchers have used computers to find similarities in the writings of these two authors. This exercise examines three methods for analyzing texts with a computer.

a) Write a program that reads several lines of text and prints a table indicating the number of occurrences of each letter of the alphabet in the text. For example, the phrase

```
To be, or not to be: that is the question:
```

contains one "a," two "b's," no "c's," and so on.

b) Write a program that reads several lines of text and prints a table indicating the number of one-letter words, two-letter words, three-letter words, and so on, appearing in the text. For example, the phrase

```
Whether 'tis nobler in the mind to suffer
```

contains

Word length	Occurrences
1	0
2	2
3	1
4	2 (including 'tis)
5	0
6	2
7	1

c) Write a program that reads several lines of text and prints a table indicating the number of occurrences of each different word in the text. The program should include the words in the table in the same order in which they appear in the text. For example, the lines

```
To be, or not to be: that is the question:
Whether 'tis nobler in the mind to suffer
```

contain the words "to" three times, "be" two times, "or" once, and so on.

8.32   *(Printing Dates in Various Formats)* Dates are commonly printed in several different formats in business correspondence. Two of the more common formats are

```
07/21/2003 and July 21, 2003
```

Write a program that reads a date in the first format and prints it in the second format.

8.33   *(Check Protection)* Computers are frequently used in check-writing systems, such as payroll and accounts payable applications. Many stories circulate regarding weekly paychecks being printed (by mistake) for amounts in excess of $1 million. Weird amounts are printed by computerized check-writing systems because of human error and/or machine failure. Systems designers, of course, make every effort to build controls into their systems to prevent erroneous checks from being issued.

Another serious problem is the intentional alteration of a check amount by someone who intends to cash it fraudulently. To prevent a dollar amount from being altered, most computerized check-writing systems employ a technique called *check protection*.

Checks designed for imprinting by computer contain a fixed number of spaces in which the computer may print an amount. Suppose a paycheck contains nine blank spaces in which the computer is supposed to print the amount of a weekly paycheck. If the amount is large, then all nine of those spaces will be filled—for example:

```
11,230.60  (check amount)
---------
123456789  (position numbers)
```

On the other hand, if the amount is less than $1000, then several of the spaces will ordinarily be left blank—for example,

```
    99.87
---------
123456789
```

contains four blank spaces. If a check is printed with blank spaces, it's easier for someone to alter the amount of the check. To prevent such alteration, many check-writing systems insert *leading asterisks* to protect the amount as follows:

```
****99.87
---------
123456789
```

Write a program that inputs a dollar amount to be printed on a check and then prints the amount in check-protected format with leading asterisks if necessary. Assume that nine spaces are available for printing an amount.

8.34   *(Writing the Word Equivalent of a Check Amount)* Continuing the discussion of the previous exercise, we reiterate the importance of designing check-writing systems to prevent alteration of check amounts. One common security method requires that the check amount be both written in numbers and "spelled out" in words. Even if someone is able to alter the numerical amount of the check, it's extremely difficult to change the amount in words. Write a program that inputs a numeric check amount and writes the word equivalent of the amount. For example, the amount 52.43 should be written as

```
FIFTY TWO and 43/100
```

8.35   *(Project: A Metric Conversion Program)* Write a program that will assist the user with metric conversions. Your program should allow the user to specify the names of the units as strings (i.e., centimeters, liters, grams, and so on for the metric system and inches, quarts, pounds, and so on for the English system) and should respond to simple questions such as

```
"How many inches are in 2 meters?"
"How many liters are in 10 quarts?"
```

Your program should recognize invalid conversions. For example, the question

```
"How many feet are in 5 kilograms?"
```

is not meaningful, because "feet" are units of length while "kilograms" are units of mass.

A Challenging String-Manipulation Project

8.36   *(Project: A Crossword-Puzzle Generator)* Most people have worked a crossword puzzle at one time or another, but few have ever attempted to generate one. Generating a crossword puzzle is a difficult problem. It's suggested here as a string-manipulation project requiring substantial sophistication and effort. There are many issues you must resolve to get even the simplest crossword-puzzle generator program working. For example, how does one represent the grid of a crossword puzzle inside the computer? Should one use a series of strings, or perhaps double-subscripted arrays? You need a source of words (i.e., a computerized dictionary) that can be directly referenced by the program. In what form should these words be stored to facilitate the complex manipulations required by the program? The really ambitious reader will want to generate the "clues" portion of the puzzle in which the brief hints for each "across" word and each "down" word are printed for the puzzle worker. Merely printing a version of the blank puzzle itself is not a simple problem.

Making a Difference

8.37   *(Cooking with Healthier Ingredients)* Obesity in America is increasing at an alarming rate. Check the map from the Centers for Disease Control and Prevention (CDC) at `www.cdc.gov/nccdphp/dnpa/Obesity/trend/maps/index.htm`, which shows obesity trends in the United States over the last 20 years. As obesity increases, so do occurrences of related problems (e.g., heart disease, high blood pressure, high cholesterol, type 2 diabetes). Write a program that helps users choose healthier ingredients when cooking, and helps those allergic to certain foods (e.g., nuts, gluten) find substitutes. The program should read a recipe from the user and suggest healthier replacements for some of the ingredients. For simplicity, your program should assume the recipe has no abbreviations for measures such as teaspoons, cups, and tablespoons, and uses numerical digits for quantities (e.g., 1 egg, 2 cups) rather than spelling them out (one egg, two cups). Some common substitutions are shown in Fig. 8.36. Your program should display a warning such as, "Always consult your physician before making significant changes to your diet."

Your program should take into consideration that replacements are not always one-for-one. For example, if a cake recipe calls for three eggs, it might reasonably use six egg whites instead. Conversion data for measurements and substitutes can be obtained at websites such as:

```
chinesefood.about.com/od/recipeconversionfaqs/f/usmetricrecipes.htm
www.pioneerthinking.com/eggsub.html
www.gourmetsleuth.com/conversions.htm
```

Your program should consider the user's health concerns, such as high cholesterol, high blood pressure, weight loss, gluten allergy, and so on. For high cholesterol, the program should suggest substitutes for eggs and dairy products; if the user wishes to lose weight, low-calorie substitutes for ingredients such as sugar should be suggested.

Ingredient	Substitution
1 cup sour cream	1 cup yogurt
1 cup milk	1/2 cup evaporated milk and 1/2 cup water
1 teaspoon lemon juice	1/2 teaspoon vinegar
1 cup sugar	1/2 cup honey, 1 cup molasses or 1/4 cup agave nectar
1 cup butter	1 cup margarine or yogurt
1 cup flour	1 cup rye or rice flour
1 cup mayonnaise	1 cup cottage cheese or 1/8 cup mayonnaise and 7/8 cup yogurt

Fig. 8.36 | Common ingredient substitutions. (Part 1 of 2.)

Ingredient	Substitution
1 egg	2 tablespoons cornstarch, arrowroot flour or potato starch or 2 egg whites or 1/2 of a large banana (mashed)
1 cup milk	1 cup soy milk
1/4 cup oil	1/4 cup applesauce
white bread	whole-grain bread

Fig. 8.36 | Common ingredient substitutions. (Part 2 of 2.)

8.38 *(Spam Scanner)* Spam (or junk e-mail) costs U.S. organizations billions of dollars a year in spam-prevention software, equipment, network resources, bandwidth, and lost productivity. Research online some of the most common spam e-mail messages and words, and check your own junk e-mail folder. Create a list of 30 words and phrases commonly found in spam messages. Write a program in which the user enters an e-mail message. Read the message into a large character array and ensure that the program does not attempt to insert characters past the end of the array. Then scan the message for each of the 30 keywords or phrases. For each occurrence of one of these within the message, add a point to the message's "spam score." Next, rate the likelihood that the message is spam, based on the number of points it received.

8.39 *(SMS Language)* Short Message Service (SMS) is a communications service that allows sending text messages of 160 or fewer characters between mobile phones. With the proliferation of mobile phone use worldwide, SMS is being used in many developing nations for political purposes (e.g., voicing opinions and opposition), reporting news about natural disasters, and so on. For example, check out comunica.org/radio2.0/archives/87. Because the length of SMS messages is limited, SMS Language—abbreviations of common words and phrases in mobile text messages, e-mails, instant messages, etc.—is often used. For example, "in my opinion" is "IMO" in SMS Language. Research SMS Language online. Write a program that lets the user enter a message using SMS Language, then the program translates it into English (or your own language). Also provide a mechanism to translate text written in English (or your own language) into SMS Language. One potential problem is that one SMS abbreviation could expand into a variety of phrases. For example, IMO (as used above) could also stand for "International Maritime Organization," "in memory of," etc.

8.40 *(Gender Neutrality)* In Exercise 1.15, you researched eliminating sexism in all forms of communication. You then described the algorithm you'd use to read through a paragraph of text and replace gender-specific words with gender-neutral equivalents. Create a program that reads a paragraph of text, then replaces gender-specific words with gender-neutral ones. Display the resulting gender-neutral text.

C Formatted Input/Output

All the news that's fit to print.
—Adolph S. Ochs

What mad pursuit? What struggle to escape?
—John Keats

Objectives

In this chapter, you'll:

- Use input and output streams.

- Use all print formatting capabilities.

- Use all input formatting capabilities.

- Print with field widths and precisions.

- Use formatting flags in the `printf` format control string.

- Output literals and escape sequences.

- Format input using `scanf`.

9.1 Introduction

An important part of the solution to any problem is the *presentation* of the results. In this chapter, we discuss in depth the formatting features of `scanf` and `printf`. These functions input data from the **standard input stream** and output data to the standard output stream. Include the header `<stdio.h>` in programs that call these functions. Chapter 11 discusses several additional functions included in the standard input/output (`<stdio.h>`) library.

9.2 Streams

All input and output is performed with **streams**, which are sequences of bytes. In *input* operations, the bytes flow *from a device* (e.g., a keyboard, a disk drive, a network connection) *to main memory*. In output operations, bytes flow *from main memory to a device* (e.g., a display screen, a printer, a disk drive, a network connection, and so on).

When program execution begins, three streams are connected to the program automatically. Normally, the *standard input stream* is connected to the *keyboard* and the *standard output stream* is connected to the *screen*. Operating systems often allow these streams to be *redirected* to other devices. A third stream, the **standard error stream**, is connected to the *screen*. We'll show how to output error messages to the *standard error stream* in Chapter 11, C File Processing. Streams are discussed in detail in Chapter 11.

9.3 Formatting Output with `printf`

Precise output formatting is accomplished with `printf`. Every `printf` call contains a format control string that describes the output format. The format control string consists of **conversion specifiers**, **flags**, **field widths**, **precisions** and **literal characters**. Together with the percent sign (%), these form **conversion specifications**. Function `printf` can perform the following formatting capabilities, each of which is discussed in this chapter:

1. Rounding floating-point values to an indicated number of decimal places.

2. Aligning a column of numbers with decimal points appearing one above the other.

3. Right justification and left justification of outputs.

4. Inserting literal characters at precise locations in a line of output.

5. Representing floating-point numbers in exponential format.

6. Representing unsigned integers in octal and hexadecimal format. See Appendix C for more information on octal and hexadecimal values.

7. Displaying all types of data with fixed-size field widths and precisions.

The `printf` function has the form

```
printf( format-control-string, other-arguments );
```

format-control-string describes the output format, and *other-arguments* (which are optional) correspond to each conversion specification in *format-control-string*. Each conversion specification begins with a percent sign and ends with a conversion specifier. There can be many conversion specifications in one format control string.

Common Programming Error 9.1

Forgetting to enclose a format-control-string in quotation marks is a syntax error.

9.4 Printing Integers

An integer is a whole number, such as 776, 0 or –52. Integer values are displayed in one of several formats. Figure 9.1 describes the **integer conversion specifiers**.

Conversion specifier	Description
d	Display as a *signed decimal integer*.
i	Display as a *signed decimal integer*. [*Note:* The i and d specifiers are *different* when used with `scanf`.]
o	Display as an *unsigned octal integer*.
u	Display as an *unsigned decimal integer*.
x or X	Display as an *unsigned hexadecimal integer*. X causes the digits 0-9 and the uppercase letters A-F to be displayed and x causes the digits 0-9 and the lowercase letters a-f to be displayed.
h, l or ll (letter "ell")	Place *before* any integer conversion specifier to indicate that a short, long or long long integer is displayed, respectively. These are called length modifiers.

Fig. 9.1 | Integer conversion specifiers.

Figure 9.2 prints an integer using each of the integer conversion specifiers. Only the minus sign prints; plus signs are normally suppressed. Later in this chapter we'll see how to force plus signs to print. Also, the value -455, when read by %u (line 15), is interpreted as an unsigned value 4294966841.

Common Programming Error 9.2

Printing a negative value with a conversion specifier that expects an unsigned value.

```
1   // Fig. 9.2: fig09_02.c
2   // Using the integer conversion specifiers
3   #include <stdio.h>
4
5   int main( void )
6   {
7      printf( "%d\n", 455 );
8      printf( "%i\n", 455 ); // i same as d in printf
9      printf( "%d\n", +455 ); // plus sign does not print
10     printf( "%d\n", -455 ); // minus sign prints
11     printf( "%hd\n", 32000 );
12     printf( "%ld\n", 2000000000L ); // L suffix makes literal a long int
13     printf( "%o\n", 455 ); // octal
14     printf( "%u\n", 455 );
15     printf( "%u\n", -455 );
16     printf( "%x\n", 455 ); // hexadecimal with lowercase letters
17     printf( "%X\n", 455 ); // hexidecimal with uppercase letters
18  } // end main
```

```
455
455
455
-455
32000
2000000000
707
455
4294966841
1c7
1C7
```

Fig. 9.2 | Using the integer conversion specifiers.

9.5 Printing Floating-Point Numbers

A floating-point value contains a decimal point as in 33.5, 0.0 or -657.983. Floating-point values are displayed in one of several formats. Figure 9.3 describes the floating-point conversion specifiers. The **conversion specifiers e and E** display floating-point values in exponential notation—the computer equivalent of *scientific notation* used in mathematics. For example, the value 150.4582 is represented in scientific notation as

$$1.504582 \times 10^2$$

and in exponential notation as

$$1.504582\text{E}+02$$

by the computer. This notation indicates that 1.504582 is multiplied by 10 raised to the second power (E+02). The E stands for "exponent."

Values displayed with the conversion specifiers e, E and f show *six digits of precision* to the right of the decimal point by default (e.g., 1.04592); other precisions can be specified explicitly. Conversion specifier f always prints at least one digit to the *left* of the decimal point. Conversion specifiers e and E print *lowercase* e and *uppercase* E, respectively, preceding the exponent, and print *exactly one* digit to the left of the decimal point.

Conversion specifier	Description
e or E	Display a floating-point value in *exponential notation*.
f or F	Display floating-point values in *fixed-point notation* (F is not supported in the Visual C++ compiler).
g or G	Display a floating-point value in either the *floating-point form* f or the exponential form e (or E), based on the magnitude of the value.
L	Place before any floating-point conversion specifier to indicate that a long double floating-point value is displayed.

Fig. 9.3 | Floating-point conversion specifiers.

Conversion specifier g (or G) prints in either e (E) or f format with *no trailing zeros* (1.234000 is printed as 1.234). Values are printed with e (E) if, after conversion to exponential notation, the value's exponent is less than -4, or the exponent is greater than or equal to the specified precision (*six significant digits* by default for g and G). Otherwise, conversion specifier f is used to print the value. Trailing zeros are *not* printed in the fractional part of a value output with g or G. At least one decimal digit is required for the decimal point to be output. The values 0.0000875, 8750000.0, 8.75 and 87.50 are printed as 8.75e-05, 8.75e+06, 8.75 and 87.5 with the conversion specifier g. The value 0.0000875 uses e notation because, when it's converted to exponential notation, its exponent (-5) is less than -4. The value 8750000.0 uses e notation because its exponent (6) is equal to the default precision.

The precision for conversion specifiers g and G indicates the maximum number of significant digits printed, *including* the digit to the *left* of the decimal point. The value 1234567.0 is printed as 1.23457e+06, using conversion specifier %g (remember that all floating-point conversion specifiers have a *default precision of 6*). There are six significant digits in the result. The difference between g and G is identical to the difference between e and E when the value is printed in exponential notation—*lowercase* g causes a *lowercase* e to be output, and *uppercase* G causes an *uppercase* E to be output.

Error-Prevention Tip 9.1

When outputting data, be sure that the user is aware of situations in which data may be imprecise due to formatting (e.g., rounding errors from specifying precisions).

Figure 9.4 demonstrates each of the floating-point conversion specifiers. The **%E**, **%e** and %g conversion specifiers cause the value to be *rounded* in the output and the conversion specifier %f does *not*. [*Note:* With some compilers, the exponent in the outputs will be shown with two digits to the right of the + sign.]

```
1    // Fig. 9.4: fig09_04.c
2    // Using the floating-point conversion specifiers
3    #include <stdio.h>
4
```

Fig. 9.4 | Using the floating-point conversion specifiers. (Part 1 of 2.)

```
5   int main( void )
6   {
7      printf( "%e\n", 1234567.89 );
8      printf( "%e\n", +1234567.89 ); // plus does not print
9      printf( "%e\n", -1234567.89 ); // minus prints
10     printf( "%E\n", 1234567.89 );
11     printf( "%f\n", 1234567.89 );
12     printf( "%g\n", 1234567.89 );
13     printf( "%G\n", 1234567.89 );
14  } // end main
```

```
1.234568e+006
1.234568e+006
-1.234568e+006
1.234568E+006
1234567.890000
1.23457e+006
1.23457E+006
```

Fig. 9.4 | Using the floating-point conversion specifiers. (Part 2 of 2.)

9.6 Printing Strings and Characters

The c and s conversion specifiers are used to print individual characters and strings, respectively. **Conversion specifier c** requires a char argument. **Conversion specifier s** requires a pointer to char as an argument. Conversion specifier s causes characters to be printed until a terminating null ('\0') character is encountered. The program shown in Fig. 9.5 displays characters and strings with conversion specifiers c and s.

```
1   // Fig. 9.5: fig09_05c
2   // Using the character and string conversion specifiers
3   #include <stdio.h>
4
5   int main( void )
6   {
7      char character = 'A'; // initialize char
8      char string[] = "This is a string"; // initialize char array
9      const char *stringPtr = "This is also a string"; // char pointer
10
11     printf( "%c\n", character );
12     printf( "%s\n", "This is a string" );
13     printf( "%s\n", string );
14     printf( "%s\n", stringPtr );
15  } // end main
```

```
A
This is a string
This is a string
This is also a string
```

Fig. 9.5 | Using the character and string conversion specifiers.

Common Programming Error 9.3

Using %c to print a string is an error. The conversion specifier %c expects a char argument. A string is a pointer to char (i.e., a char *).

Common Programming Error 9.4

Using %s to print a char argument often causes a fatal execution-time error called an access violation. The conversion specifier %s expects an argument of type pointer to char.

Common Programming Error 9.5

Using single quotes around character strings is a syntax error. Character strings must be enclosed in double quotes.

Common Programming Error 9.6

Using double quotes around a character constant creates a pointer to a string consisting of two characters, the second of which is the terminating null.

9.7 Other Conversion Specifiers

Figure 9.6 shows the p and % conversion specifiers. Figure 9.7's **%p** prints the value of ptr and the address of x; these values are identical because ptr is assigned the address of x. The last printf statement uses **%%** to print the % character in a character string.

Portability Tip 9.1

The conversion specifier p displays an address in an implementation-defined manner (on many systems, hexadecimal notation is used rather than decimal notation).

Common Programming Error 9.7

Trying to print a literal percent character using % rather than %% in the format control string. When % appears in a format control string, it must be followed by a conversion specifier.

Conversion specifier	Description
p	Display a pointer value in an implementation-defined manner.
%	Display the percent character.

Fig. 9.6 | Other conversion specifiers.

```
1   // Fig. 9.7: fig09_07.c
2   // Using the p and % conversion specifiers
3   #include <stdio.h>
4
5   int main( void )
6   {
7      int *ptr; // define pointer to int
```

Fig. 9.7 | Using the p and % conversion specifiers. (Part 1 of 2.)

```
 8      int x = 12345; // initialize int x
 9
10      ptr = &x; // assign address of x to ptr
11      printf( "The value of ptr is %p\n", ptr );
12      printf( "The address of x is %p\n\n", &x );
13
14      puts( "Printing a %% in a format control string" );
15   } // end main
```

```
The value of ptr is 002EF778
The address of x is 002EF778

Printing a % in a format control string
```

Fig. 9.7 | Using the p and % conversion specifiers. (Part 2 of 2.)

9.8 Printing with Field Widths and Precision

The exact size of a field in which data is printed is specified by a *field width*. If the field width is larger than the data being printed, the data will normally be *right justified* within that field. An integer representing the field width is inserted between the percent sign (%) and the conversion specifier (e.g., %4d). Figure 9.8 prints two groups of five numbers each, *right justifying* those numbers that contain fewer digits than the field width. The field width is increased to print values wider than the field. Note that the minus sign for a negative value uses one character position in the field width. Field widths can be used with all conversion specifiers.

Common Programming Error 9.8

Not providing a sufficiently large field width to handle a value to be printed can offset other data being printed and can produce confusing outputs. Know your data!

```
 1   // Fig. 9.8: fig09_08.c
 2   // Right justifying integers in a field
 3   #include <stdio.h>
 4
 5   int main( void )
 6   {
 7      printf( "%4d\n", 1 );
 8      printf( "%4d\n", 12 );
 9      printf( "%4d\n", 123 );
10      printf( "%4d\n", 1234 );
11      printf( "%4d\n\n", 12345 );
12
13      printf( "%4d\n", -1 );
14      printf( "%4d\n", -12 );
15      printf( "%4d\n", -123 );
16      printf( "%4d\n", -1234 );
17      printf( "%4d\n", -12345 );
18   } // end main
```

Fig. 9.8 | Right justifying integers in a field. (Part 1 of 2.)

```
    1
   12
  123
 1234
12345

   -1
  -12
 -123
-1234
-12345
```

Fig. 9.8 | Right justifying integers in a field. (Part 2 of 2.)

Function printf also enables you to specify the *precision* with which data is printed. Precision has different meanings for different data types. When used with integer conversion specifiers, precision indicates the *minimum number of digits to be printed*. If the printed value contains fewer digits than the specified precision and the precision value has a leading zero or decimal point, zeros are prefixed to the printed value until the total number of digits is equivalent to the precision. If neither a zero nor a decimal point is present in the precision value, spaces are inserted instead. The default precision for integers is 1. When used with floating-point conversion specifiers e, E and f, the precision is the *number of digits to appear after the decimal point*. When used with conversion specifiers g and G, the precision is the *maximum number of significant digits to be printed*. When used with conversion specifier s, the precision is the *maximum number of characters to be written from the string*.

To use precision, place a decimal point (.), followed by an integer representing the precision between the percent sign and the conversion specifier. Figure 9.9 demonstrates the use of precision in format control strings. When a floating-point value is printed with a precision smaller than the original number of decimal places in the value, the value is *rounded*.

```
 1  // Fig. 9.9: fig09_09.c
 2  // Printing integers, floating-point numbers and strings with precisions
 3  #include <stdio.h>
 4
 5  int main( void )
 6  {
 7     int i = 873; // initialize int i
 8     double f = 123.94536; // initialize double f
 9     char s[] = "Happy Birthday"; // initialize char array s
10
11     puts( "Using precision for integers" );
12     printf( "\t%.4d\n\t%.9d\n\n", i, i );
13
14     puts( "Using precision for floating-point numbers" );
15     printf( "\t%.3f\n\t%.3e\n\t%.3g\n\n", f, f, f );
16
17     puts( "Using precision for strings" );
18     printf( "\t%.11s\n", s );
19  } // end main
```

Fig. 9.9 | Printing integers, floating-point numbers and strings with precisions. (Part 1 of 2.)

```
Using precision for integers
        0873
        000000873

Using precision for floating-point numbers
        123.945
        1.239e+002
        124

Using precision for strings
        Happy Birth
```

Fig. 9.9 | Printing integers, floating-point numbers and strings with precisions. (Part 2 of 2.)

The field width and the precision can be combined by placing the field width, followed by a decimal point, followed by a precision between the percent sign and the conversion specifier, as in the statement

```
printf( "%9.3f", 123.456789 );
```

which displays 123.457 with three digits to the right of the decimal point right justified in a nine-digit field.

It's possible to specify the field width and the precision using integer expressions in the argument list following the format control string. To use this feature, insert an asterisk (*) in place of the field width or precision (or both). The matching int argument in the argument list is evaluated and used in place of the asterisk. A field width's value may be either positive or negative (which causes the output to be left justified in the field, as described in the next section). The statement

```
printf( "%*.*f", 7, 2, 98.736 );
```

uses 7 for the field width, 2 for the precision and outputs the value 98.74 right justified.

9.9 Using Flags in the printf Format Control String

Function printf also provides *flags* to supplement its output formatting capabilities. Five flags are available for use in format control strings (Fig. 9.10). To use a flag in a format control string, place the flag immediately to the right of the percent sign. Several flags may be combined in one conversion specifier.

Figure 9.11 demonstrates right justification and left justification of a string, an integer, a character and a floating-point number.

Flag	Description
- (minus sign)	*Left justify* the output within the specified field.
+ (plus sign)	Display a *plus sign* preceding positive values and a *minus sign* preceding negative values.
space	Print a space before a positive value not printed with the + flag.

Fig. 9.10 | Format control string flags. (Part 1 of 2.)

Flag	Description
#	Prefix 0 to the output value when used with the octal conversion specifier o. Prefix 0x or 0X to the output value when used with the hexadecimal conversion specifiers x or X. *Force a decimal point* for a floating-point number printed with e, E, f, g or G that does *not* contain a fractional part. (Normally the decimal point is printed *only* if a digit follows it.) For g and G specifiers, trailing zeros are not eliminated.
0 (zero)	Pad a field with *leading zeros*.

Fig. 9.10 | Format control string flags. (Part 2 of 2.)

```
1   // Fig. 9.11: fig09_11.c
2   // Right justifying and left justifying values
3   #include <stdio.h>
4
5   int main( void )
6   {
7      printf( "%10s%10d%10c%10f\n\n", "hello", 7, 'a', 1.23 );
8      printf( "%-10s%-10d%-10c%-10f\n", "hello", 7, 'a', 1.23 );
9   } // end main
```

```
     hello         7         a  1.230000

hello      7         a         1.230000
```

Fig. 9.11 | Right justifying and left justifying values.

Figure 9.12 prints a positive number and a negative number, each with and without the + flag. The minus sign is displayed in both cases, but the plus sign is displayed only when the + flag is used.

```
1   // Fig. 9.12: fig09_12.c
2   // Printing positive and negative numbers with and without the + flag
3   #include <stdio.h>
4
5   int main( void )
6   {
7      printf( "%d\n%d\n", 786, -786 );
8      printf( "%+d\n%+d\n", 786, -786 );
9   } // end main
```

```
786
-786
+786
-786
```

Fig. 9.12 | Printing positive and negative numbers with and without the + flag.

Figure 9.13 prefixes a space to the positive number with the **space flag**. This is useful for aligning positive and negative numbers with the same number of digits. The value -547 is not preceded by a space in the output because of its minus sign.

```
1   // Fig. 9.13: fig09_13.c
2   // Using the space flag
3   // not preceded by + or -
4   #include <stdio.h>
5
6   int main( void )
7   {
8      printf( "% d\n% d\n", 547, -547 );
9   } // end main
```

```
 547
-547
```

Fig. 9.13 | Using the space flag.

Figure 9.14 uses the # flag to prefix 0 to the octal value and 0x and 0X to the hexadecimal values, and to force the decimal point on a value printed with g.

```
1   // Fig. 9.14: fig09_14.c
2   // Using the # flag with conversion specifiers
3   // o, x, X and any floating-point specifier
4   #include <stdio.h>
5
6   int main( void )
7   {
8      int c = 1427; // initialize c
9      double p = 1427.0; // initialize p
10
11     printf( "%#o\n", c );
12     printf( "%#x\n", c );
13     printf( "%#X\n", c );
14     printf( "\n%g\n", p );
15     printf( "%#g\n", p );
16  } // end main
```

```
02623
0x593
0X593

1427
1427.00
```

Fig. 9.14 | Using the # flag with conversion specifiers.

Figure 9.15 combines the + flag and the 0 (zero) flag to print 452 in a 9-space field with a + sign and leading zeros, then prints 452 again using only the 0 flag and a 9-space field.

```
1    // Fig. 9.15: fig09_15.c
2    // Using the 0( zero ) flag
3    #include <stdio.h>
4
5    int main( void )
6    {
7       printf( "%+09d\n", 452 );
8       printf( "%09d\n", 452 );
9    } // end main
```

```
+00000452
000000452
```

Fig. 9.15 | Using the 0 (zero) flag.

9.10 Printing Literals and Escape Sequences

Most literal characters to be printed in a printf statement can simply be included in the format control string. However, there are several "problem" characters, such as the *quotation mark (")* that delimits the format control string itself. Various control characters, such as *newline* and *tab*, must be represented by escape sequences. An escape sequence is represented by a backslash (\), followed by a particular escape character. Figure 9.16 lists the escape sequences and the actions they cause.

Escape sequence	Description
\' (single quote)	Output the single quote (') character.
\" (double quote)	Output the double quote (") character.
\? (question mark)	Output the question mark (?) character.
\\ (backslash)	Output the backslash (\) character.
\a (alert or bell)	Cause an audible (bell) or visual alert.
\b (backspace)	Move the cursor back one position on the current line.
\f (new page or form feed)	Move the cursor to the start of the next logical page.
\n (newline)	Move the cursor to the beginning of the *next* line.
\r (carriage return)	Move the cursor to the beginning of the *current* line.
\t (horizontal tab)	Move the cursor to the next horizontal tab position.
\v (vertical tab)	Move the cursor to the next vertical tab position.

Fig. 9.16 | Escape sequences.

9.11 Reading Formatted Input with scanf

Precise *input formatting* can be accomplished with scanf. Every scanf statement contains a format control string that describes the format of the data to be input. The format control string consists of conversion specifiers and literal characters. Function scanf has the following input formatting capabilities:

1. Inputting all types of data.
2. Inputting specific characters from an input stream.
3. Skipping specific characters in the input stream.

Function scanf is written in the following form:

```
scanf( format-control-string, other-arguments );
```

format-control-string describes the formats of the input, and *other-arguments* are pointers to variables in which the input will be stored.

Good Programming Practice 9.1

When inputting data, prompt the user for one data item or a few data items at a time. Avoid asking the user to enter many data items in response to a single prompt.

Good Programming Practice 9.2

Always consider what the user and your program will do when (not if) incorrect data is entered—for example, a value for an integer that's nonsensical in a program's context, or a string with missing punctuation or spaces.

Figure 9.17 summarizes the conversion specifiers used to input all types of data. The remainder of this section provides programs that demonstrate reading data with the various scanf conversion specifiers.

Conversion specifier	Description
Integers	
d	Read an *optionally signed decimal integer.* The corresponding argument is a pointer to an int.
i	Read an *optionally signed decimal, octal or hexadecimal integer.* The corresponding argument is a pointer to an int.
o	Read an *octal integer.* The corresponding argument is a pointer to an unsigned int.
u	Read an *unsigned decimal integer.* The corresponding argument is a pointer to an unsigned int.
x or X	Read a *hexadecimal integer.* The corresponding argument is a pointer to an unsigned int.
h, l and ll	Place before any of the integer conversion specifiers to indicate that a short, long or long long integer is to be input, respectively.
Floating-point numbers	
e, E, f, g or G	Read a *floating-point value.* The corresponding argument is a pointer to a floating-point variable.
l or L	Place before any of the floating-point conversion specifiers to indicate that a double or long double value is to be input. The corresponding argument is a pointer to a double or long double variable.

Fig. 9.17 | Conversion specifiers for scanf. (Part 1 of 2.)

Conversion specifier	Description
Characters and strings	
c	Read a *character*. The corresponding argument is a pointer to a char; no null ('\0') is added.
s	Read a *string*. The corresponding argument is a pointer to an array of type char that's large enough to hold the string and a terminating null ('\0') character—which is automatically added.
Scan set	
[*scan characters*]	Scan a string for a set of characters that are stored in an array.
Miscellaneous	
p	Read an *address* of the same form produced when an address is output with %p in a printf statement.
n	Store the number of characters input so far in this call to scanf. The corresponding argument is a pointer to an int.
%	Skip a percent sign (%) in the input.

Fig. 9.17 | Conversion specifiers for scanf. (Part 2 of 2.)

Figure 9.18 reads integers with the various integer conversion specifiers and displays the integers as decimal numbers. Conversion specifier **%i** can input decimal, octal and hexadecimal integers.

```
1   // Fig. 9.18: fig09_18.c
2   // Reading input with integer conversion specifiers
3   #include <stdio.h>
4
5   int main( void )
6   {
7      int a;
8      int b;
9      int c;
10     int d;
11     int e;
12     int f;
13     int g;
14
15     puts( "Enter seven integers: " );
16     scanf( "%d%i%i%i%o%u%x", &a, &b, &c, &d, &e, &f, &g );
17
18     puts( "\nThe input displayed as decimal integers is:" );
19     printf( "%d %d %d %d %d %d %d\n", a, b, c, d, e, f, g );
20  } // end main
```

Fig. 9.18 | Reading input with integer conversion specifiers. (Part 1 of 2.)

```
Enter seven integers:
-70 -70 070 0x70 70 70 70

The input displayed as decimal integers is:
-70 -70 56 112 56 70 112
```

Fig. 9.18 | Reading input with integer conversion specifiers. (Part 2 of 2.)

When inputting floating-point numbers, any of the floating-point conversion specifiers e, E, f, g or G can be used. Figure 9.19 reads three floating-point numbers, one with each of the three types of floating conversion specifiers, and displays all three numbers with conversion specifier f. The program output confirms the fact that floating-point values are imprecise—this is highlighted by the third value printed.

```
1    // Fig. 9.19: fig09_19.c
2    // Reading input with floating-point conversion specifiers
3    #include <stdio.h>
4
5    // function main begins program execution
6    int main( void )
7    {
8       double a;
9       double b;
10      double c;
11
12      puts( "Enter three floating-point numbers:" );
13      scanf( "%le%lf%lg", &a, &b, &c );
14
15      puts( "\nHere are the numbers entered in plain:" );
16      puts( "floating-point notation:\n" );
17      printf( "%f\n%f\n%f\n", a, b, c );
18   } // end main
```

```
Enter three floating-point numbers:
1.27987 1.27987e+03 3.38476e-06

Here are the numbers entered in plain
floating-point notation:
1.279870
1279.870000
0.000003
```

Fig. 9.19 | Reading input with floating-point conversion specifiers.

Characters and strings are input using the conversion specifiers c and s, respectively. Figure 9.20 prompts the user to enter a string. The program inputs the first character of the string with **%c** and stores it in the character variable x, then inputs the remainder of the string with **%s** and stores it in character array y.

```
1   // Fig. 9.20: fig09_20.c
2   // Reading characters and strings
3   #include <stdio.h>
4
5   int main( void )
6   {
7      char x;
8      char y[ 9 ];
9
10     printf( "%s", "Enter a string: " );
11     scanf( "%c%8s", &x, y );
12
13     puts( "The input was:\n" );
14     printf( "the character \"%c\" and the string \"%s\"\n", x, y );
15  } // end main
```

```
Enter a string: Sunday
The input was:
the character "S" and the string "unday"
```

Fig. 9.20 | Reading characters and strings.

A sequence of characters can be input using a **scan set**. A scan set is a set of characters enclosed in square brackets, [], and preceded by a percent sign in the format control string. A scan set scans the characters in the input stream, looking only for those characters that match characters contained in the scan set. Each time a character is matched, it's stored in the scan set's corresponding argument—a pointer to a character array. The scan set stops inputting characters when a character that's not contained in the scan set is encountered. If the first character in the input stream does *not* match a character in the scan set, the array is not modified. Figure 9.21 uses the scan set [aeiou] to scan the input stream for vowels. Notice that the first seven letters of the input are read. The eighth letter (h) is not in the scan set and therefore the scanning is terminated.

```
1   // Fig. 9.21: fig09_21.c
2   // Using a scan set
3   #include <stdio.h>
4
5   // function main begins program execution
6   int main( void )
7   {
8      char z[ 9 ]; // define array z
9
10     printf( "%s", "Enter string: " );
11     scanf( "%8[aeiou]", z ); // search for set of characters
12
13     printf( "The input was \"%s\"\n", z );
14  } // end main
```

Fig. 9.21 | Using a scan set. (Part 1 of 2.)

```
Enter string: ooeeooahah
The input was "ooeeooa"
```

Fig. 9.21 | Using a scan set. (Part 2 of 2.)

The scan set can also be used to scan for characters not contained in the scan set by using an inverted scan set. To create an inverted scan set, place a caret (^) in the square brackets before the scan characters. This causes characters not appearing in the scan set to be stored. When a character contained in the inverted scan set is encountered, input terminates. Figure 9.22 uses the inverted scan set [^aeiou] to search for consonants—more properly to search for "nonvowels."

```
 1   // Fig. 9.22: fig09_22.c
 2   // Using an inverted scan set
 3   #include <stdio.h>
 4
 5   int main( void )
 6   {
 7      char z[ 9 ];
 8
 9      printf( "%s", "Enter a string: " );
10      scanf( "%8[^aeiou]", z ); // inverted scan set
11
12      printf( "The input was \"%s\"\n", z );
13   } // end main
```

```
Enter a string: String
The input was "Str"
```

Fig. 9.22 | Using an inverted scan set.

A field width can be used in a scanf conversion specifier to *read a specific number of characters* from the input stream. Figure 9.23 inputs a series of consecutive digits as a two-digit integer and an integer consisting of the remaining digits in the input stream.

```
 1   // Fig. 9.23: fig09_23.c
 2   // inputting data with a field width
 3   #include <stdio.h>
 4
 5   int main( void )
 6   {
 7      int x;
 8      int y;
 9
10      printf( "%s", "Enter a six digit integer: " );
11      scanf( "%2d%d", &x, &y );
12
13      printf( "The integers input were %d and %d\n", x, y );
14   } // end main
```

Fig. 9.23 | Inputting data with a field width. (Part 1 of 2.)

```
Enter a six digit integer: 123456
The integers input were 12 and 3456
```

Fig. 9.23 | Inputting data with a field width. (Part 2 of 2.)

Often it's necessary to *skip* certain characters in the input stream. For example, a date could be entered as

11-10-1999

Each number in the date needs to be stored, but the dashes that separate the numbers can be discarded. To eliminate unnecessary characters, include them in the format control string of `scanf` (whitespace characters—such as space, newline and tab—skip all leading whitespace). For example, to skip the dashes in the input, use the statement

scanf("%d-%d-%d", &month, &day, &year);

Although this `scanf` *does* eliminate the dashes in the preceding input, it's possible that the date could be entered as

10/11/1999

In this case, the preceding `scanf` would *not* eliminate the unnecessary characters. For this reason, `scanf` provides the **assignment suppression character** *. This character enables `scanf` to read any type of data from the input and discard it without assigning it to a variable. Figure 9.24 uses the assignment suppression character in the %c conversion specifier to indicate that a character appearing in the input stream should be read and discarded. Only the month, day and year are stored. The values of the variables are printed to demonstrate that they're in fact input correctly. The argument lists for each `scanf` call do not contain variables for the conversion specifiers that use the assignment suppression character. The corresponding characters are simply discarded.

```
1   // Fig. 9.24: fig09_24.c
2   // Reading and discarding characters from the input stream
3   #include <stdio.h>
4
5   int main( void )
6   {
7      int month1;
8      int day1;
9      int year1;
10     int month2;
11     int day2;
12     int year2;
13
14     printf( "%s", "Enter a date in the form mm-dd-yyyy: " );
15     scanf( "%d%*c%d%*c%d", &month1, &day1, &year1 );
16
17     printf( "month = %d  day = %d  year = %d\n\n", month1, day1, year1 );
18
```

Fig. 9.24 | Reading and discarding characters from the input stream. (Part 1 of 2.)

```
19      printf( "%s", "Enter a date in the form mm/dd/yyyy: " );
20      scanf( "%d%*c%d%*c%d", &month2, &day2, &year2 );
21
22      printf( "month = %d  day = %d  year = %d\n", month2, day2, year2 );
23   } // end main
```

```
Enter a date in the form mm-dd-yyyy: 11-18-2012
month = 11   day = 18   year = 2012

Enter a date in the form mm/dd/yyyy: 11/18/2012
month = 11   day = 18   year = 2012
```

Fig. 9.24 | Reading and discarding characters from the input stream. (Part 2 of 2.)

9.12 Secure C Programming

The C standard lists many cases in which using incorrect library-function arguments can result in *undefined behaviors*. These can cause security vulnerabilities, so they should be avoided. Such problems can occur when using printf (or any of its variants, such as sprintf, fprintf, printf_s, etc.) with improperly formed conversion specifications. CERT rule FIO00-C (www.securecoding.cert.org) discusses these issues and presents a table showing the valid combinations of formatting flags, length modifiers and conversion-specifier characters that can be used to form conversion specifications. The table also shows the proper argument type for each valid conversion specification. In general, as you study *any* programming language, if the language specification says that doing something can lead to undefined behavior, avoid doing it to prevent security vulnerabilities.

Summary

Section 9.2 Streams

- All input and output is performed with streams—which are sequences of bytes.
- Normally, the standard input stream is connected to the keyboard, and the standard output and error streams are connected to the computer screen.
- Operating systems often allow the standard input and standard output streams to be redirected to other devices.

Section 9.3 Formatting Output with printf

- A format control string describes the formats in which the output values appear. The format control string consists of conversion specifiers, flags, field widths, precisions and literal characters.

Section 9.4 Printing Integers

- Integers are printed with the following conversion specifiers: d or i for optionally signed integers, o for unsigned integers in octal form, u for unsigned integers in decimal form and x or X for unsigned integers in hexadecimal form. The modifier h or l is prefixed to the preceding conversion specifiers to indicate a short or long integer, respectively.

Section 9.5 Printing Floating-Point Numbers

- Floating-point values are printed with the following conversion specifiers: e or E for exponential notation, f for regular floating-point notation, and g or G for either e (or E) notation or f notation. When the g (or G) conversion specifier is indicated, the e (or E) conversion specifier is used if the value's exponent is less than -4 or greater than or equal to the precision with which the value is printed.

- The precision for the g and G conversion specifiers indicates the maximum number of significant digits printed.

Section 9.6 Printing Strings and Characters
- The conversion specifier c prints a character.
- The conversion specifier s prints a string of characters ending in the null character.

Section 9.7 Other Conversion Specifiers
- The conversion specifier p displays an address in an implementation-defined manner (on many systems, hexadecimal notation is used).
- The conversion specifier %% causes a literal % to be output.

Section 9.8 Printing with Field Widths and Precision
- If the field width is larger than the object being printed, the object is right justified by default.
- Field widths can be used with all conversion specifiers.
- Precision used with integer conversion specifiers indicates the minimum number of digits printed. Zeros are prefixed to the printed value until the number of digits is equivalent to the precision.
- Precision used with floating-point conversion specifiers e, E and f indicates the number of digits that appear after the decimal point. Precision used with floating-point conversion specifiers g and G indicates the number of significant digits to appear.
- Precision used with conversion specifier s indicates the number of characters to be printed.
- The field width and the precision can be combined by placing the field width, followed by a decimal point, followed by the precision between the percent sign and the conversion specifier.
- It's possible to specify the field width and the precision through integer expressions in the argument list following the format control string. To do so, use an asterisk (*) for the field width or precision. The matching argument in the argument list is used in place of the asterisk.

Section 9.9 Using Flags in the **printf** Format Control String
- The - flag left justifies its argument in a field.
- The + flag prints a plus sign for positive values and a minus sign for negative values. The space flag prints a space preceding a positive value that's not displayed with the + flag.
- The # flag prefixes 0 to octal values and 0x or 0X to hexadecimal values, and forces the decimal point to be printed for floating-point values printed with e, E, f, g or G.
- The 0 flag prints leading zeros for a value that does not occupy its entire field width.

Section 9.10 Printing Literals and Escape Sequences
- Most literal characters to be printed in a printf statement can simply be included in the format control string. However, there are several "problem" characters, such as the quotation mark (") that delimits the format control string itself. Various control characters, such as newline and tab, must be represented by escape sequences. An escape sequence is represented by a backslash (\), followed by a particular escape character.

Section 9.11 Reading Formatted Input with **scanf**
- Precise input formatting is accomplished with the scanf library function.

- Integers are input with scanf with the conversion specifiers d and i for optionally signed integers and o, u, x or X for unsigned integers. The modifiers h and l are placed before an integer conversion specifier to input a short or long integer, respectively.

- Floating-point values are input with scanf with the conversion specifiers e, E, f, g or G. The modifiers l and L are placed before any of the floating-point conversion specifiers to indicate that the input value is a double or long double value, respectively.

- Characters are input with scanf with the conversion specifier c.

- Strings are input with scanf with the conversion specifier s.

- A scan set scans the characters in the input, looking only for those characters that match characters contained in the scan set. When a character is matched, it's stored in a character array. The scan set stops inputting characters when a character not contained in the scan set is encountered.

- To create an inverted scan set, place a caret (∧) in the square brackets before the scan characters. This causes characters input with scanf and not appearing in the scan set to be stored until a character contained in the inverted scan set is encountered.

- Address values are input with scanf with the conversion specifier p.

- Conversion specifier n stores the number of characters input previously in the current scanf. The corresponding argument is a pointer to int.

- The conversion specifier %% with scanf matches a single % character in the input.

- The assignment suppression character reads data from the input stream and discards the data.

- A field width is used in scanf to read a specific number of characters from the input stream.

Terminology

Self-Review Exercises

9.1 Fill in the blanks in each of the following:

    a) All input and output is dealt with in the form of _____.

b) The _____ stream is normally connected to the keyboard.

c) The _____ stream is normally connected to the computer screen.

d) Precise output formatting is accomplished with the _____ function.

e) The format control string may contain _____, _____, _____, _____ and _____.

f) The conversion specifier _____ or _____ may be used to output a signed decimal integer.

g) The conversion specifiers _____, _____ and _____ are used to display unsigned integers in octal, decimal and hexadecimal form, respectively.

h) The modifiers _____ and _____ are placed before the integer conversion specifiers to indicate that short or long integer values are to be displayed.

i) The conversion specifier _____ is used to display a floating-point value in exponential notation.

j) The modifier _____ is placed before any floating-point conversion specifier to indicate that a long double value is to be displayed.

k) The conversion specifiers e, E and f are displayed with _____ digits of precision to the right of the decimal point if no precision is specified.

l) The conversion specifiers _____ and _____ are used to print strings and characters, respectively.

m) All strings end in the _____ character.

n) The field width and precision in a printf conversion specifier can be controlled with integer expressions by substituting a(n) _____ for the field width or for the precision and placing an integer expression in the corresponding argument of the argument list.

o) The _____ flag causes output to be left justified in a field.

p) The _____ flag causes values to be displayed with either a plus sign or a minus sign.

q) Precise input formatting is accomplished with the _____ function.

r) A(n) _____ is used to scan a string for specific characters and store the characters in an array.

s) The conversion specifier _____ can be used to input optionally signed octal, decimal and hexadecimal integers.

t) The conversion specifiers _____ can be used to input a double value.

u) The _____ is used to read data from the input stream and discard it without assigning it to a variable.

v) A(n) _____ can be used in a scanf conversion specifier to indicate that a specific number of characters or digits should be read from the input stream.

9.2 Find the error in each of the following and explain how it can be corrected.

a) The following statement should print the character 'c'.

```
printf( "%s\n", 'c' );
```

b) The following statement should print 9.375%.

```
printf( "%.3f%", 9.375 );
```

c) The following statement should print the first character of the string "Monday".

```
printf( "%c\n", "Monday" );
```

d) puts(""A string in quotes"");

e) printf(%d%d, 12, 20);

f) printf("%c", "x");

g) printf("%s\n", 'Richard');

9.3 Write a statement for each of the following:

a) Print 1234 right justified in a 10-digit field.

b) Print 123.456789 in exponential notation with a sign (+ or -) and 3 digits of precision.

c) Read a double value into variable number.

d) Print 100 in octal form preceded by 0.

e) Read a string into character array string.

f) Read characters into array n until a nondigit character is encountered.

g) Use integer variables x and y to specify the field width and precision used to display the double value 87.4573.

h) Read a value of the form 3.5%. Store the percentage in float variable percent and eliminate the % from the input stream. Do not use the assignment suppression character.

i) Print 3.333333 as a long double value with a sign (+ or -) in a field of 20 characters with a precision of 3.

Answers to Self-Review Exercises

9.1   a) streams. b) standard input. c) standard output. d) printf. e) conversion specifiers, flags, field widths, precisions, literal characters. f) d, i. g) o, u, x (or X). h) h, l. i) e (or E). j) L. k) 6. l) s, c. m) NULL ('\0'). n) asterisk (*). o) - (minus). p) + (plus). q) scanf. r) scan set. s) i. t) 1e, 1E, 1f, 1g or 1G. u) assignment suppression character (*). v) field width.

9.2   a) Error: Conversion specifier s expects an argument of type pointer to char.
Correction: To print the character 'c', use the conversion specifier %c or change 'c' to "c".

b) Error: Trying to print the literal character % without using the conversion specifier %%.
Correction: Use %% to print a literal % character.

c) Error: Conversion specifier c expects an argument of type char.
Correction: To print the first character of "Monday" use the conversion specifier %1s.

d) Error: Trying to print the literal character " without using the \" escape sequence.
Correction: Replace each quote in the inner set of quotes with \".

e) Error: The format control string is not enclosed in double quotes.
Correction: Enclose %d%d in double quotes.

f) Error: The character x is enclosed in double quotes.
Correction: Character constants to be printed with %c must be enclosed in single quotes.

g) Error: The string to be printed is enclosed in single quotes.
Correction: Use double quotes instead of single quotes to represent a string.

9.3   a) `printf( "%10d\n", 1234 );`

b) `printf( "%+.3e\n", 123.456789 );`

c) `scanf( "%lf", &number );`

d) `printf( "%#o\n", 100 );`

e) `scanf( "%s", string );`

f) `scanf( "%[0123456789]", n );`

g) `printf( "%*.*f\n", x, y, 87.4573 );`

h) `scanf( "%f%%", &percent );`

i) `printf( "%+20.3Lf\n", 3.333333 );`

Exercises

9.4   Write a printf or scanf statement for each of the following:

a) Print unsigned integer 40000 left justified in a 15-digit field with 8 digits.

b) Read a hexadecimal value into variable hex.

c) Print 200 with and without a sign.

d) Print 100 in hexadecimal form preceded by 0x.

e) Read characters into array s until the letter p is encountered.

f) Print 1.234 in a 9-digit field with preceding zeros.

g) Read a time of the form hh:mm:ss, storing the parts of the time in the integer variables hour, minute and second. Skip the colons (:) in the input stream. Use the assignment suppression character.

h) Read a string of the form "characters" from the standard input. Store the string in character array s. Eliminate the quotation marks from the input stream.

i) Read a time of the form hh:mm:ss, storing the parts of the time in the integer variables hour, minute and second. Skip the colons (:) in the input stream. Do not use the assignment suppression character.

9.5 Show what each of the following statements prints. If a statement is incorrect, indicate why.

a) `printf( "%-10d\n", 10000 );`

b) `printf( "%c\n", "This is a string" );`

c) `printf( "%*.*1f\n", 8, 3, 1024.987654 );`

d) `printf( "%#o\n%#X\n%#e\n", 17, 17, 1008.83689 );`

e) `printf( "% 1d\n%+1d\n", 1000000, 1000000 );`

f) `printf( "%10.2E\n", 444.93738 );`

g) `printf( "%10.2g\n", 444.93738 );`

h) `printf( "%d\n", 10.987 );`

9.6 Find the error(s) in each of the following program segments. Explain how each error can be corrected.

a) `printf( "%s\n", 'Happy Birthday' );`

b) `printf( "%c\n", 'Hello' );`

c) `printf( "%c\n", "This is a string" );`

d) The following statement should print "Bon Voyage":

`printf( ""%s"", "Bon Voyage" );`

e) `char day[] = "Sunday";`

`printf( "%s\n", day[ 3 ] );`

f) `puts( 'Enter your name: ' );`

g) `printf( %f, 123.456 );`

h) The following statement should print the characters 'O' and 'K':

`printf( "%s%s\n", 'O', 'K' );`

i) `char s[ 10 ];`

`scanf( "%c", s[ 7 ] );`

9.7 *(Difference Between %o and %x)* Write a program to test the difference between the %o and %x conversion specifiers when used in scanf statements. Use the statements

```
scanf( "%o%x", &a, &b );
printf( "%d %d\n", a, b );
```

to input and print the values. Test the program with the following sets of input data:

```
112       112
-112      -112
0112      0112
0x112     0x112
```

9.8 *(Displaying Values and Number of Bits to Represent Them)* Write a program that takes integer values from the user and prints the value entered by the user along with the total number of bits required to represent that value in binary.

9.9 *(Printing Pointer Values as Floating-Point Numbers)* Write a program that prints pointer values using all the floating point conversion specifiers and the %p conversion specifier. Which ones print strange values? Which ones cause errors? In which format does the %p conversion specifier display the address on your system?

9.10 *(Right and Left Justification of Strings)* Write a program that prints the two strings "Hello" and "World" in right justified and left justified order.

9.11 *(Hollow Rectangle Using Escape Sequences)* Write a program that uses only escape sequences to print a hollow rectangle of asterisks. List the escape sequences you use in the program.

9.12 *(Printing a Single Quote)* Write a program that determines whether ' can be printed as part of a printf format control string as a literal character rather than using the \' escape sequence.

9.13 *(Reading an Integer with Each **scanf** Conversion Specifier)* Write a program that inputs the value 437 using each of the scanf integer conversion specifiers. Print each input value using all the integer conversion specifiers.

9.14 *(Outputting a Number with the Floating-Point Conversion Specifiers)* Write a program that uses each of the conversion specifiers e, f and g to input the value 1.2345. Print the values of each variable to prove that each conversion specifier can be used to input this same value.

9.15 *(Reading Strings in Quotes)* In some programming languages, strings are entered surrounded by either single *or* double quotation marks. Write a program that reads the three strings suzy, "suzy" and 'suzy'. Are the single and double quotes ignored by C or read as part of the string?

9.16 *(Printing a Question Mark as a Character Constant)* Write a program that determines whether ? can be printed as the character constant '?' rather than the character constant escape sequence '\?' using conversion specifier %c in the format control string of a printf statement.

9.17 *(Using **%g** with Various Precisions)* Write a program that uses the conversion specifier g to output the value 9876.12345. Print the value with precisions ranging from 1 to 9.

C Structures, Unions, Bit Manipulation and Enumerations

10

But yet an union in partition.
—William Shakespeare

I could never make out what those damned dots meant.
—Winston Churchill

Objectives

In this chapter, you'll:

- Create and use structures, unions and enumerations.

- Pass structures to functions by value and by reference.

- Use typedefs to create aliases for existing type names.

- Manipulate data with the bitwise operators.

- Create bit fields for storing data compactly.

10.1 Introduction

Structures—sometimes referred to as **aggregates**—are collections of related variables under one name. Structures may contain variables of many different data types—in contrast to arrays, which contain *only* elements of the same data type. Structures are commonly used to define *records* to be stored in files (see Chapter 11, C File Processing). Pointers and structures facilitate the formation of more complex data structures such as linked lists, queues, stacks and trees (see Chapter 12, C Data Structures). We'll also discuss:

- typedefs—for creating *aliases* for previously defined data types
- unions—derived data types like structures, but with members that *share* the *same* storage space
- bitwise operators—for manipulating the bits of integral operands
- bit fields—unsigned int or int members of structures or unions for which you specify the number of bits in which the members are stored, helping you pack information tightly
- enumerations—sets of integer constants represented by identifiers.

10.2 Structure Definitions

Structures are **derived data types**—they're constructed using objects of other types. Consider the following structure definition:

```
struct card {
   char *face;
   char *suit;
}; // end struct card
```

Keyword `struct` introduces a structure definition. The identifier `card` is the structure tag, which names the structure definition and is used with `struct` to declare variables of the structure type—e.g., `struct card`. Variables declared within the braces of the structure definition are the structure's members. Members of the same structure type must have unique names, but two different structure types may contain members of the same name without conflict (we'll soon see why). Each structure definition *must* end with a semicolon.

Common Programming Error 10.1

Forgetting the semicolon that terminates a structure definition is a syntax error.

The definition of `struct card` contains members `face` and `suit`, each of type `char *`. Structure members can be variables of the primitive data types (e.g., `int`, `float`, etc.), or aggregates, such as arrays and other structures. As we saw in Chapter 6, each element of an array must be of the *same* type. Structure members, however, can be of different types. For example, the following `struct` contains character array members for an employee's first and last names, an `unsigned int` member for the employee's age, a `char` member that would contain `'M'` or `'F'` for the employee's gender and a `double` member for the employee's hourly salary:

```
struct employee {
   char firstName[ 20 ];
   char lastName[ 20 ];
   unsigned int age;
   char gender;
   double hourlySalary;
}; // end struct employee
```

10.2.1 Self-Referential Structures

A structure cannot contain an instance of itself. For example, a variable of type `struct employee` cannot be declared in the definition for `struct employee`. A pointer to `struct employee`, however, may be included. For example,

```
struct employee2 {
   char firstName[ 20 ];
   char lastName[ 20 ];
   unsigned int age;
   char gender;
   double hourlySalary;
   struct employee2 person; // ERROR
   struct employee2 *ePtr; // pointer
}; // end struct employee2
```

`struct employee2` contains an instance of itself (`person`), which is an error. Because `ePtr` is a pointer (to type `struct employee2`), it's permitted in the definition. A structure containing a member that's a pointer to the *same* structure type is referred to as a self-referential structure. Self-referential structures are used in Chapter 12 to build linked data structures.

10.2.2 Defining Variables of Structure Types

Structure definitions do *not* reserve any space in memory; rather, each definition creates a new data type that's used to define variables. Structure variables are defined like variables of other types. The definition

```
struct card aCard, deck[ 52 ], *cardPtr;
```

declares aCard to be a variable of type struct card, declares deck to be an array with 52 elements of type struct card and declares cardPtr to be a pointer to struct card. Variables of a given structure type may also be declared by placing a comma-separated list of the variable names between the closing brace of the structure definition and the semicolon that ends the structure definition. For example, the preceding definition could have been incorporated into the struct card definition as follows:

```
struct card {
   char *face;
   char *suit;
} aCard, deck[ 52 ], *cardPtr;
```

10.2.3 Structure Tag Names

The structure tag name is optional. If a structure definition does not contain a structure tag name, variables of the structure type may be declared *only* in the structure definition—*not* in a separate declaration.

Good Programming Practice 10.1

Always provide a structure tag name when creating a structure type. The structure tag name is convenient for declaring new variables of the structure type later in the program.

10.2.4 Operations That Can Be Performed on Structures

The only valid operations that may be performed on structures are:

- assigning structure variables to structure variables of the *same* type
- taking the address (&) of a structure variable
- accessing the members of a structure variable (see Section 10.4)
- using the sizeof operator to determine the size of a structure variable.

Common Programming Error 10.2

Assigning a structure of one type to a structure of a different type is a compilation error.

Structures may *not* be compared using operators == and !=, because structure members are not necessarily stored in consecutive bytes of memory. Sometimes there are "holes" in a structure, because computers may store specific data types only on certain memory boundaries such as half-word, word or double-word boundaries. A word is a standard memory unit used to store data in a computer—usually 2 bytes or 4 bytes. Consider the following structure definition, in which sample1 and sample2 of type struct example are declared:

```
struct example {
   char c;
   int i;
} sample1, sample2;
```

A computer with 2-byte words may require that each member of struct example be aligned on a word boundary, i.e., at the beginning of a word (this is machine dependent). Figure 10.1 shows a sample storage alignment for a variable of type struct example that has been assigned the character `'a'` and the integer 97 (the bit representations of the values are shown). If the members are stored beginning at word boundaries, there's a 1-byte hole (byte 1 in the figure) in the storage for variables of type `struct example`. The value in the 1-byte hole is undefined. Even if the member values of `sample1` and `sample2` are in fact equal, the structures are not necessarily equal, because the undefined 1-byte holes are not likely to contain identical values.

Byte 0   1   2   3

| 01100001 | | 00000000 | 01100001 |

Fig. 10.1 | Possible storage alignment for a variable of type `struct` example showing an undefined area in memory.

Portability Tip 10.1

Because the size of data items of a particular type is machine dependent and because storage alignment considerations are machine dependent, so too is the representation of a structure.

10.3 Initializing Structures

Structures can be initialized using initializer lists as with arrays. To initialize a structure, follow the variable name in the definition with an equals sign and a brace-enclosed, comma-separated list of initializers. For example, the declaration

```
struct card aCard = { "Three", "Hearts" };
```

creates variable `aCard` to be of type `struct card` (as defined in Section 10.2) and initializes member `face` to `"Three"` and member `suit` to `"Hearts"`. If there are *fewer* initializers in the list than members in the structure, the remaining members are automatically initialized to 0 (or `NULL` if the member is a pointer). Structure variables defined outside a function definition (i.e., externally) are initialized to 0 or `NULL` if they're not explicitly initialized in the external definition. Structure variables may also be initialized in assignment statements by assigning a structure variable of the *same* type, or by assigning values to the *individual* members of the structure.

10.4 Accessing Structure Members

Two operators are used to access members of structures: the structure member operator (`.`)—also called the dot operator—and the structure pointer operator (`->`)—also called the **arrow operator**. The structure member operator accesses a structure member via the structure variable name. For example, to print member `suit` of structure variable `aCard` defined in Section 10.3, use the statement

```
printf( "%s", aCard.suit ); // displays Hearts
```

The structure pointer operator—consisting of a minus (`-`) sign and a greater than (`>`) sign with no intervening spaces—accesses a structure member via a pointer to the structure. Assume that the pointer `cardPtr` has been declared to point to `struct card` and that the address of structure aCard has been assigned to cardPtr. To print member suit of structure aCard with pointer cardPtr, use the statement

```
printf( "%s", cardPtr->suit ); // displays Hearts
```

The expression cardPtr->suit is equivalent to (*cardPtr).suit, which dereferences the pointer and accesses the member suit using the structure member operator. The parentheses are needed here because the structure member operator (.) has a higher precedence than the pointer dereferencing operator (*). The structure pointer operator and structure member operator, along with parentheses (for calling functions) and brackets ([]) used for array subscripting, have the highest operator precedence and associate from left to right.

Good Programming Practice 10.2

Do not put spaces around the -> and . operators. Omitting spaces helps emphasize that the expressions the operators are contained in are essentially single variable names.

Common Programming Error 10.3

Inserting space between the - and > components of the structure pointer operator (or between the components of any other multiple keystroke operator except ?:) is a syntax error.

Common Programming Error 10.4

Attempting to refer to a member of a structure by using only the member's name is a syntax error.

Common Programming Error 10.5

*Not using parentheses when referring to a structure member that uses a pointer and the structure member operator (e.g., *cardPtr.suit) is a syntax error.*

The program of Fig. 10.2 demonstrates the use of the structure member and structure pointer operators. Using the structure member operator, the members of structure aCard are assigned the values "Ace" and "Spades", respectively (lines 18 and 19). Pointer cardPtr is assigned the address of structure aCard (line 21). Function printf prints the members of structure variable aCard using the structure member operator with variable name aCard, the structure pointer operator with pointer cardPtr and the structure member operator with dereferenced pointer cardPtr (lines 23 through 25).

```
1   // Fig. 10.2: fig10_02.c
2   // Structure member operator and
3   // structure pointer operator
4   #include <stdio.h>
5
6   // card structure definition
7   struct card {
8      char *face; // define pointer face
9      char *suit; // define pointer suit
10  }; // end structure card
11
```

Fig. 10.2 | Structure member operator and structure pointer operator. (Part 1 of 2.)

```
12   int main( void )
13   {
14      struct card aCard; // define one struct card variable
15      struct card *cardPtr; // define a pointer to a struct card
16
17      // place strings into aCard
18      aCard.face = "Ace";
19      aCard.suit = "Spades";
20
21      cardPtr = &aCard; // assign address of aCard to cardPtr
22
23      printf( "%s%s%s\n%s%s%s\n%s%s%s\n", aCard.face, " of ", aCard.suit,
24         cardPtr->face, " of ", cardPtr->suit,
25         ( *cardPtr ).face, " of ", ( *cardPtr ).suit );
26   } // end main
```

```
Ace of Spades
Ace of Spades
Ace of Spades
```

Fig. 10.2 | Structure member operator and structure pointer operator. (Part 2 of 2.)

10.5 Using Structures with Functions

Structures may be passed to functions by passing individual structure members, by passing an entire structure or by passing a pointer to a structure. When structures or individual structure members are passed to a function, they're passed by value. Therefore, the members of a caller's structure cannot be modified by the called function. To pass a structure by reference, pass the address of the structure variable. Arrays of structures—like all other arrays—are automatically passed by reference.

In Chapter 6, we stated that an array could be passed by value by using a structure. To pass an array by value, create a structure with the array as a member. Structures are passed by value, so the array is passed by value.

Common Programming Error 10.6

Assuming that structures, like arrays, are automatically passed by reference and trying to modify the caller's structure values in the called function is a logic error.

Performance Tip 10.1

Passing structures by reference is more efficient than passing structures by value (which requires the entire structure to be copied).

10.6 typedef

The keyword **typedef** provides a mechanism for creating synonyms (or aliases) for previously defined data types. Names for structure types are often defined with **typedef** to create shorter type names. For example, the statement

```
typedef struct card Card;
```

defines the new type name `Card` as a synonym for type `struct card`. C programmers often use `typedef` to define a structure type, so a structure tag is not required. For example, the following definition

```
typedef struct {
    char *face;
    char *suit;
} Card; // end typedef of Card
```

creates the structure type `Card` without the need for a separate `typedef` statement.

Good Programming Practice 10.3

Capitalize the first letter of `typedef` names to emphasize that they're synonyms for other type names.

`Card` can now be used to declare variables of type `struct card`. The declaration

```
Card deck[ 52 ];
```

declares an array of 52 `Card` structures (i.e., variables of type `struct card`). Creating a new name with `typedef` does *not* create a new type; `typedef` simply creates a new type name, which may be used as an alias for an existing type name. A meaningful name helps make the program self-documenting. For example, when we read the previous declaration, we know "deck is an array of 52 Cards."

Often, `typedef` is used to create synonyms for the basic data types. For example, a program requiring four-byte integers may use type `int` on one system and type `long` on another. Programs designed for portability often use `typedef` to create an alias for four-byte integers, such as `Integer`. The alias `Integer` can be changed once in the program to make the program work on both systems.

Portability Tip 10.2

Use `typedef` to help make a program more portable.

Good Programming Practice 10.4

Using `typedef`s can help make a program be more readable and maintainable.

10.7 Example: High-Performance Card Shuffling and Dealing Simulation

The program in Fig. 10.3 is based on the card shuffling and dealing simulation discussed in Chapter 7. The program represents the deck of cards as an array of structures and uses high-performance shuffling and dealing algorithms. The program output is shown in Fig. 10.4.

```
1  // Fig. 10.3: fig10_03.c
2  // Card shuffling and dealing program using structures
3  #include <stdio.h>
```

Fig. 10.3 | Card shuffling and dealing program using structures. (Part 1 of 3.)

```c
4   #include <stdlib.h>
5   #include <time.h>
6
7   #define CARDS 52
8   #define FACES 13
9
10  // card structure definition
11  struct card {
12     const char *face; // define pointer face
13     const char *suit; // define pointer suit
14  }; // end struct card
15
16  typedef struct card Card; // new type name for struct card
17
18  // prototypes
19  void fillDeck( Card * const wDeck, const char * wFace[],
20     const char * wSuit[] );
21  void shuffle( Card * const wDeck );
22  void deal( const Card * const wDeck );
23
24  int main( void )
25  {
26     Card deck[ CARDS ]; // define array of Cards
27
28     // initialize array of pointers
29     const char *face[] = { "Ace", "Deuce", "Three", "Four", "Five",
30        "Six", "Seven", "Eight", "Nine", "Ten",
31        "Jack", "Queen", "King"};
32
33     // initialize array of pointers
34     const char *suit[] = { "Hearts", "Diamonds", "Clubs", "Spades"};
35
36     srand( time( NULL ) ); // randomize
37
38     fillDeck( deck, face, suit ); // load the deck with Cards
39     shuffle( deck ); // put Cards in random order
40     deal( deck ); // deal all 52 Cards
41  } // end main
42
43  // place strings into Card structures
44  void fillDeck( Card * const wDeck, const char * wFace[],
45     const char * wSuit[] )
46  {
47     size_t i; // counter
48
49     // loop through wDeck
50     for ( i = 0; i < CARDS; ++i ) {
51        wDeck[ i ].face = wFace[ i % FACES ];
52        wDeck[ i ].suit = wSuit[ i / FACES ];
53     } // end for
54  } // end function fillDeck
55
```

Fig. 10.3 | Card shuffling and dealing program using structures. (Part 2 of 3.)

```
56  // shuffle cards
57  void shuffle( Card * const wDeck )
58  {
59     size_t i; // counter
60     size_t j; // variable to hold random value between 0 - 51
61     Card temp; // define temporary structure for swapping Cards
62
63     // loop through wDeck randomly swapping Cards
64     for ( i = 0; i < CARDS; ++i ) {
65        j = rand() % CARDS;
66        temp = wDeck[ i ];
67        wDeck[ i ] = wDeck[ j ];
68        wDeck[ j ] = temp;
69     } // end for
70  } // end function shuffle
71
72  // deal cards
73  void deal( const Card * const wDeck )
74  {
75     size_t i; // counter
76
77     // loop through wDeck
78     for ( i = 0; i < CARDS; ++i ) {
79        printf( "%5s of %-8s%s", wDeck[ i ].face, wDeck[ i ].suit,
80           ( i + 1 ) % 4 ? "   " : "\n" );
81     } // end for
82  } // end function deal
```

Fig. 10.3 | Card shuffling and dealing program using structures. (Part 3 of 3.)

Three of Hearts	Jack of Clubs	Three of Spades	Six of Diamonds
Five of Hearts	Eight of Spades	Three of Clubs	Deuce of Spades
Jack of Spades	Four of Hearts	Deuce of Hearts	Six of Clubs
Queen of Clubs	Three of Diamonds	Eight of Diamonds	King of Clubs
King of Hearts	Eight of Hearts	Queen of Hearts	Seven of Clubs
Seven of Diamonds	Nine of Spades	Five of Clubs	Eight of Clubs
Six of Hearts	Deuce of Diamonds	Five of Spades	Four of Clubs
Deuce of Clubs	Nine of Hearts	Seven of Hearts	Four of Spades
Ten of Spades	King of Diamonds	Ten of Hearts	Jack of Diamonds
Four of Diamonds	Six of Spades	Five of Diamonds	Ace of Diamonds
Ace of Clubs	Jack of Hearts	Ten of Clubs	Queen of Diamonds
Ace of Hearts	Ten of Diamonds	Nine of Clubs	King of Spades
Ace of Spades	Nine of Diamonds	Seven of Spades	Queen of Spades

Fig. 10.4 | Output for the high-performance card shuffling and dealing simulation.

In the program, function fillDeck (lines 44–54) initializes the Card array in order with "Ace" through "King" of each suit. The Card array is passed (in line 39) to function shuffle (lines 57–70), where the high-performance shuffling algorithm is implemented. Function shuffle takes an array of 52 Cards as an argument. The function loops through the 52 Cards (lines 64–69). For each Card, a number between 0 and 51 is picked randomly. Next, the current Card and the randomly selected Card are swapped in the array (lines 66–68). A total of 52 swaps are made in a single pass of the entire array, and the array of Cards is shuffled! This algorithm *cannot* suffer from *indefinite postponement* like the shuffling algorithm presented in Chapter 7. Because the Cards were swapped in place in the array, the high-performance dealing algorithm implemented in function deal (lines 73–82) requires only *one* pass of the array to deal the shuffled Cards.

Common Programming Error 10.7

Forgetting to include the array subscript when referring to individual structures in an array of structures is a syntax error.

10.8 Unions

A **union** is a *derived data type*—like a structure—with members that *share the same storage space*. For different situations in a program, some variables may not be relevant, but other variables are—so a union *shares* the space instead of wasting storage on variables that are not being used. The members of a union can be of *any* data type. The number of bytes used to store a union must be at least enough to hold the *largest* member. In most cases, unions contain two or more data types. Only one member, and thus one data type, can be referenced at a time. It's your responsibility to ensure that the data in a union is referenced with the proper data type.

Common Programming Error 10.8

Referencing data in a union with a variable of the wrong type is a logic error.

Portability Tip 10.3

If data is stored in a union as one type and referenced as another type, the results are implementation dependent.

10.8.1 Union Declarations

A union definition has the same format as a structure definition. The union definition

```
union number {
    int x;
    double y;
}; // end union number
```

indicates that number is a union type with members int x and double y. The union definition is normally placed in a header and included in all source files that use the union type.

Software Engineering Observation 10.1

As with a struct definition, a union definition simply creates a new type. Placing a union or struct definition outside any function does not create a global variable.

10.8.2 Operations That Can Be Performed on Unions

The operations that can be performed on a union are: assigning a union to another union of the same type, taking the address (&) of a union variable, and accessing union members using the structure member operator and the structure pointer operator. Unions may not be compared using operators == and != for the same reasons that structures cannot be compared.

10.8.3 Initializing Unions in Declarations

In a declaration, *a union may be initialized with a value of the same type as the first union member*. For example, with the union in Section 10.8.1, the statement

```
union number value = { 10 };
```

is a valid initialization of union variable value because the union is initialized with an int, but the following declaration would truncate the floating-point part of the initializer value and normally would produce a warning from the compiler:

```
union number value = { 1.43 };
```

Portability Tip 10.4
The amount of storage required to store a union is implementation dependent but will always be at least as large as the largest member of the union.

Portability Tip 10.5
Some unions may not port easily to other computer systems. Whether a union is portable or not often depends on the storage alignment requirements for the union member data types on a given system.

10.8.4 Demonstrating Unions

The program in Fig. 10.5 uses the variable value (line 13) of type union number (lines 6–9) to display the value stored in the union as both an int and a double. The program output is *implementation dependent*. The program output shows that the internal representation of a double value can be quite different from the representation of int.

```c
1   // Fig. 10.5: fig10_05.c
2   // Displaying the value of a union in both member data types
3   #include <stdio.h>
4
5   // number union definition
6   union number {
7      int x;
8      double y;
9   }; // end union number
10
11  int main( void )
12  {
13     union number value; // define union variable
14
15     value.x = 100; // put an integer into the union
16     printf( "%s\n%s\n%s\n  %d\n%s\n  %f\n\n\n",
17        "Put 100 in the integer member",
18        "and print both members.",
19        "int:", value.x,
20        "double:", value.y );
21
```

Fig. 10.5 | Displaying the value of a union in both member data types. (Part 1 of 2.)

```
22        value.y = 100.0; // put a double into the same union
23        printf( "%s\n%s\n%s\n  %d\n\n%s\n  %f\n",
24           "Put 100.0 in the floating member",
25           "and print both members.",
26           "int:", value.x,
27           "double:", value.y );
28     } // end main
```

```
Put 100 in the integer member
and print both members.
int:
  100

double:
  -9255959211743313600000000000000000000000000000000000000000000000.000000


Put 100.0 in the floating member
and print both members.
int:
  0

double:
  100.000000
```

Fig. 10.5 | Displaying the value of a union in both member data types. (Part 2 of 2.)

10.9 Bitwise Operators

Computers represent all data internally as sequences of bits. Each bit can assume the value 0 or the value 1. On most systems, a sequence of 8 bits forms a byte—the typical storage unit for a variable of type char. Other data types are stored in larger numbers of bytes. The bitwise operators are used to manipulate the bits of integral operands, both signed and unsigned. Unsigned integers are normally used with the bitwise operators.

Portability Tip 10.6
Bitwise data manipulations are machine dependent.

The bitwise operator discussions in this section show the binary representations of the integer operands. For a detailed explanation of the binary (also called base-2) number system see Appendix C. Because of the machine-dependent nature of bitwise manipulations, these programs may not work correctly on your system.

The bitwise operators are **bitwise AND (&)**, **bitwise inclusive OR (|)**, **bitwise exclusive OR (∧; also known as bitwise XOR)**, **left shift (<<)**, **right shift (>>)** and **complement (~)**. The bitwise AND, bitwise inclusive OR and bitwise exclusive OR operators compare their two operands bit by bit. The *bitwise AND operator* sets each bit in the result to 1 if the corresponding bit in both operands is 1. The *bitwise inclusive OR operator* sets each bit in the result to 1 if the corresponding bit in either (or both) operand(s) is 1. The *bitwise exclusive OR operator* sets each bit in the result to 1 if the corresponding bit in exactly one operand is 1. The *left-shift operator* shifts the bits of its left operand to the left by the number of bits specified in its right operand. The *right-shift operator* shifts the bits in its left operand to the right by the number of bits specified in its right operand. The *bitwise complement operator* sets all 0 bits in its operand to 1 in the result and sets all 1 bits to 0 in the result. Detailed discussions of each bitwise operator appear in the examples that follow. The bitwise operators are summarized in Fig. 10.6.

Operator		Description
&	bitwise AND	The bits in the result are set to 1 if the corresponding bits in the two operands are *both* 1.
|	bitwise inclusive OR	The bits in the result are set to 1 if *at least one* of the corresponding bits in the two operands is 1.
^	bitwise exclusive OR	The bits in the result are set to 1 if *exactly one* of the corresponding bits in the two operands is 1.
<<	left shift	Shifts the bits of the first operand left by the number of bits specified by the second operand; fill from the right with 0 bits.
>>	right shift	Shifts the bits of the first operand right by the number of bits specified by the second operand; the method of filling from the left is machine dependent when the left operand is negative.
~	one's complement	All 0 bits are set to 1 and all 1 bits are set to 0.

Fig. 10.6 | Bitwise operators.

10.9.1 Displaying an Unsigned Integer in Bits

When using the bitwise operators, it's useful to display values in binary to show the precise effects of these operators. The program of Fig. 10.7 prints an unsigned int in its binary representation in groups of eight bits each for readability. For the examples in this section, we assume an implementation where unsigned ints are stored in 4 bytes (32 bits) of memory.

```
1   // Fig. 10.7: fig10_07.c
2   // Displaying an unsigned int in bits
3   #include <stdio.h>
4
5   void displayBits( unsigned int value ); // prototype
6
7   int main( void )
8   {
9      unsigned int x; // variable to hold user input
10
11     printf( "%s", "Enter a nonnegative int: " );
12     scanf( "%u", &x );
13
14     displayBits( x );
15  } // end main
16
```

Fig. 10.7 | Displaying an unsigned int in bits. (Part 1 of 2.)

```
17   // display bits of an unsigned int value
18   void displayBits( unsigned int value )
19   {
20      unsigned int c; // counter
21
22      // define displayMask and left shift 31 bits
23      unsigned int displayMask = 1 << 31;
24
25      printf( "%10u = ", value );
26
27      // loop through bits
28      for ( c = 1; c <= 32; ++c ) {
29         putchar( value & displayMask ? '1' : '0' );
30         value <<= 1; // shift value left by 1
31
32         if ( c % 8 == 0 ) { // output space after 8 bits
33            putchar( ' ' );
34         } // end if
35      } // end for
36
37      putchar( '\n' );
38   } // end function displayBits
```

```
Enter a nonnegative int: 65000
    65000 = 00000000 00000000 11111101 11101000
```

Fig. 10.7 | Displaying an unsigned int in bits. (Part 2 of 2.)

Function displayBits (lines 18–38) uses the bitwise AND operator to combine variable value with variable displayMask (line 29). Often, the bitwise AND operator is used with an operand called a **mask**—an integer value with specific bits set to 1. Masks are used to *hide* some bits in a value while *selecting* other bits. In function displayBits, mask variable displayMask is assigned the value

```
1 << 31        (10000000 00000000 00000000 00000000)
```

The left-shift operator shifts the value 1 from the low-order (rightmost) bit to the high-order (leftmost) bit in displayMask and fills in 0 bits from the right. Line 29

```
putchar( value & displayMask ? '1' : '0' );
```

determines whether a 1 or a 0 should be printed for the current leftmost bit of variable value. When value and displayMask are combined using &, all the bits except the high-order bit in variable value are "masked off" (hidden), because any bit "ANDed" with 0 yields 0. If the leftmost bit is 1, value & displayMask evaluates to a nonzero (true) value and 1 is printed—otherwise, 0 is printed. Variable value is then left shifted one bit by the expression value <<= 1 (this is equivalent to value = value << 1). These steps are repeated for each bit in unsigned variable value. Figure 10.8 summarizes the results of combining two bits with the bitwise AND operator.

Common Programming Error 10.9

Using the logical AND operator (&&) for the bitwise AND operator (&) is an error.

Bit 1	Bit 2	Bit 1 & Bit 2
0	0	0
0	1	0
1	0	0
1	1	1

Fig. 10.8 | Results of combining two bits with the bitwise AND operator &.

10.9.2 Making Function displayBits More Scalable and Portable

In line 23 of Fig. 10.7, we hard coded the integer 31 to indicate that the value 1 should be shifted to the leftmost bit in the variable displayMask. Similarly, in line 28, we hard coded the integer 32 to indicate that the loop should iterate 32 times—once for each bit in variable value. We assumed that unsigned ints are always stored in 32 bits (4 bytes) of memory. Many of today's popular computers use 32-bit- or 64-bit-word hardware architectures. As a C programmer, you'll tend to work across many hardware architectures, and sometimes unsigned ints will be stored in smaller or larger numbers of bits.

We can make the program in Fig. 10.7 more scalable and more portable by replacing the integer 31 in line 23 with the expression

```
CHAR_BIT * sizeof( unsigned int ) - 1
```

and by replacing the integer 32 in line 28 with the the expression

```
CHAR_BIT * sizeof( unsigned int )
```

The symbolic constant **CHAR_BIT** (defined in <limits.h>) represents the number of bits in a byte (normally 8). As you learned in Section 7.7, operator sizeof determines the number of bytes used to store an object or type. On a computer that uses 32-bit words, the expression sizeof(unsigned int) evaluates to 4, so the two preceding expressions evaluate to 31 and 32, respectively. On a computer that uses 16-bit words, the sizeof expression evaluates to 2 and the two preceding expressions evaluate to 15 and 16, respectively.

10.9.3 Using the Bitwise AND, Inclusive OR, Exclusive OR and Complement Operators

Figure 10.9 demonstrates the use of the bitwise AND operator, the bitwise inclusive OR operator, the bitwise exclusive OR operator and the bitwise complement operator. The program uses function displayBits (lines 51–71) to print the unsigned int values. The output is shown in Fig. 10.10.

```
1   // Fig. 10.9: fig10_09.c
2   // Using the bitwise AND, bitwise inclusive OR, bitwise
3   // exclusive OR and bitwise complement operators
```

Fig. 10.9 | Using the bitwise AND, bitwise inclusive OR, bitwise exclusive OR and bitwise complement operators. (Part 1 of 3.)

```
 4   #include <stdio.h>
 5
 6   void displayBits( unsigned int value ); // prototype
 7
 8   int main( void )
 9   {
10      unsigned int number1;
11      unsigned int number2;
12      unsigned int mask;
13      unsigned int setBits;
14
15      // demonstrate bitwise AND (&)
16      number1 = 65535;
17      mask = 1;
18      puts( "The result of combining the following" );
19      displayBits( number1 );
20      displayBits( mask );
21      puts( "using the bitwise AND operator & is" );
22      displayBits( number1 & mask );
23
24      // demonstrate bitwise inclusive OR (|)
25      number1 = 15;
26      setBits = 241;
27      puts( "\nThe result of combining the following" );
28      displayBits( number1 );
29      displayBits( setBits );
30      puts( "using the bitwise inclusive OR operator | is" );
31      displayBits( number1 | setBits );
32
33      // demonstrate bitwise exclusive OR (^)
34      number1 = 139;
35      number2 = 199;
36      puts( "\nThe result of combining the following" );
37      displayBits( number1 );
38      displayBits( number2 );
39      puts( "using the bitwise exclusive OR operator ^ is" );
40      displayBits( number1 ^ number2 );
41
42      // demonstrate bitwise complement (~)
43      number1 = 21845;
44      puts( "\nThe one's complement of" );
45      displayBits( number1 );
46      puts( "is" );
47      displayBits( ~number1 );
48   } // end main
49
50   // display bits of an unsigned int value
51   void displayBits( unsigned int value )
52   {
53      unsigned int c; // counter
54
```

Fig. 10.9 | Using the bitwise AND, bitwise inclusive OR, bitwise exclusive OR and bitwise complement operators. (Part 2 of 3.)

```
55      // declare displayMask and left shift 31 bits
56      unsigned int displayMask = 1 << 31;
57
58      printf( "%10u = ", value );
59
60      // loop through bits
61      for ( c = 1; c <= 32; ++c ) {
62         putchar( value & displayMask ? '1' : '0' );
63         value <<= 1; // shift value left by 1
64
65         if ( c % 8 == 0 ) { // output a space after 8 bits
66            putchar( ' ' );
67         } // end if
68      } // end for
69
70      putchar( '\n' );
71   } // end function displayBits
```

Fig. 10.9 | Using the bitwise AND, bitwise inclusive OR, bitwise exclusive OR and bitwise complement operators. (Part 3 of 3.)

```
The result of combining the following
      65535 = 00000000 00000000 11111111 11111111
          1 = 00000000 00000000 00000000 00000001
using the bitwise AND operator & is
          1 = 00000000 00000000 00000000 00000001

The result of combining the following
         15 = 00000000 00000000 00000000 00001111
        241 = 00000000 00000000 00000000 11110001
using the bitwise inclusive OR operator | is
        255 = 00000000 00000000 00000000 11111111

The result of combining the following
        139 = 00000000 00000000 00000000 10001011
        199 = 00000000 00000000 00000000 11000111
using the bitwise exclusive OR operator ^ is
         76 = 00000000 00000000 00000000 01001100


The one's complement of
      21845 = 00000000 00000000 01010101 01010101
is
 4294945450 = 11111111 11111111 10101010 10101010
```

Fig. 10.10 | Output for the program of Fig. 10.9.

In Fig. 10.9, integer variable number1 is assigned value 65535 (00000000 00000000 11111111 11111111) in line 16 and variable mask is assigned the value 1 (00000000 00000000 00000000 00000001) in line 17. When number1 and mask are combined using the *bitwise AND operator (&)* in the expression number1 & mask (line 22), the result is 00000000 00000000 00000000 00000001. All the bits except the low-order bit in variable number1 are "masked off" (hidden) by "ANDing" with variable mask.

The *bitwise inclusive OR operator* is used to set specific bits to 1 in an operand. In Fig. 10.9, variable number1 is assigned 15 (00000000 00000000 00000000 00001111) in line 25, and variable setBits is assigned 241 (00000000 00000000 00000000 11110001) in line 26. When number1 and setBits are combined using the *bitwise inclusive OR operator* in the expression number1 | setBits (line 31), the result is 255 (00000000 00000000 00000000 11111111). Figure 10.11 summarizes the results of combining two bits with the *bitwise inclusive OR operator*.

Bit I	Bit 2	Bit I | Bit 2
0	0	0
0	1	1
1	0	1
1	1	1

Fig. 10.11 | Results of combining two bits with the bitwise inclusive OR operator |.

The *bitwise exclusive OR operator (∧)* sets each bit in the result to 1 if *exactly* one of the corresponding bits in its two operands is 1. In Fig. 10.9, variables number1 and number2 are assigned the values 139 (00000000 00000000 00000000 10001011) and 199 (00000000 00000000 00000000 11000111) in lines 34–35. When these variables are combined with the *bitwise exclusive OR operator* in the expression number1 ∧ number2 (line 40), the result is 00000000 00000000 00000000 01001100. Figure 10.12 summarizes the results of combining two bits with the *bitwise exclusive OR operator*.

Bit I	Bit 2	Bit I ∧ Bit 2
0	0	0
0	1	1
1	0	1
1	1	0

Fig. 10.12 | Results of combining two bits with the bitwise exclusive OR operator ∧.

The bitwise complement operator (~) sets all 1 bits in its operand to 0 in the result and sets all 0 bits to 1 in the result—otherwise referred to as "taking the one's complement of the value." In Fig. 10.9, variable number1 is assigned the value 21845 (00000000 00000000 01010101 01010101) in line 43. When the expression ~number1 (line 47) is evaluated, the result is 11111111 11111111 10101010 10101010.

10.9.4 Using the Bitwise Left- and Right-Shift Operators

The program of Fig. 10.13 demonstrates the *left-shift operator (<<)* and the *right-shift operator (>>)*. Function displayBits is used to print the unsigned int values.

```c
 1   // Fig. 10.13: fig10_13.c
 2   // Using the bitwise shift operators
 3   #include <stdio.h>
 4
 5   void displayBits( unsigned int value ); // prototype
 6
 7   int main( void )
 8   {
 9      unsigned int number1 = 960; // initialize number1
10
11      // demonstrate bitwise left shift
12      puts( "\nThe result of left shifting" );
13      displayBits( number1 );
14      puts( "8 bit positions using the left shift operator << is" );
15      displayBits( number1 << 8 );
16
17      // demonstrate bitwise right shift
18      puts( "\nThe result of right shifting" );
19      displayBits( number1 );
20      puts( "8 bit positions using the right shift operator >> is" );
21      displayBits( number1 >> 8 );
22   } // end main
23
24   // display bits of an unsigned int value
25   void displayBits( unsigned int value )
26   {
27      unsigned int c; // counter
28
29      // declare displayMask and left shift 31 bits
30      unsigned int displayMask = 1 << 31;
31
32      printf( "%7u = ", value );
33
34      // loop through bits
35      for ( c = 1; c <= 32; ++c ) {
36         putchar( value & displayMask ? '1' : '0' );
37         value <<= 1; // shift value left by 1
38
39         if ( c % 8 == 0 ) { // output a space after 8 bits
40            putchar( ' ' );
41         } // end if
42      } // end for
43
44      putchar( '\n' );
45   } // end function displayBits
```

```
The result of left shifting
    960 = 00000000 00000000 00000011 11000000
8 bit positions using the left shift operator << is
 245760 = 00000000 00000011 11000000 00000000
```

Fig. 10.13 | Using the bitwise shift operators. (Part 1 of 2.)

```
The result of right shifting
   960 = 00000000 00000000 00000011 11000000
8 bit positions using the right shift operator >> is
     3 = 00000000 00000000 00000000 00000011
```

Fig. 10.13 | Using the bitwise shift operators. (Part 2 of 2.)

The *left-shift operator (<<)* shifts the bits of its left operand to the left by the number of bits specified in its right operand. Bits vacated to the right are replaced with 0s; 1s shifted off the left are lost. In Fig. 10.13, variable number1 is assigned the value 960 (00000000 00000000 00000011 11000000) in line 9. The result of left shifting variable number1 8 bits in the expression number1 << 8 (line 15) is 49152 (00000000 00000011 11000000 00000000).

The *right-shift operator (>>)* shifts the bits of its left operand to the right by the number of bits specified in its right operand. Performing a right shift on an unsigned int causes the vacated bits at the left to be replaced by 0s; 1s shifted off the right are lost. In Fig. 10.13, the result of right shifting number1 in the expression number1 >> 8 (line 21) is 3 (00000000 00000000 00000000 00000011).

Common Programming Error 10.10
The result of right or left shifting a value is undefined if the right operand is negative or if the right operand is larger than the number of bits in which the left operand is stored.

Portability Tip 10.7
The result of right shifting a negative number is implementation defined.

10.9.5 Bitwise Assignment Operators

Each binary bitwise operator has a corresponding assignment operator. These bitwise assignment operators are shown in Fig. 10.14 and are used in a manner similar to the arithmetic assignment operators introduced in Chapter 3.

Bitwise assignment operators	
&=	Bitwise AND assignment operator.
|=	Bitwise inclusive OR assignment operator.
^=	Bitwise exclusive OR assignment operator.
<<=	Left-shift assignment operator.
>>=	Right-shift assignment operator.

Fig. 10.14 | The bitwise assignment operators.

Figure 10.15 shows the precedence and associativity of the various operators introduced to this point in the text. They're shown top to bottom in decreasing order of precedence.

Operator										Associativity	Type
()	[]	.	->	++ *(postfix)*	-- *(postfix)*					left to right	highest
+	-	++	--	!	&	*	~	sizeof	*(type)*	right to left	unary
*	/	%								left to right	multiplicative
+	-									left to right	additive
<<	>>									left to right	shifting
<	<=	>	>=							left to right	relational
==	!=									left to right	equality
&										left to right	bitwise AND
^										left to right	bitwise XOR
|										left to right	bitwise OR
&&										left to right	logical AND
||										left to right	logical OR
?:										right to left	conditional
=	+=	-=	*=	/=	&=	|=	^=	<<=	>>= %=	right to left	assignment
,										left to right	comma

Fig. 10.15 | Operator precedence and associativity.

10.10 Bit Fields

C enables you to specify the number of bits in which an unsigned int or int member of a structure or union is stored. This is referred to as a **bit field**. Bit fields enable better memory utilization by storing data in the minimum number of bits required. Bit field members *must* be declared as int or unsigned int.

Performance Tip 10.2

Bit fields help conserve storage.

Consider the following structure definition:

```
struct bitCard {
    unsigned int face : 4;
    unsigned int suit : 2;
    unsigned int color : 1;
}; // end struct bitCard
```

which contains three unsigned int bit fields—face, suit and color—used to represent a card from a deck of 52 cards. A bit field is declared by following an unsigned int or int member name with a colon (:) and an integer constant representing the width of the field (i.e., the number of bits in which the member is stored). The constant representing the width must be an integer between 0 and the total number of bits used to store an int on your system, inclusive. Our examples were tested on a computer with 4-byte (32-bit) integers.

The preceding structure definition indicates that member face is stored in 4 bits, member suit is stored in 2 bits and member color is stored in 1 bit. The number of bits is based on the desired range of values for each structure member. Member `face` stores values from 0 (Ace) through 12 (King)—4 bits can store values in the range 0–15. Member `suit` stores values from 0 through 3 (0 = Diamonds, 1 = Hearts, 2 = Clubs, 3 = Spades)—2 bits can store values in the range 0–3. Finally, member `color` stores either 0 (Red) or 1 (Black)—1 bit can store either 0 or 1.

Figure 10.16 (output shown in Fig. 10.17) creates array deck containing 52 `struct bitCard` structures in line 20. Function `fillDeck` (lines 27–37) inserts the 52 cards in the deck array and function `deal` (lines 41–53) prints the 52 cards. Notice that bit field members of structures are accessed exactly as any other structure member. Member `color` is included as a means of indicating the card color on a system that allows color displays. It's possible to specify an **unnamed bit field** to be used as **padding** in the structure. For example, the structure definition

```
struct example {
    unsigned int a : 13;
    unsigned int   : 19;
    unsigned int b : 4;
}; // end struct example
```

uses an unnamed 19-bit field as padding—nothing can be stored in those 19 bits. Member b (on our 4-byte-word computer) is stored in another storage unit.

```
 1   // Fig. 10.16: fig10_16.c
 2   // Representing cards with bit fields in a struct
 3   #include <stdio.h>
 4   #define CARDS 52
 5
 6   // bitCard structure definition with bit fields
 7   struct bitCard {
 8      unsigned int face : 4; // 4 bits; 0-15
 9      unsigned int suit : 2; // 2 bits; 0-3
10      unsigned int color : 1; // 1 bit; 0-1
11   }; // end struct bitCard
12
13   typedef struct bitCard Card; // new type name for struct bitCard
14
15   void fillDeck( Card * const wDeck ); // prototype
16   void deal( const Card * const wDeck ); // prototype
17
18   int main( void )
19   {
20      Card deck[ CARDS ]; // create array of Cards
21
22      fillDeck( deck );
23      deal( deck );
24   } // end main
25
26   // initialize Cards
27   void fillDeck( Card * const wDeck )
28   {
29      size_t i; // counter
```

Fig. 10.16 | Representing cards with bit fields in a struct. (Part I of 2.)

```
30
31      // loop through wDeck
32      for ( i = 0; i < CARDS; ++i ) {
33         wDeck[ i ].face = i % (CARDS / 4);
34         wDeck[ i ].suit = i / (CARDS / 4);
35         wDeck[ i ].color = i / (CARDS / 2);
36      } // end for
37   } // end function fillDeck
38
39   // output cards in two-column format; cards 0-25 subscripted with
40   // k1 (column 1); cards 26-51 subscripted with k2 (column 2)
41   void deal( const Card * const wDeck )
42   {
43      size_t k1; // subscripts 0-25
44      size_t k2; // subscripts 26-51
45
46      // loop through wDeck
47      for ( k1 = 0, k2 = k1 + 26; k1 < CARDS / 2; ++k1, ++k2 ) {
48         printf( "Card:%3d  Suit:%2d  Color:%2d    ",
49            wDeck[ k1 ].face, wDeck[ k1 ].suit, wDeck[ k1 ].color );
50         printf( "Card:%3d  Suit:%2d  Color:%2d\n",
51            wDeck[ k2 ].face, wDeck[ k2 ].suit, wDeck[ k2 ].color );
52      } // end for
53   } // end function deal
```

Fig. 10.16 | Representing cards with bit fields in a struct. (Part 2 of 2.)

```
Card:  0  Suit: 0  Color: 0    Card:  0  Suit: 2  Color: 1
Card:  1  Suit: 0  Color: 0    Card:  1  Suit: 2  Color: 1
Card:  2  Suit: 0  Color: 0    Card:  2  Suit: 2  Color: 1
Card:  3  Suit: 0  Color: 0    Card:  3  Suit: 2  Color: 1
Card:  4  Suit: 0  Color: 0    Card:  4  Suit: 2  Color: 1
Card:  5  Suit: 0  Color: 0    Card:  5  Suit: 2  Color: 1
Card:  6  Suit: 0  Color: 0    Card:  6  Suit: 2  Color: 1
Card:  7  Suit: 0  Color: 0    Card:  7  Suit: 2  Color: 1
Card:  8  Suit: 0  Color: 0    Card:  8  Suit: 2  Color: 1
Card:  9  Suit: 0  Color: 0    Card:  9  Suit: 2  Color: 1
Card: 10  Suit: 0  Color: 0    Card: 10  Suit: 2  Color: 1
Card: 11  Suit: 0  Color: 0    Card: 11  Suit: 2  Color: 1
Card: 12  Suit: 0  Color: 0    Card: 12  Suit: 2  Color: 1
Card:  0  Suit: 1  Color: 0    Card:  0  Suit: 3  Color: 1
Card:  1  Suit: 1  Color: 0    Card:  1  Suit: 3  Color: 1
Card:  2  Suit: 1  Color: 0    Card:  2  Suit: 3  Color: 1
Card:  3  Suit: 1  Color: 0    Card:  3  Suit: 3  Color: 1
Card:  4  Suit: 1  Color: 0    Card:  4  Suit: 3  Color: 1
Card:  5  Suit: 1  Color: 0    Card:  5  Suit: 3  Color: 1
Card:  6  Suit: 1  Color: 0    Card:  6  Suit: 3  Color: 1
Card:  7  Suit: 1  Color: 0    Card:  7  Suit: 3  Color: 1
Card:  8  Suit: 1  Color: 0    Card:  8  Suit: 3  Color: 1
Card:  9  Suit: 1  Color: 0    Card:  9  Suit: 3  Color: 1
Card: 10  Suit: 1  Color: 0    Card: 10  Suit: 3  Color: 1
Card: 11  Suit: 1  Color: 0    Card: 11  Suit: 3  Color: 1
Card: 12  Suit: 1  Color: 0    Card: 12  Suit: 3  Color: 1
```

Fig. 10.17 | Output of the program in Fig. 10.16.

An unnamed bit field with a zero width is used to align the next bit field on a new *storage-unit boundary*. For example, the structure definition

```
struct example {
    unsigned int a : 13;
    unsigned int   : 0;
    unsigned int : 4;
}; // end struct example
```

uses an unnamed 0-bit field to skip the remaining bits (as many as there are) of the storage unit in which a is stored and to align b on the next storage-unit boundary.

Portability Tip 10.8

Bit-field manipulations are machine dependent.

Common Programming Error 10.11

Attempting to access individual bits of a bit field as if they were elements of an array is a syntax error. Bit fields are not "arrays of bits."

Common Programming Error 10.12

Attempting to take the address of a bit field (the & operator may not be used with bit fields because they do not have addresses).

Performance Tip 10.3

Although bit fields save space, using them can cause the compiler to generate slower-executing machine-language code. This occurs because it takes extra machine-language operations to access only portions of an addressable storage unit. This is one of many examples of the kinds of space–time trade-offs that occur in computer science.

10.11 Enumeration Constants

An enumeration (discussed briefly in Section 5.11), introduced by the keyword enum, is a set of integer **enumeration constants** represented by identifiers. Values in an enum start with 0, unless specified otherwise, and are incremented by 1. For example, the enumeration

```
enum months {
    JAN, FEB, MAR, APR, MAY, JUN, JUL, AUG, SEP, OCT, NOV, DEC
}; // end enum months
```

creates a new type, enum months, in which the identifiers are set to the integers 0 to 11, respectively. To number the months 1 to 12, use the following enumeration:

```
enum months {
    JAN = 1, FEB, MAR, APR, MAY, JUN, JUL, AUG, SEP, OCT, NOV, DEC
}; // end enum months
```

Because the first value in the preceding enumeration is explicitly set to 1, the remaining values are incremented from 1, resulting in the values 1 through 12. The *identifiers* in an enumeration *must be unique*. The value of each enumeration constant of an enumeration can be set explicitly in the definition by assigning a value to the identifier. Multiple members of an enumeration *can* have the *same* constant value. In the program of

Fig. 10.18, the enumeration variable month is used in a for statement to print the months of the year from the array monthName. We've made monthName[0] the empty string "". You could set monthName[0] to a value such as ***ERROR*** to indicate that a logic error occurred.

Common Programming Error 10.13
Assigning a value to an enumeration constant after it's been defined is a syntax error.

Good Programming Practice 10.5
Use only uppercase letters in enumeration constant names. This makes these constants stand out in a program and reminds you that enumeration constants are not variables.

```
1   // Fig. 10.18: fig10_18.c
2   // Using an enumeration
3   #include <stdio.h>
4
5   // enumeration constants represent months of the year
6   enum months {
7      JAN = 1, FEB, MAR, APR, MAY, JUN, JUL, AUG, SEP, OCT, NOV, DEC
8   }; // end enum months
9
10  int main( void )
11  {
12     enum months month; // can contain any of the 12 months
13
14     // initialize array of pointers
15     const char *monthName[] = { "", "January", "February", "March",
16        "April", "May", "June", "July", "August", "September", "October",
17        "November", "December" };
18
19     // loop through months
20     for ( month = JAN; month <= DEC; ++month ) {
21        printf( "%2d%11s\n", month, monthName[ month ] );
22     } // end for
23  } // end main
```

```
1      January
2     February
3       March
4       April
5         May
6        June
7        July
8      August
9   September
10    October
11   November
12   December
```

Fig. 10.18 | Using an enumeration.

10.12 Secure C Programming

Various CERT guidelines and rules apply to this chapter's topics. For more information on each, visit www.securecoding.cert.org.

struct

As we discussed in Section 10.2.4, the boundary alignment requirements for struct members may result in extra bytes containing undefined data for each struct variable you create. Each of the following guidelines is related to this issue:

- EXP03-C: Because of *boundary alignment* requirements, the size of a struct variable is *not* necessarily the sum of its members' sizes. Always use sizeof to determine the number of bytes in a struct variable. As you'll see, we use this technique to manipulate fixed-length records that are written to and read from files in Chapter 11, and to create so-called dynamic data structures in Chapter 12.

- EXP04-C: As we discussed in Section 10.2.4, struct variables cannot be compared for equality or inequality, because they might contain bytes of undefined data. Therefore, you must compare their individual members.

- DCL39-C: In a struct variable, the undefined extra bytes could contain secure data—left over from prior use of those memory locations—that should *not* be accessible. This CERT guideline discusses compiler-specific mechanisms for *packing the data* to eliminate these extra bytes.

typedef

- DCL05-C: Complex type declarations, such as those for function pointers can be difficult to read. You should use typedef to create self-documenting type names that make your programs more readable.

Bit Manipulation

- INT02-C: As a result of the integer promotion rules (discussed in Section 5.6), performing bitwise operations on integer types smaller than int can lead to unexpected results. Explicit casts are required to ensure correct results.

- INT13-C: Some bitwise operations on *signed* integer types are *implementation defined*—this means that the operations may have different results across C compilers. For this reason, *unsigned* integer types should be used with the bitwise operators.

- EXP17-C: The logical operators && and || are frequently confused with the bitwise operators & and |, respectively. Using & and | in the condition of a conditional expression (?:) can lead to unexpected behavior, because the & and | operators do not use short-circuit evaluation.

enum

- INT09-C: Allowing multiple enumeration constants to have the *same* value can result in difficult-to-find logic errors. In most cases, an enum's enumeration constants should each have *unique* values to help prevent such logic errors.

Summary

Section 10.1 Introduction

- Structures are collections of related variables under one name. They may contain variables of many different data types.
- Structures are commonly used to define records to be stored in files.
- Pointers and structures facilitate the formation of more complex data structures such as linked lists, queues, stacks and trees.

Section 10.2 Structure Definitions

- Keyword struct introduces a structure definition.
- The identifier following keyword struct is the structure tag, which names the structure definition. The structure tag is used with the keyword struct to declare variables of the structure type.
- Variables declared within the braces of the structure definition are the structure's members.
- Members of the same structure type must have unique names.
- Each structure definition must end with a semicolon.
- Structure members can have primitive or aggregates data types.
- A structure cannot contain an instance of itself but may include a pointer to its type.
- A structure containing a member that's a pointer to the same structure type is referred to as a self-referential structure. Self-referential structures are used to build linked data structures.
- Structure definitions create new data types that are used to define variables.
- Variables of a given structure type can be declared by placing a comma-separated list of variable names between the closing brace of the structure definition and its ending semicolon.
- The structure tag name is optional. If a structure definition does not contain a structure tag name, variables of the structure type may be declared only in the structure definition.
- The only valid operations that may be performed on structures are assigning structure variables to variables of the same type, taking the address (&) of a structure variable, accessing the members of a structure variable and using the sizeof operator to determine the size of a structure variable.

Section 10.3 Initializing Structures

- Structures can be initialized using initializer lists.
- If there are fewer initializers in the list than members in the structure, the remaining members are automatically initialized to 0 (or NULL if the member is a pointer).
- Members of structure variables defined outside a function definition are initialized to 0 or NULL if they're not explicitly C initialized in the external definition.
- Structure variables may be initialized in assignment statements by assigning a structure variable of the same type, or by assigning values to the individual members of the structure.

Section 10.4 Accessing Structure Members

- The structure member operator (.) and the structure pointer operator (->) are used to access structure members.
- The structure member operator accesses a structure member via the structure variable name.
- The structure pointer operator accesses a structure member via a pointer to the structure.

Section 10.5 Using Structures with Functions

- Structures may be passed to functions by passing individual structure members, by passing an entire structure or by passing a pointer to a structure.

- Stucture variables are passed by value by default.
- To pass a structure by reference, pass its address. Arrays of structures—like all other arrays—are automatically passed by reference.
- To pass an array by value, create a structure with the array as a member. Structures are passed by value, so the array is passed by value.

Section 10.6 **typedef**

- The keyword typedef provides a mechanism for creating synonyms for previously defined types.
- Names for structure types are often defined with typedef to create shorter type names.
- Often, typedef is used to create synonyms for the basic data types. For example, a program requiring 4-byte integers may use type int on one system and type long on another. Programs designed for portability often use typedef to create an alias for 4-byte integers such as Integer. The alias Integer can be changed once in the program to make the program work on both systems.

Section 10.8 Unions

- A union is declared with keyword union in the same format as a structure. Its members share the same storage space.
- The members of a union can be of any data type. The number of bytes used to store a union must be at least enough to hold the largest member.
- Only one member of a union can be referenced at a time. It's your responsibility to ensure that the data in a union is referenced with the proper data type.
- The operations that can be performed on a union are assigning a union to another of the same type, taking the address (&) of a union variable, and accessing union members using the structure member operator and the structure pointer operator.
- A union may be initialized in a declaration with a value of the same type as the first union member.

Section 10.9 Bitwise Operators

- Computers represent all data internally as sequences of bits with the values 0 or 1.
- On most systems, a sequence of 8 bits form a byte—the standard storage unit for a variable of type char. Other data types are stored in larger numbers of bytes.
- The bitwise operators are used to manipulate the bits of integral operands (char, short, int and long; both signed and unsigned). Unsigned integers are normally used.
- The bitwise operators are bitwise AND (&), bitwise inclusive OR (|), bitwise exclusive OR (^), left shift (<<), right shift (>>) and complement (~).
- The bitwise AND, bitwise inclusive OR and bitwise exclusive OR operators compare their two operands bit by bit. The bitwise AND operator sets each bit in the result to 1 if the corresponding bit in both operands is 1. The bitwise inclusive OR operator sets each bit in the result to 1 if the corresponding bit in either (or both) operand(s) is 1. The bitwise exclusive OR operator sets each bit in the result to 1 if the corresponding bit in exactly one operand is 1.
- The left-shift operator shifts the bits of its left operand to the left by the number of bits specified in its right operand. Bits vacated to the right are replaced with 0s; 1s shifted off the left are lost.
- The right-shift operator shifts the bits in its left operand to the right by the number of bits specified in its right operand. Performing a right shift on an unsigned int causes the vacated bits at the left to be replaced by 0s; bits shifted off the right are lost.
- The bitwise complement operator sets all 0 bits in its operand to 1 and all 1 bits to 0 in the result.
- Often, the bitwise AND operator is used with an operand called a mask—an integer value with specific bits set to 1. Masks are used to hide some bits in a value while selecting other bits.

- The symbolic constant CHAR_BIT (defined in <limits.h>) represents the number of bits in a byte (normally 8). It can be used to make a bit-manipulation program more scalable and portable.

- Each binary bitwise operator has a corresponding assignment operator.

Section 10.10 Bit Fields

- C enables you to specify the number of bits in which an unsigned int or int member of a structure or union is stored. This is referred to as a bit field. Bit fields enable better memory utilization by storing data in the minimum number of bits required.

- A bit field is declared by following an unsigned int or int member name with a colon (:) and an integer constant representing the width of the field. The constant must be an integer between 0 and the total number of bits used to store an int on your system, inclusive.

- Bit-field members of structures are accessed exactly as any other structure member.

- It's possible to specify an unnamed bit field to be used as padding in the structure.

- An unnamed bit field with a zero width aligns the next bit field on a new storage unit boundary.

Section 10.11 Enumeration Constants

- An enum defines a set of integer constants represented by identifiers. Values in an enum start with 0, unless specified otherwise, and are incremented by 1.

- The identifiers in an enum must be unique.

- The value of an enum constant can be set explicitly via assignment in the enum definition.

- Multiple members of an enumeration can have the same constant value.

Terminology

. structure member operator 437
~ bitwise complement operator 451
aggregate 434
arrow operator (->) 437
bit field 454
bit field member name 454
bitwise AND (&) operator 445
bitwise assignment operator 453
bitwise complement operator (~) 451
bitwise exclusive OR (∧) operator 445
bitwise inclusive OR (|) operator 445
CHAR_BIT symbolic constant 448
complement operator (~) 445
derived data type 434
enumeration 434
enumeration constants 457
left-shift operator (<<) 445
mask 447

member 435
member name (bit field) 454
one's complement 451
padding 455
pointer to the structure 437
right-shift operator (>>) 445
self-referential structure 435
struct 435
structure 434
structure member (.) operator 437
structure pointer (->) operator 437
structure tag 435
structure type 435
typedef 439
union 443
unnamed bit field 455
unnamed bit field with a zero width 457
width of a bit field 454

Self-Review Exercises

10.1 Fill in the blanks in each of the following:
  a) A(n) _____ is a collection of related variables under one name.
  b) A(n) _____ is a collection of variables under one name in which the variables share the same storage.

c) The bits in the result of an expression using the _____ operator are set to 1 if the corresponding bits in each operand are set to 1. Otherwise, the bits are set to zero.

d) The variables declared in a structure definition are called its _____ .

e) In an expression using the _____ operator, bits are set to 1 if at least one of the corresponding bits in either operand is set to 1. Otherwise, the bits are set to zero.

f) Keyword _____ introduces a structure declaration.

g) Keyword _____ is used to create a synonym for a previously defined data type.

h) In an expression using the _____ operator, bits are set to 1 if exactly one of the corresponding bits in either operand is set to 1. Otherwise, the bits are set to zero.

i) The bitwise AND operator (&) is often used to _____ bits—that is to select certain bits while zeroing others.

j) Keyword _____ is used to introduce a union definition.

k) The name of the structure is referred to as the structure _____.

l) A structure member is accessed with either the _____ or the _____ operator.

m) The _____ and _____ operators are used to shift the bits of a value to the left or to the right, respectively.

n) A(n) _____ is a set of integers represented by identifiers.

10.2 State whether each of the following is *true* or *false*. If *false*, explain why.

a) Structures may contain variables of only one data type.

b) Two unions can be compared (using ==) to determine whether they're equal.

c) The tag name of a structure is optional.

d) Members of different structures must have unique names.

e) Keyword `typedef` is used to define new data types.

f) Structures are always passed to functions by reference.

g) Structures may not be compared by using operators == and !=.

10.3 Write code to accomplish each of the following:

a) Define a structure called `student` containing `int` variable `USN` and `char` array `Name` with values that may be as long as 25 characters (including the terminating null character).

b) Define `stu` to be a synonym for the type `struct student`.

c) Use `stu` to declare variable `m` to be of type `struct student`, array `n[ 10 ]` to be of type `struct student` and variable `stuptr` to be of type pointer to `struct student`.

d) Read a student USN and a student name from the keyboard into the individual members of variable `m`.

e) Assign the member values of variable `m` to element 1 of array `n`.

f) Assign the address of array `m` to the pointer variable `stuptr`.

g) Print the member values of element 1 of array `m` using the variable `stuptr` and the structure pointer operator to refer to the members.

10.4 Find the error in each of the following:

a) Assume that `struct card` has been defined containing two pointers to type `char`, namely `face` and `suit`. Also, the variable `c` has been defined to be of type `struct card` and the variable `cPtr` has been defined to be of type pointer to `struct card`. Variable `cPtr` has been assigned the address of `c`.

```
printf( "%s\n", *cPtr->face );
```

b) Assume that `struct card` has been defined containing two pointers to type `char`, namely `face` and `suit`. Also, the array `hearts[ 13 ]` has been defined to be of type `struct card`. The following statement should print the member `face` of array element 10.

```
printf( "%s\n", hearts.face );
```

c) ```
union values {
    char w;
    float x;
    double y;
}; // end union values

union values v = { 1.27 };
```

d) ```
struct person {
    char lastName[ 15 ];
    char firstName[ 15 ];
    unsigned int age;
} // end struct person
```

e) Assume `struct person` has been defined as in part (d) but with the appropriate correction.

```
person d;
```

f) Assume variable p has been declared as type `struct person` and variable c has been declared as type `struct card`.

```
p = c;
```

Answers to Self-Review Exercises

10.1   a) structure. b) union. c) bitwise AND (&). d) members. e) bitwise inclusive OR (|). f) struct. g) typedef. h) bitwise exclusive OR (∧). i) mask. j) union. k) tag name. l) structure member, structure pointer. m) left-shift operator (<<), right-shift operator (>>). n) enumeration.

10.2   a) False. A structure can contain variables of many data types.
b) False. Unions cannot be compared, because there might be bytes of undefined data with different values in union variables that are otherwise identical.
c) True.
d) False. The members of separate structures can have the same names, but the members of the same structure must have unique names.
e) False. Keyword typedef is used to define new names (synonyms) for previously defined data types.
f) False. Structures are always passed to functions by value.
g) True, because of alignment problems.

10.3   a) ```
struct student {
    int USN;
    char Name[26];
};
```
b) `typedef struct student stu;`
c) `stu m, n[ 10 ], *stuptr;`
d) `scanf( "%d%10s", &m.USN, &m.Name };`
e) `n[ 1 ] = m;`
f) `stuptr = m;`
g) `printf( "%d %s\n", ( stuptrr + 3 )->USN, ( stuptr + 1 )->Name);`

**10.4**    a) The parentheses that should enclose *cPtr have been omitted, causing the order of evaluation of the expression to be incorrect. The expression should be

```
cPtr->face
```
or
```
(*cPtr).face
```
```

b) The array subscript has been omitted. The expression should be
   ```
   hearts[ 10 ].face
   ```
c) A union can be initialized only with a value that has the same type as the union's first member.
d) A semicolon is required to end a structure definition.
e) Keyword struct was omitted from the variable declaration. The declaration should be
   ```
   struct person d;
   ```
f) Variables of different structure types cannot be assigned to one another.

Exercises

10.5 Provide the definition for each of the following structures and unions:
   a) Structure time containing integers hours, minutes and seconds.
   b) Union demo containing int m, double n, char o.
   c) A structure called month that contains character arrays
      monthName[30], daysOfWeek[20], and an integer variable numberOfDays.
   d) Structure employee that contains arrays firstName[20] and lastName[20] and
      address [30] variable monthOfJoining of type struct month from part (c).
   e) Structure trail containing 8 bit fields with widths of 2 bit. The names of the bit fields are the letters m to t.

10.6 Given the following structure and variable definitions,

```
struct customer {
    char lastName[ 15 ];
    char firstName[ 15 ];
    unsigned int customerNumber;

    struct {
        char phoneNumber[ 11 ];
        char address[ 50 ];
        char city[ 15 ];
        char state[ 3 ];
        char zipCode[ 6 ];
    } personal;

} customerRecord, *customerPtr;

customerPtr = &customerRecord;
```

write an expression that can be used to access the structure members in each of the following parts:
   a) Member lastName of structure customerRecord.
   b) Member lastName of the structure pointed to by customerPtr.
   c) Member firstName of structure customerRecord.
   d) Member firstName of the structure pointed to by customerPtr.
   e) Member customerNumber of structure customerRecord.
   f) Member customerNumber of the structure pointed to by customerPtr.
   g) Member phoneNumber of member personal of structure customerRecord.
   h) Member phoneNumber of member personal of the structure pointed to by customerPtr.
   i) Member address of member personal of structure customerRecord.
   j) Member address of member personal of the structure pointed to by customerPtr.
   k) Member city of member personal of structure customerRecord.
   l) Member city of member personal of the structure pointed to by customerPtr.
   m) Member state of member personal of structure customerRecord.
   n) Member state of member personal of the structure pointed to by customerPtr.

    o) Member `zipCode` of member `personal` of structure `customerRecord`.

    p) Member `zipCode` of member `personal` of the structure pointed to by `customerPtr`.

10.7 *(Card Shuffling and Dealing Modification)* Modify the program of Fig. 10.16 to shuffle the cards using a high-performance shuffle (as shown in Fig. 10.3). Print the resulting deck in two-column format as in Fig. 10.4. Precede each card with its color.

10.8 *(Assigning Structure Variables)* Create a structure with members `int a`, `int b` and `float c`. Write a program that demonstrates how a structure variable `value1` can be assigned to another structure variable `value2`. Print the value assigned to the structure variable `value2`.

10.9 *(Comparing Structure Variables)* Modify the program of Exercise 10.8 so as to demonstrate how a structure variable `value1` can be compared to another structure variable `value2`. Print whether both structure variables are equal or not.

10.10 *(Right Shifting Integers)* Write a program that right shifts an integer variable 4 bits. The program should print the integer in bits before and after the shift operation. Does your system place 0s or 1s in the vacated bits?

10.11 *(Left Shifting Integers)* Left shifting an `unsigned int` by 1 bit is equivalent to multiplying the value by 2. Write function `power2` that takes two integer arguments `number` and `pow` and calculates

    `number * 2`^{pow}

Use the shift operator to calculate the result. Print the values as integers and as bits.

10.12 *(Packing Characters into an Integer)* The left-shift operator can be used to pack four character values into a four-byte `unsigned int` variable. Write a program that inputs four characters from the keyboard and passes them to function `packCharacters`. To pack four characters into an unsigned int variable, assign the first character to the `unsigned int` variable, shift the `unsigned int` variable left by 8 bit positions and combine the `unsigned` variable with the second character using the bitwise inclusive OR operator. Repeat this process for the third and fourth characters. The program should output the characters in their bit format before and after they're packed into the unsigned int to prove that the characters are in fact packed correctly in the `unsigned int` variable.

10.13 *(Unpacking Characters from an Integer)* Using the right-shift operator, the bitwise AND operator and a mask, write function `unpackCharacters` that takes the `unsigned int` from Exercise 10.12 and unpacks it into four characters. To unpack characters from a four-byte `unsigned int`, combine the `unsigned int` with the mask 4278190080 (11111111 00000000 00000000 00000000) and right shift the result 8 bits. Assign the resulting value to a `char` variable. Then combine the unsigned int with the mask 16711680 (00000000 11111111 00000000 00000000). Assign the result to another `char` variable. Continue this process with the masks 65280 and 255. The program should print the unsigned int in bits before it's unpacked, then print the characters in bits to confirm that they were unpacked correctly.

10.14 *(Reversing the Order of an Integer's Bits)* Write a program that reverses the order of the bits in an `unsigned int` value. The program should input the value from the user and call function `reverseBits` to print the bits in reverse order. Print the value in bits both before and after the bits are reversed to confirm that the bits are reversed properly.

10.15 *(Portable `displayBits` Function)* Modify function `displayBits` of Fig. 10.7 so it's portable between systems using 2-byte integers and systems using 4-byte integers. [*Hint:* Use the `sizeof` operator to determine the size of an integer on a particular machine.]

10.16 *(What's the Value of X?)* The following program uses function `multiple` to determine if the integer entered from the keyboard is a multiple of some integer X. Examine the function multiple, then determine X's value.

```
1    // ex10_16.c
2    // This program determines whether a value is a multiple of X.
3    #include <stdio.h>
4
5    int multiple( int num ); // prototype
6
7    int main( void )
8    {
9       int y; // y will hold an integer entered by the user
10
11      puts( "Enter an integer between 1 and 32000: " );
12      scanf( "%d", &y );
13
14      // if y is a multiple of X
15      if ( multiple( y ) ) {
16         printf( "%d is a multiple of X\n", y );
17      } // end if
18      else {
19         printf( "%d is not a multiple of X\n", y );
20      } // end else
21   } // end main
22
23   // determine whether num is a multiple of X
24   int multiple( int num )
25   {
26      int i; // counter
27      int mask = 1; // initialize mask
28      int mult = 1; // initialize mult
29
30      for ( i = 1; i <= 10; ++i, mask <<= 1 ) {
31
32         if ( ( num & mask ) != 0 ) {
33            mult = 0;
34            break;
35         } // end if
36      } // end for
37
38      return mult;
39   } // end function multiple
```

10.17 What does the following program do?

```
1    #include <stdio.h>
2    int guess( unsigned int bits ); // prototype
3    int main( void )
4    {
5       unsigned int a; // a will hold an integer entered by the user
6       puts( "Enter an integer: " );
7       scanf( "%u", &a );
8       printf( "\nThe result is %d\n", guess( a ) );
9    } // end main
10   int guess( unsigned b )
11   {
12   unsigned m; /* counter */
13   unsigned mask = 1 << 31; /* initialize mask */
14   unsigned total = 0; /* initialize total */
15   for ( m = 1; m <= 32; m++, b <<= 1 ) {
```

```
16          if ( ( b & mask ) == mask ) {
17              ++total;
18          } /* end if */
19      } /* end for */
20      return total;
21   } /* end function guess */
```

Making a Difference

10.18 *(Computerization of Health Records)* A health care issue that has been in the news lately is the computerization of health records. This possibility is being approached cautiously because of sensitive privacy and security concerns, among others. Computerizing health records could make it easier for patients to share their health profiles and histories among their various health care professionals. This could improve the quality of health care, help avoid drug conflicts and erroneous drug prescriptions, reduce costs and in emergencies could save lives. In this exercise, you'll design a "starter" HealthProfile structure for a person. The structure's members should include the person's first name, last name, gender, date of birth (consisting of separate attributes for the month, day and year of birth), height (in inches) and weight (in pounds). Your program should have a function that receives this data and uses it to set the members of a HealthProfile variable. The program also should include functions that calculate and return the user's age in years, maximum heart rate and target-heart-rate range (see Exercise 3.47), and body mass index (BMI; see Exercise 2.32). The program should prompt for the person's information, create a HealthProfile variable for that person and display the information from that variable—including the person's first name, last name, gender, date of birth, height and weight—then calculate and display the person's age in years, BMI, maximum heart rate and target-heart-rate range. It should also display the "BMI values" chart from Exercise 2.32.

C File Processing

Objectives

In this chapter, you'll:

- Understand the concepts of files and streams.

- Create and read data using sequential-access file processing.

- Create, read and update data using random-access file processing.

- Develop a substantial transaction-processing program.

11.1 Introduction

You studied the *data hierarchy* in Chapter 1. Storage of data in variables and arrays is *temporary*—such data is *lost* when a program terminates. Files are used for *permanent* retention of data. Computers store files on secondary storage devices, such as hard drives, CDs, DVDs and flash drives. In this chapter, we explain how data files are created, updated and processed by C programs. We consider both sequential-access and random-access file processing.

11.2 Files and Streams

C views each file simply as a sequential stream of bytes (Fig. 11.1). Each file ends either with an **end-of-file marker** or at a specific byte number recorded in a system-maintained, administrative data structure. When a file is *opened*, a **stream** is associated with it. Three files and their associated streams are automatically opened when program execution begins—the **standard input**, the **standard output** and the **standard error**. Streams provide communication channels between files and programs. For example, the standard input stream enables a program to read data from the keyboard, and the standard output stream enables a program to print data on the screen. Opening a file returns a pointer to a FILE structure (defined in <stdio.h>) that contains information used to process the file. In some operating systems, this structure includes a **file descriptor**, i.e., an index into an operating system array called the **open file table**. Each array element contains a file **control block** (FCB)—information that the operating system uses to administer a particular file. The standard input, standard output and standard error are manipulated using file pointers **stdin**, **stdout** and **stderr**.

| 0 | 1 | 2 | 3 | 4 | 5 | 6 | 7 | 8 | 9 | ... | *n*–1 |

... end-of-file marker

Fig. 11.1 | C's view of a file of *n* bytes.

The standard library provides many functions for reading data from files and for writing data to files. Function **fgetc**, like **getchar**, reads one character from a file. Function **fgetc** receives as an argument a FILE pointer for the file from which a character will be read. The call fgetc(stdin) reads one character from stdin—the standard input. This call is equivalent to the call getchar().

Function fputc, like **putchar**, writes one character to a file. Function fputc receives as arguments a character to be written and a pointer for the file to which the character will be written. The function call fputc('a', stdout) writes the character 'a' to stdout—the standard output. This call is equivalent to putchar('a').

Several other functions used to read data from standard input and write data to standard output have similarly named file-processing functions. The **fgets** and **fputs** functions, for example, can be used to *read a line from a file* and *write a line to a file*, respectively. In the next several sections, we introduce the file-processing equivalents of functions scanf and **printf**—**fscanf** and **fprintf**. Later in the chapter we discuss functions **fread** and **fwrite**.

11.3 Creating a Sequential-Access File

C imposes no structure on a file. Thus, notions such as a record of a file do not exist as part of the C language. The following example shows how you can impose your own record structure on a file.

Figure 11.2 creates a simple sequential-access file that might be used in an accounts receivable system to keep track of the amounts owed by a company's credit clients. For each client, the program obtains an *account number*, the *client's name* and the *client's balance* (i.e., the amount the client owes the company for goods and services received in the past). The data obtained for each client constitutes a "record" for that client. The account number is used as the *record key* in this application—the file will be created and maintained in account-number order. This program assumes the user enters the records in account-number order. In a comprehensive accounts receivable system, a sorting capability would be provided so the user could enter the records in any order. The records would then be sorted and written to the file. [*Note:* Figures 11.6–11.7 use the data file created in Fig. 11.2, so you must run Fig. 11.2 before Figs. 11.6–11.7.]

```
1   // Fig. 11.2: fig11_02.c
2   // Creating a sequential file
3   #include <stdio.h>
4
5   int main( void )
6   {
7      unsigned int account; // account number
8      char name[ 30 ]; // account name
9      double balance; // account balance
10
11     FILE *cfPtr; // cfPtr = clients.dat file pointer
12
13     // fopen opens file. Exit program if unable to create file
14     if ( ( cfPtr = fopen( "clients.dat", "w" ) ) == NULL ) {
15        puts( "File could not be opened" );
16     } // end if
17     else {
```

Fig. 11.2 | Creating a sequential file. (Part 1 of 2.)

```
18          puts( "Enter the account, name, and balance." );
19          puts( "Enter EOF to end input." );
20          printf( "%s", "? " );
21          scanf( "%d%29s%lf", &account, name, &balance );
22
23          // write account, name and balance into file with fprintf
24          while ( !feof( stdin ) ) {
25             fprintf( cfPtr, "%d %s %.2f\n", account, name, balance );
26             printf( "%s", "? " );
27             scanf( "%d%29s%lf", &account, name, &balance );
28          } // end while
29
30          fclose( cfPtr ); // fclose closes file
31       } // end else
32    } // end main
```

```
Enter the account, name, and balance.
Enter EOF to end input.
? 100 Jones 24.98
? 200 Doe 345.67
? 300 White 0.00
? 400 Stone -42.16
? 500 Rich 224.62
? ^Z
```

Fig. 11.2 | Creating a sequential file. (Part 2 of 2.)

Now let's examine this program. Line 11 states that cfPtr is a *pointer to a FILE struc-ture*. A C program administers each file with a separate FILE structure. You need not know the specifics of the FILE structure to use files, but you can study the declaration in stdio.h if you like. We'll soon see precisely how the FILE structure leads *indirectly* to the operating system's file control block (FCB) for a file.

Each open file must have a separately declared pointer of type FILE that's used to refer to the file. Line 14 names the file—"clients.dat"—to be used by the program and estab-lishes a "line of communication" with the file. The file pointer cfPtr is assigned a *pointer to the FILE structure* for the file opened with fopen. Function fopen takes two arguments: a filename (which can include path information leading to the file's location) and a file open mode. The file open mode "w" indicates that the file is to be opened for writing. If a file *does not exist* and it's opened for writing, fopen *creates the file*. If an existing file is opened for writing, the contents of the file are *discarded without warning*. In the program, the if statement is used to determine whether the file pointer cfPtr is NULL (i.e., the file is not opened). If it's NULL, the program prints an error message and terminates. Other-wise, the program processes the input and writes it to the file.

Common Programming Error 11.1

Opening an existing file for writing ("w") when, in fact, the user wants to preserve the file, discards the contents of the file without warning.

Common Programming Error 11.2

Forgetting to open a file before attempting to reference it in a program is a logic error.

The program prompts the user to enter the various fields for each record or to enter *end-of-file* when data entry is complete. Figure 11.3 lists the key combinations for entering end-of-file for various computer systems.

Operating system	Key combination
Linux/Mac OS X/UNIX	*<Ctrl> d*
Windows	*<Ctrl> z*

Fig. 11.3 | End-of-file key combinations for various popular operating systems.

Line 24 uses function **feof** to determine whether the end-of-file indicator is set for the file to which stdin refers. The *end-of-file indicator* informs the program that there's no more data to be processed. In Fig. 11.2, the end-of-file indicator is set for the standard input when the user enters the *end-of-file key combination*. The argument to function feof is a pointer to the file being tested for the end-of-file indicator (stdin in this case). The function returns a nonzero (true) value when the end-of-file indicator has been set; otherwise, the function returns zero. The while statement that includes the feof call in this program continues executing while the end-of-file indicator is not set.

Line 25 writes data to the file clients.dat. The data may be retrieved later by a program designed to read the file (see Section 11.4). Function fprintf is equivalent to printf except that fprintf also receives as an argument a file pointer for the file to which the data will be written. Function fprintf can output data to the standard output by using stdout as the file pointer, as in:

```
fprintf( stdout, "%d %s %.2f\n", account, name, balance );
```

After the user enters end-of-file, the program closes the clients.dat file with **fclose** and terminates. Function fclose also receives the file pointer (rather than the filename) as an argument. *If function fclose is not called explicitly, the operating system normally will close the file when program execution terminates.* This is an example of operating system "housekeeping."

Performance Tip 11.1

Closing a file can free resources for which other users or programs may be waiting, so you should close each file as soon as it's no longer needed rather than waiting for the operating system to close it at program termination.

In the sample execution for the program of Fig. 11.2, the user enters information for five accounts, then enters end-of-file to signal that data entry is complete. The sample execution does not show how the data records actually appear in the file. To verify that the file has been created successfully, in the next section we present a program that reads the file and prints its contents.

Figure 11.4 illustrates the relationship between FILE pointers, FILE structures and FCBs. When the file "clients.dat" is opened, an FCB for the file is copied into memory. The figure shows the connection between the file pointer returned by fopen and the FCB used by the operating system to administer the file.

Fig. 11.4 | Relationship between FILE pointers, FILE structures and FCBs.

Programs may process no files, one file or several files. Each file used in a program will have a different file pointer returned by **fopen**. *All subsequent file-processing functions after the file is opened must refer to the file with the appropriate file pointer.* Files may be opened in one of several modes (Fig. 11.5). To create a file, or to discard the contents of a file before writing data, open the file for writing ("w"). To read an existing file, open it for reading ("r"). To

Mode	Description
r	Open an existing file for reading.
w	Create a file for writing. If the file already exists, discard the current contents.
a	Append: open or create a file for writing at the end of the file.
r+	Open an existing file for update (reading and writing).
w+	Create a file for update. If the file already exists, discard the current contents.
a+	Append: open or create a file for update; writing is done at the end of the file.
rb	Open an existing file for reading in binary mode.
wb	Create a file for writing in binary mode. If the file already exists, discard the current contents.
ab	Append: open or create a file for writing at the end of the file in binary mode.
rb+	Open an existing file for update (reading and writing) in binary mode.
wb+	Create a file for update in binary mode. If the file already exists, discard the current contents.
ab+	Append: open or create a file for update in binary mode; writing is done at the end of the file.

Fig. 11.5 | File opening modes.

add records to the end of an existing file, open the file for appending ("a"). To open a file so that it may be written to and read from, open the file for updating in one of the three update modes—"r+", "w+" or "a+". Mode "r+" opens an existing file for reading and writing. Mode "w+" creates a file for reading and writing. If the file already exists, it's opened and its current contents are discarded. Mode "a+" opens a file for reading and writing—all writing is done at the end of the file. If the file does not exist, it's created. Each file open mode has a corresponding binary mode (containing the letter b) for manipulating binary files. The binary modes are used in Sections 11.5–11.9 when we introduce random-access files. In addition, C11 provides *exclusive* write mode, which you indicate by adding an x to the end of the w, w+, wb or wb+ modes. In exclusive write mode, fopen will fail if the file already exists or cannot be created. If opening a file in exclusive write mode is successful and the underlying system supports exclusive file access, then *only* your program can access the file while it's open. (Some compilers and platforms do not support exclusive write mode.) If an error occurs while opening a file in any mode, fopen returns NULL.

Common Programming Error 11.3
Opening a nonexistent file for reading is an error.

Common Programming Error 11.4
Opening a file for reading or writing without having been granted the appropriate access rights to the file (this is operating-system dependent) is an error.

Common Programming Error 11.5
Opening a file for writing when no space is available is a runtime error.

Common Programming Error 11.6

Opening a file in write mode ("w") when it should be opened in update mode ("r+") causes the contents of the file to be discarded.

Error-Prevention Tip 11.1

Open a file only for reading (and not updating) if its contents should not be modified. This prevents unintentional modification of the file's contents. This is another example of the principle of least privilege.

11.4 Reading Data from a Sequential-Access File

Data is stored in files so that the data can be retrieved for processing when needed. The previous section demonstrated how to create a file for sequential access. This section shows how to read data sequentially from a file.

Figure 11.6 reads records from the file "clients.dat" created by the program of Fig. 11.2 and prints their contents. Line 11 indicates that cfPtr is a *pointer to a FILE*. Line 14 attempts to open the file "clients.dat" for reading ("r") and determines whether it opened successfully (i.e., fopen does *not* return NULL). Line 19 reads a "record" from the file. Function fscanf is equivalent to function scanf, except fscanf receives as an argument a file pointer for the file from which the data is read. After this statement executes the first time, account will have the value 100, name will have the value "Jones" and balance will have the value 24.98. Each time the *second* fscanf statement (line 24) executes, the program reads another record from the file and account, name and balance take on new values. When the program reaches the end of the file, the file is closed (line 27) and the program terminates. Function feof returns true only *after* the program attempts to read the nonexistent data following the last line.

```c
1   // Fig. 11.6: fig11_06.c
2   // Reading and printing a sequential file
3   #include <stdio.h>
4
5   int main( void )
6   {
7      unsigned int account; // account number
8      char name[ 30 ]; // account name
9      double balance; // account balance
10
11     FILE *cfPtr; // cfPtr = clients.dat file pointer
12
13     // fopen opens file; exits program if file cannot be opened
14     if ( ( cfPtr = fopen( "clients.dat", "r" ) ) == NULL ) {
15        puts( "File could not be opened" );
16     } // end if
17     else { // read account, name and balance from file
18        printf( "%-10s%-13s%s\n", "Account", "Name", "Balance" );
19        fscanf( cfPtr, "%d%29s%lf", &account, name, &balance );
20
```

Fig. 11.6 | Reading and printing a sequential file. (Part 1 of 2.)

```
21          // while not end of file
22          while ( !feof( cfPtr ) ) {
23             printf( "%-10d%-13s%7.2f\n", account, name, balance );
24             fscanf( cfPtr, "%d%29s%lf", &account, name, &balance );
25          } // end while
26
27          fclose( cfPtr ); // fclose closes the file
28       } // end else
29    } // end main
```

```
Account    Name         Balance
100        Jones          24.98
200        Doe           345.67
300        White           0.00
400        Stone         -42.16
500        Rich          224.62
```

Fig. 11.6 | Reading and printing a sequential file. (Part 2 of 2.)

Resetting the File Position Pointer

To retrieve data sequentially from a file, a program normally starts reading from the beginning of the file and reads all data consecutively until the desired data is found. It may be desirable to process the data sequentially in a file several times (from the beginning of the file) during the execution of a program. The statement

```
rewind( cfPtr );
```

causes a program's **file position pointer**—which indicates the number of the next byte in the file to be read or written—to be repositioned to the *beginning* of the file (i.e., byte 0) pointed to by cfPtr. The file position pointer is *not* really a pointer. Rather it's an integer value that specifies the byte in the file at which the next read or write is to occur. This is sometimes referred to as the **file offset**. The file position pointer is a member of the FILE structure associated with each file.

Credit Inquiry Program

The program of Fig. 11.7 allows a credit manager to obtain lists of customers with zero balances (i.e., customers who do not owe any money), customers with credit balances (i.e., customers to whom the company owes money) and customers with debit balances (i.e., customers who owe the company money for goods and services received). A credit balance is a *negative* amount; a debit balance is a *positive* amount.

```
1    // Fig. 11.7: fig11_07.c
2    // Credit inquiry program
3    #include <stdio.h>
4
5    // function main begins program execution
6    int main( void )
7    {
8       unsigned int request; // request number
```

Fig. 11.7 | Credit inquiry program. (Part 1 of 3.)

```
 9      unsigned int account; // account number
10      double balance; // account balance
11      char name[ 30 ]; // account name
12      FILE *cfPtr; // clients.dat file pointer
13
14      // fopen opens the file; exits program if file cannot be opened
15      if ( ( cfPtr = fopen( "clients.dat", "r" ) ) == NULL ) {
16         puts( "File could not be opened" );
17      } // end if
18      else {
19
20         // display request options
21         printf( "%s", "Enter request\n"
22            " 1 - List accounts with zero balances\n"
23            " 2 - List accounts with credit balances\n"
24            " 3 - List accounts with debit balances\n"
25            " 4 - End of run\n? " );
26         scanf( "%u", &request );
27
28         // process user's request
29         while ( request != 4 ) {
30
31            // read account, name and balance from file
32            fscanf( cfPtr, "%d%29s%lf", &account, name, &balance );
33
34            switch ( request ) {
35               case 1:
36                  puts( "\nAccounts with zero balances:" );
37
38                  // read file contents (until eof)
39                  while ( !feof( cfPtr ) ) {
40
41                     if ( balance == 0 ) {
42                        printf( "%-10d%-13s%7.2f\n",
43                           account, name, balance );
44                     } // end if
45
46                     // read account, name and balance from file
47                     fscanf( cfPtr, "%d%29s%lf",
48                        &account, name, &balance );
49                  } // end while
50
51                  break;
52               case 2:
53                  puts( "\nAccounts with credit balances:\n" );
54
55                  // read file contents (until eof)
56                  while ( !feof( cfPtr ) ) {
57
58                     if ( balance < 0 ) {
59                        printf( "%-10d%-13s%7.2f\n",
60                           account, name, balance );
61                     } // end if
```

Fig. 11.7 | Credit inquiry program. (Part 2 of 3.)

```
62
63                              // read account, name and balance from file
64                              fscanf( cfPtr, "%d%29s%lf",
65                                  &account, name, &balance );
66                          } // end while
67
68                          break;
69                      case 3:
70                          puts( "\nAccounts with debit balances:\n" );
71
72                          // read file contents (until eof)
73                          while ( !feof( cfPtr ) ) {
74
75                              if ( balance > 0 ) {
76                                  printf( "%-10d%-13s%7.2f\n",
77                                      account, name, balance );
78                              } // end if
79
80                              // read account, name and balance from file
81                              fscanf( cfPtr, "%d%29s%lf",
82                                  &account, name, &balance );
83                          } // end while
84
85                          break;
86                  } // end switch
87
88                  rewind( cfPtr ); // return cfPtr to beginning of file
89
90                  printf( "%s", "\n? " );
91                  scanf( "%d", &request );
92              } // end while
93
94              puts( "End of run." );
95              fclose( cfPtr ); // fclose closes the file
96          } // end else
97  } // end main
```

Fig. 11.7 | Credit inquiry program. (Part 3 of 3.)

The program displays a menu and allows the credit manager to enter one of three options to obtain credit information. Option 1 produces a list of accounts with zero balances. Option 2 produces a list of accounts with *credit balances*. Option 3 produces a list of accounts with *debit balances*. Option 4 terminates program execution. A sample output is shown in Fig. 11.8.

```
Enter request
 1 - List accounts with zero balances
 2 - List accounts with credit balances
 3 - List accounts with debit balances
 4 - End of run
? 1
```

Fig. 11.8 | Sample output of the credit inquiry program of Fig. 11.7. (Part 1 of 2.)

```
Accounts with zero balances:
300      White              0.00

? 2

Accounts with credit balances:
400      Stone            -42.16

? 3

Accounts with debit balances:
100      Jones             24.98
200      Doe              345.67
500      Rich             224.62

? 4
End of run.
```

Fig. 11.8 | Sample output of the credit inquiry program of Fig. 11.7. (Part 2 of 2.)

Data in this type of sequential file cannot be modified without the risk of destroying other data. For example, if the name "White" needs to be changed to "Worthington," the old name cannot simply be overwritten. The record for White was written to the file as

```
300 White 0.00
```

If the record is rewritten beginning at the same location in the file using the new name, the record will be

```
300 Worthington 0.00
```

The new record is larger (has more characters) than the original record. The characters beyond the second "o" in "Worthington" will *overwrite* the beginning of the next sequential record in the file. The problem here is that in the **formatted input/output model** using fprintf and fscanf, fields—and hence records—can *vary* in size. For example, the values 7, 14, –117, 2074 and 27383 are all ints stored in the same number of bytes internally, but they're different-sized fields when displayed on the screen or written to a file as text.

Therefore, sequential access with fprintf and fscanf is *not* usually used to *update records in place*. Instead, the entire file is usually *rewritten*. To make the preceding name change, the records before 300 White 0.00 in such a sequential-access file would be copied to a new file, the new record would be written and the records after 300 White 0.00 would be copied to the new file. This requires processing every record in the file to update one record.

11.5 Random-Access Files

As we stated previously, records in a file created with the formatted output function fprintf are not necessarily the same length. However, individual records of a **random-access file** are normally *fixed in length* and may be accessed directly (and thus quickly) without searching through other records. This makes random-access files appropriate for airline reservation systems, banking systems, point-of-sale systems, and other kinds of **transaction-processing systems** that require rapid access to specific data. There are other ways of implementing random-access files, but we'll limit our discussion to this straight-forward approach using fixed-length records.

Because every record in a random-access file normally has the same length, the exact location of a record relative to the beginning of the file can be calculated as a function of the record key. We'll soon see how this facilitates *immediate* access to specific records, even in large files.

Figure 11.9 illustrates one way to implement a random-access file. Such a file is like a freight train with many cars—some empty and some with cargo. Each car in the train has the same length.

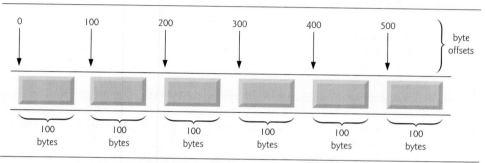

Fig. 11.9 | C's view of a random-access file.

Fixed-length records enable data to be inserted in a random-access file *without destroying other data in the file*. Data stored previously can also be updated or deleted without rewriting the entire file. In the following sections we explain how to create a random-access file, enter data, read the data both sequentially and randomly, update the data, and delete data no longer needed.

11.6 Creating a Random-Access File

Function fwrite transfers a specified number of bytes beginning at a specified location in memory to a file. The data is written beginning at the location in the file indicated by the file position pointer. Function fread transfers a specified number of bytes from the location in the file specified by the file position pointer to an area in memory beginning with a specified address. Now, when writing an integer, instead of using

```
fprintf( fPtr, "%d", number );
```

which could print a single digit or as many as 11 digits (10 digits plus a sign, each of which requires 1 byte of storage) for a four-byte integer, we can use

```
fwrite( &number, sizeof( int ), 1, fPtr );
```

which *always* writes four bytes on a system with four-byte integers from a variable number to the file represented by fPtr (we'll explain the 1 argument shortly). Later, fread can be used to read those four bytes into an integer variable number. Although fread and fwrite read and write data, such as integers, in fixed-size rather than variable-size format, the data they handle are processed in computer "raw data" format (i.e., bytes of data) rather than in printf's and scanf's human-readable text format. Because the "raw" representation of data is system dependent, "raw data" may not be readable on other systems, or by programs produced by other compilers or with other compiler options.

Functions fwrite and fread are capable of reading and writing arrays of data to and from disk. The third argument of both fread and fwrite is the number of elements in the array that should be read from or written to disk. The preceding fwrite function call writes a single integer to disk, so the third argument is 1 (as if one element of an array is being written).

File-processing programs rarely write a single field to a file. Normally, they write one struct at a time, as we show in the following examples.

Consider the following problem statement:

> *Create a credit-processing system capable of storing up to 100 fixed-length records. Each record should consist of an account number that will be used as the record key, a last name, a first name and a balance. The resulting program should be able to update an account, insert a new account record, delete an account and list all the account records in a formatted text file for printing. Use a random-access file.*

The next several sections introduce the techniques necessary to create the credit-processing program. Figure 11.10 shows how to open a random-access file, define a record format using a struct, write data to the disk and close the file. This program initializes all 100 records of the file "credit.dat" with empty structs using the function fwrite. Each empty struct contains 0 for the account number, "" (the empty string) for the last name, "" for the first name and 0.0 for the balance. The file is initialized in this manner to create space on disk in which the file will be stored and to make it possible to determine whether a record contains data.

```
1   // Fig. 11.10: fig11_10.c2
2   // Creating a random-access file sequentially
3   #include <stdio.h>
4
5   // clientData structure definition
6   struct clientData {
7      unsigned int acctNum; // account number
8      char lastName[ 15 ]; // account last name
9      char firstName[ 10 ]; // account first name
10     double balance; // account balance
11  }; // end structure clientData
12
13  int main( void )
14  {
15     unsigned int i; // counter used to count from 1-100
16
17     // create clientData with default information
18     struct clientData blankClient = { 0, "", "", 0.0 };
19
20     FILE *cfPtr; // credit.dat file pointer
21
22     // fopen opens the file; exits if file cannot be opened
23     if ( ( cfPtr = fopen( "credit.dat", "wb" ) ) == NULL ) {
```

Fig. 11.10 | Creating a random-access file sequentially. (Part 1 of 2.)

```
24        puts( "File could not be opened." );
25     } // end if
26     else {
27        // output 100 blank records to file
28        for ( i = 1; i <= 100; ++i ) {
29           fwrite( &blankClient, sizeof( struct clientData ), 1, cfPtr );
30        } // end for
31
32        fclose ( cfPtr ); // fclose closes the file
33     } // end else
34  } // end main
```

Fig. 11.10 | Creating a random-access file sequentially. (Part 2 of 2.)

Function fwrite writes a block of bytes to a file. Line 29 causes the structure blank-Client of size sizeof(struct clientData) to be written to the file pointed to by cfPtr. The operator sizeof returns the size in bytes of its operand in parentheses (in this case struct clientData).

Function fwrite can actually be used to write several elements of an array of objects. To do so, supply in the call to fwrite a pointer to an array as the first argument and the number of elements to be written as the third argument. In the preceding statement, fwrite was used to write a single object that was not an array element. Writing a single object is equivalent to writing one element of an array, hence the 1 in the fwrite call. [*Note:* Figures 11.11, 11.14 and 11.15 use the data file created in Fig. 11.10, so you must run Fig. 11.10 before Figs. 11.11, 11.14 and 11.15]

11.7 Writing Data Randomly to a Random-Access File

Figure 11.11 writes data to the file "credit.dat". It uses the combination of fseek and fwrite to store data at specific locations in the file. Function fseek sets the file position pointer to a specific position in the file, then fwrite writes the data. A sample execution is shown in Fig. 11.12.

```
1   // Fig. 11.11: fig11_11.c
2   // Writing data randomly to a random-access file
3   #include <stdio.h>
4
5   // clientData structure definition
6   struct clientData {
7      unsigned int acctNum; // account number
8      char lastName[ 15 ]; // account last name
9      char firstName[ 10 ]; // account first name
10     double balance; // account balance
11  }; // end structure clientData
12
13  int main( void )
14  {
15     FILE *cfPtr; // credit.dat file pointer
```

Fig. 11.11 | Writing data randomly to a random-access file. (Part 1 of 2.)

```
16
17      // create clientData with default information
18      struct clientData client = { 0, "", "", 0.0 };
19
20      // fopen opens the file; exits if file cannot be opened
21      if ( ( cfPtr = fopen( "credit.dat", "rb+" ) ) == NULL ) {
22         puts( "File could not be opened." );
23      } // end if
24      else {
25         // require user to specify account number
26         printf( "%s", "Enter account number"
27            " ( 1 to 100, 0 to end input )\n? " );
28         scanf( "%d", &client.acctNum );
29
30         // user enters information, which is copied into file
31         while ( client.acctNum != 0 ) {
32            // user enters last name, first name and balance
33            printf( "%s", "Enter lastname, firstname, balance\n? " );
34
35            // set record lastName, firstName and balance value
36            fscanf( stdin, "%14s%9s%lf", client.lastName,
37               client.firstName, &client.balance );
38
39            // seek position in file to user-specified record
40            fseek( cfPtr, ( client.acctNum - 1 ) *
41               sizeof( struct clientData ), SEEK_SET );
42
43            // write user-specified information in file
44            fwrite( &client, sizeof( struct clientData ), 1, cfPtr );
45
46            // enable user to input another account number
47            printf( "%s", "Enter account number\n? " );
48            scanf( "%d", &client.acctNum );
49         } // end while
50
51         fclose( cfPtr ); // fclose closes the file
52      } // end else
53   } // end main
```

Fig. 11.11 | Writing data randomly to a random-access file. (Part 2 of 2.)

Lines 40–41 position the file position pointer for the file referenced by cfPtr to the byte location calculated by (client.accountNum - 1) * sizeof(struct clientData). The value of this expression is called the **offset** or the **displacement**. Because the account number is between 1 and 100 but the byte positions in the file start with 0, 1 is subtracted from the account number when calculating the byte location of the record. Thus, for record 1, the file position pointer is set to byte 0 of the file. The symbolic constant **SEEK_SET** indicates that the file position pointer is positioned relative to the beginning of the file by the amount of the offset. As the above statement indicates, a seek for account number 1 in the file sets the file position pointer to the beginning of the file because the byte location calculated is 0. Figure 11.13 illustrates the file pointer referring to a FILE structure in memory. The file position pointer in this diagram indicates that the next byte to be read or written is 5 bytes from the beginning of the file.

```
Enter account number ( 1 to 100, 0 to end input )
? 37
Enter lastname, firstname, balance
? Barker Doug 0.00
Enter account number
? 29
Enter lastname, firstname, balance
? Brown Nancy -24.54
Enter account number
? 96
Enter lastname, firstname, balance
? Stone Sam 34.98
Enter account number
? 88
Enter lastname, firstname, balance
? Smith Dave 258.34
Enter account number
? 33
Enter lastname, firstname, balance
? Dunn Stacey 314.33
Enter account number
? 0
```

Fig. 11.12 | Sample execution of the program in Fig. 11.11.

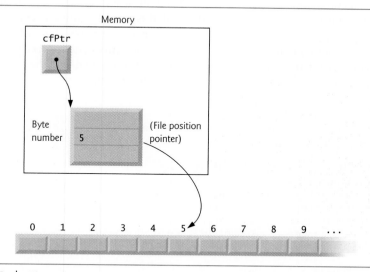

Fig. 11.13 | File position pointer indicating an offset of 5 bytes from the beginning of the file.

The function prototype for fseek is

```
int fseek( FILE *stream, long int offset, int whence );
```

where offset is the number of bytes to seek from whence in the file pointed to by stream—a positive offset seeks forward and a negative one seeks backward. Argument whence is one of the values SEEK_SET, SEEK_CUR or SEEK_END (all defined in <stdio.h>), which indicate the location from which the seek begins. SEEK_SET indicates that the seek starts at the *beginning* of the file; SEEK_CUR indicates that the seek starts at the *current location* in the file; and SEEK_END indicates that the seek starts at the *end* of the file.

For simplicity, the programs in this chapter do *not* perform error checking. Industrial-strength programs should determine whether functions such as fscanf (lines 36–37), fseek (lines 40–41) and fwrite (line 44) operate correctly by checking their return values. Function fscanf returns the number of data items successfully read or the value EOF if a problem occurs while reading data. Function fseek returns a nonzero value if the seek operation cannot be performed. Function fwrite returns the number of items it successfully output. If this number is less than the *third argument* in the function call, then a write error occurred.

11.8 Reading Data from a Random-Access File

Function fread reads a specified number of bytes from a file into memory. For example,

```
fread( &client, sizeof( struct clientData ), 1, cfPtr );
```

reads the number of bytes determined by sizeof(struct clientData) from the file referenced by cfPtr, stores the data in client and returns the number of bytes read. The bytes are read from the location specified by the file position pointer. Function fread can read several fixed-size array elements by providing a pointer to the array in which the elements will be stored and by indicating the number of elements to be read. The preceding statement reads *one* element. To read *more than one*, specify the number of elements as fread's third argument. Function fread returns the number of items it successfully input. If this number is less than the third argument in the function call, then a read error occurred.

Figure 11.14 reads sequentially every record in the "credit.dat" file, determines whether each record contains data and displays the formatted data for records containing data. Function feof determines when the end of the file is reached, and the fread function transfers data from the file to the clientData structure client.

```c
 1   // Fig. 11.14: fig11_14.c
 2   // Reading a random-access file sequentially
 3   #include <stdio.h>
 4
 5   // clientData structure definition
 6   struct clientData {
 7      unsigned int acctNum; // account number
 8      char lastName[ 15 ]; // account last name
 9      char firstName[ 10 ]; // account first name
10      double balance; // account balance
11   }; // end structure clientData
12
13   int main( void )
14   {
15      FILE *cfPtr; // credit.dat file pointer
16      int result; // used to test whether fread read any bytes
17
18      // create clientData with default information
19      struct clientData client = { 0, "", "", 0.0 };
20
```

Fig. 11.14 | Reading a random-access file sequentially. (Part 1 of 2.)

```
21        // fopen opens the file; exits if file cannot be opened
22        if ( ( cfPtr = fopen( "credit.dat", "rb" ) ) == NULL ) {
23           puts( "File could not be opened." );
24        } // end if
25        else {
26           printf( "%-6s%-16s%-11s%10s\n", "Acct", "Last Name",
27              "First Name", "Balance" );
28
29           // read all records from file (until eof)
30           while ( !feof( cfPtr ) ) {
31              result = fread( &client, sizeof( struct clientData ), 1, cfPtr );
32
33              // display record
34              if ( result != 0 && client.acctNum != 0 ) {
35                 printf( "%-6d%-16s%-11s%10.2f\n",
36                    client.acctNum, client.lastName,
37                    client.firstName, client.balance );
38              } // end if
39           } // end while
40
41           fclose( cfPtr ); // fclose closes the file
42        } // end else
43     } // end main
```

Acct	Last Name	First Name	Balance
29	Brown	Nancy	-24.54
33	Dunn	Stacey	314.33
37	Barker	Doug	0.00
88	Smith	Dave	258.34
96	Stone	Sam	34.98

Fig. 11.14 | Reading a random-access file sequentially. (Part 2 of 2.)

11.9 Case Study: Transaction-Processing Program

We now present a substantial transaction-processing program (Fig. 11.15) using random-access files. The program maintains a bank's account information—updating existing accounts, adding new accounts, deleting accounts and storing a listing of all the current accounts in a text file for printing. We assume that the program of Fig. 11.10 has been executed to create the file credit.dat.

The program has five options. Option 1 calls function textFile (lines 63–94) to store a formatted list of all the accounts (typically called a report) in a text file called accounts.txt that may be printed later. The function uses fread and the sequential file access techniques used in the program of Fig. 11.14. After option 1 is chosen, the file accounts.txt contains:

Acct	Last Name	First Name	Balance
29	Brown	Nancy	-24.54
33	Dunn	Stacey	314.33
37	Barker	Doug	0.00
88	Smith	Dave	258.34
96	Stone	Sam	34.98

Option 2 calls the function updateRecord (lines 97–141) to update an account. The function will update only a record that already exists, so the function first checks whether the record specified by the user is empty. The record is read into structure client with fread, then member acctNum is compared to 0. If it's 0, the record contains no information, and a message is printed stating that the record is empty. Then the menu choices are displayed. If the record contains information, function updateRecord inputs the transaction amount, calculates the new balance and rewrites the record to the file. A typical output for option 2 is

```
Enter account to update ( 1 - 100 ): 37
37      Barker          Doug              0.00

Enter charge ( + ) or payment ( - ): +87.99
37      Barker          Doug             87.99
```

Option 3 calls the function newRecord (lines 178–217) to add a new account to the file. If the user enters an account number for an existing account, newRecord displays an error message indicating that the record already contains information, and the menu choices are printed again. This function uses the same process to add a new account as does the program in Fig. 11.11. A typical output for option 3 is

```
Enter new account number ( 1 - 100 ): 22
Enter lastname, firstname, balance
? Johnston Sarah 247.45
```

Option 4 calls function deleteRecord (lines 144–175) to delete a record from the file. Deletion is accomplished by asking the user for the account number and reinitializing the record. If the account contains no information, deleteRecord displays an error message indicating that the account does not exist. Option 5 terminates program execution. The program is shown in Fig. 11.15. The file "credit.dat" is opened for update (reading and writing) using "rb+" mode.

```c
1   // Fig. 11.15: fig11_15.c
2   // Bank-account program reads a random-access file sequentially,
3   // updates data already written to the file, creates new data to
4   // be placed in the file, and deletes data previously in the file.
5   #include <stdio.h>
6
7   // clientData structure definition
8   struct clientData {
9      unsigned int acctNum; // account number
10     char lastName[ 15 ]; // account last name
11     char firstName[ 10 ]; // account first name
12     double balance; // account balance
13  }; // end structure clientData
14
```

Fig. 11.15 | Bank-account program. (Part 1 of 6.)

```
15    // prototypes
16    unsigned int enterChoice( void );
17    void textFile( FILE *readPtr );
18    void updateRecord( FILE *fPtr );
19    void newRecord( FILE *fPtr );
20    void deleteRecord( FILE *fPtr );
21
22    int main( void )
23    {
24       FILE *cfPtr; // credit.dat file pointer
25       unsigned int choice; // user's choice
26
27       // fopen opens the file; exits if file cannot be opened
28       if ( ( cfPtr = fopen( "credit.dat", "rb+" ) ) == NULL ) {
29          puts( "File could not be opened." );
30       } // end if
31       else {
32          // enable user to specify action
33          while ( ( choice = enterChoice() ) != 5 ) {
34             switch ( choice ) {
35                // create text file from record file
36                case 1:
37                   textFile( cfPtr );
38                   break;
39                // update record
40                case 2:
41                   updateRecord( cfPtr );
42                   break;
43                // create record
44                case 3:
45                   newRecord( cfPtr );
46                   break;
47                // delete existing record
48                case 4:
49                   deleteRecord( cfPtr );
50                   break;
51                // display message if user does not select valid choice
52                default:
53                   puts( "Incorrect choice" );
54                   break;
55             } // end switch
56          } // end while
57
58          fclose( cfPtr ); // fclose closes the file
59       } // end else
60    } // end main
61
62    // create formatted text file for printing
63    void textFile( FILE *readPtr )
64    {
65       FILE *writePtr; // accounts.txt file pointer
66       int result; // used to test whether fread read any bytes
67
```

Fig. 11.15 | Bank-account program. (Part 2 of 6.)

```
68      // create clientData with default information
69      struct clientData client = { 0, "", "", 0.0 };
70
71      // fopen opens the file; exits if file cannot be opened
72      if ( ( writePtr = fopen( "accounts.txt", "w" ) ) == NULL ) {
73         puts( "File could not be opened." );
74      } // end if
75      else {
76         rewind( readPtr ); // sets pointer to beginning of file
77         fprintf( writePtr, "%-6s%-16s%-11s%10s\n",
78            "Acct", "Last Name", "First Name","Balance" );
79
80         // copy all records from random-access file into text file
81         while ( !feof( readPtr ) ) {
82            result = fread(&client, sizeof( struct clientData ), 1, readPtr);
83
84            // write single record to text file
85            if ( result != 0 && client.acctNum != 0 ) {
86               fprintf( writePtr, "%-6d%-16s%-11s%10.2f\n",
87                  client.acctNum, client.lastName,
88                  client.firstName, client.balance );
89            } // end if
90         } // end while
91
92         fclose( writePtr ); // fclose closes the file
93      } // end else
94   } // end function textFile
95
96   // update balance in record
97   void updateRecord( FILE *fPtr )
98   {
99      unsigned int account; // account number
100     double transaction; // transaction amount
101
102     // create clientData with no information
103     struct clientData client = { 0, "", "", 0.0 };
104
105     // obtain number of account to update
106     printf( "%s", "Enter account to update ( 1 - 100 ): " );
107     scanf( "%d", &account );
108
109     // move file pointer to correct record in file
110     fseek( fPtr, ( account - 1 ) * sizeof( struct clientData ),
111        SEEK_SET );
112
113     // read record from file
114     fread( &client, sizeof( struct clientData ), 1, fPtr );
115
116     // display error if account does not exist
117     if ( client.acctNum == 0 ) {
118        printf( "Account #%d has no information.\n", account );
119     } // end if
```

Fig. 11.15 | Bank-account program. (Part 3 of 6.)

```
120      else { // update record
121         printf( "%-6d%-16s%-11s%10.2f\n\n",
122            client.acctNum, client.lastName,
123            client.firstName, client.balance );
124
125         // request transaction amount from user
126         printf( "%s", "Enter charge ( + ) or payment ( - ): " );
127         scanf( "%lf", &transaction );
128         client.balance += transaction; // update record balance
129
130         printf( "%-6d%-16s%-11s%10.2f\n",
131            client.acctNum, client.lastName,
132            client.firstName, client.balance );
133
134         // move file pointer to correct record in file
135         fseek( fPtr, ( account - 1 ) * sizeof( struct clientData ),
136            SEEK_SET );
137
138         // write updated record over old record in file
139         fwrite( &client, sizeof( struct clientData ), 1, fPtr );
140      } // end else
141   } // end function updateRecord
142
143   // delete an existing record
144   void deleteRecord( FILE *fPtr )
145   {
146      struct clientData client; // stores record read from file
147      struct clientData blankClient = { 0, "", "", 0 }; // blank client
148
149      unsigned int accountNum; // account number
150
151      // obtain number of account to delete
152      printf( "%s", "Enter account number to delete ( 1 - 100 ): " );
153      scanf( "%d", &accountNum );
154
155      // move file pointer to correct record in file
156      fseek( fPtr, ( accountNum - 1 ) * sizeof( struct clientData ),
157         SEEK_SET );
158
159      // read record from file
160      fread( &client, sizeof( struct clientData ), 1, fPtr );
161
162      // display error if record does not exist
163      if ( client.acctNum == 0 ) {
164         printf( "Account %d does not exist.\n", accountNum );
165      } // end if
166      else { // delete record
167         // move file pointer to correct record in file
168         fseek( fPtr, ( accountNum - 1 ) * sizeof( struct clientData ),
169            SEEK_SET );
170
```

Fig. 11.15 | Bank-account program. (Part 4 of 6.)

```
171          // replace existing record with blank record
172          fwrite( &blankClient,
173             sizeof( struct clientData ), 1, fPtr );
174    } // end else
175  } // end function deleteRecord
176
177  // create and insert record
178  void newRecord( FILE *fPtr )
179  {
180     // create clientData with default information
181     struct clientData client = { 0, "", "", 0.0 };
182
183     unsigned int accountNum; // account number
184
185     // obtain number of account to create
186     printf( "%s", "Enter new account number ( 1 - 100 ): " );
187     scanf( "%d", &accountNum );
188
189     // move file pointer to correct record in file
190     fseek( fPtr, ( accountNum - 1 ) * sizeof( struct clientData ),
191        SEEK_SET );
192
193     // read record from file
194     fread( &client, sizeof( struct clientData ), 1, fPtr );
195
196     // display error if account already exists
197     if ( client.acctNum != 0 ) {
198        printf( "Account #%d already contains information.\n",
199           client.acctNum );
200     } // end if
201     else { // create record
202        // user enters last name, first name and balance
203        printf( "%s", "Enter lastname, firstname, balance\n? " );
204        scanf( "%14s%9s%lf", &client.lastName, &client.firstName,
205           &client.balance );
206
207        client.acctNum = accountNum;
208
209        // move file pointer to correct record in file
210        fseek( fPtr, ( client.acctNum - 1 ) *
211           sizeof( struct clientData ), SEEK_SET );
212
213        // insert record in file
214        fwrite( &client,
215           sizeof( struct clientData ), 1, fPtr );
216     } // end else
217  } // end function newRecord
218
219  // enable user to input menu choice
220  unsigned int enterChoice( void )
221  {
222     unsigned int menuChoice; // variable to store user's choice
223
```

Fig. 11.15 | Bank-account program. (Part 5 of 6.)

```
224     // display available options
225     printf( "%s", "\nEnter your choice\n"
226        "1 - store a formatted text file of accounts called\n"
227        "    \"accounts.txt\" for printing\n"
228        "2 - update an account\n"
229        "3 - add a new account\n"
230        "4 - delete an account\n"
231        "5 - end program\n? " );
232
233     scanf( "%u", &menuChoice ); // receive choice from user
234     return menuChoice;
235 } // end function enterChoice
```

Fig. 11.15 | Bank-account program. (Part 6 of 6.)

11.10 Secure C Programming

fprintf_s and fscanf_s

The examples in Sections 11.3–11.4 used functions fprintf and fscanf to write text to and read text from files, respectively. The new standard's Annex K provides more secure versions of these functions named fprintf_s and fscanf_s that are identical to the printf_s and scanf_s functions we've previously introduced, except that you also specify a FILE pointer argument indicating the file to manipulate. If your C compiler's standard libraries include these functions, you should use them instead of fprintf and fscanf.

Chapter 9 of the CERT Secure C Coding Standard

Chapter 9 of the *CERT Secure C Coding Standard* is dedicated to input/output recommendations and rules—many apply to file processing in general and several of these apply to the file-processing functions presented in this chapter. For more information on each, visit www.securecoding.cert.org.

- FIO03-C: When opening a file for writing using the non-exclusive file-open modes (Fig. 11.5), if the file exists, function fopen opens it and truncates its contents, providing no indication of whether the file existed before the fopen call. To ensure that an existing file is *not* opened and truncated, you can use C11's new *exclusive mode* (discussed in Section 11.3), which allows fopen to open the file *only* if it does *not* already exist.

- FIO04-C: In industrial-strength code, you should always check the return values of file-processing functions that return error indicators to ensure that the functions performed their tasks correctly.

- FIO07-C. Function rewind does not return a value, so you cannot test whether the operation was successful. It's recommended instead that you use function fseek, because it returns a non-zero value if it fails.

- FIO09-C. We demonstrated both text files and binary files in this chapter. Due to differences in binary data representations across platforms, files written in binary format often are *not* portable. For more portable file representations, consider using text files or a function library that can handle the differences in binary file representations across platforms.

- FIO14-C. Some library functions do not operate identically on text files and binary files. In particular, function `fseek` is *not* guaranteed to work correctly with binary files if you seek from SEEK_END, so SEEK_SET should be used.

- FIO42-C. On many platforms, you can have only a limited number of files open at once. For this reason, you should always close a file as soon as it's no longer needed by your program.

Summary

Section 11.1 Introduction
- Files are used for permanent retention of large amounts of data.
- Computers store files on secondary storage devices, especially disk storage devices.

Section 11.2 Files and Streams
- C views each file as a sequential stream of bytes. When a file is opened, a stream is associated with the file.
- Three files and their associated streams are automatically opened when program execution begins—the standard input, the standard output and the standard error.
- Streams provide communication channels between files and programs.
- The standard input stream enables a program to read data from the keyboard, and the standard output stream enables a program to print data on the screen.
- Opening a file returns a pointer to a FILE structure (defined in <stdio.h>) that contains information used to process the file. This structure includes a file descriptor, i.e., an index into an operating-system array called the open file table. Each array element contains a file control block (FCB) that the operating system uses to administer a particular file.
- The standard input, standard output and standard error are manipulated using the file pointers `stdin`, `stdout` and `stderr`.
- Function `fgetc` reads one character from a file. It receives as an argument a FILE pointer for the file from which a character will be read.
- Function `fputc` writes one character to a file. It receives as arguments a character to be written and a pointer for the file to which the character will be written.
- The `fgets` and `fputs` functions read a line from a file or write a line to a file, respectively.

Section 11.3 Creating a Sequential-Access File
- C imposes no structure on a file. You must provide a file structure to meet the requirements of a particular application.
- A C program administers each file with a separate FILE structure.
- Each open file must have a separately declared pointer of type FILE that's used to refer to the file.
- Function `fopen` takes as arguments a filename and a file open mode and returns a pointer to the FILE structure for the file opened.
- The file open mode "w" indicates that the file is to be opened for writing. If the file does not exist, `fopen` creates it. If the file exists, the contents are discarded without warning.
- Function `fopen` returns NULL if it's unable to open a file.

- Function `feof` receives a pointer to a `FILE` and returns a nonzero (true) value when the end-of-file indicator has been set; otherwise, the function returns zero.
- Function `fprintf` is equivalent to `printf` except that `fprintf` also receives as an argument a file pointer for the file to which the data will be written.
- Function `fclose` receives a file pointer as an argument and closes the specified file.
- When a file is opened, the file control block (FCB) for the file is copied into memory. The FCB is used by the operating system to administer the file.
- To create a file, or to discard the file's contents before writing data, open the file for writing (`"w"`).
- To read an existing file, open it for reading (`"r"`).
- To add records to the end of an existing file, open the file for appending (`"a"`).
- To open a file so that it may be written to and read from, open the file for updating in one of the three update modes—`"r+"`, `"w+"` or `"a+"`. Mode `"r+"` opens a file for reading and writing. Mode `"w+"` creates a file for reading and writing. If the file already exists, it's opened and its contents are discarded. Mode `"a+"` opens a file for reading and writing—all writing is done at the end of the file. If the file does not exist, it's created.
- Each file open mode has a corresponding binary mode (containing the letter b) for manipulating binary files.
- C11 also supports exlusive write mode by appending x to the w, w+, wb and wb+ modes.

Section 11.4 Reading Data from a Sequential-Access File
- Function `fscanf` is equivalent to function `scanf` except `fscanf` receives as an argument a file pointer for the file from which the data is read.
- To retrieve data sequentially from a file, a program normally starts reading from the beginning of the file and reads all data consecutively until the desired data is found.
- Function `rewind` causes a program's file position pointer to be repositioned to the beginning of the file (i.e., byte 0) pointed to its argument.
- The file position pointer is an integer value that specifies the byte location in the file at which the next read or write is to occur. This is sometimes referred to as the file offset. The file position pointer is a member of the `FILE` structure associated with each file.
- The data in a sequential file typically cannot be modified without the risk of destroying other data in the file.

Section 11.5 Random-Access Files
- Individual records of a random-access file are normally fixed in length and may be accessed directly (and thus quickly) without searching through other records.
- Because every record in a random-access file normally has the same length, the exact location of a record relative to the beginning of the file can be calculated as a function of the record key.
- Fixed-length records enable data to be inserted in a random-access file without destroying other data. Data stored previously can also be updated or deleted without rewriting the entire file.

Section 11.6 Creating a Random-Access File
- Function `fwrite` transfers a specified number of bytes beginning at a specified location in memory to a file. The data is written beginning at the file position pointer's location.
- Function `fread` transfers a specified number of bytes from the location in the file specified by the file position pointer to an area in memory beginning with a specified address.

- Functions fwrite and fread are capable of reading and writing arrays of data from and to disk. The third argument of both fread and fwrite is the number of elements to process in the array.

- File-processing programs normally write one struct at a time.

- Function fwrite writes a block (specific number of bytes) of data to a file.

- To write several array elements, supply in the call to fwrite a pointer to an array as the first argument and the number of elements to be written as the third argument.

Section 11.7 Writing Data Randomly to a Random-Access File

- Function fseek sets the file position pointer for a given file to a specific position in the file. Its second argument indicates the number of bytes to seek and its third argument indicates the location from which to seek. The third argument can have one of three values—SEEK_SET, SEEK_CUR or SEEK_END (all defined in <stdio.h>). SEEK_SET indicates that the seek starts at the beginning of the file; SEEK_CUR indicates that the seek starts at the current location in the file; and SEEK_END indicates that the seek starts at the end of the file.

- Industrial-strength programs should determine whether functions such as fscanf, fseek and fwrite operate correctly by checking their return values.

- Function fscanf returns the number of fields successfully read or the value EOF if a problem occurs while reading data.

- Function fseek returns a nonzero value if the seek operation cannot be performed.

- Function fwrite returns the number of items it successfully output. If this number is less than the third argument in the function call, then a write error occurred.

Section 11.8 Reading Data from a Random-Access File

- Function fread reads a specified number of bytes from a file into memory.

- Function fread can be used to read several fixed-size array elements by providing a pointer to the array in which the elements will be stored and by indicating the number of elements to be read.

- Function fread returns the number of items it successfully input. If this number is less than the third argument in the function call, then a read error occurred.

Terminology

stdout (the standard output stream) 470   transaction-processing system 480
stream 470

Self-Review Exercises

11.1   Fill in the blanks in each of the following (see Section 1.4, Data Hierarchy):
   a) Ultimately, all data items processed by a computer are reduced to combinations of
       _____ and _____.
   b) The smallest data item a computer can process is called a(n) _____.
   c) A(n) _____ is a group of related records.
   d) Digits, letters and special symbols are referred to as _____.
   e) A group of related files is called a _____.
   f) Function _____ closes a file.
   g) The _____ function reads data from a file in a manner similar to how scanf reads
       from stdin.
   h) Function _____ reads a character from a specified file.
   i) Function _____ reads a line from a specified file.
   j) Function _____ opens a file.
   k) Function _____ is normally used when reading data from a file in random-access ap-
       plications.
   l) Function _____ repositions the file position pointer to a specific location in the file.

11.2   State which of the following are *true* and which are *false*. If *false*, explain why.
   a) Function fscanf cannot be used to read data from the standard input.
   b) You must explicitly use fopen to open the standard input, standard output and standard
       error streams.
   c) A program must explicitly call function fclose to close a file.
   d) If the file position pointer points to a location in a sequential file other than the begin-
       ning of the file, the file must be closed and reopened to read from the beginning of the
       file.
   e) Function fprintf can write to the standard output.
   f) Data in sequential-access files is always updated without overwriting other data.
   g) It's not necessary to search through all the records in a random-access file to find a spe-
       cific record.
   h) Records in random-access files are not of uniform length.
   i) Function fseek may seek only relative to the beginning of a file.

11.3   Write a single statement to accomplish each of the following. Assume that each of these
statements applies to the same program.
   a) Write a statement that opens the file "oldmast.dat" for reading and assigns the re-
       turned file pointer to ofPtr.
   b) Write a statement that opens the file "trans.dat" for reading and assigns the returned
       file pointer to tfPtr.
   c) Write a statement that opens the file "newmast.dat" for writing (and creation) and as-
       signs the returned file pointer to nfPtr.
   d) Write a statement that reads a record from the file "oldmast.dat". The record consists
       of integer accountNum, string name and floating-point currentBalance.
   e) Write a statement that reads a record from the file "trans.dat". The record consists of
       the integer accountNum and floating-point dollarAmount.
   f) Write statement that writes a record to the file "newmast.dat". The record consists of
       the integer accountNum, string name and floating-point currentBalance.

11.4 Find the error in each of the following program segments and explain how to correct it.

a) The file referred to by fPtr ("payables.dat") has not been opened.
```
printf( fPtr, "%d%s%d\n", account, company, amount );
```

b) `open( "receive.dat", "r+" );`

c) The following statement should read a record from the file "payables.dat". File pointer payPtr refers to this file, and file pointer recPtr refers to the file "receive.dat":
```
scanf( recPtr, "%d%s%d\n", &account, company, &amount );
```

d) The file "tools.dat" should be opened to add data to the file without discarding the current data.
```
if ( ( tfPtr = fopen( "tools.dat", "w" ) ) != NULL )
```

e) The file "courses.dat" should be opened for appending without modifying the current contents of the file.
```
if ( ( cfPtr = fopen( "courses.dat", "w+" ) ) != NULL )
```

Answers to Self-Review Exercises

11.1 a) 1s, 0s. b) bit. c) file. d) characters. e) database. f) fclose. g) fscanf. h) fgetc. i) fgets. j) fopen. k) fread. l) fseek.

11.2

a) False. Function fscanf can be used to read from the standard input by including the pointer to the standard input stream, stdin, in the call to fscanf.

b) False. These three streams are opened automatically by C when program execution begins.

c) False. The files will be closed when program execution terminates, but all files should be explicitly closed with fclose.

d) False. Function rewind can be used to reposition the file position pointer to the beginning of the file.

e) True.

f) False. In most cases, sequential file records are not of uniform length. Therefore, it's possible that updating a record will cause other data to be overwritten.

g) True.

h) False. Records in a random-access file are normally of uniform length.

i) False. It's possible to seek from the beginning of the file, from the end of the file and from the current location in the file.

11.3

a) `ofPtr = fopen( "oldmast.dat", "r" );`
b) `tfPtr = fopen( "trans.dat", "r" );`
c) `nfPtr = fopen( "newmast.dat", "w" );`
d) `fscanf( ofPtr, "%d%s%f", &accountNum, name, &currentBalance );`
e) `fscanf( tfPtr, "%d%f", &accountNum, &dollarAmount );`
f) `fprintf( nfPtr, "%d %s %.2f", accountNum, name, currentBalance );`

11.4

a) Error: The file "payables.dat" has not been opened before the reference to its file pointer.
Correction: Use fopen to open "payables.dat" for writing, appending or updating.

b) Error: Function open is not a Standard C function.
Correction: Use function fopen.

c) Error: The function scanf should be fscanf. Function fscanf uses the incorrect file pointer to refer to file "payables.dat".
Correction: Use file pointer payPtr to refer to "payables.dat".

d) Error: The contents of the file are discarded because the file is opened for writing ("w").
   Correction: To add data to the file, either open the file for updating ("r+") or open the file for appending ("a").

e) Error: File "courses.dat" is opened for updating in "w+" mode, which discards the current contents of the file.
   Correction: Open the file in "a" mode.

Exercises

11.5 Fill in the blanks in each of the following:

a) Computers store large amounts of data on secondary storage devices as _____.

b) A(n) _____ is composed of several fields.

c) To facilitate the retrieval of specific records from a file, one field in each record is chosen as a(n) _____.

d) A group of related characters that conveys meaning is called a(n) _____.

e) The file pointers for the three streams that are opened automatically when program execution begins are named _____, _____ and _____.

f) Function _____ writes a character to a specified file.

g) Function _____ writes a line to a specified file.

h) Function _____ is generally used to write data to a random-access file.

i) Function _____ repositions the file position pointer to the beginning of the file.

11.6 State which of the following are *true* and which are *false*. If *false*, explain why.

a) The impressive functions performed by computers essentially involve the manipulation of zeros and ones.

b) People prefer to manipulate bits instead of characters and fields because bits are more compact.

c) People specify programs and data items as characters; computers then manipulate and process these characters as groups of zeros and ones.

d) A person's zip code is an example of a numeric field.

e) Data items processed by a computer form a data hierarchy in which data items become larger and more complex as we progress from fields to characters to bits, and so on.

f) A record key identifies a record as belonging to a particular field.

g) Most companies store their information in a single file to facilitate computer processing.

h) Files are always referred to by name in C programs.

i) When a program creates a file, the file is automatically retained by the computer for future reference.

11.7 *(Creating Data for a File-Matching Program)* Write a simple program to create some test data for checking out the program of Exercise 11.8. Use the following sample account data:

Master File: Account number	Name	Balance
100	Alan Jones	348.17
300	Mary Smith	27.19
500	Sam Sharp	0.00
700	Suzy Green	-14.22

Transaction File: Account number	Dollar amount
100	27.14
300	62.11
400	100.56
900	82.17

11.8   *(File Matching)* Exercise 11.3 asked the reader to write a series of single statements. Actually, these statements form the core of an important type of file-processing program, namely, a file-matching program. In commercial data processing, it's common to have several files in each system. In an accounts receivable system, for example, there's generally a master file containing detailed information about each customer such as the customer's name, address, telephone number, outstanding balance, credit limit, discount terms, contract arrangements and possibly a condensed history of recent purchases and cash payments.

As transactions occur (i.e., sales are made and cash payments arrive in the mail), they're entered into a file. At the end of each business period (i.e., a month for some companies, a week for others and a day in some cases) the file of transactions (called "trans.dat" in Exercise 11.3) is applied to the master file (called "oldmast.dat" in Exercise 11.3), thus updating each account's record of purchases and payments. After each of these updates runs, the master file is rewritten as a new file ("newmast.dat"), which is then used at the end of the next business period to begin the updating process again.

File-matching programs must deal with certain problems that do not exist in single-file programs. For example, a match does not always occur. A customer on the master file might not have made any purchases or cash payments in the current business period, and therefore no record for this customer will appear on the transaction file. Similarly, a customer who did make some purchases or cash payments might have just moved to this community, and the company may not have had a chance to create a master record for this customer.

Use the statements written in Exercise 11.3 as the basis for a complete file-matching accounts receivable program. Use the account number on each file as the record key for matching purposes. Assume that each file is a sequential file with records stored in increasing account-number order.

When a match occurs (i.e., records with the same account number appear on both the master file and the transaction file), add the dollar amount on the transaction file to the current balance on the master file and write the "newmast.dat" record. (Assume that purchases are indicated by positive amounts on the transaction file, and that payments are indicated by negative amounts.) When there's a master record for a particular account but no corresponding transaction record, merely write the master record to "newmast.dat". When there's a transaction record but no corresponding master record, print the message "Unmatched transaction record for account number ..." (fill in the account number from the transaction record).

11.9   Run the program of Exercise 11.8 using the files of test data created in Exercise 11.7. Check the results carefully.

11.10   *(File Matching with Multiple Transactions)* It's possible (actually common) to have several transaction records with the same record key. This occurs because a particular customer might make several purchases and cash payments during a business period. Rewrite your accounts receivable file-matching program of Exercise 11.8 to provide for the possibility of handling several transaction records with the same record key. Modify the test data of Exercise 11.7 to include the following additional transaction records:

Account number	Dollar amount
300	83.89
700	80.78
700	1.53

11.11 Write statements that accomplish each of the following. Assume that the structure

```
struct person {
    char lastName[ 15 ];
    char firstName[ 15 ];
    char age[ 4 ];
};
```

has been defined and that the file is already open for writing.
   a) Initialize the file "nameage.dat" so that there are 100 records with lastName = "unassigned", firstname = "" and age = "0".
   b) Input 10 last names, first names and ages, and write them to the file.
   c) Update a record; if there's no information in the record, tell the user "No info".
   d) Delete a record that has information by reinitializing that particular record.

11.12 *(Outputting ASCII Values to a File)* Write a program that gives an option to the user: either to print ASCII values of lowercase characters or to print ASCII values of uppercase characters. Write the results to the file "values.dat" so you may print the results later. The format for the results in the file should be as follows:

Character	ASCII value
A	65
B	66
C	67
D	68
E	69
F	70
G	71
.	.
.	.
.	.
Z	90

11.13 *(Telephone-Number Word Generator)* Standard telephone keypads contain the digits 0 through 9. The numbers 2 through 9 each have three letters associated with them, as is indicated by the following table:

Digit	Letter	Digit	Letter
2	A B C	6	M N O
3	D E F	7	P R S
4	G H I	8	T U V
5	J K L	9	W X Y

Many people find it difficult to memorize phone numbers, so they use the correspondence between digits and letters to develop seven-letter words that correspond to their phone numbers. For example, a person whose telephone number is 686-2377 might use the correspondence indicated in the above table to develop the seven-letter word "NUMBERS."

Businesses frequently attempt to get telephone numbers that are easy for their clients to remember. If a business can advertise a simple word for its customers to dial, then, no doubt, the business will receive a few more calls.

Each seven-letter word corresponds to exactly one seven-digit telephone number. The restaurant wishing to increase its take-home business could surely do so with the number 825-3688 (i.e., "TAKEOUT").

Each seven-digit phone number corresponds to many separate seven-letter words. Unfortunately, most of these represent unrecognizable juxtapositions of letters. It's possible, however, that the owner of a barber shop would be pleased to know that the shop's telephone number, 424-7288, corresponds to "HAIRCUT." The owner of a liquor store would, no doubt, be delighted to find that the store's telephone number, 233-7226, corresponds to "BEERCAN." A veterinarian with the phone number 738-2273 would be pleased to know that the number corresponds to the letters "PETCARE."

Write a C program that, given a seven-digit number, writes to a file every possible seven-letter word corresponding to that number. There are 2187 (3 to the seventh power) such words. Avoid phone numbers with the digits 0 and 1.

11.14 *(Project: Telephone-Number Word Generator Modification)* If you have a computerized dictionary available, modify the program you wrote in Exercise 11.13 to look up the words in the dictionary. Some seven-letter combinations created by this program consist of two or more words (the phone number 843-2677 produces "THEBOSS").

11.15 Modify the program of Exercise 11.12 to use the function `fputs` rather than `fprintf`. The program should give the user the option to write to the standard output or to write to a specified file. If the user chooses the second option, have the user enter the filename for the output file.

11.16 *(Outputting Character Count to a File)* Write a program that reads a given file by using `fgetc` and counts the occurrence of each character in the file. Lowercase and uppercase characters are considered to be same. Write the results to the file "`count.dat`" so you may print the results later. The format for the results in the file should be as follows:

```
Character          Count
a                  12
b                  18
c                  9
d                  21
e                  28
f                  4
g                  7
.                  .
.                  .
.                  .
z                  0
```

11.17 Modify the program of Exercise 11.16 to give the user the option to write to the standard output or to write to a specified file. If the user chooses the second option, have the user enter the filename for the output file.

Making a Difference

11.18 *(Project: Phishing Scanner)* Phishing is a form of identity theft in which, in an e-mail, a sender posing as a trustworthy source attempts to acquire private information, such as your user names, passwords, credit-card numbers and social security number. Phishing e-mails claiming to be from popular banks, credit-card companies, auction sites, social networks and online payment services may look quite legitimate. These fraudulent messages often provide links to spoofed (fake) websites where you're asked to enter sensitive information.

Visit Security Extra (www.securityextra.com/), www.snopes.com and other websites to find lists of the top phishing scams. Also check out the Anti-Phishing Working Group (www.antiphishing.org/), and the FBI's Cyber Investigations website (www.fbi.gov/cyberinvest/cyberhome.htm), where you'll find information about the latest scams and how to protect yourself.

Create a list of 30 words, phrases and company names commonly found in phishing messages. Assign a point value to each based on your estimate of its likeliness to be in a phishing message (e.g., one point if it's somewhat likely, two points if moderately likely, or three points if highly likely). Write a program that scans a file of text for these terms and phrases. For each occurrence of a keyword or phrase within the text file, add the assigned point value to the total points for that word or phrase. For each keyword or phrase found, output one line with the word or phrase, the number of occurrences and the point total. Then show the point total for the entire message. Does your program assign a high point total to some actual phishing e-mails you've received? Does it assign a high point total to some legitimate e-mails you've received?

12

C Data Structures

*'Will you walk a little faster?'
said a whiting to a snail, 'There's
a porpoise close behind us, and
he's treading on my tail.'*
—Lewis Carroll

There is always room at the top.
—Daniel Webster

Push on — keep moving.
—Thomas Morton

*I think that I shall never see
A poem lovely as a tree.*
—Joyce Kilmer

Objectives

In this chapter, you'll:

- Allocate and free memory dynamically for data objects.

- Form linked data structures using pointers, self-referential structures and recursion.

- Create and manipulate linked lists, queues, stacks and binary trees.

- Learn important applications of linked data structures.

12.1 Introduction

We've studied fixed-size data structures such as single-subscripted arrays, double-subscripted arrays and structs. This chapter introduces **dynamic data structures** that can grow and shrink at execution time.

- **Linked lists** are collections of data items "lined up in a row"—insertions and deletions are made *anywhere* in a linked list.

- **Stacks** are important in compilers and operating systems—insertions and deletions are made *only at one end* of a stack—its **top**.

- **Queues** represent waiting lines; insertions are made *only at the back* (also referred to as the **tail**) of a queue and deletions are made *only from the front* (also referred to as the **head**) of a queue.

- **Binary trees** facilitate high-speed searching and sorting of data, efficient elimination of duplicate data items, representing file-system directories and compiling expressions into machine language.

Each of these data structures has many other interesting applications.

We'll discuss each of the major types of data structures and implement programs that create and manipulate them. In the next part of the book—the introduction to C++ and object-oriented programming—we'll study data abstraction. This technique will enable us to build these data structures in a dramatically different manner designed for producing software that's easier to maintain and reuse.

Optional Project: Building Your Own Compiler

We hope that you'll attempt the major project described in the special section entitled Building Your Own Compiler. You have been using a compiler to translate your C programs to machine language so that you could execute your programs on your computer. In this project, you'll actually build your own compiler. It will read a file of statements written in a simple, yet powerful, high-level language similar to early versions of the popular language BASIC. Your compiler will translate these statements into a file of Simpletron Machine Language (SML) instructions. SML is the language you learned in the Chapter 7 special section, Building Your Own Computer. Your Simpletron Simulator program will then execute the

SML program produced by your compiler! This project will give you a wonderful opportunity to exercise most of what you've learned in this course. The special section carefully walks you through the specifications of the high-level language and describes the algorithms you'll need to convert each type of high-level language statement into machine-language instructions. If you enjoy being challenged, you might attempt the many enhancements to both the compiler and the Simpletron Simulator suggested in the exercises.

12.2 Self-Referential Structures

Recall that a *self-referential structure* contains a pointer member that points to a structure of the *same* structure type. For example, the definition

```
struct node {
    int data;
    struct node *nextPtr;
}; // end struct node
```

defines a type, `struct node`. A structure of type `struct node` has two members—integer member `data` and pointer member `nextPtr`. Member `nextPtr` points to a structure of type `struct node`—a structure of the *same* type as the one being declared here, hence the term *self-referential structure*. Member `nextPtr` is referred to as a **link**—i.e., it can be used to "tie" a structure of type `struct node` to another structure of the same type. Self-referential structures can be *linked* together to form useful data structures such as lists, queues, stacks and trees. Figure 12.1 illustrates two self-referential structure objects linked together to form a list. A slash—representing a NULL pointer—is placed in the link member of the second self-referential structure to indicate that the link does not point to another structure. [*Note:* The slash is only for illustration purposes; it does not correspond to the backslash character in C.] A NULL pointer normally indicates the *end* of a data structure just as the null character indicates the end of a string.

Common Programming Error 12.1
Not setting the link in the last node of a list to NULL can lead to runtime errors.

Fig. 12.1 | Self-referential structures linked together.

12.3 Dynamic Memory Allocation

Creating and maintaining dynamic data structures requires **dynamic memory allocation**—the ability for a program to *obtain more memory space at execution time* to hold new nodes, and to *release space no longer needed.*

Functions `malloc` and `free`, and operator `sizeof`, are essential to dynamic memory allocation. Function `malloc` takes as an argument the number of bytes to be allocated and returns a pointer of type `void *` (pointer to void) to the allocated memory. As you recall, a `void *` pointer may be assigned to a variable of *any* pointer type. Function `malloc` is normally used with the `sizeof` operator. For example, the statement

```
newPtr = malloc( sizeof( struct node ) );
```

evaluates `sizeof(struct node)` to determine the size in bytes of a structure of type `struct node`, *allocates a new area in memory* of that number of bytes and stores a pointer to the allocated memory in variable `newPtr`. The allocated memory is *not* initialized. If no memory is available, `malloc` returns `NULL`.

Function `free` *deallocates* memory—i.e., the memory is *returned* to the system so that it can be reallocated in the future. To *free* memory dynamically allocated by the preceding `malloc` call, use the statement

```
free( newPtr );
```

C also provides functions `calloc` and `realloc` for creating and modifying *dynamic arrays*. These functions are discussed in Section 14.9. The sections that follow discuss lists, stacks, queues and trees, each of which is created and maintained with dynamic memory allocation and self-referential structures.

Portability Tip 12.1

A structure's size is not necessarily the sum of the sizes of its members. This is so because of various machine-dependent boundary alignment requirements (see Chapter 10).

Error-Prevention Tip 12.1

When using `malloc`, test for a `NULL` pointer return value, which indicates that the memory was not allocated.

Common Programming Error 12.2

Not returning dynamically allocated memory when it's no longer needed can cause the system to run out of memory prematurely. This is sometimes called a "memory leak."

Error-Prevention Tip 12.2

When memory that was dynamically allocated is no longer needed, use `free` to return the memory to the system immediately. Then set the pointer to `NULL` to eliminate the possibility that the program could refer to memory that's been reclaimed and which may have already been allocated for another purpose.

Common Programming Error 12.3

Freeing memory not allocated dynamically with `malloc` is an error.

Common Programming Error 12.4

Referring to memory that has been freed is an error that typically results in the program crashing.

12.4 Linked Lists

A **linked list** is a linear collection of self-referential structures, called **nodes**, connected by pointer **links**—hence, the term "linked" list. A linked list is accessed via a pointer to the *first* node of the list. Subsequent nodes are accessed via the *link pointer member* stored in each node. By convention, the link pointer in the last node of a list is set to NULL to mark the *end* of the list. Data is stored in a linked list dynamically—each node is created as necessary. A node can contain data of *any* type including other structs. Stacks and queues are also linear data structures, and, as we'll see, are constrained versions of linked lists. Trees are *nonlinear* data structures.

Lists of data can be stored in arrays, but linked lists provide several advantages. A linked list is appropriate when the number of data elements to be represented in the data structure is *unpredictable*. Linked lists are dynamic, so the length of a list can increase or decrease at *execution time* as necessary. The size of an array created at compile time, however, cannot be altered. Arrays can become full. Linked lists become full only when the system has *insufficient memory* to satisfy dynamic storage allocation requests.

Performance Tip 12.1
An array can be declared to contain more elements than the number of data items expected, but this can waste memory. Linked lists can provide better memory utilization in these situations.

Linked lists can be maintained in sorted order by inserting each new element at the proper point in the list.

Performance Tip 12.2
Insertion and deletion in a sorted array can be time consuming—all the elements following the inserted or deleted element must be shifted appropriately.

Performance Tip 12.3
The elements of an array are stored contiguously in memory. This allows immediate access to any array element because the address of any element can be calculated directly based on its position relative to the beginning of the array. Linked lists do not afford such immediate access to their elements.

Linked-list nodes are normally *not* stored contiguously in memory. Logically, however, the nodes of a linked list *appear* to be contiguous. Figure 12.2 illustrates a linked list with several nodes.

Performance Tip 12.4
Using dynamic memory allocation (instead of arrays) for data structures that grow and shrink at execution time can save memory. Keep in mind, however, that the pointers take up space, and that dynamic memory allocation incurs the overhead of function calls.

Fig. 12.2 | Linked list graphical representation.

Figure 12.3 (output shown in Fig. 12.4) manipulates a list of characters. You can insert a character in the list in alphabetical order (function `insert`) or delete a character from the list (function `delete`). A detailed discussion of the program follows.

```c
 1   // Fig. 12.3: fig12_03.c
 2   // Inserting and deleting nodes in a list
 3   #include <stdio.h>
 4   #include <stdlib.h>
 5
 6   // self-referential structure
 7   struct listNode {
 8      char data; // each listNode contains a character
 9      struct listNode *nextPtr; // pointer to next node
10   }; // end structure listNode
11
12   typedef struct listNode ListNode; // synonym for struct listNode
13   typedef ListNode *ListNodePtr; // synonym for ListNode*
14
15   // prototypes
16   void insert( ListNodePtr *sPtr, char value );
17   char delete( ListNodePtr *sPtr, char value );
18   int isEmpty( ListNodePtr sPtr );
19   void printList( ListNodePtr currentPtr );
20   void instructions( void );
21
22   int main( void )
23   {
24      ListNodePtr startPtr = NULL; // initially there are no nodes
25      unsigned int choice; // user's choice
26      char item; // char entered by user
27
28      instructions(); // display the menu
29      printf( "%s", "? " );
30      scanf( "%u", &choice );
31
32      // loop while user does not choose 3
33      while ( choice != 3 ) {
34
35         switch ( choice ) {
36            case 1:
37               printf( "%s", "Enter a character: " );
38               scanf( "\n%c", &item );
39               insert( &startPtr, item ); // insert item in list
40               printList( startPtr );
41               break;
42            case 2: // delete an element
43               // if list is not empty
44               if ( !isEmpty( startPtr ) ) {
45                  printf( "%s", "Enter character to be deleted: " );
46                  scanf( "\n%c", &item );
47
```

Fig. 12.3 | Inserting and deleting nodes in a list. (Part 1 of 4.)

```
48              // if character is found, remove it
49              if ( delete( &startPtr, item ) ) { // remove item
50                  printf( "%c deleted.\n", item );
51                  printList( startPtr );
52              } // end if
53              else {
54                  printf( "%c not found.\n\n", item );
55              } // end else
56          } // end if
57          else {
58              puts( "List is empty.\n" );
59          } // end else
60
61              break;
62          default:
63              puts( "Invalid choice.\n" );
64              instructions();
65              break;
66      } // end switch
67
68      printf( "%s", "? " );
69      scanf( "%u", &choice );
70  } // end while
71
72  puts( "End of run." );
73 } // end main
74
75 // display program instructions to user
76 void instructions( void )
77 {
78   puts( "Enter your choice:\n"
79       "   1 to insert an element into the list.\n"
80       "   2 to delete an element from the list.\n"
81       "   3 to end." );
82 } // end function instructions
83
84 // insert a new value into the list in sorted order
85 void insert( ListNodePtr *sPtr, char value )
86 {
87   ListNodePtr newPtr; // pointer to new node
88   ListNodePtr previousPtr; // pointer to previous node in list
89   ListNodePtr currentPtr; // pointer to current node in list
90
91   newPtr = malloc( sizeof( ListNode ) ); // create node
92
93   if ( newPtr != NULL ) { // is space available
94      newPtr->data = value; // place value in node
95      newPtr->nextPtr = NULL; // node does not link to another node
96
97      previousPtr = NULL;
98      currentPtr = *sPtr;
99
```

Fig. 12.3 | Inserting and deleting nodes in a list. (Part 2 of 4.)

```
100          // loop to find the correct location in the list
101          while ( currentPtr != NULL && value > currentPtr->data ) {
102             previousPtr = currentPtr; // walk to ...
103             currentPtr = currentPtr->nextPtr; // ... next node
104          } // end while
105
106          // insert new node at beginning of list
107          if ( previousPtr == NULL ) {
108             newPtr->nextPtr = *sPtr;
109             *sPtr = newPtr;
110          } // end if
111          else { // insert new node between previousPtr and currentPtr
112             previousPtr->nextPtr = newPtr;
113             newPtr->nextPtr = currentPtr;
114          } // end else
115       } // end if
116       else {
117          printf( "%c not inserted. No memory available.\n", value );
118       } // end else
119    } // end function insert
120
121    // delete a list element
122    char delete( ListNodePtr *sPtr, char value )
123    {
124       ListNodePtr previousPtr; // pointer to previous node in list
125       ListNodePtr currentPtr; // pointer to current node in list
126       ListNodePtr tempPtr; // temporary node pointer
127
128       // delete first node
129       if ( value == ( *sPtr )->data ) {
130          tempPtr = *sPtr; // hold onto node being removed
131          *sPtr = ( *sPtr )->nextPtr; // de-thread the node
132          free( tempPtr ); // free the de-threaded node
133          return value;
134       } // end if
135       else {
136          previousPtr = *sPtr;
137          currentPtr = ( *sPtr )->nextPtr;
138
139          // loop to find the correct location in the list
140          while ( currentPtr != NULL && currentPtr->data != value ) {
141             previousPtr = currentPtr; // walk to ...
142             currentPtr = currentPtr->nextPtr; // ... next node
143          } // end while
144
145          // delete node at currentPtr
146          if ( currentPtr != NULL ) {
147             tempPtr = currentPtr;
148             previousPtr->nextPtr = currentPtr->nextPtr;
149             free( tempPtr );
150             return value;
151          } // end if
152       } // end else
```

Fig. 12.3 | Inserting and deleting nodes in a list. (Part 3 of 4.)

```
153
154     return '\0';
155  } // end function delete
156
157  // return 1 if the list is empty, 0 otherwise
158  int isEmpty( ListNodePtr sPtr )
159  {
160     return sPtr == NULL;
161  } // end function isEmpty
162
163  // print the list
164  void printList( ListNodePtr currentPtr )
165  {
166     // if list is empty
167     if ( isEmpty( currentPtr ) ) {
168        puts( "List is empty.\n" );
169     } // end if
170     else {
171        puts( "The list is:" );
172
173        // while not the end of the list
174        while ( currentPtr != NULL ) {
175           printf( "%c --> ", currentPtr->data );
176           currentPtr = currentPtr->nextPtr;
177        } // end while
178
179        puts( "NULL\n" );
180     } // end else
181  } // end function printList
```

Fig. 12.3 | Inserting and deleting nodes in a list. (Part 4 of 4.)

```
Enter your choice:
   1 to insert an element into the list.
   2 to delete an element from the list.
   3 to end.
? 1
Enter a character: B
The list is:
B --> NULL

? 1
Enter a character: A

The list is:
A --> B --> NULL

? 1
Enter a character: C
The list is:
A --> B --> C --> NULL
```

Fig. 12.4 | Sample output for the program of Fig. 12.3. (Part 1 of 2.)

```
? 2
Enter character to be deleted: D
D not found.

? 2
Enter character to be deleted: B
B deleted.
The list is:
A --> C --> NULL

? 2
Enter character to be deleted: C
C deleted.
The list is:
A --> NULL

? 2
Enter character to be deleted: A
A deleted.
List is empty.

? 4
Invalid choice.

Enter your choice:
   1 to insert an element into the list.
   2 to delete an element from the list.
   3 to end.
? 3
End of run.
```

Fig. 12.4 | Sample output for the program of Fig. 12.3. (Part 2 of 2.)

The primary functions of linked lists are insert (lines 85–119) and delete (lines 122–155). Function isEmpty (lines 158–161) is called a **predicate function**—it does *not* alter the list in any way; rather it determines whether the list is empty (i.e., the pointer to the first node of the list is NULL). If the list is empty, 1 is returned; otherwise, 0 is returned. [*Note:* If you're using a compiler that's compliant with the C standard, you can use the _Bool type (Section 4.10) rather than int.] Function printList (lines 164–181) prints the list.

12.4.1 Function insert

Characters are inserted in the list in *alphabetical order*. Function insert (lines 85–119) receives the address of the list and a character to be inserted. The list's address is necessary when a value is to be inserted at the *start* of the list. Providing the address enables the list (i.e., the pointer to the first node of the list) to be *modified* via a call by reference. Because the list itself is a pointer (to its first element), passing its address creates a **pointer to a pointer** (i.e., **double indirection**). This is a complex notion and requires careful programming. The steps for inserting a character in the list are as follows (see Fig. 12.5):

1. *Create a node* by calling malloc, assigning to newPtr the address of the allocated memory (line 91), assigning the character to be inserted to newPtr->data (line 94), and assigning NULL to newPtr->nextPtr (line 95).

2. Initialize previousPtr to NULL (line 97) and currentPtr to *sPtr (line 98)—the pointer to the start of the list. Pointers previousPtr and currentPtr store the

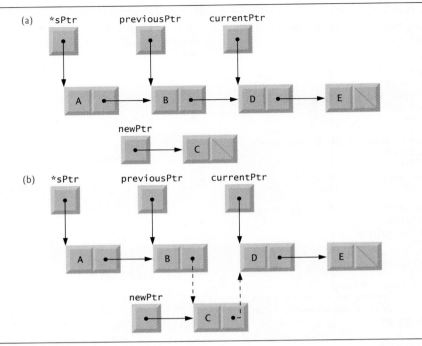

Fig. 12.5 | Inserting a node in order in a list.

locations of the node *preceding* the insertion point and the node *after* the insertion point.

3. While currentPtr is not NULL and the value to be inserted is greater than currentPtr->data (line 101), assign currentPtr to previousPtr (line 102) and advance currentPtr to the next node in the list (line 103). This locates the *insertion point* for the value.

4. If previousPtr is NULL (line 107), insert the new node as the *first* node in the list (lines 108–109). Assign *sPtr to newPtr->nextPtr (the *new node link* points to the *former first node*) and assign newPtr to *sPtr (*sPtr points to the *new node*). Otherwise, if previousPtr is not NULL, the new node is inserted in place (lines 112–113). Assign newPtr to previousPtr->nextPtr (the *previous* node points to the *new* node) and assign currentPtr to newPtr->nextPtr (the *new* node link points to the *current* node).

 Error-Prevention Tip 12.3

Assign NULL *to the link member of a new node. Pointers should be initialized before they're used.*

Figure 12.5 illustrates the insertion of a node containing the character 'C' into an ordered list. Part (a) of the figure shows the list and the new node just before the insertion. Part (b) of the figure shows the result of inserting the new node. The reassigned pointers are dotted arrows. For simplicity, we implemented function insert (and other similar functions in this chapter) with a void return type. It's possible that function malloc will *fail* to allocate the requested memory. In this case, it would be better for our insert function to return a status that indicates whether the operation was successful.

12.4.2 Function delete

Function delete (lines 122–155) receives the address of the pointer to the start of the list and a character to be deleted. The steps for deleting a character from the list are as follows (see Fig. 12.6):

1. If the character to be deleted matches the character in the *first* node of the list (line 129), assign *sPtr to tempPtr (tempPtr will be used to free the unneeded memory), assign (*sPtr)->nextPtr to *sPtr (*sPtr now points to the *second* node in the list), free the memory pointed to by tempPtr, and return the character that was deleted.

2. Otherwise, initialize previousPtr with *sPtr and initialize currentPtr with (*sPtr)->nextPtr (lines 136–137) to advance to the second node.

3. While currentPtr is not NULL and the value to be deleted is not equal to currentPtr->data (line 140), assign currentPtr to previousPtr (line 141) and assign currentPtr->nextPtr to currentPtr (line 142). This locates the character to be deleted if it's contained in the list.

4. If currentPtr is not NULL (line 146), assign currentPtr to tempPtr (line 147), assign currentPtr->nextPtr to previousPtr->nextPtr (line 148), *free* the node pointed to by tempPtr (line 149), and return the character that was deleted from the list (line 150). If currentPtr is NULL, return the null character ('\0') to signify that the character to be deleted was *not* found in the list (line 154).

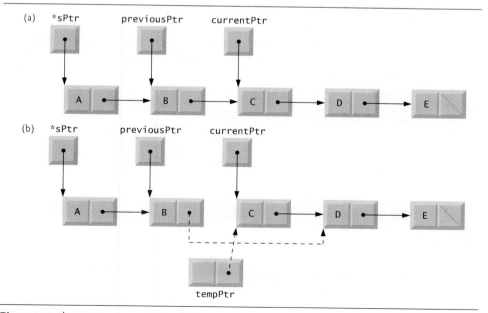

Fig. 12.6 | Deleting a node from a list.

Figure 12.6 illustrates the deletion of a node from a linked list. Part (a) of the figure shows the linked list after the preceding insert operation. Part (b) shows the reassignment of the link element of previousPtr and the assignment of currentPtr to tempPtr. Pointer tempPtr is used to *free* the memory allocated to the node that stores 'C'. Note that in lines 132 and 149 we free tempPtr. Recall that we recommended setting a freed pointer to NULL. We do not do that in these two cases, because tempPtr is a local automatic variable and the function returns immediately.

12.4.3 Function printList

Function printList (lines 164–181) receives a pointer to the start of the list as an argument and refers to the pointer as currentPtr. The function first determines whether the list is *empty* (lines 167–169) and, if so, prints "List is empty." and terminates. Otherwise, it prints the data in the list (lines 170–180). While currentPtr is not NULL, the value of currentPtr->data is printed by the function, and currentPtr->nextPtr is assigned to currentPtr to advance to the next node. If the link in the last node of the list is not NULL, the printing algorithm will try to print *past the end of the list*, and an error will occur. The printing algorithm is identical for linked lists, stacks and queues.

Exercise 12.20 asks you to implement a recursive function that prints a list backward. Exercise 12.21 asks the reader to implement a recursive function that searches a linked list for a particular data item.

12.5 Stacks

A stack can be implemented as a constrained version of a linked list. New nodes can be added to a stack and removed from a stack *only* at the *top*. For this reason, a stack is referred to as a **last-in, first-out (LIFO)** data structure. A stack is referenced via a pointer to the top element of the stack. The link member in the last node of the stack is set to NULL to indicate the bottom of the stack.

Figure 12.7 illustrates a stack with several nodes—stackPtr points to the stack's top element. Stacks and linked lists are represented identically. The difference between stacks and linked lists is that insertions and deletions may occur *anywhere* in a linked list, but *only* at the *top* of a stack.

> **Common Programming Error 12.5**
> *Not setting the link in the bottom node of a stack to NULL can lead to runtime errors.*

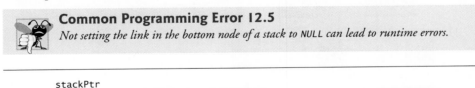

Fig. 12.7 | Stack graphical representation.

The primary functions used to manipulate a stack are push and pop. Function push creates a new node and places it on *top* of the stack. Function pop *removes* a node from the *top* of the stack, *frees* the memory that was allocated to the popped node and *returns the popped value.*

Figure 12.8 (output shown in Fig. 12.9) implements a simple stack of integers. The program provides three options: 1) push a value onto the stack (function push), 2) pop a value off the stack (function pop) and 3) terminate the program.

```c
1   // Fig. 12.8: fig12_08.c
2   // A simple stack program
3   #include <stdio.h>
4   #include <stdlib.h>
5
6   // self-referential structure
7   struct stackNode {
8      int data; // define data as an int
9      struct stackNode *nextPtr; // stackNode pointer
10  }; // end structure stackNode
11
12  typedef struct stackNode StackNode; // synonym for struct stackNode
13  typedef StackNode *StackNodePtr; // synonym for StackNode*
14
15  // prototypes
16  void push( StackNodePtr *topPtr, int info );
17  int pop( StackNodePtr *topPtr );
18  int isEmpty( StackNodePtr topPtr );
19  void printStack( StackNodePtr currentPtr );
20  void instructions( void );
21
22  // function main begins program execution
23  int main( void )
24  {
25     StackNodePtr stackPtr = NULL; // points to stack top
26     unsigned int choice; // user's menu choice
27     int value; // int input by user
28
29     instructions(); // display the menu
30     printf( "%s", "? " );
31     scanf( "%u", &choice );
32
33     // while user does not enter 3
34     while ( choice != 3 ) {
35
36        switch ( choice ) {
37           // push value onto stack
38           case 1:
39              printf( "%s", "Enter an integer: " );
40              scanf( "%d", &value );
41              push( &stackPtr, value );
42              printStack( stackPtr );
43              break;
44           // pop value off stack
45           case 2:
46              // if stack is not empty
47              if ( !isEmpty( stackPtr ) ) {
```

Fig. 12.8 | A simple stack program. (Part 1 of 3.)

```
48              printf( "The popped value is %d.\n", pop( &stackPtr ) );
49           } // end if
50
51           printStack( stackPtr );
52           break;
53        default:
54           puts( "Invalid choice.\n" );
55           instructions();
56           break;
57        } // end switch
58
59        printf( "%s", "? " );
60        scanf( "%u", &choice );
61     } // end while
62
63     puts( "End of run." );
64  } // end main
65
66  // display program instructions to user
67  void instructions( void )
68  {
69     puts( "Enter choice:\n"
70        "1 to push a value on the stack\n"
71        "2 to pop a value off the stack\n"
72        "3 to end program" );
73  } // end function instructions
74
75  // insert a node at the stack top
76  void push( StackNodePtr *topPtr, int info )
77  {
78     StackNodePtr newPtr; // pointer to new node
79
80     newPtr = malloc( sizeof( StackNode ) );
81
82     // insert the node at stack top
83     if ( newPtr != NULL ) {
84        newPtr->data = info;
85        newPtr->nextPtr = *topPtr;
86        *topPtr = newPtr;
87     } // end if
88     else { // no space available
89        printf( "%d not inserted. No memory available.\n", info );
90     } // end else
91  } // end function push
92
93  // remove a node from the stack top
94  int pop( StackNodePtr *topPtr )
95  {
96     StackNodePtr tempPtr; // temporary node pointer
97     int popValue; // node value
98
99     tempPtr = *topPtr;
100    popValue = ( *topPtr )->data;
```

Fig. 12.8 | A simple stack program. (Part 2 of 3.)

```
101        *topPtr = ( *topPtr )->nextPtr;
102        free( tempPtr );
103        return popValue;
104    } // end function pop
105
106    // print the stack
107    void printStack( StackNodePtr currentPtr )
108    {
109       // if stack is empty
110       if ( currentPtr == NULL ) {
111          puts( "The stack is empty.\n" );
112       } // end if
113       else {
114          puts( "The stack is:" );
115
116          // while not the end of the stack
117          while ( currentPtr != NULL ) {
118             printf( "%d --> ", currentPtr->data );
119             currentPtr = currentPtr->nextPtr;
120          } // end while
121
122          puts( "NULL\n" );
123       } // end else
124    } // end function printList
125
126    // return 1 if the stack is empty, 0 otherwise
127    int isEmpty( StackNodePtr topPtr )
128    {
129       return topPtr == NULL;
130    } // end function isEmpty
```

Fig. 12.8 | A simple stack program. (Part 3 of 3.)

```
Enter choice:
1 to push a value on the stack
2 to pop a value off the stack
3 to end program
? 1
Enter an integer: 5
The stack is:
5 --> NULL

? 1
Enter an integer: 6
The stack is:
6 --> 5 --> NULL

? 1
Enter an integer: 4
The stack is:
4 --> 6 --> 5 --> NULL
```

Fig. 12.9 | Sample output from the program of Fig. 12.8. (Part 1 of 2.)

```
? 2
The popped value is 4.
The stack is:
6 --> 5 --> NULL

? 2
The popped value is 6.
The stack is:
5 --> NULL

? 2
The popped value is 5.
The stack is empty.

? 2
The stack is empty.

? 4
Invalid choice.

Enter choice:
1 to push a value on the stack
2 to pop a value off the stack
3 to end program
? 3
End of run.
```

Fig. 12.9 | Sample output from the program of Fig. 12.8. (Part 2 of 2.)

12.5.1 Function push

Function push (lines 76–91) places a new node at the top of the stack. The function consists of three steps:

1. Create a *new node* by calling malloc and assign the location of the allocated memory to newPtr (line 80).

2. Assign to newPtr->data the value to be placed on the stack (line 84) and assign *topPtr (the *stack top pointer*) to newPtr->nextPtr (line 85)—the *link member* of newPtr now points to the *previous* top node.

3. Assign newPtr to *topPtr (line 86)—*topPtr now points to the *new* stack top.

Manipulations involving *topPtr change the value of stackPtr in main. Figure 12.10 illustrates function push. Part (a) of the figure shows the stack and the new node *before* the push operation. The dotted arrows in part (b) illustrate *Steps 2* and *3* of the push operation that enable the node containing 12 to become the new stack top.

12.5.2 Function pop

Function pop (lines 94–104) removes a node from the top of the stack. Function main determines whether the stack is empty before calling pop. The pop operation consists of five steps:

1. Assign *topPtr to tempPtr (line 99); tempPtr will be used to *free* the unneeded memory.

2. Assign (*topPtr)->data to popValue (line 100) to *save* the value in the top node.

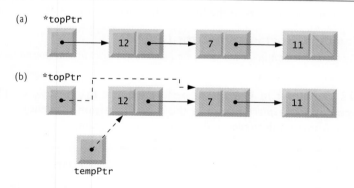

Fig. 12.10 | push operation.

3. Assign `(*topPtr)->nextPtr` to `*topPtr` (line 101) so `*topPtr` contains *address of the new top node.*

4. *Free the memory* pointed to by `tempPtr` (line 102).

5. *Return `popValue`* to the caller (line 103).

Figure 12.11 illustrates function `pop`. Part (a) shows the stack *after* the previous push operation. Part (b) shows `tempPtr` pointing to the *first node* of the stack and `topPtr` pointing to the *second node* of the stack. Function **free** is used to *free the memory* pointed to by `tempPtr`.

Fig. 12.11 | pop operation.

12.5.3 Applications of Stacks

Stacks have many interesting applications. For example, whenever a *function call* is made, the called function must know how to *return* to its caller, so the *return address* is pushed onto a stack. If a series of function calls occurs, the successive return values are pushed onto the stack in *last-in, first-out order* so that each function can return to its caller. Stacks support recursive function calls in the same manner as conventional nonrecursive calls.

Stacks contain the space created for *automatic variables* on each invocation of a function. When the function returns to its caller, the space for that function's automatic variables is popped off the stack, and these variables no longer are known to the program. Stacks are used by compilers in the process of evaluating expressions and generating machine-language code. The exercises explore several applications of stacks.

12.6 Queues

Another common data structure is the **queue**. A queue is similar to a checkout line in a grocery store—the *first* person in line is *serviced first*, and other customers enter the line only at the *end* and *wait* to be serviced. Queue nodes are removed *only* from the **head of the queue** and are inserted *only* at the **tail of the queue**. For this reason, a queue is referred to as a **first-in, first-out (FIFO)** data structure. The *insert* and *remove* operations are known as `enqueue` and `dequeue`, respectively.

Queues have many applications in computer systems. For computers that have only a single processor, only one user at a time may be serviced. Entries for the other users are placed in a queue. Each entry gradually advances to the front of the queue as users receive service. The entry at the *front* of the queue is the *next to receive service*.

Queues are also used to support *print spooling*. A multiuser environment may have only a single printer. Many users may be generating outputs to be printed. If the printer is busy, other outputs may still be generated. These are spooled to disk where they *wait* in a *queue* until the printer becomes available.

Information packets also wait in queues in computer networks. Each time a packet arrives at a network node, it must be routed to the next node on the network along the path to its final destination. The routing node routes one packet at a time, so additional packets are enqueued until the router can route them. Figure 12.12 illustrates a queue with several nodes. Note the pointers to the head of the queue and the tail of the queue.

 Common Programming Error 12.6
Not setting the link in the last node of a queue to NULL can lead to runtime errors.

Figure 12.13 (output in Fig. 12.14) performs queue manipulations. The program provides several options: *insert* a node in the queue (function **enqueue**), *remove* a node from the queue (function **dequeue**) and terminate the program.

Fig. 12.12 | Queue graphical representation.

```
1   // Fig. 12.13: fig12_13.c
2   // Operating and maintaining a queue
3   #include <stdio.h>
4   #include <stdlib.h>
5
6   // self-referential structure
7   struct queueNode {
8      char data; // define data as a char
9      struct queueNode *nextPtr; // queueNode pointer
10  }; // end structure queueNode
11
12  typedef struct queueNode QueueNode;
13  typedef QueueNode *QueueNodePtr;
14
15  // function prototypes
16  void printQueue( QueueNodePtr currentPtr );
17  int isEmpty( QueueNodePtr headPtr );
18  char dequeue( QueueNodePtr *headPtr, QueueNodePtr *tailPtr );
19  void enqueue( QueueNodePtr *headPtr, QueueNodePtr *tailPtr,
20     char value );
21  void instructions( void );
22
23  // function main begins program execution
24  int main( void )
25  {
26     QueueNodePtr headPtr = NULL; // initialize headPtr
27     QueueNodePtr tailPtr = NULL; // initialize tailPtr
28     unsigned int choice; // user's menu choice
29     char item; // char input by user
30
31     instructions(); // display the menu
32     printf( "%s", "? " );
33     scanf( "%u", &choice );
34
35     // while user does not enter 3
36     while ( choice != 3 ) {
37
38        switch( choice ) {
39           // enqueue value
40           case 1:
41              printf( "%s", "Enter a character: " );
42              scanf( "\n%c", &item );
43              enqueue( &headPtr, &tailPtr, item );
44              printQueue( headPtr );
45              break;
46           // dequeue value
47           case 2:
48              // if queue is not empty
49              if ( !isEmpty( headPtr ) ) {
50                 item = dequeue( &headPtr, &tailPtr );
51                 printf( "%c has been dequeued.\n", item );
52              } // end if
```

Fig. 12.13 | Operating and maintaining a queue. (Part 1 of 3.)

```
53
54                  printQueue( headPtr );
55                  break;
56              default:
57                  puts( "Invalid choice.\n" );
58                  instructions();
59                  break;
60          } // end switch
61
62          printf( "%s", "? " );
63          scanf( "%u", &choice );
64      } // end while
65
66      puts( "End of run." );
67  } // end main
68
69  // display program instructions to user
70  void instructions( void )
71  {
72      printf ( "Enter your choice:\n"
73              "   1 to add an item to the queue\n"
74              "   2 to remove an item from the queue\n"
75              "   3 to end\n" );
76  } // end function instructions
77
78  // insert a node in at queue tail
79  void enqueue( QueueNodePtr *headPtr, QueueNodePtr *tailPtr,
80      char value )
81  {
82      QueueNodePtr newPtr; // pointer to new node
83
84      newPtr = malloc( sizeof( QueueNode ) );
85
86      if ( newPtr != NULL ) { // is space available
87          newPtr->data = value;
88          newPtr->nextPtr = NULL;
89
90          // if empty, insert node at head
91          if ( isEmpty( *headPtr ) ) {
92              *headPtr = newPtr;
93          } // end if
94          else {
95              ( *tailPtr )->nextPtr = newPtr;
96          } // end else
97
98          *tailPtr = newPtr;
99      } // end if
100     else {
101         printf( "%c not inserted. No memory available.\n", value );
102     } // end else
103 } // end function enqueue
104
```

Fig. 12.13 | Operating and maintaining a queue. (Part 2 of 3.)

```
105  // remove node from queue head
106  char dequeue( QueueNodePtr *headPtr, QueueNodePtr *tailPtr )
107  {
108     char value; // node value
109     QueueNodePtr tempPtr; // temporary node pointer
110
111     value = ( *headPtr )->data;
112     tempPtr = *headPtr;
113     *headPtr = ( *headPtr )->nextPtr;
114
115     // if queue is empty
116     if ( *headPtr == NULL ) {
117        *tailPtr = NULL;
118     } // end if
119
120     free( tempPtr );
121     return value;
122  } // end function dequeue
123
124  // return 1 if the queue is empty, 0 otherwise
125  int isEmpty( QueueNodePtr headPtr )
126  {
127     return headPtr == NULL;
128  } // end function isEmpty
129
130  // print the queue
131  void printQueue( QueueNodePtr currentPtr )
132  {
133     // if queue is empty
134     if ( currentPtr == NULL ) {
135        puts( "Queue is empty.\n" );
136     } // end if
137     else {
138        puts( "The queue is:" );
139
140        // while not end of queue
141        while ( currentPtr != NULL ) {
142           printf( "%c --> ", currentPtr->data );
143           currentPtr = currentPtr->nextPtr;
144        } // end while
145
146        puts( "NULL\n" );
147     } // end else
148  } // end function printQueue
```

Fig. 12.13 | Operating and maintaining a queue. (Part 3 of 3.)

```
Enter your choice:
   1 to add an item to the queue
   2 to remove an item from the queue
   3 to end
```

Fig. 12.14 | Sample output from the program in Fig. 12.13. (Part 1 of 2.)

```
? 1
Enter a character: A
The queue is:
A --> NULL

? 1
Enter a character: B
The queue is:
A --> B --> NULL

? 1
Enter a character: C
The queue is:
A --> B --> C --> NULL

? 2
A has been dequeued.
The queue is:
B --> C --> NULL

? 2
B has been dequeued.
The queue is:
C --> NULL

? 2
C has been dequeued.
Queue is empty.

? 2
Queue is empty.

? 4
Invalid choice.

Enter your choice:
   1 to add an item to the queue
   2 to remove an item from the queue
   3 to end
? 3
End of run.
```

Fig. 12.14 | Sample output from the program in Fig. 12.13. (Part 2 of 2.)

12.6.1 Function enqueue

Function enqueue (lines 79–103) receives three arguments from main: the *address* of the *pointer to the head of the queue*, the *address* of the *pointer to the tail of the queue* and the *value* to be inserted in the queue. The function consists of three steps:

1. To create a new node: Call malloc, assign the allocated memory location to newPtr (line 84), assign the value to be inserted in the queue to newPtr->data (line 87) and assign NULL to newPtr->nextPtr (line 88).

2. If the queue is empty (line 91), assign newPtr to *headPtr (line 92), because the new node will be both the head and tail of the queue; otherwise, assign pointer

newPtr to (*tailPtr)->nextPtr (line 95), because the new node will be placed after the previous tail node.

3. Assign newPtr to *tailPtr (line 98), because the new node is the queue's tail.

Figure 12.15 illustrates an enqueue operation. Part (a) shows the queue and the new node *before* the operation. The dotted arrows in part (b) illustrate *Steps 2* and *3* of function enqueue that enable a new node to be added to the *end* of a queue that's not empty.

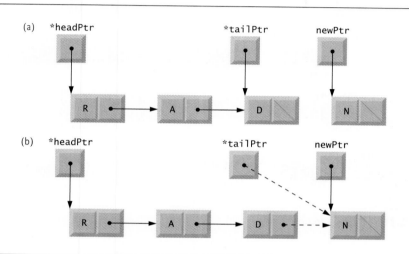

Fig. 12.15 | enqueue operation.

12.6.2 Function dequeue

Function dequeue (lines 106–122) receives the *address* of the *pointer to the head of the queue* and the *address* of the *pointer to the tail of the queue* as arguments and removes the *first* node from the queue. The dequeue operation consists of six steps:

1. Assign (*headPtr)->data to value to save the data (line 111).

2. Assign *headPtr to tempPtr (line 112), which will be used to free the unneeded memory.

3. Assign (*headPtr)->nextPtr to *headPtr (line 113) so that *headPtr now points to the new first node in the queue.

4. If *headPtr is NULL (line 116), assign NULL to *tailPtr (line 117) because the queue is now empty.

5. Free the memory pointed to by tempPtr (line 120).

6. Return value to the caller (line 121).

Figure 12.16 illustrates function dequeue. Part (a) shows the queue *after* the preceding enqueue operation. Part (b) shows tempPtr pointing to the *dequeued node*, and headPtr pointing to the *new first node* of the queue. Function free is used to *reclaim the memory* pointed to by tempPtr.

12.7 Trees

Linked lists, stacks and queues are **linear data structures**. A tree is a *nonlinear, two-dimensional data structure* with special properties. Tree nodes contain *two or more* links. This

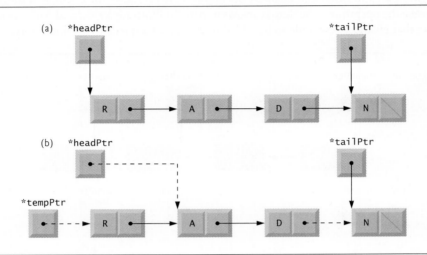

Fig. 12.16 | dequeue operation.

section discusses **binary trees** (Fig. 12.17)—trees whose nodes all contain *two* links (none, one, or both of which may be NULL). The **root node** is the *first* node in a tree. Each link in the root node refers to a **child**. The **left child** is the *first* node in the **left subtree**, and the **right child** is the *first* node in the **right subtree**. The children of a node are called **siblings**. A node with *no* children is called a **leaf node**. Computer scientists normally draw trees from the root node down—exactly the *opposite* of trees in nature.

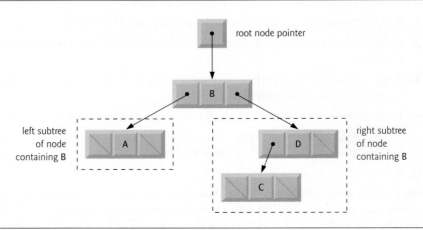

Fig. 12.17 | Binary tree graphical representation.

In this section, a special binary tree called a **binary search tree** is created. A binary search tree (with no duplicate node values) has the characteristic that the values in any left subtree are less than the value in its parent node, and the values in any right subtree are greater than the value in its **parent node**. Figure 12.18 illustrates a binary search tree with 12 values. The shape of the binary search tree that corresponds to a set of data can *vary*, depending on the *order* in which the values are *inserted* into the tree.

Common Programming Error 12.7

Not setting to NULL the links in leaf nodes of a tree can lead to runtime errors.

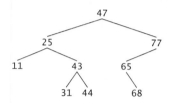

Fig. 12.18 | Binary search tree.

Figure 12.19 (output shown in Fig. 12.20) creates a binary search tree and *traverses* it three ways—**inorder, preorder** and **postorder**. The program generates 10 random numbers and inserts each in the tree, except that *duplicate* values are *discarded*.

```c
// Fig. 12.19: fig12_19.c
// Creating and traversing a binary tree
// preorder, inorder, and postorder
#include <stdio.h>
#include <stdlib.h>
#include <time.h>

// self-referential structure
struct treeNode {
   struct treeNode *leftPtr; // pointer to left subtree
   int data; // node value
   struct treeNode *rightPtr; // pointer to right subtree
}; // end structure treeNode

typedef struct treeNode TreeNode; // synonym for struct treeNode
typedef TreeNode *TreeNodePtr; // synonym for TreeNode*

// prototypes
void insertNode( TreeNodePtr *treePtr, int value );
void inOrder( TreeNodePtr treePtr );
void preOrder( TreeNodePtr treePtr );
void postOrder( TreeNodePtr treePtr );

```

Fig. 12.19 | Creating and traversing a binary tree. (Part 1 of 3.)

```
24   // function main begins program execution
25   int main( void )
26   {
27      unsigned int i; // counter to loop from 1-10
28      int item; // variable to hold random values
29      TreeNodePtr rootPtr = NULL; // tree initially empty
30
31      srand( time( NULL ) );
32      puts( "The numbers being placed in the tree are:" );
33
34      // insert random values between 0 and 14 in the tree
35      for ( i = 1; i <= 10; ++i ) {
36         item = rand() % 15;
37         printf( "%3d", item );
38         insertNode( &rootPtr, item );
39      } // end for
40
41      // traverse the tree preOrder
42      puts( "\n\nThe preOrder traversal is:" );
43      preOrder( rootPtr );
44
45      // traverse the tree inOrder
46      puts( "\n\nThe inOrder traversal is:" );
47      inOrder( rootPtr );
48
49      // traverse the tree postOrder
50      puts( "\n\nThe postOrder traversal is:" );
51      postOrder( rootPtr );
52   } // end main
53
54   // insert node into tree
55   void insertNode( TreeNodePtr *treePtr, int value )
56   {
57      // if tree is empty
58      if ( *treePtr == NULL ) {
59         *treePtr = malloc( sizeof( TreeNode ) );
60
61         // if memory was allocated, then assign data
62         if ( *treePtr != NULL ) {
63            ( *treePtr )->data = value;
64            ( *treePtr )->leftPtr = NULL;
65            ( *treePtr )->rightPtr = NULL;
66         } // end if
67         else {
68            printf( "%d not inserted. No memory available.\n", value );
69         } // end else
70      } // end if
71      else { // tree is not empty
72         // data to insert is less than data in current node
73         if ( value < ( *treePtr )->data ) {
74            insertNode( &( ( *treePtr )->leftPtr ), value );
75         } // end if
76
```

Fig. 12.19 | Creating and traversing a binary tree. (Part 2 of 3.)

```
77            // data to insert is greater than data in current node
78            else if ( value > ( *treePtr )->data ) {
79               insertNode( &( ( *treePtr )->rightPtr ), value );
80            } // end else if
81            else { // duplicate data value ignored
82               printf( "%s", "dup" );
83            } // end else
84         } // end else
85   } // end function insertNode
86
87   // begin inorder traversal of tree
88   void inOrder( TreeNodePtr treePtr )
89   {
90      // if tree is not empty, then traverse
91      if ( treePtr != NULL ) {
92         inOrder( treePtr->leftPtr );
93         printf( "%3d", treePtr->data );
94         inOrder( treePtr->rightPtr );
95      } // end if
96   } // end function inOrder
97
98   // begin preorder traversal of tree
99   void preOrder( TreeNodePtr treePtr )
100  {
101     // if tree is not empty, then traverse
102     if ( treePtr != NULL ) {
103        printf( "%3d", treePtr->data );
104        preOrder( treePtr->leftPtr );
105        preOrder( treePtr->rightPtr );
106     } // end if
107  } // end function preOrder
108
109  // begin postorder traversal of tree
110  void postOrder( TreeNodePtr treePtr )
111  {
112     // if tree is not empty, then traverse
113     if ( treePtr != NULL ) {
114        postOrder( treePtr->leftPtr );
115        postOrder( treePtr->rightPtr );
116        printf( "%3d", treePtr->data );
117     } // end if
118  } // end function postOrder
```

Fig. 12.19 | Creating and traversing a binary tree. (Part 3 of 3.)

```
The numbers being placed in the tree are:
  6   7   4 12   7dup   2   2dup   5   7dup 11

The preOrder traversal is:
  6   4   2   5   7 12 11
```

Fig. 12.20 | Sample output from the program of Fig. 12.19. (Part 1 of 2.)

```
The inOrder traversal is:
   2   4   5   6   7  11  12
The postOrder traversal is:
   2   5   4  11  12   7   6
```

Fig. 12.20 | Sample output from the program of Fig. 12.19. (Part 2 of 2.)

12.7.1 Function insertNode

The functions used in Fig. 12.19 to create a binary search tree and traverse it are *recursive*. Function insertNode (lines 55–85) receives the *address of the tree* and an *integer to be stored* in the tree as arguments. *A node can be inserted only as a leaf node in a binary search tree.* The steps for inserting a node in a binary search tree are as follows:

1. If *treePtr is NULL (line 58), create a new node (line 59). Call malloc, assign the *allocated memory* to *treePtr, assign to (*treePtr)->data the *integer to be stored* (line 63), assign to (*treePtr)->leftPtr and (*treePtr)->rightPtr the value NULL (lines 64–65, and return control to the caller (either main or a previous call to insertNode).

2. If the value of *treePtr is not NULL and the value to be inserted is *less than* (*treePtr)->data, function insertNode is called with the address of (*treePtr)->leftPtr (line 74) to insert the node in the left subtree of the node pointed to by treePtr. If the value to be inserted is *greater than* (*treePtr)->data, function insertNode is called with the address of (*treePtr)->rightPtr (line 79) to insert the node in the right subtree of the node pointed to by treePtr. Otherwise, the *recursive steps* continue until a NULL pointer is found, then *Step 1* is executed to *insert the new node.*

12.7.2 Traversals: Functions inOrder, preOrder and postOrder

Functions inOrder (lines 88–96), preOrder (lines 99–107) and postOrder (lines 110–118) each receive a *tree* (i.e., the *pointer to the root node of the tree*) and *traverse* the tree.

The steps for an inOrder traversal are:

1. Traverse the left subtree inOrder.
2. Process the value in the node.
3. Traverse the right subtree inOrder.

The value in a node is not processed until the values in its *left subtree* are processed. The inOrder traversal of the tree in Fig. 12.21 is:

```
    6  13  17  27  33  42  48
```

The inOrder traversal of a binary search tree prints the node values in *ascending* order. The process of creating a binary search tree actually sorts the data—and thus this process is called the **binary tree sort**.

The steps for a preOrder traversal are:

1. Process the value in the node.
2. Traverse the left subtree preOrder.
3. Traverse the right subtree preOrder.

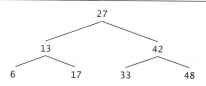

Fig. 12.21 | Binary search tree with seven nodes.

The value in each node is processed as the node is visited. After the value in a given node is processed, the values in the *left* subtree are processed, then those in the *right* subtree are processed. The preOrder traversal of the tree in Fig. 12.21 is:

```
27 13 6 17 42 33 48
```

The steps for a postOrder traversal are:

1. Traverse the left subtree postOrder.
2. Traverse the right subtree postOrder.
3. Process the value in the node.

The value in each node is not printed until the values of its children are printed. The post-Order traversal of the tree in Fig. 12.21 is:

```
6 17 13 33 48 42 27
```

12.7.3 Duplicate Elimination

The binary search tree facilitates **duplicate elimination**. As the tree is being created, an attempt to insert a duplicate value will be recognized because a duplicate will follow the *same* "go left" or "go right" decisions on each comparison as the original value did. Thus, the duplicate will eventually be compared with a node in the tree containing the same value. The duplicate value may simply be discarded at this point.

12.7.4 Binary Tree Search

Searching a binary tree for a value that matches a key value is also fast. If the tree is tightly packed, each level contains about *twice* as many elements as the previous level. So a binary search tree with n elements would have a maximum of $\log_2 n$ levels, and thus a *maximum* of $\log_2 n$ comparisons would have to be made either to find a match or to determine that no match exists. This means, for example, that when searching a (tightly packed) 1000-element binary search tree, no more than 10 comparisons need to be made because $2^{10} > 1000$. When searching a (tightly packed) 1,000,000-element binary search tree, no more than 20 comparisons need to be made because $2^{20} > 1,000,000$.

12.7.5 Other Binary Tree Operations

In the exercises, algorithms are presented for several other binary tree operations such as *deleting* an item from a binary tree, *printing* a binary tree in a two-dimensional tree format and performing a *level order traversal* of a binary tree. The level order traversal of a binary tree visits the nodes of the tree *row-by-row* starting at the root node level. On each level of the tree, the nodes are visited from left to right. Other binary tree exercises include allowing a binary search tree to contain duplicate values, inserting string values in a binary tree and determining how many levels are contained in a binary tree.

12.8 Secure C Programming

Chapter 8 of the CERT Secure C Coding Standard

Chapter 8 of the *CERT Secure C Coding Standard* is dedicated to memory-management recommendations and rules—many apply to the uses of pointers and dynamic-memory allocation presented in this chapter. For more information, visit `www.securecoding.cert.org`.

- MEM01-C/MEM30-C: Pointers should not be left uninitialized. Rather, they should be assigned either NULL or the address of a valid item in memory. When you use `free` to deallocate dynamically allocated memory, the pointer passed to `free` is *not* assigned a new value, so it still points to the memory location where the dynamically allocated memory *used* to be. Using such a pointer can lead to program crashes and security vulnerabilities. When you free dynamically allocated memory, you should immediately assign the pointer either NULL or a valid address. We chose not to do this for local pointer variables that immediately go out of scope after a call to `free`.

- MEM31-C: Undefined behavior occurs when you attempt to use `free` to deallocate dynamic memory that was already deallocated—this is known as a "double `free` vulnerability." To ensure that you don't attempt to deallocate the same memory more than once, immediately set a pointer to NULL after the call to `free`—attempting to free a NULL pointer has no effect.

- MEM32-C: Function `malloc` returns NULL if it's unable to allocate the requested memory. You should *always* ensure that `malloc` did not return NULL *before* attempting to use the pointer that stores malloc's return value.

Summary

Section 12.1 Introduction
- Dynamic data structures grow and shrink at execution time.
- Linked lists are collections of data items "lined up in a row"—insertions and deletions are made anywhere in a linked list.
- With stacks, insertions and deletions are made only at the top.
- Queues represent waiting lines; insertions are made at the back (also referred to as the tail) of a queue and deletions are made from the front (also referred to as the head) of a queue.
- Binary trees facilitate high-speed searching and sorting of data, efficient elimination of duplicate data items, representing file-system directories and compiling expressions into machine language.

Section 12.2 Self-Referential Structures
- A self-referential structure contains a pointer member that points to a structure of the same type.
- Self-referential structures can be linked together to form lists, queues, stacks and trees.
- A NULL pointer normally indicates the end of a data structure.

Section 12.3 Dynamic Memory Allocation

- Creating and maintaining dynamic data structures require dynamic memory allocation.
- Functions malloc and free, and operator sizeof, are essential to dynamic memory allocation.
- Function malloc receives the number of bytes to be allocated and returns a void * pointer to the allocated memory. A void * pointer may be assigned to a variable of any pointer type.
- Function malloc is normally used with the sizeof operator.
- The memory allocated by malloc is not initialized.
- If no memory is available, malloc returns NULL.
- Function free deallocates memory so that the memory can be reallocated in the future.
- C also provides functions calloc and realloc for creating and modifying dynamic arrays.

Section 12.4 Linked Lists

- A linked list is a linear collection of self-referential structures, called nodes, connected by pointer links.
- A linked list is accessed via a pointer to the first node. Subsequent nodes are accessed via the link pointer member stored in each node.
- By convention, the link pointer in the last node of a list is set to NULL to mark the end of the list.
- Data is stored in a linked list dynamically—each node is created as necessary.
- A node can contain data of any type including other struct objects.
- Linked lists are dynamic, so the length of a list can increase or decrease as necessary.
- Linked list nodes are normally not stored contiguously in memory. Logically, however, the nodes of a linked list appear to be contiguous.

Section 12.5 Stacks

- A stack can be implemented as a constrained version of a linked list. New nodes can be added to a stack and removed from a stack only at the top—referred to as a last-in, first-out (LIFO) data structure.
- The primary functions used to manipulate a stack are push and pop. Function push creates a new node and places it on top of the stack. Function pop removes a node from the top of the stack, frees the memory that was allocated to the popped node and returns the popped value.
- Whenever a function call is made, the called function must know how to return to its caller, so the return address is pushed onto a stack. If a series of function calls occurs, the successive return values are pushed onto the stack in last-in, first-out order so that each function can return to its caller. Stacks support recursive function calls in the same manner as conventional nonrecursive calls.
- Stacks are used by compilers in the process of evaluating expressions and generating machine-language code.

Section 12.6 Queues

- Queue nodes are removed only from the head of the queue and inserted only at the tail of the queue—referred to as a first-in, first-out (FIFO) data structure.
- The insert and remove operations for a queue are known as enqueue and dequeue.

Section 12.7 Trees

- A tree is a nonlinear, two-dimensional data structure. Tree nodes contain two or more links.
- Binary trees are trees whose nodes all contain two links.

- The root node is the first node in a tree. Each link in the root node of a binary tree refers to a child. The left child is the first node in the left subtree, and the right child is the first node in the right subtree. The children of a node are called siblings.

- A node with no children is called a leaf node.

- A binary search tree (with no duplicate node values) has the characteristic that the values in any left subtree are less than the value in its parent node, and the values in any right subtree are greater than the value in its parent node.

- A node can be inserted only as a leaf node in a binary search tree.

- The steps for an in-order traversal are: Traverse the left subtree in-order, process the value in the node, then traverse the right subtree in-order. The value in a node is not processed until the values in its left subtree are processed.

- The in-order traversal of a binary search tree processes the node values in ascending order. The process of creating a binary search tree actually sorts the data—and thus this process is called the binary tree sort.

- The steps for a pre-order traversal are: Process the value in the node, traverse the left subtree pre-order, then traverse the right subtree pre-order. The value in each node is processed as the node is visited. After the value in a given node is processed, the values in the left subtree are processed, then the values in the right subtree are processed.

- The steps for a post-order traversal are: Traverse the left subtree post-order, traverse the right subtree post-order, then process the value in the node. The value in each node is not processed until the values of its children are processed.

- A binary search tree facilitates duplicate elimination. As the tree is being created, an attempt to insert a duplicate value will be recognized because a duplicate will follow the same "go left" or "go right" decisions on each comparison as the original value did. Thus, the duplicate will eventually be compared with a node in the tree containing the same value. The duplicate value may simply be discarded at this point.

- Searching a binary tree for a value that matches a key value is fast. If the tree is tightly packed, each level contains about twice as many elements as the previous level. So a binary search tree with n elements would have a maximum of $\log_2 n$ levels, and thus a maximum of $\log_2 n$ comparisons would have to be made either to find a match or to determine that no match exists. This means that when searching a (tightly packed) 1000-element binary search tree, no more than 10 comparisons need to be made because $2^{10} > 1000$. When searching a (tightly packed) 1,000,000-element binary search tree, no more than 20 comparisons need to be made because $2^{20} > 1,000,000$.

Terminology

Self-Review Exercises

12.1   Fill in the blanks in each of the following:

a) A self-_____ structure is used to form dynamic data structures.

b) Function _____ is used to dynamically allocate memory.

c) A(n) _____ is a specialized version of a linked list in which nodes can be inserted and deleted only from the start of the list.

d) Functions that look at a linked list but do not modify it are referred to as _____.

e) A queue is referred to as a(n) _____ data structure.

f) The pointer to the next node in a linked list is referred to as a(n) _____.

g) Function _____ is used to reclaim dynamically allocated memory.

h) A(n) _____ is a specialized version of a linked list in which nodes can be inserted only at the start of the list and deleted only from the end of the list.

i) A(n) _____ is a nonlinear, two-dimensional data structure that contains nodes with two or more links.

j) A stack is referred to as a(n) _____ data structure because the last node inserted is the first node removed.

k) The nodes of a(n) _____ tree contain two link members.

l) The first node of a tree is the _____ node.

m) Each link in a tree node points to a(n) _____ or _____ of that node.

n) A tree node that has no children is called a(n) _____ node.

o) The three traversal algorithms (covered in this chapter) for a binary tree are _____, _____ and _____.

12.2   What are the differences between a linked list and a stack?

12.3   What are the differences between a stack and a queue?

12.4   Write a statement or set of statements to accomplish each of the following. Assume that all the manipulations occur in main (therefore, no addresses of pointer variables are needed), and assume the following definitions:

```
struct gradeNode {
   char lastName[ 20 ];
   double grade;
   struct gradeNode *nextPtr;
};

typedef struct gradeNode GradeNode;
typedef GradeNode *GradeNodePtr;
```

a) Create a pointer to the start of the list called startPtr. The list is empty.

b) Create a new node of type GradeNode that's pointed to by pointer newPtr of type Grade-NodePtr. Assign the string "Jones" to member lastName and the value 91.5 to member grade (use strcpy). Provide any necessary declarations and statements.

c) Assume that the list pointed to by startPtr currently consists of 2 nodes—one containing "Jones" and one containing "Smith". The nodes are in alphabetical order. Provide the statements necessary to insert in order nodes containing the following data for lastName and grade:

"Adams"	85.0
"Thompson"	73.5
"Pritchard"	66.5

Use pointers previousPtr, currentPtr and newPtr to perform the insertions. State what previousPtr and currentPtr point to before each insertion. Assume that newPtr always points to the new node, and that the new node has already been assigned the data.

d) Write a while loop that prints the data in each node of the list. Use pointer currentPtr to move along the list.

e) Write a while loop that deletes all the nodes in the list and frees the memory associated with each node. Use pointer currentPtr and pointer tempPtr to walk along the list and free memory, respectively.

12.5 *(Tree Traversals)* Provide the inorder, preorder and postorder traversals of the binary search tree shown in Fig. 12.22

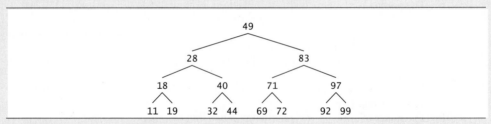

Fig. 12.22 | A 8-node tree.

Answers to Self-Review Exercises

12.1 a) referential. b) malloc. c) stack. d) predicates. e) FIFO. f) link. g) free. h) queue. i) tree. j) LIFO. k) binary. l) root. m) child, subtree. n) leaf. o) inorder, preorder, postorder.

12.2 It's possible to insert a node anywhere in a linked list and remove a node from anywhere in a linked list. However, nodes in a stack may be inserted only at the top of the stack and removed only from the top of a stack.

12.3 A queue has pointers to both its head and its tail so that nodes may be inserted at the tail and deleted from the head. A stack has a single pointer to the top of the stack where both insertion and deletion of nodes is performed.

12.4 a) GradeNodePtr startPtr = NULL;
b) GradeNodePtr newPtr;
```
newPtr = malloc( sizeof( GradeNode ) );
strcpy( newPtr->lastName, "Jones" );
newPtr->grade = 91.5;
newPtr->nextPtr = NULL;
```

c) To insert "Adams":
   previousPtr is NULL, currentPtr points to the first element in the list.
   ```
   newPtr->nextPtr = currentPtr;
   startPtr = newPtr;
   ```
   To insert "Thompson":
   previousPtr points to the last element in the list (containing "Smith")
   currentPtr is NULL.
   ```
   newPtr->nextPtr = currentPtr;
   previousPtr->nextPtr = newPtr;
   ```
   To insert "Pritchard":
   previousPtr points to the node containing "Jones"
   currentPtr points to the node containing "Smith"
   ```
   newPtr->nextPtr = currentPtr;
   previousPtr->nextPtr = newPtr;
   ```

d)
```
currentPtr = startPtr;
while ( currentPtr != NULL ) {
    printf( "Lastname = %s\nGrade = %6.2f\n",
            currentPtr->lastName, currentPtr->grade );
    currentPtr = currentPtr->nextPtr;
}
```

e)
```
currentPtr = startPtr;
while ( currentPtr != NULL ) {
    tempPtr = currentPtr;
    currentPtr = currentPtr->nextPtr;
    free( tempPtr );
}
startPtr = NULL;
```

12.5 The *inorder* traversal is:

   4,2,5,3,7,9,8,1

The *preorder* traversal is:

   7,5,4,2,3,8,9,1

The *postorder* traversal is:

   2,4,3,5,9,1,8,7

Exercises

12.6 *(Concatenating after Inserting into Lists)* Write a program that inserts 5 random characters between A and Z in one linked list and 5 random characters between a and z in another linked list. The program must concatenate these two linked lists of characters into a single linked list of characters.

12.7 *(Inserting into an Ordered List)* Write a program that inserts 10 random characters between a and z in order in a linked list. The program should print the characters of the list in uppercase.

12.8 *(Merging after Inserting into Ordered Lists)* Write a program that inserts 5 random integers between 0 and 50 in order in one linked list and 5 random integers between 0 and 100 in order in another linked list. The program must merge these two linked lists into a single ordered list of integers.

12.9 *(Creating a Linked List, Then Reversing Its Elements)* Write a program that creates a linked list of 15 integers, then creates a copy of the list in reverse order.

12.10   *(Reversing the Words of a Sentence)* Write a program that inputs a line of text and uses a stack to print the line reversed.

12.11   *(Palindrome Tester)* Write a program that uses a stack to determine whether a string is a palindrome (i.e., the string is spelled identically backward and forward). The program should ignore spaces and punctuation.

12.12   *(Infix-to-Postfix Converter)* Stacks are used by compilers to help in the process of evaluating expressions and generating machine language code. In this and the next exercise, we investigate how compilers evaluate arithmetic expressions consisting only of constants, operators and parentheses.

Humans generally write expressions like 3 + 4 and 7 / 9 in which the operator (+ or / here) is written between its operands—this is called **infix notation**. Computers "prefer" **postfix notation** in which the operator is written to the right of its two operands. The preceding infix expressions would appear in postfix notation as 3 4 + and 7 9 /, respectively.

To evaluate a complex infix expression, a compiler would first convert the expression to postfix notation, and then evaluate the postfix version. Each of these algorithms requires only a single left-to-right pass of the expression. Each algorithm uses a stack in support of its operation, and in each the stack is used for a different purpose.

In this exercise, you'll write a version of the infix-to-postfix conversion algorithm. In the next exercise, you'll write a version of the postfix-expression evaluation algorithm.

Write a program that converts an ordinary infix arithmetic expression (assume a valid expression is entered) with single-digit integers such as

    (6 + 2) * 5 - 8 / 4

to a postfix expression. The postfix version of the preceding infix expression is

    6 2 + 5 * 8 4 / -

The program should read the expression into character array `infix` and use the stack functions implemented in this chapter to help create the postfix expression in character array `postfix`. The algorithm for creating a postfix expression is as follows:

1) Push a left parenthesis `'('` onto the stack.
2) Append a right parenthesis `')'` to the end of `infix`.
3) While the stack is not empty, read `infix` from left to right and do the following:

   If the current character in `infix` is a digit, copy it to the next element of `postfix`.

   If the current character in `infix` is a left parenthesis, push it onto the stack.

   If the current character in `infix` is an operator,

   > Pop operators (if there are any) at the top of the stack while they have equal or higher precedence than the current operator, and insert the popped operators in `postfix`.

   > Push the current character in `infix` onto the stack.

   If the current character in `infix` is a right parenthesis

   > Pop operators from the top of the stack and insert them in `postfix` until a left parenthesis is at the top of the stack.

   > Pop (and discard) the left parenthesis from the stack.

The following arithmetic operations are allowed in an expression:

+	addition
-	subtraction
*	multiplication
/	division
^	exponentiation
%	remainder

The stack should be maintained with the following declarations:

```
struct stackNode {
   char data;
   struct stackNode *nextPtr;
};

typedef struct stackNode StackNode;
typedef StackNode *StackNodePtr;
```

The program should consist of main and eight other functions with the following function headers:

void convertToPostfix(**char** infix[], **char** postfix[])

Convert the infix expression to postfix notation.

int isOperator(**char** c)

Determine whether c is an operator.

int precedence(**char** operator1, **char** operator2)

Determine whether the precedence of operator1 is less than, equal to, or greater than the precedence of operator2. The function returns –1, 0 and 1, respectively.

void push(StackNodePtr *topPtr, **char** value)

Push a value on the stack.

char pop(StackNodePtr *topPtr)

Pop a value off the stack.

char stackTop(StackNodePtr topPtr)

Return the top value of the stack without popping the stack.

int isEmpty(StackNodePtr topPtr)

Determine whether the stack is empty.

void printStack(StackNodePtr topPtr)

Print the stack.

12.13   *(Postfix Evaluator)* Write a program that evaluates a postfix expression (assume it's valid) such as

6 2 + 5 * 8 4 / –

The program should read a postfix expression consisting of single digits and operators into a character array. Using the stack functions implemented earlier in this chapter, the program should scan the expression and evaluate it. The algorithm is as follows:

1) Append the null character ('\0') to the end of the postfix expression. When the null character is encountered, no further processing is necessary.
2) While '\0' has not been encountered, read the expression from left to right.
    If the current character is a digit,
        Push its integer value onto the stack (the integer value of a digit character is its value in the computer's character set minus the value of '0' in the computer's character set).
    Otherwise, if the current character is an *operator*,
        Pop the two top elements of the stack into variables x and y.
        Calculate y *operator* x.
        Push the result of the calculation onto the stack.
3) When the null character is encountered in the expression, pop the top value of the stack. This is the result of the postfix expression.

[*Note:* In 2) above, if the operator is `'/'`, the top of the stack is 2, and the next element in the stack is 8, then pop 2 into x, pop 8 into y, evaluate 8 / 2, and push the result, 4, back onto the stack. This note also applies to operator `'-'`.]

The arithmetic operations allowed in an expression are:

+ addition
- subtraction
* multiplication
/ division
^ exponentiation
% remainder

The stack should be maintained with the following declarations:

```
struct stackNode {
   int data;
   struct stackNode *nextPtr;
};

typedef struct stackNode StackNode;
typedef StackNode *StackNodePtr;
```

The program should consist of main and six other functions with the following function headers:

```
int evaluatePostfixExpression( char *expr )
```

Evaluate the postfix expression.

```
int calculate( int op1, int op2, char operator )
```

Evaluate the expression op1 operator op2.

```
void push( StackNodePtr *topPtr, int value )
```

Push a value on the stack.

```
int pop( StackNodePtr *topPtr )
```

Pop a value off the stack.

```
int isEmpty( StackNodePtr topPtr )
```

Determine whether the stack is empty.

```
void printStack( StackNodePtr topPtr )
```

Print the stack.

12.14 *(Postfix Evaluator Modification)* Modify the postfix evaluator program of Exercise 12.13 so that it can process integer operands larger than 9.

12.15 *(Supermarket Simulation)* Write a program that simulates a check-out line at a supermarket. The line is a queue. Customers arrive in random integer intervals of 1 to 4 minutes. Also, each customer is serviced in random integer intervals of 1 to 4 minutes. Obviously, the rates need to be balanced. If the average arrival rate is larger than the average service rate, the queue will grow infinitely. Even with balanced rates, randomness can still cause long lines. Run the supermarket simulation for a 12-hour day (720 minutes) using the following algorithm:

1) Choose a random integer between 1 and 4 to determine the minute at which the first customer arrives.
2) At the first customer's arrival time:
   Determine customer's service time (random integer from 1 to 4);
   Begin servicing the customer;
   Schedule arrival time of next customer (random integer 1 to 4 added to the current time).

3) For each minute of the day:
> If the next customer arrives,
>> Say so;
>> Enqueue the customer;
>> Schedule the arrival time of the next customer.
> If service was completed for the last customer,
>> Say so;
>> Dequeue next customer to be serviced;
>> Determine customer's service completion time
>>> (random integer from 1 to 4 added to the current time).

Now run your simulation for 720 minutes and answer each of the following:
  a) What's the maximum number of customers in the queue at any time?
  b) What's the longest wait any one customer experienced?
  c) What happens if the arrival interval is changed from 1 to 4 minutes to 1 to 3 minutes?

12.16 *(Allowing Duplicates in a Binary Tree)* Modify the program of Fig. 12.19 to allow the binary tree to contain duplicate values.

12.17 *(Binary Search Tree of Strings)* Write a program based on the program of Fig. 12.19 that inputs a line of text, tokenizes the sentence into separate words, inserts the words in a binary search tree, and prints the inorder, preorder, and postorder traversals of the tree.
[*Hint:* Read the line of text into an array. Use strtok to tokenize the text. When a token is found, create a new node for the tree, assign the pointer returned by strtok to member string of the new node, and insert the node in the tree.]

12.18 *(Duplicate Elimination)* We've seen that duplicate elimination is straightforward when creating a binary search tree. Describe how you would perform duplicate elimination using only a single subscripted array. Compare the performance of array-based duplicate elimination with the performance of binary-search-tree-based duplicate elimination.

12.19 *(Height of a Binary Tree)* Write a function height that receives a tree and determines the height of that tree.

12.20 *(Recursively Print a List Backward)* Write a function printListBackward that recursively outputs the items in a list in reverse order. Use your function in a test program that creates an alphabetically ordered list of characters and prints the list in reverse order.

12.21 *(Recursively Search a List)* Write a function searchList that recursively searches a linked list for a specified character. The function should return a pointer to the character if it's found; otherwise, NULL should be returned. Use your function in a test program that creates a list of characters. The program should prompt the user for a character to locate in the list.

12.22 *(Binary Tree Search)* Write function binaryTreeSearch that attempts to locate a specified value in a binary search tree. The function should take as arguments a pointer to the root node of the binary tree and a search key to be located. If the node containing the search key is found, the function should return a pointer to that node; otherwise, the function should return a NULL pointer.

12.23 *(Level Order Binary Tree Traversal)* The program of Fig. 12.19 illustrated three recursive methods of traversing a binary tree—inorder traversal, preorder traversal, and postorder traversal. This exercise presents the **level order traversal** of a binary tree in which the node values are printed level-by-level starting at the root node level. The nodes on each level are printed from left to right. The level order traversal is not a recursive algorithm. It uses the queue data structure to control the output of the nodes. The algorithm is as follows:
  1) Insert the root node in the queue

2) While there are nodes left in the queue,
   Get the next node in the queue
   Print the node's value
   If the pointer to the left child of the node is not null
    Insert the left child node in the queue
   If the pointer to the right child of the node is not null
    Insert the right child node in the queue.

Write function `levelOrder` to perform a level order traversal of a binary tree. The function should take as an argument a pointer to the root node of the binary tree. Modify the program of Fig. 12.19 to use this function. Compare the output from this function to the outputs of the other traversal algorithms to see that it worked correctly. [*Note:* You'll also need to modify and incorporate the queue-processing functions of Fig. 12.13 in this program.]

12.24 *(Printing Trees)* Write a recursive function `outputTree` to display a binary tree on the screen. The function should output the tree row-by-row with the top of the tree at the left of the screen and the bottom of the tree toward the right of the screen. Each row is output vertically. For example, the binary tree illustrated in Fig. 12.22 is output as follows:

Note that the rightmost leaf node appears at the top of the output in the rightmost column, and the root node appears at the left of the output. Each column of output starts five spaces to the right of the previous column. Function `outputTree` should receive as arguments a pointer to the root node of the tree and an integer `totalSpaces` representing the number of spaces preceding the value to be output (this variable should start at zero so that the root node is output at the left of the screen). The function uses a modified inorder traversal to output the tree—it starts at the rightmost node in the tree and works back to the left. The algorithm is as follows:

  While the pointer to the current node is not null
   Recursively call `outputTree` with the current node's right subtree and `totalSpaces` + 5.
   Use a `for` statement to count from 1 to `totalSpaces` and output spaces.
   Output the value in the current node.
   Recursively call `outputTree` with the current node's left subtree and `totalSpaces` + 5.

Special Section: Building Your Own Compiler

In Exercises 7.27–7.29, we introduced Simpletron Machine Language (SML), and you implemented a Simpletron computer simulator to execute SML programs. In Exercises 12.25–12.30, we build a compiler that converts programs written in a high-level programming language to SML. This section "ties" together the entire programming process. You'll write programs in this new high-level language, compile them on the compiler you build and run them on the simulator you built in Exercise 7.28. [*Note:* Due to the size of the descriptions for Exercises 12.25–12.30, we've posted them in a PDF document located at www.deitel.com/books/chtp7/.]

C Preprocessor

Hold thou the good; define it well.
—Alfred, Lord Tennyson

I have found you an argument; but I am not obliged to find you an understanding.
—Samuel Johnson

A good symbol is the best argument, and is a missionary to persuade thousands.
—Ralph Waldo Emerson

The partisan, when he is engaged in a dispute, cares nothing about the rights of the question, but is anxious only to convince his hearers of his own assertions.
—Plato

Objectives

In this chapter, you'll:

- Use #include to develop large programs.

- Use #define to create macros and macros with arguments.

- Use conditional compilation to specify portions of a program that should not always be compiled (such as code that assists you in debugging).

- Display error messages during conditional compilation.

- Use assertions to test whether the values of expressions are correct.

13.1 Introduction

The C preprocessor executes *before* a program is compiled. Some actions it performs are the inclusion of other files in the file being compiled, definition of symbolic constants and macros, conditional compilation of program code and conditional execution of preprocessor directives. Preprocessor directives begin with # and only whitespace characters and comments may appear before a preprocessor directive on a line.

C has perhaps the largest installed base of "legacy code" of any modern programming language. It's been in active use for four decades. As a professional C programmer, you're likely to encounter code written many years ago using older programming techniques. To help you prepare for this, we discuss a number of those techniques in this chapter and recommend some newer techniques that can replace them.

13.2 #include Preprocessor Directive

The #include preprocessor directive has been used throughout this text. The #include directive causes a *copy* of a specified file to be included in place of the directive. The two forms of the #include directive are:

```
#include <filename>
#include "filename"
```

The difference between these is the location at which the preprocessor begins searches for the file to be included. If the filename is enclosed in angle brackets (< and >)—used for standard library headers—the search is performed in an *implementation-dependent* manner, normally through predesignated compiler and system directories. If the filename is enclosed in *quotes*, the preprocessor starts searches in the *same* directory as the file being compiled for the file to be included. This method is normally used to include programmer-defined headers. If the compiler cannot find the file in the current directory, then it will search through the predesignated compiler and system directories.

The #include directive is used to include standard library headers such as stdio.h and stdlib.h (see Fig. 5.10) and with programs consisting of *multiple source files* that are to be compiled together. A header containing declarations *common* to the separate program files is often created and included in the file. Examples of such declarations are *structure and union declarations, enumerations* and *function prototypes*.

13.3 #define Preprocessor Directive: Symbolic Constants

The **#define** directive creates *symbolic constants*—constants represented as symbols—and macros—operations defined as symbols. The #define directive format is

> **#define** *identifier   replacement-text*

When this line appears in a file, all subsequent occurrences of *identifier* that do *not* appear in string literals will be replaced by **replacement text** automatically *before* the program is compiled. For example,

> **#define** PI 3.14159

replaces all subsequent occurrences of the symbolic constant PI with the numeric constant 3.14159. *Symbolic constants* enable you to create a name for a constant and use the name throughout the program. If the constant needs to be modified throughout the program, it can be modified *once* in the #define directive. When the program is recompiled, *all* occurrences of the constant in the program will be modified accordingly. [*Note:* Everything to the right of the symbolic constant name replaces the symbolic constant.] For example, #define PI = 3.14159 causes the preprocessor to replace *every* occurrence of the identifier PI with = 3.14159. This is the cause of many subtle logic and syntax errors. For this reason, you may prefer to use const variable declarations, such as

> **const double** PI = 3.14159;

in preference to the preceding #define. Redefining a symbolic constant with a new value is also an error.

Good Programming Practice 13.1
Using meaningful names for symbolic constants helps make programs self-documenting.

Good Programming Practice 13.2
By convention, symbolic constants are defined using only uppercase letters and underscores.

13.4 #define Preprocessor Directive: Macros

A macro is an identifier defined in a #define preprocessor directive. As with symbolic constants, the macro-identifier is replaced in the program with the **replacement-text** before the program is compiled. Macros may be defined with or without **arguments**. A macro without arguments is processed like a symbolic constant. In a macro with arguments, the *arguments are substituted in the replacement text*, then the macro is expanded—i.e., the replacement-text replaces the identifier and argument list in the program. A symbolic constant is a type of macro.

Consider the following *macro definition* with one *argument* for the area of a circle:

> **#define** CIRCLE_AREA(x) ((PI) * (x) * (x))

Wherever CIRCLE_AREA(y) appears in the file, the value of y is substituted for x in the replacement-text, the symbolic constant PI is replaced by its value (defined previously) and the macro is expanded in the program. For example, the statement

```
area = CIRCLE_AREA( 4 );
```

is expanded to

```
area = ( ( 3.14159 ) * ( 4 ) * ( 4 ) );
```

then, at compile time, the value of the expression is evaluated and assigned to variable area. The *parentheses* around each x in the replacement text *force the proper order of evaluation when the macro argument is an expression*. For example, the statement

```
area = CIRCLE_AREA( c + 2 );
```

is expanded to

```
area = ( ( 3.14159 ) * ( c + 2 ) * ( c + 2 ) );
```

which evaluates *correctly* because the parentheses force the proper order of evaluation. If the parentheses in the macro definition are omitted, the macro expansion is

```
area = 3.14159 * c + 2 * c + 2;
```

which evaluates *incorrectly* as

```
area = ( 3.14159 * c ) + ( 2 * c ) + 2;
```

because of the rules of operator precedence.

Common Programming Error 13.1

Forgetting to enclose macro arguments in parentheses in the replacement text can lead to logic errors.

Macro CIRCLE_AREA could be defined more safely as a function. Function circleArea

```
double circleArea( double x )
{
    return 3.14159 * x * x;
}
```

performs the same calculation as macro CIRCLE_AREA, but the function's argument is evaluated only once when the function is called.

Performance Tip 13.1

In the past, macros were often used to replace function calls with inline code *to eliminate the function-call overhead. Today's optimizing compilers often inline function calls for you, so many programmers no longer use macros for this purpose. You can also use the C standard's* inline *keyword (see Appendix F).*

The following is a macro definition with two arguments for the area of a rectangle:

```
#define RECTANGLE_AREA( x, y )  ( ( x ) * ( y ) )
```

Wherever RECTANGLE_AREA(x, y) appears in the program, the values of x and y are substituted in the macro replacement text and the macro is expanded in place of the macro name. For example, the statement

```
rectArea = RECTANGLE_AREA( a + 4, b + 7 );
```

is expanded to

```
rectArea = ( ( a + 4 ) * ( b + 7 ) );
```

The value of the expression is evaluated at runtime and assigned to variable rectArea.

The replacement text for a macro or symbolic constant is normally any text on the line after the identifier in the #define directive. If the replacement text for a macro or symbolic constant is longer than the remainder of the line, a **backslash** (\) must be placed at the end of the line, indicating that the replacement text continues on the next line.

Symbolic constants and macros can be *discarded* by using the **#undef** preprocessor directive. Directive #undef *"undefines"* a symbolic constant or macro name. The scope of a symbolic constant or macro is from its definition until it's undefined with #undef, or until the end of the file. Once undefined, a name can be redefined with #define.

Functions in the standard library sometimes are defined as macros based on other library functions. A macro commonly defined in the <stdio.h> header is

```
#define getchar() getc( stdin )
```

The macro definition of getchar uses function getc to get one character from the standard input stream. Function putchar of the <stdio.h> header and the character-handling functions of the <ctype.h> header often are implemented as macros as well.

Expressions with *side effects* (i.e., variable values are modified) should *not* be passed to a macro because macro arguments may be evaluated more than once. We'll show an example of this in the Secure C Programming section.

13.5 **Conditional Compilation**

Conditional compilation enables you to control the execution of preprocessor directives and the compilation of program code. Each conditional preprocessor directive evaluates a constant integer expression. Cast expressions, sizeof expressions and enumeration constants *cannot* be evaluated in preprocessor directives.

The conditional preprocessor construct is much like the if selection statement. Consider the following preprocessor code:

```
#if !defined(MY_CONSTANT)
    #define MY_CONSTANT 0
#endif
```

which determines whether MY_CONSTANT is *defined*—that is, whether MY_CONSTANT has already appeared in an earlier #define directive. The expression defined(MY_CONSTANT) evaluates to 1 if MY_CONSTANT is defined and 0 otherwise. If the result is 0, !defined(MY_CONSTANT) evaluates to 1 and MY_CONSTANT is defined. Otherwise, the #define directive is skipped. Every #if construct ends with **#endif**. Directives **#ifdef** and **#ifndef** are shorthand for #if defined(*name*) and #if !defined(*name*). A multiple-part conditional preprocessor construct may be tested by using the **#elif** (the equivalent of else if in an if statement) and the **#else** (the equivalent of else in an if statement) directives. These directives are frequently used to *prevent header files from being included multiple times in the same source file*. We use this technique extensively in the C++ part of this book.

During program development, it's often helpful to "comment out" portions of code to prevent them from being compiled. If the code contains multiline comments, /* and */ cannot be used to accomplish this task, because such comments cannot be nested. Instead, you can use the following preprocessor construct:

```
#if 0
    code prevented from compiling
#endif
```

To enable the code to be compiled, replace the 0 in the preceding construct with 1.

Conditional compilation is commonly used as a *debugging* aid. Many C implementations include **debuggers**, which provide much more powerful features than conditional compilation. If a debugger is not available, printf statements are often used to print variable values and to confirm the flow of control. These printf statements can be enclosed in conditional preprocessor directives so the statements are compiled only while the debugging process is *not* completed. For example,

```
#ifdef DEBUG
    printf( "Variable x = %d\n", x );
#endif
```

causes a printf statement to be compiled in the program if the symbolic constant DEBUG has been defined (#define DEBUG) before directive #ifdef DEBUG. When debugging is completed, the #define directive is removed from the source file (or commented out) and the printf statements inserted for debugging purposes are ignored during compilation. In larger programs, it may be desirable to define several different symbolic constants that control the conditional compilation in separate sections of the source file. Many compilers allow you to define and undefine symbolic constants with a compiler flag so that you do not need to change the code.

Common Programming Error 13.2

Inserting conditionally compiled printf *statements for debugging purposes in locations where C currently expects a single statement. In this case, the conditionally compiled statement should be enclosed in a compound statement, so that when the program is compiled with debugging statements, the flow of control of the program is not altered.*

13.6 #error and #pragma Preprocessor Directives

The **#error** directive

```
#error tokens
```

prints an implementation-dependent message including the *tokens* specified in the directive. The tokens are sequences of characters separated by spaces. For example,

```
#error 1 - Out of range error
```

contains 6 tokens. When a #error directive is processed on some systems, the tokens in the directive are displayed as an error message, preprocessing stops and the program does not compile.

The **#pragma** directive

```
#pragma tokens
```

causes an *implementation-defined* action. A pragma not recognized by the implementation is ignored. For more information on #error and #pragma, see the documentation for your C implementation.

13.7 # and ## Operators

The # and ## preprocessor operators are available in Standard C. The # operator causes a replacement text token to be converted to a string surrounded by quotes. Consider the following macro definition:

```
#define HELLO(x) puts( "Hello, " #x );
```

When HELLO(John) appears in a program file, it's expanded to

```
puts( "Hello, " "John" );
```

The string "John" replaces #x in the replacement text. Strings separated by white space are concatenated during preprocessing, so the preceding statement is equivalent to

```
puts( "Hello, John" );
```

The # operator must be used in a macro with arguments because the operand of # refers to an argument of the macro.

The ## operator *concatenates two tokens*. Consider the following macro definition:

```
#define TOKENCONCAT(x, y)  x ## y
```

When TOKENCONCAT appears in the program, its arguments are concatenated and used to replace the macro. For example, TOKENCONCAT(O, K) is replaced by OK in the program. The ## operator must have two operands.

13.8 Line Numbers

The #line preprocessor directive causes the subsequent source code lines to be renumbered starting with the specified constant integer value. The directive

```
#line 100
```

starts line numbering from 100 beginning with the next source code line. A filename can be included in the #line directive. The directive

```
#line 100 "file1.c"
```

indicates that lines are numbered from 100 beginning with the next source code line and that the name of the file for the purpose of any compiler messages is "file1.c". The directive normally is used to help make the messages produced by syntax errors and compiler warnings more meaningful. The line numbers do not appear in the source file.

13.9 Predefined Symbolic Constants

Standard C provides predefined symbolic constants, several of which are shown in Fig. 13.1—the rest are in Section 6.10.8 of the C standard document. The identifiers for each of the predefined symbolic constants begin and end with *two* underscores. These identifiers and the defined identifier (used in Section 13.5) cannot be used in #define or #undef directives.

Symbolic constant	Explanation
__LINE__	The line number of the current source code line (an integer constant).
__FILE__	The presumed name of the source file (a string).
__DATE__	The date the source file was compiled (a string of the form "Mmm dd yyyy" such as "Jan 19 2002").
__TIME__	The time the source file was compiled (a string literal of the form "hh:mm:ss").
__STDC__	The value 1 if the compiler supports Standard C.

Fig. 13.1 | Some predefined symbolic constants.

13.10 Assertions

The **assert** macro—defined in the **<assert.h>** header—tests the value of an expression at execution time. If the value is false (0), assert prints an error message and calls function **abort** (of the general utilities library—<stdlib.h>) to terminate program execution. This is a useful *debugging tool* for testing whether a variable has a correct value. For example, suppose variable x should never be larger than 10 in a program. An assertion may be used to test the value of x and print an error message if the value of x is incorrect. The statement would be

```
assert( x <= 10 );
```

If x is greater than 10 when the preceding statement is encountered in a program, an error message containing the line number and filename is printed and the program *terminates*. You may then concentrate on this area of the code to find the error. If the symbolic constant NDEBUG is defined, subsequent assertions will be *ignored*. Thus, when assertions are no longer needed, the line

```
#define NDEBUG
```

is inserted in the program file rather than each assertion being deleted manually.

Software Engineering Observation 13.1

Assertions are not meant as a substitute for error handling during normal runtime conditions. Their use should be limited to finding logic errors during program development.

[*Note:* The new C standard includes a capability called _Static_assert, which is essentially a compile-time version of assert that produces a *compilation error* if the assertion fails. We discuss _Static_assert in Appendix F.]

13.11 Secure C Programming

The CIRCLE_AREA macro defined in Section 13.4

```
#define CIRCLE_AREA( x ) ( ( PI ) * ( x ) * ( x ) )
```

is considered to be an *unsafe macro* because it evaluates its argument x *more than once*. This can cause subtle errors. If the macro argument contains *side effects*—such as incrementing a variable or calling a function that modifies a variable's value—those side effects would be performed *multiple* times.

For example, if we call CIRCLE_AREA as follows:

```
result = CIRCLE_AREA( ++radius );
```

the call to the macro CIRCLE_AREA is expanded to:

```
result = ( ( 3.14159 ) * ( ++radius ) * ( ++radius ) );
```

which increments radius *twice* in the statement. In addition, the result of the preceding statement is *undefined* because C allows a variable to be modified *only once* in a statement. In a function call, the argument is evaluated *only once before* it's passed to the function. So, functions are always preferred to unsafe macros.

Summary

Section 13.1 Introduction
- The preprocessor executes before a program is compiled.
- All preprocessor directives begin with #.
- Only whitespace characters and comments may appear before a preprocessor directive on a line.

Section 13.2 #include Presprocessor Directive
- The #include directive includes a copy of the specified file. If the filename is enclosed in quotes, the preprocessor begins searching in the same directory as the file being compiled for the file to be included. If the filename is enclosed in angle brackets (< and >), the search is performed in an implementation-defined manner.

Section 13.3 #define Preprocessor Directive: Symbolic Constants
- The #define preprocessor directive is used to create symbolic constants and macros.
- A symbolic constant is a name for a constant.
- A macro is an operation defined in a #define preprocessor directive. Macros may be defined with or without arguments.

Section 13.4 #define Preprocessor Directive: Macros
- The replacement text for a macro or symbolic constant is any text remaining on the line after the identifier in the #define directive. If the replacement text for a macro or symbolic constant is longer than the remainder of the line, a backslash (\) is placed at the end of the line, indicating that the replacement text continues on the next line.
- Symbolic constants and macros can be discarded by using the #undef preprocessor directive. Directive #undef "undefines" the symbolic constant or macro name.
- The scope of a symbolic constant or macro is from its definition until it's undefined with #undef or until the end of the file.

Section 13.5 Conditional Compilation
- Conditional compilation enables you to control the execution of preprocessor directives and the compilation of program code.
- The conditional preprocessor directives evaluate constant integer expressions. Cast expressions, sizeof expressions and enumeration constants cannot be evaluated in preprocessor directives.
- Every #if construct ends with #endif.

- Directives `#ifdef` and `#ifndef` are provided as shorthand for `#if defined(`*name*`)` and `#if !defined(`*name*`)`.
- Multiple-part conditional preprocessor constructs may be tested with directives `#elif` and `#else`.

Section 13.6 #error and #pragma Preprocessor Directives
- The `#error` directive prints an implementation-dependent message that includes the tokens specified in the directive.
- The `#pragma` directive causes an implementation-defined action. If the pragma is not recognized by the implementation, the pragma is ignored.

Section 13.7 # and ## Operators
- The `#` operator causes a *replacement-text* token to be converted to a string surrounded by quotes. The `#` operator must be used in a macro with arguments, because the operand of `#` must be an argument of the macro.
- The `##` operator concatenates two tokens. The `##` operator must have two operands.

Section 13.8 Line Numbers
- The `#line` preprocessor directive causes the subsequent source code lines to be renumbered starting with the specified constant integer value.

Section 13.9 Predefined Symbolic Constants
- Constant `__LINE__` is the line number (an integer) of the current source code line. Constant `__FILE__` is the presumed name of the file (a string). Constant `__DATE__` is the date the source file is compiled (a string). Constant `__TIME__` is the time the source file is compiled (a string). Constant `__STDC__` indicates whether the compiler supports Standard C. Each of the predefined symbolic constants begins and ends with two underscores.

Section 13.10 Assertions
- Macro `assert`—defined in the `<assert.h>` header—tests the value of an expression. If the value is 0 (false), `assert` prints an error message and calls function `abort` to terminate program execution.

Terminology

abort function 552
arguments 547
assert macro 552
`<assert.h>` 552
backslash (\) 549
C preprocessor 546
conditional compilation 546
debugger 550
`#define` preprocessor directive 547
`#elif` preprocessor directive 549
`#endif` preprocessor directive 549
`#error` preprocessor directive 550
expand a macro 547
`#if` preprocessor directive 549

`#ifdef` preprocessor directive 549
`#ifndef` preprocessor directive 549
`#include` preprocessor directive 546
`#line` preprocessor directive 551
macro 546
macro identifier 547
macro with an argument 547
`#pragma` preprocessor directive 550
predefined symbolic constant 551
preprocessor directive 546
replacement text 547
scope 549
symbolic constant 546
`#undef` preprocessor directive 549

Self-Review Exercises

13.1 Fill in the blanks in each of the following:
   a)   Every preprocessor directive must begin with _____.

b) The conditional compilation construct may be extended to test for multiple cases by using the _____ and _____ directives.

c) The _____ directive creates macros and symbolic constants.

d) Only _____ characters may appear before a preprocessor directive on a line.

e) The _____ directive discards symbolic constant and macro names.

f) The _____ and _____ directives are provided as shorthand notation for #if defined(*name*) and #if !defined(*name*).

g) _____ enables you to control the execution of preprocessor directives and the compilation of program code.

h) The _____ macro prints a message and terminates program execution if the value of the expression the macro evaluates is 0.

i) The _____ directive inserts a file in another file.

j) The _____ operator concatenates its two arguments.

k) The _____ operator converts its operand to a string.

l) The character _____ indicates that the replacement text for a symbolic constant or macro continues on the next line.

m) The _____ directive causes the source code lines to be numbered from the indicated value beginning with the next source code line.

13.2 Write a program to print the values of the predefined symbolic constants listed in Fig. 13.1.

13.3 Write a preprocessor directive to accomplish each of the following:

a) If symbolic constant Matrix is defined, undefine it and redefine it as 20. Do not use #ifdef.

b) Define symbolic constant MAX to have the value 50.

c) Define macro SQUARE_NUMBER that computes the square of a number. The macro takes one argument.

d) Include the header splash.h. The header is found in the same directory as the file being compiled.

e) If symbolic constant YES is defined, undefine it and redefine it as 5. Use the #ifdef preprocessor directive.

f) Define symbolic constant VALUE to have the value 2.

g) Renumber the remaining lines in the file beginning with line number 350.

h) Define macro AREA_RECTANGLE that computes the area of rectangle of two numbers. The macro takes two arguments.

Answers to Self-Review Exercises

13.1 a) #. b) #elif, #else. c) #define. d) white-space. e) #undef. f) #ifdef, #ifndef. g) Conditional compilation. h) assert. i) #include. j) ##. k) #. l) \. m) #line.

13.2 See below.

```
 1   // Print the values of the predefined macros
 2   #include <stdio.h>
 3   int main( void )
 4   {
 5      printf( "__LINE__ = %d\n", __LINE__ );
 6      printf( "__FILE__ = %s\n", __FILE__ );
 7      printf( "__DATE__ = %s\n", __DATE__ );
 8      printf( "__TIME__ = %s\n", __TIME__ );
 9      printf( "__STDC__ = %s\n", __STDC__ );
10   }
```

```
__LINE__  = 5
__FILE__  = ex13_02.c
__DATE__  = Jan  5 2012
__TIME__  = 09:38:58
__STDC__  = 1
```

13.3 a) `#if defined( Matrix )`
          `#undef Matrix`
          `#define Matrix 20`
          `#endif`
      b) `#define MAX 50`
      c) `#define SQUARE_NUMBER ( a ) ( ( a ) * ( a ))`
      d) `#include " splash.h "`
      e) `#ifdef YES`
          `#undef YES`
          `#define YES 5`
          `#endif`
      f) `#define VALUE 2`
      g) `#line 350`
      h) `#define AREA_RECTANGLE ( a, b ) ( ( a ) * ( b ))`

Exercises

13.4 *(Area of a Circle)* Write a program that defines a macro with one argument to compute the area of circle. The program should compute the area for circles of radius 5 to 15 and print the results in tabular format. The formula for the area of a circle is

$$\pi * r^2$$

where π is `3.14159`.

13.5 *(Adding Three Numbers)* Write a program that produces the following output:

```
The sum of a, b and c is 16.8
```

The program should define macro ADD with three arguments, a, b and c, and use ADD to produce the output.

13.6 *(Cube of a Number)* Write a program that defines and uses macro CUBE to determine the cube of a number. Input the values from the keyboard.

13.7 *(Largest of Three Numbers)* Write a program that defines and uses macro Largest3 to determine the largest of three numeric values. Macro Largest3 should use macro Largest2 which gives largest of two numbers, to determine the largest number. Input the values from the keyboard.

13.8 *(Printing a String)* Write a program that defines and uses macro PRINT to print a string value.

13.9 *(Printing an Array)* Write a program that defines and uses macro PRINTARRAY to print an array of integers. The macro should receive the array and the number of elements in the array as arguments.

13.10 *(Averaging the Contents of Array)* Write a program that defines and uses macro AVGARRAY to sum and average the values in a numeric array. The macro should receive the array and the number of elements in the array as arguments.

Other C Topics

*We'll use a signal I have tried
and found far-reaching and
easy to yell. Waa-hoo!*
—Zane Grey

It is quite a three-pipe problem.
—Sir Arthur Conan Doyle

Objectives

In this chapter, you'll:

- Redirect keyboard input to come from a file.

- Redirect screen output to be placed in a file.

- Write functions that use variable-length argument lists.

- Process command-line arguments.

- Compile multiple-source-file programs.

- Assign specific types to numeric constants.

- Process external asynchronous events in a program.

- Dynamically allocate arrays and resize memory that was dynamically allocated previously.

14.1 Introduction

This chapter presents several additional topics not ordinarily covered in introductory courses. Many of the capabilities discussed here are specific to particular operating systems, especially Linux/UNIX and Windows.

14.2 Redirecting I/O

In command-line applications, normally the input is received from the *keyboard* (standard input), and the output is displayed on the *screen* (standard output). On most computer systems—Linux/UNIX, Mac OS X and Windows systems in particular—it's possible to **redirect** inputs to come from a *file* rather than the keyboard and redirect outputs to be placed in a *file* rather than on the screen. Both forms of redirection can be accomplished without using the file-processing capabilities of the standard library.

There are several ways to redirect input and output from the command line—that is, a **Command Prompt** window in Windows, a shell in Linux or a **Terminal** window in Mac OS X. Consider the executable file `sum` (on Linux/UNIX systems) that inputs integers one at a time and keeps a running total of the values until the end-of-file indicator is set, then prints the result. Normally the user inputs integers from the keyboard and enters the end-of-file key combination to indicate that no further values will be input. With input redirection, the input can be stored in a file. For example, if the data is stored in file `input`, the command line

```
$ sum < input
```

executes the program `sum`; the **redirect input symbol** (<) indicates that the data in file `input` is to be used as input by the program. Redirecting input on a Windows system is performed identically.

The character `$` is a typical Linux/UNIX command-line prompt (some systems use a `%` prompt or other symbol). Students often find it difficult to understand that redirection is an operating system function, not another C feature.

The second method of redirecting input is **piping**. A **pipe** (|) causes the output of one program to be redirected as the input to another program. Suppose program `random` outputs a series of random integers; the output of `random` can be "piped" directly to program `sum` using the command line

```
$ random | sum
```

This causes the sum of the integers produced by random to be calculated. Piping is performed identically in Linux/UNIX and Windows.

The standard output stream can be redirected to a file by using the **redirect output symbol** (>). For example, to redirect the output of program random to file out, use

```
$ random > out
```

Finally, program output can be appended to the end of an existing file by using the **append output symbol** (>>). For example, to append the output from program random to file out created in the preceding command line, use the command line

```
$ random >> out
```

14.3 Variable-Length Argument Lists

It's possible to create functions that receive an unspecified number of arguments. Most programs in the text have used the standard library function printf, which, as you know, takes a variable number of arguments. As a minimum, printf must receive a string as its first argument, but printf can receive any number of additional arguments. The function prototype for printf is

```
int printf( const char *format, ... );
```

The ellipsis (...) in the function prototype indicates that the function receives a *variable number of arguments of any type*. The ellipsis must always be placed at the *end* of the parameter list.

The macros and definitions of the variable arguments headers <stdarg.h> (Fig. 14.1) provide the capabilities necessary to build functions with variable-length argument lists. Figure 14.2 demonstrates function average (lines 25–40) that receives a variable number of arguments. The first argument of average is always the number of values to be averaged.

Identifier	Explanation
va_list	A *type* suitable for holding information needed by macros va_start, va_arg and va_end. To access the arguments in a variable-length argument list, an object of type va_list must be defined.
va_start	A *macro* that's invoked before the arguments of a variable-length argument list can be accessed. The macro initializes the object declared with va_list for use by the va_arg and va_end macros.
va_arg	A *macro* that expands to the value of the next argument in the variable-length argument list—the value has the type specified as the macro's second argument. Each invocation of va_arg modifies the object declared with va_list so that it points to the next argument in the list.
va_end	A *macro* that facilitates a normal return from a function whose variable-length argument list was referred to by the va_start macro.

Fig. 14.1 | stdarg.h variable-length argument-list type and macros.

```
 1   // Fig. 14.2: fig14_02.c
 2   // Using variable-length argument lists
 3   #include <stdio.h>
 4   #include <stdarg.h>
 5
 6   double average( int i, ... ); // prototype
 7
 8   int main( void )
 9   {
10      double w = 37.5;
11      double x = 22.5;
12      double y = 1.7;
13      double z = 10.2;
14
15      printf( "%s%.1f\n%s%.1f\n%s%.1f\n%s%.1f\n\n",
16         "w = ", w, "x = ", x, "y = ", y, "z = ", z );
17      printf( "%s%.3f\n%s%.3f\n%s%.3f\n",
18         "The average of w and x is ", average( 2, w, x ),
19         "The average of w, x, and y is ", average( 3, w, x, y ),
20         "The average of w, x, y, and z is ",
21         average( 4, w, x, y, z ) );
22   } // end main
23
24   // calculate average
25   double average( int i, ... )
26   {
27      double total = 1; // initialize total
28      int j; // counter for selecting arguments
29      va_list ap; // stores information needed by va_start and va_end
30
31      va_start( ap, i ); // initializes the va_list object
32
33      // process variable-length argument list
34      for ( j = 1; j <= i; ++j ) {
35         total += va_arg( ap, double );
36      } // end for
37
38      va_end( ap ); // clean up variable-length argument list
39      return total / i; // calculate average
40   } // end function average
```

```
w = 37.5
x = 22.5
y = 1.7
z = 10.2

The average of w and x is 30.000
The average of w, x, and y is 20.567
The average of w, x, y, and z is 17.975
```

Fig. 14.2 | Using variable-length argument lists.

Function average (lines 25–40) uses all the definitions and macros of header <stdarg.h>. Object ap, of type **va_list** (line 29), is used by macros **va_start**, **va_arg** and **va_end** to process the variable-length argument list of function average. The function begins by invoking macro va_start (line 31) to initialize object ap for use in va_arg and va_end. The macro receives two arguments—object ap and the identifier of the rightmost argument in the argument list *before* the ellipsis—i in this case (va_start uses i here to determine where the variable-length argument list begins). Next, function average repeatedly adds the arguments in the variable-length argument list to variable total (lines 34–36). The value to be added to total is retrieved from the argument list by invoking macro va_arg. Macro va_arg receives two arguments—object ap and the *type* of the value expected in the argument list—double in this case. The macro returns the value of the argument. Function average invokes macro va_end (line 38) with object ap as an argument to facilitate a normal return to main from average. Finally, the average is calculated and returned to main.

> **Common Programming Error 14.1**
> *Placing an ellipsis in the middle of a function parameter list is a syntax error—an ellipsis may be placed only at the end of the parameter list.*

The reader may question how function printf and function scanf know what type to use in each va_arg macro. The answer is that they scan the format conversion specifiers in the format control string to determine the type of the next argument to be processed.

14.4 Using Command-Line Arguments

On many systems, it's possible to pass arguments to main from a command line by including parameters int argc and char *argv[] in the parameter list of main. Parameter **argc** receives the number of command-line arguments that the user has entered. Parameter **argv** is an array of strings in which the actual command-line arguments are stored. Common uses of command-line arguments include passing options to a program and passing filenames to a program.

Figure 14.3 copies a file into another file one character at a time. We assume that the executable file for the program is called mycopy. A typical command line for the mycopy program on a Linux/UNIX system is

```
$ mycopy input output
```

This command line indicates that file input is to be copied to file output. When the program is executed, if argc is not 3 (mycopy counts as one of the arguments), the program prints an error message and terminates. Otherwise, array argv contains the strings "mycopy", "input" and "output". The second and third arguments on the command line are used as file names by the program. The files are opened using function fopen. If both files are opened successfully, characters are read from file input and written to file output until the end-of-file indicator for file input is set. Then the program terminates. The result is an exact copy of file input (if no errors occur during processing). See your system documentation for more information on command-line arguments. [*Note:* In Visual C++, you can specify the command-line arguments by right clicking the project name in the Solution Explorer and selecting **Properties**, then expanding **Configuration Properties**, selecting **Debugging** and entering the arguments in the textbox to the right of **Command Arguments**.]

```
 1   // Fig. 14.3: fig14_03.c
 2   // Using command-line arguments
 3   #include <stdio.h>
 4
 5   int main( int argc, char *argv[] )
 6   {
 7      FILE *inFilePtr; // input file pointer
 8      FILE *outFilePtr; // output file pointer
 9      int c; // define c to hold characters read from the source file
10
11      // check number of command-line arguments
12      if ( argc != 3 ) {
13         puts( "Usage: mycopy infile outfile" );
14      } // end if
15      else {
16         // if input file can be opened
17         if ( ( inFilePtr = fopen( argv[ 1 ], "r" ) ) != NULL ) {
18            // if output file can be opened
19            if ( ( outFilePtr = fopen( argv[ 2 ], "w" ) ) != NULL ) {
20               // read and output characters
21               while ( ( c = fgetc( inFilePtr ) ) != EOF ) {
22                  fputc( c, outFilePtr );
23               } // end while
24
25               fclose( outFilePtr ); // close the output file
26            } // end if
27            else { // output file could not be opened
28               printf( "File \"%s\" could not be opened\n", argv[ 2 ] );
29            } // end else
30
31            fclose( inFilePtr ); // close the input file
32         } // end if
33         else { // input file could not be opened
34            printf( "File \"%s\" could not be opened\n", argv[ 1 ] );
35         } // end else
36      } // end else
37   } // end main
```

Fig. 14.3 | Using command-line arguments.

14.5 Notes on Compiling Multiple-Source-File Programs

It's possible to build programs that consist of multiple source files. There are several considerations when creating programs in multiple files. For example, the definition of a function must be entirely contained in one file—it cannot span two or more files.

In Chapter 5, we introduced the concepts of storage class and scope. We learned that variables declared *outside* any function definition are referred to as *global variables*. Global variables are accessible to any function defined in the same file after the variable is declared. Global variables also are accessible to functions in other files. However, the global variables must be declared in each file in which they're used. For example, to refer to global integer variable flag in another file, you can use the declaration

```
extern int flag;
```

This declaration uses the storage-class specifier **extern** to indicate that variable flag is defined either *later in the same file or in a different file*. The compiler informs the linker that unresolved references to variable flag appear in the file. If the linker finds a proper global definition, the linker resolves the references by indicating where flag is located. If the linker cannot locate a definition of flag, it issues an error message and does not produce an executable file. Any identifier that's declared at file scope is extern by default.

Software Engineering Observation 14.1

Global variables should be avoided unless application performance is critical because they violate the principle of least privilege.

Just as **extern** declarations can be used to declare *global variables* to other program files, *function prototypes can extend the scope of a function beyond the file in which it's defined* (the extern specifier is not required in a function prototype). Simply include the function prototype in each file in which the function is invoked and compile the files together (see Section 13.2). Function prototypes indicate to the compiler that the specified function is defined either later in the *same* file or in a *different* file. Again, the compiler does *not* attempt to resolve references to such a function—that task is left to the linker. If the linker cannot locate a proper function definition, the linker issues an error message.

As an example of using function prototypes to extend the scope of a function, consider any program containing the preprocessor directive #include <stdio.h>, which includes a file containing the function prototypes for functions such as printf and scanf. Other functions in the file can use printf and scanf to accomplish their tasks. The printf and scanf functions are defined in other files. We do *not* need to know *where* they're defined. We're simply reusing the code in our programs. The linker resolves our references to these functions automatically. This process enables us to use the functions in the standard library.

Software Engineering Observation 14.2

Creating programs in multiple source files facilitates software reusability and good software engineering. Functions may be common to many applications. In such instances, those functions should be stored in their own source files, and each source file should have a corresponding header file containing function prototypes. This enables programmers of different applications to reuse the same code by including the proper header file and compiling their applications with the corresponding source file.

It's possible to restrict the scope of a global variable or a function to the file in which it's defined. The storage-class specifier **static**, when applied to a global variable or a function, prevents it from being used by any function that's not defined in the same file. This is referred to as **internal linkage**. Global variables and functions that are *not* preceded by static in their definitions have **external linkage**—they can be accessed in other files if those files contain proper declarations and/or function prototypes.

The global variable declaration

```
static const double PI = 3.14159;
```

creates constant variable PI of type double, initializes it to 3.14159 and indicates that PI is known *only* to functions in the file in which it's defined.

The static specifier is commonly used with utility functions that are called only by functions in a particular file. If a function is not required outside a particular file, the principle of least privilege should be enforced by using static. If a function is defined *before* it's used in a file, static should be applied to the function definition. Otherwise, static should be applied to the function prototype.

When building large programs in multiple source files, compiling the program becomes tedious if small changes are made to one file and the entire program must be recompiled. Many systems provide special utilities that recompile *only* the modified program file. On Linux/UNIX systems the utility is called **make**. Utility make reads a file called **makefile** that contains instructions for compiling and linking the program. Products such as Eclipse™ and Microsoft® Visual C++® provide similar utilities as well.

14.6 Program Termination with exit and atexit

The general utilities library (<stdlib.h>) provides methods of terminating program execution by means other than a conventional return from function main. Function **exit** causes a program to terminate. The function often is used to terminate a program when an input error is detected, or when a file to be processed by the program cannot be opened. Function **atexit** registers a function that should be called upon *successful termination* of the program—i.e., either when the program terminates by reaching the end of main, or when exit is invoked.

Function atexit takes as an argument a pointer to a function (i.e., the *function name*). *Functions called at program termination cannot have arguments and cannot return a value.*

Function exit takes one argument. The argument is normally the symbolic constant **EXIT_SUCCESS** or the symbolic constant **EXIT_FAILURE**. If exit is called with EXIT_SUCCESS, the implementation-defined value for successful termination is returned to the calling environment. If exit is called with EXIT_FAILURE, the implementation-defined value for unsuccessful termination is returned. When function exit is invoked, any functions previously registered with atexit are invoked in the *reverse* order of their registration, all streams associated with the program are flushed and closed, and control returns to the host environment.

Figure 14.4 tests functions exit and atexit. The program prompts the user to determine whether the program should be terminated with exit or by reaching the end of main. Function print is executed at program termination in each case.

```
1   // Fig. 14.4: fig14_04.c
2   // Using the exit and atexit functions
3   #include <stdio.h>
4   #include <stdlib.h>
5
6   void print( void ); // prototype
7
8   int main( void )
9   {
10      int answer; // user's menu choice
11
```

Fig. 14.4 | Using the exit and atexit functions. (Part 1 of 2.)

```
12        atexit( print ); // register function print
13        puts( "Enter 1 to terminate program with function exit"
14            "\nEnter 2 to terminate program normally" );
15        scanf( "%d", &answer );
16
17        // call exit if answer is 1
18        if ( answer == 1 ) {
19            puts( "\nTerminating program with function exit" );
20            exit( EXIT_SUCCESS );
21        } // end if
22
23        puts( "\nTerminating program by reaching the end of main" );
24    } // end main
25
26    // display message before termination
27    void print( void )
28    {
29        puts( "Executing function print at program "
30            "termination\nProgram terminated" );
31    } // end function print
```

```
Enter 1 to terminate program with function exit
Enter 2 to terminate program normally
1

Terminating program with function exit
Executing function print at program termination
Program terminated
```

```
Enter 1 to terminate program with function exit
Enter 2 to terminate program normally
2

Terminating program by reaching the end of main
Executing function print at program termination
Program terminated
```

Fig. 14.4 | Using the exit and atexit functions. (Part 2 of 2.)

14.7 Suffixes for Integer and Floating-Point Literals

C provides integer and floating-point *suffixes* for explicitly specifying the data types of integer and floating-point literal values. (The C standard refers to such literal values as constants). If an integer literal is *not* suffixed, its type is determined by the first type capable of storing a value of that size (first int, then long int, then unsigned long int, etc.). A floating-point literal that's *not* suffixed is automatically of type double.

The integer suffixes are: **u** or **U** for an unsigned int, **l** or **L** for a long int, and **ll** or **LL** for a long long int. You can combine u or U with those for long int and long long int to create unsigned literals for the larger integer types. The following literals are of type unsigned int, long int, unsigned long int and unsigned long long int, respectively:

```
174u
8358L
28373ul
987654321011u
```

The floating-point suffixes are: **f** or **F** for a **float**, and **l** or **L** for a **long double**. The following constants are of type **float** and **long double**, respectively:

```
1.28f
3.14159L
```

14.8 Signal Handling

An *external asynchronous* event, or **signal**, can cause a program to terminate prematurely. Some events include **interrupts** (typing *<Ctrl> c* on a Linux/UNIX or Windows system), **illegal instructions**, **segmentation violations**, termination orders from the operating system and **floating-point exceptions** (division by zero or multiplying large floating-point values). The **signal-handling library** (**<signal.h>**) provides the capability to **trap** unexpected events with function **signal**. Function **signal** receives two arguments—an integer *signal number* and a *pointer to the signal-handling function*. Signals can be generated by function **raise**, which takes an integer signal number as an argument. Figure 14.5 summarizes the *standard signals* defined in header file <signal.h>.

Signal	Explanation
SIGABRT	Abnormal termination of the program (such as a call to function abort).
SIGFPE	An erroneous arithmetic operation, such as a divide-by-zero or an operation resulting in overflow.
SIGILL	Detection of an illegal instruction.
SIGINT	Receipt of an interactive attention signal.
SIGSEGV	An attempt to access to memory that is not allocated to a program.
SIGTERM	A termination request sent to the program.

Fig. 14.5 | signal.h standard signals.

Figure 14.6 uses function signal to *trap* a SIGINT. Line 15 calls signal with SIGINT and a pointer to function signalHandler (remember that the name of a function is a pointer to the beginning of the function). When a signal of type SIGINT occurs, control passes to function signalHandler, which prints a message and gives the user the option to continue normal execution of the program. If the user wishes to continue execution, the signal handler is reinitialized by calling signal again and control returns to the point in the program at which the signal was detected. In this program, function raise (line 24) is used to simulate a SIGINT. A random number between 1 and 50 is chosen. If the number is 25, raise is called to generate the signal. Normally, SIGINTs are initiated outside the program. For example, typing *<Ctrl> c* during program execution on a Linux/UNIX or Windows system generates a SIGINT that *terminates* program execution. Signal handling can be used to trap the SIGINT and prevent the program from being terminated.

```c
 1  // Fig. 14.6: fig14_06.c
 2  // Using signal handling
 3  #include <stdio.h>
 4  #include <signal.h>
 5  #include <stdlib.h>
 6  #include <time.h>
 7
 8  void signalHandler( int signalValue ); // prototype
 9
10  int main( void )
11  {
12     int i; // counter used to loop 100 times
13     int x; // variable to hold random values between 1-50
14
15     signal( SIGINT, signalHandler ); // register signal handler
16     srand( time( NULL ) );
17
18     // output numbers 1 to 100
19     for ( i = 1; i <= 100; ++i ) {
20        x = 1 + rand() % 50; // generate random number to raise SIGINT
21
22        // raise SIGINT when x is 25
23        if ( x == 25 ) {
24           raise( SIGINT );
25        } // end if
26
27        printf( "%4d", i );
28
29        // output \n when i is a multiple of 10
30        if ( i % 10 == 0 ) {
31           printf( "%s", "\n" );
32        } // end if
33     } // end for
34  } // end main
35
36  // handles signal
37  void signalHandler( int signalValue )
38  {
39     int response; // user's response to signal (1 or 2)
40
41     printf( "%s%d%s\n%s",
42        "\nInterrupt signal ( ", signalValue, " ) received.",
43        "Do you wish to continue ( 1 = yes or 2 = no )? " );
44
45     scanf( "%d", &response );
46
47     // check for invalid responses
48     while ( response != 1 && response != 2 ) {
49        printf( "%s", "( 1 = yes or 2 = no )? " );
50        scanf( "%d", &response );
51     } // end while
52
```

Fig. 14.6 | Using signal handling. (Part 1 of 2.)

```
53      // determine whether it's time to exit
54      if ( response == 1 ) {
55         // reregister signal handler for next SIGINT
56         signal( SIGINT, signalHandler );
57      } // end if
58      else {
59         exit( EXIT_SUCCESS );
60      } // end else
61   } // end function signalHandler
```

```
  1   2   3   4   5   6   7   8   9  10
 11  12  13  14  15  16  17  18  19  20
 21  22  23  24  25  26  27  28  29  30
 31  32  33  34  35  36  37  38  39  40
 41  42  43  44  45  46  47  48  49  50
 51  52  53  54  55  56  57  58  59  60
 61  62  63  64  65  66  67  68  69  70
 71  72  73  74  75  76  77  78  79  80
 81  82  83  84  85  86  87  88  89  90
 91  92  93
Interrupt signal ( 2 ) received.
Do you wish to continue ( 1 = yes or 2 = no )? 1
 94  95  96
Interrupt signal ( 2 ) received.
Do you wish to continue ( 1 = yes or 2 = no )? 2
```

Fig. 14.6 | Using signal handling. (Part 2 of 2.)

14.9 Dynamic Memory Allocation: Functions calloc and realloc

Chapter 12 introduced the notion of dynamically allocating memory using function malloc. As we stated in Chapter 12, arrays are better than linked lists for rapid sorting, searching and data access. However, arrays are normally **static data structures**. The general utilities library (**stdlib.h**) provides two other functions for dynamic memory allocation—**calloc** and **realloc**. These functions can be used to create and modify **dynamic arrays**. As shown in Chapter 7, a pointer to an array can be subscripted like an array. Thus, a pointer to a contiguous portion of memory created by calloc can be manipulated as an array. Function calloc dynamically allocates memory for an array. The prototype for calloc is

```
void *calloc( size_t nmemb, size_t size );
```

Its two arguments represent the *number of elements* (nmemb) and the *size* of each element (size). Function calloc also initializes the elements of the array to zero. The function returns a pointer to the allocated memory, or a NULL pointer if the memory is *not* allocated. The primary difference between malloc and calloc is that calloc *clears the memory* it allocates and malloc *does not*.

Function realloc *changes the size* of an object allocated by a previous call to malloc, calloc or realloc. The original object's contents are *not modified* provided that the amount of memory allocated is *larger* than the amount allocated previously. Otherwise, the contents are unchanged up to the size of the new object. The prototype for realloc is

```
void *realloc( void *ptr, size_t size );
```

The two arguments are a pointer to the original object (ptr) and the *new size* of the object (size). If ptr is NULL, realloc works identically to malloc. If ptr is not NULL and size is greater than zero, realloc tries to *allocate a new block of memory* for the object. If the new space *cannot* be allocated, the object pointed to by ptr is unchanged. Function realloc returns either a pointer to the reallocated memory, or a NULL pointer to indicate that the memory was not reallocated.

Error-Prevention Tip 14.1
Avoid zero-sized allocations in calls to malloc, calloc *and* realloc.

14.10 Unconditional Branching with goto

Throughout the text we've stressed the importance of using structured programming techniques to build reliable software that's easy to debug, maintain and modify. In some cases, performance is more important than strict adherence to structured programming techniques. In these cases, some unstructured programming techniques may be used. For example, we can use break to terminate execution of a repetition structure before the loop-continuation condition becomes false. This saves unnecessary repetitions of the loop if the task is completed *before* loop termination.

Another instance of unstructured programming is the **goto** statement—an unconditional branch. The result of the goto statement is a change in the flow of control to the first statement after the label specified in the goto statement. A label is an identifier followed by a colon. A label must appear in the same function as the goto statement that refers to it. Figure 14.7 uses goto statements to loop ten times and print the counter value each time. After initializing count to 1, line 11 tests count to determine whether it's greater than 10 (the label start: is skipped because labels do not perform any action). If so, control is transferred from the goto to the first statement after the label end: (which appears at line 20). Otherwise, lines 15–16 print and increment count, and control transfers from the goto (line 18) to the first statement after the label start: (which appears at line 9).

```c
1   // Fig. 14.7: fig14_07.c
2   // Using the goto statement
3   #include <stdio.h>
4
5   int main( void )
6   {
7      int count = 1; // initialize count
8
9      start: // label
10
11        if ( count > 10 ) {
12           goto end;
13        } // end if
14
15        printf( "%d  ", count );
16        ++count;
```

Fig. 14.7 | Using the goto statement. (Part 1 of 2.)

```
17
18          goto start; // goto start on line 9
19
20      end: // label
21          putchar( '\n' );
22  } // end main
```

```
1  2  3  4  5  6  7  8  9  10
```

Fig. 14.7 | Using the goto statement. (Part 2 of 2.)

In Chapter 3, we stated that only three control structures are required to write any program—sequence, selection and repetition. When the rules of structured programming are followed, it's possible to create deeply nested control structures from which it's difficult to escape efficiently. Some programmers use goto statements in such situations as a quick exit from a deeply nested structure. This eliminates the need to test multiple conditions to escape from a control structure. There are some additional situations where goto is actually recommended—see, for example, CERT recommendation MEM12-C, "Consider using a Goto-Chain when leaving a function on error when using and releasing resources."

Performance Tip 14.1

The goto statement can be used to exit deeply nested control structures efficiently.

Software Engineering Observation 14.3

The goto statement is unstructured and can lead to programs that are more difficult to debug, maintain and modify.

Summary

Section 14.2 Redirecting I/O
- On many computer systems it's possible to redirect input to a program and output from a program.
- Input is redirected from the command line using the redirect input symbol (<) or a pipe (|).
- Output is redirected from the command line using the redirect output symbol (>) or the append output symbol (>>). The redirect output symbol simply stores the program output in a file, and the append output symbol appends the output to the end of a file.

Section 14.3 Variable-Length Argument Lists
- The macros and definitions of the variable arguments header <stdarg.h> provide the capabilities necessary to build functions with variable-length argument lists.
- An ellipsis (...) in a function prototype indicates a variable number of arguments.
- Type va_list is suitable for holding information needed by macros va_start, va_arg and va_end. To access the arguments in a variable-length argument list, an object of type va_list must be declared.
- Invoke macro va_start before accessing the arguments of a variable-length argument list. The macro initializes the object declared with va_list for use by the va_arg and va_end macros.

- Macro va_arg expands to an expression of the value and type of the next argument in the variable-length argument list. Each invocation of va_arg modifies the object declared with va_list so that the object points to the next argument in the list.

- Macro va_end facilitates a normal return from a function whose variable-length argument list was referred to by the va_start macro.

Section 14.4 Using Command-Line Arguments

- On many systems it's possible to pass arguments to main from the command line by including the parameters int argc and char *argv[] in the parameter list of main. Parameter argc receives the number of command-line arguments. Parameter argv is an array of strings in which the actual command-line arguments are stored.

Section 14.5 Notes on Compiling Multiple-Source-File Programs

- A function definition must be entirely contained in one file—it cannot span two or more files.

- Global variables must be declared in each file in which they're used.

- Function prototypes can extend the scope of a function beyond the file in which it's defined. This is accomplished by including the function prototype in each file in which the function is invoked and compiling the files together.

- The storage-class specifier static, when applied to a global variable or a function, prevents it from being used by any function that's not defined in the same file. This is referred to as internal linkage. Global variables and functions that are not preceded by static in their definitions have external linkage—they can be accessed in other files if those files contain proper declarations or function prototypes.

- The static specifier is commonly used with utility functions that are called only by functions in a particular file. If a function is not required outside a particular file, the principle of least privilege should be enforced by using static.

- The storage-class specifier extern indicates that a variable is defined either later in the same file or in a different file.

- When building large programs in multiple source files, compiling the program becomes tedious if small changes are made to one file and the entire program must be recompiled. Many systems provide special utilities that recompile only the modified program file. On Linux/UNIX systems the utility is called make. Utility make reads a file called makefile that contains instructions for compiling and linking the program.

Section 14.6 Program Termination with *exit* and *atexit*

- Function exit forces a program to terminate.

- Function atexit registers a function to be called upon normal termination of the program—i.e., either when the program terminates by reaching the end of main or when exit is invoked.

- Function atexit takes a pointer to a function as an argument. Functions called at program termination cannot have arguments and cannot return a value.

- Function exit takes one argument. The argument is normally the symbolic constant EXIT_SUCCESS or the symbolic constant EXIT_FAILURE. If exit is called with EXIT_SUCCESS, the implementation-defined value for successful termination is returned to the calling environment. If exit is called with EXIT_FAILURE, the implementation-defined value for unsuccessful termination is returned.

- When function exit is invoked, any functions registered with atexit are invoked in the reverse order of their registration, all streams associated with the program are flushed and closed, and control returns to the host environment.

Section 14.7 Suffixes for Integer and Floating-Point Literals

- C provides integer and floating-point suffixes for specifying the types of integer and floating-point constants. The integer suffixes are: u or U for an unsigned integer, l or L for a long integer, and ul or UL for an unsigned long integer. If an integer constant is not suffixed, its type is determined by the first type capable of storing a value of that size (first int, then long int, then unsigned long int). The floating-point suffixes are: f or F for a float, and l or L for a long double. A floating-point constant that's not suffixed is of type double.

Section 14.8 Signal Handling

- The signal-handling library enables trapping of unexpected events with function signal. Function signal receives two arguments—an integer signal number and a pointer to the signal-handling function.
- Signals can also be generated with function raise and an integer argument.

Section 14.9 Dynamic Memory Allocation: Functions `calloc` and `realloc`

- The general utilities library (<stdlib.h>) provides two functions for dynamic memory allocation—calloc and realloc. These functions can be used to create dynamic arrays.
- Function calloc receives two arguments—the number of elements (nmemb) and the size of each element (size)—and initializes the elements of the array to zero. The function returns either a pointer to the allocated memory, or a NULL pointer if the memory is not allocated.
- Function realloc changes the size of an object allocated by a previous call to malloc, calloc or realloc. The original object's contents are not modified, provided that the amount of memory allocated is larger than the amount allocated previously.
- Function realloc takes two arguments—a pointer to the original object (ptr) and the new size of the object (size). If ptr is NULL, realloc works identically to malloc. If size is 0 and the pointer received is not NULL, the memory for the object is freed. Otherwise, if ptr is not NULL and size is greater than zero, realloc tries to allocate a new block of memory for the object. If the new space cannot be allocated, the object pointed to by ptr is unchanged. Function realloc returns either a pointer to the reallocated memory, or a NULL pointer.

Section 14.10 Unconditional Branching with `goto`

- The result of the goto statement is a change in the flow of control of the program. Program execution continues at the first statement after the label specified in the goto statement.
- A label is an identifier followed by a colon. A label must appear in the same function as the goto statement that refers to it.

Terminology

makefile 564
pipe symbol (|) 558
raise 566
redirect input from a file 558
redirect input symbol < 558
redirect output symbol > 559
segmentation violation 566
signal 566
signal-handling library 566
<signal.h> 566
static keyword 895

<stdlib.h> header file 568
trap 566
unsigned integer 898
unsigned long int 899
va_arg 560
va_end 561
va_list 560
va_start 560
variable arguments header <stdarg.h> 559
variable-length argument list 559

Self-Review Exercise

14.1   Fill in the blanks in each of the following:

a) The _____ symbol redirects input data from a file rather than the keyboard.

b) The _____ symbol is used to redirect the screen output so that it's placed in a file.

c) The _____ symbol is used to append the output of a program to the end of a file.

d) A(n) _____ directs the output of one program to be the input of another program.

e) A(n) _____ in the parameter list of a function indicates that the function can receive a variable number of arguments.

f) Macro _____ must be invoked before the arguments in a variable-length argument list can be accessed.

g) Macro _____ accesses the individual arguments of a variable-length argument list.

h) Macro _____ facilitates a normal return from a function whose variable-length argument list was referred to by macro va_start.

i) Argument _____ of main receives the number of arguments in a command line.

j) Argument _____ of main stores command-line arguments as character strings.

k) Linux/UNIX utility _____ reads a file called _____ that contains instructions for compiling and linking a program consisting of multiple source files.

l) Function _____ forces a program to terminate execution.

m) Function _____ registers a function to be called upon normal program termination.

n) An integer or floating-point _____ can be appended to an integer or floating-point constant to specify the exact type of the constant.

o) Function _____ can be used to trap unexpected events.

p) Function _____ generates a signal from within a program.

q) Function _____ dynamically allocates memory for an array and initializes the elements to zero.

r) Function _____ changes the size of a block of previously allocated dynamic memory.

Answers to Self-Review Exercise

14.1   a) redirect input (<). b) redirect output (>). c) append output (>>). d) pipe (|). e) ellipsis (...). f) va_start. g) va_arg. h) va_end. i) argc. j) argv. k) make, makefile. l) exit. m) atexit. n) suffix. o) signal. p) raise. q) calloc. r) realloc.

Exercises

14.2   *(Variable-Length Argument List: Calculating Sums)* Write a program that calculates the sum of a series of double numbers that are passed to a function sum using a variable-length argument list. Test your function with several calls, each with a different number of arguments.

14.3   *(Printing Command-Line Arguments)* Write a program that prints the command-line arguments of the program in reverse order.

14.4   *(Printing Characters)* Write a program that prints the characters from a to z using user instructions. Use command-line arguments to pass either argument -u for upper case or -1 for lower case. [*Note:* This is the standard format for passing options to a program in UNIX.]

14.5   *(Signal Handling)* Read the documentation for your compiler to determine what signals are supported by the signal handling library (`<signal.h>`). Write a program that contains signal handlers for the standard signals SIGABRT and SIGINT. The program should test the trapping of these signals by calling function abort to generate a signal of type SIGABRT and by having the user type *<Ctrl>* c to generate a signal of type SIGINT.

14.6   *(Dynamic Array Allocation)* Write a program that dynamically allocates an array of characters. The size of the array should be input from the keyboard. The elements of the array should be assigned characters input from the keyboard. Print the characters in the array. Next, reallocate the memory for the array to 40% of the current number of elements. Print the characters remaining in the array to confirm that they match the first 40% of the characters in the original array.

14.7   *(Command-Line Arguments)* Write a program that takes two command-line arguments that are file names, reads the characters from the first file one at a time and prints them in uppercase in the second file.

14.8   *(goto Statement)* Write a program that uses goto statements and only the following three printf statements to simulate a nested looping structure that prints a rectangle of asterisks as shown below:

```
printf( "%s", "*" );
printf( "%s", " " );
printf( "%s", "\n" )
```

```
********
*      *
*      *
********
```

C++ as a Better C; Introducing Object Technology

15

Objectives

In this chapter you'll learn:

- C++ enhancements to C.
- The header files of the C++ Standard Library.
- To use `inline` functions.
- To use references.
- To use default arguments.
- To use the unary scope resolution operator to access a global variable.
- To overload functions.
- To create and use function templates that perform identical operations on data of different types.

15.1 Introduction

We now begin the second section of this unique text. The first 14 chapters presented a thorough treatment of procedural programming and top-down program design with C. The C++ section (Chapters 15–24) introduces two additional programming paradigms—**object-oriented programming** (with classes, encapsulation, objects, operator overloading, inheritance and polymorphism) and **generic programming** (with function templates and class templates). These chapters emphasize "crafting valuable classes" to create reusable software componentry.

15.2 C++

C++ improves on many of C's features and provides object-oriented-programming (OOP) capabilities that increase software productivity, quality and reusability. This chapter discusses many of C++'s enhancements to C.

C's designers and early implementers never anticipated that the language would become such a phenomenon. When a programming language becomes as entrenched as C, new requirements demand that the language evolve rather than simply be displaced by a new language. C++ was developed by Bjarne Stroustrup at Bell Laboratories and was originally called "C with classes." The name C++ includes C's increment operator (++) to indicate that C++ is an enhanced version of C.

Chapters 15–24 provide an introduction to the version of C++ standardized in the United States through the American National Standards Institute (ANSI) and worldwide through the International Standards Organization (ISO). We have done a careful walk-through of the ANSI/ISO C++ standard document and audited our presentation against it for completeness and accuracy. However, C++ is a rich language, and there are some subtleties in the language and some advanced subjects that we have not covered. If you need additional technical details on C++, we suggest that you read the C++ standard document "Programming languages—C++" (document number ISO/IEC 14882:2011), which can be purchased from various standards organization websites, such as ansi.org and iso.org.

15.3 A Simple Program: Adding Two Integers

This section revisits the addition program of Fig. 2.5 and illustrates several important features of the C++ language as well as some differences between C and C++. C file names have the .c (lowercase) extension. C++ file names can have one of several extensions, such as .cpp, .cxx or .C (uppercase). We use the extension .cpp.

Figure 15.1 uses C++-style input and output to obtain two integers typed by a user at the keyboard, computes the sum of these values and outputs the result. Lines 1 and 2 each begin with //, indicating that the remainder of each line is a comment. C++ allows you to begin a comment with // and use the remainder of the line as comment text. A // comment is a maximum of one line long. C++ programmers may also use /*...*/ C-style comments, which can be more than one line long.

```
1   // Fig. 15.1: fig15_01.cpp
2   // Addition program that displays the sum of two numbers.
3   #include <iostream> // allows program to perform input and output
4
5   int main()
6   {
7      int number1; // first integer to add
8
9      std::cout << "Enter first integer: "; // prompt user for data
10     std::cin >> number1; // read first integer from user into number1
11
12     int number2; // second integer to add
13     int sum; // sum of number1 and number2
14
15     std::cout << "Enter second integer: "; // prompt user for data
16     std::cin >> number2; // read second integer from user into number2
17     sum = number1 + number2; // add the numbers; store result in sum
18     std::cout << "Sum is " << sum << std::endl; // display sum; end line
19  } // end function main
```

```
Enter first integer: 45
Enter second integer: 72
Sum is 117
```

Fig. 15.1 | Addition program that displays the sum of two numbers.

The C++ preprocessor directive in line 3 exhibits the standard C++ style for including header files from the standard library. This line tells the C++ preprocessor to include the contents of the input/output stream header file <iostream>. This file must be included for any program that outputs data to the screen or inputs data from the keyboard using C++-style stream input/output. We discuss iostream's many features in detail in Chapter 23, Stream Input/Output.

As in C, every C++ program begins execution with function main (line 5). Keyword int to the left of main indicates that main returns an integer value. C++ requires you to specify the return type, possibly void, for all functions. In C++, specifying a parameter list with empty parentheses is equivalent to specifying a void parameter list in C. In C, using empty parentheses in a function definition or prototype is dangerous. It disables compile-time argument checking in function calls, which allows the caller to pass any arguments to the function. This could lead to runtime errors.

Common Programming Error 15.1

Omitting the return type in a C++ function definition is a syntax error.

Line 7 is a familiar variable declaration. Declarations can be placed almost anywhere in a C++ program, but they must appear before their corresponding variables are used in the program. For example, in Fig. 15.1, the declaration in line 7 could have been placed immediately before line 10, the declaration in line 12 could have been placed immediately before line 16 and the declaration in line 13 could have been placed immediately before line 17.

Good Programming Practice 15.1

Always place a blank line between a declaration and adjacent executable statements. This makes the declarations stand out in the program, enhancing program clarity.

Line 9 uses the **standard output stream object**—`std::cout`—and the **stream insertion operator**, `<<`, to display the string `"Enter first integer: "`. Output and input in C++ are accomplished with streams of characters. Thus, when line 9 executes, it sends the stream of characters `"Enter first integer: "` to `std::cout`, which is normally "connected" to the screen. We like to pronounce the preceding statement as "`std::cout` *gets* the character string `"Enter first integer: "`."

Line 10 uses the **standard input stream object**—`std::cin`—and the **stream extraction operator**, `>>`, to obtain a value from the keyboard. Using the stream extraction operator with `std::cin` takes character input from the standard input stream, which is usually the keyboard. We like to pronounce the preceding statement as, "`std::cin` *gives* a value to `number1`" or simply "`std::cin` *gives* `number1`."

When the computer executes the statement in line 10, it waits for the user to enter a value for variable `number1`. The user responds by typing an integer (as characters), then pressing the *Enter* key. The computer converts the character representation of the number to an integer and assigns this value to the variable `number1`.

Line 15 displays `"Enter second integer: "` on the screen, prompting the user to take action. Line 16 obtains a value for variable `number2` from the user.

The assignment statement in line 17 calculates the sum of the variables `number1` and `number2` and assigns the result to variable `sum`. Line 18 displays the character string `Sum is` followed by the numerical value of variable `sum` followed by `std::endl`—a so-called **stream manipulator**. The name `endl` is an abbreviation for "end line." The `std::endl` stream manipulator outputs a newline, then "flushes the output buffer." This simply means that, on some systems where outputs accumulate in the machine until there are enough to "make it worthwhile" to display on the screen, `std::endl` forces any accumulated outputs to be displayed at that moment. This can be important when the outputs are prompting the user for an action, such as entering data.

We place `std::` before `cout`, `cin` and `endl`. This is required when we use standard C++ header files. The notation `std::cout` specifies that we're using a name, in this case `cout`, that belongs to "namespace" `std`. Namespaces are an advanced C++ feature that we do not discuss in these introductory C++ chapters. For now, you should simply remember to include `std::` before each mention of `cout`, `cin` and `endl` in a program. This can be cumbersome—in Fig. 15.3, we introduce the using statement, which will enable us to avoid placing std:: before each use of a namespace std name.

The statement in line 18 outputs values of different types. The stream insertion operator "knows" how to output each type of data. Using multiple stream insertion operators (<<) in a single statement is referred to as **concatenating, chaining** or **cascading stream insertion operations.**

Calculations can also be performed in output statements. We could have combined the statements in lines 17 and 18 into the statement

```
std::cout << "Sum is " << number1 + number2 << std::endl;
```

thus eliminating the need for the variable sum.

You'll notice that we did not have a return 0; statement at the end of main in this example. According to the C++ standard, if program execution reaches the end of main without encountering a return statement, it's assumed that the program terminated successfully—exactly as when the last statement in main is a return statement with the value 0. For that reason, we omit the return statement at the end of main in our C++ programs.

A powerful C++ feature is that users can create their own types called classes (we introduce this capability in Chapter 16 and explore it in depth in Chapters 17–18). Users can then "teach" C++ how to input and output values of these new data types using the >> and << operators (this is called **operator overloading**—a topic we explore in Chapter 19).

15.4 C++ Standard Library

C++ programs consist of pieces called **classes** and functions. You can program each piece that you may need to form a C++ program. Instead, most C++ programmers take advantage of the rich collections of existing classes and functions in the **C++ Standard Library.** Thus, there are really two parts to learning the C++ "world." The first is learning the C++ language itself; the second is learning how to use the classes and functions in the C++ Standard Library. Throughout the book, we discuss many of these classes and functions. P J. Plauger's book, *The Standard C Library* (Englewood Cliffs, NJ: Prentice Hall PTR, 1992), is a must read for programmers who need a deep understanding of the Standard C library functions that are included in C++, how to implement them and how to use them to write portable code. The standard class libraries generally are provided by compiler vendors. Many special-purpose class libraries are supplied by independent software vendors.

Software Engineering Observation 15.1

Use a "building-block" approach to create programs. Avoid reinventing the wheel. Use existing pieces wherever possible. Called software reuse, this practice is central to object-oriented programming.

Software Engineering Observation 15.2

When programming in C++, you typically will use the following building blocks: classes and functions from the C++ Standard Library, classes and functions you and your colleagues create and classes and functions from various popular third-party libraries.

The advantage of creating your own functions and classes is that you'll know exactly how they work. You'll be able to examine the C++ code. The disadvantage is the time-consuming and complex effort that goes into designing, developing and maintaining new functions and classes that are correct and that operate efficiently.

Performance Tip 15.1

Using C++ Standard Library functions and classes instead of writing your own versions can improve program performance, because they are written to perform efficiently. This technique also shortens program development time.

Portability Tip 15.1

Using C++ Standard Library functions and classes instead of writing your own improves program portability, because they are included in every C++ implementation.

15.5 Header Files

The C++ Standard Library is divided into many portions, each with its own header file. The header files contain the function prototypes for the related functions that form each portion of the library. The header files also contain definitions of various class types and functions, as well as constants needed by those functions. A header file "instructs" the compiler on how to interface with library and user-written components.

Figure 15.2 lists some common C++ Standard Library header files. Header file names ending in .h are "old-style" header files that have been superceded by the C++ Standard Library header files.

C++ Standard Library header file	Explanation
`<iostream>`	Contains function prototypes for the C++ standard input and standard output functions. This header file replaces header file `<iostream.h>`. This header is discussed in detail in Chapter 23, Stream Input/Output.
`<iomanip>`	Contains function prototypes for stream manipulators that format streams of data. This header file replaces header file `<iomanip.h>`. This header is used in Chapter 23.
`<cmath>`	Contains function prototypes for math library functions. This header file replaces header file `<math.h>`.
`<cstdlib>`	Contains function prototypes for conversions of numbers to text, text to numbers, memory allocation, random numbers and various other utility functions. This header file replaces header file `<stdlib>`.
`<ctime>`	Contains function prototypes and types for manipulating the time and date. This header file replaces header file `<time.h>`.
`<vector>`, `<list>`, `<deque>`, `<queue>`, `<stack>`, `<map>`, `<set>`, `<bitset>`	These header files contain classes that implement the C++ Standard Library containers. Containers store data during a program's execution.

Fig. 15.2 | C++ Standard Library header files. (Part 1 of 2.)

C++ Standard Library header file	Explanation
`<cctype>`	Contains function prototypes for functions that test characters for certain properties (such as whether the character is a digit or a punctuation), and function prototypes for functions that can be used to convert lowercase letters to uppercase letters and vice versa. This header file replaces header file `<ctype.h>`.
`<cstring>`	Contains function prototypes for C-style string-processing functions. This header file replaces header file `<string.h>`.
`<typeinfo>`	Contains classes for runtime type identification (determining data types at execution time).
`<exception>`, `<stdexcept>`	These header files contain classes that are used for exception handling (discussed in Chapter 24).
`<memory>`	Contains classes and functions used by the C++ Standard Library to allocate memory to the C++ Standard Library containers. This header is used in Chapter 24.
`<fstream>`	Contains function prototypes for functions that perform input from files on disk and output to files on disk. This header file replaces header file `<fstream.h>`.
`<string>`	Contains the definition of class `string` from the C++ Standard Library.
`<sstream>`	Contains function prototypes for functions that perform input from strings in memory and output to strings in memory.
`<functional>`	Contains classes and functions used by C++ Standard Library algorithms.
`<iterator>`	Contains classes for accessing C++ Standard Library container data.
`<algorithm>`	Contains functions for manipulating container data.
`<cassert>`	Contains macros for adding diagnostics that aid program debugging. This replaces header file `<assert.h>` from pre-standard C++.
`<cfloat>`	Contains the floating-point size limits of the system. This header file replaces header file `<float.h>`.
`<climits>`	Contains the integral size limits of the system. This header file replaces header file `<limits.h>`.
`<cstdio>`	Contains function prototypes for the C-style standard input/output library functions and information used by them. This header file replaces header file `<stdio.h>`.
`<locale>`	Contains classes and functions normally used by stream processing to process data in the natural form for different languages (e.g., monetary formats, sorting strings, character presentation, and so on).
`<limits>`	Contains classes for defining the numerical data type limits on each computer platform.
`<utility>`	Contains classes and functions that are used by many C++ Standard Library header files.

Fig. 15.2 | C++ Standard Library header files. (Part 2 of 2.)

You can create custom header files. Programmer-defined header files should end in .h. A programmer-defined header file can be included by using the #include preprocessor directive. For example, the header file square.h can be included in a program by placing the directive #include "square.h" at the beginning of the program.

15.6 Inline Functions

Implementing a program as a set of functions is good from a software engineering standpoint, but function calls involve execution-time overhead. C++ provides **inline functions** to help reduce function call overhead—especially for small functions. Placing the qualifier **inline** before a function's return type in the function definition "advises" the compiler to generate a copy of the function's code in place (when appropriate) to avoid a function call. The trade-off is that multiple copies of the function code are inserted in the program (often making the program larger) rather than there being a single copy of the function to which control is passed each time the function is called. The compiler can ignore the inline qualifier and typically does so for all but the smallest functions.

Software Engineering Observation 15.3
Changing to an inline function could require clients of the function to be recompiled. This can be significant in program development and maintenance situations.

Performance Tip 15.2
Using inline functions can reduce execution time but may increase program size.

Software Engineering Observation 15.4
The inline qualifier should be used only with small, frequently used functions.

Figure 15.3 uses inline function cube (lines 11–14) to calculate the volume of a cube of side length side. Keyword const in the parameter list of function cube tells the compiler that the function does not modify variable side. This ensures that the value of side is not changed by the function when the calculation is performed. Notice that the complete definition of function cube appears before it's used in the program. This is required so that the compiler knows how to expand a cube function call into its inlined code. For this reason, reusable inline functions are typically placed in header files, so that their definitions can be included in each source file that uses them.

Software Engineering Observation 15.5
The const qualifier should be used to enforce the principle of least privilege. Using the principle of least privilege to properly design software can greatly reduce debugging time and improper side effects, and can make a program easier to modify and maintain.

```
1   // Fig. 15.3: fig15_03.cpp
2   // inline function that calculates the volume of a cube.
3   #include <iostream>
```

Fig. 15.3 | inline function that calculates the volume of a cube. (Part 1 of 2.)

```
 4    using std::cout;
 5    using std::cin;
 6    using std::endl;
 7
 8    // Definition of inline function cube. Definition of function appears
 9    // before function is called, so a function prototype is not required.
10    // First line of function definition acts as the prototype.
11    inline double cube( const double side )
12    {
13       return side * side * side; // calculate the cube of side
14    } // end function cube
15
16    int main()
17    {
18       double sideValue; // stores value entered by user
19
20       for ( int i = 1; i <= 3; i++ )
21       {
22          cout << "\nEnter the side length of your cube: ";
23          cin >> sideValue; // read value from user
24
25          // calculate cube of sideValue and display result
26          cout << "Volume of cube with side "
27             << sideValue << " is " << cube( sideValue ) << endl;
28       }
29    } // end main
```

```
Enter the side length of your cube: 1.0
Volume of cube with side 1 is 1

Enter the side length of your cube: 2.3
Volume of cube with side 2.3 is 12.167

Enter the side length of your cube: 5.4
Volume of cube with side 5.4 is 157.464
```

Fig. 15.3 | inline function that calculates the volume of a cube. (Part 2 of 2.)

Lines 4–6 are using statements that help us eliminate the need to repeat the std:: prefix. Once we include these using statements, we can write cout instead of std::cout, cin instead of std::cin and endl instead of std::endl, in the remainder of the program. From this point forward, each C++ example contains one or more using statements.

In place of lines 4–6, many programmers prefer to use the declaration

```
using namespace std;
```

which enables a program to use all the names in any standard C++ header file (such as <iostream>) that a program might include. From this point forward in our C++ programs, we'll use the preceding declaration in our programs.

The for statement's condition (line 20) evaluates to either 0 (false) or nonzero (true). This is consistent with C. C++ also provides type **bool** for representing boolean (true/false) values. The two possible values of a bool are the keywords **true** and **false**. When true and `false` are converted to integers, they become the values 1 and 0, respectively. When non-boolean values are converted to type `bool`, non-zero values become `true`, and zero or null pointer values become `false`. Figure 15.4 lists the keywords common to C and C++ and the keywords unique to C++.

C++ keywords				
Keywords common to the C and C++ programming languages				
auto	break	case	char	const
continue	default	do	double	else
enum	extern	float	for	goto
if	int	long	register	return
short	signed	sizeof	static	struct
switch	typedef	union	unsigned	void
volatile	while			
C++-only keywords				
and	and_eq	asm	bitand	bitor
bool	catch	class	compl	const_cast
delete	dynamic_cast	explicit	export	false
friend	inline	mutable	namespace	new
not	not_eq	operator	or	or_eq
private	protected	public	reinterpret_cast	static_cast
template	this	throw	true	try
typeid	typename	using	virtual	wchar_t
xor	xor_eq			

Fig. 15.4 | C++ keywords.

15.7 References and Reference Parameters

Two ways to pass arguments to functions in many programming languages are pass-by-value and pass-by-reference. When an argument is passed by value, a *copy* of the argument's value is made and passed (on the function call stack) to the called function. Changes to the copy do not affect the original variable's value in the caller. This prevents the accidental side effects that so greatly hinder the development of correct and reliable software systems. Each argument that has been passed in the programs in this chapter so far has been passed by value.

Performance Tip 15.3
One disadvantage of pass-by-value is that, if a large data item is being passed, copying that data can take a considerable amount of execution time and memory space.

Reference Parameters
This section introduces reference parameters—the first of two means that C++ provides for performing pass-by-reference. With pass-by-reference, the caller gives the called function the ability to access the caller's data directly, and to modify that data if the called function chooses to do so.

Performance Tip 15.4

Pass-by-reference is good for performance reasons, because it can eliminate the pass-by-value overhead of copying large amounts of data.

Software Engineering Observation 15.6

Pass-by-reference can weaken security; the called function can corrupt the caller's data.

Later, we'll show how to achieve the performance advantage of pass-by-reference while simultaneously achieving the software engineering advantage of protecting the caller's data from corruption.

A reference parameter is an alias for its corresponding argument in a function call. To indicate that a function parameter is passed by reference, simply follow the parameter's type in the function prototype by an ampersand (&); use the same notation when listing the parameter's type in the function header. For example, the following declaration in a function header

```
int &count
```

when read from right to left is pronounced "count is a reference to an int." In the function call, simply mention the variable by name to pass it by reference. Then, mentioning the variable by its parameter name in the body of the called function actually refers to the original variable in the calling function, and the original variable can be modified directly by the called function. As always, the function prototype and header must agree.

Passing Arguments by Value and by Reference
Figure 15.5 compares pass-by-value and pass-by-reference with reference parameters. The "styles" of the arguments in the calls to function squareByValue (line 17) and function squareByReference (line 22) are identical—both variables are simply mentioned by name in the function calls. Without checking the function prototypes or function definitions, it's not possible to tell from the calls alone whether either function can modify its arguments. Because function prototypes are mandatory, however, the compiler has no trouble resolving the ambiguity. Recall that a function prototype tells the compiler the type of data returned by the function, the number of parameters the function expects to receive, the types of the parameters, and the order in which they are expected. The compiler uses this information to validate function calls. In C, function prototypes are not required. Making them mandatory in C++ enables **type-safe linkage**, which ensures that the types of the arguments conform to the types of the parameters. Otherwise, the compiler reports an error. Locating such type errors at compile time helps prevent the runtime errors that can occur in C when arguments of incorrect data types are passed to functions.

```
1   // Fig. 15.5: fig15_05.cpp
2   // Comparing pass-by-value and pass-by-reference with references.
3   #include <iostream>
4   using namespace std;
5
6   int squareByValue( int ); // function prototype (value pass)
```

Fig. 15.5 | Comparing pass-by-value and pass-by-reference with references. (Part 1 of 2.)

```
 7   void squareByReference( int & ); // function prototype (reference pass)
 8
 9   int main()
10   {
11      int x = 2; // value to square using squareByValue
12      int z = 4; // value to square using squareByReference
13
14      // demonstrate squareByValue
15      cout << "x = " << x << " before squareByValue\n";
16      cout << "Value returned by squareByValue: "
17         << squareByValue( x ) << endl;
18      cout << "x = " << x << " after squareByValue\n" << endl;
19
20      // demonstrate squareByReference
21      cout << "z = " << z << " before squareByReference" << endl;
22      squareByReference( z );
23      cout << "z = " << z << " after squareByReference" << endl;
24   } // end main
25
26   // squareByValue multiplies number by itself, stores the
27   // result in number and returns the new value of number
28   int squareByValue( int number )
29   {
30      return number *= number; // caller's argument not modified
31   } // end function squareByValue
32
33   // squareByReference multiplies numberRef by itself and stores the result
34   // in the variable to which numberRef refers in the caller
35   void squareByReference( int &numberRef )
36   {
37      numberRef *= numberRef; // caller's argument modified
38   } // end function squareByReference
```

```
x = 2 before squareByValue
Value returned by squareByValue: 4
x = 2 after squareByValue

z = 4 before squareByReference
z = 16 after squareByReference
```

Fig. 15.5 | Comparing pass-by-value and pass-by-reference with references. (Part 2 of 2.)

Common Programming Error 15.2

Because reference parameters are mentioned only by name in the body of the called function, you might inadvertently treat reference parameters as pass-by-value parameters. This can cause unexpected side effects if the original copies of the variables are changed by the function.

Performance Tip 15.5

For passing large objects efficiently, use a constant reference parameter to simulate the appearance and security of pass-by-value and avoid the overhead of passing a copy of the large object. The called function will not be able to modify the object in the caller.

Software Engineering Observation 15.7

Many programmers do not declare parameters passed by value as const, even when the called function should not modify the passed argument. Keyword const in this context would protect only a copy of the original argument, not the original argument itself, which when passed by value is safe from modification by the called function.

To specify a reference to a constant, place the const qualifier before the type specifier in the parameter declaration. Note in line 35 of Fig. 15.5 the placement of & in the parameter list of function squareByReference. Some C++ programmers prefer to write int& numberRef with the ampersand abutting int—both forms are equivalent to the compiler.

Software Engineering Observation 15.8

For the combined reasons of clarity and performance, many C++ programmers prefer that modifiable arguments be passed to functions by using pointers, small nonmodifiable arguments be passed by value and large nonmodifiable arguments be passed by using references to constants.

References as Aliases within a Function

References can also be used as aliases for other variables within a function (although they typically are used with functions as shown in Fig. 15.5). For example, the code

```
int count = 1; // declare integer variable count
int &cRef = count; // create cRef as an alias for count
cRef++; // increment count (using its alias cRef)
```

increments variable count by using its alias cRef. Reference variables must be initialized in their declarations, as we show in line 9 of both Fig. 15.6 and Fig. 15.7, and cannot be reassigned as aliases to other variables. Once a reference is declared as an alias for a variable, all operations "performed" on the alias (i.e., the reference) are actually performed on the original variable. The alias is simply another name for the original variable. Taking the address of a reference and comparing references do not cause syntax errors; rather, each operation occurs on the variable for which the reference is an alias. Unless it's a reference to a constant, a reference argument must be an *lvalue* (e.g., a variable name), not a constant or expression that returns an *rvalue* (e.g., the result of a calculation).

```
1   // Fig. 15.6: fig15_06.cpp
2   // Initializing and using a reference.
3   #include <iostream>
4   using namespace std;
5
6   int main()
7   {
8      int x = 3;
9      int &y = x; // y refers to (is an alias for) x
10
11     cout << "x = " << x << endl << "y = " << y << endl;
12     y = 7; // actually modifies x
13     cout << "x = " << x << endl << "y = " << y << endl;
14  } // end main
```

Fig. 15.6 | Initializing and using a reference. (Part 1 of 2.)

```
x = 3
y = 3
x = 7
y = 7
```

Fig. 15.6 | Initializing and using a reference. (Part 2 of 2.)

```
 1   // Fig. 15.7: fig15_07.cpp
 2   // Uninitialized reference is a syntax error.
 3   #include <iostream>
 4   using namespace std;
 5
 6   int main()
 7   {
 8      int x = 3;
 9      int &y; // Error: y must be initialized
10
11      cout << "x = " << x << endl << "y = " << y << endl;
12      y = 7;
13      cout << "x = " << x << endl << "y = " << y << endl;
14   } // end main
```

Microsoft Visual C++ compiler error message:

```
C:\examples\ch15\fig15_07\fig15_07.cpp(10) : error C2530: 'y' :
   references must be initialized
```

GNU C++ compiler error message:

```
fig15_07.cpp:10: error: 'y' declared as a reference but not initialized
```

Fig. 15.7 | Uninitialized reference is a syntax error.

Returning a Reference from a Function

Returning references from functions can be dangerous. When returning a reference to a variable declared in the called function, the variable should be declared static within that function. Otherwise, the reference refers to an automatic variable that is discarded when the function terminates; such a variable is "undefined," and the program's behavior is unpredictable. References to undefined variables are called **dangling references**.

Common Programming Error 15.3

Not initializing a reference variable when it's declared is a compilation error, unless the declaration is part of a function's parameter list. Reference parameters are initialized when the function in which they're declared is called.

Common Programming Error 15.4

Attempting to reassign a previously declared reference to be an alias to another variable is a logic error. The value of the other variable is simply assigned to the variable for which the reference is already an alias.

Common Programming Error 15.5

Returning a reference to an automatic variable in a called function is a logic error. Some compilers issue a warning when this occurs.

Error Messages for Uninitialized References

The C++ standard does not specify the error messages that compilers use to indicate particular errors. For this reason, we show in Fig. 15.7 the error messages produced by several compilers when a reference is not initialized.

15.8 Empty Parameter Lists

C++, like C, allows you to define functions with no parameters. In C++, an empty parameter list is specified by writing either void or nothing at all in parentheses. The prototypes

```
void print();
void print( void );
```

each specify that function print does not take arguments and does not return a value. These prototypes are equivalent.

Portability Tip 15.2

The meaning of an empty function parameter list in C++ is dramatically different than in C. In C, it means all argument checking is disabled (i.e., the function call can pass any arguments it wants). In C++, it means that the function takes no arguments. Thus, C programs using this feature might cause compilation errors when compiled in C++.

15.9 Default Arguments

It's not uncommon for a program to invoke a function repeatedly with the same argument value for a particular parameter. In such cases, you can specify that such a parameter has a **default argument**, i.e., a default value to be passed to that parameter. When a program omits an argument for a parameter with a default argument in a function call, the compiler rewrites the function call and inserts the default value of that argument to be passed as an argument in the function call.

Default arguments must be the rightmost (trailing) arguments in a function's parameter list. When calling a function with two or more default arguments, if an omitted argument is not the rightmost argument in the argument list, then all arguments to the right of that argument also must be omitted. Default arguments should be specified with the first occurrence of the function name—typically, in the function prototype. If the function prototype is omitted because the function definition also serves as the prototype, then the default arguments should be specified in the function header. Default values can be any expression, including constants, global variables or function calls. Default arguments also can be used with inline functions.

Figure 15.8 demonstrates using default arguments in calculating the volume of a box. The function prototype for boxVolume (line 7) specifies that all three parameters have been given default values of 1. We provided variable names in the function prototype for readability, but these are not required.

```
1  // Fig. 15.8: fig15_08.cpp
2  // Using default arguments.
3  #include <iostream>
4  using namespace std;
5
6  // function prototype that specifies default arguments
7  int boxVolume( int length = 1, int width = 1, int height = 1 );
8
9  int main()
10 {
11    // no arguments--use default values for all dimensions
12    cout << "The default box volume is: " << boxVolume();
13
14    // specify length; default width and height
15    cout << "\n\nThe volume of a box with length 10,\n"
16       << "width 1 and height 1 is: " << boxVolume( 10 );
17
18    // specify length and width; default height
19    cout << "\n\nThe volume of a box with length 10,\n"
20       << "width 5 and height 1 is: " << boxVolume( 10, 5 );
21
22    // specify all arguments
23    cout << "\n\nThe volume of a box with length 10,\n"
24       << "width 5 and height 2 is: " << boxVolume( 10, 5, 2 )
25       << endl;
26 } // end main
27
28 // function boxVolume calculates the volume of a box
29 int boxVolume( int length, int width, int height )
30 {
31    return length * width * height;
32 } // end function boxVolume
```

```
The default box volume is: 1

The volume of a box with length 10,
width 1 and height 1 is: 10

The volume of a box with length 10,
width 5 and height 1 is: 50

The volume of a box with length 10,
width 5 and height 2 is: 100
```

Fig. 15.8 | Using default arguments.

 Common Programming Error 15.6
It's a compilation error to specify default arguments in both a function's prototype and header.

The first call to boxVolume (line 12) specifies no arguments, thus using all three default values of 1. The second call (line 16) passes a length argument, thus using default values of 1 for the width and height arguments. The third call (line 20) passes arguments for length and width, thus using a default value of 1 for the height argument. The last call (line 24) passes arguments for length, width and height, thus using no default values. Any arguments passed to the function explicitly are assigned to the function's parameters from left to right. Therefore, when boxVolume receives one argument, the function assigns the value of that argument to its length parameter (i.e., the leftmost parameter in the parameter list). When boxVolume receives two arguments, the function assigns the values of those arguments to its length and width parameters in that order. Finally, when box-Volume receives all three arguments, the function assigns the values of those arguments to its length, width and height parameters, respectively.

Good Programming Practice 15.2

Using default arguments can simplify writing function calls. However, some programmers feel that explicitly specifying all arguments is clearer.

Software Engineering Observation 15.9

If the default values for a function change, all client code must be recompiled.

Common Programming Error 15.7

In a function definition, specifying and attempting to use a default argument that is not a rightmost (trailing) argument (while not simultaneously defaulting all the rightmost arguments) is a syntax error.

15.10 Unary Scope Resolution Operator

It's possible to declare local and global variables of the same name. This causes the global variable to be "hidden" by the local variable in the local scope. C++ provides the **unary scope resolution operator** (::) to access a global variable when a local variable of the same name is in scope. The unary scope resolution operator cannot be used to access a local variable of the same name in an outer block. A global variable can be accessed directly without the unary scope resolution operator if the name of the global variable is not the same as that of a local variable in scope.

Figure 15.9 demonstrates the unary scope resolution operator with global and local variables of the same name (lines 6 and 10, respectively). To emphasize that the local and global versions of variable number are distinct, the program declares one variable of type int and the other double.

```
1   // Fig. 15.9: fig15_09.cpp
2   // Using the unary scope resolution operator.
3   #include <iostream>
4   using namespace std;
5
6   int number = 7; // global variable named number
7
8   int main()
9   {
10      double number = 10.5; // local variable named number
```

Fig. 15.9 | Using the unary scope resolution operator. (Part 1 of 2.)

```
11
12      // display values of local and global variables
13      cout << "Local double value of number = " << number
14          << "\nGlobal int value of number = " << ::number << endl;
15  } // end main
```

```
Local double value of number = 10.5
Global int value of number = 7
```

Fig. 15.9 | Using the unary scope resolution operator. (Part 2 of 2.)

Using the unary scope resolution operator (::) with a given variable name is optional when the only variable with that name is a global variable.

Common Programming Error 15.8

It's an error to attempt to use the unary scope resolution operator (::) to access a nonglobal variable in an outer block. If no global variable with that name exists, a compilation error occurs. If a global variable with that name exists, this is a logic error, because the program will refer to the global variable when you intended to access the nonglobal variable in the outer block.

Good Programming Practice 15.3

Always using the unary scope resolution operator (::) to refer to global variables makes programs easier to read and understand, because it makes it clear that you intend to access a global variable rather than a nonglobal variable.

Software Engineering Observation 15.10

Always using the unary scope resolution operator (::) to refer to global variables makes programs easier to modify by reducing the risk of name collisions with nonglobal variables.

Error-Prevention Tip 15.1

Always using the unary scope resolution operator (::) to refer to a global variable eliminates logic errors that might occur if a nonglobal variable hides the global variable.

Error-Prevention Tip 15.2

Avoid using variables of the same name for different purposes in a program. Although this is allowed in various circumstances, it can lead to errors.

15.11 Function Overloading

C++ enables several functions of the same name to be defined, as long as these functions have different sets of parameters (at least as far as the parameter types or the number of parameters or the order of the parameter types are concerned). This capability is called function overloading.[1] When an overloaded function is called, the C++ compiler selects the proper function by examining the number, types and order of the arguments in the

---

1. The C++ standard requires float, double and long double overloaded versions of the math library functions discussed in Section 5.3.

call. Function overloading is commonly used to create several functions of the same name that perform similar tasks, but on data of different types. For example, many functions in the math library are overloaded for different numeric data types.

Good Programming Practice 15.4

Overloading functions that perform closely related tasks can make programs more readable and understandable.

Overloaded *square* Functions

Figure 15.10 uses overloaded square functions to calculate the square of an int (lines 7–11) and the square of a double (lines 14–18). Line 22 invokes the int version of function square by passing the literal value 7. C++ treats whole-number literal values as type int by default. Similarly, line 24 invokes the double version of function square by passing the literal value 7.5, which C++ treats as a double value by default. In each case the compiler chooses the proper function to call, based on the type of the argument. The outputs confirm that the proper function was called in each case.

```
1   // Fig. 15.10: fig15_10.cpp
2   // Overloaded square functions.
3   #include <iostream>
4   using namespace std;
5
6   // function square for int values
7   int square( int x )
8   {
9      cout << "square of integer " << x << " is ";
10     return x * x;
11  } // end function square with int argument
12
13  // function square for double values
14  double square( double y )
15  {
16     cout << "square of double " << y << " is ";
17     return y * y;
18  } // end function square with double argument
19
20  int main()
21  {
22     cout << square( 7 ); // calls int version
23     cout << endl;
24     cout << square( 7.5 ); // calls double version
25     cout << endl;
26  } // end main
```

```
square of integer 7 is 49
square of double 7.5 is 56.25
```

Fig. 15.10 | Overloaded square functions.

How the Compiler Differentiates Overloaded Functions

Overloaded functions are distinguished by their signatures—a combination of a function's name and its parameter types (in order). The compiler encodes each function identifier with the number and types of its parameters (sometimes referred to as **name mangling** or **name decoration**) to enable type-safe linkage. This ensures that the proper overloaded function is called and that the argument types conform to the parameter types.

Figure 15.11 was compiled with GNU C++. Rather than showing the execution output of the program (as we normally would), we show the mangled function names produced in assembly language by GNU C++. Each mangled name (other than main) begins with two underscores (__) followed by the letter Z, a number and the function name. The number that follows Z specifies how many characters are in the function's name. For example, function square has 6 characters in its name, so its mangled name is prefixed with __Z6. The function name is then followed by an encoding of its parameter list. In the parameter list for function nothing2 (line 25; see the fourth output line), c represents a char, i represents an int, Rf represents a float & (i.e., a reference to a float) and Rd represents a double & (i.e., a reference to a double). In the parameter list for function nothing1, i represents an int, f represents a float, c represents a char and Ri represents an int &. The two square functions are distinguished by their parameter lists; one specifies d for double and the other specifies i for int. The return types of the functions are not specified in the mangled names. Overloaded functions can have different return types, but if they do, they must also have different parameter lists. Again, you cannot have two functions with the same signature and different return types. Function-name mangling is compiler specific. Also, function main is not mangled, because it cannot be overloaded.

```
1    // Fig. 15.11: fig15_11.cpp
2    // Name mangling to enable type-safe linkage.
3
4    // function square for int values
5    int square( int x )
6    {
7       return x * x;
8    } // end function square
9
10   // function square for double values
11   double square( double y )
12   {
13      return y * y;
14   } // end function square
15
16   // function that receives arguments of types
17   // int, float, char and int &
18   void nothing1( int a, float b, char c, int &d )
19   {
20      // empty function body
21   } // end function nothing1
22
23   // function that receives arguments of types
24   // char, int, float & and double &
25   int nothing2( char a, int b, float &c, double &d )
26   {
27      return 0;
28   } // end function nothing2
```

Fig. 15.11 | Name mangling to enable type-safe linkage. (Part 1 of 2.)

```
29
30   int main()
31   {
32      return 0; // indicates successful termination
33   } // end main
```

```
__Z6squarei
__Z6squared
__Z8nothing1ifcRi
__Z8nothing2ciRfRd
_main
```

Fig. 15.11 | Name mangling to enable type-safe linkage. (Part 2 of 2.)

Common Programming Error 15.9

Creating overloaded functions with identical parameter lists and different return types is a compilation error.

The compiler uses only the parameter lists to distinguish between functions of the same name. Overloaded functions need not have the same number of parameters. Programmers should use caution when overloading functions with default parameters, because this may cause ambiguity.

Common Programming Error 15.10

A function with default arguments omitted might be called identically to another overloaded function; this is a compilation error. For example, having in a program both a function that explicitly takes no arguments and a function of the same name that contains all default arguments results in a compilation error when an attempt is made to use that function name in a call passing no arguments. The compiler does not know which version of the function to choose.

Overloaded Operators

In Chapter 19, we discuss how to overload operators to define how they should operate on objects of user-defined data types. (In fact, we've been using overloaded operators, including the stream insertion operator << and the stream extraction operator >>, each of which is overloaded to be able to display data of all the fundamental types. We say more about overloading << and >> to be able to handle objects of user-defined types in Chapter 19.) Section 15.12 introduces function templates for automatically generating overloaded functions that perform identical tasks on data of different types.

15.12 Function Templates

Overloaded functions are used to perform similar operations that may involve different program logic on different data types. If the program logic and operations are identical for each data type, overloading may be performed more compactly and conveniently by using **function templates**. You write a single function template definition. Given the argument types provided in calls to this function, C++ automatically generates separate **function template specializations** to handle each type of call appropriately. Thus, defining a single function template essentially defines a whole family of overloaded functions.

Figure 15.12 contains the definition of a function template (lines 4–18) for a maximum function that determines the largest of three values. All function template definitions begin with the template keyword (line 4) followed by a **template parameter list** to the function template enclosed in angle brackets (< and >). Every parameter in the template parameter list (each is referred to as a **formal type parameter**) is preceded by keyword typename or keyword class (which are synonyms). The formal type parameters are place-holders for fundamental types or user-defined types. These placeholders are used to specify the types of the function's parameters (line 5), to specify the function's return type and to declare variables within the body of the function definition (line 7). A function template is defined like any other function, but uses the formal type parameters as placeholders for actual data types.

The function template in Fig. 15.12 declares a single formal type parameter T (line 4) as a placeholder for the type of the data to be tested by function maximum. The name of a type parameter must be unique in the template parameter list for a particular template definition. When the compiler detects a maximum invocation in the program source code, the type of the data passed to maximum is substituted for T throughout the template defini-tion, and C++ creates a complete source-code function for determining the maximum of three values of the specified data type. Then the newly created function is compiled. Thus, templates are a means of code generation.

```
 1   // Fig. 15.12: maximum.h
 2   // Function template maximum header file.
 3
 4   template < class T >  // or template< typename T >
 5   T maximum( T value1, T value2, T value3 )
 6   {
 7      T maximumValue = value1; // assume value1 is maximum
 8
 9      // determine whether value2 is greater than maximumValue
10      if ( value2 > maximumValue )
11         maximumValue = value2;
12
13      // determine whether value3 is greater than maximumValue
14      if ( value3 > maximumValue )
15         maximumValue = value3;
16
17      return maximumValue;
18   } // end function template maximum
```

Fig. 15.12 | Function template maximum header file.

Common Programming Error 15.11
Not placing keyword class or keyword typename before every formal type parameter of a function template (e.g., writing < class S, T > instead of < class S, class T >) is a syntax error.

Figure 15.13 uses the maximum function template (lines 18, 28 and 38) to determine the largest of three int values, three double values and three char values.

```
 1   // Fig. 15.13: fig15_13.cpp
 2   // Demonstrating function template maximum.
 3   #include <iostream>
 4   using namespace std;
 5
 6   #include "maximum.h" // include definition of function template maximum
 7
 8   int main()
 9   {
10      // demonstrate maximum with int values
11      int int1, int2, int3;
12
13      cout << "Input three integer values: ";
14      cin >> int1 >> int2 >> int3;
15
16      // invoke int version of maximum
17      cout << "The maximum integer value is: "
18         << maximum( int1, int2, int3 );
19
20      // demonstrate maximum with double values
21      double double1, double2, double3;
22
23      cout << "\n\nInput three double values: ";
24      cin >> double1 >> double2 >> double3;
25
26      // invoke double version of maximum
27      cout << "The maximum double value is: "
28         << maximum( double1, double2, double3 );
29
30      // demonstrate maximum with char values
31      char char1, char2, char3;
32
33      cout << "\n\nInput three characters: ";
34      cin >> char1 >> char2 >> char3;
35
36      // invoke char version of maximum
37      cout << "The maximum character value is: "
38         << maximum( char1, char2, char3 ) << endl;
39   } // end main
```

```
Input three integer values: 1 2 3
The maximum integer value is: 3

Input three double values: 3.3 2.2 1.1
The maximum double value is: 3.3

Input three characters: A C B
The maximum character value is: C
```

Fig. 15.13 | Demonstrating function template `maximum`.

In Fig. 15.13, three functions are created as a result of the calls in lines 18, 28 and 38—expecting three `int` values, three `double` values and three `char` values, respectively. For example, the function template specialization created for type `int` replaces each occurrence of `T` with `int` as follows:

```
int maximum( int value1, int value2, int value3 )
{
   int maximumValue = value1; // assume value1 is maximum

   // determine whether value2 is greater than maximumValue
   if ( value2 > maximumValue )
      maximumValue = value2;

   // determine whether value3 is greater than maximumValue
   if ( value3 > maximumValue )
      maximumValue = value3;

   return maximumValue;
} // end function template maximum
```

15.13 Introduction to C++ Standard Library Class Template vector

We now introduce C++ Standard Library class template **vector**, which represents a more robust type of array featuring many additional capabilities. As you'll see in later chapters, C-style pointer-based arrays (i.e., the type of arrays presented thus far) have great potential for errors. For example, as mentioned earlier, a program can easily "walk off" either end of an array, because C++ does not check whether subscripts fall outside the range of an array. Two arrays cannot be meaningfully compared with equality operators or relational operators. As you learned in Chapter 7, pointer variables (known more commonly as pointers) contain memory addresses as their values. Array names are simply *pointers* to where the arrays begin in memory, and, of course, two arrays will always be at different memory locations. When an array is passed to a general-purpose function designed to handle arrays of any size, the size of the array must be passed as an additional argument. Furthermore, one array cannot be assigned to another with the assignment operator(s)—array names are const pointers, so they cannot be used on the left side of an assignment operator. These and other capabilities certainly seem like "naturals" for dealing with arrays, but C++ does not provide such capabilities. However, the C++ Standard Library provides class template vector to allow you to create a more powerful and less error-prone alternative to arrays. In Chapter 19, we present the means to implement such array capabilities as those provided by vector. You'll learn how to customize operators for use with your own classes (a technique known as *operator overloading*).

The vector class template is available to anyone building applications with C++. The notations that the vector example uses might be unfamiliar to you, because vectors use template notation. In the previous section, we discussed function templates. In Chapter 22, we discuss class templates. For now, you should feel comfortable using class template vector by mimicking the syntax in the example we show in this section. Chapter 22 presents class template vector (and several other standard C++ container classes) in detail.

The program of Fig. 15.14 demonstrates capabilities provided by C++ Standard Library class template vector that are not available for C-style pointer-based arrays. Standard class template vector provides many of the same features as the Array class that we construct in Chapter 19. Standard class template vector is defined in header <vector> (line 5) and belongs to namespace std. Chapter 22 discusses the full functionality of vector. At the end of this section, we'll demonstrate class vector's bounds checking capabilities and introduce C++'s exception-handling mechanism, which can be used to detect and handle an out-of-bounds vector index.

```cpp
1   // Fig. 15.14: fig15_14.cpp
2   // Demonstrating C++ Standard Library class template vector.
3   #include <iostream>
4   #include <iomanip>
5   #include <vector>
6   using namespace std;
7
8   void outputVector( const vector< int > & ); // display the vector
9   void inputVector( vector< int > & ); // input values into the vector
10
11  int main()
12  {
13     vector< int > integers1( 7 ); // 7-element vector< int >
14     vector< int > integers2( 10 ); // 10-element vector< int >
15
16     // print integers1 size and contents
17     cout << "Size of vector integers1 is " << integers1.size()
18        << "\nvector after initialization:" << endl;
19     outputVector( integers1 );
20
21     // print integers2 size and contents
22     cout << "\nSize of vector integers2 is " << integers2.size()
23        << "\nvector after initialization:" << endl;
24     outputVector( integers2 );
25
26     // input and print integers1 and integers2
27     cout << "\nEnter 17 integers:" << endl;
28     inputVector( integers1 );
29     inputVector( integers2 );
30
31     cout << "\nAfter input, the vectors contain:\n"
32        << "integers1:" << endl;
33     outputVector( integers1 );
34     cout << "integers2:" << endl;
35     outputVector( integers2 );
36
37     // use inequality (!=) operator with vector objects
38     cout << "\nEvaluating: integers1 != integers2" << endl;
39
40     if ( integers1 != integers2 )
41        cout << "integers1 and integers2 are not equal" << endl;
42
43     // create vector integers3 using integers1 as an
44     // initializer; print size and contents
45     vector< int > integers3( integers1 ); // copy constructor
46
47     cout << "\nSize of vector integers3 is " << integers3.size()
48        << "\nvector after initialization:" << endl;
49     outputVector( integers3 );
```

Fig. 15.14 | Demonstrating C++ Standard Library class template vector. (Part 1 of 4.)

```
50
51      // use overloaded assignment (=) operator
52      cout << "\nAssigning integers2 to integers1:" << endl;
53      integers1 = integers2; // assign integers2 to integers1
54
55      cout << "integers1:" << endl;
56      outputVector( integers1 );
57      cout << "integers2:" << endl;
58      outputVector( integers2 );
59
60      // use equality (==) operator with vector objects
61      cout << "\nEvaluating: integers1 == integers2" << endl;
62
63      if ( integers1 == integers2 )
64         cout << "integers1 and integers2 are equal" << endl;
65
66      // use square brackets to create rvalue
67      cout << "\nintegers1[5] is " << integers1[ 5 ];
68
69      // use square brackets to create lvalue
70      cout << "\n\nAssigning 1000 to integers1[5]" << endl;
71      integers1[ 5 ] = 1000;
72      cout << "integers1:" << endl;
73      outputVector( integers1 );
74
75      // attempt to use out-of-range subscript
76      try
77      {
78         cout << "\nAttempt to display integers1.at( 15 )" << endl;
79         cout << integers1.at( 15 ) << endl; // ERROR: out of range
80      } // end try
81      catch ( out_of_range &ex )
82      {
83         cout << "An exception occurred: " << ex.what() << endl;
84      } // end catch
85   } // end main
86
87   // output vector contents
88   void outputVector( const vector< int > &array )
89   {
90      size_t i; // declare control variable
91
92      for ( i = 0; i < array.size(); ++i )
93      {
94         cout << setw( 12 ) << array[ i ];
95
96         if ( ( i + 1 ) % 4 == 0 ) // 4 numbers per row of output
97            cout << endl;
98      } // end for
99
100     if ( i % 4 != 0 )
101        cout << endl;
102  } // end function outputVector
```

Fig. 15.14 | Demonstrating C++ Standard Library class template vector. (Part 2 of 4.)

```
103
104  // input vector contents
105  void inputVector( vector< int > &array )
106  {
107     for ( size_t i = 0; i < array.size(); ++i )
108        cin >> array[ i ];
109  } // end function inputVector
```

```
Size of vector integers1 is 7
vector after initialization:
        0            0          0          0
        0            0          0

Size of vector integers2 is 10
vector after initialization:
        0            0          0          0
        0            0          0          0
        0            0

Enter 17 integers:
1 2 3 4 5 6 7 8 9 10 11 12 13 14 15 16 17

After input, the vectors contain:
integers1:
        1            2          3          4
        5            6          7
integers2:
        8            9         10         11
       12           13         14         15
       16           17

Evaluating: integers1 != integers2
integers1 and integers2 are not equal

Size of vector integers3 is 7
vector after initialization:
        1            2          3          4
        5            6          7

Assigning integers2 to integers1:
integers1:
        8            9         10         11
       12           13         14         15
       16           17
integers2:
        8            9         10         11
       12           13         14         15
       16           17

Evaluating: integers1 == integers2
integers1 and integers2 are equal

integers1[5] is 13
```

Fig. 15.14 | Demonstrating C++ Standard Library class template vector. (Part 3 of 4.)

```
Assigning 1000 to integers1[5]
integers1:
          8           9          10          11
         12        1000          14          15
         16          17

Attempt to display integers1.at( 15 )
An exception occurred: invalid vector<T> subscript
```

Fig. 15.14 | Demonstrating C++ Standard Library class template `vector`. (Part 4 of 4.)

Creating vector Objects

Lines 13–14 create two `vector` objects that store values of type `int`—`integers1` contains seven elements, and `integers2` contains 10 elements. By default, all the elements of each `vector` object are set to 0. Note that `vector`s can be defined to store *any* data type, by replacing `int` in `vector<int>` with the appropriate data type. This notation, which specifies the type stored in the `vector`, is similar to the template notation that Section 15.12 introduced with function templates.

vector Member Function size; Function outputVector

Line 17 uses `vector` member function `size` to obtain the size (i.e., the number of elements) of `integers1`. Line 19 passes `integers1` to function `outputVector` (lines 88–102), which uses square brackets, `[]` (line 94), to obtain the value in each element of the `vector` for output. Note the resemblance of this notation to that used to access the value of an array element. Lines 22 and 24 perform the same tasks for `integers2`.

Member function `size` of class template `vector` returns the number of elements in a `vector` as a value of type `size_t` (which represents the type `unsigned int` on many systems). As a result, line 90 declares the control variable `i` to be of type `size_t`, too. On some compilers, declaring `i` as an `int` causes the compiler to issue a warning message, since the loop-continuation condition (line 92) would compare a `signed` value (i.e., `int i`) and an `unsigned` value (i.e., a value of type `size_t` returned by function `size`).

Function inputVector

Lines 28–29 pass `integers1` and `integers2` to function `inputVector` (lines 105–109) to read values for each `vector`'s elements from the user. The function uses square brackets (`[]`) to form *lvalues* that are used to store the input values in each `vector` element.

Comparing vector Objects for Inequality

Line 40 demonstrates that `vector` objects can be compared with one another using the `!=` operator. If the contents of two `vector`s are not equal, the operator returns `true`; otherwise, it returns `false`.

Initializing One vector with the Contents of Another

The C++ Standard Library class template `vector` allows you to create a new `vector` object that is initialized with the contents of an existing `vector`. Line 45 creates a `vector` object `integers3` and initializes it with a copy of `integers1`. This invokes `vector`'s so-called copy constructor to perform the copy operation. You'll learn about copy constructors in detail in Chapter 19. Lines 47–49 output the size and contents of `integers3` to demonstrate that it was initialized correctly.

Assigning *vectors* and Comparing *vectors* for Equality
Line 53 assigns integers2 to integers1, demonstrating that the assignment (=) operator can be used with vector objects. Lines 55–58 output the contents of both objects to show that they now contain identical values. Line 63 then compares integers1 to integers2 with the equality (==) operator to determine whether the contents of the two objects are equal after the assignment in line 53 (which they are).

Using the *[]* Operator to Access and Modify *vector* Elements
Lines 67 and 71 use square brackets ([]) to obtain a vector element as an *rvalue* and as an *lvalue*, respectively. Recall that an *rvalue* cannot be modified, but an *lvalue* can. As is the case with C-style pointer-based arrays, *C++ does not perform any bounds checking when vector elements are accessed with square brackets*. Therefore, you must ensure that operations using [] do not accidentally attempt to manipulate elements outside the bounds of the vector. Standard class template vector does, however, provide bounds checking in its member function at, which we use at line 79 and discuss shortly.

Exception Handling: Processing an Out-of-Range Subscript
An **exception** indicates a problem that occurs while a program executes. The name "exception" suggests that the problem occurs infrequently—if the "rule" is that a statement normally executes correctly, then the problem represents the "exception to the rule." **Exception handling** enables you to create **fault-tolerant programs** that can resolve (or handle) exceptions. In many cases, this allows a program to continue executing as if no problems were encountered. For example, Fig. 15.14 still runs to completion, even though an attempt was made to access an out-of-range subscript. More severe problems might prevent a program from continuing normal execution, instead requiring the program to notify the user of the problem, then terminate. When a function detects a problem, such as an invalid array subscript or an invalid argument, it **throws** an exception—that is, an exception occurs. Here we introduce exception handling briefly. We'll discuss it in detail in Chapter 24.

The *try* Statement
To handle an exception, place any code that might throw an exception in a **try statement** (lines 76–84). The **try block** (lines 76–80) contains the code that might *throw* an exception, and the **catch block** (lines 81–84) contains the code that *handles* the exception if one occurs. You can have many catch blocks to handle different types of exceptions that might be thrown in the corresponding try block. If the code in the try block executes successfully, lines 81–84 are ignored. The braces that delimit try and catch blocks' bodies are required.

The vector member function **at** provides bounds checking and throws an exception if its argument is an invalid subscript. By default, this causes a C++ program to terminate. If the subscript is valid, function at returns the element at the specified location as a modifiable *lvalue* or an unmodifiable *lvalue*, depending on the context in which the call appears. An unmodifiable *lvalue* is an expression that identifies an object in memory (such as an element in a vector), but cannot be used to modify that object.

Executing the *catch* Block
When the program calls vector member function at with the argument 15 (line 79), the function attempts to access the element at location 15, which is *outside* the vector's bounds—integers1 has only 10 elements at this point. Because bounds checking is per-

formed at execution time, vector member function at generates an exception—specifically line 79 throws an **out_of_range** exception (from header <stdexcept>) to notify the program of this problem. At this point, the try block terminates immediately and the catch block begins executing—if you declared any variables in the try block, they're now out of scope and are not accessible in the catch block. [*Note:* To avoid compilation errors with GNU C++, you may need to include header <stdexcept> to use class out_of_range.]

The catch block declares a type (out_of_range) and an exception parameter (ex) that it receives as a reference. The catch block can handle exceptions of the specified type. Inside the block, you can use the parameter's identifier to interact with a caught exception object.

what *Member Function of the Exception Parameter*

When lines 81–84 *catch* the exception, the program displays a message indicating the problem that occurred. Line 83 calls the exception object's **what** member function to get the error message that is stored in the exception object and display it. Once the message is displayed in this example, the exception is considered handled and the program continues with the next statement after the catch block's closing brace. In this example, the end of the program is reached, so the program terminates. We use exception handling throughout our treatment of C++; Chapter 24 presents a deeper look at exception handling.

Summary of This Example

In this section, we demonstrated the C++ Standard Library class template vector, a robust, reusable class that can replace C-style pointer-based arrays. In Chapter 19, you'll see that vector achieves many of its capabilities by "overloading" C++'s built-in operators, and you'll learn how to customize operators for use with your own classes in similar ways. For example, we create an Array class that, like class template vector, improves upon basic array capabilities. Our Array class also provides additional features, such as the ability to input and output entire arrays with operators >> and <<, respectively.

15.14 Introduction to Object Technology and the UML

Now we introduce object orientation, a natural way of thinking about the world and writing computer programs. Our goal here is to help you develop an object-oriented way of thinking and to introduce you to the **Unified Modeling Language™** (**UML™**)—a graphical language that allows people who design object-oriented software systems to use an industry-standard notation to represent them. In this section, we introduce basic object-oriented concepts and terminology.

Basic Object Technology Concepts

We begin our introduction to object orientation with some key terminology. Everywhere you look in the real world you see **objects**—people, animals, plants, cars, planes, buildings, computers and so on. Humans think in terms of objects. Telephones, houses, traffic lights, microwave ovens and water coolers are just a few more objects we see around us every day.

Objects have some things in common. They all have **attributes** (e.g., size, shape, color and weight), and they all exhibit **behaviors** (e.g., a ball rolls, bounces, inflates and deflates; a baby cries, sleeps, crawls, walks and blinks; a car accelerates, brakes and turns; a towel absorbs water). We'll study the kinds of attributes and behaviors that software objects have.

Humans learn about existing objects by studying their attributes and observing their behaviors. Different objects can have similar attributes and can exhibit similar behaviors.

Comparisons can be made, for example, between babies and adults and between humans and chimpanzees.

Object-oriented design (OOD) models software in terms similar to those that people use to describe real-world objects. It takes advantage of class relationships, where objects of a certain class, such as a class of vehicles, have the same characteristics—cars, trucks, little red wagons and roller skates have much in common. OOD takes advantage of **inheritance** relationships, where new classes of objects are derived by absorbing characteristics of existing classes and adding unique characteristics of their own. An object of class "convertible" certainly has the characteristics of the more general class "automobile," but more specifically, the roof goes up and down.

Object-oriented design provides a natural and intuitive way to view the software design process—namely, modeling objects by their attributes, behaviors and interrelationships just as we describe real-world objects. OOD also models communication between objects. Just as people send messages to one another (e.g., a sergeant commands a soldier to stand at attention), objects also communicate via messages. A bank account object may receive a message to decrease its balance by a certain amount because the customer has withdrawn that amount of money.

OOD **encapsulates** (i.e., wraps) attributes and **operations** (behaviors) into objects—an object's attributes and operations are intimately tied together. Objects have the property of **information hiding**. This means that objects may know how to communicate with one another across well-defined **interfaces**, but normally they're not allowed to know how other objects are implemented—implementation details are hidden within the objects themselves. We can drive a car effectively, for instance, without knowing the details of how engines, transmissions, brakes and exhaust systems work internally—as long as we know how to use the accelerator pedal, the brake pedal, the steering wheel and so on. Information hiding, as we'll see, is crucial to good software engineering.

Languages like C++ are **object oriented**. Programming in such a language is called **object-oriented programming (OOP)**, and it allows you to implement an object-oriented design as a working software system. Languages like C, on the other hand, are **procedural**, so programming tends to be **action oriented**. In C, the unit of programming is the function. In C++, the unit of programming is the "class" from which objects are eventually **instantiated** (an OOP term for "created"). C++ classes contain functions that implement operations and data that implements attributes.

C programmers concentrate on writing functions. Programmers group actions that perform some common task into functions, and group functions to form programs. Data is certainly important in C, but the view is that data exists primarily in support of the actions that functions perform. The verbs in a system specification help you determine the set of functions that will work together to implement the system.

Classes, Data Members and Member Functions

C++ programmers concentrate on creating their own user-defined types called classes. Each class contains data as well as the set of functions that manipulate that data and provide services to **clients** (i.e., other classes or functions that use the class). The data components of a class are called **data members**. For example, a bank account class might include an account number and a balance. The function components of a class are called **member functions** (typically called **methods** in other object-oriented programming languages such as Java). For example, a bank account class might include member functions to make a deposit (increasing the balance), make a withdrawal (decreasing the balance) and inquire what the current balance is. You use built-in types (and other user-defined types) as the "building blocks" for constructing new user-defined types (classes). The nouns in a system specification help the C++ programmer determine the set of classes from which objects are created that work together to implement the system.

Classes are to objects as blueprints are to houses—a class is a "plan" for building an object of the class. Just as we can build many houses from one blueprint, we can instantiate (create) many objects from one class. You cannot cook meals in the kitchen of a blueprint; you can cook meals in the kitchen of a house. You cannot sleep in the bedroom of a blueprint; you can sleep in the bedroom of a house.

Classes can have relationships with other classes. In an object-oriented design of a bank, the "bank teller" class relates to other classes, such as the "customer" class, the "cash drawer" class, the "safe" class, and so on. These relationships are called **associations**. Packaging software as classes makes it possible for future software systems to **reuse** the classes.

Software Engineering Observation 15.11

Reuse of existing classes when building new classes and programs saves time, money and effort. Reuse also helps you build more reliable and effective systems, because existing classes often have gone through extensive testing, debugging and performance tuning.

Indeed, with object technology, you can build much of the new software you'll need by combining existing classes, just as automobile manufacturers combine interchangeable parts. Each new class you create can become a valuable software asset that you and others can reuse to speed and enhance the quality of future software development efforts.

Introduction to Object-Oriented Analysis and Design (OOAD)

Soon you'll be writing programs in C++. How will you create the code for your programs? Perhaps, like many beginning programmers, you'll simply turn on your computer and start typing. This approach may work for small programs, but what if you were asked to create a software system to control thousands of automated teller machines for a major bank? Or what if you were asked to work on a team of 1000 software developers building the next generation of the U.S. air traffic control system? For projects so large and complex, you could not simply sit down and start writing programs.

To create the best solutions, you should follow a detailed process for **analyzing** your project's **requirements** (i.e., determining *what* the system is supposed to do) and developing a **design** that satisfies them (i.e., deciding *how* the system should do it). Ideally, you would go through this process and carefully review the design (or have your design reviewed by other software professionals) before writing any code. If this process involves analyzing and designing your system from an object-oriented point of view, it's called **object-oriented analysis and design** (OOAD). Experienced programmers know that analysis and design can save many hours by helping avoid an ill-planned system development approach that has to be abandoned partway through its implementation, possibly wasting considerable time, money and effort.

OOAD is the generic term for the process of analyzing a problem and developing an approach for solving it. Small problems like the ones discussed in the next few chapters do not require an exhaustive OOAD process.

As problems and the groups of people solving them increase in size, the methods of OOAD quickly become more appropriate than pseudocode. Ideally, a group should agree on a strictly defined process for solving its problem and a uniform way of communicating the results of that process to one another. Although many different OOAD processes exist, a single graphical language for communicating the results of *any* OOAD process has come into wide use. This language, known as the Unified Modeling Language (UML), was developed in the mid-1990s under the initial direction of three software methodologists: Grady Booch, James Rumbaugh and Ivar Jacobson.

History of the UML

In the 1980s, increasing numbers of organizations began using OOP to build their applications, and a need developed for a standard OOAD process. Many methodologists—including Booch, Rumbaugh and Jacobson—individually produced and promoted separate processes to satisfy this need. Each process had its own notation, or "language" (in the form of graphical diagrams), to convey the results of analysis and design.

In 1994, James Rumbaugh joined Grady Booch at Rational Software Corporation (now a division of IBM), and the two began working to unify their popular processes. They soon were joined by Ivar Jacobson. In 1996, the group released early versions of the UML to the software engineering community and requested feedback. Around the same time, an organization known as the **Object Management Group™** (**OMG™**) invited submissions for a common modeling language. The OMG (www.omg.org) is a nonprofit organization that promotes the standardization of object-oriented technologies by issuing guidelines and specifications, such as the UML. Several corporations—among them HP, IBM, Microsoft, Oracle and Rational Software—had already recognized the need for a common modeling language. In response to the OMG's request for proposals, these companies formed **UML Partners**—the consortium that developed the UML version 1.1 and submitted it to the OMG. The OMG accepted the proposal and, in 1997, assumed responsibility for the continuing maintenance and revision of the UML. We present the terminology and notation of the current version of the UML—UML version 2—throughout the C++ section of this book.

What Is the UML?

The Unified Modeling Language is now the most widely used graphical representation scheme for modeling object-oriented systems. Those who design systems use the language (in the form of diagrams) to model their systems, as we do throughout the C++ section of this book. An attractive feature of the UML is its flexibility. The UML is **extensible** (i.e., capable of being enhanced with new features) and is independent of any particular OOAD process. UML modelers are free to use various processes in designing systems, but all developers can now express their designs with one standard set of graphical notations. For more information, visit our UML Resource Center at www.deitel.com/UML/.

15.15 Wrap-Up

In this chapter, you learned several of C++'s enhancements to C. We presented basic C++-style input and output with cin and cout and overviewed the C++ Standard Library header files. We discussed inline functions for improving performance by eliminating the overhead of function calls. You learned how to use pass-by-reference with C++'s reference parameters, which enable you to create aliases for existing variables. You learned that multiple functions can be overloaded by providing functions with the same name and different signatures; such functions can be used to perform the same or similar tasks, using different types or different numbers of parameters. We then demonstrated a simpler way of overloading functions using function templates, where a function is defined once but can be used for several different types. You learned the basic terminology of object technology and were introduced to the UML—the most widely used graphical representation scheme for modeling OO systems. In Chapter 16, you'll learn how to implement your own classes and use objects of those classes in applications.

Summary

Section 15.2 C++

- C++ improves on many of C's features and provides object-oriented-programming (OOP) capabilities that increase software productivity, quality and reusability.
- C++ was developed by Bjarne Stroustrup at Bell Labs and was originally called "C with classes."

Section 15.3 A Simple Program: Adding Two Integers

- C++ filenames can have one of several extensions, such as .cpp, .cxx or .C (uppercase).
- C++ allows you to begin a comment with // and use the remainder of the line as comment text. C++ programmers may also use C-style comments.
- The input/output stream header file <iostream> must be included for any program that outputs data to the screen or inputs data from the keyboard using C++-style stream input/output.
- As in C, every C++ program begins execution with function main. Keyword int to the left of main indicates that main "returns" an integer value.
- In C, you need not specify a return type for functions. However, C++ requires you to specify the return type, possibly void, for all functions; otherwise, a syntax error occurs.
- Declarations can be placed almost anywhere in a C++ program, but they must appear before their corresponding variables are used in the program.
- The standard output stream object (std::cout) and the stream insertion operator (<<) are used to display text on the screen.
- The standard input stream object (std::cin) and the stream extraction operator (>>) are used to obtain values from the keyboard.
- The stream manipulator std::endl outputs a newline, then "flushes the output buffer."
- The notation std::cout specifies that we're using a name, in this case cout, that belongs to "namespace" std.
- Using multiple stream insertion operators (<<) in a single statement is referred to as concatenating, chaining or cascading stream insertion operations.

Section 15.4 C++ Standard Library

- C++ programs consist of pieces called classes and functions. You can program each piece you may need to form a C++ program. However, most C++ programmers take advantage of the rich collections of existing classes and functions in the C++ Standard Library.

Section 15.5 Header Files

- The C++ Standard Library is divided into many portions, each with its own header file. The header files contain the function prototypes for the related functions that form each portion of the library. The header files also contain definitions of various class types and functions, as well as constants needed by those functions.

- Header file names ending in .h are "old-style" header files that have been superceded by the C++ Standard Library header files.

Section 15.6 Inline Functions

- C++ provides inline functions to help reduce function call overhead—especially for small functions. Placing the qualifier inline before a function's return type in the function definition "advises" the compiler to generate a copy of the function's code in place to avoid a function call.

Section 15.7 References and Reference Parameters

- Two ways to pass arguments to functions in many programming languages are pass-by-value and pass-by-reference.

- When an argument is passed by value, a *copy* of its value is made and passed (on the function call stack) to the called function. Changes to the copy do not affect the original in the caller.

- With pass-by-reference, the caller gives the called function the ability to access the caller's data directly and to modify it if the called function chooses to do so.

- A reference parameter is an alias for its corresponding argument in a function call.

- To indicate that a function parameter is passed by reference, simply follow the parameter's type in the function prototype by an ampersand (&); use the same notation when listing the parameter's type in the function header.

- Once a reference is declared as an alias for another variable, all operations supposedly performed on the alias (i.e., the reference) are actually performed on the original variable. The alias is simply another name for the original variable.

Section 15.8 Empty Parameter Lists

- In C++, an empty parameter list is specified by writing either void or nothing in parentheses.

Section 15.9 Default Arguments

- It's not uncommon for a program to invoke a function repeatedly with the same argument value for a particular parameter. In such cases, the programmer can specify that such a parameter has a default argument, i.e., a default value to be passed to that parameter.

- When a program omits an argument for a parameter with a default argument, the compiler inserts the default value of that argument to be passed as an argument in the function call.

- Default arguments must be the rightmost (trailing) arguments in a function's parameter list.

- Default arguments should be specified with the first occurrence of the function name—typically, in the function prototype.

Section 15.10 Unary Scope Resolution Operator

- C++ provides the unary scope resolution operator (::) to access a global variable when a local variable of the same name is in scope.

Section 15.11 Function Overloading

- C++ enables several functions of the same name to be defined, as long as they have different sets of parameters (by number, type and/or order). This capability is called function overloading.

- When an overloaded function is called, the C++ compiler selects the proper function by examining the number, types and order of the arguments in the call.

- Overloaded functions are distinguished by their signatures.

- The compiler encodes each function identifier with the number and types of its parameters to enable type-safe linkage. Type-safe linkage ensures that the proper overloaded function is called and that the types of the arguments conform to the types of the parameters.

Section 15.12 Function Templates

- Overloaded functions are used to perform similar operations that may involve different program logic on data of different types. If the program logic and operations are identical for each data type, overloading may be performed more compactly and conveniently using function templates.

- The programmer writes a single function template definition. Given the argument types provided in calls to this function, C++ automatically generates separate function template specializations to handle each type of call appropriately. Thus, defining a single function template essentially defines a family of overloaded functions.

- All function template definitions begin with the `template` keyword followed by a template parameter list to the function template enclosed in angle brackets (< and >).

- The formal type parameters are placeholders for fundamental types or user-defined types. These placeholders are used to specify the types of the function's parameters, to specify the function's return type and to declare variables within the body of the function definition.

Section 15.13 Introduction to C++ Standard Library Class Template `vector`

- C++ Standard Library class template `vector` represents a more robust alternative to arrays featuring many capabilities that are not provided for C-style pointer-based arrays.

- By default, all the elements of an integer `vector` object are set to 0.

- A `vector` can be defined to store any data type using a declaration of the form

    vector< *type* > *name*(*size*);

- Member function `size` of class template `vector` returns the number of elements in the `vector` on which it's invoked.

- The value of an element of a `vector` can be accessed or modified using square brackets ([]).

- Objects of standard class template `vector` can be compared directly with the equality (==) and inequality (!=) operators. The assignment (=) operator can also be used with `vector` objects.

- An unmodifiable *lvalue* is an expression that identifies an object in memory (such as an element in a vector), but cannot be used to modify that object. A modifiable *lvalue* also identifies an object in memory, but can be used to modify the object.

- An exception indicates a problem that occurs while a program executes. The name "exception" suggests that the problem occurs infrequently—if the "rule" is that a statement normally executes correctly, then the problem represents the "exception to the rule."

- Exception handling enables you to create fault-tolerant programs that can resolve exceptions.

- To handle an exception, place any code that might throw an exception in a `try` statement.

- The `try` block contains the code that might throw an exception, and the `catch` block contains the code that handles the exception if one occurs.

- When a `try` block terminates any variables declared in the `try` block go out of scope.

- A `catch` block declares a type and an exception parameter. Inside the `catch` block, you can use the parameter's identifier to interact with a caught exception object.

- An exception object's `what` method returns the exception's error message.

Section 15.14 Introduction to Object Technology and the UML

- The Unified Modeling Language (UML) is a graphical language that allows people who build systems to represent their object-oriented designs in a common notation.

- Object-oriented design (OOD) models software components in terms of real-world objects. It takes advantage of class relationships, where objects of a certain class have the same characteristics. It also takes advantage of inheritance relationships, where newly created classes of objects are derived by absorbing characteristics of existing classes and adding unique characteristics of their own. OOD encapsulates data (attributes) and functions (behavior) into objects—the data and functions of an object are intimately tied together.

- Objects have the property of information hiding—objects normally are not allowed to know how other objects are implemented.

- Object-oriented programming (OOP) allows programmers to implement object-oriented designs as working systems.

- C++ programmers create their own user-defined types called classes. Each class contains data (known as data members) and the set of functions (known as member functions) that manipulate that data and provide services to clients.

- Classes can have relationships with other classes. These relationships are called associations.

- Packaging software as classes makes it possible for future software systems to reuse the classes. Groups of related classes are often packaged as reusable components.

- An instance of a class is called an object.

- With object technology, programmers can build much of the software they will need by combining standardized, interchangeable parts called classes.

- The process of analyzing and designing a system from an object-oriented point of view is called object-oriented analysis and design (OOAD).

Terminology

Self-Review Exercises

15.1   Answer each of the following:
    a) In C++, it's possible to have various functions with the same name that operate on different types or numbers of arguments. This is called function _____ .
    b) The _____ enables access to a global variable with the same name as a variable in the current scope.
    c) A function _____ enables a single function to be defined to perform the same task on data of many different types.
    d) _____ is the most widely used graphical representation scheme for OO modeling.
    e) _____ models software components in terms of real-world objects.
    f) C++ programmers create their own user-defined types called _____ .

15.2   Why would a function prototype contain a parameter type declaration such as double &?

15.3   (True/False) All arguments to function calls in C++ are passed by value.

15.4   Write a complete program that prompts the user for the side of a square, and calculates and prints the area of that square. Use an inline function squareArea that returns the result of the following expression: (side * side).

Answers to Self-Review Exercises

15.1   a) overloading. b) unary scope resolution operator (::). c) template. d) The UML. e) Object-oriented design (OOD). f) classes.

15.2   This creates a reference parameter of type "reference to double" that enables the function to modify the original variable in the calling function.

15.3   False. C++ enables pass-by-reference using reference parameters.

15.4   See the following program:

```
1    // Exercise 15.4 Solution
2    // Inline function that calculates the area of a square.
3    #include <iostream>
4    #include <cmath>
5    using namespace std;
6
7    // calculates area of a square
8    inline int squareArea( const int side )
9    {
10       return (side * side);
11   } // end inline function squareArea
12
```

```
13   int main()
14   {
15       int side;
16
17       // prompt user for side
18       cout << "Enter the side of your square: ";
19       cin >> side; // input side
20
21       // use side to calculate area of a square and display result
22       cout << "Area of the square with side " << side
23           << " is " << squareArea(side) << endl;
24   } // end main
```

```
Enter the side of your square: 9
Area of the square with side 9 is 81
```

Exercises

15.5   Write a C++ program that prompts the user for the length and the breadth of a rectangle, then calls `inline` function `rectanglePerimeter` to calculate the perimeter of that rectangle.

15.6   Write a complete C++ program with the two alternate functions specified below, each of which simply calculates the perimeter of a square. Then compare and contrast the two approaches. These two functions are

a) function `squarePerimeterByValue` that passes a copy of the side of a square by value, quadruples the copy and returns the new value and

b) function `squarePerimeterByReference` that passes the side of a square by reference via a reference parameter and quadruples the original value of `side` through its alias (i.e., the reference parameter).

15.7   What is the purpose of the unary scope resolution operator?

15.8   Write a program that uses a function template called `sum` to determine the sum of three arguments. Test the program using integer and floating-point number arguments.

15.9   Write a program that uses a function template called `product` to determine the product of two arguments. Test the program using integer and floating-point number arguments.

15.10   Determine whether the following program segments contain errors. For each error, explain how to correct it. [*Note:* It's possible that no errors are present in the segment.]

a)
```
template < class A >
int sum( int num1, int num2, int num3 )
{
    return num1 + num2 + num3;
}
```

b)
```
void printResults( int x, int y )
{
    cout << "The sum is " << x + y << '\n';
    return x + y;
}
```

c)
```
template < A >
A product( A num1, A num2, A num3 )
{
    return num1 * num2 * num3;
}
```

d)
```
double cube( int );
int cube( int );
```

16

Introduction to Classes, Objects and Strings

Nothing can have value without being an object of utility.
—Karl Marx

Your public servants serve you right.
—Adlai E. Stevenson

Knowing how to answer one who speaks, To reply to one who sends a message.
—Amenemopel

Objectives

In this chapter you'll learn:

- How to define a class and use it to create an object.

- How to implement a class's behaviors as member functions.

- How to implement a class's attributes as data members.

- How to call a member function of an object to perform a task.

- The differences between data members of a class and local variables of a function.

- How to use a constructor to initialize an object's data when the object is created.

- How to engineer a class to separate its interface from its implementation and encourage reuse.

- How to use objects of class `string`.

16.1 Introduction

In this chapter, you'll begin writing programs that employ the basic concepts of *object-oriented programming* that we introduced in Section 15.14. One common feature of every program in Chapter 15 was that all the statements that performed tasks were located in function main. Typically, the programs you develop in C++ will consist of function main and one or more *classes*, each containing *data members* and *member functions*. If you become part of a development team in industry, you might work on software systems that contain hundreds, or even thousands, of classes. In this chapter, we develop a simple, well-engineered framework for organizing object-oriented programs in C++.

We present a carefully paced sequence of complete working programs to demonstrate creating and using your own classes. These examples begin our integrated case study on developing a grade-book class that instructors can use to maintain student test scores. We also introduce the C++ standard library class string.

16.2 Defining a Class with a Member Function

We begin with an example (Fig. 16.1) that consists of class GradeBook (lines 8–16)—which will represent a grade book that an instructor can use to maintain student test scores—and a main function (lines 19–23) that creates a GradeBook object. Function main uses this object and its member function to display a message on the screen welcoming the instructor to the grade-book program.

```
1   // Fig. 16.1: fig16_01.cpp
2   // Define class GradeBook with a member function displayMessage,
3   // create a GradeBook object, and call its displayMessage function.
4   #include <iostream>
5   using namespace std;
```

Fig. 16.1 | Define class GradeBook with a member function displayMessage, create a GradeBook object and call its displayMessage function. (Part 1 of 2.)

```
 6
 7    // GradeBook class definition
 8    class GradeBook
 9    {
10    public:
11       // function that displays a welcome message to the GradeBook user
12       void displayMessage()
13       {
14          cout << "Welcome to the Grade Book!" << endl;
15       } // end function displayMessage
16    }; // end class GradeBook
17
18    // function main begins program execution
19    int main()
20    {
21       GradeBook myGradeBook; // create a GradeBook object named myGradeBook
22       myGradeBook.displayMessage(); // call object's displayMessage function
23    } // end main
```

```
Welcome to the Grade Book!
```

Fig. 16.1 | Define class GradeBook with a member function displayMessage, create a GradeBook object and call its displayMessage function. (Part 2 of 2.)

Class *GradeBook*

Before function main (lines 19–23) can create a GradeBook object, we must tell the compiler what member functions and data members belong to the class. The GradeBook **class definition** (lines 8–16) contains a member function called displayMessage (lines 12–15) that displays a message on the screen (line 14). We need to make an object of class GradeBook (line 21) and call its displayMessage member function (line 22) to get line 14 to execute and display the welcome message. We'll soon explain lines 21–22 in detail.

The class definition begins in line 8 with the keyword class followed by the class name GradeBook. By convention, the name of a user-defined class begins with a capital letter, and for readability, each subsequent word in the class name begins with a capital letter. This capitalization style is often referred to as **Camel case**, because the pattern of uppercase and lowercase letters resembles the silhouette of a camel.

Every class's **body** is enclosed in a pair of left and right braces ({ and }), as in lines 9 and 16. The class definition terminates with a semicolon (line 16).

Common Programming Error 16.1

Forgetting the semicolon at the end of a class definition is a syntax error.

Recall that the function main is always called automatically when you execute a program. Most functions do *not* get called automatically. As you'll soon see, you must call member function displayMessage *explicitly* to tell it to perform its task.

Line 10 contains the keyword **public**, which is an **access specifier**. Lines 12–15 define member function displayMessage. This member function appears after access specifier public: to indicate that the function is "available to the public"—that is, it can be called by other functions in the program (such as main), and by member functions of other classes (if there are any). Access specifiers are always followed by a colon (:). For the remainder of the text, when we refer to the access specifier public, we'll omit the colon as we did in this sentence. Section 16.4 introduces the access specifier, private. Later in the book we'll study the access specifier protected.

Each function in a program performs a task and may *return a value* when it completes its task—for example, a function might perform a calculation, then return the result of that calculation. When you define a function, you must specify a **return type** to indicate the type of the value returned by the function when it completes its task. In line 12, keyword **void** to the left of the function name displayMessage is the function's return type. Return type void indicates that displayMessage will *not* return any data to its **calling function** (in this example, line 22 of main, as we'll see in a moment) when it completes its task. In Fig. 16.5, you'll see an example of a function that *does* return a value.

The name of the member function, displayMessage, follows the return type (line 12). By convention, function names begin with a *lowercase* first letter and all subsequent words in the name begin with a capital letter. The parentheses after the member function name indicate that this is a function. An empty set of parentheses, as shown in line 12, indicates that this member function does *not* require additional data to perform its task. You'll see an example of a member function that *does* require additional data in Section 16.3. Line 12 is commonly referred to as a **function header**. Every function's *body* is delimited by left and right braces ({ and }), as in lines 13 and 15.

The *body of a function* contains statements that perform the function's task. In this case, member function displayMessage contains one statement (line 14) that displays the message "Welcome to the Grade Book!". After this statement executes, the function has completed its task.

Testing Class *GradeBook*

Next, we'd like to use class GradeBook in a program. As you know, the function main (lines 19–23) begins the execution of every program.

In this program, we'd like to call class GradeBook's displayMessage member function to display the welcome message. Typically, you cannot call a member function of a class until you create an object of that class. (As you'll learn in Section 18.6, static member functions are an exception.) Line 21 creates an object of class GradeBook called myGradeBook. The variable's type is GradeBook—the class we defined in lines 8–16. When we declare variables of type int, the compiler knows what int is—it's a *fundamental type* that's "built into" C++. In line 21, however, the compiler does *not* automatically know what type GradeBook is—it's a user-defined type. We tell the compiler what GradeBook is by including the *class definition* (lines 8–16). If we omitted these lines, the compiler would issue an error message. Each class you create becomes a new *type* that can be used to create objects. You can define new class types as needed; this is one reason why C++ is known as an extensible language.

Line 22 *calls* the member function displayMessage using variable myGradeBook followed by the **dot operator** (.), the function name displayMessage and an empty set of parentheses. This call causes the displayMessage function to perform its task. At the beginning of line 22, "myGradeBook." indicates that main should use the GradeBook object that was created in line 21. The empty parentheses in line 12 indicate that member function displayMessage does *not* require additional data to perform its task, which is why we called this function with empty parentheses in line 22. (In Section 16.3, you'll see how to pass data to a function.) When displayMessage completes its task, the program reaches the end of main (line 23) and terminates.

UML Class Diagram for Class GradeBook

Recall from Section 15.14 that the UML is a standardized graphical language used by software developers to represent their object-oriented systems. In the UML, each class is modeled in a UML **class diagram** as a rectangle with three compartments. Figure 16.2 presents a class diagram for class GradeBook (Fig. 16.1). The *top compartment* contains the class's name centered horizontally and in boldface type. The *middle compartment* contains the class's attributes, which correspond to data members in C++. This compartment is currently empty, because class GradeBook does not have any attributes. (Section 16.4 presents a version of class GradeBook with an attribute.) The *bottom compartment* contains the class's operations, which correspond to member functions in C++. The UML models operations by listing the operation name followed by a set of parentheses. Class GradeBook has only one member function, displayMessage, so the bottom compartment of Fig. 16.2 lists one operation with this name. Member function displayMessage does *not* require additional information to perform its tasks, so the parentheses following displayMessage in the class diagram are *empty*, just as they are in the member function's header in line 12 of Fig. 16.1. The *plus sign (+)* in front of the operation name indicates that displayMessage is a *public* operation in the UML (i.e., a public member function in C++).

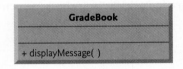

Fig. 16.2 | UML class diagram indicating that class GradeBook has a public displayMessage operation.

16.3 Defining a Member Function with a Parameter

In our car analogy from Section 1.9, we mentioned that pressing a car's gas pedal sends a message to the car to perform a task—make the car go faster. But *how fast* should the car accelerate? As you know, the farther down you press the pedal, the faster the car accelerates. So the message to the car includes *both* the *task to perform* and *additional information that helps the car perform the task*. This additional information is known as a parameter—the *value* of the parameter helps the car determine how fast to accelerate. Similarly, a member function can require one or more parameters that represent additional data it needs to perform its task. A function call supplies values—called **arguments**—for each of the function's parameters. For example, to make a deposit into a bank account, suppose a deposit member function of an Account class specifies a parameter that represents the *deposit amount*. When the deposit member function is called, an argument value representing the deposit amount is copied to the member function's parameter. The member function then adds that amount to the account balance.

Defining and Testing Class *GradeBook*

Our next example (Fig. 16.3) redefines class GradeBook (lines 9–18) with a display-Message member function (lines 13–17) that displays the course name as part of the welcome message. The new version of displayMessage requires a parameter (courseName in line 13) that represents the course name to output.

```cpp
1   // Fig. 16.3: fig16_03.cpp
2   // Define class GradeBook with a member function that takes a parameter,
3   // create a GradeBook object and call its displayMessage function.
4   #include <iostream>
5   #include <string> // program uses C++ standard string class
6   using namespace std;
7
8   // GradeBook class definition
9   class GradeBook
10  {
11  public:
12     // function that displays a welcome message to the GradeBook user
13     void displayMessage( string courseName )
14     {
15        cout << "Welcome to the grade book for\n" << courseName << "!"
16           << endl;
17     } // end function displayMessage
18  }; // end class GradeBook
19
20  // function main begins program execution
21  int main()
22  {
23     string nameOfCourse; // string of characters to store the course name
24     GradeBook myGradeBook; // create a GradeBook object named myGradeBook
25
26     // prompt for and input course name
27     cout << "Please enter the course name:" << endl;
28     getline( cin, nameOfCourse ); // read a course name with blanks
29     cout << endl; // output a blank line
30
31     // call myGradeBook's displayMessage function
32     // and pass nameOfCourse as an argument
33     myGradeBook.displayMessage( nameOfCourse );
34  } // end main
```

```
Please enter the course name:
CS101 Introduction to C++ Programming

Welcome to the grade book for
CS101 Introduction to C++ Programming!
```

Fig. 16.3 | Define class GradeBook with a member function that takes a parameter, create a GradeBook object and call its displayMessage function.

Before discussing the new features of class GradeBook, let's see how the new class is used in main (lines 21–34). Line 23 creates a variable of type **string** called nameOfCourse that will be used to store the course name entered by the user. A variable of type `string` represents a string of characters such as "CS101 Introduction to C++ Programming". A string is actually an *object* of the C++ Standard Library class `string`. This class is defined in **header <string>**, and the name `string`, like `cout`, belongs to namespace `std`. To enable lines 13 and 23 to compile, line 5 includes the `<string>` header. The `using` directive in line 6 allows us to simply write `string` in line 23 rather than `std::string`. For now, you can think of `string` variables like variables of other types such as `int`. You'll learn additional `string` capabilities in Section 16.8.

Line 24 creates an object of class `GradeBook` named `myGradeBook`. Line 27 prompts the user to enter a course name. Line 28 reads the name from the user and assigns it to the `nameOfCourse` variable, using the library function **getline** to perform the input. Before we explain this line of code, let's explain why we cannot simply write

```
cin >> nameOfCourse;
```

to obtain the course name. In our sample program execution, we use the course name "CS101 Introduction to C++ Programming," which contains multiple words separated by blanks. (Recall that we highlight user-supplied input in bold.) When `cin` is used with the stream extraction operator, it reads characters *until the first white-space character is reached*. Thus, only "CS101" would be read by the preceding statement. The rest of the course name would have to be read by subsequent input operations.

In this example, we'd like the user to type the complete course name and press *Enter* to submit it to the program, and we'd like to store the entire course name in the `string` variable `nameOfCourse`. The function call `getline( cin, nameOfCourse )` in line 28 reads characters (*including* the space characters that separate the words in the input) from the standard input stream object `cin` (i.e., the keyboard) until the newline character is encountered, places the characters in the `string` variable `nameOfCourse` and *discards* the newline character. When you press *Enter* while typing program input, a newline is inserted in the input stream. The `<string>` header must be included in the program to use function `getline`, which belongs to namespace `std`.

Line 33 calls `myGradeBook`'s `displayMessage` member function. The `nameOfCourse` variable in parentheses is the *argument* that's passed to member function `displayMessage` so that it can perform its task. The value of variable `nameOfCourse` in `main` is copied to member function `displayMessage`'s parameter `courseName` in line 13. When you execute this program, member function `displayMessage` outputs as part of the welcome message the course name you type (in our sample execution, CS101 Introduction to C++ Programming).

More on Arguments and Parameters

To specify in a function definition that the function requires data to perform its task, you place additional information in the function's **parameter list**, which is located in the parentheses following the function name. The parameter list may contain any number of parameters, including none at all (represented by empty parentheses as in Fig. 16.1, line 12) to indicate that a function does *not* require any parameters. Member function `displayMessage`'s parameter list (Fig. 16.3, line 13) declares that the function requires one parameter. Each parameter specifies a *type* and an *identifier*. The type `string` and the identifier `courseName` indicate that member function `displayMessage` requires a `string` to perform its task. The member function body uses the parameter `courseName` to access the value that's passed to the function in the function call (line 33 in `main`). Lines 15–16 display parameter `courseName`'s value as part of the welcome message. The parameter variable's name (`courseName` in line 13) can be the *same* as or *different* from the argument variable's name (`nameOfCourse` in line 33).

A function can specify multiple parameters by separating each from the next with a comma. The number and order of arguments in a function call *must match* the number and order of parameters in the parameter list of the called member function's header. Also, the argument types in the function call must be consistent with the types of the corresponding parameters in the function header. (As you'll learn in subsequent chapters, an argument's type and its corresponding parameter's type need not always be *identical*, but they must be "consistent.") In our example, the one `string` argument in the function call (i.e., `nameOfCourse`) *exactly matches* the one `string` parameter in the member-function definition (i.e., `courseName`).

Updated UML Class Diagram for Class *GradeBook*

The UML class diagram of Fig. 16.4 models class `GradeBook` of Fig. 16.3. Like the class `GradeBook` defined in Fig. 16.1, this `GradeBook` class contains `public` member function `displayMessage`. However, this version of `displayMessage` has a parameter. The UML models a parameter by listing the parameter name, followed by a colon and the parameter type in the parentheses following the operation name. The UML has its own data types similar to those of C++. The UML is language independent—it's used with many different programming languages—so its terminology does not exactly match that of C++. For example, the UML type `String` corresponds to the C++ type `string`. Member function `displayMessage` of class GradeBook (Fig. 16.3, lines 13–17) has a `string` parameter named `courseName`, so Fig. 16.4 lists `courseName : String` between the parentheses following the operation name `displayMessage`. This version of the GradeBook class still does *not* have any data members.

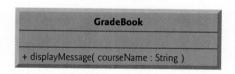

Fig. 16.4 | UML class diagram indicating that class `GradeBook` has a public `displayMessage` operation with a `courseName` parameter of UML type `String`.

16.4 Data Members, *set* Functions and *get* Functions

Variables declared in a function definition's body are known as **local variables** and can be used *only* from the line of their declaration in the function to closing right brace (}) of the block in which they're declared. A local variable must be declared *before* it can be used in a function. A local variable cannot be accessed outside the function in which it's declared. *When a function terminates, the values of its local variables are lost.*

A class normally consists of one or more member functions that manipulate the attributes that belong to a particular object of the class. Attributes are represented as variables in a class definition. Such variables are called **data members** and are declared *inside* a class definition but *outside* the bodies of the class's member-function definitions. Each object of a class maintains its own copy of its attributes in memory. These attributes exist throughout the life of the object. The example in this section demonstrates a GradeBook class that contains a courseName data member to represent a particular GradeBook object's course name.

GradeBook *Class with a Data Member, a* set *Function and a* get *Function*

In our next example, class GradeBook (Fig. 16.5) maintains the course name as a *data member* so that it can be used or modified at any time during a program's execution. The class contains member functions setCourseName, getCourseName and displayMessage. Member function setCourseName stores a course name in a GradeBook data member. Member function getCourseName obtains the course name from that data member. Member function displayMessage—which now specifies no parameters—still displays a welcome message that includes the course name. However, as you'll see, the function now obtains the course name by calling another function in the same class—getCourseName.

```cpp
 1   // Fig. 16.5: fig16_05.cpp
 2   // Define class GradeBook that contains a courseName data member
 3   // and member functions to set and get its value;
 4   // Create and manipulate a GradeBook object with these functions.
 5   #include <iostream>
 6   #include <string> // program uses C++ standard string class
 7   using namespace std;
 8
 9   // GradeBook class definition
10   class GradeBook
11   {
12   public:
13      // function that sets the course name
14      void setCourseName( string name )
15      {
16         courseName = name; // store the course name in the object
17      } // end function setCourseName
18
19      // function that gets the course name
20      string getCourseName()
21      {
22         return courseName; // return the object's courseName
23      } // end function getCourseName
24
25      // function that displays a welcome message
26      void displayMessage()
27      {
28         // this statement calls getCourseName to get the
29         // name of the course this GradeBook represents
30         cout << "Welcome to the grade book for\n" << getCourseName() << "!"
31            << endl;
32      } // end function displayMessage
```

Fig. 16.5 | Defining and testing class GradeBook with a data member and *set* and *get* functions. (Part 1 of 2.)

```
33    private:
34       string courseName; // course name for this GradeBook
35    }; // end class GradeBook
36
37    // function main begins program execution
38    int main()
39    {
40       string nameOfCourse; // string of characters to store the course name
41       GradeBook myGradeBook; // create a GradeBook object named myGradeBook
42
43       // display initial value of courseName
44       cout << "Initial course name is: " << myGradeBook.getCourseName()
45          << endl;
46
47       // prompt for, input and set course name
48       cout << "\nPlease enter the course name:" << endl;
49       getline( cin, nameOfCourse ); // read a course name with blanks
50       myGradeBook.setCourseName( nameOfCourse ); // set the course name
51
52       cout << endl; // outputs a blank line
53       myGradeBook.displayMessage(); // display message with new course name
54    } // end main
```

```
Initial course name is:

Please enter the course name:
CS101 Introduction to C++ Programming

Welcome to the grade book for
CS101 Introduction to C++ Programming!
```

Fig. 16.5 | Defining and testing class GradeBook with a data member and *set* and *get* functions. (Part 2 of 2.)

A typical instructor teaches multiple courses, each with its own course name. Line 34 declares that courseName is a variable of type string. Because the variable is declared in the class definition (lines 10–35) but outside the bodies of the class's member-function definitions (lines 14–17, 20–23 and 26–32), the variable is a *data member*. Every instance (i.e., object) of class GradeBook contains one copy of each of the class's data members—if there are two GradeBook objects, each has its *own* copy of courseName (one per object), as you'll see in the example of Fig. 16.7. A benefit of making courseName a data member is that all the member functions of the class can manipulate any data members that appear in the class definition (in this case, courseName).

Access Specifiers public *and* private

Most data-member declarations appear after the **private** access specifier. Variables or functions declared after access specifier private (and before the next access specifier if there is one) are accessible only to member functions of the class for which they're declared (or to "friends" of the class, as you'll see in Chapter 18, Classes: A Deeper Look, Part 2). Thus, data member courseName can be used only in member functions setCourseName, getCourseName and displayMessage of class GradeBook (or to "friends" of the class, if there were any).

Software Engineering Observation 16.1

Generally, data members should be declared `private` *and member functions should be declared* `public`.

Error-Prevention Tip 16.1

Make the data members of a class `private` *and the member functions of the class* `public`. *This facilitates debugging because problems with data manipulations are localized to either the class's member functions or the friends of the class.*

Common Programming Error 16.2

An attempt by a function, which is not a member of a particular class (or a friend of that class) to access a `private` *member of that class is a compilation error.*

The *default access* for class members is `private` so all members after the class header and before the first access specifier (if there are any) are `private`. The access specifiers `public` and `private` may be repeated, but this is unnecessary and can be confusing.

Declaring data members with access specifier `private` is known as **data hiding**. When a program creates a GradeBook object, data member courseName is *encapsulated* (hidden) in the object and can be accessed only by member functions of the object's class. In class GradeBook, member functions setCourseName and getCourseName manipulate the data member courseName directly.

Member Functions *setCourseName and getCourseName*

Member function setCourseName (lines 14–17) does not return any data when it completes its task, so its return type is void. The member function receives one parameter—name—which represents the course name that will be passed to it as an argument (as we'll see in line 50 of main). Line 16 assigns name to data member courseName. In this example, setCourseName does not *validate* the course name—i.e., the function does *not* check that the course name adheres to any particular format or follows any other rules regarding what a "valid" course name looks like. Suppose, for instance, that a university can print student transcripts containing course names of only 25 characters or fewer. In this case, we might want class GradeBook to ensure that its data member courseName never contains more than 25 characters. We discuss validation in Section 16.8.

Member function getCourseName (lines 20–23) returns a particular GradeBook object's courseName. The member function has an empty parameter list, so it does *not* require additional data to perform its task. The function specifies that it returns a string. When a function that specifies a return type other than void is called and completes its task, the function uses a **return statement** (as in line 22) to *return a result* to its calling function. For example, when you go to an automated teller machine (ATM) and request your account balance, you expect the ATM to give you back a value that represents your balance. Similarly, when a statement calls member function getCourseName on a GradeBook object, the statement expects to receive the GradeBook's course name (in this case, a string, as specified by the function's return type).

If you have a function square that returns the square of its argument, the statement

```
result = square( 2 );
```

returns 4 from function `square` and assigns to variable `result` the value 4. If you have a function `maximum` that returns the largest of three integer arguments, the statement

```
biggest = maximum( 27, 114, 51 );
```

returns 114 from function `maximum` and assigns to variable `biggest` the value 114.

The statements in lines 16 and 22 each use variable `courseName` (line 34) even though it was *not* declared in any of the member functions. We can do this because `courseName` is a *data member* of the class.

Member Function `displayMessage`

Member function `displayMessage` (lines 26–32) does *not* return any data when it completes its task, so its return type is `void`. The function does *not* receive parameters, so its parameter list is empty. Lines 30–31 output a welcome message that includes the value of data member `courseName`. Line 30 calls member function `getCourseName` to obtain the value of `courseName`. Member function `displayMessage` could also access data member `courseName` directly, just as member functions `setCourseName` and `getCourseName` do. We explain shortly why it's preferable to call member function `getCourseName` to obtain the value of `courseName`.

Testing Class *GradeBook*

The `main` function (lines 38–54) creates one object of class `GradeBook` and uses each of its member functions. Line 41 creates a `GradeBook` object named `myGradeBook`. Lines 44–45 display the initial course name by calling the object's `getCourseName` member function. The first line of the output does not show a course name, because the object's `courseName` data member (i.e., a `string`) is initially empty—by default, the initial value of a `string` is the so-called **empty string**, i.e., a string that does not contain any characters. Nothing appears on the screen when an empty string is displayed.

Line 48 prompts the user to enter a course name. Local `string` variable `nameOfCourse` (declared in line 40) is set to the course name entered by the user, which is obtained by the call to the `getline` function (line 49). Line 50 calls object `myGradeBook`'s `setCourseName` member function and supplies `nameOfCourse` as the function's argument. When the function is called, the argument's value is copied to parameter `name` (line 14) of member function `setCourseName`. Then the parameter's value is assigned to data member `courseName` (line 16). Line 52 skips a line; then line 53 calls object `myGradeBook`'s `displayMessage` member function to display the welcome message containing the course name.

Software Engineering with Set and Get Functions

A class's `private` data members can be manipulated only by member functions of that class (and by "friends" of the class). So a **client of an object**—that is, any statement that calls the object's member functions from *outside* the object—calls the class's `public` member functions to request the class's services for particular objects of the class. This is why the statements in function `main` call member functions `setCourseName`, `getCourseName` and `displayMessage` on a `GradeBook` object. Classes often provide `public` member functions to allow clients of the class to *set* (i.e., assign values to) or *get* (i.e., obtain the values of) `private` data members. These member function names need not begin with `set` or `get`, but this naming convention is common. In this example, the member function that *sets* the `courseName` data member is called `setCourseName`, and the member function that *gets* the value of the `courseName` data member is called `getCourseName`. *Set* functions are sometimes called **mutators** (because they mutate, or change, values), and *get* functions are also called **accessors** (because they access values).

Recall that declaring data members with access specifier `private` enforces data hiding. Providing `public` *set* and *get* functions allows clients of a class to access the hidden data, but only *indirectly*. The client knows that it's attempting to modify or obtain an object's data, but the client does *not* know *how* the object performs these operations. In some cases, a class may internally represent a piece of data one way, but expose that data to clients in a different way. For example, suppose a `Clock` class represents the time of day as a `private int` data member `time` that stores the number of seconds since midnight. However, when a client calls a `Clock` object's `getTime` member function, the object could return the time with hours, minutes and seconds in a `string` in the format `"HH:MM:SS"`. Similarly, suppose the `Clock` class provides a *set* function named `setTime` that takes a `string` parameter in the `"HH:MM:SS"` format. Using `string` class capabilities, the `setTime` function could convert this `string` to a number of seconds, which the function stores in its `private` data member. The *set* function could also check that the value it receives represents a valid time (e.g., `"12:30:45"` is valid but `"42:85:70"` is not). The *set* and *get* functions allow a client to interact with an object, but the object's `private` data remains safely encapsulated (i.e., hidden) in the object itself.

The *set* and *get* functions of a class also should be used by other member functions *within* the class to manipulate the class's `private` data, although these member functions *can* access the `private` data directly. In Fig. 16.5, member functions `setCourseName` and `getCourseName` are `public` member functions, so they're accessible to clients of the class, as well as to the class itself. Member function `displayMessage` calls member function `getCourseName` to obtain the value of data member `courseName` for display purposes, even though `displayMessage` can access `courseName` directly—accessing a data member via its *get* function creates a better, more robust class (i.e., a class that's easier to maintain and less likely to malfunction). If we decide to change the data member `courseName` in some way, the `displayMessage` definition will *not* require modification—only the bodies of the *get* and *set* functions that directly manipulate the data member will need to change. For example, suppose we want to represent the course name as two separate data members— `courseNumber` (e.g., `"CS101"`) and `courseTitle` (e.g., `"Introduction to C++ Programming"`). Member function `displayMessage` can still issue a single call to member function `getCourseName` to obtain the full course name to display as part of the welcome message. In this case, `getCourseName` would need to build and return a `string` containing the `courseNumber` followed by the `courseTitle`. Member function `displayMessage` could continue to display the complete course title "CS101 Introduction to C++ Programming." The benefits of calling a *set* function from another member function of the same class will become clear when we discuss validation in Section 16.8.

Good Programming Practice 16.1
Always try to localize the effects of changes to a class's data members by accessing and manipulating the data members through their get and set functions.

Software Engineering Observation 16.2
Write programs that are clear and easy to maintain. Change is the rule rather than the exception. You should anticipate that your code will be modified.

GradeBook's UML Class Diagram with a Data Member and set and get Functions
Figure 16.6 contains an updated UML class diagram for the version of class GradeBook in
Fig. 16.5. This diagram models GradeBook's data member courseName as an attribute in
the middle compartment. The UML represents data members as attributes by listing the
attribute name, followed by a colon and the attribute type. The UML type of attribute
courseName is String, which corresponds to string in C++. Data member courseName is
private in C++, so the class diagram lists a minus sign (–) in front of the corresponding
attribute's name. The minus sign in the UML is equivalent to the private access specifier
in C++. Class GradeBook contains three public member functions, so the class diagram
lists three operations in the third compartment. Operation setCourseName has a String
parameter called name. The UML indicates the return type of an operation by placing a
colon and the return type after the parentheses following the operation name. Member
function getCourseName of class GradeBook has a string return type in C++, so the class
diagram shows a String return type in the UML. Operations setCourseName and displayMessage do not return values (i.e., they return void in C++), so the UML class diagram does not specify a return type after the parentheses of these operations.

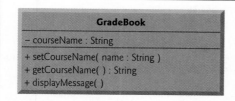

Fig. 16.6 | UML class diagram for class GradeBook with a private courseName attribute and
public operations setCourseName, getCourseName and displayMessage.

16.5 Initializing Objects with Constructors

As mentioned in Section 16.4, when an object of class GradeBook (Fig. 16.5) is created, its
data member courseName is initialized to the empty string by default. What if you want
to provide a course name when you *create* a GradeBook object? Each class you declare can
provide a **constructor** that can be used to initialize an object of the class when the object
is created. A constructor is a special member function that must be defined with the same
name as the class, so that the compiler can distinguish it from the class's other member
functions. An important difference between constructors and other functions is that *constructors cannot return values*, so they *cannot* specify a return type (not even void). Normally, constructors are declared public.

C++ requires a constructor call for each object that's created, which helps ensure that
each object is initialized properly before it's used in a program. The constructor call occurs
implicitly when the object is created. If a class does not *explicitly* include a constructor, the
compiler provides a **default constructor**—that is, a constructor with *no* parameters. For
example, when line 41 of Fig. 16.5 creates a GradeBook object, the default constructor is
called. The default constructor provided by the compiler creates a GradeBook object
without giving any initial values to the object's fundamental type data members. [*Note:*
For data members that are objects of other classes, the default constructor implicitly calls
each data member's default constructor to ensure that the data member is initialized prop-

erly. This is why the `string` data member `courseName` (in Fig. 16.5) was initialized to the empty string—the default constructor for class `string` sets the `string`'s value to the empty string. You'll learn more about initializing data members that are objects of other classes in Section 18.3.]

In the example of Fig. 16.7, we specify a course name for a `GradeBook` object when the object is created (e.g., line 46). In this case, the argument `"CS101 Introduction to C++ Programming"` is passed to the `GradeBook` object's constructor (lines 14–17) and used to initialize the `courseName`. Figure 16.7 defines a modified `GradeBook` class containing a constructor with a `string` parameter that receives the initial course name.

```cpp
1   // Fig. 16.7: fig16_07.cpp
2   // Instantiating multiple objects of the GradeBook class and using
3   // the GradeBook constructor to specify the course name
4   // when each GradeBook object is created.
5   #include <iostream>
6   #include <string> // program uses C++ standard string class
7   using namespace std;
8
9   // GradeBook class definition
10  class GradeBook
11  {
12  public:
13     // constructor initializes courseName with string supplied as argument
14     GradeBook( string name )
15     {
16        setCourseName( name ); // call set function to initialize courseName
17     } // end GradeBook constructor
18
19     // function to set the course name
20     void setCourseName( string name )
21     {
22        courseName = name; // store the course name in the object
23     } // end function setCourseName
24
25     // function to get the course name
26     string getCourseName()
27     {
28        return courseName; // return object's courseName
29     } // end function getCourseName
30
31     // display a welcome message to the GradeBook user
32     void displayMessage()
33     {
34        // call getCourseName to get the courseName
35        cout << "Welcome to the grade book for\n" << getCourseName()
36           << "!" << endl;
37     } // end function displayMessage
38  private:
39     string courseName; // course name for this GradeBook
40  }; // end class GradeBook
```

Fig. 16.7 | Instantiating multiple objects of the `GradeBook` class and using the `GradeBook` constructor to specify the course name when each `GradeBook` object is created. (Part 1 of 2.)

```
41
42   // function main begins program execution
43   int main()
44   {
45      // create two GradeBook objects
46      GradeBook gradeBook1( "CS101 Introduction to C++ Programming" );
47      GradeBook gradeBook2( "CS102 Data Structures in C++" );
48
49      // display initial value of courseName for each GradeBook
50      cout << "gradeBook1 created for course: " << gradeBook1.getCourseName()
51         << "\ngradeBook2 created for course: " << gradeBook2.getCourseName()
52         << endl;
53   } // end main
```

```
gradeBook1 created for course: CS101 Introduction to C++ Programming
gradeBook2 created for course: CS102 Data Structures in C++
```

Fig. 16.7 | Instantiating multiple objects of the GradeBook class and using the GradeBook constructor to specify the course name when each GradeBook object is created. (Part 2 of 2.)

Defining a Constructor

Lines 14–17 of Fig. 16.7 define a constructor for class GradeBook. Notice that the constructor has the *same* name as its class, GradeBook. A constructor specifies in its parameter list the data it requires to perform its task. When you create a new object, you place this data in the parentheses that follow the object name (as we did in lines 46–47). Line 14 indicates that class GradeBook's constructor has a string parameter called name. Line 14 does not specify a return type, because constructors *cannot* return values (or even void).

Line 16 in the constructor's body passes the constructor's parameter name to member function setCourseName (lines 20–23), which simply assigns the value of its parameter to data member courseName. You might be wondering why we make the call to setCourseName in line 16—the constructor certainly could perform the assignment courseName = name. In Section 16.8, we modify setCourseName to perform validation (ensuring that, in this case, the courseName is 25 or fewer characters in length). At that point the benefits of calling setCourseName from the constructor will become clear. Both the constructor (line 14) and the setCourseName function (line 20) use a parameter called name. You can use the same parameter names in different functions because the parameters are *local* to each function; they do not interfere with one another.

Testing Class *GradeBook*

Lines 43–53 of Fig. 16.7 define the main function that tests class GradeBook and demonstrates initializing GradeBook objects using a constructor. Line 46 creates and initializes GradeBook object gradeBook1. When this line executes, the GradeBook constructor (lines 14–17) is called (implicitly by C++) with the argument "CS101 Introduction to C++ Programming" to initialize gradeBook1's course name. Line 47 repeats this process for GradeBook object gradeBook2, this time passing the argument "CS102 Data Structures in C++" to initialize gradeBook2's course name. Lines 50–51 use each object's getCourseName member function to obtain the course names and show that they were indeed initialized when the objects were created. The output confirms that each GradeBook object maintains its *own* copy of data member courseName.

Two Ways to Provide a Default Constructor for a Class

Any constructor that takes no arguments is called a default constructor. A class can get a default constructor in one of two ways:

1. The compiler implicitly creates a default constructor in a class that does not define a constructor. Such a constructor does *not* initialize the class's data members, but *does* call the default constructor for each data member that's an object of another class. An uninitialized variable typically contains a "garbage" value.

2. You explicitly define a constructor that takes no arguments. Such a default constructor will call the default constructor for each data member that's an object of another class and will perform additional initialization specified by you.

If you define a constructor with arguments, C++ will not implicitly create a default constructor for that class. For each version of class GradeBook in Fig. 16.1, Fig. 16.3 and Fig. 16.5 the compiler *implicitly* defined a default constructor.

Error-Prevention Tip 16.2

Unless no initialization of your class's data members is necessary (almost never), provide a constructor to ensure that your class's data members are initialized with meaningful values when each new object of your class is created.

Software Engineering Observation 16.3

Data members can be initialized in a constructor, or their values may be set *later after the object is created. However, it's a good software engineering practice to ensure that an object is fully initialized before the client code invokes the object's member functions. You should not rely on the client code to ensure that an object gets initialized properly.*

*Adding the Constructor to Class **GradeBook**'s UML Class Diagram*

The UML class diagram of Fig. 16.8 models the GradeBook class of Fig. 16.7, which has a constructor with a name parameter of type string (represented by type String in the UML). Like operations, the UML models constructors in the third compartment of a class in a class diagram. To distinguish a constructor from a class's operations, the UML places the word "constructor" between guillemets (« and ») before the constructor's name. By convention, you list the class's constructor before other operations in the third compartment.

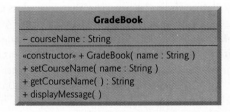

Fig. 16.8 | UML class diagram indicating that class GradeBook has a constructor with a name parameter of UML type String.

16.6 Placing a Class in a Separate File for Reusability

One of the benefits of creating class definitions is that, when packaged properly, your classes can be *reused* by other programmers. For example, you can reuse C++ Standard Library type string in any C++ program by including the header <string> (and, as you'll see, by being able to link to the library's object code).

Programmers who wish to use our GradeBook class cannot simply include the file from Fig. 16.7 in another program. As you know, function main begins the execution of every program, and every program must have *exactly one* main function. If other programmers include the code from Fig. 16.7, they get extra "baggage"—our main function—and their programs will then have two main functions. Attempting to compile a program with two main functions produces an error when the compiler tries to compile the second main function it encounters. So, placing main in the same file with a class definition *prevents that class from being reused* by other programs. In this section, we demonstrate how to make class GradeBook reusable by *separating it into another file* from the main function.

Headers

Each of the previous examples in the chapter consists of a single .cpp file, also known as a source-code file, that contains a GradeBook class definition and a main function. When building an object-oriented C++ program, it's customary to define *reusable* source code (such as a class) in a file that by convention has a .h filename extension—known as a header. Programs use #include preprocessor directives to include headers and take advantage of reusable software components, such as type string provided in the C++ Standard Library and user-defined types like class GradeBook.

Our next example separates the code from Fig. 16.7 into two files—GradeBook.h (Fig. 16.9) and fig16_10.cpp (Fig. 16.10). As you look at the header in Fig. 16.9, notice that it contains only the GradeBook class definition (lines 8–38), the appropriate headers and a using directive. The main function that *uses* class GradeBook is defined in the source-code file fig16_10.cpp (Fig. 16.10) in lines 8–18. To help you prepare for the larger programs you'll encounter later in this book and in industry, we often use a separate source-code file containing function main to test our classes (this is called a **driver program**). You'll soon learn how a source-code file with main can use the class definition found in a header to create objects of a class.

```
1   // Fig. 16.9: GradeBook.h
2   // GradeBook class definition in a separate file from main.
3   #include <iostream>
4   #include <string> // class GradeBook uses C++ standard string class
5   using namespace std;
6
7   // GradeBook class definition
8   class GradeBook
9   {
10  public:
11     // constructor initializes courseName with string supplied as argument
12     GradeBook( string name )
13     {
```

Fig. 16.9 | GradeBook class definition in a separate file from main. (Part 1 of 2.)

```
14          setCourseName( name ); // call set function to initialize courseName
15       } // end GradeBook constructor
16
17       // function to set the course name
18       void setCourseName( string name )
19       {
20          courseName = name; // store the course name in the object
21       } // end function setCourseName
22
23       // function to get the course name
24       string getCourseName()
25       {
26          return courseName; // return object's courseName
27       } // end function getCourseName
28
29       // display a welcome message to the GradeBook user
30       void displayMessage()
31       {
32          // call getCourseName to get the courseName
33          cout << "Welcome to the grade book for\n" << getCourseName()
34             << "!" << endl;
35       } // end function displayMessage
36    private:
37       string courseName; // course name for this GradeBook
38    }; // end class GradeBook
```

Fig. 16.9 | GradeBook class definition in a separate file from main. (Part 2 of 2.)

```
1    // Fig. 16.10: fig16_10.cpp
2    // Including class GradeBook from file GradeBook.h for use in main.
3    #include <iostream>
4    #include "GradeBook.h" // include definition of class GradeBook
5    using namespace std;
6
7    // function main begins program execution
8    int main()
9    {
10      // create two GradeBook objects
11      GradeBook gradeBook1( "CS101 Introduction to C++ Programming" );
12      GradeBook gradeBook2( "CS102 Data Structures in C++" );
13
14      // display initial value of courseName for each GradeBook
15      cout << "gradeBook1 created for course: " << gradeBook1.getCourseName()
16         << "\ngradeBook2 created for course: " << gradeBook2.getCourseName()
17         << endl;
18    } // end main
```

```
gradeBook1 created for course: CS101 Introduction to C++ Programming
gradeBook2 created for course: CS102 Data Structures in C++
```

Fig. 16.10 | Including class GradeBook from file GradeBook.h for use in main.

Including a Header That Contains a User-Defined Class

A header such as GradeBook.h (Fig. 16.9) cannot be used as a complete program, because it does not contain a main function. If you try to compile and link GradeBook.h by itself to create an executable application, Microsoft Visual C++ 2010 produces the linker error message:

```
error LNK2001: unresolved external symbol _mainCRTStartup
```

To compile and link with GNU C++ on Linux, you must first include the header in a .cpp source-code file, then GNU C++ produces a linker error message containing:

```
undefined reference to 'main'
```

This error indicates that the linker could not locate the program's main function. To test class GradeBook (defined in Fig. 16.9), you must write a separate source-code file containing a main function (such as Fig. 16.10) that instantiates and uses objects of the class.

The compiler doesn't know what a GradeBook is because it's a user-defined type. In fact, the compiler doesn't even know the classes in the C++ Standard Library. To help it understand how to use a class, we must explicitly provide the compiler with the class's definition—that's why, for example, to use type string, a program must include the <string> header. This enables the compiler to determine the amount of memory that it must reserve for each string object and ensure that a program calls a string's member functions correctly.

To create GradeBook objects gradeBook1 and gradeBook2 in lines 11–12 of Fig. 16.10, the compiler must know the *size* of a GradeBook object. While objects conceptually contain data members and member functions, C++ objects actually contain *only* data. The compiler creates only *one* copy of the class's member functions and *shares* that copy among all the class's objects. Each object, of course, needs its own copy of the class's data members, because their contents can vary among objects (such as two different BankAccount objects having two different balances). The member-function code, however, is *not modifiable*, so it can be shared among all objects of the class. Therefore, the size of an object depends on the amount of memory required to store the class's data members. By including GradeBook.h in line 4, we give the compiler access to the information it needs (Fig. 16.9, line 37) to determine the size of a GradeBook object and to determine whether objects of the class are used correctly (in lines 11–12 and 15–16 of Fig. 16.10).

Line 4 instructs the C++ preprocessor to replace the directive with a copy of the contents of GradeBook.h (i.e., the GradeBook class definition) *before* the program is compiled. When the source-code file fig16_10.cpp is compiled, it now contains the GradeBook class definition (because of the #include), and the compiler is able to determine how to create GradeBook objects and see that their member functions are called correctly. Now that the class definition is in a header (without a main function), we can include that header in *any* program that needs to reuse our GradeBook class.

How Headers Are Located

Notice that the name of the GradeBook.h header in line 4 of Fig. 16.10 is enclosed in quotes (" ") rather than angle brackets (< >). Normally, a program's source-code files and user-defined headers are placed in the *same* directory. When the preprocessor encounters a header name in quotes, it attempts to locate the header in the same directory as the file in which the #include directive appears. If the preprocessor cannot find the header in that directory, it searches for it in the same location(s) as the C++ Standard Library headers. When the preprocessor encounters a header name in angle brackets (e.g., <iostream>), it assumes that the header is part of the C++ Standard Library and does *not* look in the directory of the program that's being preprocessed.

Error-Prevention Tip 16.3

To ensure that the preprocessor can locate headers correctly, #include preprocessor directives should place user-defined headers names in quotes (e.g., "GradeBook.h") and place C++ Standard Library headers names in angle brackets (e.g., <iostream>).

Additional Software Engineering Issues

Now that class GradeBook is defined in a header, the class is *reusable*. Unfortunately, placing a class definition in a header as in Fig. 16.9 still *reveals the entire implementation of the class to the class's clients*—GradeBook.h is simply a text file that anyone can open and read. Conventional software engineering wisdom says that to use an object of a class, the client code needs to know only what member functions to call, what arguments to provide to each member function and what return type to expect from each member function. *The client code does not need to know how those functions are implemented.*

If client code *does* know how a class is implemented, the programmer might write client code based on the class's implementation details. Ideally, if that implementation changes, the class's clients should not have to change. *Hiding the class's implementation details makes it easier to change the class's implementation while minimizing, and hopefully eliminating, changes to client code.*

In Section 16.7, we show how to break up the GradeBook class into two files so that

1. the class is *reusable*,

2. the clients of the class know what member functions the class provides, how to call them and what return types to expect, and

3. the clients do *not* know how the class's member functions are implemented.

16.7 Separating Interface from Implementation

In the preceding section, we showed how to promote software reusability by separating a class definition from the client code (e.g., function main) that uses the class. We now introduce another fundamental principle of good software engineering—separating interface from implementation.

Interface of a Class

Interfaces define and standardize the ways in which things such as people and systems interact with one another. For example, a radio's controls serve as an interface between the radio's users and its internal components. The controls allow users to perform a limited set of operations (such as changing the station, adjusting the volume, and choosing between AM and FM stations). Various radios may implement these operations differently—some provide push buttons, some provide dials and some support voice commands. The interface specifies *what* operations a radio permits users to perform but does not specify *how* the operations are implemented inside the radio.

Similarly, the interface of a class describes *what* services a class's clients can use and how to *request* those services, but not *how* the class carries out the services. A class's public interface consists of the class's public member functions (also known as the class's **public** services). For example, class GradeBook's interface (Fig. 16.9) contains a constructor and member functions setCourseName, getCourseName and displayMessage. GradeBook's clients (e.g., main in Fig. 16.10) *use* these functions to request the class's services. As you'll soon see, you can specify a class's interface by writing a class definition that lists *only* the member-function names, return types and parameter types.

Separating the Interface from the Implementation

In our prior examples, each class definition contained the complete definitions of the class's public member functions and the declarations of its private data members. However, it's better software engineering to define member functions *outside* the class definition, so that their implementation details can be *hidden* from the client code. This practice *ensures* that you do not write client code that depends on the class's implementation details. If you were to do so, the client code would be more likely to "break" if the class's implementation changed. Given that one class could have many clients, such a change could cause wide-ranging problems in a software system.

The program of Figs. 16.11–16.13 separates class GradeBook's interface from its implementation by splitting the class definition of Fig. 16.9 into two files—the header GradeBook.h (Fig. 16.11) in which class GradeBook is defined, and the source-code file GradeBook.cpp (Fig. 16.12) in which GradeBook's member functions are defined. By convention, member-function definitions are placed in a source-code file of the same base name (e.g., GradeBook) as the class's header but with a .cpp filename extension. The source-code file fig16_13.cpp (Fig. 16.13) defines function main (the client code). The code and output of Fig. 16.13 are identical to that of Fig. 16.10. Figure 16.14 shows how this three-file program is compiled from the perspectives of the GradeBook class programmer and the client-code programmer—we'll explain this figure in detail.

GradeBook.h: Defining a Class's Interface with Function Prototypes

Header GradeBook.h (Fig. 16.11) contains another version of GradeBook's class definition (lines 9–18). This version is similar to the one in Fig. 16.9, but the function definitions in Fig. 16.9 are replaced here with **function prototypes** (lines 12–15) that *describe the class's public interface without revealing the class's member-function implementations*. A function prototype is a *declaration* of a function that tells the compiler the function's name, its return type and the types of its parameters. Also, the header still specifies the class's private data member (line 17) as well. Again, the compiler must know the data members of the class to determine how much memory to reserve for each object of the class. Including the header GradeBook.h in the client code (line 5 of Fig. 16.13) provides the compiler with the information it needs to ensure that the client code calls the member functions of class GradeBook correctly.

The function prototype in line 12 (Fig. 16.11) indicates that the constructor requires one string parameter. Recall that constructors don't have return types, so no return type appears in the function prototype. Member function setCourseName's function prototype indicates that setCourseName requires a string parameter and does not return a value (i.e., its return type is void). Member function getCourseName's function prototype indicates that the function does not require parameters and returns a string. Finally, member

```
 1   // Fig. 16.11: GradeBook.h
 2   // GradeBook class definition. This file presents GradeBook's public
 3   // interface without revealing the implementations of GradeBook's member
 4   // functions, which are defined in GradeBook.cpp.
 5   #include <string> // class GradeBook uses C++ standard string class
 6   using namespace std;
 7
 8   // GradeBook class definition
 9   class GradeBook
10   {
11   public:
12      GradeBook( string ); // constructor that initializes courseName
13      void setCourseName( string ); // function that sets the course name
14      string getCourseName(); // function that gets the course name
15      void displayMessage(); // function that displays a welcome message
16   private:
17      string courseName; // course name for this GradeBook
18   }; // end class GradeBook
```

Fig. 16.11 | GradeBook class definition containing function prototypes that specify the interface of the class.

function displayMessage's function prototype (line 15) specifies that displayMessage does not require parameters and does not return a value. These function prototypes are the same as the corresponding function headers in Fig. 16.9, except that the parameter names (which are *optional* in prototypes) are not included and each function prototype *must* end with a semicolon.

Good Programming Practice 16.2

Although parameter names in function prototypes are optional (they're ignored by the compiler), many programmers use these names for documentation purposes.

Error-Prevention Tip 16.4

Parameter names in a function prototype (which, again, are ignored by the compiler) can be misleading if the names used do not match those used in the function definition. For this reason, many programmers create function prototypes by copying the first line of the corresponding function definitions (when the source code for the functions is available), then appending a semicolon to the end of each prototype.

GradeBook.cpp: *Defining Member Functions in a Separate Source-Code File*
Source-code file GradeBook.cpp (Fig. 16.12) *defines* class GradeBook's member functions, which were *declared* in lines 12–15 of Fig. 16.11. The definitions appear in lines 9–32 and are nearly identical to the member-function definitions in lines 12–35 of Fig. 16.9.

Each member-function name in the function headers (lines 9, 15, 21 and 27) is preceded by the class name and ::, which is known as the **binary scope resolution operator**. This "ties" each member function to the (now separate) GradeBook class definition (Fig. 16.11), which declares the class's member functions and data members. Without "GradeBook::" preceding each function name, these functions would *not* be recognized by the compiler as member functions of class GradeBook—the compiler would consider them

```
1    // Fig. 16.12: GradeBook.cpp
2    // GradeBook member-function definitions. This file contains
3    // implementations of the member functions prototyped in GradeBook.h.
4    #include <iostream>
5    #include "GradeBook.h" // include definition of class GradeBook
6    using namespace std;
7
8    // constructor initializes courseName with string supplied as argument
9    GradeBook::GradeBook( string name )
10   {
11      setCourseName( name ); // call set function to initialize courseName
12   } // end GradeBook constructor
13
14   // function to set the course name
15   void GradeBook::setCourseName( string name )
16   {
17      courseName = name; // store the course name in the object
18   } // end function setCourseName
19
20   // function to get the course name
21   string GradeBook::getCourseName()
22   {
23      return courseName; // return object's courseName
24   } // end function getCourseName
25
26   // display a welcome message to the GradeBook user
27   void GradeBook::displayMessage()
28   {
29      // call getCourseName to get the courseName
30      cout << "Welcome to the grade book for\n" << getCourseName()
31         << "!" << endl;
32   } // end function displayMessage
```

Fig. 16.12 | GradeBook member-function definitions represent the implementation of class GradeBook.

"free" or "loose" functions, like main. These are also called *global functions*. Such functions cannot access GradeBook's private data or call the class's member functions, without specifying an object. So, the compiler would *not* be able to compile these functions. For example, lines 17 and 23 that access variable courseName would cause compilation errors because courseName is not declared as a local variable in each function—the compiler would not know that courseName is already declared as a data member of class GradeBook.

 Common Programming Error 16.3
When defining a class's member functions outside that class, omitting the class name and binary scope resolution operator (::) preceding the function names causes errors.

To indicate that the member functions in GradeBook.cpp are part of class GradeBook, we must first include the GradeBook.h header (line 5 of Fig. 16.12). This allows us to access the class name GradeBook in the GradeBook.cpp file. When compiling Grade-Book.cpp, the compiler uses the information in GradeBook.h to ensure that

1. the first line of each member function (lines 9, 15, 21 and 27) matches its prototype in the GradeBook.h file—for example, the compiler ensures that getCourseName accepts no parameters and returns a string, and that

2. each member function knows about the class's data members and other member functions—for example, lines 17 and 23 can access variable courseName because it's declared in GradeBook.h as a data member of class GradeBook, and lines 11 and 30 can call functions setCourseName and getCourseName, respectively, because each is declared as a member function of the class in GradeBook.h (and because these calls conform with the corresponding prototypes).

*Testing Class **GradeBook***

Figure 16.13 performs the same GradeBook object manipulations as Fig. 16.10. Separating GradeBook's interface from the implementation of its member functions does *not* affect the way that this client code uses the class. It affects only how the program is compiled and linked, which we discuss in detail shortly.

```cpp
1   // Fig. 16.13: fig16_13.cpp
2   // GradeBook class demonstration after separating
3   // its interface from its implementation.
4   #include <iostream>
5   #include "GradeBook.h" // include definition of class GradeBook
6   using namespace std;
7
8   // function main begins program execution
9   int main()
10  {
11     // create two GradeBook objects
12     GradeBook gradeBook1( "CS101 Introduction to C++ Programming" );
13     GradeBook gradeBook2( "CS102 Data Structures in C++" );
14
15     // display initial value of courseName for each GradeBook
16     cout << "gradeBook1 created for course: " << gradeBook1.getCourseName()
17        << "\ngradeBook2 created for course: " << gradeBook2.getCourseName()
18        << endl;
19  } // end main
```

```
gradeBook1 created for course: CS101 Introduction to C++ Programming
gradeBook2 created for course: CS102 Data Structures in C++
```

Fig. 16.13 | GradeBook class demonstration after separating its interface from its implementation.

As in Fig. 16.10, line 5 of Fig. 16.13 includes the GradeBook.h header so that the compiler can ensure that GradeBook objects are created and manipulated correctly in the client code. Before executing this program, the source-code files in Fig. 16.12 and Fig. 16.13 must both be compiled, then linked together—that is, the member-function calls in the client code need to be tied to the implementations of the class's member functions—a job performed by the linker.

The Compilation and Linking Process

The diagram in Fig. 16.14 shows the compilation and linking process that results in an executable GradeBook application that can be used by instructors. Often a class's interface and implementation will be created and compiled by one programmer and used by a separate programmer who implements the client code that uses the class. So, the diagram shows what's required by both the class-implementation programmer and the client-code programmer. The dashed lines in the diagram show the pieces required by the class-implementation programmer, the client-code programmer and the GradeBook application user, respectively. [*Note:* Figure 16.14 is *not* a UML diagram.]

A class-implementation programmer responsible for creating a reusable GradeBook class creates the header GradeBook.h and the source-code file GradeBook.cpp that

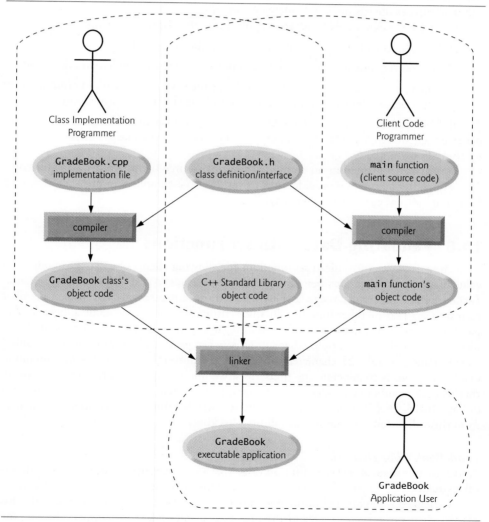

Fig. 16.14 | Compilation and linking process that produces an executable application.

`#includes` the header, then compiles the source-code file to create GradeBook's object code. To hide the class's member-function implementation details, the class-implementation programmer would provide the client-code programmer with the header Grade-Book.h (which specifies the class's interface and data members) and the GradeBook object code (i.e., the machine-language instructions that represent GradeBook's member functions). The client-code programmer is *not* given GradeBook.cpp, so the client remains unaware of how GradeBook's member functions are implemented.

The client code needs to know only GradeBook's interface to use the class and must be able to link its object code. Since the interface of the class is part of the class definition in the GradeBook.h header, the client-code programmer must have access to this file and must #include it in the client's source-code file. When the client code is compiled, the compiler uses the class definition in GradeBook.h to ensure that the main function creates and manipulates objects of class GradeBook correctly.

To create the executable GradeBook application, the last step is to link

1. the object code for the main function (i.e., the client code),

2. the object code for class GradeBook's member-function implementations and

3. the C++ Standard Library object code for the C++ classes (e.g., string) used by the class-implementation programmer and the client-code programmer.

The linker's output is the *executable* GradeBook application that instructors can use to manage their students' grades. Compilers and IDEs typically invoke the linker for you after compiling your code.

For further information on compiling multiple-source-file programs, see your compiler's documentation. We provide links to various C++ compilers in our C++ Resource Center at www.deitel.com/cplusplus/.

16.8 Validating Data with *set* Functions

In Section 16.4, we introduced *set* functions for allowing clients of a class to modify the value of a private data member. In Fig. 16.5, class GradeBook defines member function setCourseName to simply assign a value received in its parameter name to data member courseName. This member function does not ensure that the course name adheres to any particular format or follows any other rules regarding what a "valid" course name looks like. As we stated earlier, suppose that a university can print student transcripts containing course names of only 25 characters or less. If the university uses a system containing GradeBook objects to generate the transcripts, we might want class GradeBook to ensure that its data member courseName never contains more than 25 characters. The program of Figs. 16.15–16.17 enhances class GradeBook's member function setCourseName to perform this **validation** (also known as **validity checking**).

GradeBook Class Definition
Notice that GradeBook's class definition (Fig. 16.15)—and hence, its interface—is identical to that of Fig. 16.11. Since the interface remains unchanged, clients of this class need not be changed when the definition of member function setCourseName is modified. This enables clients to take advantage of the improved GradeBook class simply by linking the client code to the updated GradeBook's object code.

```
 1   // Fig. 16.15: GradeBook.h
 2   // GradeBook class definition presents the public interface of
 3   // the class. Member-function definitions appear in GradeBook.cpp.
 4   #include <string> // program uses C++ standard string class
 5   using namespace std;
 6
 7   // GradeBook class definition
 8   class GradeBook
 9   {
10   public:
11      GradeBook( string ); // constructor that initializes a GradeBook object
12      void setCourseName( string ); // function that sets the course name
13      string getCourseName(); // function that gets the course name
14      void displayMessage(); // function that displays a welcome message
15   private:
16      string courseName; // course name for this GradeBook
17   }; // end class GradeBook
```

Fig. 16.15 | GradeBook class definition.

Validating the Course Name with **GradeBook** *Member Function* ***setCourseName***

The enhancement to class GradeBook is in the definition of setCourseName (Fig. 16.16, lines 16–29). The if statement in lines 18–19 determines whether parameter name contains a valid course name (i.e., a string of 25 or fewer characters). If the course name is valid, line 19 stores it in data member courseName. Note the expression name.length() in line 18. This is a member-function call just like myGradeBook.displayMessage(). The C++ Standard Library's string class defines a member function **length** that returns the number of characters in a string object. Parameter name is a string object, so the call name.length() returns the number of characters in name. If this value is less than or equal to 25, name is valid and line 19 executes.

```
 1   // Fig. 16.16: GradeBook.cpp
 2   // Implementations of the GradeBook member-function definitions.
 3   // The setCourseName function performs validation.
 4   #include <iostream>
 5   #include "GradeBook.h" // include definition of class GradeBook
 6   using namespace std;
 7
 8   // constructor initializes courseName with string supplied as argument
 9   GradeBook::GradeBook( string name )
10   {
11      setCourseName( name ); // validate and store courseName
12   } // end GradeBook constructor
13
14   // function that sets the course name;
15   // ensures that the course name has at most 25 characters
16   void GradeBook::setCourseName( string name )
17   {
```

Fig. 16.16 | Member-function definitions for class GradeBook with a *set* function that validates the length of data member courseName. (Part 1 of 2.)

```
18    if ( name.length() <= 25 ) // if name has 25 or fewer characters
19        courseName = name; // store the course name in the object
20
21    if ( name.length() > 25 ) // if name has more than 25 characters
22    {
23        // set courseName to first 25 characters of parameter name
24        courseName = name.substr( 0, 25 ); // start at 0, length of 25
25
26        cout << "Name \"" << name << "\" exceeds maximum length (25).\n"
27            << "Limiting courseName to first 25 characters.\n" << endl;
28    } // end if
29 } // end function setCourseName
30
31 // function to get the course name
32 string GradeBook::getCourseName()
33 {
34    return courseName; // return object's courseName
35 } // end function getCourseName
36
37 // display a welcome message to the GradeBook user
38 void GradeBook::displayMessage()
39 {
40    // call getCourseName to get the courseName
41    cout << "Welcome to the grade book for\n" << getCourseName()
42        << "!" << endl;
43 } // end function displayMessage
```

Fig. 16.16 | Member-function definitions for class GradeBook with a *set* function that validates the length of data member courseName. (Part 2 of 2.)

The if statement in lines 21–28 handles the case in which setCourseName receives an invalid course name (i.e., a name that is more than 25 characters long). Even if parameter name is too long, we still want to leave the GradeBook object in a **consistent state**—that is, a state in which the object's data member courseName contains a valid value (i.e., a string of 25 characters or less). Thus, we truncate the specified course name and assign the first 25 characters of name to the courseName data member (unfortunately, this could truncate the course name awkwardly). Standard class string provides member function **substr** (short for "substring") that returns a new string object created by copying part of an existing string object. The call in line 24 (i.e., name.substr(0, 25)) passes two integers (0 and 25) to name's member function substr. These arguments indicate the portion of the string name that substr should return. The first argument specifies the starting position in the original string from which characters are copied—the first character in every string is considered to be at position 0. The second argument specifies the number of characters to copy. Therefore, the call in line 24 returns a 25-character substring of name starting at position 0 (i.e., the first 25 characters in name). For example, if name holds the value "CS101 Introduction to Programming in C++", substr returns "CS101 Introduction to Pro". After the call to substr, line 24 assigns the substring returned by substr to data member courseName. In this way, setCourseName ensures that courseName is always assigned a string containing 25 or fewer characters. If the member function has to truncate the course name to make it valid, lines 26–27 display a warning message.

The `if` statement in lines 21–28 contains two body statements—one to set the courseName to the first 25 characters of parameter name and one to print an accompanying message to the user. Both statements should execute when name is too long, so we place them in a pair of braces, { }.

The statement in lines 26–27 could also appear without a stream insertion operator at the start of the second line of the statement, as in:

```
cout << "Name \"" << name << "\" exceeds maximum length (25).\n"
     "Limiting courseName to first 25 characters.\n" << endl;
```

The C++ compiler combines adjacent string literals, even if they appear on separate lines of a program. Thus, in the statement above, the C++ compiler would combine the string literals "\" exceeds maximum length (25).\n" and "Limiting courseName to first 25 characters.\n" into a single string literal that produces output identical to that of lines 26–27 in Fig. 16.16. This behavior allows you to print lengthy strings by breaking them across lines in your program without including additional stream insertion operations.

Testing Class *GradeBook*

Figure 16.17 demonstrates the modified version of class GradeBook (Figs. 16.15–16.16) featuring validation. Line 12 creates a GradeBook object named gradeBook1. Recall that the GradeBook constructor calls setCourseName to initialize data member courseName. In previous versions of the class, the benefit of calling setCourseName in the constructor was not evident. Now, however, *the constructor takes advantage of the validation* provided by setCourseName. The constructor simply calls setCourseName, *rather than duplicating* its validation code. When line 12 of Fig. 16.17 passes an initial course name of "CS101 Introduction to Programming in C++" to the GradeBook constructor, the constructor passes this value to setCourseName, where the actual initialization occurs. Because this course name contains more than 25 characters, the body of the second `if` statement executes, causing courseName to be initialized to the truncated 25-character course name "CS101 Introduction to Pro". The output in Fig. 16.17 contains the warning message output by lines 26–27 of Fig. 16.16 in member function setCourseName. Line 13 creates another GradeBook object called gradeBook2—the valid course name passed to the constructor is exactly 25 characters.

Lines 16–19 of Fig. 16.17 display the truncated course name for gradeBook1 (we highlight this in blue in the program output) and the course name for gradeBook2. Line 22 calls gradeBook1's setCourseName member function directly, to change the course name in the GradeBook object to a shorter name that does not need to be truncated. Then, lines 25–28 output the course names for the GradeBook objects again.

```
1   // Fig. 16.17: fig16_17.cpp
2   // Create and manipulate a GradeBook object; illustrate validation.
3   #include <iostream>
4   #include "GradeBook.h" // include definition of class GradeBook
5   using namespace std;
```

Fig. 16.17 | Create and manipulate a GradeBook object; illustrate validation. (Part 1 of 2.)

```
 6
 7   // function main begins program execution
 8   int main()
 9   {
10      // create two GradeBook objects;
11      // initial course name of gradeBook1 is too long
12      GradeBook gradeBook1( "CS101 Introduction to Programming in C++" );
13      GradeBook gradeBook2( "CS102 C++ Data Structures" );
14
15      // display each GradeBook's courseName
16      cout << "gradeBook1's initial course name is: "
17         << gradeBook1.getCourseName()
18         << "\ngradeBook2's initial course name is: "
19         << gradeBook2.getCourseName() << endl;
20
21      // modify myGradeBook's courseName (with a valid-length string)
22      gradeBook1.setCourseName( "CS101 C++ Programming" );
23
24      // display each GradeBook's courseName
25      cout << "\ngradeBook1's course name is: "
26         << gradeBook1.getCourseName()
27         << "\ngradeBook2's course name is: "
28         << gradeBook2.getCourseName() << endl;
29   } // end main
```

```
Name "CS101 Introduction to Programming in C++" exceeds maximum length (25).
Limiting courseName to first 25 characters.

gradeBook1's initial course name is: CS101 Introduction to Pro
gradeBook2's initial course name is: CS102 C++ Data Structures

gradeBook1's course name is: CS101 C++ Programming
gradeBook2's course name is: CS102 C++ Data Structures
```

Fig. 16.17 | Create and manipulate a GradeBook object; illustrate validation. (Part 2 of 2.)

Additional Notes on Set Functions

A public *set* function such as setCourseName should carefully scrutinize any attempt to modify the value of a data member (e.g., courseName) to ensure that the new value is appropriate for that data item. For example, an attempt to *set* the day of the month to 37 should be rejected, an attempt to *set* a person's weight to zero or a negative value should be rejected, an attempt to *set* a grade on an exam to 185 (when the proper range is zero to 100) should be rejected, and so on

Software Engineering Observation 16.4

Making data members private and controlling access, especially write access, to those data members through public member functions helps ensure data integrity.

Error-Prevention Tip 16.5

The benefits of data integrity are not automatic simply because data members are made private—you must provide appropriate validity checking and report the errors.

A class's *set* functions can return values to the class's clients indicating that attempts were made to assign invalid data to objects of the class. A client can test the return value of a *set* function to determine whether the attempt to modify the object was successful and to take appropriate action. In C++, clients of objects can be notified of invalid values via the *exception-handling mechanism*, which we discuss in Chapter 24. To keep the program of Figs. 16.15–16.17 simple at this point, `setCourseName` in Fig. 16.16 just prints an appropriate message.

16.9 Wrap-Up

In this chapter, you created user-defined classes, and created and used objects of those classes. We declared data members of a class to maintain data for each object of the class. We also defined member functions that operate on that data. You learned how to call an object's member functions to request the services the object provides and how to pass data to those member functions as arguments. We discussed the difference between a local variable of a member function and a data member of a class. We also showed how to use a constructor to specify initial values for an object's data members. You learned how to separate the interface of a class from its implementation to promote good software engineering. We presented a diagram that shows the files that class-implementation programmers and client-code programmers need to compile the code they write. We demonstrated how *set* functions can be used to validate an object's data and ensure that objects are maintained in a consistent state. UML class diagrams were used to model classes and their constructors, member functions and data members. In the next chapter, we take a deeper look at classes.

Summary

Section 16.2 Defining a Class with a Member Function

- A class definition (p. 616) contains the data members and member functions that define the class's attributes and behaviors, respectively.
- A class definition begins with the keyword `class` followed immediately by the class name.
- By convention, the name of a user-defined class (p. 617) begins with a capital letter and, for readability, each subsequent word in the class name begins with a capital letter.
- Every class's body (p. 616) is enclosed in a pair of braces ({ and }) and ends with a semicolon.
- Member functions that appear after access specifier `public` (p. 616) can be called by other functions in a program and by member functions of other classes.
- Access specifiers are always followed by a colon (:).
- Keyword `void` (p. 617) is a special return type which indicates that a function will perform a task but will not return any data to its calling function when it completes its task.
- By convention, function names (p. 617) begin with a lowercase first letter and all subsequent words in the name begin with a capital letter.
- An empty set of parentheses after a function name indicates that the function does not require additional data to perform its task.
- Every function's body is delimited by left and right braces ({ and }).
- Typically, you cannot call a member function until you create an object of its class.
- Each new class you create becomes a new type in C++.

- In the UML, each class is modeled in a class diagram (p. 618) as a rectangle with three compartments, which (top to bottom) contain the class's name, attributes and operations, respectively.

- The UML models operations as the operation name followed by parentheses. A plus sign (+) preceding the name indicates a `public` operation (i.e., a `public` member function in C++).

Section 16.3 Defining a Member Function with a Parameter

- A member function can require one or more parameters (p. 618) that represent additional data it needs to perform its task. A function call supplies an argument (p. 618) for each function parameter.

- A member function is called by following the object name with a dot (.) operator (p. 617), the function name and a set of parentheses containing the function's arguments.

- A variable of C++ Standard Library class `string` (p. 619) represents a string of characters. This class is defined in header `<string>`, and the name `string` belongs to namespace `std`.

- Function `getline` (from header `<string>`, p. 620) reads characters from its first argument until a newline character is encountered, then places the characters (not including the newline) in the `string` variable specified as its second argument. The newline character is discarded.

- A parameter list (p. 620) may contain any number of parameters, including none at all (represented by empty parentheses) to indicate that a function does not require any parameters.

- The number of arguments in a function call must match the number of parameters in the parameter list of the called member function's header. Also, the argument types in the function call must be consistent with the types of the corresponding parameters in the function header.

- The UML models a parameter of an operation by listing the parameter name, followed by a colon and the parameter type between the parentheses following the operation name.

- The UML has its own data types. Not all the UML data types have the same names as the corresponding C++ types. The UML type `String` corresponds to the C++ type `string`.

Section 16.4 Data Members, set Functions and get Functions

- Variables declared in a function's body are local variables (p. 621) and can be used only from the point of their declaration in the function to the immediately following closing right brace (}).

- A local variable must be declared before it can be used in a function. A local variable cannot be accessed outside the function in which it's declared.

- Data members (p. 621) normally are `private` (p. 623). Variables or functions declared `private` are accessible only to member functions of the class in which they're declared, or to friends of the class.

- When a program creates (instantiates) an object, its `private` data members are encapsulated (hidden, p. 624) in the object and can be accessed only by member functions of the object's class.

- When a function that specifies a return type other than `void` is called and completes its task, the function returns a result to its calling function.

- By default, the initial value of a `string` is the empty string (p. 625)—i.e., a string that does not contain any characters. Nothing appears on the screen when an empty string is displayed.

- A class often provides `public` member functions to allow the class's clients to *set* or *get* (p. 625) `private` data members. The names of these member functions normally begin with *set* or *get*.

- *Set* and *get* functions allow clients of a class to indirectly access the hidden data. The client does not know how the object performs these operations.

- A class's *set* and *get* functions should be used by other member functions of the class to manipulate the class's `private` data. If the class's data representation is changed, member functions that access the data only via the *set* and *get* functions will not require modification.

- A `public` *set* function should carefully scrutinize any attempt to modify the value of a data member to ensure that the new value is appropriate for that data item.

- The UML represents data members as attributes by listing the attribute name, followed by a colon and the attribute type. Private attributes are preceded by a minus sign (–) in the UML.
- The UML indicates the return type of an operation by placing a colon and the return type after the parentheses following the operation name.
- UML class diagrams do not specify return types for operations that do not return values.

Section 16.5 Initializing Objects with Constructors
- Each class should provide a constructor (p. 627) to initialize an object of the class when the object is created. A constructor must be defined with the same name as the class.
- A difference between constructors and functions is that constructors cannot return values, so they cannot specify a return type (not even void). Normally, constructors are declared public.
- C++ requires a constructor call at the time each object is created, which helps ensure that every object is initialized before it's used in a program.
- A constructor with no parameters is a default constructor (p. 627). If you do not provide a constructor, the compiler provides a default constructor. You can also define a default constructor explicitly. If you define a constructor for a class, C++ will not create a default constructor.
- The UML models constructors as operations in a class diagram's third compartment with the word "constructor" between guillemets (« and ») before the constructor's name.

Section 16.6 Placing a Class in a Separate File for Reusability
- Class definitions, when packaged properly, can be reused by programmers worldwide.
- It's customary to define a class in a header (p. 631) that has a .h filename extension.

Section 16.7 Separating Interface from Implementation
- If the class's implementation changes, the class's clients should not be required to change.
- Interfaces define and standardize the ways in which things such as people and systems interact.
- A class's public interface (p. 635) describes the public member functions that are made available to the class's clients. The interface describes *what* services (p. 635) clients can use and how to *request* those services, but does not specify *how* the class carries out the services.
- Separating interface from implementation (p. 634) makes programs easier to modify. Changes in the class's implementation do not affect the client as long as the class's interface remains unchanged.
- A function prototype (p. 635) contains a function's name, its return type and the number, types and order of the parameters the function expects to receive.
- Once a class is defined and its member functions are declared (via function prototypes), the member functions should be defined in a separate source-code file.
- For each member function defined outside of its corresponding class definition, the function name must be preceded by the class name and the binary scope resolution operator (::, p. 636).

Section 16.8 Validating Data with set Functions
- Class string's length member function (p. 641) returns the number of characters in a string.
- Class string's member function substr (p. 642) returns a new string containing a copy of part of an existing string. The first argument specifies the starting position in the original string. The second specifies the number of characters to copy.

Self-Review Exercises

16.1   Fill in the blanks in each of the following:
   a)   Every class definition contains the keyword _____ followed immediately by the class's name.
   b)   A class definition is typically stored in a file with the _____ filename extension.

c) Each parameter in a function header specifies both a(n) _____ and a(n) _____.

d) When each object of a class maintains its own copy of an attribute, the variable that represents the attribute is also known as a(n) _____.

e) Keyword `public` is a(n) _____.

f) Return type _____ indicates that a function will perform a task but will not return any information when it completes its task.

g) Function _____ from the `<string>` library reads characters until a newline character is encountered, then copies those characters into the specified `string`.

h) When a member function is defined outside the class definition, the function header must include the class name and the _____, followed by the function name to "tie" the member function to the class definition.

i) The source-code file and any other files that use a class can include the class's header via a(n) _____ preprocessor directive.

16.2 State whether each of the following is *true* or *false*. If *false*, explain why.

a) By convention, function names begin with a capital letter and all subsequent words in the name begin with a capital letter.

b) Empty parentheses following a function name in a function prototype indicate that the function does not require any parameters to perform its task.

c) Data members or member functions declared with access specifier `private` are accessible to member functions of the class in which they're declared.

d) Variables declared in the body of a particular member function are known as data members and can be used in all member functions of the class.

e) Every function's body is delimited by left and right braces ({ and }).

f) Any source-code file that contains `int main()` can be used to execute a program.

g) The types of arguments in a function call must be consistent with the types of the corresponding parameters in the function prototype's parameter list.

16.3 What is data hiding?

16.4 Explain the purpose of a function parameter. What's the difference between a parameter and an argument?

Answers to Self-Review Exercises

16.1 a) `class`. b) `.h`. c) type, name. d) data member. e) access specifier. f) `void`. g) `getline`. h) binary scope resolution operator (`::`). i) `#include`.

16.2 a) False. Function names begin with a lowercase letter and all subsequent words in the name begin with a capital letter. b) True. c) True. d) False. Such variables are local variables and can be used only in the member function in which they're declared. e) True. f) True. g) True.

16.3 Declaring data members with access specifier 'private' is known as data hiding since those data members are accessible only to the member functions of the class for which they are declared.

16.4 A parameter represents additional information that a function requires to perform its task. Each parameter required by a function is specified in the function header. An argument is the value supplied in the function call. When the function is called, the argument value is passed into the function parameter so that the function can perform its task.

Exercises

16.5 *(Function Prototypes and Definitions)* Explain the difference between a function prototype and a function definition.

16.6 *(Constructor)* How does a compiler distinguish between a constructor and other member functions of the class? Can a constructor return any value?

16.7 *(Member Functions)* Explain the purpose of member functions.

16.8 *(User-defined Header File)* What is a user-defined header file? How is it located?

16.9 *(Using a Class Without a using Directive)* Explain how a program could use class string without inserting a using directive.

16.10 *(Set and Get Functions)* Explain why a class might provide a *set* function and a *get* function for a data member.

16.11 *(Modifying Class GradeBook)* Modify class GradeBook (Figs. 16.11–16.12) as follows:
  a) Include a second string data member that represents the course instructor's name.
  b) Provide a *set* function to change the instructor's name and a *get* function to retrieve it.
  c) Modify the constructor to specify course name and instructor name parameters.
  d) Modify function displayMessage to output the welcome message and course name, then the string "This course is presented by: " followed by the instructor's name.

Use your modified class in a test program that demonstrates the class's new capabilities.

16.12 *(Account Class)* Create an Account class that a bank might use to represent customers' bank accounts. Include a data member of type int to represent the account balance. Provide a constructor that receives an initial balance and uses it to initialize the data member. The constructor should validate the initial balance to ensure that it's greater than or equal to 0. If not, set the balance to 0 and display an error message indicating that the initial balance was invalid. Provide three member functions. Member function credit should add an amount to the current balance. Member function debit should withdraw money from the Account and ensure that the debit amount does not exceed the Account's balance. If it does, the balance should be left unchanged and the function should print a message indicating "Debit amount exceeded account balance." Member function getBalance should return the current balance. Create a program that creates two Account objects and tests the member functions of class Account.

16.13 *(Invoice Class)* Create a class called Invoice that a hardware store might use to represent an invoice for an item sold at the store. An Invoice should include four data members—a part number (type string), a part description (type string), a quantity of the item being purchased (type int) and a price per item (type int). Your class should have a constructor that initializes the four data members. Provide a *set* and a *get* function for each data member. In addition, provide a member function named getInvoiceAmount that calculates the invoice amount (i.e., multiplies the quantity by the price per item), then returns the amount as an int value. If the quantity is not positive, it should be set to 0. If the price per item is not positive, it should be set to 0. Write a test program that demonstrates class Invoice's capabilities.

16.14 *(Student Class)* Create a class called Student that includes five pieces of information as data members—a first name (type string), a last name (type string) and marks in three subjects (all of type int). Your class should have a constructor that initializes the five data members. Provide a *set* and a *get* function for each data member. Write a test program that demonstrates class Student's capabilities. Create two Student objects and display each object's marks in three subjects. Then scale down the marks in every subject by 50% for each student and display each student's marks again.

16.15 *(Time Class)* Create a class called Time that includes three pieces of information as data members – an hour (type int), a minute (type int) and a second (type int). Your class should have a constructor with three parameters that uses the parameters to initialize the three data members. For the purpose of this exercise, assume that the values provided for the minute and second are correct, but ensure that the hour value is in the range 0–23; if it isn't, set the hour to 0. Provide a *set* and a *get* function for each data member. Provide a member function displayTime that displays the hour, minute and second separated by a colon (:). Write a test program that demonstrates class Time's capabilities.

Making a Difference

16.16   *(Target-Heart-Rate Calculator)* While exercising, you can use a heart-rate monitor to see that your heart rate stays within a safe range suggested by your trainers and doctors. According to the American Heart Association (AHA) (www.americanheart.org/presenter.jhtml?identifier=4736), the formula for calculating your *maximum heart rate* in beats per minute is 220 minus your age in years. Your *target heart rate* is a range that is 50–85% of your maximum heart rate. [Note: *These formulas are estimates provided by the AHA. Maximum and target heart rates may vary based on the health, fitness and gender of the individual. Always consult a physician or qualified health care professional before beginning or modifying an exercise program.*] Create a class called HeartRates. The class attributes should include the person's first name, last name and date of birth (consisting of separate attributes for the month, day and year of birth). Your class should have a constructor that receives this data as parameters. For each attribute provide *set* and *get* functions. The class also should include a function getAge that calculates and returns the person's age (in years), a function getMaxiumumHeartRate that calculates and returns the person's maximum heart rate and a function getTargetHeartRate that calculates and returns the person's target heart rate. Since you do not yet know how to obtain the current date from the computer, function getAge should prompt the user to enter the current month, day and year before calculating the person's age. Write an application that prompts for the person's information, instantiates an object of class HeartRates and prints the information from that object— including the person's first name, last name and date of birth—then calculates and prints the person's age in (years), maximum heart rate and target-heart-rate range.

16.17   *(Computerization of Health Records)* A health care issue that has been in the news lately is the computerization of health records. This possibility is being approached cautiously because of sensitive privacy and security concerns, among others. Computerizing health records could make it easier for patients to share their health profiles and histories among their various health care professionals. This could improve the quality of health care, help avoid drug conflicts and erroneous drug prescriptions, reduce costs and in emergencies, could save lives. In this exercise, you'll design a "starter" HealthProfile class for a person. The class attributes should include the person's first name, last name, gender, date of birth (consisting of separate attributes for the month, day and year of birth), height (in inches) and weight (in pounds). Your class should have a constructor that receives this data. For each attribute, provide *set* and *get* functions. The class also should include functions that calculate and return the user's age in years, maximum heart rate and target-heart-rate range (see Exercise 16.16), and body mass index (BMI; see Exercise 2.32). Write an application that prompts for the person's information, instantiates an object of class HealthProfile for that person and prints the information from that object—including the person's first name, last name, gender, date of birth, height and weight—then calculates and prints the person's age in years, BMI, maximum heart rate and target-heart-rate range. It should also display the "BMI values" chart from Exercise 2.32. Use the same technique as Exercise 16.16 to calculate the person's age.

Classes: A Deeper Look, Part 1

17

My object all sublime
I shall achieve in time.
—W. S. Gilbert

Is it a world to hide virtues in?
—William Shakespeare

Don't be "consistent," but be
simply true.
—Oliver Wendell Holmes, Jr.

Objectives

In this chapter you'll learn:

- How to use a preprocessor wrapper to prevent multiple definition errors.

- To understand class scope and accessing class members via the name of an object, a reference to an object or a pointer to an object.

- To define constructors with default arguments.

- How destructors are used to perform "termination housekeeping" on an object before it's destroyed.

- When constructors and destructors are called and the order in which they're called.

- The logic errors that may occur when a `public` member function returns a reference to `private` data.

- To assign the data members of one object to those of another object by default memberwise assignment.

Outline

17.1 Introduction

In the preceding chapters, we introduced many basic terms and concepts of C++ object-oriented programming. We also discussed our program development methodology: We selected appropriate attributes and behaviors for each class and specified the manner in which objects of our classes collaborated with objects of C++ Standard Library classes to accomplish each program's overall goals.

In this chapter, we take a deeper look at classes. We use an integrated Time class case study in both this chapter and Chapter 18, Classes: A Deeper Look, Part 2, to demonstrate several class construction capabilities. We begin with a Time class that reviews several of the features presented in the preceding chapters. The example also demonstrates an important C++ software engineering concept—using a "preprocessor wrapper" in headers to prevent the code in the header from being included into the same source code file more than once. Since a class can be defined only once, using such preprocessor directives prevents multiple definition errors.

Next, we discuss class scope and the relationships among class members. We demonstrate how client code can access a class's public members via three types of "handles"—the name of an object, a reference to an object or a pointer to an object. As you'll see, object names and references can be used with the dot (.) member selection operator to access a public member, and pointers can be used with the arrow (->) member selection operator.

We discuss access functions that can read or display data in an object. A common use of access functions is to test the truth or falsity of conditions—such functions are known as *predicate functions*. We also demonstrate the notion of a utility function (also called a *helper function*)—a private member function that supports the operation of the class's public member functions, but is not intended for use by clients of the class.

In the second Time class case study example, we demonstrate how to pass arguments to constructors and show how default arguments can be used in a constructor to enable client code to initialize objects using a variety of arguments. Next, we discuss a special member function called a *destructor* that's part of every class and is used to perform "termination housekeeping" on an object before the object is destroyed. We then demonstrate the *order* in which constructors and destructors are called, because your programs' correctness depends on using properly initialized objects that have not yet been destroyed.

Our last example of the Time class case study in this chapter shows a dangerous programming practice in which a member function returns a reference to private data. We discuss how this *breaks the encapsulation of a class* and allows client code to directly access an object's data. This last example shows that objects of the same class can be assigned to one another using default memberwise assignment, which copies the data members in the object on the right side of the assignment into the corresponding data members of the object on the left side of the assignment.

17.2 Time Class Case Study

Our first example (Figs. 17.1–17.3) creates class Time and a driver program that tests the class. We demonstrate an important C++ software engineering concept—using a "preprocessor wrapper" in headers to prevent the code in the header from being included into the same source code file more than once. Since a class can be defined only once, using such preprocessor directives prevents multiple-definition errors.

```
 1   // Fig. 17.1: Time.h
 2   // Time class definition.
 3   // Member functions are defined in Time.cpp
 4
 5   // prevent multiple inclusions of header
 6   #ifndef TIME_H
 7   #define TIME_H
 8
 9   // Time class definition
10   class Time
11   {
12   public:
13      Time(); // constructor
14      void setTime( int, int, int ); // set hour, minute and second
15      void printUniversal(); // print time in universal-time format
16      void printStandard(); // print time in standard-time format
17   private:
18      int hour; // 0 - 23 (24-hour clock format)
19      int minute; // 0 - 59
20      int second; // 0 - 59
21   }; // end class Time
22
23   #endif
```

Fig. 17.1 | Time class definition.

Time Class Definition
The class definition (Fig. 17.1) contains prototypes (lines 13–16) for member functions Time, setTime, printUniversal and printStandard, and includes private integer members hour, minute and second (lines 18–20). Class Time's private data members can be accessed *only* by its four public member functions. Chapter 20 introduces a third access specifier, protected, as we study inheritance and the part it plays in object-oriented programming.

Good Programming Practice 17.1

For clarity and readability, use each access specifier only once in a class definition. Place public *members first, where they're easy to locate.*

Software Engineering Observation 17.1

Each element of a class should have private *visibility unless it can be proven that the element needs* public *visibility. This is another example of the principle of least privilege.*

In Fig. 17.1, the class definition is enclosed in the following **preprocessor wrapper** (lines 6, 7 and 23):

```
// prevent multiple inclusions of header
#ifndef TIME_H
#define TIME_H
   ...
#endif
```

When we build larger programs, other definitions and declarations will also be placed in headers. The preceding preprocessor wrapper prevents the code between **#ifndef** (which means "if not defined") and **#endif** from being included if the name TIME_H has been defined. If the header has *not* been included previously in a file, the name TIME_H is defined by the **#define** directive and the header statements *are* included. If the header has been included previously, TIME_H *is defined* already and the header is *not* included again. Attempts to include a header multiple times (inadvertently) typically occur in large programs with many headers that may themselves include other headers.

Error-Prevention Tip 17.1

Use #ifndef, #define *and* #endif *preprocessor directives to form a preprocessor wrapper that prevents headers from being included more than once in a program.*

Good Programming Practice 17.2

By convention, use the name of the header in upper case with the period replaced by an underscore in the #ifndef *and* #define *preprocessor directives of a header.*

Time Class Member Functions

In Fig. 17.2, the Time constructor (lines 11–14) initializes the data members to 0—the universal-time equivalent of 12 AM. Invalid values cannot be stored in the data members of a Time object, because the constructor is called when the Time object is created, and all subsequent attempts by a client to modify the data members are scrutinized by function setTime (discussed shortly). Finally, it's important to note that you can define several *overloaded constructors* for a class.

```
1   // Fig. 17.2: Time.cpp
2   // Time class member-function definitions.
3   #include <iostream>
4   #include <iomanip>
5   #include <stdexcept> // for invalid_argument exception class
```

Fig. 17.2 | Time class member-function definitions. (Part 1 of 2.)

```
6   #include "Time.h" // include definition of class Time from Time.h
7
8   using namespace std;
9
10  // Time constructor initializes each data member to zero.
11  Time::Time()
12  {
13     hour = minute = second = 0;
14  } // end Time constructor
15
16  // set new Time value using universal time
17  void Time::setTime( int h, int m, int s )
18  {
19     // validate hour, minute and second
20     if ( ( h >= 0 && h < 24 ) && ( m >= 0 && m < 60 ) &&
21        ( s >= 0 && s < 60 ) )
22     {
23        hour = h;
24        minute = m;
25        second = s;
26     } // end if
27     else
28        throw invalid_argument(
29           "hour, minute and/or second was out of range" );
30  } // end function setTime
31
32  // print Time in universal-time format (HH:MM:SS)
33  void Time::printUniversal()
34  {
35     cout << setfill( '0' ) << setw( 2 ) << hour << ":"
36        << setw( 2 ) << minute << ":" << setw( 2 ) << second;
37  } // end function printUniversal
38
39  // print Time in standard-time format (HH:MM:SS AM or PM)
40  void Time::printStandard()
41  {
42     cout << ( ( hour == 0 || hour == 12 ) ? 12 : hour % 12 ) << ":"
43        << setfill( '0' ) << setw( 2 ) << minute << ":" << setw( 2 )
44        << second << ( hour < 12 ? " AM" : " PM" );
45  } // end function printStandard
```

Fig. 17.2 | Time class member-function definitions. (Part 2 of 2.)

With the exception of static const int *data members, a class's data members cannot (in many current C++ compilers) be initialized where they're declared in the class body—but this is allowed in the new C++ standard. It's strongly recommended that these data members be initialized by the class's constructor as* there is no default initialization for fundamental-type data members. *Data members can also be assigned values by* Time's *set functions.*

Common Programming Error 17.1

*Attempting to initialize a non-*static *data member of a class explicitly in the class definition is a syntax error.*

Time Class Member Function `setTime` and Throwing Exceptions

Function `setTime` (lines 17–30) is a `public` function that declares three `int` parameters and uses them to set the time. Lines 20–21 test each argument to determine whether the value is in range, and, if so, lines 23–25 assign the values to the `hour`, `minute` and `second` data members. The `hour` value must be greater than or equal to 0 and less than 24, because universal-time format represents hours as integers from 0 to 23 (e.g., 1 PM is hour 13 and 11 PM is hour 23; midnight is hour 0 and noon is hour 12). Similarly, both `minute` and `second` must be greater than or equal to 0 and less than 60. For values outside these ranges, `setTime` **throws an exception** of type `invalid_argument` (lines 28–29), which notifies the client code that an invalid argument was received. As you've learned, you can use `try...catch` to catch exceptions and attempt to recover from them, which we'll do in Fig. 17.3. The **throw statement** (lines 28–29) creates a new object of type `invalid_argument`. The parentheses following the class name indicate a call to the `invalid_argument` constructor that allows us to specify a custom error message string. After the exception object is created, the `throw` statement immediately terminates function `setTime` and the exception is returned to the code that attempted to set the time. [*Note:* To avoid compilation errors with GNU C++, you may need to include header `<stdexcept>` to use class `invalid_argument`.]

Time Class Member Function `printUniversal`

Function `printUniversal` (lines 33–37 of Fig. 17.2) takes no arguments and outputs the time in universal-time format, consisting of three colon-separated pairs of digits for the hour, minute and second. For example, if the time were 1:30:07 PM, function `printUniversal` would return 13:30:07. Line 35 uses parameterized stream manipulator **setfill** to specify the **fill character** that's displayed when an integer is output in a field wider than the number of digits in the value. By default, the fill characters appear to the left of the digits in the number. In this example, if the `minute` value is 2, it will be displayed as 02, because the fill character is set to zero (`'0'`). If the number being output fills the specified field, the fill character will *not* be displayed. Once the fill character is specified with `setfill`, it applies for all subsequent values that are displayed in fields wider than the value being displayed (i.e., `setfill` is a "sticky" setting). This is in contrast to `setw`, which applies only to the next value displayed (`setw` is a "nonsticky" setting).

> **Error-Prevention Tip 17.2**
>
> *Each sticky setting (such as a fill character or floating-point precision) should be restored to its previous setting when it's no longer needed. Failure to do so may result in incorrectly formatted output later in a program. Chapter 23, Stream Input/Output, discusses how to reset the fill character and precision.*

Time Class Member Function `printStandard`

Function `printStandard` (lines 40–45) takes no arguments and outputs the date in standard-time format, consisting of the `hour`, `minute` and `second` values separated by colons and followed by an AM or PM indicator (e.g., 1:27:06 PM). Like function `printUniversal`, function `printStandard` uses `setfill('0')` to format the `minute` and `second` as two digit values with leading zeros if necessary. Line 42 uses the conditional operator (`?:`) to determine the value of `hour` to be displayed—if the `hour` is 0 or 12 (AM or PM), it appears as 12; otherwise, the `hour` appears as a value from 1 to 11. The conditional operator in line 44 determines whether AM or PM will be displayed.

Defining Member Functions Outside the Class Definitiogn; Class Scope

Even though a member function declared in a class definition may be defined outside that class definition (and "tied" to the class via the *scope resolution operator*), that member function is still within that class's scope—that is, its name is known to other members of the class. We'll say more about class scope shortly.

If a member function is defined in the body of a class definition, the member function is implicitly declared inline. Remember that the compiler reserves the right not to inline any function.

Performance Tip 17.1

Defining a member function inside the class definition inlines the member function (if the compiler chooses to do so). This can improve performance.

Software Engineering Observation 17.2

Defining a small member function inside the class definition does not promote the best software engineering, because clients of the class will be able to see the implementation of the function, and the client code must be recompiled if the function definition changes.

Software Engineering Observation 17.3

Only the simplest and most stable member functions (i.e., whose implementations are unlikely to change) should be defined in the class header.

Member Functions vs. Global Functions

The `printUniversal` and `printStandard` member functions take no arguments, because these member functions implicitly know that they're to print the data members of the particular `Time` object for which they're invoked. This can make member function calls more concise than conventional function calls in procedural programming.

Software Engineering Observation 17.4

Using an object-oriented programming approach often simplifies function calls by reducing the number of parameters. This benefit of object-oriented programming derives from the fact that encapsulating data members and member functions within an object gives the member functions the right to access the data members.

Software Engineering Observation 17.5

Member functions are usually shorter than functions in non-object-oriented programs, because the data stored in data members have ideally been validated by a constructor or by member functions that store new data. Because the data is already in the object, the member-function calls often have no arguments or fewer arguments than function calls in non-object-oriented languages. Thus, the calls, the function definitions and the function prototypes are shorter. This improves many aspects of program development.

Error-Prevention Tip 17.3

The fact that member function calls generally take either no arguments or substantially fewer arguments than conventional function calls in non-object-oriented languages reduces the likelihood of passing the wrong arguments, the wrong types of arguments or the wrong number of arguments.

*Using Class **Time***

Once defined, Time can be used as a type in declarations as follows:

```
Time sunset; // object of type Time
Time arrayOfTimes[ 5 ]; // array of 5 Time objects
Time &dinnerTime = sunset; // reference to a Time object
Time *timePtr = &dinnerTime; // pointer to a Time object
```

Figure 17.3 uses class Time. Line 10 instantiates a single object of class Time called t. When the object is instantiated, the Time constructor is called to initialize each private data member to 0. Then, lines 14 and 16 print the time in universal and standard formats, respectively, to confirm that the members were initialized properly. Line 18 sets a new time by calling member function setTime, and lines 22 and 24 print the time again in both formats.

```
 1   // Fig. 17.3: fig17_03.cpp
 2   // Program to test class Time.
 3   // NOTE: This file must be compiled with Time.cpp.
 4   #include <iostream>
 5   #include "Time.h" // include definition of class Time from Time.h
 6   using namespace std;
 7
 8   int main()
 9   {
10      Time t; // instantiate object t of class Time
11
12      // output Time object t's initial values
13      cout << "The initial universal time is ";
14      t.printUniversal(); // 00:00:00
15      cout << "\nThe initial standard time is ";
16      t.printStandard(); // 12:00:00 AM
17
18      t.setTime( 13, 27, 6 ); // change time
19
20      // output Time object t's new values
21      cout << "\n\nUniversal time after setTime is ";
22      t.printUniversal(); // 13:27:06
23      cout << "\nStandard time after setTime is ";
24      t.printStandard(); // 1:27:06 PM
25
26      // attempt to set the time with invalid values
27      try
28      {
29         t.setTime( 99, 99, 99 ); // all values out of range
30      } // end try
31      catch ( invalid_argument &e )
32      {
33         cout << "Exception: " << e.what() << endl << endl;
34      } // end catch
35
36      // output t's values after specifying invalid values
37      cout << "\n\nAfter attempting invalid settings:"
38         << "\nUniversal time: ";
```

Fig. 17.3 | Program to test class Time. (Part 1 of 2.)

```
39      t.printUniversal(); // 00:00:00
40      cout << "\nStandard time: ";
41      t.printStandard(); // 12:00:00 AM
42      cout << endl;
43   } // end main
```

```
The initial universal time is 00:00:00
The initial standard time is 12:00:00 AM

Universal time after setTime is 13:27:06
Standard time after setTime is 1:27:06 PM

Exception: hour, minute and/or second was out of range

After attempting invalid settings:
Universal time: 13:27:06
Standard time: 1:27:06 PM
```

Fig. 17.3 | Program to test class Time. (Part 2 of 2.)

Calling *setTime* with Invalid Values

To illustrate that method setTime validates its arguments, line 29 calls setTime with invalid arguments of 99 for the hour, minute and second. This statement is placed in a try block (lines 27–30) in case setTime throws an invalid_argument exception, which it will do since the arguments are all invalid. When this occurs, the exception is caught at lines 31–34 and line 33 displays the exception's error message by calling its what member function. Lines 37–41 output the time again in both formats to confirm that setTime did not change the time when invalid arguments were supplied.

Looking Ahead to Composition and Inheritance

Often, classes do not have to be created "from scratch." Rather, they can include objects of other classes as members or they may be **derived** from other classes that provide attributes and behaviors the new classes can use. Such software reuse can greatly enhance productivity and simplify code maintenance. Including class objects as members of other classes is called **composition** and is discussed in Chapter 18. Deriving new classes from existing classes is called **inheritance** and is discussed in Chapter 20.

Object Size

People new to object-oriented programming often suppose that objects must be quite large because they contain data members and member functions. Logically, this is true—you may think of objects as containing data and functions (and our discussion has certainly encouraged this view); physically, however, this is not true.

Performance Tip 17.2

Objects contain only data, so objects are much smaller than if they also contained member functions. Applying operator sizeof to a class name or to an object of that class will report only the size of the class's data members. The compiler creates one copy (only) of the member functions separate from all objects of the class. All objects of the class share this one copy. Each object, of course, needs its own copy of the class's data, because the data can vary among the objects. The function code is nonmodifiable and, hence, can be shared among all objects of one class.

17.3 Class Scope and Accessing Class Members

A class's data members (variables declared in the class definition) and member functions (functions declared in the class definition) belong to that class's scope. Nonmember functions are defined at *global namespace scope*.

Within a class's scope, class members are immediately accessible by all of that class's member functions and can be referenced by name. Outside a class's scope, public class members are referenced through one of the **handles** on an object—an object name, a reference to an object or a pointer to an object. The type of the object, reference or pointer specifies the interface (i.e., the member functions) accessible to the client. [We'll see in Chapter 18 that an *implicit handle* is inserted by the compiler on every reference to a data member or member function from within an object.]

Member functions of a class can be overloaded, but only by other member functions of that class. To overload a member function, simply provide in the class definition a prototype for each version of the overloaded function, and provide a separate function definition for each version of the function. This also applies to the class's constructors.

Variables declared in a member function have *local scope* and are known only to that function. If a member function defines a variable with the same name as a variable with class scope, the class-scope variable is *hidden* by the block-scope variable in the local scope. Such a hidden variable can be accessed by preceding the variable name with the class name followed by the scope resolution operator (::). Hidden global variables can be accessed with the scope resolution operator.

The dot member selection operator (.) is preceded by an object's name or with a reference to an object to access the object's members. The **arrow member selection operator** (->) is preceded by a pointer to an object to access the object's members.

Figure 17.4 uses a simple class called Count (lines 7–24) with private data member x of type int (line 23), public member function setX (lines 11–14) and public member function print (lines 17–20) to illustrate accessing class members with the member-selection operators. For simplicity, we've included this small class in the same file as main. Lines 28–30 create three variables related to type Count—counter (a Count object), counterPtr (a pointer to a Count object) and counterRef (a reference to a Count object). Variable counterRef *refers to* counter, and variable counterPtr *points to* counter. In lines 33–34 and 37–38, note that the program invokes member functions setX and print by using the dot (.) member selection operator preceded by either the name of the object (counter) or a reference to the object (counterRef, which is an alias for counter). Similarly, lines 41–42 demonstrate that the program can invoke member functions setX and print by using a pointer (countPtr) and the arrow (->) member-selection operator.

```
1   // Fig. 17.4: fig17_04.cpp
2   // Demonstrating the class member access operators . and ->
3   #include <iostream>
4   using namespace std;
5
```

Fig. 17.4 | Demonstrating the class member access operators . and ->. (Part 1 of 2.)

```
 6   // class Count definition
 7   class Count
 8   {
 9   public: // public data is dangerous
10      // sets the value of private data member x
11      void setX( int value )
12      {
13         x = value;
14      } // end function setX
15
16      // prints the value of private data member x
17      void print()
18      {
19         cout << x << endl;
20      } // end function print
21
22   private:
23      int x;
24   }; // end class Count
25
26   int main()
27   {
28      Count counter; // create counter object
29      Count *counterPtr = &counter; // create pointer to counter
30      Count &counterRef = counter; // create reference to counter
31
32      cout << "Set x to 1 and print using the object's name: ";
33      counter.setX( 1 ); // set data member x to 1
34      counter.print(); // call member function print
35
36      cout << "Set x to 2 and print using a reference to an object: ";
37      counterRef.setX( 2 ); // set data member x to 2
38      counterRef.print(); // call member function print
39
40      cout << "Set x to 3 and print using a pointer to an object: ";
41      counterPtr->setX( 3 ); // set data member x to 3
42      counterPtr->print(); // call member function print
43   } // end main
```

```
Set x to 1 and print using the object's name: 1
Set x to 2 and print using a reference to an object: 2
Set x to 3 and print using a pointer to an object: 3
```

Fig. 17.4 | Demonstrating the class member access operators . and ->. (Part 2 of 2.)

17.4 Separating Interface from Implementation

In Chapter 16, we began by including a class's definition and member-function definitions in *one* file. We then demonstrated separating this code into *two* files—a header for the class definition (i.e., the class's *interface*) and a source code file for the class's member-function definitions (i.e., the class's *implementation*). This makes it easier to modify programs—as far as clients of a class are concerned, changes in the class's implementation do not affect the client as long as the class's interface originally provided to the client remains unchanged.

Software Engineering Observation 17.6

Clients of a class do not need access to the class's source code in order to use the class. The clients do, however, need to be able to link to the class's object code (i.e., the compiled version of the class). This encourages independent software vendors (ISVs) to provide class libraries for sale or license. The ISVs provide in their products only the headers and the object modules. No proprietary information is revealed—as would be the case if source code were provided. The C++ user community benefits by having more ISV-produced class libraries available.

Actually, things are not quite this rosy. Headers do contain some portions of the implementation and hints about others. Inline member functions, for example, should be in a header, so that when the compiler compiles a client, the client can include the `inline` function definition in place. A class's `private` members are listed in the class definition in the header, so these members are visible to clients even though the clients may not access the `private` members. In Chapter 18, we show how to use a *proxy class* to hide even the `private` data of a class from clients of the class.

Software Engineering Observation 17.7

Information important to the interface of a class should be included in the header. Information that will be used only internally in the class and will not be needed by clients of the class should be included in the unpublished source file. This is yet another example of the principle of least privilege.

17.5 Access Functions and Utility Functions

Access functions can read or display data. Another common use for access functions is to test the truth or falsity of conditions—such functions are often called **predicate functions**. An example of a predicate function would be an `isEmpty` function for any container class—a class capable of holding many objects, like a `vector`. A program might test `isEmpty` before attempting to read another item from the container object. An `isFull` predicate function might test a container-class object to determine whether it has no additional room. Useful predicate functions for our `Time` class might be `isAM` and `isPM`.

The program of Figs. 17.5–17.7 demonstrates the notion of a **utility function** (also called a **helper function**). A utility function is *not* part of a class's `public` interface; rather, it's a `private` member function that supports the operation of the class's other member functions. Utility functions are not intended to be used by clients of a class (but can be used by *friends* of a class, as we'll see in Chapter 18).

Class `SalesPerson` (Fig. 17.5) declares an array of 12 monthly sales figures (line 17) and the prototypes for the class's constructor and member functions that manipulate the array.

```
1   // Fig. 17.5: SalesPerson.h
2   // SalesPerson class definition.
3   // Member functions defined in SalesPerson.cpp.
```

Fig. 17.5 | `SalesPerson` class definition. (Part 1 of 2.)

```
4    #ifndef SALESPERSON_H
5    #define SALESPERSON_H
6
7    class SalesPerson
8    {
9    public:
10      static const int monthsPerYear = 12; // months in one year
11      SalesPerson(); // constructor
12      void getSalesFromUser(); // input sales from keyboard
13      void setSales( int, double ); // set sales for a specific month
14      void printAnnualSales(); // summarize and print sales
15   private:
16      double totalAnnualSales(); // prototype for utility function
17      double sales[ monthsPerYear ]; // 12 monthly sales figures
18   }; // end class SalesPerson
19
20   #endif
```

Fig. 17.5 | SalesPerson class definition. (Part 2 of 2.)

In Fig. 17.6, the SalesPerson constructor (lines 9–13) initializes array sales to zero. The public member function setSales (lines 30–37) sets the sales figure for one month in array sales. The public member function printAnnualSales (lines 40–45) prints the total sales for the last 12 months. The private utility function totalAnnualSales (lines 48–56) totals the 12 monthly sales figures for the benefit of printAnnualSales. Member function printAnnualSales edits the sales figures into monetary format.

```
1    // Fig. 17.6: SalesPerson.cpp
2    // SalesPerson class member-function definitions.
3    #include <iostream>
4    #include <iomanip>
5    #include "SalesPerson.h" // include SalesPerson class definition
6    using namespace std;
7
8    // initialize elements of array sales to 0.0
9    SalesPerson::SalesPerson()
10   {
11      for ( int i = 0; i < monthsPerYear; ++i )
12         sales[ i ] = 0.0;
13   } // end SalesPerson constructor
14
15   // get 12 sales figures from the user at the keyboard
16   void SalesPerson::getSalesFromUser()
17   {
18      double salesFigure;
19
20      for ( int i = 1; i <= monthsPerYear; ++i )
21      {
22         cout << "Enter sales amount for month " << i << ": ";
23         cin >> salesFigure;
```

Fig. 17.6 | SalesPerson class member-function definitions. (Part 1 of 2.)

```
24          setSales( i, salesFigure );
25      } // end for
26  } // end function getSalesFromUser
27
28  // set one of the 12 monthly sales figures; function subtracts
29  // one from month value for proper subscript in sales array
30  void SalesPerson::setSales( int month, double amount )
31  {
32      // test for valid month and amount values
33      if ( month >= 1 && month <= monthsPerYear && amount > 0 )
34          sales[ month - 1 ] = amount; // adjust for subscripts 0-11
35      else // invalid month or amount value
36          cout << "Invalid month or sales figure" << endl;
37  } // end function setSales
38
39  // print total annual sales (with the help of utility function)
40  void SalesPerson::printAnnualSales()
41  {
42      cout << setprecision( 2 ) << fixed
43          << "\nThe total annual sales are: $"
44          << totalAnnualSales() << endl; // call utility function
45  } // end function printAnnualSales
46
47  // private utility function to total annual sales
48  double SalesPerson::totalAnnualSales()
49  {
50      double total = 0.0; // initialize total
51
52      for ( int i = 0; i < monthsPerYear; ++i ) // summarize sales results
53          total += sales[ i ]; // add month i sales to total
54
55      return total;
56  } // end function totalAnnualSales
```

Fig. 17.6 | SalesPerson class member-function definitions. (Part 2 of 2.)

In Fig. 17.7, notice that the application's main function includes only a simple sequence of member-function calls—there are no control statements. The logic of manipulating the sales array is completely encapsulated in class SalesPerson's member functions.

Software Engineering Observation 17.8

A phenomenon of object-oriented programming is that once a class is defined, creating and manipulating objects of that class often involve issuing only a simple sequence of member-function calls—few, if any, control statements are needed. By contrast, it's common to have control statements in the implementation of a class's member functions.

```
1   // Fig. 17.7: fig17_07.cpp
2   // Utility function demonstration.
3   // Compile this program with SalesPerson.cpp
4
```

Fig. 17.7 | Utility function demonstration. (Part 1 of 2.)

```
 5    // include SalesPerson class definition from SalesPerson.h
 6    #include "SalesPerson.h"
 7
 8    int main()
 9    {
10       SalesPerson s; // create SalesPerson object s
11
12       s.getSalesFromUser(); // note simple sequential code; there are
13       s.printAnnualSales(); // no control statements in main
14    } // end main
```

```
Enter sales amount for month 1: 5314.76
Enter sales amount for month 2: 4292.38
Enter sales amount for month 3: 4589.83
Enter sales amount for month 4: 5534.03
Enter sales amount for month 5: 4376.34
Enter sales amount for month 6: 5698.45
Enter sales amount for month 7: 4439.22
Enter sales amount for month 8: 5893.57
Enter sales amount for month 9: 4909.67
Enter sales amount for month 10: 5123.45
Enter sales amount for month 11: 4024.97
Enter sales amount for month 12: 5923.92

The total annual sales are: $60120.59
```

Fig. 17.7 | Utility function demonstration. (Part 2 of 2.)

17.6 Time Class Case Study: Constructors with Default Arguments

The program of Figs. 17.8–17.10 enhances class Time to demonstrate how arguments are implicitly passed to a constructor. The constructor defined in Fig. 17.2 initialized hour, minute and second to 0 (i.e., midnight in universal time). Like other functions, constructors can specify *default arguments*. Line 13 of Fig. 17.8 declares the Time constructor to include default arguments, specifying a default value of zero for each argument passed to the constructor. In Fig. 17.9, lines 10–13 define the new version of the Time constructor that receives values for parameters hour, minute and second that will be used to initialize private data members hour, minute and second, respectively. Class Time provides *set* and *get* functions for each data member. The Time constructor now calls setTime, which calls the setHour, setMinute and setSecond functions to validate and assign values to the data members. The default arguments to the constructor ensure that, even if no values are provided in a constructor call, the constructor still initializes the data members. *A constructor that defaults all its arguments is also a default constructor—that is, a constructor that can be invoked with no arguments. There can be at most one default constructor per class.*

Software Engineering Observation 17.9

Any change to the default argument values of a function requires the client code to be recompiled (to ensure that the program still functions correctly).

```
1   // Fig. 17.8: Time.h
2   // Time class containing a constructor with default arguments.
3   // Member functions defined in Time.cpp.
4
5   // prevent multiple inclusions of header
6   #ifndef TIME_H
7   #define TIME_H
8
9   // Time abstract data type definition
10  class Time
11  {
12  public:
13     Time( int = 0, int = 0, int = 0 ); // default constructor
14
15     // set functions
16     void setTime( int, int, int ); // set hour, minute, second
17     void setHour( int ); // set hour (after validation)
18     void setMinute( int ); // set minute (after validation)
19     void setSecond( int ); // set second (after validation)
20
21     // get functions
22     int getHour(); // return hour
23     int getMinute(); // return minute
24     int getSecond(); // return second
25
26     void printUniversal(); // output time in universal-time format
27     void printStandard(); // output time in standard-time format
28  private:
29     int hour; // 0 - 23 (24-hour clock format)
30     int minute; // 0 - 59
31     int second; // 0 - 59
32  }; // end class Time
33
34  #endif
```

Fig. 17.8 | Time class containing a constructor with default arguments.

In Fig. 17.9, line 12 of the constructor calls member function setTime with the values passed to the constructor (or the default values). Function setTime calls setHour to ensure that the value supplied for hour is in the range 0–23, then calls setMinute and setSecond to ensure that the values for minute and second are each in the range 0–59. Functions setHour (lines 24–30), setMinute (lines 33–39) and setSecond (lines 42–48) each throw an exception if an out-of-range argument is received.

```
1   // Fig. 17.9: Time.cpp
2   // Time class member-function definitions.
3   #include <iostream>
4   #include <iomanip>
```

Fig. 17.9 | Time class member-function definitions including a constructor that takes arguments. (Part 1 of 3.)

```cpp
5   #include <stdexcept>
6   #include "Time.h" // include definition of class Time from Time.h
7   using namespace std;
8
9   // Time constructor initializes each data member to zero
10  Time::Time( int hour, int minute, int second )
11  {
12     setTime( hour, minute, second ); // validate and set time
13  } // end Time constructor
14
15  // set new Time value using universal time
16  void Time::setTime( int h, int m, int s )
17  {
18     setHour( h ); // set private field hour
19     setMinute( m ); // set private field minute
20     setSecond( s ); // set private field second
21  } // end function setTime
22
23  // set hour value
24  void Time::setHour( int h )
25  {
26     if ( h >= 0 && h < 24 )
27        hour = h;
28     else
29        throw invalid_argument( "hour must be 0-23" );
30  } // end function setHour
31
32  // set minute value
33  void Time::setMinute( int m )
34  {
35     if ( m >= 0 && m < 60 )
36        minute = m;
37     else
38        throw invalid_argument( "minute must be 0-59" );
39  } // end function setMinute
40
41  // set second value
42  void Time::setSecond( int s )
43  {
44     if ( s >= 0 && s < 60 )
45        second = s;
46     else
47        throw invalid_argument( "second must be 0-59" );
48  } // end function setSecond
49
50  // return hour value
51  int Time::getHour()
52  {
53     return hour;
54  } // end function getHour
55
```

Fig. 17.9 | Time class member-function definitions including a constructor that takes arguments. (Part 2 of 3.)

```
56   // return minute value
57   int Time::getMinute()
58   {
59      return minute;
60   } // end function getMinute
61
62   // return second value
63   int Time::getSecond()
64   {
65      return second;
66   } // end function getSecond
67
68   // print Time in universal-time format (HH:MM:SS)
69   void Time::printUniversal()
70   {
71      cout << setfill( '0' ) << setw( 2 ) << getHour() << ":"
72         << setw( 2 ) << getMinute() << ":" << setw( 2 ) << getSecond();
73   } // end function printUniversal
74
75   // print Time in standard-time format (HH:MM:SS AM or PM)
76   void Time::printStandard()
77   {
78      cout << ( ( getHour() == 0 || getHour() == 12 ) ? 12 : getHour() % 12 )
79         << ":" << setfill( '0' ) << setw( 2 ) << getMinute()
80         << ":" << setw( 2 ) << getSecond() << ( hour < 12 ? " AM" : " PM" );
81   } // end function printStandard
```

Fig. 17.9 | Time class member-function definitions including a constructor that takes arguments. (Part 3 of 3.)

Function main in Fig. 17.10 initializes five Time objects—one with all three arguments defaulted in the implicit constructor call (line 10), one with one argument specified (line 11), one with two arguments specified (line 12), one with three arguments specified (line 13) and one with three invalid arguments specified (line 38). The program displays each object in universal-time and standard-time formats. For Time object t5 (line 38), the program displays an error message because the constructor arguments are out of range.

```
1    // Fig. 17.10: fig17_10.cpp
2    // Constructor with default arguments for class Time.
3    #include <iostream>
4    #include <stdexcept>
5    #include "Time.h" // include definition of class Time from Time.h
6    using namespace std;
7
8    int main()
9    {
10      Time t1; // all arguments defaulted
11      Time t2( 2 ); // hour specified; minute and second defaulted
12      Time t3( 21, 34 ); // hour and minute specified; second defaulted
13      Time t4( 12, 25, 42 ); // hour, minute and second specified
```

Fig. 17.10 | Constructor with default arguments for class Time. (Part 1 of 2.)

```
14
15       cout << "Constructed with:\n\nt1: all arguments defaulted\n   ";
16       t1.printUniversal(); // 00:00:00
17       cout << "\n   ";
18       t1.printStandard(); // 12:00:00 AM
19
20       cout << "\n\nt2: hour specified; minute and second defaulted\n   ";
21       t2.printUniversal(); // 02:00:00
22       cout << "\n   ";
23       t2.printStandard(); // 2:00:00 AM
24
25       cout << "\n\nt3: hour and minute specified; second defaulted\n   ";
26       t3.printUniversal(); // 21:34:00
27       cout << "\n   ";
28       t3.printStandard(); // 9:34:00 PM
29
30       cout << "\n\nt4: hour, minute and second specified\n   ";
31       t4.printUniversal(); // 12:25:42
32       cout << "\n   ";
33       t4.printStandard(); // 12:25:42 PM
34
35       // attempt to initialize t6 with invalid values
36       try
37       {
38          Time t5( 27, 74, 99 ); // all bad values specified
39       } // end try
40       catch ( invalid_argument &e )
41       {
42          cout << "\n\nException while initializing t5: " << e.what() << endl;
43       } // end catch
44    } // end main
```

```
Constructed with:

t1: all arguments defaulted
   00:00:00
   12:00:00 AM

t2: hour specified; minute and second defaulted
   02:00:00
   2:00:00 AM

t3: hour and minute specified; second defaulted
   21:34:00
   9:34:00 PM

t4: hour, minute and second specified
   12:25:42
   12:25:42 PM

Exception while initializing t5: hour must be 0-23
```

Fig. 17.10 | Constructor with default arguments for class Time. (Part 2 of 2.)

*Notes Regarding Class **Time***'s* Set *and* Get *Functions and Constructor*

Time's *set* and *get* functions are called throughout the class's body. In particular, function setTime (lines 17–22 of Fig. 17.9) calls functions setHour, setMinute and setSecond, and functions printUniversal and printStandard call functions getHour, getMinute and getSecond in line 72–73 and lines 79–81, respectively. In each case, these functions could have accessed the class's private data directly. However, consider changing the representation of the time from three int values (requiring 12 bytes of memory) to a single int value representing the total number of seconds that have elapsed since midnight (requiring only four bytes of memory). If we made such a change, only the bodies of the functions that access the private data directly would need to change—in particular, the individual *set* and *get* functions for the hour, minute and second. There would be no need to modify the bodies of functions setTime, printUniversal or printStandard, because they do *not* access the data directly. Designing the class in this manner reduces the likelihood of programming errors when altering the class's implementation.

Similarly, the Time constructor could be written to include a copy of the appropriate statements from function setTime. Doing so may be slightly more efficient, because the extra constructor call and call to setTime are eliminated. However, duplicating statements in multiple functions or constructors makes changing the class's internal data representation more difficult. Having the Time constructor call setTime and having setTime call setHour, setMinute and setSecond enables us to limit the changes to code that validates the hour, minute or second to the corresponding *set* function. This reduces the likelihood of errors when altering the class's implementation. Also, the performance of the Time constructor and setTime can (possibly) be enhanced by explicitly declaring them inline or by defining them in the class definition (which implicitly inlines the function definition).

Software Engineering Observation 17.10

If a member function of a class already provides all or part of the functionality required by a constructor (or other member function) of the class, call that member function from the constructor (or other member function). This simplifies the maintenance of the code and reduces the likelihood of an error if the implementation of the code is modified. As a general rule: Avoid repeating code.

Common Programming Error 17.2

A constructor can call other member functions of the class, such as set or get functions, but because the constructor is initializing the object, the data members may not yet be initialized. Using data members before they have been properly initialized can cause logic errors.

17.7 Destructors

A **destructor** is another type of special member function. The name of the destructor for a class is the **tilde character** (~) followed by the class name. This naming convention has intuitive appeal, because as we'll see in a later chapter, the tilde operator is the bitwise complement operator, and, in a sense, the destructor is the complement of the constructor.

A class's destructor is called *implicitly* when an object is destroyed. This occurs, for example, as an automatic object is destroyed when program execution leaves the scope in which that object was instantiated. *The destructor itself does not actually release the object's memory*—it performs termination housekeeping before the object's memory is reclaimed, so the memory may be reused to hold new objects.

> **Common Programming Error 17.3**
>
> *It's a syntax error to attempt to pass arguments to a destructor, to specify a return type for a destructor (even* void *cannot be specified), to return values from a destructor or to overload a destructor.*

Even though destructors have not been provided for the classes presented so far, *every class has a destructor.* If you do not explicitly provide a destructor, the compiler creates an "empty" destructor. [*Note:* We'll see that such an implicitly created destructor does, in fact, perform important operations on objects that are created through composition (Chapter 18) and inheritance (Chapter 20).] In Chapter 19, we'll build destructors appropriate for classes whose objects contain dynamically allocated memory (e.g., for arrays and strings) or use other system resources (e.g., files on disk. We discuss how to dynamically allocate and deallocate memory in Chapter 18.

17.8 When Constructors and Destructors Are Called

Constructors and destructors are called *implicitly* by the compiler. The order in which these function calls occur depends on the order in which execution enters and leaves the scopes where the objects are instantiated. Generally, destructor calls are made in the *reverse order* of the corresponding constructor calls, but as we'll see in Figs. 17.11–17.13, the storage classes of objects can alter the order in which destructors are called.

Constructors and Destructors for Objects in Global Scope

Constructors are called for objects defined in global scope *before* any other function (including main) in that file begins execution (although the order of execution of global object constructors between files is *not* guaranteed). The corresponding destructors are called when main terminates. Function **exit** forces a program to terminate immediately and does *not* execute the destructors of automatic objects. The function often is used to terminate a program when an error is detected in the input or if a file to be processed by the program cannot be opened. Function **abort** performs similarly to function exit but forces the program to terminate *immediately*, without allowing the destructors of any objects to be called. Function abort is usually used to indicate an abnormal termination of the program.

Constructors and Destructors for Local Automatic Objects

The constructor for an automatic local object is called when execution reaches the point where that object is defined—the corresponding destructor is called when execution leaves the object's scope (i.e., the block in which that object is defined has finished executing). Constructors and destructors for automatic objects are called each time execution enters and leaves the scope of the object. Destructors are not called for automatic objects if the program terminates with a call to function exit or function abort.

Constructors and Destructors for static Local Objects

The constructor for a static local object is called only *once*, when execution first reaches the point where the object is defined—the corresponding destructor is called when main terminates or the program calls function `exit`. Global and `static` objects are destroyed in the *reverse* order of their creation. Destructors are *not* called for `static` objects if the program terminates with a call to function `abort`.

Demonstrating When Constructors and Destructors Are Called

The program of Figs. 17.11–17.13 demonstrates the order in which constructors and destructors are called for objects of class `CreateAndDestroy` (Fig. 17.11 and Fig. 17.12) of various storage classes in several scopes. Each object of class `CreateAndDestroy` contains an integer (`objectID`) and a `string` (`message`) that are used in the program's output to identify the object (Fig. 17.11 lines 16–17). This mechanical example is purely for pedagogic purposes. For this reason, line 21 of the destructor in Fig. 17.12 determines whether the object being destroyed has an `objectID` value 1 or 6 and, if so, outputs a newline character. This line makes the program's output easier to follow.

```
1   // Fig. 17.11: CreateAndDestroy.h
2   // CreateAndDestroy class definition.
3   // Member functions defined in CreateAndDestroy.cpp.
4   #include <string>
5   using namespace std;
6
7   #ifndef CREATE_H
8   #define CREATE_H
9
10  class CreateAndDestroy
11  {
12  public:
13     CreateAndDestroy( int, string ); // constructor
14     ~CreateAndDestroy(); // destructor
15  private:
16     int objectID; // ID number for object
17     string message; // message describing object
18  }; // end class CreateAndDestroy
19
20  #endif
```

Fig. 17.11 | CreateAndDestroy class definition.

```
1   // Fig. 17.12: CreateAndDestroy.cpp
2   // CreateAndDestroy class member-function definitions.
3   #include <iostream>
4   #include "CreateAndDestroy.h"// include CreateAndDestroy class definition
5   using namespace std;
6
7   // constructor
8   CreateAndDestroy::CreateAndDestroy( int ID, string messageString )
9   {
10     objectID = ID; // set object's ID number
11     message = messageString; // set object's descriptive message
12
```

Fig. 17.12 | CreateAndDestroy class member-function definitions. (Part 1 of 2.)

```
13        cout << "Object " << objectID << "   constructor runs    "
14           << message << endl;
15     } // end CreateAndDestroy constructor
16
17     // destructor
18     CreateAndDestroy::~CreateAndDestroy()
19     {
20        // output newline for certain objects; helps readability
21        cout << ( objectID == 1 || objectID == 6 ? "\n" : "" );
22
23        cout << "Object " << objectID << "   destructor runs    "
24           << message << endl;
25     } // end ~CreateAndDestroy destructor
```

Fig. 17.12 | CreateAndDestroy class member-function definitions. (Part 2 of 2.)

Figure 17.13 defines object first (line 10) in global scope. Its constructor is actually called *before* any statements in main execute and its destructor is called at program termination *after* the destructors for all other objects have run.

Function main (lines 12–23) declares three objects. Objects second (line 15) and fourth (line 21) are local automatic objects, and object third (line 16) is a static local object. The constructor for each of these objects is called when execution reaches the point where that object is declared. The destructors for objects fourth then second are called (i.e., the *reverse* of the order in which their constructors were called) when execution reaches the end of main. Because object third is static, it exists until program termination. The destructor for object third is called *before* the destructor for global object first, but *after* all other objects are destroyed.

Function create (lines 26–33) declares three objects—fifth (line 29) and seventh (line 31) as local automatic objects, and sixth (line 30) as a static local object. The destructors for objects seventh then fifth are called (i.e., the *reverse* of the order in which their constructors were called) when create terminates. Because sixth is static, it exists until program termination. The destructor for sixth is called *before* the destructors for third and first, but *after* all other objects are destroyed.

```
 1     // Fig. 17.13: fig17_13.cpp
 2     // Order in which constructors and
 3     // destructors are called.
 4     #include <iostream>
 5     #include "CreateAndDestroy.h" // include CreateAndDestroy class definition
 6     using namespace std;
 7
 8     void create( void ); // prototype
 9
10     CreateAndDestroy first( 1, "(global before main)" ); // global object
11
12     int main()
13     {
14        cout << "\nMAIN FUNCTION: EXECUTION BEGINS" << endl;
```

Fig. 17.13 | Order in which constructors and destructors are called. (Part 1 of 2.)

```
15      CreateAndDestroy second( 2, "(local automatic in main)" );
16      static CreateAndDestroy third( 3, "(local static in main)" );
17
18      create(); // call function to create objects
19
20      cout << "\nMAIN FUNCTION: EXECUTION RESUMES" << endl;
21      CreateAndDestroy fourth( 4, "(local automatic in main)" );
22      cout << "\nMAIN FUNCTION: EXECUTION ENDS" << endl;
23   } // end main
24
25   // function to create objects
26   void create( void )
27   {
28      cout << "\nCREATE FUNCTION: EXECUTION BEGINS" << endl;
29      CreateAndDestroy fifth( 5, "(local automatic in create)" );
30      static CreateAndDestroy sixth( 6, "(local static in create)" );
31      CreateAndDestroy seventh( 7, "(local automatic in create)" );
32      cout << "\nCREATE FUNCTION: EXECUTION ENDS" << endl;
33   } // end function create
```

```
Object 1    constructor runs    (global before main)

MAIN FUNCTION: EXECUTION BEGINS
Object 2    constructor runs    (local automatic in main)
Object 3    constructor runs    (local static in main)

CREATE FUNCTION: EXECUTION BEGINS
Object 5    constructor runs    (local automatic in create)
Object 6    constructor runs    (local static in create)
Object 7    constructor runs    (local automatic in create)

CREATE FUNCTION: EXECUTION ENDS
Object 7    destructor runs     (local automatic in create)
Object 5    destructor runs     (local automatic in create)

MAIN FUNCTION: EXECUTION RESUMES
Object 4    constructor runs    (local automatic in main)

MAIN FUNCTION: EXECUTION ENDS
Object 4    destructor runs     (local automatic in main)
Object 2    destructor runs     (local automatic in main)

Object 6    destructor runs     (local static in create)
Object 3    destructor runs     (local static in main)

Object 1    destructor runs     (global before main)
```

Fig. 17.13 | Order in which constructors and destructors are called. (Part 2 of 2.)

17.9 Time Class Case Study: A Subtle Trap—Returning a Reference to a private Data Member

A reference to an object is an alias for the name of the object and, hence, may be used on the left side of an assignment statement. In this context, the reference makes a perfectly acceptable *lvalue* that can receive a value. One way to use this capability (unfortunately!)

is to have a `public` member function of a class return a reference to a `private` data member of that class. If a function returns a `const` reference, that reference cannot be used as a modifiable *lvalue*.

The program of Figs. 17.14–17.16 uses a simplified `Time` class (Fig. 17.14 and Fig. 17.15) to demonstrate returning a reference to a `private` data member with member function `badSetHour` (declared in Fig. 17.14 in line 15 and defined in Fig. 17.15 in lines 37–45). Such a reference return actually makes a call to member function `badSetHour` an alias for `private` data member `hour`! The function call can be used in any way that the `private` data member can be used, including as an *lvalue* in an assignment statement, thus *enabling clients of the class to clobber the class's private data at will!* The same problem would occur if a pointer to the `private` data were to be returned by the function.

```
1   // Fig. 17.14: Time.h
2   // Time class declaration.
3   // Member functions defined in Time.cpp
4
5   // prevent multiple inclusions of header
6   #ifndef TIME_H
7   #define TIME_H
8
9   class Time
10  {
11  public:
12     Time( int = 0, int = 0, int = 0 );
13     void setTime( int, int, int );
14     int getHour();
15     int &badSetHour( int ); // DANGEROUS reference return
16  private:
17     int hour;
18     int minute;
19     int second;
20  }; // end class Time
21
22  #endif
```

Fig. 17.14 | Time class declaration.

```
1   // Fig. 17.15: Time.cpp
2   // Time class member-function definitions.
3   #include <stdexcept>
4   #include "Time.h" // include definition of class Time
5   using namespace std;
6
7   // constructor function to initialize private data; calls member function
8   // setTime to set variables; default values are 0 (see class definition)
9   Time::Time( int hr, int min, int sec )
10  {
11     setTime( hr, min, sec );
12  } // end Time constructor
```

Fig. 17.15 | Time class member-function definitions. (Part 1 of 2.)

```
13
14    // set values of hour, minute and second
15    void Time::setTime( int h, int m, int s )
16    {
17       // validate hour, minute and second
18       if ( ( h >= 0 && h < 24 ) && ( m >= 0 && m < 60 ) &&
19          ( s >= 0 && s < 60 ) )
20       {
21          hour = h;
22          minute = m;
23          second = s;
24       } // end if
25       else
26          throw invalid_argument(
27             "hour, minute and/or second was out of range" );
28    } // end function setTime
29
30    // return hour value
31    int Time::getHour()
32    {
33       return hour;
34    } // end function getHour
35
36    // POOR PRACTICE: Returning a reference to a private data member.
37    int &Time::badSetHour( int hh )
38    {
39       if ( hh >= 0 && hh < 24 )
40          hour = hh;
41       else
42          throw invalid_argument( "hour must be 0-23" );
43
44       return hour; // DANGEROUS reference return
45    } // end function badSetHour
```

Fig. 17.15 | Time class member-function definitions. (Part 2 of 2.)

Figure 17.16 declares Time object t (line 10) and reference hourRef (line 13), which is initialized with the reference returned by the call t.badSetHour(20). Line 15 displays the value of the alias hourRef. This shows how hourRef *breaks the encapsulation of the class*—statements in main should not have access to the private data of the class. Next, line 16 uses the alias to set the value of hour to 30 (an invalid value) and line 17 displays the value returned by function getHour to show that assigning a value to hourRef actually modifies the private data in the Time object t. Finally, line 21 uses the badSetHour function call itself as an *lvalue* and assigns 74 (another invalid value) to the reference returned by the function. Line 26 again displays the value returned by function getHour to show that assigning a value to the result of the function call in line 21 modifies the private data in the Time object t.

Error-Prevention Tip 17.4

Returning a reference or a pointer to a private data member breaks the encapsulation of the class and makes the client code dependent on the representation of the class's data; this is a dangerous practice that should be avoided.

```
1   // Fig. 17.16: fig17_16.cpp
2   // Demonstrating a public member function that
3   // returns a reference to a private data member.
4   #include <iostream>
5   #include "Time.h" // include definition of class Time
6   using namespace std;
7
8   int main()
9   {
10     Time t; // create Time object
11
12     // initialize hourRef with the reference returned by badSetHour
13     int &hourRef = t.badSetHour( 20 ); // 20 is a valid hour
14
15     cout << "Valid hour before modification: " << hourRef;
16     hourRef = 30; // use hourRef to set invalid value in Time object t
17     cout << "\nInvalid hour after modification: " << t.getHour();
18
19     // Dangerous: Function call that returns
20     // a reference can be used as an lvalue!
21     t.badSetHour( 12 ) = 74; // assign another invalid value to hour
22
23     cout << "\n\n****************************************************\n"
24        << "POOR PROGRAMMING PRACTICE!!!!!!!!\n"
25        << "t.badSetHour( 12 ) as an lvalue, invalid hour: "
26        << t.getHour()
27        << "\n****************************************************" << endl;
28  } // end main
```

```
Valid hour before modification: 20
Invalid hour after modification: 30

****************************************************
POOR PROGRAMMING PRACTICE!!!!!!!!
t.badSetHour( 12 ) as an lvalue, invalid hour: 74
****************************************************
```

Fig. 17.16 | Demonstrating a public member function that returns a reference to a private data member.

17.10 Default Memberwise Assignment

The assignment operator (=) can be used to assign an object to another object of the same type. By default, such assignment is performed by **memberwise assignment**—each data member of the object on the right of the assignment operator is assigned individually to the *same* data member in the object on the left of the assignment operator. Figures 17.17–17.18 define class Date for use in this example. Line 18 of Fig. 17.19 uses **default memberwise assignment** to assign the data members of Date object date1 to the corresponding data members of Date object date2. In this case, the month member of date1 is assigned to the month member of date2, the day member of date1 is assigned to the day member of date2 and the year member of date1 is assigned to the year member of date2. [*Caution:* Memberwise assignment can cause serious problems when used with a class whose data members contain pointers to dynamically allocated memory; we discuss these problems in Chapter 19 and show how to deal with them.] The Date constructor does not contain any error checking; we leave this to the exercises.

Objects may be passed as function arguments and may be returned from functions. Such passing and returning is performed using pass-by-value by default—a copy of the object is passed or returned. In such cases, C++ creates a new object and uses a **copy constructor** to copy the original object's values into the new object. For each class, the compiler provides a default copy constructor that copies each member of the original object

```cpp
1  // Fig. 17.17: Date.h
2  // Date class declaration. (Member functions are defined in Date.cpp.)
3
4  // prevent multiple inclusions of header
5  #ifndef DATE_H
6  #define DATE_H
7
8  // class Date definition
9  class Date
10 {
11 public:
12    Date( int = 1, int = 1, int = 2000 ); // default constructor
13    void print();
14 private:
15    int month;
16    int day;
17    int year;
18 }; // end class Date
19
20 #endif
```

Fig. 17.17 | Date class declaration. (Member functions are defined in Data.cpp.)

```cpp
1  // Fig. 17.18: Date.cpp
2  // Date class member-function definitions.
3  #include <iostream>
4  #include "Date.h" // include definition of class Date from Date.h
5  using namespace std;
6
7  // Date constructor (should do range checking)
8  Date::Date( int m, int d, int y )
9  {
10    month = m;
11    day = d;
12    year = y;
13 } // end constructor Date
14
15 // print Date in the format mm/dd/yyyy
16 void Date::print()
17 {
```

Fig. 17.18 | Date class member-function definitions. (Part 1 of 2.)

```
18        cout << month << '/' << day << '/' << year;
19    } // end function print
```

Fig. 17.18 | Date class member-function definitions. (Part 2 of 2.)

```
1    // Fig. 17.19: fig17_19.cpp
2    // Demonstrating that class objects can be assigned
3    // to each other using default memberwise assignment.
4    #include <iostream>
5    #include "Date.h" // include definition of class Date from Date.h
6    using namespace std;
7
8    int main()
9    {
10       Date date1( 7, 4, 2004 );
11       Date date2; // date2 defaults to 1/1/2000
12
13       cout << "date1 = ";
14       date1.print();
15       cout << "\ndate2 = ";
16       date2.print();
17
18       date2 = date1; // default memberwise assignment
19
20       cout << "\n\nAfter default memberwise assignment, date2 = ";
21       date2.print();
22       cout << endl;
23    } // end main
```

```
date1 = 7/4/2004
date2 = 1/1/2000

After default memberwise assignment, date2 = 7/4/2004
```

Fig. 17.19 | Demonstrating that class objcts can be assigned to each other by default memberwise assignment.

into the corresponding member of the new object. Like memberwise assignment, copy constructors can cause serious problems when used with a class whose data members contain pointers to dynamically allocated memory. Chapter 19 discusses how to define customized copy constructors that properly copy objects containing pointers to dynamically allocated memory.

Performance Tip 17.3

Passing an object by value is good from a security standpoint, because the called function has no access to the original object in the caller, but pass-by-value can degrade performance when making a copy of a large object. An object can be passed by reference by passing either a pointer or a reference to the object. Pass-by-reference offers good performance but is weaker from a security standpoint, because the called function is given access to the original object. Pass-by-const-reference is a safe, good-performing alternative (this can be implemented with a const reference parameter or with a pointer-to-const-data parameter).

17.11 Wrap-Up

This chapter deepened our coverage of classes, using a rich Time class case study to introduce several new features. You saw that member functions are usually shorter than global functions because member functions can directly access an object's data members, so the member functions can receive fewer arguments than functions in procedural programming languages. You learned how to use the arrow operator to access an object's members via a pointer of the object's class type.

You learned that member functions have class scope—the member function's name is known only to the class's other members unless referred to via an object of the class, a reference to an object of the class, a pointer to an object of the class or the scope resolution operator. We also discussed access functions (commonly used to retrieve the values of data members or to test the truth or falsity of conditions) and utility functions (private member functions that support the operation of the class's public member functions).

You learned that a constructor can specify default arguments that enable it to be called in a variety of ways. You also learned that any constructor that can be called with no arguments is a default constructor and that there can be at most one default constructor per class. We discussed destructors and their purpose of performing termination housekeeping on an object of a class before that object is destroyed. We also demonstrated the order in which an object's constructors and destructors are called.

We demonstrated the problems that can occur when a member function returns a reference to a private data member, which breaks the encapsulation of the class. We also showed that objects of the same type can be assigned to one another using default memberwise assignment. We also discussed the benefits of using class libraries to enhance the speed with which code can be created and to increase the quality of software.

Chapter 18 presents additional class features. We'll demonstrate how const can be used to indicate that a member function does not modify an object of a class. You'll build classes with composition, which allows a class to contain objects of other classes as members. We'll show how a class can allow friend functions to access the class's non-public members. We'll also show how a class's non-static member functions can use a special pointer named this to access an object's members.

Summary

Section 17.2 *Time Class Case Study*
- Preprocessor directives #ifndef (which means "if not defined"; p. 654) and #endif (p. 654) are used to prevent multiple inclusions of a header. If the code between these directives has not previously been included in an application, #define (p. 654) defines a name that can be used to prevent future inclusions, and the code is included in the source code file.

- Data members cannot be initialized where they're declared in the class body (except for a class's static const data members of integral or enum types). Initialize these data members in the class's constructor (as there is no default initialization for data members of fundamental types).

- A class's functions can throw (p. 656) exceptions (such as invalid_argument; p. 656) to indicate invalid data.

- Stream manipulator setfill (p. 656) specifies the fill character (p. 656) that's displayed when an integer is output in a field that's wider than the number of digits in the value.

- By default, the fill characters appear before the digits in the number.
- Stream manipulator `setfill` is a "sticky" setting, meaning that once the fill character is set, it applies for all subsequent fields being printed.
- Even though a member function declared in a class definition may be defined outside that class definition (and "tied" to the class via the scope resolution operator), that member function is still within that class's scope.
- If a member function is defined in the body of a class definition, the member function is implicitly declared inline.
- Classes can include objects of other classes as members or they may be derived (p. 659) from other classes that provide attributes and behaviors the new classes can use.

Section 17.3 Class Scope and Accessing Class Members
- A class's data members and member functions belong to that class's scope.
- Nonmember functions are defined at global namespace scope.
- Within a class's scope, class members are immediately accessible by all of that class's member functions and can be referenced by name.
- Outside a class's scope, class members are referenced through one of the handles on an object—an object name, a reference to an object or a pointer to an object.
- Member functions of a class can be overloaded, but only by other member functions of that class.
- To overload a member function, provide in the class definition a prototype for each version of the overloaded function, and provide a separate definition for each version of the function.
- Variables declared in a member function have local scope and are known only to that function.
- If a member function defines a variable with the same name as a variable with class scope (p. 657), the class-scope variable is hidden by the block-scope variable in the local scope.
- The dot member selection operator (`.`) is preceded by an object's name or by a reference to an object to access the object's `public` members.
- The arrow member selection operator (`->`; p. 660) is preceded by a pointer to an object to access that object's `public` members.

Section 17.4 Separating Interface from Implementation
- Headers contain some portions of a class's implementation and hints about others. Inline member functions, for example, should be in a header, so that when the compiler compiles a client, the client can include the `inline` function definition in place.
- A class's `private` members that are listed in the class definition in the header are visible to clients, even though the clients may not access the `private` members.

Section 17.5 Access Functions and Utility Functions
- A utility function is a `private` member function that supports the operation of the class's `public` member functions. Utility functions are not intended to be used by clients of a class.

Section 17.6 Time Class Case Study: Constructors with Default Arguments
- Like other functions, constructors can specify default arguments.

Section 17.7 Destructors
- A class's destructor (p. 670) is called implicitly when an object of the class is destroyed.
- The name of the destructor for a class is the tilde (~) character followed by the class name.
- A destructor does not release an object's storage—it performs termination housekeeping (p. 671) before the system reclaims an object's memory, so the memory may be reused to hold new objects.

- A destructor receives no parameters and returns no value. A class may have only one destructor.

- If you do not explicitly provide a destructor, the compiler creates an "empty" destructor, so every class has exactly one destructor.

Section 17.8 When Constructors and Destructors Are Called

- The order in which constructors and destructors are called depends on the order in which execution enters and leaves the scopes where the objects are instantiated.

- Generally, destructor calls are made in the reverse order of the corresponding constructor calls, but the storage classes of objects can alter the order in which destructors are called.

Section 17.9 Time Class Case Study: A Subtle Trap—Returning a Reference to a private Data Member

- A reference to an object is an alias for the name of the object and, hence, may be used on the left side of an assignment statement. In this context, the reference makes a perfectly acceptable *lvalue* that can receive a value.

- If the function returns a const reference, then the reference cannot be used as a modifiable *lvalue*.

Section 17.10 Default Memberwise Assignment

- The assignment operator (=) can be used to assign an object to another object of the same type. By default, such assignment is performed by memberwise assignment (p. 677).

- Objects may be passed by value to or returned by value from functions. C++ creates a new object and uses a copy constructor (p. 678) to copy the original object's values into the new object.

- For each class, the compiler provides a default copy constructor that copies each member of the original object into the corresponding member of the new object.

Self-Review Exercises

17.1   Fill in the blanks in each of the following:

    a) Class members are accessed via the _____ operator in conjunction with the name of an object (or reference to an object) of the class or via the _____ operator in conjunction with a pointer to an object of the class.

    b) Class members specified as _____ are accessible only to member functions of the class and friends of the class.

    c) Class members specified as _____ are accessible anywhere an object of the class is in scope.

    d) _____ can be used to assign an object of a class to another object of the same class.

17.2   Find the error(s) in each of the following and explain how to correct it (them):

    a) Assume the class Rectangle is declared as below:

```
class Rectangle
{
float m=9.56;
int z;
Rectangle()
{}
};
```

    b) Assume the following prototype is declared in class Rectangle:

```
float Rectangle( int, int );
```

c) The following is a partial definition of class `Rectangle`:

```
class Rectangle
{
Rectangle()
{}
~()
{}
}; // end class Rectangle
```

Answers to Self-Review Exercises

17.1 a) dot (.), arrow (->). b) `private`. c) `public`. d) Default memberwise assignment (performed by the assignment operator).

17.2 a) *Error:* Data members cannot be initialized within the class.
Correction: Replace `float m=9.56` with `float m`.
b) *Error:* Constructors are not allowed to return values.
Correction: Remove the return type `float` from the declaration.
c) *Error:* Name of the destructor is missing.
Correction: `~Rectangle(){}`

Exercises

17.3 *(Scope Resolution Operator)* What's the purpose of the scope resolution operator?

17.4 *(Enhancing Class `Time`)* Provide a constructor that's capable of using the current time from the `time` and `localtime` functions—declared in the C++ Standard Library header `<ctime>`—to initialize an object of the `Time` class.

17.5 *(Complex Class)* Create a class called `Complex` for performing arithmetic with complex numbers. Write a program to test your class. Complex numbers have the form

```
realPart + imaginaryPart * i
```

where *i* is

$$\sqrt{-1}$$

Use double variables to represent the `private` data of the class. Provide a constructor that enables an object of this class to be initialized when it's declared. The constructor should contain default values in case no initializers are provided. Provide `public` member functions that perform the following tasks:

a) Multiplying two `Complex` numbers: The real parts are multiplied together and the imaginary parts are multiplied together.
b) Dividing two `Complex` numbers: The numerator and denominator are multiplied with the conjugant of the denominator.
c) Printing `Complex` numbers in the form (x, y), where x is the real part and y is the imaginary part.

17.6 *(Rational Class)* Create a class called `Rational` for performing arithmetic with fractions. Write a program to test your class.

Use integer variables to represent the `private` data of the class—the numerator and the denominator. Provide a constructor that enables an object of this class to be initialized when it's declared. The constructor should contain default values in case no initializers are provided and should store the fraction in reduced form. For example, the fraction

$$\frac{2}{4}$$

would be stored in the object as 1 in the numerator and 2 in the denominator. Provide public member functions that perform each of the following tasks:

a) Adding two Rational numbers. The result should be stored in reduced form.
b) Subtracting two Rational numbers. The result should be stored in reduced form.
c) Multiplying two Rational numbers. The result should be stored in reduced form.
d) Dividing two Rational numbers. The result should be stored in reduced form.
e) Printing Rational numbers in the form a/b, where a is the numerator and b is the denominator.
f) Printing Rational numbers in floating-point format.

17.7 *(Enhancing Class Time)* Modify the Time class of Figs. 17.8–17.9 to include a tick member function that increments the time stored in a Time object by one second. Write a program that tests the tick member function in a loop that prints the time in standard format during each iteration of the loop to illustrate that the tick member function works correctly. Be sure to test the following cases:

a) Incrementing into the next minute.
b) Incrementing into the next hour.
c) Incrementing into the next day (i.e., 11:59:59 PM to 12:00:00 AM).

17.8 *(Enhancing Class Date)* Modify the Date class of Figs. 17.17–17.18 to perform error checking on the initializer values for data members month, day and year. Also, provide a member function nextDay to increment the day by one. Write a program that tests function nextDay in a loop that prints the date during each iteration to illustrate that nextDay works correctly. Be sure to test the following cases:

a) Incrementing into the next month.
b) Incrementing into the next year.

17.9 *(Combining Class Time and Class Date)* Combine the modified Time class of Exercise 17.7 and the modified Date class of Exercise 17.8 into one class called DateAndTime. (In Chapter 20, we'll discuss inheritance, which will enable us to accomplish this task quickly without modifying the existing class definitions.) Modify the tick function to call the nextDay function if the time increments into the next day. Modify functions printStandard and printUniversal to output the date and time. Write a program to test the new class DateAndTime. Specifically, test incrementing the time into the next day.

17.10 *(Returning Error Indicators from Class Time's set Functions)* Modify the *set* functions in the Time class of Figs. 17.8–17.9 to return appropriate error values if an attempt is made to *set* a data member of an object of class Time to an invalid value. Write a program that tests your new version of class Time. Display error messages when *set* functions return error values.

17.11 *(Square Class)* Create a class Square with attribute side, with the default value 10. Provide member functions that calculate the perimeter and the area of the square. Also, provide *set* and *get* functions for the side attribute. The *set* function should verify that side is an integer number larger than 0 and less than 50.

17.12 *(Enhancing Class Square)* Create a more sophisticated Square class than the one you created in Exercise 17.11. This class stores only the Cartesian coordinates of the four corners of the square. The constructor calls a *set* function that accepts four sets of coordinates and verifies that none of these *x*- or *y*-coordinate is larger than 20. The *set* function also verifies that the supplied coordinates do, in fact, specify a square. Provide member functions that calculate the side, perimeter and area.

17.13 *(Enhancing Class Square)* Modify class Square from Exercise 17.12 to include a draw function that displays the square inside a 25-by-25 box enclosing the portion of the first quadrant in which the square resides. Include a setFillCharacter function to specify the character out of which the body of the square will be drawn. Include a setPerimeterCharacter function to specify the character that will be used to draw the border of the square. If you feel ambitious, you might include functions to scale the size of the square, rotate it, and move it around within the designated portion of the first quadrant.

17.14 *(HugeInteger Class)* Create a class HugeInteger that uses a 40-element array of digits to store integers as large as 40 digits each. Provide member functions input, output, add and subtract. For comparing HugeInteger objects, provide functions isEqualTo, isNotEqualTo, isGreaterThan, isLessThan, isGreaterThanOrEqualTo and isLessThanOrEqualTo—each of these is a "predicate" function that simply returns true if the relationship holds between the two HugeIntegers and returns false if the relationship does not hold. Also, provide a predicate function isZero. If you feel ambitious, provide member functions multiply, divide and modulus.

17.15 *(TicTacToe Class)* Create a class TicTacToe that will enable you to write a complete program to play the game of tic-tac-toe. The class contains as private data a 3-by-3 two-dimensional array of integers. The constructor should initialize the empty board to all zeros. Allow two human players. Wherever the first player moves, place a 1 in the specified square. Place a 2 wherever the second player moves. Each move must be to an empty square. After each move, determine whether the game has been won or is a draw. If you feel ambitious, modify your program so that the computer makes the moves for one of the players. Also, allow the player to specify whether he or she wants to go first or second. If you feel exceptionally ambitious, develop a program that will play three-dimensional tic-tac-toe on a 4-by-4-by-4 board. [*Caution:* This is an extremely challenging project that could take many weeks of effort!]

18

Classes: A Deeper Look, Part 2

But what, to serve our private ends,
Forbids the cheating of our friends?
—Charles Churchill

Instead of this absurd division into sexes they ought to class people as static and dynamic.
—Evelyn Waugh

Have no friends not equal to yourself.
—Confucius

Objectives

In this chapter you'll learn:

- To specify **const** (constant) objects and **const** member functions.

- To create objects composed of other objects.

- To use **friend** functions and **friend** classes.

- To use the **this** pointer.

- To use **static** data members and member functions.

- The concept of a container class.

- To use proxy classes to hide implementation details from a class's clients.

18.1   Introduction

In this chapter, we continue our study of classes with several more advanced topics. We use const objects and const member functions to prevent modifications of objects and enforce the principle of least privilege. We discuss *composition*—a form of reuse in which a class can have objects of other classes as members. Next, we introduce *friendship*, which enables a class designer to specify nonmember functions that can access a class's non-public members—a technique that is often used in operator overloading (Chapter 19) for performance reasons. We discuss a special pointer (called this), which is an *implicit* argument to each of a class's non-static member functions. It allows those member functions to access the correct object's data members and non-static member functions. We motivate the need for static class members and show how to use static data members and member functions in your own classes. Finally, we show how to create a proxy class to hide a class's implementation details (including its private data) from its clients.

18.2   const (Constant) Objects and const Member Functions

Let's see how the principle of least privilege applies to objects. Some objects need to be modifiable and some do not. You may use keyword const to specify that an object *is not* modifiable and that any attempt to modify the object should result in a compilation error. The statement

```
const Time noon( 12, 0, 0 );
```

declares a const object noon of class Time and initializes it to 12 noon.

Software Engineering Observation 18.1

Attempts to modify a const object are caught at compile time rather than causing execution-time errors.

Performance Tip 18.1

Declaring variables and objects const when appropriate can improve performance—compilers can perform optimizations on constants that cannot be performed on variables.

C++ disallows member function calls for const objects unless the member functions themselves are also declared const. This is true even for *get* member functions that do not modify the object.

A member function is specified as const *both* in its prototype by inserting the keyword const after the function's parameter list and, in the case of the function definition, before the left brace that begins the function body.

Common Programming Error 18.1

Defining as const a member function that modifies a data member of the object is a compilation error.

Common Programming Error 18.2

Defining as const a member function that calls a non-const member function of the class on the same object is a compilation error.

Common Programming Error 18.3

Invoking a non-const member function on a const object is a compilation error.

Software Engineering Observation 18.2

A const member function can be overloaded with a non-const version. The compiler chooses which overloaded member function to use based on the object on which the function is invoked. If the object is const, the compiler uses the const version. If the object is not const, the compiler uses the non-const version.

An interesting problem arises for constructors and destructors, each of which typically modifies objects. A constructor *must* be allowed to modify an object so that the object can be initialized properly. A destructor must be able to perform its termination housekeeping chores before an object's memory is reclaimed by the system.

Common Programming Error 18.4

Attempting to declare a constructor or destructor const is a compilation error.

Defining and Using const Member Functions

The program of Figs. 18.1–18.3 modifies class Time of Figs. 17.8–17.9 by making its *get* functions and printUniversal function const. In the header Time.h (Fig. 18.1), lines 19–21 and 24 now include keyword const after each function prototype's parameter list. The corresponding definition of each function in Fig. 18.2 (lines 53, 59, 65 and 71, respectively) also specifies keyword const after each function's parameter list.

```
1   // Fig. 18.1: Time.h
2   // Time class definition with const member functions.
3   // Member functions defined in Time.cpp.
4   #ifndef TIME_H
5   #define TIME_H
6
7   class Time
8   {
```

Fig. 18.1 | Time class definition with const member functions. (Part 1 of 2.)

```
 9   public:
10      Time( int = 0, int = 0, int = 0 ); // default constructor
11
12      // set functions
13      void setTime( int, int, int ); // set time
14      void setHour( int ); // set hour
15      void setMinute( int ); // set minute
16      void setSecond( int ); // set second
17
18      // get functions (normally declared const)
19      int getHour() const; // return hour
20      int getMinute() const; // return minute
21      int getSecond() const; // return second
22
23      // print functions (normally declared const)
24      void printUniversal() const; // print universal time
25      void printStandard(); // print standard time (should be const)
26   private:
27      int hour; // 0 - 23 (24-hour clock format)
28      int minute; // 0 - 59
29      int second; // 0 - 59
30   }; // end class Time
31
32   #endif
```

Fig. 18.1 | Time class definition with const member functions. (Part 2 of 2.)

```
 1   // Fig. 18.2: Time.cpp
 2   // Time class member-function definitions.
 3   #include <iostream>
 4   #include <iomanip>
 5   #include <stdexcept>
 6   #include "Time.h" // include definition of class Time
 7   using namespace std;
 8
 9   // constructor function to initialize private data;
10   // calls member function setTime to set variables;
11   // default values are 0 (see class definition)
12   Time::Time( int hour, int minute, int second )
13   {
14      setTime( hour, minute, second );
15   } // end Time constructor
16
17   // set hour, minute and second values
18   void Time::setTime( int hour, int minute, int second )
19   {
20      setHour( hour );
21      setMinute( minute );
22      setSecond( second );
23   } // end function setTime
24
```

Fig. 18.2 | Time class member-function definitions. (Part 1 of 3.)

```
25    // set hour value
26    void Time::setHour( int h )
27    {
28       if ( h >= 0 && h < 24 )
29          hour = h;
30       else
31          throw invalid_argument( "hour must be 0-23" );
32    } // end function setHour
33
34    // set minute value
35    void Time::setMinute( int m )
36    {
37       if ( m >= 0 && m < 60 )
38          minute = m;
39       else
40          throw invalid_argument( "minute must be 0-59" );
41    } // end function setMinute
42
43    // set second value
44    void Time::setSecond( int s )
45    {
46       if ( s >= 0 && s < 60 )
47          second = s;
48       else
49          throw invalid_argument( "second must be 0-59" );
50    } // end function setSecond
51
52    // return hour value
53    int Time::getHour() const // get functions should be const
54    {
55       return hour;
56    } // end function getHour
57
58    // return minute value
59    int Time::getMinute() const
60    {
61       return minute;
62    } // end function getMinute
63
64    // return second value
65    int Time::getSecond() const
66    {
67       return second;
68    } // end function getSecond
69
70    // print Time in universal-time format (HH:MM:SS)
71    void Time::printUniversal() const
72    {
73       cout << setfill( '0' ) << setw( 2 ) << hour << ":"
74          << setw( 2 ) << minute << ":" << setw( 2 ) << second;
75    } // end function printUniversal
76
```

Fig. 18.2 | Time class member-function definitions. (Part 2 of 3.)

```
77   // print Time in standard-time format (HH:MM:SS AM or PM)
78   void Time::printStandard() // note lack of const declaration
79   {
80      cout << ( ( hour == 0 || hour == 12 ) ? 12 : hour % 12 )
81         << ":" << setfill( '0' ) << setw( 2 ) << minute
82         << ":" << setw( 2 ) << second << ( hour < 12 ? " AM" : " PM" );
83   } // end function printStandard
```

Fig. 18.2 | Time class member-function definitions. (Part 3 of 3.)

Figure 18.3 instantiates two Time objects—non-const object wakeUp (line 7) and const object noon (line 8). The program attempts to invoke non-const member functions setHour (line 13) and printStandard (line 20) on the const object noon. In each case, the compiler generates an error message. The program also illustrates the three other member-function-call combinations on objects—a non-const member function on a non-const object (line 11), a const member function on a non-const object (line 15) and a const member function on a const object (lines 17–18). The error messages generated for non-const member functions called on a const object are shown in the output window.

```
1    // Fig. 18.3: fig18_03.cpp
2    // Attempting to access a const object with non-const member functions.
3    #include "Time.h" // include Time class definition
4
5    int main()
6    {
7       Time wakeUp( 6, 45, 0 ); // non-constant object
8       const Time noon( 12, 0, 0 ); // constant object
9
10                                 // OBJECT     MEMBER FUNCTION
11      wakeUp.setHour( 18 );      // non-const  non-const
12
13      noon.setHour( 12 );        // const      non-const
14
15      wakeUp.getHour();          // non-const  const
16
17      noon.getMinute();          // const      const
18      noon.printUniversal();     // const      const
19
20      noon.printStandard();      // const      non-const
21   } // end main
```

Microsoft Visual C++ compiler error messages:

```
C:\examples\ch18\fig18_01_03\fig18_03.cpp(13) : error C2662:
   'Time::setHour' : cannot convert 'this' pointer from 'const Time' to 'Time &'
      Conversion loses qualifiers
C:\examples\ch18\fig18_01_03\fig18_03.cpp(20) : error C2662:
   'Time::printStandard' : cannot convert 'this' pointer from 'const Time' to
'Time &'
      Conversion loses qualifiers
```

Fig. 18.3 | Attempting to access a const objects with non-const member functions.

A constructor must be a non-const member function (Fig. 18.2, lines 11–14), but it can still be used to initialize a const object (Fig. 18.3, line 8). The Time constructor's definition (Fig. 18.2, lines 11–14) shows that it calls another non-const member function—setTime (lines 17–22)—to perform the initialization of a Time object. Invoking a non-const member function from the constructor call as part of the initialization of a const object is allowed. The "constness" of a const object is enforced from the time the constructor *completes* initialization of the object until that object's destructor is called.

Line 20 in Fig. 18.3 generates a compilation error even though member function printStandard of class Time *does not* modify the object on which it's invoked. The fact that a member function does not modify an object is not sufficient to indicate that the function is a constant function—the function must *explicitly* be declared const.

Initializing a const Data Member with a Member Initializer

The program of Figs. 18.4–18.6 introduces using **member initializer syntax**. All data members *can* be initialized using member initializer syntax, but const data members and data members that are references *must* be initialized using member initializers. Later in this chapter, we'll see that member objects must be initialized this way as well.

```
1   // Fig. 18.4: Increment.h
2   // Definition of class Increment.
3   #ifndef INCREMENT_H
4   #define INCREMENT_H
5
6   class Increment
7   {
8   public:
9      Increment( int c = 0, int i = 1 ); // default constructor
10
11     // function addIncrement definition
12     void addIncrement()
13     {
14        count += increment;
15     } // end function addIncrement
16
17     void print() const; // prints count and increment
18  private:
19     int count;
20     const int increment; // const data member
21  }; // end class Increment
22
23  #endif
```

Fig. 18.4 | Increment class definition containing non-const data member count and const data member increment.

```
1   // Fig. 18.5: Increment.cpp
2   // Member-function definitions for class Increment demonstrate using a
3   // member initializer to initialize a constant of a built-in data type.
```

Fig. 18.5 | Member initializer used to initialize a constant of a built-in data type. (Part 1 of 2.)

```
4    #include <iostream>
5    #include "Increment.h" // include definition of class Increment
6    using namespace std;
7
8    // constructor
9    Increment::Increment( int c, int i )
10      : count( c ), // initializer for non-const member
11        increment( i ) // required initializer for const member
12   {
13      // empty body
14   } // end constructor Increment
15
16   // print count and increment values
17   void Increment::print() const
18   {
19      cout << "count = " << count << ", increment = " << increment << endl;
20   } // end function print
```

Fig. 18.5 | Member initializer used to initialize a constant of a built-in data type. (Part 2 of 2.)

```
1    // Fig. 18.6: fig18_06.cpp
2    // Program to test class Increment.
3    #include <iostream>
4    #include "Increment.h" // include definition of class Increment
5    using namespace std;
6
7    int main()
8    {
9       Increment value( 10, 5 );
10
11      cout << "Before incrementing: ";
12      value.print();
13
14      for ( int j = 1; j <= 3; ++j )
15      {
16         value.addIncrement();
17         cout << "After increment " << j << ": ";
18         value.print();
19      } // end for
20   } // end main
```

```
Before incrementing: count = 10, increment = 5
After increment 1: count = 15, increment = 5
After increment 2: count = 20, increment = 5
After increment 3: count = 25, increment = 5
```

Fig. 18.6 | Invoking an Increment object's print and addIncrement member functions.

The constructor definition (Fig. 18.5, lines 9–14) uses a **member initializer list** to initialize class Increment's data members—non-const integer count and const integer increment (declared in lines 19–20 of Fig. 18.4). *Member initializers* appear between a constructor's parameter list and the left brace that begins the constructor's body. The member initializer list (Fig. 18.5, lines 10–11) is separated from the parameter list with a colon (:). Each member initializer consists of the data member name followed by parentheses containing the member's initial value. In this example, count is initialized with the value of constructor parameter c and increment is initialized with the value of constructor parameter i. Multiple member initializers are separated by commas. Also, the member initializer list executes *before* the body of the constructor executes.

Software Engineering Observation 18.3

A const object cannot be modified by assignment, so it must be initialized. When a data member of a class is declared const, a member initializer must be used to provide the constructor with the initial value of the data member for an object of the class. The same is true for references.

Why Is Function **print** Declared **const**?

Function print (Fig. 18.5, lines 17–20) is declared const. It might seem strange to label this function const, because a program probably will never have a const Increment object. However, it's possible that a program will have a const reference to an Increment object or a pointer to const that points to an Increment object. Typically, this occurs when objects of class Increment are passed to functions or returned from functions. In these cases, only class Increment's const member functions can be called through the reference or pointer. Thus, it's reasonable to declare function print as const—doing so prevents errors in these situations where an Increment object is treated as a const object.

Error-Prevention Tip 18.1

Declare as const all of a class's member functions that do not modify the object in which they operate. Occasionally this may seem inappropriate, because you'll have no intention of creating const objects of that class or accessing objects of that class through const references or pointers to const. Declaring such member functions const does offer a benefit, though. If the member function is inadvertently written to modify the object, the compiler will issue an error message.

Erroneously Attempting to Initialize a **const** Data Member with an Assignment

Figure 18.7 shows the compilation errors caused by attempting to initialize const data member increment with an assignment statement in the Increment constructor's body rather than with a member initializer.

Microsoft Visual C++ compiler error messages:

```
C:\examples\ch18\consterror\Increment.cpp(10) : error C2758:
   'Increment::increment' : must be initialized in constructor base/member
   initializer list
      C:\examples\ch18\consterror\increment.h(20) : see
         declaration of 'Increment::increment'
C:\examples\ch18\consterror\Increment.cpp(12) : error C2166:
   l-value specifies const object
```

Fig. 18.7 | Compilation errors generated by attempting to initialize a const data member in the constructor's body rather than in the member initializer list. (Part 1 of 2.)

GNU C++ compiler error messages:

```
Increment.cpp:9: error: uninitialized member 'Increment::increment' with
   'const' type 'const int'
Increment.cpp:12: error: assignment of read-only data-member
   'Increment::increment'
```

Fig. 18.7 | Compilation errors generated by attempting to initialize a `const` data member in the constructor's body rather than in the member initializer list. (Part 2 of 2.)

Common Programming Error 18.5

Not providing a member initializer for a `const` data member is a compilation error.

18.3 Composition: Objects as Members of Classes

An `AlarmClock` object needs to know when it's supposed to sound its alarm, so why not include a `Time` object as a member of the `AlarmClock` class? Such a capability is called composition and is sometimes referred to as a *has-a* relationship—*a class can have objects of other classes as members.*

Software Engineering Observation 18.4

A common form of software reusability is composition, in which a class has objects of other classes as members.

Previously, we saw how to pass arguments to the constructor of an object we created in main. Now we show how *an object's constructor can pass arguments to member-object constructors via member initializers.*

Software Engineering Observation 18.5

Member objects are constructed in the order in which they're declared in the class definition (not in the order they're listed in the constructor's member initializer list) and before their enclosing class objects (sometimes called host objects) are constructed.

The next program uses classes `Date` (Figs. 18.8–18.9) and `Employee` (Figs. 18.10–18.11) to demonstrate composition. Class `Employee`'s definition (Fig. 18.10) contains `private` data members `firstName`, `lastName`, `birthDate` and `hireDate`. Members `birthDate` and `hireDate` are `const` objects of class `Date`, which contains `private` data members `month`, `day` and `year`. The `Employee` constructor's header (Fig. 18.11, lines 10–11) specifies that the constructor has four parameters (`first`, `last`, `dateOfBirth` and `dateOfHire`). The first two parameters are passed via member initializers to the `string` class constructor. The last two are passed via member initializers to the `Date` class constructor.

```
1   // Fig. 18.8: Date.h
2   // Date class definition; member functions defined in Date.cpp
3   #ifndef DATE_H
```

Fig. 18.8 | Date class definition; member functions defined in `Date.cpp` (Part 1 of 2.)

```
4   #define DATE_H
5
6   class Date
7   {
8   public:
9      static const int monthsPerYear = 12; // number of months in a year
10     Date( int = 1, int = 1, int = 1900 ); // default constructor
11     void print() const; // print date in month/day/year format
12     ~Date(); // provided to confirm destruction order
13  private:
14     int month; // 1-12 (January-December)
15     int day; // 1-31 based on month
16     int year; // any year
17
18     // utility function to check if day is proper for month and year
19     int checkDay( int ) const;
20  }; // end class Date
21
22  #endif
```

Fig. 18.8 | Date class definition; member functions defined in `Date.cpp` (Part 2 of 2.)

```
1   // Fig. 18.9: Date.cpp
2   // Date class member-function definitions.
3   #include <iostream>
4   #include <stdexcept>
5   #include "Date.h" // include Date class definition
6   using namespace std;
7
8   // constructor confirms proper value for month; calls
9   // utility function checkDay to confirm proper value for day
10  Date::Date( int mn, int dy, int yr )
11  {
12     if ( mn > 0 && mn <= monthsPerYear ) // validate the month
13        month = mn;
14     else
15        throw invalid_argument( "month must be 1-12" );
16
17     year = yr; // could validate yr
18     day = checkDay( dy ); // validate the day
19
20     // output Date object to show when its constructor is called
21     cout << "Date object constructor for date ";
22     print();
23     cout << endl;
24  } // end Date constructor
25
26  // print Date object in form month/day/year
27  void Date::print() const
28  {
29     cout << month << '/' << day << '/' << year;
30  } // end function print
```

Fig. 18.9 | Date class member-function definitions. (Part 1 of 2.)

```
31
32   // output Date object to show when its destructor is called
33   Date::~Date()
34   {
35      cout << "Date object destructor for date ";
36      print();
37      cout << endl;
38   } // end ~Date destructor
39
40   // utility function to confirm proper day value based on
41   // month and year; handles leap years, too
42   int Date::checkDay( int testDay ) const
43   {
44      static const int daysPerMonth[ monthsPerYear + 1 ] =
45         { 0, 31, 28, 31, 30, 31, 30, 31, 31, 30, 31, 30, 31 };
46
47      // determine whether testDay is valid for specified month
48      if ( testDay > 0 && testDay <= daysPerMonth[ month ] )
49         return testDay;
50
51      // February 29 check for leap year
52      if ( month == 2 && testDay == 29 && ( year % 400 == 0 ||
53         ( year % 4 == 0 && year % 100 != 0 ) ) )
54         return testDay;
55
56      throw invalid_argument( "Invalid day for current month and year" );
57   } // end function checkDay
```

Fig. 18.9 | Date class member-function definitions. (Part 2 of 2.)

```
1    // Fig. 18.10: Employee.h
2    // Employee class definition showing composition.
3    // Member functions defined in Employee.cpp.
4    #ifndef EMPLOYEE_H
5    #define EMPLOYEE_H
6
7    #include <string>
8    #include "Date.h" // include Date class definition
9    using namespace std;
10
11   class Employee
12   {
13   public:
14      Employee( const string &, const string &,
15         const Date &, const Date & );
16      void print() const;
17      ~Employee(); // provided to confirm destruction order
18   private:
19      string firstName; // composition: member object
20      string lastName; // composition: member object
21      const Date birthDate; // composition: member object
```

Fig. 18.10 | Employee class definition showing composition. (Part 1 of 2.)

```
22       const Date hireDate; // composition: member object
23   }; // end class Employee
24
25   #endif
```

Fig. 18.10 | Employee class definition showing composition. (Part 2 of 2.)

```
 1   // Fig. 18.11: Employee.cpp
 2   // Employee class member-function definitions.
 3   #include <iostream>
 4   #include "Employee.h" // Employee class definition
 5   #include "Date.h" // Date class definition
 6   using namespace std;
 7
 8   // constructor uses member initializer list to pass initializer
 9   // values to constructors of member objects
10   Employee::Employee( const string &first, const string &last,
11      const Date &dateOfBirth, const Date &dateOfHire )
12      : firstName( first ), // initialize firstName
13        lastName( last ), // initialize lastName
14        birthDate( dateOfBirth ), // initialize birthDate
15        hireDate( dateOfHire ) // initialize hireDate
16   {
17      // output Employee object to show when constructor is called
18      cout << "Employee object constructor: "
19         << firstName << ' ' << lastName << endl;
20   } // end Employee constructor
21
22   // print Employee object
23   void Employee::print() const
24   {
25      cout << lastName << ", " << firstName << "  Hired: ";
26      hireDate.print();
27      cout << "  Birthday: ";
28      birthDate.print();
29      cout << endl;
30   } // end function print
31
32   // output Employee object to show when its destructor is called
33   Employee::~Employee()
34   {
35      cout << "Employee object destructor: "
36         << lastName << ", " << firstName << endl;
37   } // end ~Employee destructor
```

Fig. 18.11 | Employee class member-function definitions, including constructor with a member initializer list.

Employee Constructor's Member Initializer List

The colon (:) following the constructor's header (Fig. 18.11, line 12) begins the member initializer list. The member initializers specify the Employee constructor parameters being passed to the constructors of the string and Date data members. Parameters first, last, dateOf-

Birth and dateOfHire are passed to the constructors for objects firstName's (Fig. 18.11, line 12), lastName (Fig. 18.11, line 13), birthDate (Fig. 18.11, line 14) and hireDate (Fig. 18.11, line 15), respectively. Again, member initializers are separated by commas.

Date Class's Default Copy Constructor

As you study class Date (Fig. 18.8), notice that the class does not provide a constructor that receives a parameter of type Date. So, why can the Employee constructor's member initializer list initialize the birthDate and hireDate objects by passing Date object's to their Date constructors? As we mentioned in Chapter 17, the compiler provides each class with a *default copy constructor* that copies each data member of the constructor's argument object into the corresponding member of the object being initialized. Chapter 19 discusses how you can define customized copy constructors.

Testing Classes Date and Employee

Figure 18.12 creates two Date objects (lines 9–10) and passes them as arguments to the constructor of the Employee object created in line 11. Line 14 outputs the Employee object's data. When each Date object is created in lines 9–10, the Date constructor defined in lines 10–24 of Fig. 18.9 displays a line of output to show that the constructor was called (see the first two lines of the sample output). [*Note:* Line 11 of Fig. 18.12 causes two additional Date constructor calls that do not appear in the program's output. When each of the Employee's Date member object's is initialized in the Employee constructor's

```
1   // Fig. 18.12: fig18_12.cpp
2   // Demonstrating composition--an object with member objects.
3   #include <iostream>
4   #include "Employee.h" // Employee class definition
5   using namespace std;
6
7   int main()
8   {
9      Date birth( 7, 24, 1949 );
10     Date hire( 3, 12, 1988 );
11     Employee manager( "Bob", "Blue", birth, hire );
12
13     cout << endl;
14     manager.print();
15  } // end main
```

```
Date object constructor for date 7/24/1949
Date object constructor for date 3/12/1988
Employee object constructor: Bob Blue

Blue, Bob  Hired: 3/12/1988  Birthday: 7/24/1949
Employee object destructor: Blue, Bob
Date object destructor for date 3/12/1988
Date object destructor for date 7/24/1949
Date object destructor for date 3/12/1988
Date object destructor for date 7/24/1949
```

There are actually five constructor calls when an **Employee** is constructed—two calls to the **string** class's constructor (lines 12–13 of Fig. 18.11), two calls to the **Date** class's default copy constructor (lines 14–15 of Fig. 18.11) and the call to the **Employee** class's constructor.

Fig. 18.12 | Demonstrating composition—an object with member objects.

member initializer list (Fig. 18.11, lines 14–15), the default copy constructor for class Date is called. Since this constructor is defined implicitly by the compiler, it does not contain any output statements to demonstrate when it's called.]

Class Date and class Employee each include a destructor (lines 33–38 of Fig. 18.9 and lines 33–37 of Fig. 18.11, respectively) that prints a message when an object of its class is destructed. This enables us to confirm in the program output that objects are constructed from the *inside out* and destroyed in the *reverse* order, from the *outside in* (i.e., the Date member objects are destroyed after the Employee object that contains them). Notice the last four lines in the output of Fig. 18.12. The last two lines are the outputs of the Date destructor running on Date objects hire (line 10) and birth (line 9), respectively. These outputs confirm that the three objects created in main are destructed in the *reverse* of the order in which they were constructed. The Employee destructor output is five lines from the bottom. The fourth and third lines from the bottom of the output window show the destructors running for the Employee's member objects hireDate (Fig. 18.10, line 22) and birthDate (Fig. 18.10, line 21). These outputs confirm that the Employee object is destructed from the *outside in*—i.e., the Employee destructor runs first (output shown five lines from the bottom of the output window), then the member objects are destructed in the *reverse order* from which they were constructed. Class string's destructor does not contain output statements, so we do not see the firstName and lastName objects being destructed. Again, Fig. 18.12's output did not show the constructors running for member objects birthDate and hireDate, because these objects were initialized with the default Date class copy constructors provided by the compiler.

What Happens When I Do Not Use the Member Initializer List?

If a member object is *not* initialized through a member initializer, the member object's default constructor will be called implicitly. Values, if any, established by the default constructor can be overridden by *set* functions. However, for complex initialization, this approach may require significant additional work and time.

Common Programming Error 18.6

A compilation error occurs if a member object is not initialized with a member initializer and the member object's class does not provide a default constructor (i.e., the member object's class defines one or more constructors, but none is a default constructor).

Performance Tip 18.2

Initialize member objects explicitly through member initializers. This eliminates the overhead of "doubly initializing" member objects—once when the member object's default constructor is called and again when set *functions are called in the constructor body (or later) to initialize the member object.*

Software Engineering Observation 18.6

If a class member is an object of another class, making that member object public *does not violate the encapsulation and hiding of that member object's* private *members. But, it does violate the encapsulation and hiding of the containing class's implementation, so member objects of class types should still be* private, *like all other data members.*

18.4 friend Functions and friend Classes

A friend function of a class is defined outside that class's scope, yet has the right to access the non-public (and public) members of the class. Standalone functions, entire classes or member functions of other classes may be declared to be friends of another class.

Using friend functions can enhance performance. This section presents a mechanical example of how a friend function works. Later in the book, friend functions are used to overload operators for use with class objects (Chapter 19) and to create iterator classes. Objects of an iterator class can successively select items or perform an operation on items in a container class object. Objects of container classes can store items. Using friends is often appropriate when a member function cannot be used for certain operations, as we'll see in Chapter 19.

To declare a function as a friend of a class, precede the function prototype in the class definition with keyword friend. To declare all member functions of class ClassTwo as friends of class ClassOne, place a declaration of the form

```
friend class ClassTwo;
```

in the definition of class ClassOne.

Software Engineering Observation 18.7

Even though the prototypes for friend functions appear in the class definition, friends are not member functions.

Software Engineering Observation 18.8

Member access notions of private, protected and public are not relevant to friend declarations, so friend declarations can be placed anywhere in a class definition.

Good Programming Practice 18.1

Place all friendship declarations first inside the class definition's body and do not precede them with any access specifier.

Friendship is granted, *not* taken—i.e., for class B to be a friend of class A, class A must explicitly declare that class B is its friend. Also, the friendship relation is neither symmetric nor transitive; i.e., if class A is a friend of class B, and class B is a friend of class C, you cannot infer that class B is a friend of class A (again, friendship is not symmetric), that class C is a friend of class B (also because friendship is not symmetric), or that class A is a friend of class C (friendship is not transitive).

Software Engineering Observation 18.9

Some people in the OOP community feel that "friendship" corrupts information hiding and weakens the value of the object-oriented design approach. We will provide several examples of responsible friendship use.

Modifying a Class's **private** Data with a Friend Function

Figure 18.13 is a mechanical example in which we define friend function setX to set the private data member x of class Count. The friend declaration (line 9) appears first (by convention) in the class definition, even before public member functions are declared. Again, this friend declaration can appear *anywhere* in the class.

```
1    // Fig. 18.13: fig18_13.cpp
2    // Friends can access private members of a class.
3    #include <iostream>
4    using namespace std;
5
6    // Count class definition
7    class Count
8    {
9       friend void setX( Count &, int ); // friend declaration
10   public:
11      // constructor
12      Count()
13         : x( 0 ) // initialize x to 0
14      {
15         // empty body
16      } // end constructor Count
17
18      // output x
19      void print() const
20      {
21         cout << x << endl;
22      } // end function print
23   private:
24      int x; // data member
25   }; // end class Count
26
27   // function setX can modify private data of Count
28   // because setX is declared as a friend of Count (line 9)
29   void setX( Count &c, int val )
30   {
31      c.x = val; // allowed because setX is a friend of Count
32   } // end function setX
33
34   int main()
35   {
36      Count counter; // create Count object
37
38      cout << "counter.x after instantiation: ";
39      counter.print();
40
41      setX( counter, 8 ); // set x using a friend function
42      cout << "counter.x after call to setX friend function: ";
43      counter.print();
44   } // end main
```

```
counter.x after instantiation: 0
counter.x after call to setX friend function: 8
```

Fig. 18.13 │ Friends can access private members of a class.

Function setX (lines 29–32) is a C-style, stand-alone function—it isn't a member function of class Count. For this reason, when setX is invoked for object counter, line 41 passes counter as an argument to setX rather than using a handle (such as the name of the object) to call the function, as in

```
counter.setX( 8 );
```

If you remove the friend declaration in line 9, you'll receive error messages indicating that function setX cannot modify class Count's private data member x.

As we mentioned, Fig. 18.13 is a mechanical example of using the friend construct. It would normally be appropriate to define function setX as a member function of class Count. It would also normally be appropriate to separate the program of Fig. 18.13 into three files:

1. A header (e.g., Count.h) containing the Count class definition, which in turn contains the prototype of friend function setX

2. An implementation file (e.g., Count.cpp) containing the definitions of class Count's member functions and the definition of friend function setX

3. A test program (e.g., fig18_15.cpp) with main.

Overloaded *friend* Functions

It's possible to specify overloaded functions as friends of a class. Each function intended to be a friend must be explicitly declared in the class definition as a friend of the class.

18.5 Using the this Pointer

We've seen that an object's member functions can manipulate the object's data. How do member functions know *which* object's data members to manipulate? Every object has access to its own address through a pointer called this (a C++ keyword). The this pointer is *not* part of the object itself—i.e., the memory occupied by the this pointer is not reflected in the result of a sizeof operation on the object. Rather, the this pointer is passed (by the compiler) as an *implicit* argument to each of the object's non-static member functions. Section 18.6 introduces static class members and explains why the this pointer is *not* implicitly passed to static member functions.

Objects use the this pointer *implicitly* (as we've done to this point) or *explicitly* to reference their data members and member functions. The type of the this pointer depends on the type of the object and whether the member function in which this is used is declared const. For example, in a nonconstant member function of class Employee, the this pointer has type Employee * const (a constant pointer to a nonconstant Employee object). In a constant member function of the class Employee, the this pointer has the data type const Employee * const (a constant pointer to a constant Employee object).

The next example shows implicit and explicit use of the this pointer; later in this chapter and in Chapter 19, we show some substantial and subtle examples of using this.

Implicitly and Explicitly Using the *this* Pointer to Access an Object's Data Members

Figure 18.14 demonstrates the implicit and explicit use of the this pointer to enable a member function of class Test to print the private data x of a Test object.

For illustration purposes, member function print (lines 24–36) first prints x by using the this pointer *implicitly* (line 27)—only the name of the data member is specified. Then print uses two different notations to access x through the this pointer—the arrow operator (->) off the this pointer (line 31) and the dot operator (.) off the dereferenced this

```cpp
 1   // Fig. 18.14: fig18_14.cpp
 2   // Using the this pointer to refer to object members.
 3   #include <iostream>
 4   using namespace std;
 5
 6   class Test
 7   {
 8   public:
 9      Test( int = 0 ); // default constructor
10      void print() const;
11   private:
12      int x;
13   }; // end class Test
14
15   // constructor
16   Test::Test( int value )
17      : x( value ) // initialize x to value
18   {
19      // empty body
20   } // end constructor Test
21
22   // print x using implicit and explicit this pointers;
23   // the parentheses around *this are required
24   void Test::print() const
25   {
26      // implicitly use the this pointer to access the member x
27      cout << "        x = " << x;
28
29      // explicitly use the this pointer and the arrow operator
30      // to access the member x
31      cout << "\n  this->x = " << this->x;
32
33      // explicitly use the dereferenced this pointer and
34      // the dot operator to access the member x
35      cout << "\n(*this).x = " << ( *this ).x << endl;
36   } // end function print
37
38   int main()
39   {
40      Test testObject( 12 ); // instantiate and initialize testObject
41
42      testObject.print();
43   } // end main
```

```
        x = 12
  this->x = 12
(*this).x = 12
```

Fig. 18.14 | using the this pointer to refer to object members.

pointer (line 35). Note the parentheses around *this (line 35) when used with the dot member selection operator (.). The parentheses are required because the dot operator has higher precedence than the * operator. Without the parentheses, the expression *this.x would be evaluated as if it were parenthesized as *(this.x), which is a compilation error, because the dot operator cannot be used with a pointer.

> **Common Programming Error 18.7**
> *Attempting to use the member selection operator (.) with a pointer to an object is a compilation error—the dot member selection operator may be used only with an lvalue such as an object's name, a reference to an object or a dereferenced pointer to an object.*

One interesting use of the this pointer is to prevent an object from being assigned to itself. As we'll see in Chapter 19, *self-assignment* can cause serious errors when the object contains pointers to dynamically allocated storage.

Using the **this** Pointer to Enable Cascaded Function Calls

Another use of the this pointer is to enable **cascaded member-function calls**—that is, invoking multiple functions in the same statement (as in line 12 of Fig. 18.17). The program of Figs. 18.15–18.17 modifies class Time's *set* functions setTime, setHour, setMinute and setSecond such that each returns a reference to a Time object to enable cascaded member-function calls. Notice in Fig. 18.16 that the last statement in the body of each of these member functions returns *this (lines 22, 33, 44 and 55) into a return type of Time &.

```
1   // Fig. 18.15: Time.h
2   // Time class modified to enable cascaded member function calls.
3
4   // Time class definition.
5   // Member functions defined in Time.cpp.
6   #ifndef TIME_H
7   #define TIME_H
8
9   class Time
10  {
11  public:
12     Time( int = 0, int = 0, int = 0 ); // default constructor
13
14     // set functions (the Time & return types enable cascading)
15     Time &setTime( int, int, int ); // set hour, minute, second
16     Time &setHour( int ); // set hour
17     Time &setMinute( int ); // set minute
18     Time &setSecond( int ); // set second
19
20     // get functions (normally declared const)
21     int getHour() const; // return hour
22     int getMinute() const; // return minute
23     int getSecond() const; // return second
24
25     // print functions (normally declared const)
26     void printUniversal() const; // print universal time
27     void printStandard() const; // print standard time
28  private:
29     int hour; // 0 - 23 (24-hour clock format)
30     int minute; // 0 - 59
```

Fig. 18.15 | Time class modified to enable cascaded member-function calls. (Part 1 of 2.)

```
31      int second; // 0 - 59
32   }; // end class Time
33
34   #endif
```

Fig. 18.15 | Time class modified to enable cascaded member-function calls. (Part 2 of 2.)

```
1    // Fig. 18.16: Time.cpp
2    // Time class member-function definitions.
3    #include <iostream>
4    #include <iomanip>
5    #include "Time.h" // Time class definition
6    using namespace std;
7
8    // constructor function to initialize private data;
9    // calls member function setTime to set variables;
10   // default values are 0 (see class definition)
11   Time::Time( int hr, int min, int sec )
12   {
13      setTime( hr, min, sec );
14   } // end Time constructor
15
16   // set values of hour, minute, and second
17   Time &Time::setTime( int h, int m, int s ) // note Time & return
18   {
19      setHour( h );
20      setMinute( m );
21      setSecond( s );
22      return *this; // enables cascading
23   } // end function setTime
24
25   // set hour value
26   Time &Time::setHour( int h ) // note Time & return
27   {
28      if ( h >= 0 && h < 24 )
29         hour = h;
30      else
31         throw invalid_argument( "hour must be 0-23" );
32
33      return *this; // enables cascading
34   } // end function setHour
35
36   // set minute value
37   Time &Time::setMinute( int m ) // note Time & return
38   {
39      if ( m >= 0 && m < 60 )
40         minute = m;
41      else
42         throw invalid_argument( "minute must be 0-59" );
43
```

Fig. 18.16 | Time class member-function definitions modified to enable cascaded member-function calls. (Part 1 of 2.)

```
44      return *this; // enables cascading
45   } // end function setMinute
46
47   // set second value
48   Time &Time::setSecond( int s ) // note Time & return
49   {
50      if ( s >= 0 && s < 60 )
51         second = s;
52      else
53         throw invalid_argument( "second must be 0-59" );
54
55      return *this; // enables cascading
56   } // end function setSecond
57
58   // get hour value
59   int Time::getHour() const
60   {
61      return hour;
62   } // end function getHour
63
64   // get minute value
65   int Time::getMinute() const
66   {
67      return minute;
68   } // end function getMinute
69
70   // get second value
71   int Time::getSecond() const
72   {
73      return second;
74   } // end function getSecond
75
76   // print Time in universal-time format (HH:MM:SS)
77   void Time::printUniversal() const
78   {
79      cout << setfill( '0' ) << setw( 2 ) << hour << ":"
80         << setw( 2 ) << minute << ":" << setw( 2 ) << second;
81   } // end function printUniversal
82
83   // print Time in standard-time format (HH:MM:SS AM or PM)
84   void Time::printStandard() const
85   {
86      cout << ( ( hour == 0 || hour == 12 ) ? 12 : hour % 12 )
87         << ":" << setfill( '0' ) << setw( 2 ) << minute
88         << ":" << setw( 2 ) << second << ( hour < 12 ? " AM" : " PM" );
89   } // end function printStandard
```

Fig. 18.16 | Time class member-function definitions modified to enable cascaded member-function calls. (Part 2 of 2.)

The program of Fig. 18.17 creates Time object t (line 9), then uses it in *cascaded member-function calls* (lines 12 and 24). Why does the technique of returning *this as a reference work? The dot operator (.) associates from left to right, so line 12 first evaluates

```
 1   // Fig. 18.17: fig18_17.cpp
 2   // Cascading member-function calls with the this pointer.
 3   #include <iostream>
 4   #include "Time.h" // Time class definition
 5   using namespace std;
 6
 7   int main()
 8   {
 9      Time t; // create Time object
10
11      // cascaded function calls
12      t.setHour( 18 ).setMinute( 30 ).setSecond( 22 );
13
14      // output time in universal and standard formats
15      cout << "Universal time: ";
16      t.printUniversal();
17
18      cout << "\nStandard time: ";
19      t.printStandard();
20
21      cout << "\n\nNew standard time: ";
22
23      // cascaded function calls
24      t.setTime( 20, 20, 20 ).printStandard();
25      cout << endl;
26   } // end main
```

```
Universal time: 18:30:22
Standard time: 6:30:22 PM

New standard time: 8:20:20 PM
```

Fig. 18.17 | Cascading member-function calls with the this pointer.

t.setHour(18), then returns a reference to object t as the value of this function call. The remaining expression is then interpreted as

        t.setMinute(30).setSecond(22);

The t.setMinute(30) call executes and returns a reference to the object t. The remaining expression is interpreted as

        t.setSecond(22);

Line 24 also uses cascading. The calls must appear in the order shown in line 24, because printStandard as defined in the class does *not* return a reference to t. Placing the call to printStandard before the call to setTime in line 24 results in a compilation error. Chapter 19 presents several practical examples of using cascaded function calls. One such example uses multiple << operators with cout to output multiple values in a single statement.

18.6 static Class Members

There is an important exception to the rule that each object of a class has its own copy of all the data members of the class. In certain cases, only *one* copy of a variable should be *shared* by *all* objects of a class. A **static** data member is used for these and other reasons. Such a variable represents "class-wide" information (i.e., a property that is shared by all instances and is not specific to any one object of the class).

Motivating Class-Wide Data

Let's further motivate the need for static class-wide data with an example. Suppose that we have a video game with Martians and other space creatures. Each Martian tends to be brave and willing to attack other space creatures when the Martian is aware that there are at least five Martians present. If fewer than five are present, each Martian becomes cowardly. So each Martian needs to know the martianCount. We could endow each instance of class Martian with martianCount as a data member. If we do, every Martian will have a *separate* copy of the data member. Every time we create a new Martian, we'll have to update the data member martianCount in all Martian objects. Doing this would require every Martian object to have, or have access to, handles to all other Martian objects in memory. This wastes space with the redundant copies and wastes time in updating the separate copies. Instead, we declare martianCount to be static. This makes martianCount class-wide data. Every Martian can access martianCount as if it were a data member of the Martian, but only one copy of the static variable martianCount is maintained by C++. This saves space. We save time by having the Martian constructor increment static variable martianCount and having the Martian destructor decrement martianCount. Because there's only one copy, we do not have to increment or decrement separate copies of martianCount for each Martian object.

Performance Tip 18.3

Use static data members to save storage when a single copy of the data for all objects of a class will suffice.

Scope and Initialization of static Data Members

Although they may seem like global variables, a class's static data members have class scope. Also, static members can be declared public, private or protected. A fundamental-type static data member is initialized by default to 0. If you want a different initial value, a static data member can be initialized *once*. A static const data member of int or enum type can be initialized in its declaration in the class definition. However, all other static data members must be defined *at global namespace scope* (i.e., outside the body of the class definition) and can be initialized only in those definitions—again, the next version of the C++ standard will allow initialization where these variables are declared in the class definition. If a static data member is an object of a class that provides a default constructor, the static data member need not be initialized because its default constructor will be called.

Accessing static Data Members

A class's private and protected static members are normally accessed through the class's public member functions or friends. *A class's static members exist even when no objects of that class exist.* To access a public static class member when no objects of the class exist, simply prefix the class name and the scope resolution operator (::) to the name of the data member. For example, if our preceding variable martianCount is public, it can be accessed with the expression `Martian::martianCount` when there are no `Martian` objects. (Of course, using `public` data is discouraged.)

To access a `private` or `protected` `static` class member when *no* objects of the class exist, provide a `public` **static** member function and call the function by prefixing its name with the class name and scope resolution operator. A `static` member function is a service of the *class*, *not* of a specific object of the class.

Software Engineering Observation 18.10

A class's `static` data members and `static` member functions exist and can be used even if no objects of that class have been instantiated.

Demonstrating static *Data Members*

The program of Figs. 18.18–18.20 demonstrates a `private` `static` data member called count (Fig. 18.18, line 25) and a `public` `static` member function called `getCount` (Fig. 18.18, line 19). In Fig. 18.19, line 8 defines and initializes the data member count to zero *at global namespace scope* and lines 12–15 define `static` member function get-Count. Notice that neither line 8 nor line 12 includes keyword `static`, yet both lines refer to `static` class members. When `static` is applied to an item at global namespace scope, that item becomes known only in that file. The `static` class members need to be available to any client code that uses the class, so we declare them `static` only in the `.h` file. Data member count maintains a count of the number of objects of class `Employee` that have been instantiated. When objects of class `Employee` exist, member count can be referenced through any member function of an `Employee` object—in Fig. 18.19, count is referenced by both line 22 in the constructor and line 32 in the destructor.

Common Programming Error 18.8

It's a compilation error to include keyword `static` in the definition of a `static` data member at global namespace scope.

```
1   // Fig. 18.18: Employee.h
2   // Employee class definition with a static data member to
3   // track the number of Employee objects in memory
4   #ifndef EMPLOYEE_H
5   #define EMPLOYEE_H
6
7   #include <string>
8   using namespace std;
9
10  class Employee
11  {
12  public:
13     Employee( const string &, const string & ); // constructor
14     ~Employee(); // destructor
15     string getFirstName() const; // return first name
16     string getLastName() const; // return last name
```

Fig. 18.18 | `Employee` class definition with a static data member to track the number of `Employee` objects in memory. (Part 1 of 2.)

```
17
18      // static member function
19      static int getCount(); // return number of objects instantiated
20   private:
21      string firstName;
22      string lastName;
23
24      // static data
25      static int count; // number of objects instantiated
26   }; // end class Employee
27
28   #endif
```

Fig. 18.18 | Employee class definition with a static data member to track the number of Employee objects in memory. (Part 2 of 2.)

```
1    // Fig. 18.19: Employee.cpp
2    // Employee class member-function definitions.
3    #include <iostream>
4    #include "Employee.h" // Employee class definition
5    using namespace std;
6
7    // define and initialize static data member at global namespace scope
8    int Employee::count = 0; // cannot include keyword static
9
10   // define static member function that returns number of
11   // Employee objects instantiated (declared static in Employee.h)
12   int Employee::getCount()
13   {
14      return count;
15   } // end static function getCount
16
17   // constructor initializes non-static data members and
18   // increments static data member count
19   Employee::Employee( const string &first, const string &last )
20      : firstName( first ), lastName( last )
21   {
22      ++count; // increment static count of employees
23      cout << "Employee constructor for " << firstName
24         << ' ' << lastName << " called." << endl;
25   } // end Employee constructor
26
27   // destructor deallocates dynamically allocated memory
28   Employee::~Employee()
29   {
30      cout << "~Employee() called for " << firstName
31         << ' ' << lastName << endl;
32      --count; // decrement static count of employees
33   } // end ~Employee destructor
34
```

Fig. 18.19 | Employee class member-function definitions. (Part 1 of 2.)

```
35  // return first name of employee
36  string Employee::getFirstName() const
37  {
38     return firstName; // return copy of first name
39  } // end function getFirstName
40
41  // return last name of employee
42  string Employee::getLastName() const
43  {
44     return lastName; // return copy of last name
45  } // end function getLastName
```

Fig. 18.19 | Employee class member-function definitions. (Part 2 of 2.)

Figure 18.20 uses static member function getCount to determine the number of Employee objects in memory at various points in the program. The program calls Employee::getCount() before any Employee objects have been created (line 12), after two Employee objects have been created (line 23) and after those Employee objects have been destroyed (line 34). Lines 16–29 in main define a *nested scope*. Recall that local variables exist until the scope in which they're defined terminates. In this example, we create two Employee objects in lines 17–18 inside the nested scope. As each constructor executes, it increments class Employee's static data member count. These Employee objects are destroyed when the program reaches line 29. At that point, each object's destructor executes and decrements class Employee's static data member count.

```
1   // Fig. 18.20: fig18_20.cpp
2   // static data member tracking the number of objects of a class.
3   #include <iostream>
4   #include "Employee.h" // Employee class definition
5   using namespace std;
6
7   int main()
8   {
9      // no objects exist; use class name and binary scope resolution
10     // operator to access static member function getCount
11     cout << "Number of employees before instantiation of any objects is "
12        << Employee::getCount() << endl; // use class name
13
14     // the following scope creates and destroys
15     // Employee objects before main terminates
16     {
17        Employee e1( "Susan", "Baker" );
18        Employee e2( "Robert", "Jones" );
19
20        // two objects exist; call static member function getCount again
21        // using the class name and the scope resolution operator
22        cout << "Number of employees after objects are instantiated is "
23           << Employee::getCount();
24
```

Fig. 18.20 | static data member tracking the number of objects of a class. (Part 1 of 2.)

```
25          cout << "\n\nEmployee 1: "
26             << e1.getFirstName() << " " << e1.getLastName()
27             << "\nEmployee 2: "
28             << e2.getFirstName() << " " << e2.getLastName() << "\n\n";
29      } // end nested scope in main
30
31      // no objects exist, so call static member function getCount again
32      // using the class name and the scope resolution operator
33      cout << "\nNumber of employees after objects are deleted is "
34             << Employee::getCount() << endl;
35  } // end main
```

```
Number of employees before instantiation of any objects is 0
Employee constructor for Susan Baker called.
Employee constructor for Robert Jones called.
Number of employees after objects are instantiated is 2

Employee 1: Susan Baker
Employee 2: Robert Jones

~Employee() called for Robert Jones
~Employee() called for Susan Baker

Number of employees after objects are deleted is 0
```

Fig. 18.20 | static data member tracking the number of objects of a class. (Part 2 of 2.)

A member function should be declared static if it does *not* access non-static data members or non-static member functions of the class. Unlike non-static member functions, *a static member function does not have a this pointer*, because static *data members and static member functions exist independently of any objects of a class*. The this pointer *must* refer to a specific object of the class, and when a static member function is called, there might *not* be any objects of its class in memory.

Common Programming Error 18.9
Using the this pointer in a static member function is a compilation error.

Common Programming Error 18.10
Declaring a static member function const is a compilation error. The const qualifier indicates that a function cannot modify the contents of the object in which it operates, but static member functions exist and operate independently of any objects of the class.

18.7 Proxy Classes

Two of the fundamental principles of good software engineering are *separating interface from implementation* and *hiding implementation details*. We strive to achieve these goals by defining a class in a header and implementing its member functions in a separate implementation file. As we pointed out in Chapter 17, however, *headers do contain a portion of a class's implementation and hints about others*. For example, a class's private members are listed in the class definition in a header, so these members are visible to clients, even though the clients may not access the private members. *Revealing a class's private data in this manner potentially exposes proprietary information to clients of the class.* We now introduce the notion of a **proxy class** that allows you to hide even the private data of a class from clients of the class. Providing clients of your class with a *proxy class* that knows only the public interface to your class enables the clients to use your class's services without giving the clients access to your class's implementation details.

Implementing a proxy class requires several steps, which we demonstrate in Figs. 18.21–18.24. First, we create the class definition for the class that contains the proprietary implementation we would like to hide. Our example class, called Implementation, is shown in Fig. 18.21. The proxy class Interface is shown in Figs. 18.22–18.23. The test program and sample output are shown in Fig. 18.24.

Class Implementation (Fig. 18.21) provides a single private data member called value (the data we would like to hide from the client), a constructor to initialize value and functions setValue and getValue.

```cpp
 1   // Fig. 18.21: Implementation.h
 2   // Implementation class definition.
 3
 4   class Implementation
 5   {
 6   public:
 7      // constructor
 8      Implementation( int v )
 9         : value( v ) // initialize value with v
10      {
11         // empty body
12      } // end constructor Implementation
13
14      // set value to v
15      void setValue( int v )
16      {
17         value = v; // should validate v
18      } // end function setValue
19
20      // return value
21      int getValue() const
22      {
23         return value;
24      } // end function getValue
25   private:
26      int value; // data that we would like to hide from the client
27   }; // end class Implementation
```

Fig. 18.21 | Implementation class definition.

We define a proxy class called Interface (Fig. 18.22) with an identical public interface (except for the constructor and destructor names) to that of class Implementation. The proxy class's only private member is a pointer to an Implementation object. Using a pointer in this manner allows us to hide class Implementation's implementation details from the client. Notice that the only mentions in class Interface of the proprietary Implementation class are in the pointer declaration (line 17) and in line 6, a **forward class** declaration. When a class definition uses only a pointer or reference to an object of another class (as in this case), the class header for that other class (which would ordinarily reveal the private data of that class) is *not* required to be included with #include. This is because the compiler doesn't need to reserve space for an *object* of the class. The compiler *does* need to reserve space for the *pointer* or *reference*. The sizes of pointers and references are characteristics of the hardware platform on which the compiler runs, so the compiler already knows those sizes. You can simply declare that other class as a data type with a *forward class declaration* (line 6) before the type is used in the file.

```
1   // Fig. 18.22: Interface.h
2   // Proxy class Interface definition.
3   // Client sees this source code, but the source code does not reveal
4   // the data layout of class Implementation.
5
6   class Implementation; // forward class declaration required by line 17
7
8   class Interface
9   {
10  public:
11     Interface( int ); // constructor
12     void setValue( int ); // same public interface as
13     int getValue() const; // class Implementation has
14     ~Interface(); // destructor
15  private:
16     // requires previous forward declaration (line 6)
17     Implementation *ptr;
18  }; // end class Interface
```

Fig. 18.22 | Proxy class Interface definition.

The member-function implementation file for proxy class Interface (Fig. 18.23) is the only file that includes the header Implementation.h (line 5) containing class Implementation. The file Interface.cpp (Fig. 18.23) is provided to the client as a precompiled object code file along with the header Interface.h that includes the function prototypes of the services provided by the proxy class. Because file Interface.cpp is made available to the client only as object code, the client is not able to see the interactions between the proxy class and the proprietary class (lines 9, 17, 23 and 29). The proxy class imposes an extra "layer" of function calls as the "price to pay" for hiding the private data of class Implementation. Given the speed of today's computers and the fact that many compilers can *inline* simple function calls automatically, the effect of these extra function calls on performance is often negligible.

```
1   // Fig. 18.23: Interface.cpp
2   // Implementation of class Interface--client receives this file only
3   // as precompiled object code, keeping the implementation hidden.
4   #include "Interface.h" // Interface class definition
5   #include "Implementation.h" // Implementation class definition
6
```

Fig. 18.23 | Interface class member-function definitions. (Part 1 of 2.)

```
7   // constructor
8   Interface::Interface( int v )
9      : ptr ( new Implementation( v ) ) // initialize ptr to point to
10  {                                    // a new Implementation object
11     // empty body
12  } // end Interface constructor
13
14  // call Implementation's setValue function
15  void Interface::setValue( int v )
16  {
17     ptr->setValue( v );
18  } // end function setValue
19
20  // call Implementation's getValue function
21  int Interface::getValue() const
22  {
23     return ptr->getValue();
24  } // end function getValue
25
26  // destructor
27  Interface::~Interface()
28  {
29     delete ptr;
30  } // end ~Interface destructor
```

Fig. 18.23 | Interface class member-function definitions. (Part 2 of 2.)

Figure 18.24 tests class Interface. Notice that only the header for Interface is included in the client code (line 4)—there is no mention of the existence of a separate class called Implementation. Thus, the client never sees the private data of class Implementation, nor can the client code become dependent on the Implementation code.

Software Engineering Observation 18.11

A proxy class insulates client code from implementation changes.

```
1   // Fig. 18.24: fig18_24.cpp
2   // Hiding a class's private data with a proxy class.
3   #include <iostream>
4   #include "Interface.h" // Interface class definition
5   using namespace std;
6
7   int main()
8   {
9      Interface i( 5 ); // create Interface object
10
11     cout << "Interface contains: " << i.getValue()
12        << " before setValue" << endl;
13
14     i.setValue( 10 );
```

Fig. 18.24 | Hiding a class's private data with a proxy class. (Part 1 of 2.)

```
15
16      cout << "Interface contains: " << i.getValue()
17          << " after setValue" << endl;
18  } // end main
```

```
Interface contains: 5 before setValue
Interface contains: 10 after setValue
```

Fig. 18.24 | Hiding a class's private data with a proxy class. (Part 2 of 2.)

18.8 Wrap-Up

This chapter introduced several advanced topics related to classes and data abstraction. You learned how to specify const objects and const member functions to prevent modifications to objects, thus enforcing the principle of least privilege. You also learned that, through composition, a class can have objects of other classes as members. We introduced the topic of friendship and demonstrated how to use friend functions.

You learned that the this pointer is passed as an implicit argument to each of a class's non-static member functions, allowing the functions to access the correct object's data members and other non-static member functions. You also saw explicit use of the this pointer to access the class's members and to enable cascaded member-function calls. We motivated the need for static data members and demonstrated how to declare and use static data members and static member functions in your own classes. Finally, we showed how to create a proxy class to hide the implementation details of a class from the class's clients.

In Chapter 19, we continue our study of classes and objects by showing how to enable C++'s operators to work with objects—a process called operator overloading. For example, you'll see how to overload the << operator so it can be used to output a complete array without explicitly using a repetition statement.

Summary

Section 18.2 const (Constant) Objects and const Member Functions

- The keyword const can be used to specify that an object is not modifiable and that any attempt to modify the object should result in a compilation error.
- C++ compilers disallow non-const member function calls on const objects.
- An attempt by a const member function to modify an object of its class is a compilation error.
- A member function is specified as const both in its prototype and in its definition.
- A const object must be initialized.
- Constructors and destructors cannot be declared const.
- const data member and reference data members *must* be initialized using member initializers (p. 692).

Section 18.3 Composition: Objects as Members of Classes

- A class can have objects of other classes as members—this concept is called composition.

- Member objects (p. 695) are constructed in the order in which they're declared in the class definition and before their enclosing class objects are constructed.

- If a member initializer is not provided for a member object, the member object's default constructor (p. 695) will be called implicitly.

Section 18.4 **friend** Functions and **friend** Classes

- A friend function (p. 701) of a class is defined outside that class's scope, yet has the right to access all of the class's members. Stand-alone functions or entire classes may be declared to be friends.

- A friend declaration can appear anywhere in the class.

- The friendship relation is neither symmetric nor transitive.

Section 18.5 Using the **this** Pointer

- Every object has access to its own address through the this pointer (p. 703).

- An object's this pointer is not part of the object itself—i.e., the size of the memory occupied by the this pointer is not reflected in the result of a sizeof operation on the object.

- The this pointer is passed as an implicit argument to each non-static member function.

- Objects use the this pointer implicitly (as we've done to this point) or explicitly to reference their data members and member functions.

- The this pointer enables cascaded member-function calls (p. 705) in which multiple functions are invoked in the same statement.

Section 18.6 **static** Class Members

- A static data member (p. 709) represents "class-wide" information (i.e., a property of the class shared by all instances, not a property of a specific object of the class).

- static data members have class scope and can be declared public, private or protected.

- A class's static members exist even when no objects of that class exist.

- To access a public static class member when no objects of the class exist, simply prefix the class name and the scope resolution operator (::) to the name of the data member.

- A member function should be declared static (p. 710) if it does not access non-static data members or non-static member functions of the class. Unlike non-static member functions, a static member function does not have a this pointer, because static data members and static member functions exist independently of any objects of a class.

Section 18.7 Proxy Classes

- Providing clients of your class with a proxy class (p. 714) that knows only the public interface to your class enables the clients to use your class's services without giving the clients access to your class's implementation details, such as its private data.

- When a class definition uses only a pointer or reference to an object of another class, the class header for that other class (which would ordinarily reveal the private data of that class) is not required to be included with #include. You can simply declare that other class as a data type with a forward class declaration (p. 715) before the type is used in the file.

- The implementation file containing the member functions for a proxy class is the only file that includes the header for the class whose private data we would like to hide.

- The implementation file containing the member functions for the proxy class is provided to the client as a precompiled object code file along with the header that includes the function prototypes of the services provided by the proxy class.

Self-Review Exercises

18.1   Fill in the blanks in each of the following:

a) _____ must be used to initialize constant members of a class.

b) A nonmember function must be declared as a(n) _____ of a class to have access to that class's `private` data members.

c) A constant object must be _____; it cannot be modified after it's created.

d) A(n) _____ data member represents class-wide information.

e) An object's non-`static` member functions have access to a "self pointer" to the object called the _____ pointer.

f) Keyword _____ specifies that an object or variable is not modifiable.

g) If a member initializer is not provided for a member object of a class, the object's _____ is called.

h) A member function should be `static` if it does not access _____ class members.

i) Member objects are constructed _____ their enclosing class object.

18.2   Find the errors in the following class and explain how to correct them:

```
class Demo
{
public:
    int Demo( int a = 100 )
        : b( a )
    {
        // empty body
    } // end Example constructor

    int getData()
    {
        return ++b;
    } // end function getData

    int putData()
    {
        cout << "Data is " << b << endl;
        return b;
    } // end function putData
private:
    int b;

} // end class Example
```

Answers to Self-Review Exercises

18.1   a) Member initializers. b) `friend`. c) initialized. d) `static`. e) `this`. f) `const`. g) default constructor. h) non-`static`. i) before.

18.2   This code has two errors.

Error: The `Demo` constructor returns a value. Constructors cannot return values.

Correction 1: Remove `int` from the constructor `Demo`.

Error: No end for class `Demo`.

Correction: Put ; after } where the class ends.

Exercises

18.3   *(this Pointer)* What is the `this` pointer? In how many ways can the `this` pointer be used by objects?

18.4 *(Constructor Overloading)* Can a correct `Complex` class definition include both of the following constructors? If not, explain why not.

```
Complex ( int x = 10, int y = 10 );
Complex ( float x = 30.00, float y = 20.00);
```

18.5 *(Right to Access)* Which function of a class is defined outside that class's scope, yet has the right to access the non-public (and public) members of the class?

18.6 *(`Date` Class Modification)* Modify class `Date` in Fig. 18.8 to have the following capabilities:
a) Output the date in multiple formats such as

```
DDD YYYY
MM/DD/YY
June 14, 1992
```

b) Use overloaded constructors to create `Date` objects initialized with dates of the formats in part (a).
c) Create a `Date` constructor that reads the system date using the standard library functions of the `<ctime>` header and sets the `Date` members. (See your compiler's reference documentation or www.cplusplus.com/ref/ctime/index.html for information on the functions in header `<ctime>`.)

In Chapter 19, we'll be able to create operators for testing the equality of two dates and for comparing dates to determine whether one date is prior to, or after, another.

18.7 *(`FixedDeposit` Class)* Create a `FixedDeposit` class. Use a `static` data member `annualInterestRate` to store the interest rate for each of the depositors. Each member of the class contains a `private` data member `fixedBalance` indicating the amount the depositor currently has as a fixed deposit. Provide member function `calculateSixMonthlyInterest` that calculates the interest for six months by multiplying the `balance` by `annualInterestRate` divided by 2; this interest should be added to `fixedBalance`. Provide a `static` member function `modifyInterestRate` that sets the `static` `annualInterestRate` to a new value. Write a driver program to test class `FixedDeposit`. Instantiate two different objects of class `FixedDeposit`, `depositor1` and `depositor2`, with fixed deposits of $10000.00 and $60000.00, respectively. Set the `InterestRate` to 9 percent. Then calculate the six monthly interest and print the new balances for each of the depositors. Then set the `annualInterestRate` to 10 percent, calculate the next six months' interest and print the new balances for each of the depositors.

18.8 *(`IntegerSet` Class)* Create class `IntegerSet` for which each object can hold integers in the range 0 through 100. Represent the set internally as a `vector` of `bool` values. Element a[i] is `true` if integer i is in the set. Element a[j] is `false` if integer j is not in the set. The default constructor initializes a set to the so-called "empty set," i.e., a set for which all elements contain `false`.

Provide member functions for the common set operations. For example, provide a `unionOfSets` member function that creates a third set that is the set-theoretic union of two existing sets (i.e., an element of the result is set to `true` if that element is `true` in either or both of the existing sets, and an element of the result is set to `false` if that element is `false` in each of the existing sets).

Provide an `intersectionOfSets` member function which creates a third set which is the set-theoretic intersection of two existing sets (i.e., an element of the result is set to `false` if that element is `false` in either or both of the existing sets, and an element of the result is set to `true` if that element is `true` in each of the existing sets).

Provide an `insertElement` member function that places a new integer k into a set by setting a[k] to `true`. Provide a `deleteElement` member function that deletes integer m by setting a[m] to `false`.

Provide a `printSet` member function that prints a set as a list of numbers separated by spaces. Print only those elements that are present in the set (i.e., their position in the `vector` has a value of `true`). Print `---` for an empty set.

Provide an `isEqualTo` member function that determines whether two sets are equal.

Provide an additional constructor that receives an array of integers and the size of that array and uses the array to initialize a set object.

Now write a driver program to test your `IntegerSet` class. Instantiate several `IntegerSet` objects. Test that all your member functions work properly.

18.9 *(Time Class Modification)* It would be perfectly reasonable for the `Time` class of Figs. 18.15–18.16 to represent the time internally as the number of seconds since midnight rather than the three integer values `hour`, `minute` and `second`. Clients could use the same `public` methods and get the same results. Modify the `Time` class of Fig. 18.15 to implement the time as the number of seconds since midnight and show that there is no visible change in functionality to the clients of the class. [*Note:* This exercise nicely demonstrates the virtues of implementation hiding.]

18.10 *(Card Shuffling and Dealing)* Create a program to shuffle and deal a deck of cards. The program should consist of class `Card`, class `DeckOfCards` and a driver program. Class `Card` should provide:

a) Data members `face` and `suit` of type `int`.

b) A constructor that receives two `int`s representing the face and suit and uses them to initialize the data members.

c) Two `static` arrays of `string`s representing the faces and suits.

d) A `toString` function that returns the `Card` as a `string` in the form "*face* of *suit*." You can use the + operator to concatenate `string`s.

Class `DeckOfCards` should contain:

a) A `vector` of `Card`s named `deck` to store the `Card`s.

b) An integer `currentCard` representing the next card to deal.

c) A default constructor that initializes the `Card`s in the deck. The constructor should use `vector` function `push_back` to add each `Card` to the end of the `vector` after the `Card` is created and initialized. This should be done for each of the 52 `Card`s in the deck.

d) A `shuffle` function that shuffles the `Card`s in the deck. The shuffle algorithm should iterate through the `vector` of `Card`s. For each `Card`, randomly select another `Card` in the deck and swap the two `Card`s.

e) A `dealCard` function that returns the next `Card` object from the deck.

f) A `moreCards` function that returns a `bool` value indicating whether there are more `Card`s to deal.

The driver program should create a `DeckOfCards` object, shuffle the cards, then deal the 52 cards.

18.11 *(Card Shuffling and Dealing)* Modify the program you developed in Exercise 18.10 so that it deals a five-card poker hand. Then write functions to accomplish each of the following:

a) Determine whether the hand contains a pair.

b) Determine whether the hand contains two pairs.

c) Determine whether the hand contains three of a kind (e.g., three jacks).

d) Determine whether the hand contains four of a kind (e.g., four aces).

e) Determine whether the hand contains a flush (i.e., all five cards of the same suit).

f) Determine whether the hand contains a straight (i.e., five cards of consecutive face values).

Card Shuffling and Dealing Projects

18.12 *(Card Shuffling and Dealing)* Use the functions from Exercise 18.11 to write a program that deals two five-card poker hands, evaluates each hand and determines which is the better hand.

18.13 *(Card Shuffling and Dealing)* Modify the program you developed in Exercise 18.12 so that it can simulate the dealer. The dealer's five-card hand is dealt "face down" so the player cannot see it. The program should then evaluate the dealer's hand, and, based on the quality of the hand, the dealer should draw one, two or three more cards to replace the corresponding number of unneeded cards in the original hand. The program should then reevaluate the dealer's hand.

18.14   *(Card Shuffling and Dealing)* Modify the program you developed in Exercise 18.13 so that it handles the dealer's hand, but the player is allowed to decide which cards of the player's hand to replace. The program should then evaluate both hands and determine who wins. Now use this new program to play 20 games against the computer. Who wins more games, you or the computer? Have one of your friends play 20 games against the computer. Who wins more games? Based on the results of these games, make appropriate modifications to refine your poker-playing program. Play 20 more games. Does your modified program play a better game?

Making a Difference

18.15   *(Project: Emergency Response Class)* The North American emergency response service, *9-1-1*, connects callers to a *local* Public Service Answering Point (PSAP). Traditionally, the PSAP would ask the caller for identification information—including the caller's address, phone number and the nature of the emergency, then dispatch the appropriate emergency responders (such as the police, an ambulance or the fire department). *Enhanced 9-1-1 (or E9-1-1)* uses computers and databases to determine the caller's physical address, directs the call to the nearest PSAP, and displays the caller's phone number and address to the call taker. *Wireless Enhanced 9-1-1* provides call takers with identification information for wireless calls. Rolled out in two phases, the first phase required carriers to provide the wireless phone number and the location of the cell site or base station transmitting the call. The second phase required carriers to provide the location of the caller (using technologies such as GPS). To learn more about 9-1-1, visit `www.fcc.gov/pshs/services/911-services/Welcome.html` and `people.howstuffworks.com/9-1-1.htm`.

An important part of creating a class is determining the class's attributes (instance variables). For this class design exercise, research 9-1-1 services on the Internet. Then, design a class called `Emergency` that might be used in an object-oriented 9-1-1 emergency response system. List the attributes that an object of this class might use to represent the emergency. For example, the class might include information on who reported the emergency (including their phone number), the location of the emergency, the time of the report, the nature of the emergency, the type of response and the status of the response. The class attributes should completely describe the nature of the problem and what's happening to resolve that problem.

Operator Overloading; Class string

There are two men inside the artist, the poet and the craftsman. One is born a poet. One becomes a craftsman.
—Emile Zola

A thing of beauty is a joy forever.
—John Keats

Objectives

In this chapter you'll learn:

- How operator overloading can help you craft valuable classes.

- To overload unary and binary operators.

- To convert objects from one class to another class.

- To use overloaded operators and additional features of C++'s **string** class.

- To create **PhoneNumber**, **Date** and **Array** classes that provide overloaded operators.

- To use keyword **explicit** to indicate that a constructor cannot be used for implicit conversions.

- To experience a "light-bulb moment" when you'll truly appreciate the value of the class concept.

19.1 Introduction

This chapter shows how to enable C++'s operators to work with class objects—a process called **operator overloading**. One example of an overloaded operator built into C++ is <<, which is used *both* as the stream insertion operator *and* as the bitwise left-shift operator. Similarly, >> also is overloaded; it's used both as the stream extraction operator and the bitwise right-shift operator. Both of these operators are overloaded in the C++ Standard Library. You've been using overloaded operators since early in the book. The overloads are built into the base C++ language itself. For example, C++ overloads the addition operator (+) and the subtraction operator (-) to perform differently, depending on their context in integer, floating-point and pointer arithmetic with data of fundamental types.

You can overload *most* operators to be used with class objects—the compiler generates the appropriate code based on the *types* of the operands. The jobs performed by overloaded operators also can be performed by explicit function calls, but operator notation is often more natural.

Our examples start by demonstrating the C++ Standard Library's class `string`, which has lots of overloaded operators. This enables you to see overloaded operators in use before implementing your own overloaded operators. Next, we create a `PhoneNumber` class that enables us to use overloaded operators << and >> to conveniently output and input fully formatted, 10-digit phone numbers. We then present a `Date` class that overloads the prefix and postfix increment (++) operators to add one day to the value of a `Date`. The class also overloads the += operator to allow a program to increment a `Date` by the number of days specified on the right side of the operator.

Next, we present a capstone case study—an `Array` class that uses overloaded operators and other capabilities to solve various problems with pointer-based arrays. This is one of the most important case studies in the book. Many of our students have indicated that the `Array` case study is their "light bulb moment" in truly understanding what classes and object technology are all about. As part of this class, we'll overload stream insertion, stream extraction, assignment, equality, relational and subscript operators. Once you master this

Array class, you'll indeed understand the essence of object technology—crafting, using and reusing valuable classes.

The chapter concludes with discussions of how you can convert between types (incuding class types), problems with certain implicit conversions and how to prevent those problems.

19.2 Using the Overloaded Operators of Standard Library Class `string`

Figure 19.1 demonstrates many of class `string`'s overloaded operators and several other useful member functions, including `empty`, `substr` and `at`. Function `empty` determines whether a `string` is empty, function `substr` returns a `string` that represents a portion of an existing `string` and function `at` returns the character at a specific index in a `string` (after checking that the index is in range).

```cpp
1   // Fig. 19.1: fig19_01.cpp
2   // Standard Library string class test program.
3   #include <iostream>
4   #include <string>
5   using namespace std;
6
7   int main()
8   {
9      string s1( "happy" );
10     string s2( " birthday" );
11     string s3;
12
13     // test overloaded equality and relational operators
14     cout << "s1 is \"" << s1 << "\"; s2 is \"" << s2
15        << "\"; s3 is \"" << s3 << '\"'
16        << "\n\nThe results of comparing s2 and s1:"
17        << "\ns2 == s1 yields " << ( s2 == s1 ? "true" : "false" )
18        << "\ns2 != s1 yields " << ( s2 != s1 ? "true" : "false" )
19        << "\ns2 >  s1 yields " << ( s2 > s1 ? "true" : "false" )
20        << "\ns2 <  s1 yields " << ( s2 < s1 ? "true" : "false" )
21        << "\ns2 >= s1 yields " << ( s2 >= s1 ? "true" : "false" )
22        << "\ns2 <= s1 yields " << ( s2 <= s1 ? "true" : "false" );
23
24     // test string member-function empty
25     cout << "\n\nTesting s3.empty():" << endl;
26
27     if ( s3.empty() )
28     {
29        cout << "s3 is empty; assigning s1 to s3;" << endl;
30        s3 = s1; // assign s1 to s3
31        cout << "s3 is \"" << s3 << "\"";
32     } // end if
33
34     // test overloaded string concatenation operator
35     cout << "\n\ns1 += s2 yields s1 = ";
```

Fig. 19.1 | Standard Library `string` class test program. (Part 1 of 3.)

```
36      s1 += s2; // test overloaded concatenation
37      cout << s1;
38
39      // test overloaded string concatenation operator with a char * string
40      cout << "\n\ns1 += \" to you\" yields" << endl;
41      s1 += " to you";
42      cout << "s1 = " << s1 << "\n\n";
43
44      // test string member function substr
45      cout << "The substring of s1 starting at location 0 for\n"
46         << "14 characters, s1.substr(0, 14), is:\n"
47         << s1.substr( 0, 14 ) << "\n\n";
48
49      // test substr "to-end-of-string" option
50      cout << "The substring of s1 starting at\n"
51         << "location 15, s1.substr(15), is:\n"
52         << s1.substr( 15 ) << endl;
53
54      // test copy constructor
55      string s4( s1 );
56      cout << "\ns4 = " << s4 << "\n\n";
57
58      // test overloaded assignment (=) operator with self-assignment
59      cout << "assigning s4 to s4" << endl;
60      s4 = s4;
61      cout << "s4 = " << s4 << endl;
62
63      // test using overloaded subscript operator to create lvalue
64      s1[ 0 ] = 'H';
65      s1[ 6 ] = 'B';
66      cout << "\ns1 after s1[0] = 'H' and s1[6] = 'B' is: "
67         << s1 << "\n\n";
68
69      // test subscript out of range with string member function "at"
70      try
71      {
72         cout << "Attempt to assign 'd' to s1.at( 30 ) yields:" << endl;
73         s1.at( 30 ) = 'd'; // ERROR: subscript out of range
74      } // end try
75      catch ( out_of_range &ex )
76      {
77         cout << "An exception occurred: " << ex.what() << endl;
78      } // end catch
79   } // end main
```

```
s1 is "happy"; s2 is " birthday"; s3 is ""

The results of comparing s2 and s1:
s2 == s1 yields false
s2 != s1 yields true
s2 >  s1 yields false
s2 <  s1 yields true
```

Fig. 19.1 | Standard Library `string` class test program. (Part 2 of 3.)

```
s2 >= s1 yields false
s2 <= s1 yields true

Testing s3.empty():
s3 is empty; assigning s1 to s3;
s3 is "happy"

s1 += s2 yields s1 = happy birthday

s1 += " to you" yields
s1 = happy birthday to you

The substring of s1 starting at location 0 for
14 characters, s1.substr(0, 14), is:
happy birthday

The substring of s1 starting at
location 15, s1.substr(15), is:
to you

s4 = happy birthday to you

assigning s4 to s4
s4 = happy birthday to you

s1 after s1[0] = 'H' and s1[6] = 'B' is: Happy Birthday to you

Attempt to assign 'd' to s1.at( 30 ) yields:
An exception occurred: invalid string position
```

Fig. 19.1 | Standard Library string class test program. (Part 3 of 3.)

Lines 9–11 create three string objects—s1 is initialized with the literal "happy", s2 is initialized with the literal " birthday" and s3 uses the default string constructor to create an empty string. Lines 14–15 output these three objects, using cout and operator <<, which the string class designers overloaded to handle string objects. Then lines 16–22 show the results of comparing s2 to s1 by using class string's overloaded equality and relational operators, which perform lexicographical comparisons using the numerical values of the characters (see Appendix B, ASCII Character Set) in each string.

Class string provides member function **empty** to determine whether a string is empty, which we demonstrate in line 27. Member function empty returns true if the string is empty; otherwise, it returns false.

Line 30 demonstrates class string's overloaded assignment operator by assigning s1 to s3. Line 31 outputs s3 to demonstrate that the assignment worked correctly.

Line 36 demonstrates class string's overloaded += operator for string concatenation. In this case, the contents of s2 are appended to s1. Then line 37 outputs the resulting string that's stored in s1. Line 41 demonstrates that a string literal can be appended to a string object by using operator +=. Line 42 displays the result.

Class string provides member function **substr** (lines 47 and 52) to return a portion of a string as a string object. The call to substr in line 47 obtains a 14-character substring (specified by the second argument) of s1 starting at position 0 (specified by the first argument). The call to substr in line 52 obtains a substring starting from position 15 of s1.

When the second argument is not specified, substr returns the *remainder* of the string on which it's called.

Line 55 creates string object s4 and initializes it with a copy of s1. This results in a call to class string's copy constructor. Line 60 uses class string's overloaded = operator to demonstrate that it handles *self-assignment* properly—we'll see when we build class Array later in the chapter that self-assignment can be dangerous and we'll show how to deal with the issues.

Lines 64–65 use class string's overloaded [] operator to create *lvalues* that enable new characters to replace existing characters in s1. Line 67 outputs the new value of s1. *Class string's overloaded [] operator does not perform any bounds checking.* Therefore, *you must ensure that operations using standard class string's overloaded [] operator do not accidentally manipulate elements outside the bounds of the string.* Class string *does* provide bounds checking in its member function at, which throws an exception if its argument is an invalid subscript. By default, this causes a C++ program to terminate and display a system-specific error message. If the subscript is valid, function at returns the character at the specified location as a modifiable *lvalue* or an unmodifiable *lvalue* (i.e., a const reference), depending on the context in which the call appears. Line 73 demonstrates a call to function at with an invalid subscript; this throws an out_of_range exception.

19.3 Fundamentals of Operator Overloading

As you saw in Fig. 19.1, operators provide a concise notation for manipulating string objects. You can use operators with your own user-defined types as well. Although C++ does *not* allow *new* operators to be created, it *does* allow most existing operators to be overloaded so that, when they're used with objects, they have meaning appropriate to those objects.

Operator overloading is not automatic—you must write operator-overloading functions to perform the desired operations. An operator is overloaded by writing a non-static member function definition or non-member function definition as you normally would, except that the function name starts with the keyword operator followed by the symbol for the operator being overloaded. For example, the function name operator+ would be used to overload the addition operator (+) for use with objects of a particular class. When operators are overloaded as member functions, they must be non-static, because *they must be called on an object of the class* and operate on that object.

To use an operator on an object of a class, the operator must be overloaded for that class—with three exceptions:

- The assignment operator (=) may be used with *every* class to perform *memberwise assignment* of the class's data members—each data member is assigned from the assignment's "source" object (on the right) to the "target" object (on the left). *Memberwise assignment is dangerous for classes with pointer members*, so we'll explicitly overload the assignment operator for such classes.

- The address (&) operator returns a pointer to the object; this operator also can be overloaded.

- The comma operator evaluates the expression to its left then the expression to its right, and returns the value of the latter expression. This operator also can be overloaded.

Operators That Cannot Be Overloaded

Most of C++'s operators can be overloaded. Figure 19.2 shows the operators that cannot be overloaded.

Fig. 19.2 | Operators that cannot be overloaded.

Rules and Restrictions on Operator Overloading

As you prepare to overload operators with your own classes, there are several rules and restrictions you should keep in mind:

- *The precedence of an operator cannot be changed by overloading.* However, parentheses can be used to *force* the order of evaluation of overloaded operators in an expression.

- *The associativity of an operator cannot be changed by overloading*—if an operator normally associates from left to right, then so do all of its overloaded versions.

- *You cannot change the "arity" of an operator* (that is, the number of operands an operator takes)—overloaded unary operators remain unary operators; overloaded binary operators remain binary operators. Operators &, *, + and - all have both unary and binary versions; these unary and binary versions can be separately overloaded.

- *You cannot create new operators; only existing operators can be overloaded.*

- The meaning of how an operator works on values of fundamental types *cannot* be changed by operator overloading. For example, you cannot make the + operator subtract two ints. Operator overloading works only with *objects of user-defined types or with a mixture of an object of a user-defined type and an object of a fundamental type.*

- *Related operators, like + and +=, must be overloaded separately.*

- When overloading (), [], -> or any of the assignment operators, the operator overloading function *must* be declared as a class member. For all other overloadable operators, the operator overloading functions can be member functions or non-member functions.

19.4 Overloading Binary Operators

A binary operator can be overloaded as a non-static member function with one parameter or as a non-member function with two parameters (one of those parameters must be either a class object or a reference to a class object). A non-member operator function is often declared as friend of a class for performance reasons.

Binary Overloaded Operators as Member Functions

Consider using < to compare two objects of a String class that you define. When overloading binary operator < as a non-static member function of a String class, if y and z are String-class objects, then y < z is treated as if y.operator<(z) had been written, invoking the operator< member function with one argument declared below:

```
class String
{
public:
    bool operator<( const String & ) const;
    ...
}; // end class String
```

Overloaded operator functions for binary operators can be member functions *only* when the *left* operand is an object of the class in which the function is a member.

Binary Overloaded Operators as Non-Member Functions

As a non-member function, binary operator < must take two arguments—one of which must be an object (or a reference to an object) of the class. If y and z are String-class objects or references to String-class objects, then y < z is treated as if the call operator<(y, z) had been written in the program, invoking function operator< which is declared as follows:

```
bool operator<( const String &, const String & );
```

Performance Tip 19.1

It's possible to overload an operator as a non-member, non-friend function, but such a function requiring access to a class's private or protected data would need to use set or get functions provided in that class's public interface. The overhead of calling these functions could cause poor performance, so these functions can be inlined to improve performance.

19.5 Overloading the Binary Stream Insertion and Stream Extraction Operators

You can input and output fundamental-type data using the stream extraction operator >> and the stream insertion operator <<. The C++ class libraries overload these binary operators for each fundamental type, including pointers and char * strings. You can also overload these operators to perform input and output for your own types. The program of Figs. 19.3–19.5 overloads these operators to input and output PhoneNumber objects in the format "(000) 000-0000." The program assumes telephone numbers are input correctly.

```
1   // Fig. 19.3: PhoneNumber.h
2   // PhoneNumber class definition
3   #ifndef PHONENUMBER_H
4   #define PHONENUMBER_H
5
6   #include <iostream>
7   #include <string>
8   using namespace std;
9
10  class PhoneNumber
11  {
```

Fig. 19.3 | PhoneNumber class with overloaded stream insertion and stream extraction operators as friend functions. (Part 1 of 2.)

```
12        friend ostream &operator<<( ostream &, const PhoneNumber & );
13        friend istream &operator>>( istream &, PhoneNumber & );
14    private:
15       string areaCode; // 3-digit area code
16       string exchange; // 3-digit exchange
17       string line; // 4-digit line
18    }; // end class PhoneNumber
19
20    #endif
```

Fig. 19.3 | PhoneNumber class with overloaded stream insertion and stream extraction operators as friend functions. (Part 2 of 2.)

```
 1    // Fig. 19.4: PhoneNumber.cpp
 2    // Overloaded stream insertion and stream extraction operators
 3    // for class PhoneNumber.
 4    #include <iomanip>
 5    #include "PhoneNumber.h"
 6    using namespace std;
 7
 8    // overloaded stream insertion operator; cannot be
 9    // a member function if we would like to invoke it with
10    // cout << somePhoneNumber;
11    ostream &operator<<( ostream &output, const PhoneNumber &number )
12    {
13       output << "(" << number.areaCode << ") "
14          << number.exchange << "-" << number.line;
15       return output; // enables cout << a << b << c;
16    } // end function operator<<
17
18    // overloaded stream extraction operator; cannot be
19    // a member function if we would like to invoke it with
20    // cin >> somePhoneNumber;
21    istream &operator>>( istream &input, PhoneNumber &number )
22    {
23       input.ignore(); // skip (
24       input >> setw( 3 ) >> number.areaCode; // input area code
25       input.ignore( 2 ); // skip ) and space
26       input >> setw( 3 ) >> number.exchange; // input exchange
27       input.ignore(); // skip dash (-)
28       input >> setw( 4 ) >> number.line; // input line
29       return input; // enables cin >> a >> b >> c;
30    } // end function operator>>
```

Fig. 19.4 | Overloaded stream insertion and stream extraction operators for class PhoneNumber.

```
 1    // Fig. 19.5: fig19_05.cpp
 2    // Demonstrating class PhoneNumber's overloaded stream insertion
 3    // and stream extraction operators.
```

Fig. 19.5 | Overloaded stream insertion and stream extraction operators. (Part 1 of 2.)

```
 4    #include <iostream>
 5    #include "PhoneNumber.h"
 6    using namespace std;
 7
 8    int main()
 9    {
10       PhoneNumber phone; // create object phone
11
12       cout << "Enter phone number in the form (123) 456-7890:" << endl;
13
14       // cin >> phone invokes operator>> by implicitly issuing
15       // the non-member function call operator>>( cin, phone )
16       cin >> phone;
17
18       cout << "The phone number entered was: ";
19
20       // cout << phone invokes operator<< by implicitly issuing
21       // the non-member function call operator<<( cout, phone )
22       cout << phone << endl;
23    } // end main
```

```
Enter phone number in the form (123) 456-7890:
(800) 555-1212
The phone number entered was: (800) 555-1212
```

Fig. 19.5 | Overloaded stream insertion and stream extraction operators. (Part 2 of 2.)

Overloading the Stream Extraction (>>) Operator

The stream extraction operator function `operator>>` (Fig. 19.4, lines 21–30) takes the `istream` reference `input` and the `PhoneNumber` reference `number` as arguments and returns an `istream` reference. Operator function `operator>>` inputs phone numbers of the form

```
(800) 555-1212
```

into objects of class `PhoneNumber`. When the compiler sees the expression

```
cin >> phone
```

in line 16 of Fig. 19.5, the compiler generates the *non-member function call*

```
operator>>( cin, phone );
```

When this call executes, reference parameter `input` (Fig. 19.4, line 21) becomes an alias for `cin` and reference parameter `number` becomes an alias for `phone`. The operator function reads as `string`s the three parts of the telephone number into the `areaCode` (line 24), exchange (line 26) and `line` (line 28) members of the `PhoneNumber` object referenced by parameter `number`. Stream manipulator `setw` limits the number of characters read into each `string`. *When used with* `cin` *and* `string`s, *setw restricts the number of characters read to the number of characters specified by its argument* (i.e., `setw(3)` allows three characters to be read). The parentheses, space and dash characters are skipped by calling `istream` member function `ignore` (Fig. 19.4, lines 23, 25 and 27), which discards the specified number of characters in the input stream (one character by default). Function `operator>>` returns `istream` reference `input` (i.e., `cin`). This enables input operations on `PhoneNumber` objects to be cascaded with input operations on other `PhoneNumber` objects or other data types. For example, a program can input two `PhoneNumber` objects in one statement as follows:

```
cin >> phone1 >> phone2;
```

First, the expression `cin >> phone1` executes by making the non-member function call

```
operator>>( cin, phone1 );
```

This call then returns a reference to `cin` as the value of `cin >> phone1`, so the remaining portion of the expression is interpreted simply as `cin >> phone2`. This executes by making the non-member function call

```
operator>>( cin, phone2 );
```

Good Programming Practice 19.1

Overloaded operators should mimic the functionality of their built-in counterparts—for example, the + operator should be overloaded to perform addition, not subtraction. Avoid excessive or inconsistent use of operator overloading, as this can make a program cryptic and difficult to read.

Overloading the Stream Insertion (<<) Operator

The stream insertion operator function (Fig. 19.4, lines 11–16) takes an `ostream` reference (`output`) and a `const PhoneNumber` reference (`number`) as arguments and returns an `ostream` reference. Function `operator<<` displays objects of type `PhoneNumber`. When the compiler sees the expression

```
cout << phone
```

in line 22 of Fig. 19.5, the compiler generates the non-member function call

```
operator<<( cout, phone );
```

Function `operator<<` displays the parts of the telephone number as `strings`, because they're stored as `string` objects.

Error-Prevention Tip 19.1

Returning a reference from an overloaded << or >> operator function is typically successful because cout, cin and most stream objects are global, or at least long-lived. Returning a reference to an automatic variable or other temporary object is dangerous—this can create "dangling references" to nonexisting objects.

Overloaded Operators as Non-Member **friend** Functions

The functions `operator>>` and `operator<<` are declared in `PhoneNumber` as non-member, `friend` functions (Fig. 19.3, lines 12–13). They're non-member functions because the object of class `PhoneNumber` must be the operator's *right* operand. If these were to be `PhoneNumber` member functions, the following awkward statements would have to be used to output and input an `Array`:

```
phone << cout;
phone >> cin;
```

Such statements would be confusing to most C++ programmers, who are familiar with `cout` and `cin` appearing as the *left* operands of `<<` and `>>`, respectively.

Overloaded operator functions for binary operators can be member functions only when the left operand is an object of the class in which the function is a member. *Overloaded input and output operators are declared as `friend`s if they need to access non-`public` class members directly for performance reasons or because the class may not offer appropriate get functions.* Also, the `PhoneNumber` reference in function `operator<<`'s parameter list (Fig. 19.4, line 11) is `const`, because the `PhoneNumber` will simply be output, and the `PhoneNumber` reference in function `operator>>`'s parameter list (line 21) is non-`const`, because the `PhoneNumber` object must be modified to store the input telephone number in the object.

 Software Engineering Observation 19.1

New input/output capabilities for user-defined types are added to C++ without modifying standard input/output library classes. This is another example of C++'s extensibility.

Why Overloaded Stream Insertion and Stream Extraction Operators Are Overloaded as Non-Member Functions

The overloaded stream insertion operator (`<<`) is used in an expression in which the left operand has type `ostream &`, as in `cout << classObject`. To use the operator in this manner where the *right* operand is an object of a user-defined class, it must be overloaded as a non-member function. To be a member function, operator `<<` would have to be a member of the `ostream` class. This is not possible for user-defined classes, since we are *not allowed to modify C++ Standard Library classes*. Similarly, the overloaded stream extraction operator (`>>`) is used in an expression in which the left operand has the type `istream &`, as in the expression `cin >> classObject`, and the *right* operand is an object of a user-defined class, so it, too, must be a non-member function. Also, each of these overloaded operator functions may require access to the `private` data members of the class object being output or input, so these overloaded operator functions can be made `friend` functions of the class for *performance* reasons.

19.6 Overloading Unary Operators

A unary operator for a class can be overloaded as a non-`static` member function with no arguments or as a non-member function with one argument that must be an object (or a reference to an object) of the class. Member functions that implement overloaded operators must be non-`static` so that they can access the non-`static` data in each object of the class.

Unary Overloaded Operators as Member Functions

Consider overloading unary operator `!` to test whether an object of your own `String` class is empty. Such a function would return a `bool` result. When a unary operator such as `!` is overloaded as a member function with no arguments and the compiler sees the expression `!s` (in which `s` is an object of class `String`), the compiler generates the function call `s.operator!()`. The operand `s` is the `String` object for which the `String` class member function `operator!` is being invoked. The function is declared as follows:

```
class String
{
public:
   bool operator!() const;
   ...
}; // end class String
```

Unary Overloaded Operators as Non-Member Functions

A unary operator such as ! may be overloaded as a non-member function with one parameter in two different ways—either with a parameter that's an object (this requires a copy of the object, so the side effects of the function are *not* applied to the original object), or with a parameter that's a reference to an object (no copy of the original object is made, so all side effects of this function are applied to the original object). If s is a String class object (or a reference to a String class object), then !s is treated as if the call operator!(s) had been written, invoking the non-member operator! function that's declared as follows:

```
bool operator!( const String & );
```

19.7 Overloading the Unary Prefix and Postfix ++ and -- Operators

The prefix and postfix versions of the increment and decrement operators can all be overloaded. We'll see how the compiler distinguishes between the prefix version and the postfix version of an increment or decrement operator.

To overload the prefix and postfix increment operators, each overloaded operator function must have a distinct signature, so that the compiler will be able to determine which version of ++ is intended. The prefix versions are overloaded exactly as any other prefix unary operator would be. Everything stated in this section for overloading prefix and postfix increment operators applies to overloading predecrement and postdecrement operators. In the next section, we examine a Date class with overloaded prefix and postfix increment operators.

Overloading the Prefix Increment Operator

Suppose, that we want to add 1 to the day in Date object d1. When the compiler sees the preincrementing expression ++d1, the compiler generates the *member-function call*

```
d1.operator++()
```

The prototype for this operator member function would be

```
Date &operator++();
```

If the prefix increment operator is implemented as a *non-member function*, then, when the compiler sees the expression ++d1, the compiler generates the function call

```
operator++( d1 )
```

The prototype for this non-member operator function would be declared as

```
Date &operator++( Date & );
```

Overloading the Postfix Increment Operator

Overloading the postfix increment operator presents a challenge, because the compiler must be able to distinguish between the signatures of the overloaded prefix and postfix increment operator functions. The *convention* that has been adopted is that, when the compiler sees the postincrementing expression d1++, it generates the *member-function call*

```
d1.operator++( 0 )
```

The prototype for this operator member function is

```
Date operator++( int )
```

The argument 0 is strictly a "dummy value" that enables the compiler to distinguish between the prefix and postfix increment operator functions. The same syntax is used to differentiate between the prefix and postfix decrement operator functions.

If the postfix increment is implemented as a *non-member function*, then, when the compiler sees the expression d1++, the compiler generates the function call

```
operator++( d1, 0 )
```

The prototype for this function would be

```
Date operator++( Date &, int );
```

Once again, the 0 argument is used by the compiler to distinguish between the prefix and postfix increment operators implemented as non-member functions. Note that the *postfix increment operator* returns `Date` objects *by value*, whereas the prefix increment operator returns `Date` objects *by reference*—the postfix increment operator typically returns a temporary object that contains the original value of the object before the increment occurred. C++ treats such objects as *rvalues*, which *cannot be used on the left side of an assignment*. The prefix increment operator returns the actual incremented object with its new value. Such an object *can* be used as an *lvalue* in a continuing expression.

Performance Tip 19.2

The extra object that's created by the postfix *increment (or decrement) operator can result in a performance problem—especially when the operator is used in a loop. For this reason, you should prefer the overloaded* prefix *increment and decrement operators.*

19.8 Case Study: A Date Class

The program of Figs. 19.6–19.8 demonstrates a `Date` class, which uses overloaded prefix and postfix increment operators to add 1 to the day in a `Date` object, while causing appropriate increments to the month and year if necessary. The `Date` header (Fig. 19.6) specifies that `Date`'s `public` interface includes an overloaded stream insertion operator (line 11), a default constructor (line 13), a `setDate` function (line 14), an overloaded prefix increment operator (line 15), an overloaded postfix increment operator (line 16), an overloaded += addition assignment operator (line 17), a function to test for leap years (line 18) and a function to determine whether a day is the last day of the month (line 19).

```
1   // Fig. 19.6: Date.h
2   // Date class definition with overloaded increment operators.
3   #ifndef DATE_H
4   #define DATE_H
5
6   #include <iostream>
7   using namespace std;
8
9   class Date
10  {
11     friend ostream &operator<<( ostream &, const Date & );
```

Fig. 19.6 | Date class definition with overloaded increment operators. (Part 1 of 2.)

```
12    public:
13       Date( int m = 1, int d = 1, int y = 1900 ); // default constructor
14       void setDate( int, int, int ); // set month, day, year
15       Date &operator++(); // prefix increment operator
16       Date operator++( int ); // postfix increment operator
17       const Date &operator+=( int ); // add days, modify object
18       static bool leapYear( int ); // is date in a leap year?
19       bool endOfMonth( int ) const; // is date at the end of month?
20    private:
21       int month;
22       int day;
23       int year;
24
25       static const int days[]; // array of days per month
26       void helpIncrement(); // utility function for incrementing date
27    }; // end class Date
28
29    #endif
```

Fig. 19.6 | Date class definition with overloaded increment operators. (Part 2 of 2.)

```
1     // Fig. 19.7: Date.cpp
2     // Date class member- and friend-function definitions.
3     #include <iostream>
4     #include <string>
5     #include "Date.h"
6     using namespace std;
7
8     // initialize static member; one classwide copy
9     const int Date::days[] =
10       { 0, 31, 28, 31, 30, 31, 30, 31, 31, 30, 31, 30, 31 };
11
12    // Date constructor
13    Date::Date( int month, int day, int year )
14    {
15       setDate( month, day, year );
16    } // end Date constructor
17
18    // set month, day and year
19    void Date::setDate( int mm, int dd, int yy )
20    {
21       if ( mm >= 1 && mm <= 12 )
22          month = mm;
23       else
24          throw invalid_argument( "Month must be 1-12" );
25
26       if ( yy >= 1900 && yy <= 2100 )
27          year = yy;
28       else
29          throw invalid_argument( "Year must be >= 1900 and <= 2100" );
```

Fig. 19.7 | Date class member- and friend-function definitions. (Part 1 of 3.)

```
30
31      // test for a leap year
32      if ( ( month == 2 && leapYear( year ) && dd >= 1 && dd <= 29 ) ||
33          ( dd >= 1 && dd <= days[ month ] ) )
34        day = dd;
35      else
36        throw invalid_argument(
37           "Day is out of range for current month and year" );
38   } // end function setDate
39
40   // overloaded prefix increment operator
41   Date &Date::operator++()
42   {
43      helpIncrement(); // increment date
44      return *this; // reference return to create an lvalue
45   } // end function operator++
46
47   // overloaded postfix increment operator; note that the
48   // dummy integer parameter does not have a parameter name
49   Date Date::operator++( int )
50   {
51      Date temp = *this; // hold current state of object
52      helpIncrement();
53
54      // return unincremented, saved, temporary object
55      return temp; // value return; not a reference return
56   } // end function operator++
57
58   // add specified number of days to date
59   const Date &Date::operator+=( int additionalDays )
60   {
61      for ( int i = 0; i < additionalDays; ++i )
62        helpIncrement();
63
64      return *this; // enables cascading
65   } // end function operator+=
66
67   // if the year is a leap year, return true; otherwise, return false
68   bool Date::leapYear( int testYear )
69   {
70      if ( testYear % 400 == 0 ||
71          ( testYear % 100 != 0 && testYear % 4 == 0 ) )
72        return true; // a leap year
73      else
74        return false; // not a leap year
75   } // end function leapYear
76
77   // determine whether the day is the last day of the month
78   bool Date::endOfMonth( int testDay ) const
79   {
80      if ( month == 2 && leapYear( year ) )
81        return testDay == 29; // last day of Feb. in leap year
```

Fig. 19.7 | Date class member- and `friend`-function definitions. (Part 2 of 3.)

```
82          else
83              return testDay == days[ month ];
84      } // end function endOfMonth
85
86      // function to help increment the date
87      void Date::helpIncrement()
88      {
89          // day is not end of month
90          if ( !endOfMonth( day ) )
91              ++day; // increment day
92          else
93              if ( month < 12 ) // day is end of month and month < 12
94              {
95                  ++month; // increment month
96                  day = 1; // first day of new month
97              } // end if
98              else // last day of year
99              {
100                 ++year; // increment year
101                 month = 1; // first month of new year
102                 day = 1; // first month of new month
103             } // end else
104     } // end function helpIncrement
105
106     // overloaded output operator
107     ostream &operator<<( ostream &output, const Date &d )
108     {
109         static string monthName[ 13 ] = { "", "January", "February",
110             "March", "April", "May", "June", "July", "August",
111             "September", "October", "November", "December" };
112         output << monthName[ d.month ] << ' ' << d.day << ", " << d.year;
113         return output; // enables cascading
114     } // end function operator<<
```

Fig. 19.7 | Date class member- and `friend`-function definitions. (Part 3 of 3.)

```
1   // Fig. 19.08: fig19_08.cpp
2   // Date class test program.
3   #include <iostream>
4   #include "Date.h" // Date class definition
5   using namespace std;
6
7   int main()
8   {
9       Date d1( 12, 27, 2010 ); // December 27, 2010
10      Date d2; // defaults to January 1, 1900
11
12      cout << "d1 is " << d1 << "\nd2 is " << d2;
13      cout << "\n\nd1 += 7 is " << ( d1 += 7 );
14
15      d2.setDate( 2, 28, 2008 );
16      cout << "\n\n  d2 is " << d2;
```

Fig. 19.8 | Date class test program. (Part 1 of 2.)

```
17        cout << "\n++d2 is " << ++d2 << " (leap year allows 29th)";
18
19        Date d3( 7, 13, 2010 );
20
21        cout << "\n\nTesting the prefix increment operator:\n"
22           << "  d3 is " << d3 << endl;
23        cout << "++d3 is " << ++d3 << endl;
24        cout << "  d3 is " << d3;
25
26        cout << "\n\nTesting the postfix increment operator:\n"
27           << "  d3 is " << d3 << endl;
28        cout << "d3++ is " << d3++ << endl;
29        cout << "  d3 is " << d3 << endl;
30    } // end main
```

```
d1 is December 27, 2010
d2 is January 1, 1900

d1 += 7 is January 3, 2011

  d2 is February 28, 2008
++d2 is February 29, 2008 (leap year allows 29th)

Testing the prefix increment operator:
  d3 is July 13, 2010
++d3 is July 14, 2010
  d3 is July 14, 2010

Testing the postfix increment operator:
  d3 is July 14, 2010
d3++ is July 14, 2010
  d3 is July 15, 2010
```

Fig. 19.8 | Date class test program. (Part 2 of 2.)

Function main (Fig. 19.8) creates two Date objects (lines 9–10)—d1 is initialized to December 27, 2010 and d2 is initialized by default to January 1, 1900. The Date constructor (defined in Fig. 19.7, lines 13–16) calls setDate (defined in Fig. 19.7, lines 19–38) to validate the month, day and year specified. Invalid values for the month, day or year result in invalid_argument exceptions.

Line 12 of main outputs each of the Date objects, using the overloaded stream insertion operator (defined in Fig. 19.7, lines 107–114). Line 13 of main uses the overloaded operator += (defined in Fig. 19.7, lines 59–65) to add seven days to d1. Line 15 uses function setDate to set d2 to February 28, 2008, which is a leap year. Then, line 17 preincrements d2 to show that the date increments properly to February 29. Next, line 19 creates a Date object, d3, which is initialized with the date July 13, 2010. Then line 23 increments d3 by 1 with the overloaded prefix increment operator. Lines 21–24 output d3 before and after the preincrement operation to confirm that it worked correctly. Finally, line 28 increments d3 with the overloaded postfix increment operator. Lines 26–29 output d3 before and after the postincrement operation to confirm that it worked correctly.

Date *Class Prefix Increment Operator*
Overloading the prefix increment operator is straightforward. The prefix increment operator (defined in Fig. 19.7, lines 41–45) calls utility function helpIncrement (defined in

Fig. 19.7, lines 87–104) to increment the date. This function deals with "wraparounds" or "carries" that occur when we increment the last day of the month. These carries require incrementing the month. If the month is already 12, then the year must also be incremented and the month must be set to 1. Function `helpIncrement` uses function `endOfMonth` to increment the day correctly.

The overloaded prefix increment operator returns a reference to the current `Date` object (i.e., the one that was just incremented). This occurs because the current object, `*this`, is returned as a `Date &`. This enables a preincremented `Date` object to be used as an *lvalue*, which is how the built-in prefix increment operator works for fundamental types.

Date Class Postfix Increment Operator

Overloading the postfix increment operator (defined in Fig. 19.7, lines 49–56) is trickier. To emulate the effect of the postincrement, we must return an unincremented copy of the `Date` object. For example, if `int` variable x has the value 7, the statement

```
cout << x++ << endl;
```

outputs the original value of variable x. So we'd like our postfix increment operator to operate the same way on a `Date` object. On entry to `operator++`, we save the current object (`*this`) in `temp` (line 51). Next, we call `helpIncrement` to increment the current `Date` object. Then, line 55 returns the unincremented copy of the object previously stored in `temp`. This function cannot return a reference to the local `Date` object `temp`, because a local variable is destroyed when the function in which it's declared exits. Thus, declaring the return type to this function as `Date &` would return a reference to an object that no longer exists. *Returning a reference (or a pointer) to a local variable is a common error for which most compilers will issue a warning.*

19.9 Dynamic Memory Management

A standard C++ array data structure is fixed in size once it's created. The size is specified with a constant at compile time. Sometimes it's useful to determine the size of an array *dynamically* at execution time and then create the array. C++ enables you to control the *allocation* and *deallocation* of memory in a program for objects and for arrays of any built-in or user-defined type. This is known as **dynamic memory management** and is performed with the operators **new** and **delete**. We'll use these capabilities to implement our `Array` class in the next section.

You can use the `new` operator to dynamically **allocate** (i.e., reserve) the exact amount of memory required to hold an object or array at execution time. The object or array is created in the **free store** (also called the **heap**)—*a region of memory assigned to each program for storing dynamically allocated objects.* Once memory is allocated in the free store, you can access it via the pointer that operator `new` returns. When you no longer need the memory, you can return it to the free store by using the `delete` operator to **deallocate** (i.e., release) the memory, which can then be *reused* by future new operations.

Obtaining Dynamic Memory with new
Consider the following statement:

```
Time *timePtr = new Time;
```

The new operator allocates storage of the proper size for an object of type Time, calls the default constructor to initialize the object and returns a pointer to the type specified to the right of the new operator (i.e., a Time *). If new is unable to find sufficient space in memory for the object, it indicates that an error occurred by throwing an exception.

Releasing Dynamic Memory with **delete**

To destroy a dynamically allocated object and free the space for the object, use the delete operator as follows:

```
delete timePtr;
```

This statement first *calls the destructor for the object to which* timePtr *points, then deallocates the memory associated with the object, returning the memory to the free store.*

Common Programming Error 19.1

Not releasing dynamically allocated memory when it's no longer needed can cause the system to run out of memory prematurely. This is sometimes called a "memory leak."

Initializing Dynamic Memory

You can provide an initializer for a newly created fundamental-type variable, as in

```
double *ptr = new double( 3.14159 );
```

which initializes a newly created double to 3.14159 and assigns the resulting pointer to ptr. The same syntax can be used to specify a comma-separated list of arguments to the constructor of an object. For example,

```
Time *timePtr = new Time( 12, 45, 0 );
```

initializes a new Time object to 12:45 PM and assigns the resulting pointer to timePtr.

Dynamically Allocating Arrays with **new []**

You can also use the new operator to allocate arrays dynamically. For example, a 10-element integer array can be allocated and assigned to gradesArray as follows:

```
int *gradesArray = new int[ 10 ];
```

which declares int pointer gradesArray and assigns to it a pointer to the first element of a dynamically allocated 10-element array of ints. The size of an array created at compile time must be specified using a constant integral expression; however, a dynamically allocated array's size can be specified using *any* non-negative integral expression that can be evaluated at execution time. Also, when allocating an array of objects dynamically, you *cannot* pass arguments to each object's constructor—each object is initialized by its default constructor. For fundamental types, the elements are initialized to 0 or the equivalent of 0 (e.g., chars are initialized to the null character, '\0'). Since an array name is a constant pointer to the array's first element, the following is not allowed for dynamically allocated memory:

```
int gradesArray[] = new int[ 10 ];
```

Releasing Dynamically Allocated Arrays with **delete []**

To deallocate the memory to which gradesArray points, use the statement

```
delete [] gradesArray;
```

If the pointer points to an array of objects, the statement first calls the destructor for every object in the array, then deallocates the memory. If the preceding statement did not include the square brackets ([]) and `gradesArray` pointed to an array of objects, the result is *undefined. Some compilers call the destructor only for the first object in the array.* Using `delete` on a null pointer (i.e., a pointer with the value 0) has no effect.

Common Programming Error 19.2

Using `delete` instead of `delete []` for arrays of objects can lead to runtime logic errors. To ensure that every object in the array receives a destructor call, always delete memory allocated as an array with operator `delete []`. Similarly, always delete memory allocated as an individual element with operator `delete`—the result of deleting a single object with operator `delete []` is undefined.

19.10 Case Study: Array Class

We discussed arrays in Chapter 6. An array is not much more than a pointer to some space in memory. Pointer-based arrays have many problems, including:

- A program can easily "walk off" either end of an array, because *C++ does not check whether subscripts fall outside the range of an array* (though you can still do this explicitly).

- Arrays of size *n* must number their elements 0, ..., *n* – 1; alternate subscript ranges are *not* allowed.

- An entire array cannot be input or output at once; each array element must be read or written individually (unless the array is a null-terminated `char *` string).

- Two arrays cannot be meaningfully compared with equality or relational operators (because the array names are simply pointers to where the arrays begin in memory and two arrays will always be at different memory locations).

- When an array is passed to a general-purpose function designed to handle arrays of any size, the array's *size* must be passed as an additional argument.

- One array cannot be assigned to another with the assignment operator(s) (because array names are `const` pointers and a *constant* pointer cannot be used on the left side of an assignment operator).

Class development is an interesting, creative and intellectually challenging activity—always with the goal of "crafting valuable classes." With C++, you can implement more robust array capabilities via classes and operator overloading. You can develop an array class that's preferable to "raw" arrays.

In this example, we create a powerful `Array` class that performs range checking to ensure that subscripts remain within the bounds of the `Array`. The class allows one array object to be assigned to another with the assignment operator. `Array` objects know their size, so the size does not need to be passed separately to functions that receive `Array` parameters. Entire `Array`s can be input or output with the stream extraction and stream insertion operators, respectively. You can compare `Array`s with the equality operators `==` and `!=`. Recall that C++ Standard Library class template `vector` provides many of these capabilities as well.

19.10.1 Using the Array Class

The program of Figs. 19.9–19.11 demonstrates class `Array` and its overloaded operators. First we walk through main (Fig. 19.9) and the program's output, then we consider the class definition (Fig. 19.10) and each of its member-function definitions (Fig. 19.11).

```cpp
 1    // Fig. 19.9: fig19_09.cpp
 2    // Array class test program.
 3    #include <iostream>
 4    #include "Array.h"
 5    using namespace std;
 6
 7    int main()
 8    {
 9       Array integers1( 7 ); // seven-element Array
10       Array integers2; // 10-element Array by default
11
12       // print integers1 size and contents
13       cout << "Size of Array integers1 is "
14          << integers1.getSize()
15          << "\nArray after initialization:\n" << integers1;
16
17       // print integers2 size and contents
18       cout << "\nSize of Array integers2 is "
19          << integers2.getSize()
20          << "\nArray after initialization:\n" << integers2;
21
22       // input and print integers1 and integers2
23       cout << "\nEnter 17 integers:" << endl;
24       cin >> integers1 >> integers2;
25
26       cout << "\nAfter input, the Arrays contain:\n"
27          << "integers1:\n" << integers1
28          << "integers2:\n" << integers2;
29
30       // use overloaded inequality (!=) operator
31       cout << "\nEvaluating: integers1 != integers2" << endl;
32
33       if ( integers1 != integers2 )
34          cout << "integers1 and integers2 are not equal" << endl;
35
36       // create Array integers3 using integers1 as an
37       // initializer; print size and contents
38       Array integers3( integers1 ); // invokes copy constructor
39
40       cout << "\nSize of Array integers3 is "
41          << integers3.getSize()
42          << "\nArray after initialization:\n" << integers3;
43
44       // use overloaded assignment (=) operator
45       cout << "\nAssigning integers2 to integers1:" << endl;
46       integers1 = integers2; // note target Array is smaller
```

Fig. 19.9 | Array class test program. (Part 1 of 3.)

```
47
48        cout << "integers1:\n" << integers1
49          << "integers2:\n" << integers2;
50
51        // use overloaded equality (==) operator
52        cout << "\nEvaluating: integers1 == integers2" << endl;
53
54        if ( integers1 == integers2 )
55          cout << "integers1 and integers2 are equal" << endl;
56
57        // use overloaded subscript operator to create rvalue
58        cout << "\nintegers1[5] is " << integers1[ 5 ];
59
60        // use overloaded subscript operator to create lvalue
61        cout << "\n\nAssigning 1000 to integers1[5]" << endl;
62        integers1[ 5 ] = 1000;
63        cout << "integers1:\n" << integers1;
64
65        // attempt to use out-of-range subscript
66        try
67        {
68          cout << "\nAttempt to assign 1000 to integers1[15]" << endl;
69          integers1[ 15 ] = 1000; // ERROR: subscript out of range
70        } // end try
71        catch ( out_of_range &ex )
72        {
73          cout << "An exception occurred: " << ex.what() << endl;
74        } // end catch
75    } // end main
```

```
Size of Array integers1 is 7
Array after initialization:
            0              0              0              0
            0              0              0

Size of Array integers2 is 10
Array after initialization:
            0              0              0              0
            0              0              0              0
            0              0

Enter 17 integers:
1 2 3 4 5 6 7 8 9 10 11 12 13 14 15 16 17

After input, the Arrays contain:
integers1:
            1              2              3              4
            5              6              7
integers2:
            8              9             10             11
           12             13             14             15
           16             17
```

Fig. 19.9 | Array class test program. (Part 2 of 3.)

```
Evaluating: integers1 != integers2
integers1 and integers2 are not equal

Size of Array integers3 is 7
Array after initialization:
           1               2               3               4
           5               6               7

Assigning integers2 to integers1:
integers1:
           8               9              10              11
          12              13              14              15
          16              17
integers2:
           8               9              10              11
          12              13              14              15
          16              17

Evaluating: integers1 == integers2
integers1 and integers2 are equal

integers1[5] is 13

Assigning 1000 to integers1[5]
integers1:
           8               9              10              11
          12            1000              14              15
          16              17

Attempt to assign 1000 to integers1[15]
An exception occurred: Subscript out of range
```

Fig. 19.9 | Array class test program. (Part 3 of 3.)

Creating Arrays, Outputting Their Size and Displaying Their Contents

The program begins by instantiating two objects of class Array—integers1 (Fig. 19.9, line 9) with seven elements, and integers2 (line 10) with the default Array size—10 elements (specified by the Array default constructor's prototype in Fig. 19.10, line 14). Lines 13–15 use member function getSize to determine the size of integers1 then output integers1's contents, using the Array overloaded stream insertion operator. The sample output confirms that the Array elements were set correctly to zeros by the constructor. Next, lines 18–20 output the size of Array integers2 then output integers2's contents, using the Array overloaded stream insertion operator.

Using the Overloaded Stream Insertion Operator to Fill an Array

Line 23 prompts the user to input 17 integers. Line 24 uses the Array overloaded stream extraction operator to read the first seven values into integers1 and the remaining 10 values into integers2. Lines 26–28 output the two arrays with the overloaded Array stream insertion operator to confirm that the input was performed correctly.

Using the Overloaded Inequality Operator

Line 33 tests the overloaded inequality operator by evaluating the condition

```
integers1 != integers2
```

The program output shows that the Arrays are not equal.

Initializing a New *Array* with a Copy of an Existing *Array's* Contents

Line 38 instantiates a third Array called integers3 and initializes it with a copy of Array integers1. This invokes class Array's **copy constructor** to copy the elements of integers1 into integers3. We discuss the details of the copy constructor shortly. The copy constructor can also be invoked by writing line 38 as follows:

```
Array integers3 = integers1;
```

The equal sign in the preceding statement is *not* the assignment operator. When an equal sign appears in the declaration of an object, it invokes a constructor for that object. This form can be used to pass only a single argument to a constructor—specifically, the value on the right side of the = symbol.

Lines 40–42 output the size of integers3 then output integers3's contents, using the Array overloaded stream insertion operator to confirm that integers3's elements were set correctly by the copy constructor.

Using the Overloaded Assignment Operator

Line 46 tests the overloaded assignment operator (=) by assigning integers2 to integers1. Lines 48–49 display both Array objects' contents to confirm that the assignment was successful. Array integers1 originally held 7 integers, but was resized to hold a copy of the 10 elements in integers2. As we'll see, the overloaded assignment operator performs this resizing operation in a manner that's transparent to the client code.

Using the Overloaded Equality Operator

Line 54 uses the overloaded equality operator (==) to confirm that objects integers1 and integers2 are indeed identical after the assignment in line 46.

Using the Overloaded Subscript Operator

Line 58 uses the overloaded subscript operator to refer to integers1[5]—an in-range element of integers1. This subscripted name is used as an *rvalue* to print the value stored in integers1[5]. Line 62 uses integers1[5] as a modifiable *lvalue* on the left side of an assignment statement to assign a new value, 1000, to element 5 of integers1. We'll see that operator[] returns a reference to use as the modifiable *lvalue* after the operator confirms that 5 is a valid subscript for integers1.

Line 69 attempts to assign the value 1000 to integers1[15]—an *out-of-range* element. In this example, operator[] determines that the subscript is out of range and throws an out_of_range exception.

Interestingly, *the array subscript operator [] is not restricted for use only with arrays*; it also can be used, for example, to select elements from other kinds of *container classes*, such as linked lists, strings and dictionaries. Also, when overloaded operator[] functions are defined, *subscripts no longer have to be integers*—characters, strings or even objects of user-defined classes also could be used.

19.10.2 Array Class Definition

Now that we've seen how this program operates, let's walk through the class header (Fig. 19.10). As we refer to each member function in the header, we discuss that function's implementation in Fig. 19.11. In Fig. 19.10, lines 34–35 represent the private data members of class Array. Each Array object consists of a size member indicating the number of elements in the `Array` and an `int` pointer—`ptr`—that points to the dynamically allocated pointer-based array of integers managed by the `Array` object.

```cpp
1   // Fig. 19.10: Array.h
2   // Array class definition with overloaded operators.
3   #ifndef ARRAY_H
4   #define ARRAY_H
5
6   #include <iostream>
7   using namespace std;
8
9   class Array
10  {
11     friend ostream &operator<<( ostream &, const Array & );
12     friend istream &operator>>( istream &, Array & );
13  public:
14     Array( int = 10 ); // default constructor
15     Array( const Array & ); // copy constructor
16     ~Array(); // destructor
17     int getSize() const; // return size
18
19     const Array &operator=( const Array & ); // assignment operator
20     bool operator==( const Array & ) const; // equality operator
21
22     // inequality operator; returns opposite of == operator
23     bool operator!=( const Array &right ) const
24     {
25        return ! ( *this == right ); // invokes Array::operator==
26     } // end function operator!=
27
28     // subscript operator for non-const objects returns modifiable lvalue
29     int &operator[]( int );
30
31     // subscript operator for const objects returns rvalue
32     int operator[]( int ) const;
33  private:
34     int size; // pointer-based array size
35     int *ptr; // pointer to first element of pointer-based array
36  }; // end class Array
37
38  #endif
```

Fig. 19.10 | Array class definition with overloaded operators.

```cpp
1   // Fig 19.11: Array.cpp
2   // Array class member- and friend-function definitions.
3   #include <iostream>
4   #include <iomanip>
5   #include <cstdlib> // exit function prototype
6   #include "Array.h" // Array class definition
```

Fig. 19.11 | Array class member- and `friend`-function definitions. (Part 1 of 4.)

```cpp
 7   using namespace std;
 8
 9   // default constructor for class Array (default size 10)
10   Array::Array( int arraySize )
11   {
12      // validate arraySize
13      if ( arraySize > 0 )
14         size = arraySize;
15      else
16         throw invalid_argument( "Array size must be greater than 0" );
17
18      ptr = new int[ size ]; // create space for pointer-based array
19
20      for ( int i = 0; i < size; ++i )
21         ptr[ i ] = 0; // set pointer-based array element
22   } // end Array default constructor
23
24   // copy constructor for class Array;
25   // must receive a reference to prevent infinite recursion
26   Array::Array( const Array &arrayToCopy )
27      : size( arrayToCopy.size )
28   {
29      ptr = new int[ size ]; // create space for pointer-based array
30
31      for ( int i = 0; i < size; ++i )
32         ptr[ i ] = arrayToCopy.ptr[ i ]; // copy into object
33   } // end Array copy constructor
34
35   // destructor for class Array
36   Array::~Array()
37   {
38      delete [] ptr; // release pointer-based array space
39   } // end destructor
40
41   // return number of elements of Array
42   int Array::getSize() const
43   {
44      return size; // number of elements in Array
45   } // end function getSize
46
47   // overloaded assignment operator;
48   // const return avoids: ( a1 = a2 ) = a3
49   const Array &Array::operator=( const Array &right )
50   {
51      if ( &right != this ) // avoid self-assignment
52      {
53         // for Arrays of different sizes, deallocate original
54         // left-side array, then allocate new left-side array
55         if ( size != right.size )
56         {
57            delete [] ptr; // release space
58            size = right.size; // resize this object
```

Fig. 19.11 | Array class member- and friend-function definitions. (Part 2 of 4.)

```
59          ptr = new int[ size ]; // create space for array copy
60       } // end inner if
61
62       for ( int i = 0; i < size; ++i )
63          ptr[ i ] = right.ptr[ i ]; // copy array into object
64    } // end outer if
65
66    return *this; // enables x = y = z, for example
67 } // end function operator=
68
69 // determine if two Arrays are equal and
70 // return true, otherwise return false
71 bool Array::operator==( const Array &right ) const
72 {
73    if ( size != right.size )
74       return false; // arrays of different number of elements
75
76    for ( int i = 0; i < size; ++i )
77       if ( ptr[ i ] != right.ptr[ i ] )
78          return false; // Array contents are not equal
79
80    return true; // Arrays are equal
81 } // end function operator==
82
83 // overloaded subscript operator for non-const Arrays;
84 // reference return creates a modifiable lvalue
85 int &Array::operator[]( int subscript )
86 {
87    // check for subscript out-of-range error
88    if ( subscript < 0 || subscript >= size )
89       throw out_of_range( "Subscript out of range" );
90
91    return ptr[ subscript ]; // reference return
92 } // end function operator[]
93
94 // overloaded subscript operator for const Arrays
95 // const reference return creates an rvalue
96 int Array::operator[]( int subscript ) const
97 {
98    // check for subscript out-of-range error
99    if ( subscript < 0 || subscript >= size )
100       throw out_of_range( "Subscript out of range" );
101
102    return ptr[ subscript ]; // returns copy of this element
103 } // end function operator[]
104
105 // overloaded input operator for class Array;
106 // inputs values for entire Array
107 istream &operator>>( istream &input, Array &a )
108 {
109    for ( int i = 0; i < a.size; ++i )
110       input >> a.ptr[ i ];
111
```

Fig. 19.11 | Array class member- and friend-function definitions. (Part 3 of 4.)

```
112        return input; // enables cin >> x >> y;
113    } // end function operator>>
114
115    // overloaded output operator for class Array
116    ostream &operator<<( ostream &output, const Array &a )
117    {
118        int i;
119
120        // output private ptr-based array
121        for ( i = 0; i < a.size; ++i )
122        {
123            output << setw( 12 ) << a.ptr[ i ];
124
125            if ( ( i + 1 ) % 4 == 0 ) // 4 numbers per row of output
126                output << endl;
127        } // end for
128
129        if ( i % 4 != 0 ) // end last line of output
130            output << endl;
131
132        return output; // enables cout << x << y;
133    } // end function operator<<
```

Fig. 19.11 | Array class member- and friend-function definitions. (Part 4 of 4.)

Overloading the Stream Insertion and Stream Extraction Operators as *friends*

Lines 11–12 of Fig. 19.10 declare the overloaded stream insertion operator and the overloaded stream extraction operator as friends of class Array. When the compiler sees an expression like cout << arrayObject, it invokes non-member function operator<< with the call

```
operator<<( cout, arrayObject )
```

When the compiler sees an expression like cin >> arrayObject, it invokes non-member function operator>> with the call

```
operator>>( cin, arrayObject )
```

Again, these stream insertion and stream extraction operator functions cannot be members of class Array, because the Array object is always mentioned on the *right* side of the stream insertion or stream extraction operator.

Function operator<< (defined in Fig. 19.11, lines 116–133) prints the number of elements indicated by size from the integer array to which ptr points. Function operator>> (defined in Fig. 19.11, lines 107–113) inputs directly into the array to which ptr points. Each of these operator functions returns an appropriate reference to enable *cascaded* output or input statements, respectively. These functions have access to an Array's private data because they're declared as friends of class Array. We could have used class Array's getSize and operator[] functions in the bodies of operator<< and operator>>, in which case these operator functions would not need to be friends of class Array. However, the additional function calls might degrade performance.

Array Default Constructor

Line 14 of Fig. 19.10 declares the *default constructor* for the class and specifies a default size of 10 elements. When the compiler sees a declaration like line 10 in Fig. 19.9, it invokes class `Array`'s default constructor to set the size of the `Array` to 10 elements. The default constructor (defined in Fig. 19.11, lines 10–22) validates and assigns the argument to data member `size`, uses `new` to obtain the memory for the internal pointer-based representation of this array and assigns the pointer returned by `new` to data member `ptr`. Then the constructor uses a `for` statement to set all the elements of the array to zero. It's possible to have an `Array` class that does not initialize its members if, for example, these members are to be read at some later time; but this is considered to be a poor programming practice. *Arrays, and objects in general, should be properly initialized as they're created.*

Array Copy Constructor
Line 15 of Fig. 19.10 declares a *copy constructor* (defined in Fig. 19.11, lines 26–33) that initializes an `Array` by making a copy of an existing `Array` object. *Such copying must be done carefully to avoid the pitfall of leaving both `Array` objects pointing to the same dynamically allocated memory.* This is exactly the problem that would occur with default memberwise copying, if the compiler is allowed to define a default copy constructor for this class. Copy constructors are invoked whenever a copy of an object is needed, such as in

- passing an object by value to a function,
- returning an object by value from a function or
- initializing an object with a copy of another object of the same class.

The copy constructor is called in a declaration when an object of class `Array` is instantiated and initialized with another object of class `Array`, as in the declaration in line 38 of Fig. 19.9.

The copy constructor for `Array` uses a member initializer (Fig. 19.11, line 27) to copy the `size` of the initializer `Array` into data member `size`, uses `new` (line 29) to obtain the memory for the internal pointer-based representation of this `Array` and assigns the pointer returned by `new` to data member `ptr`.[1] Then the copy constructor uses a `for` statement to copy all the elements of the initializer `Array` into the new `Array` object. An object of a class can look at the `private` data of any other object of that class (using a handle that indicates which object to access).

Software Engineering Observation 19.2
The argument to a copy constructor should be a `const` reference to allow a `const` object to be copied.

Common Programming Error 19.3
A copy constructor must *receive its argument by reference, not by value. Otherwise, the copy constructor call results in* infinite recursion *(a fatal logic error) because receiving an object by value requires the copy constructor to make a copy of the argument object. Recall that any time a copy of an object is required, the class's copy constructor is called. If the copy constructor received its argument by value, the copy constructor would call itself recursively to make a copy of its argument!*

---

1. Operator `new` could fail to obtain the needed memory, in which case a `bad_alloc` exception will occur. We deal with `new` failures in Chapter 24.

Common Programming Error 19.4

If the copy constructor simply copied the pointer in the source object to the target object's pointer, then both would point to the same *dynamically allocated memory. The first destructor to execute would delete the dynamically allocated memory, and the other object's* ptr *would be* undefined, *a situation called a* dangling pointer—*this would likely result in a serious runtime error (such as early program termination) when the pointer was used.*

Array Destructor

Line 16 of Fig. 19.10 declares the class's destructor (defined in Fig. 19.11, lines 36–39). The destructor is invoked when an object of class Array goes out of scope. The destructor uses delete [] to release the memory allocated dynamically by new in the constructor.

Error-Prevention Tip 19.2

If after deleting dynamically allocated memory, the pointer will continue to exist in memory, set the pointer's value to 0 to indicate that the pointer no longer points to memory in the free store. By setting the pointer to 0, the program loses access to that free-store space, which could be reallocated for a different purpose. If you do not set the pointer to 0, your code *could* inadvertently *access the reallocated memory, causing subtle, nonrepeatable logic errors.*

getSize *Member Function*

Line 17 of Fig. 19.10 declares function getSize (defined in Fig. 19.11, lines 42–45) that returns the number of elements in the Array.

Overloaded Assignment Operator

Line 19 of Fig. 19.10 declares the overloaded assignment operator function for the class. When the compiler sees the expression integers1 = integers2 in line 46 of Fig. 19.9, the compiler invokes member function operator= with the call

```
integers1.operator=( integers2 )
```

Member function operator='s implementation (Fig. 19.11, lines 49–67) tests for **self-assignment** (line 51) in which an Array object is being assigned to itself. When this is equal to the right operand's address, a self-assignment is being attempted, so the assignment is skipped (i.e., the object already is itself; in a moment we'll see why self-assignment is dangerous). If it isn't a self-assignment, then the function determines whether the sizes of the two arrays are identical (line 55); in that case, the original array of integers in the left-side Array object is not reallocated. Otherwise, operator= uses delete (line 57) to release the memory originally allocated to the target array, copies the size of the source array to the size of the target array (line 58), uses new to allocate the memory for the target array and places the pointer returned by new into the array's ptr member. Then the for statement in lines 62–63 copies the array elements from the source array to the target array. Regardless of whether this is a self-assignment, the member function returns the current object (i.e., *this in line 66) as a constant reference; this enables cascaded Array assignments such as x = y = z, but prevents ones like (x = y) = z because z cannot be assigned to the const Array reference that's returned by (x = y). If self-assignment occurs, and function operator= did not test for this case, operator= would unnecessarily copy the elements of the Array into itself.

Software Engineering Observation 19.3

A copy constructor, a destructor and an overloaded assignment operator are usually provided as a group for any class that uses dynamically allocated memory.

Common Programming Error 19.5

Not providing an overloaded assignment operator and a copy constructor for a class when objects of that class contain pointers to dynamically allocated memory is a logic error.

Software Engineering Observation 19.4

It's possible to prevent one object of a class from being assigned to another. This is done by declaring the assignment operator as a `private` member of the class.

Software Engineering Observation 19.5

It's possible to prevent class objects from being copied; to do this, simply make both the overloaded assignment operator and the copy constructor of that class `private`.

Overloaded Equality and Inequality Operators

Line 20 of Fig. 19.10 declares the overloaded equality operator (==) for the class. When the compiler sees the expression `integers1 == integers2` in line 54 of Fig. 19.9, the compiler invokes member function `operator==` with the call

```
integers1.operator==( integers2 )
```

Member function `operator==` (defined in Fig. 19.11, lines 71–81) immediately returns `false` if the `size` members of the arrays are not equal. Otherwise, `operator==` compares each pair of elements. If they're all equal, the function returns `true`. The first pair of elements to differ causes the function to return `false` immediately.

Lines 23–26 of the header define the overloaded inequality operator (!=) for the class. Member function `operator!=` uses the overloaded `operator==` function to determine whether one `Array` is equal to another, then returns the *opposite* of that result. Writing `operator!=` in this manner enables you to *reuse* `operator==`, which *reduces the amount of code that must be written in the class.* Also, the full function definition for `operator!=` is in the `Array` header. This allows the compiler to *inline* the definition of `operator!=` to eliminate the overhead of the extra function call.

Overloaded Subscript Operators

Lines 29 and 32 of Fig. 19.10 declare two overloaded subscript operators (defined in Fig. 19.11 in lines 85–92 and 95–103, respectively). When the compiler sees the expression `integers1[5]` (Fig. 19.9, line 58), it invokes the appropriate overloaded `operator[]` member function by generating the call

```
integers1.operator[]( 5 )
```

The compiler creates a call to the `const` version of `operator[]` (Fig. 19.11, lines 95–103) when the subscript operator is used on a `const Array` object. For example, if `const` object z is instantiated with the statement

```
const Array z( 5 );
```

then the `const` version of `operator[]` is required to execute a statement such as

```
cout << z[ 3 ] << endl;
```

Remember, a program can invoke only the `const` member functions of a `const` object.

Each definition of `operator[]` determines whether the subscript it receives as an argument is *in range* and—if not, each throws an `out_of_range` exception. If the subscript is in range, the non-`const` version of `operator[]` returns the appropriate array element as a reference so that it may be used as a modifiable *lvalue* (e.g., on the left side of an assignment statement). If the subscript is in range, the `const` version of `operator[]` returns a copy of the appropriate element of the array. The returned character is an *rvalue*.

19.11 Operators as Member Functions vs. Non-Member Functions

Whether an operator function is implemented as a member function or as a non-member function, the operator is still used the same way in expressions. So which is best?

When an operator function is implemented as a member function, the leftmost (or only) operand must be an object (or a reference to an object) of the operator's class. If the left operand *must* be an object of a different class or a fundamental type, this operator function *must* be implemented as a non-member function (as we did in Section 19.5 when overloading `<<` and `>>` as the stream insertion and stream extraction operators, respectively). A non-member operator function can be made a `friend` of a class if that function must access `private` or `protected` members of that class directly.

Operator member functions of a specific class are called (implicitly by the compiler) only when the *left* operand of a binary operator is specifically an object of that class, or when the *single operand of a unary operator* is an object of that class.

Commutative Operators

Another reason why you might choose a non-member function to overload an operator is to enable the operator to be *commutative*. For example, suppose we have a *fundamental type variable*, number, of type `long int`, and an *object* `bigInteger1`, of class `HugeInteger` (a class in which integers may be arbitrarily large rather than being limited by the machine word size of the underlying hardware; class `HugeInteger` is developed in the chapter exercises). The addition operator (+) produces a *temporary* `HugeInteger` object as the sum of a `HugeInteger` and a `long int` (as in the expression `bigInteger1 + number`), *or* as the sum of a `long int` and a `HugeInteger` (as in the expression `number + bigInteger1`). Thus, we require the addition operator to be *commutative* (exactly as it is with two fundamental-type operands). The problem is that the class object *must* appear on the *left* of the addition operator if that operator is to be overloaded as a member function. So, we *also* overload the operator as a non-member function to allow the `HugeInteger` to appear on the *right* of the addition. The `operator+` function that deals with the `HugeInteger` on the left can still be a member function. The non-member function can simply swap its arguments and call the member function.

19.12 Converting between Types

Most programs process information of many types. Sometimes all the operations "stay within a type." For example, adding an `int` to an `int` produces an `int`. It's often necessary, however, to convert data of one type to data of another type. This can happen in assignments, in calculations, in passing values to functions and in returning values from functions. The compiler knows how to perform certain conversions among fundamental types. You can use *cast operators* to *force* conversions among fundamental types.

But what about user-defined types? The compiler cannot know in advance how to convert among user-defined types, and between user-defined types and fundamental types, so you must specify how to do this. Such conversions can be performed with **conversion constructors—single-argument constructors** that turn objects of other types (including fundamental types) into objects of a particular class.

A **conversion operator** (also called a *cast operator*) can be used to convert an object of one class into an object of another class or into an object of a fundamental type. Such a conversion operator must be a non-`static` member function. The function prototype

```
A::operator char *() const;
```

declares an overloaded cast operator function for converting an object of user-defined type A into a temporary `char *` object. The operator function is declared `const` because it does not modify the original object. An overloaded **cast operator function** does not specify a return type—the return type is the type to which the object is being converted. If `s` is a class object, when the compiler sees the expression `static_cast< char * >( s )`, the compiler generates the call

```
s.operator char *()
```

The operand `s` is the class object `s` for which the member function `operator char *` is being invoked.

Overloaded cast operator functions can be defined to convert objects of user-defined types into fundamental types or into objects of other user-defined types. The prototypes

```
A::operator int() const;
A::operator OtherClass() const;
```

declare *overloaded cast operator functions* that can convert an object of user-defined type A into an integer or into an object of user-defined type OtherClass, respectively.

One of the nice features of cast operators and conversion constructors is that, when necessary, the compiler can call these functions implicitly to create temporary objects. For example, if an object `s` of a user-defined `String` class appears in a program at a location where an ordinary `char *` is expected, such as

```
cout << s;
```

the compiler can call the overloaded cast-operator function `operator char *` to convert the object into a `char *` and use the resulting `char *` in the expression. With this cast operator provided for a `String` class, the stream insertion operator does not have to be overloaded to output a `String` using `cout`.

Software Engineering Observation 19.6

When a conversion constructor is used to perform an implicit conversion, *C++ can apply only one* implicit constructor call *(i.e., a single user-defined conversion) to try to match the needs of another overloaded operator.* The compiler will not satisfy an overloaded operator's needs by performing a series of implicit, user-defined conversions.

19.13 explicit Constructors

Any single-argument constructor—except a copy constructor—can be used by the compiler to perform an implicit conversion. The constructor's argument is converted to an object of the class in which the constructor is defined. The conversion is automatic and you need not use a cast operator. *In some situations, implicit conversions are undesirable or error-prone.* For example, our Array class in Fig. 19.10 defines a constructor that takes a single int argument. The intent of this constructor is to create an Array object containing the number of elements specified by the int argument. However, this constructor can be misused by the compiler to perform an *implicit conversion.*

Common Programming Error 19.6
Unfortunately, the compiler might use implicit conversions in cases that you do not expect, resulting in ambiguous expressions that generate compilation errors or result in execution-time logic errors.

Accidentally Using a Single-Argument Constructor as a Conversion Constructor
The program (Fig. 19.12) uses the Array class of Figs. 19.10–19.11 to demonstrate an improper implicit conversion.

```cpp
1   // Fig. 19.12: fig19_12.cpp
2   // Single-argument constructors and implicit conversions.
3   #include <iostream>
4   #include "Array.h"
5   using namespace std;
6
7   void outputArray( const Array & ); // prototype
8
9   int main()
10  {
11     Array integers1( 7 ); // 7-element array
12     outputArray( integers1 ); // output Array integers1
13     outputArray( 3 ); // convert 3 to an Array and output Array's contents
14  } // end main
15
16  // print Array contents
17  void outputArray( const Array &arrayToOutput )
18  {
19     cout << "The Array received has " << arrayToOutput.getSize()
20        << " elements. The contents are:\n" << arrayToOutput << endl;
21  } // end outputArray
```

```
The Array received has 7 elements. The contents are:
    0           0           0           0
    0           0           0

The Array received has 3 elements. The contents are:
    0           0           0
```

Fig. 19.12 | Single-argument constructors and implicit conversions.

Line 11 in `main` instantiates `Array` object `integers1` and calls the single argument constructor with the `int` value 7 to specify the number of elements in the `Array`. Recall from Fig. 19.11 that the `Array` constructor that receives an `int` argument initializes all the array elements to 0. Line 12 calls function `outputArray` (defined in lines 17–21), which receives as its argument a `const Array &` to an `Array`. The function outputs the number of elements in its `Array` argument and the contents of the `Array`. In this case, the size of the `Array` is 7, so seven 0s are output.

Line 13 calls function `outputArray` with the `int` value 3 as an argument. However, this program does *not* contain a function called `outputArray` that takes an `int` argument. So, the compiler determines whether class `Array` provides a *conversion constructor* that can convert an `int` into an `Array`. Since the `Array` constructor receives one `int` argument, the compiler assumes that the constructor is a conversion constructor that can be used to convert the argument 3 into a temporary `Array` object containing three elements. Then, the compiler passes the temporary `Array` object to function `outputArray` to output the `Array`'s contents. Thus, even though we do not explicitly provide an `outputArray` function that receives an `int` argument, the compiler is able to compile line 13. The output shows the contents of the three-element `Array` containing 0s.

Preventing Implicit Conversions with Single-Argument Constructors

C++ provides the keyword **explicit** to *suppress implicit conversions via conversion constructors when such conversions should not be allowed*. A constructor that's declared `explicit` *cannot* be used in an implicit conversion. In the example of Figure 19.13, the only modification to the included file `Array.h` from Fig. 19.10 was the addition of the keyword `explicit` to the declaration of the single-argument constructor in line 14, as in

```
explicit Array( int = 10 ); // default constructor
```

No modifications are required to the source-code file containing class `Array`'s member-function definitions.

Figure 19.13 presents a slightly modified version of the program in Fig. 19.12. When this program is compiled, the compiler produces an error message indicating that the integer value passed to `outputArray` in line 13 cannot be converted to a `const Array &`. The compiler error message (from Visual C++) is shown in the output window. Line 14 demonstrates how the explicit constructor can be used to create a temporary `Array` of 3 elements and pass it to function `outputArray`.

> **Error-Prevention Tip 19.3**
> *Use the `explicit` keyword on single-argument constructors that should not be used by the compiler to perform implicit conversions.*

```
1   // Fig. 19.13: fig19_13.cpp
2   // Driver for simple class Array; demonstrating an explicit constructor.
3   #include <iostream>
4   #include "Array.h"
5   using namespace std;
6
```

Fig. 19.13 | Driver for simple class `Array`; demonstrating an `explicit` constructor. (Part 1 of 2.)

```
 7   void outputArray( const Array & ); // prototype
 8
 9   int main()
10   {
11      Array integers1( 7 ); // 7-element array
12      outputArray( integers1 ); // output Array integers1
13      outputArray( 3 ); // convert 3 to an Array and output Array's contents
14      outputArray( Array( 3 ) ); // explicit single-argument constructor call
15   } // end main
16
17   // print array contents
18   void outputArray( const Array &arrayToOutput )
19   {
20      cout << "The Array received has " << arrayToOutput.getSize()
21         << " elements. The contents are:\n" << arrayToOutput << endl;
22   } // end outputArray
```

```
c:\examples\ch19\fig19_13\fig19_13.cpp(13) : error C2664:
'outputArray' : cannot convert parameter 1 from 'int' to 'const Array &'
      Reason: cannot convert from 'int' to 'const Array'
      Constructor for class 'Array' is declared 'explicit'
```

Fig. 19.13 | Driver for simple class `Array`; demonstrating an `explicit` constructor. (Part 2 of 2.)

19.14 Building a String Class

We've discussed C-style, pointer-based string processing with character arrays. As part of our coverage of crafting valuable classes, we implement our own `String` class that encapsulates a dynamically allocated `char *` string and provides many capabilities that are similar to those we introduced in the `Array` class. Because classes `Array` and `String` are so similar, we placed our `String` class's code and discussion online at www.deitel.com/books/chtp7/ under **Downloads and Resources for Registered Users**. The C++ standard library includes the similar, more robust class `string`, which we demonstrated in Section 19.2. In this section, we discuss one key feature of our `String` class.

Overloaded Function Call Operator
Overloading the **function call operator ()** is powerful, because functions can take an *arbitrary* number of parameters. In our `String` class, we overload this operator to select a substring from a `String`. The operator's two integer parameters specify the start location and the length of the substring to be selected. If the start location is out of range or the substring length is negative, the operator simply returns an empty `String`. If the substring length is 0, then the substring is selected to the end of the `String` object. Suppose `string1` is a `String` object containing the string "AEIOU". When the compiler encounters the expression `string1(2, 2)`, it generates the member-function call

```
string1.operator()( 2, 2 )
```

which returns a `String` containing "IO".

19.15 Wrap-Up

In this chapter, you learned how to overload operators to work with class objects. We demonstrated standard C++ class `string`, which makes extensive use of overloaded operators to create a robust, reusable class that can replace C-style, pointer-based strings. Next, we discussed several restrictions that the C++ standard places on overloaded operators. We then presented a PhoneNumber class that overloaded operators << and >> to conveniently output and input phone numbers. You also saw a Date class that overloaded the prefix and postfix increment (++) operators and we showed a special syntax that's required to differentiate between the prefix and postfix versions of the increment (++) operator.

Next, we introduced the concept of dynamic memory management. You learned that you can create and destroy objects dynamically with the `new` and `delete` operators, respectively. Then, we presented a capstone Array class case study that used overloaded operators and other capabilities to solve various problems with pointer-based arrays. This case study helped you truly understand what classes and object technology are all about—crafting, using and reusing valuable classes. As part of this class, you saw overloaded stream insertion, stream extraction, assignment, equality, relational and subscript operators.

You learned reasons for implementing overloaded operators as member functions or as non-member functions. The chapter concluded with discussions of converting between types (incuding class types), problems with certain implicit conversions defined by single-argument constructors and how to prevent those problems by using `explicit` constructors.

In the next chapter, we continue our discussion of classes by introducing a form of software reuse called inheritance. We'll see that when classes share common attributes and behaviors, it's possible to define those attributes and behaviors in a common "base" class and "inherit" those capabilities into new class definitions, enabling you to create the new classes with a minimal amount of code.

Summary

Section 19.1 Introduction
- C++ enables you to overload most operators to be sensitive to the context in which they're used—the compiler generates the appropriate code based on the types of the operands.
- One example of an overloaded operator built into C++ is operator <<, which is used both as the stream insertion operator and as the bitwise left-shift operator. Similarly, >> is also overloaded; it's used both as the stream extraction operator and as the bitwise right-shift operator. Both of these operators are overloaded in the C++ Standard Library.
- C++ overloads + and - to perform differently, depending on their context in integer arithmetic, floating-point arithmetic and pointer arithmetic.
- The jobs performed by overloaded operators can also be performed by explicit function calls, but operator notation is often more natural.

Section 19.2 Using the Overloaded Operators of Standard Library Class `string`
- Standard class `string` is defined in header `<string>` and belongs to namespace `std`.
- Class `string` provides many overloaded operators, including equality, relational, assignment, addition assignment (for concatenation) and subscript operators.
- Class `string` provides member function empty (p. 727), which returns `true` if the `string` is empty; otherwise, it returns `false`.

- Standard class string member function substr (p. 727) obtains a substring of a length specified by the second argument, starting at the position specified by the first argument. When the second argument is not specified, substr returns the remainder of the string on which it's called.

- Class string's overloaded [] operator does not perform any bounds checking. Therefore, you must ensure that operations using standard class string's overloaded [] operator do not accidentally manipulate elements outside the bounds of the string.

- Standard class string provides bounds checking with member function at (p. 728), which "throws an exception" if its argument is an invalid subscript. By default, this causes the program to terminate. If the subscript is valid, function at returns a reference or a const reference to the character at the specified location depending on the context.

Section 19.3 Fundamentals of Operator Overloading

- An operator is overloaded by writing a non-static member-function definition or non-member function definition in which the function name is the keyword operator followed by the symbol for the operator being overloaded.

- When operators are overloaded as member functions, they must be non-static, because they must be called on an object of the class and operate on that object.

- To use an operator on class objects, that operator *must* be overloaded, with three exceptions—the assignment operator (=), the address operator (&) and the comma operator (,).

- You cannot change the precedence and associativity of an operator by overloading.

- You cannot change the "arity" of an operator (i.e., the number of operands an operator takes).

- You cannot create new operators—only existing operators can be overloaded.

- You cannot change the meaning of how an operator works on objects of fundamental types.

- Overloading an assignment operator and an addition operator for a class does not imply that the += operator is also overloaded. Such behavior can be achieved only by explicitly overloading operator += for that class.

- Overloaded (), [], -> and assignment operators must be declared as class members. For the other operators, the operator overloading functions can be class members or non-member functions.

Section 19.4 Overloading Binary Operators

- A binary operator can be overloaded as a non-static member function with one argument or as a non-member function with two arguments (one of those arguments must be either a class object or a reference to a class object).

Section 19.5 Overloading the Binary Stream Insertion and Stream Extraction Operators

- The overloaded stream insertion operator (<<) is used in an expression in which the left operand has type ostream &. For this reason, it must be overloaded as a non-member function. To be a member function, operator << would have to be a member of the ostream class, but this is not possible, since we are not allowed to modify C++ Standard Library classes. Similarly, the overloaded stream extraction operator (>>) must be a non-member function.

- Another reason to choose a non-member function to overload an operator is to enable the operator to be commutative.

- When used with cin, setw restricts the number of characters read to the number of characters specified by its argument.

- istream member function ignore discards the specified number of characters in the input stream (one character by default).

- Overloaded input and output operators are declared as `friends` if they need to access non-`public` class members directly for performance reasons.

Section 19.6 Overloading Unary Operators

- A unary operator for a class can be overloaded as a non-`static` member function with no arguments or as a non-member function with one argument; that argument must be either an object of the class or a reference to an object of the class.

- Member functions that implement overloaded operators must be non-`static` so that they can access the non-`static` data in each object of the class.

Section 19.7 Overloading the Unary Prefix and Postfix ++ and -- Operators

- The prefix and postfix increment and decrement operators can all be overloaded.

- To overload the pre- and post-increment operators, each overloaded operator function must have a distinct signature. The prefix versions are overloaded like any other unary operator. The postfix increment operator's unique signature is accomplished by providing a second argument, which must be of type `int`. This argument is not supplied in the client code. It's used implicitly by the compiler to distinguish between the prefix and postfix versions of the increment operator. The same syntax is used to differentiate between the prefix and postfix decrement operator functions.

Section 19.9 Dynamic Memory Management

- Dynamic memory management (p. 741) enables you to control the allocation and deallocation of memory in a program for any built-in or user-defined type.

- The free store (sometimes called the heap; p. 741) is a region of memory assigned to each program for storing objects dynamically allocated at execution time.

- The `new` operator (p. 741) allocates storage of the proper size for an object, runs the object's constructor and returns a pointer of the correct type. The `new` operator can be used to dynamically allocate (p. 741) any fundamental type (such as `int` or `double`) or class type. If `new` is unable to find space in memory for the object, it indicates that an error occurred by "throwing" an "exception." This usually causes the program to terminate immediately, unless the exception is handled.

- To destroy a dynamically allocated object and free its space, use the `delete` operator (p. 741).

- An array of objects can be allocated dynamically with `new` as in

      `int *ptr = new int[ 100 ];`

  which allocates an array of 100 integers and assigns the starting location of the array to `ptr`. The preceding array of integers is deleted (p. 741) with the statement

      `delete [] ptr;`

Section 19.10 Case Study: Array Class

- A copy constructor initializes a new object of a class by copying the members of an existing one. Classes that contain dynamically allocated memory typically provide a copy constructor, a destructor and an overloaded assignment operator.

- The implementation of member function `operator=` should test for self-assignment (p. 753), in which an object is being assigned to itself.

- The compiler calls the `const` version of `operator[]` when the subscript operator is used on a `const` object and calls the non-`const` version of the operator when it's used on a non-`const` object.

- The array subscript operator (`[]`) can be used to select elements from other types of containers. Also, with overloading, the index values no longer need to be integers.

Section 19.11 Operators as Member Functions vs. Non-Member Functions

- Operator functions can be member functions or non-member functions—non-member functions are often made friends for performance reasons. Member functions use the this pointer implicitly to obtain one of their class object arguments (the left operand for binary operators). Arguments for both operands of a binary operator must be explicitly listed in a non-member function call.

- When an operator function is implemented as a member function, the leftmost (or only) operand must be an object (or a reference to an object) of the operator's class.

- If the left operand must be an object of a different class or a fundamental type, this operator function must be implemented as a non-member function.

- A non-member operator function can be made a friend of a class if that function must access private or protected members of that class directly.

Section 19.12 Converting between Types

- The compiler cannot know in advance how to convert among user-defined types, and between user-defined types and fundamental types, so you must specify how to do this. Such conversions can be performed with conversion constructors (p. 756)—single-argument constructors (p. 756) that turn objects of other types (including fundamental types) into objects of a particular class.

- Any single-argument constructor can be thought of as a conversion constructor.

- A conversion operator (p. 756) must be a non-static member function. Overloaded cast-operator functions (p. 756) can be defined for converting objects of user-defined types into fundamental types or into objects of other user-defined types.

- An overloaded cast operator function does not specify a return type—the return type is the type to which the object is being converted.

- When necessary, the compiler can call cast operators and conversion constructors implicitly to create temporary objects.

Section 19.13 explicit Constructors

- C++ provides the keyword explicit (p. 758) to suppress implicit conversions via conversion constructors when such conversions should not be allowed. A constructor that's declared explicit cannot be used in an implicit conversion.

Section 19.14 Building a String Class

- Overloading the function call operator () (p. 759) is powerful, because functions can take an arbitrary number of parameters.

Self-Review Exercises

19.1 Fill in the blanks in each of the following:

    a) Suppose a and b are integer variables and we form the sum a + b. Now suppose c and d are floating-point variables and we form the sum c + d. The two + operators here are clearly being used for different purposes. This is an example of _____.

    b) Keyword _____ introduces an overloaded-operator function definition.

    c) To use operators on class objects, they must be overloaded, with the exception of operators _____, _____ and _____.

    d) The _____, _____ and _____ of an operator cannot be changed by overloading the operator.

    e) The operators that cannot be overloaded are _____, _____, _____ and _____.

    f) The _____ operator reclaims memory previously allocated by new.

g) The _____ operator dynamically allocates memory for an object of a specified type and returns a(n) _____ to that type.

19.2 Explain the multiple meanings of the operators + and -.

19.3 In what context might the name `operator/` be used?

19.4 (True/False) When operators are overloaded as member functions, they must be non-static.

19.5 How does the precedence of an overloaded operator compare with the precedence of the original operator?

Answers to Self-Review Exercises

19.1 a) operator overloading. b) `operator`. c) assignment (=), address (&), comma (,). d) precedence, associativity, "arity." e) ., ?:, .*, and ::. f) `delete`. g) new, pointer.

19.2 The + operator is used for addition and the – operator is used for subtraction. C++ overloads the addition operator (+) and the subtraction operator (-) to perform differently, depending on their context in integer, floating-point and pointer arithmetic with data of fundamental types.

19.3 For operator overloading: It would be the name of a function that would provide an overloaded version of the / operator for a specific class.

19.4 True.

19.5 The precedence is identical.

Exercises

19.6 *(Rules and Restrictions)* Discuss the rules and restrictions of operator overloading.

19.7 *(Overloading the Parentheses Operator)* One nice example of overloading the function call operator () is to allow another form of double-array subscripting popular in some programming languages. Instead of saying

```
chessBoard[ row ][ column ]
```

for an array of objects, overload the function call operator to allow the alternate form

```
chessBoard( row, column )
```

Create a class `DoubleSubscriptedArray` that has similar features to class `Array` in Figs. 19.10–19.11. At construction time, the class should be able to create an array of any number of rows and any number of columns. The class should supply `operator()` to perform double-subscripting operations. For example, in a 3-by-5 `DoubleSubscriptedArray` called a, the user could write a(1, 3) to access the element at row 1 and column 3. Remember that `operator()` can receive any number of arguments. The underlying representation of the double-subscripted array should be a single-subscripted array of integers with *rows * columns* number of elements. Function `operator()` should perform the proper pointer arithmetic to access each element of the array. There should be two versions of `operator()`—one that returns `int &` (so that an element of a `DoubleSubscriptedArray` can be used as an *lvalue*) and one that returns `const int &`. The class should also provide the following operators: ==, !=, =, << (for outputting the array in row and column format) and >> (for inputting the entire array contents).

19.8 *(Complex Class)* Consider class `Complex` shown in Figs. 19.14–19.16. The class enables operations on so-called *complex numbers*. These are numbers of the form realPart + imaginaryPart * *i*, where *i* has the value

$$\sqrt{-1}$$

a) Modify the class to enable input and output of complex numbers via overloaded >> and
<< operators, respectively (you should remove the print function from the class).

b) Overload the multiplication operator to enable multiplication of two complex numbers
as in algebra.

c) Overload the == and != operators to allow comparisons of complex numbers.

```
1   // Fig. 19.14: Complex.h
2   // Complex class definition.
3   #ifndef COMPLEX_H
4   #define COMPLEX_H
5
6   class Complex
7   {
8   public:
9      Complex( double = 0.0, double = 0.0 ); // constructor
10     Complex operator+( const Complex & ) const; // addition
11     Complex operator-( const Complex & ) const; // subtraction
12     void print() const; // output
13  private:
14     double real; // real part
15     double imaginary; // imaginary part
16  }; // end class Complex
17
18  #endif
```

Fig. 19.14 | Complex class definition.

```
1   // Fig. 19.15: Complex.cpp
2   // Complex class member-function definitions.
3   #include <iostream>
4   #include "Complex.h" // Complex class definition
5   using namespace std;
6
7   // Constructor
8   Complex::Complex( double realPart, double imaginaryPart )
9      : real( realPart ),
10     imaginary( imaginaryPart )
11  {
12     // empty body
13  } // end Complex constructor
14
15  // addition operator
16  Complex Complex::operator+( const Complex &operand2 ) const
17  {
18     return Complex( real + operand2.real,
19        imaginary + operand2.imaginary );
20  } // end function operator+
21
22  // subtraction operator
23  Complex Complex::operator-( const Complex &operand2 ) const
24  {
25     return Complex( real - operand2.real,
26        imaginary - operand2.imaginary );
27  } // end function operator-
28
```

Fig. 19.15 | Complex class member-function definitions. (Part 1 of 2.)

```
29    // display a Complex object in the form: (a, b)
30    void Complex::print() const
31    {
32       cout << '(' << real << ", " << imaginary << ')';
33    } // end function print
```

Fig. 19.15 | Complex class member-function definitions. (Part 2 of 2.)

```
1    // Fig. 19.16: fig19_16.cpp
2    // Complex class test program.
3    #include <iostream>
4    #include "Complex.h"
5    using namespace std;
6
7    int main()
8    {
9       Complex x;
10      Complex y( 4.3, 8.2 );
11      Complex z( 3.3, 1.1 );
12
13      cout << "x: ";
14      x.print();
15      cout << "\ny: ";
16      y.print();
17      cout << "\nz: ";
18      z.print();
19
20      x = y + z;
21      cout << "\n\nx = y + z:" << endl;
22      x.print();
23      cout << " = ";
24      y.print();
25      cout << " + ";
26      z.print();
27
28      x = y - z;
29      cout << "\n\nx = y - z:" << endl;
30      x.print();
31      cout << " = ";
32      y.print();
33      cout << " - ";
34      z.print();
35      cout << endl;
36    } // end main
```

```
x: (0, 0)
y: (4.3, 8.2)
z: (3.3, 1.1)

x = y + z:
(7.6, 9.3) = (4.3, 8.2) + (3.3, 1.1)

x = y - z:
(1, 7.1) = (4.3, 8.2) - (3.3, 1.1)
```

Fig. 19.16 | Complex class test program.

19.9   *(HugeInt Class)* A machine with 32-bit integers can represent integers in the range of approximately –2 billion to +2 billion. This fixed-size restriction is rarely troublesome, but there are applications in which we would like to be able to use a much wider range of integers. This is what

C++ was built to do, namely, create powerful new data types. Consider class HugeInt of Figs. 19.17–19.19. Study the class carefully, then answer the following:

a) Describe precisely how it operates.
b) What restrictions does the class have?
c) Overload the * multiplication operator.
d) Overload the / division operator.
e) Overload all the relational and equality operators.

[*Note:* We do not show an assignment operator or copy constructor for class HugeInteger, because the assignment operator and copy constructor provided by the compiler are capable of copying the entire array data member properly.]

```
1    // Fig. 19.17: Hugeint.h
2    // HugeInt class definition.
3    #ifndef HUGEINT_H
4    #define HUGEINT_H
5
6    #include <iostream>
7    #include <string>
8    using namespace std;
9
10   class HugeInt
11   {
12      friend ostream &operator<<( ostream &, const HugeInt & );
13   public:
14      static const int digits = 30; // maximum digits in a HugeInt
15
16      HugeInt( long = 0 ); // conversion/default constructor
17      HugeInt( const string & ); // conversion constructor
18
19      // addition operator; HugeInt + HugeInt
20      HugeInt operator+( const HugeInt & ) const;
21
22      // addition operator; HugeInt + int
23      HugeInt operator+( int ) const;
24
25      // addition operator;
26      // HugeInt + string that represents large integer value
27      HugeInt operator+( const string & ) const;
28   private:
29      short integer[ digits ];
30   }; // end class HugetInt
31
32   #endif
```

Fig. 19.17 | HugeInt class definition.

```
1    // Fig. 19.18: Hugeint.cpp
2    // HugeInt member-function and friend-function definitions.
3    #include <cctype> // isdigit function prototype
4    #include "Hugeint.h" // HugeInt class definition
5    using namespace std;
6
7    // default constructor; conversion constructor that converts
8    // a long integer into a HugeInt object
9    HugeInt::HugeInt( long value )
10   {
```

Fig. 19.18 | HugeInt member-function and friend-function definitions. (Part 1 of 3.)

```
11      // initialize array to zero
12      for ( int i = 0; i < digits; ++i )
13         integer[ i ] = 0;
14
15      // place digits of argument into array
16      for ( int j = digits - 1; value != 0 && j >= 0; j-- )
17      {
18         integer[ j ] = value % 10;
19         value /= 10;
20      } // end for
21   } // end HugeInt default/conversion constructor
22
23   // conversion constructor that converts a character string
24   // representing a large integer into a HugeInt object
25   HugeInt::HugeInt( const string &number )
26   {
27      // initialize array to zero
28      for ( int i = 0; i < digits; ++i )
29         integer[ i ] = 0;
30
31      // place digits of argument into array
32      int length = number.size();
33
34      for ( int j = digits - length, k = 0; j < digits; ++j, ++k )
35         if ( isdigit( number[ k ] ) ) // ensure that character is a digit
36            integer[ j ] = number[ k ] - '0';
37   } // end HugeInt conversion constructor
38
39   // addition operator; HugeInt + HugeInt
40   HugeInt HugeInt::operator+( const HugeInt &op2 ) const
41   {
42      HugeInt temp; // temporary result
43      int carry = 0;
44
45      for ( int i = digits - 1; i >= 0; i-- )
46      {
47         temp.integer[ i ] = integer[ i ] + op2.integer[ i ] + carry;
48
49         // determine whether to carry a 1
50         if ( temp.integer[ i ] > 9 )
51         {
52            temp.integer[ i ] %= 10;   // reduce to 0-9
53            carry = 1;
54         } // end if
55         else // no carry
56            carry = 0;
57      } // end for
58
59      return temp; // return copy of temporary object
60   } // end function operator+
61
62   // addition operator; HugeInt + int
63   HugeInt HugeInt::operator+( int op2 ) const
64   {
65      // convert op2 to a HugeInt, then invoke
66      // operator+ for two HugeInt objects
67      return *this + HugeInt( op2 );
68   } // end function operator+
69
```

Fig. 19.18 | HugeInt member-function and friend-function definitions. (Part 2 of 3.)

```
70     // addition operator;
71     // HugeInt + string that represents large integer value
72     HugeInt HugeInt::operator+( const string &op2 ) const
73     {
74        // convert op2 to a HugeInt, then invoke
75        // operator+ for two HugeInt objects
76        return *this + HugeInt( op2 );
77     } // end operator+
78
79     // overloaded output operator
80     ostream& operator<<( ostream &output, const HugeInt &num )
81     {
82        int i;
83
84        for ( i = 0; ( num.integer[ i ] == 0 ) && ( i <= HugeInt::digits ); ++i )
85           ; // skip leading zeros
86
87        if ( i == HugeInt::digits )
88           output << 0;
89        else
90           for ( ; i < HugeInt::digits; ++i )
91              output << num.integer[ i ];
92
93        return output;
94     } // end function operator<<
```

Fig. 19.18 | HugeInt member-function and friend-function definitions. (Part 3 of 3.)

```
1     // Fig. 19.19: fig19_19.cpp
2     // HugeInt test program.
3     #include <iostream>
4     #include "Hugeint.h"
5     using namespace std;
6
7     int main()
8     {
9        HugeInt n1( 7654321 );
10       HugeInt n2( 7891234 );
11       HugeInt n3( "99999999999999999999999999999" );
12       HugeInt n4( "1" );
13       HugeInt n5;
14
15       cout << "n1 is " << n1 << "\nn2 is " << n2
16          << "\nn3 is " << n3 << "\nn4 is " << n4
17          << "\nn5 is " << n5 << "\n\n";
18
19       n5 = n1 + n2;
20       cout << n1 << " + " << n2 << " = " << n5 << "\n\n";
21
22       cout << n3 << " + " << n4 << "\n= " << ( n3 + n4 ) << "\n\n";
23
24       n5 = n1 + 9;
25       cout << n1 << " + " << 9 << " = " << n5 << "\n\n";
26
27       n5 = n2 + "10000";
28       cout << n2 << " + " << "10000" << " = " << n5 << endl;
29    } // end main
```

Fig. 19.19 | HugeInt test program. (Part 1 of 2.)

```
n1 is 7654321
n2 is 7891234
n3 is 99999999999999999999999999999
n4 is 1
n5 is 0

7654321 + 7891234 = 15545555

99999999999999999999999999999 + 1
= 100000000000000000000000000000

7654321 + 9 = 7654330

7891234 + 10000 = 7901234
```

Fig. 19.19 | HugeInt test program. (Part 2 of 2.)

19.10 *(NaturalNumber Class)* Create a class `NaturalNumber` with the following capabilities:
    a) Create a constructor that verifies whether the given number is a natural number and sets the number to 1 if it is not a natural number.
    b) Overload the addition and multiplication operators for this class.
    c) Overload the relational and equality operators for this class.

19.11 *(Polynomial Class)* Develop class `Polynomial`. The internal representation of a `Polynomial` is an array of terms. Each term contains a coefficient and an exponent, e.g., the term

$$2x^4$$

has the coefficient 2 and the exponent 4. Develop a complete class containing proper constructor and destructor functions as well as *set* and *get* functions. The class should also provide the following overloaded operator capabilities:
    a) Overload the addition operator (+) to add two `Polynomial`s.
    b) Overload the subtraction operator (-) to subtract two `Polynomial`s.
    c) Overload the assignment operator to assign one `Polynomial` to another.
    d) Overload the multiplication operator (*) to multiply two `Polynomial`s.
    e) Overload the addition assignment operator (+=), subtraction assignment operator (-=), and multiplication assignment operator (*=).

Object-Oriented Programming: Inheritance

20

Objectives

In this chapter you'll learn:

- What inheritance is and how it promotes software reuse.
- The notions of base classes and derived classes and the relationships between them.
- The **protected** member access specifier.
- The use of constructors and destructors in inheritance hierarchies.
- The order in which constructors and destructors are called in inheritance hierarchies.
- The differences between `public`, `protected` and `private` inheritance.
- To use inheritance to customize existing software.

20.1 Introduction

This chapter continues our discussion of object-oriented programming (OOP) by introducing inheritance—a form of software reuse in which you create a class that absorbs an existing class's capabilities, then *customizes* or enhances them. Software reuse saves time during program development by taking advantage of proven, high-quality software.

When creating a class, instead of writing completely new data members and member functions, you can specify that the new class should inherit the members of an existing class. This existing class is called the base class, and the new class is called the derived class. Other programming languages, such as Java and C#, refer to the base class as the superclass and the derived class as the subclass. A derived class represents a *more specialized* group of objects.

C++ offers public, protected and private inheritance. In this chapter, we concentrate on public inheritance and briefly explain the other two. *With public inheritance, every object of a derived class is also an object of that derived class's base class.* However, base-class objects are *not* objects of their derived classes. For example, if we have Vehicle as a base class and Car as a derived class, then all Cars are Vehicles, but not all Vehicles are Cars—for example, a Vehicle could also be a Truck or a Boat.

We distinguish between the *is-a* relationship and the *has-a* relationship. The *is-a* relationship represents inheritance. In an *is-a* relationship, an object of a derived class also can be treated as an object of its base class—for example, a Car *is a* Vehicle, so any attributes and behaviors of a Vehicle are also attributes and behaviors of a Car. By contrast, the *has-a* relationship represents *composition*, which was discussed in Chapter 18. In a *has-a* relationship, an object *contains* one or more objects of other classes as members. For example, a Car has many components—it *has a* steering wheel, *has a* brake pedal, *has a* transmission, etc.

20.2 Base Classes and Derived Classes

Figure 20.1 lists several simple examples of base classes and derived classes. Base classes tend to be *more general* and derived classes tend to be *more specific*.

Base class	Derived classes
Student	GraduateStudent, UndergraduateStudent
Shape	Circle, Triangle, Rectangle, Sphere, Cube
Loan	CarLoan, HomeImprovementLoan, MortgageLoan
Employee	Faculty, Staff
Account	CheckingAccount, SavingsAccount

Fig. 20.1 | Inheritance examples.

Because every derived-class object *is an* object of its base class, and one base class can have *many* derived classes, the set of objects represented by a base class typically is *larger* than the set of objects represented by any of its derived classes. For example, the base class Vehicle represents all vehicles, including cars, trucks, boats, airplanes, bicycles and so on. By contrast, derived class Car represents a *smaller, more specific* subset of all vehicles.

Inheritance relationships form class hierarchies. A base class exists in a hierarchical relationship with its derived classes. Although classes can exist independently, once they're employed in inheritance relationships, they become affiliated with other classes. A class becomes either a base class—supplying members to other classes, a derived class—inheriting its members from other classes, or *both*.

CommunityMember Class Hierarchy

Let's develop a simple inheritance hierarchy with five levels (represented by the UML class diagram in Fig. 20.2). A university community has thousands of CommunityMembers. These CommunityMembers consist of Employees, Students and alumni (each of class Alumnus). Employees are either Faculty or Staff. Faculty are either Administrators or

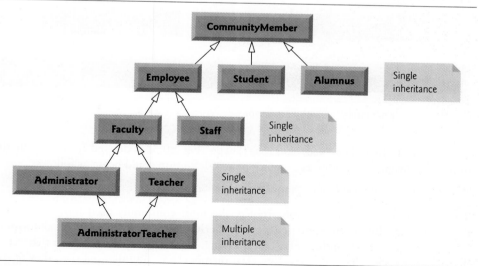

Fig. 20.2 | Inheritance hierarchy for university CommunityMembers.

Teachers. Some Administrators, however, are also Teachers. We've used *multiple inheritance* to form class AdministratorTeacher. With single inheritance, a class is derived from *one* base class. With **multiple inheritance**, a derived class inherits from *two or more* (possibly unrelated) base classes.

Each arrow in the hierarchy (Fig. 20.2) represents an *is-a* relationship. For example, as we follow the arrows in this class hierarchy, we can state "an Employee *is a* CommunityMember" and "a Teacher *is a* Faculty member." CommunityMember is the direct base class of Employee, Student and Alumnus. In addition, CommunityMember is an indirect base class of all the other classes in the diagram. An indirect base class is inherited from two or more levels up the class hierarchy.

Starting from the bottom of the diagram, you can follow the arrows upwards and apply the *is-a* relationship to the topmost base class. For example, an AdministratorTeacher *is an* Administrator, *is a* Faculty member, *is an* Employee and *is a* CommunityMember.

Shape Class Hierarchy

Now consider the Shape inheritance hierarchy in Fig. 20.3. This hierarchy begins with base class Shape. Classes TwoDimensionalShape and ThreeDimensionalShape derive from base class Shape—a Shape *is a* TwoDimensionalShape or *is a* ThreeDimensionalShape. The third level of this hierarchy contains *more specific* types of TwoDimensionalShapes and ThreeDimensionalShapes. As in Fig. 20.2, we can follow the arrows from the bottom of the diagram upwards to the topmost base class in this hierarchy to identify several *is-a* relationships. For instance, a Triangle *is a* TwoDimensionalShape and *is a* Shape, while a Sphere *is a* ThreeDimensionalShape and *is a* Shape.

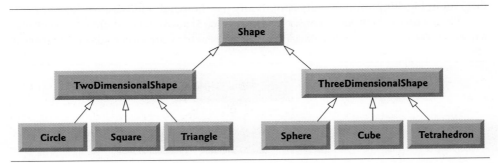

Fig. 20.3 | Inheritance hierarchy for Shapes.

To specify that class TwoDimensionalShape (Fig. 20.3) is derived from (or inherits from) class Shape, class TwoDimensionalShape's definition could begin as follows:

```
class TwoDimensionalShape : public Shape
```

This is an example of **public** inheritance, the most commonly used form. We'll also discuss **private** inheritance and **protected** inheritance (Section 20.6). With all forms of inheritance, private members of a base class are *not* accessible directly from that class's derived classes, but these private base-class members are still inherited (i.e., they're still considered parts of the derived classes). With public inheritance, all other base-class members retain their original member access when they become members of the derived class (e.g., public members of the base class become public members of the derived class, and, as we'll soon see, protected members of the base class become protected members of the derived class). Through these inherited base-class members, the derived class can manipulate private members of the base class (if these inherited members provide such functionality in the base class). Note that friend functions are *not* inherited.

Inheritance is not appropriate for every class relationship. In Chapter 18, we discussed the *has-a* relationship, in which classes have members that are objects of other classes. Such relationships create classes by *composition* of existing classes. For example, given the classes Employee, BirthDate and TelephoneNumber, it's improper to say that an Employee *is a* BirthDate or that an Employee *is a* TelephoneNumber. However, it is appropriate to say that an Employee *has a* BirthDate and that an Employee *has a* TelephoneNumber.

It's possible to treat base-class objects and derived-class objects similarly; their commonalities are expressed in the members of the base class. Objects of all classes derived from a common base class can be treated as objects of that base class (i.e., such objects have an *is-a* relationship with the base class). In Chapter 21, we consider many examples that take advantage of this relationship.

20.3 protected Members

Chapter 16 introduced access specifiers public and private. A base class's public members are accessible within its body and anywhere that the program has a handle (i.e., a name, reference or pointer) to an object of that class or one of its derived classes. A base class's private members are accessible only within its body and to the friends of that base class. In this section, we introduce the access specifier **protected**.

Using protected access offers an intermediate level of protection between public and private access. A base class's protected members can be accessed within the body of that base class, by members and friends of that base class, and by members and friends of any classes derived from that base class.

Derived-class member functions can refer to public and protected members of the base class simply by using the member names. When a derived-class member function *redefines* a base-class member function, the base-class member can still be accessed from the derived class by preceding the base-class member name with the base-class name and the scope resolution operator (::). We discuss accessing redefined members of the base class in Section 20.4.5 and using protected data in Section 20.4.4.

20.4 Relationship between Base Classes and Derived Classes

In this section, we use an inheritance hierarchy containing types of employees in a company's payroll application to discuss the relationship between a base class and a derived class. Commission employees (who will be represented as objects of a base class) are paid a percentage of their sales, while base-salaried commission employees (who will be represented as objects of a derived class) receive a base salary plus a percentage of their sales. We divide our discussion of the relationship between commission employees and base-salaried commission employees into a carefully paced series of five examples.

20.4.1 Creating and Using a CommissionEmployee Class

Let's examine CommissionEmployee's class definition (Figs. 20.4–20.5). The Commission-Employee header (Fig. 20.4) specifies class CommissionEmployee's public services, which include a constructor (lines 12–13) and member functions earnings (line 30) and print (line 31). Lines 15–28 declare public *get* and *set* functions that manipulate the class's data members (declared in lines 33–37) firstName, lastName, socialSecurityNumber, grossSales and commissionRate. Member functions setGrossSales (defined in lines 56–62 of Fig. 20.5) and setCommissionRate (defined in lines 71–77 of Fig. 20.5), for example, validate their arguments before assigning the values to data members grossSales and commissionRate, respectively.

```cpp
1   // Fig. 20.4: CommissionEmployee.h
2   // CommissionEmployee class header.
3   #ifndef COMMISSION_H
4   #define COMMISSION_H
5
6   #include <string> // C++ standard string class
7   using namespace std;
8
9   class CommissionEmployee
10  {
11  public:
12     CommissionEmployee( const string &, const string &, const string &,
13        double = 0.0, double = 0.0 );
14
15     void setFirstName( const string & ); // set first name
16     string getFirstName() const; // return first name
17
18     void setLastName( const string & ); // set last name
19     string getLastName() const; // return last name
20
21     void setSocialSecurityNumber( const string & ); // set SSN
22     string getSocialSecurityNumber() const; // return SSN
23
24     void setGrossSales( double ); // set gross sales amount
25     double getGrossSales() const; // return gross sales amount
26
27     void setCommissionRate( double ); // set commission rate (percentage)
28     double getCommissionRate() const; // return commission rate
29
30     double earnings() const; // calculate earnings
31     void print() const; // print CommissionEmployee object
32  private:
33     string firstName;
34     string lastName;
35     string socialSecurityNumber;
36     double grossSales; // gross weekly sales
37     double commissionRate; // commission percentage
38  }; // end class CommissionEmployee
39
40  #endif
```

Fig. 20.4 | CommissionEmployee class header.

```cpp
1   // Fig. 20.5: CommissionEmployee.cpp
2   // Class CommissionEmployee member-function definitions.
3   #include <iostream>
4   #include "CommissionEmployee.h" // CommissionEmployee class definition
5   using namespace std;
6
7   // constructor
8   CommissionEmployee::CommissionEmployee(
9      const string &first, const string &last, const string &ssn,
10     double sales, double rate )
11  {
12     firstName = first; // should validate
13     lastName = last; // should validate
14     socialSecurityNumber = ssn; // should validate
15     setGrossSales( sales ); // validate and store gross sales
16     setCommissionRate( rate ); // validate and store commission rate
17  } // end CommissionEmployee constructor
18
19  // set first name
20  void CommissionEmployee::setFirstName( const string &first )
21  {
22     firstName = first; // should validate
23  } // end function setFirstName
24
25  // return first name
26  string CommissionEmployee::getFirstName() const
27  {
28     return firstName;
29  } // end function getFirstName
30
31  // set last name
32  void CommissionEmployee::setLastName( const string &last )
33  {
34     lastName = last; // should validate
35  } // end function setLastName
36
37  // return last name
38  string CommissionEmployee::getLastName() const
39  {
40     return lastName;
41  } // end function getLastName
42
43  // set social security number
44  void CommissionEmployee::setSocialSecurityNumber( const string &ssn )
45  {
46     socialSecurityNumber = ssn; // should validate
47  } // end function setSocialSecurityNumber
48
49  // return social security number
50  string CommissionEmployee::getSocialSecurityNumber() const
51  {
```

Fig. 20.5 | Class CommissionEmployee member-function definitions. (Part 1 of 2.)

```
52       return socialSecurityNumber;
53    } // end function getSocialSecurityNumber
54
55    // set gross sales amount
56    void CommissionEmployee::setGrossSales( double sales )
57    {
58       if ( sales >= 0.0 )
59          grossSales = sales;
60       else
61          throw invalid_argument( "Gross sales must be >= 0.0" );
62    } // end function setGrossSales
63
64    // return gross sales amount
65    double CommissionEmployee::getGrossSales() const
66    {
67       return grossSales;
68    } // end function getGrossSales
69
70    // set commission rate
71    void CommissionEmployee::setCommissionRate( double rate )
72    {
73       if ( rate > 0.0 && rate < 1.0 )
74          commissionRate = rate;
75       else
76          throw invalid_argument( "Commission rate must be > 0.0 and < 1.0" );
77    } // end function setCommissionRate
78
79    // return commission rate
80    double CommissionEmployee::getCommissionRate() const
81    {
82       return commissionRate;
83    } // end function getCommissionRate
84
85    // calculate earnings
86    double CommissionEmployee::earnings() const
87    {
88       return commissionRate * grossSales;
89    } // end function earnings
90
91    // print CommissionEmployee object
92    void CommissionEmployee::print() const
93    {
94       cout << "commission employee: " << firstName << ' ' << lastName
95          << "\nsocial security number: " << socialSecurityNumber
96          << "\ngross sales: " << grossSales
97          << "\ncommission rate: " << commissionRate;
98    } // end function print
```

Fig. 20.5 | Class CommissionEmployee member-function definitions. (Part 2 of 2.)

CommissionEmployee *Constructor*

The CommissionEmployee constructor definition purposely does not use member-initializer syntax in the first several examples of this section, so that we can demonstrate how private and protected specifiers affect member access in derived classes. As shown in

Fig. 20.5, lines 12–14, we assign values to data members firstName, lastName and socialSecurityNumber in the constructor body. Later in this section, we'll return to using member-initializer lists in the constructors.

We do not validate the values of the constructor's arguments first, last and ssn before assigning them to the corresponding data members. We certainly could validate the first and last names—perhaps by ensuring that they're of a reasonable length. Similarly, a social security number could be validated to ensure that it contains nine digits, with or without dashes (e.g., 123-45-6789 or 123456789).

CommissionEmployee *Member Functions* earnings *and* print

Member function earnings (lines 86–89) calculates a CommissionEmployee's earnings. Line 88 multiplies the commissionRate by the grossSales and returns the result. Member function print (lines 92–98) displays the values of a CommissionEmployee object's data members.

Testing Class CommissionEmployee

Figure 20.6 tests class CommissionEmployee. Lines 11–12 instantiate object employee of class CommissionEmployee and invoke CommissionEmployee's constructor to initialize the object with "Sue" as the first name, "Jones" as the last name, "222-22-2222" as the social security number, 10000 as the gross sales amount and .06 as the commission rate. Lines 19–24 use employee's *get* functions to display the values of its data members. Lines 26–27 invoke the object's member functions setGrossSales and setCommissionRate to change the values of data members grossSales and commissionRate, respectively. Line 31 then calls employee's print member function to output the updated CommissionEmployee information. Finally, line 34 displays the CommissionEmployee's earnings, calculated by the object's earnings member function using the updated values of data members grossSales and commissionRate.

```cpp
1   // Fig. 20.6: fig20_06.cpp
2   // CommissionEmployee class test program..
3   #include <iostream>
4   #include <iomanip>
5   #include "CommissionEmployee.h" // CommissionEmployee class definition
6   using namespace std;
7
8   int main()
9   {
10      // instantiate a CommissionEmployee object
11      CommissionEmployee employee(
12         "Sue", "Jones", "222-22-2222", 10000, .06 );
13
14      // set floating-point output formatting
15      cout << fixed << setprecision( 2 );
16
17      // get commission employee data
18      cout << "Employee information obtained by get functions: \n"
19         << "\nFirst name is " << employee.getFirstName()
```

Fig. 20.6 | CommissionEmployee class test program. (Part 1 of 2.)

```
20            << "\nLast name is " << employee.getLastName()
21            << "\nSocial security number is "
22            << employee.getSocialSecurityNumber()
23            << "\nGross sales is " << employee.getGrossSales()
24            << "\nCommission rate is " << employee.getCommissionRate() << endl;
25
26       employee.setGrossSales( 8000 ); // set gross sales
27       employee.setCommissionRate( .1 ); // set commission rate
28
29       cout << "\nUpdated employee information output by print function: \n"
30            << endl;
31       employee.print(); // display the new employee information
32
33       // display the employee's earnings
34       cout << "\n\nEmployee's earnings: $" << employee.earnings() << endl;
35    } // end main
```

```
Employee information obtained by get functions:

First name is Sue
Last name is Jones
Social security number is 222-22-2222
Gross sales is 10000.00
Commission rate is 0.06

Updated employee information output by print function:

commission employee: Sue Jones
social security number: 222-22-2222
gross sales: 8000.00
commission rate: 0.10

Employee's earnings: $800.00
```

Fig. 20.6 | CommissionEmployee class test program. (Part 2 of 2.)

20.4.2 Creating a BasePlusCommissionEmployee Class Without Using Inheritance

We now discuss the second part of our introduction to inheritance by creating and testing (a completely new and independent) class BasePlusCommissionEmployee (Figs. 20.7–20.8), which contains a first name, last name, social security number, gross sales amount, commission rate *and* base salary.

```
1   // Fig. 20.7: BasePlusCommissionEmployee.h
2   // BasePlusCommissionEmployee class definition represents an employee
3   // that receives a base salary in addition to commission.
4   #ifndef BASEPLUS_H
5   #define BASEPLUS_H
6
7   #include <string> // C++ standard string class
8   using namespace std;
9
```

Fig. 20.7 | BasePlusCommissionEmployee class header. (Part 1 of 2.)

```
10   class BasePlusCommissionEmployee
11   {
12   public:
13      BasePlusCommissionEmployee( const string &, const string &,
14         const string &, double = 0.0, double = 0.0, double = 0.0 );
15
16      void setFirstName( const string & ); // set first name
17      string getFirstName() const; // return first name
18
19      void setLastName( const string & ); // set last name
20      string getLastName() const; // return last name
21
22      void setSocialSecurityNumber( const string & ); // set SSN
23      string getSocialSecurityNumber() const; // return SSN
24
25      void setGrossSales( double ); // set gross sales amount
26      double getGrossSales() const; // return gross sales amount
27
28      void setCommissionRate( double ); // set commission rate
29      double getCommissionRate() const; // return commission rate
30
31      void setBaseSalary( double ); // set base salary
32      double getBaseSalary() const; // return base salary
33
34      double earnings() const; // calculate earnings
35      void print() const; // print BasePlusCommissionEmployee object
36   private:
37      string firstName;
38      string lastName;
39      string socialSecurityNumber;
40      double grossSales; // gross weekly sales
41      double commissionRate; // commission percentage
42      double baseSalary; // base salary
43   }; // end class BasePlusCommissionEmployee
44
45   #endif
```

Fig. 20.7 | BasePlusCommissionEmployee class header. (Part 2 of 2.)

```
1    // Fig. 20.8: BasePlusCommissionEmployee.cpp
2    // Class BasePlusCommissionEmployee member-function definitions.
3    #include <iostream>
4    #include "BasePlusCommissionEmployee.h"
5    using namespace std;
6
7    // constructor
8    BasePlusCommissionEmployee::BasePlusCommissionEmployee(
9       const string &first, const string &last, const string &ssn,
10      double sales, double rate, double salary )
11   {
```

Fig. 20.8 | BasePlusCommissionEmployee class represents an employee who receives a base salary in addition to a commission. (Part 1 of 4.)

```
12      firstName = first; // should validate
13      lastName = last; // should validate
14      socialSecurityNumber = ssn; // should validate
15      setGrossSales( sales ); // validate and store gross sales
16      setCommissionRate( rate ); // validate and store commission rate
17      setBaseSalary( salary ); // validate and store base salary
18   } // end BasePlusCommissionEmployee constructor
19
20   // set first name
21   void BasePlusCommissionEmployee::setFirstName( const string &first )
22   {
23      firstName = first; // should validate
24   } // end function setFirstName
25
26   // return first name
27   string BasePlusCommissionEmployee::getFirstName() const
28   {
29      return firstName;
30   } // end function getFirstName
31
32   // set last name
33   void BasePlusCommissionEmployee::setLastName( const string &last )
34   {
35      lastName = last; // should validate
36   } // end function setLastName
37
38   // return last name
39   string BasePlusCommissionEmployee::getLastName() const
40   {
41      return lastName;
42   } // end function getLastName
43
44   // set social security number
45   void BasePlusCommissionEmployee::setSocialSecurityNumber(
46      const string &ssn )
47   {
48      socialSecurityNumber = ssn; // should validate
49   } // end function setSocialSecurityNumber
50
51   // return social security number
52   string BasePlusCommissionEmployee::getSocialSecurityNumber() const
53   {
54      return socialSecurityNumber;
55   } // end function getSocialSecurityNumber
56
57   // set gross sales amount
58   void BasePlusCommissionEmployee::setGrossSales( double sales )
59   {
60      if ( sales >= 0.0 )
61         grossSales = sales;
```

Fig. 20.8 | BasePlusCommissionEmployee class represents an employee who receives a base salary in addition to a commission. (Part 2 of 4.)

```
62         else
63            throw invalid_argument( "Gross sales must be >= 0.0" );
64      } // end function setGrossSales
65
66      // return gross sales amount
67      double BasePlusCommissionEmployee::getGrossSales() const
68      {
69         return grossSales;
70      } // end function getGrossSales
71
72      // set commission rate
73      void BasePlusCommissionEmployee::setCommissionRate( double rate )
74      {
75         if ( rate > 0.0 && rate < 1.0 )
76            commissionRate = rate;
77         else
78            throw invalid_argument( "Commission rate must be > 0.0 and < 1.0" );
79      } // end function setCommissionRate
80
81      // return commission rate
82      double BasePlusCommissionEmployee::getCommissionRate() const
83      {
84         return commissionRate;
85      } // end function getCommissionRate
86
87      // set base salary
88      void BasePlusCommissionEmployee::setBaseSalary( double salary )
89      {
90         if ( salary >= 0.0 )
91            baseSalary = salary;
92         else
93            throw invalid_argument( "Salary must be >= 0.0" );
94      } // end function setBaseSalary
95
96      // return base salary
97      double BasePlusCommissionEmployee::getBaseSalary() const
98      {
99         return baseSalary;
100     } // end function getBaseSalary
101
102     // calculate earnings
103     double BasePlusCommissionEmployee::earnings() const
104     {
105        return baseSalary + ( commissionRate * grossSales );
106     } // end function earnings
107
108     // print BasePlusCommissionEmployee object
109     void BasePlusCommissionEmployee::print() const
110     {
111        cout << "base-salaried commission employee: " << firstName << ' '
112           << lastName << "\nsocial security number: " << socialSecurityNumber
```

Fig. 20.8 | BasePlusCommissionEmployee class represents an employee who receives a base salary in addition to a commission. (Part 3 of 4.)

```
113            << "\ngross sales: " << grossSales
114            << "\ncommission rate: " << commissionRate
115            << "\nbase salary: " << baseSalary;
116 } // end function print
```

Fig. 20.8 | BasePlusCommissionEmployee class represents an employee who receives a base salary in addition to a commission. (Part 4 of 4.)

Defining Class BasePlusCommissionEmployee

The BasePlusCommissionEmployee header (Fig. 20.7) specifies class BasePlusCommissionEmployee's public services, which include the BasePlusCommissionEmployee constructor (lines 13–14) and member functions earnings (line 34) and print (line 35). Lines 16–32 declare public *get* and *set* functions for the class's private data members (declared in lines 37–42) firstName, lastName, socialSecurityNumber, grossSales, commissionRate and baseSalary. These variables and member functions encapsulate all the necessary features of a base-salaried commission employee. Note the similarity between this class and class CommissionEmployee (Figs. 20.4–20.5)—in this example, we do not yet exploit that similarity.

Class BasePlusCommissionEmployee's earnings member function (defined in lines 100–103 of Fig. 20.8) computes the earnings of a base-salaried commission employee. Line 102 returns the result of adding the employee's base salary to the product of the commission rate and the employee's gross sales.

Testing Class BasePlusCommissionEmployee

Figure 20.9 tests class BasePlusCommissionEmployee. Lines 11–12 instantiate object employee of class BasePlusCommissionEmployee, passing "Bob", "Lewis", "333-33-3333", 5000, .04 and 300 to the constructor as the first name, last name, social security number, gross sales, commission rate and base salary, respectively. Lines 19–25 use BasePlusCommissionEmployee's *get* functions to retrieve the values of the object's data members for output. Line 27 invokes the object's setBaseSalary member function to change the base salary. Member function setBaseSalary (Fig. 20.8, lines 88–94) ensures that data member baseSalary is not assigned a negative value, because an employee's base salary cannot be negative. Line 31 of Fig. 20.9 invokes the object's print member function to output the updated BasePlusCommissionEmployee's information, and line 34 calls member function earnings to display the BasePlusCommissionEmployee's earnings.

```
1  // Fig. 20.9: fig20_09.cpp
2  // Testing class BasePlusCommissionEmployee.
3  #include <iostream>
4  #include <iomanip>
5  #include "BasePlusCommissionEmployee.h"
6  using namespace std;
7
8  int main()
9  {
```

Fig. 20.9 | BasePlusCommissionEmployee class test program. (Part 1 of 2.)

```
10      // instantiate BasePlusCommissionEmployee object
11      BasePlusCommissionEmployee
12         employee( "Bob", "Lewis", "333-33-3333", 5000, .04, 300 );
13
14      // set floating-point output formatting
15      cout << fixed << setprecision( 2 );
16
17      // get commission employee data
18      cout << "Employee information obtained by get functions: \n"
19         << "\nFirst name is " << employee.getFirstName()
20         << "\nLast name is " << employee.getLastName()
21         << "\nSocial security number is "
22         << employee.getSocialSecurityNumber()
23         << "\nGross sales is " << employee.getGrossSales()
24         << "\nCommission rate is " << employee.getCommissionRate()
25         << "\nBase salary is " << employee.getBaseSalary() << endl;
26
27      employee.setBaseSalary( 1000 ); // set base salary
28
29      cout << "\nUpdated employee information output by print function: \n"
30         << endl;
31      employee.print(); // display the new employee information
32
33      // display the employee's earnings
34      cout << "\n\nEmployee's earnings: $" << employee.earnings() << endl;
35   } // end main
```

```
Employee information obtained by get functions:

First name is Bob
Last name is Lewis
Social security number is 333-33-3333
Gross sales is 5000.00
Commission rate is 0.04
Base salary is 300.00

Updated employee information output by print function:

base-salaried commission employee: Bob Lewis
social security number: 333-33-3333
gross sales: 5000.00
commission rate: 0.04
base salary: 1000.00

Employee's earnings: $1200.00
```

Fig. 20.9 | BasePlusCommissionEmployee class test program. (Part 2 of 2.)

Exploring the Similarities Between Class BasePlusCommissionEmployee and Class CommissionEmployee

Most of the code for class BasePlusCommissionEmployee (Figs. 20.7–20.8) is similar, if not identical, to the code for class CommissionEmployee (Figs. 20.4–20.5). For example, in class BasePlusCommissionEmployee, private data members firstName and lastName and member functions setFirstName, getFirstName, setLastName and getLastName are identical to those of class CommissionEmployee. Classes CommissionEmployee and Base-PlusCommissionEmployee also both contain private data members socialSecurity-Number, commissionRate and grossSales, as well as *get* and *set* functions to manipulate these members. In addition, the BasePlusCommissionEmployee constructor is *almost* identical to that of class CommissionEmployee, except that BasePlusCommissionEmployee's constructor also sets the baseSalary. The other additions to class BasePlusCommission-Employee are private data member baseSalary and member functions setBaseSalary and getBaseSalary. Class BasePlusCommissionEmployee's print member function is *nearly identical* to that of class CommissionEmployee, except that BasePlusCommissionEmployee's print also outputs the value of data member baseSalary.

We literally *copied* code from class CommissionEmployee and *pasted* it into class Base-PlusCommissionEmployee, then modified class BasePlusCommissionEmployee to include a base salary and member functions that manipulate the base salary. This *copy-and-paste approach* is error prone and time consuming.

Software Engineering Observation 20.1

Copying and pasting code *from one class to another can spread many physical* copies of the same code *and can spread* errors *throughout a system, creating a code-maintenance nightmare. To avoid duplicating code (and possibly errors), use* inheritance, *rather than the "copy-and-paste" approach, in situations where you want one class to "absorb" the data members and member functions of another class.*

Software Engineering Observation 20.2

With inheritance, the common data members and member functions of all the classes in the hierarchy are declared in a base class. When changes are required for these common features, you need to make the changes only *in the base class—derived classes then inherit the changes. Without inheritance, changes would need to be made to* all *the source code files that contain a copy of the code in question.*

20.4.3 Creating a CommissionEmployee–BasePlusCommissionEmployee Inheritance Hierarchy

Now we create and test a new BasePlusCommissionEmployee class (Figs. 20.10–20.11) that *derives from* class CommissionEmployee (Figs. 20.4–20.5). In this example, a BasePlus-CommissionEmployee object *is a* CommissionEmployee (because inheritance passes on the capabilities of class CommissionEmployee), but class BasePlusCommissionEmployee *also* has data member baseSalary (Fig. 20.10, line 23). The *colon (:)* in line 11 of the class definition indicates inheritance. Keyword public indicates the *type of inheritance*. As a derived class (formed with public inheritance), BasePlusCommissionEmployee inherits *all* the members of class CommissionEmployee, *except* for the constructor—each class provides its *own* constructors that are specific to the class. (Destructors, too, are not inherited.) Thus, the public services of BasePlusCommissionEmployee include its constructor (lines 14–15) and the public member functions inherited from class CommissionEmployee—*although we cannot see these inherited member functions* in BasePlusCommissionEmployee's source code, they're nevertheless a part of derived class BasePlusCommissionEmployee. The derived class's public services also include member functions setBaseSalary, getBaseSalary, earnings and print (lines 17–21).

```
1    // Fig. 20.10: BasePlusCommissionEmployee.h
2    // BasePlusCommissionEmployee class derived from
3    // class CommissionEmployee.
4    #ifndef BASEPLUS_H
5    #define BASEPLUS_H
6
7    #include <string> // C++ standard string class
8    #include "CommissionEmployee.h" // CommissionEmployee class declaration
9    using namespace std;
10
11   class BasePlusCommissionEmployee : public CommissionEmployee
12   {
13   public:
14      BasePlusCommissionEmployee( const string &, const string &,
15         const string &, double = 0.0, double = 0.0, double = 0.0 );
16
17      void setBaseSalary( double ); // set base salary
18      double getBaseSalary() const; // return base salary
19
20      double earnings() const; // calculate earnings
21      void print() const; // print BasePlusCommissionEmployee object
22   private:
23      double baseSalary; // base salary
24   }; // end class BasePlusCommissionEmployee
25
26   #endif
```

Fig. 20.10 | BasePlusCommissionEmployee class derived from class CommissionEmployee.

```
1    // Fig. 20.11: BasePlusCommissionEmployee.cpp
2    // Class BasePlusCommissionEmployee member-function definitions.
3    #include <iostream>
4    #include "BasePlusCommissionEmployee.h"
5    using namespace std;
6
7    // constructor
8    BasePlusCommissionEmployee::BasePlusCommissionEmployee(
9       const string &first, const string &last, const string &ssn,
10      double sales, double rate, double salary )
11      // explicitly call base-class constructor
12      : CommissionEmployee( first, last, ssn, sales, rate )
13   {
14      setBaseSalary( salary ); // validate and store base salary
15   } // end BasePlusCommissionEmployee constructor
16
17   // set base salary
18   void BasePlusCommissionEmployee::setBaseSalary( double salary )
19   {
```

Fig. 20.11 | Class BasePlusCommissionEmployee member-function definitions: private base-class data cannot be accessed from derived class. (Part 1 of 3.)

```
20       if ( salary >= 0.0 )
21          baseSalary = salary;
22       else
23          throw invalid_argument( "Salary must be >= 0.0" );
24    } // end function setBaseSalary
25
26    // return base salary
27    double BasePlusCommissionEmployee::getBaseSalary() const
28    {
29       return baseSalary;
30    } // end function getBaseSalary
31
32    // calculate earnings
33    double BasePlusCommissionEmployee::earnings() const
34    {
35       // derived class cannot access the base class's private data
36       return baseSalary + ( commissionRate * grossSales );
37    } // end function earnings
38
39    // print BasePlusCommissionEmployee object
40    void BasePlusCommissionEmployee::print() const
41    {
42       // derived class cannot access the base class's private data
43       cout << "base-salaried commission employee: " << firstName << ' '
44          << lastName << "\nsocial security number: " << socialSecurityNumber
45          << "\ngross sales: " << grossSales
46          << "\ncommission rate: " << commissionRate
47          << "\nbase salary: " << baseSalary;
48    } // end function print
```

```
C:\examples\ch20\Fig20_10_11\BasePlusCommissionEmployee.cpp(36) :
   error C2248: 'CommissionEmployee::commissionRate' :
   cannot access private member declared in class 'CommissionEmployee'

C:\examples\ch20\Fig20_10_11\BasePlusCommissionEmployee.cpp(36) :
   error C2248: 'CommissionEmployee::grossSales' :
   cannot access private member declared in class 'CommissionEmployee'

C:\examples\ch20\Fig20_10_11\BasePlusCommissionEmployee.cpp(43) :
   error C2248: 'CommissionEmployee::firstName' :
   cannot access private member declared in class 'CommissionEmployee'

C:\examples\ch20\Fig20_10_11\BasePlusCommissionEmployee.cpp(44) :
   error C2248: 'CommissionEmployee::lastName' :
   cannot access private member declared in class 'CommissionEmployee'

C:\examples\ch20\Fig20_10_11\BasePlusCommissionEmployee.cpp(44) :
   error C2248: 'CommissionEmployee::socialSecurityNumber' :
   cannot access private member declared in class 'CommissionEmployee'

C:\examples\ch20\Fig20_10_11\BasePlusCommissionEmployee.cpp(45) :
   error C2248: 'CommissionEmployee::grossSales' :
   cannot access private member declared in class 'CommissionEmployee'
```

Fig. 20.11 | Class `BasePlusCommissionEmployee` member-function definitions: `private` base-class data cannot be accessed from derived class. (Part 2 of 3.)

```
C:\examples\ch20\Fig20_10_11\BasePlusCommissionEmployee.cpp(46) :
    error C2248: 'CommissionEmployee::commissionRate' :
    cannot access private member declared in class 'CommissionEmployee'
```

Fig. 20.11 | Class `BasePlusCommissionEmployee` member-function definitions: `private` base-class data cannot be accessed from derived class. (Part 3 of 3.)

Figure 20.11 shows `BasePlusCommissionEmployee`'s member-function implementations. The constructor (lines 8–15) introduces base-class initializer syntax (line 12), which uses a member initializer to pass arguments to the base-class (`CommissionEmployee`) constructor. C++ requires that a derived-class constructor call its base-class constructor to initialize the base-class data members that are inherited into the derived class. Line 12 does this by *explicitly* invoking the `CommissionEmployee` constructor by name, passing the constructor's parameters `first`, `last`, `ssn`, `sales` and `rate` as arguments to initialize the base-class data members `firstName`, `lastName`, `socialSecurityNumber`, `grossSales` and `commissionRate`. If `BasePlusCommissionEmployee`'s constructor did *not* invoke class `CommissionEmployee`'s constructor *explicitly*, C++ would attempt to invoke class `CommissionEmployee`'s default constructor implicitly—but the class does *not* have such a constructor, so the compiler would issue an error. Recall from Chapter 16 that the compiler provides a default constructor with no parameters in any class that does *not* explicitly include a constructor. However, `CommissionEmployee` *does* explicitly include a constructor, so a default constructor is *not* provided

Common Programming Error 20.1

When a derived-class constructor calls a base-class constructor, the arguments passed to the base-class constructor must be consistent with the number and types of parameters specified in one of the base-class constructors; otherwise, a compilation error occurs.

Performance Tip 20.1

In a derived-class constructor, invoking base-class constructors and initializing member object explicitly in the member initializer list prevents duplicate initialization in which a default constructor is called, then data members are modified again in the derived-class constructor's body.

Compilation Errors from Accessing Base-Class **private** *Members*

The compiler generates errors for line 36 of Fig. 20.11 because base class `CommissionEmployee`'s data members `commissionRate` and `grossSales` are `private`—derived class `BasePlusCommissionEmployee`'s member functions are *not* allowed to access base class `CommissionEmployee`'s private data. The compiler issues additional errors in lines 43–46 of `BasePlusCommissionEmployee`'s print member function for the same reason. As you can see, C++ rigidly enforces restrictions on accessing `private` data members, so that *even a derived class (which is intimately related to its base class) cannot access the base class's* `private` *data.*

Preventing the Errors in **BasePlusCommissionEmployee**

We purposely included the erroneous code in Fig. 20.11 to emphasize that a derived class's member functions cannot access its base class's `private` data. The errors in `BasePlusCom-`

missionEmployee could have been prevented by using the *get* member functions inherited from class CommissionEmployee. For example, line 36 could have invoked getCommissionRate and getGrossSales to access CommissionEmployee's private data members commissionRate and grossSales, respectively. Similarly, lines 43–46 could have used appropriate *get* member functions to retrieve the values of the base class's data members. In the next example, we show how using protected data *also* allows us to avoid the errors encountered in this example.

Including the Base-Class Header in the Derived-Class Header with #include

Notice that we #include the base class's header in the derived class's header (line 8 of Fig. 20.10). This is necessary for three reasons. First, for the derived class to use the base class's name in line 11, we must tell the compiler that the base class exists—the class definition in CommissionEmployee.h does exactly that.

The second reason is that the compiler uses a class definition to determine the *size* of an object of that class (as we discussed in Section 16.6). A client program that creates an object of a class must #include the class definition to enable the compiler to reserve the proper amount of memory for the object. When using inheritance, a derived-class object's size depends on the data members declared explicitly in its class definition *and* the data members inherited from its direct and indirect base classes. Including the base class's definition in line 8 allows the compiler to determine the memory requirements for the base class's data members that become part of a derived-class object and thus contribute to the total size of the derived-class object.

The last reason for line 8 is to allow the compiler to determine whether the derived class uses the base class's inherited members properly. For example, in the program of Figs. 20.10–20.11, the compiler uses the base-class header to determine that the data members being accessed by the derived class are private in the base class. Since these are *inaccessible* to the derived class, the compiler generates errors. The compiler also uses the base class's *function prototypes* to *validate* function calls made by the derived class to the inherited base-class functions.

Linking Process in an Inheritance Hierarchy

In Section 16.7, we discussed the linking process for creating an executable GradeBook application. In that example, you saw that the client's object code was linked with the object code for class GradeBook, as well as the object code for any C++ Standard Library classes used in either the client code or in class GradeBook.

The linking process is similar for a program that uses classes in an inheritance hierarchy. The process requires the object code for all classes used in the program and the object code for the direct and indirect base classes of any derived classes used by the program. Suppose a client wants to create an application that uses class BasePlusCommissionEmployee, which is a derived class of CommissionEmployee (we'll see an example of this in Section 20.4.4). When compiling the client application, the client's object code must be linked with the object code for classes BasePlusCommissionEmployee and CommissionEmployee, because BasePlusCommissionEmployee inherits member functions from its base class CommissionEmployee. The code is also linked with the object code for any C++ Standard Library classes used in class CommissionEmployee, class BasePlusCommissionEmployee or the client code. This provides the program with access to the implementations of all of the functionality that the program may use.

20.4.4 CommissionEmployee–BasePlusCommissionEmployee Inheritance Hierarchy Using protected Data

To enable class BasePlusCommissionEmployee to directly access CommissionEmployee data members firstName, lastName, socialSecurityNumber, grossSales and commission-Rate, we can declare those members as protected in the base class. As we discussed in Section 20.3, a base class's protected members can be accessed by members and friends of the base class and by members and friends of any classes derived from that base class.

Defining Base Class *CommissionEmployee with protected Data*

Class CommissionEmployee (Fig. 20.12) now declares data members firstName, last-Name, socialSecurityNumber, grossSales and commissionRate as protected (lines 32–37) rather than private. The member-function implementations are identical to those in Fig. 20.5, so CommissionEmployee.cpp is not shown here.

```
1   // Fig. 20.12: CommissionEmployee.h
2   // CommissionEmployee class definition with protected data.
3   #ifndef COMMISSION_H
4   #define COMMISSION_H
5
6   #include <string> // C++ standard string class
7   using namespace std;
8
9   class CommissionEmployee
10  {
11  public:
12     CommissionEmployee( const string &, const string &, const string &,
13        double = 0.0, double = 0.0 );
14
15     void setFirstName( const string & ); // set first name
16     string getFirstName() const; // return first name
17
18     void setLastName( const string & ); // set last name
19     string getLastName() const; // return last name
20
21     void setSocialSecurityNumber( const string & ); // set SSN
22     string getSocialSecurityNumber() const; // return SSN
23
24     void setGrossSales( double ); // set gross sales amount
25     double getGrossSales() const; // return gross sales amount
26
27     void setCommissionRate( double ); // set commission rate
28     double getCommissionRate() const; // return commission rate
29
30     double earnings() const; // calculate earnings
31     void print() const; // print CommissionEmployee object
32  protected:
33     string firstName;
34     string lastName;
35     string socialSecurityNumber;
```

Fig. 20.12 | CommissionEmployee class definition that declares protected data to allow access by derived classes. (Part 1 of 2.)

```
36        double grossSales; // gross weekly sales
37        double commissionRate; // commission percentage
38   }; // end class CommissionEmployee
39
40   #endif
```

Fig. 20.12 | CommissionEmployee class definition that declares protected data to allow access by derived classes. (Part 2 of 2.)

Class *BasePlusCommissionEmployee*

The definition of class BasePlusCommissionEmployee from Figs. 20.10–20.11 remains unchanged, so we do not show it again here. Now that BasePlusCommissionEmployee inherits from the updated class CommissionEmployee Fig. 20.12, BasePlusCommissionEmployee objects can access inherited data members that are declared protected in class CommissionEmployee (i.e., data members firstName, lastName, socialSecurityNumber, grossSales and commissionRate). As a result, the compiler does *not* generate errors when compiling the BasePlusCommissionEmployee earnings and print member-function definitions in Fig. 20.11 (lines 33–37 and 40–48, respectively). This shows the special privileges that a derived class is granted to access protected base-class data members. Objects of a derived class also can access protected members in *any* of that derived class's *indirect* base classes.

Class BasePlusCommissionEmployee does *not* inherit class CommissionEmployee's constructor. However, class BasePlusCommissionEmployee's constructor (Fig. 20.11, lines 8–15) calls class CommissionEmployee's constructor explicitly with member initializer syntax (line 12). Recall that BasePlusCommissionEmployee's constructor must explicitly call the constructor of class CommissionEmployee, because CommissionEmployee does not contain a default constructor that could be invoked implicitly.

Testing the Modified *BasePlusCommissionEmployee* Class

To test the updated class hierarchy, we reused the test program from Fig. 20.9. As shown in Fig. 20.13, the output is identical to that of Fig. 20.9. We created the first class Base-PlusCommissionEmployee *without using inheritance* and created this version of Base-PlusCommissionEmployee *using inheritance*; however, both classes provide the *same* functionality. The code for class BasePlusCommissionEmployee (i.e., the header and implementation files), which is 74 lines, is considerably *shorter* than the code for the noninherited version of the class, which is 161 lines, because the inherited version absorbs part of its functionality from CommissionEmployee, whereas the noninherited version does not absorb any functionality. Also, there is now only *one* copy of the CommissionEmployee functionality declared and defined in class CommissionEmployee. This makes the source code easier to maintain, modify and debug, because the source code related to a CommissionEmployee exists only in the files CommissionEmployee.h and CommissionEmployee.cpp.

```
Employee information obtained by get functions:

First name is Bob
Last name is Lewis
Social security number is 333-33-3333
```

Fig. 20.13 | protected base-class data can be accessed from derived class. (Part 1 of 2.)

```
Gross sales is 5000.00
Commission rate is 0.04
Base salary is 300.00

Updated employee information output by print function:

base-salaried commission employee: Bob Lewis
social security number: 333-33-3333
gross sales: 5000.00
commission rate: 0.04
base salary: 1000.00

Employee's earnings: $1200.00
```

Fig. 20.13 | protected base-class data can be accessed from derived class. (Part 2 of 2.)

Notes on Using **protected** Data

In this example, we declared base-class data members as protected, so derived classes can modify the data directly. Inheriting protected data members slightly improves performance, because we can directly access the members without incurring the overhead of calls to *set* or *get* member functions.

Software Engineering Observation 20.3

In most cases, it's better to use private data members to encourage proper software engineering, and leave code optimization issues to the compiler. Your code will be easier to maintain, modify and debug.

Using protected data members creates two serious problems. First, the derived-class object does *not* have to use a member function to set the value of the base class's protected data member. An invalid value can easily be assigned to the protected data member, thus leaving the object in an *inconsistent* state—e.g., with CommissionEmployee's data member grossSales declared as protected, a derived-class object can assign a negative value to grossSales. The second problem with using protected data members is that derived-class member functions are more likely to be written so that they *depend on the base-class implementation*. Derived classes should depend only on the base-class services (i.e., non-private member functions) and *not* on the base-class implementation. With protected data members in the base class, if the base-class implementation changes, we may need to modify *all* derived classes of that base class. For example, if for some reason we were to change the names of data members firstName and lastName to first and last, then we'd have to do so for all occurrences in which a derived class references these base-class data members directly. Such software is said to be fragile or brittle, because a small change in the base class can "break" derived-class implementation. You should be able to change the base-class implementation while still providing the same services to derived classes. Of course, if the base-class services change, we must reimplement our derived classes—good object-oriented design attempts to prevent this.

Software Engineering Observation 20.4

It's appropriate to use the protected access specifier when a base class should provide a service (i.e., a member function) only to its derived classes and friends.

Software Engineering Observation 20.5

Declaring base-class data members private *(as opposed to declaring them* protected*) enables you to change the base-class implementation without having to change derived-class implementations.*

20.4.5 CommissionEmployee–BasePlusCommissionEmployee Inheritance Hierarchy Using private Data

We now reexamine our hierarchy once more, this time using the best software engineering practices. Class CommissionEmployee now declares data members firstName, lastName, socialSecurityNumber, grossSales and commissionRate as private as shown previously in lines 32–37 of Fig. 20.4.

*Changes to Class **CommissionEmployee**'s Member Function Definitions*
In the CommissionEmployee constructor implementation (Fig. 20.14, lines 8–15), we use member initializers (line 11) to set the values of the members firstName, lastName and socialSecurityNumber. We show how the derived-class BasePlusCommissionEmployee (Fig. 20.15) can invoke non-private base-class member functions (setFirstName, get-FirstName, setLastName, getLastName, setSocialSecurityNumber and getSocialSecurityNumber) to manipulate these data members.

In the body of the constructor and in the bodies of member function's earnings (lines 84–87) and print (lines 90–97), we call the class's *set* and *get* member functions to access the class's private data members. If we decide to change the data member names, the earnings and print definitions will *not* require modification—only the definitions of the *get* and *set* member functions that directly manipulate the data members will need to change. These changes occur solely within the base class—no changes to the derived class are needed. Localizing the effects of changes like this is a good software engineering practice.

Performance Tip 20.2

Using a member function to access a data member's value can be slightly slower than accessing the data directly. However, today's optimizing compilers perform many optimizations implicitly (such as inlining set *and* get *member-function calls). You should write code that adheres to proper software engineering principles, and leave optimization to the compiler. A good rule is: "Do not second-guess the compiler."*

```
1   // Fig. 20.14: CommissionEmployee.cpp
2   // Class CommissionEmployee member-function definitions.
3   #include <iostream>
4   #include "CommissionEmployee.h" // CommissionEmployee class definition
5   using namespace std;
6
7   // constructor
8   CommissionEmployee::CommissionEmployee(
9      const string &first, const string &last, const string &ssn,
10     double sales, double rate )
```

Fig. 20.14 | CommissionEmployee class implementation file: CommissionEmployee class uses member functions to manipulate its private data. (Part 1 of 3.)

```
11          : firstName( first ), lastName( last ), socialSecurityNumber( ssn )
12      {
13          setGrossSales( sales ); // validate and store gross sales
14          setCommissionRate( rate ); // validate and store commission rate
15      } // end CommissionEmployee constructor
16
17      // set first name
18      void CommissionEmployee::setFirstName( const string &first )
19      {
20          firstName = first; // should validate
21      } // end function setFirstName
22
23      // return first name
24      string CommissionEmployee::getFirstName() const
25      {
26          return firstName;
27      } // end function getFirstName
28
29      // set last name
30      void CommissionEmployee::setLastName( const string &last )
31      {
32          lastName = last; // should validate
33      } // end function setLastName
34
35      // return last name
36      string CommissionEmployee::getLastName() const
37      {
38          return lastName;
39      } // end function getLastName
40
41      // set social security number
42      void CommissionEmployee::setSocialSecurityNumber( const string &ssn )
43      {
44          socialSecurityNumber = ssn; // should validate
45      } // end function setSocialSecurityNumber
46
47      // return social security number
48      string CommissionEmployee::getSocialSecurityNumber() const
49      {
50          return socialSecurityNumber;
51      } // end function getSocialSecurityNumber
52
53      // set gross sales amount
54      void CommissionEmployee::setGrossSales( double sales )
55      {
56          if ( sales >= 0.0 )
57              grossSales = sales;
58          else
59              throw invalid_argument( "Gross sales must be >= 0.0" );
60      } // end function setGrossSales
61
```

Fig. 20.14 | CommissionEmployee class implementation file: CommissionEmployee class uses member functions to manipulate its private data. (Part 2 of 3.)

```
62   // return gross sales amount
63   double CommissionEmployee::getGrossSales() const
64   {
65      return grossSales;
66   } // end function getGrossSales
67
68   // set commission rate
69   void CommissionEmployee::setCommissionRate( double rate )
70   {
71      if ( rate > 0.0 && rate < 1.0 )
72         commissionRate = rate;
73      else
74         throw invalid_argument( "Commission rate must be > 0.0 and < 1.0" );
75   } // end function setCommissionRate
76
77   // return commission rate
78   double CommissionEmployee::getCommissionRate() const
79   {
80      return commissionRate;
81   } // end function getCommissionRate
82
83   // calculate earnings
84   double CommissionEmployee::earnings() const
85   {
86      return getCommissionRate() * getGrossSales();
87   } // end function earnings
88
89   // print CommissionEmployee object
90   void CommissionEmployee::print() const
91   {
92      cout << "commission employee: "
93         << getFirstName() << ' ' << getLastName()
94         << "\nsocial security number: " << getSocialSecurityNumber()
95         << "\ngross sales: " << getGrossSales()
96         << "\ncommission rate: " << getCommissionRate();
97   } // end function print
```

Fig. 20.14 | CommissionEmployee class implementation file: CommissionEmployee class uses member functions to manipulate its private data. (Part 3 of 3.)

Changes to Class BasePlusCommissionEmployee's Member Function Definitions

Class BasePlusCommissionEmployee inherits CommissionEmployee's public member functions and can access the private base-class members via the inherited member functions. Class BasePlusCommissionEmployee's header remains unchanged from Fig. 20.10. The class has several changes to its member-function implementations (Fig. 20.15) that distinguish it from the previous version of the class (Figs. 20.10–20.11). Member functions earnings (Fig. 20.15, lines 33–36) and print (lines 39–47) each invoke member function getBaseSalary to obtain the base salary value, rather than accessing baseSalary directly. This insulates earnings and print from potential changes to the implementation of data member baseSalary. For example, if we decide to rename data member baseSalary or change its type, only member functions setBaseSalary and getBaseSalary will need to change.

```
1   // Fig. 20.15: BasePlusCommissionEmployee.cpp
2   // Class BasePlusCommissionEmployee member-function definitions.
3   #include <iostream>
4   #include "BasePlusCommissionEmployee.h"
5   using namespace std;
6
7   // constructor
8   BasePlusCommissionEmployee::BasePlusCommissionEmployee(
9      const string &first, const string &last, const string &ssn,
10     double sales, double rate, double salary )
11     // explicitly call base-class constructor
12     : CommissionEmployee( first, last, ssn, sales, rate )
13  {
14     setBaseSalary( salary ); // validate and store base salary
15  } // end BasePlusCommissionEmployee constructor
16
17  // set base salary
18  void BasePlusCommissionEmployee::setBaseSalary( double salary )
19  {
20     if ( salary >= 0.0 )
21        baseSalary = salary;
22     else
23        throw invalid_argument( "Salary must be >= 0.0" );
24  } // end function setBaseSalary
25
26  // return base salary
27  double BasePlusCommissionEmployee::getBaseSalary() const
28  {
29     return baseSalary;
30  } // end function getBaseSalary
31
32  // calculate earnings
33  double BasePlusCommissionEmployee::earnings() const
34  {
35     return getBaseSalary() + CommissionEmployee::earnings();
36  } // end function earnings
37
38  // print BasePlusCommissionEmployee object
39  void BasePlusCommissionEmployee::print() const
40  {
41     cout << "base-salaried ";
42
43     // invoke CommissionEmployee's print function
44     CommissionEmployee::print();
45
46     cout << "\nbase salary: " << getBaseSalary();
47  } // end function print
```

Fig. 20.15 | BasePlusCommissionEmployee class that inherits from class
CommissionEmployee but cannot directly access the class's private data.

BasePlusCommissionEmployee *Member Function* earnings

Class BasePlusCommissionEmployee's earnings function (Fig. 20.15, lines 33–36) redefines class CommissionEmployee's earnings member function (Fig. 20.14, lines 84–87) to

calculate the earnings of a base-salaried commission employee. Class BasePlusCommis-sionEmployee's version of earnings obtains the portion of the employee's earnings based on commission alone by calling base-class CommissionEmployee's earnings function with the expression CommissionEmployee::earnings() (Fig. 20.15, line 35). BasePlus-CommissionEmployee's earnings function then adds the base salary to this value to calculate the total earnings of the employee. Note the syntax used to invoke a redefined base-class member function from a derived class—place the base-class name and the scope resolution operator (::) before the base-class member-function name. This member-function invocation is a good software engineering practice: Recall that, if an object's member function performs the actions needed by another object, we should call that member function rather than duplicating its code body. By having BasePlusCommissionEmployee's earnings function invoke CommissionEmployee's earnings function to calculate part of a BasePlusCommissionEmployee object's earnings, we avoid duplicating the code and reduce code-maintenance problems.

Common Programming Error 20.2

When a base-class member function is redefined in a derived class, the derived-class version often calls the base-class version to do additional work. Failure to use the :: operator prefixed with the name of the base class when referencing the base class's member function causes infinite recursion, *because the derived-class member function would then call itself.*

BasePlusCommissionEmployee *Member Function* print

Similarly, BasePlusCommissionEmployee's print function (Fig. 20.15, lines 39–47) redefines class CommissionEmployee's print function (Fig. 20.14, lines 90–97) to output the appropriate base-salaried commission employee information. The new version displays part of a BasePlusCommissionEmployee object's information (i.e., the string "commission employee" and the values of class CommissionEmployee's private data members) by calling CommissionEmployee's print member function with the qualified name Commission-Employee::print() (Fig. 20.15, line 44). BasePlusCommissionEmployee's print function then outputs the remainder of a BasePlusCommissionEmployee object's information (i.e., the value of class BasePlusCommissionEmployee's base salary).

Testing the Modified Class Hierarchy

Once again, this example uses the BasePlusCommissionEmployee test program from Fig. 20.9 and produces the same output. Although each "base-salaried commission employee" class behaves identically, the version in this example is the best engineered. *By using inheritance and by calling member functions that hide the data and ensure consistency, we've efficiently and effectively constructed a well-engineered class.*

Summary of the CommissionEmployee–BasePlusCommissionEmployee *Examples*

In this section, you saw an evolutionary set of examples that was carefully designed to teach key capabilities for good software engineering with inheritance. You learned how to create a derived class using inheritance, how to use protected base-class members to enable a derived class to access inherited base-class data members and how to redefine base-class functions to provide versions that are more appropriate for derived-class objects. In addition, you learned how to apply various software engineering techniques to create classes that are easy to maintain, modify and debug.

20.5 **Constructors and Destructors in Derived Classes**

As we explained in the preceding section, instantiating a derived-class object begins a chain of constructor calls in which the derived-class constructor, before performing its own tasks, invokes its direct base class's constructor either explicitly (via a base-class member initializer) or implicitly (calling the base class's default constructor). Similarly, if the base class is derived from another class, the base-class constructor is required to invoke the constructor of the next class up in the hierarchy, and so on. The last constructor called in this chain is the one of the class at the base of the hierarchy, whose body actually finishes executing *first*. The original derived-class constructor's body finishes executing *last*. Each base-class constructor initializes the base-class data members that the derived-class object inherits. In the Commission-Employee/BasePlusCommissionEmployee hierarchy that we've been studying, when a program creates an object of class BasePlusCommissionEmployee, the CommissionEmployee constructor is called. Since class CommissionEmployee is at the base of the hierarchy, its constructor executes, initializing the private data members of CommissionEmployee that are part of the BasePlusCommissionEmployee object. When CommissionEmployee's constructor completes execution, it returns control to BasePlusCommissionEmployee's constructor, which initializes the BasePlusCommissionEmployee object's baseSalary.

Software Engineering Observation 20.6

When a program creates a derived-class object, the derived-class constructor immediately calls the base-class constructor, the base-class constructor's body executes, then the derived class's member initializers execute and finally the derived-class constructor's body executes. This process cascades up the hierarchy if it contains more than two levels.

When a derived-class object is destroyed, the program calls that object's destructor. This begins a chain (or cascade) of destructor calls in which the derived-class destructor and the destructors of the direct and indirect base classes and the classes' members execute in *reverse* of the order in which the constructors executed. When a derived-class object's destructor is called, the destructor performs its task, then invokes the destructor of the next base class up the hierarchy. This process repeats until the destructor of the final base class at the top of the hierarchy is called. Then the object is removed from memory.

Software Engineering Observation 20.7

Suppose that we create an object of a derived class where both the base class and the derived class contain (via composition) objects of other classes. When an object of that derived class is created, first the constructors for the base class's member objects execute, then the base-class constructor body executes, then the constructors for the derived class's member objects execute, then the derived class's constructor body executes. Destructors for derived-class objects are called in the reverse of the order in which their corresponding constructors are called.

Base-class constructors, destructors and overloaded assignment operators (Chapter 19) are *not* inherited by derived classes. Derived-class constructors, destructors and overloaded assignment operators, however, can call base-class versions.

20.6 **public, protected and private Inheritance**

When deriving a class from a base class, the base class may be inherited through public, protected or private inheritance. We normally use public inheritance in this book. Use of protected inheritance is rare. private inheritance is sometimes used as an alternative to composition. Figure 20.16 summarizes for each type of inheritance the accessibility of base-class members in a derived class. The first column contains the base-class access specifiers.

Base-class member-access specifier	Type of inheritance		
	public inheritance	protected inheritance	private inheritance
public	public in derived class. Can be accessed directly by member functions, friend functions and nonmember functions.	protected in derived class. Can be accessed directly by member functions and friend functions.	private in derived class. Can be accessed directly by member functions and friend functions.
protected	protected in derived class. Can be accessed directly by member functions and friend functions.	protected in derived class. Can be accessed directly by member functions and friend functions.	private in derived class. Can be accessed directly by member functions and friend functions.
private	Hidden in derived class. Can be accessed by member functions and friend functions through public or protected member functions of the base class.	Hidden in derived class. Can be accessed by member functions and friend functions through public or protected member functions of the base class.	Hidden in derived class. Can be accessed by member functions and friend functions through public or protected member functions of the base class.

Fig. 20.16 | Summary of base-class member accessibility in a derived class.

When deriving a class from a public base class, public members of the base class become public members of the derived class, and protected members of the base class become protected members of the derived class. A base class's private members are *never* accessible directly from a derived class, but can be accessed through calls to the public and protected members of the base class.

When deriving from a protected base class, public and protected members of the base class become protected members of the derived class. When deriving from a private base class, public and protected members of the base class become private members (e.g., the functions become utility functions) of the derived class. Private and protected inheritance are not *is-a* relationships.

20.7 Software Engineering with Inheritance

Sometimes it's difficult for students to appreciate the scope of problems faced by designers who work on large-scale software projects in industry. People experienced with such projects say that effective software reuse improves the software development process. Object-oriented programming facilitates software reuse, thus shortening development times and enhancing software quality.

When we use inheritance to create a new class from an existing one, the new class inherits the data members and member functions of the existing class, as described in Fig. 20.16. We can customize the new class to meet our needs by redefining base-class members and by including additional members. The derived-class programmer does this in C++ *without* accessing the base class's source code (the derived class must be able to *link* to the base class's object code). This powerful capability is attractive to software developers. They can develop proprietary classes for sale or license and make these classes available to users in object-code format. Users then can derive new classes from these library classes rapidly and without accessing the proprietary source code. The software developers need to supply the headers along with the object code

The availability of substantial and useful class libraries delivers the maximum benefits of software reuse through inheritance. Interest in creating and selling class libraries is growing exponentially. The standard C++ libraries tend to be general purpose and limited in scope. There is a worldwide commitment to the development of class libraries for a huge variety of application arenas.

Software Engineering Observation 20.8

At the design stage in an object-oriented system, the designer often determines that certain classes are closely related. The designer should "factor out" common attributes and behaviors and place these in a base class, then use inheritance to form derived classes.

Software Engineering Observation 20.9

Creating a derived class does not affect its base class's source code. Inheritance preserves the integrity of a base class.

20.8 Wrap-Up

This chapter introduced inheritance—the ability to create a class by absorbing an existing class's data members and member functions and embellishing them with new capabilities. Through a series of examples using an employee inheritance hierarchy, you learned the notions of base classes and derived classes and used `public` inheritance to create a derived class that inherits members from a base class. The chapter introduced the access specifier `protected`—derived-class member functions can access `protected` base-class members. You learned how to access redefined base-class members by qualifying their names with the base-class name and scope resolution operator (`::`). You also saw the order in which constructors and destructors are called for objects of classes that are part of an inheritance hierarchy. Finally, we explained the three types of inheritance—`public`, `protected` and `private`—and the accessibility of base-class members in a derived class when using each type.

In Chapter 21, we build on our discussion of inheritance by introducing polymorphism—an object-oriented concept that enables us to write programs that handle, in a more general manner, objects of a wide variety of classes related by inheritance. When you complete Chapter 21, you'll be familiar with classes, objects, encapsulation, inheritance and polymorphism—the essential concepts of object-oriented programming.

Summary

Section 20.1 Introduction

- Software reuse reduces program development time and cost.

- Inheritance (p. 772) is a form of software reuse in which you create a class that absorbs an existing class's capabilities, then customizes or enhances them. The existing class is called the base class (p. 772), and the new class is referred to as the derived class (p. 772).

- Every object of a derived class is also an object of that class's base class. However, a base-class object is not an object of that class's derived classes.

- The *is-a* relationship (p. 772) represents inheritance. In an *is-a* relationship, an object of a derived class also can be treated as an object of its base class.

- The *has-a* relationship (p. 772) represents composition—an object contains one or more objects of other classes as members, but does not disclose their behavior directly in its interface.

Section 20.2 Base Classes and Derived Classes

- A direct base class (p. 774) is the one from which a derived class explicitly inherits. An indirect base class (p. 774) is inherited from two or more levels up the class hierarchy (p. 773).

- With single inheritance (p. 774), a class is derived from one base class. With multiple inheritance (p. 774), a class inherits from multiple (possibly unrelated) base classes.

- A derived class represents a more specialized group of objects.

- Inheritance relationships form class hierarchies.

- It's possible to treat base-class objects and derived-class objects similarly; the commonality shared between the object types is expressed in the base class's data members and member functions.

Section 20.3 protected Members

- A base class's public members are accessible anywhere that the program has a handle to an object of that base class or to an object of one of that base class's derived classes—or, when using the scope resolution operator, whenever the class's name is in scope.

- A base class's private members are accessible only within the base class or from its friends.

- A base class's protected members can be accessed by members and friends of that base class and by members and friends of any classes derived from that base class.

- When a derived-class member function redefines a base-class member function, the base-class member function can still be accessed from the derived class by qualifying the base-class member function name with the base-class name and the scope resolution operator (::).

Section 20.5 Constructors and Destructors in Derived Classes

- When an object of a derived class is instantiated, the base class's constructor is called immediately to initialize the base-class data members in the derived-class object, then the derived-class constructor initializes the additional derived-class data members.

- When a derived-class object is destroyed, the destructors are called in the reverse order of the constructors—first the derived-class destructor is called, then the base-class destructor is called.

Section 20.6 public, protected and private Inheritance

- Declaring data members private, while providing non-private member functions to manipulate and perform validity checking on this data, enforces good software engineering.

- When deriving a class, the base class may be declared as either public, protected or private.

- When deriving a class from a `public` base class (p. 774), `public` members of the base class become `public` members of the derived class, and `protected` members of the base class become `protected` members of the derived class.
- When deriving a class from a `protected` base class (p. 774), `public` and `protected` members of the base class become `protected` members of the derived class.
- When deriving a class from a `private` base class (p. 774), `public` and `protected` members of the base class become `private` members of the derived class.

Self-Review Exercises

20.1   Fill in the blanks in each of the following statements:
  a) _____ is a form of software reuse in which new classes absorb the data and behaviors of existing classes and embellish these classes with new capabilities.
  b) A base class's _____ members can be accessed in the base-class definition, in derived-class definitions and in `friends` of the base class its derived classes.
  c) In a(n) _____ relationship, an object of a derived class also can be treated as an object of its base class.
  d) In a(n) _____ relationship, a class object has one or more objects of other classes as members.
  e) In single inheritance, a class exists in a(n) _____ relationship with its derived classes.
  f) A base class's _____ members are accessible within that base class and anywhere that the program has a handle to an object of that class or one of its derived classes.
  g) A base class's `protected` access members have a level of protection between those of `public` and _____ access.
  h) C++ provides for _____, which allows a derived class to inherit from many base classes, even if the base classes are unrelated.
  i) When an object of a derived class is instantiated, the base class's _____ is called implicitly or explicitly to do any necessary initialization of the base-class data members in the derived-class object.
  j) When deriving a class from a base class with `public` inheritance, `public` members of the base class become _____ members of the derived class, and `protected` members of the base class become _____ members of the derived class.
  k) When deriving a class from a base class with `protected` inheritance, `public` members of the base class become _____ members of the derived class, and `protected` members of the base class become _____ members of the derived class.

20.2   State whether each of the following is *true* or *false*. If *false*, explain why.
  a) Base-class constructors are not inherited by derived classes.
  b) A *has-a* relationship is implemented via inheritance.
  c) A `Car` class has an *is-a* relationship with the `SteeringWheel` and `Brakes` classes.
  d) Inheritance encourages the reuse of proven high-quality software.
  e) When a derived-class object is destroyed, the destructors are called in the reverse order of the constructors.

Answers to Self-Review Exercises

20.1   a) Inheritance. b) `protected`. c) *is-a* or inheritance (for `public` inheritance). d) *has-a* or composition. e) hierarchical. f) `public`. g) `private`. h) multiple inheritance. i) constructor. j) `public`, `protected`. k) `protected`, `protected`.

20.2   a) True. b) False. A *has-a* relationship is implemented via composition. An *is-a* relationship is implemented via inheritance. c) False. This is an example of a *has-a* relationship. Class Car has an *is-a* relationship with class `Vehicle`. d) True. e) True.

Exercises

20.3 *(Composition as an Alternative to Inheritance)* Many programs written with inheritance could be written with composition instead, and vice versa. Rewrite class BasePlusCommissionEmployee of the CommissionEmployee–BasePlusCommissionEmployee hierarchy to use composition rather than inheritance. After you do this, assess the relative merits of the two approaches for designing classes CommissionEmployee and BasePlusCommissionEmployee, as well as for object-oriented programs in general. Which approach is more natural? Why?

20.4 *(Inheriting Constructors and Destructors)* Describe the order in which constructors and destructors are invoked for the base class and derived class.

20.5 *(Accessing Private Data Members of Base Class)* How can a derived class access private data members of the base class?

20.6 *(Vehicle Inheritance Hierarchy)* Draw an inheritance hierarchy for vehicles. Use Vehicle as the base class of the hierarchy, then include classes FourWheeler and TwoWheeler that derive from Vehicle. Continue to extend the hierarchy as deep (i.e., as many levels) as possible. For example, LightWeight and HeavyWeight vehicles might derive from FourWheeler, and MotorBike might derive from TwoWheeler. After drawing the hierarchy, discuss the relationships that exist between the classes. [*Note:* You do not need to write any code for this exercise.]

20.7 *(Richer Shape Hierarchy)* The world of shapes is much richer than the shapes included in the inheritance hierarchy of Fig. 20.3. Write down all the shapes you can think of—both two-dimensional and three-dimensional—and form them into a more complete Shape hierarchy with as many levels as possible. Your hierarchy should have the base class Shape from which class TwoDimensionalShape and class ThreeDimensionalShape are derived. [*Note:* You do not need to write any code for this exercise.] We'll use this hierarchy in the exercises of Chapter 21 to process a set of distinct shapes as objects of base-class Shape. (This technique, called polymorphism, is the subject of Chapter 21.)

20.8 *(Triangle Inheritance Hierarchy)* Draw an inheritance hierarchy for classes Triangle, Isosceles Triangle and Equilateral Triangle. Use Triangle as the base class of the hierarchy. Make the hierarchy as deep as possible.

20.9 (*Package Inheritance Hierarchy*) Package-delivery services, such as FedEx®, DHL® and UPS®, offer a number of different shipping options, each with specific costs associated. Create an inheritance hierarchy to represent various types of packages. Use class Package as the base class of the hierarchy, then include classes TwoDayPackage and OvernightPackage that derive from Package. Base class Package should include data members representing the name, address, city, state and ZIP code for both the sender and the recipient of the package, in addition to data members that store the weight (in ounces) and cost per ounce to ship the package. Package's constructor should initialize these data members. Ensure that the weight and cost per ounce contain positive values. Package should provide a public member function calculateCost that returns a double indicating the cost associated with shipping the package. Package's calculateCost function should determine the cost by multiplying the weight by the cost per ounce. Derived class TwoDayPackage should inherit the functionality of base class Package, but also include a data member that represents a flat fee that the shipping company charges for two-day-delivery service. TwoDayPackage's constructor should receive a value to initialize this data member. TwoDayPackage should redefine member function calculateCost so that it computes the shipping cost by adding the flat fee to the weight-based cost calculated by base class Package's calculateCost function. Class OvernightPackage should inherit directly from class Package and contain an additional data member representing an additional fee per ounce charged for overnight-delivery service. OvernightPackage should redefine member function calculateCost so that it adds the additional fee per ounce to the standard cost per ounce before calculating the shipping cost. Write a test program that creates objects of each type of Package and tests member function calculateCost.

20.10 *(Account Inheritance Hierarchy)* Create an inheritance hierarchy that a bank might use to represent customers' bank accounts. All customers at this bank can deposit (i.e., credit) money into their accounts and withdraw (i.e., debit) money from their accounts. More specific types of accounts also exist. Savings accounts, for instance, earn interest on the money they hold. Checking accounts, on the other hand, charge a fee per transaction (i.e., credit or debit).

Create an inheritance hierarchy containing base class Account and derived classes Savings-Account and CheckingAccount that inherit from class Account. Base class Account should include one data member of type double to represent the account balance. The class should provide a constructor that receives an initial balance and uses it to initialize the data member. The constructor should validate the initial balance to ensure that it's greater than or equal to 0.0. If not, the balance should be set to 0.0 and the constructor should display an error message, indicating that the initial balance was invalid. The class should provide three member functions. Member function credit should add an amount to the current balance. Member function debit should withdraw money from the Account and ensure that the debit amount does not exceed the Account's balance. If it does, the balance should be left unchanged and the function should print the message "Debit amount exceeded account balance." Member function getBalance should return the current balance.

Derived class SavingsAccount should inherit the functionality of an Account, but also include a data member of type double indicating the interest rate (percentage) assigned to the Account. SavingsAccount's constructor should receive the initial balance, as well as an initial value for the SavingsAccount's interest rate. SavingsAccount should provide a public member function calculateInterest that returns a double indicating the amount of interest earned by an account. Member function calculateInterest should determine this amount by multiplying the interest rate by the account balance. [*Note:* SavingsAccount should inherit member functions credit and debit as is without redefining them.]

Derived class CheckingAccount should inherit from base class Account and include an additional data member of type double that represents the fee charged per transaction. CheckingAccount's constructor should receive the initial balance, as well as a parameter indicating a fee amount. Class CheckingAccount should redefine member functions credit and debit so that they subtract the fee from the account balance whenever either transaction is performed successfully. CheckingAccount's versions of these functions should invoke the base-class Account version to perform the updates to an account balance. CheckingAccount's debit function should charge a fee only if money is actually withdrawn (i.e., the debit amount does not exceed the account balance). [*Hint:* Define Account's debit function so that it returns a bool indicating whether money was withdrawn. Then use the return value to determine whether a fee should be charged.]

After defining the classes in this hierarchy, write a program that creates objects of each class and tests their member functions. Add interest to the SavingsAccount object by first invoking its calculateInterest function, then passing the returned interest amount to the object's credit function.

21

Object-Oriented Programming: Polymorphism

The silence often of pure innocence
Persuades when speaking fails.
—William Shakespeare

General propositions do not decide concrete cases.
—Oliver Wendell Holmes

A philosopher of imposing stature doesn't think in a vacuum. Even his most abstract ideas are, to some extent, conditioned by what is or is not known in the time when he lives.
—Alfred North Whitehead

Objectives

In this chapter you'll learn:

- How polymorphism makes programming more convenient and systems more extensible.

- The distinction between abstract and concrete classes and how to create abstract classes.

- To use runtime type information (RTTI).

- How C++ implements virtual functions and dynamic binding.

- How virtual destructors ensure that all appropriate destructors run on an object.

21.1 Introduction

We now continue our study of OOP by explaining and demonstrating polymorphism with inheritance hierarchies. Polymorphism enables you to "program in the general" rather than "program in the specific." In particular, polymorphism enables you to write programs that process objects of classes that are part of the same class hierarchy as if they were all objects of the hierarchy's base class. As we'll soon see, polymorphism works off base-class pointer handles and base-class reference handles, but not off name handles.

Implementing for Extensibility

With polymorphism, you can design and implement systems that are easily *extensible*—new classes can be added with little or no modification to the general portions of the program, as long as the new classes are part of the inheritance hierarchy that the program processes generically. The only parts of a program that must be altered to accommodate new classes are those that require direct knowledge of the new classes that you add to the hierarchy. For example, if we create class `Tortoise` that inherits from class `Animal` (which might respond to a move message by crawling one inch), we need to write only the `Tortoise` class and the part of the simulation that instantiates a `Tortoise` object. The portions of the simulation that process each `Animal` generically can remain the same.

Optional Discussion of Polymorphism "Under the Hood"

A key feature of this chapter is its (optional) detailed discussion of polymorphism, `virtual` functions and dynamic binding "under the hood," which uses a detailed diagram to explain how polymorphism can be implemented in C++.

21.2 Introduction to Polymorphism: Polymorphic Video Game

Suppose that we design a video game that manipulates objects of many different types, including objects of classes Martian, Venutian, Plutonian, SpaceShip and LaserBeam. Imagine that each of these classes inherits from the common base class SpaceObject, which contains member function draw. Each derived class implements this function in a manner appropriate for that class. A screen-manager program maintains a container (e.g., a vector) that holds SpaceObject pointers to objects of the various classes. To refresh the screen, the screen manager periodically sends each object the same message—namely, draw. Each type of object responds in a unique way. For example, a Martian object might draw itself in red with the appropriate number of antennae, a SpaceShip object might draw itself as a silver flying saucer, and a LaserBeam object might draw itself as a bright red beam across the screen. The *same* message (in this case, draw) sent to a variety of objects has *many forms* of results—hence the term polymorphism.

A polymorphic screen manager facilitates adding new classes to a system with minimal modifications to its code. Suppose that we want to add objects of class Mercurian to our video game. To do so, we must build a class Mercurian that inherits from SpaceObject, but provides its own definition of member function draw. Then, when pointers to objects of class Mercurian appear in the container, you do not need to modify the code for the screen manager. The screen manager invokes member function draw on every object in the container, regardless of the object's type, so the new Mercurian objects simply "plug right in." Thus, without modifying the system (other than to build and include the classes themselves), you can use polymorphism to accommodate additional classes, including ones that were *not even envisioned* when the system was created.

Software Engineering Observation 21.1

Polymorphism enables you to deal in generalities *and let the execution-time environment concern itself with the* specifics. *You can direct a variety of objects to behave in manners appropriate to those objects* without even knowing their types—*as long as those objects belong to the same inheritance hierarchy and are being accessed off a common base-class pointer or a common base-class reference.*

Software Engineering Observation 21.2

Polymorphism promotes extensibility: Software written to invoke polymorphic behavior is written independently of the types of the objects to which messages are sent. Thus, new *types of objects that can respond to* existing *messages can be incorporated into such a system without modifying the base system. Only client code that instantiates new objects must be modified to accommodate new types.*

21.3 Relationships Among Objects in an Inheritance Hierarchy

Section 20.4 created an employee class hierarchy, in which class BasePlusCommission-Employee inherited from class CommissionEmployee. The Chapter 20 examples manipulated CommissionEmployee and BasePlusCommissionEmployee objects by using the objects' names to invoke their member functions. We now examine the relationships among classes in a hierarchy more closely. The next several sections present a series of examples that demonstrate how base-class and derived-class pointers can be aimed at base-class and derived-class objects, and how those pointers can be used to invoke member functions that manipulate those objects.

- In Section 21.3.1, we assign the address of a derived-class object to a base-class pointer, then show that invoking a function via the base-class pointer invokes the base-class functionality in the derived-class object—i.e., the *type of the handle determines which function is called.*

- In Section 21.3.2, we assign the address of a base-class object to a derived-class pointer, which results in a compilation error. We discuss the error message and investigate why the compiler does not allow such an assignment.

- In Section 21.3.3, we assign the address of a derived-class object to a base-class pointer, then examine how the base-class pointer can be used to invoke only the base-class functionality—*when we attempt to invoke derived-class member functions through the base-class pointer, compilation errors occur.*

- Finally, in Section 21.3.4, we demonstrate how to get polymorphic behavior from base-class pointers aimed at derived-class objects. We introduce virtual functions and polymorphism by declaring a base-class function as virtual. We then assign the address of a derived-class object to the base-class pointer and use that pointer to invoke derived-class functionality—*precisely the capability we need to achieve polymorphic behavior.*

A key concept in these examples is to demonstrate that with public inheritance *an object of a derived class can be treated as an object of its base class.* This enables various interesting manipulations. For example, a program can create an array of base-class pointers that point to objects of many derived-class types. Despite the fact that the derived-class objects are of *different types,* the compiler allows this because each derived-class object *is an* object of its base class. However, *we cannot treat a base-class object as an object of any of its derived classes.* For example, a CommissionEmployee is not a BasePlusCommissionEmployee in the hierarchy defined in Chapter 20—a CommissionEmployee does *not* have a baseSalary data member and does *not* have member functions setBaseSalary and getBaseSalary. The *is-a* relationship applies only from a derived class to its direct and indirect base classes.

21.3.1 Invoking Base-Class Functions from Derived-Class Objects

The example in Fig. 21.1 reuses the final versions of classes CommissionEmployee and BasePlusCommissionEmployee from Section 20.4.5. The example demonstrates three ways to aim base and derived-class pointers at base and derived-class objects. The first two are straightforward—we aim a base-class pointer at a base-class object and invoke base-class functionality, and we aim a derived-class pointer at a derived-class object and invoke derived-class functionality. Then, we demonstrate the relationship between derived classes and base classes (i.e., the *is-a* relationship of inheritance) by aiming a base-class pointer at a derived-class object and showing that the base-class functionality is indeed available in the derived-class object.

```cpp
1   // Fig. 21.1: fig21_01.cpp
2   // Aiming base-class and derived-class pointers at base-class
3   // and derived-class objects, respectively.
4   #include <iostream>
5   #include <iomanip>
6   #include "CommissionEmployee.h"
7   #include "BasePlusCommissionEmployee.h"
8   using namespace std;
9
10  int main()
11  {
12     // create base-class object
13     CommissionEmployee commissionEmployee(
14        "Sue", "Jones", "222-22-2222", 10000, .06 );
15
16     // create base-class pointer
17     CommissionEmployee *commissionEmployeePtr = 0;
18
19     // create derived-class object
20     BasePlusCommissionEmployee basePlusCommissionEmployee(
21        "Bob", "Lewis", "333-33-3333", 5000, .04, 300 );
22
23     // create derived-class pointer
24     BasePlusCommissionEmployee *basePlusCommissionEmployeePtr = 0;
25
26     // set floating-point output formatting
27     cout << fixed << setprecision( 2 );
28
29     // output objects commissionEmployee and basePlusCommissionEmployee
30     cout << "Print base-class and derived-class objects:\n\n";
31     commissionEmployee.print(); // invokes base-class print
32     cout << "\n\n";
33     basePlusCommissionEmployee.print(); // invokes derived-class print
34
35     // aim base-class pointer at base-class object and print
36     commissionEmployeePtr = &commissionEmployee; // perfectly natural
37     cout << "\n\n\nCalling print with base-class pointer to "
38        << "\nbase-class object invokes base-class print function:\n\n";
39     commissionEmployeePtr->print(); // invokes base-class print
40
41     // aim derived-class pointer at derived-class object and print
42     basePlusCommissionEmployeePtr = &basePlusCommissionEmployee; // natural
43     cout << "\n\n\nCalling print with derived-class pointer to "
44        << "\nderived-class object invokes derived-class "
45        << "print function:\n\n";
46     basePlusCommissionEmployeePtr->print(); // invokes derived-class print
47
48     // aim base-class pointer at derived-class object and print
49     commissionEmployeePtr = &basePlusCommissionEmployee;
50     cout << "\n\n\nCalling print with base-class pointer to "
51        << "derived-class object\ninvokes base-class print "
```

Fig. 21.1 | Assigning addresses of base-class and derived-class objects to base-class and derived-class pointers. (Part 1 of 2.)

```
52              << "function on that derived-class object:\n\n";
53        commissionEmployeePtr->print(); // invokes base-class print
54        cout << endl;
55   } // end main
```

```
Print base-class and derived-class objects:

commission employee: Sue Jones
social security number: 222-22-2222
gross sales: 10000.00
commission rate: 0.06

base-salaried commission employee: Bob Lewis
social security number: 333-33-3333
gross sales: 5000.00
commission rate: 0.04
base salary: 300.00


Calling print with base-class pointer to
base-class object invokes base-class print function:

commission employee: Sue Jones
social security number: 222-22-2222
gross sales: 10000.00
commission rate: 0.06


Calling print with derived-class pointer to
derived-class object invokes derived-class print function:

base-salaried commission employee: Bob Lewis
social security number: 333-33-3333
gross sales: 5000.00
commission rate: 0.04
base salary: 300.00


Calling print with base-class pointer to derived-class object
invokes base-class print function on that derived-class object:

commission employee: Bob Lewis
social security number: 333-33-3333
gross sales: 5000.00
commission rate: 0.04
```

Fig. 21.1 | Assigning addresses of base-class and derived-class objects to base-class and derived-class pointers. (Part 2 of 2.)

Recall that each BasePlusCommissionEmployee object *is a* CommissionEmployee that also has a base salary. Class BasePlusCommissionEmployee's earnings member function (lines 33–36 of Fig. 20.15) redefines class CommissionEmployee's earnings member function (lines 84–87 of Fig. 20.14) to include the object's base salary. Class BasePlusCommissionEmployee's print member function (lines 39–47 of Fig. 20.15) redefines class CommissionEmployee's version (lines 90–97 of Fig. 20.14) to display the same information plus the employee's base salary.

Creating Objects and Displaying Their Contents
In Fig. 21.1, lines 13–14 create a CommissionEmployee object and line 17 creates a pointer to a CommissionEmployee object; lines 20–21 create a BasePlusCommissionEmployee object and line 24 creates a pointer to a BasePlusCommissionEmployee object. Lines 31 and 33 use each object's name to invoke its print member function.

Aiming a Base-Class Pointer at a Base-Class Object
Line 36 assigns the address of base-class object commissionEmployee to base-class pointer commissionEmployeePtr, which line 39 uses to invoke member function print on that CommissionEmployee object. This invokes the version of print defined in base class CommissionEmployee.

Aiming a Derived-Class Pointer at a Derived-Class Object
Similarly, line 42 assigns the address of derived-class object basePlusCommissionEmployee to derived-class pointer basePlusCommissionEmployeePtr, which line 46 uses to invoke member function print on that BasePlusCommissionEmployee object. This invokes the version of print defined in derived class BasePlusCommissionEmployee.

Aiming a Base-Class Pointer at a Derived-Class Object
Line 49 then assigns the address of derived-class object basePlusCommissionEmployee to base-class pointer commissionEmployeePtr, which line 53 uses to invoke member function print. This "crossover" is allowed because an object of a derived class *is an* object of its base class. Despite the fact that the base class CommissionEmployee pointer points to a derived class BasePlusCommissionEmployee object, the base class CommissionEmployee's print member function is invoked (rather than BasePlusCommissionEmployee's print function). The output of each print member-function invocation in this program reveals that *the invoked functionality depends on the type of the pointer (or reference) used to invoke the function, not the type of the object for which the member function is called*. In Section 21.3.4, when we introduce virtual functions, we demonstrate that it's possible to invoke the object type's functionality, rather than invoke the handle type's functionality. We'll see that this is crucial to implementing polymorphic behavior—the key topic of this chapter.

21.3.2 Aiming Derived-Class Pointers at Base-Class Objects

In Section 21.3.1, we assigned the address of a derived-class object to a base-class pointer and explained that the C++ compiler allows this assignment, because a derived-class object *is a* base-class object. We take the opposite approach in Fig. 21.2, as we aim a derived-class pointer at a base-class object. [*Note:* This program reuses the final versions of classes CommissionEmployee and BasePlusCommissionEmployee from Section 20.4.5.] Lines 8–9 of Fig. 21.2 create a CommissionEmployee object, and line 10 creates a BasePlusCommissionEmployee pointer. Line 14 attempts to assign the address of base-class object commissionEmployee to derived-class pointer basePlusCommissionEmployeePtr, but the compiler generates an error. The compiler prevents this assignment, because a CommissionEmployee is *not* a BasePlusCommissionEmployee. Consider the consequences if the compiler were to allow this assignment. Through a BasePlusCommissionEmployee pointer, we can invoke *every* BasePlusCommissionEmployee member function, including setBaseSalary, for the object to which the pointer points (i.e., the base-class object commissionEmployee). However, the CommissionEmployee object does *not* provide a set-

BaseSalary member function, *nor* does it provide a baseSalary data member to set. This could lead to problems, because member function setBaseSalary would assume that there is a baseSalary data member to set at its "usual location" in a BasePlusCommission-Employee object. This memory does not belong to the CommissionEmployee object, so member function setBaseSalary might overwrite other important data in memory, possibly data that belongs to a different object.

```
1   // Fig. 21.2: fig21_02.cpp
2   // Aiming a derived-class pointer at a base-class object.
3   #include "CommissionEmployee.h"
4   #include "BasePlusCommissionEmployee.h"
5
6   int main()
7   {
8      CommissionEmployee commissionEmployee(
9         "Sue", "Jones", "222-22-2222", 10000, .06 );
10     BasePlusCommissionEmployee *basePlusCommissionEmployeePtr = 0;
11
12     // aim derived-class pointer at base-class object
13     // Error: a CommissionEmployee is not a BasePlusCommissionEmployee
14     basePlusCommissionEmployeePtr = &commissionEmployee;
15  } // end main
```

Microsoft Visual C++ compiler error message:

```
C:\examples\ch21\Fig21_02\fig21_02.cpp(14) : error C2440: '=' :
   cannot convert from 'CommissionEmployee *' to 'BasePlusCommissionEmployee *'
      Cast from base to derived requires dynamic_cast or static_cast
```

Fig. 21.2 | Aiming a derived-class pointer at a base-class object.

21.3.3 Derived-Class Member-Function Calls via Base-Class Pointers

Off a base-class pointer, the compiler allows us to invoke *only* base-class member functions. Thus, if a base-class pointer is aimed at a derived-class object, and an attempt is made to access a *derived-class-only member function*, a compilation error will occur.

Figure 21.3 shows the consequences of attempting to invoke a derived-class member function off a base-class pointer. [*Note:* We're again reusing the versions of classes CommissionEmployee and BasePlusCommissionEmployee from Section 20.4.5.] Line 9 creates commissionEmployeePtr—a pointer to a CommissionEmployee object—and lines 10–11 create a BasePlusCommissionEmployee object. Line 14 aims commissionEmployeePtr at derived-class object basePlusCommissionEmployee. Recall from Section 21.3.1 that this is allowed, because a BasePlusCommissionEmployee *is a* CommissionEmployee (in the sense that a BasePlusCommissionEmployee object contains all the functionality of a Commission-Employee object). Lines 18–22 invoke base-class member functions getFirstName, get-LastName, getSocialSecurityNumber, getGrossSales and getCommissionRate off the base-class pointer. All of these calls are legitimate, because BasePlusCommissionEmployee inherits these member functions from CommissionEmployee. We know that commission-EmployeePtr is aimed at a BasePlusCommissionEmployee object, so in lines 26–27 we attempt to invoke BasePlusCommissionEmployee member functions getBaseSalary and setBaseSalary. The compiler generates errors on both of these calls, because they're *not* made to member functions of base-class CommissionEmployee. The handle can be used to invoke *only* those functions that are members of that handle's associated class type. (In this case, off a CommissionEmployee *, we can invoke only CommissionEmployee member functions setFirstName, getFirstName, setLastName, getLastName, setSocialSecurityNumber, getSocialSecurityNumber, setGrossSales, getGrossSales, setCommissionRate, getCommissionRate, earnings and print.)

```
 1   // Fig. 21.3: fig21_03.cpp
 2   // Attempting to invoke derived-class-only member functions
 3   // through a base-class pointer.
 4   #include "CommissionEmployee.h"
 5   #include "BasePlusCommissionEmployee.h"
 6
 7   int main()
 8   {
 9      CommissionEmployee *commissionEmployeePtr = 0; // base class
10      BasePlusCommissionEmployee basePlusCommissionEmployee(
11         "Bob", "Lewis", "333-33-3333", 5000, .04, 300 ); // derived class
12
13      // aim base-class pointer at derived-class object
14      commissionEmployeePtr = &basePlusCommissionEmployee;
15
16      // invoke base-class member functions on derived-class
17      // object through base-class pointer (allowed)
18      string firstName = commissionEmployeePtr->getFirstName();
19      string lastName = commissionEmployeePtr->getLastName();
20      string ssn = commissionEmployeePtr->getSocialSecurityNumber();
21      double grossSales = commissionEmployeePtr->getGrossSales();
22      double commissionRate = commissionEmployeePtr->getCommissionRate();
23
24      // attempt to invoke derived-class-only member functions
25      // on derived-class object through base-class pointer (disallowed)
26      double baseSalary = commissionEmployeePtr->getBaseSalary();
27      commissionEmployeePtr->setBaseSalary( 500 );
28   } // end main
```

Microsoft Visual C++ compiler error messages:

```
C:\examples\ch21\Fig21_03\fig21_03.cpp(26) : error C2039:
   'getBaseSalary' : is not a member of 'CommissionEmployee'
      C:\examples\ch21\Fig21_03\CommissionEmployee.h(10) :
      see declaration of 'CommissionEmployee'
C:\examples\ch21\Fig21_03\fig21_03.cpp(27) : error C2039:
   'setBaseSalary' : is not a member of 'CommissionEmployee'
      C:\examples\ch21\Fig21_03\CommissionEmployee.h(10) :
      see declaration of 'CommissionEmployee'
```

GNU C++ compiler error messages:

```
fig21_03.cpp:26: error: 'getBaseSalary' undeclared (first use this function)
fig21_03.cpp:27: error: 'setBaseSalary' undeclared (first use this function)
```

Fig. 21.3 | Attempting to invoke derived-class-only functions through a base-class pointer.

The compiler will allow access to derived-class-only members from a base-class pointer that's aimed at a derived-class object *if* we explicitly cast the base-class pointer to a derived-class pointer—this is known as **downcasting**. As you know, it's possible to aim a base-class pointer at a derived-class object. However, as we demonstrated in Fig. 21.3, a base-class pointer can be used to invoke *only* the functions declared in the base class. Downcasting allows a derived-class-specific operation on a derived-class object pointed to by a base-class pointer. After a downcast, the program *can* invoke derived-class functions that are not in the base class. Downcasting is a potentially dangerous operation. Section 21.8 demonstrates how to *safely* use downcasting.

Software Engineering Observation 21.3

If the address of a derived-class object has been assigned to a pointer of one of its direct or indirect base classes, it's acceptable to cast that base-class pointer back to a pointer of the derived-class type. In fact, this must *be done to send that derived-class object messages that do not appear in the base class.*

21.3.4 Virtual Functions

In Section 21.3.1, we aimed a base-class `CommissionEmployee` pointer at a derived-class `BasePlusCommissionEmployee` object, then invoked member function `print` through that pointer. Recall that the *type of the handle* determined which class's functionality to invoke. In that case, the `CommissionEmployee` pointer invoked the `CommissionEmployee` member function `print` on the `BasePlusCommissionEmployee` object, even though the pointer was aimed at a `BasePlusCommissionEmployee` object that has its own custom `print` function.

Software Engineering Observation 21.4

With `virtual` *functions, the type of the object, not the type of the handle used to invoke the member function, determines which version of a* `virtual` *function to invoke.*

First, we consider why `virtual` functions are useful. Suppose that shape classes such as `Circle`, `Triangle`, `Rectangle` and `Square` are all derived from base class `Shape`. Each of these classes might be endowed with the ability to draw itself via a member function `draw`. Although each class has its own `draw` function, the function for each shape is quite different. In a program that draws a set of shapes, it would be useful to be able to treat all the shapes generically as objects of the base class `Shape`. Then, to draw any shape, we could simply use a base-class `Shape` pointer to invoke function `draw` and let the program determine *dynamically* (i.e., at runtime) which derived-class `draw` function to use, based on the type of the object to which the base-class `Shape` pointer points at any given time.

To enable this behavior, we declare `draw` in the base class as a **virtual** function, and we **override** `draw` in each of the derived classes to draw the appropriate shape. From an implementation perspective, *overriding* a function is no different than *redefining* one (which is the approach we've been using until now). An overridden function in a derived class has the *same signature and return type* (i.e., *prototype*) as the function it overrides in its base class. If we do not declare the base-class function as `virtual`, we can redefine that function. By contrast, if we declare the base-class function as `virtual`, we can override that function to enable polymorphic behavior. We declare a `virtual` function by preceding the function's prototype with the keyword `virtual` in the base class. For example,

```
virtual void draw() const;
```

would appear in base class `Shape`. The preceding prototype declares that function `draw` is a `virtual` function that takes no arguments and returns nothing. This function is declared `const` because a `draw` function typically would not make changes to the `Shape` object on which it's invoked—virtual functions do *not* have to be `const` functions.

Software Engineering Observation 21.5

Once a function is declared `virtual`, it remains `virtual` all the way down the inheritance hierarchy from that point, even if that function is not explicitly declared `virtual` when a derived class overrides it.

Good Programming Practice 21.1

Even though certain functions are implicitly `virtual` because of a declaration made higher in the class hierarchy, explicitly declare these functions `virtual` at every level of the class hierarchy to promote program clarity.

Error-Prevention Tip 21.1

When you browse a class hierarchy to locate a class to reuse, it's possible that a function in that class will exhibit `virtual` function behavior even though it isn't explicitly declared `virtual`. This happens when the class inherits a `virtual` function from its base class, and it can lead to subtle logic errors. Such errors can be avoided by explicitly declaring all `virtual` functions `virtual` throughout the inheritance hierarchy.

Software Engineering Observation 21.6

When a derived class chooses not to override a `virtual` function from its base class, the derived class simply inherits its base class's `virtual` function implementation.

If a program invokes a `virtual` function through a base-class pointer to a derived-class object (e.g., `shapePtr->draw()`) or a base-class reference to a derived-class object (e.g., `shapeRef.draw()`), the program will choose the correct derived-class `draw` function dynamically (i.e., at execution time) *based on the object type—not the pointer or reference type*. Choosing the appropriate function to call at execution time (rather than at compile time) is known as **dynamic binding** or **late binding**.

When a `virtual` function is called by referencing a specific object by *name* and using the dot member-selection operator (e.g., `squareObject.draw()`), the function invocation is resolved at compile time (this is called **static binding**) and the `virtual` function that's called is the one defined for (or inherited by) the class of that particular object—this is not polymorphic behavior. Thus, dynamic binding with `virtual` functions occurs only off pointer (and, as we'll soon see, reference) handles.

Now let's see how `virtual` functions can enable polymorphic behavior in our employee hierarchy. Figures 21.4–21.5 are the headers for classes `CommissionEmployee` and `BasePlusCommissionEmployee`, respectively. The only new features in these files is that we specify each class's `earnings` and `print` member functions as `virtual` (lines 30–31 of Fig. 21.4 and lines 20–21 of Fig. 21.5). Because functions `earnings` and `print` are `virtual` in class `CommissionEmployee`, class `BasePlusCommissionEmployee`'s `earnings` and `print` functions override class `CommissionEmployee`'s. Now, if we aim a base-class `CommissionEmployee` pointer at a derived-class `BasePlusCommissionEmployee` object, and the program uses that pointer to call either function `earnings` or `print`, the `BasePlusCommissionEmployee` object's corresponding function will be invoked. There were no changes to the member-function implementations of classes CommissionEmployee and BasePlusCommissionEmployee, so we reuse the versions of Figs. 20.14 and 20.15.

```
1   // Fig. 21.4: CommissionEmployee.h
2   // CommissionEmployee class definition represents a commission employee.
3   #ifndef COMMISSION_H
4   #define COMMISSION_H
5
6   #include <string> // C++ standard string class
7   using namespace std;
8
9   class CommissionEmployee
10  {
11  public:
12     CommissionEmployee( const string &, const string &, const string &,
13        double = 0.0, double = 0.0 );
14
15     void setFirstName( const string & ); // set first name
16     string getFirstName() const; // return first name
17
18     void setLastName( const string & ); // set last name
19     string getLastName() const; // return last name
20
21     void setSocialSecurityNumber( const string & ); // set SSN
22     string getSocialSecurityNumber() const; // return SSN
23
24     void setGrossSales( double ); // set gross sales amount
25     double getGrossSales() const; // return gross sales amount
26
27     void setCommissionRate( double ); // set commission rate
28     double getCommissionRate() const; // return commission rate
29
30     virtual double earnings() const; // calculate earnings
31     virtual void print() const; // print CommissionEmployee object
32  private:
33     string firstName;
34     string lastName;
35     string socialSecurityNumber;
36     double grossSales; // gross weekly sales
37     double commissionRate; // commission percentage
38  }; // end class CommissionEmployee
39
40  #endif
```

Fig. 21.4 | CommissionEmployee class header declares earnings and print as virtual.

```
1   // Fig. 21.5: BasePlusCommissionEmployee.h
2   // BasePlusCommissionEmployee class derived from class
3   // CommissionEmployee.
4   #ifndef BASEPLUS_H
5   #define BASEPLUS_H
```

Fig. 21.5 | BasePlusCommissionEmployee class header declares earnings and print functions as virtual. (Part I of 2.)

```
6
7    #include <string> // C++ standard string class
8    #include "CommissionEmployee.h" // CommissionEmployee class declaration
9    using namespace std;
10
11   class BasePlusCommissionEmployee : public CommissionEmployee
12   {
13   public:
14      BasePlusCommissionEmployee( const string &, const string &,
15         const string &, double = 0.0, double = 0.0, double = 0.0 );
16
17      void setBaseSalary( double ); // set base salary
18      double getBaseSalary() const; // return base salary
19
20      virtual double earnings() const; // calculate earnings
21      virtual void print() const; // print BasePlusCommissionEmployee object
22   private:
23      double baseSalary; // base salary
24   }; // end class BasePlusCommissionEmployee
25
26   #endif
```

Fig. 21.5 | BasePlusCommissionEmployee class header declares earnings and print functions as virtual. (Part 2 of 2.)

We modified Fig. 21.1 to create the program of Fig. 21.6. Lines 40–51 demonstrate again that a CommissionEmployee pointer aimed at a CommissionEmployee object can be used to invoke CommissionEmployee functionality, and a BasePlusCommissionEmployee pointer aimed at a BasePlusCommissionEmployee object can be used to invoke BasePlusCommissionEmployee functionality. Line 54 aims the base-class pointer commissionEmployeePtr at derived-class object basePlusCommissionEmployee. Note that when line 61 invokes member function print off the base-class pointer, the derived-class BasePlusCommissionEmployee's print member function is invoked, so line 61 outputs different text than line 53 does in Fig. 21.1 (when member function print was *not* declared virtual). We see that declaring a member function virtual causes the program to dynamically determine which function to invoke *based on the type of object to which the handle points, rather than on the type of the handle*. Note again that when commissionEmployeePtr points to a CommissionEmployee object (line 40), class CommissionEmployee's print function is invoked, and when CommissionEmployeePtr points to a BasePlusCommissionEmployee object, class BasePlusCommissionEmployee's print function is invoked. Thus, the same message—print, in this case—sent (off a base-class pointer) to a variety of objects related by inheritance to that base class, takes on many forms—this is polymorphic behavior.

```
1    // Fig. 21.6: fig21_06.cpp
2    // Introducing polymorphism, virtual functions and dynamic binding.
3    #include <iostream>
```

Fig. 21.6 | Demonstrating polymorphism by invoking a derived-class virtual function via a base-class pointer to a derived-class object. (Part 1 of 3.)

```
 4   #include <iomanip>
 5   #include "CommissionEmployee.h"
 6   #include "BasePlusCommissionEmployee.h"
 7   using namespace std;
 8
 9   int main()
10   {
11      // create base-class object
12      CommissionEmployee commissionEmployee(
13         "Sue", "Jones", "222-22-2222", 10000, .06 );
14
15      // create base-class pointer
16      CommissionEmployee *commissionEmployeePtr = 0;
17
18      // create derived-class object
19      BasePlusCommissionEmployee basePlusCommissionEmployee(
20         "Bob", "Lewis", "333-33-3333", 5000, .04, 300 );
21
22      // create derived-class pointer
23      BasePlusCommissionEmployee *basePlusCommissionEmployeePtr = 0;
24
25      // set floating-point output formatting
26      cout << fixed << setprecision( 2 );
27
28      // output objects using static binding
29      cout << "Invoking print function on base-class and derived-class "
30         << "\nobjects with static binding\n\n";
31      commissionEmployee.print(); // static binding
32      cout << "\n\n";
33      basePlusCommissionEmployee.print(); // static binding
34
35      // output objects using dynamic binding
36      cout << "\n\n\nInvoking print function on base-class and "
37         << "derived-class \nobjects with dynamic binding";
38
39      // aim base-class pointer at base-class object and print
40      commissionEmployeePtr = &commissionEmployee;
41      cout << "\n\nCalling virtual function print with base-class pointer"
42         << "\nto base-class object invokes base-class "
43         << "print function:\n\n";
44      commissionEmployeePtr->print(); // invokes base-class print
45
46      // aim derived-class pointer at derived-class object and print
47      basePlusCommissionEmployeePtr = &basePlusCommissionEmployee;
48      cout << "\n\nCalling virtual function print with derived-class "
49         << "pointer\nto derived-class object invokes derived-class "
50         << "print function:\n\n";
51      basePlusCommissionEmployeePtr->print(); // invokes derived-class print
52
53      // aim base-class pointer at derived-class object and print
54      commissionEmployeePtr = &basePlusCommissionEmployee;
```

Fig. 21.6 | Demonstrating polymorphism by invoking a derived-class virtual function via a base-class pointer to a derived-class object. (Part 2 of 3.)

```
55          cout << "\n\nCalling virtual function print with base-class pointer"
56             << "\nto derived-class object invokes derived-class "
57             << "print function:\n\n";
58
59          // polymorphism; invokes BasePlusCommissionEmployee's print;
60          // base-class pointer to derived-class object
61          commissionEmployeePtr->print();
62          cout << endl;
63     } // end main
```

```
Invoking print function on base-class and derived-class
objects with static binding

commission employee: Sue Jones
social security number: 222-22-2222
gross sales: 10000.00
commission rate: 0.06

base-salaried commission employee: Bob Lewis
social security number: 333-33-3333
gross sales: 5000.00
commission rate: 0.04
base salary: 300.00


Invoking print function on base-class and derived-class
objects with dynamic binding

Calling virtual function print with base-class pointer
to base-class object invokes base-class print function:

commission employee: Sue Jones
social security number: 222-22-2222
gross sales: 10000.00
commission rate: 0.06

Calling virtual function print with derived-class pointer
to derived-class object invokes derived-class print function:

base-salaried commission employee: Bob Lewis
social security number: 333-33-3333
gross sales: 5000.00
commission rate: 0.04
base salary: 300.00

Calling virtual function print with base-class pointer
to derived-class object invokes derived-class print function:

base-salaried commission employee: Bob Lewis
social security number: 333-33-3333
gross sales: 5000.00
commission rate: 0.04
base salary: 300.00
```

Fig. 21.6 | Demonstrating polymorphism by invoking a derived-class virtual function via a base-class pointer to a derived-class object. (Part 3 of 3.)

21.4 Type Fields and switch Statements

One way to determine the type of an object is to use a switch statement to check the value of a field in the object. This allows us to distinguish among object types, then invoke an appropriate action for a particular object. For example, in a hierarchy of shapes in which each shape object has a shapeType attribute, a switch statement could check the object's shapeType to determine which print function to call.

Using switch logic exposes programs to a variety of potential problems. For example, you might forget to include a type test when one is warranted, or might forget to test all possible cases in a switch statement. When modifying a switch-based system by adding new types, you might forget to insert the new cases in *all* relevant switch statements. Every addition or deletion of a class requires the modification of every switch statement in the system; tracking these statements down can be time consuming and error prone.

Software Engineering Observation 21.7

Polymorphic programming can eliminate the need for switch logic. By using the polymorphism mechanism to perform the equivalent logic, you can avoid the kinds of errors typically associated with switch logic.

Software Engineering Observation 21.8

An interesting consequence of using polymorphism is that programs take on a simplified appearance. They contain less branching logic and simpler sequential code. This simplification facilitates testing, debugging and program maintenance.

21.5 Abstract Classes and Pure virtual Functions

When we think of a class as a type, we assume that programs will create objects of that type. However, there are cases in which it's useful to define *classes from which you never intend to instantiate any objects*. Such classes are called abstract classes. Because these classes normally are used as base classes in inheritance hierarchies, we refer to them as abstract base classes. These classes cannot be used to instantiate objects, because, as we'll soon see, abstract classes are *incomplete*—derived classes must define the "missing pieces" before objects of these classes can be instantiated. We build programs with abstract classes in Section 21.6.

An abstract class provides a base class from which other classes can inherit. Classes that can be used to instantiate objects are called concrete classes. Such classes define or inherit implementations for every member function they declare. We could have an *abstract* base class TwoDimensionalShape and derive such *concrete* classes as Square, Circle and Triangle. We could also have an *abstract* base class ThreeDimensionalShape and derive such *concrete* classes as Cube, Sphere and Cylinder. Abstract base classes are *too generic* to define real objects; we need to be *more specific* before we can think of instantiating objects. For example, if someone tells you to "draw the two-dimensional shape," what shape would you draw? Concrete classes provide the *specifics* that make it reasonable to instantiate objects.

An inheritance hierarchy does not need to contain any abstract classes, but many object-oriented systems have class hierarchies headed by abstract base classes. In some cases, abstract classes constitute the top few levels of the hierarchy. A good example of this is the shape hierarchy in Fig. 20.3, which begins with abstract base class Shape. On the next level of the hierarchy we have two more abstract base classes—TwoDimensionalShape and ThreeDimensionalShape. The next level of the hierarchy defines *concrete* classes for two-dimensional shapes (namely, Circle, Square and Triangle) and for three-dimensional shapes (namely, Sphere, Cube and Tetrahedron).

Pure Virtual Functions
A class is made abstract by declaring one or more of its virtual functions to be "pure." A pure virtual function is specified by placing "= 0" in its declaration, as in

```
virtual void draw() const = 0; // pure virtual function
```

The "= 0" is a pure specifier. Pure virtual functions do *not* provide implementations. Every concrete derived class *must override all* base-class pure virtual functions with concrete implementations of those functions. The difference between a virtual function and a pure virtual function is that a virtual function has an implementation and gives the derived class the *option* of overriding the function; by contrast, a pure virtual function does *not* provide an implementation and *requires* the derived class to override the function for that derived class to be concrete; otherwise the derived class remains *abstract*.

Pure virtual functions are used when it does *not* make sense for the base class to have an implementation of a function, but you want all concrete derived classes to implement the function. Returning to our earlier example of space objects, it does not make sense for the base class SpaceObject to have an implementation for function draw (as there is no way to draw a generic space object without having more information about what type of space object is being drawn). An example of a function that would be defined as virtual (and not pure virtual) would be one that returns a name for the object. We can name a generic SpaceObject (for instance, as "space object"), so a default implementation for this function can be provided, and the function does not need to be pure virtual. The function is still declared virtual, however, because it's expected that derived classes will override this function to provide *more specific* names for the derived-class objects.

Software Engineering Observation 21.9
An abstract class defines a common public interface for the various classes in a class hierarchy. An abstract class contains one or more pure virtual functions that concrete derived classes must *override.*

Common Programming Error 21.1
Failure to override a pure virtual function in a derived class makes that class abstract. Attempting to instantiate an object of an abstract class causes a compilation error.

Software Engineering Observation 21.10
An abstract class has at least one pure virtual function. An abstract class also can have data members and concrete functions (including constructors and destructors), which are subject to the normal rules of inheritance by derived classes.

Although we *cannot* instantiate objects of an abstract base class, we *can* use the abstract base class to declare pointers and references that can refer to objects of any concrete classes derived from the abstract class. Programs typically use such pointers and references to manipulate derived-class objects polymorphically.

Device Drivers and Polymorphism

Polymorphism is particularly effective for implementing layered software systems. In operating systems, for example, each type of physical device could operate quite differently from the others. Even so, commands to *read* or *write* data from and to devices may have a certain uniformity. The *write* message sent to a device-driver object needs to be interpreted specifically in the context of that device driver and how that device driver manipulates devices of a specific type. However, the *write* call itself really is no different from the *write* to any other device in the system—place some number of bytes from memory onto that device. An object-oriented operating system might use an abstract base class to provide an interface appropriate for all device drivers. Then, through inheritance from that abstract base class, derived classes are formed that all operate similarly. The capabilities (i.e., the public functions) offered by the device drivers are provided as pure virtual functions in the abstract base class. The implementations of these pure virtual functions are provided in the derived classes that correspond to the specific types of device drivers. This architecture also allows new devices to be added to a system easily, even after the operating system has been defined. The user can just plug in the device and install its new device driver. The operating system "talks" to this new device through its device driver, which has the same public member functions as all other device drivers—those defined in the device driver abstract base class.

Iterators and Polymorphism

It's common in object-oriented programming to define an *iterator class* that can traverse all the objects in a container (such as an array). For example, a program can print a list of objects in a vector by creating an iterator object, then using the iterator to obtain the next element of the list each time the iterator is called. Iterators often are used in polymorphic programming to traverse an array or a linked list of pointers to objects from various levels of a hierarchy. The pointers in such a list are all base-class pointers. A list of pointers to objects of thebase class TwoDimensionalShape could contain pointers to objects of the classes Square, Circle, Triangle and so on. Using polymorphism to send a draw message, off a TwoDimensionalShape * pointer, to each object in the list would draw them correctly on the screen.

21.6 Case Study: Payroll System Using Polymorphism

This section reexamines the CommissionEmployee-BasePlusCommissionEmployee hierarchy that we explored throughout Section 20.4. In this example, we use an abstract class and polymorphism to perform payroll calculations based on the type of employee. We create an enhanced employee hierarchy to solve the following problem:

> *A company pays its employees weekly. The employees are of three types: Salaried employees are paid a fixed weekly salary regardless of the number of hours worked, commission employees are paid a percentage of their sales and base-salary-plus-commission employees receive a base salary plus a percentage of their sales. For the current pay period, the company has decided to reward base-salary-plus-commission employees by adding 10 percent to their base salaries. The company wants to implement a C++ program that performs its payroll calculations polymorphically.*

We use abstract class Employee to represent the general concept of an employee. The classes that derive directly from Employee are SalariedEmployee and CommissionEmployee. Class BasePlusCommissionEmployee—derived from CommissionEmployee—represents the last employee type. The UML class diagram in Fig. 21.7 shows the inheritance

hierarchy for our polymorphic employee payroll application. The abstract class name
Employee is italicized, as per the convention of the UML.

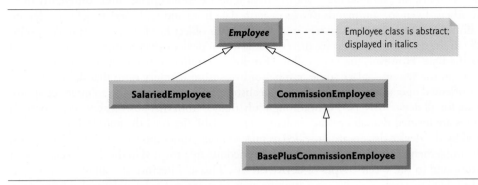

Fig. 21.7 | Employee hierarchy UML class diagram.

Abstract base class Employee declares the "interface" to the hierarchy—that is, the set
of member functions that a program can invoke on all Employee objects. Each employee,
regardless of the way his or her earnings are calculated, has a first name, a last name and a
social security number, so private data members firstName, lastName and socialSecurityNumber appear in abstract base class Employee.

Software Engineering Observation 21.11

*A derived class can inherit interface and/or implementation from a base class. Hierarchies
designed for* implementation inheritance *tend to have their functionality high in the
hierarchy—each new derived class inherits one or more member functions that were
defined in a base class, and the derived class uses the base-class definitions. Hierarchies
designed for* interface inheritance *tend to have their functionality lower in the
hierarchy—a base class specifies one or more functions that should be defined for each class
in the hierarchy (i.e., they have the same prototype), but the individual derived classes
provide their own implementations of the function(s).*

The following sections implement the Employee class hierarchy. The first five each
implement one of the abstract or concrete classes. The last section implements a test program that builds objects of all these classes and processes the objects polymorphically.

21.6.1 Creating Abstract Base Class Employee

Class Employee (Figs. 21.9–21.10, discussed in further detail shortly) provides functions
earnings and print, in addition to various *get* and *set* functions that manipulate Employee's data members. An earnings function certainly applies generically to all employees,
but each earnings calculation depends on the employee's class. So we declare earnings as
pure virtual in base class Employee because *a default implementation does not make sense*
for that function—there is not enough information to determine what amount earnings
should return. Each derived class *overrides* earnings with an appropriate implementation.
To calculate an employee's earnings, the program assigns the address of an employee's object to a base class Employee pointer, then invokes the earnings function on that object.

We maintain a vector of Employee pointers, each of which points to an Employee object. *Of course, there cannot be Employee objects, because Employee is an abstract class—because of inheritance, however, all objects of all derived classes of Employee may nevertheless be thought of as Employee objects.* The program iterates through the vector and calls function earnings for each Employee object. C++ processes these function calls *polymorphically.* Including earnings as a pure virtual function in Employee forces every direct derived class of Employee that wishes to be a *concrete* class to *override* earnings.

Function print in class Employee displays the first name, last name and social security number of the employee. As we'll see, each derived class of Employee overrides function print to output the employee's type (e.g., "salaried employee:") followed by the rest of the employee's information. Function print in the derived classes could also call earnings, even though earnings is a pure-virtual function in base class Employee.

The diagram in Fig. 21.8 shows each of the four classes in the hierarchy down the left side and functions earnings and print across the top. For each class, the diagram shows the desired results of each function. Class Employee specifies "= 0" for function earnings to indicate that this is a pure virtual function and hence has *no* implementation. Each derived class overrides this function to provide an appropriate implementation. We do not list base class Employee's *get* and *set* functions because they're not overridden in any of the derived classes—each of these functions is inherited and used "as is" by each of the derived classes.

	earnings	print
Employee	= 0	*firstName lastName* social security number: *SSN*
Salaried-Employee	*weeklySalary*	salaried employee: *firstName lastName* social security number: *SSN* weekly salary: *weeklySalary*
Commission-Employee	*commissionRate * grossSales*	commission employee: *firstName lastName* social security number: *SSN* gross sales: *grossSales*; commission rate: *commissionRate*
BasePlus-Commission-Employee	*(commissionRate * grossSales) + baseSalary*	base-salaried commission employee: *firstName lastName* social security number: *SSN* gross sales: *grossSales*; commission rate: *commissionRate*; base salary: *baseSalary*

Fig. 21.8 | Polymorphic interface for the Employee hierarchy classes.

Employee Class Header

Let's consider class Employee's header (Fig. 21.9). The public member functions include a constructor that takes the first name, last name and social security number as arguments (line 12); *set* functions that set the first name, last name and social security number (lines

14, 17 and 20, respectively); *get* functions that return the first name, last name and social security number (lines 15, 18 and 21, respectively); pure virtual function earnings (line 24) and virtual function print (line 25).

```cpp
1   // Fig. 21.9: Employee.h
2   // Employee abstract base class.
3   #ifndef EMPLOYEE_H
4   #define EMPLOYEE_H
5
6   #include <string> // C++ standard string class
7   using namespace std;
8
9   class Employee
10  {
11  public:
12     Employee( const string &, const string &, const string & );
13
14     void setFirstName( const string & ); // set first name
15     string getFirstName() const; // return first name
16
17     void setLastName( const string & ); // set last name
18     string getLastName() const; // return last name
19
20     void setSocialSecurityNumber( const string & ); // set SSN
21     string getSocialSecurityNumber() const; // return SSN
22
23     // pure virtual function makes Employee an abstract base class
24     virtual double earnings() const = 0; // pure virtual
25     virtual void print() const; // virtual
26  private:
27     string firstName;
28     string lastName;
29     string socialSecurityNumber;
30  }; // end class Employee
31
32  #endif // EMPLOYEE_H
```

Fig. 21.9 | Employee abstract base class.

Recall that we declared earnings as a pure virtual function because first we must know the *specific* Employee type to determine the appropriate earnings calculations. Declaring this function as pure virtual indicates that each concrete derived class *must* provide an earnings implementation and that a program can use base-class Employee pointers to invoke function earnings *polymorphically* for any type of Employee.

Employee *Class Member-Function Definitions*
Figure 21.10 contains the member-function implementations for class Employee. No implementation is provided for virtual function earnings. The Employee constructor (lines 9–14) does not validate the social security number. Normally, such validation should be provided.

```
1    // Fig. 21.10: Employee.cpp
2    // Abstract-base-class Employee member-function definitions.
3    // Note: No definitions are given for pure virtual functions.
4    #include <iostream>
5    #include "Employee.h" // Employee class definition
6    using namespace std;
7
8    // constructor
9    Employee::Employee( const string &first, const string &last,
10      const string &ssn )
11      : firstName( first ), lastName( last ), socialSecurityNumber( ssn )
12   {
13      // empty body
14   } // end Employee constructor
15
16   // set first name
17   void Employee::setFirstName( const string &first )
18   {
19      firstName = first;
20   } // end function setFirstName
21
22   // return first name
23   string Employee::getFirstName() const
24   {
25      return firstName;
26   } // end function getFirstName
27
28   // set last name
29   void Employee::setLastName( const string &last )
30   {
31      lastName = last;
32   } // end function setLastName
33
34   // return last name
35   string Employee::getLastName() const
36   {
37      return lastName;
38   } // end function getLastName
39
40   // set social security number
41   void Employee::setSocialSecurityNumber( const string &ssn )
42   {
43      socialSecurityNumber = ssn; // should validate
44   } // end function setSocialSecurityNumber
45
46   // return social security number
47   string Employee::getSocialSecurityNumber() const
48   {
49      return socialSecurityNumber;
50   } // end function getSocialSecurityNumber
51
```

Fig. 21.10 | Employee class implementation file. (Part 1 of 2.)

```
52   // print Employee's information (virtual, but not pure virtual)
53   void Employee::print() const
54   {
55      cout << getFirstName() << ' ' << getLastName()
56         << "\nsocial security number: " << getSocialSecurityNumber();
57   } // end function print
```

Fig. 21.10 | Employee class implementation file. (Part 2 of 2.)

The virtual function print (Fig. 21.10, lines 53–57) provides an *implementation* that will be *overridden* in each of the derived classes. Each of these functions will, however, use the abstract class's version of print to print information *common to all classes* in the Employee hierarchy.

21.6.2 Creating Concrete Derived Class SalariedEmployee

Class SalariedEmployee (Figs. 21.11–21.12) derives from class Employee (line 8 of Fig. 21.11). The public member functions include a constructor that takes a first name, a last name, a social security number and a weekly salary as arguments (lines 11–12); a *set* function to assign a new nonnegative value to data member weeklySalary (line 14); a *get* function to return weeklySalary's value (line 15); a virtual function earnings that calculates a SalariedEmployee's earnings (line 18) and a virtual function print (line 19) that outputs the employee's type, namely, "salaried employee: " followed by employee-specific information produced by base class Employee's print function and SalariedEmployee's getWeeklySalary function.

```
 1   // Fig. 21.11: SalariedEmployee.h
 2   // SalariedEmployee class derived from Employee.
 3   #ifndef SALARIED_H
 4   #define SALARIED_H
 5
 6   #include "Employee.h" // Employee class definition
 7
 8   class SalariedEmployee : public Employee
 9   {
10   public:
11      SalariedEmployee( const string &, const string &,
12         const string &, double = 0.0 );
13
14      void setWeeklySalary( double ); // set weekly salary
15      double getWeeklySalary() const; // return weekly salary
16
17      // keyword virtual signals intent to override
18      virtual double earnings() const; // calculate earnings
19      virtual void print() const; // print SalariedEmployee object
20   private:
21      double weeklySalary; // salary per week
22   }; // end class SalariedEmployee
23
24   #endif // SALARIED_H
```

Fig. 21.11 | SalariedEmployee class derived from Employee.

SalariedEmployee Class Member-Function Definitions

Figure 21.12 contains the member-function implementations for SalariedEmployee. The class's constructor passes the first name, last name and social security number to the Employee constructor (line 10) to initialize the private data members that are inherited from the base class, but not directly accessible in the derived class. Function earnings (lines 32–35) overrides pure virtual function earnings in Employee to provide a *concrete* implementation that returns the SalariedEmployee's weekly salary. If we did not implement earnings, class SalariedEmployee would be an *abstract* class, and any attempt to instantiate an object of the class would result in a compilation error (and, of course, we want SalariedEmployee here to be a concrete class). In class SalariedEmployee's header, we declared member functions earnings and print as virtual (lines 18–19 of Fig. 21.11)—actually, placing the virtual keyword before these member functions is *redundant*. We defined them as virtual in base class Employee, so they remain virtual functions throughout the class hierarchy. Explicitly declaring such functions virtual at every level of the hierarchy can promote program clarity. Not declaring earnings as pure virtual signals our intent to provide an implementation in this concrete class.

```cpp
1   // Fig. 21.12: SalariedEmployee.cpp
2   // SalariedEmployee class member-function definitions.
3   #include <iostream>
4   #include "SalariedEmployee.h" // SalariedEmployee class definition
5   using namespace std;
6
7   // constructor
8   SalariedEmployee::SalariedEmployee( const string &first,
9      const string &last, const string &ssn, double salary )
10     : Employee( first, last, ssn )
11  {
12     setWeeklySalary( salary );
13  } // end SalariedEmployee constructor
14
15  // set salary
16  void SalariedEmployee::setWeeklySalary( double salary )
17  {
18     if ( salary >= 0.0 )
19        weeklySalary = salary;
20     else
21        throw invalid_argument( "Weekly salary must be >= 0.0" );
22  } // end function setWeeklySalary
23
24  // return salary
25  double SalariedEmployee::getWeeklySalary() const
26  {
27     return weeklySalary;
28  } // end function getWeeklySalary
29
30  // calculate earnings;
31  // override pure virtual function earnings in Employee
32  double SalariedEmployee::earnings() const
33  {
```

Fig. 21.12 | SalariedEmployee class implementation file. (Part 1 of 2.)

```
34       return getWeeklySalary();
35   } // end function earnings
36
37   // print SalariedEmployee's information
38   void SalariedEmployee::print() const
39   {
40       cout << "salaried employee: ";
41       Employee::print(); // reuse abstract base-class print function
42       cout << "\nweekly salary: " << getWeeklySalary();
43   } // end function print
```

Fig. 21.12 | SalariedEmployee class implementation file. (Part 2 of 2.)

Function print of class SalariedEmployee (lines 38–43 of Fig. 21.12) overrides Employee function print. If class SalariedEmployee did not override print, SalariedEmployee would inherit the Employee version of print. In that case, SalariedEmployee's print function would simply return the employee's full name and social security number, which does not adequately represent a SalariedEmployee. To print a SalariedEmployee's complete information, the derived class's print function outputs "salaried employee: " followed by the base-class Employee-specific information (i.e., first name, last name and social security number) printed by invoking the base class's print function using the scope resolution operator (line 41)—this is a nice example of code reuse. Without the scope resolution operator, the print call would cause *infinite recursion*. The output produced by SalariedEmployee's print function contains the employee's weekly salary obtained by invoking the class's getWeeklySalary function.

21.6.3 Creating Concrete Derived Class CommissionEmployee

Class CommissionEmployee (Figs. 21.13–21.14) derives from Employee (Fig. 21.13, line 8). The member-function implementations (Fig. 21.14) include a constructor (lines 8–14) that takes a first name, last name, social security number, sales amount and commission rate; *set* functions (lines 17–23 and 32–38) to assign new values to data members commissionRate and grossSales, respectively; *get* functions (lines 26–29 and 41–44) that retrieve their values; function earnings (lines 47–50) to calculate a CommissionEmployee's earnings; and function print (lines 53–59) to output the employee's type, namely, "commission employee: " and employee-specific information. The constructor passes the first name, last name and social security number to the Employee constructor (line 10) to initialize Employee's private data members. Function print calls base-class function print (line 56) to display the Employee-specific information.

```
1    // Fig. 21.13: CommissionEmployee.h
2    // CommissionEmployee class derived from Employee.
3    #ifndef COMMISSION_H
4    #define COMMISSION_H
5
6    #include "Employee.h" // Employee class definition
7
```

Fig. 21.13 | CommissionEmployee class header. (Part 1 of 2.)

```
8    class CommissionEmployee : public Employee
9    {
10   public:
11      CommissionEmployee( const string &, const string &,
12         const string &, double = 0.0, double = 0.0 );
13
14      void setCommissionRate( double ); // set commission rate
15      double getCommissionRate() const; // return commission rate
16
17      void setGrossSales( double ); // set gross sales amount
18      double getGrossSales() const; // return gross sales amount
19
20      // keyword virtual signals intent to override
21      virtual double earnings() const; // calculate earnings
22      virtual void print() const; // print CommissionEmployee object
23   private:
24      double grossSales; // gross weekly sales
25      double commissionRate; // commission percentage
26   }; // end class CommissionEmployee
27
28   #endif // COMMISSION_H
```

Fig. 21.13 | CommissionEmployee class header. (Part 2 of 2.)

```
1    // Fig. 21.14: CommissionEmployee.cpp
2    // CommissionEmployee class member-function definitions.
3    #include <iostream>
4    #include "CommissionEmployee.h" // CommissionEmployee class definition
5    using namespace std;
6
7    // constructor
8    CommissionEmployee::CommissionEmployee( const string &first,
9       const string &last, const string &ssn, double sales, double rate )
10      : Employee( first, last, ssn )
11   {
12      setGrossSales( sales );
13      setCommissionRate( rate );
14   } // end CommissionEmployee constructor
15
16   // set gross sales amount
17   void CommissionEmployee::setGrossSales( double sales )
18   {
19      if ( sales >= 0.0 )
20         grossSales = sales;
21      else
22         throw invalid_argument( "Gross sales must be >= 0.0" );
23   } // end function setGrossSales
24
25   // return gross sales amount
26   double CommissionEmployee::getGrossSales() const
27   {
```

Fig. 21.14 | CommissionEmployee class implementation file. (Part 1 of 2.)

```
28        return grossSales;
29   } // end function getGrossSales
30
31   // set commission rate
32   void CommissionEmployee::setCommissionRate( double rate )
33   {
34        if ( rate > 0.0 && rate < 1.0 )
35            commissionRate = rate;
36        else
37            throw invalid_argument( "Commission rate must be > 0.0 and < 1.0" );
38   } // end function setCommissionRate
39
40   // return commission rate
41   double CommissionEmployee::getCommissionRate() const
42   {
43        return commissionRate;
44   } // end function getCommissionRate
45
46   // calculate earnings; override pure virtual function earnings in Employee
47   double CommissionEmployee::earnings() const
48   {
49        return getCommissionRate() * getGrossSales();
50   } // end function earnings
51
52   // print CommissionEmployee's information
53   void CommissionEmployee::print() const
54   {
55        cout << "commission employee: ";
56        Employee::print(); // code reuse
57        cout << "\ngross sales: " << getGrossSales()
58            << "; commission rate: " << getCommissionRate();
59   } // end function print
```

Fig. 21.14 | CommissionEmployee class implementation file. (Part 2 of 2.)

21.6.4 Creating Indirect Concrete Derived Class BasePlusCommissionEmployee

Class BasePlusCommissionEmployee (Figs. 21.15–21.16) directly inherits from class CommissionEmployee (line 8 of Fig. 21.15) and therefore is an *indirect* derived class of class Employee. Class BasePlusCommissionEmployee's member-function implementations include a constructor (lines 8–14 of Fig. 21.16) that takes as arguments a first name, a last name, a social security number, a sales amount, a commission rate and a base salary. It then passes the first name, last name, social security number, sales amount and commission rate to the CommissionEmployee constructor (line 11) to initialize the inherited members. BasePlusCommissionEmployee also contains a *set* function (lines 17–23) to assign a new value to data member baseSalary and a *get* function (lines 26–29) to return baseSalary's value. Function earnings (lines 33–36) calculates a BasePlusCommissionEmployee's earnings. Line 35 in function earnings calls base-class CommissionEmployee's earnings function to calculate the commission-based portion of the employee's earnings. This is another nice example of code reuse. BasePlusCommissionEmployee's print function (lines 39–44) outputs "base-salaried", followed by the output of base-class CommissionEmployee's print function (another example of code reuse), then the base salary. The resulting output begins with "base-salaried commission employee: " followed by the rest of the Base-PlusCommissionEmployee's information. Recall that CommissionEmployee's print displays the employee's first name, last name and social security number by invoking the print function of its base class (i.e., Employee)—yet another example of code reuse. Base-PlusCommissionEmployee's print initiates a chain of functions calls that spans *all three levels* of the Employee hierarchy.

```cpp
1   // Fig. 21.15: BasePlusCommissionEmployee.h
2   // BasePlusCommissionEmployee class derived from CommissionEmployee.
3   #ifndef BASEPLUS_H
4   #define BASEPLUS_H
5
6   #include "CommissionEmployee.h" // CommissionEmployee class definition
7
8   class BasePlusCommissionEmployee : public CommissionEmployee
9   {
10  public:
11     BasePlusCommissionEmployee( const string &, const string &,
12        const string &, double = 0.0, double = 0.0, double = 0.0 );
13
14     void setBaseSalary( double ); // set base salary
15     double getBaseSalary() const; // return base salary
16
17     // keyword virtual signals intent to override
18     virtual double earnings() const; // calculate earnings
19     virtual void print() const; // print BasePlusCommissionEmployee object
20  private:
21     double baseSalary; // base salary per week
22  }; // end class BasePlusCommissionEmployee
23
24  #endif // BASEPLUS_H
```

Fig. 21.15 | BasePlusCommissionEmployee class header.

```cpp
1   // Fig. 21.16: BasePlusCommissionEmployee.cpp
2   // BasePlusCommissionEmployee member-function definitions.
3   #include <iostream>
4   #include "BasePlusCommissionEmployee.h"
5   using namespace std;
6
7   // constructor
8   BasePlusCommissionEmployee::BasePlusCommissionEmployee(
9      const string &first, const string &last, const string &ssn,
10     double sales, double rate, double salary )
11     : CommissionEmployee( first, last, ssn, sales, rate )
12  {
13     setBaseSalary( salary ); // validate and store base salary
14  } // end BasePlusCommissionEmployee constructor
15
```

Fig. 21.16 | BasePlusCommissionEmployee class implementation file. (Part 1 of 2.)

```
16   // set base salary
17   void BasePlusCommissionEmployee::setBaseSalary( double salary )
18   {
19      if ( salary >= 0.0 )
20         baseSalary = salary;
21      else
22         throw invalid_argument( "Salary must be >= 0.0" );
23   } // end function setBaseSalary
24
25   // return base salary
26   double BasePlusCommissionEmployee::getBaseSalary() const
27   {
28      return baseSalary;
29   } // end function getBaseSalary
30
31   // calculate earnings;
32   // override virtual function earnings in CommissionEmployee
33   double BasePlusCommissionEmployee::earnings() const
34   {
35      return getBaseSalary() + CommissionEmployee::earnings();
36   } // end function earnings
37
38   // print BasePlusCommissionEmployee's information
39   void BasePlusCommissionEmployee::print() const
40   {
41      cout << "base-salaried ";
42      CommissionEmployee::print(); // code reuse
43      cout << "; base salary: " << getBaseSalary();
44   } // end function print
```

Fig. 21.16 | BasePlusCommissionEmployee class implementation file. (Part 2 of 2.)

21.6.5 Demonstrating Polymorphic Processing

To test our Employee hierarchy, the program in Fig. 21.17 creates an object of each of the three concrete classes SalariedEmployee, CommissionEmployee and BasePlusCommissionEmployee. The program manipulates these objects, first with *static binding*, then *polymorphically*, using a vector of Employee pointers. Lines 22–27 create objects of each of the three concrete Employee derived classes. Lines 32–38 output each Employee's information and earnings. Each member-function invocation in lines 32–37 is an example of static binding—at *compile time*, because we are using *name handles* (not *pointers* or *references* that could be set at *execution time*), the *compiler* can identify each object's type to determine which print and earnings functions are called.

```
1   // Fig. 21.17: fig21_17.cpp
2   // Processing Employee derived-class objects individually
3   // and polymorphically using dynamic binding.
4   #include <iostream>
5   #include <iomanip>
6   #include <vector>
```

Fig. 21.17 | Employee class hierarchy driver program. (Part 1 of 4.)

```cpp
7   #include "Employee.h"
8   #include "SalariedEmployee.h"
9   #include "CommissionEmployee.h"
10  #include "BasePlusCommissionEmployee.h"
11  using namespace std;
12
13  void virtualViaPointer( const Employee * const ); // prototype
14  void virtualViaReference( const Employee & ); // prototype
15
16  int main()
17  {
18     // set floating-point output formatting
19     cout << fixed << setprecision( 2 );
20
21     // create derived-class objects
22     SalariedEmployee salariedEmployee(
23        "John", "Smith", "111-11-1111", 800 );
24     CommissionEmployee commissionEmployee(
25        "Sue", "Jones", "333-33-3333", 10000, .06 );
26     BasePlusCommissionEmployee basePlusCommissionEmployee(
27        "Bob", "Lewis", "444-44-4444", 5000, .04, 300 );
28
29     cout << "Employees processed individually using static binding:\n\n";
30
31     // output each Employee's information and earnings using static binding
32     salariedEmployee.print();
33     cout << "\nearned $" << salariedEmployee.earnings() << "\n\n";
34     commissionEmployee.print();
35     cout << "\nearned $" << commissionEmployee.earnings() << "\n\n";
36     basePlusCommissionEmployee.print();
37     cout << "\nearned $" << basePlusCommissionEmployee.earnings()
38        << "\n\n";
39
40     // create vector of three base-class pointers
41     vector < Employee * > employees( 3 );
42
43     // initialize vector with Employees
44     employees[ 0 ] = &salariedEmployee;
45     employees[ 1 ] = &commissionEmployee;
46     employees[ 2 ] = &basePlusCommissionEmployee;
47
48     cout << "Employees processed polymorphically via dynamic binding:\n\n";
49
50     // call virtualViaPointer to print each Employee's information
51     // and earnings using dynamic binding
52     cout << "Virtual function calls made off base-class pointers:\n\n";
53
54     for ( size_t i = 0; i < employees.size(); ++i )
55        virtualViaPointer( employees[ i ] );
56
57     // call virtualViaReference to print each Employee's information
58     // and earnings using dynamic binding
59     cout << "Virtual function calls made off base-class references:\n\n";
```

Fig. 21.17 | Employee class hierarchy driver program. (Part 2 of 4.)

```
60
61      for ( size_t i = 0; i < employees.size(); ++i )
62         virtualViaReference( *employees[ i ] ); // note dereferencing
63   } // end main
64
65   // call Employee virtual functions print and earnings off a
66   // base-class pointer using dynamic binding
67   void virtualViaPointer( const Employee * const baseClassPtr )
68   {
69      baseClassPtr->print();
70      cout << "\nearned $" << baseClassPtr->earnings() << "\n\n";
71   } // end function virtualViaPointer
72
73   // call Employee virtual functions print and earnings off a
74   // base-class reference using dynamic binding
75   void virtualViaReference( const Employee &baseClassRef )
76   {
77      baseClassRef.print();
78      cout << "\nearned $" << baseClassRef.earnings() << "\n\n";
79   } // end function virtualViaReference
```

```
Employees processed individually using static binding:

salaried employee: John Smith
social security number: 111-11-1111
weekly salary: 800.00
earned $800.00

commission employee: Sue Jones
social security number: 333-33-3333
gross sales: 10000.00; commission rate: 0.06
earned $600.00

base-salaried commission employee: Bob Lewis
social security number: 444-44-4444
gross sales: 5000.00; commission rate: 0.04; base salary: 300.00
earned $500.00

Employees processed polymorphically using dynamic binding:

Virtual function calls made off base-class pointers:

salaried employee: John Smith
social security number: 111-11-1111
weekly salary: 800.00
earned $800.00

commission employee: Sue Jones
social security number: 333-33-3333
gross sales: 10000.00; commission rate: 0.06
earned $600.00

base-salaried commission employee: Bob Lewis
social security number: 444-44-4444
gross sales: 5000.00; commission rate: 0.04; base salary: 300.00
earned $500.00
```

Fig. 21.17 | Employee class hierarchy driver program. (Part 3 of 4.)

```
Virtual function calls made off base-class references:

salaried employee: John Smith
social security number: 111-11-1111
weekly salary: 800.00
earned $800.00

commission employee: Sue Jones
social security number: 333-33-3333
gross sales: 10000.00; commission rate: 0.06
earned $600.00

base-salaried commission employee: Bob Lewis
social security number: 444-44-4444
gross sales: 5000.00; commission rate: 0.04; base salary: 300.00
earned $500.00
```

Fig. 21.17 | Employee class hierarchy driver program. (Part 4 of 4.)

Line 41 allocates vector employees, which contains three Employee pointers. Line 44 aims employees[0] at object salariedEmployee. Line 45 aims employees[1] at object commissionEmployee. Line 46 aims employee[2] at object basePlusCommissionEmployee. The compiler allows these assignments, because a SalariedEmployee *is an* Employee, a CommissionEmployee *is an* Employee and a BasePlusCommissionEmployee *is an* Employee. Therefore, we can assign the addresses of SalariedEmployee, CommissionEmployee and BasePlusCommissionEmployee objects to base-class Employee pointers, even though Employee is an *abstract* class.

The loop in lines 54–55 traverses vector employees and invokes function virtualViaPointer (lines 67–71) for each element in employees. Function virtualViaPointer receives in parameter baseClassPtr the address stored in an employees element. Each call to virtualViaPointer uses baseClassPtr to invoke virtual functions print (line 69) and earnings (line 70). Function virtualViaPointer does not contain any SalariedEmployee, CommissionEmployee or BasePlusCommissionEmployee type information. The function knows only about base-class type Employee. Therefore, the compiler *cannot know* which concrete class's functions to call through baseClassPtr. Yet at execution time, each virtual-function invocation calls the function on the object to which baseClassPtr points at that moment. The output illustrates that *the appropriate functions for each class are indeed invoked* and that each object's proper information is displayed. For instance, the weekly salary is displayed for the SalariedEmployee, and the gross sales are displayed for the CommissionEmployee and BasePlusCommissionEmployee. Also, obtaining the earnings of each Employee polymorphically in line 70 produces the same results as obtaining these employees' earnings via static binding in lines 33, 35 and 37. All virtual function calls to print and earnings are resolved at runtime with dynamic binding.

Finally, another for statement (lines 61–62) traverses employees and invokes function virtualViaReference (lines 75–79) for each element in the vector. Function virtualViaReference receives in its parameter baseClassRef (of type const Employee &) a *reference* to the object obtained by *dereferencing the pointer* stored in each employees element (line 62). Each call to virtualViaReference invokes virtual functions print (line

77) and earnings (line 78) via reference baseClassRef to demonstrate that *polymorphic processing occurs with base-class references as well*. Each virtual-function invocation calls the function on the object to which baseClassRef refers at runtime. This is another example of *dynamic binding*. The output produced using base-class references is identical to the output produced using base-class pointers.

21.7 (Optional) Polymorphism, Virtual Functions and Dynamic Binding "Under the Hood"

C++ makes polymorphism easy to program. It's certainly possible to program for polymorphism in non-object-oriented languages such as C, but doing so requires complex and potentially dangerous pointer manipulations. This section discusses how C++ can implement polymorphism, virtual functions and dynamic binding internally. This will give you a solid understanding of how these capabilities really work. More importantly, it will help you appreciate the overhead of polymorphism—in terms of additional memory consumption and processor time. This will help you determine when to use polymorphism and when to avoid it.

First, we'll explain the data structures that the compiler builds at *compile time* to support polymorphism at execution time. You'll see that polymorphism is accomplished through three levels of pointers, i.e., *triple indirection*. Then we'll show how an executing program uses these data structures to execute virtual functions and achieve the dynamic binding associated with polymorphism. Our discussion explains one possible implementation; this is not a language requirement.

When C++ compiles a class that has one or more virtual functions, it builds a **virtual function table** (*vtable*) for that class. An executing program uses the *vtable* to select the proper function implementation each time a virtual function of that class is called. The leftmost column of Fig. 21.18 illustrates the *vtables* for the classes Employee, SalariedEmployee, CommissionEmployee and BasePlusCommissionEmployee.

Employee *Class* vtable

In the *vtable* for class Employee, the first function pointer is set to 0 (i.e., the null pointer). This is done because function earnings is a pure virtual function and therefore *lacks an implementation*. The second function pointer points to function print, which displays the employee's full name and social security number. [*Note:* We've abbreviated the output of each print function in this figure to conserve space.] Any class that has one or more null pointers in its *vtable* is an *abstract* class. Classes without any null *vtable* pointers (such as SalariedEmployee, CommissionEmployee and BasePlusCommissionEmployee) are *concrete* classes.

SalariedEmployee *Class* vtable

Class SalariedEmployee overrides function earnings to return the employee's weekly salary, so the function pointer points to the earnings function of class SalariedEmployee. SalariedEmployee also overrides print, so the corresponding function pointer points to the SalariedEmployee member function that prints "salaried employee: " followed by the employee's name, social security number and weekly salary.

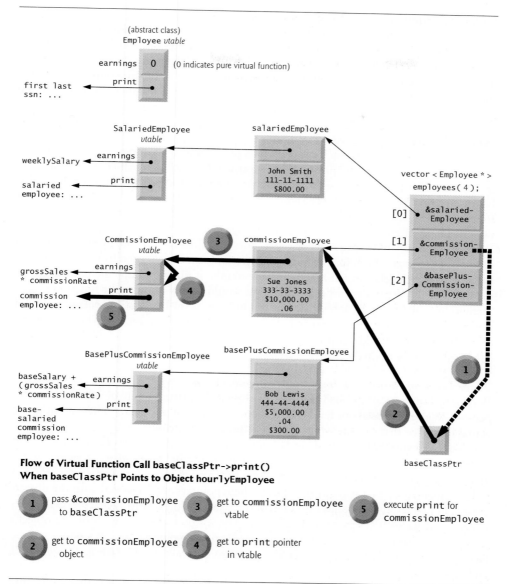

Fig. 21.18 | How virtual function calls work.

CommissionEmployee *Class* vtable

The earnings function pointer in the *vtable* for class CommissionEmployee points to CommissionEmployee's earnings function that returns the employee's gross sales multiplied by the commission rate. The print function pointer points to the CommissionEmployee version of the function, which prints the employee's type, name, social security number, commission rate and gross sales. As in class HourlyEmployee, both functions override the functions in class Employee.

BasePlusCommissionEmployee Class vtable

The earnings function pointer in the *vtable* for class BasePlusCommissionEmployee points to the BasePlusCommissionEmployee's earnings function, which returns the employee's base salary plus gross sales multiplied by commission rate. The print function pointer points to the BasePlusCommissionEmployee version of the function, which prints the employee's base salary plus the type, name, social security number, commission rate and gross sales. Both functions override the functions in class CommissionEmployee.

Inheriting Concrete *virtual* Functions

In our Employee case study, each concrete class provides its own implementation for virtual functions earnings and print. You've learned that each class which inherits directly from abstract base class Employee *must implement earnings* in order to be a concrete class, because earnings is a pure virtual function. These classes do *not* need to implement function print, however, to be considered concrete—print is not a pure virtual function and derived classes can inherit class Employee's implementation of print. Furthermore, class BasePlusCommissionEmployee does *not* have to implement either function print or earnings—both function implementations can be inherited from class CommissionEmployee. If a class in our hierarchy were to inherit function implementations in this manner, the *vtable* pointers for these functions would simply point to the function implementation that was being inherited. For example, if BasePlusCommissionEmployee did not override earnings, the earnings function pointer in the *vtable* for class BasePlusCommissionEmployee would point to the same earnings function as the *vtable* for class CommissionEmployee points to.

Three Levels of Pointers to Implement Polymorphism

Polymorphism is accomplished through an elegant data structure involving *three levels of pointers*. We've discussed one level—the function pointers in the *vtable*. These point to the actual functions that execute when a virtual function is invoked.

Now we consider the second level of pointers. *Whenever an object of a class with one or more virtual functions is instantiated, the compiler attaches to the object a pointer to the* vtable *for that class.* This pointer is normally at the front of the object, but it isn't required to be implemented that way. In Fig. 21.18, these pointers are associated with the objects created in Fig. 21.17 (one object for each of the types SalariedEmployee, CommissionEmployee and BasePlusCommissionEmployee). The diagram displays each of the object's data member values. For example, the salariedEmployee object contains a pointer to the SalariedEmployee *vtable*; the object also contains the values John Smith, 111-11-1111 and $800.00.

The third level of pointers simply contains the handles to the objects that receive the virtual function calls. The handles in this level may also be references. Fig. 21.18 depicts the vector employees that contains Employee pointers.

Now let's see how a typical virtual function call executes. Consider the call baseClassPtr->print() in function virtualViaPointer (line 69 of Fig. 21.17). Assume that baseClassPtr contains employees[1] (i.e., the address of object commissionEmployee in employees). When the compiler compiles this statement, it determines that the call is indeed being made via a base-class pointer and that print is a virtual function.

The compiler determines that print is the *second* entry in each of the *vtables*. To locate this entry, the compiler notes that it will need to skip the first entry. Thus, the compiler compiles an **offset** or **displacement** into the table of machine-language object-code pointers to find the code that will execute the `virtual` function call. The size in bytes of the offset depends on the number of bytes used to represent a pointer on an individual platform. For example, on a 32-bit platform, a pointer is typically stored in 4 bytes, whereas on a 64-bit platform, a pointer could be stored in 8 bytes.

The compiler generates code that performs the following operations [*Note:* The numbers in the list correspond to the circled numbers in Fig. 21.18]:

1. Select the *i*th entry of `employees` (in this case, the address of object `commission-Employee`), and pass it as an argument to function `virtualViaPointer`. This sets parameter `baseClassPtr` to point to `commissionEmployee`.

2. *Dereference* that pointer to get to the `commissionEmployee` object—which, as you recall, begins with a pointer to the `CommissionEmployee` *vtable*.

3. *Dereference* `commissionEmployee`'s *vtable* pointer to get to the `CommissionEmployee` *vtable*.

4. Skip the offset of four bytes to select the `print` function pointer.

5. *Dereference* the `print` function pointer to form the "name" of the actual function to execute, and use the function call operator () to execute the appropriate `print` function, which in this case prints the employee's type, name, social security number, gross sales and commission rate.

Fig. 21.18's data structures may appear to be complex, but this complexity is managed by the compiler and hidden from you, making polymorphic programming straightforward. The pointer dereferencing operations and memory accesses that occur on every `virtual` function call require some additional execution time. The *vtables* and the *vtable* pointers added to the objects require some additional memory. You now have enough information to determine whether `virtual` functions are appropriate for your programs.

Performance Tip 21.1

Polymorphism, as typically implemented with `virtual` functions and dynamic binding in C++, is efficient. You can use these capabilities with nominal impact on performance.

Performance Tip 21.2

Virtual functions and dynamic binding enable polymorphic programming as an alternative to `switch` logic programming. Optimizing compilers normally generate polymorphic code that runs as efficiently as hand-coded `switch`-based logic. Polymorphism's overhead is acceptable for most applications. But in some situations—such as real-time applications with stringent performance requirements—polymorphism's overhead may be too high.

21.8 Case Study: Payroll System Using Polymorphism and Runtime Type Information with Downcasting, `dynamic_cast`, `typeid` and `type_info`

Recall from the problem statement at the beginning of Section 21.6 that, for the current pay period, our fictitious company has decided to reward `BasePlusCommissionEmployees` by adding 10 percent to their base salaries. When processing `Employee` objects polymorphically in Section 21.6.5, we did not need to worry about the "specifics." Now, however, to adjust the base salaries of BasePlusCommissionEmployees, we have to determine the specific type of each Employee object at execution time, then act appropriately. This section demonstrates the powerful capabilities of **runtime type information (RTTI)** and dynamic casting, which enable a program to determine the type of an object at execution time and act on that object accordingly.

[*Note:* Some compilers require that RTTI be enabled before it can be used in a program. In Visual C++ 2010, this option is enabled by default.]

Figure 21.19 uses the Employee hierarchy developed in Section 21.6 and increases by 10 percent the base salary of each BasePlusCommissionEmployee. Line 21 declares three-element vector employees that stores pointers to Employee objects. Lines 24–29 populate the vector with the addresses of dynamically allocated objects of classes SalariedEmployee (Figs. 21.11–21.12), CommissionEmployee (Figs. 21.13–21.14) and BasePlusCommissionEmployee (Figs. 21.15–21.16).

```cpp
1   // Fig. 21.19: fig21_19.cpp
2   // Demonstrating downcasting and runtime type information.
3   // NOTE: You may need to enable RTTI on your compiler
4   // before you can execute this application.
5   #include <iostream>
6   #include <iomanip>
7   #include <vector>
8   #include <typeinfo>
9   #include "Employee.h"
10  #include "SalariedEmployee.h"
11  #include "CommissionEmployee.h"
12  #include "BasePlusCommissionEmployee.h"
13  using namespace std;
14
15  int main()
16  {
17     // set floating-point output formatting
18     cout << fixed << setprecision( 2 );
19
20     // create vector of three base-class pointers
21     vector < Employee * > employees( 3 );
22
23     // initialize vector with various kinds of Employees
24     employees[ 0 ] = new SalariedEmployee(
25        "John", "Smith", "111-11-1111", 800 );
26     employees[ 1 ] = new CommissionEmployee(
27        "Sue", "Jones", "333-33-3333", 10000, .06 );
28     employees[ 2 ] = new BasePlusCommissionEmployee(
29        "Bob", "Lewis", "444-44-4444", 5000, .04, 300 );
30
31     // polymorphically process each element in vector employees
32     for ( size_t i = 0; i < employees.size(); ++i )
33     {
34        employees[ i ]->print(); // output employee information
35        cout << endl;
36
```

Fig. 21.19 | Demonstrating downcasting and runtime type information. (Part 1 of 2.)

```
37        // downcast pointer
38        BasePlusCommissionEmployee *derivedPtr =
39           dynamic_cast < BasePlusCommissionEmployee * >
40              ( employees[ i ] );
41
42        // determine whether element points to base-salaried
43        // commission employee
44        if ( derivedPtr != 0 ) // 0 if not a BasePlusCommissionEmployee
45        {
46           double oldBaseSalary = derivedPtr->getBaseSalary();
47           cout << "old base salary: $" << oldBaseSalary << endl;
48           derivedPtr->setBaseSalary( 1.10 * oldBaseSalary );
49           cout << "new base salary with 10% increase is: $"
50              << derivedPtr->getBaseSalary() << endl;
51        } // end if
52
53        cout << "earned $" << employees[ i ]->earnings() << "\n\n";
54     } // end for
55
56     // release objects pointed to by vector's elements
57     for ( size_t j = 0; j < employees.size(); ++j )
58     {
59        // output class name
60        cout << "deleting object of "
61           << typeid( *employees[ j ] ).name() << endl;
62
63        delete employees[ j ];
64     } // end for
65  } // end main
```

```
salaried employee: John Smith
social security number: 111-11-1111
weekly salary: 800.00
earned $800.00

commission employee: Sue Jones
social security number: 333-33-3333
gross sales: 10000.00; commission rate: 0.06
earned $600.00

base-salaried commission employee: Bob Lewis
social security number: 444-44-4444
gross sales: 5000.00; commission rate: 0.04; base salary: 300.00
old base salary: $300.00
new base salary with 10% increase is: $330.00
earned $530.00

deleting object of class SalariedEmployee
deleting object of class CommissionEmployee
deleting object of class BasePlusCommissionEmployee
```

Fig. 21.19 | Demonstrating downcasting and runtime type information. (Part 2 of 2.)

The `for` statement in lines 32–54 iterates through the `employees` vector and displays each `Employee`'s information by invoking member function `print` (line 34). Recall that because `print` is declared `virtual` in base class `Employee`, the system invokes the appropriate derived-class object's `print` function.

In this example, as we encounter `BasePlusCommissionEmployee` objects, we wish to increase their base salary by 10 percent. Since we process the employees generically (i.e., polymorphically), we cannot (with the techniques we've learned) be certain as to which type of `Employee` is being manipulated at any given time. This creates a problem, because `BasePlusCommissionEmployee` employees *must* be identified when we encounter them so they can receive the 10 percent salary increase. To accomplish this, we use operator **dynamic_cast** (line 39) to determine whether the type of each object is `BasePlusCommissionEmployee`. This is the *downcast* operation we referred to in Section 21.3.3. Lines 38–40 dynamically downcast `employees[i]` from type `Employee *` to type `BasePlusCommissionEmployee *`. If the `vector` element points to an object that *is a* `BasePlusCommissionEmployee` object, then that object's address is assigned to `commissionPtr`; otherwise, 0 is assigned to derived-class pointer `derivedPtr`.

If the value returned by the `dynamic_cast` operator in lines 38–40 *is not* 0, the object *is* the correct type, and the `if` statement (lines 44–51) performs the special processing required for the `BasePlusCommissionEmployee` object. Lines 46, 48 and 50 invoke `BasePlusCommissionEmployee` functions `getBaseSalary` and `setBaseSalary` to retrieve and update the employee's salary.

Line 53 invokes member function `earnings` on the object to which `employees[i]` points. Recall that `earnings` is declared `virtual` in the base class, so the program invokes the derived-class object's `earnings` function—another example of dynamic binding.

Lines 57–64 display each employee's object type and uses the `delete` operator to deallocate the dynamic memory to which each `vector` element points. Operator **typeid** (line 61) returns a reference to an object of class **type_info** that contains the information about the type of its operand, including the name of that type. When invoked, `type_info` member function **name** (line 51) returns a pointer-based string that contains the type name (e.g., `"class BasePlusCommissionEmployee"`) of the argument passed to `typeid`. To use `typeid`, the program must include header **<typeinfo>** (line 8).

Portability Tip 21.1

The string returned by type_info *member function* name *may vary by compiler.*

We avoid several compilation errors in this example by *downcasting* an `Employee` pointer to a `BasePlusCommissionEmployee` pointer (lines 38–40). If we remove the `dynamic_cast` from line 39 and attempt to assign the current `Employee` pointer directly to `BasePlusCommissionEmployee` pointer `derivedPtr`, we'll receive a compilation error. C++ does not allow a program to assign a base-class pointer to a derived-class pointer because the *is-a* relationship does not apply—a `CommissionEmployee` is *not* a `BasePlusCommissionEmployee`. The *is-a* relationship applies only between the derived class and its base classes, not vice versa.

Similarly, if lines 46, 48 and 50 used the current base-class pointer from `employees`, rather than derived-class pointer `derivedPtr`, to invoke derived-class-only functions `getBaseSalary` and `setBaseSalary`, we would receive a compilation error at each of these lines. As you learned in Section 21.3.3, attempting to invoke derived-class-only functions through a base-class pointer is not allowed. Although lines 46, 48 and 50 execute only if `commissionPtr` is not 0 (i.e., if the cast *can* be performed), we *cannot* attempt to invoke derived-class `BasePlusCommissionEmployee` functions `getBaseSalary` and `setBaseSalary` on the base-class `Employee` pointer. Recall that, using a base class `Employee` pointer, we can invoke only functions found in base class `Employee`—`earnings`, `print` and `Employee`'s *get* and *set* functions.

21.9   Virtual Destructors

A problem can occur when using polymorphism to process dynamically allocated objects of a class hierarchy. So far you've seen **nonvirtual destructors**—destructors that are not declared with keyword `virtual`. If a derived-class object with a nonvirtual destructor is destroyed explicitly by applying the `delete` operator to a base-class pointer to the object, the C++ standard specifies that the behavior is *undefined*.

The simple solution to this problem is to create a **virtual destructor** (i.e., a destructor that is declared with keyword `virtual`) in the base class. This makes all derived-class destructors `virtual` *even though they do not have the same name as the base-class destructor*. Now, if an object in the hierarchy is destroyed explicitly by applying the `delete` operator to a base-class pointer, the destructor for the appropriate class is called based on the object to which the base-class pointer points. Remember, when a derived-class object is destroyed, the base-class part of the derived-class object is also destroyed, so it's important for the destructors of both the derived class and base class to execute. The base-class destructor automatically executes after the derived-class destructor.

Error-Prevention Tip 21.2

If a class has `virtual` functions, provide a `virtual` destructor, even if one is not required for the class. This ensures that a custom derived-class destructor (if there is one) will be invoked when a derived-class object is deleted via a base class pointer.

Common Programming Error 21.2

Constructors cannot be `virtual`. Declaring a constructor `virtual` is a compilation error.

21.10   Wrap-Up

In this chapter we discussed polymorphism, which enables us to "program in the general" rather than "program in the specific," and we showed how this makes programs more extensible. We began with an example of how polymorphism would allow a screen manager to display several "space" objects. We then demonstrated how base-class and derived-class pointers can be aimed at base-class and derived-class objects. We said that aiming base-class pointers at base-class objects is natural, as is aiming derived-class pointers at derived-class objects. Aiming base-class pointers at derived-class objects is also natural because a derived-class object *is an* object of its base class. You learned why aiming derived-class pointers at base-class objects is dangerous and why the compiler disallows such assignments. We introduced `virtual` functions, which enable the proper functions to be called when objects at various levels of an inheritance hierarchy are referenced (at execution time) via base-class pointers or references. This is known as dynamic or late binding. We then discussed pure `virtual` functions and abstract classes (classes with one or more pure `vir`-

tual functions). You learned that abstract classes cannot be used to instantiate objects, while concrete classes can. We then demonstrated using abstract classes in an inheritance hierarchy. You learned how polymorphism works "under the hood" with *vtables* that are created by the compiler. We used runtime type information (RTTI) and dynamic casting to determine the type of an object at execution time and act on that object accordingly. The chapter concluded with a discussion of virtual destructors, and how they ensure that all appropriate destructors in an inheritance hierarchy run on a derived-class object when that object is deleted via a base-class pointer or reference.

In the next chapter, we discuss templates, a sophisticated feature of C++ that enables you to define a family of related classes or functions with a single code segment.

Summary

Section 21.1 Introduction

- Polymorphism (p. 807) enables us to "program in the general" rather than "program in the specific."

- Polymorphism enables us to write programs that process objects of classes that are part of the same class hierarchy as if they were all objects of the hierarchy's base class.

- With polymorphism, we can design and implement systems that are easily extensible—new classes can be added with little or no modification to the general portions of the program. The only parts of a program that must be altered to accommodate new classes are those that require direct knowledge of the new classes that you add to the hierarchy.

Section 21.2 Introduction to Polymorphism: Polymorphic Video Game

- With polymorphism, one function can cause different actions to occur, depending on the type of the object on which the function is invoked.

- This makes it possible to design and implement more extensible systems. Programs can be written to process objects of types that may not exist when the program is under development.

Section 21.3 Relationships Among Objects in an Inheritance Hierarchy

- C++ enables polymorphism—the ability for objects of different classes related by inheritance to respond differently to the same member-function call.

- Polymorphism is implemented via virtual functions (p. 815) and dynamic binding (p. 816).

- When a base-class pointer or reference is used to call a virtual function, C++ chooses the correct overridden function in the appropriate derived class associated with the object.

- If a virtual function is called by referencing a specific object by name and using the dot member-selection operator, the reference is resolved at compile time (this is called static binding; p. 816); the virtual function that is called is the one defined for the class of that particular object.

- Derived classes can provide their own implementations of a base-class virtual function if necessary, but if they do not, the base class's implementation is used.

Section 21.4 Type Fields and switch Statements

- Polymorphic programming with virtual functions can eliminate the need for switch logic. You can use the virtual function mechanism to perform the equivalent logic automatically, thus avoiding the kinds of errors typically associated with switch logic.

Section 21.5 Abstract Classes and Pure **virtual** Functions

- Abstract classes (p. 821) are typically used as base classes, so we refer to them as abstract base classes (p. 821). No objects of an abstract class may be instantiated.

- Classes from which objects can be instantiated are concrete classes (p. 821).

- You create an abstract class by declaring one or more pure virtual functions (p. 822) with pure specifiers (= 0) in their declarations.

- If a class is derived from a class with a pure virtual function and that derived class does not supply a definition for that pure virtual function, then that virtual function remains pure in the derived class. Consequently, the derived class is also an abstract class.

- Although we cannot instantiate objects of abstract base classes, we can declare pointers and references to objects of abstract base classes. Such pointers and references can be used to enable polymorphic manipulations of derived-class objects instantiated from concrete derived classes.

Section 21.7 (Optional) Polymorphism, Virtual Functions and Dynamic Binding "Under the Hood"

- Dynamic binding requires that at runtime, the call to a virtual member function be routed to the virtual function version appropriate for the class. A virtual function table called the *vtable* (p. 838) is implemented as an array containing function pointers. Each class with virtual functions has a *vtable*. For each virtual function in the class, the *vtable* has an entry containing a function pointer to the version of the virtual function to use for an object of that class. The virtual function to use for a particular class could be the function defined in that class, or it could be a function inherited either directly or indirectly from a base class higher in the hierarchy.

- When a base class provides a virtual member function, derived classes can override the virtual function, but they do not have to override it.

- Each object of a class with virtual functions contains a pointer to the *vtable* for that class. When a function call is made from a base-class pointer to a derived-class object, the appropriate function pointer in the *vtable* is obtained and dereferenced to complete the call at execution time.

- Any class that has one or more 0 pointers in its *vtable* is an abstract class. Classes without any 0 *vtable* pointers are concrete classes.

- New kinds of classes are regularly added to systems and accommodated by dynamic binding.

Section 21.8 Case Study: Payroll System Using Polymorphism and Runtime Type Information with Downcasting, **dynamic_cast**, **typeid** and **type_info**

- Operator dynamic_cast (p. 842) checks the type of the object to which a pointer points, then determines whether the type has an *is-a* relationship with the type to which the pointer is being converted. If so, dynamic_cast returns the object's address. If not, dynamic_cast returns 0.

- Operator typeid (p. 844) returns a reference to a type_info object (p. 844) that contains information about the operand's type, including the type name. To use typeid, the program must include header <typeinfo> (p. 844).

- When invoked, type_info member function name (p. 844) returns a pointer-based string that contains the name of the type that the type_info object represents.

- Operators dynamic_cast and typeid are part of C++'s runtime type information (RTTI; p. 842) feature, which allows a program to determine an object's type at runtime.

Section 21.9 Virtual Destructors

- Declare the base-class destructor virtual (p. 845) if the class contains virtual functions. This makes all derived-class destructors virtual, even though they do not have the same name as the base-class destructor. If an object in the hierarchy is destroyed explicitly by applying the delete operator to a base-class pointer to a derived-class object, the destructor for the appropriate class is called. After a derived-class destructor runs, the destructors for all of that class's base classes run all the way up the hierarchy.

Self-Review Exercises

21.1   Fill in the blanks in each of the following statements:
  a) Treating a base-class object as a(n) _____ can cause errors.
  b) Polymorphism helps eliminate _____ logic.
  c) If a class contains at least one pure virtual function, it's a(n) _____ class.
  d) Classes from which objects can be instantiated are called _____ classes.
  e) Operator _____ can be used to downcast base-class pointers safely.
  f) Operator typeid returns a reference to a(n) _____ object.
  g) _____ involves using a base-class pointer or reference to invoke virtual functions on base-class and derived-class objects.
  h) Overridable functions are declared using keyword _____.
  i) Casting a base-class pointer to a derived-class pointer is called _____.

21.2   State whether each of the following is *true* or *false*. If *false*, explain why.
  a) All virtual functions in an abstract base class must be declared as pure virtual functions.
  b) Referring to a derived-class object with a base-class handle is dangerous.
  c) A class is made abstract by declaring that class virtual.
  d) If a base class declares a pure virtual function, a derived class must implement that function to become a concrete class.
  e) Polymorphic programming can eliminate the need for switch logic.

Answers to Self-Review Exercises

21.1   a) derived-class object. b) switch. c) abstract. d) concrete. e) dynamic_cast. f) type_info. g) Polymorphism. h) virtual. i) downcasting.

21.2   a) False. An abstract base class can include virtual functions with implementations. b) False. Referring to a base-class object with a derived-class handle is dangerous. c) False. Classes are never declared virtual. Rather, a class is made abstract by including at least one pure virtual function in the class. d) True. e) True.

Exercises

21.3   *(Programming in the General)* How is it that polymorphism enables you to program "in the general" rather than "in the specific"? Discuss the key advantages of programming "in the general."

21.4   *(Polymorphism vs. switch logic)* Discuss the problems of programming with switch logic. Explain why polymorphism can be an effective alternative to using switch logic.

21.5   *(Inheriting Interface vs. Implementation)* Distinguish between inheriting interface and inheriting implementation. How do inheritance hierarchies designed for inheriting interface differ from those designed for inheriting implementation?

21.6   *(Virtual Destructors)* What are virtual destructors? Can constructors be virtual?

21.7   *(Dynamic Binding vs. Static Binding)* Distinguish between static binding and dynamic binding. Explain the use of virtual functions and the *vtable* in dynamic binding.

21.8 *(Abstract and Concrete Classes)* Distinguish between abstract classes and concrete classes.

21.9 *(Abstract Base Classes)* Suggest one or more levels of abstract base classes for the Shape hierarchy discussed in this chapter and shown in Fig. 20.3. (The first level is Shape, and the second level consists of the classes TwoDimensionalShape and ThreeDimensionalShape.)

21.10 *(Extensibility)* How can you design and implement systems that are easily extensible?

21.11 *(Polymorphic Application)* You've been asked to develop a flight simulator that will have elaborate graphical outputs. Explain why polymorphic programming could be especially effective for a problem of this nature.

21.12 *(Payroll System Modification)* Modify the payroll system of Figs. 21.9–21.17 to include private data member birthDate in class Employee. Use class Date from Figs. 19.6–19.7 to represent an employee's birthday. Assume that payroll is processed once per month. Create a vector of Employee references to store the various employee objects. In a loop, calculate the payroll for each Employee (polymorphically), and add a $100.00 bonus to the person's payroll amount if the current month is the month in which the Employee's birthday occurs.

21.13 *(Shape Hierarchy)* Implement the Shape hierarchy designed in Exercise 20.7 (which is based on the hierarchy in Fig. 20.3). Each TwoDimensionalShape should contain function getArea to calculate the area of the two-dimensional shape. Each ThreeDimensionalShape should have member functions getArea and getVolume to calculate the surface area and volume, respectively, of the three-dimensional shape. Create a program that uses a vector of Shape pointers to objects of each concrete class in the hierarchy. The program should print the object to which each vector element points. Also, in the loop that processes all the shapes in the vector, determine whether each shape is a TwoDimensionalShape or a ThreeDimensionalShape. If a shape is a TwoDimensionalShape, display its area. If a shape is a ThreeDimensionalShape, display its area and volume.

21.14 *(Project: Polymorphic Screen Manager Using Shape Hierarchy)* Develop a basic graphics package. Use the Shape hierarchy implemented in Exercise 21.13. Limit yourself to two-dimensional shapes such as squares, rectangles, triangles and circles. Interact with the user. Let the user specify the position, size, shape and fill characters to be used in drawing each shape. The user can specify more than one of the same shape. As you create each shape, place a Shape * pointer to each new Shape object into an array. Each Shape class should now have its own draw member function. Write a polymorphic screen manager that walks through the array, sending draw messages to each object in the array to form a screen image. Redraw the screen image each time the user specifies an additional shape.

21.15 *(Package Inheritance Hierarchy)* Use the Package inheritance hierarchy created in Exercise 20.9 to create a program that displays the address information and calculates the shipping costs for several Packages. The program should contain a vector of Package pointers to objects of classes TwoDayPackage and OvernightPackage. Loop through the vector to process the Packages polymorphically. For each Package, invoke *get* functions to obtain the address information of the sender and the recipient, then print the two addresses as they would appear on mailing labels. Also, call each Package's calculateCost member function and print the result. Keep track of the total shipping cost for all Packages in the vector, and display this total when the loop terminates.

21.16 *(Polymorphic Banking Program Using Account Hierarchy)* Develop a polymorphic banking program using the Account hierarchy created in Exercise 20.10. Create a vector of Account pointers to SavingsAccount and CheckingAccount objects. For each Account in the vector, allow the user to specify an amount of money to withdraw from the Account using member function debit and an amount of money to deposit into the Account using member function credit. As you process each Account, determine its type. If an Account is a SavingsAccount, calculate the amount of interest owed to the Account using member function calculateInterest, then add the interest to the account balance using member function credit. After processing an Account, print the updated account balance obtained by invoking base-class member function getBalance.

21.17   *(Payroll System Modification)* Modify the payroll system of Figs. 21.9–21.17 to include an additional Employee subclasses PieceWorker and HourlyWorker. A PieceWorker represents an employee whose pay is based on the number of pieces of merchandise produced. An HourlyWorker represents an employee whose pay is based on an hourly wage and the number of hours worked. Hourly workers receive overtime pay (1.5 times the hourly wage) for all hours worked in excess of 40 hours.

Class PieceWorker should contain private instance variables wage (to store the employee's wage per piece) and pieces (to store the number of pieces produced). Class HourlyWorker should contain private instance variables wage (to store the employee's wage per hour) and hours (to store the hours worked). In class PieceWorker, provide a concrete implementation of method earnings that calculates the employee's earnings by multiplying the number of pieces produced by the wage per piece. In class HourlyWorker, provide a concrete implementation of method earnings that calculates the employee's earnings by multiplying the number of hours worked by the wage per hour. If the number of hours worked is over 40, be sure to pay the HourlyWorker for the overtime hours. Add a pointer to an object of each new class into the vector of Employee pointers in main. For each Employee, display its string representation and earnings.

Making a Difference

21.18   *(CarbonFootprint Abstract Class: Polymorphism)* Using an abstract class with only pure virtual functions, you can specify similar behaviors for possibly disparate classes. Governments and companies worldwide are becoming increasingly concerned with carbon footprints (annual releases of carbon dioxide into the atmosphere) from buildings burning various types of fuels for heat, vehicles burning fuels for power, and the like. Many scientists blame these greenhouse gases for the phenomenon called global warming. Create three small classes unrelated by inheritance—classes Building, Car and Bicycle. Give each class some unique appropriate attributes and behaviors that it does not have in common with other classes. Write an abstract class CarbonFootprint with only a pure virtual getCarbonFootprint method. Have each of your classes inherit from that abstract class and implement the getCarbonFootprint method to calculate an appropriate carbon footprint for that class (check out a few websites that explain how to calculate carbon footprints). Write an application that creates objects of each of the three classes, places pointers to those objects in a vector of CarbonFootprint pointers, then iterates through the vector, polymorphically invoking each object's getCarbonFootprint method. For each object, print some identifying information and the object's carbon footprint.

Templates

*Behind that outside
pattern the dim shapes
get clearer every day.
It is always the same shape,
only very numerous.*
—Charlotte Perkins Gilman

*Every man of genius sees the
world at a different angle from
his fellows.*
—Havelock Ellis

*…our special individuality, as
distinguished from our generic
humanity.*
—Oliver Wendell Holmes, Sr.

Objectives

In this chapter you'll learn:

- To use function templates to conveniently create a group of related (overloaded) functions.

- To distinguish between function templates and function-template specializations.

- To use class templates to create groups of related types.

- To distinguish between class templates and class-template specializations.

- To overload function templates.

22.1 Introduction

In this chapter, we discuss one of C++'s more powerful software reuse features, namely templates. **Function templates** and **class templates** enable you to specify, with a single code segment, an entire range of related (overloaded) functions—called **function-template specializations**—or an entire range of related classes—called **class-template specializations**. This technique is called **generic programming**.

We might write a single function template for an array-sort function, then have C++ generate separate function-template specializations that will sort `int` arrays, `float` arrays, `string` arrays and so on. We've introduced function templates. We present an additional discussion and example in this chapter.

We might write a single class template for a stack class, then have C++ generate separate class-template specializations, such as a stack-of-`int` class, a stack-of-`float` class, a stack-of-`string` class and so on.

Note the distinction between templates and template specializations: Function templates and class templates are like stencils out of which we trace shapes; function-template specializations and class-template specializations are like the separate tracings that all have the same shape, but could, for example, be drawn in different colors. In this chapter, we present a function template and a class template.

Software Engineering Observation 22.1

Most C++ compilers require the complete definition of a template to appear in the client source-code file that uses the template. For this reason and for reusability, templates are often defined in headers, which are then #included in the appropriate client source-code files. For class templates, this means that the member functions are also defined in the header.

22.2 Function Templates

Overloaded functions normally perform *similar* or *identical* operations on *different* types of data. If the operations are *identical* for each type, they can be expressed more compactly and conveniently using function templates. Initially, you write a single function-template definition. Based on the argument types provided explicitly or inferred from calls to this function, the compiler generates separate source-code functions (i.e., *function-template specializations*) to handle each function call appropriately. In the C programming language, this task can be performed using **macros** created with the preprocessor directive `#define`.

However, macros can have serious *side effects* and do *not* enable the compiler to perform *type checking*.

Error-Prevention Tip 22.1

Function templates, like macros, enable software reuse. Unlike macros, function templates help eliminate many types of errors through the scrutiny of full C++ type checking.

All function-template definitions begin with keyword `template` followed by a list of template parameters to the function template enclosed in angle brackets (< and >); each template parameter that represents a type *must* be preceded by either of the interchangeable keywords `class` or `typename`, as in

```
template< typename T >
```

or

```
template< class ElementType >
```

or

```
template< typename BorderType, typename FillType >
```

The type template parameters of a function-template definition are used to specify the types of the function's parameters, to specify the return type of the function and to declare variables within the function. The function definition follows and appears like any other function definition. Keywords `typename` and `class` used to specify function-template parameters actually mean "any fundamental type or user-defined type."

Common Programming Error 22.1

Not placing keyword `class` or keyword `typename` before each type template parameter of a function template is a syntax error.

Example: Function Template `printArray`

Let's examine function template `printArray` in Fig. 22.1, lines 7–14. Function template `printArray` declares (line 7) a single template parameter T (T can be any valid identifier) for the type of the array to be printed by function `printArray`; T is referred to as a type template parameter, or type parameter. You'll see nontype template parameters in Section 22.5.

```
1   // Fig. 22.1: fig22_01.cpp
2   // Function-template specializations of function template printArray.
3   #include <iostream>
4   using namespace std;
5
6   // function template printArray definition
7   template< typename T >
8   void printArray( const T * const array, int count )
9   {
10      for ( int i = 0; i < count; ++i )
11         cout << array[ i ] << " ";
```

Fig. 22.1 | Function-template specializations of function template `printArray`. (Part 1 of 2.)

```
12
13        cout << endl;
14   } // end function template printArray
15
16   int main()
17   {
18        const int aCount = 5; // size of array a
19        const int bCount = 7; // size of array b
20        const int cCount = 6; // size of array c
21
22        int a[ aCount ] = { 1, 2, 3, 4, 5 };
23        double b[ bCount ] = { 1.1, 2.2, 3.3, 4.4, 5.5, 6.6, 7.7 };
24        char c[ cCount ] = "HELLO"; // 6th position for null
25
26        cout << "Array a contains:" << endl;
27
28        // call integer function-template specialization
29        printArray( a, aCount );
30
31        cout << "Array b contains:" << endl;
32
33        // call double function-template specialization
34        printArray( b, bCount );
35
36        cout << "Array c contains:" << endl;
37
38        // call character function-template specialization
39        printArray( c, cCount );
40   } // end main
```

```
Array a contains:
1 2 3 4 5
Array b contains:
1.1 2.2 3.3 4.4 5.5 6.6 7.7
Array c contains:
H E L L O
```

Fig. 22.1 | Function-template specializations of function template printArray. (Part 2 of 2.)

When the compiler detects a printArray function invocation in the client program (e.g., lines 29 and 34), the compiler uses its overload resolution capabilities to find a definition of function printArray that best matches the function call. In this case, the only printArray function with the appropriate number of parameters is the printArray function template (lines 7–14). Consider the function call at line 29. The compiler compares the type of printArray's first argument (int * at line 29) to the printArray function template's first parameter (const T * const at line 8) and deduces that replacing the type parameter T with int would make the argument consistent with the parameter. Then, the compiler substitutes int for T throughout the template definition and compiles a printArray specialization that can display an array of int values. In Fig. 22.1, the compiler creates two printArray specializations—one that expects an int array and one that expects a double array. For example, the function-template specialization for type int is

```
void printArray( const int * const array, int count )
{
    for ( int i = 0; i < count; ++i )
        cout << array[ i ] << " ";

    cout << endl;
} // end function printArray
```

As with function parameters, the names of template parameters must be *unique* inside a template definition. Template parameter names need not be unique across *different* function templates.

Figure 22.1 demonstrates function template printArray (lines 7–14). The program begins by declaring five-element int array a and seven-element double array b (lines 22–23). Then, the program outputs each array by calling printArray—once with a first argument a of type int * (line 29) and once with a first argument b of type double * (line 34). The call in line 29, for example, causes the compiler to infer that T is int and to instantiate a printArray function-template specialization, for which type parameter T is int. The call in line 34 causes the compiler to infer that T is double and to instantiate a second printArray function-template specialization, for which type parameter T is double. It's important to note that if T (line 7) represents a user-defined type (which it does not in Fig. 22.1), there must be an overloaded stream insertion operator for that type; otherwise, the first stream insertion operator in line 11 will not compile.

Common Programming Error 22.2

If a template is invoked with a user-defined type, and if that template uses functions or operators (e.g., ==, +, <=) with objects of that class type, then those functions and operators must be overloaded for the user-defined type. Forgetting to overload such operators causes compilation errors.

In this example, the template mechanism saves you from having to write two separate overloaded functions with prototypes

```
void printArray( const int * const, int );
void printArray( const double * const, int );
void printArray( const char * const, int );
```

that all use the same code, except for type T (as used in line 8).

Performance Tip 22.1

Although templates offer software-reusability benefits, remember that multiple function-template specializations and class-template specializations are instantiated in a program (at compile time), despite the fact that the templates are written only once. These copies can consume considerable memory. This is not normally an issue, though, because the code generated by the template is the same size as the code you'd have written to produce the separate overloaded functions.

22.3 Overloading Function Templates

Function templates and overloading are intimately related. The function-template specializations generated from a function template all have the same name, so the compiler uses overload resolution to invoke the proper function.

A function template may be overloaded in several ways. We can provide other function templates that specify the same function name but different function parameters. For example, function template printArray of Fig. 22.1 could be overloaded with another printArray function template with additional parameters lowSubscript and highSubscript to specify the portion of the array to output (see Exercise 22.4).

A function template also can be overloaded by providing nontemplate functions with the same function name but different function arguments. For example, function template printArray of Fig. 22.1 could be overloaded with a nontemplate version that specifically prints an array of character strings in neat, tabular format (see Exercise 22.5).

The compiler performs a matching process to determine what function to call when a function is invoked. First, the compiler tries to find and use a precise match in which the function names and argument types are consistent with those of the function call. If this fails, the compiler determines whether a function template is available that can be used to generate a function-template specialization with a precise match of function name and argument types that are consistent with those of the function call. If such a template is found, the compiler generates and uses the appropriate function-template specialization. If not, the compiler generates an error message. Also, if there are multiple matches for the function call, the compiler attempts to determine the best match. If there is more than one best match, the call is ambiguous and the compiler generates an error message.

Common Programming Error 22.3

A compilation error occurs if no matching function definition can be found for a particular function call or if there are multiple matches that the compiler considers ambiguous.

22.4 Class Templates

It's possible to understand the concept of a "stack" (a data structure into which we insert items at the top and retrieve those items in last-in, first-out order) *independent of the type of the items* being placed in the stack. However, to instantiate a stack, a data type must be specified. This creates a wonderful opportunity for software reusability. We need the means for describing the notion of a stack *generically* and instantiating classes that are *type-specific* versions of this generic stack class. C++ provides this capability through **class templates**.

Software Engineering Observation 22.2

Class templates encourage software reusability by enabling type-specific versions of generic classes to be instantiated.

Class templates are called **parameterized types**, because they require one or more *type parameters* to specify how to customize a "generic class" template to form a class-template specialization. To produce many specializations you write only one class-template definition. When an additional specialization is needed, you use a concise, simple notation, and the compiler writes the source code for that specialization. One Stack class template, for example, could thus become the basis for creating many Stack classes (such as "Stack of double," "Stack of int," "Stack of char," "Stack of Employee," etc.) used in a program.

Creating Class Template *Stack< T >*
Note the Stack class-template definition in Fig. 22.2. It looks like a conventional class definition, except that it's preceded by the header (line 6)

```
template< typename T >
```

to specify a class-template definition with type parameter T which acts as a placeholder for the type of the Stack class to be created. You need not specifically use identifier T—any valid identifier can be used. The type of element to be stored on this Stack is mentioned generically as T throughout the Stack class header and member-function definitions. We'll show how T becomes associated with a specific type, such as double or int. Due to the way this class template is designed, there are two constraints for class types used with this Stack—they must have a *default constructor* (for use in line 44 to create the array that stores the stack elements), and their *assignment operators* must properly copy objects into the Stack (lines 56 and 70).

```
 1  // Fig. 22.2: Stack.h
 2  // Stack class template.
 3  #ifndef STACK_H
 4  #define STACK_H
 5
 6  template< typename T >
 7  class Stack
 8  {
 9  public:
10     explicit Stack( int = 10 ); // default constructor (Stack size 10)
11
12     // destructor
13     ~Stack()
14     {
15        delete [] stackPtr; // deallocate internal space for Stack
16     } // end ~Stack destructor
17
18     bool push( const T & ); // push an element onto the Stack
19     bool pop( T & ); // pop an element off the Stack
20
21     // determine whether Stack is empty
22     bool isEmpty() const
23     {
24        return top == -1;
25     } // end function isEmpty
26
27     // determine whether Stack is full
28     bool isFull() const
29     {
30        return top == size - 1;
31     } // end function isFull
32
33  private:
34     int size; // # of elements in the Stack
35     int top; // location of the top element (-1 means empty)
36     T *stackPtr; // pointer to internal representation of the Stack
37  }; // end class template Stack
38
```

Fig. 22.2 | Stack class template. (Part 1 of 2.)

```
39   // constructor template
40   template< typename T >
41   Stack< T >::Stack( int s )
42      : size( s > 0 ? s : 10 ), // validate size
43        top( -1 ), // Stack initially empty
44        stackPtr( new T[ size ] ) // allocate memory for elements
45   {
46      // empty body
47   } // end Stack constructor template
48
49   // push element onto Stack;
50   // if successful, return true; otherwise, return false
51   template< typename T >
52   bool Stack< T >::push( const T &pushValue )
53   {
54      if ( !isFull() )
55      {
56         stackPtr[ ++top ] = pushValue; // place item on Stack
57         return true; // push successful
58      } // end if
59
60      return false; // push unsuccessful
61   } // end function template push
62
63   // pop element off Stack;
64   // if successful, return true; otherwise, return false
65   template< typename T >
66   bool Stack< T >::pop( T &popValue )
67   {
68      if ( !isEmpty() )
69      {
70         popValue = stackPtr[ top-- ]; // remove item from Stack
71         return true; // pop successful
72      } // end if
73
74      return false; // pop unsuccessful
75   } // end function template pop
76
77   #endif
```

Fig. 22.2 | Stack class template. (Part 2 of 2.)

The member-function definitions of a class template are function templates. The member-function definitions that appear outside the class template definition each begin with the header

```
template< typename T >
```

(lines 40, 51 and 65). Thus, each definition resembles a conventional function definition, except that the Stack element type always is listed generically as type parameter T. The scope resolution operator is used with the class-template name Stack<T> (lines 41, 52 and 66) to tie each member-function definition to the class template's scope. In this case, the generic class name is Stack<T>. When doubleStack is instantiated as type Stack<double>, the Stack constructor function-template specialization uses new to create an array of elements of type double to represent the stack (line 44). The statement

```
stackPtr( new T[ size ] );
```

in the Stack class-template definition is generated by the compiler in the class-template specialization Stack<double> as

```
stackPtr( new double[ size ] );
```

Driver to Test Class Template Stack< T >

Now, let's consider the driver (Fig. 22.3) that exercises the Stack class template. The driver begins by instantiating object doubleStack of size 5 (line 9). This object is declared to be of class Stack< double > (pronounced "Stack of double"). The compiler associates type double with type parameter T in the class template to produce the source code for a Stack class of type double. Although templates offer software-reusability benefits, remember that multiple class-template specializations are instantiated in a program (at compile time), even though the template is written only once.

```cpp
1   // Fig. 22.3: fig22_03.cpp
2   // Stack class template test program.
3   #include <iostream>
4   #include "Stack.h" // Stack class template definition
5   using namespace std;
6
7   int main()
8   {
9      Stack< double > doubleStack( 5 ); // size 5
10     double doubleValue = 1.1;
11
12     cout << "Pushing elements onto doubleStack\n";
13
14     // push 5 doubles onto doubleStack
15     while ( doubleStack.push( doubleValue ) )
16     {
17        cout << doubleValue << ' ';
18        doubleValue += 1.1;
19     } // end while
20
21     cout << "\nStack is full. Cannot push " << doubleValue
22        << "\n\nPopping elements from doubleStack\n";
23
24     // pop elements from doubleStack
25     while ( doubleStack.pop( doubleValue ) )
26        cout << doubleValue << ' ';
27
28     cout << "\nStack is empty. Cannot pop\n";
29
30     Stack< int > intStack; // default size 10
31     int intValue = 1;
32     cout << "\nPushing elements onto intStack\n";
```

Fig. 22.3 | Stack class template test program. (Part 1 of 2.)

```
33
34       // push 10 integers onto intStack
35       while ( intStack.push( intValue ) )
36       {
37          cout << intValue++ << ' ';
38       } // end while
39
40       cout << "\nStack is full. Cannot push " << intValue
41          << "\n\nPopping elements from intStack\n";
42
43       // pop elements from intStack
44       while ( intStack.pop( intValue ) )
45          cout << intValue << ' ';
46
47       cout << "\nStack is empty. Cannot pop" << endl;
48    } // end main
```

```
Pushing elements onto doubleStack
1.1 2.2 3.3 4.4 5.5
Stack is full. Cannot push 6.6

Popping elements from doubleStack
5.5 4.4 3.3 2.2 1.1
Stack is empty. Cannot pop

Pushing elements onto intStack
1 2 3 4 5 6 7 8 9 10
Stack is full. Cannot push 11

Popping elements from intStack
10 9 8 7 6 5 4 3 2 1
Stack is empty. Cannot pop
```

Fig. 22.3 | Stack class template test program. (Part 2 of 2.)

Lines 15–19 invoke push to place the double values 1.1, 2.2, 3.3, 4.4 and 5.5 onto doubleStack. The while loop terminates when the driver attempts to push a sixth value onto doubleStack (which is full, because it holds a maximum of five elements). Function push returns false when it's unable to push a value onto the stack.[1]

Lines 25–26 invoke pop in a while loop to remove the five values from the stack (note, in the output of Fig. 22.3, that the values do pop off in *last-in, first-out order*). When the driver attempts to pop a sixth value, the doubleStack is empty, so the pop loop terminates.

Line 30 instantiates integer stack intStack with the declaration

```
Stack< int > intStack;
```

---

1. Class Stack (Fig. 22.2) provides the function isFull, which you can use to determine whether the stack is full before attempting a push operation. This avoids the potential error of pushing onto a full stack. We could also have function push throw an exception. You could catch that exception, then decide how to handle it appropriately for the application. The same technique can be used with function pop when an attempt is made to pop an element from an empty stack.

(pronounced "intStack is a Stack of int"). Because no size is specified, the size defaults to 10 as specified in the default constructor (Fig. 22.2, line 10). Lines 35–38 loop and invoke push to place values onto intStack until it's full, then lines 44–45 loop and invoke pop to remove values from intStack until it's empty. Once again, notice in the output that the values pop off in last-in, first-out order.

Creating Function Templates to Test Class Template Stack< T >

Notice that the code in function main of Fig. 22.3 is *almost identical* for both the double-Stack manipulations in lines 9–28 and the intStack manipulations in lines 30–47. This presents another opportunity to use a function template. Figure 22.4 defines function template testStack (lines 10–34) to perform the same tasks as main in Fig. 22.3—push a series of values onto a Stack< T > and pop the values off a Stack< T >. Function template testStack uses template parameter T (specified at line 10) to represent the data type stored in the Stack< T >. The function template takes four arguments (lines 12–15)—a reference to an object of type Stack< T >, a value of type T that will be the first value pushed onto the Stack< T >, a value of type T used to increment the values pushed onto the Stack< T > and a string that represents the name of the Stack< T > object for output purposes. Function main (lines 36–43) instantiates an object of type Stack< double > called doubleStack (line 38) and an object of type Stack< int > called intStack (line 39) and uses these objects in lines 41 and 42. The compiler infers the type of T for testStack from the type used to instantiate the function's first argument (i.e., the type used to instantiate doubleStack or intStack). The output of Fig. 22.4 precisely matches the output of Fig. 22.3.

```cpp
1   // Fig. 22.4: fig22_04.cpp
2   // Stack class template test program. Function main uses a
3   // function template to manipulate objects of type Stack< T >.
4   #include <iostream>
5   #include <string>
6   #include "Stack.h" // Stack class template definition
7   using namespace std;
8
9   // function template to manipulate Stack< T >
10  template< typename T >
11  void testStack(
12     Stack< T > &theStack, // reference to Stack< T >
13     T value, // initial value to push
14     T increment, // increment for subsequent values
15     const string stackName ) // name of the Stack< T > object
16  {
17     cout << "\nPushing elements onto " << stackName << '\n';
18
19     // push element onto Stack
20     while ( theStack.push( value ) )
21     {
22        cout << value << ' ';
23        value += increment;
24     } // end while
25
```

Fig. 22.4 | Passing a Stack template object to a function template. (Part 1 of 2.)

```
26         cout << "\nStack is full. Cannot push " << value
27             << "\n\nPopping elements from " << stackName << '\n';
28
29     // pop elements from Stack
30     while ( theStack.pop( value ) )
31         cout << value << ' ';
32
33     cout << "\nStack is empty. Cannot pop" << endl;
34 } // end function template testStack
35
36 int main()
37 {
38     Stack< double > doubleStack( 5 ); // size 5
39     Stack< int > intStack; // default size 10
40
41     testStack( doubleStack, 1.1, 1.1, "doubleStack" );
42     testStack( intStack, 1, 1, "intStack" );
43 } // end main
```

```
Pushing elements onto doubleStack
1.1 2.2 3.3 4.4 5.5
Stack is full. Cannot push 6.6

Popping elements from doubleStack
5.5 4.4 3.3 2.2 1.1
Stack is empty. Cannot pop

Pushing elements onto intStack
1 2 3 4 5 6 7 8 9 10
Stack is full. Cannot push 11

Popping elements from intStack
10 9 8 7 6 5 4 3 2 1
Stack is empty. Cannot pop
```

Fig. 22.4 | Passing a Stack template object to a function template. (Part 2 of 2.)

22.5 Nontype Parameters and Default Types for Class Templates

Class template Stack of Section 22.4 used only a type parameter in the template header (Fig. 22.2, line 6). It's also possible to use non-type template parameters, which can have default arguments and are treated as consts. For example, the template header could be modified to take an int elements parameter as follows:

```
template< typename T, int elements > // nontype parameter elements
```

Then, a declaration such as

```
Stack< double, 100 > mostRecentSalesFigures;
```

could be used to instantiate (at compile time) a 100-element Stack class-template specialization of double values named mostRecentSalesFigures; this class-template specialization would be of type Stack<double, 100>. The class definition then might contain a private data member with an array declaration such as

```
T stackHolder[ elements ]; // array to hold Stack contents
```
In addition, a type parameter can specify a **default type**. For example,

```
template< typename T = string > // defaults to type string
```
might specify that a Stack contains string objects by default. Then, a declaration such as

```
Stack<> jobDescriptions;
```
could be used to instantiate a Stack class-template specialization of strings named job-Descriptions; this class-template specialization would be of type Stack<string>. Default type parameters must be the *rightmost* (trailing) parameters in a template's type-parameter list. When one is instantiating a class with two or more default types, if an omitted type is not the rightmost type parameter in the type-parameter list, then all type parameters to the right of that type also must be omitted.

Performance Tip 22.2
When appropriate, specify the size of a container class (such as an array class or a stack class) at compile time (possibly through a nontype template parameter). This eliminates the execution-time overhead of using new to create the space dynamically.

Software Engineering Observation 22.3
Specifying the size of a container at compile time avoids the potentially fatal execution-time error if new is unable to obtain the needed memory.

In the exercises, you'll be asked to use a nontype parameter to create a template for our class Array from Chapter 19. This template will enable Array objects to be instantiated with a specified number of elements of a specified type at compile time, rather than creating space for the Array objects at execution time.

In some cases, it may not be possible to use a particular type with a class template. For example, our Stack template (Fig. 22.2) requires that class types that will be stored in a Stack must provide a default constructor and an assignment operator that properly copies objects. If a particular user-defined type will not work with our Stack template or requires customized processing, you can define an **explicit specialization** of the class template for a particular type. Let's assume we want to create an explicit specialization Stack for Employee objects. To do this, form a new class with the name Stack<Employee> as follows:

```
template<>
class Stack< Employee >
{
    // body of class definition
};
```
The Stack<Employee> explicit specialization is a complete replacement for the Stack class template that is specific to type Employee—it does *not* use anything from the original class template and can even have different members.

22.6 Wrap-Up

This chapter presented one of C++'s most powerful features—templates. You learned how to use function templates to enable the compiler to produce a set of function-template specializations that represent a group of related overloaded functions. We also discussed how to overload a function template to create a specialized version of a function that handles a particular data type's processing in a manner that differs from the other function-template specializations. Next, you learned about class templates and class-template specializations. You saw examples of how to use a class template to create a group of related types that each perform identical processing on different data types. In the next chapter, we discuss many of C++'s I/O capabilities and demonstrate several stream manipulators that perform various formatting tasks.

Summary

Section 22.1 Introduction

- Templates (p. 852) enable us to specify a range of related (overloaded) functions—called function-template specializations—or a range of related classes—called class-template specializations.

Section 22.2 Function Templates

- To use function-template specializations (p. 852), you write a single function-template definition (p. 853). Based on the argument types provided in calls to this function, C++ generates separate specializations to handle each type of call appropriately.

- All function-template definitions begin with the keyword `template` (p. 852) followed by template parameters (p. 853) enclosed in angle brackets (< and >); each template parameter that represents a type must be preceded by keyword `class` or `typename` (p. 853). Keywords `typename` and `class` used to specify function-template parameters mean "any fundamental type or user-defined type."

- Template-definition template parameters are used to specify the kinds of arguments to the function, the return type of the function and to declare variables in the function.

- As with function parameters, the names of template parameters must be unique inside a template definition. Template parameter names need not be unique across different function templates.

Section 22.3 Overloading Function Templates

- A function template may be overloaded in several ways. We can provide other function templates that specify the same function name but different function parameters. A function template can also be overloaded by providing other nontemplate functions with the same function name, but different function parameters. If both the template and non-template versions match a call, the non-template version will be used.

Section 22.4 Class Templates

- Class templates provide the means for describing a class generically and for instantiating classes that are type-specific versions of this generic class.

- Class templates are called parameterized types (p. 856); they require type parameters to specify how to customize a generic class template to form a specific class-template specialization.

- To use class-template specializations you write one class template. When you need a new type-specific class, the compiler writes the source code for the class-template specialization.

- A class-template definition (p. 856) looks like a conventional class definition, but it's preceded by `template<typename T>` (or `template<class T>`) to indicate this is a class-template definition. Type parameter `T` acts as a placeholder for the type of the class to create. The type `T` is mentioned throughout the class definition and member-function definitions as a generic type name.

- Member-function definitions outside a class template each begin with `template<typename T>` (or `template<class T>`). Then, each function definition resembles a conventional function definition, except that the generic data in the class always is listed generically as type parameter T. The binary scope-resolution operator is used with the class-template name to tie each member-function definition to the class template's scope.

Section 22.5 Nontype Parameters and Default Types for Class Templates

- It's possible to use nontype parameters (p. 862) in the header of a class or function template.
- You can specify a default type (p. 863) for a type parameter in the type-parameter list.
- An explicit specialization (p. 863) of a class template overrides a class template for a specific type.

Self-Review Exercises

22.1 State which of the following are *true* and which are *false*. If *false*, explain why.
  a) The template parameters of a function-template definition are used to specify the types of the arguments to the function, to specify the return type of the function and to declare variables within the function.
  b) Keywords `typename` and `class` as used with a template type parameter specifically mean "any user-defined class type."
  c) A function template can be overloaded by another function template with the same function name.
  d) Template parameter names among template definitions must be unique.
  e) Each member-function definition outside a class template must begin with a template header.

22.2 Fill in the blanks in each of the following:
  a) Templates enable us to specify, with a single code segment, an entire range of related functions called _____, or an entire range of related classes called _____.
  b) All function-template definitions begin with the keyword _____, followed by a list of template parameters to the function template enclosed in _____.
  c) The related functions generated from a function template all have the same name, so the compiler uses _____ resolution to invoke the proper function.
  d) Class templates also are called _____ types.
  e) The _____ operator is used with a class-template name to tie each member-function definition to the class template's scope.

Answers to Self-Review Exercises

22.1 a) True. b) False. Keywords `typename` and `class` in this context also allow for a type parameter of a fundamental type. c) True. d) False. Template parameter names among function templates need not be unique. e) True.

22.2 a) function-template specializations, class-template specializations. b) `template`, angle brackets (< and >). c) overload. d) parameterized. e) scope resolution.

Exercises

22.3 *(Selection Sort Function Template)* Write a function template `selectionSort` based on Fig. E.1. Write a driver program that inputs, sorts and outputs an `int` array and a `float` array.

22.4 *(Print Array Range)* Overload function template `printArray` of Fig. 22.1 so that it takes two additional integer arguments, namely `int lowSubscript` and `int highSubscript`. A call to this function will print only the designated portion of the array. Validate `lowSubscript` and `highSub-`

script; if either is out of range or if highSubscript is less than or equal to lowSubscript, the overloaded printArray function should return 0; otherwise, printArray should return the number of elements printed. Then modify main to exercise both versions of printArray on arrays a, b and c (lines 22–24 of Fig. 22.1). Be sure to test all capabilities of both versions of printArray.

22.5 *(Function Template Overloading)* Overload function template printArray of Fig. 22.1 with a nontemplate version that prints an array of natural numbers in neat, tabular, column format.

22.6 *(Operator Overloading in Templates)* Write a simple function template for predicate function isEqualTo that compares its two arguments of the same type with the equality operator (==) and returns true if they are equal and false otherwise. Use this function template in a program that calls isEqualTo only with a variety of fundamental types. Now write a separate version of the program that calls isEqualTo with a user-defined class type, but does not overload the equality operator. What happens when you attempt to run this program? Now overload the equality operator (with the operator function) operator==. Now what happens when you attempt to run this program?

22.7 *(Array Class Template)* Reimplement class Array from Figs. 19.10–19.11 as a class template. Demonstrate the new Array class template in a program.

22.8 Distinguish between the terms "function template" and "function-template specialization."

22.9 Explain which is more like a stencil—a class template or a class-template specialization?

22.10 What's the relationship between function templates and overloading?

22.11 Why might you choose to use a function template instead of a macro?

22.12 What performance problem can result from using function templates and class templates?

22.13 The compiler performs a matching process to determine which function-template specialization to call when a function is invoked. Under what circumstances does an attempt to make a match result in a compile error?

22.14 Why is it appropriate to refer to a class template as a parameterized type?

22.15 Explain why a C++ program would use the statement

```
Array< Student > studentNumber( 60 );
```

22.16 Review your answer to Exercise 22.15. Explain why a C++ program might use the statement

```
Array< Student > studentNumber;
```

22.17 Explain the use of the following notation in a C++ program:

```
template< typename T > Array< T >::Array( char p )
```

22.18 Why might you use a nontype parameter with a class template for a container such as an array or stack?

Stream Input/Output

*Consciousness ... does not
appear to itself chopped up in
bits ... A "river" or a "stream"
are the metaphors by which it is
most naturally described.*
—William James

Objectives

In this chapter you'll learn:

- To use C++ object-oriented stream input/output.

- To format input and output.

- The stream-I/O class hierarchy.

- To use stream manipulators.

- To control justification and padding.

- To determine the success or failure of input/output operations.

- To tie output streams to input streams.

Outline

23.1 Introduction

The C++ standard libraries provide an extensive set of input/output capabilities. This chapter discusses a range of capabilities sufficient for performing most common I/O operations and overviews the remaining capabilities. We discussed some of these features earlier in the text; now we provide a more complete treatment. Many of the I/O features that we'll discuss are object oriented. This style of I/O makes use of other C++ features, such as references, function overloading and operator overloading.

C++ uses **type-safe I/O**. Each I/O operation is executed in a manner sensitive to the data type. If an I/O function has been defined to handle a particular data type, then that member function is called to handle that data type. If there is no match between the type of the actual data and a function for handling that data type, the compiler generates an error. Thus, improper data cannot "sneak" through the system (as can occur in C, allowing for some subtle and bizarre errors).

Users can specify how to perform I/O for objects of user-defined types by overloading the stream insertion operator (<<) and the stream extraction operator (>>). This **extensibility** is one of C++'s most valuable features.

Software Engineering Observation 23.1

Use the C++-style I/O exclusively in C++ programs, even though C-style I/O is available to C++ programmers.

Error-Prevention Tip 23.1

C++ I/O is type safe.

Software Engineering Observation 23.2

C++ enables a common treatment of I/O for predefined types and user-defined types. This commonality facilitates software development and reuse.

23.2 Streams

C++ I/O occurs in **streams**, which are sequences of bytes. In input operations, the bytes flow from a device (e.g., a keyboard, a disk drive, a network connection, etc.) to main memory. In output operations, bytes flow from main memory to a device (e.g., a display screen, a printer, a disk drive, a network connection, etc.).

An application associates meaning with bytes. The bytes could represent characters, raw data, graphics images, digital speech, digital video or any other information an application may require. The system I/O mechanisms should transfer bytes from devices to memory (and vice versa) consistently and reliably. Such transfers often involve some mechanical motion, such as the rotation of a disk or a tape, or the typing of keystrokes at a keyboard. The time these transfers take typically is much greater than the time the processor requires to manipulate data internally. Thus, I/O operations require careful planning and tuning to ensure optimal performance.

C++ provides both "low-level" and "high-level" I/O capabilities. Low-level I/O capabilities (i.e., **unformatted I/O**) specify that some number of bytes should be transferred device-to-memory or memory-to-device. In such transfers, the individual byte is the item of interest. Such low-level capabilities provide high-speed, high-volume transfers but are not particularly convenient.

Programmers generally prefer a higher-level view of I/O (i.e., **formatted I/O**), in which bytes are grouped into meaningful units, such as integers, floating-point numbers, characters, strings and user-defined types. These type-oriented capabilities are satisfactory for most I/O other than high-volume file processing.

Performance Tip 23.1

Use unformatted I/O for the best performance in high-volume file processing.

Portability Tip 23.1

Using unformatted I/O can lead to portability problems, because unformatted data is not portable across all platforms.

23.2.1 Classic Streams vs. Standard Streams

In the past, the C++ **classic stream** libraries enabled input and output of chars. Because a char normally occupies one byte, it can represent only a limited set of characters (such as those in the ASCII character set used by most readers of this book, or other popular character sets). However, many languages use alphabets that contain more characters than a single-byte char can represent. The ASCII character set does not provide these characters;

the Unicode® character set does. Unicode is an extensive international character set that represents the majority of the world's "commercially viable" languages, mathematical symbols and much more. For more information on Unicode, visit www.unicode.org.

C++ includes the **standard stream libraries**, which enable developers to build systems capable of performing I/O operations with Unicode characters. For this purpose, C++ includes an additional character type called wchar_t, which among other uses can store Unicode characters. The C++ standard also redesigned the classic C++ stream classes, which processed only chars, as class templates with separate specializations for processing characters of types char and wchar_t, respectively. We use the char type of class templates throughout this book.

23.2.2 iostream Library Headers

The C++ iostream library provides hundreds of I/O capabilities. Several headers contain portions of the library interface.

Most C++ programs include the <iostream> header, which declares basic services required for all stream-I/O operations. The <iostream> header defines the cin, cout, cerr and clog objects, which correspond to the standard input stream, the standard output stream, the unbuffered standard error stream and the buffered standard error stream, respectively. (cerr and clog are discussed in Section 23.2.3.) Both unformatted- and formatted-I/O services are provided.

The <iomanip> header declares services useful for performing formatted I/O with so-called **parameterized stream manipulators**, such as setw and setprecision.

The <fstream> header declares services for file processing.

C++ implementations generally contain other I/O-related libraries that provide system-specific capabilities, such as the controlling of special-purpose devices for audio and video I/O.

23.2.3 Stream Input/Output Classes and Objects

The iostream library provides many templates for handling common I/O operations. For example, class template **basic_istream** supports stream-input operations, class template **basic_ostream** supports stream-output operations, and class template **basic_iostream** supports both stream-input and stream-output operations. Each template has a predefined template specialization that enables char I/O. In addition, the iostream library provides a set of typedefs that provide aliases for these template specializations. The **typedef** specifier declares synonyms (aliases) for data types. We introduced typedef in the C portion of the book. You'll sometimes use typedef to create shorter or more readable type names. For example, the statement

```
typedef Card *CardPtr;
```

defines an additional type name, CardPtr, as a synonym for type Card *. Creating a name using typedef does not create a data type; typedef creates only a type name. The typedef istream represents a specialization of basic_istream that enables char input. Similarly, the typedef **ostream** represents a specialization of basic_ostream that enables char output. Also, the typedef **iostream** represents a specialization of basic_iostream that enables both char input and output. We use these typedefs throughout this chapter.

Stream-I/O Template Hierarchy and Operator Overloading

Templates `basic_istream` and `basic_ostream` both derive through single inheritance from base template `basic_ios`.[1] Template `basic_iostream` derives through multiple inheritance from templates `basic_istream` and `basic_ostream`. The UML class diagram of Fig. 23.1 summarizes these inheritance relationships.

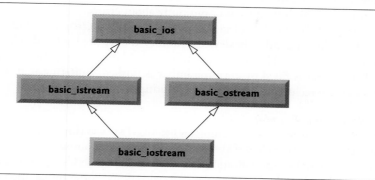

Fig. 23.1 | Stream-I/O template hierarchy portion.

Operator overloading provides a convenient notation for performing input/output. The left-shift operator (<<) is overloaded to designate stream output and is referred to as the stream insertion operator. The right-shift operator (>>) is overloaded to designate stream input and is referred to as the stream extraction operator. These operators are used with the standard stream objects `cin`, `cout`, `cerr` and `clog` and, commonly, with user-defined stream objects.

Standard Stream Objects *cin, cout, cerr and clog*

Predefined object `cin` is an `istream` instance and is said to be "connected to" (or attached to) the standard input device, which usually is the keyboard. The stream extraction operator (>>) as used in the following statement causes a value for integer variable `grade` (assuming that `grade` has been declared as an `int` variable) to be input from `cin` to memory:

```
cin >> grade; // data "flows" in the direction of the arrows
```

The compiler determines the data type of `grade` and selects the appropriate overloaded stream extraction operator. Assuming that `grade` has been declared properly, the stream extraction operator does not require additional type information (as is the case, for example, in C-style I/O). The >> operator is overloaded to input data items of fundamental types, strings and pointer values.

The predefined object `cout` is an `ostream` instance and is said to be "connected to" the standard output device, which usually is the display screen. The stream insertion operator (<<), as used in the following statement, causes the value of variable `grade` to be output from memory to the standard output device:

```
cout << grade; // data "flows" in the direction of the arrows
```

---

1. This chapter discusses templates only in the context of the template specializations for `char` I/O.

The compiler determines the data type of `grade` (assuming `grade` has been declared properly) and selects the appropriate stream insertion operator. The << operator is overloaded to output data items of fundamental types, strings and pointer values.

The predefined object `cerr` is an `ostream` instance and is said to be "connected to" the standard error device, normally the screen. Outputs to object `cerr` are **unbuffered**, implying that each stream insertion to `cerr` causes its output to appear immediately—this is appropriate for notifying a user promptly about errors.

The predefined object `clog` is an instance of the `ostream` class and is said to be "connected to" the standard error device. Outputs to `clog` are **buffered**. This means that each insertion to `clog` could cause its output to be held in a buffer (that is, an area in memory) until the buffer is filled or until the buffer is flushed. Buffering is an I/O performance-enhancement technique discussed in operating-systems courses.

File-Processing Templates

C++ file processing uses class templates **basic_ifstream** (for file input), **basic_ofstream** (for file output) and **basic_fstream** (for file input and output). Each class template has a predefined template specialization that enables char I/O. C++ provides a set of `typedef`s that provide aliases for these template specializations. For example, the `typedef` **ifstream** represents a specialization of `basic_ifstream` that enables char input from a file. Similarly, `typedef` **ofstream** represents a specialization of `basic_ofstream` that enables char output to a file. Also, `typedef` **fstream** represents a specialization of `basic_fstream` that enables char input from, and output to, a file. Template `basic_ifstream` inherits from `basic_istream`, `basic_ofstream` inherits from `basic_ostream` and `basic_fstream` inherits from `basic_iostream`. The UML class diagram of Fig. 23.2 summarizes the various inheritance relationships of the I/O-related classes. The full stream-I/O class hierarchy provides most of the capabilities that you need. Consult the class-library reference for your C++ system for additional file-processing information.

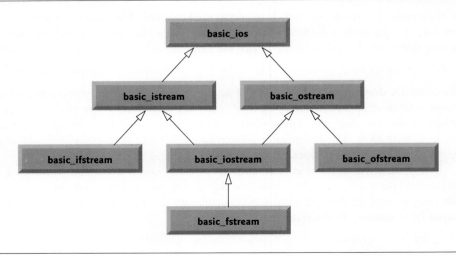

Fig. 23.2 | Stream-I/O template hierarchy portion showing the main file-processing templates.

23.3 Stream Output

Formatted and unformatted output capabilities are provided by ostream. Capabilities include output of standard data types with the stream insertion operator (<<); output of characters via the put member function; unformatted output via the write member function (Section 23.5); output of integers in decimal, octal and hexadecimal formats (Section 23.6.1); output of floating-point values with various precision (Section 23.6.2), with forced decimal points (Section 23.7.1), in scientific notation and in fixed notation (Section 23.7.5); output of data justified in fields of designated widths (Section 23.7.2); output of data in fields padded with specified characters (Section 23.7.3); and output of uppercase letters in scientific notation and hexadecimal notation (Section 23.7.6).

23.3.1 Output of char * Variables

C++ determines data types automatically—an improvement over C. This feature sometimes "gets in the way." For example, suppose we want to print the address stored in a char * pointer. The << operator has been overloaded to output a char * as a *null-terminated string*. To output the *address*, you can cast the char * to a void * (this can be done to any pointer variable). Figure 23.3 demonstrates printing a char * variable in both string and address formats. The address prints here as a hexadecimal (base-16) number—in general, the way addresses print is implementation dependent. To learn more about hexadecimal numbers, read Appendix C. We say more about controlling the bases of numbers in Section 23.6.1 and Section 23.7.4.

```
1   // Fig. 23.3: fig23_03.cpp
2   // Printing the address stored in a char * variable.
3   #include <iostream>
4   using namespace std;
5
6   int main()
7   {
8      const char *const word = "again";
9
10     // display value of char *, then display value of char *
11     // static_cast to void *
12     cout << "Value of word is: " << word << endl
13        << "Value of static_cast< void * >( word ) is: "
14        << static_cast< void * >( word ) << endl;
15  } // end main
```

```
Value of word is: again
Value of static_cast< void * >( word ) is: 00428300
```

Fig. 23.3 | Printing the address stored in a char * variable.

23.3.2 Character Output Using Member Function put

We can use the put member function to output characters. For example, the statement

```
cout.put( 'A' );
```

displays a single character A. Calls to put may be cascaded, as in the statement

```
cout.put( 'A' ).put( '\n' );
```

which outputs the letter A followed by a newline character. As with <<, the preceding statement executes in this manner, because the dot operator (.) associates from left to right, and the put member function returns a reference to the ostream object (cout) that received the put call. The put function also may be called with a numeric expression that represents an ASCII value, as in the following statement, which also outputs A:

```
cout.put( 65 );
```

23.4 Stream Input

Now let's consider stream input. Formatted and unformatted input capabilities are provided by istream. The stream extraction operator (>>) normally skips whitespace characters (such as blanks, tabs and newlines) in the input stream; later we'll see how to change this behavior. After each input, the stream extraction operator returns a *reference* to the stream object that received the extraction message (e.g., cin in the expression cin >> grade). If that reference is used as a condition (e.g., in a while statement's loop-continuation condition), the stream's overloaded void * cast operator function is implicitly invoked to convert the reference into a non-null pointer value or the null pointer based on the success or failure of the last input operation. A non-null pointer converts to the bool value true to indicate success and the null pointer converts to the bool value false to indicate failure. When an attempt is made to read past the end of a stream, the stream's overloaded void * cast operator returns the null pointer to indicate end-of-file.

Each stream object contains a set of **state bits** used to control the stream's state (i.e., formatting, setting error states, etc.). These bits are used by the stream's overloaded void * cast operator to determine whether to return a non-null pointer or the null pointer. Stream extraction causes the stream's **failbit** to be set if data of the wrong type is input and causes the stream's **badbit** to be set if the operation fails. Section 23.7 and Section 23.8 discuss stream state bits in detail, then show how to test these bits after an I/O operation.

23.4.1 get and getline Member Functions

The **get** member function with no arguments inputs one character from the designated stream (including white-space characters and other nongraphic characters, such as the key sequence that represents end-of-file) and returns it as the value of the function call. This version of get returns EOF when end-of-file is encountered on the stream.

Using Member Functions eof, get and put
Figure 23.4 demonstrates the use of member functions eof and get on input stream cin and member function put on output stream cout. The program first prints the value of cin.eof()—i.e., false (0 on the output)—to show that end-of-file has not occurred on cin. The user enters a line of text and presses *Enter* followed by end-of-file (*<Ctrl>-z* on Microsoft Windows systems, *<Ctrl>-d* on UNIX and Macintosh systems). Line 15 reads each character, which line 16 outputs to cout using member function put. When end-of-file is encountered, the while statement ends, and line 20 displays the value of cin.eof(), which is now true (1 on the output), to show that end-of-file has been set on cin. This program uses the version of istream member function get that takes no arguments and

returns the character being input (line 15). Function `eof` returns `true` only after the program attempts to read past the last character in the stream.

The `get` member function with a character-reference argument inputs the next character from the input stream (even if this is a white-space character) and stores it in the character argument. This version of `get` returns a reference to the `istream` object for which the `get` member function is being invoked.

A third version of `get` takes three arguments—a character array, a size limit and a delimiter (with default value `'\n'`). This version reads characters from the input stream. It either reads one fewer than the specified maximum number of characters and terminates or terminates as soon as the delimiter is read. A null character is inserted to terminate the input string in the character array used as a buffer by the program. The delimiter is not placed in the character array but *does remain in the input stream* (the delimiter will be the next character read). Thus, the result of a second consecutive `get` is an empty line, unless the delimiter character is removed from the input stream (possibly with `cin.ignore()`).

```cpp
 1   // Fig. 23.4: fig23_04.cpp
 2   // Using member functions get, put and eof.
 3   #include <iostream>
 4   using namespace std;
 5
 6   int main()
 7   {
 8      int character; // use int, because char cannot represent EOF
 9
10      // prompt user to enter line of text
11      cout << "Before input, cin.eof() is " << cin.eof() << endl
12         << "Enter a sentence followed by end-of-file:" << endl;
13
14      // use get to read each character; use put to display it
15      while ( ( character = cin.get() ) != EOF )
16         cout.put( character );
17
18      // display end-of-file character
19      cout << "\nEOF in this system is: " << character << endl;
20      cout << "After input of EOF, cin.eof() is " << cin.eof() << endl;
21   } // end main
```

```
Before input, cin.eof() is 0
Enter a sentence followed by end-of-file:
Testing the get and put member functions
Testing the get and put member functions
^Z

EOF in this system is: -1
After input of EOF, cin.eof() is 1
```

Fig. 23.4 | Using member functions `get`, `put` and `eof`.

Comparing `cin` and `cin.get`

Figure 23.5 compares input using stream extraction with `cin` (which reads characters until a white-space character is encountered) and input using `cin.get`. The call to `cin.get` (line 22) does not specify a delimiter, so the default `'\n'` character is used.

```cpp
 1   // Fig. 23.5: fig23_05.cpp
 2   // Contrasting input of a string via cin and cin.get.
 3   #include <iostream>
 4   using namespace std;
 5
 6   int main()
 7   {
 8      // create two char arrays, each with 80 elements
 9      const int SIZE = 80;
10      char buffer1[ SIZE ];
11      char buffer2[ SIZE ];
12
13      // use cin to input characters into buffer1
14      cout << "Enter a sentence:" << endl;
15      cin >> buffer1;
16
17      // display buffer1 contents
18      cout << "\nThe string read with cin was:" << endl
19         << buffer1 << endl << endl;
20
21      // use cin.get to input characters into buffer2
22      cin.get( buffer2, SIZE );
23
24      // display buffer2 contents
25      cout << "The string read with cin.get was:" << endl
26         << buffer2 << endl;
27   } // end main
```

```
Enter a sentence:
Contrasting string input with cin and cin.get

The string read with cin was:
Contrasting

The string read with cin.get was:
 string input with cin and cin.get
```

Fig. 23.5 | Contrasting input of a string via cin and cin.get.

Using Member Function getline

Member function **getline** operates similarly to the third version of the get member function and inserts a null character after the line in the character array. The getline function removes the delimiter from the stream (i.e., reads the character and discards it), but does not store it in the character array. The program of Fig. 23.6 demonstrates the use of the getline member function to input a line of text (line 13).

```cpp
 1   // Fig. 23.6: fig23_06.cpp
 2   // Inputting characters using cin member function getline.
 3   #include <iostream>
 4   using namespace std;
 5
```

Fig. 23.6 | Inputting characters with cin member function getline. (Part 1 of 2.)

```
 6    int main()
 7    {
 8        const int SIZE = 80;
 9        char buffer[ SIZE ]; // create array of 80 characters
10
11        // input characters in buffer via cin function getline
12        cout << "Enter a sentence:" << endl;
13        cin.getline( buffer, SIZE );
14
15        // display buffer contents
16        cout << "\nThe sentence entered is:" << endl << buffer << endl;
17    } // end main
```

```
Enter a sentence:
Using the getline member function

The sentence entered is:
Using the getline member function
```

Fig. 23.6 | Inputting characters with `cin` member function `getline`. (Part 2 of 2.)

23.4.2 `istream` Member Functions `peek`, `putback` and `ignore`

The **ignore** member function of `istream` reads and discards a designated number of characters (the default is one) or terminates upon encountering a designated delimiter (the default is EOF, which causes `ignore` to skip to the end of the file when reading from a file).

The **putback** member function places the previous character obtained by a `get` from an input stream back into that stream. This function is useful for applications that scan an input stream looking for a field beginning with a specific character. When that character is input, the application returns the character to the stream, so the character can be included in the input data.

The **peek** member function returns the next character from an input stream but does not remove the character from the stream.

23.4.3 Type-Safe I/O

C++ offers *type-safe I/O*. The << and >> operators are overloaded to accept data items of specific types. If unexpected data is processed, various error bits are set, which the user may test to determine whether an I/O operation succeeded or failed. If operators << and >> have not been overloaded for a user-defined type and you attempt to input into or output the contents of an object of that user-defined type, the compiler reports an error. This enables the program to "stay in control." We discuss these error states in Section 23.8.

23.5 Unformatted I/O Using `read`, `write` and `gcount`

Unformatted input/output is performed using the **read** and **write** member functions of `istream` and `ostream`, respectively. Member function `read` inputs bytes to a character array in memory; member function `write` outputs bytes from a character array. These bytes are not formatted in any way. They're input or output as raw bytes. For example, the call

```
char buffer[] = "HAPPY BIRTHDAY";
cout.write( buffer, 10 );
```

outputs the first 10 bytes of buffer (including null characters, if any, that would cause output with cout and << to terminate). The call

```
cout.write( "ABCDEFGHIJKLMNOPQRSTUVWXYZ", 10 );
```

displays the first 10 characters of the alphabet.

The read member function inputs a designated number of characters into a character array. If fewer than the designated number of characters are read, failbit is set. Section 23.8 shows how to determine whether failbit has been set. Member function **gcount** reports the number of characters read by the last input operation.

Figure 23.7 demonstrates istream member functions read and gcount, and ostream member function write. The program inputs 20 characters (from a longer input sequence) into the array buffer with read (line 13), determines the number of characters input with gcount (line 17) and outputs the characters in buffer with write (line 17).

```
 1   // Fig. 23.7: fig23_07.cpp
 2   // Unformatted I/O using the read, gcount and write member functions.
 3   #include <iostream>
 4   using namespace std;
 5
 6   int main()
 7   {
 8      const int SIZE = 80;
 9      char buffer[ SIZE ]; // create array of 80 characters
10
11      // use function read to input characters into buffer
12      cout << "Enter a sentence:" << endl;
13      cin.read( buffer, 20 );
14
15      // use functions write and gcount to display buffer characters
16      cout << endl << "The sentence entered was:" << endl;
17      cout.write( buffer, cin.gcount() );
18      cout << endl;
19   } // end main
```

```
Enter a sentence:
Using the read, write, and gcount member functions
The sentence entered was:
Using the read, writ
```

Fig. 23.7 | Unformatted I/O using the read, gcount and write member functions.

23.6 Introduction to Stream Manipulators

C++ provides various **stream manipulators** that perform formatting tasks. The stream manipulators provide capabilities such as setting field widths, setting precision, setting and unsetting format state, setting the fill character in fields, flushing streams, inserting a newline into the output stream (and flushing the stream), inserting a null character into the output stream and skipping white space in the input stream. These features are described in the following sections.

23.6.1 Integral Stream Base: dec, oct, hex and setbase

Integers are interpreted normally as decimal (base-10) values. To change the base in which integers are interpreted on a stream, insert the **hex** manipulator to set the base to hexadecimal (base 16) or insert the **oct** manipulator to set the base to octal (base 8). Insert the **dec** manipulator to reset the stream base to decimal. These are all sticky manipulators.

A stream's base also may be changed by the **setbase** stream manipulator, which takes an int argument of 10, 8, or 16 to set the base to decimal, octal or hexadecimal, respectively. Because setbase takes an argument, it's called a parameterized stream manipulator. Using setbase (or any other parameterized manipulator) requires the inclusion of the <iomanip> header. The stream base value remains the same until changed explicitly; setbase settings are "sticky." Figure 23.8 demonstrates stream manipulators hex, oct, dec and setbase.

```cpp
1   // Fig. 23.8: fig23_08.cpp
2   // Using stream manipulators hex, oct, dec and setbase.
3   #include <iostream>
4   #include <iomanip>
5   using namespace std;
6
7   int main()
8   {
9      int number;
10
11     cout << "Enter a decimal number: ";
12     cin >> number; // input number
13
14     // use hex stream manipulator to show hexadecimal number
15     cout << number << " in hexadecimal is: " << hex
16        << number << endl;
17
18     // use oct stream manipulator to show octal number
19     cout << dec << number << " in octal is: "
20        << oct << number << endl;
21
22     // use setbase stream manipulator to show decimal number
23     cout << setbase( 10 ) << number << " in decimal is: "
24        << number << endl;
25  } // end main
```

```
Enter a decimal number: 20
20 in hexadecimal is: 14
20 in octal is: 24
20 in decimal is: 20
```

Fig. 23.8 | Using stream manipulators hex, oct, dec and setbase.

23.6.2 Floating-Point Precision (precision, setprecision)

We can control the **precision** of floating-point numbers (i.e., the number of digits to the right of the decimal point) by using either the setprecision stream manipulator or the **precision** member function of ios_base. A call to either of these sets the precision for all subsequent output operations until the next precision-setting call. A call to member function `precision` with no argument returns the current precision setting (this is what you need to use so that you can restore the original precision eventually after a "sticky" setting is no longer needed). The program of Fig. 23.9 uses both member function `precision` (line 22) and the `setprecision` manipulator (line 31) to print a table that shows the square root of 2, with precision varying from 0 to 9.

```cpp
1   // Fig. 23.9: fig23_09.cpp
2   // Controlling precision of floating-point values.
3   #include <iostream>
4   #include <iomanip>
5   #include <cmath>
6   using namespace std;
7
8   int main()
9   {
10     double root2 = sqrt( 2.0 ); // calculate square root of 2
11     int places; // precision, vary from 0-9
12
13     cout << "Square root of 2 with precisions 0-9." << endl
14        << "Precision set by ios_base member function "
15        << "precision:" << endl;
16
17     cout << fixed; // use fixed-point notation
18
19     // display square root using ios_base function precision
20     for ( places = 0; places <= 9; ++places )
21     {
22        cout.precision( places );
23        cout << root2 << endl;
24     } // end for
25
26     cout << "\nPrecision set by stream manipulator "
27        << "setprecision:" << endl;
28
29     // set precision for each digit, then display square root
30     for ( places = 0; places <= 9; ++places )
31        cout << setprecision( places ) << root2 << endl;
32   } // end main
```

```
Square root of 2 with precisions 0-9.
Precision set by ios_base member function precision:
1
1.4
1.41
1.414
1.4142
1.41421
1.414214
1.4142136
1.41421356
1.414213562
```

Fig. 23.9 | Controlling precision of floating-point values. (Part 1 of 2.)

```
Precision set by stream manipulator setprecision:
1
1.4
1.41
1.414
1.4142
1.41421
1.414214
1.4142136
1.41421356
1.414213562
```

Fig. 23.9 | Controlling precision of floating-point values. (Part 2 of 2.)

23.6.3 Field Width (width, setw)

The **width** member function (of base class ios_base) sets the field width (i.e., the number of character positions in which a value should be output or the maximum number of characters that should be input) and returns the previous width. If values output are narrower than the field width, **fill characters** are inserted as **padding**. A value wider than the designated width will not be truncated—the full number will be printed. The width function with no argument returns the current setting.

Common Programming Error 23.1

The width setting applies only for the next insertion or extraction (i.e., the width setting is not "sticky"); afterward, the width is set implicitly to 0 (that is, input and output will be performed with default settings). Assuming that the width setting applies to all subsequent outputs is a logic error.

Common Programming Error 23.2

When a field is not sufficiently wide to handle outputs, the outputs print as wide as necessary, which can yield confusing outputs.

Figure 23.10 demonstrates the use of the width member function on both input and output. On input into a char array, *a maximum of one fewer characters than the width will be read*, because provision is made for the null character to be placed in the input string. Remember that stream extraction terminates when nonleading white space is encountered. The setw stream manipulator also may be used to set the field width. [*Note:* When prompted for input in Fig. 23.10, the user should enter a line of text and press *Enter* followed by end-of-file (*<Ctrl>-z* on Microsoft Windows systems and *<Ctrl>-d* on UNIX and Macintosh systems).]

```
1   // Fig. 23.10: fig23_10.cpp
2   // Demonstrating the width member function of class ios_base.
3   #include <iostream>
4   using namespace std;
```

Fig. 23.10 | Demonstrating the width member function of class ios_base. (Part 1 of 2.)

```
5
6   int main()
7   {
8       int widthValue = 4;
9       char sentence[ 10 ];
10
11      cout << "Enter a sentence:" << endl;
12      cin.width( 5 ); // input only 5 characters from sentence
13
14      // set field width, then display characters based on that width
15      while ( cin >> sentence )
16      {
17          cout.width( widthValue++ );
18          cout << sentence << endl;
19          cin.width( 5 ); // input 5 more characters from sentence
20      } // end while
21  } // end main
```

```
Enter a sentence:
This is a test of the width member function
This
   is
      a
   test
      of
      the
      widt
         h
        memb
           er
         func
         tion
```

Fig. 23.10 | Demonstrating the width member function of class ios_base. (Part 2 of 2.)

23.6.4 User-Defined Output Stream Manipulators

You can create your own stream manipulators.[2] Figure 23.11 shows the creation and use of new nonparameterized stream manipulators bell (lines 8–11), carriageReturn (lines 14–17), tab (lines 20–23) and endLine (lines 27–30). For output stream manipulators, the return type and parameter must be of type ostream &. When line 35 inserts the endLine manipulator in the output stream, function endLine is called and line 29 outputs the escape sequence \n and the flush manipulator to the standard output stream cout. Similarly, when lines 35–44 insert the manipulators tab, bell and carriageReturn in the output stream, their corresponding functions—tab (line 20), bell (line 8) and carriage-Return (line 14) are called, which in turn output various escape sequences.

---

2. You can also create your own parameterized stream manipulators. This capability is beyond the scope of this book.

```cpp
1   // Fig. 23.11: fig23_11.cpp
2   // Creating and testing user-defined, nonparameterized
3   // stream manipulators.
4   #include <iostream>
5   using namespace std;
6
7   // bell manipulator (using escape sequence \a)
8   ostream& bell( ostream& output )
9   {
10     return output << '\a'; // issue system beep
11  } // end bell manipulator
12
13  // carriageReturn manipulator (using escape sequence \r)
14  ostream& carriageReturn( ostream& output )
15  {
16     return output << '\r'; // issue carriage return
17  } // end carriageReturn manipulator
18
19  // tab manipulator (using escape sequence \t)
20  ostream& tab( ostream& output )
21  {
22     return output << '\t'; // issue tab
23  } // end tab manipulator
24
25  // endLine manipulator (using escape sequence \n and member
26  // function flush)
27  ostream& endLine( ostream& output )
28  {
29     return output << '\n' << flush; // issue endl-like end of line
30  } // end endLine manipulator
31
32  int main()
33  {
34     // use tab and endLine manipulators
35     cout << "Testing the tab manipulator:" << endLine
36        << 'a' << tab << 'b' << tab << 'c' << endLine;
37
38     cout << "Testing the carriageReturn and bell manipulators:"
39        << endLine << "..........";
40
41     cout << bell; // use bell manipulator
42
43     // use carriageReturn and endLine manipulators
44     cout << carriageReturn << "-----" << endLine;
45  } // end main
```

```
Testing the tab manipulator:
a       b       c
Testing the carriageReturn and bell manipulators:
-----.....
```

Fig. 23.11 | Creating and testing user-defined, nonparameterized stream manipulators.

23.7 Stream Format States and Stream Manipulators

Various stream manipulators can be used to specify the kinds of formatting to be performed during stream-I/O operations. Stream manipulators control the output's format settings. Figure 23.12 lists each stream manipulator that controls a given stream's format state. All these manipulators belong to class ios_base. We show examples of most of these stream manipulators in the next several sections.

Manipulator	Description
skipws	Skip white-space characters on an input stream. This setting is reset with stream manipulator noskipws.
left	Left justify output in a field. Padding characters appear to the right if necessary.
right	Right justify output in a field. Padding characters appear to the left if necessary.
internal	Indicate that a number's sign should be left justified in a field and a number's magnitude should be right justified in that same field (i.e., padding characters appear between the sign and the number).
boolalpha	Specify that bool values should be displayed as the word true or false. The manipulator noboolalpha sets the stream back to displaying bool values as 1 (true) and 0 (false).
dec	Specify that integers should be treated as decimal (base 10) values.
oct	Specify that integers should be treated as octal (base 8) values.
hex	Specify that integers should be treated as hexadecimal (base 16) values.
showbase	Specify that the base of a number is to be output ahead of the number (a leading 0 for octals; a leading 0x or 0X for hexadecimals). This setting is reset with stream manipulator noshowbase.
showpoint	Specify that floating-point numbers should be output with a decimal point. This is used normally with fixed to guarantee a certain number of digits to the right of the decimal point, even if they're zeros. This setting is reset with stream manipulator noshowpoint.
uppercase	Specify that uppercase letters (i.e., X and A through F) should be used in a hexadecimal integer and that uppercase E should be used when representing a floating-point value in scientific notation. This setting is reset with stream manipulator nouppercase.
showpos	Specify that positive numbers should be preceded by a plus sign (+). This setting is reset with stream manipulator noshowpos.
scientific	Specify output of a floating-point value in scientific notation.
fixed	Specify output of a floating-point value in fixed-point notation with a specific number of digits to the right of the decimal point.

Fig. 23.12 | Format state stream manipulators from <iostream>.

23.7.1 Trailing Zeros and Decimal Points (showpoint)

Stream manipulator **showpoint** forces a floating-point number to be output with its decimal point and trailing zeros. For example, the floating-point value 79.0 prints as 79 without using `showpoint` and prints as `79.000000` (or as many trailing zeros as are specified by the current precision) using `showpoint`. To reset the `showpoint` setting, output the stream manipulator **`noshowpoint`**. The program in Fig. 23.13 shows how to use stream manipulator `showpoint` to control the printing of trailing zeros and decimal points for floating-point values. Recall that the default precision of a floating-point number is 6. When neither the `fixed` nor the `scientific` stream manipulator is used, the precision represents the number of significant digits to display (i.e., the total number of digits to display), not the number of digits to display after decimal point.

```
 1   // Fig. 23.13: fig23_13.cpp
 2   // Controlling the printing of trailing zeros and
 3   // decimal points in floating-point values.
 4   #include <iostream>
 5   using namespace std;
 6
 7   int main()
 8   {
 9      // display double values with default stream format
10      cout << "Before using showpoint" << endl
11         << "9.9900 prints as: " << 9.9900 << endl
12         << "9.9000 prints as: " << 9.9000 << endl
13         << "9.0000 prints as: " << 9.0000 << endl << endl;
14
15      // display double value after showpoint
16      cout << showpoint
17         << "After using showpoint" << endl
18         << "9.9900 prints as: " << 9.9900 << endl
19         << "9.9000 prints as: " << 9.9000 << endl
20         << "9.0000 prints as: " << 9.0000 << endl;
21   } // end main
```

```
Before using showpoint
9.9900 prints as: 9.99
9.9000 prints as: 9.9
9.0000 prints as: 9

After using showpoint
9.9900 prints as: 9.99000
9.9000 prints as: 9.90000
9.0000 prints as: 9.00000
```

Fig. 23.13 | Controlling the printing of trailing zeros and decimal points in floating-point values.

23.7.2 Justification (`left`, `right` and `internal`)

Stream manipulators **`left`** and **`right`** enable fields to be left justified with padding characters to the right or right justified with padding characters to the left, respectively. The padding character is specified by the `fill` member function or the `setfill` parameterized stream manipulator (which we discuss in Section 23.7.3). Figure 23.14 uses the `setw`, `left` and `right` manipulators to left justify and right justify integer data in a field.

```
1   // Fig. 23.14: fig23_14.cpp
2   // Left and right justification with stream manipulators left and right.
3   #include <iostream>
4   #include <iomanip>
5   using namespace std;
6
7   int main()
8   {
9      int x = 12345;
10
11     // display x right justified (default)
12     cout << "Default is right justified:" << endl
13        << setw( 10 ) << x;
14
15     // use left manipulator to display x left justified
16     cout << "\n\nUse std::left to left justify x:\n"
17        << left << setw( 10 ) << x;
18
19     // use right manipulator to display x right justified
20     cout << "\n\nUse std::right to right justify x:\n"
21        << right << setw( 10 ) << x << endl;
22  } // end main
```

```
Default is right justified:
     12345

Use std::left to left justify x:
12345

Use std::right to right justify x:
     12345
```

Fig. 23.14 | Left and right justification with stream manipulators `left` and `right`.

Stream manipulator **internal** indicates that a number's sign (or base when using stream manipulator showbase) should be left justified within a field, that the number's magnitude should be right justified and that intervening spaces should be padded with the fill character. Figure 23.15 shows the internal stream manipulator specifying internal spacing (line 10). Note that showpos forces the plus sign to print (line 10). To reset the showpos setting, output the stream manipulator **noshowpos**.

```
1   // Fig. 23.15: fig23_14.cpp
2   // Printing an integer with internal spacing and plus sign.
3   #include <iostream>
4   #include <iomanip>
5   using namespace std;
6
7   int main()
8   {
9      // display value with internal spacing and plus sign
10     cout << internal << showpos << setw( 10 ) << 123 << endl;
11  } // end main
```

Fig. 23.15 | Printing an integer with internal spacing and plus sign. (Part 1 of 2.)

+	123

Fig. 23.15 | Printing an integer with internal spacing and plus sign. (Part 2 of 2.)

23.7.3 Padding (`fill`, `setfill`)

The `fill` member function specifies the fill character to be used with justified fields; spaces are used for padding by default. The function returns the prior padding character. The `setfill` manipulator also sets the padding character. Figure 23.16 demonstrates function `fill` (line 30) and stream manipulator `setfill` (lines 34 and 37) to set the fill character.

```
1   // Fig. 23.16: fig23_16.cpp
2   // Using member function fill and stream manipulator setfill to change
3   // the padding character for fields larger than the printed value.
4   #include <iostream>
5   #include <iomanip>
6   using namespace std;
7
8   int main()
9   {
10      int x = 10000;
11
12      // display x
13      cout << x << " printed as int right and left justified\n"
14          << "and as hex with internal justification.\n"
15          << "Using the default pad character (space):" << endl;
16
17      // display x with base
18      cout << showbase << setw( 10 ) << x << endl;
19
20      // display x with left justification
21      cout << left << setw( 10 ) << x << endl;
22
23      // display x as hex with internal justification
24      cout << internal << setw( 10 ) << hex << x << endl << endl;
25
26      cout << "Using various padding characters:" << endl;
27
28      // display x using padded characters (right justification)
29      cout << right;
30      cout.fill( '*' );
31      cout << setw( 10 ) << dec << x << endl;
32
33      // display x using padded characters (left justification)
34      cout << left << setw( 10 ) << setfill( '%' ) << x << endl;
35
36      // display x using padded characters (internal justification)
37      cout << internal << setw( 10 ) << setfill( '^' ) << hex
38          << x << endl;
39   } // end main
```

Fig. 23.16 | Using member function `fill` and stream manipulator `setfill` to change the padding character for fields larger than the values being printed. (Part 1 of 2.)

```
10000 printed as int right and left justified
and as hex with internal justification.
Using the default pad character (space):
     10000
10000
0x     2710

Using various padding characters:
*****10000
10000%%%%%
0x^^^^2710
```

Fig. 23.16 | Using member function `fill` and stream manipulator `setfill` to change the padding character for fields larger than the values being printed. (Part 2 of 2.)

23.7.4 Integral Stream Base (dec, oct, hex, showbase)

C++ provides stream manipulators **dec**, **hex** and **oct** to specify that integers are to be displayed as decimal, hexadecimal and octal values, respectively. Stream insertions default to decimal if none of these manipulators is used. With stream extraction, integers prefixed with 0 (zero) are treated as octal values, integers prefixed with 0x or 0X are treated as hexadecimal values, and all other integers are treated as decimal values. Once a particular base is specified for a stream, all integers on that stream are processed using that base until a different base is specified or until the program terminates.

Stream manipulator **showbase** forces the base of an integral value to be output. Decimal numbers are output by default, octal numbers are output with a leading 0, and hexadecimal numbers are output with either a leading 0x or a leading 0X (as we discuss in Section 23.7.6, stream manipulator **uppercase** determines which option is chosen). Figure 23.17 demonstrates the use of stream manipulator **showbase** to force an integer to print in decimal, octal and hexadecimal formats. To reset the **showbase** setting, output the stream manipulator **noshowbase**.

```
1   // Fig. 23.17: fig23_17.cpp
2   // Using stream manipulator showbase.
3   #include <iostream>
4   using namespace std;
5
6   int main()
7   {
8      int x = 100;
9
10     // use showbase to show number base
11     cout << "Printing integers preceded by their base:" << endl
12        << showbase;
13
14     cout << x << endl; // print decimal value
15     cout << oct << x << endl; // print octal value
16     cout << hex << x << endl; // print hexadecimal value
17  } // end main
```

Fig. 23.17 | Using stream manipulator `showbase`. (Part 1 of 2.)

```
Printing integers preceded by their base:
100
0144
0x64
```

Fig. 23.17 | Using stream manipulator showbase. (Part 2 of 2.)

23.7.5 Floating-Point Numbers; Scientific and Fixed Notation (scientific, fixed)

Stream manipulators scientific and fixed control the output format of floating-point numbers. Stream manipulator scientific forces the output of a floating-point number to display in scientific format. Stream manipulator fixed forces a floating-point number to display a specific number of digits (as specified by member function precision or stream manipulator setprecision) to the right of the decimal point. Without using another manipulator, the floating-point-number value determines the output format.

Figure 23.18 demonstrates displaying floating-point numbers in fixed and scientific formats using stream manipulators scientific (line 18) and fixed (line 22). The exponent format in scientific notation might differ across different compilers.

```
 1   // Fig. 23.18: fig23_18.cpp
 2   // Floating-point values dsplayed in default,
 3   // scientific and fixed formats.
 4   #include <iostream>
 5   using namespace std;
 6
 7   int main()
 8   {
 9      double x = 0.001234567;
10      double y = 1.946e9;
11
12      // display x and y in default format
13      cout << "Displayed in default format:" << endl
14         << x << '\t' << y << endl;
15
16      // display x and y in scientific format
17      cout << "\nDisplayed in scientific format:" << endl
18         << scientific << x << '\t' << y << endl;
19
20      // display x and y in fixed format
21      cout << "\nDisplayed in fixed format:" << endl
22         << fixed << x << '\t' << y << endl;
23   } // end main
```

```
Displayed in default format:
0.00123457      1.946e+009

Displayed in scientific format:
1.234567e-003   1.946000e+009
```

Fig. 23.18 | Floating-point values displayed in default, scientific and fixed formats. (Part 1 of 2.)

```
Displayed in fixed format:
0.001235        1946000000.000000
```

Fig. 23.18 | Floating-point values displayed in default, scientific and fixed formats. (Part 2 of 2.)

23.7.6 Uppercase/Lowercase Control (uppercase)

Stream manipulator **uppercase** outputs an uppercase X or E with hexadecimal-integer values or with scientific notation floating-point values, respectively (Fig. 23.19). Using stream manipulator **uppercase** also causes all letters in a hexadecimal value to be uppercase. By default, the letters for hexadecimal values and the exponents in scientific notation floating-point values appear in lowercase. To reset the **uppercase** setting, output the stream manipulator **nouppercase**.

```
 1   // Fig. 23.19: fig23_19.cpp
 2   // Stream manipulator uppercase.
 3   #include <iostream>
 4   using namespace std;
 5
 6   int main()
 7   {
 8      cout << "Printing uppercase letters in scientific" << endl
 9         << "notation exponents and hexadecimal values:" << endl;
10
11      // use std:uppercase to display uppercase letters; use std::hex and
12      // std::showbase to display hexadecimal value and its base
13      cout << uppercase << 4.345e10 << endl
14         << hex << showbase << 123456789 << endl;
15   } // end main
```

```
Printing uppercase letters in scientific
notation exponents and hexadecimal values:
4.345E+010
0X75BCD15
```

Fig. 23.19 | Stream manipulator uppercase.

23.7.7 Specifying Boolean Format (boolalpha)

C++ provides data type **bool**, whose values may be **false** or **true**, as a preferred alternative to the old style of using 0 to indicate **false** and nonzero to indicate **true**. A **bool** variable outputs as 0 or 1 by default. However, we can use stream manipulator **boolalpha** to set the output stream to display **bool** values as the strings "true" and "false". Use stream manipulator **noboolalpha** to set the output stream to display **bool** values as integers (i.e., the default setting). The program of Fig. 23.20 demonstrates these stream manipulators. Line 11 displays the **bool** value, which line 8 sets to **true**, as an integer. Line 15 uses manipulator **boolalpha** to display the **bool** value as a string. Lines 18–19 then change the **bool**'s value and use manipulator **noboolalpha**, so line 22 can display the **bool** value as an integer. Line 26 uses manipulator **boolalpha** to display the **bool** value as a string. Both **boolalpha** and **noboolalpha** are "sticky" settings.

Good Programming Practice 23.1

Displaying bool values as true or false, rather than nonzero or 0, respectively, makes program outputs clearer.

```cpp
1   // Fig. 23.20: fig23_20.cpp
2   // Using stream manipulators boolalpha and noboolalpha.
3   #include <iostream>
4   using namespace std;
5
6   int main()
7   {
8      bool booleanValue = true;
9
10     // display default true booleanValue
11     cout << "booleanValue is " << booleanValue << endl;
12
13     // display booleanValue after using boolalpha
14     cout << "booleanValue (after using boolalpha) is "
15        << boolalpha << booleanValue << endl << endl;
16
17     cout << "switch booleanValue and use noboolalpha" << endl;
18     booleanValue = false; // change booleanValue
19     cout << noboolalpha << endl; // use noboolalpha
20
21     // display default false booleanValue after using noboolalpha
22     cout << "booleanValue is " << booleanValue << endl;
23
24     // display booleanValue after using boolalpha again
25     cout << "booleanValue (after using boolalpha) is "
26        << boolalpha << booleanValue << endl;
27  } // end main
```

```
booleanValue is 1
booleanValue (after using boolalpha) is true

switch booleanValue and use noboolalpha

booleanValue is 0
booleanValue (after using boolalpha) is false
```

Fig. 23.20 | Using stream manipulators boolalpha and noboolalpha.

23.7.8 Setting and Resetting the Format State via Member Function flags

Throughout Section 23.7, we've been using stream manipulators to change output format characteristics. We now discuss how to return an output stream's format to its default state after having applied several manipulations. Member function **flags** without an argument returns the current format settings as a **fmtflags** data type (of class ios_base), which represents the format state. Member function flags with a fmtflags argument sets the format state as specified by the argument and returns the prior state settings. The initial settings of the value that flags returns might differ across several systems. The program of Fig. 23.21 uses member function `flags` to save the stream's original format state (line 17), then restore the original format settings (line 25).

```cpp
1  // Fig. 23.21: fig23_21.cpp
2  // Demonstrating the flags member function.
3  #include <iostream>
4  using namespace std;
5
6  int main()
7  {
8     int integerValue = 1000;
9     double doubleValue = 0.0947628;
10
11    // display flags value, int and double values (original format)
12    cout << "The value of the flags variable is: " << cout.flags()
13       << "\nPrint int and double in original format:\n"
14       << integerValue << '\t' << doubleValue << endl << endl;
15
16    // use cout flags function to save original format
17    ios_base::fmtflags originalFormat = cout.flags();
18    cout << showbase << oct << scientific; // change format
19
20    // display flags value, int and double values (new format)
21    cout << "The value of the flags variable is: " << cout.flags()
22       << "\nPrint int and double in a new format:\n"
23       << integerValue << '\t' << doubleValue << endl << endl;
24
25    cout.flags( originalFormat ); // restore format
26
27    // display flags value, int and double values (original format)
28    cout << "The restored value of the flags variable is: "
29       << cout.flags()
30       << "\nPrint values in original format again:\n"
31       << integerValue << '\t' << doubleValue << endl;
32 } // end main
```

```
The value of the flags variable is: 513
Print int and double in original format:
1000    0.0947628

The value of the flags variable is: 012011
Print int and double in a new format:
01750    9.476280e-002

The restored value of the flags variable is: 513
Print values in original format again:
1000    0.0947628
```

Fig. 23.21 | Demonstrating the `flags` member function.

23.8 Stream Error States

The state of a stream may be tested through bits in class `ios_base`. In a moment, we show how to test these bits, in the example of Fig. 23.22.

```
 1   // Fig. 23.22: fig23_22.cpp
 2   // Testing error states.
 3   #include <iostream>
 4   using namespace std;
 5
 6   int main()
 7   {
 8      int integerValue;
 9
10      // display results of cin functions
11      cout << "Before a bad input operation:"
12         << "\ncin.rdstate(): " << cin.rdstate()
13         << "\n    cin.eof(): " << cin.eof()
14         << "\n   cin.fail(): " << cin.fail()
15         << "\n    cin.bad(): " << cin.bad()
16         << "\n   cin.good(): " << cin.good()
17         << "\n\nExpects an integer, but enter a character: ";
18
19      cin >> integerValue; // enter character value
20      cout << endl;
21
22      // display results of cin functions after bad input
23      cout << "After a bad input operation:"
24         << "\ncin.rdstate(): " << cin.rdstate()
25         << "\n    cin.eof(): " << cin.eof()
26         << "\n   cin.fail(): " << cin.fail()
27         << "\n    cin.bad(): " << cin.bad()
28         << "\n   cin.good(): " << cin.good() << endl << endl;
29
30      cin.clear(); // clear stream
31
32      // display results of cin functions after clearing cin
33      cout << "After cin.clear()" << "\ncin.fail(): " << cin.fail()
34         << "\ncin.good(): " << cin.good() << endl;
35   } // end main
```

```
Before a bad input operation:
cin.rdstate(): 0
    cin.eof(): 0
   cin.fail(): 0
    cin.bad(): 0
   cin.good(): 1

Expects an integer, but enter a character: A

After a bad input operation:
cin.rdstate(): 2
    cin.eof(): 0
   cin.fail(): 1
    cin.bad(): 0
   cin.good(): 0

After cin.clear()
cin.fail(): 0
cin.good(): 1
```

Fig. 23.22 | Testing error states.

The **eofbit** is set for an input stream after end-of-file is encountered. A program can use member function eof to determine whether end-of-file has been encountered on a stream after an attempt to extract data beyond the end of the stream. The call

```
cin.eof()
```

returns true if end-of-file has been encountered on cin and false otherwise.

The failbit is set for a stream when a format error occurs on the stream and no characters are input (e.g., when you attempt to read a number and the user enters a string). When such an error occurs, the characters are not lost. The **fail** member function reports whether a stream operation has failed. Usually, recovering from such errors is possible.

The badbit is set for a stream when an error occurs that results in the loss of data. The **bad** member function reports whether a stream operation failed. Generally, such serious failures are nonrecoverable.

The **goodbit** is set for a stream if none of the bits eofbit, failbit or badbit is set for the stream.

The **good** member function returns true if the bad, fail and eof functions would all return false. I/O operations should be performed only on "good" streams.

The **rdstate** member function returns the stream's error state. Calling cout.rdstate, for example, would return the stream's state, which then could be tested by a switch statement that examines eofbit, badbit, failbit and goodbit. The preferred means of testing the state of a stream is to use member functions eof, bad, fail and good—using these functions does not require you to be familiar with particular status bits.

The **clear** member function is used to restore a stream's state to "good," so that I/O may proceed on that stream. The default argument for clear is goodbit, so the statement

```
cin.clear();
```

clears cin and sets goodbit for the stream. The statement

```
cin.clear( ios::failbit )
```

sets the failbit. You might want to do this when performing input on cin with a user-defined type and encountering a problem. The name clear might seem inappropriate in this context, but it's correct.

The program of Fig. 23.22 demonstrates member functions rdstate, eof, fail, bad, good and clear. The actual values output may differ across different compilers.

The operator! member function of basic_ios returns true if the badbit is set, the failbit is set or both are set. The operator void * member function returns false (0) if the badbit is set, the failbit is set or both are set. These functions are useful in file processing when a true/false condition is being tested under the control of a selection statement or repetition statement.

23.9 Tying an Output Stream to an Input Stream

Interactive applications generally involve an istream for input and an ostream for output. When a prompting message appears on the screen, the user responds by entering the appropriate data. Obviously, the prompt needs to appear before the input operation proceeds. With output buffering, outputs appear only when the buffer fills, when outputs are flushed explicitly by the program or automatically at the end of the program. C++ provides member function **tie** to synchronize (i.e., "tie together") the operation of an `istream` and an `ostream` to ensure that outputs appear before their subsequent inputs. The call

```
cin.tie( &cout );
```

ties `cout` (an `ostream`) to `cin` (an `istream`). Actually, this particular call is redundant, because C++ performs this operation automatically to create a user's standard input/output environment. However, the user would tie other `istream`/`ostream` pairs explicitly. To untie an input stream, `inputStream`, from an output stream, use the call

```
inputStream.tie( 0 );
```

23.10 Wrap-Up

This chapter summarized how C++ performs input/output using streams. You learned about the stream-I/O classes and objects, as well as the stream I/O template class hierarchy. We discussed `ostream`'s formatted and unformatted output capabilities performed by the `put` and `write` functions. You saw examples using `istream`'s formatted and unformatted input capabilities performed by the `eof`, `get`, `getline`, `peek`, `putback`, `ignore` and `read` functions. We discussed stream manipulators and member functions that perform formatting tasks—`dec`, `oct`, `hex` and `setbase` for displaying integers; `precision` and `setprecision` for controlling floating-point precision; and `width` and `setw` for setting field width. You also learned additional formatting `iostream` manipulators and member functions—`showpoint` for displaying decimal point and trailing zeros; `left`, `right` and `internal` for justification; `fill` and `setfill` for padding; `scientific` and `fixed` for displaying floating-point numbers in scientific and fixed notation; `uppercase` for uppercase/lowercase control; `boolalpha` for specifying boolean format; and `flags` and `fmtflags` for resetting the format state.

We introduced exception handling earlier in the book. In the next chapter, we take a deeper look at C++'s rich set of exception handling capabilities.

Summary

Section 23.1 Introduction
- I/O operations are performed in a manner sensitive to the type of the data.

Section 23.2 Streams
- C++ I/O occurs in streams (p. 869). A stream is a sequence of bytes.
- Low-level I/O-capabilities specify that bytes should be transferred device-to-memory or memory-to-device. High-level I/O is performed with bytes grouped into meaningful units such as integers, strings and user-defined types.
- C++ provides both unformatted-I/O and formatted-I/O operations. Unformatted-I/O (p. 869) transfers are fast, but process raw data that is difficult for people to use. Formatted I/O processes data in meaningful units, but requires extra processing time that can degrade the performance.
- The `<iostream>` header declares all stream-I/O operations (p. 870).
- The `<iomanip>` header declares the parameterized stream manipulators (p. 870).
- The `<fstream>` header declares file-processing operations (p. 872).
- The `basic_istream` template (p. 870) supports stream-input operations.

- The `basic_ostream` template (p. 870) supports stream-output operations.
- The `basic_iostream` template supports both stream-input and stream-output operations.
- Templates `basic_istream` and the `basic_ostream` each derive from the `basic_ios` (p. 871) template.
- Template `basic_iostream` derives from both the `basic_istream` and `basic_ostream` templates.
- The `istream` object `cin` is tied to the standard input device, normally the keyboard.
- The `ostream` object `cout` is tied to the standard output device, normally the screen.
- The `ostream` object `cerr` is tied to the standard error device, normally the screen. Outputs to `cerr` are unbuffered (p. 872)—each insertion to `cerr` appears immediately.
- The `ostream` object `clog` is tied to the standard error device, normally the screen. Outputs to `clog` are buffered (p. 872).
- The C++ compiler determines data types automatically for input and output.

Section 23.3 Stream Output
- Addresses are displayed in hexadecimal format by default.
- To print the address in a pointer variable, cast the pointer to `void *`.
- Member function `put` outputs one character. Calls to `put` may be cascaded.

Section 23.4 Stream Input
- Stream input is performed with the stream extraction operator `>>`, which automatically skips whitespace characters (p. 874) in the input stream and returns `false` after end-of-file is encountered.
- Stream extraction causes `failbit` (p. 874) to be set for improper input and `badbit` (p. 874) to be set if the operation fails.
- A series of values can be input using the stream extraction operation in a `while` loop header. The extraction returns 0 when end-of-file is encountered or an error occurs.
- The `get` member function (p. 874) with no arguments inputs one character and returns the character; `EOF` is returned if end-of-file is encountered on the stream.
- Member function `get` with a character-reference argument inputs the next character from the input stream and stores it in the character argument. This version of `get` returns a reference to the `istream` object (p. 870) for which the `get` member function is being invoked.
- Member function `get` with three arguments—a character array, a size limit and a delimiter (with default value newline)—reads characters from the input stream up to a maximum of limit – 1 characters, or until the delimiter is read. The input string is terminated with a null character. The delimiter is not placed in the character array but remains in the input stream.
- Member function `getline` (p. 876) operates like the three-argument `get` member function. The `getline` function removes the delimiter from the input stream but does not store it in the string.
- Member function `ignore` (p. 877) skips the specified number of characters (the default is 1) in the input stream; it terminates if the specified delimiter is encountered (the default delimiter is `EOF`).
- The `putback` member function (p. 877) places the previous character obtained by a `get` on a stream back into that stream.
- The `peek` member function (p. 877) returns the next character from an input stream but does not extract (remove) the character from the stream.
- C++ offers type-safe I/O (p. 868). If unexpected data is processed by the `<<` and `>>` operators, various error bits are set, which can be tested to determine whether an I/O operation succeeded or failed. If operator `<<` has not been overloaded for a user-defined type, a compiler error is reported.

Section 23.5 Unformatted I/O Using `read`, `write` and `gcount`

- Unformatted I/O is performed with member functions read and write (p. 877). These input or output bytes to or from memory, beginning at a designated memory address.

- The gcount member function (p. 878) returns the number of characters input by the previous read operation on that stream.

- Member function read inputs a specified number of characters into a character array. failbit is set if fewer than the specified number of characters are read.

Section 23.6 Introduction to Stream Manipulators

- To change the base in which integers output, use the manipulator hex (p. 879) to set the base to hexadecimal (base 16) or oct (p. 879) to set the base to octal (base 8). Use manipulator dec (p. 879) to reset the base to decimal. The base remains the same until changed explicitly.

- The parameterized stream manipulator setbase (p. 879) also sets the base for integer output. setbase takes one integer argument of 10, 8 or 16 to set the base.

- Floating-point precision can be controlled with the setprecision stream manipulator or the precision member function (p. 879). Both set the precision for all subsequent output operations until the next precision-setting call. The precision member function with no argument returns the current precision value.

- Parameterized manipulators require the inclusion of the <iomanip> header.

- Member function width sets the field width and returns the previous width. Values narrower than the field are padded with fill characters (p. 881). The field-width setting applies only for the next insertion or extraction; the field width is set to 0 implicitly (subsequent values will be output as large as necessary). Values wider than a field are printed in their entirety. Function width with no argument returns the current width setting. Manipulator setw also sets the width.

- For input, the setw stream manipulator establishes a maximum string size; if a larger string is entered, the larger line is broken into pieces no larger than the designated size.

- You can create your own stream manipulators.

Section 23.7 Stream Format States and Stream Manipulators

- Stream manipulator showpoint (p. 884) forces a floating-point number to be output with a decimal point and with the number of significant digits specified by the precision.

- Stream manipulators left and right (p. 885) cause fields to be left justified with padding characters to the right or right justified with padding characters to the left.

- Stream manipulator internal (p. 886) indicates that a number's sign (or base when using stream manipulator showbase; p. 888) should be left justified within a field, its magnitude should be right justified and intervening spaces should be padded with the fill character.

- Member function fill (p. 887) specifies the fill character to be used with stream manipulators left, right and internal (space is the default); the prior padding character is returned. Stream manipulator setfill (p. 887) also sets the fill character.

- Stream manipulators oct, hex and dec specify that integers are to be treated as octal, hexadecimal or decimal values, respectively. Integer output defaults to decimal if none of these bits is set; stream extractions process the data in the form the data is supplied.

- Stream manipulator showbase forces the base of an integral value to be output.

- Stream manipulator scientific (p. 889) is used to output a floating-point number in scientific format. Stream manipulator fixed (p. 889) is used to output a floating-point number with the precision specified by the precision member function.

- Stream manipulator uppercase (p. 884) outputs an uppercase X or E for hexadecimal integers and scientific notation floating-point values, respectively. Hexadecimal values appear in all uppercase.
- Member function flags (p. 891) with no argument returns the current format state (p. 891) as a long value. Function flags with a long argument sets the format state specified by the argument.

Section 23.8 Stream Error States
- The state of a stream may be tested through bits in class ios_base.
- The eofbit (p. 894) is set for an input stream after end-of-file is encountered during an input operation. The eof member function (p. 894) reports whether the eofbit has been set.
- A stream's failbit is set when a format error occurs. The fail member function (p. 894) reports whether a stream operation has failed; it's normally possible to recover from such errors.
- A stream's badbit is set when an error occurs that results in data loss. Member function bad reports whether a stream operation failed. Such serious failures are normally nonrecoverable.
- The good member function (p. 894) returns true if the bad, fail and eof functions would all return false. I/O operations should be performed only on "good" streams.
- The rdstate member function (p. 894) returns the error state of the stream.
- Member function clear (p. 894) restores a stream's state to "good," so that I/O may proceed.

Section 23.9 Tying an Output Stream to an Input Stream
- C++ provides the tie member function (p. 895) to synchronize istream and ostream operations to ensure that outputs appear before subsequent inputs.

Self-Review Exercises

23.1 *(Fill in the Blanks)* Answer each of the following:
   a) Input/output in C++ occurs as _____ of bytes.
   b) The stream manipulators for justification are _____, _____ and _____.
   c) Member function _____ can be used to set and reset format state.
   d) Most C++ programs that do I/O should include the _____ header that contains the declarations required for all stream-I/O operations.
   e) When using parameterized manipulators, the header _____ must be included.
   f) Header _____ contains the declarations required for file processing.
   g) The ostream member function _____ is used to perform unformatted output.
   h) Input operations are supported by class _____.
   i) Standard error stream outputs are directed to the stream objects _____ or _____.
   j) Output operations are supported by class _____.
   k) The symbol for the stream insertion operator is _____.
   l) The four objects that correspond to the standard devices on the system include _____, _____, _____ and _____.
   m) The symbol for the stream extraction operator is _____.
   n) The stream manipulators _____, _____ and _____ specify that integers should be displayed in octal, hexadecimal and decimal formats, respectively.
   o) The _____ stream manipulator causes positive numbers to display with a plus sign.

23.2 *(True or False)* State whether the following are *true* or *false*. If the answer is *false*, explain why.
   a) The stream member function flags with a long argument sets the flags state variable to its argument and returns its previous value.
   b) The stream insertion operator << and the stream extraction operator >> are overloaded to handle all standard data types—including strings and memory addresses (stream insertion only)—and all user-defined data types.

c) The stream member function flags with no arguments resets the stream's format state.

d) The stream extraction operator >> can be overloaded with an operator function that takes an istream reference and a reference to a user-defined type as arguments and returns an istream reference.

e) The stream insertion operator << can be overloaded with an operator function that takes an istream reference and a reference to a user-defined type as arguments and returns an istream reference.

f) Input with the stream extraction operator >> always skips leading white-space characters in the input stream, by default.

g) The stream member function rdstate returns the current state of the stream.

h) The cout stream normally is connected to the display screen.

i) The stream member function good returns true if the bad, fail and eof member functions all return false.

j) The cin stream normally is connected to the display screen.

k) If a nonrecoverable error occurs during a stream operation, the bad member function will return true.

l) Output to cerr is unbuffered and output to clog is buffered.

m) Stream manipulator showpoint forces floating-point values to print with the default six digits of precision unless the precision value has been changed, in which case floating-point values print with the specified precision.

n) The ostream member function put outputs the specified number of characters.

o) The stream manipulators dec, oct and hex affect only the next integer output operation.

23.3 *(Write a C++ Statement)* For each of the following, write a single statement that performs the indicated task.

a) Output the string "Enter your name: ".

b) Use a stream manipulator that causes the exponent in scientific notation and the letters in hexadecimal values to print in capital letters.

c) Output the address of the variable myString of type char *.

d) Use a stream manipulator to ensure that floating-point values print in scientific notation.

e) Output the address in variable integerPtr of type int *.

f) Use a stream manipulator such that, when integer values are output, the integer base for octal and hexadecimal values is displayed.

g) Output the value pointed to by floatPtr of type float *.

h) Use a stream member function to set the fill character to '*' for printing in field widths larger than the values being output. Repeat this statement with a stream manipulator.

i) Output the characters 'O' and 'K' in one statement with ostream function put.

j) Get the value of the next character to input without extracting it from the stream.

k) Input a single character into variable charValue of type char, using the istream member function get in two different ways.

l) Input and discard the next six characters in the input stream.

m) Use istream member function read to input 50 characters into char array line.

n) Read 10 characters into character array name. Stop reading characters if the '.' delimiter is encountered. Do not remove the delimiter from the input stream. Write another statement that performs this task and removes the delimiter from the input.

o) Use the istream member function gcount to determine the number of characters input into character array line by the last call to istream member function read, and output that number of characters, using ostream member function write.

p) Output 124, 18.376, 'Z', 1000000 and "String", separated by spaces.

q) Print the current precision setting, using a member function of object cout.

r) Input an integer value into `int` variable `months` and a floating-point value into `float` variable `percentageRate`.

s) Print `1.92`, `1.925` and `1.9258` separated by tabs and with 3 digits of precision, using a stream manipulator.

t) Print integer 100 in octal, hexadecimal and decimal, using stream manipulators and separated by tabs.

u) Print integer 100 in decimal, octal and hexadecimal separated by tabs, using a stream manipulator to change the base.

v) Print 1234 right justified in a 10-digit field.

w) Read characters into character array `line` until the character `'z'` is encountered, up to a limit of 20 characters (including a terminating null character). Do not extract the delimiter character from the stream.

x) Use integer variables `x` and `y` to specify the field width and precision used to display the `double` value `87.4573`, and display the value.

23.4 *(Find and Correct Code Errors)* Identify the error in each of the following statements and explain how to correct it.

a) The following statement should print the ASCII value of Z.

```
cout << "Z = " << 'Z';
```

b) `cout << "Employee 1 earns more than employee 2?" << emp1 > emp2;`

c) `cout << "New line character" << \n;`

23.5 *(Show Outputs)* For each of the following, show the output.

a) ```
cout.width(4);
cout << "00" << endl << "Program";
```

b) ```
int a = 2;
cout.width( ++a ); cout.fill('C');
cout << "++" << endl << "Program";
```

c) `cout << setw( 13 ) << setfill( '+' ) << "Programming";`

d) `cout << setprecision( 2 ) << 9.43 << '\t' << 8.0931;`

e) ```
int a = 2, b = 4;
cout << setw(a) << setprecision(b) << 63.5129;
```

f) `cout << 99 << '\n' << setbase( 8 ) << 99 << '\n' << setbase( 16 ) << 99;`

# Answers to Self-Review Exercises

**23.1** a) streams. b) `left`, `right` and `internal`. c) `flags`. d) `<iostream>`. e) `<iomanip>`. f) `<fstream>`. g) `write`. h) `istream`. i) `cerr` or `clog`. j) `ostream`. k) `<<`. l) `cin`, `cout`, `cerr` and `clog`. m) `>>`. n) `oct`, `hex` and `dec`. o) `showpos`.

**23.2** a) False. The stream member function `flags` with a `fmtflags` argument sets the `flags` state variable to its argument and returns the prior state settings. b) False. The stream insertion and stream extraction operators are not overloaded for all user-defined types. You must specifically provide the overloaded operator functions to overload the stream operators for use with each user-defined type you create. c) False. The stream member function `flags` with no arguments returns the current format settings as a `fmtflags` data type, which represents the format state. d) True. e) False. To overload the stream insertion operator `<<`, the overloaded operator function must take an `ostream` reference and a reference to a user-defined type as arguments and return an `ostream` reference. f) True. g) True. h) True. i) True. j) False. The `cin` stream is connected to the standard input of the computer, which normally is the keyboard. k) True. l) True. m) True. n) False. The `ostream`
```

member function put outputs its single-character argument. o) False. The stream manipulators dec, oct and hex set the output format state for integers to the specified base until the base is changed again or the program terminates.

23.3 a) `cout << "Enter your name: ";`
b) `cout << uppercase;`
c) `cout << static_cast< void * >( myString );`
d) `cout << scientific;`
e) `cout << integerPtr;`
f) `cout << showbase;`
g) `cout << *floatPtr;`
h) `cout.fill( '*' );`
   `cout << setfill( '*' );`
i) `cout.put( 'O' ).put( 'K' );`
j) `cin.peek();`
k) `charValue = cin.get();`
   `cin.get( charValue );`
l) `cin.ignore( 6 );`
m) `cin.read( line, 50 );`
n) `cin.get( name, 10, '.' );`
   `cin.getline( name, 10, '.' );`
o) `cout.write( line, cin.gcount() );`
p) `cout << 124 << ' ' << 18.376 << ' ' << "Z " << 1000000 << " String";`
q) `cout << cout.precision();`
r) `cin >> months >> percentageRate;`
s) `cout << setprecision( 3 ) << 1.92 << '\t' << 1.925 << '\t' << 1.9258;`
t) `cout << oct << 100 << '\t' << hex << 100 << '\t' << dec << 100;`
u) `cout << 100 << '\t' << setbase( 8 ) << 100 << '\t' << setbase( 16 ) << 100;`
v) `cout << setw( 10 ) << 1234;`
w) `cin.get( line, 20, 'z' );`
x) `cout << setw( x ) << setprecision( y ) << 87.4573;`

23.4 a) *Error:* In C++, characters are not treated as small integers
   Correction: To print the ASCII value of Z, it must be cast to an integer value, as shown below:

   `cout << "Z = " << static_cast< int >('Z');`
b) *Error:* The statement results in a compilation error since the precedence of `<<` is higher than that of `>`.
   Correction: Use parenthesis around `emp1 > emp2`
c) *Error:* \n here is not represented as a character
   Correction: Replace `\n` by `'\n'`

23.5 a) `00`
   `Program`
b) `C++`
   `Program`
c) `++Programming`
d) `9.4     8.1`
e) `63.51`
f) `99`
   `143`
   `63`

Exercises

23.6 *(Write C++ Statements)* Write a statement for each of the following:

a) Print integer 40000 left justified in a 15-digit field.

b) Read a string into character array variable state.

c) Print 200 with and without a sign.

d) Print the decimal value 100 in hexadecimal form preceded by 0x.

e) Read characters into array charArray until the character 'p' is encountered, up to a limit of 10 characters (including the terminating null character). Extract the delimiter from the input stream, and discard it.

f) Print 1.234 in a 9-digit field with preceding zeros.

23.7 *(Inputting Decimal, Octal and Hexadecimal Values)* Write a program to test the inputting of integer values in decimal, octal and hexadecimal formats. Output each integer read by the program in all three formats. Test the program with the following input data: 10, 010, 0x10.

23.8 *(Printing Pointer Values as Integers)* Write a program that prints pointer values, using casts to all the integer data types. Which ones print strange values? Which ones cause errors?

23.9 *(Printing with Field Widths)* Write a program to test the results of printing the strings Object, Oriented and Program in various-sized fields. What happens when the characters are printed in fields containing fewer digits than the characters?

23.10 *(Precision)* Write a program that prints the value 993.0015621 with a precision of 0, 1, 2, 3, 4, 5 and 6.

23.11 *(Length of a String)* Write a program that inputs a string from the keyboard and determines the length of the string. Print the string in a field width that is thrice the length of the string. Fill the blank spaces with *.

23.12 *(Converting Meters to Kilometers)* Write a program that converts distance in integer meters to distance in floating-point kilometers with 2 digits of precision. Use the formula

```
kilometers = meters / 1000.00;
```

to perform the calculation. The output should be printed in two columns.

23.13 In some programming languages, strings are entered surrounded by either single or double quotation marks. Write a program that reads the three strings suzy, "suzy" and 'suzy'. Are the single and double quotes ignored or read as part of the string?

23.14 *(Reading Phone Numbers with and Overloaded Stream Extraction Operator)* In Fig. 19.5, the stream extraction and stream insertion operators were overloaded for input and output of objects of the PhoneNumber class. Rewrite the stream extraction operator to perform the following error checking on input. The operator>> function will need to be reimplemented.

a) Input the entire phone number into an array. Test that the proper number of characters has been entered. There should be a total of 14 characters read for a phone number of the form (800) 555-1212. Use ios_base-member-function clear to set failbit for improper input.

b) The area code and exchange do not begin with 0 or 1. Test the first digit of the area-code and exchange portions of the phone number to be sure that neither begins with 0 or 1. Use ios_base-member-function clear to set failbit for improper input.

c) The middle digit of an area code used to be limited to 0 or 1 (though this has changed). Test the middle digit for a value of 0 or 1. Use the ios_base-member-function clear to set failbit for improper input. If none of the above operations results in failbit being set for improper input, copy the parts of the telephone number into the PhoneNumber object's areaCode, exchange and line members. If failbit has been set on the input, have the program print an error message and end, rather than print the phone number.

23.15 *(Point Class)* Write a program that accomplishes each of the following:

a) Create a user-defined class Point that contains the private integer data members xCoordinate and yCoordinate and declares stream insertion and stream extraction overloaded operator functions as friends of the class.

b) Define the stream insertion and stream extraction operator functions. The stream extraction operator function should determine whether the data entered is valid, and, if not, it should set the failbit to indicate improper input. The stream insertion operator should not be able to display the point after an input error occurred.

c) Write a main function that tests input and output of user-defined class Point, using the overloaded stream extraction and stream insertion operators.

23.16 *(Complex Class)* Write a program that accomplishes each of the following:

a) Create a user-defined class Complex that contains the private integer data members real and imaginary and declares stream insertion and stream extraction overloaded operator functions as friends of the class.

b) Define the stream insertion and stream extraction operator functions. The stream extraction operator function should determine whether the data entered is valid, and, if not, it should set failbit to indicate improper input. The input should be of the form

3 + 8i

c) The values can be negative or positive, and it's possible that one of the two values is not provided, in which case the appropriate data member should be set to 0. The stream insertion operator should not be able to display the point if an input error occurred. For negative imaginary values, a minus sign should be printed rather than a plus sign.

d) Write a main function that tests input and output of user-defined class Complex, using the overloaded stream extraction and stream insertion operators.

23.17 *(Printing a Table of ASCII Values)* Write a program that uses a for statement to print a table of ASCII values for the characters in the ASCII character set from 33 to 126. The program should print the decimal value, octal value, hexadecimal value and character value for each character. Use the stream manipulators dec, oct and hex to print the integer values.

23.18 *(String-Terminating Null Character)* Write a program to show that the getline and three-argument get istream member functions both end the input string with a string-terminating null character. Also, show that get leaves the delimiter character on the input stream, whereas getline extracts the delimiter character and discards it. What happens to the unread characters in the stream?

24

Exception Handling: A Deeper Look

It is common sense to take a method and try it. If it fails, admit it frankly and try another. But above all, try something.
—Franklin Delano Roosevelt

If they're running and they don't look where they're going I have to come out from somewhere and catch them.
—Jerome David Salinger

Objectives

In this chapter you'll learn:

- To use `try`, `catch` and `throw` to detect, handle and indicate exceptions, respectively.

- To process uncaught and unexpected exceptions.

- To declare new exception classes.

- How stack unwinding enables exceptions not caught in one scope to be caught in another.

- To handle `new` failures.

- To use `unique_ptr` to prevent memory leaks.

- To understand the standard exception hierarchy.

24.1 Introduction

As you know, an **exception** is an indication of a problem that occurs during a program's execution. **Exception handling** enables you to create applications that can resolve (or handle) exceptions. In many cases, handling an exception allows a program to continue executing as if no problem had been encountered. The features presented in this chapter enable you to write **robust** and **fault-tolerant programs** that can deal with problems continue executing or terminate gracefully.

We begin with a review of exception-handling concepts via an example that demonstrates handling an exception that occurs when a function attempts to divide by zero. We show how to handle exceptions that occur in a constructor or destructor and exceptions that occur if operator new fails to allocate memory for an object. We introduce several C++ Standard Library exception handling classes.

Software Engineering Observation 24.1

Exception handling provides a standard mechanism for processing errors. This is especially important when working on a project with a large team of programmers.

Software Engineering Observation 24.2

Incorporate your exception-handling strategy into your system from inception. Including effective exception handling after a system has been implemented can be difficult.

24.2 Example: Handling an Attempt to Divide by Zero

Let's consider a simple example of exception handling (Figs. 24.1–24.2). We show how to deal with a common arithmetic problem—division by zero. In C++, *division by zero* using integer arithmetic typically causes a program to terminate prematurely. In floating-point arithmetic, some C++ implementations allow division by zero, in which case a result of positive or negative infinity is displayed as INF or -INF, respectively.

In this example, we define a function named quotient that receives two integers input by the user and divides its first int parameter by its second int parameter. Before performing the division, the function casts the first int parameter's value to type double. Then, the second int parameter's value is (implicitly) promoted to type double for the calculation. So function quotient actually performs the division using two double values and returns a double result.

Although division by zero is often allowed in floating-point arithmetic, for the purpose of this example we treat any attempt to divide by zero as an error. Thus, function quotient tests its second parameter to ensure that it isn't zero before allowing the division to proceed. If the second parameter is zero, the function throws an exception to indicate to the caller that a problem occurred. The caller (main in this example) can then process the exception and allow the user to type two new values before calling function quotient again. In this way, the program can continue executing even after an improper value is entered, thus making the program more robust.

The example consists of two files. DivideByZeroException.h (Fig. 24.1) defines an *exception class* that represents the type of the problem that might occur in the example, and fig24_02.cpp (Fig. 24.2) defines the quotient function and the main function that calls it. Function main contains the code that demonstrates exception handling.

Defining an Exception Class to Represent the Type of Problem That Might Occur
Figure 24.1 defines class DivideByZeroException as a derived class of Standard Library class **runtime_error** (defined in header **<stdexcept>**). Class runtime_error—a derived class of Standard Library class **exception** (defined in header **<exception>**)—is the C++ standard base class for representing runtime errors. Class exception is the standard C++ base class for all exceptions. (Section 24.11 discusses class exception and its derived classes in detail.) A typical exception class that derives from the runtime_error class defines only a constructor (e.g., lines 12–13) that passes an error-message string to the base-class runtime_error constructor. Every exception class that derives directly or indirectly from exception contains the virtual function **what**, which returns an exception object's error message. You're not required to derive a custom exception class, such as DivideByZeroException, from the standard exception classes provided by C++. However, doing so allows you to use the virtual function what to obtain an appropriate error message. We use an object of this DivideByZeroException class in Fig. 24.2 to indicate when an attempt is made to divide by zero.

```
 1   // Fig. 24.1: DivideByZeroException.h
 2   // Class DivideByZeroException definition.
 3   #include <stdexcept> // stdexcept header contains runtime_error
 4   using namespace std;
 5
 6   // DivideByZeroException objects should be thrown by functions
 7   // upon detecting division-by-zero exceptions
 8   class DivideByZeroException : public runtime_error
 9   {
10   public:
11      // constructor specifies default error message
12      DivideByZeroException()
13         : runtime_error( "attempted to divide by zero" ) {}
14   }; // end class DivideByZeroException
```

Fig. 24.1 | Class DivideByZeroException definition.

Demonstrating Exception Handling
Figure 24.2 uses exception handling to wrap code that might throw a "divide-by-zero" exception and to handle that exception, should one occur. The user enters two integers, which are passed as arguments to function quotient (lines 10–18). This function divides its first

parameter (numerator) by its second parameter (denominator). Assuming that the user does not specify 0 as the denominator for the division, function quotient returns the division result. If the user inputs 0 for the denominator, quotient throws an exception. In the sample output, the first two lines show a successful calculation, and the next two show a failure due to an attempt to divide by zero. When the exception occurs, the program informs the user of the mistake and prompts the user to input two new integers. After we discuss the code, we'll consider the user inputs and flow of program control that yield these outputs.

```cpp
1   // Fig. 24.2: fig24_02.cpp
2   // A simple exception-handling example that checks for
3   // divide-by-zero exceptions.
4   #include <iostream>
5   #include "DivideByZeroException.h" // DivideByZeroException class
6   using namespace std;
7
8   // perform division and throw DivideByZeroException object if
9   // divide-by-zero exception occurs
10  double quotient( int numerator, int denominator )
11  {
12     // throw DivideByZeroException if trying to divide by zero
13     if ( denominator == 0 )
14        throw DivideByZeroException(); // terminate function
15
16     // return division result
17     return static_cast< double >( numerator ) / denominator;
18  } // end function quotient
19
20  int main()
21  {
22     int number1; // user-specified numerator
23     int number2; // user-specified denominator
24     double result; // result of division
25
26     cout << "Enter two integers (end-of-file to end): ";
27
28     // enable user to enter two integers to divide
29     while ( cin >> number1 >> number2 )
30     {
31        // try block contains code that might throw exception
32        // and code that will not execute if an exception occurs
33        try
34        {
35           result = quotient( number1, number2 );
36           cout << "The quotient is: " << result << endl;
37        } // end try
38        catch ( DivideByZeroException &divideByZeroException )
39        {
40           cout << "Exception occurred: "
41              << divideByZeroException.what() << endl;
42        } // end catch
```

Fig. 24.2 | Exception-handling example that throws exceptions on attempts to divide by zero. (Part 1 of 2.)

```
43
44            cout << "\nEnter two integers (end-of-file to end): ";
45       } // end while
46
47       cout << endl;
48   } // end main
```

```
Enter two integers (end-of-file to end): 100 7
The quotient is: 14.2857

Enter two integers (end-of-file to end): 100 0
Exception occurred: attempted to divide by zero

Enter two integers (end-of-file to end): ^Z
```

Fig. 24.2 | Exception-handling example that throws exceptions on attempts to divide by zero.
(Part 2 of 2.)

Enclosing Code in a `try` Block

The program begins by prompting the user to enter two integers. The integers are input in the condition of the `while` loop (line 29). Line 35 passes the values to function `quotient` (lines 10–18), which either divides the integers and returns a result, or **throws an exception** (i.e., indicates that an error occurred) on an attempt to divide by zero. Exception handling is geared to situations in which the function that detects an error is unable to handle it.

A `try` block encloses statements that might cause exceptions and statements that should be skipped if an exception occurs. The `try` block in lines 33–37 encloses the invocation of function `quotient` and the statement that displays the division result. In this example, because the invocation of function `quotient` (line 35) can *throw* an exception, we enclose this function invocation in a `try` block. Enclosing the output statement (line 36) in the `try` block ensures that the output will occur only if function `quotient` returns a result.

Software Engineering Observation 24.3

Exceptions may surface through explicitly mentioned code in a `try` block, through calls to other functions and through deeply nested function calls initiated by code in a `try` block.

Defining a `catch` Handler to Process a `DivideByZeroException`

Exceptions are processed by `catch` handlers. At least one `catch` handler (lines 38–42) must immediately follow each `try` block. The exception parameter is declared as a *reference* to the type of exception the `catch` handler can process (`DivideByZeroException` in this case). When an exception occurs in a `try` block, the `catch` handler that executes is the one whose type matches the type of the exception that occurred (i.e., the type in the `catch` block matches the thrown exception type exactly or is a base class of it). If an exception parameter includes an optional parameter name, the `catch` handler can use that parameter name to interact with the caught exception in the body of the `catch` handler, which is delimited by braces ({ and }). A `catch` handler typically reports the error to the user, logs it to a file, terminates the program gracefully or tries an alternate strategy to accomplish the failed task. In this example, the catch handler simply reports that the user attempted to divide by zero. Then the program prompts the user to enter two new integer values.

Common Programming Error 24.1

It's a syntax error to place code between a try block and its corresponding catch handlers or between its catch handlers.

Common Programming Error 24.2

Each catch handler can have only a single parameter—specifying a comma-separated list of exception parameters is a syntax error.

Common Programming Error 24.3

It's a logic error to catch the same type in two different catch handlers following a single try block.

Termination Model of Exception Handling

If an exception occurs as the result of a statement in a try block, the try block expires (i.e., terminates immediately). Next, the program searches for the first catch handler that can process the type of exception that occurred. The program locates the matching catch by comparing the thrown exception's type to each catch's exception-parameter type until the program finds a match. A match occurs if the types are *identical* or if the thrown exception's type is a *derived class* of the exception-parameter type. When a match occurs, the code contained in the matching catch handler executes. When a catch handler finishes processing by reaching its closing right brace (}), the exception is considered handled and the local variables defined within the catch handler (including the catch parameter) go out of scope. Program control does *not* return to the point at which the exception occurred (known as the **throw point**), because the try block has *expired*. Rather, control resumes with the first statement (line 44) after the last catch handler following the try block. This is known as the **termination model of exception handling**. Some languages use the re-sumption model of exception handling, in which, after an exception is handled, control resumes just after the throw point. As with any other block of code, when a try block terminates, local variables defined in the block go out of scope.

Common Programming Error 24.4

Logic errors can occur if you assume that after an exception is handled, control will return to the first statement after the throw point.

Error-Prevention Tip 24.1

With exception handling, a program can continue executing (rather than terminating) after dealing with a problem. This helps ensure the kind of robust applications that con-tribute to what's called mission-critical computing or business-critical computing.

If the try block completes its execution successfully (i.e., no exceptions occur in the try block), then the program ignores the catch handlers and program control continues with the first statement after the last catch following that try block.

If an exception that occurs in a try block has no matching catch handler, or if an exception occurs in a statement that is not in a try block, the function that contains the statement terminates immediately, and the program attempts to locate an enclosing `try` block in the calling function. This process is called **stack unwinding** and is discussed in Section 24.6.

Flow of Program Control When the User Enters a Nonzero Denominator

Consider the flow of control when the user inputs the numerator 100 and the denominator 7. In line 13, function `quotient` determines that the `denominator` does not equal zero, so line 17 performs the division and returns the result (14.2857) to line 35 as a `double`. Program control then continues sequentially from line 35, so line 36 displays the division result—line 37 ends the `try` block. Because the `try` block completed successfully and did not throw an exception, the program does not execute the statements contained in the `catch` handler (lines 38–42), and control continues to line 44 (the first line of code after the `catch` handler), which prompts the user to enter two more integers.

Flow of Program Control When the User Enters a Denominator of Zero

Now consider the case in which the user inputs the numerator 100 and the denominator 0. In line 13, `quotient` determines that the `denominator` equals zero, which indicates an attempt to divide by zero. Line 14 throws an exception, which we represent as an object of class `DivideByZeroException` (Fig. 24.1).

To throw an exception, line 14 uses keyword **throw** followed by an operand that represents the type of exception to throw. Normally, a `throw` statement specifies one operand. (In Section 24.4, we discuss how to use a `throw` statement with no operand.) The operand of a `throw` can be of any type. If the operand is an object, we call it an **exception object**—in this example, the exception object is an object of type `DivideByZeroException`. However, a `throw` operand also can assume other values, such as the value of an expression that does not result in an object of a class (e.g., `throw x > 5`) or the value of an `int` (e.g., `throw 5`). The examples in this chapter focus exclusively on throwing objects of exception classes.

> **Common Programming Error 24.5**
>
> *Use caution when throwing the result of a conditional expression (?:)—promotion rules could cause the value to be of a type different from the one expected. For example, when throwing an `int` or a `double` from the same conditional expression, the `int` is promoted to a `double`. So, a catch handler that catches an `int` would never execute based on such a conditional expression.*

As part of throwing an exception, the `throw` operand is created and used to initialize the parameter in the `catch` handler, which we discuss momentarily. The `throw` statement in line 14 creates a `DivideByZeroException` object. When line 14 throws the exception, function `quotient` exits immediately. So, line 14 throws the exception *before* function `quotient` can perform the division in line 17. This is a central characteristic of exception handling: *A function should throw an exception before the error has an opportunity to occur.*

Because we enclosed the call to `quotient` (line 35) in a `try` block, program control enters the `catch` handler (lines 38–42) that immediately follows the `try` block. This `catch` handler serves as the exception handler for the divide-by-zero exception. In general, when an exception is thrown within a `try` block, the exception is caught by a `catch` handler that specifies the type matching the thrown exception. In this program, the `catch` handler specifies that it catches `DivideByZeroException` objects—this type matches the object type thrown in function `quotient`. Actually, the `catch` handler catches a *reference* to the `DivideByZeroException` object created by function `quotient`'s `throw` statement (line 14), so that the `catch` handler does not make a copy of the exception object.

The `catch`'s body (lines 40–41) prints the error message returned by function `what` of base-class `runtime_error`—i.e., the string that the `DivideByZeroException` constructor (lines 12–13 in Fig. 24.1) passed to the `runtime_error` base-class constructor.

Performance Tip 24.1

Catching an exception object by reference eliminates the overhead of copying the object that represents the thrown exception.

Good Programming Practice 24.1

Associating each type of runtime error with an appropriately named exception object improves program clarity.

24.3 When to Use Exception Handling

Exception handling is designed to process **synchronous errors**, which occur when a statement executes, such as *out-of-range array subscripts*, *arithmetic overflow* (i.e., a value outside the representable range of values), *division by zero*, *invalid function parameters* and *unsuccessful memory allocation* (due to lack of memory). Exception handling is not designed to process errors associated with **asynchronous events** (e.g., disk I/O completions, network message arrivals, mouse clicks and keystrokes), which occur in parallel with, and independent of, the program's flow of control.

Software Engineering Observation 24.4

Exception handling provides a single, uniform technique for processing problems. This helps programmers on large projects understand each other's error-processing code.

Software Engineering Observation 24.5

Avoid using exception handling as an alternate form of flow of control. These "additional" exceptions can "get in the way" of genuine error-type exceptions.

Software Engineering Observation 24.6

Exception handling enables predefined software components to communicate problems to application-specific components, which can then process the problems in an application-specific manner.

Exception handling also is useful for processing problems that occur when a program interacts with software elements, such as member functions, constructors, destructors and classes. Such software elements often use exceptions to notify programs when problems occur. This enables you to implement *customized error handling* for each application.

Performance Tip 24.2

When no exceptions occur, exception-handling code incurs little or no performance penalty. Thus, programs that implement exception handling operate more efficiently than do programs that intermix error-handling code with program logic.

Software Engineering Observation 24.7

Functions with common error conditions should return 0 or NULL (or other appropriate values, such as bools) rather than throw exceptions. A program calling such a function can check the return value to determine success or failure of the function call.

Complex applications normally consist of predefined software components and application-specific components that use the predefined components. When a predefined component encounters a problem, that component needs a mechanism to communicate the problem to the application-specific component—the *predefined component cannot know in advance how each application processes a problem that occurs.*

24.4 Rethrowing an Exception

It's possible that an exception handler, upon receiving an exception, might decide either that it cannot process that exception or that it can process the exception only partially. In such cases, the exception handler can *defer the exception handling (or perhaps a portion of it) to another exception handler.* In either case, you achieve this by **rethrowing the exception** via the statement

```
throw;
```

Regardless of whether a handler can process an exception, the handler can *rethrow* the exception for further processing outside the handler. The next enclosing try block detects the rethrown exception, which a catch handler listed after that enclosing try block attempts to handle.

Common Programming Error 24.6

*Executing an empty throw statement outside a catch handler calls function **terminate**, which abandons exception processing and terminates the program immediately.*

The program of Fig. 24.3 demonstrates rethrowing an exception. In main's try block (lines 29–34), line 32 calls function throwException (lines 8–24). The throwException function also contains a try block (lines 11–15), from which the throw statement in line 14 throws an instance of standard-library-class exception. Function throwException's catch handler (lines 16–21) catches this exception, prints an error message (lines 18–19) and rethrows the exception (line 20). This terminates function throwException and returns control to line 32 in the try...catch block in main. The try block terminates (so line 33 does not execute), and the catch handler in main (lines 35–38) catches this exception and prints an error message (line 37). Since we do not use the exception parameters in the catch handlers of this example, we omit the exception parameter names and specify only the type of exception to catch (lines 16 and 35).

```
1   // Fig. 24.3: fig24_03.cpp
2   // Rethrowing an exception.
3   #include <iostream>
4   #include <exception>
5   using namespace std;
```

Fig. 24.3 | Rethrowing an exception. (Part 1 of 2.)

```
6
7    // throw, catch and rethrow exception
8    void throwException()
9    {
10       // throw exception and catch it immediately
11       try
12       {
13          cout << "  Function throwException throws an exception\n";
14          throw exception(); // generate exception
15       } // end try
16       catch ( exception & ) // handle exception
17       {
18          cout << "  Exception handled in function throwException"
19             << "\n  Function throwException rethrows exception";
20          throw; // rethrow exception for further processing
21       } // end catch
22
23       cout << "This also should not print\n";
24    } // end function throwException
25
26    int main()
27    {
28       // throw exception
29       try
30       {
31          cout << "\nmain invokes function throwException\n";
32          throwException();
33          cout << "This should not print\n";
34       } // end try
35       catch ( exception & ) // handle exception
36       {
37          cout << "\n\nException handled in main\n";
38       } // end catch
39
40       cout << "Program control continues after catch in main\n";
41    } // end main
```

```
main invokes function throwException
  Function throwException throws an exception
  Exception handled in function throwException
  Function throwException rethrows exception

Exception handled in main
Program control continues after catch in main
```

Fig. 24.3 | Rethrowing an exception. (Part 2 of 2.)

24.5 Processing Unexpected Exceptions

Function unexpected calls the function registered with function **set_unexpected** (defined in header <exception>). If no function has been registered in this manner, function terminate is called by default. Cases in which function terminate is called include:

1. the exception mechanism cannot find a matching catch for a thrown exception
2. a destructor attempts to throw an exception during stack unwinding

3. an attempt is made to rethrow an exception when there's no exception currently being handled

4. a call to function `unexpected` defaults to calling function `terminate`

(Section 15.5.1 of the C++ Standard Document discusses several additional cases.) Function `set_terminate` can specify the function to invoke when `terminate` is called. Otherwise, `terminate` calls **abort**, *which terminates the program without calling the destructors of any remaining objects of automatic or static storage class.* This could lead to resource leaks when a program terminates prematurely.

> **Common Programming Error 24.7**
>
> *Aborting a program component due to an uncaught exception could leave a resource—such as a file stream or an I/O device—in a state in which other programs are unable to acquire the resource. This is known as a resource leak.*

Function `set_terminate` and function `set_unexpected` each return a pointer to the last function called by `terminate` and `unexpected`, respectively (0, the first time each is called). This enables you to save the function pointer so it can be restored later. Functions `set_terminate` and `set_unexpected` take as arguments pointers to functions with `void` return types and no arguments.

If the last action of a programmer-defined termination function is not to exit a program, function `abort` will be called to end program execution.

24.6 Stack Unwinding

When an exception is thrown but not caught in a particular scope, the function call stack is "unwound," and an attempt is made to `catch` the exception in the next outer `try...catch` block. Unwinding the function call stack means that the function in which the exception was not caught terminates, all local variables in that function are destroyed and control returns to the statement that originally invoked that function. If a `try` block encloses that statement, an attempt is made to `catch` the exception. If a `try` block does not enclose that statement, stack unwinding occurs again. If no `catch` handler ever catches this exception, function `terminate` is called to terminate the program. The program of Fig. 24.4 demonstrates stack unwinding.

```
1   // Fig. 24.4: fig24_04.cpp
2   // Stack unwinding.
3   #include <iostream>
4   #include <stdexcept>
5   using namespace std;
6
7   // function3 throws runtime error
8   void function3() throw ( runtime_error )
9   {
10      cout << "In function 3" << endl;
11
```

Fig. 24.4 | Stack unwinding. (Part 1 of 2.)

```
12        // no try block, stack unwinding occurs, return control to function2
13        throw runtime_error( "runtime_error in function3" ); // no print
14    } // end function3
15
16    // function2 invokes function3
17    void function2() throw ( runtime_error )
18    {
19        cout << "function3 is called inside function2" << endl;
20        function3(); // stack unwinding occurs, return control to function1
21    } // end function2
22
23    // function1 invokes function2
24    void function1() throw ( runtime_error )
25    {
26        cout << "function2 is called inside function1" << endl;
27        function2(); // stack unwinding occurs, return control to main
28    } // end function1
29
30    // demonstrate stack unwinding
31    int main()
32    {
33        // invoke function1
34        try
35        {
36            cout << "function1 is called inside main" << endl;
37            function1(); // call function1 which throws runtime_error
38        } // end try
39        catch ( runtime_error &error ) // handle runtime error
40        {
41            cout << "Exception occurred: " << error.what() << endl;
42            cout << "Exception handled in main" << endl;
43        } // end catch
44    } // end main
```

```
function1 is called inside main
function2 is called inside function1
function3 is called inside function2
In function 3
Exception occurred: runtime_error in function3
Exception handled in main
```

Fig. 24.4 | Stack unwinding. (Part 2 of 2.)

In main, the try block (lines 34–38) calls function1 (lines 24–28). Next, function1 calls function2 (lines 17–21), which in turn calls function3 (lines 8–14). Line 13 of function3 throws a runtime_error object. However, because no try block encloses the throw statement in line 13, stack unwinding occurs—function3 terminates at line 13, then returns control to the statement in function2 that invoked function3 (i.e., line 20). Because no try block encloses line 20, stack unwinding occurs again—function2 terminates at line 20 and returns control to the statement in function1 that invoked function2 (i.e., line 27). Because no try block encloses line 27, stack unwinding occurs one more time—function1 terminates at line 27 and returns control to the statement in main that invoked function1 (i.e., line 37). The try block of lines 34–38 encloses this statement, so the first matching catch handler located after this try block (line 39–43) catches and processes the exception. Line 41 uses function what to display the exception message. Recall that function what is a virtual function of class exception that can be overridden by a derived class to return an appropriate error message.

24.7 Constructors, Destructors and Exception Handling

First, let's discuss an issue that we've mentioned but not yet resolved satisfactorily: What happens when an error is detected in a *constructor*? For example, how should an object's constructor respond when new fails because it was unable to allocate required memory for storing that object's internal representation? Because the constructor cannot return a value to indicate an error, we must choose an alternative means of indicating that the object has not been constructed properly. One scheme is to return the improperly constructed object and hope that anyone using it would make appropriate tests to determine that it's in an inconsistent state. Another scheme is to set some variable outside the constructor. The preferred alternative is to require the constructor to throw an exception that contains the error information, thus offering an opportunity for the program to handle the failure.

Before an exception is thrown by a constructor, destructors are called for any member objects built as part of the object being constructed. Destructors are called for every automatic object constructed in a try block before an exception is thrown. Stack unwinding is guaranteed to have been completed at the point that an exception handler begins executing. If a destructor invoked as a result of stack unwinding throws an exception, terminate is called.

If an object has member objects, and if an exception is thrown before the outer object is fully constructed, then destructors will be executed for the member objects that have been constructed prior to the occurrence of the exception. If an array of objects has been partially constructed when an exception occurs, only the destructors for the constructed objects in the array will be called.

An exception could preclude the operation of code that would normally *release a resource* (such as memory or a file), thus causing a *resource leak*. One technique to resolve this problem is to initialize a local object to acquire the resource. When an exception occurs, the destructor for that object will be invoked and can free the resource.

 Error-Prevention Tip 24.2
When an exception is thrown from the constructor for an object that's created in a new expression, the dynamically allocated memory for that object is released.

24.8 Exceptions and Inheritance

Various exception classes can be derived from a common base class, as we discussed in Section 24.2, when we created class DivideByZeroException as a derived class of class exception. If a catch handler catches a pointer or reference to an exception object of a base-class type, it also can catch a pointer or reference to all objects of classes publicly derived from that base class—this allows for polymorphic processing of related errors.

Error-Prevention Tip 24.3

Using inheritance with exceptions enables an exception handler to catch related errors with concise notation. One approach is to catch each type of pointer or reference to a derived-class exception object individually, but a more concise approach is to catch pointers or references to base-class exception objects instead. Also, catching pointers or references to derived-class exception objects individually is error prone, especially if you forget to test explicitly for one or more of the derived-class pointer or reference types.

24.9 Processing new Failures

The C++ standard specifies that, when operator new fails, it throws a **bad_alloc** exception (defined in header <new>). In this section, we present two examples of new failing. The first uses the version of new that throws a bad_alloc exception when new fails. The second uses function **set_new_handler** to handle new failures. [*Note:* The examples in Figs. 24.5–24.6 allocate large amounts of dynamic memory, which could cause your computer to become sluggish.]

new *Throwing* bad_alloc *on Failure*

Figure 24.5 demonstrates new throwing bad_alloc on failure to allocate the requested memory. The for statement (lines 16–20) inside the try block should loop 50 times and, on each pass, allocate an array of 50,000,000 double values. If new fails and throws a bad_alloc exception, the loop terminates, and the program continues in line 22, where the catch handler catches and processes the exception. Lines 24–25 print the message "Exception occurred:" followed by the message returned from the base-class-exception version of function what (i.e., an implementation-defined exception-specific message, such as "Allocation Failure" in Microsoft Visual C++). The output shows that the program performed only four iterations of the loop before new failed and threw the bad_alloc exception. Your output might differ based on the physical memory, disk space available for virtual memory on your system and the compiler you're using.

```
1   // Fig. 24.5: fig24_05.cpp
2   // Demonstrating standard new throwing bad_alloc when memory
3   // cannot be allocated.
4   #include <iostream>
5   #include <new> // bad_alloc class is defined here
6   using namespace std;
7
8   int main()
9   {
10     double *ptr[ 50 ];
11
12     // aim each ptr[i] at a big block of memory
13     try
14     {
15        // allocate memory for ptr[ i ]; new throws bad_alloc on failure
16        for ( int i = 0; i < 50; ++i )
17        {
```

Fig. 24.5 | new throwing bad_alloc when memory cannot be allocated. (Part 1 of 2.)

```
18              ptr[ i ] = new double[ 50000000 ]; // may throw exception
19              cout << "ptr[" << i << "] points to 50,000,000 new doubles\n";
20          } // end for
21      } // end try
22      catch ( bad_alloc &memoryAllocationException )
23      {
24          cerr << "Exception occurred: "
25              << memoryAllocationException.what() << endl;
26      } // end catch
27  } // end main
```

```
ptr[0] points to 50,000,000 new doubles
ptr[1] points to 50,000,000 new doubles
ptr[2] points to 50,000,000 new doubles
ptr[3] points to 50,000,000 new doubles
Exception occurred: bad allocation
```

Fig. 24.5 | new throwing bad_alloc when memory cannot be allocated. (Part 2 of 2.)

new *Returning 0 on Failure*

The C++ standard specifies that compilers can use an older version of new that returns 0 upon failure. For this purpose, header <new> defines object **nothrow** (of type nothrow_t), which is used as follows:

```
double *ptr = new( nothrow ) double[ 50000000 ];
```

The preceding statement uses the version of new that does *not* throw bad_alloc exceptions (i.e., nothrow) to allocate an array of 50,000,000 doubles.

> **Software Engineering Observation 24.8**
>
> *To make programs more robust, use the version of new that throws bad_alloc exceptions on failure.*

Handling **new** *Failures Using Function* **set_new_handler**

An additional feature for handling new failures is function set_new_handler (prototyped in standard header <new>). This function takes as its argument a pointer to a function that takes no arguments and returns void. This pointer points to the function that will be called if new fails. This provides you with a uniform approach to handling all new failures, regardless of where a failure occurs in the program. Once set_new_handler registers a **new** handler in the program, operator new does not throw bad_alloc on failure; rather, it defers the error handling to the new-handler function.

If new allocates memory successfully, it returns a pointer to that memory. If new fails to allocate memory and set_new_handler did not register a new-handler function, new throws a bad_alloc exception. If new fails to allocate memory and a new-handler function has been registered, the new-handler function is called. The C++ standard specifies that the new-handler function should perform one of the following tasks:

1. Make more memory available by deleting other dynamically allocated memory (or telling the user to close other applications) and return to operator new to attempt to allocate memory again.

2. Throw an exception of type bad_alloc.

3. Call function abort or exit (both found in header <cstdlib>) to terminate the program.

Figure 24.6 demonstrates set_new_handler. Function customNewHandler (lines 9–13) prints an error message (line 11), then calls abort (line 12) to terminate the program. The output shows that the loop iterated four times before new failed and invoked function customNewHandler. Your output might differ based on the physical memory and disk space available for virtual memory on your system and your compiler.

```cpp
 1  // Fig. 24.6: fig24_06.cpp
 2  // Demonstrating set_new_handler.
 3  #include <iostream>
 4  #include <new> // set_new_handler function prototype
 5  #include <cstdlib> // abort function prototype
 6  using namespace std;
 7
 8  // handle memory allocation failure
 9  void customNewHandler()
10  {
11     cerr << "customNewHandler was called";
12     abort();
13  } // end function customNewHandler
14
15  // using set_new_handler to handle failed memory allocation
16  int main()
17  {
18     double *ptr[ 50 ];
19
20     // specify that customNewHandler should be called on
21     // memory allocation failure
22     set_new_handler( customNewHandler );
23
24     // aim each ptr[i] at a big block of memory; customNewHandler will be
25     // called on failed memory allocation
26     for ( int i = 0; i < 50; ++i )
27     {
28        ptr[ i ] = new double[ 50000000 ]; // may throw exception
29        cout << "ptr[" << i << "] points to 50,000,000 new doubles\n";
30     } // end for
31  }  // end main
```

```
ptr[0] points to 50,000,000 new doubles
ptr[1] points to 50,000,000 new doubles
ptr[2] points to 50,000,000 new doubles
ptr[3] points to 50,000,000 new doubles
customNewHandler was called
This application has requested the Runtime to terminate it in an unusual way.
Please contact the application's support team for more information.
```

Fig. 24.6 | set_new_handler specifying the function to call when new fails.

24.10 Class unique_ptr and Dynamic Memory Allocation[1]

A common programming practice is to allocate dynamic memory, assign the address of that memory to a pointer, use the pointer to manipulate the memory and deallocate the memory with delete when the memory is no longer needed. If an exception occurs after successful memory allocation but *before* the delete statement executes, a *memory leak* could occur. The C++ standard provides class template **unique_ptr** in header **<memory>** to deal with this situation.

An object of class unique_ptr maintains a pointer to dynamically allocated memory. When a unique_ptr object destructor is called (for example, when a unique_ptr object goes out of scope), it performs a delete operation on its pointer data member. Class template unique_ptr provides overloaded operators * and -> so that a unique_ptr object can be used just as a regular pointer variable is. Figure 24.9 demonstrates a unique_ptr object that points to a dynamically allocated object of class Integer (Figs. 24.7–24.8).

```
1   // Fig. 24.7: Integer.h
2   // Integer class definition.
3
4   class Integer
5   {
6   public:
7      Integer( int i = 0 ); // Integer default constructor
8      ~Integer(); // Integer destructor
9      void setInteger( int i ); // functions to set Integer
10     int getInteger() const; // function to return Integer
11  private:
12     int value;
13  }; // end class Integer
```

Fig. 24.7 | Integer class definition.

```
1   // Fig. 24.8: Integer.cpp
2   // Member function definitions of class Integer.
3   #include <iostream>
4   #include "Integer.h"
5   using namespace std;
6
7   // Integer default constructor
8   Integer::Integer( int i )
9      : value( i )
10  {
11     cout << "Constructor for Integer " << value << endl;
12  } // end Integer constructor
13
```

Fig. 24.8 | Member function definitions of class Integer. (Part 1 of 2.)

---

1. Class unique_ptr is a part of the new C++ standard that's already implemented in Visual C++ 2010 and GNU C++. This class replaces the deprecated auto_ptr class. To compile this program in GNU C++, use the -std=C++0x compiler flag.

```
14  // Integer destructor
15  Integer::~Integer()
16  {
17     cout << "Destructor for Integer " << value << endl;
18  } // end Integer destructor
19
20  // set Integer value
21  void Integer::setInteger( int i )
22  {
23     value = i;
24  } // end function setInteger
25
26  // return Integer value
27  int Integer::getInteger() const
28  {
29     return value;
30  } // end function getInteger
```

Fig. 24.8 | Member function definitions of class `Integer`. (Part 2 of 2.)

Line 15 of Fig. 24.9 creates `unique_ptr` object `ptrToInteger` and initializes it with a pointer to a dynamically allocated `Integer` object that contains the value 7. Line 18 uses the `unique_ptr` overloaded `->` operator to invoke function `setInteger` on the `Integer` object that `ptrToInteger` manages. Line 21 uses the `unique_ptr` overloaded `*` operator to dereference `ptrToInteger`, then uses the dot (`.`) operator to invoke function `getInteger` on the `Integer` object. Like a regular pointer, a `unique_ptr`'s `->` and `*` overloaded operators can be used to access the object to which the `unique_ptr` points.

```
1   // Fig. 24.9: fig24_09.cpp
2   // unique_ptr object manages dynamically allocated memory.
3   #include <iostream>
4   #include <memory>
5   using namespace std;
6
7   #include "Integer.h"
8
9   // use unique_ptr to manipulate Integer object
10  int main()
11  {
12     cout << "Creating a unique_ptr object that points to an Integer\n";
13
14     // "aim" unique_ptr at Integer object
15     unique_ptr< Integer > ptrToInteger( new Integer( 7 ) );
16
17     cout << "\nUsing the unique_ptr to manipulate the Integer\n";
18     ptrToInteger->setInteger( 99 ); // use unique_ptr to set Integer value
19
20     // use unique_ptr to get Integer value
21     cout << "Integer after setInteger: " << ( *ptrToInteger ).getInteger()
22  } // end main
```

Fig. 24.9 | `unique_ptr` object manages dynamically allocated memory. (Part 1 of 2.)

```
Creating a unique_ptr object that points to an Integer
Constructor for Integer 7

Using the unique_ptr to manipulate the Integer
Integer after setInteger: 99

Destructor for Integer 99
```

Fig. 24.9 | unique_ptr object manages dynamically allocated memory. (Part 2 of 2.)

Because ptrToInteger is a local automatic variable in main, ptrToInteger is destroyed when main terminates. The unique_ptr destructor forces a delete of the Integer object pointed to by ptrToInteger, which in turn calls the Integer class destructor. The memory that Integer occupies is released, regardless of how control leaves the block (e.g., by a return statement or by an exception). Most importantly, using this technique can *prevent memory leaks*. For example, suppose a function returns a pointer aimed at some object. Unfortunately, the function caller that receives this pointer might not delete the object, thus resulting in *a memory leak*. However, if the function returns a unique_ptr to the object, the object will be deleted automatically when the unique_ptr object's destructor gets called.

Only one unique_ptr at a time can own a dynamically allocated object and the object cannot be an array. By using its overloaded assignment operator or copy constructor, a unique_ptr can transfer ownership of the dynamic memory it manages. The last unique_ptr object that maintains the pointer to the dynamic memory will delete the memory. This makes unique_ptr an ideal mechanism for returning dynamically allocated memory to client code. When the unique_ptr goes out of scope in the client code, the unique_ptr's destructor deletes the dynamic memory.

24.11 Standard Library Exception Hierarchy

Experience has shown that exceptions fall nicely into a number of categories. The C++ Standard Library includes a hierarchy of exception classes, some of which are shown in Fig. 24.10. As we first discussed in Section 24.2, this hierarchy is headed by base-class exception (defined in header <exception>), which contains virtual function what, which derived classes can override to issue appropriate error messages.

Immediate derived classes of base-class exception include runtime_error and **logic_error** (both defined in header <stdexcept>), each of which has several derived classes. Also derived from exception are the exceptions thrown by C++ operators—for example, bad_alloc is thrown by new (Section 24.9), **bad_cast** is thrown by dynamic_cast (Chapter 21) and **bad_typeid** is thrown by typeid (Chapter 21). Including **bad_exception** in the throw list of a function means that, if an unexpected exception occurs, function unexpected can throw bad_exception rather than terminating the program's execution (by default) or calling another function specified by set_unexpected.

Common Programming Error 24.8

Placing a catch handler that catches a base-class object before a catch that catches an object of a class derived from that base class is a logic error. The base-class catch catches all objects of classes derived from that base class, so the derived-class catch will never execute.

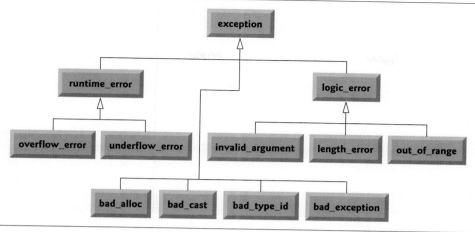

Fig. 24.10 | Some of the Standard Library exception classes.

Class `logic_error` is the base class of several standard exception classes that indicate errors in program logic. For example, class `invalid_argument` indicates that an invalid argument was passed to a function. (Proper coding can, of course, prevent invalid arguments from reaching a function.) Class `length_error` indicates that a length larger than the maximum size allowed for the object being manipulated was used for that object. Class `out_of_range` indicates that a value, such as a subscript into an array, exceeded its allowed range of values.

Class `runtime_error`, which we used briefly in Section 24.6, is the base class of several other standard exception classes that indicate execution-time errors. For example, class `overflow_error` describes an arithmetic overflow error (i.e., the result of an arithmetic operation is larger than the largest number that can be stored in the computer) and class `underflow_error` describes an arithmetic underflow error (i.e., the result of an arithmetic operation is smaller than the smallest number that can be stored in the computer).

Common Programming Error 24.9

Exception classes need not be derived from class `exception`, so catching type `exception` is not guaranteed to `catch` all exceptions a program could encounter.

Error-Prevention Tip 24.4

To catch all exceptions potentially thrown in a `try` block, use `catch(...)`. One weakness with catching exceptions in this way is that the type of the caught exception is unknown at compile time. Another weakness is that, without a named parameter, there's no way to refer to the exception object inside the exception handler.

Software Engineering Observation 24.9

The standard `exception` hierarchy is a good starting point for creating exceptions. You can build programs that can `throw` standard exceptions, `throw` exceptions derived from the standard exceptions or `throw` your own exceptions not derived from the standard exceptions.

Software Engineering Observation 24.10

Use catch(...) to perform recovery that does not depend on the exception type (e.g., releasing common resources). The exception can be rethrown to alert more specific enclosing catch handlers.

24.12 Wrap-Up

In this chapter, you learned how to use exception handling to deal with errors in a program. You learned that exception handling enables you to remove error-handling code from the "main line" of the program's execution. We demonstrated exception handling in the context of a divide-by-zero example. We reviewed how to use try blocks to enclose code that may throw an exception, and how to use catch handlers to deal with exceptions that may arise. You learned how to throw and rethrow exceptions, and how to handle the exceptions that occur in constructors. The chapter continued with discussions of processing new failures, dynamic memory allocation with class unique_ptr and the standard library exception hierarchy.

Summary

Section 24.1 Introduction
- An exception (p. 905) is an indication of a problem that occurs during a program's execution.
- Exception handling enables you to create programs that can resolve problems that occur at execution time—often allowing programs to continue executing as if no problems had been encountered. More severe problems may require a program to notify the user of the problem before terminating in a controlled manner.

Section 24.2 Example: Handling an Attempt to Divide by Zero
- Class exception is the standard base class for exceptions classes (p. 906). It provides virtual function what (p. 906) that returns an appropriate error message and can be overridden in derived classes.
- Class runtime_error (p. 906), which is defined in header <stdexcept> (p. 906), is the C++ standard base class for representing runtime errors.
- C++ uses the termination model (p. 909) of exception handling.
- A try block consists of keyword try followed by braces ({}) that define a block of code in which exceptions might occur. The try block encloses statements that might cause exceptions and statements that should not execute if exceptions occur.
- At least one catch handler must immediately follow a try block. Each catch handler specifies an exception parameter that represents the type of exception the catch handler can process.
- If an exception parameter includes an optional parameter name, the catch handler can use that parameter name to interact with a caught exception object (p. 910).
- The point in the program at which an exception occurs is called the throw point (p. 909).
- If an exception occurs in a try block, the try block expires and program control transfers to the first catch in which the exception parameter's type matches that of the thrown exception.
- When a try block terminates, local variables defined in the block go out of scope.
- When a try block terminates due to an exception, the program searches for the first catch handler that matches the type of exception that occurred. A match occurs if the types are identical

or if the thrown exception's type is a derived class of the exception-parameter type. When a match occurs, the code contained within the matching catch handler executes.

- When a catch handler finishes processing, the catch parameter and local variables defined within the catch handler go out of scope. Any remaining catch handlers that correspond to the try block are ignored, and execution resumes at the first line of code after the try...catch sequence.

- If no exceptions occur in a try block, the program ignores the catch handler(s) for that block. Program execution resumes with the next statement after the try...catch sequence.

- If an exception that occurs in a try block has no matching catch handler, or if an exception occurs in a statement that is not in a try block, the function that contains the statement terminates immediately, and the program attempts to locate an enclosing try block in the calling function. This process is called stack unwinding (p. 910).

- To throw an exception, use keyword throw followed by an operand that represents the type of exception to throw. The operand of a throw can be of any type.

Section 24.3 When to Use Exception Handling
- Exception handling is for synchronous errors (p. 911), which occur when a statement executes.
- Exception handling is not designed to process errors associated with asynchronous events (p. 911), which occur in parallel with, and independent of, the program's flow of control.

Section 24.4 Rethrowing an Exception
- The exception handler can defer the exception handling (or perhaps a portion of it) to another exception handler. In either case, the handler achieves this by rethrowing the exception (p. 912).
- Common examples of exceptions are out-of-range array subscripts, arithmetic overflow, division by zero, invalid function parameters and unsuccessful memory allocations.

Section 24.5 Processing Unexpected Exceptions
- Function unexpected calls the function registered with function set_unexpected (p. 913). If no function has been registered in this manner, function terminate (p. 912) is called by default.
- Function set_terminate (p. 914) can specify the function to invoke when terminate is called. Otherwise, terminate calls abort (p. 914), which terminates the program without calling the destructors of objects that are declared static and auto.
- Functions set_terminate and set_unexpected each return a pointer to the last function called by terminate and unexpected, respectively (0, the first time each is called). This enables you to save the function pointer so it can be restored later.
- Functions set_terminate and set_unexpected take as arguments pointers to functions with void return types and no arguments.
- If a programmer-defined termination function does not exit a program, function abort will be called after the programmer-defined termination function completes execution.

Section 24.6 Stack Unwinding
- Unwinding the function call stack means that the function in which the exception was not caught terminates, all local variables in that function are destroyed and control returns to the statement that originally invoked that function.

Section 24.7 Constructors, Destructors and Exception Handling
- Exceptions thrown by a constructor cause destructors to be called for any objects built as part of the object being constructed before the exception is thrown.
- Each automatic object constructed in a try block is destructed before an exception is thrown.

- Stack unwinding completes before an exception handler begins executing.
- If a destructor invoked as a result of stack unwinding throws an exception, terminate is called.
- If an object has member objects, and if an exception is thrown before the outer object is fully constructed, then destructors will be executed for the member objects that have been constructed before the exception occurs.
- If an array of objects has been partially constructed when an exception occurs, only the destructors for the constructed array element objects will be called.
- When an exception is thrown from the constructor for an object that is created in a new expression, the dynamically allocated memory for that object is released.

Section 24.8 Exceptions and Inheritance
- If a catch handler catches a pointer or reference to an exception object of a base-class type, it also can catch a pointer or reference to all objects of classes derived publicly from that base class—this allows for polymorphic processing of related errors.

Section 24.9 Processing new Failures
- The C++ standard document specifies that, when operator new fails, it throws a bad_alloc exception (p. 917), which is defined in header <new>.
- Function set_new_handler (p. 917) takes as its argument a pointer to a function that takes no arguments and returns void. This pointer points to the function that will be called if new fails.
- Once set_new_handler registers a new handler (p. 918) in the program, operator new does not throw bad_alloc on failure; rather, it defers the error handling to the new-handler function.
- If new allocates memory successfully, it returns a pointer to that memory.
- If an exception occurs after successful memory allocation but before the delete statement executes, a memory leak could occur.

Section 24.10 Class unique_ptr and Dynamic Memory Allocation
- The C++ Standard Library provides class template unique_ptr (p. 920) to deal with memory leaks.
- An object of class unique_ptr maintains a pointer to dynamically allocated memory. A unique_ptr's destructor performs a delete operation on the unique_ptr's pointer data member.
- Class template unique_ptr provides overloaded operators * and -> so that a unique_ptr object can be used just as a regular pointer variable is. A unique_ptr also transfers ownership of the dynamic memory it manages via its copy constructor and overloaded assignment operator.

Section 24.11 Standard Library Exception Hierarchy
- The C++ Standard Library includes a hierarchy of exception classes. This hierarchy is headed by base-class exception.
- Immediate derived classes of base class exception include runtime_error and logic_error (both defined in header <stdexcept>), each of which has several derived classes.
- Several operators throw standard exceptions—operator new throws bad_alloc, operator dynamic_cast throws bad_cast (p. 922) and operator typeid throws bad_typeid (p. 922).
- Including bad_exception (p. 922) in the throw list of a function means that, if an unexpected exception occurs, function unexpected can throw bad_exception rather than terminating the program's execution or calling another function specified by set_unexpected.

Self-Review Exercises
24.1 What does exception handled code promise?

24.2   Give several reasons why exception-handling techniques should not be used for conventional program control.

24.3   Why are exceptions appropriate for dealing with errors produced by library functions?

24.4   What's a "resource leak"?

24.5   If no exceptions are thrown in a try block, where does control proceed to after the try block completes execution?

24.6   What happens if an exception is thrown outside a try block?

24.7   Give a key advantage and a key disadvantage of using catch(...).

24.8   What happens if no catch handler matches the type of a thrown object?

24.9   What happens if several handlers match the type of the thrown object?

24.10   Why would you specify a base-class type as the type of a catch handler, then throw objects of derived-class types?

24.11   Suppose a catch handler with a precise match to an exception object type is available. Under what circumstances might a different handler be executed for exception objects of that type?

24.12   Must throwing an exception cause program termination?

24.13   What happens when a catch handler throws an exception?

24.14   What does the statement throw; do?

Answers to Self-Review Exercises

24.1   It promises robust and fault-tolerant programs that can deal with problems and continue executing or terminate gracefully.

24.2   (a) Exception handling is designed to handle infrequently occurring situations that often result in program termination, so compiler writers are not required to implement exception handling to perform optimally. (b) Flow of control with conventional control structures generally is clearer and more efficient than with exceptions. (c) Problems can occur because the stack is unwound when an exception occurs and resources allocated prior to the exception might not be freed. (d) The "additional" exceptions make it more difficult for you to handle the larger number of exception cases.

24.3   It's unlikely that a library function will perform error processing that will meet the unique needs of all users.

24.4   A program that terminates abruptly could leave a resource in a state in which other programs would not be able to acquire the resource, or the program itself might not be able to reacquire a "leaked" resource.

24.5   The exception handlers (in the catch handlers) for that try block are skipped, and the program resumes execution after the last catch handler.

24.6   An exception thrown outside a try block causes a call to terminate.

24.7   The form catch(...) catches any type of exception thrown in a try block. An advantage is that all possible exceptions will be caught. A disadvantage is that the catch has no parameter, so it cannot reference information in the thrown object and cannot know the cause of the exception.

24.8   This causes the search for a match to continue in the next enclosing try block if there is one. As this process continues, it might eventually be determined that there is no handler in the program that matches the type of the thrown object; in this case, terminate is called, which by default calls abort. An alternative terminate function can be provided as an argument to set_terminate.

24.9   The first matching exception handler after the `try` block is executed.

24.10   This is a nice way to `catch` related types of exceptions.

24.11   A base-class handler would catch objects of all derived-class types.

24.12   No, but it does terminate the block in which the exception is thrown.

24.13   The exception will be processed by a `catch` handler (if one exists) associated with the `try` block (if one exists) enclosing the `catch` handler that caused the exception.

24.14   It rethrows the exception if it appears in a `catch` handler; otherwise, function `unexpected` is called.

Exercises

24.15   *(Exceptional Conditions)* List various exceptional conditions that have occurred throughout this text. List as many additional exceptional conditions as you can. For each of these exceptions, describe briefly how a program typically would handle the exception, using the exception-handling techniques discussed in this chapter. Some typical exceptions are division by zero, arithmetic overflow, array subscript out of bounds, exhaustion of the free store, etc.

24.16   *(Catch Parameter)* Under what circumstances would you not provide a parameter name when defining the type of the object that will be caught by a handler?

24.17   *(**throw** Statement)* A program contains the statement

```
throw;
```

Where would you normally expect to find such a statement? What if that statement appeared in a different part of the program?

24.18   *(Exception Handling vs. Other Schemes)* Compare and contrast exception handling with the various other error-processing schemes discussed in the text.

24.19   *(Exception Handling and Program Control)* Why should exceptions *not* be used as an alternate form of program control?

24.20   *(Operator **new** Failure)* Which exceptions are thrown if operator `new` fails?

24.21   *(Throwing Exceptions from a **catch**)* Suppose a program `throws` an exception and the appropriate exception handler begins executing. Now suppose that the exception handler itself `throws` the same exception. Does this create infinite recursion? Write a program to check your observation.

24.22   *(Catching Divide by Zero Exceptions)* Write a program that throws an exception when there is an attempt to divide a number by zero.

24.23   *(Throwing the Result of a Conditional Expression)* Throw the result of a conditional expression that returns either a `double` or an `int`. Provide an `int` catch handler and a `double` catch handler. Show that only the `double` catch handler executes, regardless of whether the `int` or the `double` is returned.

24.24   *(Local Variable Destructors)* Write a program illustrating that all destructors for objects constructed in a block are called before an exception is thrown from that block.

24.25   *(Member Object Destructors)* Write a program illustrating that member object destructors are called for only those member objects that were constructed before an exception occurred.

24.26   *(Catching All Exceptions)* Write a program that demonstrates several exception types being caught with the `catch(...)` exception handler.

24.27   *(Order of Exception Handlers)* Write a program illustrating that the order of exception handlers is important. The first matching handler is the one that executes. Attempt to compile and run your program two different ways to show that two different handlers execute with two different effects.

24.28 *(Constructors Throwing Exceptions)* Write a program that shows a constructor passing information about constructor failure to an exception handler after a try block.

24.29 *(Rethrowing Exceptions)* Write a program that illustrates rethrowing an exception.

24.30 *(Uncaught Exceptions)* Write a program that illustrates that a function with its own try block does not have to catch every possible error generated within the try. Some exceptions can slip through to, and be handled in, outer scopes.

24.31 *(Stack Unwinding)* Write a program that throws an exception from a deeply nested function and still has the catch handler following the try block enclosing the initial call in main catch the exception.

Operator Precedence Charts

Operators are shown in decreasing order of precedence from top to bottom (Figs. A.1–A.2).

C Operator	Type	Associativity
()	parentheses (function call operator)	left to right
[]	array subscript	
.	member selection via object	
->	member selection via pointer	
++	unary postincrement	
--	unary postdecrement	
++	unary preincrement	right to left
--	unary predecrement	
+	unary plus	
-	unary minus	
!	unary logical negation	
~	unary bitwise complement	
(*type*)	C-style unary cast	
*	dereference	
&	address	
sizeof	determine size in bytes	
*	multiplication	left to right
/	division	
%	modulus	
+	addition	left to right
-	subtraction	
<<	bitwise left shift	left to right
>>	bitwise right shift	
<	relational less than	left to right
<=	relational less than or equal to	
>	relational greater than	
>=	relational greater than or equal to	

Fig. A.1 | C operator precedence chart. (Part 1 of 2.)

C Operator	Type	Associativity
==	relational is equal to	left to right
!=	relational is not equal to	
&	bitwise AND	left to right
^	bitwise exclusive OR	left to right
|	bitwise inclusive OR	left to right
&&	logical AND	left to right
||	logical OR	left to right
?:	ternary conditional	right to left
=	assignment	right to left
+=	addition assignment	
-=	subtraction assignment	
*=	multiplication assignment	
/=	division assignment	
%=	modulus assignment	
&=	bitwise AND assignment	
^=	bitwise exclusive OR assignment	
|=	bitwise inclusive OR assignment	
<<=	bitwise left shift assignment	
>>=	bitwise right shift with sign	
,	comma	left to right

Fig. A.1 | C operator precedence chart. (Part 2 of 2.)

C++ Operator	Type	Associativity
::	binary scope resolution	left to right
::	unary scope resolution	
()	parentheses (function call operator)	left to right
[]	array subscript	
.	member selection via object	
->	member selection via pointer	
++	unary postincrement	
--	unary postdecrement	
typeid	runtime type information	
dynamic_cast<*type*>	runtime type-checked cast	
static_cast<*type*>	compile-time type-checked cast	
reinterpret_cast<*type*>	cast for nonstandard conversions	
const_cast<*type*>	cast away const-ness	

Fig. A.2 | C++ operator precedence chart. (Part 1 of 3.)

C++ Operator	Type	Associativity
++	unary preincrement	right to left
--	unary predecrement	
+	unary plus	
-	unary minus	
!	unary logical negation	
~	unary bitwise complement	
(*type*)	C-style unary cast	
sizeof	determine size in bytes	
&	address	
*	dereference	
new	dynamic memory allocation	
new[]	dynamic array allocation	
delete	dynamic memory deallocation	
delete[]	dynamic array deallocation	
.*	pointer to member via object	left to right
->*	pointer to member via pointer	
*	multiplication	left to right
/	division	
%	modulus	
+	addition	left to right
-	subtraction	
<<	bitwise left shift	left to right
>>	bitwise right shift	
<	relational less than	left to right
<=	relational less than or equal to	
>	relational greater than	
>=	relational greater than or equal to	
==	relational is equal to	left to right
!=	relational is not equal to	
&	bitwise AND	left to right
^	bitwise exclusive OR	left to right
|	bitwise inclusive OR	left to right
&&	logical AND	left to right
||	logical OR	left to right
?:	ternary conditional	right to left

Fig. A.2 | C++ operator precedence chart. (Part 2 of 3.)

C++ Operator	Type	Associativity
=	assignment	right to left
+=	addition assignment	
-=	subtraction assignment	
*=	multiplication assignment	
/=	division assignment	
%=	modulus assignment	
&=	bitwise AND assignment	
^=	bitwise exclusive OR assignment	
|=	bitwise inclusive OR assignment	
<<=	bitwise left shift assignment	
>>=	bitwise right shift with sign	
,	comma	left to right

Fig. A.2 | C++ operator precedence chart. (Part 3 of 3.)

B

ASCII Character Set

ASCII character set

	0	1	2	3	4	5	6	7	8	9
0	nul	soh	stx	etx	eot	enq	ack	bel	bs	ht
1	lf	vt	ff	cr	so	si	dle	dc1	dc2	dc3
2	dc4	nak	syn	etb	can	em	sub	esc	fs	gs
3	rs	us	sp	!	"	#	$	%	&	'
4	(	)	*	+	,	-	.	/	0	1
5	2	3	4	5	6	7	8	9	:	;
6	<	=	>	?	@	A	B	C	D	E
7	F	G	H	I	J	K	L	M	N	O
8	P	Q	R	S	T	U	V	W	X	Y
9	Z	[	\	]	^	_	'	a	b	c
10	d	e	f	g	h	i	j	k	l	m
11	n	o	p	q	r	s	t	u	v	w
12	x	y	z	{	|	}	~	del		

Fig. B.1 | ASCII Character Set.

The digits at the left of the table are the left digits of the decimal equivalent (0–127) of the character code, and the digits at the top of the table are the right digits of the character code. For example, the character code for "F" is 70, and the character code for "&" is 38.

Number Systems

Here are only numbers ratified.
—William Shakespeare

Objectives

In this appendix, you'll learn:

- To understand basic number systems concepts such as base, positional value and symbol value.

- To understand how to work with numbers represented in the binary, octal and hexadecimal number systems

- To be able to abbreviate binary numbers as octal numbers or hexadecimal numbers.

- To be able to convert octal numbers and hexadecimal numbers to binary numbers.

- To be able to convert back and forth between decimal numbers and their binary, octal and hexadecimal equivalents.

- To understand binary arithmetic and how negative binary numbers are represented using two's complement notation.

C.1 Introduction

In this appendix, we introduce the key number systems that programmers use, especially when they are working on software projects that require close interaction with machine-level hardware. Projects like this include operating systems, computer networking software, compilers, database systems and applications requiring high performance.

When we write an integer such as 227 or –63 in a program, the number is assumed to be in the **decimal (base 10) number system**. The **digits** in the decimal number system are 0, 1, 2, 3, 4, 5, 6, 7, 8 and 9. The lowest digit is 0 and the highest digit is 9—one less than the **base** of 10. Internally, computers use the **binary (base 2) number system**. The binary number system has only two digits, namely 0 and 1. Its lowest digit is 0 and its highest digit is 1—one less than the base of 2.

As we'll see, binary numbers tend to be much longer than their decimal equivalents. Programmers who work in assembly languages and in high-level languages like C that enable programmers to reach down to the machine level, find it cumbersome to work with binary numbers. So two other number systems—the **octal number system (base 8)** and the **hexadecimal number system (base 16)**—are popular primarily because they make it convenient to abbreviate binary numbers.

In the octal number system, the digits range from 0 to 7. Because both the binary number system and the octal number system have fewer digits than the decimal number system, their digits are the same as the corresponding digits in decimal.

The hexadecimal number system poses a problem because it requires 16 digits—a lowest digit of 0 and a highest digit with a value equivalent to decimal 15 (one less than the base of 16). By convention, we use the letters A through F to represent the hexadecimal digits corresponding to decimal values 10 through 15. Thus in hexadecimal we can have numbers like 876 consisting solely of decimal-like digits, numbers like 8A55F consisting of digits and letters and numbers like FFE consisting solely of letters. Occasionally, a hexadecimal number spells a common word such as FACE or FEED—this can appear strange to programmers accustomed to working with numbers. The digits of the binary, octal, decimal and hexadecimal number systems are summarized in Figs. C.1–C.2.

Each of these number systems uses **positional notation**—each position in which a digit is written has a different **positional value**. For example, in the decimal number 937 (the 9, the 3 and the 7 are referred to as **symbol values**), we say that the 7 is written in the ones position, the 3 is written in the tens position and the 9 is written in the hundreds position. Each of these positions is a power of the base (base 10) and these powers begin at 0 and increase by 1 as we move left in the number (Fig. C.3).

Binary digit	Octal digit	Decimal digit	Hexadecimal digit
0	0	0	0
1	1	1	1
	2	2	2
	3	3	3
	4	4	4
	5	5	5
	6	6	6
	7	7	7
		8	8
		9	9
			A (decimal value of 10)
			B (decimal value of 11)
			C (decimal value of 12)
			D (decimal value of 13)
			E (decimal value of 14)
			F (decimal value of 15)

Fig. C.1 | Digits of the binary, octal, decimal and hexadecimal number systems.

Attribute	Binary	Octal	Decimal	Hexadecimal
Base	2	8	10	16
Lowest digit	0	0	0	0
Highest digit	1	7	9	F

Fig. C.2 | Comparing the binary, octal, decimal and hexadecimal number systems.

Positional values in the decimal number system			
Decimal digit	9	3	7
Position name	Hundreds	Tens	Ones
Positional value	100	10	1
Positional value as a power of the base (10)	10^2	10^1	10^0

Fig. C.3 | Positional values in the decimal number system.

For longer decimal numbers, the next positions to the left would be the thousands position (10 to the 3rd power), the ten-thousands position (10 to the 4th power), the hundred-thousands position (10 to the 5th power), the millions position (10 to the 6th power), the ten-millions position (10 to the 7th power) and so on.

In the binary number 101, the rightmost 1 is written in the ones position, the 0 is written in the twos position and the leftmost 1 is written in the fours position. Each position is a power of the base (base 2) and these powers begin at 0 and increase by 1 as we move left in the number (Fig. C.4). So, $101 = 1 * 2^2 + 0 * 2^1 + 1 * 2^0 = 4 + 0 + 1 = 5$.

Positional values in the binary number system			
Binary digit	1	0	1
Position name	Fours	Twos	Ones
Positional value	4	2	1
Positional value as a power of the base (2)	2^2	2^1	2^0

Fig. C.4 | Positional values in the binary number system.

For longer binary numbers, the next positions to the left would be the eights position (2 to the 3rd power), the sixteens position (2 to the 4th power), the thirty-twos position (2 to the 5th power), the sixty-fours position (2 to the 6th power) and so on.

In the octal number 425, we say that the 5 is written in the ones position, the 2 is written in the eights position and the 4 is written in the sixty-fours position. Each of these positions is a power of the base (base 8) and that these powers begin at 0 and increase by 1 as we move left in the number (Fig. C.5).

Positional values in the octal number system			
Decimal digit	4	2	5
Position name	Sixty-fours	Eights	Ones
Positional value	64	8	1
Positional value as a power of the base (8)	8^2	8^1	8^0

Fig. C.5 | Positional values in the octal number system.

For longer octal numbers, the next positions to the left would be the five-hundred-and-twelves position (8 to the 3rd power), the four-thousand-and-ninety-sixes position (8 to the 4th power), the thirty-two-thousand-seven-hundred-and-sixty-eights position (8 to the 5th power) and so on.

In the hexadecimal number 3DA, we say that the A is written in the ones position, the D is written in the sixteens position and the 3 is written in the two-hundred-and-fifty-sixes position. Each of these positions is a power of the base (base 16) and these powers begin at 0 and increase by 1 as we move left in the number (Fig. C.6).

For longer hexadecimal numbers, the next positions to the left would be the four-thousand-and-ninety-sixes position (16 to the 3rd power), the sixty-five-thousand-five-hundred-and-thirty-sixes position (16 to the 4th power) and so on.

Positional values in the hexadecimal number system			
Decimal digit	3	D	A
Position name	Two-hundred-and-fifty-sixes	Sixteens	Ones
Positional value	256	16	1
Positional value as a power of the base (16)	16^2	16^1	16^0

Fig. C.6 | Positional values in the hexadecimal number system.

C.2 Abbreviating Binary Numbers as Octal and Hexadecimal Numbers

The main use for octal and hexadecimal numbers in computing is for abbreviating lengthy binary representations. Figure C.7 highlights the fact that lengthy binary numbers can be expressed concisely in number systems with higher bases than the binary number system.

Decimal number	Binary representation	Octal representation	Hexadecimal representation
0	0	0	0
1	1	1	1
2	10	2	2
3	11	3	3
4	100	4	4
5	101	5	5
6	110	6	6
7	111	7	7
8	1000	10	8
9	1001	11	9
10	1010	12	A
11	1011	13	B
12	1100	14	C
13	1101	15	D
14	1110	16	E
15	1111	17	F
16	10000	20	10

Fig. C.7 | Decimal, binary, octal and hexadecimal equivalents.

A particularly important relationship that both the octal number system and the hexadecimal number system have to the binary system is that the bases of octal and hexadecimal (8 and 16 respectively) are powers of the base of the binary number system (base 2). Consider the following 12-digit binary number and its octal and hexadecimal equivalents. See if you can determine how this relationship makes it convenient to abbreviate binary numbers in octal or hexadecimal. The answer follows the numbers.

Binary number	Octal equivalent	Hexadecimal equivalent
100011010001	4321	8D1

To see how the binary number converts easily to octal, simply break the 12-digit binary number into groups of three consecutive bits each and write those groups over the corresponding digits of the octal number as follows:

100	011	010	001
4	3	2	1

The octal digit you have written under each group of three bits corresponds precisely to the octal equivalent of that 3-digit binary number, as shown in Fig. C.7.

The same kind of relationship can be observed in converting from binary to hexadecimal. Break the 12-digit binary number into groups of four consecutive bits each and write those groups over the corresponding digits of the hexadecimal number as follows:

1000	1101	0001
8	D	1

The hexadecimal digit you wrote under each group of four bits corresponds precisely to the hexadecimal equivalent of that 4-digit binary number as shown in Fig. C.7.

C.3 Converting Octal and Hexadecimal Numbers to Binary Numbers

In the previous section, we saw how to convert binary numbers to their octal and hexadecimal equivalents by forming groups of binary digits and simply rewriting them as their equivalent octal digit values or hexadecimal digit values. This process may be used in reverse to produce the binary equivalent of a given octal or hexadecimal number.

For example, the octal number 653 is converted to binary simply by writing the 6 as its 3-digit binary equivalent 110, the 5 as its 3-digit binary equivalent 101 and the 3 as its 3-digit binary equivalent 011 to form the 9-digit binary number 110101011.

The hexadecimal number FAD5 is converted to binary simply by writing the F as its 4-digit binary equivalent 1111, the A as its 4-digit binary equivalent 1010, the D as its 4-digit binary equivalent 1101 and the 5 as its 4-digit binary equivalent 0101 to form the 16-digit 1111101011010101.

C.4 Converting from Binary, Octal or Hexadecimal to Decimal

We're accustomed to working in decimal, and therefore it's often convenient to convert a binary, octal, or hexadecimal number to decimal to get a sense of what the number is "really" worth. Our tables in Section C.1 express the positional values in decimal. To convert a number to decimal from another base, multiply the decimal equivalent of each digit by its positional value and sum these products. For example, the binary number 110101 is converted to decimal 53, as shown in Fig. C.8.

Converting a binary number to decimal					
Postional values:	32	16	8	4	2	1
Symbol values:	1	1	0	1	0	1
Products:	1*32=32	1*16=16	0*8=0	1*4=4	0*2=0	1*1=1
Sum:	= 32 + 16 + 0 + 4 + 0 + 1 = 53					

Fig. C.8 | Converting a binary number to decimal.

To convert octal 7614 to decimal 3980, we use the same technique, this time using appropriate octal positional values, as shown in Fig. C.9.

Converting an octal number to decimal			
Positional values:	512	64	8	1
Symbol values:	7	6	1	4
Products	7*512=3584	6*64=384	1*8=8	4*1=4
Sum:	= 3584 + 384 + 8 + 4 = 3980			

Fig. C.9 | Converting an octal number to decimal.

To convert hexadecimal AD3B to decimal 44347, we use the same technique, this time using appropriate hexadecimal positional values, as shown in Fig. C.10.

Converting a hexadecimal number to decimal			
Postional values:	4096	256	16	1
Symbol values:	A	D	3	B
Products	A*4096=40960	D*256=3328	3*16=48	B*1=11
Sum:	= 40960 + 3328 + 48 + 11 = 44347			

Fig. C.10 | Converting a hexadecimal number to decimal.

C.5 Converting from Decimal to Binary, Octal or Hexadecimal ·

The conversions in Section C.4 follow naturally from the positional notation conventions. Converting from decimal to binary, octal, or hexadecimal also follows these conventions.

Suppose we wish to convert decimal 57 to binary. We begin by writing the positional values of the columns right to left until we reach a column whose positional value is greater than the decimal number. We do not need that column, so we discard it. Thus, we first write:

Positional values:	64	32	16	8	4	2	1

Then we discard the column with positional value 64, leaving:

Positional values:	32	16	8	4	2	1

Next we work from the leftmost column to the right. We divide 32 into 57 and observe that there is one 32 in 57 with a remainder of 25, so we write 1 in the 32 column. We divide 16 into 25 and observe that there is one 16 in 25 with a remainder of 9 and write 1 in the 16 column. We divide 8 into 9 and observe that there is one 8 in 9 with a remainder of 1. The next two columns each produce quotients of 0 when their positional values are divided into 1, so we write 0s in the 4 and 2 columns. Finally, 1 into 1 is 1, so we write 1 in the 1 column. This yields:

Positional values:	32	16	8	4	2	1
Symbol values:	1	1	1	0	0	1

and thus decimal 57 is equivalent to binary 111001.

To convert decimal 103 to octal, we begin by writing the positional values of the columns until we reach a column whose positional value is greater than the decimal number. We do not need that column, so we discard it. Thus, we first write:

Positional values:	512	64	8	1

Then we discard the column with positional value 512, yielding:

Positional values:		64	8	1

Next we work from the leftmost column to the right. We divide 64 into 103 and observe that there is one 64 in 103 with a remainder of 39, so we write 1 in the 64 column. We divide 8 into 39 and observe that there are four 8s in 39 with a remainder of 7 and write 4 in the 8 column. Finally, we divide 1 into 7 and observe that there are seven 1s in 7 with no remainder, so we write 7 in the 1 column. This yields:

Positional values:	64	8	1
Symbol values:	1	4	7

and thus decimal 103 is equivalent to octal 147.

To convert decimal 375 to hexadecimal, we begin by writing the positional values of the columns until we reach a column whose positional value is greater than the decimal number. We do not need that column, so we discard it. Thus, we first write:

Positional values:	4096	256	16	1

Then we discard the column with positional value 4096, yielding:

Positional values:		256	16	1

Next we work from the leftmost column to the right. We divide 256 into 375 and observe that there is one 256 in 375 with a remainder of 119, so we write 1 in the 256 column. We divide 16 into 119 and observe that there are seven 16s in 119 with a remainder of 7 and write 7 in the 16 column. Finally, we divide 1 into 7 and observe that there are seven 1s in 7 with no remainder, so we write 7 in the 1 column. This yields:

Positional values:	256	16	1
Symbol values:	1	7	7

and thus decimal 375 is equivalent to hexadecimal 177.

C.6 Negative Binary Numbers: Two's Complement Notation

The discussion so far in this appendix has focused on positive numbers. In this section, we explain how computers represent negative numbers using two's complement notation. First we explain how the two's complement of a binary number is formed, then we show why it represents the negative value of the given binary number.

Consider a machine with 32-bit integers. Suppose

```
int value = 13;
```

The 32-bit representation of value is

```
00000000 00000000 00000000 00001101
```

To form the negative of value we first form its one's complement by applying C's bitwise complement operator (~):

```
onesComplementOfValue = ~value;
```

Internally, ~value is now value with each of its bits reversed—ones become zeros and zeros become ones, as follows:

```
value:
00000000 00000000 00000000 00001101
~value  (i.e., value's ones complement):
11111111 11111111 11111111 11110010
```

To form the two's complement of value, we simply add 1 to value's one's complement. Thus

```
Two's complement of value:
11111111 11111111 11111111 11110011
```

Now if this is in fact equal to −13, we should be able to add it to binary 13 and obtain a result of 0. Let's try this:

```
 00000000 00000000 00000000 00001101
+11111111 11111111 11111111 11110011
-------------------------------------
 00000000 00000000 00000000 00000000
```

The carry bit coming out of the leftmost column is discarded and we indeed get 0 as a result. If we add the one's complement of a number to the number, the result would be all 1s. The key to getting a result of all zeros is that the twos complement is one more than the one's complement. The addition of 1 causes each column to add to 0 with a carry of 1. The carry keeps moving leftward until it's discarded from the leftmost bit, and thus the resulting number is all zeros.

Computers actually perform a subtraction, such as

```
x = a - value;
```

by adding the two's complement of value to a, as follows:

```
x = a + (~value + 1);
```

Suppose a is 27 and `value` is 13 as before. If the two's complement of `value` is actually the negative of `value`, then adding the two's complement of `value` to a should produce the result 14. Let's try this:

```
a (i.e., 27)        00000000 00000000 00000000 00011011
+(~value + 1)      +11111111 11111111 11111111 11110011
                   ------------------------------------
                    00000000 00000000 00000000 00001110
```

which is indeed equal to 14.

Summary

- An integer such as 19 or 227 or −63 in a program is assumed to be in the decimal (base 10) number system. The digits in the decimal number system are 0, 1, 2, 3, 4, 5, 6, 7, 8 and 9. The lowest digit is 0 and the highest digit is 9—one less than the base of 10.

- Internally, computers use the binary (base 2) number system. The binary number system has only two digits, namely 0 and 1. Its lowest digit is 0 and its highest digit is 1—one less than the base of 2.

- The octal number system (base 8) and the hexadecimal number system (base 16) are popular primarily because they make it convenient to abbreviate binary numbers.

- The digits of the octal number system range from 0 to 7.

- The hexadecimal number system poses a problem because it requires 16 digits—a lowest digit of 0 and a highest digit with a value equivalent to decimal 15 (one less than the base of 16). By convention, we use the letters A through F to represent the hexadecimal digits corresponding to decimal values 10 through 15.

- Each number system uses positional notation—each position in which a digit is written has a different positional value.

- A particularly important relationship of both the octal number system and the hexadecimal number system to the binary system is that the bases of octal and hexadecimal (8 and 16 respectively) are powers of the base of the binary number system (base 2).

- To convert an octal to a binary number, replace each octal digit with its three-digit binary equivalent.

- To convert a hexadecimal number to a binary number, simply replace each hexadecimal digit with its four-digit binary equivalent.

- Because we're accustomed to working in decimal, it's convenient to convert a binary, octal or hexadecimal number to decimal to get a sense of the number's "real" worth.

- To convert a number to decimal from another base, multiply the decimal equivalent of each digit by its positional value and sum the products.

- Computers represent negative numbers using two's complement notation.

- To form the negative of a value in binary, first form its one's complement by applying C's bitwise complement operator (~). This reverses the bits of the value. To form the two's complement of a value, simply add one to the value's one's complement.

Terminology

base 936	base 8 number system 936
base 2 number system 936	base 10 number system 936

Self-Review Exercises

C.1   Fill in the blanks in each of the following statements:

a) The bases of the decimal, binary, octal and hexadecimal number systems are _____, _____, _____ and _____ respectively.

b) The positional value of the rightmost digit of any number in either binary, octal, decimal or hexadecimal is always _____.

c) The positional value of the digit to the left of the rightmost digit of any number in binary, octal, decimal or hexadecimal is always equal to _____.

C.2   State whether each of the following is *true* or *false*. If *false*, explain why.

a) A popular reason for using the decimal number system is that it forms a convenient notation for abbreviating binary numbers simply by substituting one decimal digit per group of four binary bits.

b) The highest digit in any base is one more than the base.

c) The lowest digit in any base is one less than the base.

C.3   In general, the decimal, octal and hexadecimal representations of a given binary number contain (more/fewer) digits than the binary number contains.

C.4   The (octal / hexadecimal / decimal) representation of a large binary value is the most concise (of the given alternatives).

C.5   Fill in the missing values in this chart of positional values for the rightmost four positions in each of the indicated number systems:

	1000	100	10	1
decimal	1000	100	10	1
hexadecimal	...	256	...	...
binary	...	...	...	...
octal	512	...	8	...

C.6   Convert binary 110101011000 to octal and to hexadecimal.

C.7   Convert hexadecimal FACE to binary.

C.8   Convert octal 7316 to binary.

C.9   Convert hexadecimal 4FEC to octal. [*Hint:* First convert 4FEC to binary, then convert that binary number to octal.]

C.10   Convert binary 1101110 to decimal.

C.11   Convert octal 317 to decimal.

C.12   Convert hexadecimal EFD4 to decimal.

C.13   Convert decimal 177 to binary, to octal and to hexadecimal.

C.14   Show the binary representation of decimal 417. Then show the one's complement of 417 and the two's complement of 417.

C.15   What is the result when a number and its two's complement are added to each other?

Answers to Self-Review Exercises

C.1 a) 10, 2, 8, 16. b) 1 (the base raised to the zero power). c) The base of the number system.

C.2 a) False. Hexadecimal does this. b) False. The highest digit in any base is one less than the base. c) False. The lowest digit in any base is zero.

C.3 Fewer.

C.4 Hexadecimal.

C.5

decimal	1000	100	10	1
hexadecimal	4096	256	16	1
binary	8	4	2	1
octal	512	64	8	1

C.6 Octal 6530; Hexadecimal D58.

C.7 Binary 1111 1010 1100 1110.

C.8 Binary 111 011 001 110.

C.9 Binary 0 100 111 111 101 100; Octal 47754.

C.10 Decimal 2+4+8+32+64=110.

C.11 Decimal 7+1*8+3*64=7+8+192=207.

C.12 Decimal 4+13*16+15*256+14*4096=61396.

C.13 Decimal 177
to binary:

```
256 128 64 32 16 8 4 2 1
128 64 32 16 8 4 2 1
(1*128)+(0*64)+(1*32)+(1*16)+(0*8)+(0*4)+(0*2)+(1*1)
10110001
```

to octal:

```
512 64 8 1
64 8 1
(2*64)+(6*8)+(1*1)
261
```

to hexadecimal:

```
256 16 1
16 1
(11*16)+(1*1)
(B*16)+(1*1)
B1
```

C.14 Binary:

```
512 256 128 64 32 16 8 4 2 1
256 128 64 32 16 8 4 2 1
(1*256)+(1*128)+(0*64)+(1*32)+(0*16)+(0*8)+(0*4)+(0*2)+(1*1)
110100001
```

```
One's complement: 001011110
Two's complement: 001011111
Check: Original binary number + its two's complement
```

```
110100001
001011111
---------
000000000
```

C.15 Zero.

Exercises

C.16 Some people argue that many of our calculations would be easier in the base 12 number system because 12 is divisible by so many more numbers than 10 (for base 10). What is the lowest digit in base 12? What would be the highest symbol for the digit in base 12? What are the positional values of the rightmost four positions of any number in the base 12 number system?

C.17 Complete the following chart of positional values for the rightmost four positions in each of the indicated number systems:

decimal	1000	100	10	1
base 6	. . .	. . .	6	. . .
base 13	. . .	169	. . .	. . .
base 3	27	. . .	. . .	. . .

C.18 Convert binary 100101111010 to octal and to hexadecimal.

C.19 Convert hexadecimal 3A7D to binary.

C.20 Convert hexadecimal 765F to octal. (*Hint:* First convert 765F to binary, then convert that binary number to octal.)

C.21 Convert binary 1011110 to decimal.

C.22 Convert octal 426 to decimal.

C.23 Convert hexadecimal FFFF to decimal.

C.24 Convert decimal 299 to binary, to octal and to hexadecimal.

C.25 Show the binary representation of decimal 779. Then show the one's complement of 779 and the two's complement of 779.

C.26 Show the two's complement of integer value −1 on a machine with 32-bit integers.

Game Programming: Solving Sudoku

D.1 Introduction

The game of Sudoku exploded in popularity worldwide in 2005. Almost every major newspaper now publishes a Sudoku puzzle daily. Handheld game players let you play anytime, anywhere and create puzzles on demand at various levels of difficulty.

A completed **Sudoku puzzle** is a 9×9 grid (i.e., a two-dimensional array) in which the digits 1 through 9 appear once and only once in each row, each column and each of nine 3×3 grids. In the partially completed 9×9 grid of Fig. D.1, row 1, column 1, and the 3×3 grid in the upper-left corner of the board each contain the digits 1 through 9 once and only once. We use C's two-dimensional array row and column-numbering conventions, but we're ignoring row 0 and column 0 in conformance with Sudoku community conventions.

	1	2	3	4	5	6	7	8	9
1	5	1	3	4	9	7	6	2	8
2	4	6	8						
3	7	9	2						
4	2								
5	9								
6	3								
7	8								
8	1								
9	6								

Fig. D.1 | Partially completed 9×9 Sudoku grid. Note the nine 3×3 grids.

The typical Sudoku puzzle provides many filled-in cells and many blanks, often arranged in a symmetrical pattern as is typical with crossword puzzles. The player's task is to fill in the blanks to complete the puzzle. Some puzzles are easy to solve; some are quite difficult, requiring sophisticated solution strategies.

We'll discuss various simple solution strategies, and suggest what to do when these fail. We'll also present approaches for programming Sudoku puzzle creators and solvers in C. Unfortunately,

Standard C does not include graphics and GUI (graphical user interface) capabilities, so our representation of the board won't be as elegant as we could make it in Java and other programming languages that support these capabilities. You may want to revisit your Sudoku programs after you study a game programming library, such as Allegro, which offers capabilities for adding graphics and sounds to your programs.

D.2 Deitel Sudoku Resource Center

Check out our Sudoku Resource Center at www.deitel.com/sudoku. It contains downloads, tutorials, books, e-books and more that will help you master the game. Trace the history of Sudoku from its origin in the eighth century through modern times. Download free Sudoku puzzles at various levels of difficulty, enter daily game contests to win Sudoku books, and get a daily Sudoku puzzle to post on your web site. Get great beginner's resources—learn the rules of Sudoku, receive hints on solving sample puzzles, learn the best solution strategies and get free Sudoku solvers—just type in the puzzle from your newspaper or favorite Sudoku site and get an immediate solution; some Sudoku solvers even provide detailed step-by-step explanations. Get mobile device Sudoku games that can be installed on cell phones, Palm® devices, Game Boy® players and Java-enabled devices. Some Sudoku sites have timers, signal when an incorrect number is placed and provide hints. Purchase T-shirts and coffee mugs with Sudoku puzzles on them, participate in Sudoku player forums, get blank Sudoku worksheets that can be printed and check out hand-held Sudoku game players—one offers a million puzzles at five levels of difficulty. Download free Sudoku puzzle maker software. And not for the faint of heart—try fiendishly difficult Sudokus with tricky twists, a circular Sudoku and a variant of the puzzle with five interlocking grids.

D.3 Solution Strategies

When we refer to a Sudoku 9×9 grid, we'll call it array s. By looking at all the filled-in cells in the row, column and 3×3 grid that includes a particular empty cell, the value for that cell might become obvious. Trivially, cell s[1][7] in Fig. D.2 *must* be 6.

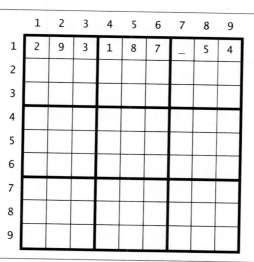

Fig. D.2 | Determining the value of a cell by checking all filled-in cells in the same row.

Less trivially, to determine the value of s[1][7] in Fig. D.3, you have to pick up hints from row 1 (i.e., the digits 3, 6 and 9 are taken), column 7 (i.e., the digits 4, 7 and 1 are taken) and the upper-right 3×3 grid (i.e., the digits 9, 8, 4 and 2 are taken). Here the empty cell s[1][7] *must* be 5—the only number not already mentioned in row 1, column 7 or the upper-right 3×3 grid.

Fig. D.3 | Determining the value of a cell by checking all filled-in cells in the same row, column and 3×3 grid.

Singletons

The strategies we've discussed so far can easily determine the final digits for some open cells, but you'll often have to dig deeper. Column 6 of Fig. D.4 shows cells with already determined values (e.g., s[1][6] is a 9, s[3][6] is a 6, etc.), and cells indicating the set of values (which we call "possibles") that at this point are still possible for that cell.

Cell s[6][6] contains 257, indicating that only the values 2, 5 or 7 can eventually be assigned to this cell. The other two open cells in column 6—s[2][6] and s[5][6]—are both 27, indicating that *only* the values 2 or 7 can eventually be assigned to these cells. Thus s[6][6], the only cell in column 6 that lists 5 as a remaining possible value, *must* be 5. We call that value 5 a **singleton**. So we can commit cell s[6][6] to a 5 (Fig. D.5), somewhat simplifying the puzzle.

Doubles

Consider the upper-right 3×3 grid in Fig. D.6. The dashed cells could already be committed or could have lists of possible values. Notice the **doubles**—the two cells s[1][9] and s[2][7] containing only the two possibilities 15. If s[1][9] ultimately becomes 1, then s[2][7] *must* be 5; if s[1][9] ultimately becomes 5, then s[2][7] *must* be 1. So between them, those two cells will definitely "use up" the 1 and the 5. Thus 1 and 5 can be eliminated from cell s[3][9] that contains the possible values 1357, so we can rewrite its contents as 37, simplifying the puzzle a bit. If cell s[3][9] had originally contained only 135, then eliminating the 1 and the 5 would enable us to force the cell to the value 3.

Doubles can be more subtle. For example, suppose two cells of a row, column or 3×3 grid have possibles lists of 2467 and 257 and that no other cell in that row, column or 3×3 grid mentions 2 or 7 as a possible value. Then, 27 is a **hidden double**—one of those two cells must be 2 and the other must be 7, so all digits other than 2 and 7 can be removed from the possibles lists of those two cells (i.e., 2467 becomes 27 and 257 becomes 27—creating a pair of doubles—thus somewhat simplifying the puzzle).

Fig. D.4 | Notation showing the complete sets of possible values for open cells.

Fig. D.5 | Committing cell s[6][6] to the singleton value 5.

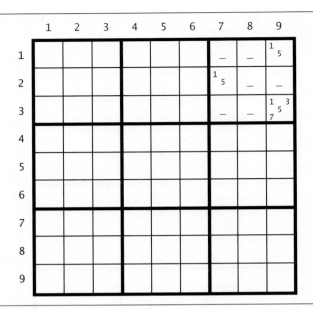

Fig. D.6 | Using doubles to simplify a puzzle.

Triples

Consider column 5 of Fig. D.7. The dashed cells could already be committed or could have lists of possible values. Notice the **triples**—the three cells containing the exact same three possibilities 467, namely cells s[1][5], s[6][5] and s[9][5]. If one of those three cells ultimately becomes 4, then

Fig. D.7 | Using triples to simplify a puzzle.

the others reduce to doubles of 67; if one of those three cells ultimately becomes 6, then the others reduce to doubles of 47; and if one of those three cells ultimately becomes 7, then the others reduce to doubles of 46. Among the three cells containing 467, one must ultimately be 4, one must be 6, and one must be 7. Thus the 4, 6 and 7 can be eliminated from cell s[4][5] that contains the possibles 14567, so we can rewrite its contents as 15, simplifying the puzzle a bit. If cell s[4][5] had originally contained 1467, then eliminating the 4, 6 and 7 would enable us to force the value 1 in that cell.

Triples can be more subtle. Suppose a row, column or 3×3 grid contains cells with possibles lists of 467, 46, and 67. Clearly one of those cells must be 4, one must be 6 and one must be 7. Thus 4, 6 and 7 can be removed from all the other possibles lists in that row, column or 3×3 grid.

Triples can also be hidden. Suppose that a row, column or 3×3 grid contains the possibles lists 5789, 259 and 13789, and that no other cell in that row, column or 3×3 grid mentions 5, 7 or 9. Then one of those cells must be 5, one must be 7 and one must be 9. We call 579 a **hidden triple** and all possibles other than 5, 7 and 9 can be deleted from those three cells (i.e., 5789 becomes 579, 259 becomes 59 and 13789 becomes 79), thus somewhat simplifying the puzzle.

Other Sudoku Solution Strategies

There are a number of other Sudoku solution strategies. Here are two of the many sites we recommend in our Sudoku Resource Center (www.deitel.com/sudoku) that will help you dig deeper:

```
www.sudokuoftheday.com/pages/techniques-overview.php
www.angusj.com/sudoku/hints.php
```

D.4 Programming Sudoku Puzzle Solvers

In this section we suggest how to program Sudoku solvers. We use a variety of approaches. Some may seem unintelligent, but if they can solve Sudokus faster than any human on the planet, then perhaps they are in some sense intelligent.

If you've done our Knight's Tour exercises (Exercises 6.24, 6.25 and 6.29) and Eight Queens exercises (Exercises 6.26 and 6.27), you've implemented various brute force and heuristic problem-solving approaches. In the next several sections, we suggest brute force and heuristic Sudoku-solving strategies. You should try programming them, as well as creating and programming your own. Our goal is simply to acquaint you with Sudoku, and some of its challenges and problem-solving strategies. Along the way, you'll become more facile with manipulating two-dimensional arrays and with nested iteration structures. We've made no attempt to produce optimal strategies, so once you analyze our strategies, you'll want to consider how you can improve upon them.

Programming a Solution for "Easy" Sudokus

The strategies we've shown—eliminating possibilities based on values already committed in a cell's row, column and 3×3 grid; and simplifying a puzzle using singletons, doubles (and hidden doubles) and triples (and hidden triples)—are sometimes sufficient to solve a puzzle. You can program the strategies then iterate on them until all 81 squares are filled. To confirm that the filled puzzle is a valid Sudoku, you can write a function to check that each row, column and 3×3 grid contains the digits 1 through 9 once and only once. Your program should apply the strategies in order. Each of them either forces a digit in a cell or simplifies the puzzle a bit. When any one of the strategies works, return to the beginning of your loop and reapply the strategies in order. When a strategy doesn't work, try the next. For "easy" Sudokus, these techniques should generate a solution.

Programming a Solution for Harder Sudokus

For harder Sudokus, your program will eventually reach a point where it still has uncommitted cells with possibles lists, and none of the simple strategies we've discussed will work. If this happens, first save the state of the board, then generate the next move by randomly choosing one of the possible values in any of the remaining cells. Then reevaluate the board, enumerating the remaining possibilities for each cell. Then try the basic strategies again, looping through them repeatedly, until either the Sudoku is solved, or the strategies once again no longer improve the board, at which point you can again try another move at random. If you reach a point where there are still empty cells, but no possible digits for at least one of those cells, the program should abandon that attempt, restore the board state that you saved, and begin the random approach again. Keep looping until a solution is found.

D.5 Generating New Sudoku Puzzles

First, let's consider approaches for generating valid finished 9×9 Sudokus with all 81 squares filled in. Then, we'll suggest how to empty some cells to create puzzles that people can attempt.

Brute Force Approaches

When personal computers appeared in the late 1970s, they processed tens of thousands of instructions per second. Today's desktop computers commonly process *billions* of instructions per second and the world's fastest supercomputers can process *trillions* of instructions per second! Brute force approaches that might have required months of computing in the 1970s can now produce solutions in seconds! This encourages people who need results quickly to program simple brute force approaches and get solutions sooner than by taking the time to develop more sophisticated "intelligent" problem solving strategies. Although our brute force approaches may seem ponderous, they will mechanically grind out solutions.

For these approaches you'll need some utility functions. Create the function

```
int validSudoku( int sudokuBoard[ 10 ][ 10 ] );
```

which receives a Sudoku board as a two-dimensional array of integers (recall that we're ignoring row 0 and column 0). This function should return 1 if a completed board is valid, 2 if a partially completed board is valid and 0 otherwise.

An Exhaustive Brute Force Approach

One brute force approach is simply to select all possible placements of the digits 1 through 9 in every cell. This could be done with 81 nested for statements that each loop from 1 through 9. The number of possibilities (9^{81}) is so vast that you might say it's not worth trying. But this approach does have the advantage that it will eventually stumble onto *every* possible solution, some of which could show up fortuitously early on.

A slightly more intelligent version of this exhaustive brute-force approach would be to check each digit you're about to place to see if it leaves the board in a valid state. If it does, then move on to placing a digit in the next cell. If the digit you're attempting to place leaves the board in an invalid state, then try all other eight digits on that cell in order. If one of them works, then move on to the next cell. If none of them works, then move back up to the previous cell and try its next value. Nested for statements can handle this automatically.

Brute Force Approach with Randomly Selected Row Permutations

Every row, column, and 3×3 grid on a valid Sudoku contains a permutation of the digits 1 through 9. There are 9! (i.e., 9·8·7·6·5·4·3·2·1 = 362,880) such permutations. Write a function

```
void permutations( int sudokuBoard[ 10 ][ 10 ] );
```

that receives a 10×10 two-dimensional array and in the 9×9 portion of it that corresponds to a Sudoku grid fills each of the nine rows with a randomly selected permutation of the digits 1 through 9.

Here's one way to generate a random permutation of the digits 1 through 9—for the first digit, simply choose a random digit from 1 through 9; for the second digit, use a loop to repeatedly generate a random digit from 1 through 9 until a digit *different* from the first digit is selected; for the third digit, use a loop to repeatedly generate a random digit from 1 through 9 until a digit different from the first two digits is selected; and so on.

After placing nine randomly selected permutations into the nine rows of your Sudoku array, run function validSudoku on the array. If it returns 1, you're done. If it returns 0, simply loop again, generating another nine randomly selected permutations of the digits 1 through 9 into the nine successive rows of the array Sudoku. The simple process will generate valid Sudokus. By the way, this approach guarantees that all the rows are valid permutations of the digits 1 through 9, so you should add an option to your function validSudoku that will have it check only columns and 3×3 grids.

Heuristic Solution Strategies

When we studied the Knight's Tour in Exercises 6.24, 6.25 and 6.29, we developed a "keep your options open" heuristic. To review, a heuristic is a guideline. It "sounds good" and seems like a reasonable rule to follow. It's programmable, so it gives us a way to direct a computer to attempt to solve a problem. But heuristic approaches don't necessarily guarantee success. For complex problems like solving a Sudoku puzzle, the number of possible placements of the digits 1–9 is enormous, so the hope in using a reasonable heuristic is that it will avoid wasting time on fruitless possibilities and instead focus on solution attempts much more likely to yield success.

A "Keep Your Options Open" Sudoku-Solving Heuristic

Let's develop a "keep your options open" heuristic for solving Sudokus. At any point in solving a Sudoku, we can categorize the board by listing in each empty cell the digits from 1 to 9 which are still open possibilities for that cell. For example, if a cell contains 3578, then the cell must eventually become 3, 5, 7 or 8. When attempting to solve a Sudoku, we reach a dead end when the number of possible digits that can be placed in an empty cell becomes zero. So, consider the following strategy:

1. Associate with every empty square a possibles list of the digits that can still be placed in that square.

2. Characterize the state of the board by simply counting the number of possible placements for the entire board.

3. For each possible placement for each empty cell, associate with that placement the count that would characterize the state of the board after that placement.

4. Then, place the particular digit in the particular empty square (of all those that remain) that leaves the board count the highest (in case of a tie, pick one at random). This is a key to "keeping your options open."

Lookahead Heuristic

This is simply an embellishment of our "keep your options open" heuristic. In case of a tie, look ahead one more placement. Place the particular digit in the particular square whose subsequent placement leaves the board count the highest after two moves out.

Forming Sudoku Puzzles with Empty Cells

Once you get your Sudoku generator program running, you should be able to generate lots of valid Sudokus quickly. To form a puzzle, save the solved grid, then empty some cells. One way to do this is to empty randomly chosen cells. A general observation is that Sudokus tend to become more difficult as the empty cells increase (there are exceptions to this).

Another approach is to empty the cells in a manner that leaves the resulting board symmetric. This can be done programmatically by randomly picking a cell to empty, then emptying its "reflecting cell." For example, if you empty the top-left cell s[1][1], you might empty the bottom-left cell s[9][1] as well. Such reflections are calculated by presenting the column, but determining the row by subtracting the initial row from 10. You could also do the reflections by subtracting both the row and column of the cell you're emptying from 10. Hence, the reflecting cell to s[1][1] would be s[10-1][10-1] or s[9][9].

A Programming Challenge

Published Sudoku puzzles typically have exactly one solution, but it's still satisfying to solve any Sudoku, even ones that have multiple solutions. Develop a means of demonstrating that a particular Sudoku puzzle has *exactly one* solution.

D.6 Conclusion

This appendix on solving and programming Sudoku puzzles has presented you with many challenges. Be sure to check out our Sudoku Resource Center (www.deitel.com/sudoku/) for numerous web resources that will help you master Sudoku and develop various approaches for writing programs to create and solve existing Sudoku puzzles.

Appendices on the Web

The following appendices are available as PDF documents from this book's Companion Website (www.pearsoninternationaleditions.com/deitel/):

- Appendix E, Sorting: A Deeper Look
- Appendix F, Introduction to the New C Standard
- Appendix G, Using the Visual Studio Debugger
- Appendix H, Using the GNU Debugger

These files can be viewed in Adobe® Reader® (get.adobe.com/reader). The index entries for these appendices have uppercase Roman numeral page numbers.

Index